A TREATISE OF THE LAWS OF NATURE

NATURAL LAW AND
ENLIGHTENMENT CLASSICS

Knud Haakonssen
General Editor

Richard Cumberland

NATURAL LAW AND
ENLIGHTENMENT CLASSICS

A Treatise of the Laws of Nature

Richard Cumberland

Translated, with Introduction and Appendix,
by John Maxwell (1727)

Edited and with a Foreword by
Jon Parkin

LIBERTY FUND

Indianapolis

This book is published by Liberty Fund, Inc., a foundation established to encourage study of the ideal of a society of free and responsible individuals.

© 2005 Liberty Fund, Inc.

09   08   07   06   05   C   5   4   3   2   1
09   08   07   06   05   P   5   4   3   2   1

Frontispiece: Portrait of Richard Cumberland used by permission of the Master and Fellows of Magdalene College, Cambridge.

Library of Congress Cataloging-in-Publication Data
Cumberland, Richard, 1631–1718.
[De legibus naturae. English]
A treatise of the laws of nature / Richard Cumberland;
translated, with introduction and appendix by John Maxwell (1727);
edited and with a foreword by Jon Parkin.
p.   cm.—(Natural law and enlightenment classics)
Includes bibliographical references and index.
ISBN 0-86597-472-1 (alk. paper)   ISBN 0-86597-473-X (pbk.: alk. paper)
1. Ethics.   2. Christian ethics.
I. Parkin, Jon (Jonathan Bruce), 1969–   .   II. Title.   III. Series.
B1201.C83D423 2005
171'.2—dc22

2004048750

LIBERTY FUND, INC.
8335 Allison Pointe Trail, Suite 300
Indianapolis, Indiana 46250-1684

CONTENTS

Appendixes

FOREWORD

The seventeenth century witnessed what has been called the "heroic" period in the development of modern natural law theory.[1] Beginning with Hugo Grotius, Protestant thinkers began to experiment with scholastic natural law ideas to produce a distinctive and highly successful tradition of natural jurisprudence that would come to dominate European political thought. Viewed from the eighteenth century, the success of the tradition could be, and often was, taken for granted, but such retrospective views could often conceal the extent to which the early pioneers faced real challenges in their attempts to reconcile natural law ideas with the rigors of Protestant theology. In this context, Richard Cumberland is perhaps one of the great unsung heroes of the natural law tradition. Cumberland's *De Legibus Naturae* constituted a critical intervention in the early debate over the role of natural jurisprudence at a moment when the natural law project was widely suspected of heterodoxy and incoherence.

Hugo Grotius's work undoubtedly generated a great deal of interest among Protestant thinkers, but it also occasioned a critical response that threatened to undermine the whole project. The most dangerous writer in this respect was Thomas Hobbes. Hobbes simultaneously adapted and subverted the new jurisprudence, producing a theory that would become notorious for its apparent atheism and absolutism. As a result,

---

1. For discussion of the "modern" theory of natural law, see Tuck, *Natural Rights Theories: Their Origin and Development* (1979), and also his "The 'Modern' Theory of Natural Law" (1987), 99–122. For more recent discussions of the same tradition, see Haakonssen, *Natural Law and Modern Philosophy* (1996); and Hochstrasser, *Natural Law Theories in the Early Enlightenment* (2000).

early natural law writers were dogged by accusations of Hobbism, the charge that behind their attempts to forge a new tradition lay the reduction of moral and political obligation to self-interest alone. Cumberland's *De Legibus Naturae,* with its sustained assault on Hobbes's ideas, constituted one of the most important and influential responses to this damaging accusation. Cumberland not only produced one of the most effective critiques of Hobbes's ideas, but he also used the opportunity to propose a new and distinctively scientific approach to questions of moral and political obligation. Cumberland's achievement was to provide a much-needed defense of the natural jurisprudential project while laying important theoretical foundations for the work of such later writers as Clarke, Shaftesbury, and Hutcheson.[2]

Richard Cumberland (1632–1718)[3]

Cumberland was born in London, the son of a Salisbury Court tailor. He attended St. Paul's School, and in June 1649, barely five months after the execution of Charles I, he entered Magdalene College, Cambridge. At Magdalene, Cumberland supplemented his regular studies with a rich diet of natural philosophy, developing the scientific knowledge that in-

2. For Cumberland's contribution to the natural law tradition, see Parkin, *Science, Religion and Politics in Restoration England: Richard Cumberland's "De Legibus Naturae"* (1999), especially ch. 7; Kirk, *Richard Cumberland and Natural Law* (1987); Haakonssen, "The Character and Obligation of Natural Law According to Richard Cumberland" (2001), pp. 29–47; Schneider, *Justitia Universalis* (1967), pp. 166–75; Darwall, *The British Moralists and the Internal "Ought"* (1995), pp. 80–108; and Schneewind, *The Invention of Autonomy* (1998), pp. 101–17. For Cumberland's influence upon Scottish Enlightenment thought, see Forbes, "Natural Law and the Scottish Enlightenment" (1982), pp. 186–204. See also Forbes, *Hume's Philosophical Politics* (1975), pp. 18–26; Moore and Silverthorne, "Gerschom Carmichael and the Natural Jurisprudence Tradition in Eighteenth-Century Scotland" (1983), pp. 73–88.

3. The main source for Cumberland's life is a short biography written by his son-in-law Squire Payne: "Brief Account of the Life . . . of the Author," prefaced to Cumberland's *Sanchoniatho's Phoenician History* (1720). Linda Kirk has produced the best modern account in "Richard Cumberland (1632–1718) and His Political Theory," Ph.D. diss., University of London, 1976. Kirk's discussion forms the basis for ch. 1 of her *Richard Cumberland and Natural Law.* Some additional information is provided in Parkin, *Science, Religion and Politics,* Introduction.

forms almost every page of the *De Legibus*. Cumberland's interest in the new science was crucial to his natural law theory; the union of natural philosophy and natural theology created the basis for his science of morality and his logical demonstration of divine obligation.

Cumberland left Cambridge after receiving his master of arts in 1656, becoming rector of the small Northamptonshire parish of Brampton Ash in 1658. This rural posting might have marked the end of Cumberland's significance, but in 1667 he became a client of, and possibly domestic chaplain to, Sir Orlando Bridgeman, formerly lord chief justice of the Common Pleas and now in 1667 newly appointed lord keeper of the Great Seal.[4] An ex-Magdalene man himself, Bridgeman employed a number of Cumberland's colleagues, including Cumberland's friend Hezekiah Burton. It is likely that Burton's recommendation secured Cumberland's new and politically important patronage.

The connection with Bridgeman placed Cumberland at the center of English politics in the later 1660s and led directly to the publication of *De Legibus Naturae*. During this period, Bridgeman sponsored Hezekiah Burton and another of Cumberland's friends, John Wilkins, in their attempts to construct a religious compromise with Presbyterian nonconformists. Although the negotiations ultimately failed, the discussion of the role of natural law in such a settlement formed the immediate political context to Cumberland's work on the subject. In 1670, Bridgeman established the newly married Cumberland in comparatively affluent livings in Stamford, enabling him to complete *De Legibus Naturae*. Burton supervised the publication of the work, which was dedicated to Bridgeman. The book was published in the spring of 1672.

The same year would see Bridgeman resign in protest at Charles II's

---

4. The lord keeper of the Great Seal was the judicial officer appointed in lieu of the lord chancellor. As well as being the head of the legal side of the government and the senior judge in the Court of Chancery, the lord keeper authorized grants of offices, privileges, and royal charters. Virtually indistinguishable from the office of lord chancellor in theory and practice, the post was abolished in 1760. See G. E. Aylmer, *The Crown's Servants* (2002), p. 18.

decision to issue the Declaration of Indulgence, suspending the penal laws against Catholic and Protestant dissenters. Cumberland appears to have survived his patron's fall, devoting himself to his parochial duties. In 1680 he proceeded to a doctorate at Cambridge University. His thesis maintained (against the Roman Catholic position) that St. Peter had no jurisdiction over the other apostles and (against the nonconformist position) that separation from the Anglican Church was schismatic.[5] In the 1680s, Cumberland produced two works. The first was a pamphlet dedicated to his school friend Samuel Pepys, by this time president of the Royal Society, entitled *An Essay Towards the Recovery of Jewish Measures and Weights* (1686). The *Essay*, originally designed as an appendix to a new edition of the Bible, was widely respected for its scholarship. During the same time, Cumberland also produced *Sanchoniatho's Phoenician History* in manuscript. This work claimed to find the sources of Roman Catholic idolatry in the Phoenician corruption of sacred history. The anti-Catholic bias of the work was such that, on the eve of the Glorious Revolution of 1688, Cumberland's publisher felt that the manuscript was too inflammatory to be released. The book appeared posthumously, in 1720.

In the wake of the revolution, Cumberland was called upon to replace the nonjuring bishop of Peterborough, Thomas White.[6] Cumberland was consecrated in July 1691, at age fifty-nine. From this time until his death, Cumberland administered his diocese diligently but with declining efficiency as old age took its toll. He attended the House of Lords regularly until 1716, a loyal Whig supporter of Archbishop Tenison. Intellectually, Cumberland busied himself with studies in ancient chronology. He died after suffering a stroke on October 9, 1718.[7]

5. Squire Payne, "Brief Account," p. ix; Cambridge University Library Grace Book, Supplicats 1677–80.

6. The nonjurors were the eight bishops and some four hundred priests who, because of their belief in the divine right of kings, continued to see the Stuarts as the legitimate monarchs and hence refused to take the oath of allegiance to William and Mary.

7. Payne, "Brief Account," p. xxvi.

De Legibus Naturae

De Legibus Naturae was a theoretical response to a range of issues that came together during the later 1660s. The immediate political circumstances were English debates over the toleration of religious dissent. Cumberland's Latitudinarian friends sought to reach an accommodation with moderate nonconformists based upon an appeal to natural law ideas.[8] If the nonconformists could accept that the magistrate had a natural right to regulate adiaphora (religious ritual not prescribed by Scripture), intractable theological disputes might be avoided, which would open the way for accommodation within the church. The negotiations failed, resulting in the rise of more strident demands from dissenters for a pluralist, toleration-based settlement. For some Latitudinarian Anglicans, notably Samuel Parker, such demands were unacceptable. For Parker, natural law required nonconformists to submit to the legal requirements imposed by the sovereign for the common good. Parker's illiberal use of the natural law argument soon attracted accusations that he was following the arguments of Thomas Hobbes. Notoriously, Hobbes's political theory had appeared to pay lip service to the obligations imposed by natural law, whereas in practice vesting all practical authority in the hands of an arbitrary and absolute sovereign. Although Parker and others attempted to demonstrate that they were not Hobbists, their attempt to justify extensive sovereign power appeared to undermine their avowed commitment to natural obligation. By the time Cumberland began to write *De Legibus Naturae,* there was a clear need to separate the Anglican use of the natural law argument from Hobbes's account. Such a project required a decisive attack upon Hobbes's subversive natural law theory, but it also provided an opportunity to demonstrate the character of the obligation to natural law. Cumberland sought to do both in *De Legibus Naturae.*

The question of moral obligation lies at the heart of Cumberland's treatise, and it was a question that created profound difficulties for Prot-

8. For a discussion of the political context, see Parkin, *Science, Religion and Politics,* ch. 1.

estant natural law theorists.[9] Protestant thinkers were skeptical about Grotius's appropriation of scholastic ideas. John Selden in particular was scathing about the Dutchman's apparent assumption that conclusions of reason alone could have the force of law. A law was properly the command of a superior, in this case God. How, then, could it be shown naturally that the conclusions of reason or empirically observed norms were the will of God and thus properly obligatory laws? Hobbes made the same criticism: If the laws of nature are simply rational theorems, then they are not properly laws at all and need the command of a superior to give them obligatory force. Hobbes's deeply skeptical answer was that providing such obligatory force was the role of the sovereign, a position that potentially ruled out the possibility of divine moral obligation altogether.

Cumberland accepted the force of this critique but rejected Hobbes's destructive conclusion, turning instead to a solution indicated by Selden. Selden preferred to sidestep the problem by arguing that God had spoken directly to Adam and Noah; the natural law precepts delivered were handed down within the rabbinical tradition. His second, rather underdeveloped, suggestion was that individuals might be capable of apprehending God's will more directly, but he was understandably reluctant to develop a theory that blurred the distinction between reason and command. Like many readers of Selden, Cumberland was less convinced by the first solution, but he saw the potential in the second argument.[10]

Cumberland's optimism about Selden's hint derived from two related sources. The first was the revaluation of man's rational capacity encouraged by such Cambridge thinkers as Benjamin Whichcote and Nathaniel Culverwell, both of whom sought an enhanced role for reason and empirical observation in Protestant natural law discourse.[11] The sec-

9. Ibid., ch. 2.

10. See below, Cumberland's "Introduction," sect. III.

11. Parkin, *Science, Religion and Politics,* ch. 2, especially pp. 72–87; see also Haakonssen, "Moral Philosophy and Natural Law: From the Cambridge Platonists to the Scottish Enlightenment" (1988), pp. 97–110.

ond major influence was Cumberland's conviction that science might offer a more effective means of demonstrating both the contents and the obligatory force of the law of nature. At a time when Hobbes's work appeared to suggest that the appliance of science undermined rather than supported the idea of obligatory natural law, Cumberland's *De Legibus* would recover a godly role for natural philosophy.[12]

To this end, Cumberland deployed the latest scientific evidence to reject Hobbes's narrow emphasis upon self-preservation as the beginning and end of natural obligation. Cumberland used evidence from "the nature of things" to show that an awareness of self-preservation is merely the starting point in developing an awareness of the natural duty of sociability. The logical consequence of such evidence is to reinforce the idea that individuals are bound, both by their limitations and their potentiality, to a common social good. Given that the pursuit of the common good results in a greater fulfillment of human nature than the narrow pursuit of individual self-interest, the pursuit of the common good presents itself as the logical priority for individuals, given that their own interests will be best served as a result. Such a proposition offered the prospect of a handy summary of the law of nature in one universal formula: Man's proper action should be an endeavor to promote the common good of the whole system of rational agents.

Although Cumberland had derived this practical proposition from a scientific examination of the nature of things, he still needed to demonstrate that such a proposition could be considered the will of God. His solution to this problem, discussed at length in chapter 5 of *De Legibus,* is Cumberland's most distinctive theoretical move. Cumberland argued that it was possible to identify the sanctions attached to the law of nature, namely the structures of reward and punishment that God had ordained for the observance and dereliction of the law of nature. Punishments take various forms, ranging from the traditional scourges

---

12. For discussion of Cumberland's science, see Parkin, *Science, Religion and Politics,* chs. 4–6; Forsyth, "The Place of Richard Cumberland in the History of Natural Law Doctrine," pp. 23–42; Stewart, *The Rise of Public Science: Rhetoric, Technology and Natural Philosophy in Newtonian Britain 1660–1750* (1992), pp. 37–39.

of conscience through to the state of war, a natural punishment for un-reasonable, Hobbesian behavior. Rewards include simple happiness through to the benefits of peace, prosperity, and security. Cumberland stressed that such sanctions are not in themselves the causes of moral obligation. They are merely clues indicating that the practical proposition concerning the common good is indeed the basic principle of God's justice. The knowledge that such a proposition is God's will gives the proposition the force of law. Cumberland's theory of obligation risked the suggestion that God himself is bound by the laws of nature, but Cumberland avoided the implication by arguing that an essentially free God binds himself to the observance of the regularities in his creation. Although not an unproblematic solution, Cumberland's scheme allowed a reconciliation between natural law and the requirements of Protestant theology, one of the many reasons for Cumberland's profound influence upon later writers in the tradition.

The practical implications of Cumberland's solution are scattered throughout the book but particularly in chapter 9, where the political implications of his argument are made clear. Having clarified the differences between Hobbes's natural law theory and his own, Cumberland attempted to show that his position sustains a more durable account of sovereignty justified by the common good. The magistrate's competence extends "universally to things divine and human, of foreigners and fellow-subjects, of peace and war."[13] Cumberland's sovereign possesses extensive civil and ecclesiastical jurisdiction, all warranted by divinely ordained natural law. Paradoxically, one of Cumberland's major achievements was to demonstrate that an almost Hobbesian sovereignty could be part of an orthodox natural law theory.[14]

Reception

The reception of *De Legibus* gives some indication of its impact upon the natural law tradition. Cumberland's thesis was particularly impor-

---

13. Ch. 9, sect. VIII.
14. Kirk, *Richard Cumberland,* ch. 4; Parkin, *Science, Religion and Politics,* ch. 1, pp. 48–55.

tant for Samuel Pufendorf, whose *De Jure Naturae et Gentium* was published in the same year. Pufendorf was accused of Hobbism and in response deployed Cumberland's arguments in his own defense. The second edition of *De Jure Naturae* (1684) included no fewer than forty references to *De Legibus,* reinforcing Pufendorf's anti-Hobbesian credentials but also adding weight to his theory of obligation.[15] In England it is perhaps no surprise to find Samuel Parker freely adapting the central argument of *De Legibus* in his *Demonstration of the Divine Authority of the Law of Nature* (1681). James Tyrrell, who had urged John Locke to publish something similar, produced an English abridgement of the work (with Cumberland's approval) under the title *A Brief Disquisition of the Law of Nature* (1692). Cumberland's combination of positive theory and anti-Hobbesian critique ensured that the work would continue to find an audience until the early eighteenth century. After that time, Cumberland's ideas were developed by writers like Samuel Clarke; Anthony Ashley Cooper, third earl of Shaftesbury; and Francis Hutcheson; but the waning of the Hobbesian threat and Cumberland's outmoded science made the book itself less urgent and rather dated to an audience that had become used to more sophisticated treatments of natural law.[16]

Editions

The original Latin edition was published by the Little Britain bookseller Nathaneal Hooke and seen through the press by Hezekiah Burton; but as Burton admitted in his address to the reader, the job was not well done.[17] The text is littered with transcription errors allegedly perpetrated by an unnamed youth who did the typesetting. The first edition was

15. For discussion of Pufendorf's critics, see Palladini, *Discussioni Seicentesche su Samuel Pufendorf* (1978), pp. 99–122, and Haakonssen, *Natural Law and Modern Philosophy,* pp. 43–46. For Cumberland's influence, see Kirk, *Richard Cumberland,* ch. 5; and Parkin, *Science, Religion and Politics,* ch. 7. For another view, see Palladini's discussion in *Samuel Pufendorf: Discepolo di Hobbes* (1990).

16. For Cumberland's impact upon these writers, see Kirk, *Richard Cumberland,* chs. 5 and 6. For Cumberland's place in the wider tradition, see Darwall, *The British Moralists and the Internal "Ought"*; and Schneewind, *The Invention of Autonomy.*

17. A translation of Burton's "Alloquium ad Lectorem" (Address to the Reader) is reproduced as an appendix to this edition.

licensed by Samuel Parker on July 25, 1671, and the work was advertised
in the term catalogues in February 1671/72. As Linda Kirk has established, there are two variants of this edition, with slightly different definitions of the law of nature at the beginning of chapter 5.[18] The possible
significance of these differences is discussed in this edition in the notes
to that chapter. A second edition of the Latin text was published in Lübeck and Frankfurt a.d.O. by Samuel Otto and Johann Wiedermeyer
in 1683, followed by a third in the same places in 1694. A fourth edition
of the Latin text, based upon the 1672 edition, was published in 1720 by
James Carson in Dublin.

In terms of translations, Cumberland's text was, as we have seen,
adapted by Samuel Parker and James Tyrrell, whose *Brief Disquisition*
went into a second edition in 1701. Cumberland's work would have to
wait until 1727 for a full translation into English, by John Maxwell, the
text used in this edition. Maxwell was prebendary of Connor and chaplain to Lord Carteret, then lord lieutenant of Ireland. Maxwell's preface
makes it clear that his intention was to produce a full translation for the
first time, given that Cumberland's original Latin text was both difficult
to acquire and complicated to read. Cumberland's anti-Hobbism may
have appealed at a time when Bernard Mandeville's *Fable of the Bees*
(1714, 1723) appeared to revive central Hobbesian arguments. Maxwell's
project was probably also occasioned by discussions of natural law inspired by Francis Hutcheson's work. Hutcheson headed a private academy in Dublin during the early 1720s and developed his own natural
law position in his *Inquiry into the Original of Our Ideas of Beauty and
Virtue* (1725), a work critical of some aspects of Cumberland's project
but with clear debts to the argument of *De Legibus*. Maxwell was familiar
with Hutcheson's work and saw the latter's project as a supplement to
Cumberland's own.[19]

Whatever the gains Maxwell hoped for, his *Treatise of the Laws of
Nature* also registers considerable anxieties about the text. The translation comes with two introductory essays and lengthy appendixes by

18. Kirk, *Richard Cumberland,* ch. 2.
19. Ibid., ch. 6.

Maxwell, all of which are designed to head off wayward readings of Cumberland's work.[20] The opening essays, in particular, qualify Cumberland's use of pagan philosophy, both by rejecting deist assumptions that might flow from such sources but also by asserting the importance of revelation in guiding the use of natural reason. The appendices carry out the same task with lengthy extracts from Samuel Clarke's defenses of the immateriality of a thinking substance and Maxwell's own essay on obligation, which reinforces the orthodox character of Cumberland's theory of obligation. Cumberland's work, so advanced for its own time, contained rather too many hostages to fortune to be published on its own in the very different world of the 1720s.

The next major translation of Cumberland's work produced what is undoubtedly the best edition of *De Legibus,* Jean Barbeyrac's *Traité Philosophique des Loix Naturelles,* published in Amsterdam in 1744. Barbeyrac was able to obtain a transcript of Cumberland's manuscript alterations, together with Richard Bentley's corrections,[21] and these were incorporated into extensive notes, together with commentaries on the text and even on Maxwell's English translation. As a critical edition, Barbeyrac's work is an astonishing feat of scholarship, an essential starting point for a modern editor.

The last edition of Cumberland's work was produced in Dublin in 1750 by John Towers. Towers produced a new but rather wayward translation and annotation inferior to Maxwell's earlier attempt. Towers also included considerable ancillary material, including translations of prefatory addresses that Maxwell had left out. These pieces have been included in appendixes 1 and 2 of this edition.

---

20. Maxwell borrowed most of this material from Richard Brocklesby's *An Explication of the Gospel—Theism and the Divinity of the Christian Religion* (1706). On some copies Maxwell acknowledged his debt to the obscure Brocklesby on the title page, but the most common state of the work lacks any reference to the earlier writer.

21. Cumberland's son Richard had supplied Bentley with his father's interleaved copy (Trinity College, Cambridge, MS. adv.c.2.4), containing Cumberland's own revisions for future publication of a corrected Latin edition. The project never came to fruition. For Barbeyrac's account of how he came by this material, see his *Traité Philosophique des Loix Naturelles* (1744), pp. v–viii.

A NOTE ON THIS EDITION

The current edition reproduces Maxwell's complete text, together with additional material taken from Cumberland's copy of *De Legibus,* Barbeyrac's *Traité Philosophique,* and Towers's *Philosophical Enquiry.* The only substantial changes to Maxwell's text are to the footnotes. Maxwell's footnotes use a variety of conventions, but they are unnumbered and in the introductory essays and appendixes consist usually of very general abbreviated references that provide hardly any guidance for a non-specialist modern reader.

For ease of reference, Maxwell's footnote callouts (normally asterisks) in the text have been silently deleted and replaced by arabic-numbered footnotes for each essay or chapter. In some instances multiple references occurring close together have been rationalized into one note. In Maxwell's supplementary essays, the notes have been expanded to include the full title of the work referred to and, where it can be identified, the edition used. Book, chapter, page, and section numbers have been left in the form of the original note. In his supplementary essays, Maxwell often both loosely paraphrases his source and quotes it verbatim in the original Greek or Latin; in those cases, the quotation is left out and only the reference is retained.

In the translation of Cumberland's text, Maxwell supplemented Cumberland's brief textual references (mostly to Hobbes's works) with notes of his own. Maxwell's comments are identified in the notes to this edition, as is material taken from Barbeyrac's notes and Cumberland's manuscript. Additional information is the work of the current editor. In order to facilitate comparison, references to appropriate modern editions of Hobbes's major works have been used.

A TREATISE OF THE LAWS OF NATURE

A

TREATISE

OF THE

LAWS of NATURE.

By the Right Reverend Father in God,
RICHARD CUMBERLAND, Lord Bishop of *Peterborough*.

Made *English* from the *Latin* by JOHN MAXWELL, M. A.
Prebendary of *Connor,* and Chaplain to his Excellency
the Lord CARTERET, Lord Lieutenant of *Ireland*.

To which is prefix'd,

An *Introduction* concerning the *mistaken Notions* which the
Heathens had of the DEITY, and the *Defects* in their MORAL-
ITY, whence the *Usefulness* of REVELATION may appear.

At the End is subjoin'd,

An *Appendix,* containing two *Discourses,* 1. Concerning the *Im-
materiality* of THINKING SUBSTANCE. 2. Concerning the
OBLIGATION, PROMULGATION, and OBSERVANCE, of the
LAW of NATURE, by the *Translator.*[1]

LONDON:

Printed by R. PHILLIPS; and Sold by J. KNAPTON, in St. *Paul's* Church-
Yard, J. SENEX, over against St. *Dunstan's* Church, in *Fleet-Street,* F.
FAYRAM, at the *South-Entrance* of the *Royal-Exchange,* J. OSBORNE, and
T. LONGMAN, in *Pater-Noster-Row,* and T. OSBORNE, by *Gray's-Inn-
Walks.* 1727.

1. In some copies the following variant text replaces "by the Translator": "the
Introduction and latter part of the Appendix being chiefly extracted out of the writings of the learned Mr. Brocklesby, by the translator." Richard Brocklesby (1636–
1714) was the author of *An Explication of the Gospel—Theism and the Divinity of the
Christian Religion* (1706). Maxwell makes liberal use of Brocklesby's text, particularly
books I and V, adapting, paraphrasing, and sometimes plagiarizing the text without
reference.

His EXCELLENCY,
JOHN,
Lord CARTERET,
Lord Lieutenant of *IRELAND*.[1]

May it please your Excellency,

When I was to publish the following Sheets, I knew not under the Authority of what great Name so properly to introduce them to the Publick as your Excellency's, and that for several Reasons.

The Design of the Work, is, to enforce the Obligation of the Dictates of REASON, and the Necessity of REVELATION, the Practice of VIRTUE and RELIGION, to Mankind; which could, with no Propriety, be address'd to a Person of an exceptionable Character.

How I have succeeded in my Performance, no one is a better Judge than your Excellency, who have made the Authors of Antiquity, which I have made use of in the following Work, the Diversion and Improvement of your retir'd Hours.

The Relation also, which you bear to my native Country, which is happy under your Excellency's Administration, was another Inducement to my taking the Liberty of this Address, to which I was the more embolden'd, by having had the Honour of being receiv'd into your Excellency's Service.

That your Country may long enjoy the Advantage of your Example and your Counsels; that you and your Family may be long Happy in one another; and that, after a long and prosperous Life here, you may receive an eternal Reward of all your Labours hereafter, is the sincere Prayer of him, who is, with the profoundest respect,

May it please your Excellency,
your most devoted, and
most faithful humble
Servant and Chaplain,

London March
8th, 1726–7.   JOHN MAXWELL.

---

1. John Carteret (1690–1763), 1st earl of Granville, but more commonly known as Lord Carteret, was lord lieutenant of Ireland between 1724 and 1730. Maxwell was Carteret's domestic chaplain.

THE TRANSLATOR'S PREFACE

The Original of MORAL OBLIGATION, *and the fundamental Principles of* LAWS *Divine and Human, of* SOCIETY, *of* VIRTUE, *and of* RELIGION, *are Points, which, in my Opinion, best deserve our Consideration, of any, which the Mind of Man can contemplate. 'Tis to these we chiefly owe all the Happiness we enjoy here, or hope for hereafter. 'Tis from Enquiries of* this *kind, that we learn our* Duties *of every sort, to* God, *our Creator and supreme Governor, our* Fellow-creatures, *and* Ourselves; *that we learn that unerring Rule and Standard of* right Reason, *by pursuing whose Dictates we regulate our* Passions, *and preserve them in a due Subordination. Whilst we preserve them under the Conduct of that governing Principle in the Mind of Man, which they were form'd to obey, they are our chief Instruments of* Happiness; *as, when they grow exorbitant, headstrong, and irregular, they are the Causes of all our* Misery.

For these Reasons, being led as much by Inclination, *as in pursuance of the* Profession *which I have undertaken, I was willing to inquire into what those Authors had offer'd, who had treated upon this Subject, among whom Bishop* CUMBERLAND *seems to me, to have handled it in the most masterly and rational Manner, and to have gone farthest in the Argument, of any I have had the good Fortune to meet with. But at the same time that I own myself an Admirer of his* Reasoning *in the main, I cannot but acknowledge, that his* Periods *are very perplex'd and intricate, and that his* Language *is too Scholastick and Philosophical; which have deterr'd many from reading him, and have been the Occasion of his valuable Work's not being so universally known as it deserv'd. His Book labour'd also under another Disadvantage; his Manuscript was transcrib'd for the Press (as he himself says) by a Person unskillful in such Matters, whose Performance was, in conse-*

4

quence, very incorrect;[1] *and the Author, living in the Country at a distance from* London, *where the Book was printed, left the Care of the Edition to a Friend, who was not at sufficient Pains, to see that it came out* correctly,[2] *as whoever examines the Original with attention, will perceive in every Sheet of the Book, in which many of the* Errata *are more than literal Mistakes, or Mispointings, and disturb the Sense extremely, which are a great Hinderance to the Reader, especially in an Argument otherwise intricate. This Fault has not been corrected in the subsequent Editions, but in the last greatly increas'd.*[3] *His* Paragraphs *also, in many places, are not divided in such a manner as to give the most Light to his Argument, sometimes joining them where they should be divided, and dividing them where the Reasoning requires that they should be join'd. All these Circumstances conspire to make the Reading of his valuable Work, a laborious Task, which, therefore, few Readers will be at the Pains to do. This I thought well deserv'd a helping Hand, to which I have, therefore, contributed what lay in my power.*

In order to remedy these Inconveniences, I thought it would be no disservice to the Publick, to publish his Work in English; *Morality and the Law of Nature being Subjects, which many, who don't understand* Latin, *would willingly inquire into; and the Poison, which Mr.* Hobbes *and other Writers of his Stamp, have spread far and wide, subversive of the Principles of all Morality and all Religion, having strongly infected many, who don't understand that Language; beside, that many, who are conversant in other* Latin *Authors, don't care to be at the Pains of reading* CUMBERLAND.

In my Translation I have us'd my utmost Endeavours, throughout, religiously to preserve my Author's Sense, and at the same time to free him from as many of his Scholastick Terms *as I could, without hurting the Sense,*

---

1. In the errata to the first edition of *De Legibus Naturae,* Cumberland blames the inaccuracies upon the youth who did the typesetting.

2. Cumberland lived in Stamford in the early 1670s and left the printing in the hands of his friend Hezekiah Burton. See also Burton's "Alloquium ad Lectorem," reproduced as appendix 2 to the current volume.

3. Maxwell refers to subsequent editions of the Latin text; slightly improved second and third editions were published in Lübeck and Frankfurt by Samuel Otto and Johann Wiedermeyer in 1683 and 1694. The problematic fourth edition, based upon the 1672 edition, was published in Dublin by James Carson in 1720.

explaining such of the rest as seem'd most to require it, altering and increasing the Breaks *into Paragraphs, where it seem'd necessary, and giving the* Heads *of each Section at the Beginning of it, in order to render more clear the Connexion of the Author's Reasoning, and his Transitions; for which purpose I have likewise frequently made use of* "inverted Commas" *and a* difference of Character, *adding at the End a particular* Analysis *of the whole Work, and a copious* Index. *In the* Notes *at the Bottom of the Page, I have endeavour'd, either to explain, illustrate, or confirm, what the Author has advanc'd, and in some places where I differ'd from him, to give my Reasons for it, which are submitted to the Judgment of the Reader, with all due deference to the Character of so Judicious and Learned a Writer. I have added, likewise, at the End of most of the Chapters general* Remarks, *with the same View.*

The Appendix *which I have added, consists of* two Parts. *The Author, in the Beginning of his second Chapter, which is concerning* the Nature of Man, *where he comes to touch upon the* Distinctness of the Soul from the Body, *refers, for the Proof of it, to Several Authors,* DES-CARTES, MORE, DIGBY, *and* WARD, *whom the Reader may, perhaps, not have at hand, nor Leisure and Inclination to consult 'em, if he had:*[4] *And, as that is a most important Point in the present Inquiry, and has, in my Opinion, been set in a clearer and stronger Light by Dr.* Clark, *than by any other Writer I have met with, I have reduc'd into as narrow a Compass as I could, the Substance of his Controversy upon that Head, with an Anonymous Adversary; as to which, I dare venture to appeal to both the Gentlemen themselves, whether or no I have not fairly represented their Arguments.*[5] *The* second Part *of the* Appendix *is a Discourse concerning* the Promulgation, Obligation, and Observance of the Law of Nature, *in which I have endeavour'd to supply what seem'd to me wanting in* CUMBERLAND'*s Scheme, in order to render it more compleat.*

---

4. René Descartes, Henry More, Kenelm Digby, and Seth Ward. For the works referred to, see ch. 2, n. 2.

5. Maxwell's piece summarizes the arguments that emerged from Samuel Clarke's attack upon Henry Dodwell; the anonymous adversary was Anthony Collins, who attacked Clarke's work in turn. See "A Summary of the Controversy Between Dr. Samuel Clark &c.," in Cumberland's appendix 1, below, pp. 759–93.

Inquiries of the present kind and upon the present Argument, are such as can be made concerning the Will of God, as discoverable by the Light of Nature; but yet, tho', by the help of Reason only, we may discover many *and important Truths, with respect to our moral and religious Conduct,* Human Reason alone *and* unassisted *is not sufficient to inform us of* all *those Truths, which it greatly concerns us to know, with such* a degree of Certainty, *as that the Mind of Man can acquiesce therein with Satisfaction; and, consequently, a farther Light, the Light of* Revelation *I mean, must be added to crown our Inquiries, without which we do but still grope in the Dark, as I have endeavour'd clearly to make out in my* Introduction; *for I would lay no greater stress upon any thing, no, not even upon Reason itself, than I think it can bear. If we strain the String too high, it will crack, and then it is of no farther Service. In order to discover the true Foundation of all Religion and Piety, and* what *our Duty to God is, we must first know* who *he is; that is to say, we must first learn so to distinguish him from all other Beings, whether Real or Imaginary, as not to* give his Glory to another. *The* Heathens, *indeed, plainly discover'd, what it was impossible they should avoid discovering, that there was a* God, *a wise, powerful, and good Governor of the World, but yet they did not discover* the one true God; *for their supreme God was only the Imperial Head of their Polity of Gods, whom they set at the Head of their* Heathen *Religion; so that their supreme God was as different from the true God, as their* Heathen *Religion was from the true Religion. And the better Sects of the* Heathen *Philosophers, such as the* Pythagoreans, Platonists, *and* Stoicks, *made* God *no better than* the Soul of the World, *so deifying the World as a part of God, and his Body; and this Notion introduc'd the Worship of the* Universe, *and of the* Heavenly Bodies *among them. And as for* Aristotle, *he made no more of Religion, than a mere Civil or Political Institution. Thus the true God and the true Religion were Strangers among them all. As for their Morality, I have likewise shewn how imperfect that was. Thus were their Notions defective, with respect to God, Religion, and Morality; and without the Knowledge of the true God it is as impossible to form a true Religion, as it is impossible for a blind Man to take a true Aim, or for an Architect to raise a firm Building without a Foundation. This, therefore, is the Scope of my* Introduction; *for, as great a value as I set upon Reason, I would not over-rate her: Where she convinces me, that she is a sufficient Guide, I will follow her Directions; but where she owns herself at a loss, and that another Guide is necessary, I will follow her Directions in the Choice of that Guide, among the Pretenders, and in explaining the Directions and Institutions given me by that Guide. Thus is Reason justly subservient to, and consistent with, Religion; and thus, if our Practice be suitable, we make a right Use of both.*

There is only one thing more, with which I think it proper to acquaint the Reader, and I have done. In the last Page but one of the Introduction *I affirm, "That the Knowledge of the Being and Attributes of God are previously necessary to the Belief of a Revelation;" and I have before in the same* Introduction *prov'd, "That the* Heathens *were ignorant of the true God;" my Meaning, which is perfectly consistent, is this. It is plain, that they may believe in* a God, *who are ignorant of* the true God, *as was the Case of the* Heathens. *All that is necessary for me to know, in order to give a firm Assent to a Revelation, is, to be convinc'd that the Revelation comes from one, who neither can be deceiv'd himself, nor will deceive me; for, otherwise, how can I give a firm Assent to any thing upon his Testimony, if either He himself may be mistaken, or He be willing to misguide me? But more than this is not necessary, in order to the Belief of a Revelation. And so far the* Heathens *might and did know without the help of Revelation, by the Light of Nature only, tho' at the same time they were ignorant of the true God. For tho' they believ'd in a wise, powerful, and good Governor of the World, in consequence of which they must believe, that his Wisdom could not be deceiv'd, and that his Goodness would not suffer him to deceive; and tho' all this was* a true Notion of God, *yet it was* not a Notion of the true God, *because they tack'd to it one or both of these Notions, "That he was the Soul of the World;" and, "That he was the supreme of their* Heathen *Deities;" both which, being equally* false, *could be no parts of the Notion of the* true God. *If then this wise and good Governor of the World, in whom they before believ'd without a Revelation, thought fit to give proper Credentials to any Missionaries, as coming from him, by whom they were inform'd, that this Governor of the World was the* supreme *God (contrary to what* PLATO *taught,) and that he was the* only *God (contrary to what was taught by the* PLATONISTS *and* STOICKS,*) and that he was the* Creator of the World, not *the* Soul *of it (contrary to what was taught by the* PLATONISTS, PYTHAG-

OREANS, *and* STOICKS;*) and if these Missionaries should likewise inform them, that Religion was not a merely Civil and* Political Institution *(as* ARISTOTLE *made it;) would not they, in Reason and Duty, be bound to believe all this, and to practice accordingly? Yes undoubtedly. And thus both parts of my Assertion are very consistent.*

I know not, whether it be worth while to take notice here of a Passage in Page 12*th of the* Introduction,[6] *where I say,* "*That the* Canaanites, *among whom the Patriarchs sojourn'd 'till their Descent into* Aegypt, *were all of them Idolatrous Nations;" I do not mean, that* all *the* Canaanites *were then Idolaters, but only* all the *Canaanites,* among whom the Patriarchs sojourn'd; *because it is certain, that* Melchizedek, *and probably his People, were no Idolaters then; but then we have no Account that the Patriarchs ever sojourn'd in* Salem.

---

6. Maxwell refers to p. xii of his opening essay (p. 39 of this work).

NAMES OF SUBSCRIBERS

Those mark'd with * are for large
Paper.

A.

His Grace the A. Bp. of Ardmagh.
Sir Arthur Atcheson.
The Rev. Mr. Abbot.
Mr. John Abernethy.
Mr. Nathaniel Adams.
The Rev. Mr. John Addenbrooke.
The Rev. Mr. Alexander Alcock,
    Dean of Limerick.
Edmund Allen, *Esq;*
*Francis Allen, *Esq;*
*James Anderson, *Esq;*
John Arbuthnot, *M. D.*
Mr. Charles Arbuthnot.
Henry Arkwright, *Esq; Collector of*
    Dublin.
*Margeston Armar, *Esq;*
The Rev. Mr. Edward Arrowsmith.
*Benjamin Arthur, *Esq;*
Capt. Beaumont Astle.
*William Aston, *Esq;*
* *The Rev. Mr.* Walter Atkin, *Vicar-
    general of* Cloyne.
The Rev. Mr. John Thomas Atkin.
Mr. Henry Aubin.
Mr. Richard Auchmooty.
Capt. Sheffield Austen.
Nicholas Aylward, *Esq;*

B.

The Rt. Hon. the E. of Barkshire.
The Hon. William Brabazon, *Esq;*
The Hon. Mr. Justice Bernard.
Montague Bacon, *Esq;*
John Bailie, *Esq;*
William Baker, *Esq;*
Seignior Beneditti Baldassari.
* *The Rev. Dr.* Richard Baldwin,
    Provost of Dublin-College.
William Balfour, *Esq;*
Mr. Samuel Ballard.
Mr. Thomas Ballard.
Benjamin Barrington, *Esq;*
Mr. William Barwell.
Mr. Richard Baylis.
Capt. Philip Beard.
Lieut. Peter Beaver.
William Becket, *Esq;*
Mr. William Becket.
*Henry Bellingham, *Esq;*
The Rev. Mr. Edward Benson.
Mr. Bentham, *for 2 Books.*
* *The Rev. Dr.* Geo. Berkely, *Dean of*
    Derry.
William Berry, *Esq;*
Mr. David Bindon.
The Rev. Dr. Birch, *Chan. of*
    Worcester.
The Rev. Mr. George Black.
Robert Blackwood, *Esq;*

James Blackwood, *Esq;*
Francis Blake, *of the* Mid. Tem. *Esq;*
*Col. William Blakeny.
Mr. John Blackley.
The Rev. Mr. Francis Bland.
Arthur Blenerhasset, *Esq;*
The Rev. Mr. Richard Bolton.
Mr. Sam. Bonamy *Jun. of* Guernsey.
Edward Bond, *Esq;*
Mr. Arden Bonell.
Mr. John Bonvill.
The Rev. Mr. Peter Bonworth.
*The Rev. Mr. Booth.
Mr. John Boushman.
Mr. Bowles.
Mr. David Boyd.
Mr. Will. Boyle, *of* Cork, *Merchant.*
*The Rev. Mr. Alexander Bradford.
Mr. William Bradford.
Mr. Graham Bradford.
Mr. Rowland Bradstock.
Mr. Robert Bransby.
*The Rev. Mr. Jasper Brett,
    Chancellor of Connor.
The Rev. Mr. William Brett.
Edward Brice, *Esq;*
William Bromley, *of the* Middle
    Temple, *Esq;*
*The Rev. Mr. Brooke, *Fellow of*
    Brazen-nose-College, Oxford.
Mr. John Broughton.
Mr. John Brown.
Mr. Ulick Brown.
———— Brown, *Esq;*
Mr. Daniel Brown.
Mr. Ellis Brownsword.
Charles Brumstead, *Esq;*
Eustace Budgell, *of the* Middle
    Temple, *Esq;*
The Rev. Mr. Robert Bultfell.
*Mr. Josiah Bullock.
Mr. Burchett.

Thomas Burgh, *Esq;*
William Burgh, *Esq;*
*———— Burroughs, *Esq;*
Mrs. Jane Burton.
*Francis Burton, *Esq;*
The Rev. Mr. Butler.

C.

His Grace the A. Bp. of Canter.
*His Excellency the Ld. Carteret, *Lord
    Lieut. of* Ireland.
His Grace the A. Bp. of Cashel, *for* 4.
The Rt. Rev. the Ld. Bp. of* Clogher.
*The Right Hon. Thomas
    Clutterbuck, *Esq;* 4 *Books.*
*The Rt. Hon. Marma. Coghill, *Esq;*
*The Hon. John Chichester, *Esq;*
*The Hon. Mr. Justice Caulfield.
Mr. Andrew Caldwell.
Stratford Canning, *of the* Middle
    Temple, *Esq;*
*The Rev. Mr. Robert Carlton, *Dean
    of* Cork.
*Henry Cartwright, *Esq; one of the
    Commissi. of the* Victualling
    Office.
Rev. Mr. Cartwright, *Fell.* Dub. Coll.
Mr. John Carty.
Francis Cashell, *Esq;*
Mr. John Caswell *of* London, *Merch.*
*Mr. Patrick Cassedy.
*Mr. Thomas Causlon.
Mr. Samuel Chandler.
Bejamin Chapman, *Esq;*
Capt. John Charlton.
Capt. Philip Chenevex.
Mr. Chester.
Mr. William Cheselden.
Mr. Richard Choppin.
Thomas Christmass, *Esq;*
*The Rev. Dr. Samuel Clark, *Rector of*
    St. James's.

Mr. Darby Clark.

Mr. Francis Clay.

* *The Rev. Dr.* Clayton, *Fellow of* Dublin College.

*Theophilus Clements, *Esq;*

Mr. Clements.

The Rev. Mr. Samuel Close.

The Rev. Dr. Cobden.

*William Cockburn, *M. D.*

David Cockburn, *M. D.*

John Coddington, *Esq;*

Henry Coddington, *Esq;*

Mr. Dixey Coddington.

Mrs. Mary Coghill.

*James Coghill, *L. L. D.*

Thomas Coke, *Esq;*

Mr. Thomas Colborne.

Mr. Colebatch.

Richard Colley, *Esq;*

*Anthony Collins, *Esq;*

Mr. Alexander Colvil.

The Rev. Mr. Conybeare, *Fellow of* Exeter College.

*Williams Conyngham, *Esq;*

Capt. Henry Conyngham.

Mr. Richard Conyngham.

Mr. Daniel Conyngham.

*Edward Cooke, *Esq;*

* *Mr.* Thomas Cooke.

The Rev. Mr. Thomas Cooke.

Mr. Peter Cooke.

The Rev. Mr. Thomas Cooper.

The Rev. Dr. Chidley Coote.

The Rev. Mr. Richard Corbet.

Mr. Thomas Corbet.

* *Mr.* Richard Cosins.

Rev. Mr. Cotterel, *Dean of* Raphoe.

Major John Cotterel.

Mr. Courthope.

Joshua Cox, *Esq; for* 2 *Books.*

*Richard Cox, *Esq;*

Mr. John Cox.

* *Brigadier* Creighton.

* *Mr.* Joseph Creswick.

Mr. James Croft.

Mr. Edward Crowe.

The Rev. Mr. William Crowe.

John Cuffe, *Esq;*

Maurice Cuffe, *Esq;*

Capt. Cumberland.

The Rev. Mr. James Cunningham.

George Cunningham, *Esq;*

Mr. Daniel Cunningham.

William Curtis, *Esq;*

Mr. William Curtis.

Mr. John Curtis.

Mr. Christopher Cusack.

Mr. Thomas Cutbert.

Mr. Nathaniel Cutler.

D.

His Grace the A. Bp. of Dublin.

* *The Rt. Rev. the Lord Bp. of* Derry, *for* 2 *Books.*

The Rt. Rev. the Lord Bp. of Down.

* *The Rt. Rev. the Ld. Bp. of* Dromore.

* *Sir* Francis-Henry Drake.

Mary *Lady* Dunne.

* *Mr.* Isaac Dalton.

Mr. Thomas Dance.

The Rev. Mr. Richard Daniel, *Dean of* Ardmagh.

*Gebhard D'Antheny, *Esq; for* 2.

Mr. Ferdinando Davis.

Mr. Charles Davis.

Ephraim Dawson, *Esq;*

Thomas Dawson, *Esq;*

The Rev. Mr. Thomas Dawson.

The Rev. Caleb Debutz, *L. L. D.*

Edward Deering, *Esq;*

*Stephen Delacreuze, *Esq;*

*Charles Delafay, *Esq;*

The Rev. Dr. Delany, *Fellow of* Dublin-College.

Mr. Samuel Derham.

The Rev. Mr. Benjamin Digby.

Robert Dillon, *Esq;*

Mr. Henry Dixon.

Robert Dixon, *Esq;*

Arthur Dobbs, *Esq;*

The Rev. Mr. Dobbs, *Fellow of* Dublin-College.

Mr. John Dobyns.

Mr. Robert Donaldson.

The Rev. Dr. Richard Dongworth.

The Rev. Mr. Dean Dopping.

*John Dowdall, *of the* Middle Temple, *Esq;*

Edward Dowdall, *Esq;*

The Rev. Mr. Lancelot Dowdall.

Whitfield Doyne, *Esq;*

*Montague-Gerrard Drake, *Esq;*

Mr. Francis Drake.

The Rev. Dr. Edward Drury.

Lieut. James Drysdale.

The Rev. Dr. Pascal Ducasse, *Dean of* Ferns.

Jeremiah Dummer, *Esq;*

Jeremiah Dunavan, *Esq;*

Mr. James Duncan.

The Rev. Mr. Hancock Dunbar.

The Rev. Mr. John Dunlap.

Mr. Samuel Dunlap.

John Dunne, *Esq;*

The Rev. Dr. Dunstar.

**Mr.* James Durand, *for* 4 *Books.*

**Mr.* Dynes.

E.

**Sir* Joseph Eyles.

**Sir* Laurence Esmond.

Sir Henry Echlin.

Mr. John Eastman.

The Rev. Mr. Robert Echlin.

Mr. John Eden.

Mr. William Edgell.

Mr. Thomas Edlin.

*Francis Edwards, *Esq;*

Richard Elliot, *Esq; Commissioner of the Excise.*

Mrs. Frances Empson.

Bury Erwin, *Esq;*

The Rev. Mr. Charles Este, *Student of* Christ-Church.

Eyre Evans, *Esq;*

Benjamin Everard, *Esq;*

Kingsmill Eyre, *Esq;*

F.

The Rt. Rev. the Ld. Bp. of Ferns.

**The Rt. Hon. the Lord* Ferrard.

The Rt. Hon. the Lord Fitz-Morris.

Mr. Thomas Fairchild.

**Mr.* Henry Faure, *of* Lond. *Merch.*

Mr. Francis Fayram.

Felix Feast, *Esq;*

The Rev. Mr. Philip Fernesly.

The Rev. Mr. Richard Fisher.

Michael Fleming, *Esq;*

Mr. Fletcher.

The Rev. Mr. Arthur Fletcher.

Warden Flood, *Esq;*

*Martin Folkes, *Esq;*

Mr. John Foord.

*Richard Forster, *Esq;*

Mr. John Forsyth.

James Forth, *Esq;*

**Mr.* Nathaniel France.

The Rev. Mr. Thomas Frazier.

**Mr.* Stephen Freeman.

The Rev. Mr. William Freeman.

**Mr.* Edmund French.

Nicholas-Ambrose French, *Esq;*

Mr. William French.

John Fuller, *Esq;*

Samuel Fuller.

G.

*The Hon. Mr. Justice Gore,
  for 2.

*Sir Ralph Gore.

Arthur Gahegan, Esq; for 5 Books.

The Rev. Mr. Gale.

*Luke Gardiner, Esq;

The Rev. Mr. Nicholas Garnett.

Mr. John Garnett.

The Rev. Mr. Garwood.

Mr. William Gavan.

The Rev. Mr. John Giffard.

The Rev. Dr. Gilbert, Vice-Provost
  of Dublin-College.

Mr. Henry Gill.

Mr. Thomas Gladstanes.

Mr. Thomas Glen.

Philip Glover, Esq;

Mr. John Glover.

The Rev. Mr. Goolat.

Mr. Hugh Gordon.

Mr. John Gore.

Mr. Robert Gosling.

*Mr. Nathaniel Gould, of London,
  Merchant.

The Rev. Mr. John Graham.

Mr. George Graham.

*Mr. Hugh Granger.

——— Granger, Esq;

James Gratton, M. D.

The Rev. Mr. Robert Gratton.

Mr. William Graves, of Drogheda,
  Merchant.

Mr. William Green, of the Post-
  Office, for 2 Books.

Mr. William Green, Surgeon.

Mr. Thomas Green.

The Rev. Mr. Benjamin Gregory.

Mr. John Gregory, for 2 Books.

Mr. John Griffitt, for 2 Books.

Mr. William Grigson.

Mr. Groenewege.

Mr. Nicholas Groubere.

Mr. Fletcher Gyles.

H.

The Rt. Hon. the Ld. Vis. Hatton.

*The Rt. Hon. the Ld. C. B. Hale.

Mr. Samuel Haliday.

Mr. John Hall.

The Rev. Dr. Hall.

Mr. Hannibal Hall.

Edward Hamage, Esq;

Mr. Henry Hamage.

Mr. Alexander Hamilton.

*John Hamilton, Esq;

The Rev. Mr. John Hamilton.

The Rev. Mr. Hamilton, Arch-Deacon
  of Ardmagh.

Mr. William Hamilton.

Anthony Hammond, Esq;

Mr. James Haning.

*Mr. Nicholas Hansard.

The Rev. Mr. Ralph Hansard.

Mr. John Hara.

Ambrose Harding, Esq;

The Rev. Mr. John Hare.

Mr. Harper.

Mr. Samuel Harper.

Mr. John Harris.

Nicholas Harris, of the Inner-
  Temple, Esq;

The Rev. Mr. Harrison.

William Harrison, Esq; Commissioner
  of the Revenue in Ireland.

*Francis Harrison, Esq;

Marsh Harrison, Esq;

*The Rev. Mr. Henry Harrison.

The Rev. Mr. Hartson.

*Pryce Harstonge, Esq;

Mr. John Hasty.

The Rev. Mr. William Hatsell.

Mr. Francis Hauksbee.

John Hawkshaw, L. L. D.

The Rev. Mr. Heald, *Fellow of St.*
John'*s* Cambridge, *and Curate of*
St. George'*s,* Southwark.
*Mr. Paul Heeger.
*Hugh Henry *Esq;*
Mr. Henry.
The Rev. Mr. Henry Herbert.
The Rev. Mr. John Herbert.
Mr. Philip-Parry Hetherington.
**Mr.* Richard Hewerdine.
Mr. Robert Higinbothom.
Mr. Rowley Hill.
Major Edward Hill.
*Henry Hoare, *Esq;*
* *The Rev. Mr.* Samuel Holt.
**Mr.* Christopher Hopkins.
The Rev. Mr. Richard Hopkins.
Mr. John Horan.
James Horn, *Esq;*
The Rev. Dr. Howard, *Dean of*
Ardagh.
Jabez Hughes, *Esq;*
Mr. Hughes, *of* Wadham-College.
The Rev. Mr. Bartholomew Hughes.
The Rev. Mr. Thomas Hunt.
Miler Hussey, *Esq;*
Mr. Hans Hutcheson.
The Rev. Mr. John Hutchinson, 2.
The Rev. Mr. Samuel Hutchinson.
The Rev. Mr. Charles Huxley, *Fellow*
of Brazen-nose.
**Mr.* Thomas Hyam.

I.

Thomas Jacomb, *Esq;*
The Rev. Dr. Jenkins.
Mr. Thomas Ingram.
Thomas Jobber, *Esq;*
Mr. Serjeant Jocelyn.
Robert Johnson, *Esq;*
George Johnston, *Esq;*
Mr. Hugh Johnston.

The Rev. Mr. Thomas Johnston.
The Rev. Mr. Jones, *Fellow of* Baliol-
College.
Mr. Lewis Jones.
Roger Jones, *Esq;*
Valentine Jones, *Esq;*
The Rev. Mr. Walter Jones.
Mr. William Jones.
Mr. Matthew Jones.
Mr. Talbot Jones.
James Jurin, *M. D. Secretary to the*
Royal-Society.

K.

The Rt. Rev. the Lord Bp. of Kilmore.
* *The Rt. Rev. the Lord Bp. of* Killala.
* *The Rt. Rev. the Ld. Bp. of* Killaloo.
Mr. Nathaniel Kane.
The Rev. Dr. Kearny.
Col. Maurice Keatinge.
Maurice Keatinge, *Jun. Esq;*
William Keatinge, *Esq;*
Mr. Samuel Keeling.
Benjamin Keene, *Esq; Consul at*
Madrid.
John Kelly *Esq;*
The Rev. Mr. Daniel Kemble.
Mr. Robert Kendal.
John Kennedy, *M. D.*
John Ker, *Esq;*
Col. Peter Ker.
*Abel Kettleby, *Esq;*
Mr. Benjamin King.
The Rev. Mr. Oliver King.
The Rev. Mr. James King.
The Rev. Mr. Thomas Kinnersly.
Mr. James Kirkpatrick.
Mr. James Knapton.
Mrs. Anne Knight.
Mr. William Knight.
The Rev. Mr. Knipe.
Mr. Ralph Knox, *of* London, *Merch.*

L.

*The Rt. Rev. the Lord Bp. of London.

Sir Richard Levinge.

Montague Lambert, Esq;

Mr. James Lancashire.

The Rev. Mr. Vere-Essex Lanergan.

The Rev. Mr. La Placette.

The Rev. Mr. Leche, Fellow of Brazen-nose.

——— Lee, of the Mid. Tem. Esq;

Thomas Le Hunt, Esq;

Mr. Leigh, Fellow-commoner of Wadham-College, Oxford.

*The Rev. Mr. Theophilus Leigh, Head of Baliol-College.

Mr. John Leland.

Mr. John Lennox.

Capt. Edmund Lesly.

The Rev. Mr. Lewis, Arch-Deacon of Kells.

The Rev. Mr. William Lewes.

Mr. Thomas Lewes.

Mr. Lindsay.

Mr. William Lingen.

The Rev. Mr. Richard Lisset.

Mr. John Lisset.

Mr. William Livingstone.

The Rev. Dr. Anthony Locay.

Mr. Christopher Lock.

The Rev. Dr. Edward Lovell.

Robert Lowry, Esq;

The Rev. Mr. Richard Lucas.

Mr. Cornelius Lyde.

The Rev. Mr. Roger Lynden.

The Rev. Mr. Patrick Lyon.

*Colley Lyons, of River-Lyons Esq;

Capt. John Lyons.

M.

*The Rt. Hon. the E. of Meath.

*The Rt. Hon. the Ld. Mountjoy.

*The Rt. Rev. the Ld Bp. of Meath.

*The Hon. Mr. Justice Maccartney.

The Hon. Edward Moore, Esq;

The Rev. Mr. John Mac Arthur.

Mr. Alexander Mac Aulay.

George Maccartney, Esq;

Mr. Isaac Macartney of Belfast, Mer.

Major John Maccollum.

*Mr. Richard Macguire.

Mr. Archibald Maclane.

James Macmanus, Esq;

Mr. Bartholomew Macneighten.

Mr. Edmund Macneighten.

Mr. Archibald Macneile.

The Rev. Mr. John Maddin.

Mr. John Mairs.

Mr. William Maple.

Thomas Marley, Esq; Sollicitor-general of Ireland.

The Rev. Mr. George Marley.

The Rev. Mr. Able Marmyon.

*Jeremiah Marsh, D. D. Dean of Kilmore.

*John Marsh, Esq; Recorder of Rochester.

*Robert Marshall, Esq; Recorder of Clonmell.

George Martin, M. D.

Mr. John Martin.

Mr. Adam Martin.

Mr. Enoch Mason.

Mr. John Mason.

The Rev. Mr. Charles Massy.

The Rev. Mr. Thomas Mathers.

Mr. Edward Matthews.

The Rev. Dr. Mawl, Dean of Cloyne.

Colin Maxwell, M. D.

*Henry Maxwell, Esq;

*Hugh Maxwell, Esq;

John Maxwell, Esq;

*Mr. John Maxwell.

The Rev. Dr. Robert Maxwell, *of*
  Fellows hall, *for* 8 *Books.*
The Rev. Dr. Rob. Maxwell, *of*
  Graies.
Robert Maxwell, *Esq;*
Capt. Robert Maxwell.
Mr. Nathaniel May.
*William Maynard, *Esq; Collector of*
  Cork.
*Edward Maynard, *Esq;*
The Rev. Mr. Mears.
Mr. Roger Medcalf.
Thomas Medlicott, *Esq;*
  Comissioner of the Revenue in
  Ireland.
The Rev. Mr. Medlicott.
**Mr.* Charles Mein.
*Thomas Meredith, *Esq;*
Mr. William Meredith.
Mr. Jean-Baptist Meulenaer.
Mr. Samuel Mills.
Charles Milne, *Esq;*
Pooley Molyneux, *Esq;*
William Monsell, *Esq;*
*Alexander Montgomery, *Esq;*
William Montgomery, *Esq;*
Charles Moore, *of the* Middle-
  Temple, *Esq;*
Mr. John Moore.
*William Moore, *Esq; Commissary-*
  general of Ireland.
The Rev. Mr. John Morgan.
Mr. Richard Morgan.
Richard Morley, *of* Gray's-Inn, *Esq;*
Mr. Thomas Mosely.
Mr. John Murry *of* Chester, *Merch.*

N.
*Sir Isaac Newton.
The Rev. Mr. Arthur Nevin.
Mr. Thomas Nevin.
Brabazon Newcomen, *Esq;*

Mr. Newton.
The Rev. Mr. Nicholson.
Mr. John Noon.
Mr. Robert Norman.
Mr. William Norman.
Mr. Richard Norris.
The Rev. Mr. Bernard Northcote.
Mr. Richard Nuttall.

O.
*Sir John Osborne.
**Mrs.* Susannah OBryen
*George Ogle, *Esq;*
*Charles O Hara, *Esq;*
The Rev. Mr. Felix Oneile.
*Arthur Onslow, *Esq;*
*Richard Ord, *Esq;*
Mr. John Orr.
Mr. John Osborne.
Mr. Thomas Osborne.
Mr. Osborne *of* Eaton.
Mr. Henry Overton.
The Rev. Mr. John Owen.

P.
**The Rt. Hon. the E. of* Pembroke.
**The Rt. Hon.* Benja. Parry, *Esq;*
The Hon. Mr. Baron Pocklington.
Sir Charles Potts.
*Sir Henry Piers.
Mr. Thomas Page.
Laurence Paine, *Esq;*
The Rev. Mr. William Paine.
Mr. Samuel Palmer.
Mrs. Mary Parker.
Mr. James Parker, *Fellow of* Oriel
  and Brazen-nose Colleges.
Mr. Richard Parker.
Robert Parkinson, *Esq;*
*Robert Paul, *Esq;*
Edward Palwet, *Esq;*
The Rev. Mr. Francis Peck.

Mr. William Peers.
Mrs. Pendarvis.
Col. Matthew Pennyfather.
The Rev. Mr. Thomas Penwarne.
Mr. George Pepyard.
Mr. William Peters.
Mr. James Petit.
*Ambrose Philips, *Esq;*
Chichester Philips, *Esq;*
Thomas Philips, *Esq;*
The Rev. Mr. Marmaduke Philips.
Mr. David Philips.
Southwell Piggott, *Esq;*
The Rev. Mr. Pilkington.
**Mr.* Thomas Pocklington.
Col. Thomas Pollexsen.
The Rev. Mr. Edward Pordage.
Mr. John Porter.
Mr. Joseph Pote.
Mr. John Power.
*Benjamin Prat, *Esq;*
Col. John Preston.
Daniel Preverau, *Esq;*
Brigadier Nicholas Price.
*Cromwell Price, *Esq;*
William Price, *Esq;*
Mr. Thomas Prior.
Thomas Proby, *Esq; Surgeon-general of* Ireland.
George Purdon, *Esq;*
The Rev. Mr. Edward Purdon.
Mr. William Pyms.
The Rev. Mr. Cornelius Pyne.

Q.
The Rev. Mr. Questburn.

R.
* *The Rt. Hon. the Bp. of* Raphoe, *for 2 Books.*
Dorothy *Lady* Rawdon.
*Matthew Raper, *Esq; for 3 Books.*

The Rev. Mr. John Ratcliffe, *Fellow of* Pembroke-College, Oxford.
The Rev. Mr. Gersham Rawlins.
Mr. Edward Raymond.
James Reilly, *Esq;*
Mr. Reynolds, *for 3 Books.*
The Rev. Mr. Thomas Rice.
**Mr.* Thomas Richardson 7 *Books.*
*William Richardson, *Esq;*
Edward Richardson, *Esq;*
Mr. Robert Rigmaiden.
Mr. Patrick Riley.
The Rev. Mr. David Roberts.
Col. George Robinson.
Tancred Robinson, *M. D. Physician in Ordinary to his Majesty.*
The Rev. Mr. Rogers, *Fellow of* Dublin-College.
Mr. Rogers, *Commoner of* Wadham-College.
Woods Rogers, *Esq;*
*William Rogerson, *Esq; Attorney-general of* Ireland.
Edward Roome, *of* Lincoln's Inn, *Esq;*
Dr. William Rowen, *Fellow of* Dublin-College.
*Hercules Rowley, *Esq;*
The Rev. Dr. Rundle.

S.
* *The Rt. Rev. the Lord Bp. of* Salisbury.
* *The Rt. Hon. the Ld.* Southwell.
The Rt. Hon. Edw. Southwell, *Esq;*
* *The Rt. Hon.* Oliver St. George, *Esq;*
The Hon. Henry Southwell, *Esq;*
* *The Hon. Mrs.* Wargaretta Sabine.
* *The Lady* Stanley.
Sir George Savil.
Oliver St. John, *Esq;*

Mrs. Elizabeth St. John.
The Rev. Mr. St. Paul.
*John Sale, *Esq;*
Mrs. Judith Sambrooke.
Francis Savage, *Esq;*
Dr. Sayer.
The Rev. Mr. Sayer.
John Gasper Scheuchzer, *M. D.*
**Mr.* David Scott.
Mr. Hewit Scriven.
Mr. John Senex.
Capt. Shakleton.
Mr. Francis Shaw.
Mr. Hugh Shaw.
Mr. Thomas Shaw.
*Abraham Sherigly, *Esq;*
Mr. Edward Shewell.
Mr. John Shipton, *Surgeon.*
**Mr.* John Shipton, *for* 7 *Books.*
Thomas Shrewsbridge, *Esq; Consul at*
    Cyprus.
Stephen Sibthorp, *Esq;*
**Mr.* Isaac Sierra.
Mr. Henry Sisson.
The Rev. Dr. Skerret.
William Sloan, *Esq;*
The Rev. Mr. Archdeacon Smith.
The Rev. Dr. Smith.
Mr. Christopher Smith.
Mr. John Smith.
Mr. Patrick Smith, *of* Belfast, *Mer.*
**Mr.* Ralph Smith.
Mr. William Smith, *of* Amsterdam.
The Rev. Mr. William Smith.
William Smith, *M. D.*
Mr. Samuel Smyth.
Mr. Ralph Snow.
The Rev. Mr. Philip Speke, *Fellow of*
    Wadham College, Oxon.
The Rev. Mr. Soley.
*Edward Southwell, *Esq;*

The Rev. Mr. Thomas Squire.
Mrs. Anne Stafford.
Henry Stafford, *Esq; for* 2 *Books.*
Kennedy Stafford, *Esq;*
Mr. John Standish.
Mrs. Sarah Stephens.
Col. John Sterling.
* *The Rev. Mr.* Luke Sterling.
*James Stevenson, *Esq;*
The Rev. Dr. Archibald Stewart.
The Rev. Mr. Stewart, *Fellow of*
    Dublin-College.
Mr. James Stewart.
The Rev. Mr. Edward Stillingfleet.
Mr. John Stones.
Jonas Stowell, *Esq;*
Mr. George Strahan.
Mr. John Stratford.
*Mark Strother, *Esq; for* 2 *Books.*
*Samuel Stroud, *Esq;*
The Rev. Mr. Edward Synge.
The Rev. Mr. Nicholas Synge.

       T.

His Grace the A. Bp. of Tuam.
* *The Rt. Hon. the Ld.* Tyrawley.
* *The Rt. Hon.* Richard Tighe, *Esq;*
The Rt. Hon. Sir Thomas Taylor.
The Rt. Hon. James Tynte, *Esq;*
Charles Talbot, *Esq; Solicitor-general.*
Thomas Taylor, *Esq;*
The Rev. Mr. Archdeacon Taylor.
Mr. David Tew.
The Rev. Mr. Robert Thistlethwayte.
The Rev. Mr. Aaron Thompson.
William Thornton, *Esq;*
The Rev. Mr. John Throp. ·
Mr. Roger Throp.
*Thomas Tickell, *Esq;*
Mr. Samuel Tickner, *for* 2 *Books.*
**Mrs.* Tilier.

Mr. John Tod.
The Rev. Mr. William Tod.
Mr. John Tooker.
Blaney Townley, *Esq;*
Henry Townley, *Esq;*
Col. Thomas Townsend.
Frederick Trench, *Esq;*
Mrs. Mary Trenchard.
Thomas Trotter, *L. L. D.*
William Trumball, *Esq;*
Mr. John Tulidge.

U.

* The Rt. Hon. the Lady Grace
Vane.
Mr. John Vandeleur.
*Mr. Francis Vanhemer.
The Rev. Mr. John Veal.
Mr. John Verdon.
George-Venables Vernon, *Esq;*
William Vesey, *Esq;*
Mr. Philip Vincent.
*Col. John Upton.
The Rev. Mr. Samuel Usher.

W.

* The Rt. Hon. Thomas West, *Esq;*
Ld. Chancellor of Ireland.
The Rt. Hon. the Ld. Chief Justice
Whitshead.
The Rt. Hon. the Lord C. Justice
Wyndham.
* The Rt. Hon. Maj. General Wynne.
The Hon. Sir Charles Wager, *one of
the Commissioners of the
Admiralty.*
*Captain William Wade.
Mr. William Wahup.
Mrs. Sarah Wahup.
Mr. Henry Walker.
*Col. John Waller.

***Robert Waller, *Esq;*
Robert Waller, *Esq;*
Capt. George Walsh.
Capt. John Walsh.
The Rev. Mr. Thomas Walsh.
Philip Walsh, *Esq;*
*Mr. Jacob Walton.
***Richard Warburton, *Esq; for 6.*
The Rev. Mr. James Ward, *Dean of*
Cloyne.
Michael Ward, *Esq; for* 2 *Books.*
Nicholas Ward, *Esq;*
Henry Ware, *Esq;*
Samuel Waring, *Esq;*
Mr. Thomas Warner.
The Rev. Mr. Simon Warner.
Mr. John Warren.
Richard Wastfield, *Esq;*
John Webber, *Esq;*
The Rev. Mr. William Webster.
Paul Whichcote, *Esq;*
* The Rev. Mr. John Whitcombe,
Fellow of Dublin-College.
***John White, *Esq;*
Boyle White, *Esq;*
The Rev. Mr. William White.
*Mr. Conway Whithorne.
Mr. John Whitlock.
The Rev. Mr. Peter Wibrants.
The Rev. Mr. Wigget.
Mr. Wilford.
The Rev. Mr. George Wilkins.
The Rev. Mr. Charles Wilkinson.
*Mr. Roger Williams.
Hugh Willoughby, *Esq;*
***James Wills, *Esq;*
*Col. Thomas Wilson.
* The Rev. Mr. Thomas Wilson, *Dean
of* Baliol-College.
Thomas Wilson, *Esq;*
Ezekiel. Davys Wilson.

The Rev. Mr. William Wilson *of*
    Shinglis.
Joseph Wilson, *Esq;*
The Rev. Mr. Winter, *Dean of*
    Kildare.
Mr. George Woodcraft.
Mr. Thomas Woodward.
Mr. Thomas Worrall.
William Worth, *Esq;*
Mr. Bruen Worthington.
The Rev. Mr. Henry Wright.
Mr. Thomas Wyat.
The Rev. Mr. Wyat.
The Rev. Dr. Mossum Wye.
*Thomas Wylde, *Esq; Commissioner*
    of the Revenue in Ireland.
The Rev. Mr. John Wynne.

Y.
* *The Rt. Hon. Sir* Will. Yonge,
    one of the Lords of the
    Treasury.
The Rev. Mr. Francis Yarborough,
    Fellow of Brazen-nose-College.
The Rev. Mr. Young.

    NAMES omitted.
The Rev. Mr. Bennet.
The Rev. Mr. Benson.
Mr. John Brindley.
Mrs. Mary Brown.
The Rt. Rev. the Lord Bp. of
    Durham.
The Library of the Chapter of
    Durham.

TWO
Introductory ESSAYS

I. Concerning the CITY, or KINGDOM, of GOD in the Rational World, and the Defects in HEATHEN DEISM.

II. Concerning the Imperfectness of the HEATHEN MORALITY; from both which, the Usefulness of REVELATION may appear.

LONDON:

Printed in the YEAR, MDCCXXVII.

Of the City, or Kingdom, of God in the Rational World, and the Defects in Heathen Deism

"*Know thy-self*," was certainly the Wisest of the Sayings of the seven Wise-Men of *Greece;* that Knowledge being the greatest Wisdom, as being the only Method, by which we are enabled to *discharge* those *Duties* and *Obligations* we lie under, and to *obtain Happiness*.

Man con-
sider'd in his
various Capaci-
ties.

Man is consider'd, in a double Capacity, *Natural* and *Political*.

Man, in his natural Capacity, is compos'd of two Parts, *Body* and *Mind*.

His Body is consider'd, by the *Anatomist*, as it is an *Organiz'd* Body; and by the *Physician*, and *Surgeon*, as it is a Body *liable to Distempers, that may be prevented, or remedied*.

The *Natural Philosopher*, commonly so call'd, considers the *Nature* of the human *Mind*, and of its *Faculties;* of which the two Principal are the *Understanding* and the *Will*, the Object of the former being *Truth;* and of the latter, *Good*. *Logick* conducts our *Understanding* in the *Search* after, and *Delivery* of, *Truth*.[1] *Morality* and *Religion* conduct our *Will* in the Pursuit of *Good*.

Man *Political* is consider'd, as a *Member of Society*.

The *Societies* are various, of which a Man may at the same Time be

---

1. [Maxwell] "I take *Logick* here, not in the common restrain'd Sense, but so as to comprise all Arts, or *Methods of Reasoning,* such as the *Algebraical, Geometrical, Metaphysical,* &c."

25

a Member, who may, therefore, be considered in as many various *Political* Lights.

Oeconomics regulate his Conduct, as Member of a *Family;* the *Laws of his Country,* as Member of the *Common-Wealth;* the *Laws of Nature,* as he is a Member of *Human Society;* and *Religion,* as he is a Member of a *holy Society of rational Agents, with God at their Head,* which constitute what we call *a Church.*

The Denyers of Providence, Atheists.

§II. Whoever *does not consider himself, as Member of a Society, at whose Head God is,* seems to me, to be truly an *Atheist.* For, whoever pretends to acknowledge a *God,* or universal Mind, considering him only *Naturally,* as the *Soul of the World,* and not *Politically,* as the supreme *Governor* thereof, and so not acknowledging a *Providence,* (a *particular* Providence, for, without that, a *general* Providence is an unintelligible Notion;) as he cannot prove the Being of such a God, so neither does the Acknowledging him influence our Conduct, or answer any valuable Purpose in Life. If God were the *Soul of the World,* and *not* its *supreme Governor,* it would be impossible for us to prove his *Being,* which we can discover, only from the Effects of his *Wisdom, Power,* and *Goodness,* in Forming and Governing the World. If you take away these, you may as well call him by the empty *Names* of *Chance,* or *Fate,* or *Nature,* or any Thing else, as well as *God:* Nor could the Acknowledgment of *such* a God influence our Conduct, any more than the Gods of *Epicurus* did his.

Future Rewards, and Punishments, prov'd.

§III. Now every *Wise, Good,* and *Powerful Governor,* must be a *Law-Giver;* for, without Laws, there is no Government: Such a Law-Giver must therefore have *promulg'd* his Laws, which God has done by *Reason* only, to those, to whom he has not afforded *Revelation;* and they can oblige *no farther,* than they have been *promulg'd.* Such a Law-Giver must also have fenc'd his Laws, with the *Sanction* of sufficient Rewards and Punishments, otherwise his Laws were *in vain;* but a *wise* Being does *nothing in vain.* Right Reason, from Experience, *pronounces,* "That the Rewards, and Punishments, *naturally* connected with the Observance, or Non-Observance, of the Laws of Nature, are not a *sufficient* Sanction." Human Wisdom has, therefore, every where guarded such of the Laws of Nature as could properly fall within their Cognizance, with the additional Sanction of *positive* Rewards, and Punishments; which, however, tho' they pretty well support Civil Society, are by no Means a sufficient Fence to the Law of Nature, and that upon several Accounts, 1. Many of the Laws of Nature are of such a Kind, as not properly to fall within the *Design* of human Laws, such as those, which enjoyn *Gratitude, Veracity,* in many Cases, *Temperance, Liberality, Courtesy,* &c. 2. Other Crimes, of which human Laws can take Notice, are sometimes committed so *secretly,* as to escape the Knowledge of those, who should put the Laws in Execution. 3. Others, sometimes, escape unpunish'd, for want of a *sufficient Power* to enforce the Laws; the Crimes of some being of such a Kind, as, in their own Nature, tend to enable the Criminal to *trample* upon the *Power* of the Laws, as the *unjust Acquisition of Arbitrary Power.* 4. Human Wisdom cannot *proportion* Punishments to Crimes, because that depends upon such a through Knowledge, both of Things and Circumstances, as none but God has; the *Pillory,* being a far greater Punishment to some, than the *Gallows* is to others. It is, therefore, incumbent upon the supreme Law-Giver, and Governor of the World, as he would effectually Vindicate the Honour of his Laws, and promote the publick Happiness, to let *no Crime* pass unpunish'd; but that a super-added Punishment should await Criminals after this Life, of what Kind soever these Punishments may be; whether such as are *naturally* Connected with evil Habits, and the evil Company of the Wicked, with one another, or by the farther Addition of Punishments *positively* inflicted, as the Nature of the Case and of Things requires. All Crimes fall properly within his Cognizance; no Privacy excludes him; no Power can resist him; no Prejudice can byass him; and he, and he *only,* knows how to proportion Punishments to the Crimes, and to the Nature of the Sufferer, and to what the greatest Good of the Whole requires, which seems to be the Measure of the Intenseness and Duration of Punishments.

If it be *objected,* "That future Rewards and Punishments, super-added to those of this Life, are not sufficient, if by the Word [*Sufficient*] be meant, what fully prevents the Transgression of the Law, in all the Members of the Society. But that if by [*Sufficient*] be meant, that which renders the Observance of the Law more eligible, than the Breach, to a well-inform'd Mind; the natural Consequences of Action, without any future Rewards, or Punishments, super-added, are, in this Sense, *Sufficient.*" I *answer,* "That, according to this Reasoning, all civil Sanctions, super-added to those of Nature, would be unnecessary, Minds well-inform'd not needing such Motives, and wicked Men, not being restrain'd by these Sanctions super-added to those of Nature; yet we see, that Civil Laws and Sanctions, are of great Use, notwithstanding the Appearance of this Reasoning to the contrary, many being mov'd by *both* Sanctions, that would not be mov'd by *one* only, as also others by the *treble* Sanction of natural Rewards and Punishments, positive Rewards and Punishments, inflicted by Men, and by the super-added Rewards and Punishments of another Life, who would not be influenc'd by the former *Two.*"

Without such a State of *future Rewards and Punishments,* no End can be assign'd, why *such* a Maker and Governor of the World should have placed us here, *such* as we are. Upon that Supposition, the *Shortness* and *Uncertainty* of human Life is unaccountable, and our *Reason* is often a disadvantage; the Bulk of Mankind losing Life, before they come to the full and true Exercise of their Reason; and when we do, to what purpose is this Mind possess'd of it, and of so many exalted and capacious Faculties, but, *"like the Soul of a Swine,"* (as our *Author* well observes,) *"instead of Salt to preserve the Body from Putrefaction";* [2] which, without that Reason, and those Faculties, it might support much longer than it does; several *Brutes,* without them, living longer than Man, and many *Vegetables,* without even a Sensitive Soul, much more without a Rational One, longer than either. Could *such* a Creator and Governor of the World, have given us *Reason* and *Reflexion,* with *unbounded Prospects* and Desires, with respect to Futurity and Eternity, with Anxieties and Doubts from thence arising innumerable, at the End of a short Farce to shut up the Scene in Death? A *Farce,* where the Wicked often thrive by their Vice, and the Good suffer, even on account of their Virtue. And

---

2. Cumberland, *A Treatise of the Laws of Nature* (1727), 1.29. For the source of Cumberland's analogy, see Cicero, *De Natura Deorum,* II.64; *De Finibus,* V.13.

Wisdom, united with Goodness, would rather have so ordered it, that we should neither have fear'd to die, nor desir'd to live beyond the Time appointed by Nature, as it is with the Beasts of the Field, often the Happier of the Two, if that were the Case, neither knowing, nor caring, whence they come, or whither they go. The many and grievous Calamities, (beyond what the Brutes are subject to,) lengthen'd out by the Memory of what is past, and the Fears of what is to come, can fairly be accounted for, if this Life be a State of Probation, and there be a Retribution afterwards, otherwise not, under the Conduct of a Wise and Good Governor of the World, and he would have made us satisfy'd with, and acquiesce under, our present Lot, whatever it were, like the Brute Creation, who when they suffer, do not redouble the Force of it by Reflexion; and if we were like them in the one Circumstance, why not in the other so? Why were we so made, that the Remembrance of certain past Actions creates in us Grief, Fear, and Horror, from which neither the Tyrant, nor the Politician, can free himself, if our Maker had not design'd us for *accountable* Creatures, in giving us such an Idea of *Guilt,* and Punishment, even for the most secret Crimes?

But I would not be mis-understood here, as if I *thought,* "That human Affairs were so disorderly, as not clearly to shew plain Marks of a governing Providence." To say, "That the present moral Appearances are *all* regular and good," is false. But, "That there is *no* moral Order visible in the Constitution of Nature," is equally false. The Truth seems this, "Moral Order is prevalent in Nature; Virtue is constituted, at present, the supreme Happiness, and the Virtuous generally have the happiest Share of Life." The few Disorders, which are exceptions to this general Proposition, are probably left to us as Evidences, or Arguments, for a future State. This Argument has been finely touch'd upon by Lord *Shaftsbury,* in his *Rhapsody,* thus. *"If Virtue be to it-self no small Reward, and Vice, in a great Measure, its own Punishment, we have a solid Ground to go upon. The plain Foundations of a distributive Justice, and due Order in this World, may lead us to conceive a further Building. We apprehend a larger Scheme, and easily resolve ourselves, why Things were not compleated in this State; but their Accomplishments reserv'd rather to some further Period. For, had the Good and Virtuous of Mankind been wholly prosperous*

in this Life; had Goodness never met with Opposition, nor Merit ever lain
under a Cloud; where had been the Trial, Victory, or Crown of Virtue?
Where had the Virtues had their Theater, or whence their Names? Where
had been Temperance, or Self-denial? Where Patience, Meekness, Magna-
nimity? Whence have these their Being? What Merit, except from Hardship?
What Virtue without a Conflict, and the Encounter of such Enemies as arise
both within, and from abroad?

"But *as many as are the Difficulties which Virtue has to encounter in this*
World, her Force is yet superior. Expos'd as she is here, she is not however
abandon'd, or left miserable. She has enough to raise her above Pity, tho' not
above our Wishes: And as happy as we see her here, we have room for further
Hopes in her behalf. Her present Portion is sufficient to shew Providence
already ingag'd on her side. And since there is such Provision for her here,
such Happiness, and such Advantages, even in this Life; how probable must
it appear, that this providential Care is yet extended further to a succeeding
Life and perfected Hereafter?" [3]

Antient, Current, and Famous, were the Notices in *Paganism*, touching *the Soul's Immortality, the Rewards and Punishments of another Life,*
touching *Hades, Elysium, the Isles of the Blessed, Orcus, Erebus, Tartarus,*
Mercury the Soul-Carrier, the Judges of Hell, which the *Stoicks* laugh'd
at, as *vulgar Errors,* because they were the Doctrines of *vulgar Paganism.*
But without them *Natural Religion* would be but *Matter of Ridicule.*
And, accordingly, it is an Article of natural Religion, which is antecedent
to any Institution of *Paganism, Judaism,* or *Christianity.* And the *Chris-*
tian Doctrine, touching the Rewards and Punishments of a future Life,
is so con-natural to the Mind of Man, (which hath the Conscience of
Good and Evil,) so agreeable to his Reason, and his Notions of a God
and Providence, that it has met with a general Reception, and Approbation. Agreeably to these Sentiments, the generality of *Pagan Religion-*
ists stiled the Soul *Divine, of Kin to the Gods, a Part and Particle of God,*
deducing it from Heaven, and reducing it thither again, worshipping
their *Heroes* and *Benefactors.* All which imply'd, that their Religion had

---

3. Shaftesbury, *The Moralists, a Philosophical Rhapsody* (1714), p. 275. The first
edition was published in 1709; Maxwell is using the second edition.

this generous Sentiment in it, which *Cicero* (*de Leg.* 2.) accounteth one of its Principles, *"That Virtue and Piety are Things which raise Men unto Heaven."*[4] The *Egyptians* are particularly fam'd for their Doctrine of *the Soul's Immortality,* and *the Rewards* of the Pious in another Life, as is most conspicuous, from a Funeral Rite of theirs recorded by *Porphyry,* and which deserveth to be everlastingly remember'd. When they embalm'd one of their Nobles, they took out the Belly, (which it is hence plain, they did not make a God of,) and put it into a Chest, which they held up to the Sun, one of the Embalmers making this Oration for the Dead Man. *Porphyry* de abst. L. 4. §. 10

"O LORD the Sun, and all ye Gods that give Life to Men, receive me, and transmit me into Consortship with the eternal Gods; for so long as I liv'd in the World, I piously worshipp'd the Gods, whom my Parents shewed me; those that generated my Body I always honoured; I neither kill'd any Man, nor defrauded any of what was committed to my Trust; nor have I done any Thing else of an atrocious Nature. If, in my Life-Time, I committed any Offence in Eating and Drinking what was not Lawful, the Offence was not done by my-self, but by those," pointing at, or shewing, the Chest, wherein the Belly was. And having so said, he threw it into the River. The Rest of the Body was embalm'd apart, as Pure.[5]

§IV. It is evident, that his making us capable of Happiness, was the Effect of his Goodness. It will therefore, from thence, and from the Immutability of his Nature, necessarily *follow,* "That he, who will'd us once into Being, will always Will the Continuance of our Being, and that too in a happy State, except where the Vindication of the Honour of his Laws, and the Common Good requires the contrary."

The Immortality of the Soul, agreeable to the Notions we naturally Form of the Deity.

§V. God, the Author of Nature, has imprinted Characters of his independent Power, Wisdom, Goodness, Providence, &c. upon his Works; he has given us Reason, by which we cannot but discover, if we attend, these his Attributes, and the Relation we bear to him. It is, there-

It is the Will of God, that we should practise Religion.

---

4. Cicero, *De Legibus,* II.19.
5. Porphyry, *De Abstinentia* (in *Select Works of Porphyry*), IV.10.

fore, his Will, that we should know, and, knowing, acknowledge these his Perfections, and the Relation HE and WE, his dependent Creatures, bear to one another; that is, that we should pursue and promote, to our Power, those beneficent Ends, which he had in creating us, and other Beings like our-selves, capable of Happiness, and give him the Honour due to him, that is, that we should practise Virtue and Religion, which are, therefore, his Laws to us.

A View of the *Pagan* System of the Rational World.

II. Let us, in the next Place, consider the several Parts of that Society of Rational Agents, of which God is at the Head; first, according to the Notion of the *Pagans,* and next, according to the Idea we have of it, by *Revelation,* and the Scriptures; for Truth, and Error, like all other Opposites, will best illustrate each other. For we can no otherwise come to the Knowledge of *our-selves,* in the *political* Sense, of our *Duty,* and the *Obligations* we lie under, without considering the *Relation* we stand in to the *Kingdom of God,* that great and holy Society, of which we are a Part; and to any other Society, if such there be, with which we may have to do; for it is impossible, to understand a Duty which is *Relative,* without first understanding the *Terms* of the Relation, (to make use of a *Logical* Expression.) To begin then with the *Pagan* System.

In which they consider'd, 1. One intellectual Head of the Universe.

The *Heathen* Philosophers, who acknowledg'd a Deity, acknowledg'd but *one single intellectual Head of the Universe,* (whom they call'd *Jupiter, Zeus, Baal,* &c.) and but *one Universe;* not such a One as the *Epicureans* imagin'd, who incoherently talk'd of infinite incoherent Worlds in infinite Space, but one total universal System, made up of several coherent subordinate Systems.

This one Universe is capable of being consider'd *Politically* and *Naturally:* Politically, the *Heathens* consider'd it as a *Universe of Rational Agents.*

Whom they suppos'd also the Soul of the World.

The Universe was *Politically* considered by the *Heathen Theologers;* for they suppos'd it to be a *Political System,* or *Monarchy,* having the foremention'd intellectual Head presiding in and over it. But they consider'd it also *Naturally,* supposing it to be an *Animated System,* or *Mundan Animal,* with the fore-mention'd intellectual Head, as the *Soul* thereof; yet so, as to be also the imperial Head of the Monarchy of the Universe.

§II. The *Heathen* Theologers, who do not acknowledge any such Society as the *Church of God,* represented the *Universe of Rational Agents,* as but *one Political System,* which is their prime fundamental Mistake. For, in this Scheme, *God* and the *Creature* are not sufficiently distinguish'd, but criminally confounded by deifying Creatures. The Kingdoms of *Good* and *Bad Angels* (or Demons) are not distinguish'd. The *Church* and the *World* are not distinguish'd, but confounded, or rather, the Church is shut out of Being, for which there is no Place in the *Heathen* System. *Heaven, Earth,* and *Hell,* are not duly distinguish'd, but confounded into one Political Society, under one Monarch; and they are suppos'd, as *friendly conspiring together,* whence they thought themselves secure from any Disaster after Death. And, because they thought themselves *by Nature,* the Citizens of God's Kingdom already, they could not be prevail'd with, to enter into the *real* Kingdom of God, when the Gospel was preach'd, which they oppos'd, as opposite to their System. Upon this fundamental Error, was grounded their whole Morality; and upon this Notion, *That they were Fellow-Citizens with the Gods,* their Practice was, doubtless, grounded of *making new Gods,* as it were by a right of Suffrage in Heaven it-self.

Representing the Universe of rational Agents as but one political System, which is a fundamental Mistake.

§III. Some *Christian* Writers have, in great Measure, adopted these Sentiments, not discerning the Difference between a *Holy Divine Republick,* and a *Heathen Mundan System,* heedlesly entertaining false Notions of the State of the Universe, and speaking the Language of *Heathen* Philosophers, which is irreconcileable with the *Jewish,* and *Christian* Religion.

The Worshippers of the true God indeed are, in a large Sense, Citizens of this lower World; they have a Duty to discharge as such, and must not fail of a dutiful and virtuous Correspondence with Nature, and common Providence; but the proper Design, and Effect of God's *reveal'd* Laws, was not to instate men Citizens of the World at large, nor was it the proper Law of that Estate of Life, nor was it the Law of Nature governing all Things as such, but it was the Law of that King, who governeth all Things as *Law-Giver of his Church.*

From which
our *Author* is
not free. The foregoing *Language of the* Heathen *Philosophers,* our *Author* usually speaketh, *"The most ample Society of all rational Agents, the City of God. The System of all rational Agents, or the whole natural City of God. The whole Aggregate of rational Beings, or the whole City, the Head whereof is God. The System of all rational Agents, the Kingdom of God. God, the Head and Father of all rational Beings, and other rational Agents, as his Sons. All men, altho' they are not under the same human imperial Power, yet are in the most ample City of God. In the City of God, or in the Universe, they are Subjects, that in a human City are Supreme. This Law of Nature, Care of the publick Good, is the natural Law, uniting all rational Beings. The Summary of the Laws of rational Nature, or of the City of God, which is the Aggregate of Mankind, subordinate to God the Rector, his City constituted by the Nature of it. The whole System of rational Beings, that City, the Head of which is God; the Members, all his Subjects."* [6] Such *Christian* Doctrines, in their Scheme, *agree* with the *Heathens,* in making the *Universe of rational Agents a Kingdom;* in making it *one* Kingdom; in making *common* Reason, which directeth to *common* Good, to be the *common* Law, which uniteth the Universe of rational Agents into one Kingdom; and in making *degenerate* Mankind to be *by Nature,* in the State of Society with God, the Citizens of the City of God, and the Subjects of his Kingdom. But in these Respects they *differ.* The *Heathens deify'd subordinate rational Agents,* which these *Christian* Divines do not; as the *Heathens* were much more Curious than the *Christians,* in *distinguishing several Orders* in their Kingdom of rational Beings, which they generally divided into 6 Classes.

6. Cumberland, *De Legibus Naturae* (1672), VII.9, p. 350; V.48, p. 296; V.49, p. 300; V.3, p. 190; I.14, p. 22; V.50, p. 303; IX.7, p. 388; II.8, p. 88; I.19, p. 28.

§IV. 1. The *supreme* God. 2. *Subordinate* Gods *Invisible.* 3. *Visible,* such as the 12 *Dij majorum Gentium,* namely, the 7 Planets, the 4 Elements, and the Earth, and such like. 4. *Demons.* 5. *Heroes,* or Souls of illustrious Men deify'd. 6. *Men.*

In a large Sense they call'd every Thing *Superior to Man,* a *God,* as in Ovid, "*Deus & melior Natura,*" are the same; and *Cicero argueth,* "*There is something Superior to Man, therefore there is a God.*"[7] But in their classing, or distinguishing, the System of rational Agents, they took the Word *God* in a restrain'd Sense.

The *Heathens* divided their system of rational Agents into 6 Classes, 1. The supreme God. 2. Subordinate Gods Invisible. 3. Visible. 4. Demons. 5. Heroes. 6. Men. The Word *God,* taken by the *Heathens* in a larger, and more refrained Sense.

Of the Order of *Demons.*

§V. These several Orders of rational Beings, the *Heroes* only excepted, belong to the original Constitution of the Universe, in the *Heathen* Scheme. The middle Order of *Demons* does not proceed from any fall of *Angels,* as *Revelation* informs us, but is suppos'd originally necessary to the Polity of the Universe. 1. That all the Regions of the Universe may be replenished with proper Animals, and rational Inhabitants. 2. That there may be due Order amongst rational Agents, which requires some First, some Last, and some Middle, according to the usual Method of Nature, which gradually ascends. 3. That the Gods might not be polluted, as it were, nor descend beneath their Majesty, in managing human Affairs by themselves. 4. For the Management of the Affairs of their Religion and Virtue, and rendering their Souls more Happy, presiding over Oracles, and managing the Affairs of Prophecy and Divination. Hence that Prayer in the Golden Verses of *Pythagoras,* as they are call'd.

Ζεῦ πάτερ, ἤ πολλῶν τε κακῶν λύσειας ἄπαντας
Ἤ πᾶσιν δ εἴξαις οἴῳ τῷ δαίμονι χρῶνται

"Jupiter *Father, either do thou thy-self loose all Men from those manifold Evils, or shew them all what Demon is to be made use of for that Purpose.*"[8] 5. For carrying on an Intercourse between Gods and Men, and to be

---

7. Ovid, *Metamorphoses,* I.21; Cicero, *De Natura Deorum,* II.16.
8. Maxwell quotes from Hierocles's *Golden Verses of Pythagoras,* lines 61–62. As with so many of Maxwell's citations, it is not clear which edition or collection the quotation comes from.

Mediators between them. 6. To manage (in subserviency to the Gods) Nature, Providence, and human Affairs.

The Universe of rational Agents, being thus united into one friendly and harmonious System, constitutes one Monarchy thereof, which is a fundamental *Pagan* Mistake.

Of Demons Good and Evil, and a Good and Evil Principle.

III. These *Demons*, the *Heathens* distributed into *Good* and *Evil*, (call'd *Vejoves*.) the former worshipp'd in hopes of their Help, the latter, lest they should Hurt. At the Head of the Good *Demons*, some set a *Good Principle*, at the Head of the Evil, an *Evil*. This Doctrine was embrac'd by the antient *Persians*, of which *Prideaux* giveth the following Account.

The Doctrine of the *Magi* reform'd by *Zoroastres*.

"Zoroastres *did not found a new Religion, but only took upon him to revive and reform an old one, that of the* Magians, *which had been, for many Ages past, the antient national Religion of the* Medes *as well as of the* Persians.———*The chief Reformation which he made in the* Magian *Religion, was in the first Principle of it. For, whereas before they held the Being of two first Causes, the First, Light, or the good God, who was the Author of all Good; and the other, Darkness, or the evil God, who was the Author of all Evil; and that of the Mixture of these two, as they were in a continual Struggle with each other, all Things were made; he introduc'd a Principle superior to them both, one supreme God, who created both Light and Darkness, and out of these two, according to the alone Pleasure of his own Will, made all Things else that are.———But to avoid making God the Author of Evil, his Doctrine was, that God originally and directly created only Light, or Good, and that Darkness, or Evil, follow'd it by Consequence, as the Shadow doth the Person; that Light, or Good, hath only a real Production from God, and the other afterwards resulted from it, as the Defect thereof.———That, in the Struggle between them, where the Angel of Light prevails, there the most is Good, and where the Angel of Darkness prevails, there the most is Evil: That this Struggle shall continue to the End of the World: That there shall be a general Resurrection, and a Day of Judgment, wherein just Retribution shall be rendered to all, according to their Works. After which the Angel of Darkness, and his Disciples, shall go into a World of their own, where they shall receive the Punishments of their evil Deeds. And the Angel of Light, and his Disciples, shall go into a World of their own, where they shall receive, in everlasting Light, the Reward due unto their good Deeds; and that after this they shall remain separated for ever, and Light, and Darkness, be no more annex'd together to all Eternity. And all this, the Remainder of that Sect, which is in* India *and* Persia, *do, without any variation, after so many Ages, still hold even to this Day,"*[9] as is affirm'd by *Ovington,* in his *Travels,* Lord in his *Discovery of the Sects of the* Banians, *and* Persees, and other Travellers.[10] The good Principle they call'd *Oromasdes,* the evil Principle, *Arimanius;* to both which *Zoroastres* taught them to Sacrifice, as *Plutarch* relates.[11] This Doctrine of two Principles was introduc'd, in order to account for the Evil observ'd in the World, and as it stood before *Zoroastres* reform'd it as above, was the most evident Ditheism, or acknowledgment of two supreme co-ordinate independent Deities, that ever was, or that can be imagin'd; in whom there was not so much as an Unity of Will, their Wills being always in direct Opposition to one another. Upon this Occasion, I cannot but take Notice of a remarkable Passage, in *A Discourse of the Grounds and Reasons of the* Christian Religion, P. 139, 140. *"It is to be observ'd, that the* Jews, *who were greatly departed from the* Law of Moses, *and especially from the Doctrine of the* Unity of God, *went* Idolaters *into Captivity; that they went into* Chaldea, *a Country, where* one God *had from remote Antiquity been believ'd and worshipp'd; that the religious Books of that Nation give a Relation of Matters from the Creation to the Time of* Abraham, *so little different from that contain'd in the* Pentateuch, *that one of the Accounts must, in all probability, be borrow'd from the other. That particular Care was taken among the* Chaldees, *to instruct the* Jewish *Youths of Quality and Parts, in the* Chaldean *Discipline and Learning; that the* Jews *came out at different Times from* Chaldea, *such firm Believers and Worshippers of* one God, *and that under the high Patronage and Protection of the Kings of* Chaldea, *ordaining such Belief and Worship among them, that they have continu'd*

A mistake of the Author of the *Grounds,* &c. corrected.

9. Prideaux, *The Old and New Testament Connected in the History of the Jews and Neighbouring Nations* (1717), pt. I, bk. IV, p. 169.

10. Ovington, *Voyages to Suratt in 1689* (1696); Lord, *A Display of Two Forraigne Sects in the East Indies* (1630).

11. Plutarch, *De Iside et Osiride* (in *Moralia*).

in that Belief and Worship ever since; that it seems more Natural for a Body
of Slaves and Captives to be form'd by their Masters and Conquerors, than
that the Conquerors should be form'd by them; and that the Slave should
rather receive Histories, and Antiquities, from the Master, than the Master
from the Slave; that, particularly, it seems improbable, that the Jews, *who*
chang'd their own idolatrous Notions and Practices for those of the Chaldeans, *should have so much Credit with the* Chaldeans, *as to introduce new*
History and Antiquities among them; and that it seems more probable, that
the Jews, *who became compleat Converts to the Notion of* one God, *receiv'd*
among the Chaldeans, *and were, in many Respects, form'd and disciplin'd*
by them, should receive their History and Antiquities from the Chaldeans."[12] Thus far the *Author of the Grounds,* &c. Let us now examine upon
what Authority he has advanc'd this Assertion. "That the *Chaldeans*
were, from remote Antiquity, Worshippers of *one God* only," he advances upon the Authorities of *Hyde,* in his Account of the Religion of
the antient *Persians;* of *Prideaux,* in his Connexion, Vol. 1. of *Lord,* in
his Account of the Religion of the *Persees;* of *Pocock,* in his Specimen
of the History of the *Arabians,* P. 148.[13]

Now all these Authors speak there only of the Religion of the *Per-*
sians, but not a Syllable of the Religion of the *Chaldeans,* or *Babylonians,*
concerning which is the present Question.

That those different Nations did not profess the same Religion, we
shall see presently, the *Persians* being *Magians,* and the *Chaldeans,* or
Babylonians, Sabians. But, if the *Babylonians,* to whom the *Jews* were
Captives, had been of the same Religion with the *Persians* of that Time,
I do not see how it would prove the *Babylonians,* Worshippers of *one*
God only, at that Time; for the *Persians* were then *Magians,* and *Ditheists;*
Zoroastres not having reform'd *Magianism* 'till after the *Babylonian* Cap-
tivity, as above.

12. Collins, *A Discourse of the Grounds and Reasons of the Christian Religion* (1724),
pp. 139, 140.

13. Hyde, *Historia religionis veterum Persorum* (1700); Prideaux, *Old and New Tes-*
tament; Lord, *A Display of Two Forraigne Sects in the East Indies* (1630), vol. I; Pocock,
Specimen Historiae Arabum (1650), p. 148.

Therefore it does not appear, that even the *Persians* believ'd in *one first Cause, and supreme Governor of the World,* 'till after the *Babylonian* Captivity; asserting two first and independent Principles, the one *Good,* and the other *Evil,* as above, 'till *Zoroastres* reform'd *Magianism,* and establish'd one first and good Principle, which, according to Dr. *Prideaux,* and Sir *Isaac Newton* was not 'till the Days of *Darius Hystaspes,* about 492 Years before *Christ.*[14] Now *Cyrus* put an End to the 70 Years Captivity of the *Jews,* in, or about, the Year before *Christ* 536, that is, 44 Years before the first Appearance of *Zoroastres* at the *Persian* Court.

Now it does not appear, that the *Babylonians* were ever of the *Magian* Sect; but that, from the earliest Times we have any Account of them, they were *Polytheists,* and *Idolaters;* and, more particularly, during the Time of the *Jewish* Captivity under them; how then could the *Jews* imbibe their Notion of the *Unity of God,* and *aversion to Idolatry,* from those who were themselves *Polytheists,* and *Idolaters?*

The *Chaldeans,* from among whom God call'd *Abraham,* were an Idolatrous Nation. *Joshua* (24. 2) thus accosteth the Children of *Israel,* "*Your Fathers dwelt on the other Side of the Flood* (*i.e.* of the River *Euphrates*) *in old Time, even* Terah, *the Father of* Abraham, *and the Father of* Nahor, *and they serv'd other Gods.*" The *Canaanites,* among whom the Patriarchs sojourn'd, 'till their Descent into *Egypt,* were all of them Idolatrous Nations, as were the *Egyptians,* to whom they were so long in Bondage. *Rachel* Stole the Gods of her Father *Laban* the *Syrian.* And, as for the *Babylonians* particularly, it is so far from being true, that the *Jews* ow'd their Belief of the *Unity of God,* and *Detestation of Images,* to them; that we have undoubted Proof, of their being an Idolatrous Nation at that Time. When the ten Tribes were carried away Captive by the King of *Assyria,* he planted *Samaria* with Colonies from his other Dominions. We are told (2 *Kings* 17. 28.) that these Colonies did not

---

14. [Maxwell cites Prideaux] "In the Passage above quoted, and in his Defence of it, in the Letters which pass'd between him and Mr. *Moyle,* in *Moyle's* works, Vol. 2d." See n. 9 (above) and his defense of his ideas in Moyle, *The Works of Walter Moyle* (1726), vol. II. The work by Newton is the unauthorized *Abregé de la Chronologie de M. le Chevalier Newton* (1725).

"*Fear the Lord,*" that is, *the one God;* but that, when they settled in *Samaria,* they set up and worshipp'd their own Idols. "*The Men of* Babylon *made* Succoth-Benoth, *the Men of* Cuth *made* Nergal, &c. 2 *Kings* 17. 30." which Images, we are told *v.* 41. that their Fathers before them had worshipp'd. We find likewise *Sennacherib,* King of *Assyria,* "*Worshipping in the House of* Nisroch, *his God,* 2 *Kings* 19. 37." We are likewise told by *Ezra,* (1. 7.) That "Cyrus *the King brought forth the Vessels of the House of the Lord, which* Nebuchadnezzar *had brought forth out of* Jerusalem, and had put them in the House of his *Gods.*" *Nebuchadnezzar,* King of *Babylon,* set up a Golden Image, in the Plain of *Dura,* to be worshipp'd by all his Subjects, under Pain of Death, for refusing to comply with which, *Shadrach, Meshach,* and *Abed-nego,* were cast into the Fiery Furnace, *Dan.* Chap. 3. which, I think, is a pretty plain Proof, that the *Jews* did not learn their *Aversion to Idolatry* from the *Babylonians,* their Masters. *Belshazzar,* the Son of *Nebuchadnezzar,* and his Princes, in a remarkable Feast, "*Drank Wine, and prais'd the Gods of Gold, and of Silver, of Brass, of Iron, of Wood, and of Stone,*" *Dan.* 5. 4. Upon which Occasion, *Daniel* delivers himself thus to *Belshazzar,* (23.) "*Thou hast prais'd the Gods of Silver, and Gold, of Brass, Iron, Wood, and Stone, which see not, nor hear, nor know; and the God in whose Hand thy Breath is, and whose are all thy Ways, hast thou not glorify'd.*" Great Marks of the *Babylonians* attachment to the Belief of the *Unity of God,* and *Aversion to Idolatry!* The Occasion also of *Daniel*'s being thrown into the Lyons Den, is another Proof of the like Kind. "Babylon *is fallen, is fallen, and all the graven Images of her Gods he hath broken unto the Ground.*" *Is.* 21. 9. "Bel *boweth down,* Nebo *stoopeth,* their Idols were upon the Beasts, and upon the Cattle," saith *Isaiah* (46. 1.) speaking of the Idols of *Babylon.* "Babylon *is taken,* Bell *is confounded,* Merodach *is broken in Pieces, her Idols are confounded, her Images are broken in Pieces.*" *Jer.* 50. 2. "*A Sword is upon the* Chaldeans, *saith the Lord, and upon the Inhabitants of* Babylon, *and upon her Princes, and upon her Wise-Men:—A Drought is upon her Waters, and they shall be dry'd up; for it is the Land of graven Images, and they are mad upon their Idols.*" *Jer.* 50. 35–38. "*I will do Judgment upon the graven Images of* Babylon." *Jer.* 51. 47. 52.

Thus, therefore, I think it *evident,* "That the *Author of the Grounds,*

&c. has not given a probable Account, how the *Jews* came out of the *Babylonian* Captivity, more firm Believers of the Unity of God, and more averse to Idolatry, than they were, when they went into Captivity; Dr. *Prideaux,* in his Connexion, seems to me, to have given a much more probable Solution of that Affair.[15]

As for what *the Author of the Grounds,* &c. affirms, (from *Berosus* in *Josephus,* against *Apion,* Book 1.) That *"the religious Books of the* Chaldeans *give a Relation of Matters* FROM THE CREATION, *to the Time of* Abraham, *so little different from that contain'd in the* Pentateuch, *that one of the Accounts must, in all probability, be borrowed from the other."*[16] *Josephus* is here quoted, for what he does not say, who expresses himself only thus. "Berosus, *after the Manner of the most antient Historians, treats of the* DELUGE, *and the Destruction of Mankind, just as* Moses *reports it; and of the* ARK *also; and how the first Father of our Race was preserv'd in it a-float upon the Mountains of* Armenia. *He runs thro' the Genealogy likewise of the Sons of* Noah, *their Names, and their Ages; and so carries on the Train, from* Noah *himself to* Nabulassar." Now an Account from the *Creation,* and from the *Deluge,* are two very different Things; nor do I see any Reason, which makes it probable, that *Moses* borrow'd his Account of the Origin of Things from the *Chaldeans,* as this *Author* would insinuate; *Moses* having had no intercourse, that we know of, with the *Chaldeans;* nor the *Jewish* Nation, indeed, 'till after the Building of *Solomon's* Temple, to which, both their Civil and Religious Establishments, and, consequently, their Accounts of Things, were long prior. The *Chaldean* Account, from the Flood downward, agreeing with the *Mosaick,* is, indeed, a very good Proof of the Truth of the *Chaldean* Accounts of those Affairs; but no Proof at all, that *Moses,* who had no intercourse with the *Chaldeans,* borrow'd his Accounts of the Creation and downwards, from them. Besides, *Josephus* affirms, "That most antient Historians agreed with the *Mosaick* Account of the *Deluge"*; which is no more a Proof, that *Moses* borrow'd his Account from the *Chaldeans,* than from the *Aegyptians,* or *Phoenicians,* with whom *Moses,* and the

15. Prideaux, *Old and New Testament.*
16. Collins, *A Discourse of the Grounds and Reasons.*

Jews, had then much more intercourse. All that we can fairly infer from the Passage quoted, I think, is this, "That most antient Historians agreeing with the *Mosaick* Account of the *Deluge,* shews, that the Tradition of that Affair was pretty General, and, consequently, that it is very probable, that it was true"; which is a great Confirmation of the Truth of the *Mosaick* Account of Things. But so much for this *Digression,* which I hope the Reader will pardon.

The *Egyptian Typhon.*
  The *Aegyptian Typhon* seems to have been of the same Stamp with the *Persian Arimanius.* And *Plutarch* says, That "Typhon *begat two Sons,* Hierosolymus, *and* Judaeus";[17] which is a small Sample of the Kindness the *Aegyptians* had for the *Hebrews:* He also Interprets the antient Stories of *Giants,* and *Titans,* concerning evil Demons; for he, with some other *Grecian* Philosophers, acknowledg'd such, which the *Stoicks,* as well as *Epicureans,* utterly deny'd, deriding the Punishments of another Life.

The Doctrine of Evil Demons, according to the *Heathens.*
  §II. *Plutarch* acknowledges *powerful and surly evil Demons,* who were the Authors of unlucky Days, who were worshipp'd by Beating, Lamentations, and Fasting, obscene Words, and contumelious Speeches, by which their Fury was appeas'd, contrary to the Nature of the good Demons.[18] These *Demons,* they conceiv'd to have Bodies, and some of them so gross, that they might be wounded with a Sword, whence *Spencer* explains a Magical Rite, mention'd *Ezek.* 33. 26. *Ye stand upon your Swords.*[19] For they had their Swords in readiness drawn and glittering, to keep the Ghosts and Demons in awe, whom they had conjur'd up. Which is not a more unphilosophical Notion, than that of several of the *Hebrew* Doctors, "*That the* Aerial *Demons, Eat, and Drink, Generate, and Die, as Men.*"[20] Nor than that *Conceit* of several of the Fathers, "That the Fall of Angels, was their falling in Love with Women, and having impure Commerce with them," whence the *Giants* were begotten, as some of them say; *Demons,* as others. Most of the Fathers *believ'd,*

---

17. Plutarch, *De Iside et Osiride* (in *Moralia*).
18. Plutarch, *De Defectu Oraculorum* (in *Moralia*).
19. Spencer, *De Legibus Hebraeorum Ritualibus* (1685), II.11.
20. Münster, *Biblia Hebraica* (1534–35), Leviticus 17.7n.

"That they had Bodies of a purer Kind." The *Heathens* generally *believ'd,* "That the *Demons* were pleas'd and allur'd by the Scent and Fumes of the Sacrifices they offer'd to them, and which they thought a Sort of Food to them"; whence it was customary for the Sacrificers, to pour the Blood upon the Ground, or into a Ditch, to entice the *Demons* to come, themselves Banquetting, about the Blood, upon the Sacrifice, that so they might gain the Friendship and Society of the *Demons,* and the Faculty of *Divination.* Whence the *Jews* were commanded to bring the Animals, which they sacrific'd, *unto the Door of the Tabernacle of the Congregation,* and their Blood was to be *sprinkled upon the Altar,* that the Children of *Israel* might *no more offer their Sacrifices to Devils,* Sehirim, *to hairy, or Goat-like Demons. Lev.* 17. 7.[21] This Kind of Idolatry, amongst others, the *Israelites* learn'd from the *Aegyptians,* who had a mighty Veneration for the Goat, which they religiously abstain'd from killing; and the *Mendesians* (a People of *Aegypt*) thought it an Honour to bear the Name of *Mendes,* a *Goat* in their Language, which they deify'd, and to which they built Temples.

§III. A SECOND Class of *Evil Demons,* or *Genij,* is acknowledg'd by some later *Heathen* Writers, (who, probably, took the Hint from the *Christians,* whose Doctrines were then well known;) these were said to be *vitious in their Nature,* and *to tempt Men to vice.* "*There are differences of Virtue and Vice among Demons, as among Men,*" says *Plutarch.*[22] The same Author, in the Life of *Galba,* relates the Speech of an Officer to his Soldiers, then about to revolt, wherein he represents the Fickleness of their Temper, *"That chang'd so often in so short a Time, not upon any rational Consideration, but by the impulse of some Demon, that hurried them from one Treason to another."* As the former Class of *Evil Demons* were suppos'd to bring upon Men *Natural Evils,* so the latter were suppos'd to tempt them to *Moral Evil.*

Now this Doctrine of the *Pagans,* concerning *Evil Demons,* must, of necessity, fall in, either with the *Manichean,* or with the *Christian,*

21. Ibid.
22. Plutarch, *De Iside et Osiride* (in *Moralia*).

Scheme; with the *Manichean,* if they were originally constituted Evil; with the *Christian,* if they became such by an abuse of their own Liberty.

Petavius saith, that several of the Fathers *suppose,* "That, when the World was made, the several Parts of it were committed to several Orders of Angels, that he who is now the *Devil,* was the Chief of the Terrestrial Order, and that his Sin was this, that, *He envy'd and could not brook the Dignity bestow'd upon Man.*"[23] Which Conceit of theirs, *That Envy was the Devil's Sin,* has been entertain'd by many.

Of Nemesis and the *Furies,* Ministers of divine Vengeance. §IV. A THIRD Class of *Evil Demons,* but not so reputed upon account of their vitious Nature, are the *Ministers of divine Vengeance,* call'd *Furies, Dirae, Erynnyes, Alastores, Dii impii, Hecate, Proserpina,* with *Nemesis* at their Head. So, according to some Expositors, the *Evil Angels,* mention'd *Psal.* 78. 49. were not *morally* Evil, but are denominated *Evil,* as being Angels of Punishment. Such were those, which *Atteius* invok'd by Name, when he curs'd *Crassus,* as *Plutarch* relates in his Life.[24] Some of these they suppos'd, to go about and punish enormous Crimes in this World, (which seem to be no more than the Stings of *Conscience,*) supposing it inconsistent with the Nature of the Gods, to be themselves the Punishers of wicked Men; but not so, to appoint these their Executioners upon such Occasions. For *Plutarch,* enquiring the Reason, why the *Romans* cloath'd their *Lares,* or domestick Gods, with Dog-Skins, makes this Conjecture. "*As* Chrysippus *supposeth, that certain evil Genij go about, which the Gods make use of, to do the Work of Executioners upon impious and unjust Men; so the Lares may be thought certain direful and punitive Genij.*" In this *Author's* Description of the Punishments of another Life, certain Lakes are said to be there, "*and certain Demons stand by, which plunge Souls in, and draw them out.*"[25] As in the famous Apologue of *Er* in *Plato,* there are "*Men ferine and of igneous Aspect,*" the Tormentors of Souls.[26] This Sort of *Evil Demons* is acknowledg'd by

---

23. Pétau (Petavius), *Opus de Theologicis Dogmatibus* (1644), vol. 3, III.2.8–9, 3.5.
24. Plutarch, *Vitae Parallelae* (*Parallel Lives*), XIV.6.
25. [Maxwell] "In his Treatise, *concerning such whom God is slow to punish.*" Maxwell refers to Plutarch's *De Sera Numinis Vindicta* (in *Moralia*).
26. Plato, *Republic,* X, 613e–621d.

Plato; and one of his School (who acknowledgeth no *Demons* morally Evil, yet) affirmeth, *"That there are Demons, which punish Souls; that the Sins of Men make the Gods their Enemies, not that the Gods are angry, but they separate them from the Gods, and joyn them to the punitive Demons; that the Souls of the Flagitious, after their departure from the Body, are tormented by them, and that there are, for separate Souls, expiatory Gods and Demons, who purge them from their Sins."* [27] It was this Sort of *Demons,* which the *Pagans* suppos'd maleficent *Magicians* to hold Correspondence with.

§V. The *Jews* are said by *Hulsius*[28] and others, to acknowledge Angels of 3 Classes, 1. *Separate Intelligences,* who appear not in a corporeal Form, nor can be comprehended by bodily Senses, but only by prophetick Vision, and incompass the Throne of the Divine Majesty, such as *Michael, Gabriel, Raphael.* 2. *Angels of Ministry,* created by God for the Welfare and Ministry of Men. 3. *Angels of Punishment,* or *Torment, Destruction, Mischief,* and *Death;* possessing the Sublunary and Infernal Mansions, whose Head is *Samael,* the Angel of Death, as the *Jews* call him, who is suppos'd to kill Mankind, and other Animals.[29] But these *Angels of Punishment,* are consider'd by the *Jews,* not as *Tormentors* only, but as *morally Evil,* and *Tempters* also of Mankind. For they affirm, "That Mankind Sin by the Seduction of the Serpent;[30] That *Samael* rode upon the Serpent, for bigness like a Camel, when he tempted *Eve;*[31] That *Satan* has his Name from שטה (*Satah,*) for he it is that *causeth Man to* DECLINE *from the Way of Truth."* *Asmodeus,* whom the *Jews* suppose the King of the Tempters, is by *Graves* suppos'd probably to be deriv'd from the *Persian* Word *Azmoud,* he *tempted,* or *solicited to Evil,* and therefore signifieth the *Tempters.*[32] *Moses* in *Deut.* 32. 17. saith of the *Israelites,* that they

Of the Sentiments of the Jews concerning evil Demons.

27. Sallust (the Platonist), *De Diis et Mundo,* chs. 12, 14, 19.

28. Hulsius, *Theologiae Judaicae* (1653), pt. 1, bk. 1, pp. 71, 72.

29. Lightfoot, *Horae Hebraicae et Talmudicae* (1664), p. 59, on 1 Corinthians 10.10.

30. Hulsius, *Theologiae Judaicae,* p. 169.

31. Maimonides, *Moreh Nevuchim,* pt. II, ch. 30.

32. Maxwell is probably referring to Greaves's *Anonymus Persa de Siglis Arabum & Persarum Astronomicis* (1648).

sacrific'd unto Devils, שדים (*Sheddim*,) which *Fagius* upon the Place saith, that the *Jews* suppose to be evil Spirits, that come out of the Waters, and are said to have their Name from שדד (*Shadad*) *Vastavit* because they *devastate* a good Mind with bad Opinions and Affections. There are several Passages cited by *Windet, Spencer,* and *Hoornbeck,* from the *Hebrew* Doctors, insinuating, or acknowledging, the *Fall of Angels;*[33] such as these of Rabbi *Eleazar, "The evil Angels were driven out of Heaven by a fiery Scepter.* Samael *and his Armies, God cast them out of Heaven.* Aza and Azael *were the two Angels that accus'd their Lord, and God cast them Head-long out of the Holy Place."* The Book *Zohar* says, *"God threw* Aza and Azael *down Head-long, bound and chain'd."* And, in another antient Book (of the Death of *Moses,*) it is said of them, *"Descending from Heaven, they corrupted their Way."* So in *Jonathan's* Targum, *Samcha, Zai,* and *Uziel,* (the same with *Aza,* and *Azael,*) are said to *have fallen from Heaven,* and are suppos'd to have begotten Giants. Also the *Rabbinical* Name of their Prince מרוד (*Marod*) signifieth an *Apostate,*[34] who is call'd by several other *Rabbinical* Names,[35] which likewise imply the *Fall of Angels,* such as, *"The Prince of* Gehennah, *the Head of the Satanae."* The common Name, among the *Jews* in our Saviour's Time, for the *Prince of the Devils,* was *Beelzebub,* or *Beelzebul,* which may signify *Lord of Matter,* that is, *the presidentiary Ruler of the material World;* for זבול (*Zebul*) is the same with κόπρος which, in the *Orphic* Verses, signifieth *the Matter;*

Ζεῦ κύδιϛε, μέγιϛε Θεῶν, εἰλύμενε κόπρῳ

Jupiter, most Illustrious, the greatest of the Gods, involv'd in Dung, or the Matter.

Empedocles's Doctrine of Demons, which fell from

As among the *Jewish* Doctors, so among the *Heathen* Philosophers, a fall of *Demons,* or *Angels* from Heaven, is, in some Measure, acknowledg'd; for some of them discourse of a Sort of *evil Genij, passively and*

33. Windet, *De Vita Functorum Statu* (1663), sect. 13; Spencer, *De Legibus Hebraeorum* (1686), bk. III, diss. 8, p. 457; Hoornbeck, *Pro Convincendis et Convertendis Judaeis Libri Octo* (1655), IV.2, p. 309.

34. Spencer, *De Legibus Hebraeorum,* p. 455.

35. Windet, *De Vita Functorum Statu,* p. 126.

penally such, which are called by *Plutarch, "The Demons of* Empedocles, *who are agitated by the Gods, and have fallen from Heaven,"*[36] *whom Empedocles* thus describes;

Αἰθέριον μὲν γὰρ σφε μένος πόντονδε διώκει,
Πόντος δ᾽ ἐς χθονὸς οὖδας ᾽απεπτυσε, γαῖα δ᾽ ἐς αὐγας
Ἡελίου φαέθοντος, ὁ δ᾽ αἰθέρος ἔμβαλε δίναις·
Ἄλλος δ᾽ ἐξ ἄλλου δέχεται, στυγέουσι δὲ πάντες

> *From the Etherial Region down*
> *Into the Sea in Rage they're thrown.*
> *The raging Sea rejects this Rout*
> *Unto the Land, and Spews them out.*
> *The Land unto the Sun them Hurls,*
> *The Sun into the Ether's Whirles.*
> *Thus they are toss'd (the Out-Law's Fate!)*
> *By universal Nature's Hate.*[37]

The Heaven-Fallen *Demons of* Empedocles, *pursu'd by the Vengeance of the Gods,* altho' they are an approach to the *Christian* Doctrine, cannot reasonably be thought a Tradition from the *Jews,* who themselves then talked not so clearly upon this Head. 1. This Doctrine of *Empedocles* greatly befriends the common *Hypothesis* of the *Lapse of Angels from Heaven,* which must be call'd the *Christian Hypothesis,* tho' it has been weakly oppos'd by some *Christian* Writers, who have asserted the *Evil Angels,* to be, originally, the Inhabitants of the Air and Earth, and never to have been in Heaven, and enjoy'd the Beatifick Vision there. For their height of Felicity might be so far from securing them from a Fall, that it might occasion it, thro' Pride, Self-Admiration, and Self-Love; and, in consequence, affecting a Dominion over Subjects withdrawn from the Subjection of God, agreeably to the Heads of Empire, which *Satan* usually setteth up in the World, that usually affect an unbounded Liberty. And that himself, in Consort with his Fellow-Rebels, should be

---

36. Plutarch, *De Vitando Aere Alieno* and *De Iside et Osiride* (both in *Moralia*).
37. Maxwell's source is not indicated; for a modern edition of the passage quoted, see Wright, *Empedocles: The Extant Fragments* (1981), pp. 138, 270–75.

like-minded, and therefore should chuse to make a total Revolt from God and their Duty, was not incompatible with their coelestial Condition; nor is it at all incredible, the like prodigiously-frantick Enormities being no Rarities amongst intelligent Agents. Wherefore the usual Doctrine is unexceptionable, which is clearly enough express'd in H. Scriptures, which represent the Holy Angels, as originally the Inhabitants of Heaven. *Matt.* 22. 30. *Luc.* 20. 36. *Heb.* 12. 22. And the laps'd Angels, originally, of the Number of the Holy Angels, 2 *Pet.* 2. 5. *Jud.* 6. 2. 2. The *Heathen* Doctrine of *Demons* befriends the *Christian Hypothesis* of a *Kingdom of evil Angels.* For the *Heathen Demonologists suppos'd,* "That the *Evil Demons* have an imperial Head over them." Therefore, in consistence with themselves, they ought to have *suppos'd,* "That there is a distinct Kingdom, or Polity, of *Evil Demons,*" as *Christianity* asserteth. But they have so qualify'd this Doctrine of *Evil Demons,* as to make it no Contradiction to their Doctrine of the Unity of the Monarchy of the Universe, or their *City of God;* for they were Gods themselves, and Part of the common Polity of their Gods, which is monstrously, both Absurd and Impious. For whoever has any Veneration for God, will not count it a small Matter, to *deify Evil Demons,* and to pay them religious Worship. Yet this Worship of *Demons* was the Religion of popular Societies amongst the *Heathens,* as *Plutarch* plainly acknowledges,[38] thereby giving a great Attestation to the Truth of *Christianity,* (which chargeth upon *Paganism,* the *Sacrificing unto, and having Fellowship with, Devils;*) and to the peculiar Excellency of the *Christian* Learning, which alone, to the Purpose, discovereth *Satan.* For both *Jews* and *Pagans* (notwithstanding their slender Notice of *Evil Angels*) are far from knowing him as they ought, and so far as is needful to the Purpose of Piety and Sanctity. 3. The *Heathen* Doctrine of *Demons* greatly befriends the *Christian,* by asserting and ascertaining (in Consort with it) the *Existence* of *Evil Demons.* They were assured of their Existence from their Operations and Effects; and, from this *Hypothesis, Plutarch* gives an Account of the Apparitions to *Brutus* and *Dio,* upon which, after his Manner, he reflects finely. *"If* Brutus *and* Dio," (saith he,) *"Philosophical*

---

38. Plutarch, *De Iside et Osiride* and *De Defectu Oraculorum* (both in *Moralia*).

Men, of great Strength of Mind, and not apt to fancy horrible Appearances, were put into such Commotion by Apparitions, that they solicitously related them to their Friends; perhaps we may be forc'd to embrace that (seemingly) most absurd Opinion of the Antients, That there are Evil and Envious Demons, that, envying good Men, and withstanding their Actions, raise Fears and Troubles to them, to shake and overthrow their Virtue; lest, if they should persist stedfast and uncorrupted in Good, they should, after their Decease, enjoy a better Condition than theirs." The Laws of the XII Tables, in condemning and punishing hurtful Magick, acknowledge the Being of *evil Demons.* And who can doubt, but that those Learned *Heathen* Philosophers were in the Right, who suppose the antick and barbarous Rites of their Religion, to be the Worship of powerful *evil Demons.* For the *Pagan* Religion is a Demonstration of the Being of *evil Demons,* because it cannot be suppos'd, that any Power, but a Diabolical, could have subjected the World, for so many Ages, to such an Institution as *Paganism* is. The *Heathens* justly argued for the Existence of *Aerial Demons,* in this Manner, "Would Nature, that has replenish'd all other Regions with Inhabitants, suffer the spacious Air to be an uninhabited Waste?" With whom, in this, both *Jewish* and *Christian* Divines agree, whence the Chief of them is call'd by the Apostle, *the Prince of the Power of the Air,* and the Rulers of his Empire are call'd Spiritual Wickedness (ὸν τοῖς ἐπουρανίοις) *in Heavenly,* or *Aerial, Places.* But yet these Aerial Demons are sometimes under penal Confinement in the Subterraneous Regions, as that Petition of theirs implies, *Luk.* 8. 31. *They besought him, that he would not command them to go out into the Deep,* or *Abyss,* the same with *the bottomless Pit,* mention'd *Rev.* 20. 3. where *Satan* was chain'd.

In this Doctrine then of *Evil Spirits, Pagans, Jews, Mahometans,* and *Christians,* agree, the common Sense of Mankind concurring with *Revelation.*

IV. The *Pagans agreed,* "That *Good Demons* are *Guardian-Genij,* which, tho' Servants to the supreme God, or subordinate Deities, are Patrons of particular Persons, Nations, or Societies; of Things, and of Places." So *Servius,* "The Genius, according to the Sense of the Antients, is the natural God of every Place, or Thing, or Person." And this was a common

Of *Genij,* or Guardian Angels.

antient Inscription, *"To* Jupiter *the Best and Greatest, and to the* Genius *of the Place."* The *Genius* of the *Roman* People, (distinct from the tutelar God of the City, whose Name was kept secret,) was call'd the *Publick Genius,* and is usual in antient Coins. So the *Trojan Palladium* was not *a Thing that fell from Heaven,* but a *Telesm,* or Image, made by a Philosopher and Astrologer, *under a most fortunate Horoscope,* and enclosing the *Genius,* or Fortune, of the City, by Virtue of Astrological Magick. So the *Lares* were look'd upon, as the proper *Guardian-Genij* of their Houses, whence they were call'd *Prestites,* and, as *Plutarch* tells us, cloath'd with Dog-Skins. Among the personal Guardian-Genij, that of the Prince was thought by far the most August, whence arose a Custom among the *Romans,* of swearing by *Caesar's Genius,* which if any did forswear by in a Suit, he was *Bastinadoed,* but Perjury, by the Name of God, was not punish'd, they supposing that God would sufficiently avenge the Abuse of his own Deity. It was a receiv'd *Opinion* "That every Nation had a Tutelar-Deity, with subordinate *Demons."* The *Nomes,* or Prefectures of *Aegypt,* had each their distinct God, whilst *Isis* and *Osiris* were worshipp'd over the Whole, see Sir *Is. Newton's* Chronology.[39]

With respect to this Doctrine, the *Heathens* were divided in their Sentiments, some allowing a *good-Genius,* only to every Man,[40] others a *good* and a *bad* to each,[41] which Doctrine *Mahomet* has adopted. Many *Christians,* especially they of the Church of *Rome,* have embrac'd the Doctrine of *good-Genij,* converting them into *Guardian-Angels.* The determining every Man's *Genius* at his Birth, those who gave into the *Astrological* Scheme, ascrib'd to the Stars, and to every Man's Horoscope at his Birth.

Geminos, Horoscope, varo Producis Genio.[42]

The Horoscope produceth Twins of diversity of Genius.

39. Newton, *Abregé de la Chronologie.*

40. Iamblichus, *De Mysteriis* (1678), p. 170; Plutarch, *De Stoicorum Repugnantiis* (in *Moralia*), p. 1051.

41. Plutarch, *De Tranquillitate Animi* (in *Moralia*), p. 474; Iamblichus, *De Mysteriis* (1678), p. 317.

42. Persius, *Satirae,* VI.18.

§II. This Doctrine of *Genij,* the *Heathens* ow'd to their Notion of the *Polity* of the Universe; every thing superior to Man, and subordinate to the supreme Deity, being with them a *Genius,* each other *Being,* nay, and *Mode* of Being, having their *Genius. Jupiter* was the President, or *Genius,* of *Heaven, Neptune* of the *Sea, Pluto* of the *Infernal Regions,* a Triumvirate. The *Planets* had each their *Genius,* the *Elements* theirs: *Nations, Societies,* and *individual Persons,* had theirs. *Venus* was *Goddess* of the *Passion* of *Love; Mars* and *Bellona* were *Patrons* of the *State* of *War; Janus* of *Peace; Terminus* of *Bounds; Mercury, Apollo,* and the *Muses,* of the *Professions* of *Eloquence, Poetry,* and several Parts of *Learning; Esculapius,* of *Physick; Vulcan,* of *Smiths;* and *Minerva,* of the *Faculty* of *Prudence.*

Heathenism, a Religion of Patron-Deities, and their Clients.

Hence it *appears,* "That the Religion of the *Heathens* is a *Religion of Patron-Deities and of their Clients, in subordination to the supreme God.*" Herein consisted their Polytheism: How much, in this respect, *Christian-Rome* has borrow'd from *Heathen-Rome,* is but too obvious; pursuant to which the *Romanists* pray to one *Saint* in *Child-Bed;* to another, in the *Tooth-Ach;* to a third, when they are Travelling by *Land;* to a fourth, by *Water:* as if the Providence of the one God, supreme over All, did not extend over *All,* and *equally* over All: as if he were not the *God,* both of *Land* and *Sea, Hills* and *Valleys;* and as if he had not appointed *one Mediator* and *Intercessor,* sufficient for *All;* who has requir'd these Things at their Hands?

With which the Church of *Rome* greatly Symbolizes.

The Word *Demon* is sometimes taken in a larger, sometimes in a stricter, Sense; sometimes as extensively as *God* in the largest Sense: So *Homer* calls his *Gods, Demons;* and the *Pagans* say of St. *Paul,* Act. 17. 18. *He seemeth to be a setter forth of strange Demons,* that is, *Gods.* Sometimes it is taken in a stricter Sense, for a class of Beings between *Gods* and *Heroes.* Thus, according to the *Heathens,* were all things full, not of *God,* but of *Gods;* and they were guilty of the Worship of *Demons,* in both Senses of the Word, from which neither the *Platonists,* nor *Pythagoreans,* were free; but were great Promoters of it.

Different Senses of the Word, *Demon.*

§III. The *Jews* fell into the *Heathen* Notion of the Government of the World, *believing,* "That their Nation had a *Guardian-Angel,* who could

The *Jewish* Notion of the

Government of
the Universe,
falls in with
that of the
Heathens, in
great Measure;

transact nothing without leave of the Divine Providence"; *supposing*, "That all other *Nations* were committed to the care of their *Angels*, who were to them as *Gods*"; *believing* also *"Bread,* the *Water,* the *Fire,* the *Hail,* the *Winds,* &c. had each their *Angel*-President over them." They *assign* "Seven *President-Angels* to the seven *Days* of the *Week,* twelve to the twelve *Months,* and four to the four *Seasons;*[43] 7 *Arch-Angels* to the 7 *Planets;*[44] every Nation, the *Israelites* excepted, being subject to its particular *Planet."*[45] Also, with allusion to the Government of the Nations by *Angels* in Stars and Constellations, and not by immediate Divine Providence, the *Jews,* in their Liturgy, give to God the Name of the *King of Kings,* that is, the King of those *Angelical Powers,* who rule over the Potentates of the Earth. They are also of *Opinion,* "That the Number of *Nations* and *Languages* upon Earth is 70, having 70 *President-Angels,* by whom the Division of Languages was made at *Babel."*[46] This their Opinion is visible in the *Septuagint*-Translation of *Deut.* 32. 8. *"When the most High divided the Nations, when he separated the Sons of* Adam, *he set the Bounds of the People, according to the Number"* [not of *the Children of* Israel, as the *Hebrew* hath it, but] *"of the Angels of God";* which they say are 70, and whom they call the *Sanhedrim above.*

As does that of
many *Christian*
Divines.

§IV. This Notion, which transforms the *Universe* into a *Paganlike Republick,* and the *holy Angels* into *Pagan Gods* and Demons, has been embrac'd by many of the *Christian* Fathers, modern Divines, and Philosophers; allowing, among other Parts of their Scheme, each of the heavenly Bodies their *Intelligence,* as they call it. Upon this Plan has *Idolatry* principally prevail'd, both among *Heathens* and *Christians:* Upon this Plan also, the *Devil,* with his Angels under him, was suppos'd by some to have been *President* of our *Earth,* and never to have been an Inhabitant above, the Disagreement of which with Scripture is above

---

43. Selden, *De Jure Naturali et Gentium* (1640), bk. IV, ch. 7.
44. Mede, on Zechariah 4.10, in *Diatribae. Discourses on Divers Texts of Scripture* (1642).
45. Tenison, *Of Idolatry* (1678), p. 106.
46. Ibid.

shewn. The above-mention'd Mistranslation of the *Septuagint* seems, to have been a leading Cause of Error, in this Point, to the Fathers, who generally did not understand *Hebrew,* but made use of that Translation. This Notion was at last enlarg'd by many, even to the Assigning a *Guardian-Angel* to every individual of Mankind, which is nothing but the *Heathen* Doctrine of *Demon-Genij* with a new Name, and must have given the *Heathens* a great Advantage against those *Christians,* when they charg'd the *Heathens* with the Worshipping of *many Gods* and of *Demons.*

§V. The Scriptures, indeed, do acknowledge the *holy Angels* as a sort of *Potentates superior to Man,* and as *occasionally subservient to the Divine Providence in the Government of the World;* but not as *sublunary Prefects of various Faculties, Offices, Places, Stations, and Persons, residing upon their several Charges.* A misunderstanding of *Dan.* 4. 17. *"This Matter"* (the Judgment upon *Nebuchadnezzar*) *"is by the Decree of the Watchers, and the Demand"* (or Ordinance) *"by the Word of the holy Ones,"* seems to have led many into various and gross Mistakes upon this Head. This Text seems to be rightly thus explain'd. *This Matter is by more than human Appointment, it is nothing less than the Decree of the most High.* For thus the Prophet, in his Interpretation of the Dream, interpreteth the Angels saying *v.* 24. *This is the Decree of the most High, which is come upon my Lord the King.* Therefore the Angels saying is a Mode of expressing the *Decree of the most High.* For the *Decree of the Watchers,* and the *Word of the holy Ones,* are not their own Decree and Word, but God's, whose Agents they are. This remarkable Scripture is, therefore, no Foundation for that *Jewish* Notion of God's consulting with his *Sanhedrim above,* or that the *President-Angels* of the *Babylonian* Monarchy decreed the Matter, at the Petition of the Tutelar-Angels of the several Provinces, who complain'd of *Nebuchadnezzar's* Tyranny; or that the greater Angels made this Decree, at the Request of the inferior Angels. But here is a clear express Testimony for the *Superintendence* of the Holy Angels, *in subordination to the divine Providence.* So the *Elect Angels* are consider'd by the Apostle, as the *Spectators of our Actions,* along with God and Christ, 1 Tim. 5. 21. *"I charge thee before God and the Lord Jesus, and the*

The Scripture-Notion of the Holy Angels, who have no Prefecture, nor Magistracy, in the Government of the World; nor are employ'd, as Guardian-Angels to particular Persons.

elect Angels." And, agreeably to the Name of *Watchers* in *Daniel,* we read, in the *Revelations,* of the "*7 Lamps of Fire burning before the Throne of God, which are the 7 Spirits of God*"; of "*seven Angels, which are and stand before the Throne*"; of "*the 7 Horns, and the 7 Eyes of the Lamb, which are the 7 Spirits of God, sent forth into all the Earth*";[47] so, in the Prophet *Zechariah,* (as Interpreters have observ'd,[48]) 7 Angels are represented by the Candlestick of 7 *Lamps,* which burn'd continually in the Temple; and those *seven Angels* (because appointed to exercise, both in Heaven and in this World, an inspection and superintendence over us and our Affairs) are styled "*the 7 Eyes of the Lord, which run to and fro, through the whole Earth.*" The Scripture, therefore, describeth the *Court of Heaven* conformably to the *Persian Court,*[49] where there were 7 *Princes, who saw the King's Face, and sat first in the Kingdom,* (to be Officers of the Presence, such as see the King's Face, denoteth the principal Persons at Court, *Jer.* 52. 25.) who are sometimes styled *the King's seven Coun-sellors.* And, because these 7 Angels in the *Court of Heaven* are plainly Analogical, or Correspondent, to the 7 Princes in the *Persian Court;* because we read of *Angelical chief Princes;*[50] therefore some of the Holy Angels are consider'd as a sort of *Heavenly Potentates,* agreeably to the Style of the New-Testament.

For, in the New-Testament, some of the Holy Angels are usually in-tituled *Authorities, Thrones, Dominions, Principalities,* and *Powers,*[51] with Christ, who created them, at their head; between which the Dif-ference is no greater than this, that the Apostle considers them, as the *several general Names and Notions of the most Eminent created Potentates in the Universe.* So the highest Rank of Potentates, in *Satan's* Kingdom, are call'd *Principalities* and *Powers.*[52] Wherefore it seems a great Mistake of many, to *suppose,* "That the Apostle maketh a distribution of the Holy Angels into four or five subordinate Ranks, Orders, and Classes, which

47. Revelations 1.4, 4.5, 5.6, 8.2.
48. Mede, on Zechariah 4.10, in *Diatribae.*
49. Esther 1.14; Ezra 7.14.
50. Daniel 10.13.
51. I Peter 3.22; Ephesians 1.21; Colossians 1.16.
52. Ephesians 6.13; Colossians 2.15.

are signify'd by so many Names," whereas he *means*, only in general, "Whatever is high and eminent in Government." Had the Apostle made a *distribution* of human, or angelical, Authority, into several subordinate ranks, he must have noted them by proper Names of *Distinction*, which these are evidently not, according to any Rules of Criticism, any Model of Government, or any Titles of Honour. There is, however, a *Subordination* of Angels, for we read of *Michael, and his Angels*, Apoc. 12. 7.

"In Scripture the *holy Angels* are represented as the *occasional Missionary Ministers of God's governing Providence*, and the Works thereof are represented as done by their Ministry"; which their very *Name* denotes, and the many Instances of their being employ'd, in God's Appearances, in making Revelations, and bringing Messages to Mankind; in guiding, succouring, and defending, the Just; in opposing the Enmity and Malice of evil Spirits; in dispensing Benefits to, and executing Judgments upon, the World, at the End of which they are to be the Reapers. But this their *occasional Ministry*, at the immediate and particular Command of God upon every Occasion, is far from vesting them with such a *Magistracy in the Government of the World*, as the *Heathens* ascrib'd to their Deities; the Church of *Rome*, to the Virgin *Mary*, St. *Peter*, St. *Paul*, &c. nor does infer a *Guardian-Angel*, as will appear from a View of the Texts quoted for that purpose.

So *Act.* 12. 15. where the *Christians* at *Jerusalem* say of *Peter* knocking at the Gate, *"It is his Angel,"* Dr. *Hammond* renders the Word *Messenger*, or one that came from him, or made use of his Name; because the *Faithful* cannot be suppos'd so ignorant as to think, that an Angel would not come in without knocking, or having the Door open'd.[53] Others suppose, That it is St. *Peter's Guardian-Angel*, in the usual Sense, which they meant. But 1. It does not appear, That the *Jews* then embrac'd that Notion; nor 2. Will it follow, That the Notion was true, if they did believe it. But 3. What need was there, that an Angel should be sent to deliver St. *Peter* out of Prison, or St. *Paul* from Shipwreck, or to strengthen our Lord in his Agony, if an Angel-Guardian were their inseparable At-

---

53. Hammond, *A Paraphrase and Annotations upon All the Books of the New Testament* (1659), p. 384.

tendant? Beside, 4. If they did not believe it a *Messenger,* but an *Angel,* they might have suppos'd it an *Angelical Appearance, in his Likeness, and Personating him,* whom they might have styled *his Angel,* as *Lightfoot* supposes.[54] To as little Purpose do they quote *Matt.* 18. 10. *"Take heed"* (saith Christ) *"that ye despise not one of these little Ones; for I say unto you, that, in Heaven, their Angels do always behold the Face of my Father, which is in Heaven."* Our Saviour *sheweth,* That the Sin and Danger of despising his little Ones, is not little; because, tho' they be little in the eye of the World, yet really they are of so great Quality and Value, that *their Angels,* (that is, not their Guardian-Angels, but the Spirits that Minister unto them, which is the Apostles Notion of Angels, *Heb.* 1. 13.) *always behold the Face of his Father in Heaven.* This Place also speaketh not of inferior Angels, but of the *Angels of Presence,* which correspond to those in Power next to the Prince, who have always the Privilege to see the King's Face. But it cannot be thought, that *every pious Person* hath an *Arch-Angel* for his *Guardian;* therefore our Saviour speaketh not of such *Guardian-Angels.*

The Angel of the Name and Presence of God.   From *Jacob's* Prayer, *Gen.* 48. 16. *The Angel, which redeem'd me from all Evil, bless the Lads.* And from *Eccles.* 5. 6. *Neither say thou before the Angel, that it was an Error; wherefore should God be angry at thy Voice, and destroy the Work of thine Hands?* Some infer a *Guardian-Angel,* but not justly. For the Angel, which the *Preacher* speaketh of, is the *Angel of the Name and Presence of God;* the Difference between whom and a mere Angel, is visible in the *Israelites* Case, who, before their Idolatry of the Calf, had an Angel to conduct them, of whom God saith, *Exo.* 23. 21. *"My Name is in him."* But, after that Idolatry of theirs, God threateneth, That he *"will send an Angel before them, but himself will not go up in the Midst of them."*[55] As the *Angel of the Name of God,* so the *Angel of his Presence,* transcendeth a mere Angel; for *Moses* would not be satisfy'd with the Guardianship of a mere Angel, but petitioneth for the Contin-

---

54. Lightfoot, *A Commentary upon the Acts of the Apostles* (1645), p. 324.
55. Exodus 33.2, 3.

uance of God's Presence,[56] *The Angel of his Presence,*[57] which is manifestly the same with the *Angel of God's Name.* Such an Angel, because
God's Name is in him, is more than a mere Creature; and therefore great
charge is given to the *Israelites,* to revere and obey him.[58] By such an
Angel God exhibited his own Presence, and a Declaration of his Mind
by the Angel's Voice, who bears the Name, and sustains the Person of
God, speaketh and is spoken to as God, as appears from many Instances
in the Old-Testament. For this Reason, this Angel is to be look'd upon,
as *God exhibiting himself by an Angel;* therefore the Name of God is in
him; and God may be fitly styled *the Angel,* which may therefore be one
of the Names of God, not simply, but as exhibiting himself by an Angel;
and thus it is to be understood in the two Texts now under consideration.
And that this is the *Preacher's* Sense, appears from the Context, *"Neither
say thou before the* Angel, *that it was an Error; wherefore should God be
angry at thy Voice?"* The 70 also render that which is in the *Hebrew,*
"Before the Angel" [πρὸ προσώπου τοῦ θέου] *in the Sight of God.* Agreeably hereunto, when *Jehovah,* or the *Lord,* is said to do any Thing, the
Arabick Version saith, the *Angel of the Lord* did such a Thing; see
Walton's Polyglot.[59]

Some *Prophetick* Parts of holy Writ are alledg'd, in favour of a sub-
lunary Magistracy of the holy Angels. In *Zech.* 6. 1. There is a four-fold
Division of the Angelick Host, concern'd in the Affairs of the World,
into 4 Chariots, as in antient Times their Hosts consisted of Chariots.
These are said, to *"Come out from between two Mountains, to go forth from
standing before the Lord of the whole Earth, into the four Quarters of the
World, to execute God's Judgments,"* v. 1–5. Of these 4 Chariots the
Prophet enquireth, *"What are these, my Lord?"* The Angel answereth,
"These are the four Spirits" (or Winds) *"of Heaven";* like that of the *Apoc-
alypse* 7. 1. where there is mention of 4 Angels at the 4 Corners of the
Earth, holding the four Winds of the Earth, that they should not blow

56. Exodus 33.15.
57. Isaiah 63.9.
58. Exodus 23.21.
59. Walton, *Biblia Sacra Polyglotta* (1657).

on the Earth, nor Sea. The Name of *Winds,* given to the *Angels,* denoteth their Subtilty and Agility, according to the *Psalmists* Description of them,[60] *"Who maketh his Angels"* (Messengers) *"Spirits"* (Winds,) *"his Ministers a flaming Fire."* It denoteth also their *Activity,* in the Commotions and Changes of human Affairs, in raising new Empires, and demolishing the old; for *that the great things, in the Vicissitude of Kingdoms and Empires, are done by the Angels, is an Hypothesis, that both* Daniel *and the* Revelations *plainly suppose.*

This plain *Hypothesis* will enable us to form a true Notion of the Princes of *Persia* and *Grecia,* which are Parties in the Conflict of the Angelical Powers, which are spoken of in *Daniel* 10. 13, 20, 21. As *Michael* there, the *Jews* Prince, is an Angel, so, doubtless, the Princes of *Persia* and *Grecia* are Angels also, not evil, but good, Angels (v. 21. *There is none that holdeth with me in these things, but* Michael *your Prince.)* And these Angels conflict with each other,[61] as opposite Parties at Court, that have an Interest there. Here is therefore an *Appearance,* "That the *Court of Heaven* resembleth the *Court of Rome,* where several Nations have their several *Cardinal-Protectors,* as their Patrons and Tutelar-Angels." And, because *Michael* is usually thought the Presidentiary-Angel of the *Jewish* Nation, and, because the Prince of the Kingdom of *Persia* is certainly an Angel; hence some infer, *It is plain, that there are Presidentiary-Angels of all Kingdoms, Nations, and Countries,* which are suppos'd to have a settled Prefecture over them. Whereas it is plainly incongruous to *suppose,* "That the Nations of *Greece,* usually at War with one another, and not united into one Estate, are the Prefecture of one Angel; and that the holy Angels bandy against, and conflict with, each other, in behalf of their several Nations and Countries"; which is as unlikely, as that they should fight with each other, when those Nations fight.

It is incongruous also to *suppose,* "That two great *Pagan* Nations have two angelical Princes, or chieftain Angels, for their Prefects, unless all such other *Pagan* Nations have the like"; and to *suppose,* "holy Angels the Prefects of unholy *Pagan* Nations," is incongruous; and it is much

---

60. Psalms 104.4.
61. Grotius, *Annotationes ad Vetus Testamentum* (1644), on Daniel 10.13 and 10.20.

more incongruous, to infer this from the Names of *Persia* and *Grecia,* in the Prophecy, which do not signify two *Nations,* but two great *Monarchies,* wherein the fate of God's People was involv'd. The Princes of *Grecia* and *Persia,* (understood according to the Hypothesis abovemention'd,) are the angelical Agents of raising those two Empires, (as the Arch-Angel *Michael* is, by divine Appointment, the Agent of the *Jews* deliverance out of captivity, and of re-erecting their Government;) which imperial Administration of theirs, maketh them adverse and punitive to the *Jews;* for the Prince of the Kingdom of *Persia* withstandeth the *Jews* Deliverance out of Captivity, (probably pleading the demerit of their Crimes,) and withstandeth the Angel, that spake to *Daniel* 21 Days. To this Account of these Princes, it may be proper to *add;* That *as* "The seven Arch-Angels, or 7 Eyes of the Lord, *Zech.* 4. 10. are usually employ'd in the affairs of the several parts of the World, (inspecting, superintending, administring them, *Zech.* 1. 10) as *occasional Missionaries* of Providence only, without being constituted the *Presidentiary-Angels* of any parts of the World"; and *as* "The Angel *Gabriel* is usually employ'd in the Affairs of Prophecy, and of the Prophets, as an *occasional Missionary of Providence only,* without being constituted the *Presidentiary-Angel of Prophecy,* or Prophets, like *Mercury* the *Heathen President of Eloquence"; so* we may reasonably *suppose,* "That the Prince of *Persia* and his Angels, (which are thought to have the Name of *Kings, Dan.* 10. 13.) were usually employ'd in the Affairs of *Persia:* That *Michael* and his Angels were usually employ'd in the Affairs of the *Jews,* without being constituted the Presidents, or Prefects, over *Persia* and the *Jewish* Nation." They were no more, than occasional Missionaries[62] of Providence, God's Messengers and Ministers, that do nothing but by his Command, *Angels employ'd in such an imperial, national, Administration.*

§VI. The *holy Angels* belong not to the Polity of this World, of which they are, therefore, *no Magistrates;* which if they were, this World would be the City of God, and his Republick: *Nor* are they *Guardian-Angels,*

Arguments against their subordinate mundan Mag-

---

62. [Maxwell] "In this Notion *Cyrenius* is call'd Governor of *Syria.*" The reader is referred to Hammond's *Paraphrase* on Luke 2.2.

inseparably attending upon Men all their Days. But they are *occasional Missionaries* (*"Ministring Spirits sent forth,"* Heb. 1. 14.) they are the *"Angels of God in Heaven,"*[63] they are the Courtiers and Citizens of Heaven; and such are the *Guardian-Angels,* which our Saviour speaketh of, that *"always"* (save only when they are sent abroad) *"behold his Father's Face in Heaven,"* and have their abode and dwelling there.

In *Ezek.* Chap. 1, and 10. the holy Angels (which are signify'd by the hieroglyphical figures of *Cherubims*) are represented, as the imperial Chariot of the God of *Israel;* which *importeth,* "That he is the supreme Governor in Power *Imperial,* thro' their *ministerial* Power, *flying,* as it were, *upon their Wings";* agreeably to which, the God of *Israel* is usually describ'd, as *"sitting upon the Cherubims, dwelling between the Cherubims,"* and the holy Angels are represented as his regial Seat, or Throne; the Posture of the Cherubims, in the Tabernacle and Temple, was standing; they were furnish'd with Wings, and their Faces were towards the Mercy-Seat; all which Notices of the holy Angels (and many more) represent them, as Ministers of, and constant Attendants upon, the Divine Majesty, not as Magistrates of this World, attending upon their Charges.

As God has appointed, *by Nature, all* Men to live in *civil Society;* so hath he ordain'd, *by Grace,* that his *holy People* should live in *holy Society,* under the Guidance of publick Officers, which Body-Politick is *the Church.* Agreeably whereunto, the invisible World is constituted; for the holy Angels are Sons of the divine *Family,* and live in Society as other Families do.[64] They are Members of the *Church*-Triumphant, and live in Communion with it as Church-Members.[65] They are Citizens of the *heavenly-Jerusalem,* there bearing Offices, and enjoying Honours. How else can they constitute a *Family,* a *City,* a *Church?* They are the *Host of Heaven,* and therefore live in angelical Society, residing in Heaven; which is inconsistent with their *sublunary Magistracy* in this World, (which was a fundamental Error of *Paganism,* embrac'd by many *Jews*

63. Matthew 22.30; Luke 15.10.
64. Ephesians 3.15.
65. Hebrews 12.22, 23.

and *Christians,*) and with the *Hypothesis* of the *Guardian-Angel,* for such an Angel liveth out of angelical Society.

The Angels, which minister to the welfare of the Just, usually go forth by Troops and Bands.[66] And, agreeably to the *Platonick* Notion,[67] *Christianity* allotteth a Convoy of Angels for the departing Soul of one pious Man, *Lazarus,* to conduct him to Paradise; which Office the *Heathen Poets* assign'd to *Mercury;* which is also agreeable to the Notion of the *Jews.* But, if they convey single departed Souls in Troops, they, doubtless, minister to their welfare in this Life, in Troops also. Numbers of them associate with us in our religious Assemblies, and are inspectors of our Behaviour there.[68] When the *Jews* were the *holy People,* the *holy Angels,* in some sort, resided among them; to which some, reasonably enough, refer that Voice, which was heard in the Temple, immediately before its Destruction, *"Let us go hence";* those Angels of the *Shechinah,* or Divine Majestick Presence, then leaving the *Jews* naked and expos'd to all Calamities.

The company and custody of the holy Angels is, according to the Scriptures, a principal Privilege of God's People, and a *Privilege* is an *uncommon Right.* This Principle, therefore, destroys the *Heathenish* sublunary *Magistracy* of the holy Angels, and of the *Angel-Guardian,* common to all Mankind. Yet we must acknowledge the holy Angels *general* Guardianship of Mankind in *general.* The *evil Demons* are under Laws and Government; God is the Founder and supreme Governor of the World; as he hath an universal Dominion, so he exercises that Right in a Superintendence of all, as the Sovereign Disposer of the private and publick Affairs of Men. In which Administration of Things, the holy Angels are employ'd in defence of Mankind in general, of publick Persons, and publick Societies of Men, which are not wholly abandon'd to the will of Satan and his Partisans, unless sometimes for their Punishment.

---

66. Luke 2.13; I Corinthians 11.10; Matthew 13.41; Revelations 12.7; Psalms 91.11, 34.7.

67. Windet, *De Vita Functorum Statu* (1664), 2d ed., pp. 116, 119, 120.

68. I Corinthians 11.10.

If we suppose the *holy Angels* to be *sublunary Rectors and Magistrates, Lords and Rulers of this World,* in their several Provinces, to whom Mankind are rightfully subjected; if our good and evil Things, our Welfare and Punishment, are in their Hands to dispense: This is that Notion, which the *Pagan-*Theology supposeth, a *delegated Providence, whereby the World is govern'd.* Whereas the Providence, which the *Scripture-*Theology supposeth and teacheth, is *God's own undelegated Exercise of Providence,* in his divine Decrees, and the Execution of them. The *Scripture-*Theology representeth *God,* as the universal Inspector, (to the meanest Sparrow,) Protector, and Benefactor; the sole Arbiter of our Fate, upon whose Pleasure our well, or ill, being intirely depends. Pious Men submit to Afflictions, as to God's Hand, give *him* Thanks for Mercies, as *his* Gifts, in Wants and Dangers, they trust to *his* Aid, and in all their Ways and Enterprizes, the Eye of their Observance and Regard is upon *him* alone, and their Service is to this their sole Lord.[69] The holy Angels, indeed, are sent to execute his Commands. *Psa.* 103. 20, 21.

If the holy Angels are *sublunary Magistrates and Rectors,* they are, to Mankind, governing authoritative Powers; they must resemble Kings and civil Governors, God's Vicegerents, but excelling them in Dignity; there must be Societies, consisting of the holy Angels, as Regents, and of Mankind, as Subjects; and the Societies of the World must be such Societies, more than human, or civil, Power and Authority belonging to such Rectors. But of such Political Societies, the Scriptures know nothing, unless we suppose them in the Kingdom of Darkness, which consisteth of *Heathen* Mankind, and of the Rulers of the Darkness of this World; nor are these Political Societies consistent with true Religion, for they manifestly imply and introduce *Idolatry,* and *Demonolatry,* by appropriating to them divine Honours, and subjecting themselves to them, taking them from their immediate Dependence upon, and Addresses to, God.

69. Genesis 15.1, 24.7; I Samuel 2.6–9; Job 34.29; Psalms 16.8, 44.4, 62.11–12, 75.7, 119.11; Proverbs 3.6; Isaiah 5.12, 26.12, 14, 45.7; Acts 4.28; I Corinthians 16.2; James 4.12, etc.

§VII. To bring what I have been laying down to a point. From what I have said, and, from a through Consideration of the *Pagan* Religion, it *appears*, "That the Kingdom of God does not consist of all rational Agents, as of one political System, with God at their Head"; there being a Kingdom of Darkness too, and a divided State of rational Beings: And it also *appears*, "That the *Heathens* were so far ignorant of the true God, that he is not to be found amongst their Deities," notwithstanding what has been advanc'd by many *Christian* Divines to the contrary.

1. *The supreme Deity, in the* Heathen *Religion, is the supreme among* Heathen *Deities.* The *Heathens* acknowledg'd *a supreme God,* but not *the true kind of supreme God.* "*This is Life Eternal, that they might know thee, the only true God, and Jesus Christ, whom thou hast sent," Joh. 27. 3.* They Atheistically explain'd away the true Deity of God, into a *Jupiter* of the *Heroe*-kind, sometimes into a *mystical first Nature,* sometimes into the *Soul of the World,* and sometimes into *infinite Matter.* "*It is much more easy, to deviate from the true God, than from the true*" [partial] "*Notion of the Deity; for the* Gentiles, *how good soever their Notion of the Divinity was, which they had in their Mind, yet in this they seem to have miscarried in the first Place, they did not attribute it to him, to whom it belong'd.*"[70] Many of the *Heathens* had a true Notion of the Deity; they suppos'd him to be the *great Father of Nature,* the *Former* and *Governor of the Universe;* yet every imaginary Deity, that has these Attributes, is not the true God, nor is the *Heathen* Deity such.

2. *The true God was not the Deity of Religion amongst the* Heathens. Among the *Romans, Capitoline Jove* was the supreme Deity of their Religion, with *Augurs* for his Prophets, and *Juno* and *Minerva* for his Coassessors; attended by a *Nurse* too, so confounding *Cretan* and *Cosmical Jupiter. Capitoline Jove* was the same with *Babylonian Bel,* threaten'd by God, *Jer.* 51. 44. The same with *Jupiter Olympius,* whom *Antiochus Epiphanes* endeavour'd to substitute instead of the true God, and to have the Temple in *Jerusalem,* call'd the Temple of *Jupiter Olympius,* who is therefore call'd *the Abomination that maketh desolate.*[71] The same with

70. Arminius, *Orationes* (1611), I.
71. Daniel 11.31; 2 Maccabees 6.2.

Baal and *Moloch,* which are Names too that signify a supreme God, but extremely different from the true God. *Summanus* (*Summus deorum Manium*) was the proper Name of *Jupiter Capitolinus* himself; and denoteth what he was in the best Notion of him, only *the chief of the* Heathen *Gods.* Accordingly, in Scripture, the *Gentiles* are said to worship Idols, but never to be God's Worshippers; the *Assyrian* Colonies, in their *Heathenism, "feared not the Lord";*[72] all the Deities of Religion amongst them, are constantly intitul'd *no-Gods, Idols, other Gods, strange Gods.* The Apostle saith, *"When they knew God,"* (had natural Notices of the true God of Religion,) *"they glorify'd him not as God,"*[73] (they did not acknowledge him for their God, the Object of their religious Worship,) worshipping the Creature instead of the Creator. This the Apostle affirms of them, *v.* 25. ἐσεβάσησαν καὶ ἐλάτρευσαν τῇ κτίσει παρὰ τὸν κτίσαντα, which our Translation thus renders, *They worshipp'd and serv'd the Creature, more than the Creator.* The Words are also capable of this other rendering; *They worshipp'd and serv'd the Creature besides the Creator.* And, according to either of these Versions, as some observe, *"It is suppos'd, that the* Pagans *did worship the true God, though they worshipped the Creature also besides him, or perhaps in some sense above him, and more than him also."*[74] But the Words are capable of a third rendering, which is probably the true, for παρὰ is here render'd in the *vulgar Latin, potius quam, rather than,* as it usually signifieth, and, in this Version, there will be no difficulty, if the Word [*Creature*] be understood to signify [*that which is not the Creator;*] and then the Words will run thus, *"They worshipp'd and serv'd that which is not the Creator, rather than the Creator";* which is perfectly agreeable to the following Words, *v.* 28. *"They did not like to retain God in their knowledge."* Therefore they chose to worship the Creature, rather than the Creator.

3. *The supreme Deity, among the* Heathens, *is the Deity of a* Heathen *Religion;* which the true God is not. Accordingly, the *Apostle* argueth, that the religious Service of the *Heathens* was a false religious Service:

72. 2 Kings 17.25.
73. Romans 1.21.
74. Cudworth, *The True Intellectual System of the Universe* (1678), pp. 472–73.

"God, that made the World and all the Things therein, seeing that he is Lord of Heaven and Earth, dwelleth not in Temples made with Hands. Neither is worshipp'd with Mens Hands, as though he needed any Thing, seeing he giveth to all Life, and Breath, and all Things. For as much then as we are the Offspring of God, we ought not to think, that the God-head is like unto Gold, or Silver, or Stone, graven by Art, or Man's Device."[75] In which the Drift of the *Apostles* Discourse is, to persuade the *Athenians* to change the great Object of their Worship, not their corrupt Manner of Worshipping him; otherwise the *Apostle* would not have preach'd to them in such a style as he does, telling them of *their profound Ignorance of God,* that his design was *to declare God to them,* and exhorting them *to seek the Lord, if happily they might feel after him and find him.*[76]

4. *The true God is intituled the unknown God at* Athens; UNKNOWN, as when we say, a Thing is *Foreign, Alien,* and *not of our acquaintance;* not in such an *honourary* Sense, as when the *Platonists* call their first Deity, *altogether unknown;* or as if the *Athenians* design'd it to signify, *the Deity invisible and incomprehensible by Mortals. "Most learn'd Expositors probably think that Altar, which St.* Paul *found at* Athens, *had been erected upon occasion of some famous Victory, whose procurement the* Athenians *not knowing, by any Circumstance, unto what known God it might be ascrib'd; and hence fearing, left by attributing it to any of those Gods whom they worshipp'd, the true Author of it might be wrong'd, or neglected, they ascrib'd it to an unknown God."*[77] Whence will follow,

First, "That the true God was not one of the *Athenian* Deities"; for all these were sufficiently well known to themselves. All the Deities of the *Athenian* Religion were to them well known; therefore the true God, whom St. *Paul* intitul'd *the unknown God at* Athens, could not be one of them.

Secondly, "That the unknown God at *Athens* was not the same with *Zeus,* or *Jupiter,*" as some imagine. The *Apostle* citing *Aratus, "for we are his Offspring,"* is by them said to interpret it of the true God; which is

75. Acts 17.24, 25, 29.
76. Acts 17:23, 27, 30.
77. Jackson, *A Treatise Containing the Originall of Unbeliefe* (1625).

suppos'd to be a *plain Scripture-acknowledgment, that by the* Zeus *of the*
Greekish Pagans *was, sometimes at least, meant the true God.* But, if *Ju-*
piter is the true God, he is necessarily the same with the *unknown God*
at Athens, and it *follows,* "That the *Athenians* were in profound Ignorance of their own *Jupiter;* that they worshipp'd him, not knowing him;
that they ought to have grop'd after him, and that St. *Paul's* Business
at *Athens* was to preach up the *Pagan Jupiter,* to those too, that knew
him at least as well as himself; and that the *Pagan Jupiter* is the very same
Deity, who set up an Anti-*Pagan* Religion in *Judaism* and *Christianity;*
that the great Crime of the *Gentiles* was, they knew not their own *Jupiter,*
nor glorify'd him as God, nor made him their God, whose Oracles,
therefore, Priests, and Temples, were the Oracles, Priests, and Temples,
of the true God." Fine Consequences! The *Apostle* discourseth of the
Deity, from an *Heathen* Author, to *Heathen* Auditors; citeth the Saying
of a Poet touching the Deity, as a true Notice of him, that is of kind
and quality the true God, (which is ill apply'd to, and understood of, an
Heathen kind of Deity, but is rightly apply'd to, and interpreted of, him
that is the true God,) representeth him according to their own Notices;
but doth not affirm, or intend to say, that by *God, the supreme God, Zeus,*
Jupiter, or *Dios,* the *Poet* meaneth determinately him that is the true
God, or that an *Anima Mundi* (which is *Jupiter* in the best Notion of
him) is *God blessed for evermore.*

5. The Difference between the *Heathen* and the *true* Theology, is a
Dispute between two pretending *Wholes,* the *Church* and the *World.*
Both Theologies have the same Notion of a City, Polity, and Kingdom;
both agree touching the Rules and Measures of Duty to the Whole;
and both agree, that there is a System, which is the City and Kingdom
of God. But these Attributes the *Pagan* Theology attributeth to the
World; the *Christian,* to the *Church.* The Dispute between these two
Theologies, is a Dispute to which of these two *Catholick* Systems the
true supreme God belongeth. Both Theologies agree, that he cannot be-
long to both these *Catholick* Systems, which are manifestly inconsistent.
The *Pagan Catholick* System shutteth out of Being that *holy Society,* the
Church of God. And the Hypothesis of this holy Society is of a ruinous
Nature to their Whole, to the supreme Deity of their Religion, to their

native State of Mankind, which they suppose to be by Nature that of Fellow-Citizens with, Domesticks and Sons of, God; which is built upon a false imaginary State of the Universe.

6. "The *Heathens,* therefore, *knew not God,*" in the truly religious Sense of knowing him, in which consists the whole of true Piety, in order to recover Mankind out of which unenlighten'd State, the Revelation, contain'd in the holy Scriptures, which God has been pleas'd to make of himself to Mankind, has been a favour of the highest Kind, as it is of the utmost Importance.

Concerning the Imperfectness of the Heathen Morality

The Rules of Piety among the *Stoicks.*

I. To begin with the *Stoicks,* whose pretentions ran highest in this way, and who acknowledg'd *Virtue* to be the *only Good.* Their Principles shall be extracted from *Epictetus, M. Antoninus, Seneca,* and *Plutarch;* and, to do them Justice, we shall begin with what is excellent in their Doctrine.

The State of Life which they propose to themselves, is that of *Jupiter's Subjects, Friends, Ministers, Soldiers, Citizens, Sons;* to be, and to be in-titul'd, Θεῖοι *Divine.* The Law of their Subjection to *Jupiter* they consider as an Obligation, both to *active* and *passive Obedience,* discarding all Externals, the Body, Riches, Fame, Empire; they made it their Business to be, and to do, what was *agreeable to Nature,* to our proper Nature, which is Rational, Social, Human; to the Will of the governing Nature of the Universe; to the governing right Reason of *Jove,* which is a Law; and being *Philosophers,* they were the *Interpreters of Nature, and of the Will of God.* They thought themselves unconcern'd in the Applause, or Contumelies, in the Approbation, or Reprehensions, of Men, as having no Power to do them Good, or Hurt. As good and dutiful Subjects, they profess themselves Friends to God in the first Place, chiefly to regard his Eye over them, whom they ought to please; to concern themselves about this only, how to fulfil their own Province orderly and obediently to God; to understand and mind his Commands and Interdicts, and to be conversant in his Affairs; in all their Actions to have respect to him; to desire to seem fair to him, and to be pure with themselves and with God; in all Circumstances to enquire, what God would have them to do, and to divine (if it be possible) what his Will is; to imitate him in Faithfulness, Beneficence, Liberality, Magnanimity; continually to praise and celebrate, and to give Thanks to, the Divinity; to give Thanks for all Things, especially for their virtuous Living without their former Vices and Crimes; for the Sustenance of Life, but especially for the Faculty of understanding and using Things; to submit their Minds to the Governor of all Things, as good Citizens to the Laws of the City; not only to obey, but to approve and praise his Administration of Things; to will the Things that happen in the World, the Estate, or Usage, that is allotted them, because God willeth them; to will nothing, but what God willeth; to be devoted to his Commands; so to eat, as to please the Gods; to confide in the Governor of all; to live in mindfulness of him; to worship the Gods, and to invoke them in all Affairs; for Man is made to worship the Gods. To them that ask, where hast thou seen the Gods, or whence is thine Assurance of their Existence whom thou worshippest? From those Things that are Indications of the Power of the Gods, I am assured of their Existence, and therefore worship them. These are their Rules of *Piety;* their Rules of *Duty to themselves,* and of *Humanity* follow.

§II. What (say the *Stoicks*) doth the divine Law command? To keep the Things that are our own, and not to challenge to our-selves the Things of others; but, if granted to us, to use them; if not granted to us, not to desire them; when taken away, to restore them cheerfully, and to be thankful for the Time that we have had the Use of them. Hast thou not a Commandment from *Jupiter?* Hath he not given thee thine own Things, exempt from Prohibition and Impediment, the other Things, which are not thine own, liable to Prohibition and Impediment? What Commandment therefore, what Prescript hast thou brought from him? The Things that are thine own, keep by all means, desire not the Things that belong to others. Faithfulness is thine own, who can take away such Things as these, who shall hinder thee from using them beside thy-self? When thou mindest the Things that are not thine own, thou hast lost the Things that are thine own. Man must do what his Reason and Mind enjoyneth, which is a Decerption from *Jupiter,* and which *Jupiter* (a severe Exacter of Virtue) hath given him to be his Leader and Prefect.

Their Rules of Duty to themselves.

Their Rules of
Humanity. From the same Principle (the Laws of Subjection to the Governor of
the World) the *Stoicks* infer various Rules of Duty to Mankind. For (say
they) Man is not absolute and unbound, but a Part of a certain Whole,
a Member of the one universal System of rational Agents, a Citizen of
the World, and, therefore, he is an intellectual social Animal, in conjunction with his Fellow-Rationals, that are of the same Nature and
Kind, of one Tribe, or Alliance, his Kinsmen, Fellows, Associates,
Neighbours, Brothers, (not as deriving their Origin from the same
Blood, or Seed, but from the same parental Mind, of which their Minds
are so many Branches pluck'd off,) Fellow-Members of one Body, that
are born to be Fellow-Workers, (as the Feet, the Hands, the Eye-Lids,
the Rows of the upper and under Teeth,) and by Nature Friends. Let
this be laid down in the first place; I am a Part of the Whole, which is
govern'd by Nature. In the next place, I am nearly allied to those other
Parts, that are of the same Kind. The Mind of the Universe[1] is Social;
wherefore the principal thing intended in the Constitution of Men, is
the social Design, which is the End and Good, and ought to be the Scope,
of Man; and whatever Practice of his hath not reference (immediately,
or remotely) to the social Design, destroyeth the Uniformity of Life, and
is Seditious; as a factious Person, among the People, divideth his own
Party from the common Consent. We ought not to be hurried away by
such Motions, as are unsocial, but to pass from one social Practice to
another, with mindfulness of God; to treat Men socially, according to
the natural Law of Fellowship, kindly and justly. What do I care for more
than this, that my present Action be the proper Action of one that is
Rational, one that is Social, and that is govern'd by the same Law of
right Reason with God?

To Man that is rational and social, it is proper to do nothing, but what
the Reason of his regial and legislative part suggests for the Good of
Men. He ought to love them truly and from the heart, to take care of
the Welfare of all Men, to worship and praise the Gods, and to do good
to Men, to bear with them, forbearing to injure them, to do them good
unweariedly, persisting in an uninterrupted Series of good Actions, ac-

---

1. [Maxwell] "God."

counting Beneficence to others, his own Emolument and (because they are Members of the same Body) a doing good to himself. The Joy of a Man is to do what properly belongeth to a Man; and it properly belongeth to a Man, to be kindly affected to those of the same Tribe, or Kindred. It is proper and agreeable to a Man, to love those that offend against him, (for by Nature they are his Friends and Kinsmen;) to bear good-Will to them that hate and disparage him; not to be angry with the Stupid and Ungrateful, but to take care of them; to be friendly and benevolent to every Man: Men are made for one another; teach them better, or bear with them. A Branch, cut off from Continuity with its Neighbour-Branch, is necessarily cut off from the whole Tree; a Man divideth himself from his Neighbour, hating him, and having an Aversion from him, yet knoweth not, that at the same Time he divideth himself from the whole Body. As a Citizen of the World, and a part of the whole, Man is oblig'd to have no private Self-Interest, or Advantage, to consult about nothing, as unbound; but, as the Hand, or Feet, if they had Reason and Understanding of the natural Order, should have no Motions, nor desire any Thing, but with respect to the whole; to direct his whole Endeavour to the common Good, and to abstain from the contrary; for the whole is of greater regard than a part, and a City than a Citizen. He that is unjust to any, is impious; for the Nature of the Universe having made all rational Animals one for another, that they should benefit one another, according to every one's Worth, but in no wise hurt one another; he that transgresseth this her Will, is manifestly guilty of Impiety towards the most antient and venerable of the Gods.

§III. So far excellently well, and the bright Side of *Stoicism;* but now follows its dark Side, which, in consequence at least, destroyeth its better part. For one great Article of *natural Religion* is, *the Immortality of human Souls; that after this Life they exist in a happy, or calamitous, State; and that Mankind ought to be govern'd by hope of Reward, or fear of Punishment;* the two chief Pillars of all Society, whether civil, or religious; of which, amongst others, *Lucretius* and the *Epicureans* were very sensible.

But their Institution is, in great Measure, unpopular and irreligious, subverting Religion, 1. By discarding future Rewards and Punishments.

But these grand Articles of *natural Religion,* the *Stoicks* discard as vulgar Errors, designing to rid themselves of the *Passions,* to rescue themselves intirely from all Bondage of Mind, and to enjoy perfect Liberty and Tranquility; designing to institute a *Philosopher,* (a whimsical Kind of Virtuoso, by them call'd *a Wise-Man,* and his Institution, *Wisdom,*) they undermine the Fundamentals of Religion; they conspire with the *Epicureans,* in razing and demolishing the principal Pillars of it; and make their own *Laws,* the Law of Subjection to the Governor of the World, *not Law,* but an *extravagant Hypothesis.* They *suppose,* "That an imperial Head presideth over an Universe of *rational Agents,* which must be govern'd by *Law,* but without the *Sanction of Rewards and Punishments;* That the Virtuous must hope for no other Reward, the Vicious need to fear no other Punishment, but their being such; That no thing must be thought our Good or Evil, save only the things that are in the Power of our own Will, lest we curse the Gods, when they seem to neglect, or cross us." Upon which Terms there can be no dutiful Submission to divine Chastisements and Punishments, no pious Addresses for preventing, or removing, them, and for promoting the external Blessings of this, or a better, Life. According to them, "It is of no concern, for how long you shall Practice virtuously; three Hours are sufficient. Prorogation of Life conduceth nothing to Felicity; a blessed Life that is short, is no less desirable than that which is long; both are alike; Happiness is not encreas'd by length, nor diminish'd by shortness, of Time; Time is of no Moment to happiness; there is no difference between a Day and an Age; Life by that is made longer, but not happier." An Institution, which, at this rate, affronteth the common-Reason of Mankind, corrupteth their natural Notions, quencheth their innate Desires and noble Breathings after Immortality, to which an Institution of Virtue ought to conduct Men, and is doubtless, in great Measure, no Institution of serious Virtue, but of unpopular and irreligious Humour.

The *Stoicks* are also extremely *Irreligious,* in depriving the *supreme Governor* of *distributive Justice;* in ascribing to him an extravagant indulgent Goodness, destructive to the true Use of Sacrifices, methods of Atonement, penitential Sorrow, and the pious Fear of a Deity. For, altho' they sometimes acknowledge, that the Governor of the World inflicteth *castigatory Punishments* in this Life, yet they do not suppose, that he inflicteth any properly *penal Evils.* Hence it is with them a Maxim, *"The State of absolute Liberty, is, neither to fear Men, nor God."*[2] So, according to *Zeno,* one thing requisite in an happy Man, is, *"Not to fear the Gods."* The *Platonists* agree with the *Stoicks,* in attributing an irreligious Kind of Goodness to the Deity, yet they suppose *castigatory Punishments* in a future Life. The Gods themselves, all the subordinate Deities, are suppos'd by the *Stoicks,* to be *Mortal* and *Corruptible,* and they are all to be swallow'd up in the universal Conflagration: Nor is their *Jupiter* absolutely *indissoluble, indiscerpible,* and *incorruptible,* being nothing better than a corporeal fiery Nature.

§IV. Secondly, they *ridicule the Fear of Death,* explode the laudable Usage of *Burying the Dead,* and of *Mourning for them;* all which is absurdly unpopular and irreligious. Nor could the World be govern'd, if all Men entertain'd a persuasion, That Death, and, consequently, the Execution of Criminals, is no penal Evil, no Evil at all, as the *Stoicks* suppose. According to them, *"All ways of dying are alike,"* and so there is no difference between the easiest natural Death, and Death aggravated by horrible Tortures, Modes, and Circumstances, of Dying. *Plato* also and *Socrates* affirm, *"That Death is good, and better than Living with the Body, not to some only, but simply unto all."*[3]

2. By ridiculing the Fear of Death,

 If the *Wise-Man* be in tragical Circumstances, and weary of Life, their Philosophy alloweth and enjoyneth "an Exit agreeable to Reason (that is, Self-Murder.) The Gate is open, none hath Reason to complain of Life, for none is forc'd to live against his Will; if he liveth miserably, it is his own Fault; doth it please you? Live; doth it not please you? You may return whence you came." This Doctrine was practis'd by several of the *Philosophick Pagans,* and the School of *Plato* became somewhat infected with it, notwithstanding he himself has reason'd so well against it; but the *Popular Pagans,* following Nature, were of better Principles.

And allowing, nay, in some Cases, enjoyning Self-murder.

---

2. Seneca, *Epistulae Morales,* LXXV.
3. Simplicius, *Commentarius in Epicteti Enchiridion,* ch. 10, p. 58.

3. By their
denying Pain
to be an Evil.

§V. The *Stoical* Doctrine of Pain, Sickness, & c. is so far from being
Wisdom, that it is an *unpopular irreligious* and *paradoxical Humour,* or
Madness, shall I rather call it? Their magnificent Pretentions are, "That
Pain and Torture of Body are not Evil; or, if it be Evil, it is another's
Evil, not ours, the Body being no part of us, but our Organ only. *Socrates*
affirm'd, that Pain remain'd in the Foot, it doth not affect the Mind
with Evil. They can live in great hilarity of Mind, altho' the wild Beasts
pull in sunder their bodily Members. Men of Learning are furnish'd with
Fortitude against things Painful and Dolorous, which suffereth them not
to pass within the Porch of the Soul, but, considering them as a propos'd
Exercise, beareth them without Grief and Affliction. Doth sensitive
Pain, or Pleasure, touch thee? Let Sense look to it, let the Body and bodily
Members make it their care, if they can, that they suffer not; and when
they suffer, let them complain, if they can, and judge that Pain is Evil.
The Soul may keep her proper Tranquillity and Serenity, and not suppose it Evil. Not Fire, nor Iron, nor a Tyrant, nor contumelious Language, can touch the Mind." Noble Rant this! But, if they really can
abstract the Mind from all sympathizing with the Body, and from uneasiness by the Pains of it, whence is it, that they cannot keep her from
Disturbance by the Humours of the Body? For they acknowledge themselves as liable as other Mortals to Fevers, Ravings, and Madness.
Whence is it, that, upon account of extremity of Pain, they think it
decent, to take away their own Lives? And why do they talk of Pain
intolerable, and make use of the *Epicurean* Consolation, *"If Pain be intolerable, it is not long; if it be long, it is not intolerable?"* Such Philosophy
does little more for the Cure of human Evils, than to make Men wran-
glers about Names and Terms, as if changing the Names chang'd the
Natures of Things.

    Externals, and whatever Things do not depend upon our own Will,
they will not have call'd *human Goods,* but *Things indifferent;* but, "altho' the Things be indifferent, the Use of them is not indifferent: As
Children, when they play with Shells, their Sollicitude is, not about the
Shells, but to play with them dextrously." Upon which Terms there may
be *Well-doing,* but no such Thing as *doing Good* to others, in the Use
of Externals; yet the *Stoicks* pretend to *Beneficence,* and write Books *con-*

cerning Benefits: Altho' they are like a Physitian, whose Care and Concern is, not the Life and Welfare of his Patient, but only, that his own Management may be *according to Art.* They most inconsistently exhort Mankind to be *Thankful* for their *Life,* and the *Helps* of Life, the Fruits of the Earth, when they are at the same Time instituting them to an *indifference* as to "Life and Death, Health and Sickness, bodily Pain, or Pleasure, Honour, or Ignominy, Plenty, or Penury, Wife, Children, Country, Fame, Possessions, Friends, and their own Bodies." *"If a Tyrant threatneth me with Bonds,"* (saith *Epictetus*[4]) *"I say, he threatneth the Hands and the Feet: If to cut of my Head, I say, he threatneth the Neck: If to Imprison me, the Body. Doth he therefore threaten nothing to me? If I look upon these Things as nothing to me, he threatneth nothing to me. But, if I fear any of them, he threatneth me. Is thy Son dead? What hath happen'd? Thy Son is dead. Is that all? That is all. That Ill hath happen'd, is thine own additional. If thine Hearing he incommoded, what is that to thee? No ill News can come to thee from* Rome, *for what Evil can befal thee there, where thou art not? Banishment is but to be elsewhere. Dost thou want Bread? The Door is open, thou may'st go out of a smoaky House."* (But, if these Things be no Evils, what meaneth that sovereign Antidote against them, *To die readily?*) *"But is not Life a Good? No. May we not desire Health? No, by no means, nor any Thing else of the* Aliena,[5] *from which the Appetite must be far remov'd; or else thou submittest thy Neck to Servitude, to the Things first, and next to the Men, who have the Disposal of them. Health is not Good, nor Sickness Evil; the Good is, to be Healthful as you ought: In like Manner, be Sick as you ought, and Sickness becometh Good and Profitable. The right Use of the Externals which present themselves, is a* MERCURY's *Rod, which turneth every Thing that it toucheth into Gold. Sickness, Death, Penury, Contumely, capital Sentence, touch them with the Rod of* MERCURY, *and they all become Profitable. Why then should we seek our Good and Evil in Externals, seeing it is in our own Power, to make all Externals Good?"* But, in order to rectify their Phi-

---

4. Epictetus, *Discourses,* II.6, III.20.
5. [Maxwell] "Those Things which are not in our own Power, *as they stand distinguish'd from* those Things which are in our own Power."

losophy of Good and Evil, it ought to be consider'd, That good Things are of two Kinds. For some Things are Good, as constituent Parts of our true Perfection and Happiness of Life, and these we call *the End.* Other Things are Good, as conducive thereto, and these are call'd *the Means.* In the first Notion, the good Things, commonly so reputed, (Life, Health, Honour, Plenty, &c.) cannot be Evils, consider'd in the Nature of an *End;* and the Evils, commonly so reputed, (Death, Sickness, Infamy, Penury, &c.) cannot be Good. In the second Notion of *Means,* the Evils, commonly so reputed, may be Good, and the good Things, commonly so reputed, may be Evils; and usually are, not helps, but hindrances, to our true Perfection and Happiness in a future State.

Their regal and happy Estate, and Self-sufficiency.

§VI. The *Stoick's Wise-Man,* according to their Institution, is Noble, Brave, Rich, Prosperous, free from Servitude and Misery; but quite out of the Road, both of civil and religious Society. For they suppose, "That nothing but our intelligent Nature is *our-self,* and that those Things only, which properly belong thereto, and fall within the Power of our own Wills, do concern us, or are our Good and Evil Things. Discarding, therefore, the many Things, they place their one Thing, and their All, in cultivating their intelligent free-agent Nature; in its being Virtuous, and such as the proper Nature of Man requireth; thus attaining a State of Felicity without Impediment, or danger of Misfortune, never failing of what they desire, nor falling into what they have an Aversion to; living, therefore, in a State of *perfect Liberty,* which they account the greatest Good. Being obnoxious to no superior Power, they are all *Kings.* Having dismiss'd the desire and fear of Externals, none can hurt them, they inhabit an impregnable City, none can have access to their Riches, they have no Enemy, they complain of none, criminate no Body. Hearken to me," (saith *Epictetus,*) "and you shall never live in Envy, nor be in Anger, Grief, or Fear, never be prohibited, or hinder'd, nor ever Flatter any. To me" (continueth he) "no Evil can happen, to me there is no Thief" (he that stole his Lamp was no Thief to him) "nor any Earthquake; but all Things are full of Peace and Undisturbance. I seek Good and Evil within, only in mine own Things, (*i.e.* in judging aright of Things, in having my Desires and Aversions right, and in the right Use of Externals,) not giving the Name of Good, or Evil, of Utility, or Damage, or any thing of that Nature, to Things not in my own Power." Such are the Principles of the *Stoicks* in their Schools, which they relinquish, or dissemble, when they betake themselves to the management of publick Affairs. For these they manage, (as *Plutarch* well observes,) as if they accounted Externals (Health, Riches, and Glory,) good Things; for how can they be throughly concern'd, to avert publick Calamities, if they suppose them no Evils, or not their Concern?

"The Body" (saith the *Stoick*) "is nothing to me; the Parts of it are nothing to me; Death is nothing to me. This is the State and Character of a Philosopher, he looketh for all his Utility and Damage from himself. If another can hurt me, then I do nothing: If I expect that another help me, then I am nothing. The Mind devoid of Passions is inexpugnable, collected into it self, it is self-content, a Cittadel; a stronger Place, whereunto to make his Refuge, and so to become Impregnable, and better fortify'd than this, hath no Man. So that" (as *Plutarch* has observ'd) "if he be Imprison'd, he suffereth no Prohibition; if thrown down a Precipice, he suffereth no Constraint; if Tortur'd, he is not Tormented; if Bound, he is not Hurt; if he falleth in Wrestling, yet he cannot be Vanquish'd; if encompass'd by a Wall, yet he cannot be Besieged; and if he be sold by Enemies, yet he cannot be Captivated; he hath Riches and a Kingdom, and is Fortunate and Prosperous, Unindigent and Self-sufficient, without a Penny in his Purse. The Wise-Man" (saith the *Stoick*) "hath created Peace to himself, by fearing nothing, and Riches, by not desiring any Thing: Altho' without City, House, or Harbour, yet he wanteth nothing. He can be happy by himself in a State of Solitude, as being happy and sufficient from himself," without the innumerable and inestimable Benefits of Society. And, because he liveth in the Perfection of Virtue and Happiness, neither publick nor private Calamities do at all diminish the Wise-Man's Happiness. Not *publick Calamities,* for "the overturning and ruin of his City, will he count it any great Thing? If he supposeth it a grand Evil, or any Evil at all, he will be ridiculous, and no more Virtuous, accounting Wood and Stone, and the Death of Mortals, some great Matters. Wars, Sedition, the Death of Multitudes of Men, the Overturning and Burning of Cities, are no great

Things: As the Death of Multitudes of Cattle, the Overturning and
Burning of Birds nests, are no great Matters. Not *private Calamities,*
that befall himself, or his Relations. For, without any title to a future
Happiness, the Wise-Man is happy in the midst of Torments; his Happiness receives no addition from Health, Ease, and Pleasures, nor any
diminution from their opposites." Is such an Institution as this fit for
human Minds?

Apathy. §VII. Not less extravagant is their Doctrine of *Apathy,* or being free from
animal Affections and Passions, which at once discards all things external, whether Good or Evil, both of this and another World, substituting
certain mental Operations, instead of the Passions of the lower or animal
Soul; "Will, instead of the Passion of Desire; mental Joy, instead of the
Passion of Joy; Caution, instead of the Passion of Fear; but, instead of
Grief, or Sorrow, they substitute nothing, because they deny any such
Thing in a Wise-Man." If *Ulysses* (said *Epictetus*) in truth lamented for
his Wife, was he not unhappy? "But what good Man is unfortunate, or
unhappy? Therefore, if he cri'd and lamented, he was not a good Man."
Sorrow for the Death of Friends, they account a very bad Thing, their
Philosophy being a contrivance to live in perfect Indolence: Nor alloweth it Sorrow for our Sins and Vices, as *Plutarch* charges them. But, if
this be Philosophy, the old Man had great Reason to tell his Son, *"Hear
me, my Son! you must Philosophize, but you must have Brains too: These
are egregious Fooleries."* As likewise are these their Maxims. "The Wise-
Man is never mov'd by Grace, or Favour; never pardoneth the Crimes
of any. None commiserate, but the Vain and Foolish. It is not the Property of a Man, to be exorable, or placable."

But, doubtless, it would be better for Mankind to be left to the Sentiments of Nature, than to be instituted to such a harden'd Virtue, that
is neither *possible,* nor *tolerable,* being absolutely Destructive, both of
Good-Nature, and of the Exercise of divine and gracious Affections and
Passions. For Fear and Desire are truly said to be divine Virtues, if their
Objects be Things divine; and to sympathize with others in their Joys
and Sorrows, is inseparable from true Benevolence. But the *Stoicks* admit
of no sympathizing Sorrow, but in political Appearance. "If you see a

Man" (saith *Epictetus*) "lamenting his Misfortunes, you may in Words accommodate your-self to him, and, if you be so dispos'd, lament with him: But take care, that you do not internally lament."

§VIII. The *Pagans* charg'd the *Stoicks* with *Arrogance,* and not without great Reason; for it was but a natural Consequence of their extravagant *Liberty, Security, Tranquillity, Self-Sufficiency, Wisdom, Royalty,* and *Apathy;* insomuch that their Wise-Man is no less than one of *Jove's Peers, that liveth as well as the Gods live. "And, as it is agreeable to* Jove" (saith *Chrysippus*) *"to elate himself upon account of his Life, to think great, and (if I may so speak) to lift up his Head, to glory, and magnify himself, living worthy of a magnifying Elation: So these Things agree to all good Men, that in nothing come behind* Jove. *As to the Body,"* (saith *Epictetus,*) *"thou art a small part of the Universe. But in respect of the Mind, or Reason, not worse, nor less, than the Gods; for the greatness of the Mind is not to be judg'd of by Longitude, nor Altitude, but by decretory Sentiments."* In this Philosophy, one of the fundamental Maxims is, *"That all the Wise and Good are Equal,"* being all of them happy to the height of Bliss. For Virtue, the true and the sole cause of Happiness, is equal in them all; it is not capable of increase, nor diminution, and as for Externals, which are of no consideration, they make no disparity. Time also maketh no disparity. Whence it follows, "That *Jupiter* and *Dio,* being both Wise, are equals. In Virtue *Jupiter* doth not transcend *Dio.* In Felicity God doth not transcend the Wise-Man, although he surmounteth him in Age," which maketh no disparity. But is not *Jupiter* the more Powerful and Opulent? "Sextius *was wont to equalize* Jupiter *and the good Man;* Jupiter *indeed hath more, and can do more for Mankind: But between two that are Good, the Richer is not the Better. Do you inquire of the difference between a Wise-Man and the Gods? The Gods will exist a longer Time. But it is a great Artifice, to inclose the whole in a little Room,"* [6] *i.e.* for a Wise-Man to have the whole in his Age, which God hath in a long Succession of Ages. In this and some other respects, the Wise-Man transcendeth *Jupiter,* and he admireth himself above him. *"There is something wherein*

Arrogance, with respect to the Gods, as well as Men.

6. Seneca, *Epistulae Morales,* LXXIII.

the Wise-Man may have the Precedence of God: He is one of the Wise, by the Benefit of Nature, not by his own Efficiency, as the Wise-Man is. The Wise-Man seeeth and contemneth all Things which others possess, with as equal a Mind as Jupiter: *And upon this Account more admireth himself;* Jupiter *cannot make use of them, the Wise-Man will not."*[7] Very modest and pious Doctrines! If this be not rampant Luciferian Pride, I know not what is.

"The Wise-Man" (say they) "is always alike, and of the same Countenance, as *Socrates* was, in all Circumstances. He doth not assent to any Opinion, is ignorant of nothing, never deceiv'd, never unsuccessful, never repenteth of any Undertaking, wondereth at nothing, nothing befalleth him contrary to Opinion. The good Man is perfect, sinneth in nothing, is impeccable, suffereth no Injury, is not mad, altho' maniacal, is inebriated, yet not drunk. All Things are the *Stoical* Wise-Man's, he is the only King and Freeman; he alone is rich, beauteous, noble, the only Citizen, Magistrate, Judge, Orator, Poet, Priest, Prophet." Fine Prerogatives! The *Popular Pagans* fell so far short of *Stoical* Wisdom, as to acknowledge *their good Endowments the Gift of God:* But the *Stoicks* say of their Wisdom, "Every one that hath it, oweth it to himself." Sometimes they huff at praying for the divine Aid. *"What need is there of Prayers? make thy-self Happy."*[8] In a better Humour they assert the Concurrence of divine Assistance with human Endeavours; they exhort us to pray for *Virtue,* a good Mind, and *the divine Aid.* "But so, that the Effect is properly to be ascrib'd to our own Power, because it is a Thing which properly belongeth to our own Power." For this Philosophy distinguishes *Things that properly belong to our own Power,* from *the Things that do not properly belong to our own Power:* The Works of Providence are not the Things that properly belong to our own Power; they are properly to be ascrib'd to the Gods: But the *Stoicks* Virtue, and its consequent Felicity, are Things that properly belong to our own Power; according to that of *Cotta* in *Cicero,* "All Mankind ascribe the Commodity and Pros-

---

7. Ibid., LIII, LXXIV.
8. Gataker, *Markou Antoninou tou autokratoros ton eis heauton* (1653), p. 65.

perity of Life to the Gods, but none ever ascrib'd his Virtue to the Diety." [9]
So the Poet, speaking the Sense of the *Stoical* Philosopher, ascribeth
Life and Riches to *Jove,* but not a virtuous Mind; for that is an Effect,
which properly belongeth to his own Power. *"Let him give Life and Riches,
I will get to my-self a good Mind."* [10] But as Riches are the Gift of Providence, yet not exclusively to human Endeavours, so the Virtue of our
Mind belongeth to our own Power, yet not exclusively to divine Assistance; "for who hath told thee" (saith *M. Antoninus,*) "that the Gods do
not help us even to those Things, that they have put in our own Power?"
Whence an appearing inconsistency in another Poet, who also speaketh
the Sense of the *Stoical* Philosopher, is easily reconcileable.

> *Orandum est, ut sit Mens sana in corpore sano,*
> *Monstro quod tibi ipsi possis dare.*   Juvenal. [11]

Because the Gods help us in those Things that properly belong to our
own Power, therefore the Poet saith, *"Pray for a virtuous Mind"*: Yet,
because the Virtues of the Mind are Things that properly belong to our
own Power, and must be ascrib'd thereto, therefore the Poet saith, *"I tell
thee of that which thou mayst bestow upon thy-self."* For the help of the
Gods is not requisite in any great Degree, nor otherwise than as a less
Principal, and adjuvant Cause: Nor is Man suppos'd to be impotent for
Virtue and Happiness in any great Degree. Thus the Spirit of *Stoicism*
is that of a criminal Self-sufficiency, Self-confidence, Self-dependence,
and Boasting. *"He thanketh the Gods, but with audacious Gloriation."* [12]
His Joy is an elation of Mind, "trusting to his own Possessions and Abilities." "He knoweth his own Strength, and that no Burden is too much
for him." "The Agency of his Free-will, *Jupiter* cannot vanquish."

Their haughty Temper appears, not only in their Demeanour towards
Jupiter, but in their carriage to their Civil Governors. For they suppos'd,
That no Man had Dominion over them, being *Jupiter's Sons and Subjects,*

---

9. Cicero, *De Natura Deorum,* III.86.
10. Horace, *Epistles,* I.18.
11. Juvenal, *Satires,* X.356, 363, pp. 219, 221: "You should pray for a sound mind
in a sound body . . . what I commend to you, you can give to yourself."
12. Seneca, *Epistulae Morales,* XCIII.

set at liberty by him from all Servitude and Constraint. And having discarded all regard to Rewards and Punishments, whereby Societies are govern'd, they discarded therewith their due Subjection and Reverence to the Civil Power, which was very unbecoming the Citizens of the Universe, as they call'd themselves. "How do I (saith the *Cynick*) treat those as Slaves, whom you fear and admire? Who is there, that when he seeth me, doth not suppose, that he seeth his Lord and King? What is *Caesar* to a *Cynick,* or the Proconsul, or any other, save only *Jupiter,* that sent him down, and whom he serveth?"

Of their Tran-
scendentals
and passive
Obedience to
the divine Will.

§IX. Instead of *sober Morality,* they deal much in *superlative Extravagancies;* for such is their *superlative Strictness, "not to move a Finger, unless Reason dictateth,"*

(*Ni tibi concessit Ratio, digitum exere, peccas.*)

Their *Severity* of Temper, *"never speaking any thing for pleasure, nor admitting any thing of that kind spoken by others,"* which is Sowrness and supercilious Gravity. Their enjoyning *"silence for the most part, and speaking seldom,"* is an *Excess;* also their conformity to the *Pharisees* in a *supercilious Contempt of the Vulgar.* The *Patience,* which they prescribe, is nothing better than a *haughty sullen Insensibility,* for he *"must seem to the Vulgar, devoid of Sense and a Stone."* Their invariable *Constancy of Temper* was no Virtue, but an inconsistency with true Virtue, which exerciseth various Affections and Passions upon various Occasions, *Anger, Mildness, Boldness, Fearfulness, Joy, Sorrow.* But the *Stoical* Wise-Man is criminally *uniform of Countenance;* none ever saw *Socrates* more joyous, or more sad; agreeably to the Conceit of *Aristo Chius,* That the final Good is, *"To live in an absolute indifferency of Mind, without any Variation, or Motion either way, carrying ones self with the same equal Tenour always."* [13] *"The Wise-Man"* (saith *Epictetus*) *"must be always alike, in acute Pains, in the loss of Children, in Chronical Diseases."* Their *Passive Obedience* also, and *Conformity of Will to the divine Will,* is a superlative Extravagance. "How" (saith *Epictetus*) "shall I become of free-Estate? For he is

13. Diogenes Laertius, *Lives and Opinions of Eminent Philosophers,* VII.

a Free-Man, to whom all Things happen according to his Mind, and none can be his hindrance; naturally I would have all Things to happen, as I please; but to be learned, is to learn to will all Things to be as they are. Will nothing but what God willeth, and none can hinder thee; none can force thee, no more than *Jupiter.* I was never hindred in my Desires, nor necessitated in my Aversions, because I have render'd my Appetite accommodate to God. Is it his Will, that I should be in a Fever? It is my Will. Is it his Will, that I should obtain any Thing? It is my Will. Is it not his Will? It is not mine. Who can now hinder me, or force me against mine own Mind? Seek not, that Events should be as thou willest; but will them to be as they are, and thou canst not fail to be prosperous."[14]

How Specious soever such a conformity of Will to the Divine may seem, it will be found, if examin'd, far from Pious. For it is not pious to pray with the dying *Stoick,* "Place me in what Region thou pleasest. Take me and throw me where thou wilt, I am indifferent." It is not pious, to entertain all afflictive Providences with a *Stoical Indifference.* It is not pious in him, notwithstanding all his own Sins and Sufferings, the Sins and Miseries of Mankind, *"to be devoid of Sorrow, Fear, Passion, Perturbation, nor to Grieve upon any one's Account."* It cannot be thought a due Conformity to the divine Will, to discard the humbling Methods of Piety, for the Cure, or Removal, of the disastrous Events of Providence, such as afflicting the Soul, Deprecation, Intercession, and to substitute in their stead that magnanimous Voice, "With God I affect and pursue, with him I desire, my Volitions are simply and absolutely co-incident with the supreme Volitions." For these settled Maxims of the *Stoick* are irreligious Errors, "That the divine Nature cannot be angry, and that the Events of Providence are Fatalities." Beside; they that will all Things to be as they are, must necessarily will the State of Things in the World to as bad as it is, which is repugnant to all true Virtue, to the use of Prayer, and to the *Stoicks* Desires and Endeavours for the amendment of Mankind. Their *Passive Obedience* teaches them, indeed, to *suffer* Afflictions, but not to *act* in a becoming Manner in such a State, in

14. A composite quotation including sections from Epictetus, *Discourses,* I.1 and I.6.

which the grand Duties of Piety are, the humbling our-selves under the divine Hand, searching and trying our Ways, practice of Repentance, and improving in Devotion. Their *Passive Obedience* is of a spurious Kind, the insolent Boldness of an affected Liberty, (which rivals *Jove,*) and the Stoutness of a Bravo. "Look" (saith *Epictetus*) "at the Powers which thou art furnish'd with, and, having view'd them, say, Bring upon me, O *Jupiter,* what Hardship thou wilt, I am sufficiently furnish'd by what thou hast given me, to make whatever happeneth Ornamental to me. At length erect thy Neck, as one out of Servitude, fearing nothing that can happen: Dare to lift up thine Eyes to God and say, Use me hereafter to whatsoever thou pleasest, I am of the same Mind with thee, I am equal to any Thing." Their running the Pit and slinking out of harm's Way, by taking away their Lives in bad Circumstances, is Heroism and Passive Valour of the illegitimate Kind. *Diogenes, Heraclitus,* and *Socrates* himself, should have consider'd, that there may be such a Conformity to the *divine Will of Events,* as may clash with the *divine Will of Duty and Precept.* Their Passive Obedience is founded upon bad Principles. "Dost thou call that a Mischance to a Man, which is no Mischance to the proper Nature of Men? Let that part which judgeth of Things be at rest, altho' the Body, which is next the Thing, be cut, or burn'd, suffer Corruption, or Putrefaction. That which maketh not the Man worse, which doth not involve him in any Crime, doth not make his Life the worse, nor can it hurt him. All Things that befall Men, are allotted them by that Whole, or Universe, whereof they are a part; and that is good for every one, which the Nature of the whole bringeth upon every one. Whatever shall come to pass, the World loveth to have it so: I say therefore to the World, I concur with thee in Affection, and love to have it so." Which cannot be thought a very virtuous Saying; for what Virtue is there in deifying this Region of Sin and Mortality, and Misery, the Laws of whose Administration are manifestly Penal and Calamitous?

Altho' the *Stoicks* pretended to *follow Nature,* and altho' they call their Philosophy *Moral,* yet their Morality is extremely different from the institution of Nature, being that of *unpopular Humorists,* of *abstract Mentalists,* and *Enthusiasts.* "Shew me a Man" (saith the *Stoick*) "that desireth to be made a God of a Man, and in this mortal Body to have consortship with *Jove?"* The Religion, therefore, and Piety of *Stoicism,* is not *Natural Religion,* but a jumble of *Self-sufficiency, Independency, Liberty, Apathy, Prosperity, and undisturb'd Tranquillity.* It is not hard to determine, which were the better sort of Religionists; whither the *Popular Pagans,* who complain'd, when they were hurt, (provided they abstain'd from cursing their Deities,) were touch'd with their Afflictions, and looked upon mournful Spectacles with the Eyes of Mourners: Or the strutting *Philosophers,* who took a Pride in trusting to their own Strength and invincible Maxims, deriding all Events; that were to live at the rate of *Pagan* Deities, who are above Passion, in Human Flesh. Agreeably to their *Hypothesis,* "That the Perfection of Felicity is attainable in this Life," they contriv'd a method of arriving at so transcendent a condition; which was by placing all their good in *their own things only, that are in the disposal of their own Wills,* contemning all that *belong not to their own Free-agent Nature.* Being thus instituted to live in *Safety, Liberty, Independence upon Others, not liable to be constrain'd, hurt, or hindred by any, never failing of prosperous Success, never being unfortunate, nor conflicting with any Adversity;* they could bear *whatever happen'd without Humiliation, or brokenness of Mind.* They assumed to themselves a greatness of Mind, (as supposing that nothing could hurt them, and that they were beyond the power of Evil,) and were able to make this resignation to Providence from their whole Soul, "Carry me, O *Jupiter!* and thou, O Fate! whithersoever I am destin'd by you."

Such is the *Stoicks Passive Obedience,* neither *Natural,* nor *Christian.* And, if we agree not with the *Stoicks* touching *Passive Obedience,* (which is the top flower of their Philosophy,) nor think it safe to rely upon the Maxims of the *Heathen Philosophers,* (both because they are *Heathens* and *Philosophers,* i.e. Teachers of unpopular Doctrines,) we are not likely to entertain a late Conceit, *That all the Agenda in Christianity, the two Sacraments excepted, are nothing but what was taught before by the Moral Philosophers.* For, altho' of all things in our Religion, there are Affinities and Resemblances in their Religion and Institutions of Learning and Virtue; yet the best of them must be thought bad Teachers of Duty and Virtue, all of them being Aliens from true Piety, and some of them extremely deficient in Philosophizing.

§X. For, as to their *Natural* Philosophy, the Sun, Moon and Stars are
nourish'd by Vapours; and when these fail, there will be a Conflagration
of the Universe, a resolution of the Gods (*Jupiter* only excepted) and
of Men into their first Elements, *God* and *Matter;* after which there will
be a Restauration of the same World, and the same Men, and so in endless Rounds. The Night, Day, Evening, Morning, our Arts, Memories,
Fancies, Assents, Passions, Virtues, Vices, Wisdom also and Good, are
all Bodies; nay, and Animals too. An Imagination so wild could never
have enter'd into the Head of any Man, but a Philosopher, or a Rabbi.
"Virtue is nothing else but the Mind modified, therefore it is an Animal,"
saith *Seneca.*[15] Agreeably to their Notion of the Soul of the World, who,
in this Philosophy, is a subtle fiery Body, the Mind of Man is a Body,
"a part of God, and a God too." And this deified Mind of Man is that,
which they mean by their *Holy* or *Divine Spirit in Man.* "Reason in
Men" (saith *Seneca*) "is nothing else but a part of the Divine Spirit im-
mers'd in a Human Body." At the same rate the *Pythagoreans* and *Platonists* deify the Human Nature, forbidding Man to pollute, by corporeal
Passions, their *Domestick God.*[16] The *Platonists* suppos'd the Souls of all
Animals to be parts of the Divine Substance; the *Stoicks,* the Minds of
Men only; the more tolerable *Hypothesis* of the two; yet, because it supposes a Separation of the parts of the Deity, and that the parts of God
may be miserable, it is to be rejected with Indignation.

A like intermixture of absurd Fancies has overspread their *Moral* Philosophy; "That all Sins are equal; That all, who are not of the Wise of
the first Form, are equally foolish, bad, vicious, morbid, miserable,
mad." This earthly Region is visibly a *Region of Sin and Suffering;* But
in *Stoicism,* which is a sullen and surly contempt of Human Calamities,
the State of the World is a *Festival Solemnity. Death* is the *Nature* of
Man, *not Punishment;* and the serious Calamities of Mankind, "Deaths,
Rapines, the slaughtering Men and sacking Cities, are to be contemplated as the scenical Shiftings on the Theatres; the Tears of Mourners
as shews of Lamentations, and (the affairs of Life being a Play) as Chil-

15. Seneca, *Epistulae Morales,* CXIII.
16. Gataker, *Markou Antoninou,* p. 201.

drens crying." They are not troubled for their own Vices, "for who hindreth them from rectifying their own Principles?" Nor are they troubled at the Impieties of others, or angry and offended at their Sins and Injuries. "If any one hath sinn'd" (saith the *Stoick*) "the hurt is only his own. Wickedness doth not at all hurt the World. *Jupiter* hath so dispos'd things, that there should be Summer and Winter, Fruitfulness and Barrenness, Virtue and Wickedness, and all such contrarieties, for the good and symphony of the Universe. The worst of Men do but act according to their own Opinion, and are to be rectify'd, not destroy'd. All that offend, it is against their Will. All Men miss of the Truth against their Will. Nothing is hurtful to a part, which is for the good of the whole. What is not hurtful to the City, hurteth not a Citizen. Bad Men are neither affected with Benefits, nor have they any Benefactors, nor are they guilty of neglecting their Benefactors."

§XI. The great Imperfection of the *Stoical* Institution (applicable also to the other *Pagan* Institutions) appears from the gross Immoralities wherein they liv'd; for they were not well disciplin'd against the foul Vices of *Drunkenness, Uncleanness,* and *irreligious Swearing. Seneca* pleadeth for *Drunkenness, Zeno* liv'd in it, and *Chrysippus* died by it.[17] The great *Hercules,* celebrated for a great Drinker, (his Cup also is celebrated,) is a Divine Man in the Style of *Epictetus's* Dissertations; and *Cato,* a *Stoical* Wise-Man of the first Form, is of the same Character: But No-Body must call his Drunkenness a Crime; "for it is easier" (saith *Seneca*) "to make it no Crime, than *Cato* a Criminal." But, as a *Stoick* is extravagant in his Supposition, "That he remaineth safe and unhurt *in Drink and in Melancholy;* that his Body may be in Drink as to all its Senses and Powers, yet his Mind remain unprejudic'd," (which is the meaning of that Maxim, *The Wise-Man is liable to be inebriated, but not drunk;*) so it is a wild kind of Virtue, that is consistent with so great a Vice, which is indeed all Vices in one, and the Mother of all Wickedness. But these impure *Heathens* suppos'd, "That there is a right and prudent use of Drunkenness, which contributeth to Virtue, and that it ought not

Their gross Immoralities.

---

17. Plutarch, *De Tranquillitate Animi* (in *Moralia*), ultimate chapter.

to be extirpated from a well-govern'd City." "Plato *forbiddeth Children
to drink any Wine, before they be* 18, *and to be drunk before they come to*
40. *But such he is content to pardon, if they chance to delight themselves
with it, and alloweth them somewhat largely, to blend the influence of* BAC-
CHUS *in their Banquets, that good God who bestoweth cheerfulness upon
Men, and Youth unto aged Men, who allayeth and asswageth the Passions
of the Mind,* (*even as Iron is made flexible by the Fire;*) *and, in his profitable
Laws, drinking-Meetings are look'd upon as necessary and commendable,*
(*always provided there be a chief Leader among them, to contain and order
them;*) *Drunkenness being a good and certain Tryal of every Man's Nature,
and therewithal proper to give aged Men the courage to make merry in Danc-
ing and in Musick, things allowable and profitable, and such as they dare
not undertake being sober and settled.*"[18] *Anacharsis* was addicted to
Drunkenness, as *Plutarch* informs us; and the Prince of *Philosophical
Heathen* Saints, even *Socrates* himself, "tho' he was not forward to drink
at Banquets" (as we are inform'd by one of his Scholars,) "when he was
compell'd, master'd all; and, which is most to be wondred at, no Man
ever saw *Socrates* drunk." We are told, that he spent whole Nights in
drinking, and that the *Greeks* praise him exceedingly, that having spent
a whole long Night, drinking for Victory with *Aristophanes,* he was able
at Day-break, to delineate and demonstrate a subtil geometrical Problem, thereby shewing, that the Wine had no noxious Effect upon him.[19]

Socrates was a great Lover; and it was in his Time so genteel for Men
to be Lovers of Boys, that it was forbidden to Slaves; tho' at *Athens* the
Laws prohibited the Practice universally, but ineffectually. *Socratici Ci-
naedi* were proverbial. Both the *Popular* and *Philosophical Pagans* were
addicted to this Vice. Such Love of Boys as was at *Thebes, Elis,* and in
Crete, is condemn'd by *Plutarch* in his Treatise *of Education,* who alloweth that which was at *Lacedaemon* and *Athens;* yet we are assured,
that it prevail'd criminally in all parts of *Greece,* but at *Athens* most.
Euripides, being invited to a Banquet by King *Archelaus,* became Drunk,
and in that Mood kiss'd the Poet *Agatho* (who sat next him) being then

18. Montaigne, *Essays,* II.2.
19. Della Casa, *Galateus de Moribus* (1653), ch. 29, p. 123.

40 Years old. Whereupon the King ask'd him, if his Paramour were yet delectable? To which *Euripides* answer'd, That *not only the Spring, but the Autumn of the Fair, is delectable.* It is certain, That *Socrates, Plato, Xenophon, Cebes, Cicero,* approv'd the Masculine Amours, which among the Philosophers was without Disgrace, or Reprehension.[20] It was they which wrote Love-Dialogues and Discourses, which the Coelestial *Venus* never inspired. *Socrates* and *Cato* communicated their Wives to their Friends. *"All manner of Incest, Adultery, and Masculine Mixtures, some of the famous antient Philosophers accounted Things indifferent."*[21] Some of the *Stoicks* befriended Chastity at an extraordinary Rate, commending chast Eyes, forbidding obscene Speech, advising Men to be Pure, as much as may be, from Things Venereal before Marriage;[22] yet most of them agreeing with the *Popular Pagans,* amongst whom the Harlotry of simple Fornication was accounted no Crime, and which almost all the great Philosophers are known to have liv'd in.[23] But the generality of that Sect are prodigiously Paradoxical in their Unchastities; Teaching the Father to commit Incest with the Daughter, the Son with the Mother, and the Brother with the Sister; Men and Women to wear the same Garments; that no Speeches are obscene, and that every Thing should be call'd by its own Name, themselves not scrupling the most immodest Actions.[24] *Zeno* (as *Laertius* informs us) was a lover of Boys, made use of both Sexes, and sware by a *He-Goat,* a lascivious Animal. As for *Socrates,* he has had the Happiness of eloquent Apologists. As for *Plato,* he is charg'd with Unchastity by some of his greatest Admirers, who own'd, that the subject Matter of his *Convivium* is not the Love of Men and Women, but the Love of Men towards Boys, and that not merely as a *Platonick* Lover. When it was objected to *Apuleius,* that his Love-Verses were not suitable to a *Platonick* Philosopher, he justifies himself by *Plato's* Practice, who had no Verses extant, but Love-Verses upon the

20. Maimonides, *De Idolatria,* ed. Vossius (1641), I.4.

21. Marsham, *Chronicus Canon Aegypticus, Ebraicus, Graecus, et Disquisitiones* (1676), p. 172.

22. Marcus Antoninus and Epictetus.

23. Grotius, *De Veritate Religionis Christianae* (1627), II.18.

24. Sextus Empiricus, *Hypotyposeon,* III.24, 25.

Boys *After, Alexis, Phadrus,* and *Dion:* And *Ficinus (in Argum. in Char-*
mid.) changeth and omitteth part of the amatorious Things in *Plato's*
Charmides, as offensive to chast Ears.[25] *Plato* will have young Soldiers
that behave themselves Valiantly, gratify'd in their Amours, *whether Mas-*
culine, or Feminine. Following *Lycurgus's* Institution, he will have *Women*
expos'd Naked to the Eyes of Men. Transcending *Lycurgus's* Institution,
and the Impieties of the *Popular Pagans,* he abolisheth Marriage, and
instituteth the Community of Women; which was likewise the Doctrine
of *Zeno* and *Chrysippus,* the Founders of *Stoicism.* Such are the unpopular and irreligious Institutions of the *Heathen Philosophers;* which are
partly to be attributed to the Spirit of Uncleanness, predominant in the
Philosophick Pagans, (insomuch that *Lais* once laughed, to see more of
the Philosophers with her, than of any other sort of Men;) and partly
to their cross-grain'd unpopular Humour, express'd by *Diogenes,* who
entering into the Theater opposite to the People that were coming out,
was ask'd, why he did so. *"This,"* said he, *"I study to do thro' my whole*
Life"; as *Laertius* relates in his Life.[26] But, altho' the *Philosophers* had a
great Affectation, to distinguish themselves from the *Popular Pagans,* yet
they transcend them in the absurdity of their Institutes; and the *Popular*
Pagan Doctors may at least vie with them for sound Morality, whence
Horace prefers *Homer* before them.

> *Qui quid sit pulchrum, quid turpe, quid utile, quid non,*
> *Plenius & Melius Chrysippo & Crantore dicit.*[27]

   Christianity forbiddeth common and *customary Swearing,* whether by
Creatures, or by the Deity; and all *irreligious Swearing.* But no *Moral*
Philosophers ever prohibited Swearing by the *Creatures.* *Socrates* ordi-
narily practis'd it, (doubtless out of Reverence to the Gods,) sometimes
Swearing by Animals, a Dog, a Goose, a Goat, and sometimes by Plants,
an Oak, or a Plane-Tree. Nor is this the only Defect in their Discipline

   25. Maxwell is referring to Marsilio Ficino's edition of Plato's works, *Platonis*
Opera Omnia (1484).
   26. Diogenes Laertius, *Lives,* VI.
   27. Horace, *Epistles,* I.2.3–5, p. 263: "Who tells us what is fair, what is foul, what
is helpful, what not, more plainly and better than Chrysippus or Crantor."

touching *Oaths;* for being Separatists from the *Popular Pagans,* whom they contemn'd at a great Rate, and no great Friends to their Civil Government, they were shy of *solemn judicial Oaths,* which are of all other the most allowable and needful, but made no scruple of idle criminal Swearing. *Clinias* the *Pythagorean,* in a Suit depending before the Judge, might have freed himself from a Fine of three Talents, by taking a true and just Oath: But he chose rather to pay the Mulct, than to take the Oath; so great a respect had these *Pythagoreans* for their own Philosophical Institution, and so little for Civil Government. For it is well known, that they were not so shy of *Swearing by the Master of their Institution,* as Religionists Swear by their God: And *Hierocles,* who hath given many wise Cautions touching the Use of Oaths, with respect to the Honour of the Gods, justifieth their Practice. Touching a solemn judicial Oath *Epictetus* saith, *Refuse it altogether, if it be possible: If not, "as much as may be";* yet himself ordinarily swears in his Dissertations, *"I swear to you"* (saith he) *"by all the Gods."*

§XII. So much for the *Stoicks,* who "plac'd Happiness in Virtue only." The *Epicurean* Scheme, which makes the whole Man to be only a corporeal Engine, may be dispatch'd (from Bp. *Parker*) in a few Words.[28] For *Epicurus,* consistently with that Principle, "plac'd all Happiness in the Pleasure of the Body alone," which Doctrine at once destroys all Obligations to Virtue and Honesty, and to Religion, which he trampled under Foot. *Epicurus* himself plac'd all Happiness in the Enjoyments of the Palate, and such like. *Metrodorus,* his favourite Disciple, made the Belly, the only Seat of Happiness. In freedom from Pain, in sensual Enjoyments, and in Reflexions upon them, he plac'd the whole of Happiness. *Indolence* is the Happiness of *Stones,* and *Sensual Pleasures,* of *Swine,* in as great perfection as *Epicurus* himself enjoy'd them, for ought we know. So that all the boasted Happiness of the *Epicureans,* without a future State, was equally *vain* and *insecure,* which at once effectually overthrows it; shocking us, even in the Enjoyment of what is mean and low, with the Fears of losing even that. And then, to comfort us under

The Epicurean *Tenets of Morality.*

28. Parker, *Disputationes de Deo et Providentia Divina* (1678).

all the Miseries of Life, they throw out a parcel of Falshoods and Subtleties. As that *Length of Time doth not increase Happiness; as if either*
Happiness, or Misery, for 2 Hours were not twice as great as Happiness,
or Misery, for one Hour. That *Pain is short, if great; light, if long,* which
will afford but very little Relief to a Man under those Chronical Diseases
of great Torture, *Gout* and *Stone.* That *we must lop off the Fear of future*
Evils, and the Remembrance of those which are past. Easily said! The Difficulty lies in the Application. That *we are to resist Pain with all our Power;*
for, if we fly, we shall be conquer'd, if we stand our Ground, we shall gain
the Victory. As if we could either fly from, or resist, Pain, as a Man does
his Enemy.

Of a piece with these, are their *Consolations against the Fear of Death;*
against which nothing is a solid Comfort, in the midst of our present
Enjoyments, but the well-grounded Hopes of a happy Immortality.
How ridiculous an Antidote is it against that which takes away all our
Enjoyments, to tell us, That, *when that comes, it cannot hurt us, because*
when that is, we are not? Self-Love and the Fear of Annihilation are Instincts too powerful to be baffled by such a subtlety. Just (as *Plutarch*
well observes) as if you should tell a Man in a Storm at Sea, that your
Ship has no Pilot, and that there is no hope of allaying the Tempest; but
yet, however, be not afraid, for in a little Time the Ship shall split and
sink, and, when you are drown'd, the Storm will trouble you no longer.
According to this Scheme, if we have all the Enjoyment in Life we can
expect, we lose Happiness in a little Time after we come to know what
it is, of which too we are in continual Apprehensions; but the Wretched
come into the World, only to lament and leave it; than which how much
better would it be, not to have been born. But, say they, *we ought to bear*
with Patience what we cannot avoid. But the Fear of it, upon their
Scheme of Annihilation, is as Death it-self is, tho' the Philosopher
should take ever so much Pains to expose it as foolish; whose Rules cannot take away what is Natural, and, consequently, not in our Power. "In
the next Place," say they, "we are already Dead to so much of our Life
as is past and gone; so that so much as we live, we die, and that which
we call *Death,* is but our last Death; and, therefore, as we fear not our
Death that is past, why should we that which is to come?" But, if we

have been dying ever since we were born, that is it which grieves us, that we cannot be doing so for ever. Such was the Reasoning of the *Epicurean* Old Man, who reconcil'd himself to his approaching Death, because "it is as absurd to fear Death as old Age, which yet all desire, in that as old Age follows Youth, so Death follows old Age." For old Age is desirable, not because it follows Youth, but because it defers Death. "Such is that other Reasoning, that, whereas we now count our-selves Happy, if we live to an hundred Years, yet, if the natural Course of our Lives were as much shorter, we should be as much satisfy'd with twenty; and, if our natural Course reach'd to a thousand Years, we should then be as much troubled to die at 600, as now at 60, and so forward." Which proves nothing, but that there is no Time, in which an *Epicurean* can be content to die. No better is that Device of *Gassendus,* "though a Man's Life may be short in it-self, yet may he make it equal with the Duration of the whole World, because he may converse with the Transactions of all former Times, and be as well acquainted with them, as if himself had then actually liv'd. And, as for the Time to come, he, knowing that nothing shall be but what has been, understands all future Events as if present; so that a wise Man, partly by Memory, partly by Foresight, may extend his short Life to all Ages of the World."[29] But, if he could, unless he could make himself Immortal too, the Objection would still be as strong as ever. His other Arguments, to persuade us to be content with our Condition, are as ineffectual. As first, that "otherwise we forget our mortal Nature expos'd to Misery," that is, that a Man must be content with his Condition, because he knows his Condition to be miserable. And, secondly, that "it is some Comfort, that, when all Men are expos'd to Misery, you are less miserable than others," that is, that, tho' I endure most of the Calamities of human Life, yet I am happy, if I think one more miserable; according to which there can be no Misery, but the greatest.

Secondly, The *Epicureans* destroy all *Virtue,* by making it wholly subservient to sensual Pleasure, making *Virtue* the *Means,* and *Sensuality*

---

29. Maxwell is referring to Pierre Gassendi, whose *Syntagma Philosophicum* (1658) revived neo-Epicurean philosophy.

the *End;* so that what we now call *Vice* would be Virtue, if it promoted the Delights of the Body the more effectually of the two. A hopeful Foundation of Morality!

If *Epicurus* liv'd *soberly* and *abstemiously,* on coarse Bread and Water, and sometimes Sallet, it was more owing to the Weakness of his Stomach and Constitution, than to the Strength of his Principles, which were as much in contradiction to that method of living, as his denying Providence, with his pretending, that he had left Devotion; his teaching, that all Friendship is for Self-interest, and yet that Men are bound to undergo even Death for the sake of Friends. If sensual Pleasures be the *chief Good,* he must be happiest, that enjoys them most, and wisest, that procures them most; and then *Apicius* will be a happier and wiser Man than *Pythagoras, Socrates,* or *Plato.*

As for *Justice,* it is no farther a Virtue, upon the *Epicurean* Scheme, which turns to ridicule the Ties and Checks of *Conscience,* than as it promotes bodily Pleasures; that is, we are not oblig'd to act according to Justice, when we can promote them by any Action, which we are *cunning* enough to *conceal,* or *powerful* enough to *support.* All Virtue, according to them, any farther than it promotes their own sensual Pleasure, is owing only to Custom, popular Opinion, and the Prejudices of Education, which a wise Man, say they, must comply with, in order to promote his own Ends. If this were the Case, the Encouragement to Virtue, and Restraints upon Vice, are not sufficient.

And, if there be no obligation to Justice, there can be no place for *Fortitude,* which is only in defence of an honest and a just Cause, *separated* from which it is *Folly,* and in *opposition* to it, *Oppression.* But, upon the *Epicurean* Scheme, every thing ought to be sacrific'd to the preservation of Life, and the enjoyment of sensual Pleasure, which it would, therefore, be folly to hazard, and madness to sacrifice, in defence of either Friends, or Country; for Religion is with them out of the Question.

It may justly be question'd, Whether the *Heathen* Philosophers, in §XIII. The *Philosophers,* amongst the *Greeks,* succeeded the *Poets* in the profession of teaching Virtue; and they certainly made improvements in *moral Discipline,* they reduc'd it into the form of an Art, enrich'd it with variety of Arguments, fortified its Precepts with great Reasons, pro-

pos'd many wise Considerations for subduing exorbitant Affections and
Passions; they set forth the praises of Virtue, its excellency and importance, with great Vigour and Eloquence; and, in several instances, excellently declaim'd against Vice with great Wit and Judgment; they dis-
parag'd the Vanities of the World, and the Follies of human Life. There
is amongst them an unpopular kind of Virtue, which, altho' greatly distant from the holy Life, yet, in several respects, does resemble it. Their
Discipline and Institution had a considerable effect upon some of themselves; some of the Philosophers were great Examples of the Virtue
which they taught, and they made some few Converts from Debauchery
to Philosophy; and some few Common-wealths have had their Laws
from Philosophers. The Philosophers, therefore, may seem to have done
a great deal of Service to the Interest of Virtue; but, if their Disservices
be set against their Services; if their Ignorance, Vice, and Extravagance,
be compar'd with their Virtue; it may justly be doubted, upon a full
Comparison, whether they have done any real Service at all to the Cause
of *Virtue* and *Goodness*. The mighty Prejudices, which they have done
to the Interests of it, clearly enough appear in the accounts already given;
for the further setting of which in a clear Light, we will here take a brief
Survey, both of their *moral Learning* and of their *Life*.

the whole, were of Service to the Cause of Virtue.

1. The sublimer sort of them distributed the Virtues into three Kinds,
the *Ethical, Political,* and *Divine*. The Ethical and Political Virtue may
be called the common Morality, which constitutes a *good* Man; but the
Divine Virtue is suppos'd to be his *Assimilation to God,* and his *Deification*. This Divine Virtue is *Philosophic-Pagan,* the *Popular-Pagans* having no concern in it, and was the invention of Philosophy, but was not
for the Interest of Virtue, but was rather to its Prejudice and Disservice;
for it is not truly *Divine Moral Virtue,* constituting a divinely-good Man,
but an Imposture, unpopular Humour, Fancy; and a wicked sort of
Bravery is made the End, the Chief Good, the Divine Virtue, and the
Happiness, of Man, his Assimilation to God, and his Deification. *Apollonius* ask'd the *Brachmans, "What they were"? Jarchas,* the Prince of
them, answer'd, *"They thought themselves Gods."* Apathy they thought a
great and a Divine Thing, *"To live in the Body, as the Soul of the World
in the World, which cannot be struck, or impress'd upon, from without. He*

As appears, from a Consid-eration of the Divine Virtue of the Philoso-phick Pagans;

is devoid of Grief; is not a compound of Soul and Body; accounteth not the Death of Mortals, or the Ruin of his Country, any great Matter; he is above the Fear of any thing; trusteth to himself, that he shall have nothing of Evil, so he shall be fearless of any thing," saith *Plotinus.*[30] Thus they oppose the sufficiency of Virtue against all Externals. But to be thus unapprehensive of Danger, is Folly and Fool-hardiness; it is as unnatural, as it is irreligious, and ruinous to all true Virtue and Goodness. They thus impiously deified themselves, and their Virtue, by their *self-Sufficiency, self-Security,* and *Confidence.* *"They that are furnish'd with the Virtues, living in greatness and celsitude of Mind, are always in Happiness. Philosophy setteth them intirely in the Fortress of Virtue, above Grief and Fear."*[31]

And from the excessive Pride of the Stoicks.

2. There is much of *Pride* and *Arrogance,* complicated with other Vices, in the *Philosophick Pagans* rampant *Affectation of Divinity.* They were as highly conceited of their own Merits, as *Diogenes* was, who fancied, that he merited his Alms. In *Aristotle's* Composition of *Magnanimity*[32] there is a large Dose of Pride, and *Celsus's Generosity*[33] is of the same Character. Much of the *Stoical* Philosophy is a rant and huff of Pride; the *greatness* and *height* of Mind, to which they pretend, is bloated and unsound; and the *Constancy of their Wise-Man* is a System of such Maxims, as are the very Quintessence of Pride. *"The Wise-Man is not obnoxious to any Injury. The Wise-Man can suffer no Evil. An Injury detracteth and diminisheth, whereas nothing can be taken from the Wise-Man,"* who hath all in himself. *"Wickedness is not so strong as Virtue, therefore the Wise-Man is not hurt by Malice. None can benefit the Wise-Man,"* who wanteth nothing, *"therefore none can hurt him. An Injury is from Hope, or Fear; the Wise-Man is touch'd with neither. None receiveth an Injury unmov'd, the Wise-Man is not mov'd. A Contumely is a Contempt, and thence hath its Name; which the Wise-Man doth not look upon as belonging to him, who knows his own Greatness. He thinketh also, that*

---

30. Maxwell provides no source for this quotation, but very similar sentiments can be found in Plotinus, *Enneads,* I.4.4 and I.4.7.

31. Cicero, *De Finibus,* V.

32. Aristotle, *Nicomachean Ethics,* III.5, IV.7, 8.

33. Origen, *Contra Celsum,* I.

*all others are so much inferiour, that they have not boldness to despise Things
so high above them. If he once debaseth himself, so as to be mov'd with Injury,
or Contumely, he can never be secure; whereas Security is the proper Good
of the Wise-Man."* [34] If Pride and Stomachfulness had not been one of
the *Stoicks* Cardinal Virtues, they could not have applauded *Cato's* barbarous *Self-Murder, "who scorn'd to be a Petitioner to any, either for his
Death, or his Life, and was a contemner of all Powers."* [35] They call themselves *great Men,* and accordingly found their Happiness, not upon the
Favours of God and true Piety, but upon their *Greatness of Spirit, the
Greatness and Stoutness of an high invincible Mind;*[36] whence their Virtue
becomes a sort of Self-magnifying and Self-deifying, which is but an
illegitimate kind of Bravery of Spirit, incongruous to their Condition
as Creatures, much more incongruous to frail miserable Men, and most
of all incongruous to wicked miserable Sinners. Nor is there any Thing
more distastful to a truly pious Mind, than the haughty *Pharisaical* Humour of these *Philosophick-Pagan* Magnificoes swaggering with their
Virtue, their *Magnitude,* their *Celsitude,* their *Altitude,* their *Fortitude,*
their *Beatitude.* Pride suggested that *Stoical* Maxim of *Heraclitus. "The
Wise need not any Friends."* Whence all the wonderful Provision, which
Divine Grace has made for a World of wicked Sinners, was lost upon
these Philosophers; for they that need no Friend, need no Saviour, or
Salvation. They were able to live of themselves, and had an imaginary
Happiness of their own making, wherein they took Satisfaction and
Content; they look'd upon their Philosophy as the Perfection of Wisdom and Virtue, in it-self and to them; and thought, both themselves
and their Institution, far Superiour to *Popular* Mankind; and, therefore,
it was but agreeable to their *Philosophick* Grandeur and Magnificence,
to contemn *Christianity,* which is *a popular Institution, design'd for, and
adapted to, the Salvation of miserable Sinners;* whereas they were rais'd
to a Superiority above Sin and Misery, and suppos'd themselves nothing
less than *Divine Men,* and *Kings,* Jupiter's *Sons* and *Peers,* and *petty De-*

34. Seneca, *De Constantia Sapientis.*
35. Seneca, *De Providentia,* ch. 2; *Epistulae Morales* XXIV.
36. Ibid. XCII; Cicero, *Tusculan Disputations,* V.

ities. "*It must be something Super-Human, Celestial, and Magnificent, that constituteth the Wise-Man. If thou ask, What that is? As God and his Beatitude is Constituted, so is the Wise-Man.*"[37] *Chrysippus* affirmed, "*That the Happiness of* Jove *is in no respect more Eligible, nor more Fair, nor more Venerable, than that of the Wise-Man.*" Virtues are thought to be true and genuine, when they are lov'd and desir'd for their own sake; but it appears, from the *Stoicks* Elation of Mind, that when Virtues are desir'd for their own sake, in a way of Separation from God, and without any Relation to him, they are proud and tumid, and are rather Vice than Virtue. *Plato* is much more modest in his Accounts of Virtue, than the strutting *Stoicks;* yet some of the *Stoick's* principal Maxims, which nothing but Pride inspir'd, particularly that eminent One, "*The Wise-Man is self-sufficient,*" are derived from *Socrates* and *Plato.* Pride made *Plato* an envious Man, *Socrates* an ireful Man, the *Cynick* a Boaster in his great Atchievements in the Conquest of Vice. The best of these Masters alloweth us μεγαλοφρονεῖν, "*to be proud of the Conquest of any Vice.*"[38] And, "*We rightly glory in our Virtue,*" saith *Cicero,* a great Wit, but a very vain-glorious Man, who also complaineth to his Wife, "*Neither the Gods, whom thou hast most chastly serv'd, nor Men, whom I have constantly sav'd, have requited us.*"[39]

These Philosophers have been justly call'd, what they certainly were to a Crime, *Animals of Glory,* and *Traffickers for Fame;* yet so, as to be *great Adversaries to the Appetite of Vain-Glory,* as appeareth from the Tenor of their Philosophy. They despis'd the *Popular Pagans,* their Judgment, Fame, Pomp, Acclamations, and Applause, at a great Rate; they expatiate upon the *Emptiness* of *Fame,* as also, how narrow, inconstant, and devoid of Judgment it is; and the *Folly* and *Iniquity* of those who affect it; that we ought to consider the Quality of Persons that praise, or dispraise; that Fame is one of those Things, which are *not in our power,*

---

37. Seneca, *Epistulae Morales,* XCVII.

38. Crinitus, *De Honesta Disciplina* (1508), III.1; Grotius, *De Veritate Religionis Christianae,* II, annotations to sect. 18; Gataker in *Markou Antoninou,* p. 94; Epictetus, *Dissertationes,* II.18.

39. Cicero, *Letters to Friends,* XIV.4.

which others give and take away at pleasure; and therefore, say they, they are Fools who affect it, that desire to be esteem'd Beneficent for doing Good; who suppose, that the Applause of such is of great Moment, that know not themselves, and would be had in Admiration by those, who themselves call *Mad:* That Fame and Honour is not worth the while, being but a mere noise and clattering of Tongues, some Body telling these Things to some Body; they that praise another, soon dispraising him, and both being quickly buried in Oblivion: Good is not the better for being prais'd; we should be indifferent whether we do our Duty, disprais'd, or prais'd: The Lovers of Good practise it, as Lovers enjoy one another, secretly, without desiring any Hearers, or Spectators, to praise them: That we ought not to accept the Praise and Approbation of ill Men, nor guide our Life by the Opinion of the Injudicious, nor place our Happiness in the Minds and Thoughts of others, nor so much as take into our Thoughts what others say, or think, of us. Some that were not *Stoicks*[40] count themselves mean Proficients, except a Reproach be as welcome to them, as a Mark of hearty Approbation. The *Stoicks* exercise themselves to an indifferency as to Praise and Dispraise; and, not withstanding their *Pharisaical* Humour in other respects, in all Things to avoid *Ostentation,* and to do nothing for Opinion. They are urgent with Men, to chuse that which is Good, because it is Good, and not for popular Opinion; and some of them will not stretch out a Finger for a good Fame.[41] They deride the Ambitious and Vain Glorious, ridicule their Folly, who are puffed up with Honour, neither admire, nor desire Greatness, (some thinking Riches and Principalities inconsistent with virtuous Living,[42]) hugely disparage a great Name and Fame after Death; forewarn all that will be Philosophers, to expect Derision and Reproaches at their Entrance upon the Philosophick Life; teach them to bear Reproaches well, with great Equanimity and Benevolence; to do well, tho' it expose them to Disgrace, and not to desist from good Practice, nor to fear Contempt, but to contemn Infamy. In this their Doc-

40. Plutarch, *De Profectibus in Virtute* (in *Moralia*), p.m. 82.
41. Gataker in *Markou Antoninou,* p. 138.
42. Simplicius, *Commentarius in Epicteti Enchiridion,* p. 69.

trine they were much more severe, than those who suppose, *"Ambition to be of use in correcting the other vicious Affections, but must itself be put off in the last Place, as* Plato *hath call'd it the last Coat."* [43] But their *Pride* and *Arrogance* was of an unpopular Kind, mix'd with a *vicious Affectation of Vain-Glory;* for the *Greek* Philosophers usually reproach'd one another with their Vain-Glory;[44] thus *Antisthenes, Crates, Diogenes, Plato, Pyrrho,* were reproach'd by their Fellow-Philosophers; *Socrates* espied it thro' the Holes of *Antisthenes's* Cloak; and of *Socrates* himself, perhaps, *Cardan* has made a right Judgment, *"That he was extremely desirous of Glory, altho' he most of all dissembled this."* [45] They glory'd in their contempt of Glory, supposing that a contempt of Glory was the best way to obtain it. Therefore, tho' they may justly be accounted *Animals of popular Glory,* yet their Philosophy was a great Adversary to the Appetite of it, and they reproach'd one another with it, as a vicious Affection.

The *Stoicks,* in consequence of their excessive Pride, were too stout to humble themselves under the afflicting hand of Providence. The *Platonists* will not always allow this Supposition, "That Calamities are from a divine Hand," or, "That God is the Dispenser, both of Things Good and Evil to us."[46] But the *Popular Pagans* were not too high to be humbled; they looked upon their Calamities, as the Effects of the Anger of their Gods, acknowledg'd their Dependence upon them, and, in any great Distress of their Affairs, betook themselves to their most humble Supplications, in order to atone their Displeasure, and gain their Favour.

One of the bravest Exploits, which the *Philosophick Pagans* constantly celebrate, is the killing of Tyrants, and delivering Cities and Nations from them. The Practice of this applauded Virtue occasion'd the Torture of *Zeno Eleates,* who is said, to have kept the Doctrine of *Parmeendes* inviolate as Gold in the Fire, "And by his Deeds he shew'd, that a *great Man feareth nothing but to be base; that it is Children and Women, and*

---

43. Ibid., p. 95.
44. Gataker in *Markou Antoninou,* pp. 434, 435.
45. Cardan, *De Rerum Varietate* (1557), XVI.93.
46. Porphyry, *De Abstinentia,* II.38, 41.

Men, who have the Souls of Women, that are afraid of Pain."[47] From which Idea of a great Man it appeareth, that the *Fortitude* of the *Heathen Philosophers* is of no better Kind than the common Military Fortitude, or the Fortitude of those celebrated *Popular Pagans, Mutius* and *Regulus,* of *Cleopatra* and *Asdrubals* Wife, who threw her-self and her Children into the Fire; or of that famous Harlot at *Athens,* who, knowing of a Conspiracy against the Life of the Tyrant there, with great Bravery suffer'd her-self to be tortur'd to Death, rather than she would discover the Conspirators, and, biting off a piece of her Tongue, spit it out into the Tyrant's Face.

Philosophy cannot boast of many great Examples of *Patience;* the Grandees of the *Stoical* Family, *Cato* and *Brutus,* falling into Troubles fell into transports of Rage and Impatience. So *Hierocles,* according to *Saidas,* being whipp'd at *Byzantium* 'till the Blood came, took the Blood in the Hollow of his Hand, and threw it upon the Judge, saying, *"Cyclops, there is Wine for you, seeing you have eaten Man's Flesh."* Some, indeed, of the *Philosophick Pagans* have express'd an admirable Constancy of Mind in shaking Circumstances. As *Cleanthes,* who stood unmov'd without changing Countenance, when he was publickly reproach'd in the Theatre by the Poet *Sositheus.*[48] And *Polemo* did not so much as wax Pale, when his Leg was torn by mad Dogs. Yet, because this Philosophick Firmness was but of the same Kind with *Epicurus's* in his Strangury, or the Sceptick *Pyrrho's,* who endur'd cuttings and burnings with great constancy of Mind; or that of well disciplin'd *Gladiators,* and the *Spartan* Boys, who were whipp'd at the Altar, 'till the Blood gush'd out of their Bowels, without whimpering; therefore some have rightly pronounc'd concerning that *Patience* which *Philosophy* professeth, that it is *Spurious,* only a *proud Sullenness;* so much the more Spurious, as it is the more Proud. *Lipsius* therefore, otherwise an extravagant Admirer of *Stoicism,* lying upon his Sick-Bed, and strugling with grievous Pain, discarded the *Stoical* Patience, and having our Saviour's Picture hanging near his Bed,

---

47. Plutarch, *Adversus Colotem* (in *Moralia*), p.m. 1126.
48. The life of Cleanthes in Diogenes Laertius, *Lives,* VIII.

he pointed to it, and gave his Patience its due Character, *"That is the true Patience."*[49]

Several of the *Philosophers* have discours'd against Revenge, or *retaliating Injuries,* for the bearing them with Meekness, and for universal Benevolence;[50] and there are several Instances of these Virtues amongst the *Greek Philosophers.*[51] But their Practice of them looks more like *unpopular* Humour, than serious Goodness; in laying the Foundation of them, they intermix much of Pride, and Paradoxical *Stoical* Conceit, *That the Wise-Man can suffer no Injury:* And the most considerable Instances of these mighty Virtues are *Aristides* and *Phocion,* who may justly be reckon'd among the *Popular Pagans. Aristides,* after great Services, being banish'd by his Citizens unjustly, at his Departure pray'd the Gods, that the *Athenians* might never, by any Trouble, or Distress, be forc'd to recal him. And *Phocion,* being unjustly condemn'd, charg'd his Son *Phocas,* that he should never revenge his Death. But these Resemblances of *Christian* Virtue in *Heathen* good Men, did not issue from a *divine Kind of Charity,* but were Branches of their *Human-Social Virtue,* and issued from a mighty Love to their Country, which is most eminent in *Heathens.* The Virtue of these *Popular Pagans* pretendeth not to be *Divine,* nor do they, therefore, deserve to be celebrated as *divine* Men upon account of it: But the *Philosophick Pagans,* by far lesser Matters than these, got the Reputation of *divine* Men. One of their principal Virtues was their *abandoning the Superfluities of Life.* Whence *Diogenes,* seeing one take Water out of a River with his Hand, and drinking it out of his Hand, threw away his Dish, which he us'd to carry about him to drink Water in, resolving thenceforth to drink it out of the hollow of his Hand; and for this *Freak,* with others of like Nature, this *unpopular Humourist* is celebrated by his *Fellow-Philosophers* as a *"Divine Man."*

The *Philosophick Pagans* were like the *Popular,* in not discerning what

49. The source of this anecdote is Woverius's *Assertio Lipsiani Donari* (1607); the piece appears in *Iusti Lipsii Opera Omnia* (1675), I., pp. 184–86.

50. Simplicius, *Commentarius in Epicteti Enchiridion,* p. 140; Grotius, *Annotationes in Novum Testamentum* (1646) on Matthew 5.44, 45.

51. The note refers the reader to Benjamin Oley's note on bk. X of Oley's edition of Thomas Jackson's *Works* (1653).

is truly *Divine* and *Holy,* from what is *Atheous* and *Unholy.* Altho' they liv'd in gross Crimes, beside their *Pagan* Religion, yet they did not discern between Sin and Holiness. They were *Self-justifiers* at the Rate of the *Pharisees,* and, therefore, perfectly indispos'd for such a Religion, that is a Religion for Sinners; and they were too high for Repentance, which the *Popular Pagans* were not, who had a Sense of Sin, and of their need of Pardon, which they often express'd at Death: But *Apuleius*[52] pretends, *"That he always accounted all Sin a Thing detestable"; Xenophon* saith, *"No one ever saw* Socrates *do, or heard him speak, any Thing that was Impious and Irreligious":* Socrates himself had no Sense of Sin at his Death, nor express'd any Repentance; nor is there any Appearance of either in *Epictetus's* Preparatives for Death.[53] Such mistaken Teachers of Virtue were these Sages of this World, that they thought themselves made Gods by such a Virtue, that could not make them the People of God, which was a very gross Mistake, and speaketh their *Philosophy* to be no better, than a *worldly Kind of Wisdom,* and their *Virtue* could be of no better a Character than their *Philosophy.* By their introducing their Philosophy, true Religion was much more prejudic'd, than it was before by their *Pagan* Religion, they made an additional Prejudice to it, they rais'd up a new Enemy, they introduc'd a Mountebank, who pretendeth to do all Cures, that a divine Physician might be thought needless.

3. The *Super-Ethical,* as they are called, or the *Divine Virtues* of the *Platonists* are of the spurious and illegitimate kind, and so blended with what is fanciful, or bad, that, in the whole, they signify little or nothing to the constituting a Divinely-good Man. This is the Character, not only of the *Stoicks,* but of the *Platonists Divine Virtue,* in all these Parts of it.

3. The Spuriousness of the divine Virtues of the Platonists.

Such is their Divine Virtue, as it is their *intellectual Form of Life, contemplative of the Platonick Intelligibles,* and *visionary of their T'Agathon,*[54] which cannot be discern'd but by a *boniform Light, which is beyond all that is intellectual.*

52. Apuleius, *Apology,* p. 450.
53. Epictetus, *Discourses,* III.5.
54. *T'Agathon,* meaning "the Good."

Such is their Divine Virtue, as it is *Theurgick;*[55] for they pretend by a converse with the Gods in Theurgy, to be freed from Passion, to partake of Divine Perfections, and to have, what in their Dialect they call, a *Deifick Union;* which one Party of them pretendeth to in the Mystick-Metaphysical Way. And these say, *"The End and Scope is, not to be without Sin, but to be a God."*[56]

Such is their Divine Virtue, as it is the *Platonick Faith* and *Love;* for this Love is only an *Amatorious Madness.* *"When the Mind becometh Un-mental"* (or Mad) *"being drunk with Nectar, this is the Mind, that is in Love."*[57] Much of this sort of Divine Virtue there is in *Platonism;* an Ignorance, that is better than Knowledge; a Madness, that is better than Sobriety of Mind, a *Divine Madness.*

Such is their Divine Virtue, as it is the Virtue of the *Mysticks* and *Quietists,* *"Who being seated in the Bay of super-essential Goodness, enjoy a super-natural Quietism";*[58] to which *Isidore* the *Platonist* pretended. He said, *"That his Soul itself, in sacred Prayers, became wholly a Divine Sea, having in the first Place collected her-self from the Body into her-self, having in the next place"* (extatically) *"parted with her own Morals, and betaken herself from rational Notions to those that are Congenial to Intellect; and in the third place being possess'd with Divine Afflation, and chang'd into an extraordinary Serenity, deiform, not human.*

Such is their Divine Virtue, as it is an Aversation from Terrestrial, Material, and Mortal, Nature, and an Affectation of being wholly in-corporeal and immaterial; for this Affectation of Immaterial Intellectual Nature, and to be mere intellectual Souls, is an irreligious *Philosophick* Vanity and Extravagance, not intirely free from *Magick.* For, in order to the Purity of the Soul, *Pythagoras* prescrib'd strict Abstinence from several sorts of Meats.

The *Platonists* agree, that, according to *Plato* in his *Theaetetus,* Virtue

55. [Maxwell] *"Theurgy* is a kind of super-natural Magick, procuring an extraordinary and immediate intercourse with the Gods, by means of particular Rites and Ceremonies."

56. Plotinus, *Enneads,* I.2.6.

57. Ibid., VI.7.35.

58. Proclus, *In Platonis Theologiam,* I.25.

is a Similitude to God, or the Gods; *"which Assimilation"* (saith *Plato*) *"consisteth in becoming Holy and Just with Prudence."* But to what God, or Gods, this divine Similitude relateth, in this they do not agree, nor wherein this Similitude consisteth. For some say, That this divine Similitude relateth to the *Pagan* Deities in general; others say, That it relateth to the *Platonists* divine Intellect; and others are of Opinion, That it relateth to their *T'Agathon*. Some place this divine Similitude in the speculative Virtue, and intellectual Form of Life; others place it in the practick Virtue, (Ethical and Political,) which seemeth to be the Sense of *Plato;* for *Prudence, Holiness,* and *Justice,* are practical Virtues. In his *Fourth of Laws,* he placeth the divine Similitude in *Temperance,* and in his *Phaedo,* he placeth it in *Temperance* and *Justice;* thus saying, *"Are not they most Happy and Blessed, and such as go to the best Place, that have exercis'd the popular and political Virtues, which we call Temperance and Justice?"* *Plato,* therefore, seemeth to place the divine Similitude in the *Popular Pagans* Holiness and Justice; which the generality of his Followers will not admit, counting the Civil Virtues only the Way to get the divine Similitude, and that this was the Sense of *Plato.* But, whatever may be thought of his Sense, his Account of Virtue, and of the divine Similitude, is an Instance, that the *Philosophick-Pagans* may in Words agree with our Religion, when in Sense there is an extreme Disagreement. For *Plato's* divine Similitude, however it may be interpreted by his Followers, is extremely alien from, and opposite to, that truly divine Similitude, which is *Wisdom, Righteousness,* and *true Holiness,* wherewith he had no Acquaintance. For, had he been acquainted with that truly divine Kind of *Justice,* which is *Righteousness,* he could not have been a *Pagan*-Religionist; nor could he have instituted a Community of Women and of Goods in his Republick; nor would he have taken care to regulate the Drinking in the Feasts of *Bacchus,* without endeavouring to abolish them; nor could he so grosly have mistaken himself, as in a Book of Justice (his *Fifth de Republicâ,*) to discourse in this manner touching the *Greeks* and *Barbarians.* *"All* Greeks *are near of Kin, but extraneous and different from* Barbarians. *When the* Grecians *and* Barbarians *Fight with one another, this is properly called Fighting, for they are Enemies by Nature, and such a Feud must be called a War: But, if* Grecians, *that are Friends by Nature, quarrel with* Grecians, *this is an unnatural Distemper, and* Greece *must be said to be troubled with Sedition, and such a Feud must not be called a War, but a Sedition.*"[59] The *Greeks* had their Philosophy from the *Barbarians,* as they call'd them, and yet they commonly reproach'd them, and, usually, were so uncivil and unjust towards them, that they look'd upon them as *"Enemies by Nature and wild Beasts."*[60] *Plato* follow'd the *Popular Pagans* in their Injustice, as well as in their irreligious Religion. So *Plutarch,* in the Life of *Lycurgus,* can find no Injustice in the *Lacedamonians* Commonwealth, which was instituted for War, and fighting, not for Peace, as *Aristotle* observeth and blameth;[61] the *Spartan* Virtue was the Love of Glory; they were train'd up and exercis'd to be expert Thieves; exposed and murder'd their weak and deform'd Infants, and even this horrible Injustice *Plutarch* approveth. *Aristotle,* also, is known to teach, *"To expose Children that are maimed, and Women to cause Abortions, that they may not exceed their Number";*[62] and he agrees with *Plato* in supposing, *"That War is a natural Thing between the* Greeks *and* Barbarians."[63] *Plato* is justly chargeable with Injustice, in patronizing Lying, wherein he follows the general Sense of the *Heathens,* which was, that a Lye is not bad, if it be expedient, and not pernicious in the Affairs of Men. So, in his *Third* and *Fifth de Republicà, Plato* would have Governours, *"To make use of frequent Lying and Deceit for the Benefit of the Subjects; this must be granted to publick Governours, but not be touch'd by private Men."* If the *Platonists human Justice* is so bad, it is reasonable to suppose, that in their *Divine,* or superhuman *Virtue,* they were not very good.

Aristotle pretended not to an Institution of Divine Virtue.

4. *Aristotle* pretendeth not to an Institution of *Divine Virtue,* or to institute a *Divine-Good Man.* For, altho' he acknowledges a *Divine Virtue,* yet it is in so slender a Degree, that he denies, that there can be any Friendship between God and Man; the Happiness that he insisteth on,

---

59. Grotius, *Annotationes in Novum Testamentum* (1646) on Matthew 5.43.
60. Isocrates, *Panathenaicus,* p.m. 572.
61. Grotius, *De Veritate Religionis Christianae,* bk. II, sects. 12, 14.
62. Aristotle, *Politics,* VII.16.
63. Grotius, *De Veritate Religionis Christianae,* bk. II, sects. 12, 14.

is but the Civil; as the Virtue that he insisteth on, is but the Civil and Military;[64] his Ethicks are but a Branch of worldly Politicks; his active Virtue consisteth in that *Mean,* which the worldly Man's Prudence determineth; and what can *living well* signify, in a Civil Worldly Mans Institution of Virtue, but to live without Vice, or Crime, in the Notion of the Civil World? Therefore it is not to be wonder'd at, that *Aristotle,* differently from the Sense of other Philosophers, patronizeth *Revenge;*[65] or that *Cicero* agrees with him in this Point, (for this must be acknowledg'd, notwithstanding what a learned Bishop hath said to the contrary;[66]) for the former of these did not pretend to be a Religionist, and the latter of them, altho' a Philosopher, yet was not of any Philosophick Institution, and was so uncertain an Admirer of Philosophy, that sometimes he preferreth that one little Book of the XII Tables, before the Libraries of all the Philosophers, both for Utility and weight of Authority. The Lawyers, not without Reason, prefer their Institution to their *Civil* Virtue, before the Philosopher's Institutions to their *Divine* Virtue; which yet must be acknowledg'd, to have a limited agreeableness to the truly *Divine moral* Virtue; but so that, in the whole, the Disagreement is far greater than the Agreement.

5. Whence we may make a Judgment of this Saying of the same learned Bishop; *"All the* Agenda *of Christianity are so far from being opposite, that they are most agreeable to Human Reason, as 'tis cultivated and heighten'd to its utmost Improvement by Philosophy."*[67] If this Saying be converted thus, *All the Philosophers improv'd Reason* (which is their Divine Virtue) *is so far from being opposite, that it is most agreeable to the* Agenda *of Christianity,* it will be a monstrous Proposition. For nothing can be more opposite to the *Agenda* of *Christianity,* than a great part of the Philosophers Divine Virtue; therefore the *Agenda* of *Christianity* are not so suitable to the Philosophers Reason, as is pretended. That this

The *Agenda* of Christianity not agreeable to the Reason of the Philosophick Pagans.

---

64. Aristotle, *Nicomachean Ethics,* X.7.

65. Grotius, *De Veritate Religionis Christianae,* bk. II, sects. 12, 14.

66. Wilkins, Sermon on Romans 12.19 in *Sermons Preached upon Several Occasions by the Right Reverend Father in God, John Wilkins* (1682), pp. 429–56.

67. Ibid., p. 442.

Saying may have any Appearance of Truth, it must be limited to the particular *Agenda* of *Christianity;* for these general *Agenda* of *Christianity* (which are also in part the general *Agenda* of *Judaism*) are directly and expressly opposite to the Philosophers improv'd Reason. *"To have no other Gods but me; to worship the Lord thy God, and to serve him alone; to seek the Kingdom of God and his Righteousness; to take the Kingdom, enter into it, and buy it at any rate; to put off the Heathen Old Man, and to put on the New Man, in the* (Christian) *New Birth, in the New Covenant; to come out of the mundane Society, and the state of Sin and of Death, to pass into the state of Life, to incorporate with the Divine Family, and become a Citizen of the Holy Empire; not to adhere to, but to abandon the Kingdom of Darkness, and to manage an Holy War against its Powers, Interest, and Adherents; to live to him that died for us and rose again; to live for God and his Service, and to make it our daily Care and Prayer, that his Name may be hallow'd, and his Kingdom come."* All which Fundamental *Agenda* of the *Christian* Institution, and such like, are altogether alien from, and opposite to, the *Philosophick Pagans* Sentiments, as they are *Pagans;* nor is that plain Principle and summary of Piety, *the Fear of God,* suitable to their Reason; for they destroy'd it, which the *Popular Pagans* did not, by their Maxims, *"Ira Deorum nulla est,"*[68] *The Gods are never angry,* yet a learned Man saith, *"He knows not any Evangelical Precept or Duty belonging to a Christian's Practice, which natural Men of best Account"* (the Philosophers) *"by the mere Strength of Human Reason have not taught and taken upon them to maintain as Just and Reasonable."*[69] But it would be far better to say; there are not any of the particular *Agenda* of *Christianity,* the Reasonableness whereof may not be illustrated, by what they have suppos'd to be Just and Reasonable: So the *Christian* Martyrs Contempt of Death may be shew'd to be reasonable, which yet was so unsuitable to their improv'd Reason, that it is call'd by one of

---

68. Cicero, *De Officiis,* III.

69. Marcus Aurelius, *Marcus Aurelius Antoninus, the Roman Emperor, His Meditations Concerning Himselfe* [hereafter *Meditations*], translated by Casaubon (1634), preface.

them[70] *"mere Obstinacy"; and* another of them imputeth it to *"Madness and Custom."*[71] The Agreement, therefore, between *Christianity* and *Philosophy* touching this Virtue, *the Contempt of Death,* is complicated with such Disagreement, that the *Christians* Virtue, of that Name, *Philosophy* discardeth as Vice and Folly; and the *Philosophers* Virtue, of that Name, *Christians* discard as Self-Murder, or profane Bravery.

There is, therefore, a want of Judgment and Piety in many of our Modern Elogies of the *Christian* Religion, and Vindications of its Morality, as in this following. *"Christ Jesus taught Morality,* viz. *the Way of living like Men, and the fifth Chapter of* Matthew *is an excellent Lecture of this Kind."*[72] To *live like Men* is a general ambiguous Expression, and to make it of a determinate Signification, it must be understood, to signify in a Sense of Disparagement, *To live as mere Men;* or in a Sense of Excellency, *To live as more than mere Men.* If in the former Sense our Saviour hath taught us, *To live like Men;* he was a Teacher of Morality, at the same rate with *Homer,* of whom *Cicero* complaineth, *"He maketh the Gods to live like Men, whereas he ought to make Men live like the Gods."*[73] So our Saviour is suppos'd, to teach *Christians* to live like *Men;* whereas his Business was, to teach *Men* to live like *Christians.* Things more Vulgar, and accommodate to the human Size, have the Name of *Man* call'd upon them in Scripture; but they are Things great and extraordinary, that have the Name of God call'd upon them, *Job* 1. 6. *Psal.* 65. 9. 104. 16. *Isa.* 8. 1. *Gal.* 1. 7, 11. To live like *Men,* therefore, is far from being expressive of the *Christian* Godliness, which is a *living according to God,* and to sink it into such a Morality, is a *debasing the Divinity of the Christian Religion.* Whose holy Laws are *Christianity,* which cannot be of one Piece with the Moralities of *Jews* and *Heathens,* and, therefore, must not be call'd Morality, merely such, but the *Divine,* or *Christian* Kind of *Morality,* which ought to be contradistinguish'd to mere *Heathen Morality.* And what can be more apparent, than that our

70. Marcus Aurelius, *Meditations,* XI.3.
71. Epictetus, *Discourses,* IV.7.
72. Glanvill, *The Way to Happiness* (1670), pp. 113, 114.
73. Cicero, *Tusculan Disputations,* I.

Saviour's *Beatitudes, "Blessed are the Poor in Spirit, blessed are they that Mourn,"* are not Rules of mere Morality, teaching to live like Men, but are Rules initiative into the *Christian* Sanctity, which is the Life of the regenerate Children of God? So the following Precepts, *"Ye are the Salt of the Earth, the Light of the World, let your Light shine before Men, that they may glorify your Father which is in Heaven,"* are not Precepts of Morality, enjoining nothing more than to live like mere Men. And, in the Progress of a Sinner's Conversion to Godliness, such Difficulties and Conflicts usually occur, that speak it a sort of Virtue, greatly distant from, and transcendent to, ordinary Moral Virtue, which is so remote from it, that it may indispose Men to the Acquisition of it. *"For Men, never much affrighted with the Danger, wherein all by Nature stand, nor inflam'd with the Love of a better Country than they enjoy, cannot address themselves to any resolute, or speedy Departure out of the Territories of Civil Moralities, within which, if Satan hold us, he maketh full reckoning of us, as of his Civil, or Natural, Subjects."*[74] Therefore, to the way of removing out of Satan's Territories to the Territories of Godliness, the Civil Moralities may, by Accident, be a great Impediment. For the Way is a duly humbling Repentance. The high and brave Spirit of Man must be broken; it must be Poor, that he may be Rich; empty, that he may be filled; have nothing, that he may possess all Things; be Condemn'd, that he may be Pardon'd; be a Fool, that he may be Wise; and Die, that he may be made Alive. All Virtue, which is not the *Christian,* is but that of the *Will of Man,* of Mind and Quality, the *Human. Inter Ethnicam Philosophiam & Christianam tantum interest, quantum a divino Spiritu humanum abest ingenium.*[75]

The Virtue and Religion of the Heathen Philosophers, were of so spurious a kind, as, in part, to cause

The Sufferings of the Primitive *Christians* may reasonably be thought an Effect, not only of the *Popular Pagan's* Vice and Folly, but of the *Philosophick Pagans* Wisdom and Virtue; for their truly great and generous Maxims of Virtue, in their Sense and Application, lead to the Persecution of the *Christian* Church and Religion, and make it Virtue and

---

74. Jackson, *A Treatise Containing the Originall of Unbeliefe,* sect. 1, ch. 5.

75. Maxwell does not cite a source for the quotation: "Between Pagan and Christian Philosophy there is as much difference as exists between the Holy Spirit and human intelligence."

Duty. Their most noble and generous Maxims of Virtue, are touching the social Duty of Man, Duty to the *Publick,* to the *Whole,* to the *Universe* of rational Beings. For they suppos'd, "That every particular Man is a Member of the *Publick,* and of the *Whole* consisting of *Heathen* Gods and Men, a Part of that Whole; and that, as a Part, he is for the Whole intirely, (for himself, only as a Part of the Whole,) for its Being and Well-being, to Constitute and Preserve it, and to be Useful and Subservient to its Interest. But the Physician cutteth off distemper'd Parts of the Body, for the Safety and Welfare of the Whole. As particular Men, and lesser Systems, must suffer for the Whole; so they are design'd and oblig'd, faithfully to take care of, and co-operate to, the Welfare of the Whole, of their Fellow-Members and Fellow-Citizens, wherein their own Welfare is involv'd, as a Part in the Whole. The Publick and Universal Good, is the great Good. As *Cato* was minded," the unjust Persecution of the Primitive *Christians.*

Non sibi, sed toto genitum se credere Mundo.   Lucan.[76]

"He believ'd, That he was not born for his own private Advantage, but for that of the whole World. And, on the contrary, base Selfishness is the Sum of all Evil. *Because I am of Kin* (saith *Marcus Antoninus*) *to those Parts of the Universe, that are of the same kind, I will Practise nothing unsocial: But rather, I will take care of those that are my Kindred, and incline my whole Man to the common Utility, and avoid the contrary; often say to thy-self, I am a Member of the System of Rational Beings. But, if thou say, I am a distinct Part of that System, thou dost not love Men from the Heart, nor considerest thy-self as comprehended in the Whole.*[77] And he that is not thus affected, is not *naturally* affected, is not *well,* nor *justly,* nor *charitably,* nor *sociably,* nor *honourably,* nor *humanly,* affected; he hath *put off the Man,* as the *Philosophers* suppose."

But, altho' these Notions and Maxims of theirs touching *Virtue* and *Duty to the Whole,* are, all of them, extremely Solid and truly Generous, if applied and determin'd to a genuine and legitimate *Whole,* or *Universe;* yet, in their *Pagan* Application and Determination of them to

76. Lucan, *Pharsalia,* II.383.
77. Marcus Aurelius, *Meditations,* X.6, VII.13.

their *Whole, Universe,* or *Catholick System,* consisting of *Heathen Gods* and *Men,* they are extremely false and wicked, and manifestly lead them to Persecute the *Christian* Church and Religion. For the *Christians* were a People separated or broken off from their *Whole,* or *Universe;* and, consequently, were such as *Marcus Antoninus* calls *Apostems of the World.* Therefore it was but to their own mundane Tribe, that the *Popular* and *Philosophick Pagans* were charitably and sociably Affected; the World will love its own; the *Christians* that were Aliens, and who profess'd, that *Jerusalem* was their Country, they treated as those, who were *no longer Men.* The Philosophers thought themselves oblig'd, *to have regard for rational Beings who were Congenial and Cognate to them;* and, accordingly, they thought themselves oblig'd, to take care of their Gods and Demons; for these they look'd upon as Congenial and Cognate. But *Christ* and *Christians* erected and constituted a *Whole,* or *Universe,* opposite and destructive to their *Whole Universe,* or *Catholick System,* which if they look'd upon themselves oblig'd to take care of and uphold, they must necessarily think themselves oblig'd to destroy *Christianity.* Every Man must strenuously endeavour to maintain the old Religion of their Ancestors, succour the ruinous Empire of the Gods, which Christianity came to demolish, and to restore it to its Grandeur and Magnificence.

The supreme God, who was the chief Object of the religious Worship of the *Heathens,* was the Soul of the World.

6. In the *Pagan System of the Universe,* one of their supreme Deities, altho' it was not absolutely their supreme Deity, may be justly called *the supreme Deity of their Religion and Laws.* This Name, a *supreme Deity,* is ambiguous, with respect to *Heathens* and *Christians.* For, if it be understood in a general and indeterminate Notion, it is Matter of Agreement between them both; but, when once it comes to a particular Determination, it is not Matter of Agreement, but of Difference between the *Pagan* and *Christian* Theists; and, in some sort, among the *Pagan* Theists themselves, they understanding *the supreme Deity* in various Notions, and, so far, making various supreme Deities. But, as the Name, *Prince of Philosophers,* in the Schools of the *Aristotelians,* must be understood of *their Prince of Philosophers,* reputed such, the *Platonists* and *Epicureans* have *another Prince of Philosophers:* So this Name, *the supreme Deity,* amongst the *Pagan* Theists, and the several sorts of *Pagan* Theists,

must be understood of *their supreme Deity,* reputed such, several sorts of *Pagan* Theists having several sorts of supreme Deities. So that the Epithet, which they gave to the *Jews* supreme Deity, properly belongs to their own.

——— *Dedita Sacris*
Incerti Judaea Dei ———   Lucan.[78]

Judaea, *the Worshipper of an uncertain God.*

The supreme Deity, among the *Pagans,* is of this particular Determination, not merely, *a Deity Supreme,* but the *supreme of their Pagan Deities, Summus Deorum.* A usual Form of Invocation amongst them was, *O Jove, and the Gods,* understanding by *Jove, the God of the Gods.* Their Prayers were made *to Jupiter the King, and to the other Gods.* He is usually styl'd in *Homer, Virgil,* and the other Poets, *the Father and King of the Gods.* By *the Gods* they understand *the supreme Deity and the other Deities,* and, for that Reason, they speak of *God* and *the Gods* promiscuously, because they consider them as *one System.* They consider'd their Deities collectively, celebrated a Festival of them all in common, called θεοξενία, and consecrated Altars to *all the Gods and Goddesses.* They are his Associates, Collegues, and Allies, and he is the Head of the Family of *Pagan* Deities. It is the Title of a Chapter in *Eugubinus,*[79] *"That* Aristotle *affirmeth with* Homer, *that the supreme God is the Father of the Gods and of Men, of the same Kind, Kindred, and Family with them,"* as Sons and Father.

Homer, therefore, and *Aristotle,* the Poets and the Philosophers, the *Popular* and the *Philosophick Pagans,* agree in the Acknowledgment of a *supreme Deity,* in the Way of *Polytheism,* and with Relation to subordinate Deities. They agree, therefore, in the Acknowledgment of a supreme Deity, in the Sense of their Religion and Laws, but not in the Sense of their Schools. When the Philosophers speak of the supreme Deity, in the peculiar Sense of their Schools, they mean one supreme

78. Lucan, *Pharsalia,* II.592–93.
79. Eugubinus, or Steuchus, *De Perenni Philosophia* (1540).

Deity; and when they speak of the supreme Deity popularly, in the Sense of their Religion and Laws, they mean another.

The *Pagans Theism* being their *Polytheism,* and the *supreme Deity* being a Term of their *Polytheism,* it is manifestly inconsistent with the Acknowledgment of the true God, to whose Supremacy and Sovereignty it belongeth, to subsist in the Quality and Condition of *God alone.* The Atheism charg'd upon *Anaxagoras,* (for which the *Athenians* banish'd him, fin'd him five Talents, and had put him to Death, if his Scholar *Pericles* had not interpos'd,) was only a denying *the Deity of the Earth, the Sun, the Moon, the Stars,* shutting out of Being *the Soul of the World, destroying the Deity of the World, and the Parts thereof,* making them inanimate and unintelligent, calling *the Moon an Earth, and the Sun a Mass of Fire;* whilst at the same time he acknowledg'd a *single supreme Deity existing separately,* whilst he discarded the Soul of the World, which deified all the Parts thereof, which was no less than a Subversion of the main of the *Pagan* Theism; for which *Plato* charges him with Atheism. And *Ficinus*[80] affirms, "That *Plato* in his *Book of Laws* asserts the Coelestial Gods only, because the Contemplation of the higher Deities is very foreign to the matter of Laws." Which is an Insinuation, that those higher Deities in *Platonism* are properly Gods of Philosophical Speculation only, no Deities of Religion and Laws. Nor could the *Platonists* suppose their first Principle a Deity of Religion and Laws; for they look upon it, as quite above all external Adoration; and such was *Numa's* Deity, to whom he would neither allow Image, nor material Sacrifice. "Plato" (saith *Eugubinus*[81]) *"did not so clearly propose the greatest God as an Object of Worship, because he could not be worshipp'd; what he is, and how to be worshipp'd, cannot be describ'd, or declar'd. In three Places he calleth him undeclarable, in the* Timaeus, *difficult for Thought, undeclarable by Speech, or Word. According to* Philo *also he is unconceivable, unthinkable, undeclarable; being thus unspeakable and inexplicable, and such as the old Theologers call innominable, some invisible, others to be worshipp'd in silence, others uninvestigable; therefore* Plato *hath said nothing*

---

80. Maxwell refers to Plato, *Laws,* X, in Ficino's *Platonis Opera Omnia.*
81. Eugubinus, *De Perenni Philosophia,* V.3.

of him in his Book of Laws, nor set down any Thing concerning his Worship, because he could not, this Deity being unknowable, both as to Name and Nature." If *Plato*'s supreme Deity is of no *Religion;* if all *Understanding, Conception, Name, Word, Speech,* be utterly incompetible and unapplicable to this first Principle; if there be no *Doctrine,* no *Learning,* no *Discipline,* or *Institution,* touching such a Deity, and, consequently, no *Religion;* this is not discoursing, nor reasoning, but dreaming of such a Deity; for there can be no Proof of the Being of such a Deity, neither *à Priori,* nor *à Posteriori,* no more than could be given of such Gods as *Epicurus* suppos'd, who *did nothing,* and who could not be known, either *directly,* or *by their Works.*

However, the Followers of *Plato* thought this *supreme Deity* was to be worshipp'd, but *by Silence, pure Cogitation, and Assimilation to him, which is the Sacrificing our Life to him.* But such a kind of Deity and his Worship being foreign from matter of Law, and altogether unsuitable to the generality of Mankind, *Plato* thought it a Solecism to mention him in his Book of Laws. *"He taketh care that the Matters of his Acroamatical Theology, his Acroamatical Deity, do not fall into the Hands of unskilful Men; for scarce any Thing, as I suppose, would be Matter of more Derision amongst the common People. From* Plato, *therefore, you have the true Cause, why we may not speak of the first Deity amongst the Vulgar, why it is not lawful to publish to the Vulgar the Parent of the Universe: For, not understanding the Things that are said of him, they deride them, being Things remote from popular Custom, and gross Ears; therefore, treating of Laws which ought to be publish'd to the People, he spake nothing of that great uninvestigable Deity, proposing only the Worship of Heaven to the People, to whom he must speak only of that, which they thought certain Religion."* [82]

The *Platonists,* therefore, tho' they had higher Deities in their School, do yet agree, *That the supreme Deity of their Religion and Laws, is the Soul of the World, or the Mundane System as animated by a governing Mind, which Deifies it,* the supreme Deity of the *Popular Pagans,* and the same with *Zeus,* or *Jupiter. Speusippus,* also, agreeable to *Plato,* is said by *Cicero*

---

82. Ibid.

to have held *"a certain Force, or Power, whereby all Things are govern'd, and that Animal."* [83] Such also was *Pythagoras's* Notion of the Deity, as others, and *Cicero* also in the same Treatise relates; *"Pythagoras also acknowledg'd one God, an incorporeal Mind, diffus'd thro' the whole Nature of Things, the Origin of vital Sense to all Animals."* In like manner *Onatus* the *Pythagorean* defines *"God, the Mind and Soul, and Ruler of the whole World."* The *Jove* of the *Orphick* Theology is *the mundane Soul and System.*

Πάντα γδ ρν μεγάλῳ Ζῆνος τάδε σώ ματι κεῖται.

All these Things lie in the great Body of Jove.

"A Spirit that pervadeth the whole World," was one of the *Aegyptian* Notices of *God.* [84] The Supreme Deity of the *Peruvians* was of the same kind, as appeareth from his Name *Pachacamac,* which signifieth *the Soul, or Life, of the World.* The *Stoicks* usually intitle the Supreme Deity, *The Mind and Understanding of the Whole, the common, or universal, Mundane Nature, and the common Reason of Nature, the ruling Principle of the World;* and, as *Zeno* defin'd *God, a Spirit pervading the whole World.* And the *Indians,* according to *Megasthenes, suppos'd, That the God, who is the Maker and Governour of the World, pervadeth the Whole of it.* Agreeably to these Sentiments, the *Romans* styled *Capitoline Jove, "the Mind and Spirit, the Guardian and Governour of the Universe, the Artificer and Lord of this Mundane Fabrick, to whom every Name, Fate, Providence, Nature, the World, is agreeable."* [85] So true is that of *Macrobius;* "Jupiter *among the Theologers is the Soul of the World."* [86] The Soul moveth and governeth the Body, which it presideth over, saith *Cicero, "As that chief God governeth the World."* [87] St. *Austin* saith thus of *Varro;* "When Varro *elsewhere calleth the rational Soul of every one a Genius, and affirmeth such a Mind, or Soul, of the whole World to be God; he plainly implieth that*

---

83. Cicero, *De Natura Deorum,* I.32.
84. Horapollo, *Hieroglyphica,* bk. I, n. 61.
85. Seneca, *Naturales Quaestiones,* II.40.
86. Cicero, *In Somnium Scipionis,* I.17.
87. Ibid., II.12.

God is the Universal Genius of the World, and that this is he, whom they call Jove. *Those only seem to* Varro *to have understood what God is, who thought him a Soul governing the World by Motion and Reason."* [88] Such a Soul of the World the *Stoicks* call'd, *The artificial Fire orderly proceeding to the Generation of the Things of the World.*

Many *Christian* Writers have grossly symboliz'd with the aforesaid Doctrine of the *Pagans;* and, particularly, all those *Christian* Divines, who account the *Platonists* Triad the same with the *Christian* Trinity, if they are consistent with themselves, suppose the H. Ghost, to be the same with the *Platonists Soul of the World,* which is the *Pagan Jove,* thus perverting the Scriptures, confounding Things Sacred and Profane, Human and Divine, God and the World, God and Belial, the Kingdom of Darkness and of Light, *Paganizing Christianity.* It is one Thing to say, That *mundane, animative, intelligent Nature* is God, as being somewhat, that he *inclusively* is; and another Thing to say, That *mundane, animative, intelligent Nature,* form'd by the *Pagans* into a *Jove,* is, as such, God. The former Assertion is legitimate Theism, the latter is Heathenism.

This *Jupiter* of the *Popular Pagans,* the *Soul of the World,* may justly be thought the best sort of *Jupiter* in the *Pagan* Theology. But the *Heathenism* of the Notion will, in great Measure, appear from the Original of it. For the *Heathens* were carried to this Notion of the Supreme Deity, partly by the *first Original Theism of their Institution,* and partly by *their Method of proving the Existence of a Deity against Atheism.* The first Original Theism of their Institution, or their eldest Idolatry, was the deifying the *visible Heaven,* or *World,* as the Supreme universal Deity, or chief God. As amongst the *Chinese,* *"Some suppose, that the Sun, Moon and Stars, and chiefly Heaven itself, whence the Earth deriveth all her Advantages, must be worshipp'd with all possible Devotion."* [89]

This *Pagan* Idea of a Supreme Deity, was also a Consequent of *their Method of proving the Existence of a Deity against Atheism;* which, tho' it hath much of true Reason and sound Philosophy in it, does also involve *the Deity of the World;* which is of the same Importance in the

88. St. Augustine, *De Civitate Dei,* VII.13.
89. Maffeius, *Historiae Indicae* (1605).

Pagan Religion, with the Existence of a Deity. *Plato's* Theism, which he asserts in his *Book of Laws,* we have already seen to be only an asserting a *Soul of the World.* So *Cicero* disputeth. *"There is assuredly a Caelestial Force, or Power Divine. An animative Principle of Life and Sense, which is in our Bodies and in our Meanness, is not wanting in the Greatness of universal Nature, and the illustrious Motion thereof; unless, perchance, they think there is no such Thing, because it is not visible, nor sensible: As if our Mind, whereby we are Wise and Provident, whereby we do and say these very Things, was Visible, or Discernible by Sense."* [90] The *Philosophick Emperour* and others argue, *"Can there be Order in Thee, and none in the World? It is absurd to say, that the Heaven, or visible World is without a Soul, seeing we, that have but a part of the Body of the Universe, have a Soul. For how could a Part have Soul, if the Universe was devoid of it?"* *Socrates's* Discourse with *Aristodemus,* against Atheism, is thus represented by *Cicero. "The Humour, and Heat, and Breath, and Earth, which is in our Body, if any one asketh, whence we have them? It is manifest, that we took one of them from the Earth, another of them from the Water, the other from the Fire and Air. But that which surmounteth all these, Reason, Mind, Counsel, Cogitation, Prudence, where found we it? Whence took we it? Whence hath Man snatch'd to himself such a Thing as this?* So *Zeno,* the Father of the *Stoicks,* discourseth against Atheism. *"What is devoid of Soul and Reason, cannot generate an Animal and a Rational. But the World generateth Animals and Rationals. Therefore the World is an Animal and Rational. That which is Rational, is better than that which is not Rational: But nothing is better than the World. Therefore the World is Rational. In like manner we may infer, that the World is Wise, that the World is Blessed, that the World is Eternal."* So *Balbus,* in *Cicero,* discourseth for the Theism of the *Pagans* (the Worshippers of the mundane System) against Atheism; *"From that Ardor, or Vital Heat, which is in the World"* (the mundane Soul of the *Stoicks*) *"all Motion ariseth: Which, because it is self-moving, is necessarily a Mind; whence it followeth, that the World is an Animal. Hence also we may infer, that it is intelligent, because the World is certainly better than any particular Nature, which is but part of the World.*

90. Cicero, *Pro T. Annio Milone Oratio.*

The World, because it comprehendeth all Things, nor is there any Thing which is not in it, is every way perfect: Nothing can be wanting to what is the best: There is nothing better than Mind and Reason: These, therefore, cannot be wanting to the World; wherefore it is Wise and Good."[91] At this rate these *Heathen* Philosophers deified the World in their Disputes against Atheism, the main Scope of which is to prove the Being of *an Animative Mind of the World;* the acknowledgment whereof constituted a *Pagan* Theist, and distinguish'd him from an Atheist. *"All others"* (saith *Plutarch) "affirm, that the World is animated and administred by Providence: But* Democritus *and* Epicurus, *and so many as introduce* Atoms *and* Vacuum, *do neither acknowledge the World to be animated, nor to be govern'd by Providence; but by an irrational Nature."*[92]

In their Disputes against Atheism the *Pagan* Theists design to establish their own Theism, which is their Religion of worshipping the *Universe, Heaven,* and the *Stars.* For their governing Mind and Soul of the World, for whose Existence they dispute is *Universal, Mundane, Animative Nature, Animative of the World,* (as the Soul of Man is of his Body,) *involv'd in the World, and deifying the World.* In the *Stoicks* Account of the Mundane System, there are various Complications of *Jupiter* and *the World;* and they are so complicated, that each communicateth to the other his Name and his Properties. For *the Deity* is called *the World. "If you call the Deity the World, you are not mistaken in so doing,"* saith *Seneca.* And as *the Deity* is call'd *the World,* both the *Whole* and the *Parts* of it, is call'd *God,* according to that of *Manilius;*

> Quâ pateat Mundum Divino Numine verti,
> Atque ipsum esse Deum ———
>
> *The World is govern'd by the Deity,*
> *And is itself the Deity.*[93]

91. Cicero, *De Natura Deorum,* II.
92. Plutarch, *De Placitis Philosophorum* (in *Moralia*), II.3.
93. Manilius, *Astronomicon,* I.

The Doctrine of *the Soul of the World* inforceth *the Unity of the Universe,* and that all Things are one, *one animated mundane System.* *"The chief Philosophers have declared, That all is one."*[94] So *Linus;*

Omnia sunt unum, sunt omnis singula partes.

All Things are Part of the Universe, and that All is One.[95]

The Unity of the Universe, which is a fundamental Mistake, and very pernicious to true Religion, is a principal Maxim among the *Stoicks.* *"This whole"* (saith *Seneca*[96]) *"in which we are contain'd, is both one Thing and God. This All, the Comprehension of divine and human Things, is one Thing. We are the Members of one great Body."* The Universe is suppos'd to be one Body, because of its informing Soul, which connecteth and holdeth the Parts of it together. So *Sextus Empiricus* represents the Sense of *Pythagoras, Empedocles,* and all the *Italick* Philosophers. *"We Men have not only a Conjunction amongst our-selves, with one another, and with the Gods above us, but also with the Brutes below us: Because there is one Spirit, which, as a Soul, pervadeth the whole World, and uniteth together all the Parts of it."*[97]

This vital Constitution of the Universe is the Origin of *Natural Magick,* which is a vital Sympathy and Antipathy, between several Things in the World. But, under the pretence of Natural Magick, Arts Magical, in the foulest Sense, were introduc'd. The *Heathens* thought, that there was a Sympathy and Consent amongst the Parts of the Universe, as being Parts of one Whole; such, as is amongst the Parts of the human Body, or the Strings of a Musical Instrument. Into this they resolv'd the Efficacy of *Charms* and *Fascinations, Mystick Ceremonies, Symbols,* and *Sacrifices,* and *Prayers to the Sun and Stars,* attracting Influences from them, in the same manner as when the lower Part of a Chord that is stretch'd, is put into Motion, the upper Part is put into Motion also. This one animated Mundane System is necessarily *One Mundane Animal,* upon

94. Macrobius, *Saturnalia,* I.7.
95. Maxwell refers to a text by Grotius.
96. Lipsius, *Physiologia Stoicorum* (1604), bk. I, diss. 8.
97. Sextus Empiricus, *Adversus Mathematicos,* p. 331.

which Account they attribute a Magical Constitution to the Universe. For they suppose, That this Universe is one, and one Animal, so that nothing is so remote, as not to be near, because of the Sympathy and Consent of Motion, which is between the Parts of one Animal. Now an Animal Fabrick must have Distinction of Parts. So the *Stoicks* say, That God is the Mind of the Universe, the Body of it is his Body, and the Sun, Moon, and Stars, are the Eyes of this great Mundane Animal, which was thought of the Hermaphrodite Kind, because it was believ'd to be a generative Animal, and therefore both Sexes are attributed to it in *Jarchas* the *Brachman*'s answer to *Apollonius*. *"The World is an Animal; for it generateth all Things, being of both Natures, Male and Female, and doing the Part, both of Father and Mother, for Generation."* Because the World consists of *active* and *passive* Principles, and, because the Virtue of *Generating* and *Conceiving*, the Masculine and Feminine Virtue, are united in universal Nature, it is not unfitly intituled ἀρρενοθηλυς, Male and Female. The *Orphick* Doctrine concerning the Deity, of which the following Lines are a remarkable Compend, assert the same Notion; ascribing both Sexes to the All-generating Deity.

> Ζεὺς πρῶτος γένετο, Ζεὺς ὕσατος ἀρχικέραυνος.
> Ζεὺς κεφαλνὶ, Ζεὺς μέσσα, διος δ' ὃκ πάντα τέτυκτὰι.
> Ζεὺς πυθμνὶν γαίης, τε καὶ οὐρανοῦ ἀσερόεντος.
> Ζεὺς ἄρσνιν γένετο, Ζεὺς ἄμζροτος ἔπλετο νύμφη.
> Ζεὺς πνοίη πάντων, ἀκαμὰ του Ζεὺς πυρὸς ὀρμη.
> Ζεὺς πόντου ῥῖζα, Ζεὺς ἥλιος, ἠδὲ σελήνη.
> Ζεὺς βασιλευς, Ζεὺς ἀρχὸς ἀπάντων ἀρχικέραυνος:
> Πάντας γάρ κρύψας ἄυτους φάος ἐς πολυγεθές,
> Ἐξ ἱεροῦς κραδίης ἀνενέγκατο, μέρμερα ῥέζων.[98]

---

98. It seems likely that Maxwell took this Greek Orphic hymn from Eusebius's *Praeparatio Evangelica*, III.9; a slightly different version can also be found in Aristotle, *De Mundo* [401a28–b7]. It is not clear where the Latin translation comes from. A full English translation of the Greek can be found in Cory, *Ancient Fragments* (1832), n.p.:

Zeus is the first. Zeus the thunderer, is the last.
Zeus is the head. Zeus is the middle, and by Zeus all things were fabricated.
Zeus is male, Immortal Zeus is female.

Primus cunctorum est & Jupiter ultimus idem.
Jupiter & caput & medium est, sunt ex Jove cuncta.
Jupiter est terra basis, & Stellantis Olympi.
Jupiter & mas est, estque idem Nympha perennis.
Spiritus est cunctis, validusque est Jupiter ignis'
Jupiter est Pelagi radix, est Lunaque, solq;
Cunctorum Rex est, Princepsque & Originis Author;
Namque sinu occultans, dulces in luminis auras,
Cuncta tulit, sacro versans sub pectore curas.

The *Popular Pagans* call their Deities sometimes by Masculine, some-times by Feminine Names, not pretending to know their Sexes;[99] or judging it matter indifferent, which of their Sexes they ascrib'd to their Deities; or, perhaps, supposing them *Hermaphrodites*. In the *Septuagint*, also, *Baal* is sometimes of the Masculine, and sometimes of the Feminine Gender.

The *one animate Mundane System* is also *one Deity,* some say the *first* God, others the *Second,* and some call it the *Third* God. In the *Stoicks* Theology the *World* is the *supreme God.* The *Platonists* usually call it the *third God:* But *Origen* saith, that they call it the *second.* Which is very agreeable to what *Plato* saith in his *Timeus,* according to *Cicero*'s Version

---

Zeus is the foundation of the earth and of the starry heaven.
Zeus is the breath of all things. Zeus is the rushing of indefatigable fire.
Zeus is the root of the sea: He is the Sun and Moon.
Zeus is the king; He is the author of universal life;
One Power, one Daemon, the mighty prince of all things:
One kingly frame, in which this universe revolves,
Fire and water, earth and ether, night and day,
And Metis (Counsel) the primeval father, and all-delightful Eros (Love).
All these things are United in the vast body of Zeus.
Would you behold his head and his fair face,
It is the resplendent heaven, round which his golden locks
Of glittering stars are beautifully exalted in the air.
On each side are the two golden taurine horns,
The risings and settings, the tracks of the celestial gods;
His eyes the sun and the Opposing moon;
His unfallacious Mind the royal incorruptible Ether.

99. Selden, *De Diis Syris Syntagma II* (1617), ch. 2.

of it, *"Deus ille aeternus hunc perfectè beatum Deum procreavit,"* The eternal *God procreated this perfectly happy God.* The visible, sensible, fabricated World, being thus confronted to an invisible, intelligible, parental, eternal Deity, in this Antithesis, it falleth to the World's Share, to be called the *second God.* So *Celsus* the *Platonist* and others have intituled the animated World, the *Son of God.*[100] And, consequently, there is in Platonism *a twofold Son of God;* the one is the *Metaphysical Intellect of the Mundane System,* the other is the *intelligent Mundane Animal,* the only-begotten *sensible Son of God.*

The *one Mundane System* is also intituled *one Temple, House,* or *Habitation,* which Appellations denote such an Unity and undivided State of the Universe as perfectly disagrees with *Christianity. The Habitation of the Immortal God,* is one of the usual Names of the World. One Philosopher calleth it, *The Temple of the Father;* another calleth it, *A most Holy and God-becoming Temple;* another styleth it, *The Fire-refulgent House of* Jove. By *Cicero* it is intituled, *The Caelestial and Divine House;* and by the *Aegyptians, The Kingly House of the Deity. "Is God shut up within the Walls of Temples?"* said *Heraclitus. "The whole World variously adorn'd with Animals, and Plants, and Stars, is his Temple."* The *Stoicks* say, *"The whole World is the Temple of the Gods, and the only Temple becoming their Amplitude and Magnificence."* Whence the *Persians* and the *Magi* condemn'd all artificial Temples; and *Xerxes,* by the Persuasion of the *Magi,* burnt the Temples of the *Greeks,* themselves doing their religious Worship to the Gods under the open Heaven; to whom they supps'd, that all Things should be open, and that this *whole World is their Temple and Habitation. Zeno,* the Father of the *Stoicks,* is likewise said, to have disallow'd the Building of Temples; and *Plato,* as some will have it, privately prohibited the having Statues of the Gods, as knowing, *"That the World is the Temple of God."* The World is call'd by *Plato, The House of the Gods,* and, *The made Image of the Eternal Gods.* Agreeably to this Notion of the *Philosophick Pagans,* the Apocryphal Book of *Baruch* (3. 24.) looks upon the visible Universe as *"The House of God."* But no such Language ever occurreth in the Holy Bible; which should have

---

100. Origen, *Contra Celsum,* I.6, p. 308.

taught *Christian* Writers so much Discretion, as not to speak the Sense and Language of the *Heathen Philosophers,* which they frequently do.

In the *Stoicks* Philosophy, the one Mundane System *Jove* is *All Things,* and *All Things are Him, as his Parts and Members.* Particularly *Souls* are *Parts of God, and Avulsions from Him.* Visible and *Corporeal* Things are the Parts of his *Body.* Thus is he *One and All Things.* Their Deity is so intimate, complicate, united, and connected with all Things, as to constitute with them *One Mundane Intelligent Animal;* therefore the whole animated World, and all the Things thereof are *Jove,* and *Jove* is the animated World, and the Things thereof.

> *Jupiter est quodcumque vides,* ———
>
> Jove is whate'er you see.

The eldest Idolatry was the Worship of *Heaven,* the *World,* and the *Stars,* as appeareth from the *Jove* of the eldest Times, and of all Nations. Of the *Persians, Herodotus* reporteth, *"That they did not, like the* Greeks, *think the Gods of human Birth and Original; but their way was, ascending to the Tops of the Mountains, they Sacrific'd to* Jove, *calling the whole Circle of the Heaven,* Jove."[101] *Strabo* saith of them, *"They Sacrifice in an high Place, thinking the Heaven,* Jove."[102] So *Plutarch* says of the *Aegyptians, "They take the first God, and the Universe, for the same Thing."* Universal Mundane Nature, the *Aegyptians* deified under the Name of *Isis,* which was their supreme Deity, as the Inscription before her Temple at *Sais* sheweth; *"I am all that hath been, is, and shall be; and my Veil no Mortal hath ever yet uncover'd:* And that other Inscription on the Altar at *Capua ("Tibi una. Quae es omnia. Dea Isis.")* which maketh her *one, and all Things.* The *Aegyptian Serapis,* another Name of their supreme Deity, is the *World,* for, "Serapis *being ask'd by* Nicocreon" (King of the *Cypriots*) *"what God he was? Made answer, I am a God, such as I describe myself. The Starry Heaven is my Head, the Sea is my Belly, the Earth is my Feet, mine Ears are in the Aether, and mine Eye is the bright Lamp of the*

---

101. Herodotus, *Historia,* I.
102. Strabo, *Geographia,* XVI.

Universe, the Sun.[103] The *Orphic* Theology makes a like Description of *Jupiter.*[104] So *Cicero* hath shew'd from *Ennius* and *Euripides*, (who is called the scenical Philosopher,) That the *Heaven*, or *circumambient Aether* is the *European Pagans Jove*, the supreme universal Deity.[105] So in the Poet *Aeschylus*, *Jupiter* is Universal Mundane Nature. "*Jupiter is Aether, and Earth, and Heaven, and all Things. And, if there be any Thing above these*, Jupiter *is it.*" "*The Naturalists*" (saith *Macrobius*[106]) "*called the Sun*" (Διόνυσον διὸς νοῦν) "Dionysus, *the Mind of* Jove, *because the Mind of the World. The World is called Heaven, which they call* Jove. *Whence* Aratus, *being to speak of Heaven, saith, Let us take our rise from* Jove." So in an antient Inscription, the visible *Heaven* is intituled, *Eternal, the best and greatest,* Jupiter.[107] Agreeably to which Sense of the antient *Pagans*, that Tradition of theirs, reported by *Aristotle*, is to be understood touching the Divinity of the Heavens. "*It hath been delivered to us by those of very antient Times, both that the Stars are Gods, and that the Divinity containeth the whole of Nature.*"[108]

This Notion was so familiar with the *Pagans*, that *Strabo*, writing of *Moses*, could not but suppose the Gods of his Religion to be of this Nature and Notion; "*That which containeth us all, and the Earth, and the Sea, which we call Heaven, and the World, and the Nature of the whole,*" Universal Mundane Nature.[109] So *Juvenal* describes the God of the *Jews*.

Nil praeter Nubes & Caeli numen adorant.

They Worship no Deity but the Clouds and the Heavens.[110]

So *Diodorus Siculus* reporteth *Moses* to have been of Opinion, "*That the Heaven which surroundeth the Earth, is the only God and Lord of*

---

103. Lipsius, *Physiologia Stoicorum*, bk. II, diss. 10.

104. Maxwell supplies an unsourced Latin quotation, which can be translated as follows: "Behold this excellent head, beautiful face, illuminating the universe."

105. Cicero, *De Natura Deorum*, II.

106. Macrobius, *Saturnalia*, I.18.

107. Maxwell supplies an unsourced Latin quotation: "Optimus Maximus, Coelus aeternus, Jupiter."

108. Aristotle, *Metaphysics*, XIV.8.

109. Cudworth, *The True Intellectual System of the Universe*, p. 516.

110. Juvenal, *Satires*, XIV.97.

all." These *Pagans* did not imagine, that the *Jews* could Worship any other God than their supreme *Jove, the Heaven,* which, in the larger Sense of the Word, signifieth the whole corporeal World.

Pliny thus; "*The World, or the Heavenly Canopy, must, in Reason, be thought a Deity.*" Such a Deity was the *European-Pagans Jove,* and such a Deity was the *Asiatick Bel,* or *Baal;* for that Name, as *Selden*[111] informs us, means *the Heaven, the Comprehension of the Aether, and the Stars;* and the Heaven was called *Bel* by the *Chaldeans,* as *Eustathius* reporteth from the Antients; and *Philo* saith of the *Chaldeans,* "*They suppos'd the visible World, or Heaven, the Supreme Deity.*"[112] The Proclivitie of *Heathen* Mankind to such a Notion of the supreme Deity is visible in a late Writer of the Affairs of *China.* "*A mighty Nation of the* Tartars, *though they are not, by what appeareth, of any particular Religion, but indifferently receive all Religions, which they are acquainted with, and conform themselves to all, not knowing, or caring to know, what it is they adore, and they have no Knowledge of the Idols, or Deities, which the Antients ador'd; nor doth it appear, that they receive, or retain those first Notions which the Instinct of Nature, without the Assistance of any supernatural Light, impresseth upon the very Breast of every Man; yet they Worship the Heavens, and to these they pay their greatest Adoration; and this maketh the greatest Impression upon the Minds of the People.*"[113] Of the barbarous Nation of the *Gallans,* bordering *Habissina,* we have this Account. "*They have no Idols, and but very little Divine Worship. If you ask them concerning God, or any supreme Deity, or who it is that governeth the Earth with so much Order and Constancy? They answer, Heaven, which embraceth in their View all the rest.*"[114] A great Nation on the North of *Japan,* are said to have no other Religion, save only the *Worship of Heaven;* and the supreme Deity of the *Chinese* is said to be *the Heaven,* which they suppose *increate, without Beginning, unbodily, and a Spirit.*[115]

---

111. Selden, *De Diis Syris,* ch. 1.
112. Philo, *De Abrahamo,* p. 244.
113. Palafox y Mendoza, *The History of the Conquest of China* (1676), p. 440.
114. Ludolf, *A New History of Ethiopia* (1682), I.16.
115. Hoffman, *Umbra in Luce sive Consensus et Dissensus Religionum Profanorum*

According to the Testimony of the *Scriptures,* and of *Heathen* Authors the consent of all the *Christian,* and the best of the *Hebrew* Writers, the first and earliest Idolatry of the Heathen, was the Worship of the *Lights of Heaven,* which inferreth the Antiquity of the *Worship of Heaven,* and that the first Original *Pagan* Theism, was the deifying *the Mundane System. Vossius* indeed affirmeth, (agreeably to their Opinion, who suppose the *Sun* to have been the *Pagans* Supreme Deity,) that their Worship of the Coelestial Lights was antecedent to the Worship of the *Aether, Heaven,* or *the World;* which is a supposition altogether as groundless, and unreasonable, as if he should suppose them the Worshippers of Mountains and Rivers, before they were the Worshippers of their great Goddess, the Earth.[116] *Plato* supposes, that the Worship of the *Heaven* and the *Stars* was the eldest Religion of the *Pagans;* and that the Worship of the *Heaven* was contemporary with that of the *Stars,* both amongst the *Greeks* and *Barbarians.* The *Greeks* receiv'd *Astronomy,* and the Knowledge of those Coelestial Deities, the *Stars,* from the *Barbarians,* those antient *Pagan* Nations, which were the Inventors of Astronomy, and which, in *Aegypt* and *Syria,* had great Advantage for the Knowledge of the Stars, because of the Serenity of their Country. The Theology, therefore, of those antient *Pagan* Nations may be understood from the *Greek* Theology of the elder Times, which *Plato,* in his *Cratylas,* thus representeth. *"The first Inhabitants of* Greece *seem, as many of the* Barbarians *now, to have thought, that the Sun, and the Moon, and the Earth, and the Stars, and the Heaven, were the only Gods. When they beheld these running round perpetually, they call'd them* Θεοὺς *from* Θέω *which signifieth, to run. Afterwards taking Notice, that there were other Gods, they called them also by the same Name."* As the first Inhabitants of *Greece* deified, not only the Sun, Moon, and Stars, but the Heaven above them: So, when *Diodorus* saith of the Men of antient Times, *"That, beholding the World and universal Mundane Nature, being struck with Admiration, they thought the prime eternal Gods were the Sun and Moon,*

(1680), p. 88; Purchas, *Purchas His Pilgrimage* (1619), pt. I, bk. IV, ch. 19, sect. 2; bk. 5, ch. 15, sect. 7.

116. Maimonides, *De Idolatria,* ed. Vossius, II.37, VII.2.

calling the one Osiris, *and the other* Isis"; this is not to be understood, as if they deified the Sun and Moon, exclusively of the rest of the World above them: But, *beholding the World and universal Mundane Nature,* and being struck with Admiration, they deified it, and such illustrious Parts of it, as the Sun and Moon. So, when *Maimonides* saith of the *Zabii,* that their Tenet was, *"There is no other God but the Stars";*[117] this is not to be understood exclusively of the *Heaven,* as if the *Zabii* did not suppose it the Supreme Deity; for the same Author saith of them; *"All the* Zabaists *held the Eternity of the World; for the Heavens, according to them, are the Deity."* So *Philo* saith of the *Chaldeans, "They suppose the Stars to be Gods, and the Heaven and the World"* (which must consequently be the Supreme) *"to which they refer the Fates of Men, acknowledging no Cause of Things abstract from Sensibles."*[118] If the first *Heathen* deified the Lights of Heaven, because of their *Amplitude, Pulchritude, Utility,* and Residence in *Heaven,* they could not fail, upon the same Account, to deify the illustrious Canopy of Heaven.

The one Mundane System *Jove* is, in some sort, the *multitude and variety of the Pagans Gods and Goddesses;* and there is a certain *Polytheism* of theirs, which is nothing more than a *Polyonymy of this one Supreme God,* or a calling him by various Names. For it is not unusual with the *Pagan* Theologers, to reduce the Multitude and Variety of their Deities to one *Jupiter,* in various Senses, and upon various Accounts. Sometimes they consider the *Mundane System Jove,* as *Originally* and *Comprehensively* the All of their Deities, as *Valerius Soranus* representeth them.

> *Jupiter Omnipotens, Regum Rex ipse deumque,*
> *Progenitor Genitrixque Deum, Deus unus & omnis.*

> Omnipotent *Jupiter,* the King of Kings and Gods,
> The Father and Mother of the Gods, one God and all Gods.[119]

Thus *Jupiter is all the Gods;* not as if there was no Polity of Gods; but as the Founder, the Father and Mother, of the Polity, and a Deity *com-*

---

117. Maimonides, *Moreh Nevuchim,* pt. 3, ch. 29.
118. Philo, *De Nobilitate,* p. 622.
119. St. Augustine, *De Civitate Dei,* I.9.

prehensive of all the Deities; for *Jupiter* is the same with *Pan,* universal mundane Nature, whom, in the *Certamina* at *Athens,* they look'd upon as a *Pantheon,* the comprehension of all the Gods. So the Author of the *Orphick* Verses, *"having suppos'd the World a great Animal, and having call'd this Mundane Animal* Jupiter," placeth Heaven, the Earth, the Sea, and the Whole of the Universe in *Jupiter's* Womb,

Πάντες τ' ἀθάνατοι μάχαρες θεοὶ, ἠδὲ θέαιναι.

And all the blessed immortal Gods and Goddesses.

The Rabble of Deities contain'd in him, are necessarily his Parts and Members, both as he is *Politically Imperial,* and as he is *Animatively Vital,* in a *Political,* and in a *Physiological* Sense; they are the Members of his *Body Politick,* and of his *living Animal-Body;* as *Seneca* saith of Mankind, *"Et socii ejus sumus & Membra,"* "We are his *Associates"* (the Members of his Body Politick) *"and the Members of his Animal-Body."* Both these Notions are glanc'd at by the Poet introducing *Jupiter,* thus speaking to the other Gods;

Coelicola mea membra Dei, quos nostra potestas
Officiis divisa facit. ————[120]

Ye Gods my Members, to whom my Imperial Power
allotteth Diversity of Offices.

The Gods, to whom *Jupiter* allotteth Diversity of Offices, are not mere *Names,* or *Virtues,* but so many *Substantial Beings, distinct Personal Deities;* yet these, being contain'd in him, are, in some sort, reducible to him; but there is another sort of Deities, which the *Stoicks* suppose to be nothing more than so many several *Names, Notions,* and *particular Considerations* of the one Supreme *Jupiter;* or, only so many several *Powers, Virtues, Functions* and *Agencies* of his, fictitiously personated and deified, which explaineth an eminent Mode of their Idolatry. Pervading, acting, and ruling in the Air, he may be call'd *Juno;* in the Earth, *Pluto;*

---

120. Maxwell's textual comments suggest that this is a quotation from Virgil, but in fact the passage comes from Maurus Servius Honoratus's commentary on the *Aeneid, In Vergili Carmina Comentarii,* IV.638.

in the inferior Parts of it, *Proserpina;* in the Sea, *Neptune;* in the lower Part of it, *Salacia;* in the Vineyards, *Liber;* in the Smith's Forges, *Vulcan;* and in the domestick Hearths, *Vesta;* as he bestows Corn, he may be called *Ceres;* Wine, *Bacchus;* Health, *Aesculapius;* as he governeth the Wars, *Mars;* and the Winds, *Aeolus. "The Names that denote a certain Force or Effect of Things Coelestial are, any of them, properly applicable to him. His Appellations may be as many as his Gifts, or Functions."* [121] Which *Polyonymy* of the one Supreme God inferreth, that the *Pagans* Polytheism was, in part, and so far, not *real,* but *apparent* only. Thus, as the *Mythical* Theology personateth and deifieth the Parts and Powers of Mundane corporeal Matter; so the *Philosophick* Theology personateth and deifieth the several Powers, Virtues, and Agencies, of the one Supreme God. By this Mythical Plea, they defended their Worship of the several Parts of the Corporeal World. For their *Polyonymy* of the one Supreme God, was not design'd to deprive the Parts of the World of their Godship, but to give a plausible Account and Reason of their Worship.

The Reason of this *Stoical Polyonymy* was double; partly, because of a Fancy which they had, to apply, to the Supreme Deity, the proper Names of other Deities; and partly, because they discarded the Deities, which they called *Mythical* and *Commentitious,* which are Things Physical represented by Fictitious Deities; which having discarded, they substituted in their stead the various *Powers, Virtues, Effects,* and *Agencies,* of the *Mundane System* Jove; *"Calling him* Minerva, *because his Rule is extended in the Aether;* Juno, *as pervading the Air;* Vulcan, Neptune, Ceres, *as pervading and acting in the Artificer's Fire, in the Sea and the Earth."* [122] So *Balbus* in *Cicero,* having rejected the Deities, which he calleth the *Mythical,* substituteth in their Room, *"God passing thro' the Nature of every Thing."* Agreeably to which *Stoical* Notion, it is most reasonable to understand the saying of *Antisthenes* the *Cynick, "Populares Deos multos, naturalem unum esse dicens,"* [123] that is, *one natural God ought*

121. Seneca, *De Beneficiis,* IV.7.
122. Life of Zeno in Diogenes Laertius, *Lives,* VII.
123. Cicero, *De Natura Deorum,* I.

to be substituted in the stead of those many Popular Deities, which the Stoicks, *and their Brethren, the* Cynicks, *rejected as Mythical and Commentitious.*

It is, however, here to be observ'd, that the *Stoicks Polyonymy* is so far from destroying the *Pagans Polytheism,* that it maketh no considerable Abatement in the Multitude of their Deities. For they deified the Parts of the Corporeal World, as living Members of the Mundane Animal, Residences of the Powers and Virtues of the Supreme God, Sections of the Soul of the World. Both *Varro* and *Balbus* plainly affirm, That the Stars are animated with intelligent Souls, (they might as well say the same of the Earth;) and, consequently, they are so many distinct Personal Deities.[124] And, accordingly, *Plutarch* representeth the *Stoical Polyonymists* as the most extravagant *Polytheists* in all the Pack, *"That filled the Air, Heaven, Earth, Sea, with Gods."*[125] Wherefore their Reduction of Deities to the *Polyonymy* of one Supreme God, signifieth nothing to the Prejudice, or Diminution of their Polity of Gods. When they call *Jove* by the proper Names of several other Deities, they must not be thought to deny the Existence of those Synonymous *Genial* Deities of the vulgar Theology, *Liber Pater, Mercury,* and the like; for in their various *Allegorizings,* Interpretations, Accommodations, and the various honourary Appellatives which they bestow upon *Jove,* they do not speak *privatively* with respect to their Genial Deities, but *Accumulatively;* not with intention to destroy them, but to super-add to them the *Polyonymy* of their Supreme God. And, if this is the true Account of the *Stoicks Polyonymy,* as certainly it is, there is no Reason imaginable, why they should condemn the vulgar *Polytheism,* as a learned Writer supposes they would have done, if fear of disturbing the Common-wealth, and creating a *Socrates*-like Danger to themselves, had not restrain'd them.[126] For the Sense of the *Stoicks,* and of all the genuine *Pagan Theologers,* must be thus represented. *The Constitution of the Universe being Politically consider'd, and* Jupiter, *as Politically Imperial, they conceiv'd* (as they usually

---

124. St. Augustine, *De Civitate Dei,* VII.6; Cicero, *De Natura Deorum,* II.
125. Plutarch, *De Communibus Notitiis Adversus Stoicos* (in *Moralia*).
126. Maimonides, *De Idolatria,* ed. Vossius, VII.7.

say) *all full of Gods and Demons: But withal, the Constitution of the Universe being* Physiologically *consider'd, and* Jupiter, *as Vital and Animative of the Whole, they conceiv'd* Jovis omnia plena, *all full of* Jove, *his various Virtues, Powers and Effects.*

The *Mundane System Jove* must be consider'd, both as *Animatively,* or *Physiologically,* and as *Politically*-Imperial to the World. For, being the Mundane Soul, he is *Animatively*-Regent and Imperial, as the Soul of Man is. *"That is a God, which is Vigent, Sentient, Reminiscent, Provident, which ruleth, and governeth, and moveth, that Body, whose Prefect it is, as the chieftain God does this World."* [127] *"As we have a Soul that is an Animative Regent: So the Government of the World is by a Soul, that containeth and keepeth it in Consistence, which is call'd* Zeus.*"* [128] Who, as an Animative Regent, is suppos'd, regularly to agitate the Mundane Matter, to form all Things Coelestial and Terrestrial, to figurate his own Animal Body, and to generate all sorts of Animals, as the Poet *Philosophizeth,*

> *Principio Coelum, ac Terras camposque liquentes,*
> *Lucentemque globum Lunae, Titaniaque Astra,*
> *Spiritus intus alit; totamque infusa per artus,*
> *Mens agitat molem, & magno se corpore miscet,*
> *Inde Hominum, Pecudamque genus, vitaeque volantûm,*
> *Et quae marmoreo fert Monstra sub aequore Pontus.* Virg. Aen. 6.

> From first, Earth, Seas, and Heavens all spangled Robe,
> The golden Stars, and Phoebe's silver Globe,
> A Spirit fed, and to the Mass conjoin'd,
> Inspiring the vast Body with a Mind.
> Hence Men, and Beasts, and Birds, derive their Strain,
> And Monsters floating in the smooth-fac'd Main.

By Physical Motion, and as Animatively-Regent, the *Mundane System Jove* steereth the World, [129] *"As a Pilot doth a Ship, or as a Charioteer doth a Chariot, circumvolving the Heavens, keeping the Earth in Consistence,*

---

127. Cicero, *In Somnium Scipionis,* II.12.
128. Phurnutus, *De Natura Deorum,* p. 4.
129. Aristotle, *De Mundo,* ch. 6.

ruling the Sea."[130] (So *Apuleius* saith of the Goddess *Isis,* "*Thou whirlest about the World, lightenest the Sun, rulest the World;*") and variously influencing the Minds of Men, according to that of *Homer,*

> Τοῖος γὰρ νόος ἐστὶν ἐπιχθονίων ἀνθρώπων,
> Οἷον ἐπ' ἦμαρ ἄνῃσι πάτηρ ἀνδρῶν τε θεῶν τε.
>
> *Men hold not constant in one Mind; such is their Sense,*
> *As daily is instill'd by* Jove*'s hid Influence.*

Because the *System-Jove* is Animatively the Regent of the World, he ought to have his Regent part seated in some principal Part of the World, (agreeably to the Soul of Man, whose rational Faculty is seated in the Head;) either in the *Aether,* as some; in the *Heaven,* as others; or in the *Sun,* as *Cleanthes* suppos'd;[131] which latter, doubtless, was the Sense of the *Pythagoreans* in those illustrious Epithets, which they gave the Sun, styling him

> Ζηνὼς πύργον, Διὸς φυλακιὼν, Διὸς θρόνον,
>
> *The Tower, Custody, or Hold, and Throne of* Jove.

But the *System-Jove* is also *Politically* the Regent of the World, the Universe being suppos'd one Imperial Polity, one common City of Gods and Men; for such a governing Power the *Pagan* Philosophers disputed with great Reason and Strength of Argument. "*Without Political Government, neither any House, nor City, nor Nation, nor Mankind in general, can subsist, nor the whole Nature of Things, nor the World itself.*"[132] "*Seeing a City, or a House, cannot continue for the least time without a Governour and Curator, how is it possible, that so great and illustrious a Structure as the World, should be so orderly administred fortuitously and by chance?*"[133] "*The Knowledge and Contemplation of Things Coelestial, the beholding how great Moderation and Order there is among the Gods, begetteth Modesty; and the beholding the Works and Facts of the Gods, causeth a Greatness*

---

130. Cicero, *De Natura Deorum,* III.
131. Ibid.
132. Cicero, *De Legibus,* III.
133. Epictetus, *Discourses,* II.14.

of Mind; and Justice also, when you understand the Supreme Rector and Lord, what his Will and Counsell is," (in the Constitution, Government, and Administration of this Universe of Things,) *"Reason suited to his Nature, being call'd by Philosophers the true and Supreme Law."* [134] As politically-Imperial, the supreme Rector appointeth to the subordinate Deities their Lots and Prefectures, and their Function and Employment is to execute his Appointments. *"For the Sun, as also the other Gods, was made for some Work, or Function."* [135]

But, in order to form a just Notion of the *Pagan Polytheism,* it is requisite to distinguish the various Acceptations of *Saturn, Jupiter,* and other Deities, in the *Gentile* Theology. Sometimes they are taken Cos-MICALLY; as when *Jupiter* is said to be the whole World, or the Soul of it, and *Saturn* is confounded with *Uranus,* or *Heaven.* Sometimes they are taken ASTRALLY; as when by *Jupiter* is meant the *Sun,* or the *Planet* so called: So the *highest* of the *Planets* is a *Saturn.* Sometimes they are taken PHYSICALLY; as when by *Saturn* is meant *Time,* and by *Jupiter* some *Elementary Nature.* So *Empedocles* calleth the igneous Nature, or *Aether, Jupiter;* the *Air, Juno;* the *Earth, Pluto;* the *Water, Nestis.* [136] Sometimes the Names of the *Pagan* Deities signify HISTORICALLY, or of the Hero-Kind, in which Notion there are many *Joves,* and not a few *Saturns.*

The Mundane-System *Jove* is Order, Law, Providence, Fate, and Fortune, amongst the *Heathens.*

7. *Jove,* the Rector of the Universe, is *Order, Law, Fate, Fortune, Providence. "Either this Universe is a mere Hotch-Potch and casual Implication of Things, which may be dis-joyn'd and dissipated; or there is in it Union, Order, and a Providence."* [137] But it could not be κόσμος, a regular and comely Piece, without *Order;* and this Order, and the *Law* that is visible in the Universe infer a *Providence, "whereby the World, and all the Parts of it, were at first constituted, and are at all Times administred.* [138] *The equable Motion and Circumvolution of the Heaven, the Sun, Moon, and all the Stars, their Distinction, Variety, and Pulchritude, Order; the Sight*

134. Cicero, *De Finibus,* IV.
135. Marcus Aurelius, *Meditations,* VIII.19.
136. Plutarch, *De Placitis Philosophorum* (in *Moralia*), I.3.
137. Marcus Aurelius, *Meditations,* IV.27, VI.10.
138. Cicero, *De Natura Deorum,* II.

of these Things sufficiently sheweth, that they are not by Chance," [139] but *"by an eternal Law, or Prescript, a Law of the World,"* [140] which the *Stoicks* call *Fate.*

> *Sed nihil in totâ magis est mirabile mole,*
> *Quam Ratio, & certis quod Legibus omnia parent.*

> The Course and Frame of this vast Bulk display
> A Reason and fix'd Laws, which all obey. *Manil.* L. 1. Astron. [141]

But, as the governing Mind, or Reason, which constituted and administreth the corporeal World, is Law to it: So all Things that befal Mankind are of his Pre-Ordination and Appointment, as the *Stoicks* suppose; and, therefore, they derive all Things *from a Law of Fate.* "*All Things proceed by a fix'd sempiternal Law; Fatality leadeth us; by a long Series and Concatenation of Causes all Things necessarily emerge; your joyous and mournful Occurrences were appointed long ago.*" [142] A wise Man will understand, "That whatever happens is a Law of" (universal) *Nature.* "*It was ordained to him, and he to it.* [143] *Whatever happens to thee, it is that which from Eternity was predestinated unto thee; thy subsistence and such an Accident are, by an implex'd Series of natural Causes from Eternity, fatally connected, or spun together.*" [144] Fatality, by this Hypothesis, is screw'd up to a high pitch of Extravagance; especially, as this their Dogma, *That all Things come to pass fatally,* is understood by the antient *Stoicks,* for they subvert, as appeareth, all contingency and human Liberty of Agency, and, consequently, all *Humanity* and *Divinity.* [145] In the Constitution of the World, they suppos'd *Jupiter* hamper'd by *material Necessity,* (that, because of the inobsequiousness of the Matter, some Men are unavoidably made of an evil Disposition, and good Men are

---

139. Ibid.

140. Seneca, *De Providentia,* ch. 1; *Quaestiones Naturales,* II.29.

141. Manilius, *Astronomica,* I.

142. Diogenes Laertius, "Zeno"; Seneca, *De Providentia,* ch. 5; *De Vita Beata,* ch. 15.

143. Marcus Aurelius, *Meditations,* XII.1.

144. Ibid., X.5.

145. Maimonides, *De Idolatria,* ed. Vossius, II.40.

obnoxious to external Evils;) and not being able to do what he would, he is willing to do what he can.[146] In his Administration of the World and Sovereign Disposal of Things, he can alter nothing of his own Fatal Decrees;[147] *Scripsit fata, sed sequitur, having once written the Fates, he always obeys them;* (some suppose, that the *three Fates* wrote his Decrees;) and, consequently, the *supreme Deity,* with respect to his Administration of Things, is nothing but INTELLIGENT FATE in himself, and to the World; (as *Plastick Natures* are nothing else but blind UNINTELLIGENT FATE in themselves, and to the World;) and unchangeable and inexorable Fate is the supreme Deity.

Μόνη γὰρ ῥν θεοῖσιν οὐ δεαπόζεται.

For Fate alone among the Gods is not subject

But, altho' their rigid Genius hath introduc'd much of extravagant Fatality, yet some of the antient *Stoicks* attempted to mollify the rigor of Fate, to accommodate it to human Liberty.[148] They refuse not the Name of *Fortune;* for they advise Men to commit Externals τω δαι-μονίῳ, τῇ τύχῃ, *To the Divinity, to Fortune,*[149] understanding thereby the Disposal of Things by Providence. Notwithstanding their rigid Genius, they are no Friends to that rigid Doctrine of *absolute Reprobation; "for God"* (as they suppose) *"hath made all Men to Felicity and good Estate of Mind, and hath given them what is requisite thereunto.*[150] *If the Gods have consulted concerning me, and those Things that ought to happen to me, they have well consulted; for a God devoid of Counsel is scarce conceivable: But to do me a Mischief, what should impel them? For what Emolument would accrue from thence, either to them, or to the Publick, which they chiefly take care of?"*[151] Inexorable Fate, according to their generally receiv'd Maxims, is their sovereign Deity, yet some of them are prone to think, that

---

146. Lipsius, *Physiologia Stoicorum,* bk. I, diss. 14.
147. Ibid., diss. 12.
148. Ibid., diss. 14.
149. Epictetus, *Discourses,* IV.4.
150. Ibid., III.25.
151. Marcus Aurelius, *Meditations,* VI.44.

there is a *placable and flexible Providence;*[152] and others of them tell us, that they had better Notices of the supreme *Jupiter.* *"They call* Jupiter *placid, being such to them who change from Injustice; for he is not irreconcileable to them, Whence their Altars to* Jupiter *placid to suppliants."*[153] They allow not God, or Man, to be properly angry with Criminals; yet suppose, that the Rector of the Universe is just and good Government to the Whole. *"That he hath made the Parts for the Use of the Whole,*[154] *and ordereth all Things, as is most conducive to the Good of the Whole.*[155] *Good Men are his Witnesses, that he existeth; and governeth the Universe of Things well, and neglecteth not human Affairs, and that nothing Evil shall happen to a good Man, either alive, or dead."*[156] He disposeth all to a good Use, as is most necessary for the Good of the World. *"For he, the Governour of the Universe, will not fail to put thee to a good Use.*[157] *Neither willingly, nor unwillingly, doth he commit any Error.*[158] *His Government is Paternal, as a Father taking care of all, that his Citizens may be happy like himself.*[159] *Making a distribution of Things as it is fit and just";*[160] (whence they style him νομος, from νέμα, *to distribute;*) the better Men have the better Part,[161] and the Good are not afflicted without great Reason, and for wise and good Ends.[162]

The Doctrine of the *Antients,* concerning *Fate,* being somewhat intricate and perplex'd; and the Reverend Mr. *John Jackson* having, in my Opinion, set that Matter in a clear Light in his *Defence of Human Liberty* P. 150, &c.[163] I believe it will not be unacceptable to the Reader, to lay it before him in Mr. *Jackson's* Words, as follows.

152. Ibid., XII.14.
153. Phurnutus, *De Natura Deorum,* p. 17.
154. Epictetus, *Discourses,* IV.7.
155. Marcus Aurelius, *Meditations,* V.8.
156. Epictetus, *Discourses,* III.26.
157. Marcus Aurelius, *Meditations,* VI.42.
158. Ibid., XII.12.
159. Epictetus, *Discourses,* ch. 24, pp. 328, 330, 331.
160. Marcus Aurelius, *Meditations,* IV.10, VII.31, X.25.
161. Epictetus, *Discourses,* III.17.
162. Seneca, *De Providentia,* III.
163. Jackson, *A Defence of Human Liberty* (1725), pp. 150–85. Maxwell inserts this

"That there is such a Thing as *Fate,* and that many Events are effected by it, was the general Opinion of all Philosophers, *Anaxagoras* amongst the *Gentiles,* and the *Sadducees* among the *Jews,* only excepted; who were both of Opinion, that nothing was the Effect of *Fate,* and that it was a mere *empty Name.* And as these wholly deny'd *Fate* in every Sense, so it must be confess'd, that there were some others, who carried the Notion of it as far in the other Extreme, and taught, that every Thing, all Events, and even *human Actions,* were effected by the impulsive *Necessity* of it. I shall, therefore, shew the Reader, who those were, who really held the Sentiments of the *Fatalists;* and then set forth distinctly and particularly that Notion of *Fate,* or *Necessity,* which was the concurrent receiv'd Opinion of all Sects of Philosophers.

"*Plutarch* tells us, that *Parmenides* and *Democritus* held, 'That all Things came to pass by *Necessity;* and that this *Necessity* was *Fate,* and *Justice,* and *Providence,* and the *Maker* of the World.'[164] *Heraclitus* was of the same Opinion.[165] To these *Cicero* joyns *Empedocles,* and, by mistake, *Aristotle.*[166] That this was a mistake of *Cicero's,* appears from *Plutarch,* in his *Treatise of the Opinions of the Antient Philosophers,* where he remarks no such Thing concerning *Aristotle,* tho' he does observe, that *Democritus* and *Heraclitus,* to whom he adds *Parmenides,* were of that Opinion, which *Cicero* ascribes to them; and had *Aristotle,* who was so much more eminent than the others, been of the same Opinion, he could hardly have neglected to have taken notice of it. But farther; *Hierocles* expressly says, that *Aristotle's* Philosophy agreed with *Plato's,* and that the most learned *Ammonius,* who perfectly understood the Philosophy of both of them, shew'd that they agreed together.[167] The concurrence of the *Platonick* and *Aristotelian* Philosophy he again insists on; and speaks with contempt of those who pretended they disagreed; and in particular declares, that they were of the same Opinion in the

---

lengthy extract of Jackson's work (ending on p. 161) and his footnotes (some of them mistranscribed) at this point.

164. Plutarch, *De Placitis Philosophorum* (in *Moralia*), p. 884.
165. Eusebius, *De Praeparatio Evangelica,* VI.7.
166. Cicero, *De Fato,* p. 359.
167. Hierocles, *De Providentia & Fato* (1673), p. 42.

Notion of *Fate,* and that he himself agreed with them.[168] 'That it was not the senseless *Necessity* of the *Fortune-tellers;* nor the *Stoical* Compulsion—but that it was the judicial Operation of the divine Power, effecting Events according to the Laws of Providence, and determining the Order and Series of our Circumstances in the World, according to the *free* Purposes of our *voluntary* Actions.'[169] And *Aristotle* himself expressly asserts and explains at large the *Freedom of human Actions.* He lays the Foundation of *Praise* and *Dispraise* in Mens *voluntary* Actions.[170] He proves Freedom from *Deliberation* and *Desire,* which he makes to be the same with *Choice.*[171] He expressly declares, that our Actions are *Voluntary* and by *Choice;* that the Practice of *Virtue* and *Vice* is *in our own Power:* And that this is evidently the Opinion, not only of all *private Persons,* but of *Legislators themselves, who punish those who commit Evil, if they do it not through Compulsion, or involuntary Ignorance; and reward those who do well.*[172] And the learned *Alexander Aphrodisius* and *Ammonius Hermias* have wrote each a Treatise, to shew the Agreement of *Aristotle* with the *Platonick* Notion of *Fate* and human *Liberty.* It appears also from *Cicero,* that the antient *Diodorus* was a *Fatalist,* maintaining, that all Truths in *Futurity,* as well as those which are *actual,* are *necessarily* such, and cannot but be.[173]

"These are the principal Asserters of the Doctrine of absolute Fatality that we know of; and they who follow'd their Opinion, all founded the Arguments and Reasons of it in the Supposition of the Truth of the *Material System,* or that nothing existed but *Body* and *Matter.*

"First; Those of the *Atomical* Sect, who follow'd the Opinion of *Democritus,* alledg'd, that all Things, even human Actions, were effected by the eternal necessary Motion, and perpendicular Impulse, of self-

---

168. Ibid., p. 46.
169. Photius, *Bibliotheca,* p. 552.
170. Aristotle, *Nicomachean Ethics,* III.1.
171. Ibid., III.5.
172. Ibid., III.7.
173. Cicero, *De Fato,* pp. 346, 349.

existent corporeal Atoms, by whose fortuitous Concourse and Union all Things were form'd.[174]

"Secondly; Those amongst the *Stoicks,* who adher'd to the Doctrine of *Heraclitus,* were of three several Opinions.

" 'Some derived all Things from the *first Cause* of the Universe, which they said pervaded all Things, and not only gave Motion to, but was the *Efficient* Cause of, every Thing; styling it *Fate,* and the Supreme Cause, and supposing it to be itself all Things; and that, not only all other Things which exist, but even the inward Purposes of our Minds also, proceeded from the efficient Power of it, as the Members of an Animal are not mov'd of themselves, but by that governing Principle, which is in every Animal.'[175] This was making no Agent in the World, but God only, and human Actions to be nothing but the Operations of God in Men, actuating them and every Thing else, as the Soul does the Body.

"Thirdly; The Astrological Notion of Fate was this; 'That the Circumvolution of the Universe effected all Things by its Motion, and by the Position and Appearances of the Planets and fix'd Stars with respect to each other; and, founding upon these the Art of Prognostication, would have it, that every Thing came to pass thereby.'[176] This is but another way of ascribing every Thing we *do,* our Purposes and Passions, our Wickedness and Appetites, to the Universe, or to God.

"Fourthly; Another Notion of Fatality was founded on the Supposition of 'a mutual eternal Concatenation and Chain of Causes, whereby Things posterior always follow those which are antecedent, and are resolv'd into them, as existing by them; and are necessarily consequent to those which precede them: This was another way of effecting an absolute Fatality.'[177] And this was the most plausible, and most insisted on by the Maintainers of *Necessity;* and was grounded on the Supposition, that every Motion was caus'd by an external impulse of Matter, and that there

---

174. Ibid., p. 352.
175. Plotinus, *Enneads,* III.1.2. Maxwell's text mistranscribes Jackson's note as I.3.
176. Ibid.
177. Ibid.

was no internal Principle, or Cause of Motion, or Action, in the Mind at all.

"These are the several Opinions of the antient *Fatalists,* which resolv'd into two; the one made every Thing the necessary Effect of the eternal Motion and Concourse of Atoms; the absurdity of which, as supposing an eternal Chain of *Effects,* without any original *Cause,* or *Agent* at all, evidently appears; and which, by inferring the Necessity of human Actions, and thereby taking away the Foundation and Distinction of *Virtue* and *Vice,* and the consequent Praise and Dispraise due unto them, was rejected by *Epicurus* himself on this very Account.[178] The other made no Agent in the World but God, who was suppos'd to be infus'd, like a Soul, thro' the whole Universe, and to act in every Thing by an eternal Chain of Causes, necessarily connected with each other; and all deriv'd from *God* (who was called *Fate*) as the original, or supreme Cause of all.

"This latter, tho' more plausible than the former, yet so plainly inferr'd such a Fate as made Mens Actions *necessary,* (as both *Plotinus* and *Cicero* observe,[179]) whereby the Nature of *Virtue* and *Vice,* of *Rewards* and *Punishments,* were so wholly destroy'd, that it made the Notion it-self *intolerable,* as *Cicero* calls it; insomuch that the Defenders of it were forc'd to allow notwithstanding, (tho' inconsistently with themselves,) that there was a *Power of Action,* or *Free-Agency* in Mens Minds; and durst not affirm, that human Actions were *necessary:* And the opposite Party was so averse to it on this Account, as to recur to the other Extreme, and maintain that the *voluntary Motion, or Exertion of the Mind was not at all influenc'd by Fate, or antecedent Causes.* These two rigid opposite Tenents, as they were thought, made the famous *Chrysippus,*[180] and the most Reasonable and Learned of the Antients of all Sects, step in as Moderators between these two Opinions, and come to an Agreement on all Sides, that on the one Hand *Necessity* was to be excluded from *human Actions,* that so the Distinction of *Virtue* and *Vice,* and the *Re-*

178. Plutarch, *De Stoicorum Repugnantiis* (in *Moralia*), p. 1050.
179. Plotinus, *Enneads,* III.1.4.
180. Cicero, *De Fato,* p. 359.

wards and *Punishments,* both of divine and human Laws, founded upon them, might be preserv'd inviolated; so on the other Hand *Fate,* even with respect to human Actions, (as well as to external Events consequent upon them, in which it was absolute and uncontroulable,) was so far to be restrain'd, as that it was to be allow'd, that *antecedent Causes* were the Motives of acting, or influenc'd the Mind to act, tho' the *principal* and *efficient* Cause of Action was a natural Power and *free Exertion* of the Mind itself.

"This Distinction of *Fate* and *Necessity,* and middle Opinion founded upon it, prevail'd amongst all sorts of Philosophers, *Stoicks* as well as *Platonicks,* &c. (excepting the ignorant Astrologers and Fortune-tellers amongst the *Stoicks;*) accordingly, we learn from *Plutarch,* that *Plato* (the great Assertor of the Freedom of the Mind) 'admitted Fate with respect to the human Soul and Life; but adds withal, that the Cause (of Action) is in ourselves. The *Stoicks,* in agreement with *Plato,* say, that *Necessity* is an invincible and compulsive Cause; but that *Fate* is the determin'd Connection of Causes, in which Connection our *Power of Action* is contain'd: So that some Things are destin'd, and others not.'[181]

"And *Austin* says, 'That the *Stoicks* distinguish'd the Causes of Things (into *antecedent* and *efficient,* as hath been before observ'd) that they might exempt some from *Necessity,* and subject others to it: And amongst those which they allow'd, not to be *under Necessity,* they plac'd our *Wills;* lest otherwise, if subjected to *Necessity,* they should not be *free.*'[182]

"Hence it appears, that there is no real Difference betwixt the *Platonical* and *Stoical* Philosophy, in the Opinion of *Fate,* and the *Freedom of human Actions;* and that which hath led Men, thro' Mistake, to think, that it was the constant and settled Doctrine of the *Stoicks,* that human Actions were subject to an absolute *Fatality,* or *Necessity,* is their asserting in general Terms, that *all* Things were originally fix'd and determin'd by the Laws, or Decrees of Fate, and are carried on and effected by an immutable Connection and Chain of Causes; whereas this *Fatality,* or *Necessity,* with respect to Men, was only understood of *external* provi-

181. Plutarch, *De Placitis Philosophorum* (in *Moralia*), pp. 884, 885.
182. St. Augustine, *The City of God,* V.10.

dential Events, which were appointed consequential to the Nature of their Actions, presuppos'd to be *free* and *in their own Power.* For the most eminent and rigid *Stoicks* plainly assert the Freedom of human Actions, as hath been prov'd above; and the *Platonicks,* who are known to be most zealous for the Cause of *Liberty,* do yet with the *Stoicks* constantly maintain *Fate,* and a determined Order and Series of antecedent Causes.

"From the preceding Observations, then, we learn what was the true Opinion, in general, both of the *Platonicks* and *Stoicks* concerning *Fate;* namely, that it was no other than the *Laws of divine Providence,* whereby all Things are govern'd, according to their *several Natures;* and therefore, particularly in respect of Men, it was understood to be the *Rules* and *Decrees* of divine Providence, determining the Events of human Life, and dispensing Rewards and Punishments, according to the Nature of Mens *voluntary* Actions.

"They thought, that God govern'd the World by his sovereign *Will,* which they call'd *Providence,* by which he made fix'd and unalterable Laws for the Administration of the whole Universe; and that he determin'd Mens Conditions, and their Happiness, or Misery, whether here, or hereafter, according as their *Actions* freely chosen, and done *voluntarily,* should be. So that *Fate,* in reality, was no other than *Providence,* [183] or the immutable Law and Rule of God's Government of the World; and which was call'd *Necessity,* (not as being suppos'd to effect *necessarily,* or to be the *necessary efficient* Cause of human Actions, but) because it was the *necessary* Law of all Nature; and the external Effects of it, or the Events produc'd by it, by a Series of antecedent Causes, in consequence of Mens *voluntary* Actions, were unavoidable and necessary.

"That this is the true antient Notion of *Fate* and *Necessity,* I shall further distinctly prove, by a brief and indisputable Deduction of Particulars.

"*Zeno,* the Father of the *Stoicks,* in his Letter to King *Antigonus* tells him, 'It is manifest, that you are not only by *Nature* inclin'd to Greatness

---

183. Chalcidius, *In Platonis Timaeum,* 7, p. 237.

of Mind, but by *Choice* also.'[184] Again; 'That which is Good is *Eligible*, as being that which is most worthy to be *chosen*.'[185]

"*Cicero* tells us, concerning *Chrysippus*, (who was a rigid *Stoick*, and whom his Adversaries charg'd as holding the *Necessity* of human Actions in consequence of his Assertion, that all Things proceeded from Fate, or a Chain of antecedent Causes) that in order 'to assail the Argument from whence *Necessity* was inferred, holding at the same time, that nothing happened without a *preceding Cause*, he distinguish'd the Kinds of Causes, that he might avoid *Necessity*, and still hold *Fate*. Of Causes, saith he, some are *perfect* and *principal*,' (efficient) 'Causes, others are assistant, and immediately precedent. Wherefore, when we say, that all Things come to pass by the *Fatality* of antecedent Causes, we do not understand this *Fatality* to belong to the *perfect* and *principal*' (efficient) 'Causes, but only to the immediately-precedent assistant Causes; upon which Distinction he thus reasons; If all Things come to pass *by Fatality*, it doth indeed follow, that they come to pass with *antecedent Causes*, but these are not the *perfect* and *principal*' (efficient) 'Causes of the Event, but only the assistant Causes, which are nearest to the other; which assistant Causes, altho' they are *not in our Power*, it does not thence follow, that our *Affections* are *not in our Power;* but this would follow, if the perfect and principal Causes were not in our Power.'[186]

"*Cicero* acknowledgeth this Reasoning of *Chrysippus* to be very *much labour'd* and *obscure;* but what he meant, he endeavoured ingeniously to explain by the *rolling of a Cylinder* and *Whipping of a Top, which, tho' they could not begin to move without being impelled by an external Force, yet, after Motion was given to them, they would continue to move, as it were, of themselves, by the Internal Power of their own Volubility, which belongs to their Nature, and was not given to them by that which was the first and immediate external Cause of their Motion.* So in like manner he suppos'd, that *external impulsive Causes,* which were Subject to *Fate,* or *out of our Power,* were the antecedent and first Causes, or Occasions, of the *inter-*

184. Diogenes Laertius, *Lives,* VII, p. 370.
185. Ibid., p. 476.
186. Cicero, *De Fato,* pp. 360, 361.

nal Motion of the Mind, i.e. that they set the Mind on Work; but yet, that our *Inclinations, Purposes* and *Actions* following, were *in our Power,* and under the Direction and *Government* of the *Will.*[187] From which Explanation it appears, that *Chrysippus* meant, by the *perfect* and *principal* Cause of Action, the *internal efficient* Cause, or the *voluntary Motion* or *Exertion* of the Mind itself into Action; and by the *Assistant precedent* Cause, he meant the *external* Cause, or *Motive,* of Action; and so his Reasoning is just and right.

"And that *Chrysippus* really meant, that Mens *Actions* were in their *own Power,* (tho' external Causes *out of their Power,* which he call'd *Fate,* concurr'd to the Production of them,) and that they were the Effects of *voluntary Choice; Gellius* informs us from his own express Words: 'Wherefore (says *Chrysippus* in *Gellius*) it is a Saying of the *Pythagoreans; you may know that Men bring Evils voluntarily upon themselves:* Mens Calamities proceeding from their *own selves;* and their *Sins* and *Vices* resulting from their own *Appetites, Intentions,* and *Purposes.* Wherefore, says *Chrysippus,* we ought not to endure or hear those *wicked, slothful, pernicious* and *audacious* Men, who, when they are convicted of a Fault, or of an Offence, fly to a *necessary Fatality* for refuge, and attribute their wicked Actions, not to their own Temerity, but to *Fate.*'[188]

"From this Explanation of the Notion of *Chrysippus* it will appear further, that the Dispute betwixt him and his learned Scholar *Carneades* and others (who deny'd there were any *antecedent Causes,* or *Fatality,* of Mens Actions, and affirmed, that the *Motion,* or *Exertion,* of the Mind was purely *voluntary*[189]) was only a Dispute about Words; each of them understanding the Word *Cause* in a different Sense. His Reasoning, which the *Epicureans* urg'd against *Chrysippus, Cicero* sets forth thus, *viz.*

" 'When they' (the *Epicureans*) 'had admitted, that there was no Motion *without a Cause,* they needed not' (*Carneades* taught them) 'grant, that all Events came to pass by *antecedent Causes:* For that there was no

187. Aulus Gellius, *Noctes Atticae,* VI [actually VII.2], p. 367.
188. Ibid., p. 366.
189. Cicero, *De Fato,* p. 359.

external and *antecedent* Cause of our *Will;* therefore the common Custom of saying, that any one *will,* or *will not,* do a Thing *without a Cause,* is an *Abuse of Speech;* for, when we say, *without a Cause,* we mean only, without an *external* and *antecedent* Cause, not without *any* Cause at all.—An *external* Cause is not requisite to the *voluntary* Motion of the Mind; for *voluntary* Motion, in the Nature of the Thing, is *in our own Power and Choice;* and that not without Cause; for the Cause of it is the Nature of the Mind itself.'[190] Presently after he shews (which was the Point of the Dispute) what is truly and properly the *Cause* of a Thing, *viz.*

"'That is the *Cause,* which *effects* that, of which it is the *Cause;* as a Wound causeth Death; ill Digestion, a Disease; Fire causeth Heat. Therefore *Cause* is not so to be understood, as if that which is *antecedent* merely to a Thing was the *Cause* of it; but that only is the *Cause,* which is the *antecedent efficient* Cause.'[191]

"Whence it is evident, as *Cicero* observes upon the matter, that they, who thought the *voluntary* Motions of the Mind were not affected by any *Fatality;*[192] and *Chrysippus,* who held a *Fate* to belong even to human Actions, tho' he allow'd them to be *voluntary,* and not effected by *Necessity,* really meant the same Thing; only those *external* Motives, which *Chrysippus* styl'd *antecedent Causes* and *Fate* (expressly declaring his meaning at the same time, that they were not the *perfect* and *principal,* i.e. *efficient,* Causes of Action) *Carneades,* and others, the *Academicks,* wou'd not allow to be properly *Causes* at all; insisting, that the *efficient* Cause, only, was the true *Cause* of Action; 'and that in what Things soever the antecedent Causes were such, that it was *not in our Power,* that the Things should be otherwise, these Things were properly effected *by Fate;* but those Things, the effecting of which are *in our own Power,* are wholly exempt from *Fate.*'[193] Understanding *Fate,* which they excluded from Mens Actions, in the Sense of a *necessary* impulsive Cause;

190. Ibid., pp. 352–53.
191. Ibid., p. 357.
192. Ibid., p. 363.
193. Ibid.

whilst *Chrysippus* understood the Fate which he ascrib'd to them, in the Sense of a concurrent Cause, or Motive, of Action only: Which shew'd, there was no real Difference in their Opinions; and that both agreed, that Mens Actions were in their *principal, perfect* or *efficient* Cause truly *voluntary.*

"And hence we may observe, That when *Plutarch* charges *Chrysippus* with holding, 'That not the least Thing, either rests, or moves, otherwise than according to the Appointment of God, whom he makes the same with *Fate*—and that he makes Fate (which he calls *Necessity,* &c.) an invincible and uncontroulable and immutable Cause;'[194] He either mistakes, or strains *Chrysippus's* Notion too far; or else *Chrysippus* is only speaking of the *Fatality,* or *Necessity,* of external Providential Events, and not of human Actions; from which *Fatality,* or *Necessity, Plutarch* himself implies, that he exempts them; owning that, with respect to Mens Actions, he (*Chrysippus*) 'made *Fate,* not the *perfect*' (i.e. the *efficient,* as hath been above observed from *Cicero*) 'but only the *precedent (i.e.)* the concurrent Cause only.'

"Again; *Cicero* himself answers the Argument against *Liberty,* which is here made, in these Words; *viz.*

" 'Altho' some are more inclin'd to some Things than others are, thro' *natural* antecedent Causes, it does not thence follow, that there are *natural* antecedent (efficient) Causes of our *Wills* and *Desires:* For, if so, nothing would be *in our own Power.* But now we readily own, that to be *acute,* or *dull,* of *strong,* or of *weak,* Constitutions, *is not in our Power:* But he that thinks it thence follows, that even to *sit,* or to *walk,* is not Matter of *Will* and *Choice,* does not perceive the Tendency of that Consequence. For, altho' there are *antecedent* Causes of Men's being born with *quick,* or *slow,* Capacities, with *robust,* or *infirm,* Constitutions; Yet it does not follow, that our *sitting* and *walking,* and *doing any Action,* is determined and appointed by these Causes.'[195] He adds presently;

" '*Vices*' (he means *vicious Inclinations,* as his preceding Instances shew) 'may grow from *natural* Causes; but to extirpate and eradicate

194. Plutarch, *De Stoicorum Repugnantiis* (in *Moralia*), p. 1056.
195. Cicero, *De Fato,* pp. 354, 355.

them, so as that he who hath these vicious Propensities may be wholly freed from them, is not in the Power of *natural Causes,* but is effected by the *Will,* by *Study* and *Discipline.*'[196] Than which Reasoning nothing can be more truly and strongly offer'd.

"To the same Argument the learned *Alexander Aphrodisius* thus replies; 'Those Things which proceed from a *Cause,* do not always proceed from an *external* Cause; on which account something is in our own Power, of which we *ourselves* are the proper Cause, and not any *external* Cause. Wherefore those Things which in this respect are *without* Cause, have yet a Cause from ourselves. For Man himself is the *original* and *Cause* of those *Actions* which are done by him, and this is properly to be a Man, to have a Principle of Action within himself, as it is the Property of a Globe to be roll'd down a steep Place. Wherefore other Things are impelled by external Causes, but Man is not; because it is essential to him, to have a Principle and Cause (of Action) within himself, so as not to be impell'd by exterior Causes. If we had one View in our judging about Actions, it might with Reason be said, that our Judgments about the same Things was always the same: But since it is not so, (for those Things we make choice of, we choose sometimes for the *Goodness,* sometimes for the *Pleasure,* sometimes for the *Profit* of them, and these do not produce the same Effects;) it happens, that we sometimes prefer the Motives to that which is good, before all others; again, at other times our Judgment leads us to prefer that which is *pleasant,* or *profitable.* For, as we seek for no other Cause, why the Earth is carried downward according to its Gravity, and why Animals act, as they do, by Appetite, than that each of these has, of itself, an efficient Cause derived from its Nature; so neither is there any other Cause to be sought of those different Actions, which we do at different Times, in different Circumstances, but only the Man himself. For this is to be a Man, namely, to be the *Original* and Cause of those Actions, which are done by him.'[197]

"To which, on the same Argument, I shall add the Opinions of the two most learned *Christian* Philosophers, *Eusebius* and *Origen.*

196. Ibid., p. 345.
197. Ibid., pp. 80, 83.

"*Eusebius* says; 'Altho' a thousand *external* fortuitous Obstacles oppose the Temper of our Bodies, and the *voluntary* Desires of our Minds, yet the *freely-exerted* Virtue of the Soul is able to withstand them all; demonstrating, that the Power, which we have within us, of *choosing* that which is good, is unmatchable and invincible.'[198]

"*Origen's* Observation is as follows, *viz.*

" 'We confess (saith he) that many Things which are *not in our Power,* are Causes of many Things that are *in our Power;* without which, namely, those Things which are *not in our Power,* other Things, which are *in our Power,* would not be done. But those Things which are *in our Power,* and are done consequentially to *antecedent* Things, which *are not in our Power,* are done so as that, notwithstanding these *antecedent* Things, we might have done *otherwise.* But, if any one would have it, that our *Free-will* is wholly independent of every Thing in the World, so as that we do not *choose* to do some Things by reason of certain (precedent) Accidents, he forgets, that he is a Part of the World, and comprehended within human Society, and the circumambient Air.'[199]

"It is evident, that after Reasons, or Motives, not in Mens Power, are offered to them to act, and they cannot help thinking it right to act upon them, and are in their last Judgment determined to act upon them, (and the Event shews that they do act upon them;) they can yet *deliberate* with themselves before they *act,* and can *suspend* the *Action* without any *external* Motive whatsoever; which clearly shews, that the *Action* proceeds from *Will* and *Choice,* and is *voluntary,* not *necessary.*

"My Adversary himself allows, That *Choice* and *Preference* imply *Doubt* and *Deliberation;* which tho' not true, as I have shewn; yet, on the other side, it is true, that *Deliberation* and *Suspension* imply *Will* and *Choice:* For it is, I think, Demonstration, that, if the Motives of acting are such as impell the Mind *necessarily* to act, *i.e.* to act, not by *Will,* but by *Necessity,* then there can be no *Suspension* of Action; but the Moment that the Mind is impelled, it must act, just as a Balance moves the Instant

198. Eusebius, *Praeparatio Evangelica,* VI, p. 252.
199. Origen in Eusebius, *Praeparatio Evangelica,* p. 290, and Commentary in *Genesis,* p. 11.

that the Weight is hung upon it: *Necessity* has no Regard to *Time,* but, if it acts at all, acts equally in every Moment of Time; and, if *it* is the immediate *efficient* Cause, or Power of Action, must act as soon as it takes place, or impells the Mind; and I would desire to be told, what Power of the Mind it is, (if it is not that which we call *Will,*) which is able perpetually to resist, without the Assistance of any external Motive, the Operations of Necessity by Suspension of Actions. That this *Suspension* is caus'd by the *Will,* and, consequently, that the Action following is *voluntary,* may farther appear by there being *no Suspension,* or *Deliberation,* where the Actions, or Effects, are not *voluntary,* as whether the *Pulse,* or *Heart,* should beat, and in the case of the Actions of *Madmen,* of Men in a *Fever,* or under a violent *Surprise,* or *Passion;* the more of *Necessity* there is, there is always the less of *Deliberation* and *Suspension;* and, if the Motive *necessarily* produces the Action, it produces it also *instantaneously.* This Argument may be worth Consideration; and to it I shall subjoin the Opinion of the great *Aristotle;* who thus argues;

"*'Deliberation* and *Choice* is one and the same Thing; for that which was *deliberated* upon is the Matter of Choice.—Now the *elective* Faculty, being *deliberative,* and that which *desires* those Things which are *in our Power,* the *Choice* itself is the *deliberative Desire* of those Things which *are in our Power:* For, judging upon Deliberation, we afterwards desire what we deliberated upon.'[200]

"And the learned *Alexander Aphrodisius* says;

"'Certainly Man hath not the Power of *Deliberation* in vain, as it must be, if he acts *by Necessity.* But it plainly appears, that Man alone hath, by Nature, this Power above the rest of Animals, that he is not like them led merely by *Sense,* but is endued with *Reason,* whereby to judge of Objects. By which Reason examining the Objects of *Sense,* if he finds them to be really what at first they appear'd to be, he assents to the Evidence of his Senses, and pursues the Objects of them. But, if he finds them different from what they appeared, he does not continue in his Conception of them, being convinc'd by *Reason,* upon Consideration, of the Falsity of them. Wherefore we *deliberate* only about such Things,

200. Aristotle, *Nicomachean Ethics,* III.5.

as are *in our Power* to do, or *not:* And, when we act without *Deliberation,* we often repent and blame our-selves for our *Inconsideration.* Also, if we see others act unadvisedly, we reprehend them as guilty of a Fault, and the Ground of our *Consultation* with others is, that Things are *in our own Power.*'[201]

"Let us proceed, farther to explain the Doctrine of *Chrysippus* and the *Stoicks,* whose Notions, concerning Human Liberty, have been much mistaken and misrepresented.

"*Chrysippus* says, 'Fate is the Reason of the World, or the Law of Providence, by which all Things in the World are govern'd.'[202] And *Gellius* tells us, that *Chrysippus* held, that the '*Order* and *Reason* and *Necessity* of Fate was a Motive of Action, to the general and efficient Causes of it; but that every one's own *Will* and Dispositions directed the Exertion of our Minds and Purposes, and the Actions of them.'[203] And *Diogenianus* the Peripatetic, writing against *Chrysippus,* says, 'It is manifest, from the Distinction which he (*Chrysippus*) makes, that the Cause (of Action) which is in us, is exempt from Fate.'[204] And he cites *Chrysippus* as declaring, 'That it is evident, that many Things are done *by our own Power,* but yet, nevertheless, that these Things are connected with Fate, by which the Universe is govern'd.'[205]

"Whence it appears, that the learned Dr. *Cudworth* is mistaken, when he says, that *the antient* Stoicks, Zeno *and* Chrysippus, *asserted, that God acted necessarily in the general Frame of Things in the World; from whence, by a Series of Causes (they thought) doth unavoidably result whatsoever is done in it. Which Fate is a Concatenation of Causes, all in themselves necessary.*[206]

"For which Opinion, concerning these two most eminent *Stoicks,* the learned *Doctor* produceth not the least Evidence. That which deceived him, and hath also deceived others, both *antients* (as *Cicero* and *Gellius*

---

201. Eusebius, *Praeparatio Evengelica,* VI, pp. 271, 272; Aphrodisius, *De Fato.*
202. Plutarch, *De Placitis Philosophorum* (in *Moralia*), p. 885.
203. Aulus Gellius, *Noctes Atticae,* VI, pp. 365, 366.
204. Eusebius, *Praeparatio Evengelica,* VI.8.
205. Ibid.
206. Cudworth, *The True Intellectual System of the Universe,* p. 4.

observe) and *moderns,* is, their Notion of a Series and Concatenation of Causes; which Causes, tho' they were supposed *necessarily* to produce each other, yet they were not supposed, to proceed *necessarily* from God, the *original* and *first* Cause, but to be derived from the perfect *Wisdom* of his Nature, and his *Will,* as *Seneca,* the *Stoick,* has informed us: And were not thought to be the *efficient Causes* of human Actions, (which they expressly exempted from the Coercion of them,) but were only understood, to be *Motives,* or *secondary Causes;* whilst they placed the *principal* and *efficient* Cause of Action within the Mind itself: So that the *Necessity* of this *Stoical* Chain of Causes was only supposed, to operate in the Production of external providential Events, consequential to Mens Actions, which were taught to be *voluntary* and in their own Power. And it plainly appears, from the Words of *Balbus,* the *Stoick,* mention'd by *Cicero* (*de nat. Deor.* L. 2.) that the *antient Stoicks* agreed with the *Platonicks,* in asserting the *free* and *voluntary* Motion, Exertion, or Agency, of the human Mind. To proceed therefore;

"*Cicero,* in the Person of *Velleius,* represents the *Stoical* Notion of Fate to be, 'That all Events proceed from the eternal Truth and Connection of Causes.'[207] *Diogenes Laertius* says it was their Opinion, 'That Fate is the Connection of the Causes of Things, or that Reason, by which the World is govern'd.'[208]

"*Seneca* (the *Stoick*) says; 'Fate is nothing else, but the Connection of Causes.'[209]

"*Marcus Antoninus* the Emperor, and *Stoical* Philosopher, frequently expresses his Notion of Fate in like manner.[210] But that in this *Fate,* or Chain of Causes, the *Power of Action* in Men was contain'd, and was (ὑπὲρ μόρον) exempt from the *Necessity of Fate,* we are assur'd (from *Plutarch*[211]) was the common Opinion of *Stoicks* and *Platonists.* And

207. Cicero, *De Natura Deorum,* I.
208. Diogenes Laertius, *Lives,* VII, pp. 459, 460.
209. Seneca, *De Beneficiis,* IV.7.
210. Marcus Aurelius, *Meditations,* V.8, X.5.
211. Plutarch, *De Placitis Philosophorum* (in *Moralia*), pp. 884, 885.

Tacitus, speaking of the *Stoicks,* says, 'They attribute, indeed, a *Fatality* unto Things, but not as proceeding from the Motion of the Planets, (which was the Astrological Notion only,) but from the Principle and Connection of natural Causes: And yet they leave the Conduct of our Life *to our own Choice,* which being *chosen,* a certain Order of Events (they think) follows.'[212]

"*Alcinous* sets forth *Plato*'s Opinion of Fate, in the following Manner: 'He understands Fate to be this; That, if any Person chooseth such a sort of Life, and will do such and such Actions, such and such Consequences will follow. Wherefore the Soul is unrestrain'd, and hath it in its own Power to act, or not, and in this respect (of any particular Action) is not compelled: But the Consequence of it's Action will be effected by Fate: As for Example, if *Paris* will carry away *Helen,* which it is in his Power to do, or not, the Event will be, that the *Grecians* will make War against the *Trojans* for her.'[213]

"*Hierocles* teacheth, that 'Fate is the judicial Operation of the Deity, effecting Events according to the Laws of Providence, and directing human Affairs in the Order and Course that is suitable to their *free* Purposes and *voluntary* Actions.'[214] The precedent Arguments, upon which he builds his Notion, are, *viz.*

" 'If (says he) bodily and external Events fall out fortuitously and by Chance, what becomes of the Superintendency of God, to judge and recompense every one according to his Deserts? For we will not suppose these Things to happen without Appointment, and say, that our just *Purposes,* and our *Judgments* and *Desires,* proceed from an overruling *Necessity:* For, if so, we should not impute Virtue and Vice to *ourselves,* but to that *Necessity.* Nor is it reasonable to suppose all Things to be the *necessary* Effects of them, I mean the Actions of the Soul, as well as the Things that are without us, and concern the Body. Nor ought we to ascribe all Things to the unintelligent and undirected Circumvolution

212. Tacitus, *Annales,* VI.
213. Albinus [not Alcinous, as Jackson states], *De Doctrina Platonis,* ch. 6.
214. Hierocles, *De Providentia et Fato,* p. 42.

of the Universe; there being a Mind, that presides over all Things, and a God, who is the Author of the World. That which necessarily remains, therefore, is, that the *Choice* we make is *in our own Power,* and that a righteous Recompense is awarded, according thereto, by coelestial Beings and Judges appointed by God, and who have the Care of us committed to them.—And the Supposition of a Recompence, according to our Merit, immediately infers a Providence and *Fate,* as the consequent of it; and judicial Providence, which orders the Events of human Affairs, according to Right and Equity, depends upon the Principle of our *Will* and *Choice:* So that *Fate* is a Part of universal Providence, and the Rule of Judgment upon the Souls of Men.'[215]

"To which he adds presently after; 'To *choose,* is in the Power of the Mind; but the Events following the *Choice,* are determined by a judicial Providence, recompensing the Purposes of the Soul, according to its Desert: And thence we are said, both to *choose* our Condition of Life, and to have it destin'd to us. For the Recompense, ordain'd to follow our Works, both manifests the *free* Motion (or Operation) of our Mind, and the divine Superintendency over us. So that it is evident, that the Motions (or Operations) of our Minds, from Beginning to End, are *free*—and that the Recompence of our Deserts is not *without Appointment,*—as neither is *Fate,* which is the Chain and Connection of the *human Will,* with the divine Judgment: So that we *choose* what we will, thro' an *unrestrain'd Liberty,* but often suffer against our Will, thro' the unavoidable Power of Providence.'[216]

"*Chalcidius* expresseth the *Platonick* Notion of *Fate* in like manner; *viz.* 'Such, (says he) in my Opinion, is that heavenly Law, which is call'd *Fate,* commanding Men that which is right, and forbidding the contrary; but to obey, *is in our own Power,* and free from the *Coercion of Fate.* To praise him that does well, is both agreeable to this Law, and to the common Judgment of all.—Moreover, *to live ill,* is in *the Power* of Man, and, therefore, Punishment proceeds from a *fatal Necessity,* in conse-

215. Ibid., pp. 26, 27.
216. Ibid., pp. 31, 32.

quence of the Law. All these Things relate to the Mind of Man, which is *free, and acts by its own Choice.*'[217]

"Again; '*Fate* is the Decree of Providence, comprehending our *voluntary* Actions, as the precedent Grounds of it; comprehending, also, the Recompence of our Deserts. *Punishment* and *Approbation,* which are by *Fatality,* and all those Things which happen fortuitously, or by Chance, are the Consequents of it.'[218]

"But, in order to understand more fully and distinctly the antient philosophical, or theological, Notion of *Fate,* or *Necessity,* we are to observe, that it was distinguished into two *Senses,* (tho' in Reality amounting to the same,) in the one of which it was understood, *substantially* to mean that *intelligent divine* Being, or Substance, which govern'd the World by the Administration of the Laws of Providence; in the other it was taken *abstractedly,* or *virtually,* for the *Laws,* or *Decrees* themselves, of the divine Government of the World.

"'Fate (says the great Philosopher *Chalcidius*) was understood by *Plato* in a two-fold Sense, the one relating to its *Substance,* the other to its *Energy* and *Power.*'[219]

"Thus also *Plutarch* represents it;[220]

"*Fate,* in the Sense of *Operation,* or *Power,* is call'd by *Plato,* 'in his Phaedrus, an unavoidable Decree; in his Timaeus, the Laws, which God endited to coelestial Beings[221] concerning the Nature of the Universe.'[222] The Sense of which he immediately explains; *viz.*

"'By unavoidable Decree, we may understand an irrepealable Law, proceeding from an irresistible Cause, (*viz.* the supreme God,) and by the Laws which God endited to (coelestial) Beings concerning the Nature of the Universe, the Law which is consequential to the Nature of the World, and by which the Universe is governed.

---

217. Chalcidius, *In Platonis Timaeum,* p. 271.
218. Ibid., p. 279.
219. Ibid., p. 236.
220. Plutarch, *De Fato* (in *Moralia*).
221. Chalcidius, *In Platonis Timaeum,* p. 236.
222. Jackson: "By coelestial Beings, *Chalcidius* seems to mean *Providence,* which he speaks of as the *second* God, and the *Soul of the World.*"

"*'Fate*, in the Sense of Substance (he proceeds to tell us) is the *Soul of the World.'*[223] Which *Plutarch* also informs us it was.[224]

"It was call'd *Lachesis*, or (ἀνάγνινι) *Necessity;* both as being supposed to be *necessarily-existent*, and the *necessary Substratum* for the Formation of rational Beings; as also, because the *Laws* of it were fix'd and *immutable*, and to which they supposed God had subjected all Beings, and even bound himself under an irreversible and *necessary* Obligation.

"*Chalcidius* styles this *Lachesis*, or *Necessity*, 'the divine Law,'[225] by which Things future are connected with Things past and present.

"And it is, with respect to the immutable Laws of Providence, that *Plotinus* calls God 'the Necessity and Law of all Things.'[226]

"*Cicero* in like manner (speaking of the *Platonick* Philosophy) observes, that this *Fate*, or *Soul* of the World, by whose *providential Wisdom* all Things, both in *Heaven* and *Earth*, are governed, is call'd *Necessity; because nothing can happen otherwise than according to the Laws of it, whereby the eternal Order of the Universe is immutably preserved by Fatality.*[227]

"The *Stoïcks* express their Notion of Fate (substantially) in Agreement with the *Platonists*.

"*'Heraclitus* styles the *Substance* of Fate, that *Reason* which pervades the Substance of the Universe; the same (he adds) is an aethereal Body, the generating Seed of the Universe.'[228]

"*Euripides* expresses the *Stoical* Sense; *'Jupiter*, or the Necessity of Nature, or the Reason of Men. For *Necessity* and Mind is the (substantial) Power, which diffuseth itself thro' the Universe.'[229]

"*Velleius*, in *Cicero*, represents the Opinion of the *Stoick Chrysippus; '*That he says; that the Power of that perpetual and eternal Law, which is, as it were, the Guide of our Life, and Director of our Duty, is *Jupiter;*

---

223. Chalcidius, *In Platonis Timaeum*, p. 237.
224. Plutarch, *De Fato* (in *Moralia*).
225. Chalcidius, *In Platonis Timaeum*, p. 237.
226. Plotinus, *Enneads*, VI, p. 743.
227. Cicero, *Academicae Quaestiones*, I.
228. Plutarch, *De Placitis Philosophorum* (in *Moralia*), p. 885.
229. Plutarch, *De Animi Procreatione* (in *Moralia*), p. 1026.

the same he also calls *Fate* and *Necessity*.'[230] Again; 'The *Stoicks* held a *Necessity*, which they called *Fate*.'[231]

"Again; *Diogenes Laertius* tells us it was the *Stoical* Notion, 'That *God*, and *Mind*, and *Fate*, and *Jupiter*, were one and the same, to which they gave many other Names also.'[232]

"*Alexander Aphrodisius* says; 'They (the *Stoicks*) say that *Fate*, and *Nature*, and *Reason*, by which the Universe is governed, is *God*.'[233]

"*Lastly*, *Seneca* the *Stoick* says; 'What else is *Nature* but *God*, and the divine Reason, which is infused into the whole World and the Parts of it?—And, if you call the same *Fate*, you will not be mistaken.'[234]

"There was no other Difference betwixt the *Platonick* and *Stoick* Notion of *Fate*, but only, that the *Stoicks* thought that *Fate* considered (*Substantia*, or κατ᾽ οὐσίαν) as a *substantial* divine Being, which was the *Soul of the World*, was the (πρῶτος θεὸς) *supreme God*, whom they styled 'The first Cause of the Universe;'[235] and 'Fate and the Necessity (or necessary Cause) of Things:'[236] Whereas the *Platonicks* made *Fate* (δεύτερον θεὸν, ἕτερον νοῦν, secundam Mentem) *a second God, a second Mind*, inferior and subservient to the *supreme God*.

"The preceeding Observations will explain the Meaning of the strong poetical Expressions of the *Gods*, or even of *Jupiter* himself, the *supreme God*, being *subject to Fate*; by which, agreeably to the *Platonical* and *Stoical* Philosophy, was understood, that all subordinate Beings, how divine soever, were subject to the *immutable Laws of Providence*, which were the *Will* and *Command* of the *supreme* God; and, according to which, God himself was determined *invariably* to act, and so was said to be bound by, and to obey, his own Laws, as being most *wise* and *perfect*.

"With respect to the Subjection of the inferior Deities to *Fate*, *Chalcidius* gives us *Plato*'s Opinion;

230. Cicero, *De Natura Deorum*, I.
231. Ibid.
232. Diogenes Laertius, *Lives*, VII, p. 450.
233. Aphrodisius, *De Fato*, p. 107.
234. Seneca, *De Beneficiis*, IV.7.
235. Plotinus, *Enneads*, III.1.
236. Tertullian, *Apologeticus*, ch. 25.

"'The Command of God, which the subordinate Gods obey, is, I think, that Reason, call'd Fate, which contains the eternal Government of Things, and is deriv'd from Providence.'[237]

"To the same purpose *Plato* himself cites *Pindar* saying, 'That the Law (of Providence) rules over all, both mortal Men, and the immortal Gods.'[238]

"And *Simonides;* 'The Gods themselves do not resist *Necessity,*' i.e. the uncontrouble Laws of divine Providence.

"And *Seneca;* 'Whatsoever it is that commands us thus to live, or die, it binds the Gods also under the same Necessity: An irrevocable Course (of Providence) carries on, both human and divine Things; the very Maker and Governor of all Things wrote indeed the Fates, but also follows them; commanded once for all, and himself always observes what he commanded.'[239]

"*Lucan* expresses the same Notion in a lively and poetical Manner.[240]

"With respect to God's being unalterably determined to act according to the fixed Laws of his Providence, and so to be, as it were, bound by them; *Seneca* styles God *his own Necessity.*[241]

"And *Cicero* interprets a *Greek* Poet, as saying; 'That the supreme *Jupiter* cannot prevent that which is decreed to come to pass.'[242]

"And *Herodotus;* 'It is impossible for God himself to avoid the destin'd Fate.' And again; 'God himself is a Servant of Necessity.'[243]

"Which Passages do not mean, as if there was thought to be any *Fate,* or *Necessity,* distinct from, and really superior to, the supreme God; but only, that the Laws of divine Providence, as being the Result of *infinite* and *perfect Wisdom,* were the immutable Rule, by which God was determined to order the Event of Things, and to act in the Government of the World. To proceed therefore:

237. Chalcidius, *In Platonis Timaeum,* p. 239.
238. Plato, *Georgias.*
239. Seneca, *De Providentia,* ch. 5.
240. Lucan, *Pharsalia,* II.
241. Seneca, *Naturales Quaestiones,* Preface.
242. Cicero, *De Divinatione,* II, p. 275.
243. Cudworth, *The True Intellectual System of the Universe,* p. 5.

"*Fate* (κατ᾽ ὀνέργειαν) in the abstract Sense, as implying *Energy, Power,* or *Operation,* 'is the Laws' (of Providence) 'with which the Soul of the World is invested, for the good Government of the Universe.'[244] Hence we see the Reason, why the *Soul of the World* is call'd *Fate, viz.* As containing in it those Laws of Providence, which are that which is call'd *Fate.*

"Again; 'It is a Decree, existent Order, and an all-comprehending Law, which derives its precedent Causes *from our Deserts,* as the Grounds' (of the Events) 'of it; and the Events, which proceed *necessarily* from it, are the *consequential* Effects of our *precedent* Merits, and of the *Necessity*' (or immutable Sanction) 'of that Law.'[245]

"*Chalcidius* goes on; 'The Foundation therefore of the divine Law, that is, of *Fate,* is *Providence:* But it is call'd *Fate,* because it contains, as in a *Decree,* the Duty of Obedience, and the Contumacy of our Disobedience to it. And Punishments and Rewards proceed from it, according to our precedent Deserts. But our precedent Deserts, whether good, or bad, are the Motion of our own Minds; and the Judgment, Consent, Desire, and Aversion of them, which are *in our own Power;* because the *Choice* of these and their contraries *is in our own Power.*— Therefore the Soul of the World is *Fate,* as it signifies a *substantial* Being; and that *Law* also, with which it is instructed for the well Governing of all Things, is that *Fate,* which consists in *Operation* and *Act,* and the Order and Consequence of it is; if we do *this, that* will follow: Therefore, the precedent Action is *in our Power;* the Event that follows it, is the Decree of Fate; which is otherwise call'd Fatal, and differs very much from *Fate.* So that there are three Things, *viz.* that which is *in our own Power;* and *Fate,*' (or the Law of Providence,) 'and the Recompence of our Deserts according to the Law of *Fate.*'[246]

"*Chalcidius* concludes the *Platonick* Notion of *Fate,* from many foregoing Arguments in these Words, *viz.*

" 'That some Things are effected by *Fate,* is true; and that some

244. Chalcidius, *In Platonis Timaeum,* p. 239.
245. Ibid., p. 240.
246. Ibid., pp. 242, 243.

Things are *in our own Power,* has been prov'd to be true also. Wherefore, they who ascribe all *Things* to *Fate,* are justly found fault with by those, who prove, that some Things are *in our own Power.* Again; they who place every Thing *in our Power,* and attribute *nothing* to *Fate,* are plainly mistaken. For who knows not, that something is effected by *Fate,* and is not *in our Power?* Therefore, that Reasoning alone is true, and that Opinion firm and solid, which teacheth, that some Things happen by *Fate,* and other Things proceed from the *Choice* and *Will* of Men.'[247]

"Thus, I think, it is clearly and indisputably prov'd, that the *Freedom of human Actions* was the general and prevailing, and almost unanimous Doctrine, of the most eminent and numerous Sects of Philosophers, particularly, the Five great Sects amongst the *Heathens,* which comprehended all the Philosophy of *Greece* and *Rome,* namely, the *Epicureans, Stoicks, Platonicks, Aristotelians,* and *Academicks;* and that the Opposers of this Doctrine were chiefly *Leucippus, Empedocles,* and *Democritus,* the first Founders of the *Epicurean* Sect, but oppos'd herein by *Epicurus* and his Followers; *Heraclitus, Diodorus,* and some *Astrologers* and *Fortune-tellers* amongst the *Stoicks,* which were greatly despised and condemned by the most learned of that Sect also. And I have also shewn distinctly, and at large, that the antient *Platonick* and *Stoical* Notion of *Fate* and *Necessity* agreed with each other, and was declar'd to be consistent with the *Liberty* of Mens Actions; and was not understood to be a *necessary efficient Cause* of human Actions at all, but only to be the determinate *Will* and *Decrees* of God, or the *Laws* of his *Providence,* by which the Universe was govern'd, and Good and Evil was dispensed unto Men, according to the *free* and *voluntary* Actions, and Conduct, of their Life.

"And, from the preceeding Proofs of the *Freedom of human Actions,* as being the Sense and Opinion of the most *Wise* and *Learned,* as well as *greatest* Part of Mankind in all Ages, I beg leave to make one Observation, namely, that upon the Supposition of the *Necessity* of Mens Actions, it must appear very extraordinary and directly absurd, that the Light of natural Reason should necessarily lead Mankind at all Times to conclude their Actions to be *in their own Power* and *Choice,* and to

247. Ibid., pp. 279, 280.

be *voluntary* and *free,* if they are indeed *necessary:* That *Necessity* should form Mens Minds and Notions so opposite to its own Operations, and make them *necessarily* think their Actions are not *necessary* but *voluntary.* To which Purpose, the learned *Ammonius Hermias* argues; 'Does this Reason, which' (as they teach) '*necessarily* effects all Things, make it *necessary* for Men to affirm, either that all Things are *necessary,* or that some Things are *in our Power?* If the latter is true, then all Things are not *necessary;* but, if the former, how come many to think the contrary, *viz.* that many Things are *in our Power?* For it is altogether absurd to suppose, that Nature, which' (they say) '*necessarily* effects all Things, should move us against Nature, to contradict the Truth of its own Operations.'"[248]

So much for the Sentiments of the *Antients* concerning *Fate, Necessity, Liberty,* and *Providence,* from the Reverend Mr. *John Jackson.*[249]

8. From what has been already laid down, and from what follows, it is *apparent,* "That the *Heathens* knew not the true God," which is their distinguishing Character, differencing them from the *true People of God.* The *not knowing God,* is distinguishable into several Sorts and Kinds; that which is *Unprophetick,* that which is *Unphilosophick,* and that which is *Irreligious.* That which is *Unprophetick,* relates only to Matters of Intercourse between God and his Prophets, and his Method of manifesting himself to them, 1 *Sam.* 3.7. "Samuel *did not yet know the Lord, neither was the Word of the Lord yet reveal'd unto him.*" That which is *Unphilosophick,* relates only to Philosophick Disquisition and Comprehension, *Job* 36. 26. "*God is great and we know him not, neither can the number of his years be searched out.*" That which is *Irreligious,* is the Opposite to *such knowing God,* which belongeth to Religionists as such, and constitutes the *true Theists of Religion.* 2 *Thess.* 1. 7, 8. "*The Lord Jesus shall be revealed from Heaven with his mighty Angels, in flaming Fire, taking Vengeance on them that know not God.*" A truly religious *knowing God,* a knowing him so as to be truly religious towards him, is the Essence and Summary of true Religion, the Whole of Piety. Therefore some judicious Interpreters expound the Knowledge of God by *Piety,* or *Godliness,*

That the Heathens knew not the true God.

248. Ammonius Hermias, *Commentaria in Aristotelem,* p. 215.
249. Jackson, *A Defence of Human Liberty,* pp. 150–85.

others by the *Fear of God,* which comes to the same Thing. *Hos.* 4. 1. "*There is no Truth, nor Mercy, nor Knowledge of God in the Land.*" Jer. 9. 6. "*They refuse to know me, saith the Lord.*" Jer. 22. 16. "*Was this to know me? saith the Lord.*" In this Sense the Knowledge of God is preferr'd before Burnt Offerings. *Hos.* 6. 6. and this Knowledge of God will make holy and happy Times, *Isa.* 11. 9. "*They shall not hurt, nor destroy in all my holy Mountain; for the Earth shall be full of the Knowledge of the Lord.*" When God foretelleth by the Prophet, *Jer.* 24. 7. "*I will give them a Heart to know me, that I am the Lord*"; the Meaning is, they shall be true *Pietists* towards him; and by another Prophet, *Hos.* 2. 20. "*Thou shalt know the Lord*"; it is to signify, that he, on his part, would enter into a League of Amity with them, and make himself known to them at a more than ordinary Rate; and they, on their Part, shall be true Pietists. But the Sons of *Eli* were monstrous *Impietists,* and their being such was a "*not knowing the Lord.*" 1 *Sam.* 2. 22. They knew not the Lord, as *David* chargeth his Son *Solomon,* "*Know the Lord God of thy Father, and serve him with a perfect Heart,*" 1 Chron. 28. 9.

Sometimes the *knowing God* must be explain'd by *Wisdom in Divine Matters.* Thus it is to be understood, *Col.* 1. 10. "*Increasing in the Knowledge of God.*" And God foretelleth by the Prophet, that the meanest *Christian* shall be *Wise in Divine Matters.* Jer. 31. 34. "*They shall teach no more every Man his Neighbour, and every Man his Brother, saying, Know the Lord, for they shall all know me, from the least of them unto the greatest of them.*" i.e. They shall all comprehend what ought to be known of God, in conjunction with Piety.

Sometimes the Phrase of *knowing God* must be explain'd by what we commonly call *Acquaintance,* in which Sense also the *Wicked* are called *Aliens.* 1 John 4. 7, 8. "*Every one that loveth, is born of God, and knoweth God. He that loveth not, knoweth not God; for God is Love.*" 1. John 2. 4. "*He that saith, I know him, and keepeth not his Commandments, is a Liar,*" and 3. 6. "*Whosoever Sinneth,*" (habitually,) "*hath not seen him, neither knoweth him.*" In the same Sense of *knowing,* the *Prophet* saith of crooked Paths, (Isa. 59. 8.) "*Whosoever goeth therein shall not know Peace,*" (so as to have any Dealings therewith;) "*the Way of Peace have they not known"; (Rom.* 3. 17.) The *Apostle* saith of *Christ,* (2 Cor. 5. 21.) *"He knew no Sin,"* so as to have any intercourse with it; and our Saviour will say to some, as being none of his Acquaintance, *"I never knew you."* Matth. 7. 23.

Sometimes the Phrase of *knowing God* is best explain'd by that *due Discernment and Understanding of God,* which constitutes Men of the Divine Family, Subjects of his Kingdom, he being to them a God, they being to him a chosen People, which is the true *Light, Wisdom* and *Knowledge* of *Believers.* 1 John 5. 20. *"The Son of God is come, and hath given us an Understanding that we may know him that is True,"* and 2. 12. *"I write unto you, Little Children, because ye have known the Father,"* and John 16. 3. *"These Things will they do unto you, because they have not known the Father, nor me."* The World is in such an Atheistical Ignorance of God. *"O righteous Father, the World hath not known thee."* John 17. 25. In the same Sense the *Psalmist* saith (9. 10.) *"They that know thy Name, will put their trust in Thee."* When our Saviour saith, *John* 17. 3. *"This is Life Eternal, that they might know thee, the only true God,"* the Meaning is, that to know God, as one of his Pietists, as wise in Divine Matters, as of his Acquaintance, as Children of his Family, and Subjects of his Kingdom, is Life eternal to a Man.

But sometimes the Phrase of *knowing God* must be explain'd by *Understanding of God and his Matters,* (speaking of God in such Sense as we speak of Kings and Governments,) as our Saviour saith, *Matth.* 11. 27. *"No Man knoweth the Son, but the Father; neither knoweth any Man the Father, save the Son, and he to whom the Son will reveal him."* As to that great and saving Revelation of himself, *the Christian Religion,* God did not make himself known to any mere Man, *"The only-begotten Son, which is in the Bosom of the Father,"* (highly beloved by him, and most intimate with him,) *he only hath declar'd him.*

And sometimes Mens *knowing God* must be explain'd, of his being barely notic'd to them, which is consistent with the greatest Atheism of Religion and Condition, as when the *Apostle* saith of the *Gentiles,* Rom. 1. 28. *"They knew God, but did not like to retain God in their Knowledge,"* or to make an acknowledgment of Him, which is a religious knowing God. But thus the *Gentiles* knew him not; for, as the acknowledg'd Deity of Religion and People, *"There is no God in all the Earth, but in* Israel." 2 *Kin.* 5. 15.

How far the
Gentiles did
know God.
The *Gentiles,* therefore, in a certain Sense *knew God,* but so as *not to know him* in the more usual, or religious, Sense. *Rom.* 1. 19, 20. *"That which may be known of God is manifest in them; for, God hath shewn it unto them; for the invisible Things of him from the Creation of the World are clearly seen, being understood by the Things that are made, even his Eternal Power and Godhead."* And, accordingly, it is generally acknowledg'd, "That God is knowable by Natural Light, and is actually known by all Nations." But this must be understood with due Distinctions and Limitations, touching the Bounds and Measures of the *Gentiles* knowledge of God, such as these following.

1. The *Heathen* World knew God, *as understood without specifick and individual Determination.* They were not so ignorant, but that they acknowledg'd one Cause, or Principle, whence all Things have their Origin. This is so conspicuous in Nature, that natural Light cannot miss of him; nor is this his Existence matter of Faith, so much as of common Reason, and Proof by Argument. *"The Pulchritude of the World, and the Order of the Coelestial Bodies, forceth an acknowledgment, that there is a certain excellent and eternal Nature, which is to be honour'd and ador'd by Mankind."*[250] The *Pagan* Theologers, in Terms, agree with the *Christian,* that the visible World proclaimeth the invisible God, and speaketh audibly, *with a Voice that is gone out through all the Earth, that God made me.* One that was no under-graduate in Atheism, yet in a lucid interval, saith; *"If any Man shall view throughly all the Organs, both of Generation and Nutrition, and doth not perceive them to have been made and order'd to their respective Offices by some Mind, he is to be reputed himself void of Mind."*[251] To suppose, therefore, that the Existence of God is not discoverable by mere Reason, or natural Light, is a great Extravagance in *Socinus,* and some others.

250. Cicero, *De Natura Deorum,* II.
251. Hobbes, *Elementorum Philosophiae Sectio Secunda De Homine* (1658) [hereafter *De Homine*], ch. 1.

2. GOD, as of the *true Specifick and individual Determination,* (being plainly notic'd unto them in the Nature of the Thing,) *was in Nature fairly notic'd to the Heathen World.* For, *as* in the Old-Testament, a *Messiah* is notic'd and reveal'd to the *Jews,* not without, but with, true Specifick and individual Determination, (the true Messiah, the true kind of Messiah, is there in good Degree reveal'd:) *So,* in Nature, God is fairly notic'd to the *Gentiles,* not without, but with true, Specifick and individual Determination. They are blind and unintelligent in the *Nature of Things,* that do not discern, in case of Competition, which is the true God. The *Jews* mundan Kind of *Christ,* is an *Anti-Christ* Kind of *Christ.* So the *Gentiles Pagan* Kind of God, their *Jove;* being in one Part merely *mundan,* and in the other, *diabolical* and wicked; and being the Deity of a Religion, that is in one Part merely *mundan,* and in the other diabolical and wicked, is an *Anti-God* kind of *God.* All these Matters are so plain in the Nature of the Thing, that it must be said, *a Christ* is in Scripture so notic'd to the *Jews,* as that the true *Christ,* the true Kind of *Christ,* is fairly notic'd unto them: A God is in Nature so notic'd to all Mankind, as that the true God, the true Kind of God, is fairly notic'd unto them. "A Philosopher is no other than a true Philosopher; but, because some counterfeit Philosophy, therefore the Epithet of true was added." So *Christ* is no other than the true *Christ,* God is no other than the true God: If God, therefore, (or a God,) was in Nature made known to the *Gentiles,* the true God must necessarily be notic'd unto them. And some learned Men somewhat mistake the Case, when they say. "As Oedipus *knew himself to have a Father, yet did not know that* Laius *was he: So the* Gentiles, *by the Light of Nature, might reach so far as to know, there is one God, and that he is the Fountain of all Good, without knowing who was this God, as suppose the God of* Israel."[252] For, in the Case of *Oedipus,* there was no Competition, there was no Competition between two pretending Fathers; whereas, in the *Gentiles* Case, there was a Competition between two pretending Gods. And *Laius,* (being but a particular Man) could not be known but by an individual Determination: Whereas, in Case of Competition, the true God is distinctly and cer-

---

252. Vossius, *Historiae de Controversiis quas Pelagius* (1618), bk. III, pt. 3, thes. 6.

tainly notic'd by a *mere Specifick Determination*. For as the *Divine-kind* of Messiah is the true Messiah: So the *Divine-kind* of God, (and the Deity of such a kind of Religion) is the true God; but the Ungodly-kind of God (and the Deity of such a Religion) is the false God. It is not *a Divine Being,* nor *a Supreme Being,* nor *a Supreme God,* but the *Divine-kind of God,* which Specifick Determination is plainly notic'd in the Nature of the Thing; and therefore God, *as of true Specifick Determination,* is in Nature, fairly *notic'd to the Reason of all Men.* For suppose, that *Oedipus* could not know, that the Man *Laius* was his Father; yet, in the Nature of the Thing, this was plainly notic'd, *That one of Mankind was his Father:* So, in the Nature of the Thing, and therefore in Nature, this is plainly notic'd to the Reason of all the World, that God is not an unholy, or ungodly, but a Divine-kind of, God. If this God, the Deity of true Holiness and Godliness, was not, as such, fairly notic'd to the *Heathen* World; if they had not much of the Knowledge of him and of his Truth, (touching his Truth, their Duty and their Sin, his Rewards and Punishments,) *this Knowledge* could not be said, *to be manifest in them, because God hath shew'd it unto them:* Nor could they be said, *to hold the Truth* (stifled, smother'd, and imprison'd) *in Unrighteousness.* This being their great Crime, from thence it appeareth, that the true God was so far notic'd to them, as that they were under an Obligation, to erect an Holy Empire, imperfectly such, by being in common his Religionists.

3. As the *Jews* reject the true Divine-Kind of Messiah, which is notic'd unto them, such not being grateful and agreeable unto them, nor what they like and love; they are for a Messiah of another Kind: So the *Gentiles* did not like that of the true Divine-Kind of God, his Truth, and his Service, which was notic'd unto them, they were for another Kind of supreme God, which was more grateful to them, because of their own Kind and Quality; and so far (in setting up their *Jove* of several Notions jumbled and confounded together) they transform'd the Godhead into their own Similitude. According to that of *Xenophanes* the *Colophonian;* "*If Horses and Oxen could draw Pictures, they would paint the Gods like Horses and Oxen, as of their own Form and Family.*" The same Philosopher observeth, "*That the* Aethiopians *paint the Gods Black, and Flat-*

Nos'd; the Thracians *paint them Reddish and Ceruleous; the* Barbarians *suppose them Wild and Ferine; the* Greeks *suppose them more Gentle and Placid."*

4. The *Heathens* having form'd their Polity of Gods, and set up *Jove* as Chieftain of their Deities, the true God was hid from the Eyes of their Mind; and, altho he was notic'd to them, and known by them, yet no otherwise than as a Stranger-Deity (foreign to the Polity of their Gods) as they were Aliens from knowing him. For such a Degree of knowing, is knowing, *not knowing,* as the *Apostle* saith, *Rom.* 10. 19. *"Did not* Israel *know?"* They knew, but so as not to know. The *Heathens* knowing, *not knowing,* constituted them the *Heathen* People. To such a Degree the *Athenians* knew God, when they erected an Altar to the unknown God. To such a Degree the Kings of the *Amorites* and the *Canaanites* knew God, whose Hearts melted, *"When they heard that the Lord had dried up the Waters of* Jordan *from before the Children of* Israel." *Josh.* 5. 1. And the God of *Israel* saith of himself, *Mal.* 1. 14. *"My Name is dreadful among the Heathen."* To such a Degree those *Pagan* Magicians knew God, who made use of his Name, *The God of* Abraham, Isaac, *and* Jacob, in their Inchantments.

That extraneous People the *Gentiles knew not God, as a People know their God;* who is the imperial Estate of their Religion, and who are *none of the Strangers, Foreigners, and Aliens from his Theology and Religion.* In such Sense the *Gentiles* Character signifieth in the Scripture, wherein *the Gentiles, that knew not God,* are oppos'd to God's People; and in such Sense the God of *Israel* saith to *Cyrus, Isa.* 45. 5. *"I girded thee, though thou hast not known me."* So in Ecclesiastical Writers, the Conversion of a *Pagan* to be one of God's People, is express'd by a Transition *from the Heathenism of the World to the Acknowledgment of the true God.* And the *Heathens* usual Quere to the Primitive *Christians, "Who is that God, which ought alone to be worshipp'd?"* shews their prodigious Alienation from the Knowledge of God, and that the true God was no Deity of their Theology. *Cicero* hath remark'd the wild Conceits of the *Stoicks* concerning the Ruler of the World, or the Godhead. "Zeno *and the generality of the* Stoicks *suppose, that the Aether is the supreme God, having a Mind whereby all Things are govern'd.* Cleanthes, *a Prime* Stoick, *and*

In what Sense they did not know God.

Scholar of Zeno, *thinketh the Sun hath the Dominion, or is Lord of us, and all, and swayeth all. Therefore, by the Dissension of the Wise, we are necessitated to be Ignorant, who is the Lord over us; for we know not, whether to pay our Service to the Sun, or Aether."* [253] The *Philosophers* had the true Knowledge of God, as some say; but the Apostle ranketh their Knowledge of God, with the *Popular-Pagan.* 1 Cor. 1. 21. *"Seeing that in the Wisdom of God"* (that instructive Wisdom which God furnisheth in Nature) *"the World by Wisdom knew not God,"* (by Philosophy, they did not attain to the Knowledge of God,) *"it pleas'd God by the Foolishness of Preaching to save them that Believe."*

This Idea *the King,* or *he that Reigneth over us,* may be understood and taken, either without, or with that individual Person, who is King, or doth Reign. He that knoweth and honoureth the King only *in general* and *indefinitely,* (to use a *Logical* Term,) knoweth and honoureth the King according to the true Idea of a King, without any true, or determinate Knowledge of the Individual, who is King, whom he may unwittingly oppose. Many are for *Truth,* for *Justice, Virtue,* and *Piety,* according to some true general Notion which they have of them, that are Adversaries to that, in particular Cases, which is *really* and *materially* the *Truth, Justice, Virtue,* and *Piety.* Thus the *Heathen* are said to know and honour God, by having this, or the like, honourary Idea of Him in their Mind, *The King of the World; The Lord of All;* but with this honourary Idea some of them invested a *Star;* others, an *Hero;* others, a *Demon;* and others, a *Platonick Idea.* Some applied it to the *visible Universe,* being *Pan-Theists;* others were altogether uncertain, to what *definite specifick individual Nature,* it ought to be applied, and, therefore, were *Theists at random,* not determin'd to any one Thing; *"Thou* Jupiter, *whether thou be the Heaven, or the Aether, or the Earth,"* saith one in the *Poet:* Such Theists, altho' they have a true Notion of God in their Mind, *The Lord of the World, The Lord of All,* or the like; yet, because they apply it not to him to whom it belongeth, they are *not Theists truly such,* they do not know, or acknowledge, him, *who is Lord of the World,* or *Lord of All.*

It is not possible, that God's Religionists should have the same Deity

253. Cicero, *Academicae Quaestiones,* IV.

of a Religion in common with the *Gentiles* that *know not God,* which being their genuin and usual Character, we may infer from it, by way of *Consectary,* these five Branches of their *Heathenism,* and of ours too, so far as we symbolize with them. 1. *Their Atheous Darkness, as to matter of Understanding.* 2. *Their Atheousness and Flagitiousness of Life.* 3. *The Agreeableness of Heathenism of Religion to them.* 4. *The Badness of their Virtue and Goodness.* 5. *The Deadliness of their State and Condition.* For all these are our criminal *not knowing God.*

    Consect. 1. *Heathenism* is the State of Atheous Ignorance. Agreeably to *Platonism,* the *Christian* Theology contradistinguisheth *two opposite States and Conditions, and two opposite Kinds of People, Parties, and Families, the one Divine and of Light, the other Atheous and of Darkness.* Matt. 5. 14. *Luk.* 4. 18. *Job* 9. 6. and 12. 46. &*c.* The *Apostle of the Gentiles* was sent upon this Errand, *"to turn them from Darkness to Light,"* (*Act.* 26. 18.) from *Heathenism* to *Theism* and *Christianism* of Condition, which was *"a calling them out of Darkness into marvellous Light."* (1 Pet. 2. 9.) *Heathenism* is the *Darkness of this World,* of which the infernal Powers are the Rulers, *Ephe.* 6. 12. and therefore the *Apostle* saith (*Ephe.* 5. 8) *"Ye were sometimes Darkness, but now are ye Light in the Lord."* And, because of the direct Opposition of these two States, therefore the *Apostle* asketh, *"What Communion hath Light with Darkness?"* 2 *Cor.* 6. 14. The Region of *outer Darkness* has been well explain'd by the *Blindness of the Wicked;* a Region of *Blindness,* or *not-discerning,* as well as of *Darkness;* and the Inhabitants of it are the *Fools and Blind,*[254] *the Blind Leaders of the Blind, the blind People that have Eyes and see not, the Wretched and Miserable, Poor and Blind. He that lacketh these Things* (Divine Graces) *is Blind,* living in a State of *Gracelessness and Wickedness,* they had need to have their Eyes open'd. *Act.* 26. 18. They were blind and unintelligent, to a prodigy, in the matters of Holiness and Salvation (*Ephe.* 4. 18.) *"walking in the"* (Heathenish, or Atheous) *"Vanity of their Mind, having the Understanding darken'd,"* (having obliterated, or at least obscured, their natural Notices of the matters of God and Godliness,) *"being alienated from the Life of God, through the"* (Atheous kind of) *"Ignorance,*

Heathenism is the State of Atheous Ignorance.

254. Matthew 13.13, 15.14, 23.19; Isaiah 43.8; Revelations 3.17.

that was in them, because of the Blindness of their Heart." Their Wise Men (*Rom.* I. 21, 22.) "*professing themselves to be Wise, became Fools,*" (unwise and unintelligent in the matters of God,) "*and becoming vain in their Imaginations,*" (full of Heathenish and Idolatrous Conceits, which are Atheous,) "*their foolish Heart was darken'd.*" The Words of *Philo* are lively expressive of the sad benighted Estate of the *Heathen* World; "*The Region of the Wicked, where there is no Sun, but depth of the Night, endless Darkness, and vast Multitude of Shades, Ghosts, and Spectres, and Dreams.*"[255] These are always stirring in the night-time of sottish Superstition, (the Day-Light banisheth them,) they are the Issue and resembling Progeny of the dark Region of *Paganism,* wherein Mankind seem "*to have been fetter'd by a long Night, as Prisoners of Darkness,*" *Wisd.* 17. 2. Had the *Aegyptians* Eyes, who deified that blind Animal *Mus Araneus,* μυγαλήν, because they suppos'd Darkness elder than Light?[256] Or the generality of the *Pagans,* were they not as blind as that *Aegyptian* Deity, who affix'd all manner of Infamy and Villainy to their Gods, yet thought themselves *Pious?* They had a Notion of *Piety, Purity, Sanctity,* and *Justice* towards their Deity; but their *Sanctity* was Sin; their *Piety* was Villainy; their *Purity,* Pollution; their *Laver* was their Stain, and their *Righteousness,* the highest Wickedness; they counted *Evil Good,* and *Good Evil; Darkness Light,* and *Light Darkness.*

All Mankind, therefore, natively and originally, *want their Eye-Sight,* and must be denoted such as are *born Blind,* an effect of Man's Fall. There would be no need of a divine Physician, to heal and open the Eyes of Men; nor of divine Illumination, nor of a new Birth, whereby we are born into the Region of Light, if Mankind were not in some degree born Blind: No Account can be given of that more-than-*Cimmerian* Darkness, which for many Ages involv'd the World of Mankind, but from this *Hypothesis,* that they are born without their Eye-Sight; as without the *Life,* so without the *Light,* Spiritual; as in some degree *Heathen* ungodly Sinners, so *Heathen* Sons of Darkness. Upon the loss of the divine Image, which is the Soul's Life and Light, an *opposite Darkness* succeed-

255. Philo, *Opuscula Tria,* p. 163.
256. Plutarch, *Symposium,* IV.5.

eth; for such is the Reign of the Animal-Sensitive Nature, the Flesh, which is blind and foolish, unintelligent and unreasonable, the occasion of Blindness, Error, and Folly, to the Mind; as suggesting atheous Conceits, (vain and heathenish Imaginations, *Rom.* 1. 21.) as being full of vile and corrupt Affections; as being productive of all Vice and Wickedness, (*"their own Wickedness hath blinded them," Wisd.* 2. 27.) and the Mind, concurring therewith, becometh *a fleshly Mind.*[257] For, being moulded *after the Flesh,* she becometh *carnally Minded,* affected, and addicted; of an atheous, carnal, and mundan Genius and Disposition; which is an Indisposition of the Soul to unite itself to God in any respect (in her Discernments, Apprehensions, and Conceits, Opinion and Judgment, Sentiment and Estimation of Things, as also in her Designs, Elections, and Pursuits;) and a Propension to the blind and carnal Conceits of mundan Religionists, and to the various sorts of Atheous Error and Folly. Such an Atheous and *Heathen*-kind of Genius, in some degree native to Mankind, is by degrees increas'd, as vitious Affections grow to greater Height, and as Sinning against God becomes their Trade and Practice. Bad Education also, Converse and Company, Example, prevailing Custom, publick reigning Error and Vice, bad Government and Laws, beget, confirm, and encrease, Atheousness of Mind. From these concurrent Causes, all, or many of them, the antient Times of the *Heathen* were *"the Times of Ignorance." (Act.* 17. 30.*)* And thence it is, that the generality of Mankind, in all Times, are criminally involv'd in Atheous Darkness, Error, Ignorance, and Foolishness, touching *Matters of Good and Evil, Right and Wrong, Just and Unjust, Virtue and Vice, Nobility and Baseness, Sanctity and Sin, God and his Service, and the divine Kind of Things, the World also and its sensitive Good and Evil, touching themselves, their Interest, and their Happiness, their Souls and their future State,* they prodigiously deceive themselves through Pride and Self-Love; *and touching* their present State, and their Ways, *"not knowing what they do, nor whither they are going, because the Darkness hath blinded their Eyes."* (Luk. 23. 34. 1 Joh. 2. 11.)

The principal and summary Reason of the *Heathens* Blindness was,

---

257. Colossians 2.18; Romans 8.5; Ephesians 2.3.

They did not emerge out of the State of Gracelessness and Wickedness; and, therefore, they were in the State of Atheous Ignorance. From whence it follows, that all Men, who are in the same State of Gracelessness and Wickedness, are in the *State of Atheous Ignorance,* and want their Eye-Sight, as well as they. Flashes of Light, and some Convictions of Mind, are consistent with this Estate; and there may be in it a superficial and ineffectual knowing the matters of Religion; yet, because all that are in it have a Veil upon their Minds, they are necessarily in the State of Atheous Ignorance. As was the Case of those false Religionists, the carnal *Jews;* who, if they had had their Eyes, must have discern'd *the Light of the World shining* in their View; could not have mistaken God for the Devil; or thought themselves Virtuous, when they were Vile; or Wise, when they were Fools; or Safe, when they were in their Sins; nor could they have made their Religion, their Sin and Delusion. Both *Jews* and *Gentiles* shew, what Man is in his Unregenerate State; that this being the State of *reigning Wickedness and Ungodliness,* is the State of *reigning Atheous Ignorance, Error and Folly.*

Atheous Mankind being themselves, in great degree, unreasonable, the things of the Holy Spirit seem to them absurd, foolish, and unreasonable, 1 *Cor.* 2. 14. *"The natural Man receiveth not the Things of the Spirit of God, for they are foolishness to him; neither can he know them, because they are Spiritually discern'd."* The Matters of the Holy *Christian* Life, have always seem'd ridiculous and foolish to Men of the Atheous, Mundan, and Prophane Genius, which so prevaileth in Nations, call'd *Christian,* that serious Piety is not matter of Honour and Estimation, but of Disparagement with the most and greatest; and to be a *Christian* indeed, is to be Vile in their Eyes; if not to have the Usage, which such as departed from Iniquity in antient Times had, *Laughter and Derision. Christians,* so call'd, suppose, that they may be Leud, Sensual, and Worldly, yet genuine *Christians;* that Sin is a very small Matter, and, accordingly, their Life is the Sinning Trade; that God is the God and Patron of the Ungodly; that it is needless, ridiculous, and a sneaking Thing, to be Religious; that Heathenish Perfunctoriness, and outside Modishness, in God's Service, is good Devotion; that high Profaneness is Gallantry; that a Life of Flesh-pleasing Vanity is better than an Holy;

that the Worlds delusive Phantasms are the great and goodly Things; that the Concerns of this Animal-sensitive Life, are chiefly to be minded; and that it is Madness to bear the Cross, and suffer for Righteousness sake.

In *Christendom,* in *reform'd Christendom,* such Atheous Ignorance, Error and Folly prevaileth, so high a Degree of *Unreasonableness,* as to be perfect *Madness* and Phrenzy. It is *Madness* for Men to dream of a worldly-happy Estate, and a sensual Felicity, and to make it their chief End and Good; to be the World's Admirers and Lovers, that are deluded by Shadows, and idolize momentary fantastick Nothings, neglecting and losing the true inestimable Possessions of the Kingdom of God and the Soul; to chuse the Evil, and refuse the Good, running counter to their own Intention, designing to be Honourable and Happy, yet making themselves Vile and Miserable to Extremity; in a State of present Danger, wherein they are surrounded with Enemies, to be regardless of their Safety; and as regardless of the future over-whelming Calamities, which few forecast to prevent; to be merry and jovial in a mournful State, and fearless and careless in a fearful Case; to lose their Salvation for want of a little Care and Pains, and to spend their Care and Time about that which is not worth the while; to part with their All for Nothing; for a momentary Folly to plunge themselves into Miseries endless; to be deluded and befool'd in the plainest Things, and in all their great Concerns, not knowing what is good for Themselves, but sporting Themselves in their own Deceiving.

Consectary 2. *In* Heathenism *we live the Atheous Life.* Atheism of Life and Practice is connected with Atheism of Understanding, both as *an Antecedent Cause, a Concomitant,* and *a Consequent thereof.* For the Atheous kind of Life, and Practice, *causeth* the Atheous kind of Ignorance, Error, and Folly, as Steams and gross Exhalations from the Earth cause a dark Air. Sins and Vices, Lusts and Passions, are to the Mind, what a Suffusion is to the Eye, or Rust to Metal; an Atheous Temper, and Disposition, is prone to Atheous Conceits, and affecteth Atheous Opinions; carnal Affections so powerfully blind the Understanding, and byass the Judgment, that evil Men must be suppos'd to have bad Notions of God. All Men judge as they are affected; he that hateth any Man, is

In Heathenism we lead the Atheous Life.

prone to believe and judge all manner of Evil of him; and when he is otherwise affected toward him, he will be apt to believe and judge the contrary: Therefore the Lovers of the World magnify the Things of the World, and form to themselves a worldly kind of Religion: So the Lovers of fleshly Pleasures are averse from believing a Resurrection and future Judgment; and (as *Chaucer* saith of the People of *England*) *"what they not like, they never understand";* the Truth is against the Wicked, and they are, therefore, against the Truth.

Ignorance is connected with Vice and Wickedness, as a *Concomitant* inseparable; for it is impossible to be Wise and Wicked at the same time. The being Wicked is to be a Fool, the greatest of Fools; reigning Wickedness is, therefore, necessarily connected with the greatest Ignorance, Error, and Folly: Nor do any commit a sinful Fact, preferring the Evil before the Good; but, upon their Repentance, they acknowledge themselves to have been deceiv'd, in making a false Valuation of some apparent Good connected with great Evil. The grosly ignorant in matters of true Religion, do not know them, nor decline the opposite Evils. Their sinful Ignorance, therefore, is, both in itself, and in its Consequences, manifest Wickedness. The whole of true Religion, Virtue, and Duty, is Matter of Wisdom and Knowledge; for they must be Men of good Understanding, that know the Divine Empire, and the Laws thereof, and understand the matters of Divine Learning and Philosophy; that know the great Things, which alone are worthy to be known, and understand the true Nature, Worth and Use of Things; that discern between Truth and Falshood, the true and false Religion, between Good and Evil, (chusing the one, and refusing the other,) between Realities and Resemblances, and are not impos'd upon by Shews and Appearances; that escape Error, Deceit, and Delusion, (in their Opinions, Elections, Hopes and Confidences,) and the many tempting Baits of Sin; that understand the true Rates of Things, and estimate them aright; that know their Bounds, and observe them; their Dangers, and avoid them; their Enemies, and how to vanquish them; their Diseases, and how to cure them; that conduct themselves by wise Maxims, and do well and wisely; that know how to demean Themselves aright in all Cases and Circumstances, and do their Business and Office well; that are not foolishly and viciously affected, but agreeably to the Nature of Things, (contemning what is Contemptible, fearing what is really Formidable, loving what is Amiable in due Degree and Measure,) that govern themselves well, and are well advis'd in their doings, foreseeing and preventing the great Evils, making sure of their true Happiness, and so successfully managing their Affairs, that they are eternally safe and secure. But they that lack Understanding, know not their Sin, fear not their Danger, regard not their great Interests, discern not the Things that differ, mistake Trash for Treasure, and Fables for Truth and Wisdom; their Designs and Elections are ignorant and unwise; they run upon their Evils, which, in general, they would desire to avoid, for they wish well to themselves; their Atheous Life engendreth Atheous Opinions and Errors, and their Atheous Opinions and Errors, necessarily lead to Atheous Life and Practice.

Not that we are to imagine, with some, "That Mankind do not sin by Will, but only by weakness of Judgment and Ignorance; that really we would not do Evil, nor do we chuse it, but through Ignorance we judge that Good, which really is Evil." For this is an extravagant Conceit; nothing being more apparent, than that Men usually *Will* and *Chuse,* Intend and Design (which is a perverse Appetite and Will) the Evil of manifest Injustice, for carnal Self-gratification and Advantage; therefore a Conceit, which supposeth all their Sins, *"to be Sins of excusable Ignorance,"* is it-self a Branch of Ignorance inexcusable: Yet, because there is Ignorance in every actual Sin, and it is in part the Principle of it, the Maxim is true, "All Sin hath its rise from Ignorance."

In *Heathenism,* the atheous Life of profane Drunkards, Swearers, Whoremongers, and Worldlings, mainly intent upon the concerns of this Animal-Sensitive Life, was the *Pagan Popular Life,* (notwithstanding the Institutions of Virtue and Philosophy, and the arcane Institutions of Religion, that were in *Paganism;*) their brutish Appetites concurr'd with the ignorant Conceits of their Minds, touching a sensitive Felicity, to instigate them to *unclean Practices;* and being past feeling (having lost the Sight and Sense of the Turpitude and Sinfulness of their Practices, which should have restrain'd them, *adimit nox atra colorem*[258]) *they gave themselves over unto Lasciviousness, to work all Uncleanness with greediness.*

258. Virgil, *Aeneid,* VI.272: "black night has stolen from the world her hues."

The Sins of Uncleanness were the *Pagans* eminent Vice; for, altho' there are among them Instances and Institutions of *Continence,* yet so generally and outrageously were those *Heathen* Sons of Darkness addicted to the Sins of Unchastity of all sorts, (some of which were not only thought allowable, but genteel and creditable,) that the *Pagan* World may justly be thought nothing better than a Brothel-House of Uncleanness. The principal *Corruption* in the World, was thro' this sort of Lust;[259] and, because of these Things principally, *"the Wrath of God came upon"* (these enormous Sinners) *"the Children of Disobedience."* The *Gentiles* are characteriz'd by the *Lust of Concupiscence,* as a Consequent of their Ignorance, and *not knowing God.* And the New-Testament, in its black Catalogues of atrocious Sins, commonly joyneth the *Sins of Uncleanness with Heathen Idolatry,* and *eating Things offer'd to Idols* with *committing Fornication* (which in a large sense signifies all Whoredom;) and the *Gentile* Converts are by a special Decree forbid Fornication, as a Rite of gross symbolizing with the *Gentiles,* who are usually call'd by the holy Writers ʽοι πορνὸι, *Fornicators,* the *Heathen* World being *a World of impure Fornicators.* Their Doctrine did not condemn *Fornication* and *Stews;* and both Sexes were prostituted in their Stews, which were every where allow'd, and paid their Tribute. The *Persians, Aegpytians,* and *Athenians,* are infamous for their infamous Marriages, the *Stoicks* and *Chrysippus,* for allowing them; they are infamous also for unnatural Lusts, their Wise-Man is not averse from Love; Community of Women was practis'd in several *Pagan* Nations; some are superlative Instances of Masculine Amours; the *Lacedaemonians* are noted for lending their Wives; *Plato,* for countenancing Perjury in Love-Matters; *Plato* and *Lycurgus* banish'd Modesty from their Commonwealth, for they will have Men Spectators of naked Women; *Plutarch* was shameless, when he wrote his *Amatorius;* the *Greek* Philosophers are remark'd for their impure Masculine Amours, to which, not only the *Athenians,* but the *Roman* Senators, were addicted, and the Oracle of *Apollo* alloweth it. The *Apostle* hath remark'd their monstrous Uncleanness, (*Rom.* 1. 28) which he looketh upon as the Consequence of *a reprobate Mind.* But these soul Carnali-

---

259. I Peter 1.14; II Peter 1.4; Ephesians 5.5, 6; I Thessalonians 4.5.

ties, the Sins of Uncleanness, are only one eminent Limb, or Member, of the *Heathen* Old-Man, that *"hath his Conversation in the Lusts of the Flesh, fulfilling the Desires of the Flesh, and of the Mind, walketh according to the Course of this World, according to the Prince of the Power of the Air, in Lasciviousness, Lusts, excess of Wine, Revelling, Banquettings, and abominable Lewdnesses,"* Ephes. 2. 2, 3. which were so fashionable in the *Heathen* World, that it was a Thing wonder'd at, that the *Christians,* who seem'd an odd out-of-the-way People, (1 Pet. 4. 3, 4.) *"Did not run with them into the same Excess of Riot. Being fill'd"* (Rom. 1. 29, &c.) *"with all Unrighteousness, Fornication, Wickedness, Covetousness, Maliciousness, full of Envy, Murder,"* (*Homicide* was the Gladiators Discipline, and matter of Glory, they slew their Slaves at pleasure, usually expos'd their Children, *Romulus* made a Law, that Children born deform'd, should be expos'd and stifled), *"Debate, Deceit, Malignity, Whisperers, Back-Biters, Haters of God, Despiteful, Proud, Boasters, Inventors of evil Things, Disobedient to Parents, without Understanding, Covenant-Breakers, without natural Affection, Implacable, Unmerciful."* Such were the worse and the greater part of them; and of all them it must be said, that by several degrees of Wickedness, they constituted a World of flagitious People, *"an evil World,"* (a World of evil Men, and a World of Evils,) *"a World of the Lust of the Flesh, and the Lust of the Eyes, and the Pride of Life, which are not of the Father, but are of the World."* 1 Joh. 2. 15.

This degenerate Condition of the World of Mankind, is an uncontroulable Evidence of *Original Sin* in some Significations of it. For, in the *first* place, *Original Sin* may signify, That *Mankind, antecedently to their being Holy,* (which prior Condition may be called their *Original Condition,*) are ungodly Sinners. Of this Original sinful State, the current of Scripture, the frame of *Christianity* and *Judaism,* the frame of Man, the degenerate Condition of the World, the Order and Course of Things in it, are an uncontroulable Evidence. For Darkness is now before Light, antecedently to Sanctification we are Unholy, and the Proselytes were first Aliens; in *Christianity,* Unregeneracy is before Regeneracy, the Old is before the New Man, Servitude is before Freedom, all the Holy People were of the World before their coming out of the World, their Original Condition is that of mere *Mundan Heathen People.* The Re-

Of Original Sin.

ligion also of a *Saviour-King,* of *Redemption,* and an *Expiatory Sacrifice,* of *Saving Faith, Repentance* and *Conversion to God,* of a *new Covenant,* and a *new Kingdom of God,* of *Regeneration* and *Remission of Sins,* of *Justification* and *Sanctification,* proclaimeth this Original sinful State, which inferreth the Existence of Original Sin in another Notion. For,

In the *second* place, *Original Sin* may signify, that *Mankind are now natively and originally ungodly Sinners, in a degree of prevalent Tendency that way:* or, that *the Original of Sin is in such Degree originally in Man.* If Mankind are now the Flesh-Born, and Mundan People in all respects; both *privatively,* being born without the Life of Grace, or the Divine Love; and *positively,* a vicious carnal selfishness of Nature, being now our Nature, which is called *Concupiscence:* If this *Original of Sin* is now natively Original to Mankind, this vicious Tendency must be counted an *Original Sin.* And an Original Sin of this Nature and Notion, must be look'd upon, not as the Whole, but as a Branch of the Article of Original Sin, and is certainly a Branch of the *Christian* Religion, *John* 3. 6, 7. *"That which is born of the Flesh, is Flesh, and that which is born of the Spirit, is Spirit. Marvel not, that I said unto thee, ye must be born again, or born from above."* Our Saviour plainly affirmeth, (as the New-Testament ordinarily doth throughout,) that there are two opposite Families of Men: The *one, those that are born of the Spirit, the Heaven-born; the other, those that are born of the Flesh only, the Earth-born.* That, by natural Generation, none are of *the Spirit-born,* or *Heaven-born,* but all are of *the Flesh born,* or *Earth-born, Family.* Man is therefore natively so constituted, as to be one of the Animal-vital, not one of the Spiritual-vital, Family. And, of Man so constituted, impartial, *Christian* Reason cannot but pronounce, "That he is natively a carnal and mundan Kind of Man, and Liver, in a Degree of prevalent Tendency that way. Agreeably to our Saviour, the Apostles establish the same Distinction of two opposite Families, *Gal.* 4. 29. *Rom.* 9. 8. *Joh.* 1. 13. Hence appeareth, that Infants, by their first Birth, belong to that Family, which is opposite to the Spiritual and Divine Family, (both as Natural and Carnal is oppos'd to Spiritual,) they belong to the Family of those that *are in the Flesh* devoid of the Holy Spirit. At the time of their Conception and Nativity, thus far they are of this *Family; they are then the carnal and mundan Kind of Livers, in a degree of prevalent Tendency that Way.* And in such Sense the *Psalmists* Words may commodiously be interpreted, 51. 5. *"Behold! I was shapen in Iniquity, and in Sin did my Mother conceive me."* The Animal Nature in Brutes, is wicked and carnal; and the Animal Nature in Mankind, is manifestly the same. Infants are therefore such, in the way of prevalent Tendency that way, and, consequently, they are, in such Degree, *by Nature the Children of Wrath.* Which is not so to be understood, as if Mankind committed Sin, *not through the Fault of their Will;* for all the Servants of Sin are more, or less, Volunteers; the Sins which they commit, at the time of their Commission, are their Will and Choice, altho' at other times (usually in their sober retired Thoughts) they are otherwise minded. But Man's Nature is full of Inclinations to that which is Evil; all sort of Wickedness issueth from the *Heart* or inward Man, and Man is warn'd to take heed of walking *"in the Ways of his Heart, and in the Sight of his Eyes."* If in fact all Men, in their unregenerate State, live in that which is Carnality and Wickedness, if they are under the Power of the Flesh, of Sin and Vice; this is a Demonstration, that Infants, at their Birth, are the Servants of Sin, *in a degree of prevalent Tendency that Way.*

All the Wickedness that is in the Animal Nature, involveth in it an *inordinate Self-Love,* whence it ariseth. Self-Love is unquestionably innate in all, and a vicious carnal Self-Love is innate in all, *in a degree of prevalent Tendency that Way,* for it is a Root of Bitterness in all Men; therefore, in that Degree, the sourse and summary of Wickedness is innate in all Men; and so are the reigning Lusts, and Passions of the Flesh, which are nothing else but its prevalent impetuous Propensions and Tendencies. Hence Conflicts between the upper and lower Soul, between Reason, and the Motions of irrational Nature; and hence it *is,* that there is in him originally a Body of Sin and Death.

Agreeably whereunto, as some of the Learned suppose,[260] the *Pythagoreans,* and *Platonists,* discourse of *a Strife innate in Man, an alien Animal of Kin to us from Generation,* which some call, *the many-headed*

---

260. Grotius, *Annotationes in Novum Testamentum* on Luke 2.2; Casaubon, *Persii Flacci Satirarum* (1605), V, p. 439.

Beast; others call it, *a moral Species of Life.* They suppose, that every Man, from his Birth, hath a bad Genius, inclining him to Evil, that a Purgation is necessary for Human Souls; that they have lost their Wings, are estrang'd from God, obnoxious to inordinate Passions; and *Archytas,* the *Pythagorean,* said, *"We cannot arrive at the top of true Good, because of a bad Nature."* So the *Hebrew* Doctors *ordinarily speak of the Ferment which is in the Mass* (evil Concupiscence,) and the *evil Formation, or Figment,* of which they say, *"The evil Figment is born with a Man, and goeth about with him all his Days, as 'tis said, The Imagination of Man's Heart is Evil from his Youth":* [261] Which Character of Mankind speaketh a powerful Proclivity in Man's Nature, to that which is Evil, which implyeth both an Aversion and Impotence to that which is Good. Agreeably whereunto the *Apostle* saith, *"The Law was weak through the Flesh,"* Rom. 8. 3. therefore the Flesh was more powerful to make Men Sinners, than the Law was to reform them. And, if they are Sinners thro' the Flesh, then they are *"Carnal, sold under Sin, not doing what they like, the Good they would, but what they hate, the Evil that they would not, a Law in their Members warring against the Law of their Mind, and bringing them into Captivity to the Law of Sin, which is in their Members."* Rom. 7. 14, 15, 19, 23. Against their Knowledge and Convictions of Mind, against the Dictates of Prudence and of Conscience, against their own Resolutions and Vows, Mankind, in their Unregeneracy, are frequently carried away captive to perpetrate Wickedness; Convictions of the Mind, against the Flesh, is an unequal Contest. Servitude under Sin, therefore, with all the other Evils of an unregenerate condition, is, as it were, our Inheritance, by our first Birth, without which *Hypothesis,* no tolerable Sense can be made of the *Christian* Religion, no tolerable Account can be given of the World's Wickedness. For what is this lower World, but a Sink of Impurity, a Sea of Wickedness, a Stie of Sensualists, a *Sodom* of Uncleanness, a Den of the Sons of Darkness, a Shop of Frauds, a Cock-pit of Contention, an *Aegypt* for Oppression, a Bedlam

261. Buxtorf, *Lexicon Talmidicum et Rabbinicum* (1639), col. 2303; Hammond, *A Paraphrase and Annotations upon the Books of the Psalm* (1659), note B; Spencer, *Origenis contra Celsum* (1658), p. 88.

of Distractions, an Amphitheatre of Gladiators, a Wilderness of noxious Animals; insomuch, that one had reason to style it *"very near to Hell."* Mankind, universally, in all times and places, are degenerate into Vice and Wickedness; it operateth early, usually it beareth down all Obstacles, frustrateth all Remedies, it floweth in upon the World, with so high a tide, and so strong a torrent, that in all Ages, not only Vice and Wickedness, but Prodigies and Outrages of Vice and Wickedness, have been current Practices. The Age of Youth is rude, unskilful, and unwise, (without governing Prudence, of little insight into Things, and less foresighted) incautious, careless and inconsiderate, rash, heady and fearless, full of Confidence and foolish Hopes, hardly governable, or manageable by the greatest Wisdom, or capable of good Counsel; of vehement and fervid Desires, Pursuits and Passions, of flagrant Lusts, enormously addicted to sensual Mirth and Pleasure, of gay and wanton Humour, averse from Seriousness, (as apt to contemn and deride serious Piety, as Dangers,) extremely Proud, and apt to take a Pride in pranks of Lewdness and Injuriousness, (nor is there any sort of Wickedness, to which untam'd Youth is not apt to be carried by Pride,) full of disorderly Motions and Appetites, and abounding with Vice, as fat and rank Grounds with Weeds. As the Age of Manhood succeedeth that of Youth, so the manly Vices succeed the Youthful; and so gross and palpable Vice gradually ariseth in the Nature and Life of Man, commencing its Reign from his Birth. Several particular Temperaments are strongly inclin'd to several Vices; some are naturally of a bad Temper, and some are observ'd to be of a natural Malignity; which common Observations befriend the *Hypothesis of Original Sin.*

Against this Name the *Pelagians object,* (their principal Objections reach not to the *Thing,* but the *Name* only,) "That no defect in Infants, without the use of Reason and Understanding, can be truly and properly Sin, for nothing can be Sin, which is not voluntary. Sin is also that, which is *the Transgression of a Law; where no Law is, there is no Transgression;* but Laws are not given to mere Infants, that are not capable of Obligation, or, as the *Jews* say, they are not *Sons of the Precept,* no more than Brutes; for Laws are not given to Infants, or those who have lost their Understanding." These Objections may be thus answer'd.

1. The inordinate Concupiscence, of which our Animal Nature is full, may be contemplated in Brutes; for in them there is a Pravity of Nature, which, being predominant, constitutes many of them *Evil Beasts;* as in Mankind there is a Pravity of Nature, which being prevalent in them, constituteth them *Evil Men.* In Brutes we may contemplate the very Nature and Idea of the several branches of Vice and Wickedness, of inordinate *Self-Love, Lust, Pride, Wrath, Cruelty,* and such like; for there the very Face and Form of them appeareth. The Morals of degenerate Mankind, that *live after the Flesh,* have the same origin with those of Brutes, which they lively resemble; some being *Wolves,* others *Foxes,* others *Serpents,* others *Neighing Horses,* others *Dogs* and *Swine.*

2. The inordinate Concupiscence, of which our Animal Nature is full, is *Sin* in a limited sense. *It is the very Nature of that which is Sin, Vice, and Wickedness, so far imputable to us, as it is in any degree Voluntary, and no farther.* As it is in the Animal Nature of Brutes, it is the very Nature of that which is Sin, Vice, and Wickedness; the Pride and Selfishness which we contemplate there, is the very Nature of the Sins of Pride and Selfishness, and sheweth the odious face of them: These, therefore, have in Brutes, the *materiality* of Sin, without the *formality,* (as the *Logicians* use to distinguish;) for they are not imputable to them as Sin, nor do they constitute them in a proper Sense, Sinners. But, in Man, inordinate Concupiscence is imputable as *Sin,* Fault and Crime, so far as it is in any degree *Voluntary.* This the *Apostle* sometimes calleth, "*Sin that dwelleth in me,*" Rom. 7. 17. and sometimes "*Sin in the Flesh*" (8. 3.) that is, in the Animal Nature.

3. This Branch of Original Sin, which we have under Consideration, does not infer, that inordinate Concupiscence is *actually* in mere Infants; much less, that it is imputable to them, as their Crime, or that they offend against any Law of God, or commanded Duty. It only supposes, that by a Fall, or Lapse, inordinate Concupiscence, and the Reign of it, is in them *in a Degree of prevalent Tendency that Way.* So that, if Grace does not interpose, the Infant will be like the rest of unregenerate Mankind, an Alien and an Enemy, living and loving the carnal and worldly kind of Life, and its Gratifications; having a Soul destitute of its true Pulchritude, Health, and Vigour; Naked, Deformed, Diseased, Weak, and Languishing.

Consectary 3. *Mundan Mankind are of a Disposition so Atheous, that Heathenism of Religion is to them agreeable.* Such as Mens State, Life, and Genius is, such is their Religion, which is a plain Demonstration of *Original Sin;* for it shews, that Mankind are born the *Heathen*-Kind of Religionists, *in a Degree of mighty tendency that Way.* All Mankind, without a preternatural adventitious Institution of Religion, would be of the *Heathen* Religion, or none at all; for other Religions were introduc'd by extraordinary supernatural methods of Providence; under the Oeconomy of mere Nature and general Providence, *Heathenism* was universal. This appeareth also from the continued History of the *Jewish* Church, the Rise and the Progress of it; for the Progeny of *Noah,* the Offspring of *Shem,* even in the Family of *Heber* (the Father of the *Hebrews*) while *Noah, Shem,* and *Heber* were yet alive, fell to *Heathen* Idolatry, *Josh.* 24. 2. *Abraham* was doubtless bred an *Heathen;* the God of *Nabor* is thought an *Heathen* Deity, *Gen.* 31. 53. *Laban's* Images, call'd his Gods, shew, that he was not clear of *Heathen* Idolatry, and *Jacob's* House was infected with it, *Gen.* 31. 30. and 35. 2. When the Children of *Israel* went into *Aegypt,* they conform'd themselves to the *Aegyptian* Idolatry, and when they came out of *Aegypt,* they did not leave it behind them, as they were charg'd, witness the Golden-Calf, their worshipping the Host of Heaven, their joyning themselves to *Baal-Peor,* and sacrificing to *Sehirim.*[262] When God had brought them out of the Wilderness into *Canaan,* and cast out the *Heathen* Nations for their Idolatries and Impieties, and warn'd the *Israelites* to take heed of their Abominations, and of doing as they had done, yet they *"forsook the Lord God of their Fathers, served* Baalim *and the Groves"* (Idols in the Groves,) and succeeded the *Heathen* Nations in their Morals, as well as in their Lands.[263] Such was their Religion, during the time that they were govern'd by *Judges;* their *Heathen* Idolatry brought them into heavy Calamities, and no sooner were they deliver'd, but they relaps'd to their old Trade again. For this was the State of Things in *Samuel's* Days. *Solomon,* the wisest of their Kings, tho' the Lord appeared unto him thrice, and warn'd him against the Idolatry of the *Heathen,* yet fell to this foul Impiety. After his days,

Mundan Mankind are of a Atheous, that Heathenism of Religion is to them agreeable.

---

262. Ezekiel 23.2, 20.7, 8; Exodus 32.31; Acts 7.43; Psalms 106.68; Leviticus 17.7.
263. Judges 2.11–19, 3.7; Ezekiel 16.3.

the ten Tribes fell to the Idolatry of *Jeroboam,* complicated with that of *Baal,* out of which they never emerg'd. Nor were things much better in the Tribe of *Judah,* that adher'd to the House of *David;* for, altho' *Rehoboam,* had lost the greatest part of his Kingdom for the *Heathenism* of his Father, yet he, together with *Maacah* his Wife, trod in his Father's Steps, as *Abijam* his Son did in his. Out of this State *Judah* could never perfectly recover. For, after *Asa's* and *Jehosaphat's* imperfect Reformation, *Jehoram* (*Jehosaphat's* Son) and *Amaziah* his Son, symboliz'd with the House of *Ahab,* the latter of them having *Athaliah* his Counsellor to do wickedly. *Joash,* who succeeded her in the Government, was courted out of his Religion by the Princes of *Judah. Amaziah* (*Joash's* Successor) after some time of reigning laps'd into *Heathen* Idolatry at a great rate. *Uzziah* and *Jotham* succeeding *Amaziah,* the affairs of Religion were in a tolerable good Posture; but *Ahaz* (*Jotham's* Son and Successor) was *mad after his Idols.* In the days of *Hezekiah,* true Religion recover'd its Lustre, (which had suffer'd a sad Eclipse in the Days of *Ahaz,*) and a considerable Reformation was made; but no sooner was *Hezekiah* dead, but all things ran to ruin again, in the days of *Manasseh,* whom *Amon* his Son imitated in his outrageous *Heathenism. Josiah* made a great Reformation, but his Reformation was a striving against the Stream; for the People still retain'd their affection for their old *Heathenism,* and those *Heathenish* Practices were in his days, which God menaceth by the Prophet, *Zeph.* 1. 4, 5. *"I will cut off the Remnant of* Baal *from this place"* (Jerusalem) *"and the Name of the* Chemarims *with the Priests; and them that worship the Host of Heaven upon the House-tops; and them that worship and swear by the Lord, and that swear by* Malcham.*"* After the Death of *Josiah,* God began to do unto *Judah,* as he had done to the Tribes of *Israel,* they being alike obstinate in their idolatrous Disposition. No Persuasions, no Menaces, no Warnings, no Punishments, or Disasters, which befel them, avail'd to reclaim them. The succeeding Kings of *Israel* took no warning by their Predecessors Calamities; the Tribe of *Judah* took no warning by the ten Tribes; they would not desist from their *Heathenism* of Religion, when they were upon the brink of Ruin; they went on in their old Track, even in the very Times of the *Babylonian* Captivity, and those of them that went into *Aegypt,* after their City and

Temple was ruin'd, were resolved *Heathen* Idolaters. *Jer.* 44. 17. The prevalency of this Religion amongst God's antient People, speaketh it a darling to Animal Nature. It is from this Nature, that Mankind are not Theists, Religionists, or Pietists, but the Atheous Kind of Theists, the irreligious Kind of Religionists, and the impious Kind of Pietists; they bestow their devotional Esteem, Affection, and Service upon what Animal Sensitive Nature liketh, and accounteth fine Things. By an Idolatrous Kind of Superstition, the adulterous Kind of Devotion, their devotional Propension is gratified, and the way of doing it is pleasing to sensitive Nature, which they follow.

As from the History of the *Jewish,* so from the History of the *Christian* Church, the proneness of Mankind to a Religion of Idolatry is apparent; for, altho' in the three first Centuries, and some time after, there is no appearance of *a lapse of the Church into Idolatry;* yet the time was not long, before *"the holy City was trodden under Foot by the Gentiles";* when the World was come into the Church, then she began, by degrees, to model Religion after the old *Heathen* manner, and degenerated at such a rate into *Paganism,* that the Religion of unreform'd *Christendom* hath been, for many Ages, *an Imitation of the Rites and Vices of that Idolatrous Religion.* It is manifestly a Parallel for old *Heathenism* in Atheous Blindness, Darkness, and Ignorance, in its Ghosts, Spectres, and Dreams; in blind *heathenish* superstitious Conceits and Opinions; in the *heathenish* Life, and all the Limbs and Branches of the Old-Man; in Swearing, Revelling, Drunkenness, Debauchery; in Fornication, Harlotry, Incest, Sodomy, Stews, Curtesans, Carnavals, and in making the World a Brothel-House, or *Sodom* of Uncleanness; in Encouragements, as well as Practices of Looseness and Lewdness of Life, and the old *heathen* Profanenesses; in *heathenish* Pretensions to Antiquity, Duration, Universality, Unity; in *heathenish* Worldliness, Pride, and Ambition, State, and Grandeur; in *heathenish* Infidelity, and traditional Kind of Faith; in *heathenish* Vice, and an *heathenish* kind of Virtue; in numerous Festivals celebrated at the *heathen* rate; in unclean Institutions of Continence and Virginity; in a pharisaical kind of Monasticks and Asceticks, the Institution whereof is originally *Pagan;* in the Theology and Devotion of the Mysticks; in lying Stories and Legends; in processionary Pomps and

Jubilees, which answer to the antient *Ludi seculares;* in slight methods of obtaining Pardon for Sin; in the extravagant Pomps of their Religious Service, the Consecration of their Altars and of their Temples, and Celebrations of the Dedication of them; in their holy Water and enjoyned Celibacy; in their Whippings and monstrous Barbarity and Cruelty; in their Purgatory and Funeral Rites; in their Reliques and Theurgical Consecrations of *Agnus Dei's* and other Trinkets; in the external Perfunctoriness of their Religious Service; in substituting silly exterior Rituality instead of true Religion, and antick instead of true Devotion; (*for such are their numerous turnings, bowings, crossings, changes of Posture, mutterings, droppings of Beads, kissing the Pix, praying in an unknown Tongue, praying for Souls in Purgatory, saying so many Masses, offering Sacrifice for the Quick and Dead, repeating the name Jesus so many Times in a breath, translating Reliques, making Pilgrimages and Shrines, and making Oblations to them; holy Vestments, holy Scapularies, holy Oil, Anointings, holy Salt and Candles,* &c.) In their Incense, lighted Candles in their Temples, Procession with burning Candles in their Hands on *Candlemas-Day,* consecrated Bells and baptismal Spittle; in the Canonizations, Patronage, and Offices, of the Tutelar Saints, or Deities; in consecrating the *Pantheon* at *Rome* to them, and the seven Hills of the City to so many Saints; in ascribing miraculous Feats to them, making magnificent Presents and Oblations to them, swearing profanely by their Names, as the *Heathens* did by their Gods; in consecrating, adorning, adoring their Images, carrying them in Procession, and concealing them in *Lent,* as the *Heathens,* for some time, conceal'd their Idols from the People; in having impure and profane Images in many of their Churches, like the *Heathen;* in the whole Affair of *Church-Demonolatry,* the Design of it, and Method of introducing it, where Idolatry recover'd its deadly Wound, and *Paganism* liv'd again. A principal Method of introducing *Paganism;* in several Branches of it, was by counterfeit Visions, Apparitions, Revelations, Miracles; and by the same Artifices *Demonolatry* was introduc'd, and *Christianity* was chang'd into *Heathenism.* So that the *Christian* Church hath imitated the antient *Jewish* Church in her lapse into a Religion of Idolatry, and hitherto she continueth to imitate her Obstinacy and Irreclaimableness.

But *Heathen Mankind,* most properly such, are those that are without the Pale of the visible Church; the Universality of Mankind in antient Times were such; whose addictedness thereto appeareth from the Antiquity of it, its wide spreading, the long uninterrupted Duration of it, the World's resolv'd and firm Adherence to it, (for the *Heathen* World resolv'd not to change the Religion of their Ancestors,) the Laws that were made in favour of it, and against the introducing of any new Religion, (which was thought a Thing not to be endur'd, according to *Mecaenas's* Advice to *Augustus,*) the many violent Persecutions, which *Christianity* suffer'd in its attempts to undermine and ruin it. Nor was it only the *Popular-Pagans,* that were so vehemently addicted to their *Heathenism* of Religion; for the *Philosophick-Pagans* were, for the main, of the same Mind in Religion with the *Popular;* their *Rule* was, "To worship the Divinity according to the Law and Rites of their Country, and the Custom of their Ancestors." Some few Branches of this *Heathen-Popular* Religion were disliked by the *Philosophers* (*Socrates, Plato, Plutarch, Cicero, Seneca, Porphyry, Varro,* and the *Stoicks;*) but themselves were in good earnest *Pagan-Religionists, Pagan-Theologers, Pagan-Saints,* and *Champions* for *Paganism.* They were far from designing a change of Religion, as *Plato* affirmeth in his Apology for *Socrates; Plutarch* styleth it the *"Pious Faith deriv'd from their Ancestors";* and again, *"The divine Dignity of Piety receiv'd from their Ancestors."* [264] He supposeth it a plain Case, that their Deities were truly such, and their Religion of right Catholick; *"That the Sun and Moon are Animals, whom all Men sacrifice, pray to, and worship."* Other of them style their *Pagan* Devotion, *"The pure Worship of the Divinity."* [265] They affect an higher strain of Devotion towards their Deities, than the *Popular Pagans;* and it was thought a grand Incongruity in a *Philosopher,* to violate their Religious Rites; whence *Stilpo,* the *Philosopher,* sleeping in the Chappel of the Mother of the Gods contrary to Law, was thus reprimanded by the Goddess in a Dream; *"Art thou a Philosopher, and dost thou Violate the sacred*

---

264. Plutarch, *De Pythiae Oraculis,* p. 402; *De Superstitione,* p. 166; *Adversus Colotem,* p. 1123 (all in *Moralia*).
265. Proclus, *In Platonis Theologiam,* V.36.

Laws?"[266] *Philosophers* were, least of any, addicted to change their Religion; yet *Plutarch,* who maketh such high Elogies of his *Heathen-Popular* Religion, sometimes saith of it: *"The ridiculous Practices and Passions of Superstition, and Speeches, and Gestures, and Inchantments, and magical Tricks, and Running about, and Drummings, and impure Lustrations, and sordid Purifications, and barbarous and absurd Castigations in the Temples, and contumelious Usages, give occasion unto some, to say, That it is better there were no Gods at all than such Deities, that accept, and are pleas'd with, such Things as these, of so petulant, so mean, so peevish an humour: Were it not better for the* Gauls *and* Scythians, *to have no Notion at all, no Imagination, no History, of Gods, than to suppose, That there are Gods which delight in the Blood of sacrific'd Men, and account that the most perfect Sacrifice and religious Service? Had it not been better for the* Carthaginians *at the first, to have taken* Critias, *or* Diagoras, *for their Lawgiver, to suppose, that there is neither God nor Demon, rather than to make such Sacrifices as they do to* Saturn?[267] *It is not easy to judge, which of these two extremes is most conducive to Mankind, some have no respect for any Gods, the God-service of others is shameful."*[268]

Such was the *Heathen* Idolatry, and their manner of serving their fictitious Deities was extremely Shameful and Abominable, as it is visible in their *Lupercalia, Floralia, Bacchanalia,* the usual Drunkenness of the Women amongst the *Romans,* when they sacrific'd to *Bona Dea;* the infamous Drunkenness, Madness, and antick Gestures of *Cybele's* Priests, *Priapus's* Sacra, their Worship of the Goddess *Venus,* their nasty *Eleusinian* Mysteries, their unclean Fables touching their Deities, and their Images of them, which sometimes represented the Painters Harlots, (and usually in their Houses they set up the representations of monstrous Lust,) the obscene Spectacles and Speeches usual in their *Sacra,* (of which their Theologers say, that they were design'd to cure them of their filthy Affections, by gratifying them,) their perpetrations of Uncleanness, and Sodomy, in honour of their Deities, and under pretext

266. Vossius, *De Idolatria,* V.46.
267. Plutarch, *De Superstitione* (in *Moralia*), p. 171.
268. Pliny, *Natural History,* II.7.

of Holiness and Religion in many Places, the Memoirs in Scripture, of *"Sodomites doing according to the Abominations of the Nations,"* and the conjoining of Idols with Sodomites, 1 *Kin.* 14. 24. and 15. 12. and 2 *Kin.* 23. 7. Uncleanness, Drunkenness, Revelling and Debauchery, were not only the Sins of their Lives, but of their Religion. The Histories of their impure Deities instigated them to the practices of Uncleanness, their shady Groves were an Invitation to them to perpetrate them, they perpetrated them in their Sacred Places, Fornication was annex'd to their revelling Idol-Feasts. As it is a false Religion, it is like the Oriental Languages, and must be read backward; for its Holiness, in many Parts of it, is the grossest Lewdness and Profaneness; its Deities are abominably Profane, as is also their Service, and their *Sacra;* it maketh the Divinity a *Drama,* Heaven a *Scene,* and Religion a *Stage-Play;* it venerateth its Deities in the Temples, and exposeth them to Derision upon the Theatre. Their Religion was, in the main, devoid of Religion, Truth and Righteousness, made up of Lies, Folly, Madness, and consummate Wickedness. Yet, this their Religion (*Religio Deorum immortalium*) the Pagans counted their Glory; not themselves, but the *Christians,* they counted Nefarious, and most Flagitious; they furiously persecuted them, calling them *the Impious,* supposing themselves *the Pious.* O unparallell'd Darkness!

The *Pagans* Religion, as bad as it was, was hugely agreeable to their Genius and Humour; which proveth the World of Mankind, a blind and wicked Generation, extremely Atheous, sunk, and degenerate from God, and such as *Seneca* calls the Herd of *Pagan-Religionists, "insanientium turba,"* a mad Rabble. For the *Pagan* Writers themselves usually impute Madness to the *Aegyptians,* (a learned Nation, but a Fountain and Store-house of Idolatry, as well as Grain,) because of their monstrous Worship of Animals. And what were *Hercules's Sacra* at *Lindus,* but height of Madness, which were celebrated with Evil-speakings and Cursings; and, if any one, by chance, let fall a good Word, it was thought a violation of them? In this wild Religion, there was a great mixture of profane Frolick and Jovialty, which rendred it hugely agreeable to the Humour of the *Popular-Pagans.* Whence it is generally reported of *Gregory Thaumaturgus,* (who, in this, was far from imitating the *Apostles,*) that he, observing that corporeal Delights and Pleasures allur'd the Vulgar, and caus'd them to persist in their Idolatry, permitted them, in lieu of their former Jollities, to jovialize in memory of the Holy Martyrs. The *Heathens* had their numerous Festivals (celebrated after the *Israelites* Mode, who *"sat down to eat and drink, and rose up to play,"* Exod. 32. 6.) with Sports, Dancings, Shews, Musick, Banquets, Drunkenness, Lasciviousness. Their Gods gave them no Precepts of good Life, but licens'd Wickedness, authoriz'd Vice, encourag'd Lewdness, (their Oracles patroniz'd it,) and therefore it was a Flesh-pleasing Kind of Religion. Which also had the Glories of Antiquity, Universality, uninterrupted Duration and Succession, and Shews of Sanctimony. It abounded with Inspirations, Visions, Revelations, Oracles, Miracles, Prophets, Saints, and, which is extremely taking and desireable, the *Pagans* had their Gods nigh unto them, to speak to them, to converse with them, to consult them in Difficulties, to have present Access to them, and their Help at hand; by visible Signs, their Gods testified their Presence, they saw them in their Effigies, and often had Appearances of the Gods themselves. Their Religion was a *Temple-kind of Religion,* the Religion of a Temple-state and Stateliness, ritual and external, Pompous and Splendid, which is a Religion, after the manner that unregenerate Mankind affecteth. Their Temples, Altars, Images, (gross and visible Objects of Worship, which sensitive Souls dote upon,) their Priests, Sacrifices, Feasts, Aspersions, Lustrations (easy Methods of cleansing themselves from Sin) belong to their Temple-State of Religion. They had their splendid and magnificent Temples, their Idols sumptuously adorn'd, their mode of God's Service Stately, with Lights, Musick, Odours, Vessels shining with Pearl, and the Priests Garments shining with pretious-Stones, the processionary Pomps of their Gods also, their Triumphs, Games, and Sights, (Sword-fightings, Scenical Plays, and *Ludi seculares,* which were in honour of their Gods,) were part of the *Pomps and Vanities of this World,* which are hugely taking to a carnal Mind. As themselves were a mundan-kind of People, so the principal Design of the *Heathen-Popular* Religion, was a mundan Felicity. The Idolatry, both of *Rome-Heathen,* and *Heathen-Christian* is, in the design of it, a worldly Religion, (it designeth to swim in worldly Felicity, and the Enjoyments of this present

Life,) both have been attended with secular Pomp and Grandeur, Plenty, and Prosperity.

Consectary 4. The *fourth Consectary,* concerning the *badness of the Heathen Virtue and Goodness,* hath been already consider'd, in the first Part of this *Essay;* after which, it may not be improper here to consider that branch of the *Pelagian* Controversy, "Whether the seeming Virtues and good Works of the *Gentiles* are true or false, Sins and Vices, or Virtues and Well-doings, in what sense, and how far they are so?" If we say, "That all their Virtues, and good Works, are in no sense true," we contradict the *Apostle,* Rom. 2. 14. *"The Gentiles do, by Nature, the Things contain'd in the Law."* But, if we say, "That the true Virtues, and good Works, are found in the *Gentile* World," we destroy the Necessity of *Christianity,* confound Nature and Grace, *Gentilism* and *Christianism,* the Atheous World with the City of God; we contradict the Nature of Things, by supposing, that Men do what is truly Holy and Pious, antecedently to the first Principles of true Piety and Sanctity; we contradict the scriptural Account of the *Heathen* State and Life, the whole Stream of the sacred Penmen, who affirm, That *"without Faith it is impossible to please God,"* Hebr. 11. 6. Which must not be understood of such a Faith as is common to Infidels, as some understand it; but of the Faith, which constituteth Divine Believers, and God's Religionists that *come unto God.* The *Gentiles "have their Hearts purified by Faith."* The Mind and Practice of Unbelievers is *"defiled, impure, and unholy. The Carnal Mind is no keeper of the Law of God; they, that are in the Flesh, cannot please God. Ye are married to another"* (saith the Apostle) *"to have your Fruit unto Holiness, and to bring forth Fruit unto God. We are created in Christ unto good Works."* The genuine kind of Virtues are, *"The Fruits of the Holy Spirit, a corrupt Tree cannot bring forth good Fruit, of Thorns Men do not gather Figs, nor of a Bramble-Bush gather they Grapes. When ye were the Servants of Sin, ye were free from Righteousness,"* the Practice whereof is *"a Walking, not after the Flesh, but after the Spirit. Every one that doth Righteousness, is born of God."* The true and genuine Kind of Virtue, Goodness, and Righteousness, is that which is of *the Kingdom of God, of the Divine Image,* and *the New-Man that is renewed in Knowledge,* (which is inconsistent with a State of Atheous Ignorance,) *which*

The badness of the *Heathen* Virtue and Goodness.

is of a new Creature, a new and divine Birth unto Righteousness, of the *new Covenant* and Dispensation of Things, of the *true Vine,* and of a *Divine Charity,* which is the Essence, and Summary, of the truly Divine Moral Virtue, and the genuine kind of good Works. *"Though I bestow all my Goods to feed the Poor, and give my Body to be burn'd, and have not Charity, it profiteth nothing."* The Natural Man's Kind of Virtue, Goodness, and Righteousness, therefore is, according to these Notices of Scripture, on this side that, which is the true and genuine Kind of Virtue, Goodness, and Righteousness; nor can the true Virtues, Goodness, and Justice, exist without being truly Virtuous, Just, and Good, as to God, which is true Piety, Sanctity; nor can that be the true Kind of Virtue, Goodness, and Justice, which cannot constitute Men of the truly Good and Virtuous Kind, God's Kind of Virtuous, Good, and Just Men, whose Judgment is according to Truth. But, as there is a *secular and mundan Kind of Wisdom* and *Prudence,* in itself laudable, ornamental and useful, (such is the common *Jurisprudence,*) yet *originally* it is Base and Vile, being but Earth-born, not Divine, and Heaven-born; *objectively* it is Base and Vile, not being conversant about Divine Things; of *Kind and Quality,* it is also Base and Vile, being of Kind common, Graceless, and Unholy; and *effectively* it is not *Wisdom,* for it cannot constitute any Man truly Wise, nor Wise as to the main, but it continueth him where it found him, in the State of Atheous Ignorance, Error and Folly: So there is a *secular and mundan Kind of Virtue and Goodness,* which, in its own Nature, is Laudable, Ornamental, and Useful at a great rate; yet *Originally, Objectively,* and also of *Kind and Quality,* it is but Base and Vile, and *effectively* it is not *Virtue, Justice,* and *Goodness;* for it cannot constitute any Man Virtuous, Just, and Good; not *Virtuous,* Just, and Good, as to the main, but it continues him where it found him, in the State of reigning Sin and Unrighteousness. His Works are not *"wrought in God,"* as our Saviour says, *Joh.* 3. 21. by which he certainly means *Theism of Religion and Condition.* The *Heathens* are not truly Holy and Religious towards God in any thing, but are Atheous, Graceless, and Unholy, not only in their indifferent Actions, and their Evil-doings (materially such,) but in their Religious Actions, in their Virtue, Goodness, and Well-doing (materially such;) these are not of Kind, and for the main, *the truly good and holy Kind of Virtues, Duties, and good Works.* Their *manner* of doing what is *materially* Good, partakes not of the truly Good and Holy in the main Principle, Motive, End, and formal Object. They are not right in those grand Ingredients, which are essential to every one of the truly good Actions; for they live not to the true God, as his Servants, in the Exercise of all Divine Virtues; they, therefore, so sin in practicing their Virtue, as to be inconsistent with Sanctity; and, therefore, they are Wicked and Ungodly in all their Virtuous Practice, and Well-doing.

With this account of the Virtues and good Works of the *Gentiles,* the general Sense of *Christians* agreeth. *"It is a plain and granted Truth among all that are truly Pious, that without true Piety, that is, the true Worship of the true God, no Man can have the true"* (kind of) *"Virtue."*[269] The *Pagan* Theologers themselves say, that Piety is μή τηρ τών ἀρετών, *the Mother of the Virtues;*[270] their Virtues, therefore, could not be of the holy and godly Kind, if their Religion and Piety was of a contrary Kind and Family. Warm have been the Disputes among *Christians,* "Whether all the Actions of Infidels be Sins, or not?" But the greater Number seem to be of Opinion, *That all the Works of the Unregenerate have the Nature of Sins* (as the Church of *England* determineth) *and are not good Works* (wanting some Essentials thereto) *but Sins in the sight of God, altho' they be materially Good.*

It is not reasonable to attempt a Reconcilement of all the jarring Accounts of the *Pagans Virtues and good Works,* for none can reconcile Contradictions; but the most of them may commodiously be reconcil'd, by considering *their Ethical and Political Virtue,* (which may be call'd the Human Moral, or Human-Social Virtue,) and representing the true Character thereof. This sort of Virtue (which separate from the true Divine-Moral Virtue is manifestly competible to *Heathen* Mankind) is an Atheous and unholy Kind of Virtue, and, therefore, is of Character *a virtue-less Kind of Virtue, and a bad Kind of Goodness.* But, amongst the sinful Kinds of doing Duty, (the evil manner of doing what is ma-

---

269. St. Augustine, *De Civitate Dei,* V.19.
270. Hierocles, *In Aureum Pythagoreorum Carmen Commentarius,* p. 126.

terially Good,) there is this remarkable Difference; in some of them, that which is materially Good, is done in so criminal a Manner, and out of Ends and Principles so Vitious, that the Nature of Virtue is intirely lost out of the Action, and it becomes (like *Pharisaical* Holiness) Vice simply so called; but it is otherwise in this alien Kind of Virtue and Well-doing, which is a different evil Kind of doing what is materially Good, for the Nature of Virtue and Well-doing is in part really preserv'd and retain'd in it, as the Nature of an Olive is in the Wild-Olive. The Virtues of the *Gentiles,* therefore, are Sin in one sense, but not in another. He that saith, They are Sin, Vice and Crime, not Righteousness and true Holiness, saith true; but he that saith, They are not any sort of Virtue, saith false. They are not so Vice, as not to be an *unholy Virtue and Well-doing.* They are not simply, either Vice, or Virtue; for they are not the true and genuine, but the spurious and illegitimate, Kind of good Works. The case is the same, if we consider them with respect to the Law, or Rule of Virtue and Duty. For, *as* the holy kind of Virtues are of kind and for the main, according to the Law of our Piety and Holiness towards God, who is the formal Object of our Obedience, whom we ought to obey out of dutiful Affection to him, and to make the pleasing him, his Honour and Service the chief End of our Doings and Business of our Lives: *So* the Atheous unholy kind of Duties, Virtues, and good Works, are, of kind and for the main, against the Law of our Piety and Holiness towards God, and, therefore, have the Nature of Sins; they are against the Law of our Piety and Holiness, both by way of *privation* and *opposition;* for the not living unto God, is an undeifying him (as far as is in our power,) a being an Enemy to him, and a living to ourselves; the not regarding and affecting him dutifully, is a disregarding him, and a disaffecting him, and a regarding and affecting somewhat else above him and against him, and therefore the natural Man, by his unholy Kind of Virtue, is no otherwise Virtuous, than so as to be an Impietist towards God. Yet it has so much in it of the Nature of Virtue, that the *Apostle* styleth it *"a doing the Things contain'd in the Law";* God himself hath so much respect to it, that he rewardeth it several ways: No Man, upon his Conversion, so repenteth of it, as he doth of his Sins simply so called. It is not only a doing what is materially Good (which is of good Example to others, and may be of great advantage to the Publick:) But in its Principle, impulsive Cause, and End, there is so much Good as serveth to constitute it *a spurious and degenerate kind of Virtue and Well-doing*, as will appear from the *Heathens* Principles of laudable Practice, which may be reduc'd to these Four. 1. *Good-Nature and natural Instinct.* 2. *Human-Socialness.* 3. *An unholy Kind of respect for Worth and Virtue, Honesty and Duty, Justice and Equity, Reason and Ingenuity, Civility, Decency, and Order, and a like respect for himself, his own Perfection and Felicity.* 4. *Religion on this side true Religion.*

In the first place, *Animal Temper and the kindly Instincts*, which are in Animal Nature, may be call'd *Good-Nature*, which is a Principle of laudable Practice; for Mankind have this in common with the Brutes, of whom some are tame, tractable, placid; others are fierce and savage, and have the Name of *Evil Beasts*, which Name implyeth, that there are good-natur'd Beasts. *Cato* was of a good Nature, if, as *Cicero* says of him, *"Nature had fram'd him to Gravity and Temperance"*; or, if, as *Velleius Paterculus* saith, *"He was therefore Virtuous, because he could not be otherwise."* Some are by natural Temper and Constitution averse from certain Vices, (Sordidness, Cruelty, Impudence;) and disposed to the contrary Virtues, (Generosity, Clemency, Modesty;) so amongst the *Romans* some Virtues are observ'd to have been Hereditary in certain Families in continued Succession, and great Vices, (Fury, Luxury, Libidinousness,) in others; *"I am of Opinion"* (saith *Quintilian Declam.* 260) *"That the Morals of all are born with them, and the proper Virtues of every Nature."* *Plato* (in his *Tenth of Laws*) speaketh of a sort of good-natur'd Atheists, *"who think that there are no Gods at all, yet are by Nature of a just Disposition, hating bad Men and Injustice, they will do no such Practices themselves, and those Men that are not just they shun, and love them that are just."* Altho' Instances of Ferity and Barbarity are no Rarities amongst Men, yet a certain Goodness, Kindness, Benignity, and Tenderness, is part of our natural Constitution, and an effect of our bodily Temper, which so far prevaileth in the World of Mankind, that it commonly beareth the Name of *Humanity*, as Cruelty is call'd *Inhumanity*, and the Rod of Mansuetude, *"the Rod of Men,"* 2 *Sam.* 7. 14. As bodily Temper, so the kindly Instincts which are in Animal Nature, are Principles of

Of the Principles of laudable Practice amongst the Heathens.

laudable Practices. Such as *natural Affection towards Children and near Kindred, Commiseration for the Afflicted, a natural Sympathy, Gratitude, and Kindness, for our Friends and Benefactors* (remarkable in Dogs, Lions, and even Birds,) *common Sociableness and Friendliness, particular Friendship, a Propension to please and oblige others, a natural Benignity and Generosity, desire of our own Welfare and Happiness, care of our Reputation, aversion from Infamy, Misery, and Death.*

A *Second* Principle of laudable Practices is *a Human-Social Disposition,* (which is a goodness of Nature, and in great degree an innate Instinct in Man;) for all the Human-Social and Human-Moral Virtue and Duty, commonly call'd the *Political* and *Ethical,* is compriz'd in, and may be inferr'd from, this one Principle. For all political Virtue and Duty towards Mankind in general, towards our Country, all Civil-Social Charity and Justice, the common Offices of Humanity and Civil Neighbourhood, the oeconomical Duties, Duties of near Relations and of Friendship, belong to Man as Social, as Human-Social, and he is not Man without the Human-Morals. In this great Law, great Virtue and Duty, of *Man's being Human-Social, Civil-Social* (not Anti-Social) is manifestly compriz'd *"a Civil-Social kind of universal Benevolence to ourselves and all Mankind, which affecteth and endeavoureth the Good of the Publick, and is opposite to what is hurtful;"*[271] from which Benevolence Universal (*"Caritas humani Generis"* Cicero calls it) all Mundan Political Virtue is deduceable. As it is also from another great Principle compriz'd in the *Pagan* Human-Social Disposition; *"The Subordination and Relation of all Men, and lesser Societies of Men, to the great Body of Mankind, as of Parts to the Whole, and of Citizens to the Mundan City."*[272] From these Principles both the *Popular* and *Philosophick Pagans* practis'd *Civil Virtue,* as the *Bees* do in some sort, that have political Order and Government amongst them: And this their Practice of *political Virtue* constituted and denominated *a good and just Man of their Idea.* One *Antenor,* who wrote the *Cretan* History, was nam'd Δέλτα (amongst the Cretans δέλτος signified *Good,*) διὰ τὸ ἀγαθὸς ἔι καὶ φιλόπολις, *"because*

271. Simplicius, *Commentarius in Epicteti Enchiridion,* p. 141.
272. Epictetus, *Discourses,* II.

he was good and a lover of his City;[273] *To live well"* (saith *Plutarch*) *"is to live Sociably and Friendly, and Temperately and Justly."*[274] The generality of the *Pagans* suppos'd, that the observance of their political Laws constituted them just Men.

A *Third* Principle of laudable Practices is *a respect for Worth and Virtue, Honesty and Duty, Justice and Equity, Reason and Ingenuity, Civility, Decency, and Order; and a like respect for ourselves, our own Perfection and Felicity, without any regard to God, or Holiness.* For, as there is a *Human-Social Virtue,* which is on this side the *Holy-Social,* so there is a regard for *Worth* and *Virtue, Honesty, Reason,* and *Justice,* which is on this side true Holiness and Godliness. The *Pagans* practis'd the Virtue which they teach, *"fugiendae turpitudinis causa, to shun that which is base and shameful,"*[275] τοῦ καλοῦ ἕνεκα *because it was Just and Good, Virtuous, or Honest."*[276] Their Maxim was *"Honestum per se expetendum, that which is Virtuous, is Self-desirable";* and some of them have said, *"A Feast is nothing else but the doing one's Duty."*[277] Out of regard to Decency and Order, they practis'd the *small Morals,* (that may well be defin'd, as the *Stoicks* define Modesty, *the Science of decent Motion,*) which are the opposites to Rudeness, Rusticity, and Impoliteness of Behaviour. And for their *great Morals,* (altho' their practice of them was without any regard to God, or Holiness,) their Notions were so high and generous, that they profess'd a contempt of Life, and *"to throw the Body into the Fire, when Reason, when Dignity, when Fidelity, requireth it,*[278] *A virtuous Man will die for his Friends and Country, he will throw away his Money and Honours, and all the Goods that Men contest about* ωριποιούμρυος ἑαυτῳ τὸ καλὸν, *acquiring, or preserving to himself that which is Beautiful in matter of Life and Practice."*[279] *Miltiades* taught the *Athenians,* "to acknowledge no Lord but the Laws, and to be afraid of nothing more than that which is Evil and

273. Photius, *Bibliotheca,* cod. 190, col. 485.
274. Plutarch, *Adversus Colotem* (in *Moralia*), p. 1108.
275. Cicero, *Tusculan Disputations,* II.
276. Aristotle, *Nicomachean Ethics.*
277. Origen, *Contra Celsum,* VIII, p. 392.
278. Seneca, *Epistulae Morales,* XIV.
279. Aristotle, *Nicomachean Ethics,* IX.8.

Unjust";[280] and of *Themistocles* the Orator saith, *"That willingly he would not set any Thing before Virtue and his Duty.*[281] *To be Virtuous is a great Accomplishment, and every Virtue is an Accomplishment."*[282] The *Philosophick Pagans,* therefore, (at least the better sort of them,) betook themselves to the Study and Exercise of Virtue out of regard to their *Perfection and Felicity,* which they suppos'd to consist in their Virtue, which in many Instances was (in some respect) very laudable and imitable. Such was the *Platonists* disaffecting τὰ τνὶδε, *the Things that are here,* the not desiring or using them any farther, than *so far as there is need;* and the *Stoicks* γαϛυρ κεκολασμένη, *restrain'd Belly,* or *narrow-bounded Appetite.* The *Pagans,* both *Popular* and *Philosophick,* had also a regard to *Self-approbation* and the Tranquillity of their own Mind. *"There is no greater Theatre"* (saith *Cicero*[283]) *"for Virtue, than our own Mind, approving and applauding."* They had also a *Self-reverence,* or regard to their own Dignity of Person.—Πάντων δὲ μάλις' ἀιοχύνεο σαυτὸν, *Above all others reverence thy-self."*[284]

A *fourth* Principle of laudable Practices is *Religion on this side true Religion;* for it was from a Principle of Religion, and out of regard to a Deity, that *Heathens* thought themselves oblig'd, to do nothing against their Consciences, but to keep them unspotted;[285] that they look'd upon the Dictates of their practical Reason as Laws;[286] that they had Hopes and Fears, Peace and Perplexity, Joys and Anxieties, from their Consciences,[287] That they look'd upon themselves as bound to *Innocence,* to *Gratitude,* to keep *Faith,* to take care of their *Children* and *Parents,* to have a *special Kindness for their near Kindred,* to do the Offices of *Humanity* towards Mankind in general, and acts of *Heroical Virtue* for the

280. Aristides, in Photius, *Bibliotheca,* cod. 246, col. 1282.
281. Ibid., col. 1292.
282. Stobaeus, *Anthologium,* pp. 185, 187.
283. Cicero, *Tusculan Disputations,* II.
284. Hierocles, *In Aureum Pythagoreorum Carmen Commentarius.*
285. Marcus Aurelius, *Meditations,* II.17.
286. Sharrock, *De Officiis Secundum Naturae Jus* (1660), p. 12.
287. Ibid., p. 22.

publick Benefit;[288] that they thought Men criminal and punishable, not only for Facts of Wickedness (such as Adultery, Theft, Homicide,) but for the Will of Evil-doing;[289] that they shun'd the perpetration of Wickedness in secret, dreaded Perjury, rever'd an Oath;[290] that they accounted Injustice towards Men, and all vicious Errors in Life and Practice, (which they called ἁμαρτνίματα, *Sins,*) nothing less than Impieties;[291] that the *Philosophick-Pagan Religionists* thought themselves oblig'd to practise all the Virtues which were in their Institution, and to shun all the Vices;[292] that they propos'd to themselves an Imitation of the Deity, and suppos'd, that nothing could be well done, *"without having respect to the Things Divine";* [293] and therefore (as some of themselves say) *"they had an Eye to the Deity in every thing great and little";* [294] and lastly, that they look'd upon themselves as bound to an intire Subjection to the Governor of the World, and to all the Branches of active and passive Obedience to him, real, or imaginary.[295] The natural Man, therefore, in a considerable degree, hath Notices of what is Good and Bad, Virtuous and Vicious, Right and Wrong, Just and Unjust (towards the Deity, as well as towards Men,) of what is Worthy and Unworthy, that some things are very Vile and Dishonourable, others are Becoming, Excellent and Honourable; and, altho' he is an Impietist, yet he hath his Virtues and Welldoings, *"that are from Conscience, not Vain-Glory."* [296] The *Heathen* joineth Religion and Justice towards Men; as *Nicias,* (of whom *Thucydides* saith, *"He was the Man of all the* Grecians *of my time, that least deserv'd to be brought to so great a degree of Misery,*[297]) who, falling into a great Calamity in *Syracuse,* told his afflicted Army, *"I have worshipp'd the Gods*

288. Ibid., chs. 3–8.
289. Ibid., p. 92.
290. Epictetus, *Discourses,* I.14.
291. Stobaeus, *Anthologium,* p. 181.
292. Ibid.
293. Marcus Aurelius, *Meditations,* III.13; Gataker, *Markou Antoninou,* note, p. 360.
294. Epictetus, *Discourses,* XII.1, 9.
295. Ibid., I.14.
296. Macrobius, *In Somnium Scipionis,* II.10.
297. Thucydides, *History of the Peloponnesian War,* VII.

frequently according to the Laws, and liv'd justly and unblameably towards Men." The *Heathen* will be just, because, in his way, he is religious. *"He that is unjust is impious. For the Nature of the Universe having made all rational Beings for one another, so as to benefit one another, as they are worthy, but in no wise to hurt; he that transgresseth the Will hereof, is manifestly impious towards the most antient of the Gods."* [298]

The Virtue of the *Heathens* was an unholy and degenerate kind of Virtue.

    It is one thing, to say, that *a Man is an ungodly Heathen;* and another thing, to say, he is *an ungodly virtuous Heathen:* And it is one thing, to say, of an Action of his, *it is an ungodly Action;* and another thing, to say, *it is an ungodly virtuous Action.* When the natural Man doth that which is materially good, it may be done, for the main, from such good Principles, and for such good Ends, as are competible to the mere natural Man. An *Heathen* may venture into the Fire, to pull his Child our, partly from a Principle of *Good-Nature, and natural Instinct,* partly for the *conservation of Human Society,* partly out of an *unholy respect to Fortitude,* and partly from *Religion on this side true Religion;* and this Action of his, in venturing into the Fire for his Child, is of an opposite Nature, both to the Sin of exposing his Child, and also to the Sin of venturing into the Fire (like the *Indians*) for Vain-Glory. Both the Actions of this latter sort are Sin, simply so call'd: But to declaim against the former as such, is the Voice of a *Barbarian,* not of a *Christian.* This Maxim, therefore, needeth a limitation, *That the same Action cannot be both morally Good and Evil.* For, altho' the same Action cannot be *a true and genuine kind of morally good Action,* and *a morally evil Action;* yet one of the *Heathen* Man's kind of good Works is therefore Sin, because it is opposite unto Holiness, and it is so far Sin (and therefore morally Evil,) as it is opposite unto Holiness, (which is not a true and genuine kind of morally good Action;) yet this hindereth it not from being *a spurious and degenerate kind of morally good Action.*

    On the other hand, altho' it is of kind, and for the main, *a sort of Virtue and Well-doing;* yet no carnal, wicked, unholy kind of Man (remaining such) doth any thing *that is, of kind and for the main, Righ-*

298. Marcus Aurelius, *Meditations,* IX.i.

teousness and true Holiness, no holy kind of Duty, or good Work: But, when he doth that which is materially good, out of his kind of virtuous Principles, and for his kind of virtuous Ends, yet he is *carnal, wicked, and unholy-virtuous* in those his Doings; and they are like himself, of kind and for the main *wicked, carnal, and unholy kind of virtuous Doings;* or they are the carnal, wicked and unholy Man's kind of Doings, not simply so; but they are the *carnal, wicked, unholy Man's kind of virtuous Doings.* His kind of living is an Atheous kind of living; his virtuous kind of living is the *Atheous-virtuous kind of living,* which is not the *living unto the true God as his Servant,* but opposite thereto, an *ungodly kind of virtuous living.* Let us suppose, that *Hercules* undertakes immense Labours, to save Mankind from Monsters and Tyrants, out of no better Principle than *Good-Nature, natural Instinct of kindness for his Relations, regard to the preservation of human Society, a regard to an unholy kind of Fortitude,* and from *something of Religion on this side true Religion,* (suppose an imitation of *Jove,* called his Father,) this the *Pagans* accounted *Heroical Virtue.*[299] But *Hercules's* kind of virtuous living was an Atheous kind of virtuous living, it was devoid of true Piety and Holiness, and repugnant to it. The Character, therefore, of the ungodly Man's virtuous Actions, or Well-doings, consisteth of two parts: For every one of them, being consider'd as a part of his whole living, appeareth to be, both depriv'd of, and opposite to, Holiness and Godliness, and so complicated with Sin, as to be only *a spurious and illegitimate kind of Virtue, rather Vice than Virtue;* because, in reference to God, it is not Virtue. And, if those virtuous Doings of the *Pagans* are so vicious, which issu'd from Principles, that ought to be conjoin'd with, and subordinate to, true Piety and Holiness, (Good-Nature, natural Instinct, and a human-social Disposition,) what foul Crimes are the greater part of their virtuous Doings, which manifestly issued from, and were subordinated to, one of the foulest of Vices, *the inordinate Appetite of Vain-Glory?* For so the Orator *Isocrates* (whom *Dionysius Halicarnasseus* preferreth before the

---

299. Cicero, *De Officiis,* III; *De Finibus,* III.

Philosophers as a Teacher of Morality,) who calleth himself a Philosopher, and a great acquaintance and admirer of *Socrates,* professedly maketh Vain-glory the Principle, End, and Rule of all his Actions, and of
other Mens.

As for the Fact of the *Aegyptian* Mid-Wives, (which is alleg'd to prove,
that mere *Heathens* do good Deeds, that are not, of kind and for the
main, sinful,) it is not difficult to answer such Allegations. For, either
the *Aegyptians* were the Religionists of the true God, or they were not.
If they were God's Religionists, (imperfectly, or more perfectly,) their
case is no parallel for mere *Heathens.* If they were not, then their Fact
was, for the main and of kind, sinful; yet being, of kind and for the
main, spurious and degenerate Virtue and Well-doing, it was rewarded
with Temporal Blessings. It is commonly said, *That God does not so much
regard what we do, as why we do it:* But we ought rather to say, *The thing
that God regardeth is, of what kind our Doings are.* For, unless we ourselves
be holy and godly Persons, of kind and for the main such, and unless
our Doings be of the same sort, neither we, nor they, otherwise than in
a limited improper sense, can be pleasing and acceptable in God's Eyes.
The *Heathen* Philosophers were not holy, or godly kind of Persons, their
divine Virtue was not the holy and godly kind of Virtue, it was not a
faithful serving and pleasing the true God; but *a self-serving, self-pleasing,
self-adorning, self-excellence, self-beatitude,* separate from, and contrary
to, the life of true Piety and Holiness. Therefore no other Virtue is competible to unregenerate Mankind, than such as is consistent with *the reign
of the inordinate carnal Self-love,* (which is the Essence and Summary of
all Wickedness, which reigneth in all that are void of the divine Love,
which is the Essence and Summary of all divine vital Virtue;) the
Atheousness of their Virtue and Well-doings is imputable to the inordinate carnal Self-love, which causeth the want of the love of God; and,
because they are devoid of the Love of God, and are none of his Servants, therefore their Virtues and Well-doings (from whatever Principle
they issue) *are a certain self-serving, and self-pleasing, not a serving and
pleasing God.* Therefore their specious Well-doings symbolize with the
rest of the specious Things of this World, they are not what at first sight
they seem to be.

The *fifth consectary* is touching *the Deadliness of our Heathen State;* for the Scripture looketh upon us, antecedently to the Life and State of true and saving Religion, as *deadly Criminals,* as *dead,* and as *the Subjects of Satan's Kingdom:* As deadly Criminals, our Character consisteth of two branches, which imply and infer one another; for, in our *Heathen* State, we are *aliens from the Life of Righteousness, deadly Sinners in Life and Practice;* and we are *not Faithful Friends to God and Holiness.*

Of the Deadliness of our *Heathen* State.

1. Mankind are, in Scripture, divided into two opposite Parties and Families (that are contrary kind of People, of a contrary Genius and Temper, that walk in contrary Ways, belonging to contrary Societies,) which are known by the Names of the *Righteous* and the *Wicked,* the *Just* and the *Unjust,* the *Godly* and the *Ungodly,* the *Pious* and the *Impious,* the *Holy* and the *Unholy,* the *Good* and the *Evil,* the *Saints* of God and *Sinners* that are *not Saints,* the *Children of Light* and the *Children of the World,* the *Children of God* and the *Children of the Devil,* the *Carnal* and the *Spiritual;* all which Distinctions and Descriptions of two opposite Parties denote their different Life and Practice. The one are *the Servants of Sin, not the Servants of God and of Righteousness;* the other are *the Servants of God and of Righteousness, not the Servants of Sin. Rom.* 6. 18, 20, 22. The one are *the Workers of Iniquity, not the Practisers of Righteousness;* the other are *the Practisers of Righteousness, not the Workers of Iniquity. Psal.* 14. 4. and 15. 2. Of this Kind, Quality, and Character, are all that are in the State and Life of the true and saving Religion; notwithstanding that they are guilty of Weaknesses, Sins of Ignorance and Surprize, altho' they have intermixtures of blemish in their Souls, and of blame in their Lives; yet their Life is not the wicked, sinning, unrighteous kind of Life, but the contrary; their tenor, course, and way of living is *the Way of Righteousness,* not only in some particular Acts, but of kind, and for the main. They perpetrate no heinous Iniquity, no deadly atrocious Sin; so far they are faultless, perfect, and undefiled. They keep no Favourite Sin, allow of no Sin, nor allow themselves in any, nor can they dispense with sinning against God; and, therefore, they are not, in any respect, *Children of Disobedience,* nor Rebels against God. They are also the Doers of Righteousness, both towards God and Man; and the Righteousness which they practise, is not the counterfeit and

illegitimate, but the true and saving kind of Righteousness, contradistinguish'd from the Righteousness of the *Scribes* and *Pharisees*. The
Wicked, in several degrees, are such as the Old-Testament characterizeth
and complaineth of; *that are estrang'd and are far from God, that forsake
him, and live in forgetfulness and contempt of God, and have not the Fear
of God before their Eyes, that are altogether become Filthy and do abominable Works, that are far from Righteousness, and desire not the knowledge
of God's Ways, presumptuous Sinners that Sin with a high hand, and make
a Mock of Sin, Sons of* Belial *that know not the Lord, lewd Debauchees,
revelling voluptuous Sensualists, Unclean, Evil-speakers, Lyars, Slanderers,
Falsifiers of Trusts, Oaths and Contracts, unjust Dealers, the Children of
Pride, Sons of Violence and of Blood, disobedient to Parents, perpetrating
the horrid Sins against God* (Atheism, Idolatry, Blasphemy, Magick,) *the
horrid Sins against Nature* (Sodomy, Bestiality, Incest,) *the horrid Sins
against human Society* (Robbery, Rapine, Murder,) *the heinous Violaters
of the Duties of both Tables, the Duties of Piety, Charity, Justice, Sobriety.*
They are not those that *walk with God* in the Duties of religious Society,
that have *clean Hands* and a *pure Heart*.

   In the New-Testament, all Mankind, antecedently to the State and
Life of true and saving Religion, are represented as deadly *"Sinners, the
Ungodly, all under Sin"* (as deadly criminal Livers are under it,) *"a guilty
World"* (subjected to Condemnation) *"before God; for all have"* (deadly)
"sinned, and come short of the Glory of God" (as to the having with him
Glory.) As we were carnal, *"those that are after the Flesh,"* so we liv'd after
it, and brought forth the Fruits of it, *"fulfilling the Desires of the Flesh,
and of the Mind,"* Eph. 2. 3. As we were those that are *"of the World,"* so
we lived *"after the course of it,"* not living a Life of doing God Service,
but of serving Sin (the Flesh) and *"diverse Lusts, the Lust of the Flesh, the
Lust of the Eyes, and the Pride of Life,"* Tit. 3. 3. which live and reign in
unregenerate Mankind, whose Life is a serving and pleasing them as a
Law. They are not of a Divine Kind of Nature, but Aliens, and at Enmity
with God, by doing evil Works, *Col.* 1. 21. not the Lovers of God, and
of their Brother, but of the World, that have not *"the Love of God in
them, Man-haters, Man-slayers,"* 1 Joh. 3. 13–17. and *"have not eternal Life
abiding in them."* And, because they are of the evil kind, (*"Dogs, Swine,*

Serpents, Vipers," Rev. 22. 15. *Mat.* 7. 6. and 3. 7. and 23. 33.) they are necessarily the Children of the Evil-one, and his resembling Off-spring, making a worldly-happy Estate, or a carnal selfish Interest of Credit, Prosperity, and sensual Delight, their chief Good, End, and Business, and preferring it before the Favour of God, the Interest of his Service and Kingdom, and their everlasting Happiness. Themselves, their Virtue and Religion, (for *all* Men pretend to Virtue, and *almost all* to Religion,) have their Character from the three grand Enemies of *Christianity* and Godliness, the Devil, the Flesh, and the World; for they are *the wicked, carnal, and worldly kind of Men, of virtuous Men, and of Religionists.* Their Virtue, Righteousness, and Religion, is of Kind illegitimate, and continueth them in their *Wickedness, Carnality,* and *mundan Alliance.*

2. Mankind, antecedently to the State and Life of true and saving Religion, are deadly Criminals also, upon account of a *second branch* of their Character; for, whether they be open Aliens and Enemies, or pretenders to God and Holiness, *they are not the faithful Friends of God and Holiness.* In all Relations of Friendship, *Unfaithfulness* is the summary of all Vice and Crime, and *Faithfulness* is the summary of all Virtue and Duty; for *Unfaithfulness* is a *failure of Duty, in Mind, Will, and Meaning;* Faithfulness, the contrary. God's People are without Guile, and, therefore, the Righteous and Uncondemnable in the judgment of Equity, no Guilt is imputable to them; they are absolutely Sinless, as in the future State, or at least unchargeable with Wickedness. *"Blessed is the Man, unto whom the Lord imputeth no Iniquity, and in whose Spirit there is no Guile."* Of this truly noble Character, is every faithful Adherent to God and Righteousness, such as *"Abraham was, whose Heart was faithful before God."* He forsaketh Iniquity, in Will and Affection, universally and unreservedly, so that he is not dead in Sin, nor in the State of reigning Sin, and his course of Life is the Holy and Sinless. Wittingly and willingly he doth no Iniquity (therefore is no Rebel, no Traitor,) practiseth no heinous deadly Sinning. His Bent, Mind, and Will, is not partially and dividedly (which is a traiterous with-holding our Love and Affection,) but fully and intirely for God and Righteousness, which have sincerely his utmost Esteem and Affection, being his chief Good, (as Sin the chief

Evil;) nothing being so dear to him, but what he will part with for them, whom he serves with his Best, and with his All, notwithstanding all Difficulties and Discouragements. And, as a Sovereign and a Master cannot repute such Men that ought to be his Subjects and Servants, *Upright, Honest, Sincere,* and *Faithful,* that are not dutifully affected and dispos'd towards Him and his Service: So God cannot repute any Man *Upright in Heart, Honest, Sincere,* and *Faithful,* that is not *dutifully, uprightly, sincerely, and faithfully* affected and dispos'd towards him and his Service. Therefore we ought to consider who they are, that may be denominated simply, and without addition, the *faithful Friends of God and Holiness;* for all others are such, that are devoid of this *intire Integrity and Faithfulness,* (which alone is constitutive of the truly Righteous,) notwithstanding a partial, or limited, Integrity and Faithfulness which they have. They are so far from being dutifully and rightly Affected, that they are the Disaffected; so far from being faithful Friends to God and Righteousness, that they are Enemies (usually deadly Enemies, and such as may be called faithful Enemies,) their Mind, Will, and Meaning is inexcusably amiss, because they are not, simply, and without addition, *The faithful Friends of God and Righteousness, and the faithful Enemies of Sin and Wickedness.*

Many are loyal and faithful to a secular Master, or Sovereign, that are not *God's faithful Servants.* Robbers (some of them) will be faithful to those of their own Gang. Many Men, of Civil-social Virtue only, will be faithful in matters of ordinary Justice, and, in some particular affair, *faithful Messengers, Servants, Soldiers.* If we suppose *Abimelech* an evil Man, as some will have him; yet, as to the business of *Abraham's* Wife (*Gen.* 20. 6.) there was no Iniquity, no Pravity in his Mind, Will, or Meaning; he meant no Wrong to *Abraham,* whose Wife she was (to him altogether unknown,) and, therefore, in that particular affair, he was "*Upright, Right, and without Iniquity.*"

There is a Faithfulness in *Judaism,* as well as in *Christianity;* for when any one will change his Religion, and become a *Proselyte of Justice,* the *Jews* require, "*that he do it, not for the Vanity of the World,*" (any secular Advantage,) "*but out of Love, and from the whole Heart.*" Such a Faithfulness and Integrity in adhering to their God, in opposition to Idols and false Gods, was requir'd of the *Jews,* in the antient times of their Common-wealth, as the Condition of their temporal Blessings. A Faithfulness to their Institution, as it was carnal *Judaism,* those *Jews* had, who thought, they did God good Service in killing *Christians, Joh.* 16. 2. And thus the *Apostle,* when he outrageously persecuted the *Christians,* was Faithful to his Institution, he never wilfully violated the Rules of Welldoing according to carnal *Judaism,* and, therefore, had the *carnal Judaical Man's good Conscience,* as he professeth, *Acts* 26. 9. *"I have lived in all good Conscience before God until this Day."*

There is a Faithfulness in *Paganism,* as well as in *Judaism.* For *Numa* consecrated a Temple to Faithfulness. *Regulus* is a known Instance of Faithfulness. *Pyrrhus* said of *Fabritius,* that it was harder to turn him out of the way of Justice, than the Sun out of his Course.[300] *Papinianus,* the Lawyer, being commanded to defend the wicked Fact of the Emperor *Caracalla,* who had barbarously killed his Brother *Geta,* he chose rather to dye than to do it.[301] In *China,* there is a Temple of Chastity, erected in commemoration of five Virgins, who, being taken by Thieves, took away their own Lives, to avoid being ravish'd.[302] Several of the *Heathens* were so far faithful and uprightly dispos'd, that, in several particular Actions, neither Shame, Torment, Exile, or Death, could prevail with them to violate the Dictates of their Minds; and several of them were true and faithful Worshippers of false Gods; they were Faithful to their Institution of *Heathenism,* and these may be said, to have *The Heathen Man's good Conscience.*

Yet, in the unsound Profession of *Christianity,* in carnal *Judaism,* and in *Heathenism,* there are no such Persons as the *Upright,* the *Sincere* and *Faithful;* and, consequently, there is no such thing as the *Uprightness* of the *Upright,* the *Sincerity* of the *Sincere,* the *Faithfulness* of the *Faithful.* For, in these Regions, all are the Wicked and the Ungodly; whereas, if any of them were the *Upright* and the *Faithful,* these must necessarily be the *Righteous,* and in the State of justified Persons. Wherefore the

300. Gataker in *Markou Antoninou,* p. 410.
301. Spartian, *Caracella.*
302. Hoffman, *Umbra in Luce,* p. 134.

Natural and *Heathen* Man's Uprightness, Sincerity, and Faithfulness, is of the same Nature and Character with the rest of his Virtue, *it is of a spurious and degenerate Kind,* (as being on this side Holiness and God-liness,) *not the intire Integrity, not the right Kind of Uprightness, not the holy and godly Kind of Sincerity,* 2 Cor. 1. 12.) *but a faithless Kind of Faith-fulness.* And this is what is meant by *"a natural and moral Integrity."* [303] Which sort of Integrity is compatible to Rebel-Sinners, to such as are revolted from God and his Kingdom, and from true Righteousness and Holiness, in whom it is necessarily complicated with the most heinous Disloyalty and Unfaithfulness; from which none can be excus'd, who are not, as his Liege-Subjects and Servants, loyally affected unto God and unsinning Righteousness towards him: The Ignorance of the *Jews* and *Gentiles* did not excuse them, because they might have known better, and would have known better, if they had been, so far as they might have been, the faithful Friends of God and Righteousness, and the faithful Enemies of Sin and Wickedness. With this Limitation the Philosopher's Rule ought to be propos'd, which otherwise is not, universally, a safe Rule of Practice. *"That which appeareth to thee"* (as a faithful Adherent to God and Righteousness) *"to be the best, let that be to thee a Law inviolable."* [304]

It is, however, to be observ'd, that some, who are not *properly* and *formally* the *Upright* and *Faithful,* are such in *aptness of Disposition,* and in an *initial* degree; being such as mean well towards God and Righ-teousness, who are out of the State and Life of true and saving Religion, but with abatement of sense. These are they, that are denominated *"Christ's Sheep,"* Joh. 10. 4, 10. those that *"are of the Truth,"* Joh. 18. 37. and *Luk.* 8. 15. those that have *"an honest and good Heart"*; which is a degree of that Integrity, which constituteth *the Faithful and Upright in Heart, simply so called.* The Phrase denoteth *an honest and good Heart,* in respect of the Word of true and saving Religion, and the receiving thereof, (an honest and good Heart so far;) by receiving which *Honestly,*

---

303. Sanderson, *Sermon Ad Populum,* on Genesis 20.6 in *XXXIV Sermons* (1671), pp. 157–86.
304. Epictetus, *Enchiridion,* ch. 75.

Sincerely, and *Faithfully* (that is, without Vice, or Crime, as to Mind, Will, or Meaning) the Receiver becomes one of the Faithful and Upright in Heart, in a plenary Sense, whereas at first he is only so *initially,* and by way of *preparatory Disposition.* The Faithful and Upright, in a plenary sense, are Religionists of several Degrees. For many holy and good Men, under the *Mosaical* Oeconomy, were the faithful Lovers of God and of Righteousness; yet were very imperfect Religionists, agreeably to that Oeconomy. Our Saviour's Disciples, while he was on Earth, that betray a great deal of Ignorance, Weakness, and many Imperfections at every turn, were the faithful and sincere Lovers of God and of Righteousness, but so as to be Religionists of a very mean Rank. And it seemeth reasonable to suppose, touching *Cornelius,* a *Gentile,* and a Proselyte, (and such like,) that God, from the Beginning of the World, having made Provision in *Christ,* that his and *Christ*'s Religionists should be in the State of Remission of Sins, *Cornelius* was imperfectly in this Divine Condition, before Conversion to *Christianity:* But, after the Gospel-settlement was made, his Conversion to *Christianity* was necessary, both for the continuance of what he had, and the completion of what he wanted.

3. The Scripture looketh upon Mankind, antecedently to the State and Life of true and saving Religion, *not as alive, but as dead, or in the State of the Dead.* So in the *Oriental* Philosophy they call'd those Men *dead,* "that are fallen from their *Dogmata,* are become Aliens from the discipline of Truth and Virtue, whence the Soul hath her Life, and have subjected their Mind to the Animal Passions."[305] As, when any one was ejected out of the *Pythagoreans* Society, they set up an empty Coffin in his Place, to signify, that he ought to be look'd upon as Dead. And the *Platonists* say, "That the Death of a rational Substance is, to be devoid of God and of Mind." The *Mahometans* use the same way of speaking. The *Hebrews* also use this Symbolical way of expressing the Condition of the Wicked.[306] Our Saviour also useth the same Mode of Expression, when he saith, *Matth.* 8. 22. *"Let the dead bury their dead,"* i.e. *leave it*

---

305. Grotius, *Annotationes in Novum Testamentum,* note on Matthew 8.22.
306. Ibid.

to them, who are in a deadly State of Sin, to busy themselves about burying the Carcases of the Dead. And, as the *Jews* will not allow the *Gentiles,* to be reckon'd amongst the Living, so the *Apostle* looketh upon the World of *Heathen* Sinners, as in the State of the Dead. 1 *Pet.* 4. 6. *"The Gospel was preach'd to them that are dead, that they might be judg'd according to Men in the Flesh,"* i.e. suffer Death, the Death of Mortification, to which they are sentenc'd by the Gospel, that they who are dead in their Carnality, by the Death of it might live Spiritually. And this plain Notion of *the Dead* sufficiently explaineth a very obscure Phrase, which this *Apostle* useth, speaking of *Christ,* 1 Pet. 3. 18, 19, 20. *"Being put to Death in the Flesh, but quicken'd by the Spirit. By which also he preach'd to the Spirits in Prison, which sometimes were Disobedient, when once the long-suffering of God waited in the Days of* Noah." If, instead of this Phrase, *the Spirits in Prison,* the *Apostle* had made use of this Expression, *those that are in the State of the Dead,* there had been no difficulty in his Words; every Interpreter would have said, *those who are in the State of the Dead,* is a Phrase expressive of the sadly-degenerate Condition of Mankind, who are dead in a moral Sense; *that this Generation, those that are in the State of the Dead, was sometimes disobedient to the preaching of* Noah, (degenerate Mankind were then incredulous, and now are so;) and that *Christ* by the Spirit, after his Resurrection, *going preach'd to them,* not in his own Person, but by his *Apostles,* in which sense St. *Paul* saith, *he came and preach'd, Ephes.* 2. 17. If there had been no difficulty in the *Apostle's* Words, supposing that he had made use of this Phrase, *those that are in the State of the Dead;* the difficulty in them must not be thought great, altho' the *Apostle* useth this Phrase, *the Spirits in Prison,* (which is of more affinity with *the Spirit* that he was speaking of, than the other;) because the *Spirits in Prison,* and *those that are in the State of the Dead* (vitiously Dead) are plainly equivalent Expressions. Now, if the *Apostle* had said, *that, by the Spirit, Christ preach'd to those that are in the State of the Dead,* every one would have said, the *Apostle* is his own Interpreter, he meaneth nothing but what himself saith in the compass of a few Verses (1 *Pet.* 4. 6.) *that the Gospel was preach'd to the Dead;* therefore, when the *Apostle* saith, *that, by the Spirit, Christ preach'd to the Spirits in Prison,* every one ought to Interpret his Meaning, by what himself saith a few Verses after, *that the Gospel was preach'd, τοῖς νεκροῖς, to them that are in the State of the Dead. The Spirits in Prison,* in a literal Meaning, are *the Dead* in a literal Meaning; *the Spirits in Prison,* in a moral Meaning, are *the Dead* in a moral Meaning.

The *Heathen,* the Wicked, tho' they live the Animal, the Human, and Human-Social, Life; tho' they are alive unto Sin, and to their worldly and fleshly Interests and Concerns; tho' they are not without their happy Life, and are alive in their own Conceit; yet they are *dead* 1. *with respect to God and the Life of living to him.* Thus the Prodigal Son was dead to his Father, who gave him over for lost. And, as they are departed from God, and, therefore, are dead to him; so God is departed from them, upon which account also they are dead, as the Body is dead, when the Soul is departed. They are dead, as to the proper Life of the Soul, the diviner Part, the only truly valuable Life, Excellency and Happiness. 2. *The Wicked, in several Respects, resemble the Dead.* They are in a Spiritual and Atheous kind of *Darkness.* "*Weep for the Dead, for he hath lost the Light; and weep for the Fool, for he wanteth Understanding,*" *Eccles.* 22. II. They have a lively Sense of their secular Interests, but have *no perception* of those Things, which are truly Good, or Evil. An *holy vital Warmth and Fervour, Liveliness* and *Vigour* is extinct in them; in Matters of true Religion, Virtue and Piety, they are *torpid* and *inactive;* their Virtue and Religion is but the *Carcass* of good Works. They are *Vile, Worthless, Useless.* "*A living Dog is better than a dead Lyon.*" Degenerate Mankind, in this respect also, resemble the *Dead,* they are *impure* and *unclean.* 3. *They are surrounded by, and are subject to, those Evils, which are Death to the Soul, deadly Enemies, deadly Sins, deadly Sentence, and deadly Punishment.* The State of the Wicked is a *privation* of true Light, Life, Truth, Wisdom, Health, Beauty, Order, Beatitude, Liberty, Nobility, Vigour, Power, Ease, Rest, Peace, Serenity, Delight, Pleasures, Goodness, Worth, Usefulness, Innocence, Purity, the Divinity, and Beatitude of the Soul; and a *position* of all the contrary Evils. This is a State of *deadly criminal Evils;* for which reason they fall into a *deadly penal State,* a penal *privation* of Remission of Sins, Peace and Reconcilement, Grace and Favour, of divine Alliance and Acceptance, of Election and Adoption, of the Inheritance, of Freedom and Citizenship in the Kingdom of God; and a *position* of the contrary.

In our *Heathen* State, we were related to God as *Aliens* and *Enemies,* and, therefore, we could have no Rights in the holy City, nor to the holy Deity thereof. Nor was it possible, that God should look upon us as his Allies, Subjects, Servants, or Liege-People; but our Estate was that of Apostates from, Traytors and open Rebels against, our Sovereign Liege-Lord, which is a State of Death. If any of the *Heathen,* remaining such, might be saved, it must be by a Deity; but there is no Deity, whereby they can be saved, who are not the People of the true God. The true God, being the Deity of true Religion and Godliness, will certainly punish the Atheous and Ungodly. And, if it be by a Deity, that Mankind must be saved, then they must be sav'd by being truly Religious. Therefore both the *Popular* and *Philosophick-Pagans,* that acknowledg'd a future Happiness, foully mistook the Way thither; for they rely'd upon their *Mystick-Metaphysical Sanctity,* their *Teletae* and the *Hieratick* Way, their *Theurgick* Method of the Souls *Purgation, Liberation, Reduction;* they promis'd themselves a future Happiness, from an Initiation into their *Mystick-Religious Institutions,* their Heathen Piety, and Civil-Social Virtue, of which their Love of their Country was a principal Branch. But the *Virtue* of the *Heathens* is far from being *saving;* something of it is found in all Men, for all are in some sort, in some degree, Virtuous, Honest, Sincere; if, therefore, it was saving to any, all Men would be saved. The Religion of the *Heathen,* which should have been saving to them, was of a contrary Nature, constituting them A-Theists and Anti-Theists, the main Branches of it being so many mortal Sins. But from this *Hypothesis* (without which the necessity of *Christianity* is not maintainable, nor can the Grace of God towards us *Christianiz'd Gentiles* be duly illustrated without it) a terrible Conclusion will be inferr'd, *That all, who are in the Heathen State, are finally lost;* which seemeth to be a grand Difficulty in Providence, and they that think it so, if they be Wise and Religious, ought to be allow'd great Liberty of Thought, to *salve the Phaenomenon.* We will content ourselves to observe, that this Dispute, touching the *Heathens Salvation,* is partly concerning *Matter of Fact,* and partly concerning *Matter of Right.*

Of the Dispute touching the Salvation of the *Heathens*

If the Salvation of any be call'd in question as *Heathens,* the Matter of Fact ought to be debated in the first place, whether they were *Heathens* in this definitive Notion, *The Theists, that do not acknowledge the true*

God? Usually, they that plead for the Salvation of *Heathens,* make them *No-Heathens* in Religion and Morality, making them God's Religionists, and as good as *Christians,* and yet suppose, that they plead for the Salvation of *Heathens,* whereas they alter the Subject of the Question, and contradict themselves, as well as apparent Matter of Fact. But some, also, of great Learning and Piety, and not guilty of the Folly of *Christianizing* gross *Heathens,* yet have thought the Condition of some of the better sort of *Pagans* not desperate, but that their future Happiness is hopeful upon account of their *Heathen* Virtue; and some doubt not of the Happiness of all of them, who were sincere. Touching which Opinion, which carrieth a great shew of Charity and Goodness, I will only say; *That our Heathen State is certainly the state of Death; that all the better Sort of Pagans are saveable, if any be so; that mere Heathen Virtue is not available to Salvation; that the Pagans Sincerity is of no better quality, than the rest of their Virtues; that we are apt to have an extravagant Esteem for their Virtue, and every one hopeth well touching his particular Favourite;* but we are incapable of pronouncing any Thing touching their future Happiness, save only, *That, in respect of us and our Notices, their Condition is not at all hopeful;* yet, *not knowing,* what Transactions there may be between God and their Souls, who, in external appearance, dye gross *Heathens; not knowing,* whether Death rendreth every one's Condition, and particularly theirs who were never tried with the Gospel, as remediless and desperate, as it doth theirs, who have been tried with it, and frustrated that Remedy; *not knowing,* but that all Ages of the World, as well as that wherein the *Apostles* preach'd (*Act.* 18. 10.) have afforded many Souls prepar'd for *Christianity,* touching whom we may doubt, whether they will finally perish, or not; *not knowing,* what their Condemnation will amount to, who have been, in all Ages, invincibly Ignorant of *Christianity,* and are, therefore, unconcern'd in the Condemnation, which it denounceth against *Hypocrites* and *Unbelievers;* we ought not to be dogmatical in such abstruse Points, or pretend to fathom the Depths of Providence.

In order to reconcile the Dispute about the *Heathens* Salvation, as it is *Matter of Right,* so far as the different Opinions about it are reconcileable, it is to be consider'd, That all *true and genuine Theists* may be call'd *Christians* in a large sense, as being the *Christian*-kind of Theists and Religionists. In this large sense it must be acknowledg'd, that the Earth and Heavens, the Sun, Moon, and Stars, the Works of Nature, and of Providence, have always preach'd *Christianity* to the World of *Heathens;* that, from the Beginning of the World, *Christianity* hath been the only way to Righteousness and Salvation; for Mankind could never attain them otherwise, than by being *God's Believers and Religionists,* the Men of Faith, and Faithful Religionists, which is to be, in great degree, *Christ's Believers and Religionists,* and thus it may be express'd. *The way to Righteousness and Salvation, from the Beginning of the World, was, to be Christ's Believers and Religionists, so far as the being God's Believers and Religionists importeth.* If, therefore, the World of Mankind which was *Heathen,* had been God's Believers and Religionists, (such as the *Apostle* speaketh of, *Heb.* 11. 6.) they could not have fail'd of a State of Alliance and Favour, of Righteousness and Salvation, more, or less perfect; for God, in providing *Christ,* had made Provision, *that his Divine Believers should be in that Divine Condition.* And, as that Divine Condition, which Divine Believers, in the antient Times, enjoy'd, was founded upon *Christ;* so the coming of *Christ* was reveal'd to these Divine Believers, and they had Prophetick Notices of it. But those Prophetick Notices cannot be called the way to Remission of Sins and Salvation, they were not propos'd as the Condition of a Treaty, or Covenant, nor was the Knowledge of them requir'd of those, to whom they were not at all reveal'd; but different Obligations arise from different Revelations. The generality of Mankind in these elder Times of the World, antecedently to any Revelation of the Messias to them, were no farther oblig'd, to be God's Believers and Religionists, than according to natural Revelation. And, because they were not so far his Believers and Religionists, the *Apostle* looketh upon them as inexcusable, *Rom.* 1. 20. for nothing hindred them from being such, but their own Wickedness, wicked Unwillingness, or Averseness from Godliness, nor could they pretend any other Impotency but the *Moral Impotency,* which is not an Excuse, but an Aggravation. *"Else how shall God Judge the World?" Rom.* 3. 6. If the Existence of the one true God be fairly notic'd to all Mankind; if they do, or may easily, know, that his being God consisteth, in having the

Rights and Dues of his God-head, (as the being King consisteth in having his Rights and Dues, which to bereave him of, is a making him no King;) if they are oblig'd to be Virtuous, Good, Just, and Grateful; and cannot but know, that of Right, and by Obligation, they are his Liege-People, Subjects, and Servants: Mankind must necessarily be inexcusable, if they do not *serve and glorify him as God,* and, if they become not his Believers and Religionists, which is a relinquishing their *Heathenism.* The *Heathen* could not plead that they were so destitute of Means, that it was naturally impossible, for them to be God's Believers and Religionists, OF that their becoming such would be in vain; for his Parental Providence towards them demonstrated, that he had not abandon'd all Care and Concern for their Welfare. *Act.* 14. 16, 17. *"In times past he suffer'd all Nations to walk in their own Ways. Nevertheless he left not himself without witness,"* (a Testimony of his Care for their Welfare, and that he had not abandoned all Concern for it, altho' he suffer'd all Nations to walk in their own Ways,) *"in that he did Good, and gave us Rain from Heaven, and fruitful Seasons, filling our Hearts with Food and Gladness."* and 1 Tim. 9. 10. *"He is the Saviour of all Men,"* (taketh care of their Welfare,) *"especially of those that believe."* *Rom.* 2. 4. His Goodness and Patience, toward the World of Mankind, hath a mighty Tendency to their Repentance, and is design'd to induce them to it; which is an Assurance, that their Repentance, if not illegitimate, shall not be ineffectual; and, if God commandeth them the Practice of the Duties of Religion in order to that End, that so they may obtain a future Happiness, they are bound to believe, that such Practice will not be in vain. *Act.* 17. 26, 27. *"They are planted on the Face of the Earth, that they should seek the Lord, if happily they might feel after him and find him."* Which demonstrateth God's Will and Intention to be found of them, if they did faithfully seek him, and his Willingness to be a God to them: Nor is it possible, that God should disown and damn any, that is a faithful Religionist towards him; *"But in every Nation he that feareth him and worketh Righteousness, is accepted with him."* (Act. 10. 35.) *"Glory, Honour, and Peace to every Man that worketh Good, to the* Jew *first, and also to the* Gentile." *Rom.* 2. 10. That is such *Gentiles,* as *Melchizedeck, Job,* the *Ninevites* and *Cornelius.* Touching the Salvation of the *Heathens,* and the Method of obtaining it, I will only add a wise and good Saying of a Divine of our own. *"If any amongst* Heathens *had done what he could, in seeking and serving God, he should either for Christ's Sake have been accepted with that little Knowledge he could attain; or else, as* Calvin *saith in his Comment on* Acts 8. 13. *Rather than he should have perish'd, God would have sent an Angel to reveal further Things to him."*[307]

In our *Heathen* State we were Subjects of *Satan*'s Kingdom.

A principal Branch of the Deadliness of our *Heathen* State, is, *our being the Subjects of* Satan's *Kingdom;* which implieth, that the *Heathen* World of Mankind were under the Imperial Rule and Domination of *Satan,* (several ways the Subjects of the Kingdom of Darkness,) constituting his Mundan Empire. His usual Names denote him an Imperial Potentate; for he is styled *"the God of this World, the Prince of this World."* Himself and his Angels are called ἀρχαὶ καὶ 'δξουσίαι, which Names denote them, *Principalities and Powers of a mundan Empire,* κοσμοκράτορες *the Rulers of this World.* Being fallen from Heaven, their Residence is now in the Air, where they constitute amongst themselves a Kingdom, or Empire, consisting of lower and higher Orders, some being of inferior, and others of superior, Rank and Condition; but all of them subjected to, and united in, one Imperial Head, their great Lord and Master, *"the Prince of Devils, the Prince of the Power"* (or Powers) *"of the Air."* The Wisdom and Justice of Providence, by banishing them out of Heaven, hath placed them in the Air, in a Region of Vicinity to, and a Station of Superiority above, Mankind; and, accordingly, maketh use of them, to do the work of *Publick Officers,* in the Polity of our System. But this Power, which the Evil Demons exercise over Mankind, (by divine *Concession,* by a probational, or penal Tradition of Men into their Hands, and sometimes by divine Mandate and Appointment,) is rather *Ministerial* than *Imperial.* 2 *Chron.* 18. 20, 21. *Job* 1. 12. and 2. 6. *Psal.* 78. 49. *Matt.* 5. 25. and 18. 34. *Luk.* 22. 31. 1 *Cor.* 5. 5. and 10. 10. 1 *Tim.* 1. 20. *Rev.* 12. 10. Besides this Power of mere *Officers* and *Executioners,* they have acquir'd a Power of Empire and Sovereignty over Mankind; which Power is, morally speaking, in great degree unavoidable, supposing their evil Neighbourhood to degenerate Mankind. For,

307. Truman, *A Discourse of Natural and Moral Impotency* (1675), p. 113.

as these Aerial Powers are, in Place and Station, superior to Mankind; so their Spiritual Nature, Angelical Order, Policy, and Strength, is superior to the Human; (spiritual unbody'd Wickedness is paramount to weak Flesh and Blood, *Ephes.* 6. 12. they are also vastly numerous and closely united amongst themselves, which addeth to their Power; and, therefore, if not confin'd by a higher Power, they can domineer and lord it over Mankind; and, doubtless, they want not Will to do it, seeing Empire and Dominion is their great Interest, Design, and Business; Strength with them is the Law of Justice, and, therefore, as amongst the Brute-Animals, the Stronger beareth Rule over the Weaker, so the Stronger Wicked Angels will have the Mastery, and bear Rule, over the Weaker Wicked Men. They are, also, the most accomplish'd Tempters imaginable, and have the greatest Advantages to make Men Wicked, (of themselves prevalently prone to be Wicked;) for they are not wanting in depth of Malice, in great intellectual Abilities, in knowledge of us and our Affairs, in large Experience, Cunning, and Dexterity, Activity and assiduous Diligence, Hypocrisy, Imposture, Closeness, and Secrecy, in variety of Methods and Artifices; they are furnish'd with all sorts of Agents and Instruments, assisted with the World's tempting Objects, and with the many and great Weaknesses and vicious Inclinations of Man's Nature; in their Temptations they are mighty in Operation, (*"working efficaciously, with strong Delusions, carrying Captive,"* Ephes. 2. 2. 2 Thess. 2. 11. 2 Tim. 3. 26.) sometimes acting the Fox, and sometimes the roaring Lion, sometimes the old Serpent, and sometimes the bloody red Dragon; upon all which accounts, what can be reasonably imagin'd, but that they will inveigle and vanquish the World of Mankind, and subject them to live under their Domination? As the Holy Ghost saith, *Rev.* 12. 9. *"The old Serpent, called the Devil and Satan, deceiveth the whole World."* The *Heathen* World, therefore, must be considered, *as Satan's mundan Empire,* which he reigneth over as an *Imperial Potentate,* and which was subject to his Rule and Domination; whence it is plain, that his magnificent Pretension to our Saviour, was not altogether groundless, or devoid of Truth, *"That the Kingdoms of the World, the Power and Glory of them was his, and at his disposal."* Luke 4. 5, 6. The Devil and his Angels are styled, *Ephes.* 6. 12. *"The Rulers of the Darkness of this World,"* to signify, that they are the Rulers of that Darkness which *Heathenism* is, and, consequently, of the dark benighted *Heathen* World. Agreeably whereunto, the Doctor of the *Gentiles* is sent to them upon this Errand, *"to open their Eyes, and to turn them from Darkness to Light, and from the Power of Satan unto God,"* Act. 26. 18. So the Converts to *Christianity,* that were translated into the Kingdom of God's Son, are said to *"be deliver'd from the Power of Darkness,"* to which they were Subject, *Col.* 1. 13. But this subjection to the *Power of Darkness,* is not to be con-fin'd to *Heathens,* commonly so called, it is the common Condition of Mankind in general, antecedently to the State and Life of true and saving Religion, as will appear from an Enumeration of the several Ways, whereby Mankind are subject to *Satan's* Kingdom and Domination, which are these *three.* 1. *By way of Penal Subjection.* 2. *By way of criminal Subjection.* 3. *By way of criminal-religious Subjection.*

1. All Mankind, antecedently to their being in a State of true Religion, belong to *Satan's* Kingdom, and are under his Domination, *by way of Penal Subjection.* For the *Apostle, Hebr.* 2. 14. expressly attributeth to the Devil, the Power, or Empire of Death (τὸ κράτος) as his Empire. Which is an Empire agreeable to his name *Apollyon,* and to those Names which the *Jews* give him, *the Destroyer, the Angel of Death.* This Empire of Death, which the *Apostle* attributeth to the Devil, *Christ died to destroy,* therefore it must not be understood of temporal Calamities, and bodily Death only: But, principally, of the penal Death of the Soul, which is Death everlasting. And, because he had this Branch of his Imperial Power by the *Law,* therefore a principal Branch of his Empire was not by mere Usurpation, but by a legal Settlement of the penal State of Death upon unrepenting Sinners, by which he had an Authority to de-tain them under his Power after Death; and even in their Life-time, so long as they continued ungodly Sinners, and, if God, in *Christ,* had not made Provision for their Freedom: This being the State of Death, *to belong to his Kingdom, and to be under his Domination and Power.* If, without being freed by the Redemption of *Christ,* Mankind would have remain'd in the State of Death, then, without this Redemption, they would have remain'd under *Satan's* Domination and Power by Law. So far as *Christ* hath redeem'd them from being in the State of Death, so

far he hath redeem'd them from being under *Satan's* Domination and Power by Law, either in this Life, or after their Death. From which plain and intelligible Explication of a principal Branch of the State of Death, the *Collect* for Easter-Day in the *Common-Prayer-Book*, becometh plain and intelligible: *Almighty God, who, through thine only-begotten Son Jesus Christ, hast overcome Death, and open'd unto us the Gate of everlasting Life.* The *Apostles* Account of *Christ's* Victory upon the Cross, becometh easy and intelligible, which otherwise is unintelligible, *Col.* 2. 15. *"Having spoil'd Principalities and Powers, he made a shew of them openly, triumphing over them in it."*

Not only the Souls of Men, but their Bodies also, are penally subjected to *Satan's* Domination and Power, as appeareth from unquestionable Instances of *diabolical Possessions and Infestations of the Body,* which have great Analogy and Agreement with Temptations of the Soul. For, as all Temptations are not from the Devil; so Bodily Diseases ordinarily are from Natural Causes. The Evil Demons are of various Kinds, adapted to various Imployments, and as their Temptations are various, so are the Impressions which they make, and the Diseases which they produce in a Human Body. As some, by their Wickedness of Nature, tempt the Tempter, invite and draw wicked Spirits to associate with them: So some are of such a Disposition of Mind and Body, that Evil Demons as naturally enter into and inhabit them, as in Pestilential times, People, that are pre-dispos'd, catch the Contagion. Sometimes it is not discernible, whether a Temptation, be merely Natural, or in part Diabolical: So, in some Cases, it is not by us discernible, whether a Disease of Mind and Body be merely Natural, or in part Diabolical; and, therefore, Diabolical Possession and Infestation is a matter liable, both to wilful Imposture and innocent Mistake. But, as some Temptations are manifestly *Satan's* Suggestions, and have the Marks and Characters of a Diabolical Original: So, in some that are Distemper'd in Mind and Body, there are evident Marks and Characters of a Diabolical Original and Infestation; as when they tell People their Secrets, discover such Things done at a distance, and Things to come, as are beyond human reach; or when they are oppress'd, afflicted, abus'd, in measure and manner beyond the reach of Natural Causes; or when from the Nature,

Symptoms, Causes, and Circumstances of a Distemper, it plainly appears to be nothing better than a Diabolical Possession and Infestation. By these Indications *Demoniacks* and Persons acted by an evil Spirit, are discernible by us, who have no extraordinary Faculty of discerning them. Ignorance, Atheism, Fanaticism, and Witchcraft (with other Vices and Diseases) abound much more in some times than others; so do Diabolical Possessions and Infestations, which Providence might permit to abound about our Saviour's Time, to give occasion for his glorious Miracles. If they had not abounded in those Times, it is not reasonable to believe, that they would have abounded then so much in the Trade of Exorcists, and that the *Jews* should generally have entertain'd this Opinion, that their more grievous Diseases were from the Operation of evil Demons or complicated with them. *"Indeed in this Distemper"* (the Epilepsy) *"there appear so obscure Footsteps, or rather none at all, of a morbifick Matter, that we may deservedly suspect here the Afflatus of a maleficent Spirit."*[308] The much greater part and most eminent sort of Demoniacks, which our Saviour had to do with, (tho' not the only,) were *Epileptical, Melancholical, Lunatic,* and *Maniacal* Persons, (as appeareth from the Gospel,) whose horrible Distempers were either originally caus'd by, or complicated with, evil Demons. He gave a Demonstration, both of his Divine Goodness and Power in giving them relief from their hideous Calamities, rescuing them from under the Domination and Power of those infernal Spirits, and therefore the *Apostles* celebrate him for this God-like Atchievement. *Act.* 10. 38. *"He went about doing Good, and healing all that were oppress'd of the Devil."* His Disciples experimented the Divinity of his Power, and that his Empire was superior to the Diabolical; and, therefore, after he had sent them abroad, they return'd to him with Exultation and Triumph, *Luk.* 10. 17. *"Lord, even the Devils are subject to us thro' thy Name."*

2. All Mankind, antecedently to their being in a State of true Religion, belong to *Satan's* Kingdom, and are under his Domination and Rule, *by way of criminal Subjection.* The Devil's usual Name, *"the Wicked and Evil One,"* (*Matth.* 13. 19. 1 *John* 2. 13.) denoteth him the Prince of all

---

308. Willis, *Pathologiae Cerebri et Nervosi Generis Specimen* (1667), ch. 2.

Wicked and Evil Ones; he the Leader, and they the Followers, *"that are turn'd aside after Satan,"* Tim. 5. 15. He ruleth them in making them Atheous and Wicked; and, when they become such, their Life is an obeying, pleasing him, doing him Service, and *"his Servants they are, to whom they obey."* His Rule and Empire, therefore, is commensurate to the Reign of Sin. They walk *"according to the Prince of the Power of the Air,"* which Prince and Power taken collectively are *"a Spirit mightily operative in the Sons of Disobedience,"* by way of Inspiration, *Afflatus,* internal Motion, Persuasion and Suggestion, *Eph.* 2. 2, 3. They are animated by the Agency of that *great one that is in the World,* 1 *John* 4. 4. who influences them, not only by tempting Objects, and external Means, but by internal Operation, *"blinding the Mind, putting into the Heart, filling the Heart"* (2 *Cor.* 4. 4. *John* 13. 2. *Act.* 5. 3.) Like a mighty *Pharaoh* he commandeth them, and putteth upon them the vilest Practices, the basest and most painful Drudgeries, and they serve and obey, not considering what a Master they serve, usually designing only to serve their own Lusts, in the Fury whereof he hurrieth them like the Swine to Perdition. He is *the Father of their Family,* they are a *Serpentine* Brood and Race,[309] and *Devils incarnate;* agreeably to which our Saviour saith of a Miscreant among his Disciples, *"Have not I chosen you twelve, and one of you is a Devil?" Joh.* 6. 70. such is a *Son of Belial* (for *Belial* is one of *Satan's* Names, 2 *Cor.* 6. 15.) and such are *the Children of the Wicked One* in various degrees, and all that belong to the Synagogue of *Satan,* who are necessarily under his Domination, *by way of criminal Subjection.*

3. Almost the whole World of Mankind were sometime under *Satan's* Domination and Power by way of *criminal-religious Subjection,* as being the Religionists of his Institution, and his religious Worshippers. One sort of these Diabolical Religionists are *Witches* and *Magicians,* whose Existence has been so well attested by Experience and by Persons of unquestionable Learning and Veracity, so acknowledg'd by *Heathens,* by all wise Laws and Governments, and by the Holy Scriptures, is of Theory so unexceptionably Rational, and the Objections against it so inconsiderable, that, notwithstanding the many Impostures and false Stories of

309. Matthew 3.7, 12.38, 23.33; John 8.44; I John 3.8, 10.

this kind, he that would reject them all, must be a *superlative Believer.* Another Instance of Diabolical Religionists are the *Heretical-Pagan-Gnosticks,* that infested the Primitive Church, who invented a Theology and Religion, which was a mixture of *Magick* and *Demonolatry;* upon which account, some part of them were called *Ophitae, Serpent-Worshippers,* others *Sataniani, Satan's Religionists;* which is the heavy Character of the whole World of *Heathen* Religionists, as appeareth from the Historical Accounts of *Heathen* Countries, from their Theology and Religion, from the Nature of *Christianity,* and the Sense of all *Christians,* and from this Testimony of the Holy Scripture, which is also the Acknowledgment of several learn'd *Pagans, That what the Gentiles and Gentilizing Israelites sacrific'd, they sacrific'd to Devils, not to God.*[310] The *Christians* usually call'd their Doctrines, *Doctrines of Devils;* their Altars, *the Devil's Altars;* their Priests, *the Devil's Priests;* their Religion, *the Devil's Institution;* their Inspirations, Afflatus's, and Methods of Divination, *Diabolical;* their Sacrifices, *the Delight of Devils;* their Gods, *unclean Demons.* Agreeably whereto, the Renunciation of *Heathenism* at *Christian* Baptism was compos'd. The *Apostle* opposeth *"the Cup and Table of the Lord to the Cup and Table of Devils,"* in the *Heathen* Idol-Feasts, 1 *Cor.* 10. 21. So the *Heathen-Roman* Empire is said to be *"subjected to Satan the Chieftain, and to his Angels the Demons, by way of Religious Subjection";*[311] by the Holy Ghost it is represented as a *Demonarchy,* (Satan and his Angels were in reigning Condition, whilst *Paganism* flourish'd, but *Christianity* threw them down, *Revel.* 12. 8.) And all that Empire's Idol-worship is styled *the Worship of Devils, Revel.* 9. 20. *Christianity* therefore supposeth, that the World of *Heathens,* thro' their own Weakness and Wickedness, and the Artifices of *Satan* (Visions, Prodigies, Oracles, Vaticinations, Healings, and moving the Images) were seduc'd into an Opinion, that the Evil Demons were Gods, that they prostituted their Souls to be corrupted by them, were enslav'd by them, and subjected to their Domination and Power, as the Religionists of *Satan,* who had at *Rome,* and in other Places, as it were, his Imperial

310. Leviticus, 17.7; Deuteronomy 32.17; Psalms 136.37; I Corinthians 10.20.
311. Mede, *Clavis Apocalyptica ex Innatis et Institis Visionem* (1627), to ch. 6.11.

Seat and Throne, *Rev.* 2. 13 and 13. 2. They invited these Evil Demons to be the Inmates and Inhabitants of their Souls; these they deputed to be the Guardians of their Life; to these they attributed a mundane Presidency, pay'd divine Honours and a Religious Subjection, managing both their Civil and Religious Affairs by their Conduct. The learn'd Writers of the *Gentiles* do not only inform us, That they worshipp'd *Arimanius, Cacodaemones, Vejoves,* whom they knew to be evil Spirits; but some of their learn'd Theologers were of Opinion, that a considerable part of their Religion was the Religion of Evil Demons, whom the generality of *Pagans* ignorantly worshipp'd.[312] *Porphyry* discourseth at large of Evil Demons, of their Religious Worship amongst the *Pagans,* and of their Delight in bloody Sacrifices.[313] *Plutarch* discourseth, that the Order of Demons is obnoxious to Passions and brutal Affections, which are Properties, *"of which there are Footsteps and Marks in their Sacrifices and Mysteries."*[314] And, having enumerated several Rites of their Religion, *"the tearing and devouring raw Flesh, and other Discerptions, Howlings, obscene Speeches in their Sacra, Madnesses excited with noise and tossing of the Neck,"* he saith of them, *"They are not the Worship of any of the Gods, but are instituted to sweeten and appease Evil Demons."*[315] These Acknowledgments of learned *Heathens* are great approaches to the *Christian Hypothesis,* that the *Heathen* World were *Satan's* Religionists, of the Truth whereof we have so many authentick Proofs.

This, therefore, seems to have been the State of the *Heathen* World. *Abraham* was educated in Idolatry, as appears from *Jos.* 24. 2. When *Abraham* was call'd out of *Ur* of the *Chaldeas,* the only Country, in which we have any account that the true Religion was profess'd, was *Salem,* afterwards call'd *Jerusalem,* of which *Melchizedek* was King and also Priest of the most high God.[316] *Job* also and his Friends worshipp'd

The great usefulness of Revelation is evident from the foregoing Consideration of the State of the Heathen *World.*

---

312. Grotius, *De Veritate Religionis Christianae,* IV.3; Windet, *De Vita Functorum Statu,* sect. 3.

313. Porphyry, *De Abstinentia,* II.42, 43.

314. Plutarch, *De Defectu Oraculorum* (in *Moralia*), p. 417.

315. Ibid.

316. [Maxwell] "It seems no improbable Conjecture, that *Melchizedek* was *Shem,* who was Contemporary with *Abraham* for 151 Years, and liv'd 66 Years after the

the one true God; which appears likewise to have been the legal Establishment in the Country where he liv'd; for, speaking of worshipping the Sun and Moon, which he disclaims the ever having been guilty of, he says, *"That were an Iniquity to be punish'd by the Judges,"* Job 31. 28. It seems also pretty plain, from another Passage (*Job* 23. 11, 12.) that *Job* had something more than the mere Light of Nature to walk by, and that he was no Stranger to supernatural Revelation; for he saith there of himself, *"My Foot hath held his Steps, his Way have I kept, and not declin'd, neither have I gone back from the Commandments of his Lips; I have esteem'd the Words of his Mouth more than my necessary Food."* Which Words some will have to be meant of the Light and Law of Nature, merely as such, which seems an extremely absurd Construction of the Place, which is plainly meant of some Law or Doctrine, that was God's Word by his Prophets, of which Number *Job* himself seems to have been One. He must also have been no Stranger to the 7 Precepts of the Sons of *Noah,* as they are called, and to the Revelations made by God to *Abraham,* if that Opinion be true, which is generally embrac'd by the most learn'd and judicious Commentators, that *Job* was a descendent of *Abraham,* probably an *Edomite,* the Land of *Uz* being part of *Idumea;*

Congress of *Melchizedek* with *Abraham,* according to Ussher's Chronology. Now it is highly probable, that *Shem* persever'd in the true Religion, having had so great Opportunities of knowing the State of the World and Mankind from the Beginning, and the two most exemplary Punishments that ever had been inflicted by God on Man for Sin, in the Fall of Man and in the Flood; for *Methusalem,* who was born 243 Years before the Death of *Adam,* did not die 'till *Shem* was 98 Years old; and he himself was a Witness of the Flood. Accordingly we find his Piety particularly taken notice of, and that he was the most highly favour'd by God among the Sons of *Noah.* It is also highly probable, that he liv'd as a Prince among such of his Posterity as were willing to persevere in the Worship of the true God; which seems perfectly to tally with the Account we have of *Melchizedek,* who was King of *Salem,* and Priest of the most high God; and it is reasonable to believe, that his Subjects profess'd the same Religion with himself, and, consequently, that the true Religion was the legal Establishment in *Salem.* The greatest Difficulty that seems to offer in supposing *Shem* to be *Melchizedek,* is, his settling in the midst of *Canaan*'s Posterity. As for the Difference of the Names, it is easily accounted for, the H. Ghost seeming designedly to have conceal'd his Parents, Birth and Death, that he might be the more remarkable Type of the Messiah. See *Heb.* 7. 3."

and that he liv'd before the giving of the Law to *Moses*. But the first Mention we find made of the Religion of the Inhabitants of *Jerusalem*, after the Children of *Israel's* coming into the Land of *Canaan*, is that they were Idolaters; as were also the Children of *Edom*, where we first find their Religion mention'd, after the *Israelites* began to have any Intercourse with them; which was also the Case of all the other Nations descended of *Abraham*, and of the several People inhabiting *Arabia* and *Canaan*. So that, when God gave his Laws to the *Israelites*, we know not of any one Nation in the World, where the Worship of the one true God was profess'd, the *Israelites* excepted. As for *Zoroastres*, who set up the Worship of the one true God in *Persia*, that was not 'till the Days of *Darius Hystaspes*, after the *Babylonian* Captivity: And that *Zoroastres* learn'd that Truth from the *Jews*, has been render'd highly probable by several who have treated of that Subject.

It appears from what hath been said, that the *Heathens* look'd upon the whole Universe of Rational Agents, consisting of Gods, Demons, (Good and Bad), Heroes, and Men, as but one Political System; and that the current Doctrine of the best Sects among them, was Polytheism and the Worship of Demons. These their Practices were in great measure owing to their believing *God* to be *the Soul of the World*, which prevail'd universally among the better sort of them; for they could never think it a Crime to worship what they thought Parts of the Deity. From this Opinion of God's being the Soul of the World, even *Socrates* himself was not free, and some modern Deists have endeavour'd to revive it.

From what has been said it appears, that the *Heathens* were universally ignorant of the one true God, who was an *unknown God* at *Athens*. The best Sects of their Philosophers, as they were Ignorant of many important Truths, so they taught many gross Errors, as well with respect to Religion, as Morality; so that it may justly be question'd, whether the *Heathen* Philosophers, in the Main, were of any real Service to the Cause of Religion and Virtue. The Bulk of Mankind have been always very careless and inconsiderate, so as not to be at the Pains of discovering those important Truths, which they might have discover'd by the Light of Nature; and from the same Causes they were not sufficiently influenc'd by those Truths, which they did come to the Knowledge of, the strong Impressions of sensual and present Objects greatly weakening or destroying the Force of more remote ones, tho' of much greater Consequence. The Prejudices of Education, as it were imbib'd with their Mother's Milk, were also so great and so many, and the perverse Customs and Opinions of those about them influenc'd them so strongly, as greatly to obscure and give a wrong Biass to that Natural Reason, which, if it had been left to itself, would have made a much greater and clearer Discovery of the Law of Nature. The Affairs of the World, the Pursuits of Ambition, the Baits of Pleasure, and the Desire of Riches, employ so much of Mens Thoughts and Time, that they cannot attend to the still and calm Voice of Reason, which is seldom heard in so tempestuous a Sea. And when once, by such means as these, evil Habits had taken deep Root in the Minds of Men, to which by an innate Concupiscence, they had a prevalent Tendency, *their Foolish Heart became darken'd,* and *they were given up to a reprobate Mind,* by which the Light of Nature was, in great measure, extinguish'd, *the Blindness of their Hearts darkening their Understandings,* and blunting the Stings of Conscience. Amidst so great Corruptions, arising from such Causes, both within and without, which had, to so great a Degree as we have seen, benighted the *Heathen* World, what Wonder is it, if those few *Heathen* Philosophers, who gave themselves up to search after Truth, and to practice the Truths they discover'd, made so small a Progress as we find they did, in reforming so degenerate and corrupt a World? Polytheism, Demonolatry, and Idolatry, we have seen how universally they prevailed; and that, with respect to the one true God, the whole *Heathen* World lay in a State of Atheous Ignorance, not excepting even the greatest of the Philosophers themselves, who were also defective, with respect to many of the Branches of Morality, as hath likewise been shewn. Of Justice, indeed, as it is a Virtue necessary to the support of Civil Society, they seem to have had very just Notions; but such Justice is only a Political, not a truly Religious Virtue, a mere Civil Institution. From what hath been said, I think it plainly appears, that all their Virtues were of the spurious and illegitimate Kind; and that for want of the true and solid Foundation of all Virtue and all Religion, *The Knowledge of the true God and his Attributes.*

Most of those who call'd themselves Philosophers, were never in ear-

nest in their pretended Researches after Virtue; they made it matter of
mere Ostentation, and to shew their Parts, and an Affair of as great Indifference, as Problems in Mathematicks, or Natural Philosophy; thinking it sufficient, if they could but amuse the Vulgar, and dispute learn-
edly about it; and accordingly in by far the greatest Number of those
who affected to distinguish themselves by that glorious Title, it reach'd
no farther than the Head, not to the Heart, as is plain from the profligate
Manners of many of them from the Accounts of their Contemporaries.
And how should Mankind be reform'd by such Instructors? They who
were influenc'd by the Truth they taught appear, upon Examination, to
be much fewer than is generally imagin'd. And even those very few, we
have seen that they grossly err'd in most important Points, as well with
respect to God, as the Cause and Cure of the present corrupt Condition
of Mankind, and the End for which our great Creator intended us. No
less Men among them than *Plato, Cicero,* and *Epictetus* advise Men to
comply, each with the establish'd Religion of his Country; but was that
the way to enlighten and reform a benighted and idolatrous World? The
Wisest of them have profess'd their Ignorance, how the Deity was to be
worshipp'd, and how those who had done amiss were to be reconcil'd
to him; of which *Plato* represents *Socrates* so sensible, as to introduce
him in one of his Dialogues, declaring his Ignorance upon these Heads,
and wishing for the Guidance of a Divine Revelation in such Matters,
for which our wiser modern Deists think there was no occasion. Those
also among the *Heathen* Philosophers, who have upon some occasions
argued the most strenuously for the Soul's Immortality, sometimes express themselves doubtfully upon the Matter. 'Tis the *Christian* Religion
only, which hath clearly *brought Life and Immortality to Light.* The refin'd Reasonings and long Deductions of acute and speculative Philosophers upon this and other important Points, the Attributes of God,
and the Obligations to Virtue, were too fine-spun, and required too long
and close an Application, to influence the generality of Mankind. None
of them was able to form any thing like a tolerable Scheme with respect
to Providence, the Forming and the Governing the World, the Dignity
and the Corruption of human Nature, whence the Obligation to Virtue
originally arises, and to what it ultimately tends, and the happy Im-

mortality of the Righteous. All of them were Ignorant of some of these
Truths, and the imperfect Truth they did discover, lies so scatered and
blended with Error, that the greatest Genius among them was never able
to collect them into one Body; and there is so strict a Dependence of
one of these Truths upon another, that it is like breaking a Link in a
Chain, or taking a Corner-Stone from the Foundation of a Building, to
separate one of them from the rest; so close is their Connexion. What
is more; whilst the Hearers of the Philosophers consider'd that these
Instructors were but Men like themselves, the Truths they were able to
discover and support by plain Reason, were able to make but a weak
Impression upon them, for want of sufficient Weight, and because they
were not enforc'd by a Divine Authority. It awakens and rouses the Attention and Consideration of Men at another sort of a rate, not only to
have it laid before them, that such a Practice is agreeable to the Dictates
of Right Reason, that it is Beautiful, Honourable, and Decorous, that
we ought to do it, and that such Advantages will naturally and necessarily
attend it; but also to have it clearly made out to 'em, that it is moreover
the Will and positive Command of the Creator and supreme Governor
of the World, to whom they owe what they are and what they have, and
at whose hands they expect all they hope for; which makes a much deeper
Impression upon them, than barely to have the fitness of the Practice
propos'd to 'em, without the Interposition of the Authority of a competent Legislator, to whom they are under the greatest Obligations in
point of Gratitude, and who will certainly vindicate the Honour of his
Laws.

After all these Considerations, let any impartial Man judge, whether
a Revelation was useful or necessary for the Reformation of Mankind.
No, says the modern Deist; for the Light and Law of Nature, Natural
Religion, and Morality are sufficient, as they have been laid down by
Plato, Aristotle, Cicero, Epictetus, M. Antoninus, and others among the
Antients; by *Grotius, Puffendorf, Crellius, Sharrock, Wilkins, Cumberland,
Clark, Wollaston,* and others among the Moderns. In answer to this, I
desire that it may be observ'd, That there is a great Difference between
mere natural Reason, and Reason assisted by Revelation, and supernat-
ural Help. Our Reason assents to many Things, when propos'd to us,

which it could never have found out. The greatest Genius's among the *Heathen* Philosophers, seem to have been extremely sensible of the Weakness, the Short-sightedness, and the Uncertainty of their Reasonings about most important Truths. Let us hear what they themselves say upon the Point, *"Nature gives many Indications of her Will; but we"* (saith *Cicero*[317]) *"are deaf, I know not how, nor hear her Voice." "Nature hath afforded us some small Sparks, which we so quickly extinguish by evil Habits and false Opinions, that the Light of Nature no where appears."*[318] *"We seem not only blind with respect to Wisdom, but dull and stupid with respect to those very Things, which in some measure we seem to see."*[319] *"Our Minds"* (saith *Aristotle*) *"with respect to those Things which are naturally the most plain of all, are like the Eyes of Bats in Day-light."*[320] *"Truly"* (saith *Cicero*) *"the so great Dissention of the most learned Men in an Affair of the utmost Importance* [the Nature of the Gods] *will stagger even those, who before thought that they had arriv'd at Certainty in the Point."* And *"I wish"* (saith *Cicero* in the same Discourse) *"that I could as easily find out the Truth, as confute Error."*[321] Even *Socrates* express'd himself with doubt concerning a Future State, tho' he seem'd strongly to incline to the Belief of it, and tho' he brought the best Arguments in support of it, as they are represented to us by *Plato,* that we meet with offered by any *Heathen* Philosopher. *Cicero,* in his *Tusculan Questions,* is still more doubtful upon that Head, tho' inclining to the same side with *Socrates. Seneca* look'd upon it as a point more desirable, than probable.[322] *"If* (says *Cicero*[323]) *in the Opinion of all Philosophers, no-one has attain'd Wisdom, we, for whose welfare you pretend the Immortal Gods have made the best Provision, are in a most wretched State; for, as there is no material Difference, whether no Man* does *enjoy his Health, or no Man* can *enjoy it; so I do not see that it is of any consequence, whether no Man* is *or* can *be made wise."* What

---

317. Cicero, *De Amicitia.*
318. Cicero, *Tusculan Disputations,* III.
319. Lactantius, *Divinarum Institutionum,* III.
320. Aristotle, *Metaphysics,* II.1.
321. Cicero, *De Natura Deorum,* I.
322. Seneca, *Epistulae Morales,* CII.
323. Cicero, *De Natura Deorum,* III.

wonder then is it, if the best and wisest of the Philosophers, thus sensible
of their own Ignorance, and of the Weakness of human Reason, with
respect to matters of the utmost Importance, (such as the Nature of the
Deity, how he would be worshipp'd, and a future State; as also the Original of Evil, and of the present corrupt Condition of Mankind, of which
they were as sensible, as they were ignorant of the Cause,) should be
sensible of the Want of a Divine Revelation, and earnestly long for it,
as has been already mention'd? Now, whoever would go about rationally
to make a comparative Judgment of *assisted* and *unassisted* Reason, let
him compare the Schemes of *Natural Religion* and of *Morality*, left us
by the *Heathens*, with those which have been publish'd by *Christians*.
Plato, Aristotle, Cicero, Plutarch, Epictetus, and *M. Antoninus*, are clearly
the greatest *Heathen* Writers upon these Subjects. How defective these
are all, I have already, in great measure, laid before the Reader, some of
them making no more of *Virtue* and of *Religion*, than mere *Civil* and
Political Institutions; all of them conforming to the Idolatrous Establishments of their several Countries, and advising others to do the like;
Polytheism and the Worship of Demons being essential Parts of the
Platonick and *Stoick* Theology, as Magick and the Worship of Demons
were of the *Pythagorean;* and yet these have been reputed the best Sects,
and to have produc'd the greatest Moral Philosophers, which *Heathen*
Antiquity could boast of. I have already observ'd, that what Truths lay
scatter'd among them, no-one of them had discernment enough to separate from the Errors, tho' that be a point which that great Genius, *Cicero,*
seems particularly to have labour'd. Now any one with half an Eye may
see, how much the Systems of Natural Religion and of Morality, deliver'd by the above-mention'd *Christian* Writers and others, exceed
those of the foregoing *Heathen* Philosophers, some of whom seem to
have been greater Genius's than any of those *Christian* Writers I have
now mention'd. To what then must the Advantage of the *Christian*
Writers upon these Subjects over the *Heathen* Philosophers be owing?
To the Assistance of Revelation certainly, which has evidently improv'd
our Notices, even of Natural Religion and Morality, as from what I have
already advanc'd, but much more by comparing the above-mention'd
two Sets of Writers, will abundantly appear. Therefore, when modern
Deists, in order to prove, that there was no Necessity or even Usefulness

of a Revelation, alledge, that Natural Religion and Morality are sufficient, let them confine themselves to any Scheme they please among the
Heathen Philosophers, among whom the latest seem plainly to have
much improv'd from Hints they had from the *Christian* Religion, to
which they were no Strangers. When once we become assur'd of the
Truth of any Doctrine, tho' merely from Testimony, it naturally puts us
upon the Inquiry, to find out Arguments from Reason, in order to prove
that Doctrine; and in such a way, and by such means, it is evident, that
the great Truths of Natural Religion, and the Fundamentals of Morality,
have been more throughly discover'd, and establishd upon better Principles, than was ever perform'd by the greatest Genius's of the *Heathen*
World, tho' they were in themselves, perhaps, the greatest the World ever
produc'd. If there had never been any Revelation, with what Vanity can
any of our Modern Deists pretend, that *they* would have had better Notions of Religion, of God, and of Morality, than *Plato, Aristotle, Cicero,*
&c.? And in how many important Points, with respect to these, were
they ignorant, and of how many more were *they* very doubtful? Nay, I
will venture to go one step farther, and to affirm, that I think it highly
probable, That our Inquiries, into the very Frame of Nature and the
Material System of the World, would not have been so successful as they
have been, were it not for the Hints we have receiv'd from a Divine
Revelation, and more particularly this, *That the World is the Creature of
God;* which is a most important Truth, that the *Heathen* Philosophers
were not very well acquainted with; of which as great a Philosophical
Genius, and as successful an Inquirer into Nature, as this Age and Nation, or, perhaps, any other, has produc'd, has made no inconsiderable
Use. All our Knowledge of Natural Religion and Morality, is ultimately
resolv'd into our Knowledge of the Frame of Nature; as our Belief of
Reveal'd Religion is founded upon the pre-suppos'd Truth of that which
is Natural. *"He that cometh to God, must first believe, that he is, and that
he is a Rewarder of them that diligently seek him." "That which may be
known of God, is manifest in them; for God hath shew'd it unto them. For
the Invisible Things of him are clearly seen from the Creation of the World,
being understood by the Things that are made, even his eternal Power and
Godhead; so that they are without Excuse."*

To conclude; there seems to me, to be two *opposite Extremes,* into

which Men have run. *Some* cry up *Reason, and the Light of Nature,* at
such a rate, as to think them alone *sufficient Guides,* in consequence of
which they think all Revelation useless and unnecessary; whose Mistake
I have at large endeavour'd to shew, and that they who wanted Revelation, were sensible of their being at a loss in most important Points, for
want of it. *Others,* with a mistaken View of magnifying Revelation and
Faith, undervalue and *vilify Reason* and the *Light of Nature* most im-
moderately, as if they were *no proper Guides at all,* nor fit to be trusted,
in Divine Matters and the Truths of God. But, if that were the Case, how
should we ever come to the Knowledge of God at all? So it is plain
St. *Paul* thought, by the Passages just now quoted from him. The Belief
of a *Revelation* is grounded upon the *Veracity of God* the Revealer, and
we must first be convinc'd by Reason of the Veracity of God, (that he
is Omniscient, and cannot be deceiv'd, that he is perfectly Good, and
cannot deceive,) before we can give a firm Assent to a Revelation, as
coming from him. So the Knowledge of the Being and Attributes of
God, are previously necessary to the Belief of a Revelation. *Socinus* indeed held, that we can no otherwise come to the Knowledge of God,
but by Revelation; but those who have follow'd him in other Matters,
have been wise enough to drop him upon that Head. Beside; without
making use of Reason in Divine Matters, how should we be able to judge
of a Revelation, or a Miracle, and distinguish the True from the False?
Or how should we judge of the Meaning of a Revelation, when we have
it? Without applying our Reason to the Discussion of Matters reveal'd,
how should we come to know, that these Words, *"This is my Body,"* are
not to be taken in a literal Sense, or those other Words, *"If thine Eye
offend thee, pluck it out?"* We must, therefore, either use our Reason in
the Study of the Scriptures, or we have no Reason to study them at all;
nor need we fear any evil Consequences from such a Practice: For all the
Doctrines of Revelation, when freed from the Errors of the mistaken,
and the Imposition of the designing, Part of its Votaries, and taken as
they stand in the Scriptures themselves, free from all human Figments
and unwarrantable Deductions, will stand the test of Reason. Nor do I
know a more disadvantageous Idea, that can be given of the *Christian*
Religion, than to decry the use of Reason in matters belonging thereto;

for does not that plainly seem to imply, that it is an unreasonable Scheme, as being what will not stand the test of Reason? several Points, indeed, there are in it, which we cannot comprehend, which yet, that they are so, we have very good Reason to believe, tho' we cannot solve all Difficulties, or answers all Objections, that may be started about them; no more than we can explain all the Difficulties that occur about *Self-existence, Eternity* and *Immensity,* which yet, we are very certain, are Attributes that belong to some Being that really exists. Such are the Difficulties about the *infinite Divisibility of Space,* which yet is demonstrated, and those about *Liberty,* of which however we have the same Proof, that we have of our own Consciousness. The Distinction, therefore, is very just and well-grounded, between Matters *above our Reason,* and *contrary to Reason.* Propositions of the former Kind, we may give an unshaken Assent to, as well in *Religion* as *Philosophy;* but Propositions of the latter Kind are equally unintelligible, incredible, and impossible. *Reason,* therefore, and *Revelation* reflect a mutual Light upon one another; *Natural* and *Reveal'd* Religion communicate such Strength and Firmness of Parts to each other, as do the several Parts of an Arch, out of which a Stone taken at the Top weakens the whole Frame, as much as one at the Bottom. Without Natural Religion, Reveal'd Religion is a Building founded upon the Sand; but by the help of it, it is a House founded upon a Rock, against which we know who has told us, That *the Gates of Hell shall not prevail;* notwithstanding all the Assaults of those, who have taken a great deal of Pains, racking their Brains for Arguments, and ransacking all Antiquity for Testimonies, in order to invalidate and depretiate that, which if we wanted, we should, with all their boast'd Light of Nature, be like a Ship at Sea out of sight of Land, and without Chart or Compass. And so much for *the System of Rational Agents, the Kingdom of God in the rational World,* and the mistaken Notions of the *Heathens,* about these Matters, in order to shew, not only the *Usefulness* of *Revelation,* but the *Necessity* of it, in order to the Reformation of Mankind, and their Increase of Happiness in this Life, but principally in that which is to come.

A PHILOSOPHICAL
INQUIRY
INTO THE
LAWS of NATURE,

In which their FORM, chief HEADS, ORDER, PROMUL-
GATION, and OBLIGATION, are deduced from the *Nature*
of *Things:* Also the Elements of Mr. *Hobbes*'s PHILOSOPHY,
as well *Moral* as *Civil,* are consider'd and refuted.

Love is the Fulfilling of the Law.—Rom. 13. 10.

*Thou shalt love the LORD thy GOD with all thy Heart, and
with all thy Soul, and with all thy Mind. This is the first Commandment; and the second is like unto it, Thou shalt love thy
Neighbour as thy self. On these two Commandments hang all the
Law and the Prophets.*—Matt. 22. 37–40.

LONDON:

Printed in the YEAR MDCCXXVII.

THE CONTENTS

Chapter I

In the first Chapter, the State of the Question is propos'd, and all the Laws of Nature are reduc'd to that one, of Benevolence towards all Rationals; and the Sanction of that Law is briefly deduc'd from the Consequences which attend such a Benevolence, at the Appointment of the Author of Nature. The Method is also shewn, by which, Conclusions, concerning the Consequences of universal Benevolence, and its several Branches, (such as a division of Things, and of human Services amongst all Men, Fidelity, Gratitude, Self-preservation, and the Care of our Off-spring,) may be reduc'd to some Analogy or Resemblance with those Propositions in the Mathesis Universalis, *which contain the Result of Mathematical Computations. Hence is inferr'd, that the Truth of these Propositions, and their Impression on our Minds by the first Cause of all necessary Effects, do both become known to us by the same way of Reasoning. This is the Subject of the first ten Sections. In the 11th and 12th, it is prov'd, that* Hobbes *contradicts both the foregoing Conclusions, and himself; advancing atheistical Principles, and denying, that any Divine Laws, properly so call'd, may be learn'd, either from the Nature of Things, or from the Sacred Scriptures, unless a particular Revelation were made to each Person, that the sacred Writers were inspir'd. Thence to the end of § 15. is taken up in proving, That the Truth of our general Proposition is manifestly deduc'd from those* Phaenomena *of Nature, which are every where known, even to the Vulgar; and that* Hobbes *himself must acknowledge thus much, if he will be consistent with himself, is prov'd § 16. It is afterwards shewn, that from an accurate Knowledge of those natural Causes, whose Concurrence is necessary to produce certain Effects, or to preserve them when produc'd, we form distinct Ideas of Things*

Good and Evil, Profitable and Hurtful, and that too, not only to one, but many. It is prov'd, § 20. That those Philosophical Principles which are embrac'd by Mr. Hobbes *himself, demonstrate, That all Motions of Bodies are capable of producing such Good or Evil. From the Knowledge of the finite Condition of all Creatures, by a like Reasoning, is deduc'd the Necessity of limiting the Uses of all Things whatsoever, as well as of human Services, to particular Persons for a certain Time; by means whereof, by the by, is deduc'd the Origin of Property and Dominion, to the end of § 23. In § 24. the chief Heads of the Laws of Nature are propos'd, and the Rank which they hold, with respect to one another, hinted at. The Method of deducing them all from the primary one, is pointed out. In § 26. is shewn, that the Observance of these Laws is always rewarded, and their Neglect always punish'd, at the Appointment of the first Cause, according to that Course of Nature, which he at first establish'd in his first forming the World, and by which he still continues to govern it: And that* Hobbes *himself does sometimes assert this, but sometimes denys it, in order to advance the Right of every Man to every Thing; which is the Foundation of his Politicks, and is confuted in §. 27. and to the end of the Chapter.*

Chapter II

In the 2d Chapter is explain'd, what is understood by the Word Man, *what by the Word* Nature; *and, in the 4th Section, are distinctly enumerated those Faculties of the human Mind, which fit Men, more than other Animals, to enter into Society with God, and the whole Body of Mankind. Right Reason is explain'd, from the 5th Section to the end of the 10th. The Usefulness of abstract Ideas, and of universal Propositions, § 11. and of our reflex Acts, in order to this End, is pointed out, § 12. Thence we proceed to the Consideration of the human Body; particularly, that in a Survey thereof there are proper Motives to persuade us to endeavour the common Good of Rationals, and our own in subordination to that; because, (1.) Our Bodies are by Nature Part of the System of the World, which perpetually depends upon the first Mover, and the Motions of all whose Parts have necessarily such a mutual Dependence upon one another, in a subordination of some to others, for the Preservation of the Whole, to § 16. (2.) They are Animals of the same kind with other Men, and therefore have their Appetites, which tend to Self-preservation, equally limited with those of other Men; which Appetites in them are therefore very consistent with a Permission to others of the same Species to preserve themselves, § 17. Moreover, the Likeness of those Images, by which Animals of the same kind are represented, disposes them to Affections, with respect to others of their own Species, like to those, by which they are inclin'd to their own Preservation, § 18. Further, the Love Animals bear to those of the same Species, is a pleasant Affection; the Exercise whereof is therefore inseparably united with their Love of themselves, § 19. The same is likewise prov'd from their natural Propension to propagate their Species, and rear their Off-spring, § 20, 21. Hobbes's Objections against this Argument, from other Animals associating themselves, are answer'd and retorted, § 22. Finally, the same is prov'd from those Circumstances which are peculiar to a human Body; such as are, 1. Some Particulars which assist the Fancy and Memory, and consequently, Prudence. Here is consider'd, that Man has a Brain, in proportion to his Bulk, much greater than other Animals; a greater Quantity, Purity, and Vigour, of Blood and Animal Spirits; and a longer Life. 2. Those Circumstances, which either enable Man better to regulate his Affections, such as the* Plexus Nervosus, *peculiar to Man; or make his Government of them more necessary to him, as the* Pericardium's *being continued with the* Diaphragm; *and those other Causes, which expose him to greater Hazards than other Animals, in violent Passions, to the end of § 27. The Propension is observ'd to be greater in Man than in other Animals, towards propagating his Species, and rearing his Off-spring, § 28. Lastly, is consider'd the Aptness of the Disposition of the Parts in the whole Man for Society, especially in his Hands and Countenance; and that the Advantages of Society and convenient Subordination, and consequently of Government, may be deduc'd from the natural Union of the Mind with, and Dominion over, the Body.*

Chapter III

In the 3d Chapter, § 1. Natural Good is defin'd, and divided into Good, proper to one, and Good, common to many. Such Acts and Habits as promote the common natural Good of All, are enforc'd by Laws, and are call'd Mor-

*ally Good, upon account of their Agreement with those Laws or moral Rules.
§. 2. The Opinion of Mr. Hobbes, computing Good in the State of Nature,[1]
solely from the Sentiments of the Speaker, is laid open and confuted, as well
from the Principles of Reason, as from his own Writings. It is shewn, that
he does not only contradict others here, but himself also.*

Chapter IV

*In the three first Sections of the fourth Chapter, Practical Rules are defin'd
to be Practical Propositions, declaring the Consequences of human Actions;
and it is shewn, that such Propositions, when they point out the proper and
necessary Cause of the design'd Effect, do, without further Trouble, shew the
sufficient and necessary means to obtain that End. The various Forms, to
which those Propositions may be reduc'd, are compar'd with one another;
among which that is preferr'd, which considers human Actions as Causes,
and all things depending on them as certain Effects; and that the other Forms
may be all finally reduc'd to this; all which is easily learn'd from Observation.
In § 4. this whole Matter is illustrated by a Comparison with Mathematical
Practice.*

Chapter V

*In the 5th Chapter, § 1. the Law of Nature is thus defin'd: It is a Proposition,
whose Knowledge we come at by the Light of Nature, declaring those Actions
which promote the publick Good; the Performance of which is naturally
attended with Rewards, their Neglect with Punishments. The first Part
points out the Precept, which is the principal end or effect of the Law; the
latter Part the Sanction, which is the subordinate Effect of the Law. In §. 2.
a Reason is assign'd, why the Law of Nature is here defin'd otherwise than
by the Civilians. In the 3d §, the Law of Nature, according to our Definition,*

---

1. [Maxwell] *"Hobbes's* Notion is, that nothing is good to any Person, but what
he himself thinks so, and which directly and immediately gives some Pleasure to
himself, for *Hobbes* allows no disinterested Affection, which should make the Happiness of one to be desir'd by another."

is shewn to have those Powers, which in the Pandects *is ascribed to Laws.*
§ 4. *Publick natural Good, the Effect of human Actions, is farther explain'd.*
§ 5. *The* Stoicks *are reprehended, for denying what we call natural Good,
to be at all Good, in order to support their Assertion, that Virtue was the
only Good.* Hobbes *also is shewn to contradict himself; who contends, that
Civil Laws are the only Rules, by which we can distinguish between Good
and Evil: and the difference between natural Good and Evil is farther explain'd, to the end of* § 9. § 10. *The Sanction is briefly handled, as far as
is necessary to explain the foregoing Definition.* § 11. Justinian's *Definition
of Obligation is examin'd, and resolv'd into the Will of the Legislator, annexing Rewards and Punishments to his Laws. Therefore in* § 12. *are traced
the Rewards, that are naturally connected with a Pursuit of the publick
Good; and, in the first place, those which are contain'd in the Happiness of
the human Mind. Here it is prov'd by many Arguments, that the greatest
Happiness of our Mind consists in the Exercise and inward Sense of universal Benevolence, to the end of* § 17. *It is afterwards prov'd, that this End
is agreeable to the Will of God, and that he will reward those who co-operate
with him, and punish those who oppose him: and* Epicurus's *Assertion, that
the World is not govern'd by Providence, is confuted from Principles known
by the Light of Nature, and often acknowledg'd by the* Epicureans *themselves, to the end of* § 23. *It is also prov'd, that Penalties, besides those inflicted by the Society, await those who attempt any thing against the common
Good, to the end of* § 31. *In* § 32. *these Conclusions are illustrated from
opposite Cases. In* § 33, 34. *from Parallel Cases. In* §. 35. *it is prov'd, that
God and Men are the chief, and in a manner the general, Causes of that
Happiness, which each Individual necessarily desires; and that therefore they
can never be safely neglected. In* § 36. *two Objections are propos'd.* 1. *That
the Punishments and Rewards seem uncertain, which we have affirm'd to
be the Sanctions of that Law, which enjoins the promoting the common
Good. Plain Proofs of these Punishments are produc'd to the end of* § 39.
In these Sections, the difference of our Method, from that of Mr. Hobbes,
*is made apparent; and it is prov'd, that no Man can have a right to claim
any thing as his Property, unless it be first granted, that the Laws of Nature
do, in a State of Nature, oblige to the performance of external Actions conformable to them; and that therefore* Hobbes *does expressly contradict him-*

self, whilst he contends, that in a State of Nature there are natural Rights binding, with respect to external Actions, and yet denies that the Laws of Nature do in that State oblige to the performance of external Actions. In § 40. it is prov'd, that Rewards or positive Advantages are necessary Consequences of promoting the publick Good; particularly, that Peace amongst Rationals does not necessarily presuppose War, as Mr. Hobbes *asserts; and that it is a Continuation only of that Concord which is natural among Rationals, agreeing in the same Means to obtain the same End; but that War is to be defin'd from its Absence, in opposition to* Hobbes. *In § 41. greater Rewards are enumerated, and the Principles of* Epicurus's *Natural Philosophy, by which he endeavours to disprove the Providence of God, are briefly refuted. In § 43. is prov'd, that a Desire of promoting the publick Good is the Foundation of all civil Societies; and that therefore all the Advantages of living under civil Government are to be reckon'd among the natural Rewards of this Desire. Hence is shewn, § 44. that it may be prov'd, that God designs to oblige Men to the performance of such Actions; the whole Argument being reduc'd to a Syllogism. In § 45. the second Objection is answer'd; and it is prov'd, that our Method of deducing the Sanction of the Laws of Nature, from the Connexion of our Happiness with such actions as promote the common Good, does not suppose, that we prefer our selves before all others. The End or adequate Effect of the Law is in all equitable Judgment to be preferr'd to the Sanction, as it respects only particular Persons; this is explain'd to the end of § 49. § 50. Examines* Hobbes's *Reason for denying, that the Laws of Nature do oblige, in a State of Nature, to the performance of external Actions, namely, for want of Security. It is prov'd, that in order to make an Obligation valid, a perfect Security from all Fear is not necessary, and that Societies themselves do not afford such a Security: But it is prov'd, that even the State of Nature affords a comparative Security, which is greater than what arises from* Hobbes's *State of War. It is shewn, that its being presum'd by Civil Laws, that Men are good, till the contrary appears, overthrows* Hobbes's *Doctrine, to the end of § 52. In § 53. it is prov'd, that* Hobbes *acknowledges, that every Man has a Right to commit Treason, in this, that he affirms it not to be a Transgression of the Law of the State, but of the Law of Nature. § 54. Proves, that by such Doctrine is taken away all Obligation, and consequently all use, of Leagues between different Empires, as being in a State of Nature and of War, with respect to one another. § 55. Hobbes destroys the Security of Ambassadors, and of all Commerce. In § 56. is shewn, that a Commonwealth cannot be fram'd or preserv'd by such Men, as Hobbes contends, that all Men are. In § 57. it is concluded from these Premises, that this is the one Fundamental Law of Nature, That the common Good of Rationals is to be promoted.*

Chapter VI

In the four first Sections are deriv'd from that general Precept, all those Laws which concern the Happiness, 1. Of different Nations, which have any mutual Intercourse. 2. Of single States. 3. Of any smaller Societies whatsoever, as of Families and Friends. In § 5. is shewn, that the same general Law directs human Actions of every kind, as well those of the Understanding and Will, as those of the Body, which are govern'd and determin'd by the Mind. Hence is prov'd, that by this Law is enjoin'd, in the Understanding, Prudence in all kinds of Actions, as well relating to God as Man; whence arise, 1. Constancy of Mind, and its several Branches. 2. True Moderation, which comprehends Integrity and Industry. In the Will, from an Union of Prudence with Benevolence, arise Equity, the Government of all the Affections, and those Virtues which regard the special Laws of Nature. In § 9. is explain'd the Difference between Actions necessary to this End, (the common Good,) and Actions indifferent; wherein there is room for Liberty, and for the Interposition of the supreme Powers.

Chapter VII

In the three first Sections is handled more at large the Origin of Dominion, as well over Things as Persons; and it is deduc'd from that Law of Nature, which enjoins the making a Division of Rights, and the preserving it when made. In § 4. is shewn, that this Law is suppos'd in the very Definition of Justice. Thence is deduc'd (§ 5.) the Difference between Things or Persons sacred, and such as are allotted to common Uses. In § 6. the Origin of the divine Dominion is deduc'd from the Judgment of the divine Wisdom, which is analogous to, or resembles, this Law of Nature. It is prov'd, that these Conclusions of human Reason agree with the Judgment which God himself makes. The 7th Section renders a Reason, why it was thought proper to add any thing to the common Doctrine, which derives God's Right of Dominion over the Creatures, from his having created them. In § 8, 9. from the Law of Nature, appointing the introducing and the preserving of Dominion, many things are deduc'd concerning a plenary Division of Dominion, as well over Things as Persons and their Labours, to be made, (either by Consent, Arbitration, or Lot,) or to be preserv'd: Concerning transferring Rights by Covenants; the Rise of their obligatory Force, and that it reaches not to Things unlawful. In § 10. is shewn, that from the same Law is deriv'd the Obligation to Benevolence, Gratitude, a limited Self-Love, and the natural Affection of Parents towards their Children, and to constitute a civil Power, (§ 11.) which may controul that of the Subject: That it is necessary (§ 12.) that the forming and preserving States be enjoin'd by a Law of Nature, obliging to the performance of external Actions, before such States are formed. Whence, in § 13. are deduc'd other Corollaries of the utmost Importance, as well in Things Sacred, as Civil.

Chapter VIII

In § 1. is shewn, that all Obligation to the exercise of moral Virtues flows immediately from hence, that such Actions are enjoin'd by the Law of Nature. From the Law, requiring the Settlement of private Dominion, or Property, in order to the common Good, are inferred (§ 2.) the Duties, 1. Of giving to others. 2. Of reserving to our selves, those things which are necessary or highly serviceable to this end. In § 3. is shewn, that the common Good of the whole System of Rationals ought necessarily in both Cases to be regarded; and that the Nature of Mediocrity consists in giving no Part more or less, than a due regard to the whole requires. From the former are deduc'd (§ 4.) Precepts; 1. Concerning Gifts, in which Liberality; and, 2. Concerning Civility or good Manners, in which the Virtues peculiar thereto are conspicuous. In § 5. Liberality is defin'd, with its subordinate Virtues, Prudence, and Frugality, and the Vices opposite to these. In § 6. the Virtues relating to Conversation or good Manners are defin'd in general; and in particular, Gravity, Courteousness, Taciturnity, Veracity and Urbanity, and the con-

trary Vices. From the latter part of the Law explain'd in the 2d Section, is deduc'd (§ 7.) the Obligation to a limited Self-Love, whose Branches take care of the Mind, and of the Body, which is chiefly provided for by Temperance; which § 8. is defin'd, and its Parts enumerated: those belonging to the Preservation of the Individual are here explain'd, as in § 9. are those that relate to the Propagation of the Species; and it is prov'd, that the same Law commands us to take care of the Education of our Children. § 10. Passes on to the Care of the Means, which are Riches and Honours; whence Occasion is taken to define Modesty, Humility and Magnanimity. In § 11, 12, 13. is explain'd the Method of deducing the practical Rules of right Reason, by which Actions are directed according to all the Virtues. In § 14, 15, 16, 17. is shewn, that the common Good, as being the greatest of all, is a Measure naturally fix'd and divided into Parts, by means whereof the value of all things Good and Evil, and consequently the measure of all Affections conversant about them, may be naturally ascertain'd and determin'd.

Chapter IX

Deduces Corollaries from what has been already deliver'd, which regard, 1. The Decalogue. 2. Civil Laws. The Decalogue is taken into Consideration, because in that God himself has collected the Fundamentals of the Jewish *Polity. But in the Fundamentals of every Polity it is necessary, that all those Laws should be comprehended, which naturally oblige all. Tho I deny not, that in those Fundamentals of the* Jewish *Polity something is contain'd peculiar to that Nation. But we have purposely omitted that in our Deduction, which is included in the four first Sections. From our Principles we do deduce more particularly (§ 5.) that it is necessary for the publick Good, that Societies with Power Imperial, or Civil Government, be establish'd and preserv'd. The first appearance of Civil Government is to be seen in a Family. The Power of the Husband over the Wife, of the Fathers over their Children; and the just Bounds of Imperial Power, are drawn from the Relation which they bear to this, as to the End intended. In § 7. it is prov'd, that supreme Powers cannot lawfully be punish'd by their Subjects. And (§ 8.) that a very extensive Power is given to Sovereigns, according to these Principles; but that* Hobbes's *Principles overthrow the Foundations of all Government.* 1st,

(§ 9.) *Because they represent the Nature of Princes as more fierce and cruel than that of wild Beasts.* 2dly, *Because he denies to all, and consequently to Princes, that right Reason, by which they might determine, according to the nature of Things, or of Causes and Effects, what sort of Actions are good or bad to any others besides themselves: And* Hobbes's *Argument is likewise refuted, by which he endeavours to prove, that we ought therefore to obey the Reason of the Commonwealth, because there is no such thing as Reason which is right, or which can judge according to a Rule establish'd and enforc'd by the Nature of things. It is shewn,* (§ 10.) *that* Hobbes's *Doctrine of the Right of every Man to every thing, would not suffer any Man to enter into Civil Society; and that his Notions excite Subjects to Rebellion: That his Doctrine, concerning Compacts and Oaths,* (§ 11.) *is dangerous to the supreme Powers. It is shewn,* (§ 12.) *that by transferring of Rights to the same Person, (by which alone* Hobbes *teaches, that a Commonwealth can be form'd,) no one is bound to yield Obedience to a Prince.* (§ 13.) *That* Hobbes *takes away from Princes, all those things, which, for Flattery's sake, he would seem to bestow upon them more than other Philosophers have done. He even accuses them of the worst of Crimes, whilst he contends, that they are bound by no Laws. He deprives Princes of all Commendation for Wisdom and Justice; and they themselves, in most States, openly and constantly reject what* Hobbes *ascribes to them; the very same things being elsewhere denied them by* Hobbes *himself, as is prov'd by undeniable Instances: as also a Confutation of his Opinion, that Compacts do not bind Supreme Powers to their Subjects, nor to other States. It is lastly shewn, that* Hobbes's *Doctrine concerning Treason, encourages Subjects to commit that Crime.*

THE INTRODUCTION

§I. It *concerns* us *both,* friendly Reader, "That you should be briefly ac-   The Design of
this Treatise.
quainted with the *Design* and *Method* of this Treatise"; for thence you
will immediately *perceive,* "What I have perform'd, or, at least, attempted; and what is further to be supply'd from your own Understanding, or the Writings of others." The *Laws of Nature* are the Foundations
of all *moral* and *civil* Knowledge, as in the following Work will at large
appear. But these, as all other Conclusions, discoverable by the Light of   Two ways of
deducing the
Laws of
Nature.
1. From their
Effects.
Nature, may be deduc'd *two* ways; either from those manifest *Effects*
which flow from them, or from the *Causes* whence they themselves arise.
I have endeavour'd to discover them in this *latter* Method, by arguing
from the Cause to the Effect. To the former Method of proving their Ob-   This insisted
on by *Grotius,*
Sharrock, &c.
ligation, (by arguing *from the Effect to the Cause,*) belongs what has been
written by *Hugo Grotius,* and by his Brother, in his Posthumous Work,
and by our Countryman *Sharrock,* who establish them from the *approv'd*
Sentiments of various *Authors* of different Nations and Ages, as also from
a *Harmony* in the *Manners* and *Laws,* if not of all, at least of the politer,
Nations.[1] Hitherto also is to be referr'd that Work of *Selden's, concerning*
the Laws of Nature and Nations, according to the Sentiments of the Hebrews.[2] And, in my Opinion, all these Authors have deserv'd well of
Mankind. But especially the Work of *Hugo Grotius,* which was the first
of the kind, I think worthy, both of the Author, and of Immortality.
For a few Slips, and those in Matters, in which the Customs of his Coun-

---

1. Grotius, *De Jure Belli ac Pacis* (1625); Grotius, *De Principis Juris Naturalis En-*
chiridion (1667); Sharrock, *De Officiis Secundum Naturae Jus* (1660).
2. Selden, *De Jure Naturali et Gentium* (1640).

try seem to have biass'd that great Man, will easily obtain Pardon from a candid Reader.

Useful, tho objected against. §II. Nor, truly, are the *Objections,* which are usually brought against *this method* of proving the Laws of Nature, (by arguing *from the Effect to the Cause,* as *Grotius* does,) of so great weight, as to prove it altogether *fallacious* and *useless;* altho I readily acknowledge, that they may so far prevail with candid Inquirers after Truth, as to convince them, That it would be *more useful and safe,* to find out a fuller Proof, by searching into the *Causes,* which produce in the Mind of Man the Knowledge of the Laws of Nature. This, however, will more plainly appear, if we briefly propose those *Objections,* with the *Answers* to them.

First Objection from insufficient Induction. In the *first* place it is *objected,* "That the Induction is weak, which infers, from the Writings or Manners of a *few* Men, or Nations, the Opinion or Judgment of *all.*" Now there is scarce any Person so well acquainted with the Laws and Customs of *any one State,* that can ever have a perfect Knowledge of them all; much less that can attain to such a Knowledge of the Laws of *all States,* still less, of the inward Sentiments of *each Individual,* as may enable him, upon a just Comparison, to conclude, what those Notions are, in which *all* agree.

To this it is *answer'd,* "That the Judgments made by different Nations concerning matters of daily publick Practice, (such are Religion, or some sort of divine Worship in general, and a degree of Humanity, sufficient to prohibit Murder, Theft, and Adultery,) may with ease be every where observ'd by any Man, without so profound a Knowledge of their Laws": and *such Judgments sufficiently declare that they agree in the Laws of Nature;* for that which we *know by Experience,* to be, as it were, naturally *acknowledg'd good by many Nations,* we presume, upon account of the *likeness of human Nature,* to be *likewise acknowledg'd good by the rest;* especially when our *Adversaries cannot produce one undoubted Instance,* to prove *any* Nation to be of *different* Sentiments. To me, truly, those Narratives of some few barbarous *Americans,* and the *Hottentots,* "That they have no religious Worship," *seem,* not suspected only but, *false;* for such a *negative* Assertion is *hardly capable* of ever being *prov'd by Tes-*

timony. Therefore *Acosta*[3] and some others seem *rashly* to have form'd a Judgment concerning those, with whose Language, Manners, and Sentiments they could not thorowly acquaint themselves in *so short a time.* For we read, that both *Jews* and *Christians* were sometimes *falsly accus'd* by many, of the greatest *Impieties,* tho their Religion was more holy than that of other Nations. But, be that as it will, it is *manifest,* "That those Truths are with sufficient Clearness propos'd to all, which are readily acknowledg'd by almost every one, altho the same should be either overlook'd, or even oppos'd, by some few." But this Observation will be the most proper, and of greatest use, when it *appears* manifestly from *other Proofs* than *Testimony* and *Custom,* "That these Propositions teach the true Means to the best End, and that all are indispensably oblig'd to pursue that End by those Means"; which may be best prov'd by a consideration of the *Causes,* which suggest such conclusions of Reason to our Minds.

§III. A *second Objection* is, "That, altho certain Conclusions of Reason are approv'd of by our own Judgment, and the Practice of many others, yet the Authority of a known Law-giver is wanting, to give them the force of Laws to all Men; for otherwise," (say they,) "whoever holds them in contempt, has the same Right to reject the Judgment of any others whomsoever, that they exercise in condemning his Opinion by their Words and Actions." To this purpose, both *Hobbes* and *Selden* object, (beside the Antients,) but with very *different Views.*[4]

Obj. 2. That they want a sufficient enacting Authority.

For, as we shall shew in the following Treatise, the Point Mr. *Hobbes* aims at, is, "That none should believe themselves oblig'd by the Conclusions of Reason, with respect to their outward Actions, before a civil Magistrate is appointed; and that all his Appointments should be look'd upon, as the perfectly obligatory Judgments of right Reason." It is to this purpose that he affirms, that *The Laws of Nature, altho they are laid*

According to Hobbes,

---

3. Acosta, *Historia Natural y Moral de las Indias* (1591).
4. Hobbes, *Elementa Philosophica De Cive* (1647); references are to *On the Citizen* (1998), 2.1, pp. 32–33; Selden, *De Jure Naturali,* I.6, pp. 75–85.

down in the Writings of Philosophers, are no more, for that Reason, to be look'd upon as written Laws, than the Opinions of Lawyers are Laws, and that for want of a sovereign Authority."[5] He would not indeed deny them the *Name* of *Laws,* which he had before vouchsafed to give them, (tho improperly, as he elsewhere confesses;)[6] he was willing however to insinuate, that they were *not promulg'd by a sufficient Authority,* tho Philosophers learn them from the *Nature of Things,* and thence *transcribe* them into their *Writings.* It is nevertheless manifest, if they be already *truly Laws* made by the Author of Nature, that they need *no new Authority,* after they are set down in *writing by any one,* to make them become *written Laws.*

And *Selden,* but with different Virtues. But Mr. *Selden denies,* "That the Conclusions of Reason, consider'd barely in themselves, have the Authority of Laws," upon no other account, than, in order to *shew* "the Necessity of having recourse to the Legislative Power of God, and of proving that God has commanded our Obedience to them, and, by making them known to us, has proclaim'd them his Laws." And indeed he has *judiciously,* as far as I can judge, *given this Hint* to the moral Philosophers, who are wont to consider the *Conclusions of their own Reason as Laws,* without due Proof, that they have the necessary *Form* of a Law, or that they are *establish'd by God.* But when he is to shew the *Manner* wherein God might manifest to Mankind, these to be his Laws, he proposes *two* ways.[7] 1. That God himself pronounc'd them with his sacred Voice to *Adam* and *Noah,* injoining them perpetual Obedience; whence these *Precepts of the Sons of* Noah were handed down to all their Posterity by Tradition only. 2. That God has endow'd rational Minds with a Faculty able, by Application of their Understanding, to discover those Laws, and to distinguish them, when discover'd, from all positive Institutions.

He only transiently *hints,* in such *general Terms,* this *latter Method,* which however to me seems to want much Explanation and Proof; but he betakes himself wholly to the *former,* and endeavours to prove, from

5. Hobbes, *On the Citizen,* 14.15, p. 161.

6. Ibid., 3.33, pp. 56–57; Hobbes, *Leviathan with Selected Variants from the Latin Edition of 1668* (1994), ch. 15, p. 100.

7. Selden, *De Jure Naturali,* I.7–9, pp. 86–108.

the Traditions of some *Jewish Rabbins,* "That God gave seven Precepts to the Sons of *Noah,* in the observance whereof all Justice amongst Men should consist." And truly he has abundantly *prov'd,*[8] "That the *Jews* thought that all Nations, altho they did not receive the Laws of *Moses,* were nevertheless oblig'd by some divine Laws, whose chief Heads they look'd upon the *Precepts of the Sons of* Noah to be." And this *proves* at least, "That, in the Opinion of that Nation, which was not inconsiderable either for Numbers or Learning, there are Laws, not made by any State, that bind all Mankind." It is likewise to be own'd, that this learned Man *chiefly aim'd at this Point,* and that with *good Success;* and that the Knowledge of this Matter is of considerable use in *Christian Divinity. Selden,* however, has *not sufficiently answer'd his own Objection,* which we before mention'd. For, altho these Jewish Traditions were thorowly known, and perhaps firmly believ'd, by *him,*[9] they were not however manifested to *all Mankind;* and those things which that Nation looks upon as the greatest Mysteries of Religion, are by many ridicul'd. And to me truly it seems *self-evident,* "That an unwritten Tradition of the learned Men of one Nation, is not a sufficient Promulgation of a Law of Nature, which is to oblige all Nations."

[marginal note: Not sufficiently answer'd by the latter.]

§IV. Wherefore, that the *Conclusions of Reason* in *moral* Matters might more evidently appear to be Laws, *Laws of God,* I have thought it proper to make a *philosophical Inquiry into their Causes,* as well Internal as External, the nearer and the more remote; for by this Method we shall at last arrive at their *first Author,* or efficient Cause, from whose essential *Perfections,* and internal *Sanction* of them by Rewards and Punishments,[10] we have shewn that their *Authority* arises. Most others have been satisfy'd with *saying* in general Terms, "That these Conclusions, or

[marginal note: To answer this Objection, the Author chuses the second Method of deducing the Laws of Nature from their Causes, by their divine-Promulgation and Sanction.]

8. [Maxwell] "In the book before-mention'd."

9. "by him": Cumberland's Latin indicates that he meant "by them" (meaning the Jews rather than Selden); Cumberland, *De Legibus Naturae,* Prolegomena, a3r.

10. [Maxwell] "The *internal* Sanction of the Laws of Nature, consists of those Rewards and Punishments, which are necessarily connected, according to the common course of Nature, at the Appointment of the first Cause, with the Observance or Non-observance of those Laws."

Actions conformable to them, are taught by Nature"; but to me it seems necessary, especially at this time, to trace more distinctly, *after what manner* the Powers of things, as well without as within us, conspire to *imprint* these Conclusions upon our Minds, and to give a *Sanction* to them. Our Countryman, the Lord *Verulam,* has reckon'd such an Inquiry among the things which are wanting.[11] This, if solidly perform'd, will therefore be of very great use; because thence will appear, both *how* our Mind is, by the Light of Nature, let into the Knowledge of the Will or Laws of God, so as that it cannot be free from the warning of Conscience; and *what* that Rule is, whereby the Justice and Rectitude of the Laws of particular States is to be measured, and their Injustice and Imperfection to be corrected and amended by the supreme Authority if they have at any time deviated from the best and greatest End. Hence also, (that it may appear, that Morality is not the Artifice of *Ecclesiastics* or *Politicians,*) is further *shewn,* "That there is something in the Nature of God, of other Men, and of our selves, which in good Actions affords present Comfort and Joy, and a well-grounded Expectation of future Rewards." On the other hand, "That there are Causes which must naturally produce the most violent Grief and Fear, after evil Actions; so that the Sentence of Conscience may be justly look'd upon as armed with Scourges against Impiety."[12]

§V. The *Platonists,* indeed, clear up this Difficulty in an easier manner, by the Supposition of *innate Ideas,* as well of the Laws of Nature themselves, as of those Matters about which they are conversant; but, truly, I have not been so happy as to learn the Laws of Nature in so short a way.[13] Nor seems it to me well advised, to build the Doctrine of *natural Religion* and *Morality* upon an *Hypothesis,* which has been *rejected* by the *generality of Philosophers,* as well *Heathen* as *Christian,* and *can never*

Without insisting on innate Ideas of them.

---

11. Bacon, *Of the Advancement and Proficience of Learning* (1640), VIII.3, p. 424.
12. An allusion to Juvenal, *Satires,* XIII.193.
13. Cumberland's rejection of innate ideas can be compared with similar positions in Pufendorf and Locke: cf. Pufendorf, *De Jure Naturae et Gentium,* II.3.13; Locke, *An Essay Concerning Human Understanding* (1690), I.

be prov'd against the *Epicureans,* with whom is our chief Controversy. I was resolv'd, however, *not to oppose* this Opinion, because it is my earnest desire, that whatever looks with a friendly Aspect upon Piety and Morality, might have its due weight; (and I look upon these *Platonists* to be favourers of their Cause;) and because it is not impossible, that such Ideas might be both *born with us,* and *afterwards impress'd* upon us from without.

§VI. Moreover, the *same Reasons,* which hinder'd us from supposing *innate Ideas* of the Laws of Nature *in our Minds,* hinder us likewise from supposing, without Proof, that these Laws have *existed* from Eternity *in the divine Mind.* I have therefore thought it necessary to remove the Difficulty, and assert and *prove* the Authority and *eternal Existence of these Conclusions in the divine Mind,* in the following Method; assuming those Notices which we have from *Sense* and daily *Experience,* I *demonstrate,* "That the Nature of things, which subsists, and is continually govern'd, by its first Cause, does necessarily imprint on our Minds some practical Propositions, (which must be always true, and cannot without a Contradiction be suppos'd otherwise,) concerning the Study of promoting the joint Felicity of all Rationals: And that the Terms of these Propositions do immediately and directly signify, that the first Cause, in his original Constitution of Things, has annex'd the greatest Rewards and Punishments to the observance and neglect of these Truths." Whence it manifestly *follows,* "That they are Laws," *Laws* being nothing but *practical Propositions, with Rewards and Punishments annex'd, promulg'd by competent Authority.* Having hence *shewn,* "That the Knowledge and Practice of these Laws, is the natural Perfection or most happy State of our rational Nature," I *infer,* "That there must be in the first Cause, (from whom proceed both this our Perfection, and that most wise Disposition which we see, every Day, of Effects without us, for the common Preservation and Perfection of the whole System,) a Perfection correspondent, but infinitely superior, to this Knowledge and Practice of the Laws of Nature." For I look upon it as most *evident,* "That we must first know what Justice is, and from whence those Laws are deriv'd, in the observance whereof it wholly consists, before we can distinctly know,

[Marginal note:] Or supposing, without Proof, their eternal Existence in the divine Mind.

[Marginal note:] Their Promulgation and Obligation, and eternal Existence in, or agreeableness to, the divine Mind, prov'd.

that Justice is to be attributed to God, and that we ought to propose his Justice as our Example." For we come not at the *Knowledge of God* by immediate *Intuition* of his Perfections, but from his Effects[14] first known by Sense and Experience; nor can we *safely* ascribe to him *Attributes,* which from other Considerations we do *not* sufficiently *comprehend.*

§VII. Having hitherto shewn, in general, the Difference between our Method and that of others, I think it proper, *to shew briefly here the chief things which are more at large and dispersedly deliver'd in the following Discourse.* Having *undertaken* only, "to deliver the Precepts of moral Philosophy, and to deduce them from some little Knowledge of Nature presuppos'd"; what *natural Philosophers,* especially those who reason upon mathematical Principles, have often *demonstrated,* I *assume,* as sufficiently prov'd. But my *principal Supposition is,* "That all Effects of corporeal Motions, which are necessary, according to the common Course of Nature, and depend not upon the Will of Man, are produc'd by the Will of the first Cause": for this comes to no more than *saying,* "That all Motions are begun by the Impression of a first Mover, and are by the same Impression continued, and perpetually determin'd, according to certain Laws." For I thought it *superfluous* to *prove* that which had been *already prov'd* by most natural Philosophers, and is plainly acknowledg'd by *Hobbes* himself, whose Doctrine I am now examining. *Leviath.* Chap. 12. After he has assign'd the Cause of Religion, among Men, to their anxious Concern about Futurity, he adds thus, (whether insidiously or no, let others judge;) *"The acknowledging of one God Eternal, Infinite and Omnipotent, may more easily be deriv'd from the Desire Men have to know the Causes of natural Bodies, and their several Virtues and Operations, than from the fear of what was to befal them in time to come: for he that from any Effect he seeth come to pass, should reason to the next and immediate Cause thereof, and from thence to the Cause of that Cause, and plunge himself profoundly in the pursuit of Causes; shall at last come to this,*

The chief Heads of the following Book.

The Effects of corporeal Motions, Effects of the divine Will.

---

14. "from his Effects": a possible mistranscription in the Latin suggests that Cumberland meant "by their effects" [the perfections].

that there must be (as even the Heathen Philosophers confess'd) one first Mover; that is, a first and eternal Cause of all things, which is that which Men mean by the Name of God." [15] But if it be *granted*, "That every natural Effect points out God as its Author," no Man can *deny*, "That all such Effects are determin'd by his Will," unless he is *inconsistent* enough to acknowledge *God* the *Cause* of those Effects, and at the same time to contend, that he is *not a voluntary Agent.*

§VIII. Moreover, "Every Motion impress'd upon our Organs of Sense," (such Motions are by the *Peripateticks* call'd *sensible Qualities,*[16]) "by which the Mind is led to apprehend Objects, and to form Judgments concerning them, is an Effect plainly natural, and therefore, whatever second Causes intervene, owes its Original to the first." And thence it *follows,* "That God, by these Motions, as by a Pencil, delineates the Ideas or Images in our Minds of all sorts of things, especially of Causes and their Effects. And, by imprinting on us, from the same Object, various Notions imperfectly representing it, he excites us to bring them together, and to compare them among themselves; and, consequently, determines us to form true Propositions concerning things understood by us." So, because an Object is sometimes expos'd to sight *whole,* and at once, and at other times is view'd narrowly, and by *parts;* and the Mind perceives that the Idea of the *Whole* plainly represents the *same* thing, with all the Ideas of the *single Parts taken together,* it is obliged to form a Proposition concerning the *Sameness* of the *Whole* and *all the Parts;* or to *affirm,* "That the Causes which preserve the Whole, preserve also all its essential Parts."

[marginal note: Apprehending, comparing, judging, the natural Effects of such Motions, and consequently of the divine Will. *]*

15. Hobbes, *Leviathan,* ch. 12, p. 64. Maxwell tends to quote from the English *Leviathan,* but Cumberland generally refers to the Latin edition of 1668, which is occasionally different. Where Maxwell's quotation has, "As even the Heathen Philosophers confess'd," the Latin edition quoted by Cumberland has, "with the sounder of the ancient philosophers," apparently an approving reference by Hobbes to Aristotle. Cumberland, *De Legibus Naturae,* Prolegomena, a4v.

16. *"species sensibiles"*: Cumberland, *De Legibus Naturae,* Prolegomena, a4v.

§IX. Lastly, upon a diligent Consideration of all those Propositions which deserve to be rank'd amongst the general Laws of Nature, I have observ'd *they may be reduc'd to one* universal one, from the just Explication whereof all the particular Laws may be both duly limited and illustrated. This general Proposition may be thus express'd. "The Endeavour, to the utmost of our power, of promoting the common Good of the whole System of rational Agents, conduces, as far as in us lies, to the good of every Part, in which our own Happiness, as that of a Part, is contain'd. But contrary Actions produce contrary Effects, and consequently our own Misery, among that of others." Wherefore the whole of this Treatise is employ'd upon these Heads, which regard either, (1.) the *Matter* of this Proposition; that is, the Knowledge of its *Terms,* to be drawn from the Nature of Things; or (2.) its *Form,* that is, the joining these Terms in such a practical Proposition as may deserve the Name of a Law, upon account of the Rewards and Punishments annex'd by the Author of Nature; or (3.) lastly, *The Deduction and natural Limitation of the other Laws of Nature,* by their Respect to the common Good or happiest State of the whole Body.

§X. To the Knowledge of the *Terms* belongs all that we have said in general of the *Nature of Things,* especially of *Man,* as also of the *common Good.* But I must ask the Reader's pardon for sometimes *ascribing Reason to God,* and ranking him amongst rational Beings; and that we are sometimes said *to bear a good Will towards God,* or to desire something agreeable to his Nature, that is, Good. For in the beginning we declare, that these Expressions are not properly, and in the same Sense said of *God,* in which we use them, when we speak of *Men.* For we suppose in him absolute Omniscience and Wisdom, which *Cicero* himself could not better express, than by the Name of *"Reason in its Perfection."* [17] Nor do we *imagine,* "That we can testify our Love of God, by adding any thing to his Perfections, which from Eternity were infinite." Yet it is not to be doubted, but that in our *Actions,* Obedience, and Imitation of his Care of the common Good of Mankind, whose Being is continued from Day

Margin notes:
All particular Laws of Nature reduc'd to one Proposition.

Its *Matter,* that is, the Terms, explain'd.

---

17. Cicero, *De Legibus,* I.vii.23.

to Day by his Favours; and also in our *Words,* and *Thoughts,* and *Affections,* Honour, Worship, and Love, are more *agreeable* to his beneficent Nature, and more acceptable to him, than Neglect or Hatred, or direct and wilful Opposition.[18] For, if we abstractedly *compare two rational Natures* between themselves, we must acknowledge a *better Agreement* when they *consent* and *co-operate,* than when they *dissent,* and the End propos'd by one of them, is oppos'd by the other. Nor do I see that it alters the Case, tho one of these rational Natures should be suppos'd to be *God,* and the other, *Man.* Therefore, as we know by the help of our *Senses,* "That it is more acceptable to any Man to be lov'd and honour'd, than to be hated and despis'd"; so it is evident to *Reason,* by a manifest Correspondence, "That it is more grateful to the supreme Rational, *God,* to be lov'd and honour'd by the Obedience of Men, than to be the Object of Hatred and Contempt." For, as it is certain, that to *desire to be belov'd,* implies *no Imperfection* in *Man;* in *God,* it is so far from carrying any Suspicion of Imperfection, that, on the contrary, it is an *Argument* of the *Benignity* of his Nature, because Men arrive at their greatest Perfection, by loving him: which being manifest, both by Reason and Experience, it thence evidently *follows,* "That God has inseparably annex'd the greatest Reward to the Love of himself"; which he never would have done, if it were not agreeable to his Will to be belov'd.[19]

But the Reader, in perusing the three Chapters of this Treatise, whose Titles I have just now mention'd, will see, that while we explain the *Terms* (to use a School-Phrase) of the foregoing Proposition, we are not busy'd about the Interpretation of *Words,* but about *Ideas,* and the Nature of those *Things* whence they arise, as far as it is necessary to our present purpose: And at the same time he will observe, that I directly and immediately explain the *Consequences* and *Necessity* of those human Ac-

---

18. "θεομαχία," Cumberland, *De Legibus Naturae,* Prolegomena, bιv.

19. [Maxwell] "If the Deity be good, he must desire the Happiness of his Creatures; this cannot be among Rationals without kind Affections: Kind Affections cannot be supposed toward indifferent Agents, where there are none towards Benefactors, and chiefly the Deity. Therefore, if the Deity love his Creatures, he must desire that they should love him; since, without loving him, they cannot be happy."

tions, which are either necessary to the common Happiness of all, or to the private Happiness of Individuals:[20] Altho it seem'd advisable to use words so general, that they might in a sound Sense be ascrib'd to the *divine Majesty;* and that to this very purpose, that by the help of Analogy, or Correspondence, prudently apply'd, not only our *Obligation to Piety,* but the Nature of the *divine Justice* and *Dominion,* might thence be understood.

Its *Form* consider'd, Practical, declaring the Cause of the best Effect.

§XI. As to the *Form* of the Proposition, (to make use of a logical Term,) it is manifest, that it is *practical,* as pronouncing concerning the Consequences of human Action.

It is, however, to be observ'd, that the *Proposition* (altho the Word [*conduces*] be used in the *present Tense,* because the Observation is collected from things present) is not limited to the *present time,* but is equally to be understood of what is *future;* and, because its Truth chiefly depends upon "the Whole's being the same with all its Parts," is as manifestly true of the *future,* (which from other Arguments we prove in this Treatise,) and with respect to Futurity, it is always by us made use of.

Moreover, this *Proposition* is the better fitted to our purpose, that it builds upon no *Hypothesis.* For it does not *suppose* Men born either in, or out of, civil Society. It does not *suppose* a Relation between all Men as born of the same common Parents, which the *Scriptures* teach us; (for the Obligation of the Laws of Nature is to be demonstrated to those who acknowledge not the sacred *Scripture:*) Nor, on the contrary, does

---

20. Cumberland, Trinity College MS.adv.c.2.4, Prolegomena, n.p.: "That is what was required by the purpose and intention of my work. For the terms, of which the general proposition encompassing all natural laws is composed are ideas which represent the natural efficiency of human actions necessarily required, according to the present system of things, to procure the good, both public and individual, which man lacks. And the words are necessary here only as familiar signs, whose purpose is to recall to mind those ideas, which might be recalled even if we made no use of such signs. For the nature of things, and of human actions, is sufficient to produce, to imprint, to perpetuate, and to recall to mind, these sorts of ideas, even if one were deaf and mute, and consequently not in a state to recognise the usage of such signs, in which the word consists."

it *suppose,* as does Mr. *Hobbes,* that *"the Earth produc'd suddenly, like Mushrooms, the Bulk of Mankind at their full Growth."* [21] But our *Proposition,* and all the Deductions from thence, might be both understood and acknowledg'd, even by our *first Parents,* considering themselves in the Relation they stood in to *God,* and to the *Posterity* which might be born of them; nor is it less easy to be understood by all those *Nations, who are unacquainted with the History of our first Parents.*

§XII. Nor shall I think it improper here to take *notice,* "That the foregoing *Proposition,* in the same words it declares the *Cause* of the greatest and best *Effect,* declares the *Means* to obtain the best *End":* for the Effect of a rational Agent, after he has consider'd it in his Mind, and has resolv'd to produce it, is call'd his *End;* and the Actions or Causes, by whose Power he endeavours to effect it, are called the *Means.* So also in geometrical Problems, the Causes of the geometrical Effects are the prescrib'd Drawings of Lines: But if such Effect is consider'd as a Problem, whose Solution is requir'd, or is propos'd to us as an End, then the words of the Problem suggest to the Geometrician, the proper Means to obtain his End. From this *Observation* the *Method* is shewn, "How to reduce whatsoever the Moralists have said concerning the Means of obtaining the best End, into *Theorems* concerning the *Power* of human Actions in producing the Effects propos'd"; in which *Form* they may *more easily* be *examin'd,* and if they be true, *more evidently demonstrated.* In like manner we *hence learn,* "How easily all Knowledge concerning the Power of Causes, (which we can any way make subservient to our Purposes,) suggests the Means to attain the End known, and so may be apply'd to Practice, as occasion requires." Lastly, it is also *hence evident,* "That the *Proposition* we are treating of, does in this respect, at least, partake of the Nature of a *Law,* that it respects an End truly worthy of a Law, *the common Good of all Beings,"* or the Honour of God, in conjunction with the Happiness of all Mankind.

And, consequently, the Means to the best End.

21. Hobbes, *On the Citizen,* 8.1, p. 102.

Proceeding
from a compe-
tent Author,
God.

§XIII. But, at first view, perhaps, these *two* necessary *Requisites* to enforce a *Law* may not be perceiv'd in that *Proposition, viz.* a competent
Author, and a sufficient *Sanction* by Rewards and Punishments. But if
it be more closely examin'd, we shall *perceive,* "That upon this very account, that the nature of things impresses it upon our Minds, it necessarily points out its Author, THE FIRST CAUSE, as of all Things, so of
all Truths arising from them"; among the *principal of which Truths* is to
be reputed this true *Proposition,* which we affirm to contain the *fundamental Law of Nature.* Nor can any one in reason desire, that it should
be more evidently *prov'd,* "That God is the Author of this *Proposition,*"
than it is *prov'd,* "That he is the Author of the Nature of Things, whence
the Truth of this Proposition arises." Wherefore, having come to the
Knowledge of its Author, it only remains that we should *shew,* "That
there is a *sufficient* Sanction annex'd by the same Author, and that it is
clearly contain'd in the said *Proposition.*"

Confirm'd by
a sufficient
Sanction.

§XIV. I am not ignorant that a *Sanction,* in the *strictest Sense* of the
Word, is call'd by *Cicero* and *Papinian,* that *Part of the Law, which inflicts
a certain Punishment upon those who have not obey'd what the Law enjoins.*[22] But I have thought it proper to use the *Word* in a *more extensive
Sense,* so as to take in the *Rewards* which the Law promises to the Obedient; for by these also are the Laws *guarded* against the Injury of Men,
and thence are styled [*Sanctae*] *Sacred,* according to *Marcian's* looser
Definition of the Word *Sacred:* "*That is sacred, which is defended and
guarded against the Injury of Men.*"[23] In which Sense it is, that, upon
account of the *Rewards* and *Punishments* wherewith they are confirm'd,
Ulpian, in the following Law, affirms them to be *sacred.*[24] Nevertheless,
if any one is unwilling to depart from the *stricter Signification* of the
Word, there is no occasion to dispute about it, provided we agree in the
Thing. I have added therefore, upon their account, this *Proposition,*
"Such Actions as are contrary to a Care of the publick Good, whether

22. Cicero, *Oratio In C. Verrem,* IV.66; Justinian, *Digest,* XLVIII.19.41.
23. Justinian, *Digest,* I.8.8.
24. Ibid., I.8.9.3.

by a Neglect or Violation thereof, bring Evil upon each part of the System of Rationals, but the greatest upon the Evil-doers themselves"; and
this plainly expresses *Punishment,* without any mention of *Reward.* But
we have almost wholly employ'd our selves in the Proof of the former
Part of the *Proposition,* which relates to the *Rewards* included in Happiness, because hence the latter is evidently demonstrated; and because
the Nature of *Punishment* includes *Evil,*[25] that is, a *Privation* of those
good things which our Nature makes necessary to our Happiness; but
these Privations cannot be understood, unless those *good* things be first
apprehended, to which they are *oppos'd.* Finally, the *Nature of Things*
(whose Footsteps were by us most carefully to be traced in this Treatise)
lays it self out almost wholly, in letting in upon our Minds the *positive*
Notion of Causes and their Effects by our outward *Senses,* which *cannot
receive Negations* and *Privations;* and we are more *early affected* with the
love of present, and hope of future *Good,* than with the hatred or fear
of *Evil:* for no Man therefore *loves Life, Health,* or such grateful Motions
to the Nerves and Spirits as we call *corporeal Pleasures,* or desires their
Causes, that he may avoid *Death, Diseases,* and *Pain;* but because of their
intrinsic Goodness, or *positive Agreement* (to borrow a Phrase from the
Schools) with the Nature of our *Body.* In like manner, no Man therefore
desires the Perfections of the Mind, (such as a more extensive and distinct
Knowledge of the noblest Objects in all respects most agreeably con-
sonant to it self, and the most grateful Perception of Benevolence, of a
well-grounded Hope, and of a Joy in the Prosperity of all Rationals;)
barely that he may *avoid the Uneasinesses* of Ignorance, Ill-will, Envy
and Commiseration; but because of that superlative *Pleasure* which we
experimentally find in such Acts and Habits, which is the *Reason* that to
be *depriv'd* of them is most *ungrateful,* and that the *Causes* of such Privations are themselves *irksome.* Hence therefore it is manifest, that even
Civil Laws, when they receive the *Sanction* of *Punishments, Death,* for
example, or *Forfeiture of Goods,* if we closely examine the Matter, do

25. [Maxwell] "See the Notion advanced here by the Author, examin'd in a Note
on chap. 5. § 40."

oblige Men to Obedience from a *Love of Life,* or of that *Wealth,* which the Laws shew us, how to preserve thereby. For an *Aversion to Death and Poverty,* is nothing but a *Love of Life and Riches;* as he that by two Negatives *says,* "That he would not want (that is, not have) Life," says but the same thing as if he *affirm'd,* "That he would enjoy Life." To which also this may be added, that *Civil Laws* themselves seem to me to be *much more establish'd* from the *End,* which as well their *Enactors* as the *best* Subjects regard, *viz.* the publick *Good* of the Society; part whereof falls to the Share of every good Subject, and therefore naturally brings along with it the Reward of Obedience; *much more,* I say, than by those *Punishments* which they threaten; the Fear whereof moves but a *few,* and those the *worst.*

And, being promulg'd, is therefore a Law. §XV. That the Summary of all the *Precepts* and *Sanctions* of the *Law of Nature,* is contain'd in our *Proposition,* and its *Corollary* concerning the opposite Behaviour, I thus briefly shew. The *Subject* (to borrow a School-Term) of the Proposition is, *an Endeavour, according to our Ability, to promote the common Good of the whole System of Rationals.* This includes our Love of God, and of all Mankind, who are the Parts of this System. God, indeed, is the principal Part; Men, the Subordinate: A Benevolence toward both includes Piety and Humanity, that is, both Tables of the Law of Nature. The *Predicate* of the Proposition (to borrow another Phrase from the Schools) is, *conducing to the good of every Part, in which our own Happiness, as of a Part, is contain'd.* In which, as all those good Things we can procure to all, are said to be the Effect of this Endeavour, so among the rest is not omitted that Collection of good Things, whence our own Happiness arises, which is the greatest Reward of Obedience; as Misery, arising from Actions of a contrary kind, is the greatest Punishment of Wickedness. But the natural *Connexion* of the *Predicate* with the *Subject,* is both the *Foundation* of the Truth of the Proposition, and the *Proof* of the natural Connexion between Obedience and Rewards, Transgression and Punishments.

Hence the Reader will easily observe the true *Reason,* why *this practical Proposition,* and all those which may be deduc'd from thence, oblige all rational Beings who understand them; whilst *other practical Propositions,*

(suppose Geometrical ones,) equally impress'd by Nature, and consequently by God, upon the Mind of Man, *do not oblige* him to conform
his Practice to them; but may *safely be neglected* by most, to whom
the Practice of Geometry is not necessary: Which is wholly owing to the
Nature of the Effects, arising from the *one* and the *other* Practice. The
Effects of the Practice of Geometry are such as most People may want
without Prejudice. But the Effects of a care of the common Good, do
so nearly concern all, of whom we our selves are a part, and upon whose
Pleasure the Happiness of each Individual does in some measure depend, that *such* care cannot be rejected, without the hazard of losing that
Happiness, or the Hope thereof: and this God has *manifested* to us, by
the very *Nature of Things,* and thereby he has sufficiently *promulg'd,* that
he himself is the Author of the Connexion of Rewards and Punishments
with our Actions; whence this *Proposition,* and all others which flow
from thence, commence *Laws* by his Authority.

§XVI. From the very *Terms* of our *Proposition,* it is *manifest,* "That the
adequate and immediate Effect of that Practice which this Law establishes, is, *that which is acceptable to God, and beneficial to all Men;* which
is the natural Good of the whole System of Rationals, even the greatest
of all those good things which can be procur'd for them, as being greater
than the like Good of any part of the same System." Moreover, it sufficiently *implies,* "That the happiness of each Individual" (from the Prospect of enjoying which, or being depriv'd of it, the whole Sanction is
taken) "is deriv'd from the best State of the whole System," as the nourishment of each Member of an Animal depends upon the nourishment
of the whole Mass of Blood diffus'd thro' the whole.

> Actions agree-
> able thereto,
> *good.*

Hence it is *manifest,* "That this greatest Effect" (not any small Portion
thereof, the private Happiness, suppose, of any single Person) "is the
principal end of the Lawgiver, and of every one who truly obeys his
Will." It is likewise hence *evident,* "That those human Actions, which,
from their own *natural* Force or Efficacy, are apt to promote the common Good, are call'd *naturally Good,* and indeed better than those Actions which are subservient to the private Good of any Individual, in
proportion, as the publick Good is greater than a private."

Right.   In like manner, "Such Actions as take the shortest way to this Effect, as to their End, are *naturally Right,* because of their natural resemblance to a right Line, which is the shortest that can be drawn between any two given Points." Nevertheless, the same Actions, afterward, when they are compar'd with the Law, whether natural or positive, which is the Rule of Morality, and they are found conformable to it; are call'd *morally Good,* as also *Right,* that is, agreeing with the Rule: but the Rule itself is call'd right, as pointing out the shortest way to the End.

Beautiful.   So also, because that State of all Men, which most abounds with all the natural Goods, both of Mind and Body, *fitly proportion'd* among themselves, and appointed to the best End, is naturally the most beautiful, (as plainly agreeing with the Definition of *Beauty,* taken from the *Figure* and *Symmetry of the Parts;*) it is *manifest,* "That those Actions which have a natural Tendency to produce or preserve such a State, may justly be call'd *Beautiful* or *Decent.*" And hence may be explain'd the τὸ καλον and τὸ πρέπον, the *Beauty* and *Decency,* which Philosophers so often celebrate in virtuous Actions.

Amiable.   Lastly, seeing in the Chapter *concerning Good* it is largely *shewn,* "That it may be distinctly understood, without any regard to our selves," the Reader cannot doubt but that we must *acknowledge,* "That the Good is in itself *Amiable,* which contains in it every particular Good of each Individual." Therefore it is very absurd, that it should be made subordinate to the Happiness of any one Man, which is so small a part of so great a Good.

Honourable.   By a like Reasoning it is *manifest,* "That Actions conducive to this End, as being the best and most beautiful, are in themselves amiable, and highly to be commended by all rational Beings, and therefore, upon account of that high *Honour,* to which their beneficent Nature intitles them, deservedly call'd *Honest* or *Honourable.*"

These Observations I thought the more necessary, lest any one should erroneously imagine, that I did not sufficiently acknowledge the *intrinsic Perfections* of Piety and Charity, because I have deduc'd the *Sanctions* of the Laws of Nature, by which such Actions are enjoin'd, from the *happiness or misery of Individuals,* consequent upon their Obedience, or

Disobedience to the said Laws. Even in *Civil Laws,* the *Sanctions* of the Laws are sufficiently *distinguish'd* from the End and *adequate Effect,* viz. The publick Good; part, however, of the Effect of a Civil Law, is the infliction of Punishments, or the conferring of Rewards, by which the Law is guarded.

§XVII. But because the *Connexion of Rewards and Punishments with such Actions as promote the public Good, or the contrary, is somewhat obscur'd* by those *evil Things* which happen to the *Good,* and those *good Things* which happen to the *Evil;* it seems necessary to our purpose, more carefully to *shew,* "That (notwithstanding these) that Connexion is sufficiently constant and manifest in human Nature, so that thence may, with certainty, be inferr'd the Sanction of the Law of Nature, commanding these Actions, and forbidding those."

> The *Evil* often happens to the observers of the general Law of Nature, and *Good* to those who violate it; the Sanction mention'd prov'd sufficient, by a general Proof.

We suppose, 1. That Punishment, or that Reward, a *sufficient* Sanction, whose Value, all things rightly consider'd, exceeds the Advantage arising from the breach of the Law.

2. In comparing the Effects of good and evil Actions, those good or evil Things, which can neither be procur'd, nor avoided, by *human Industry,* are not to be taken into the Account. Such are those which happen by natural *Necessity,* or by mere *Chance,* from external Causes: for these both may, and do, happen alike both to good and bad. We shall therefore here consider those only, which can be taken care of by *human Reason,* as in some measure *depending upon our Actions.*

Having thus premis'd a *general Proof,* deduc'd from this *Consideration,* "That the particular Persons who promote or oppose the common Good, are parts of that Whole, which their Actions either befriend or prejudice, and therefore necessarily partake of the Advantage or Disadvantage thence arising": We come to *particular Proofs* taken, partly from the *Causes* of such Actions, which are treated of in the Chapter *concerning human Nature;* partly from their *Effects* and Consequences, which are consider'd more at large in the Chapter *concerning the Obligation of the Law of Nature.* But that Chapter is more prolix, and less clear, than the rest, because therein I have been frequently forc'd to follow my *Antagonist,* into that most confus'd State which he supposes,[26] in order to *confute him from his own Concessions;* and have been oblig'd to answer many Objections, not only of his, but also of some other better Philosophers. Wherefore I shall here briefly lay before the Reader, both *what* I there aim'd at, and the *manner how* all these things make to our purpose, lest he should suspect, that I had lost my way in so great a variety of Matter.

By *particular* Proofs taken from the Causes of human Actions.

§XVIII. The *Causes* of human Actions are the Powers of the Mind and Body of Man. Wherefore, because I have observ'd it to be *manifest,* "That Happiness, or the highest Reward, is necessarily connected with the most full and constant exercise of all our Powers, about the best and greatest Objects and Effects, which are adequate and proportionable to them"; I hence *collect,* "That Men endow'd with these Faculties, are naturally bound, under the Penalty of forfeiting their Happiness, to employ or exercise them about the noblest Objects in Nature," *viz.* God, and Man his Image. Nor can it be long a *Question,* "Whether our Faculties may be more properly employ'd in cultivating Friendship or Enmity with these, in engaging with them in a State of Peace or War." For it is *plain,* "That there can be no *neutral* State, in which God and Men shall be neither lov'd, nor hated and irritated; or in which we shall act neither acceptably nor unacceptably to either, especially when we make use of things without us." For of necessity, we must *either* take care, not to deprive others of things necessary to their Happiness, which, without Benevolence, cannot be suppos'd; *or* we shall, willingly, take them away, which is a sure indication of a malicious Mind. But if it be *acknowledg'd,* "That there is an evident Necessity, in order to Happiness, of cultivating friendship with God and Man," the *Sanction* of that most general *Law of Nature,* which *alone* we are here tracing, is of course *granted.* For *that alone* establishes, both all natural Religion, and every thing that is necessary to the happiness of Mankind. Such are, beside *Piety,* (1.) A peaceful *Commerce* among different Nations, which is the Subject of the Law of Nations: (2.) The Establishment and Preservation of *civil Society,*

26. [Maxwell] "His State of Nature, which he makes a State of War."

which is the Scope of civil Laws: (3.) The Firmness of *domestic Affection* and of Friendship, which are establish'd, both by those general Rules which settle the Peace of Nations, and by the more particular Laws of *Oeconomics.* We have therefore collected very many things in the Chapter *concerning human Nature,* by which Individuals, in some measure, become capable of so great a Society,[27] and are, remotely at least, dispos'd toward it.[28] And here we *intreat* the Reader, "That he would not consider these Observations, apart only, but together, that from them all united may result *one* Argument," proving the *Sanction* of this most general Law from *this,* "That Men must necessarily fall short of their greatest Happiness, which consists in Action, or the proper and adequate use of their Faculties, unless they exercise them in cultivating a Friendship with God and Men": to produce this Effect they were most especially fitted by Nature, which truly leaves the Transgressors of the Law without excuse.

§XIX. From the *Effects* of human Actions, with respect to the common Good of rational Beings, we thus *shew,* "That a *Sanction* by Rewards and Punishments is annexed to them." It is *manifest,* "That by the above-mention'd Endeavour, in the first place, *God,* as being in the highest degree both wise and beneficent to all rational Beings, is *lov'd* and honour'd; the Life and all other *Possessions* of Men of all Nations, are safely *preserv'd,* according to the measure of our Ability; *civil Government* is readily *constituted,* where it is wanting, and as readily *preserv'd,* where it is found; and all *Advantages,* consistent with the good of the Whole, are

From the Effects of human Actions.

---

27. [Maxwell] "By the *great Society,* the Author here means the Kingdom of God, or System of Rationals."

28. Cumberland, Trinity College MS.adv.c.2.4, Prolegomena, n.p. Replacement manuscript text (to the end of the paragraph): "But, since the natural causes, as much internal, disposing man to form and maintain this universal society, as external, attracting them to do so, act conjointly: and it is through the united forces of all these causes that society is now established and preserved: I must beg the readers, who will seek the whole cause or complete reason for this effect to consider all the partial causes, which I have detailed, as joined together, and each in its rank; by which he will see, that there results from considering them in such a way, an argument which is sufficient of itself to prove the sanction of the most general law of nature."

procur'd to each, and, consequently, to our selves also; and nothing done to any one, which a regard to the Whole does not permit." In Man, nothing but a *Propension* toward the good of all, guided by the Conduct of a *prudent Understanding*, can produce so great Advantages; nor, if such an Endeavour be not wanting in us, can any thing be desir'd to obtain this End, which we are not willing, to the utmost of our power, to perform. Wherefore, since *these Effects* may be certainly foreseen to follow from *this Endeavour*, no one can be ignorant, *that* in *them* are contain'd the present Comfort and Joys of Religion, which in all places are ever join'd with the hope of a happy Immortality; *that* moreover to this Study and Endeavour are annex'd as Rewards, the many Advantages of peaceful *Commerce* with Foreigners, of *civil* and *domestic Government*, and of *Friendship;* and *that* these Advantages *cannot* be obtain'd by *any other* Method in our power: And consequently, *that* whoever rejects the care of the common Good, does so far reject the Causes of his own Happiness, and embrace the immediate Causes of his Misery and Punishment.

To be brief; seeing it is *manifest* from the Nature of Things, "That the chief Happiness which we can procure to our selves, arises jointly from promoting Piety and Peace, mutual Commerce among Nations, civil and domestic Government, and also firm Friendship; and that the care of all these things together is to be found only in his Mind, who studies the common Good of all rational Beings"; it *follows*, "That the greatest Reward which Man can procure, is the natural Consequence of this Endeavour, as the want thereof, or Punishment, is the necessary result of Actions of a contrary kind": The *former* of these, "Which assigns the Causes of that Happiness, which single Persons are wont or able to obtain," we have prov'd from Effects confirm'd by *Experience;* the *latter*, "That Piety and universal Benevolence toward all Men, are contain'd in the care of the common Good," we have shewn from its *Definition* and *Parts* in the *Corollaries*, Chap. 9. But a *Conclusion* drawn from *such Premises*, is known by the *Light of Nature*.

The contingent. §XX. I acknowledge, however, "That all these Effects are not entirely in our Power, but that many of them depend upon the Benevolence of other rational Beings." But *since* we *know* from their *Nature,* as being *analogous,* or like, to our own, "That the common Good is the best and greatest End, which they can propose to themselves; and that the Perfection of their Nature requires, both that they should act for an End, and for this, rather than for any other not so good"; and *since* moreover we *know* from *experience,* "That such Effects of universal Benevolence may generally be procur'd from others by our Actions": It is but *reasonable,* "That they should be reckon'd and esteem'd among the Effects of our Actions, or such Consequences of them, as for the most part happen." Because every one is thought to be able to do, whatsoever he can perform by the help of his Friends. The *whole Reward,* which is annex'd to good Actions by the natural Constitution of the Universe, may not unfitly be compar'd to the Treasury or *public Stock,* which does not arise *only* from *certain* Payments, but *also* from various *contingent* Taxes: Suppose the Tolls paid upon account of Harbours, High-ways, and publick Bridges, whose Value is great, tho not certainly and distinctly known, yet often farm'd out at a determin'd Price. In *like manner,* in computing the Value of this Reward, there ought to be taken into the Account, *not only* those Parts of it, which *necessarily* accompany good Actions, (such as that formal Happiness, as it is call'd, which consists in the Knowledge and Love of God, and perhaps of those Men whose Wills conspire with his, the absolute Government of all our Passions, a most pleasant Harmony and Agreement of all our Principles of Action with all the Parts of our Life, the Favour of God, and the well-grounded Hope of a happy Immortality,) *but* there ought also to be taken into the Account, the *contingent* Advantages of good Actions; such are all those Blessings, which either accrue to us from the religious Disposition of other Men, or flow from civil Society, the good Correspondence of different Nations among one another, or from private Friendship: the Interests of all these several States, being as much taken care of, and promoted, by our good Actions, as in us lies. By a *like Reasoning* we understand, of what *Parts* the *whole Punishment* consists, which is the Consequence of Actions *hurtful* to the Publick; the Law prohibiting them, receives its proper *Sanctions* from all those *Consequences,* which are opposite to those just now mention'd.

Because they
may be suffi-
ciently esti-
mated.

§XXI. We all of us learn, from the Necessity of that *Condition* to which
we are born, and in which we live, how to *estimate contingent Advantages,*
that is, such Causes as will probably benefit us; and by the hope of such
we are inclin'd to Action. For the *Air* itself, to the breathing of which
we are forc'd by an impulse which is natural, is *not always an Advantage*
to our Blood and Spirits, but is sometimes infected with a deadly Contagion; *Meat, Drink,* and *Exercise, don't always preserve Life;* even they
are often the Causes of Diseases. *Husbandry sometimes rewards* our Labours with *Loss,* instead of Gain; yet we are *naturally inclin'd* to such
Actions from the *hope* of Good thence probably arising; *as naturally,* by
a *like hope* of probable Good, are we *mov'd* to cultivate the common
Interest: which Hope, nevertheless, is of itself *neither* the *only, nor* the
principal Cause impelling, but as it *conspires* with those *other* Rewards
already mention'd, which are naturally inseparable.

But with *how great Probability* we hope, from all other Men jointly
consider'd, for a return which may repay our Labours laid out upon the
common Good; we shall *hence* form the best judgment, *if* we consider
what both the *Experience* of the present Time, and the *History* of the
past, witness concerning the Practice of *all Nations* hitherto known, with
regard to this End. Among *every one of them* we may openly observe
some *reverence* of one Deity, at least, by which when they have taken an
Oath, they are deterr'd from Perjury: You may *every where* observe an
advantageous *Commerce* carried on between such Nations as are mutually known to one another, unless it be interrupted by a formal War:
Civil Government, and a distinction of *Property* depending thereon, is
every where preserv'd: The *Ties of Blood* and *Friendship* are generally
every where observ'd. But because the *whole Endeavour to promote the
common Good,* means nothing more than the *Worship* of a *Deity,* a Care
of *Commerce* and *Peace* among Nations, of *civil* and *domestic Government,* and also of *Friendship,* as its *Parts* jointly consider'd; it is *manifest,*
"That the care of that Good is in some measure every where to be found
among Men"; whence many Advantages of Peace and mutual Aid necessarily accrue to Individuals.

Nay, it seems to me *manifest,* "That each one who has reach'd Man's
Estate, owes his past Years much more to the Pains of others, than to

any care of his own," which in his Childhood is little or nothing. For we then wholly depend on that Obedience, which others yield to those Laws, whereby the Affairs of Families, of the State; and of Religion are govern'd; all which flow from a Care of the common Good. Hence it comes to pass, "That, if afterwards we hazard, nay lose, our Lives for the publick Good, we part with less for its sake, than we had already receiv'd from it": for we lose only an *uncertain Hope* of future Joys, if we should live, nay, not that; for it is rather certain, that scarce any Hope can remain to particular Persons, where the common Good is trampled under foot. But we had *before receiv'd* from it the *real Advantages* of Life, and all those Perfections which adorn'd us.[29]

Nor doubt I, but that the *greatest Advantages* we experience from mutual Assistance in a *social State,* might have been *foreseen* from the *Nature* of Man, by our *first Parents,* if we suppose them to have *deliberated,* "Whether they should *more effectually* promote the true Happiness of their Children, by persuading them to the exercise of *Piety* towards God and their Parents, and of mutual *Benevolence* among Brethren," (which is the Summary of *Religion,* and of *civil Government,* which was first exercis'd in a single Family, as well as of the *Law of Nations,*) "than by initiating them in the Mysteries of Atheism, and exhorting each to claim every thing to himself, and so immediately to commence Robbers and Murderers of one another." But the good and bad *Consequences* (thus *naturally known* from the *Nature* of Things) of such human Actions, because they are *foreshewn* by *God,* to *Men deliberating* concerning their Actions, in order to *incline* them to, or deter them from, Action, are intirely in the Nature of *Rewards* and *Punishments,* by which a Law receives its *Sanction.*

29. Ibid. Manuscript addition: "Setting aside even the duty imposed by gratitude, this proves the sanction of the most general law of nature, as one may foresee that, from a life constantly modeled on the demands of the public good, there will be more benefit than if one follows the promptings of boundless self-consideration."

And that Esti-
mate is farther
confirm'd, by
the natural
Manner of
nourishing and
preserving Ani-
mals.

§XXII. These *Observations* seem to me most evidently *just,* because they shew a *Method of preserving the several Members of the rational System,* extremely *like* that whereby *Nature instructs all Animals* to *preserve* the Health and Strength of the *several Members of their Bodies.* Nature obliges them, in order to this End, to take Nourishment, and breathe the Air, which, tho by reason of internal Diseases, or external Hurts, (Bruises, Wounds, and Fractures) they do not always give the *Members* the intended Strength, do yet most commonly *immediately* preserve that Temper of the Blood, which is necessary to the Life of the *whole Body.* She teaches us in the *same manner,* that by Actions *immediately* promoting the common Good, the various Perfections of Individuals, (who are *Members* of the rational System,) are ordinarily to be expected, as being not less naturally deriv'd from thence, than the Strength of our Hands from a just Temper in the Mass of Blood. We must confess, however, that many things may happen, by means whereof this general *Care of the Whole* may not *always* produce the propos'd Happiness of Individuals, without allay; as breathing and eating, however necessary to the whole Body, do not ward off *all* Diseases and Accidents. For, as well by an *irregular Behaviour of our Fellow-Citizens,* like an *indisposition in the Bowels,* as by *foreign Invasion,* good Men may be depriv'd of some of the Rewards of their good Actions, and may suffer Evils from without. But *because such Evils* are generally *warded off* by the force of Concord and Government, (which always flow from a care of the publick Good,) and are often, after short suffering, remov'd by our own Strength, and the Aid of the civil Power, as *Diseases retire* upon Nature's taking a healthful turn; and are often also compensated with greater Advantages, partly by the Virtues of others, but chiefly by means of civil Government, and of foreign Leagues: *hence* it comes to pass, "That the Race of Men has in no Age been extinguish'd, and that most Societys have lasted longer than particular Men, or even the most long-liv'd Animals."

From these Considerations it is *evident,* "That the wicked Dispositions of some Men, and those Motions of the Affections, which sometimes arise in all Men, contrary to the common Good, do no more hinder us from acknowledging, That the more powerful Inclinations of all Mankind, jointly consider'd, are carried towards that which we daily see procur'd thereby, *the preservation and further perfection of the whole;*

than Diseases sometimes arising in the Parts of Animals, hinder our confessing, That the whole frame of the human Body, and the natural Functions of the Parts, are adapted to preserve Life, propagate the Species, and preserve the vigour of each Member for its usual Term of Duration." For from *hence* are not only first *constituted Societies, Embassies,* and foreign *Leagues;* but also, if at any time a *League* with any Nation be broken, even the *breaker of the League* immediately betakes himself to the Faith of other Nations, by Engagements enter'd into with them, and so *by his own Action condemns himself:* And if at any time *one Religion* is *suppress'd* in a Nation, *another* is immediately *replac'd,* in order to procure the Favour of the Deity: So when any *Commonwealth* is *dissolv'd* by Sedition or War, *another* is immediately *thence form'd* or *enlarg'd.* Now these Observations make it *manifest,* "That the whole System of Rationals, is as much, or more, form'd for its own Preservation, and the subordinate one of its Members, than the universal corporeal System is form'd for its Preservation: whilst the Generation of one Body follows from the Corruption of another; and, in the Generation of single Animals, they are form'd with Organs, by which they for some time preserve themselves, and propagate their kind."

§XXIII. I have thus briefly laid down the Method, by which I have deduc'd the Sanction of the Laws of Nature; in which I have consider'd the Happiness which naturally flows from good Actions, as the Reward annex'd to them by the Author of Nature; and the loss thereof as a Punishment, not less naturally connected with evil Actions. For whatever Good or Evil is the necessary Consequence of human Actions, must necessarily be contain'd in such practical Propositions, as truly declare the Consequences of those Actions. And God himself is suppos'd to declare those practical Propositions, which are necessarily suggested to our Minds by the Nature, as well of our own Actions, as of those of other rational Beings, and which truly foretel what Consequences will follow. But those "Advantages and Disadvantages, which God himself pronounces annex'd to human Actions, and by which we are admonish'd to pursue those, and avoid these," are really and truly *Rewards* and *Punishments.*

In *these things,* however, I *agree,* as well *with those who say,* "That Vir-

The Author's Method of deducing the Sanction of the Laws of Nature, confirm'd by universal Consent.

tue contains Happiness in itself, and so is its own Reward: as also with *those others,* who beside look for other Advantages, whether of Mind or Body; from God, their own Conscience, their Family, or their Friends, from their own Country, or from foreign Nations; whether we enjoy them in this Life, or with reason hope for them in one hereafter."[30] And our Method seems much to be confirm'd by this, that *all,* of how different Sentiments soever in Morality, yet *agree* in this, "That good Actions ought by all means to be honour'd with suitable Rewards, and that they are actually so honour'd; and that evil Actions ought necessarily to be restrain'd by Punishments, and that they are so restrain'd." In *these* Points, *Philosophers,* however otherwise differing, *agree,* as do the *Founders of all Religions,* and *all Lawgivers.*

Even they, who would seem to neglect Rewards, and would *deduce all the Virtues from Gratitude,* must needs *own,* "That Gratitude flows from the Remembrance of Benefits receiv'd." But it argues *as much Self-love,* to be excited to good Actions from *Benefits* already *receiv'd,* as to do them for the sake of the *Hopes* of such;[31] nay, even he seems to act somewhat the *more generously* of the two, who is mov'd by the *Hope* only of Good, because there is somewhat of *uncertainty* for the most part mix'd with Hope, than he who does as much for *equal Benefits,*

---

30. Stoic philosophers believed that virtue was its own reward; by those who look for goods in this life, Cumberland signals the Peripatetic philosophers. Barbeyrac, *Traité Philosophique des Loix Naturelles* (1744), p. 26, n. 2.

31. [Maxwell] "Actions from Gratitude, cannot be said to flow from Self-love, or desire of private Good to the Agent; since in a grateful Office, the Intention of the Agent, is not to obtain any farther private Advantage. 'Tis this Intention only, of obtaining private Good, which denominates an Action *Self-interested.* This is not the Case of *real* Gratitude, however it may be in some *pretended* Offices of Gratitude— The Mistakes of many Writers upon this Head, arise from the ambiguous Use of these Words, *(per, propter, ob,)* or of their corresponding *English* Words, *(for, on account of, for the sake of, in consideration of,)* a Benefit. They denote either, *First, Acting with intention to obtain a Benefit;* this is *from Self-love:* Or, *Secondly,* When remembrance of a Benefit raises Love in the Receiver toward the Benefactor, and desire to please him, without Intention of farther private Good to the Receiver; this is *not from Self-love.* We see a *like* Affection, but perhaps a little *weaker,* arises from observing Beneficence toward a Third Person. *See the true Answer to this whole Difficulty, in a Note, on* Chap. 5. § 45."

which he *already enjoys*. But besides, the *Memory of past Benefits* affects the Mind with a certain *Pleasure,* which is a part of *Happiness,* and consequently of a *Reward,* which we therefore acknowledge to be a proper motive to good Actions. Nor seems it possible, that the Consent of all Men in these Matters should be so unanimous, unless the common Nature and Reason of all *dictated* this one and the same thing to them all, "That the chief End, the common Good of all, could not otherwise be preserv'd unviolated, than by Rewards and Punishments; and that it is therefore every where guarded by them."

§XXIV. Moreover, this Method, by which I have reduc'd all the Precepts of the Law of Nature to *one,* seems useful; because the Proof of this *one* Proposition is more *easy* and expeditious, than that of those *many,* which are usually propos'd by Philosophers; and the ease of the Memory is better consulted, to which daily calling to mind a single Sentence, is not a Burden: and, (which is the greatest Advantage of all,) from the very Nature of the common Good, which in this *Proposition* we are directed to promote, a *certain Rule* or Measure is afforded to the prudent Man's Judgment, by the help whereof he may ascertain *that just Measure in his Actions and Affections,* in which Virtue consists. This Task *Aristotle* has assign'd to the *Judgment of the Prudent,* in his Definition of *Virtue,*[32] but has not pointed out the Rule by which such Judgment is to be form'd. Our *Proposition* shews, "That the Rule is to be taken from the Nature of the best and greatest End, respect being had to all the Parts of the whole System of Rationals, or of that Society of which God is the Head, the Members, all God's Subjects." For hence we shall be directed to such Acts of *Piety* towards God, as are perfectly *consistent* with that *Peace* and *Commerce,* which is to be preserv'd among all Nations, with the Establishment of *civil Government,* and with that Obedience which is to be paid to it; as also with the more private care of the *Happiness of Individuals:* And we shall likewise be directed to such Acts of the most diffusive *Humanity,* as shall be perfectly *subordinate* to true *Piety:* And *universally,* "Each of our Affections and Actions will bear that

The reduction of the Laws of Nature to one, useful.

32. Aristotle, *Nicomachean Ethics,* II.6.

Proportion to the whole of our Strength, and to one another; which that
Good, to the procuring which each of these Actions is subservient, bears
to the greatest Good of the Whole, which in the whole Course of our
Lives, we are able to effect": Whence we shall certainly *take care,* "Not
to be diligent about Matters of smaller Moment, and remiss about those
of more Importance; not slothful about Matters of publick Concern,
and earnest about those of private; but shall, in our Affections and Endeavours, take our Measures from the Value of that which is to be
effected."

Lastly, from this Fountain is to be deriv'd that *Order* among the particular Laws of Nature, according to which a former, in some measure,
limits a latter; which the learned Dr. *Sharrock* has very judiciously and
solidly observ'd in his Book *of Offices,* especially in the tenth Chapter:
so that *greater Regard ought to be had to the not invading another's Property,*
than to the keeping our Promise; to keeping a lawful Promise, than requiting
a Benefit, &c.[33] The *reason* of which is to be deduc'd from our Principle,
"Because it conduces more to the common Good, that the principal special Law of Nature, concerning dividing and preserving Property, should
not be violated by the Invasion of another's Right, than that any one
should stand to such a Promise, as could not be perform'd, without invading another's Right." And the Reason is alike in comparing the other
Laws, which I hereafter rank according to the Order of their Dignity.
He that desires more upon this Head, let him consult the Author now
cited; it is sufficient for my Purpose, to have deduc'd the Reason of the
Order that is among the Laws of Nature, from our Principle. Unless
perhaps it may seem necessary here to add, That it ought *not to seem*
strange to any, that I have *said,* "That no Right whatsoever, no Virtue,
can be fully explain'd, without respect had to the State of all rational
Beings, or of the whole intellectual System." For *we see in Natural Phi-*
losophy, "That those Accidents of Bodies which are daily obvious to our
Senses, such as the communication of Motion, Gravitation, the Action
of Light and Heat, Firmness and Fluidity, Rarefaction and Condensation, cannot be clearly explain'd, without having a respect to the whole

33. Sharrock, *De Officiis Secundum Naturae Jus,* ch. 10.

material System, and to that Motion which is to be preserv'd therein."
It is likewise *manifest in Mechanics,* "That no Effect of any Motion, connected with others, and subordinate to them in a continued Series, can
be exactly deduc'd, except all their Motions, and that according to the
Order in which they depend upon one another, be calculated and
compar'd."

Further, *from this Order* among the Laws of Nature, (by which all
particular ones are subordinate to the general Law, and among particular
ones, the latter to the former,) we may best, in my Opinion, *demonstrate,*
"That God never dispens'd with any of them; but that in such Cases,
in which the Obligation of the latter might seem taken away, the matter
was so chang'd, as that only the prior Laws took place": so it is *evident,*
"That the Law establishing a division of Property, and prohibiting to
invade what is another's, was not dispens'd with, when God gave permission to the *Israelites* to invade the Land of the *Canaanites,* who had
transgress'd his Laws."[34] For that same Law *determines,* "That it is necessary for the public Good, that God should have a Dominion paramount over all, as well Things as Persons, in right of which (whensoever
he shall judge it conducive to the common Good) he may take away any
Creature's Property in his own Life or Goods, and transfer it to another,
by a proper Signification of his Will," as we read was done in the Case
propos'd; whence it appears, that the *Israelites* only *claim'd their own,*
and were not authoriz'd to invade what was another's. In like manner
also, the *Law is not dispens'd with,* which, for the common Good, *pro-
hibits the hurting Innocents,* if at any time an *innocent* Person is commanded (when the common Good requires it) to expose himself to *Danger,* or undergo even Death, if God clearly enough reveals his Will in
the Affair: for by this means God, the Lord of All, receives his *due Honour;* and in the *properest manner,* because the *chief End is provided for,*
according to his Judgment. Therefore in *this Case,* the *Safety* of a single
Person is neither a *Part* nor a *Cause* of the *common Good;* but on the
contrary, his *Detriment* is suppos'd to be the Means necessary to that
End. This will be yet clearer, if we consider, that the Truth of this *general*

34. Deuteronomy 20.16–17.

Proposition, "The Cause, to its power, preserving the Whole, to its power preserves all the Parts," is *not chang'd* in any particular Case; altho sometimes it should happen, that a *sound Hand* expos'd to *danger,* in defence of the *Head,* should be *cut off* by outward Violence: for we have already shewn, that the perpetual Obligation of these Laws is founded on the Truth of a practical Proposition, which is founded on this, and is therefore in no case changeable.

§XXV. I shall here say nothing concerning the *Corollaries,* which I have drawn in the Close of the following Treatise, because I know of nothing, by which I might render their Proof more *concise,* or more *clear.* I will take upon me, nevertheless, to *affirm,* "That I have not pointed out all those useful Deductions, which naturally flow from our Principles"; nor truly can I enumerate them all. For in *these* are contain'd the most general Rules of *Equity,* which both Magistrates and private Persons may apply to all the new Cases that daily happen. From *these, Magistrates* may understand what civil Laws are equitable, and, consequently, fit to be retain'd; and what want to be corrected by Equity. They may likewise *thence* perceive, what Conditions of Leagues, and what Causes of foreign War, are just, what unjust. *Hence* also *private Persons* will learn always to obey the Laws, whether Divine or Human, which *thence* derive their Authority; and in those Cases, in which by these Laws they are left at liberty, (of which innumerable daily happen,) they will be directed to regard always the best End, and be restrain'd from all unlawful Methods of pursuing their private Happiness. *Both* will perceive, that they are oblig'd to make daily a greater Progress in Virtue, and that in such proportion, as their Skill and Strength to promote the publick Good become greater by Experience, and as the publick Happiness becomes capable of any farther increase.

§XXVI. The *Origin of civil Societies* I have deduc'd from *two* Laws of Nature, which are therefore to be consider'd together: (1.) From that which commands the Settlement of *Property,* as well in Things as in human Labour, where it is not found already established; but, where it is found, the Preservation of the same inviolably, as a Means principally

---

[margin notes, left column:]

More, useful, Inferences may be deduced from this general Law, than our Author has drawn.

His Account of the Origin of Societies, and Duties of Humanity, agreeable to the Scriptures.

necessary to the common Good. And, (2.) From that which enjoins a *peculiar Benevolence of Parents towards their Children;* for, in consequence of that Benevolence, our first Parents must have granted to their Children, when of Age, both a Patrimony of their own, out of that full Dominion, which they had over all things by the former of these Laws, and also a paternal Power over their own Offspring. Hence it might easily happen, when Families were increased, that *some* Heads of Families, either in their own Life time, or by their Testaments at their Death, might divide their Dominion among many Sons, by giving to each an absolute Command over his own Family, or over many; whence many *Monarchies* might arise:[35] *Other* Heads of Families might also elsewhere settle *Aristocracies, others, Democracies;* but among *all* these sovereign Powers, the *Obligation would still continue,* "To promote the common Good, and to observe those Precepts thence necessarily arising, concerning the settlement and preservation of Property, keeping Promises, requiting Benefits, a limited Care of themselves and of their Off-spring, and an universal Humanity"; which are the principal Heads of the Law of Nations. But this is only an account of a *possible* and rightful Constitution of different Commonwealths, which also exhibits all their general Properties; nor does true Philosophy *search for* other Hypotheses. The Question concerning their *actual* Formation, is wholly concerning a *Matter of Fact,* depending on free Agents, and therefore is *not demonstrable from Principles of Reason;* the Proof here is to be taken from *Testimony* only. Facts, within the Memory of Persons now living, are to be prov'd from the *personal Testimony* of Witnesses: But Matters more antient, the Wit of Man cannot hand down otherwise to Posterity, than either by *oral Tradition,* (such as is no where to be found worthy of Credit in this Affair,) or by *Writings* compos'd on purpose to preserve their Memory; such are the Monuments preserv'd in the Archives of States, and Histories.

Seeing therefore it is *manifest,* "That the Original of all States that we know, exceeds the Memory of all Men now living," the only way we have left to form a Judgment concerning their *Origin* and *Constitution,*

35. Cf. ibid., 9.6.

is from the antient *Laws* and other *Records* of each State, publickly pre-serv'd and approv'd of; or, if we would inquire farther, we must have recourse to the most authentic and credible *Histories;* but, amongst these, we find none of equal Antiquity and Credit with that of *Moses,* which acknowledges no *antienter Authority,* under God, over Things and Persons, than is that of *Fathers of Families* over their Wives and Chil-dren, and, after them, of their *eldest Sons.* We do not *read* there, "That *Adam* and *Eve* had such a Right to all things, as made it lawful for them," (if they had thro' a mistake imagin'd it conducive to their own Preser-vation,) "to wage War with GOD, and with one another, without the Provocation of an Injury; and so mutually deprive one another of Food and Life." On the contrary, there are *Intimations,* "That they knew, and acknowledg'd, the Obligation of all those things, that were then req-uisite to the common Good of the KINGDOM OF GOD in its yet Infant-state." The Exercise of the divine Dominion in giving Laws, and the Derivation of human Property from the Gift of God, both there spoken of, oblige us to acknowledge such a Division of Property, as we have affirm'd to be necessary. Nay, without violating the Donation of God, neither of our first Parents could rob the other of the Necessaries of Life, much less of Life it self. Yet farther, they were so far from entring into a State of Enmity, that we *read,* "They contracted a Friendship at first sight," which could not subsist without Fidelity and Gratitude, lim-iting their Self-love; and presently *follows,* "A Desire of propagating their Species, and consequently of preserving it." But seeing, according to this History, our first Parents had only themselves and their Children, to consider as Parts of human Kind, it is *manifest,* "That in this singular friendly Intercourse between themselves as Husband and Wife, and nat-ural Affection toward the Children to be born of them, is contain'd Hu-manity towards all, as the less is contain'd in the greater." From hence it is *evident,* "That our Philosophy does perfectly agree with the sacred History."

The Author abstains from Theological Disputes.

§XXVII. Nevertheless, I have, in the following Treatise, purposely con-tain'd myself wholly within the Bounds of Philosophy, and have there-fore altogether *abstained from Theological Questions,* concerning the

Right of the *divine Dominion* in the Affair of *Predestination,* or of the *Satisfaction* made by *Christ;* nor have I consider'd, how much the Faculties of Mankind have been impair'd by the *Transgression of our first Parents,* concerning which we ought to form our Judgment from the Testimony of Scripture; but I have endeavour'd to prove the *Law of Nature,* only from that *Reason* we find ourselves *at present* possess'd of, and from *Experience.* We are however *certain,* "That nothing contradictory to the just Conclusions of our Reason, could ever be revealed by God." And we *therefore* believe the sacred Scriptures to be the Word of God, the Author of Nature, *because* they every where illustrate, confirm, and promote the Law of Nature.

It is in consequence of this Purpose of abstaining from all Theological Controversies, that I would not dispute with Mr. *Hobbes* about the *Sense of Scripture;* which moreover seem'd therefore to me principally needless, because I cannot bring my self to believe, that he is seriously mov'd by its Authority, as being what he looks upon to be wholly deriv'd from the Will of particular States; and has in consequence taught, that it is changeable at their Pleasure; here, of Force, and elsewhere, of none.[36]

§XXVIII. I have said little or nothing of the *Eternity* of the Laws of Nature; to which, however, I have with the greatest Diligence every where had an Eye, whilst I endeavour to demonstrate the *unchangeable Truth* of those Propositions, by a *natural Connexion* between their *Terms;* for their Eternity entirely depends upon their *necessary Truth.* For there is no *doubt,* but that "Propositions which are necessarily true, are true whensoever they can be thought of"; and it is equally *evident,* "That the Truth of such was from Eternity known to the divine Mind." *Such an Eternity,* none, that I know of, denies to *mathematical Propositions,* even *newly invented* or known among Men. To this purpose I think it proper only further to *observe,* "That the Connexion is no less necessary between human Actions, however free, whenever they are perform'd, and their Effects, than between the Actions or Motions of mere Bodies,

The Laws of Nature eternally, because necessarily, true.

---

36. Cumberland may be thinking about Hobbes's argument in *Leviathan,* ch. 33.

and the Effects thence demonstrated." Three Right Lines, for example, *freely* drawn by a Man, according to the Direction of the first of *Euclid's Elements,* do not *less necessarily* form a Triangle, than if they were drawn by *necessary Causes.*[37] In *like manner,* "Love towards God, and all Men, altho most freely exerted, after it is exerted, necessarily makes any Person as happy as his Power can make him," as I have at large explain'd. Nor is it *less manifest,* "That a Consent to the Division of Property in Things themselves, and in human Labour, or to preserve the Division when made, by Innocence, Fidelity, Gratitude, a limited Care of our selves, and of our Off-spring, and Humanity exercis'd towards all, are Parts of that universal Love, and therefore proportionably conducive to the Happiness, as of the Whole, so of Individuals, especially his, in whom they are found"; *than,* "That Quadrants, or other lesser Arches, or Sectors, are Parts of a Circle." Therefore the *Eternity* is *equal,* as well of Propositions of the one Kind, as of the other.

§XXIX. So much may suffice, by way of *Preface,* as to the *Matter* treated of; as to the *Manner* of treating it, I shall add but little. There are many things in our *Style,* candid Reader, which will greatly stand in need of your favourable Construction; being extremely sollicitous about the *Matter,* I was but too negligent of its *Dress.* It was written by Starts at Intervals, such as an uncertain State of Health, and the weighty Cares of my holy Function, would permit.[38]

The Author's Manner of handling his Subject.

I have *illustrated* my *Subject* with *Comparisons* now and then taken from *Mathematicks,* because they, with whom I dispute, reject almost all the other Sciences. Moreover, it seem'd worth while to *shew,* "That the Foundations of Piety and moral Philosophy were not shaken," (as some would insinuate,) "but strengthen'd, by Mathematicks, and Natural Philosophy, that depends thereon; and that therefore those natural Phi-

37. Euclid, *Elementa Geometriae.*
38. Cumberland was rector of Brampton Ash in Northamptonshire from 1657 but in 1670 he also became vicar of All Saints, Stamford, and rector of St. Peter's church in the same town. Internal evidence suggests that *De Legibus* was prepared for publication during the later 1660s. Parkin, *Science, Religion and Politics in Restoration England,* pp. 13, 117.

losophers, who endeavour to overturn the Precepts of Morality, by Weapons drawn from Matter and Motion, may by their own Weapons be both oppos'd and confuted."

I have designedly *abstain'd from any physical Hypothesis* concerning the System of the World, as upon other Accounts, so upon this chiefly, because the Reader may, without prejudice to our Reasoning, assume any *Hypothesis* he pleases; provided it be but such a one, as, from the Order among the natural Causes of *Phaenomena,* leads us to the first Cause. I have sometimes however had respect to the *mechanical Hypothesis,* a Specimen whereof the most ingenious *Des-Cartes* has given us, (other *Hypotheses,* according to the Laws of Matter and Motion, nevertheless, may and ought to be invented, if the *Appearances* of things so require;) because it leads us the shortest way to the first Mover, and is receiv'd by most of our Adversaries.[39]

I would make this further request to the Reader, that he would not pass a severe *Censure* upon this Work, before he has thorowly *read the Whole,* and *compar'd all its Parts* together; because certainly, if there be either *Strength* or *Beauty,* in this Off-spring of our Brain, it chiefly arises from the *firm Connexion* of all the Parts, and the *apt Proportion* of each of them, as well to attain their own, as the common End. Its Face is not painted with the florid Colours of Rhetorick, nor are its Eyes sparkling and sportive, the Signs of a light Wit; it wholly applies it self, as it were, with the Composure and Sedateness of an old Man, to the Study of natural Knowledge, to gravity of Manners, and to the cultivating of severer Learning.

§XXX. Lastly, my chief *aim* in writing, was to promote the *publick Good,*   Conclusion. by plainly proposing to the Minds of Men, the *Standard* of Virtue and Society, taken from the *Nature* of all Things; for I did not think it worth while to spend the whole Book, or the greatest Part of it, in *confuting Hobbes's* Errors, tho I judg'd it necessary to be at some Pains in refuting

39. Cumberland's qualified use of Cartesian ideas was typical of his latitudinarian contemporaries; see Parkin, *Science, Religion and Politics in Restoration England,* pp. 152–53.

his *Mistakes,* which had *so grosly perverted so many.* I thought it sufficient for this Purpose, thorowly to *demolish the Foundations* of his Doctrine, which are laid down, as well in his Treatise *de Cive,* as in his *Leviathan;* and openly to *shew,* "That they are diametrically opposite, not to Religion only, but to all civil Society." These being plainly overthrown, all the wicked Doctrines, which *Hobbes* has rais'd upon them, fall at once to the Ground. But what we have *in reality* perform'd, we leave to the Reader's Judgment. As to the *Confutation* which I have given, I am not very sollicitous; nor intreat I the Reader's Favour, let him censure it as strictly as he pleases. But in the *Confirmation of my Opinion,* (because I know, that I neither do *distinctly understand* all, that the Nature of Things suggests toward our Institution in Virtue; nor could *recollect* in time all those things, which I had once distinctly consider'd, and which I was willing to have express'd in this Treatise;) I must intreat the Reader, not only to *consider my Words,* but to enquire strictly into the Nature of God and Men, and diligently to *examine his own Breast;* for thus he will daily make innumerable Observations, which will more perfectly direct him thro' the Paths of Virtue to the same End. Moreover, because I know, that I *differ* from the Sentiments of some *very learned Men,* as to the *Causes* which imprint the Laws of Nature upon our Minds, I thought fit to add, that it is nevertheless *reasonable,* that we should *love one another,* and so fulfil that Law, which we both acknowledge God has written in our Hearts. As for my own part, I never would have committed my Thoughts upon this Subject to *writing,* much less would I have made them *publick,* unless the Importunity of some Friends at *Cambridge,* (with whom I used to converse with pleasure upon this Subject,) had extorted it from me. They, who first sollicited, and have principally influenced me to this, were Dr. *Hezekiah Burton,* and Dr. *John Hollings,* two very excellent and learned Men, my worthy Friends, with whom, to my great Advantage and Satisfaction, I have cultivated a most intimate Friendship these twenty Years.[40] I pay so great a Deference to their *Judg-*

---

40. Cumberland became friends with Hezekiah Burton (1632–81) at Magdalene. Burton, a Fellow of the College, went on to become domestic chaplain to Sir Orlando Bridgeman, and Cumberland probably owed Bridgeman's patronage to his friend's

ment, and owe so much to their *Friendship,* that I thought it a Crime, any longer to resist their Importunity. Do you, courteous Reader, make use of these our Endeavours, for the Benefit of others; enjoy them to your own, and may all Happiness attend you.

---

connection with the Lord Keeper. Burton saw *De Legibus* through the press and pro-vided a prefatory *Alloquium ad Lectorem* (reprinted here in appendix 2). Dr. John Hollings (1635–1712) was also a member of Cumberland's circle at Magdalene. He eventually became a Fellow of the College and took his M.D. in 1665. He would become a successful physician based in Shrewsbury.

A PHILOSOPHICAL
INQUIRY
INTO THE
LAWS of *NATURE,* &c.

AND

A Confutation of the Elements of Mr. *Hobbes*'s
PHILOSOPHY.

Of the Nature of Things.

The Laws of Nature, defined.

Altho' the *Scepticks* and *Epicureans* of old denied, and others of like Principles still persist in denying, that there are any *Laws of Nature;*[1] we are, nevertheless, on both sides agreed, what is intended by that Name; for we both understand thereby, certain *Propositions of unchangeable Truth, which direct our voluntary Actions, about chusing Good and refusing Evil; and impose an Obligation to external Actions, even without Civil Laws, and laying aside all Consideration of those Compacts, which constitute Civil Government.* "That some such Truths are, from the Nature of Things and of Men, necessarily suggested to the Minds of Men, and by them understood and remember'd, (whilst the Faculties of their Minds continue unhurt,) and that therefore they really exist there"; *This* is what *we affirm,* and our said *Adversaries* as expressly *deny.*

The Author's Method of Inquiry, concerning their Existence.

Wherefore, that the Nature of these Propositions may more plainly appear, it is necessary, that we first examine the *Nature of Things* universally, then, of *Men,* and lastly, of *Good,* as far as they relate to this Question. We must afterwards shew, *what sort of Propositions direct Mens Actions,* and naturally carry along with them the Force and *Obligation* of Laws, as pointing out what is necessary to be done, in order to obtain that End, which Nature has determin'd Men to pursue. Lastly, that there

---

1. The ancient skeptics to whom Cumberland refers probably included Sextus Empiricus, whose works were revived in the sixteenth century. Modern skeptics included Montaigne (*Essays,* II.12) and Hobbes. For the history of skepticism in general during this period, see Popkin, *The History of Scepticism from Erasmus to Spinoza* (1979); for the relationship between skepticism and natural law ideas, see Tuck, "The 'Modern' Theory of Natural Law" (1987), pp. 99–122.

are such Laws, will sufficiently appear from the certainty and necessary influence of those Causes which produce them.

The Consideration of the Nature of Things, necessary in this Question;

§II. Nor ought it to seem strange to any, that I *said,* "That the *Nature of Things* in the Universe ought first to be consider'd"; because the extensive Faculties of Man, which need *many* Things for their Preservation and Improvement, and are excited by *all* to Action, can't be otherwise understood: For how can any one understand, what is most *agreeable,* or most *hurtful,* to the human *Mind* or *Body,* unless he considers (as far as he is able)[2] all those *Causes,* as well remote, as near, which form'd, and now preserve, Man, and may hereafter support, or destroy, him? Nor is it possible to know, what is the best Thing a Man can do, in the present Case, unless the *Effects,* as well remote as near, which may proceed from him, in all variety of Circumstances, be foreseen and compar'd among themselves. But the Consideration of the *Causes,* upon which Men depend, and of those *Effects,* which may be produc'd by the Concurrence of their Powers, will necessarily lead every Man to consider, not only *other Men,* wheresoever dispers'd, and *himself,* as a small part of Mankind, but also this whole *Frame of Nature,* and *God,* its first Founder, and supreme Governor. These things being consider'd, in the best manner we are able, our Mind may by some general Conclusions *pronounce,* "What sort of human Actions chiefly promote the Common Good of all Beings, especially such as are Rational," wherein each Man's proper Happiness is contain'd. And we shall hereafter see, that in *such Conclusions,* provided they be true and necessary, the *Law of Nature* is contain'd.

Because all moral Philosophy is finally resolved into the Knowledge of Nature.

§III. Yet the Nature of our Undertaking does *not require,* that we should take a particular View of *all* kinds of Beings. We congratulate, indeed, the happy Genius of this learned Age, that the *intellectual Part of the World* has been much illustrated by that great Accession of Light, which former Proofs of the *Being of God,* and the *Immortality of the Soul* have

---

2. [Maxwell] "Which is as far as is necessary to discover his Obligation to obey the Laws of Nature, as will appear in the Sequel of this Treatise."

receiv'd from the daily increasing Knowledge of the *inferior Part of Nature*. We also congratulate, both the present Age and Posterity, that, now at length, the *material Part of the Universe* begins to be explain'd by introducing Mathematicks into the Study of Nature. It is truly a vast *Undertaking,* "To resolve the visible World into its most simple Principles, *Matter,* variously figur'd, and *Motion,* differently compounded, and after the Geometrical Investigation of the Properties of Figures, and of compounded Motions, from *Phaenomena* faithfully observ'd, to shew the History of the whole corporeal System exactly conspiring with the Laws of Matter and Motion"; but that is an Undertaking, not only unequal to the Abilities of any *one Man,* but of *an Age.* It is, nevertheless, *worthy* of the united Endeavours, and unwearied Industry of those great Genius's of which the *Royal Society* is compos'd: *Worthy* of his most excellent Majesty, King *Charles* its Founder, Patron and Example.[3] We may therefore safely commit so important and difficult an Affair to so faithful and skilful Hands. It is sufficient for us, in the beginning of this Undertaking, to have *admonish'd* the Reader, "That the Whole of *moral Philosophy,* and of the Laws of Nature, is ultimately resolv'd into *natural Observations* known by the Experience of all Men, or into Conclusions of true *Natural Philosophy.*" But *Natural Philosophy,* in the large Sense I now use it, does not only comprehend all those *Appearances of natural Bodies,* which we know from Experiment, but also inquires into the Nature of our *Souls,* from Observations made upon their Actions and distinguishing Perfections, and at length leads Men, by the Chain of natural Causes, to the Knowledge of the *first Mover,* and acknowledges him to be the Cause of all necessary Effects. For the Nature, as well of the Creatures, as of the Creator, suggests all those *Ideas,* of which the Laws of Nature are form'd, and discovers the *Truth* of those Laws, as practical

3. The Royal Society was founded in 1660, with Charles II as patron. Cumberland was not a member of the society, which was not unusual for provincial virtuosi. Scientific references in *De Legibus Naturae* show that Cumberland kept up with the society's activities through its journal, *Philosophical Transactions.* For the history of the Royal Society and its fellows during this period, see Hunter, *Science and Society in Restoration England* (1981) and *Establishing the New Science: The Experience of the Early Royal Society* (1989).

Propositions; but their full *Authority* is deriv'd from the Knowledge of the Creator. And these things require to be a little farther explain'd in this Place.

§IV. But altho there are *innumerable* things, which, in the Knowledge of the Universe, may be made use of for the Matter of *particular Propositions,* which are to form our Manners; I have, nevertheless, thought proper to select only a *few,* and those the most *general,* which might, in some measure, explain that *general Description* of the Laws of Nature, which I at first propos'd, and are a little more manifestly contain'd in one *Proposition,* the Fountain of all Nature's Laws. Which general Proposition is this, *The greatest Benevolence of every rational Agent towards all, forms the happiest State of every, and of all the Benevolent, as far as is in their Power; and is necessarily requisite to the happiest State which they can attain, and therefore the common Good is the supreme Law.*[4]

The *Sense* of this is first rightly to be *explain'd.* Secondly, We are to shew, *how* it may be *learned* from the *Nature of Things.* Lastly, I hope it will plainly appear, from what follows in this Treatise, that it has the *Force of a Law,* and that *all* the Laws of Nature flow from it.

The Reader is to observe, that I no where understand by the Name of *Benevolence,* that languid and lifeless Volition of theirs, which *effects nothing* of what they are said to desire; but that only, by force whereof we *execute,* as speedily and thorowly as we are able, what we heartily desire. We may likewise also comprehend in this *Word,* that *Affection, by which we desire things grateful to our Superiors,* which is particularly distinguish'd by the Name of *Piety,* towards God, our Country, and our Parents; and therefore I chose to make use of the Word [*Benevolence*] rather than [*Love*], because, in virtue of its Composition, it implies an *Act of our Will,* join'd with its most *general Object,* and is never taken in a bad Sense, as the Word [*Love*] sometime is. I here use the Words, the [*greatest*] Benevolence, because I would express the intire or *adequate Cause* of the *greatest* Happiness. We shall elsewhere shew, how those

---

4. Maxwell refers the reader to his note on section VIII. The last line of Cumberland's formula adapts the Roman law maxim "salus populi suprema lex."

Scruples which some object here, may be easily solv'd. By the Word [*All*] I understand that whole System which consists of the Individuals consider'd together, in order to one End, which I there mention by the Name of [*the happiest State.*] By the Name of [*Rationals*] I beg leave to understand, as well *God* as *Man;* and I do it upon the Authority of *Cicero,* whom I think I may safely take for a Guide, as to the Propriety of a *Latin* Word. For he acknowledges *Reason,* common both to God and Men, and has taught, That *"Wisdom"* (which all ascribe to God) is nothing else but *"Reason in Perfection."*[5] I have us'd the Word [*Forms*] to intimate, that Benevolence is both the *intrinsic Cause* of *present,* and the *efficient Cause* of *future* Happiness, and is necessarily requisite in respect of both. I have added [*as far as is in their Power*] to insinuate, that the Assistance of things *external,* is *often not in our Power,* altho they are requisite to the Happiness of the animal Life; and that *no other Assistance* to a happy Life is to be expected from the Laws of Nature and moral Philosophy, than Precepts about our Actions, and those Objects of Actions, which are *in our own Power.*[6] And altho it happens, that different Men, according to their different Abilities of Mind and Body, nay, that the same Men, in different Circumstances, are not equally able to promote the public Good; nevertheless, the Law of Nature is sufficiently observ'd, and its End obtain'd, if every one performs *what he is able,* according to his present Circumstances. But of this there will be a fuller Explanation in what follows.

Rationals,

Forms the happiest State of all,

As far as is in their Power.

§V. I must now *shew,* "Both *how* the Ideas contain'd in the foregoing Proposition, *necessarily enter* into the *Minds* of Men, and that when they are there, they are *necessarily connected,* that is, that they make a *true* Proposition"; which we shall afterwards prove to be *practical,* and to have the force of a *Law.* Seeing therefore it is well known by the *Experience* of all Men, that those *Ideas* or Thoughts, which the *Logicians* call *simple Apprehensions,* are *two* ways excited in the Mind of Man; (1.) By the

How we come to the Knowledge of the Terms of the foregoing Proposition.

5. Cicero, *De Legibus,* I.vii.22–23.
6. The distinction can be found in Epictetus, *Discourses,* I.I.

immediate Presence and Operation of the Object upon the Mind; after which manner the Mind is conscious of its *own Actions,* and also of the Motions of the Imagination, or of the *Ideas* its Objects; and by Analogy to these, we judge of the Minds of other rational Beings, *God* and *Men.* (2.) By the *Means* of our external *Senses,* Nerves, and Membranes, in which manner we perceive *other Men,* and the rest of the Parts of this *visible World;* it presently appears, that the *Terms* of our *Proposition* become known, partly by *internal,* partly by *external,* Sensation. For what *Benevolence* is, and what are its *Degrees,* and, consequently, what is any ones *greatest Benevolence,* we do not otherwise understand, than by the *Mind's reflecting upon itself;* nor needs there other help; for such is the Frame of the Mind, that it cannot but be thorowly sensible of its own Actions and Affections, as being what are intimately united with it self. I *acknowledge,* however, "That it is to the Assistance of our *outward Senses,* we owe the Knowledge of *external Advantages,* which Benevolence distributes amongst all," of which hereafter. In the same manner we come to the Knowledge of *Reason,* by our *inward Sense* thereof; and we apprehend what are *rational Agents,* mention'd in the *Subject of the Proposition.* "That there are others besides our selves who have the use of Reason," we collect by Observations made by our *outward Senses.* We come at the Knowledge of the *Causes constituting* any thing, whether intrinsically, or in the way of an Efficient, generally by the Assistance of our *outward Senses,* and by *Reasoning* founded on *Appearances.* The *inward Nature* of our Mind, and its *active Powers* by which it determines the voluntary Motions of our Bodies in pursuit of apparent Good, the Mind it self perceives, partly by *reflecting* upon it self, partly by the Aid of the *Senses* observing the Effects consequent upon the Command of our Will. Lastly, we come to the Knowledge of the *State* of Men, and of their *Happiness,* by the same Means, by which we hinted, that their Nature, and those good Things, in the Enjoyment whereof their Happiness consists, were known; for the State of Things adds nothing to their Nature, besides the Notion of some *Duration,* or Continuance. And a State is called *Happy,* from the *Possession* of *good Things,* very many, and very great.

§VI. As to the *Connexion* of the *Terms* of this Proposition, in which its And of the Connexion of these Terms, or its Truth. *necessary Truth* consists, it seems to me sufficiently plain; for it signifies the same as if we should say as follows; *That the Willing, or Prosecution, of all good Things situated in our Power, which is most effectual to the Enjoyment of them by our selves and other Rationals, is the most that Men can effect, that they themselves, and others, may most happily enjoy them.* Or, *There is no Power in Men greater, by which they may procure to themselves and others a Collection of all good Things, than a Will to pursue every one his own Happiness, together with the Happiness of others.*

In which words, what is *first obvious,* is, "That there is no Power in Men greater to effect any thing, than a Will determin'd to exert its utmost Force."

In the *next place,* it is also most *evident,* "That the Happiness of single Persons, for example, of *Socrates* and *Plato,* and other Individuals," (mention'd in the *Predicate*) "cannot singly be separated from the Happiness of all," (whose Cause is contain'd in the *Subject,*) because the Whole does not differ from all the Parts taken together. This universal Proposition, pronouncing concerning the Benevolence of all, may be observ'd to agree with *Laws* from this, that it *declares,* "Not what any *one* Person, or a *few, ought* to do to procure their own Happiness, without any regard to that of others, but what both *all unitedly can* do, in order to be happy, and what *each separately,* without any Repugnancy amongst themselves, (for that is not consistent with Reason, of which all are Partakers,) *may* do, in order to obtain the common Happiness of All, in which the greatest Happiness possible to Individuals is contain'd, and most effectually promoted." It is first and *better* known, as flowing from the common and essential Attributes of human Nature, "What all in general can, or cannot, do, conducing to the common Good," *than,* "What any particular Person can do in determinate Circumstances," for these are infinite, and, consequently, impossible to be known by any Man. *As,* several Armies being brought into the Field, it is better known, that they cannot all get the Victory, than which Army shall overcome.

Thirdly, in the last place, "One or a few particular Persons can neither enjoy a present Happiness, or with probability hope for it hereafter, by acting without any regard, or in opposition, to the Happiness of all other rational Beings"; for to a Mind so affected, an essential Part of its Happiness is wanting, "That inward *Peace,* which arises from an uniform Wisdom, always agreeing with it self," for it is *inconsistent* with it self, when it determines to act after *one manner in relation to itself,* and after *another manner in relation to others,* that partake of the *same Nature:* That "great *Joy"* is also wanting, "which arises in a benevolent Mind, from a Sense of the Felicity of others." Not to say any thing at present of *Envy, Pride,* and those Legions of other Vices, which besiege the Malevolent, and necessarily render him miserable, as labouring under the worst *Distempers of the Mind.*

Beside, "No Person, in such an Attempt, can have a well-grounded *Hope* of Happiness," because in it he neglects, nay provokes to his Destruction, other external rational Causes, *God* and *Men,* upon whose Aid that Hope necessarily depends. "There is therefore no other way, which can lead *any* particular Person to his Happiness, than that which is to lead *all* to the common Happiness." Let it suffice, briefly to have hinted these things in this place, which I have done only with this View, that I might shew from such Observations as are most obvious by common Experience, that the Truth of the aforesaid *Proposition* is very evident; but these things we shall deduce more at large hereafter.

§VII. However, I acknowledge, that this *Proposition* cannot be *effectual,* to the forming any Man's Manners, before he has propos'd to himself as his *End,* the *Effect* here discoursed of, "His own Happiness in Conjunction with that of others," and has taken "those various Actions into which Benevolence is branched," for the *Means.* The *Proposition,* however, and all just Inferences from it, (such as those less general ones, which declare the Power of Fidelity, Gratitude, natural Affection, and the other particular Virtues, towards obtaining any part of human Happiness,) may, before such Proposal, be prov'd *necessarily true.* For the whole Truth, as well of that general *Proposition,* as of those which are thence deduced, depends upon the natural and *necessary Efficacy* of such Actions, as *Causes,* to produce such *Effects.* For they do not suppose, that there *are* such Actions, which, indeed, depend upon the Agency of *free*

Which kind of
Truths are as
necessary as
Mathematical
ones.

Causes. And it is sufficient to evidence this Truth, "That, whensoever there are such Causes, Effects of such a kind shall thence follow." It is an undisputed Point in the Solution of all kind of *Mathematical Problems,* in relation to which no one questions, but that we come at true Science. All *know,* "That to draw Lines, and to compare them, in Geometrical Calculation, depends upon the *Will* of Men. We *freely* add, subtract, &c. and yet whoever performs these Operations, according to the Rules prescribed, *necessarily* finds out the true Sum, which is equal to all the Parts added." The like may be said of the Remainder in Subtraction, the Product in Multiplication, the Quotient in Division, and the Root in Extractions: And in general, in every Question, whose Solution is possible from what is given, the Answer is *necessarily* found from the Operations duly perform'd. The *Connexion* is *necessary,* between the *Effect* desired, and its *Causes* assigned by this Science. According to this Pattern are other practical Arts to be modell'd, and this we have endeavour'd to attain, in delivering the Principles of Morality, *by* reducing to one general Name [*Benevolence*], all those *voluntary* Actions, which fall under the Direction of Moral Philosophy, *by* inquiring into its Branches; and lastly, *by* shewing the Connexion between this Act and the End design'd.[7]

§VIII. But seeing *only voluntary* Actions can be govern'd by human *Reason,* and *those only which regard intelligent Beings,* are consider'd in *Morality;* and seeing the Object of the Will is *Good,* (for *Evil* is rated from the Privation of Good;) it is *evident,* "That a more general Notion of such Actions cannot be form'd, than what falls under the Name of *Benevolence,*"[8] because it comprehends the *Desire* of all kinds of *good*

All those Actions which fall under the Consideration of Moral Philosophy, are comprehended in Benevolence.

7. The fascination with the possibility of a moral science was common to ethical theorists of the period. See, for example, Pufendorf, *Elementorum Jurisprudentiae Universalis* (1660), 1.3; 11.16; More, *Divine Dialogues* (1668), p. 6; Locke, *An Essay Concerning Human Understanding,* 4.3.18.

8. [Maxwell] "The *Author* here means by BENEVOLENCE, 'A Desire of Good, both Private and Publick.' In this Sense of the Word his general Proposition, § 4. amounts to no more than this; 'If all Mankind use all Means in their Power to procure the greatest Happiness to Mankind, Mankind would enjoy the greatest Happiness in

Things, and consequently the avoiding all kinds of *Evils.* But beside, the force of *Benevolence* extends it self to all the *free* Acts of the *Understanding,* (whether we consider or compare good Things among themselves, or enquire concerning the Means of obtaining them;) and of our *bodily Faculties,* which are directed by our Will in the pursuit of Good. But it is universally *true,* "That the motion of a Point does not more certainly

---

their Power,' which Proposition is indeed self-evident; but wants another Argument to make it conclusive, which Argument I shall have occasion to mention in a following *Note.* For it is *no good Consequence* to say, 'Such a Method of acting in any Individual contributes most to the Sum of the Happiness of Mankind upon the Whole; *therefore* it contributes most to the Happiness of that Individual.' Much *less, is it a Consequence* to say, 'Such a Method of acting in any Individual contributes most to the Sum of the Happiness of Mankind upon the whole; *therefore* such a Method of acting would contribute most to the Happiness of any single Person, whether the rest concurr'd or no.'

"By BENEVOLENCE, he sometimes seems to mean, 'The Instinct, or those Actions only, which proceed from the Love of others:' But, I think, the Word in his general Law, is not to be understood in this Sense; for, 'Were the Instinct or Passion of Benevolence much greater than it usually is, I believe Mankind would not be so happy as they now are, *because* private Advantage would not be sufficiently regarded, Sloth would be incourag'd, and industry discourag'd.' Nay, even as present, we have some Examples of the bad Consequences of an *excessive* Benevolence, especially in the *weaker* Sex. Neither can it be *said,* 'That the bad Consequences would be prevented, were our *Understandings enlarg'd* in proportion to our Benevolence; *for* the curbing a violent Instinct, is always very painful and disagreeable.' Upon the Whole, I *conclude,* 'That the Author of Nature, who hath done every Thing most for our Advantage, has given us *a Measure of Benevolence* most exactly suited to our Understandings and Manner of Dependence on one another.' But yet we are from *Habit* more commonly *defective* in *Benevolence,* than *Understanding;* and the *strongest Endeavour,* in a Man of tolerable Strength of Understanding, to *improve* his *Benevolence,* will *not* be able to render it *excessive.* If he here used BENEVOLENCE in this Sense, he might, with as much reason, have *said,* 'That the greatest intellectual Capacity, or Understanding, in every Person, in things that are for his private Advantage, forms the happiest State; and *therefore,* private Good is the supreme Law': For in all Cases, what is most for *private,* is most for *publick,* Advantage, and *vice versa.*

"But here I would have it *observ'd,* 'That I don't make this *Remark* with a Design to *overthrow* our *Author's Scheme,* but to render it more *intelligible,* and to guard the Reader from some Mistakes, which the *Confusion* of his Method, and some *seeming Inconsistencies* might lead him into.' In the *following Notes* also, where I *seem* to disagree with our *Author,* my *Design* is, 'Partly, to explain him, and partly, to make some small Additions, which, I think, contribute somewhat to the rendring of his Scheme more complete.'"

produce a Line, or the Addition of Numbers a Sum, than that Benevolence produces a good Effect (to the Person to whom we wish well) proportion'd to the Power and Affection of the Agent, in the given Circumstances." It is also *certain,* "That *keeping Faith, Gratitude, natural Affection,* &c. are either *Parts* or *Modes* of a most effectual *Benevolence* towards all, accommodated to particular Circumstances; and that they must certainly produce their good Effect, after the same manner, as it is certain, that Addition, Subtraction, Multiplication, and Division, are Parts or Modes of Calculation; and that a right Line, Circle, Parabola, and other Curves, do express the various Effects, which Geometry produces by the motion of a Point."

General Mathematical *Theorems,* necessary to the Construction of Problems, are freed from the *uncertainties* of such Guesses as are made concerning *future Contingencies,* "By not affirming that such Constructions shall be, only demonstrating their Properties and Effects, if ever such Constructions are produc'd"; I have thought fit to proceed in the *same* Method, and "To deliver some evident Principles, concerning the natural Effects, the Parts, and the various respects of universal Love, without affirming that there is such Love"; being, however, certain, because such Benevolence is possible, that many Consequences may be thence drawn, which may direct us in the Practice of Morality, "which is what Theorems perform in the possible Construction of Problems." I confess, notwithstanding, that whilst we, with the greatest *Prudence,* endeavour some things which require the concurrence of others, we may *sometimes not succeed* according to our wish; but this does not prove any *error in the Rules.* The Trial *shews,* "That the Effect was not in our Power," or, as the Mathematicians speak, "That the propos'd Problem could not be solved, or thorowly determin'd, from what was given"; and as they acquiesce in *such* Discovery, so in *like* Cases may prudent Minds very justly enjoy Tranquillity. But the *Experience* of past Events, and the *Observation* of our own Strength, will quickly enable us to form a *Judgment,* "whether any Effect propos'd, be in the given Circumstance in our power, or no"; and that, for the most part, without the trouble of making an Experiment. And *Reason requires,* that such *Judgment* should be made; because he can hardly avoid the Imputation of *Folly,* "Who greatly labours the gaining a Point, which he did not know, that his Strength, together with the Assistance he had reason to expect, might obtain." This, at least, is necessary, that he be *certain,* "That the probable Hope of obtaining his End, is of greater Value, than any Effect his Endeavours could produce in the same time." For I hereafter *shew,* "That some Propositions of unchangeable Truth, can be form'd concerning the Value of contingent Advantages."[9]

§IX. Moreover, the Nature of Things *instructs* us, "That we must first distinctly know, what is the *best Effect* in our Power, before we can distinctly know the *chief End* we ought to regard." For the Answer to the *former* Question consists of more simple Terms, and consequently, of more certain Signification. The Answer to the *latter,* as it ought to contain *all* that is in the former, so it *moreover denotes,* "That the rational Agent has determin'd within himself, to use the means proper to produce that Effect." But because from this *Consideration,* "That many Effects tending to the common Good are in our Power; and that they, by the Will of the first Cause, are made necessary to the Attainment of our own Happiness," there arises, both an *Obligation to intend* the producing those Effects, and the *actual Intention* it self also, whenever it is found in Men: We must of necessity lay the *Foundation* of the Laws of Nature, in *those manifest Observations* on the Powers of Men, by which duly regulated they are enabled to make each other happy, nay will certainly do so. But these Laws are all summ'd up in [*Benevolence*] or [*Universal Love.*]

> Which is the Summary of the Laws of Nature.

I have *observ'd,* "That Mathematicians, in laying down the Principles of their Science, make no mention of the *End,* which the Doctrine by them deliver'd respects"; *altho* the more eminent of them most diligently pursue a most noble End. For they propose to investigate the Proportions of all kinds of Bodies and Motions, whence arise all the *Phaenomena* of Nature we are wont to *admire,* and the *most useful* Effects in common Life. The *Mathesis universalis,* (such as *Des Cartes* and his

9. See also ch. 5, sects. 18, 43, and 58.

Commentators have deliver'd in their Geometry)[10] is however content in the beginning briefly to *suggest,* towards the establishment of its Theorems, "That all kind of Proportions may be exhibited, by the help of such right Lines as we can draw," and "That those which are unknown, may without great difficulty be investigated, by Geometrical Calculation, from those that are more easily known." But it especially *admonishes,* "That, in order to the Preparation of those Lines whose knowledge is inquir'd after, nothing else is to be done, than that some Lines should be added together, subtracted, multiplied, or divided," and "That the Extraction of Roots, which is of principal use, should be look'd upon as a kind of Division." It uses *no* long *Exhortation* to *induce* you, "To investigate an accurate knowledge of all kinds of Things, from a mutual Comparison of their Proportions," altho *that* be its principal End; but it *supposes,* "That it is desirable for its own sake, and of the greatest use in Life." It thinks that it has sufficiently *discharg'd it self,* if it has briefly *hinted,* "How such Operations may be applied to the solution of all kinds of Problems." Nor does it think it any diminution, either of its *Truth* or *Dignity,* "Tho most Men should, thro' Unskilfulness or Sloth, neglect, or even oppose, its Rules." *Just so* it is with the Doctrine of *Morality,* which is contain'd in the Laws of Nature. For it is wholly *conversant,* "In computing the several Proportions of human Powers, which at all contribute to the common Good of rational Beings," which indeed are different in all Variety of possible Cases; and it may justly be said to have *perform'd its Part,* if, having *in the Beginning, in general, hinted,* "That all those Powers are comprehended in universal Benevolence," it *afterwards particularly shews,* "That a Division of all Things, Fidelity, Gratitude, a care of our selves and of our Off-spring, is herein contain'd," and, "In what cases they are to be made use of"; and, "After what manner thence necessarily proceed, Virtue, Religion, Society, and every thing else which contributes to the Happiness of Life." For in *this* consists the *Solution of that most useful Problem, whose investigation moral*

10. For Descartes' discussion of *mathesis universalis* in the *Regulae ad Directionem Ingenii* (1628), see Cottingham, *The Philosophical Writings of Descartes* (1985), vol. I, p. 19.

Philosophy teaches. Nor is the *Truth* and *Authority* of its Precepts in any measure *diminish'd*, "Because many will not obey, or will oppose them"; this only thence *follows*, "That they will make shipwrack of their own Happiness, and perhaps, in some measure, involve others in the same Calamity." Nevertheless, after it is made *manifest*, "That so excellent an Effect may certainly be produc'd, by Actions within the compass of their own Power"; it is not to be doubted, but that Men may more easily be *persuaded*, "To propose this Effect, so far as it is in their Power, as their End; and to take those Actions, from which, as from its Causes, it is produc'd, as the necessary means." *As* Men are excited to the making *Parabolic Specula,* or *Hyperbolic Telescopes,* for the sake of the Effects which Mathematicians have demonstrated, will thence follow.[11]

Of which Laws, God is the Author. §X. Here I shall only *add*, "That *this Truth*" (as all others equally evident, but especially those which are hence necessarily deriv'd) "does proceed from *God,* and has annex'd to its Observance *Reward;* to its Transgression, *Punishment;* and is, in its own Nature, a proper *Rule* to direct our Manners." The case being such, I see not what is wanting, to give it the Force of a *Law:* However, I shall *add,* in the Conclusion of this Work, "That in this PROPOSITION is contain'd, both *Piety* towards God, and *Charity* towards Men." In which the Sum of both Tables of the Divine Law, as well *Mosaical* as *Evangelical,* is contain'd. I shall at the same time *shew,* "That from hence all *moral Virtues,* and the *Laws of Nations,* in respect both of Peace and War, may be deduc'd." That a Truth so evident, is impress'd by God as its *Author,* is very readily shewn from that natural Philosophy, which shews, *that* all *Impressions* upon our Senses are made, according to the natural Laws (as they are call'd) of *Motion;* and *that* Motion was first impress'd upon this corporeal System by God, and is by him preserv'd unchang'd. By this Method, which to me seems most certain, and is wholly built upon Demonstration, all *necessary* Effects are immediately resolv'd into the *first Mover.* But the *Impression* of the Terms of this PROPOSITION (at least as far as it proceeds from Matter and Motion) is a *natural* Effect; and the *Perception* of the *Identity,* or

11. Cumberland is referring to Christopher Wren's geometrically designed lens-grinding machine described in *Philosophical Transactions* 48 (1669), p. 961.

Coherence of these Terms, as they are in the Imagination, is nothing else than a Perception, that each Term is an *Impression* made upon us by the *same Cause*. But the *Perception* of the Mind, by which it apprehends the Terms, as they lie in the Imagination, and perceives their Connexion, and is sensible of its own Strength and Actions, so naturally and *necessarily* follows their Presence in the Imagination, and that internal, natural, and unblameable Propension of the Mind, to the Observation of those things which are plac'd before it, that they cannot but be ascribed to the Mind's *efficient Cause,* that is, to God, by him who acknowledges God to be the Creator of all Things, or the first Mover. But all other Methods of explaining Nature, how much soever they differ from the foregoing, or amongst themselves, agree in this, that they acknowledge God the *first Cause* of such *necessary Effects:* Altho many seem not to have remark'd sufficiently, that the *simple Apprehension* of Ideas, and their *Composition,* when they plainly agree, (whence arises a necessary Proposition,) are to be reckon'd amongst *necessary* Effects, that is, such as (first supposing the natural Impressions of Motion, and an intelligent Nature, to which they are clearly and distinctly propos'd) cannot but exist: which however conduces much to our Purpose, because *God* being acknowledg'd the *Author* of these *necessary* practical Truths, which point out Actions necessary to that End, which Nature has determin'd us to pursue, it gives them the Authority of *Laws.*

§XI. But what Mr. *Hobbes* thinks of the resolving such necessary Effects into God as their first Cause, and of the Authority of Laws thence arising, is not easy to affirm; for his Writings seem in *some Places* to *acknowledge* thus much, and yet there are many *other Passages* in him, which *contradict,* as well the Existence of *God,* (which is prov'd by this very Argument,) as the Authority of the *Laws of Nature,* which is establish'd by the same Reasoning. As to the first, it is certain, that the following *Syllogism* is plainly Atheistical, "Whatsoever is not Body, or an Accident thereof, does not exist. *But* God is neither Body, nor an Accident thereof. *Therefore,*" &c.[12] But altho *Hobbes* has in many Places very sollicitously *inculcated* both the *Premises,* yet he *denies* the wicked

(Hobbes contradicts himself, with respect to the Existence of God.

12. Hobbes, *Leviathan,* ch. 46, p. 459.

Conclusion, and affirms it to be only *"a Sin of Imprudence,"* either to assert it, or any otherwise to blaspheme God.[13] The *Sense* of the foregoing *Syllogism,* he does but too openly advance, where he contends, that *"Incorporeal Substance are Words, which, when join'd together, mutually destroy one another, as if any one should say, A bodiless Body";* and that, *"there is no real Part of the Universe, which is not Body."*[14] And *"what any one shall affirm to be mov'd, or produc'd, by an incorporeal Substance, is affirm'd without Grounds."*[15] But the *Minor,* that "God is not Body," he seems plainly enough to advance, where he denies, "That God has any Properties of Body; such as Figure, Place, Motion or Rest."[16] It is true, indeed, that, in the *Appendix to his Leviathan* lately publish'd, he openly declares, "God to be a Body," in the beginning of the *Third Chapter;* and he endeavours to prove it; forgetting in the mean time, that in the *First Chapter of the same Appendix* (near the end) he had promised not to deny the First *Article of the Church of* England, in which it is expresly said, that "God is without Body, and without Parts."[17] But if *that* Authority,[18] which is the *only one* for which he seems to contend, is of less weight with him, let him hearken to himself, *Lib. de Cive c.* 15. § 14. where he teaches, *"That those Philosophers spoke unworthily of God, who said, that he was either the World itself, or the Soul* (that is, a Part) *of the World; for they do not attribute any thing to him, but wholly deny his Being."*[19] But does not *Hobbes* affirm him to be *"Part of the World,"* or *"the Whole,"* when he says that he is *Body?* For it is very certain that he has asserted, *Leviath. c.* 34. *"That the Universe is an Aggregate of all Bodies, and that it has no Part, which is not it self Body; and that nothing can be properly called Body, which is not some Part of the whole Universe."*[20]

13. Hobbes, *On the Citizen,* 14.19, pp. 163–64.

14. Hobbes, *Leviathan,* ch. 34, pp. 261–62.

15. Hobbes, *Elementorum Philosophiae sectio prima De Corpore* (1655), p. 394.

16. Hobbes, *On the Citizen,* 15.14, pp. 178–79.

17. Hobbes, *Leviathan,* Appendix, ch. 3, p. 540; ibid., appendix, ch. 1, p. 519.

18. [Maxwell] "That is, the Authority of the Legislature, which establish'd the 39 *Articles,* and which he makes to be the only Standard of *Good* and *Evil."*

19. Hobbes, *On the Citizen,* 15.14, p. 178.

20. Hobbes, *Leviathan,* ch. 34, p. 261.

But that the *World* and the *Universe,* with him signify the *same* thing, any one will easily perceive, who reads these his Words of the Universe and Stars, *Every Object is "either a Part of the Universal World, or an aggregate of the Parts;* &c."[21] I am afraid therefore, that he is *convicted* by his own Authority; "Of denying the Being of God." But it is not to my purpose, to insist any longer upon these things. I do not however doubt, but that the *Properties of Body* (such are, to be capable of being measured, and to be divided into Parts, to undergo all the Changes of Generation and Corruption, and to exclude all other Bodies out of its Place) are so well known now-a-days, both to Mr. *Hobbes* and all others, *not* to be *consistent* with the *divine Perfections,* that it would be easier for him to *persuade* most Men, "That God did not at all exist," than, "That he was Corporeal." This however we are pleased with, that, in contradiction to his own Principles, he *professes* to believe the Being of God, and acknowledges the Force of the Argument, by which we discover it; for he *grants,* "That there necessarily exists one first and eternal Cause of all Things." *Leviath. c.* 12. § 6.[22]

But as to the *Authority of the Conclusions of Reason* flowing from these Principles, (which, tho immediately discover'd by Reason, yet, by the Intervention of that, must appear to proceed from God, who is the Author of that natural Necessity, by which our Reason is determin'd to acknowledge them;) *Hobbes* is *neither consistent with himself, nor with Truth.* Leviath. c. 26. § 7. *"The Laws* (saith he) *of Nature, which consist in Equity,* &c. *in a State of mere Nature, are not properly Laws, but Qualities disposing Men to Peace and Obedience."*[23] He gives a Reason for this, *"Because a Law, accurately and properly speaking, is the Speech of one, who with Right commands others, to do or forbear any thing."* Hence in the same Place he infers, that, *"As they proceed from Nature, they are not Laws."*[24] *As if* "God were not properly included in the Name of Nature"; *And the Authority of the Laws of Nature.*

---

21. Hobbes, *De Corpore,* 26.1, p. 236.
22. Hobbes, *Leviathan,* ch. 12, p. 64.
23. Ibid., ch. 26, p. 174. Maxwell notes section 7, whereas the reference should be to section 4.
24. Hobbes, *On the Citizen,* 3.33, p. 56; see also *Leviathan,* ch. 15, p. 100.

or, *as if* "a Proposition, the Scope of which consists in declaring to us, what things are to be done, or omitted, under the Reward or Punishment of having our Happiness either increas'd or diminish'd, and which is form'd in the Mind of Man by the Necessity of that Nature which he has receiv'd at the hands of God, were not a sufficient Signification of the divine Will"; or *as if* "it were not properly enough called, the Speech of him who has a Right to command." For what else does he who "commands in plain words," than "make us most assuredly understand, that he has so determin'd concerning our Affairs, that if we act thus, Punishment, if otherwise, Reward is to be the Consequence; and that, in right of the Dominion which he has over us?" In the same place he *contends,* "That they are not otherwise the Laws of God, than as they are declar'd in Scripture."[25] But if any one inquires, how it *appears,* "That the Scriptures are the Word of God," or, "That ever there was at all any Prophet, who either receiv'd them or any other Revelation from God"; in *answer* to this *Question* put by himself, he roundly *affirms,* "That it is plainly impossible, that any Person can be certain of a Revelation made to another, without a Revelation particularly given to himself; no, not even by Miracles." *Leviath. Part* 2. *c.* 26. § 40. of the *English* Edition.[26] Yet he affirms in the same place, "That it is essential to a Law, that the Person to be oblig'd by it be certain of the Authority of the Legislator":[27] And this renders what he says, in the Passage just cited, and in the last Paragraph of the *Fifteenth Chapter* of his *Leviathan,* wholly *ineffectual.* Wherefore, if we will believe him in both places, we shall *deny them to be Laws,* both as they are from *Nature,* and as they are *revealed* in Scripture, because we cannot be certain that those things were revealed; but there ought rather to be no Credit given to what *he* says, who contradicts himself: For the same Person, (as if he had done it on purpose, that his Readers might conjecture, that *one Part* of the Contradiction was advanced, out of *respect* to the Christian Magistrate, the *other,* from his own *real Sentiments,*) in the same Treatise *de Cive,* § next following, and

25. Hobbes, *On the Citizen,* 3.33, pp. 56–57.
26. Hobbes, *Leviathan,* ch. 26, pp. 186–87.
27. Ibid.

cap. 4. § 1. professes, that *"The Law, usually called Natural and Moral, is not unjustly called a divine Law; both because Reason, which is it self the Law of Nature, is immediately given by God, to every one for the Rule of his Actions; and because the Precepts of Life which are thence derived, are the same which were deliver'd from the divine Majesty, for the Laws of the Kingdom of Heaven, by our Lord Jesus Christ, and by the holy Prophets and Apostles."* [28] Here truly, (perhaps that his Reader might see how much he can *comply* with the Manners of those among whom he lives,) he *acknowledges* "Those Conclusions, not unjustly to be called Laws," which but a little before he *denied,* "To be Laws, properly and accurately speaking." *As if,* "When he, who is by right a Sovereign, gives immediately to his Subject, a Rule of his Actions with Rewards and Punishments annex'd," *he did not* "properly command him, that something should be done or forborn," *or* "ordain a Law."

§XII. But I will insist no longer on shewing these *Contradictions;* I will only give the Reader this *Hint,* (which may be every where *useful,* to his more certain *Discovery* of this Author's *real Sentiments;*) That these latter *Passages in favour of moral Rules* have this *Mark,* by which one may guess they were affirm'd for *fear* of others, he *does not offer any Reason to support* what he seems to grant. *That* "Reason was given by God for a Rule of Action," *That* "its Conclusions are promulg'd by Revelation," he elsewhere *endeavours,* as I have shewn, to *disprove* by reasoning, tho here he seems to *assert* it: But to the *contrary Positions* he has added a *Reason,* such as it is, from his Definition of a *Law;* that you might know his *real Sentiment* to be, "That the Conclusions of Reason, which direct us to Equity, Modesty, and other Virtues, are not" (as they are wont to be esteem'd) "Laws of Nature properly so called." He here seems to have done, what he says cautious Men do, in another Affair relating to Religion; they speak of God agreeably to the Sentiments of others, *"not dogmatically but piously." Leviath. c.* 12. § 7. [29]

(Nevertheless, his real Sentiments may be discover'd, which, in such Cases, are always on the impious side of the Contradiction.)

28. Hobbes, *On the Citizen,* 4.1, pp. 58–59.
29. Hobbes, *Leviathan,* ch. 12, p. 65.

Who *(viz. God)* has guarded these his Laws, by the double Sanction of Rewards, Internal or Essential, and External or Adventitious.

What I propos'd to my self to *prove,* was only this, "That as the Being of the first Cause, so the Authority, or full Power of Obligation, which the Laws of Nature derive from their Author, may be made appear from the Consideration of the Universe; from whence the first Cause of all is found out." In the mean time, I *take notice* also, "That the Laws of Nature have an *intrinsecal* and essential *Proof* of their *Obligation,* taken from the *Rewards* or Increase of Happiness which attends the benevolent Person from the natural efficacy of his Actions, and follows the Man who studiously observes these Laws; and from the *Punishments,* or Degrees of Misery, which, whether they will or no, they call upon themselves, who either do not obey, or do oppose, the Conclusions of right Reason." For the Connexion of these Rewards with Benevolence, which is the Summary of the Laws of Nature, is plainly express'd in the above-mention'd PROPOSITION, by *the most happy State of all;* and so the want thereof, and Misery, its Opposite, is sufficiently shewn to be the Consequence of the Malevolence of all towards all.

The Terms of the foregoing Proposition, and their Connexion (*i.e.* Truth,)

§XIII. These things being *suppos'd,* which I have briefly premis'd *concerning God, the Author of natural Effects,* and, in consequence, of the *Laws of Nature;* (they being by the Supposition we have just hinted at, in the present State of Things *necessarily* introduced into the Minds of Men, as soon at least as they come to Years of Discretion;) I shall now proceed to the *Distinction* and *Explanation* of the *simple Ideas,* of which this PROPOSITION and its *Corollaries* consist; and also of the *complex Truth,* which arises from the Composition of those Terms. Its *Subject* is the *greatest Benevolence towards all Rationals,* which, it is evident, does consist in a constant Volition of the greatest Good towards all, so far as the Condition of our Nature, and of other Things, makes it practicable. In this place it seems proper to consider, how, together with a Knowledge of the visible World, (of which our Body is a part,) is let in upon our Senses and Minds, the Knowledge, (1.) of *good Things;* (2.) and, more particularly, of those which are *common to many;* (3.) amongst which one is often greater than another; (and that we call the *greatest,* than which we can perceive no greater;) (4.) of which we easily perceive that some are daily in *our Power,* and therefore practicable; some, in certain Circumstances, exceed the narrow Limits of our Faculties.

But seeing we come at the Knowledge of the Nature of these Things, *two* ways, (1.) More *confusedly,* by obvious Experience and daily Observation; (2.) More *distinctly,* by Contemplation and Philosophical Enquiries, founded upon Experiments cautiously made, and diligently compar'd amongst themselves: By *both* these Methods we receive some Knowledge of the Laws of Nature. Hence it comes to pass, that they become known, even to the *Vulgar,* but *confusedly* and *imperfectly,* according to the Degree of Knowledge which they have of Nature: But *Philosophers* must more *accurately* observe, both the *Connexion* of the most general Notions, (of which they are composed,) with the universal Causes and Principles of Things, and the *Train of Consequences,* by which particular Precepts are deduced from the general Fountain of them all; as also their *mutual Relation* and *Rank,* according to which one gives place to another; when, in the same case, the Observance of several of them together seems impossible. The *former* Manner of coming at the Knowledge of the Laws of Nature, I thought not fit to be intirely slighted, because it is that by which almost all Men learn them; and because the Principles, into which Nature is to be philosophically resolved, are so much disputed, that there might be some danger, if I built the Doctrine of Morality upon those physical Principles alone, which I embrace, that many would reject it, for that very Reason, as not agreeing with me in their Natural Philosophy.[30] I shall therefore call to mind the *common Phaenomena,* in which almost all agree; and from them I shall shew briefly in this Chapter, that the *Simple Knowledge* of the *Terms* of the aforesaid Proposition, and their *Connexion* by which they are form'd into a true Proposition, may be deduced.

Become known two ways, to the Vulgar, more confusedly; to Philosophers, more distinctly.

§XIV. All daily *behold,* "That the Enjoyment of very many Things," (produc'd upon the Surface of this Earth, and compriz'd under the Name of Victuals, Clothing and Houses,) "and the mutual Assistance of one Man to another, contribute naturally to the Life, Preservation, Strength, Comfort and Tranquillity of Man." Such kind of Effects we conceive to have this in common, that they *agree* with that Nature for

The former Method.

---

30. Cumberland acknowledges that his readers might not share his preference for Cartesian natural philosophy.

whose sake they are; that is, we esteem them *Good;* and so we come to represent *that* Affection of Man, whence the external Acts, productive of these Effects, proceed, under the Notion of *Benevolence.* Again, all are *sensible,* "That this their Benevolence may profit, not themselves only, or a few, but very many, partly by Counsel, partly by Strength and Industry"; and whereas they see others altogether like themselves, they cannot but *think* "them able to make like Returns," and consequently, *see* "much Good and Advantage to each Man, arising from mutual Aid and Assistance, which all must want, and in their stead suffer innumerable Dangers, with extreme Poverty, if each, regarding himself only, were always malevolent to others." But such Endeavours, profitable to many rational Beings, necessarily produce in the Mind a Notion of *common Good,* which, from the obvious *Likeness* of Rationals among themselves, may easily *alike* regard *all,* whom we have ever an Opportunity of coming to the knowledge of. To which this also may be added, that it is most obvious, by constant *Experience,* "That we have it more in our power to assist Men, than other *Animals,*" to say nothing of the *inanimate* Kind: for the *Nature of Man* (and consequently, *his Good* and *Evil*) is most known to us, from that Knowledge of *ourselves* which we cannot avoid; and is also capable of enjoying *more good Things,* to the Attainment whereof we can lend our Aid; and liable to *greater Calamities,* in guarding against which, our Power may most usefully be employ'd. Besides, we may procure innumerable Advantages to Men, by our *Prudence* and *Counsel* communicated by proper *Signs,* of which other Animals are wholly incapable.

Moreover, because of the *Likeness* of the Nature of other rational Agents. "To will *such* things to *them, as* we are naturally inclin'd to desire for *ourselves,* Reason cannot but judge more agreeable to our inward Principles of Action," (whatever they may be,) "than to desire the *like* to Beings widely *different.*" Further, as we perceive our selves more willing to benefit others who are like our selves, we may with reason *hope,* "That they whom we benefit, will be *mov'd* with our *Benefits,* to return us the *like,* or greater, that they may likewise oblige us."

Lastly, it is well known by the *Experience* of all, "That there is no more *valuable Possession* upon Earth, no greater Ornament or Safeguard, than

is the sincere *Benevolence* of all towards all"; (which is very consistent
with a particular *Friendship* for a few select Persons;) because Men, if
they are malevolent, may easily force from others, as all other things, so
Life it self. Nor is there a more effectual *Method* to procure either of
these, than "by our Actions to shew the same Affection towards others,
that we desire from them," that is, *Benevolence,* as occasion offers, towards *all,* but a *more particular* Regard and Kindness toward chosen
Friends. But if (as is meet, and as is every where the Practice, even of
the Vulgar;) we *take care* "to sollicit the Aid of the first Cause, to the
Establishment of human Happiness," we shall find nothing in our selves
more Divine, by which we may please the Deity, than that sincere and
most extensive Love, (of which we have been hitherto discoursing,)
which reaches even God himself, as the Head and Father of rational
Beings, and all other rational Agents, as his Children, more like to himself than the rest of his Creatures are; and, in consequence, the most
dear to him: *"For we are his Offspring."* is the Saying of *Aratus* the *Ci-
lician,* approv'd by the *Athenians,* when *Heathens.*[31] I could easily quote
innumerable Testimonies to the same purpose, but 'tis folly to light a
Candle to the Sun.

§XV. The things now propos'd concerning human Happiness, appear
so *plain* by common Experience, or obvious Reasoning, that I know
nothing belonging to human Nature *more evident;* and they have the
same Respect to the Direction of our *Practice in Morality,* which the
Postulates of *Geometricians* have to the *Construction of Problems;* such
are for *plain* Problems, that *we can draw a Right Line from any one Point
to any other;* or that *we can describe a Circle with any Center and Radius:*
And other more difficult ones, for the Construction of *solid* and *linear*
Problems. In all these Cases are suppos'd Actions, depending upon the
free Powers of Men; yet *Geometry* does not become *uncertain,* by any
Disputes arising from the Explanation of *Freewill.* The like may be said
of *Arithmetical* Operations; for it is sufficient for the Truth of these
Sciences, that the *Connexion* is *inseparable* between such *Acts* (which it

*Which is as
certain and
clear, as Math-
ematical Rea-
soning.*

31. Aratus, *Phaenomena,* 5; cited by St. Paul in Acts 17.28.

supposes may be done, and which we find placed in our power, when we go about the Practice of Geometry,) and the *Effects* desir'd. And either the Pleasure arising from such Contemplations, or the manifold Uses in Life, are sufficient to invite Men to search after such Effects. By a *like* Reasoning, the *Truth* of *Moral Philosophy* is founded in the *necessary Connexion* between the *greatest Happiness* human Powers can reach, and those Acts of universal Benevolence, or of Love towards God and Men, which is branch'd out into all the moral Virtues. But in the mean time these things are *suppos'd* as *Postulates*, "That the greatest Happiness they can attain, is sought by Men"; and, "That they can exercise Love, not only towards themselves, but also towards God, and Men, partaking of the same rational Nature with themselves."

I will here only *add*,[32] "That the same Experience which proves that the Benevolence of each towards all, is the most effectual Cause of the

---

32. [Maxwell] "As common Benevolence of all towards all, is of use to Mankind, consider'd as one Body, so the several Species of Benevolence, are of use to their respective particular Societies, wherein they are found. In as much as the Members of those inferior Societies are also in divers manners dependent of one another; and as there is a more strict and necessary Dependence of the Members of those inferiour Societies upon one another, than upon the Members of the universal Body: So the Species of Benevolence, that are distributed among those lesser Societies, do each of them exceed the common Benevolence; and the Author of Nature has most exactly *proportion'd* the *Measure* of the *Benevolence* of each Society to the *Degree* of the *Dependence* of its Members upon one another. Thus the most necessary and absolute Dependence of one Person upon another that is any where to be found among Men, is that of an Infant upon its Parent; and here hath Nature provided the strongest Benevolence, which is not only absolutely necessary for the Preservation of the helpless Infant, but is productive of a grateful Return of like care and support in the old Age and Imbecillity of the Parent. In like manner there are several other things, which naturally add to common Benevolence, the chief of which are, *Benefits* receiv'd, a *Similitude* of Pursuits among Youth, and of the settled Methods of Life in middle Age, *Acquaintance, Union* of Interests, *Neighbourhood,* & c. All which, if strictly examin'd both in themselves and in their various Degrees, and applied to the several Relations among Mankind; it will be *found*, 'That they naturally produce the greatest Benevolence, where it is the most useful; that is, where there is the strictest Dependence, and where the Parties have the most frequent Occasions of mutual Assistance.'

"Nothing, but the most sottish Stupidity can be insensible of Love and Amazement, upon the most transient Glimpse of those astonishing Instances, both of the Wisdom and Benevolence of that Being, whose *Goodness is over all his Works.*"

Happiness of the Benevolent, does most necessarily prove, by a *Parity of Reason,* that the Love of any Number, towards any Number, has an Effect in proportion; and that likewise Malevolence towards all, brings most certain Destruction upon particular Persons, how much soever they may love themselves." For "what takes away the necessary Causes of Happiness, and places in their stead the Causes of all kinds of Calamities, threatens nothing short of extreme Misery."

§XVI. The *justness* of this *Consequence* is every where *acknowledg'd* by Mr. *Hobbes,* whilst from his *Supposition,* "That every one naturally provides for his own Life only, and arrogates to himself a Right over all Things and Persons," he *infers,* "A War of all against all," and then *proclaims,* "That from thence all kinds of Miseries, even Death it self, hang over the Heads of all." Nay, he *supposes,* "That all Men are sensible of this, before they consent to enter into Compacts of Society with others."[33] The Man is very *sharp-sighted,* in the Causes of *Evil,* and of *Fear;* but he is perfectly *blind,* with respect to the Causes of *Good,* and the *Hopes* of Happiness altho these *latter* are certainly *equally obvious,* nay *first* in the Order of distinct Knowledge, *because* the Causes constituting and preserving the Natures of Things, (which are *Good,*) come *first* to be discovered, *before* the Causes corrupting and dissolving the same, which are call'd *Evils.* I cannot therefore doubt, but that it is manifest, even to *Hobbes* himself, that *the Study and Pursuit of the common Good, under the prudent Conduct of Reason, avails as much toward the Security and Happiness of all, as the Neglect thereof can toward the Destruction of all, whilst every one is intent upon his own particular Advantage:* But, whatever he may think, it is certain, that from ourselves this Truth may be learn'd by every Man of common Sense, that is come to Years of Discretion. For from their *Experience,* "That the Activity of their Will in procuring Good, is, at proper times, both sufficient to benefit themselves and others," they cannot but *understand,* "That a like Will in other Men is neither less effectual, nor less necessary, to the obtaining the same

(Hobbes himself allowing the Principles, tho he overlooks their natural Consequence.)

33. This account is drawn from Hobbes, *On the Citizen,* 1.10–13, pp. 28–30; *Leviathan,* ch. 13.

end." But 'tis tedious to inculcate with many Words a thing so plain; yet I would not pass it over in silence, because all that follows is deduc'd from thence, as presupposed.

But seeing the *Deduction of the particular Laws of Nature from this general one,* is Matter of *philosophical Enquiry,* and does therefore belong to the *second* Method of deducing them, it seem'd proper to premise some *Considerations drawn from Natural Philosophy,* in order to make it *appear,* "That a philosophical Contemplation of Nature does very much assist the Minds of Men, in forming a more distinct Notion of that general Law."

§XVII. In the first place, I think it proper to *take notice,* "That those more general Notions,[34] whose use very frequently occurs in all the Laws of Nature, are observ'd in Things *corporeal,* and that the Mind may therefore perceive them, even by the assistance of their *Senses*": Such are those universal Ideas, of *Cause* and *Effect,* and of their connexion; of *Number,* compos'd of Units, and consequently of *Summ,* (whence all collective Notions,) of *Difference, &c.* of *Order,* of *Duration,* &c. But, altho I think this Observation conduces much to our present purpose, because such Notions are essential Parts of the Laws of Nature, yet because this is no matter of Debate between us and our Adversaries, and is obvious to all, there is no occasion farther to enlarge upon this Point.

2dly, Natural Philosophy does very distinctly *explain,* "What *Things,* or *Powers* and *Motions* of Things, are to others either *Good* or *Evil*"; and, "How *necessarily* and *unchangeably* this is brought about." For *seeing* it is the only *Scope* of this Science, "To discover the Causes of Generation, Duration, and Corruption," (all which we behold daily to happen to most Bodies, but especially to Men,) and "To demonstrate the necessary Connexion of such Effects with their Causes"; and *seeing* it is *certain,* "That the *Causes generating* and *preserving* Man, for *example,* by Efficacy of which he continues for some time, and flourishes with Faculties, as well of Body as Mind, enlarg'd, and determin'd to their proper

How, in pursuance of the second Method, the Mind comes to form universal ideas,

As also, of natural Good and Evil.

---

34. Cumberland refers to "transcendental notions," a scholastic usage effaced by Maxwell. Cumberland, *De Legibus Naturae,* p. 24.

Functions, are call'd *Good* to him," but "That the *Causes* of *Corruption, Grief,* and *Troubles,* are to him *naturally Evil*"; it evidently *follows,* "That Natural Philosophy *explains* what things are to him *naturally Good* and *Evil,* and *demonstrates* that they are *necessarily such.*"

I esteem as Parts of *natural Science,* the Knowledge of all those things, which Nature produces for the *Food, Cloathing, Habitation,* and *Medicine* of Man. We may also refer to *natural Science,* the Knowledge of all human *Operations* and *Effects,* of use in human Life: for, altho the voluntary Actions of Men, whose Effects are external, do not take their Rise in the same manner with Motions merely natural, from the impulse of other Bodies, but are determin'd by our Reason and Free-will; nevertheless, since they are *true Motions* produc'd by, and receive their Measure or Proportion from, the Powers of our *Body,* which are of the *same* Nature with the Powers of *other natural Bodies,* they must, after once they exist, by a *like* Necessity and altogether in the *same* manner, as other natural Motions, produce their Effects according to the Laws of Motion. This is most clearly and universally evident, in the Operations of the simple mechanical Powers, (such are the Lever, the Pully, and the Wedge, into which all the rest may be resolv'd,) which (as is well known to all) produce the same Effects, when they are enforc'd by human Strength, as, when, instead thereof, the Weight of inanimate Bodies is apply'd.

§XVIII. It is likewise commonly *known,* "That the Industry of Man, by the *Motions* of his Body," (which the Philosopher easily resolves into the *mechanic Powers,*) "is both able and wont to be subservient to the Preservation of himself and others, in preparing and preserving *Victuals, Medicine, Apparel, Houses,* and *Ships.*" Upon these Effects is laid out the whole Power of Man, exerted in *Agriculture, Architecture, Ship-building, Merchandizing,* and other *handycraft Trades,* of *Smiths, Carpenters,* and *Weavers.* Even the *Propagation of the Species,* the *Suckling* and *Nourishment* of Infants, may be resolv'd into the *same* Principles, according to *Hobbes's* own Confession, to which he has my Concurrence. Nor are those other more *liberal Arts,* in which, by the help of *sensible Signs, articulate Sounds, Letters,* and *Numbers,* the Minds of Men are enrich'd with Sciences, or directed to various Operations, wholly exempt from

Which are such necessarily, and invariably.

these *Laws of Motion;* the *natural Powers* of our Hands and Mouths, are our *Instruments,* for *Writing,* or *Speaking,* in the making Contracts, in the Distribution, Conveyance, and Preservation of Rights; in which, *Justice,* the principal Effect of Ethicks and Politicks, almost wholly consists. For, to say nothing of Action, the Power of *Words* and *Letters,* which are perform'd wholly by *bodily* Organs, is not inconsiderable, either in the *Instruction* of the *Mind,* or in the *Government* of the *Passions,* altho both the first *Institution* of Words as Signs, and their *Choice* and *Composition,* be entirely the Work of the *Mind,* directing the Imagination and the Tongue; and altho, after Men have heard Sermons, and perused the Laws, they are still left to the *free* Determination of their own Will. Let us consider, for *Example,* after what manner Laws written, or spoken, operate. How great soever the *Force* of these Laws is, it consists entirely in these *two* Things, the *Promulgation,* and foreseen Execution of them by the Distribution of the *Punishments* and *Rewards* therein express'd: but both these become known to Men, by the help of the *Senses,* which are *affected* by *corporeal* Motions *necessarily* producing their genuine Effect; which I therefore thought proper here to remark, because, *seeing* the Promulgation and Execution of Laws are *good,* that is, conducing, as efficient Causes, to the Happiness of all rational Beings; it may be *hence prov'd,* "That there are things which are good, necessarily and naturally"; and this could be certainly known, before any Laws at all were made by Men: for these *Signs*[35] conduce to the formation of Mens Manners, *after the like manner, as* the North-Star, the Observation of the Motion of the other Stars, the Mariners Compass, Sea-Charts, and other Mathematical Instruments, are of use to the Safety of Ships, altho they may thro' Carelessness be neglected. But the Operation and *Concurrence* of the *Mind* with the *bodily Powers,* to produce these Effects, may be *compar'd* with the Action of the *Steersman,* plac'd at the Ship's Helm, and of the *Merchant* carried in that Ship, *estimating* the Prices and Uses of the Lading;[36] who can do nothing without the help of an *Interpreter,* and of *Signs;* without the Conveniences of *Ports* and

35. [Maxwell] "i.e. Arbitrary Signs or Words."
36. "Load," or "cargo."

Winds; and unless the Ship be tight in the Seams, and furnish'd with Sails and Rigging; unless also different Countries produce such Merchandizes, as may relieve mutual Wants, which yet, every one must own, depend upon necessary Causes.

[37]*Altho* it cannot be *imagin'd,* "That such Arts had arriv'd to their present Perfection, or even their Improvement and bringing to Perfection could be distinctly foreseen, before Men enter'd into Societies"; *yet* Mr. *Hobbes* himself must *acknowledge,* "That all were appriz'd, mutual Assistance would prove very advantageous"; and "That all were able, sufficiently to make known their Inclinations to others by Signs": *Because* he founds Societies upon Compacts, enter'd into for that very Purpose.

By *Parity of Reason,* all *Actions* and *Motions contrary* to these, are *naturally* and *necessarily Evil;* such are those, by which human Bodies are brought to decay, either by withdrawing what is necessary to Life and Strength, as Food, Raiment, and Houses; or by introducing hurtful things in their stead: as also those Motions, by which the Minds of Men are debarr'd from Knowledge and Virtue; or, in their stead, Errors and unbridled Affections, which stand in opposition to the common Good, are introduc'd.

§XIX. When we treat of *Good* or *Evil,* with relation to the Laws of Nature, we regard not the Body or Mind of any *particular* Man, or of a *few,* (because the Suffering or Punishment of these may sometimes contribute to the public Good;) but the *collective Body* of all Mankind, as naturally subordinate to God their Governour, which will afterwards be more clearly explain'd. But the Good of the collective Body is no other, than the greatest which accrues to all, or to the major Part of the Whole.

And may be common to many.

But these things, which I have here enlarg'd upon, concerning the natural Efficacy of many human Actions, to the preserving or assisting others, I have mention'd only for this Purpose, that we might distinctly

37. In the original work, Cumberland begins section XIX here. Cumberland, *De Legibus Naturae,* p. 27.

consider, "*How* Men, from the Observation of the Faculties of others, may *naturally* come to the knowledge of *Things naturally good,* and those both great and necessary; and so be *induc'd* to do what they have in their power, for the *Benefit* of the Bodies and Minds of *other* Men." It will not now be difficult to *shew,* "That these Faculties and Actions are not so limited, as to profit *one* only, but that their Force and Benefit extends to *many;* so that the Knowledge, Art, and Industry, the Benevolence, Fidelity, or Gratitude of *one* Man, may gratify *very many;* and being themselves good and common to many, may naturally imprint upon the Minds of the Observers, an Idea of *common Good."* What is more, by means of the *Union* of the *Mind* with the human *Body,* the Power of Man reaches *farther,* and performs *greater* Things, than the much *greater* bodily Force of *other Animals.* For that Power has invented the Art of *Navigation,* knows how to enter into and observe *Compacts* with others at a great Distance, hath shewn us how, by the benefit of Letters and Numbers, to maintain *Commerce* with the *East* and *West-Indies;* and at so great a Distance, can treat of *Peace,* or wage *War:* But, of necessity, innumerable Motions must hence be determin'd. Nevertheless, it is not unusual in other *Causes,* whose Force is only *Mechanical,* to observe an evident *Efficacy,* productive of *Advantage* or Disadvantage to *many.* This is acknowledg'd, even by the *Peripatetic* Philosophy, and by common Experience, which *shews,* "That the Rays of the Sun convey vital Nourishment, to *innumerable* Vegetables over the whole Earth, and necessary Heat to the Blood of *all* Animals." But a more accurate Inquiry into Nature, does upon several Occasions *demonstrate,* "That every Motion of every corporeal Particle does very widely extend its Force, and consequently, in some measure, however little, necessarily concur with many other Causes, to produce many Effects." The Proof of this Assertion is easy, nor at all foreign to the matter before us: But because it depends upon Principles which are partly Physical and partly Mathematical, which to most would seem too remote from the Doctrines of Morality, and because it will be readily allow'd, even by our *Adversaries,* I chose to omit what I had prepar'd upon this Head.[38]

---

38. A comment indicating that Cumberland's original version contained much more by way of scientific illustration.

§XX. This, however, I have here thought fit to *take notice of,* "That *Hobbes,* in this matter, seems to grant more than sufficient," when in the last Paragraph but one, of his Treatise *De Corpore,* he expressly asserts, "That *there can be no Motion in a Medium admitting of no Vacuity, unless the next part of the Medium give way, and so on infinitely, so that the particular Motions of every particular Body contribute somewhat to every Effect.*"[39] Mean-while he is not aware, that this will thence *follow,* "That any human Action may, by its own Nature, contribute somewhat to this Effect, *viz.* The Preservation and Perfection of many, who do not desire it," that is, may be *naturally Good to many.* Otherwise, he would not so crudely assert, *"That Good respects only him who desires it";*[40] and hence infer, *"That the Nature of Good and Evil is variable, at the pleasure of single Persons in the State of Nature, and at the pleasure of the Government in every civil State."*[41] Which are the fundamental Principles of *Hobbes's* Ethicks and Politicks, as I shall shew in the Chapter *concerning Good.*[42]

(It is therefore a Mistake in *Hobbes,* to assert the variable Nature of Good and Evil, even upon his own Principles.)

I propos'd in this Place only to *shew,* "That certain Motions, Powers, and Actions of all Things whatsoever, and consequently also of Men, whence we perceive that something is done tending to the Preservation or more flourishing Condition of others, do *naturally imprint* upon us the notion of a *Good common to many";* and *because* the *Nature* of Things will not permit us, to think all kinds of Motions or Actions *equally* conducive to this End, that *therefore Nature* does sufficiently *instruct* us. "That there is a *difference* between Things *good* and *evil,* whether they relate to many, or to Individuals." Yet further, *seeing* the Generation, Preservation, and Perfection of natural Bodies, (Men for *Instance,*) and on the contrary, their Destruction and Corruption, are nothing else than certain *Motions,* variously complicated, of those Particles whereof they consist, and that all these Motions are produc'd by their Causes, according to the Laws of certain *Theorems* geometrically demonstrated; it is clearly *manifest,* "That all things are generated, preserv'd and perfected by their Causes with the *same necessity,* that these

39. Hobbes, *De Corpore,* 30.15, p. 261.
40. Hobbes, *De Homine* (1658), 11.4, p. 62.
41. Hobbes, *Leviathan,* ch. 6, pp. 28–29.
42. Ch. 3.

Theorems are geometrically demonstrated to be *true*." But the constituting, preserving, and perfecting Causes of Things or Men, are those
Things which we call *good,* and the contrary to these, *evil,* whether their
Efficacy reaches one only, many, or all. Wherefore, *supposing* "such Motions and Actions, of some Men in relation to others, as we now see tend
to their Preservation," they produce this Effect with the *same necessity,*
that the geometrical *Theorems* concerning such Motions are *true;* and
therefore they are *naturally Good,* altho no Laws were yet suppos'd, by
which they are commanded.

Therefore *Hobbes's* Fiction, "That Good and Evil are changeable," is
perfectly *inconsistent* with the necessary and *immutable Causes,* which
he every where asserts, of the Being and Preservation of *Man.* Nor can
he come off this by *saying,* (which yet he often inculcates,) "That before
civil Laws there is no *measure* of Them"; for there is the *same* measure
of *Good* and *Evil,* that there is of *Truth* and *Falshood,* in those Propositions which relate to the Efficacy of those Motions, that tend to the
Preservation or Corruption of other Things, namely, the *Nature of
Things;* and whatsoever Proposition points out the *true Cause of Preservation,* does at the same time shew, what is *true Good.*

§XXI. We have now briefly *seen,* "How the Nature of Things imprints
on us as certain and firm a Knowledge of Good and Evil, even of that
which is common to many, as is that by which we know the Causes of
Generation and Corruption." I now proceed to *consider,* "That the *Matter* and *Motion,* in which the Powers of a human Body, as of all other
parts of the visible World, do consist, *have a finite Quantity,* and certain
Limits, beyond which they cannot extend themselves." Whence flow
these most evident Axioms concerning all natural Bodies: That *the same
Bodies cannot at the same time be in more Places than one:* That *the same
Bodies cannot at the same time be mov'd toward several Places,* (especially
if contrary,) so as to be subservient to the opposite Wills of several Men; but
that *they are so limited, that they can be determin'd by the Will of one only,
unless several conspire to one and the same Effect or Use.* Nor is this peculiar
to Bodies only, but common to the Minds of Men, and to all created
Beings, as being Finite.

[margin note:] From the limited Powers of
all Finite
Beings,
appears,

From hence I would infer *two* Things, of great Consequence to our Purpose. (1.) That from the Knowledge of *Nature*, especially that of ourselves, we learn that celebrated *Distinction* of the *Stoicks*, between *those things which are in our Power*, (such are the Actions of our Mind, and some bodily Motions, both which, by the Effects we daily perceive, are obedient to the Will, and thence, by a parity of Reason, we may easily collect, what we shall be able to do hereafter;) and *those things which are not in our Power:* Such are by far the greatest, and the most, of those Motions which we daily perceive in the Universe, which we (little Animals) cannot obstruct, and by whose Force all things are in a perpetual Change, and which are the continual Sources, even to Men themselves, of the Vicissitudes of Adversity and Prosperity, Birth, Maturity, and Death.[43]

1. The Justness and Usefulness of that Distinction of the Stoicks, between *Things in our Power,* and, *out of our Power*

This *Distinction,* constantly attended to, is of *great use* in *forming* our *Manners,* and *regulating* our *Affections* and *Endeavours.* For hence we are *taught,* "Not to seek any other Happiness to *alleviate* our Labours, than that which arises from a prudent Management of our Faculties, and from those Aids, which we know the Providence of God, in the Administration of the Universe, will afford us."

Which is a great help to Prudence,

By this means we are *freed* from those *fruitless Labours,* to which *vain Hopes* sollicit most Men; nor shall we ever *disturb* our selves upon account of those *Evils,* which, *without our Fault,* have hitherto happen'd to us, or may hereafter happen; and so a great part of the Troubles, which usually arise from those *restless Affections,* Grief, Anger, and Fear, will be *prevented.* Nor shall we be hence only directed how to *avoid Evils,* but we shall also be shewn the most *compendious Way,* by which we may by degrees proceed to the *best Things,* which are possible to be obtain'd by us, namely, the *cultivating* our *Mind,* and the *Dominion* over our *Affections.* But I have no purpose to prosecute any farther, this Subject, in this Place.

And to the Government of our Passions.

43. The distinction is drawn from Epictetus, *Discourses,* I.1.

2. The Necessity of Benevolence, in order to our Happiness.

I will only make this *Observation,* which is to our present Purpose,[44] that it is well known by the Experience of all Men, "That the *Powers* of any *single* Person, in respect of that Happiness, of which from without he is both capable and stands in need, are so *small,* that he wants the *Assistance,* both of many Things and Persons, to lead his Life *happily;* but that *every one* can nevertheless *afford* many Things for the use of *others,* which himself does not at all need, and which therefore can be of no use to him." But seeing we are *certain,* from the known *limits* of our *Powers,* "That we *cannot compel* all those whose Aid we want, (*God* and *Men,*) to co-operate with us in the procuring our Happiness"; the only *Method* we have left to obtain this End, is, "To procure *their Good will,* by making a tender to them of *our Service,* and by a faithful *Performance.*" But, altho that greatest Benevolence, (mention'd in our foregoing general PROPOSITION) consists in a *hearty, constant, universal* Inclination so to act; and therefore also in Cases, where often *no Retaliation is expected,* nay, where we *know there will be no return* of reciprocal Affection: Yet it does *not hinder* us, from cultivating *Friendship chiefly* with them, from whom Reason persuades us to *hope* for the grateful *return* of a mutual Benevolence.

This is the first Conclusion which I draw from the finite Nature of all Things, of our selves especially. It thence follows,

3. The Necessity of limiting the uses of certain Things, and of human Services, to particular Persons for a limited time.

§XXII. *Secondly.* If Men, or other Things, do, or afford, any thing for the use of Men; such *Service* or *Benefit* is naturally and necessarily *limited* to certain *Persons, Times,* and *Places.* Therefore, if right Reason *enjoins,* "That the *Use of Things,* or the *Services of Men,* should be *useful* to *all* Men," it necessarily *enjoins,* "That, for a certain Time and Place, that use of Things and of human Services should be *limited* to certain Persons." The *Consequence* is *manifest, because* "That is right Reason in commanding, which commands that to be done, which is possible to be

44. [Maxwell] "This Head being a distinct one from both the precedent and subsequent, but not taken notice of as such by the Author, it would seem to be a Paragraph inserted by him, after writing the rest; which has occasion'd the Translator to make a Head more than the Author."

done, according to the Nature of Things." The Consequence tends to *prove,* "That a *Division* of Things, and of human Services, at least for the time they may be of use to others, is necessary for the Advantage of all."

And, certainly, that *necessary Limitation* of the use of *one Thing* to *one Man* for the *time* it benefits any Person, is a *natural Division,* that is, Separation from the use of any other Person for the same time. It is manifest, that I here call those things *one,* that are necessarily wholly employ'd, *in one use at one time.* For other things are likewise call'd *one,* which at the *same time* may be *of use to many,* as *one Island, one Wood,* &c. concerning whose Division I have yet affirm'd nothing. From the above-mention'd *natural Division of Things,* and its necessity to the Preservation of all, is deriv'd that *primitive Right* to Things by first *Occupancy,* (which is so frequently mention'd by *Philosophers* and *Lawyers,* and which they teach is to take place, supposing all things *common;*) for *Right* is the *Liberty of acting any thing, granted by a Law:* But in *that* suppos'd *State* there is *no other Law,* but *the Conclusions of right Reason, concerning Actions necessary to the common Good, promulgated by God.* Therefore, because *right Reason grants,* as necessary to the common Good, to every Man the use of Things and human Services, for so long time as such Use is beneficial to him, by that *Grant* a *Right* is given him (the first *Occupant*) to the use of that Thing or Person, for that time. The *Will* or *Benevolence* conformable to this Conclusion, is as truly *Justice,* as *that* which gives every one his Rights afterwards arising in civil Society. And the *same Benevolence,* as far as it permits such Rights to every one, and restrains those Affections which have a contrary Tendency, is laudable *Innocence.* But it is most evident, that no one can in any measure promote the publick Good, except he preserve *his* Life, Health, and Strength, by the use of Things, and of human Labour; and that therefore such *Occupancy* of Necessaries is a means plainly necessary to that End. For the Preservation of a *Whole,* consisting of mutually *divided Parts,* (such as Mankind is,) consists in the Preservation of the *divided Parts,* (not to mention any thing now of the Order to be preserv'd among them:) But the Preservation of the *divided* Parts, that is, of particular Men, requires the *divided* use of Things and of human

(Which overthrows *Hobbes's* fundamental Principle, of every Man's Right to every Thing.)

Labour; therefore that is necessary to the Preservation of the Whole. Such *Division,* which is a kind of *Property,* after things are occupied and applied to uses truly necessary, is very consistent with some *Community,* like that in *Feasts* and *Theatres;* such as several of the antient *Philosophers* have suppos'd,[45] not contrary to Reason indeed, but not very consistent with the sacred History; and directly *inconsistent* with that *Right of all to all,* which *Hobbes* has feign'd, in order to *prove,* "That, before the Institution of civil Government, preceded a State of universal War, of every Man against every Man; and that then a License of doing any thing against any Man, was both just and necessary."[46]

Here may be *collected,* by the way, *"How* every Man comes to have a right to preserve his own Life and Limbs," from this, that these are his most certain *Means* of serving God and Men, in which consists that *common Good,* I have been treating of. It is also plain, that the Right of every one is under these Restrictions: (1.) That if Religion, or the publick Welfare of Men, requires it, we be ready to part with the last drop of our Blood: And, (2.) That no innocent Person is to be hurt, to procure to our selves any Advantage.

This is most clearly deduc'd from the Principles which I have here briefly touch'd upon, and overthrows *Hobbes's* whole Doctrine of the Laws of Nature and Empire. For the whole of that does first *suppose* (not prove, nor limit) "A right to preserve this mortal Life, as the Foundation of all natural Laws, and of Society"; and then is intirely *employ'd,* "In applying to that End some Means, which are often most enormous." *Lib. de Cive,* c. i. §. 7. and elsewhere.[47]

And this is what we must assert, concerning the Original of *Meum* and *Tuum,* of *Property* and *Dominion,* (in the large Sense of the Words,) without taking into consideration what is reveal'd in the *Mosaic* History, as those *Philosophers* necessarily did, who had not receiv'd that Account. But this *Example* of introducing a *Division* being given by *Nature,* it is

---

45. For example, Epictetus, *Discourses,* II.4; Diogenes Laertius, *Lives,* VI.72, II.4; Cicero, *De Finibus,* III.20; Seneca, *De Beneficiis,* VII.12.

46. A paraphrase of the argument from ch. 13 of *Leviathan.*

47. Hobbes, *On the Citizen,* 1.7, p. 27.

easy, and agreeable to the Genius of a human Mind, by a *parity of Reason,* from observing those *Inconveniences,* which every Man experiences, of holding *all things in common,* to proceed (for the benefit of all) to a *further Division* of Things and human Services, and to introduce a more *complete Dominion* or *Property* in both, that might be in some respect *perpetual.*

§XXIII. The Reader, I believe, will not *expect,* "That I should recite all the most grievous *Mischiefs,* that would arise from a *Parity* introduc'd amongst all, or from having in common, Wives, Children, and all other Goods," for of these Mischiefs, others have abundantly treated. See *Aristotle,* in the *second Book* of his *Politicks,* and his *Commentators.*[48] For what he had said of a *particular Society,* may be easily applied to the *general Society,* made up of Mankind, the Subjects, and God, the Governour. It is sufficient, that the common Experience of the World *teaches* us, "That, where any thing is *yet* left *in common,* that thing generally comes to a Division, to avoid *needless Contentions*": And "That it is a natural Vice, to *neglect* that which is possess'd in common, and to think he has nothing, that has not the Whole."[49] For the *Dangers* of Contentions, and *Want,* the Effect of neglecting to cultivate the Earth, would (especially after Mankind grew numerous, and Vices, arising from Ignorance and a neglect of Discipline, became prevalent) reduce human Affairs to such a *State,* "That *all* must see it *equally* necessary to their common Happiness, to make a Distribution of Things and the Services of Men, which shall be *fix'd* and valid for the time to come, *as* to permit the present enjoyment of them to him, who first gets them into his Possession."

From whence it *follows,* "That as Nature" (according to what we have above shewn) "confers the right of using Necessaries present, so she does, in the *same manner,* grant the right of a stated and durable Division of Things, and Offices, which is call'd direct *Dominion.*" For nothing is more *evident,* "Than that the future use of Things, or of human Labour,

Whence also is deduc'd the Origin of Property and Dominion.

---

48. Aristotle, *Politics,* II.
49. Justinian, *Digest,* 8.2.26; Justinian, *Code,* 10.34.2.

has the same relation to future Life or Health, which the present Enjoyment has to present Life"; there is in both the relation of a *necessary Cause.* Wherefore the Case is almost the same in this, as in *Geometrical Propositions,* where from *three* given *Terms* a *fourth* is found; and we may justly think, that Mankind, in a *State of Nature,* (which *Hobbes* himself supposes,) may thus reason: *As a right to the Life of this Day, proves a right to its necessary preserving Causes,* viz. *A limited and divided use of Things and of human Labour, whilst they are now at hand; so also a right to Life for the time to come, shews a right to limit the use of Things and Persons for the future.* There is no occasion here for *artificial* Multiplication and Division, which are requisite to find out a *fourth Proportional* in large Numbers; for *such reasoning* is *obvious* to every Man in his Senses, and is daily practis'd by all, even whilst they are not aware of it, nor distinctly dispose the Terms into such an order. I have shewn, that the *two first Terms* are *given by Nature.* And it is evident, that the *third Term* also is *given,* because it contains nothing that is not known by all. For all Men provide for the future, and suppose it probable, that themselves and other Men, or even their own Posterity, and that of others, shall hereafter continue some time upon the Earth, and have a right of preserving their Life. Nay, *to* foresee Things future at a great Distance, *to* be very sollicitous about them, and *to* inquire into the Causes of such Things as present themselves to his Thoughts, is *peculiar to Man* above other Animals.[50] They will therefore come at the above-mention'd *fourth Proportional,* which is *the certain and limited Causes of preserving their Life for the future,* which are no other, than "The *divided use of Things,* and of human Labour, to be ratify'd and ascertain'd by common Consent for the future," *avoiding* all the Hazards of *Contention,* and *banishing* that *Scarcity,* which we suppose Experience taught them to have taken its Rise from a Neglect of the Cultivation of Things.

But such Reasoning from an exact *Similitude of Cases* is so *strong,* that in evidence it *rivals Euclid*'s Method (*Elem. 6.*) *of finding a fourth Pro-*

---

50. Cf. Cicero, *De Officiis,* I.4.

portional, by drawing a Parallel to a Line given, and *in easiness exceeds* it; which yet no one will deny to be suggested by *natural Reason.*[51]

From this *Example* of a further Division, *appears* first, *"How* from a *Change of Circumstances,"* (or from a Consideration of some Things, which, not being essential, are not contain'd in the primary and universal Notion of Mankind;) "human Actions of a *new kind* may become *necessary* to the publick Good": And secondly, *"After what manner,* from such *Necessity,* arises a *Right,"* (antecedent to the Institution of Civil Government,) "to perform such Actions."

Nor *upon these Suppositions,* will there be *any Right to do any thing,* except what right *Reason* declares to be *necessary to the common Good,* or at least *consistent with it;* of which the *first* is therefore *commanded* by Reason, the *last permitted,* which I shall explain more at large in the *Chapter of the Law of Nature.* This, however, I thought proper here carefully to *inculcate,* "That *all Right,* even to the Use of those Things, which are absolutely necessary to every one's Preservation," (as it is distinguish'd from the mere *force* of seizing those Things, in which Sense only its Original is here inquir'd into,) "is founded in the Command, or at least in the Permission, of the Law of Nature," that is, of right Reason, pronouncing concerning those things which are necessary to the common Good, according to the Nature of Things; and that therefore it *cannot be known,* "That any one has a Right to preserve himself, *unless it be known,* 'That this will contribute to the common Good,' or That it is at least consistent with it." But, if this be the Rise of our Right to our own Preservation, our *Powers* will be hereby so *limited,* that we may not invade the *equal Rights* of others, nor break forth into a War against all; that is, make an Attempt towards the Destruction of all.

In short, I *affirm first,* "That a *Right,"* (distinguish'd from mere *Power,*) "even to *Self-defence,* cannot be understood without Respect had to the Concessions of the Law of Nature, which consults the Good of all"; and that all solid *Arguments,* "by which any one can claim any Right to himself," do *prove,* "That there is such a *Law,* and that it is at the same time of *equal Force* to the Protection of *others."* But *secondly,* since

[margin: And of a Right to self-preservation, and self-defence.]

---

51. Euclid, *Elementa Geometriae,* VI, prop. 12.

the Right to the making such a Division can only be deduc'd from a Care of the common Good, it manifestly follows, that the *Dominion of God over all Things* is preserv'd unviolated; and that, from this Principle, *no Right of Dominion* can accrue to *any* Man over others, which will license him to take from the *Innocent* their Necessaries; but on the contrary, that the *Right of Empire* is *therefore* given to them, that the *Rights* of *all* may be *protected* from the Evils of Contention, and may be encreased, as far as the Nature of Things, assisted by human Industry, will permit.

§XXIV. Having already briefly *deduced,* from the Law which commands an Endeavour to promote the *common Good,* the *Property* of particular rational Beings, at least in things necessary, some *Right* is granted, which every one may justly call *his own;* and, by the *same Law,* all *others* will be *obliged to yield that to him,* which is usually included in the Definition of *Justice.*[52]

It seems moreover proper, more distinctly to *shew,* "what kind of Actions have a natural Tendency to promote the publick Happiness"; for thence will appear, both what Actions are *commanded,* and what *permitted* to Individuals.

It is manifest, *First,* That *to abstain from hurting any innocent Person,* is necessary: For the Damage of any Part is a detriment to the Whole, unless it be inflicted as a Punishment, for some Crime committed against the publick Welfare. Hence all *Invasion* of another's *Property,* is prohibited; for all Damage done to the Mind, Body, Goods, or good Name of any Person, is a Loss to the Publick.

Hence also the same natural Law, which requires to give every one his own, must, for the publick Good, command *Reparation of Injuries.*

Secondly, It is manifest, that this greatest and noblest End cannot be obtain'd by a bare *Abstaining from doing Evil;* but it is necessary, that every one *contribute his Share,* by a true, certain, and constant Application, as well of Things external, as of his Powers, towards the gaining this Point. For, otherwise, neither will the publick Happiness, nor our

A brief Deduction of the principal particular Laws of Nature.

Justice;

Abstaining from,

And repairing, Injuries;

52. Cf. Justinian, *Digest,* 1.1.10.

own, be the greatest we can effect.[53] It is upon this account a natural Precept, that if at any time, (the Nature of the chief End so requiring it,) we should *transfer to another some Right of ours,* either by *Gift,* at present, or by *Promise,* or *Compact,* afterwards to be perform'd; we make that Transfer *validly* and *faithfully,* and not with an Intention to deceive; for it is only such a firm transferring of any Thing, or of our Services, to the Use of another, as I have mention'd, which can at all conduce to the End commanded us. Hence arises the obligation to make and keep promises; but our Pains is most wisely and happily laid out, in the prosecution of the common Good of all rational Beings, if we observe the following *Order* in our Actions.

Liberality; making, and faithfully performing Promises and Compacts;

We should, *first,* perform what is acceptable to the intelligent Agents,[54] who are Causes of the common Good, and, consequently, of our own; that is, every one should take care to make himself *acceptable* to *God,* to *Princes,* and the whole Body of the State, (upon supposition that there are such in being,) to *Parents,* to *Benefactors;* but especially to Negotiators of *Peace,* or *Ambassadors.*

Piety, Loyalty, Gratitude to Parents, Benefactors, and Ambassadors;

Secondly, Every one should study *his own Preservation,* and further *Perfection;* but always preserving the Rights of others, by that Innocence which I have already shewn to be commanded. Hither I refer our being oblig'd to study the *Improvement* of our *Minds,* with all useful *Knowledge* and *Virtue,* and to *preserve* the *Life, Health,* and *Chastity* of our *Bodies.*

Self-Preservation and Improvement;

Thirdly, Men should *provide* for their *Families* and *Offspring,* because (to omit, that they are the Substance of their Parents, form'd into the same Species with them, whence they may justly claim to themselves the Rights of human Nature) they are the only Prop of the approaching old Age of the present Set of Men, and by them only we can hope to raise a succeeding Generation. To this Care of our Offspring, I refer *Love*

Natural Affection;

---

53. [Maxwell]. "That is, we shall be wanting, both to the publick Happiness, and to our own."

54. The original text has "Causis perceptivis boni communis . . ." (p. 39). Barbeyrac (*Traité Philosophique,* p. 74, n. 3) plausibly argues that Cumberland intended "praecipuis" rather than "perceptivis"; the amended passage would be: "We should first perform what is agreeable to the principal causes of the common good."

towards our *Kindred,* (who are the Offspring of our Parents,) and towards our whole *Posterity.*

And Human-
ity, towards
All;

Fourthly, Every one should study to make himself *acceptable to all*
others, by good Offices, and to benefit others, without the detriment of
any, by all Acts of *Humanity,* as they are called, such as, *to shew the way,
to raise the Fallen,* &c. in proof whereof there is no Occasion to add any
thing farther, than that, *in order to the preservation of any aggregate Body,*
whose Parts are transient, (as is the Case of all Mankind,) it is *necessary,*
"*That* the Causes of its Corruption, especially those which happen to
its inward Parts, be taken away; *that* there be a certain Communication
of Motion between its Parts; *that* its Causes of Preservation, and all its
essential Parts, be cherish'd, not only those which are at present, but also
those which shall hereafter be produc'd, by the Motion which is intrinsick to that aggregate Body; and *that* its Parts and Motions, which have
a less Proportion to the Whole, give way to those which have a greater
Proportion to the same." For scarce any thing can be prov'd more plainly,
than this *general Proposition,* which immediately flows from the *Definitions* of Things *preservative* and *destructive,*[55] of *Whole* and *Part,* of
Cause and *Effect;* and yet in all things suits with those *Particulars,* which,
in the foregoing Section, I affirm'd to be necessary to the Preservation
of Mankind.

This illustrated
by various
Examples from
Nature, of the
Contrivance of
its Author, for
the Preserva-
tion of the
whole, with
respect, 1. To
Individuals;

§XXV. But, lest any thing should be wanting, which might suggest such
Thoughts to the Minds of Men, and might *demonstrate their necessary
Connexion among themselves,* Nature lays before us a sufficient Number
of *Examples,* in Beings of various Kinds. Let the Nature of any *Animal*
be consider'd, as an Aggregate made up of Parts very different, that defends it self, for the time appointed by universal Nature, by the Methods
already mention'd; (1.) By *expelling,* according to its Power, those *Things*
which are *hurtful,* which it diligently separates from the vital Nourish-

---

55. Maxwell notes that he corrects "Contrariorum seu Corrumpentium" to "Conservantium et Corrumpentium." Barbeyrac agrees (*Traité Philosophique,* p. 75, n. 4)
although the phrase is left uncorrected in Cumberland's interleaved edition (p. 41).

ment; (2.) by *circulating the Blood*, and perhaps other useful Fluids, as the *Lymph*, the *Bile*, and the *nervous Juices*; (3.) by *repairing* what is *wasted*, by a new Succession of like Parts; (4.) and by the *mutual good Offices* of every Part, perform'd according to the general Laws of Motion, which nevertheless hinder not, but that each may take to themselves what is sufficient for their proper Nourishment and Strength.

If we turn our Eyes to the *mutual* Behaviour of *different Animals*, but of the *same Kind*; it is evident, that they continue their Species, by a certain kind of *Innocence*, *Retaliation* of Benefits, limited *Self-Love*, and a most powerful *Love of their Offspring*.

2. To Animals of the same Species;

> *Parcit cognatis maculis similis fera.*   Juv. Sat. 15.[56]

i.e. Wild Beasts of the same Kind do not fight with one another.

Lastly, If we consider this *visible World*, with *Des-Cartes* and others,[57] as a most exquisite *Machine*, we may perceive, that this our Vortex is no otherwise daily preserv'd, than by *resisting* some *contrary Motions* of the neighbouring Vortices; by *changing* or *removing Bodies of Figures or Motions less agreeable*; by a *circular Motion* of the Parts; by *propagating* the different Species of Things, by such kind of Motions, as those by which it has produc'd the Individuals which now are; and by causing its Parts to *yield to one another*, according to the Proportion which their Dimensions and Motions have to one another, and to the Whole. But I am determin'd, not to insist upon such *Hypotheses*, altho I know, that we may fairly reason from them, provided the natural Laws of Motion be exactly observ'd in them; and I dare affirm, that has been perform'd by *Des-Cartes*, with great Care and Exactness, in most Parts of his *Hypothesis*. Howbeit, whatsoever *Hypothesis* be assum'd, in order to explain the *Phaenomena* of Nature, such Laws of Motion must of necessity be allow'd, as, amidst all natural Changes, preserve the State of the *System of the World*, by such Methods as I have mention'd. Such being the Case,

3. To the Frame of the visible World.

56. Juvenal, *Satires*, XV.159.
57. Cumberland's reference to vortices indicates his familiarity with Descartes, *Principia Philosophica* (1644).

it is manifested by a most *illustrious Example,* what things are necessary to the Preservation of the *greatest and most beautiful aggregate Body;* the Consideration whereof cannot but most certainly *convince* Men, "That human Actions, not unlike these, may be the no less proper Causes of preserving the whole System of Mankind, and making them happy." Upon which account I am of opinion, that it would not be unprofitable to consider the *special Laws of Motion,* from the necessary Observance whereof the above-mention'd general Effects arise: But because this is too remote from my present chief Aim, the Philosophical Reader is referr'd, either to his own Experience, or to *Galileus, Des-Cartes, Wallis, Wren,* and *Huygens,* all celebrated Writers.[58] But all these Theorems, or Laws of Motion, may be deduced from this *Supposition,* "That Motion is not annihilated, after it has been impress'd upon Matter by the first Cause": And for this very *Reason.* "That it exists in a World that admits no *Vacuum,* it is necessarily still further propagated, till it return into it self":[59] And, on the contrary, the Truth of this *Supposition* is demonstrated, by all the Theorems of Motion observ'd in Nature, by the help of the Senses. It is sufficient for my present purpose, that, in what State soever Men are suppos'd to exist, the *Power* of doing those things which I have mention'd is plainly necessary to be permitted them, that the collective Body or Race of Men *may* be preserv'd; and that the *Will* to do so is no less necessary to the *actual* Happiness of Men: And to these Heads may be reduc'd whatever is necessary to this Effect.

58. Galileo Galilei (1564–1642); René Descartes (1596–1640); John Wallis (1616–1703); Christopher Wren (1632–1723); Christiaan Huygens (1629–95).

59. Cumberland's discussion is based upon Cartesian conservation theory. He makes similar use of the theory in 2.15. It is worth noting that at the time he was writing, Wren and Huygens's experiments were revealing evidence of entropic tendencies in ballistic impacts, which undermined the analogy Cumberland sought to draw. See Scott, *The Conflict Between Atomism and Conservation Theory 1644–1860* (1970), pp. 6–13. Barbeyrac (*Traité Philosophique,* p. 77, n. 2) also notes that by the eighteenth century, plenism had been abandoned by the best philosophers, especially in England.

§XXVI. What I have hitherto said, concerning the *necessary Connexion between the aforesaid Actions and the common Good,* is advanc'd with this *View,* "To fix unchangeably, by their Relation to this Effect, the Nature of those human Actions, wherein Piety, Probity, and every Virtue consists"; for the *Relation* between entire *adequate Causes* (that is, Causes consider'd in all their Circumstances requisite to Action) and their *Effects,* is wholly *immutable.* In *every State,* as well of holding Things in common, as of divided Property, *such a Course of Life, as* deceives no Man by Lyes or Perfidiousness, *as* injures no Man in his Life, Reputation, or Chastity, *as* makes Returns of Gratitude to Benefactors, and provides for himself or his Posterity, without hurting another, always has been, and will be, a Cause of the common Good, and is therefore to be distinguish'd by the Name of Virtue. This is only to be taken care of, that we have in view an *Effect great enough,* that is, that some *Advantage* accrue to the *Whole,* or, at least, that it suffer *no Damage,* whilst we endeavour to *gratify a Part;* whatsoever is acted otherwise, is to be look'd upon as Vice. And because the Nature of Things makes known to Men, "That by such Actions the common Good" (in which their own proper Happiness is contain'd) "may be obtain'd, and that in the highest degree, that is to them singly possible; but that contrary Actions do likewise make Men miserable; and that these things are so, because of the *Connexion* made by the *Will* of the *First Cause,* between such Actions and their Effects"; it evidently *follows,* "That Men are *oblig'd,* by the same Will of the *First Cause,* to *exercise Virtue,* and *Shun Vice;* under the Penalty of losing Happiness, or for the Hope of acquiring it."

How it appears to be the Will of God, that we should promote the publick Good, *i.e.* be Virtuous.

Innumerable *Evils,* to the Doer himself, *naturally attend* every Action *injurious* to others; for he himself, because he contradicts better practical Principles, (which are known to himself,) sets his own Mind at variance with itself, so as to be *Self-condemn'd;* and he that but once delivers himself up to the Conduct of Rashness and of blind Affections, rather than to the Counsel of his own Reason, will, for the future, be *more easily* hurried away by them, whence he will at last with ease procure his own Ruin: He sets others also an *Example,* which may be highly prejudicial to himself: He increases *Suspicion* and the Causes of *Distrust,* the Inconveniencies of which he will some time or other experience. Nay, fur-

1. From the Evils necessarily connected with a vicious Action.

ther, every vicious Action may be said to contain all that *Punishment,* to inflict which, it will excite any rational Agents, out of their regard to publick or private Good, in order to restrain Malefactors.

2. From the Punishments inflicted, for evil Actions, by other rational Beings, Now this Influence of Actions, to excite Observers to inflict Punishment, tho it extends *only* to *rational Natures,* God and Men, yet is of great moment, and ought always to be consider'd, before we undertake any Action, lest we should thereby, even unwillingly, draw Destruction upon our own heads; because our *whole Hope* depends upon *God* and *Men,* who judge of the Merit or Demerit of our Actions, by their Relation to the common Good.

Whether God, "That *God* is privy to, and punishes, the most concealed Wickedness," perhaps I should seem impertinent, if I went about to *prove,* after so many *Philosophers,* antient and modern, and also so many *Christian Fathers;* especially since *he,* whose Opinions I am now examining, does no where, that I know of, deny it. Nevertheless, the manner, by which we naturally come to the Knowledge of this, I shew afterwards, where I more fully set forth my Opinion, concerning *the Obligation of the Laws of Nature.*[60]

or Men. Besides, *the Author of no Villany can be secure;* because *Men* (whose Interest it is universally, that a most extensive Benevolence, and that Justice should take place) may come to the Knowledge of, and punish, the most secret Crimes, which may be discover'd a thousand ways, that no one can avoid. Wicked Persons have often betray'd themselves in their *Dreams,* in their *Ravings,* in their *Cups,* or in a sudden Fit of *Passion.*[61] And this even *Epicurus* and his Followers have confess'd; *they,* who have used great Endeavours to shake off the *Fears of a divine Providence,* have yet frequently own'd, that the *Fear of Man* cannot be shook off: The Reader may have recourse to the *fundamental Maxims* of *Epicurus,* with *Gassendus's* Notes.[62] I will add only this, that, beside the divine Vengeance, which the Conscience of almost all wicked Men

60. Chapter 5.
61. Cf. Lucretius, *De Rerum Natura,* III.1155.
62. Gassendi, *Animadversiones in Decimum Librum Diogenis Laertii* (1649), vol. III, p. 1758.

dread, as the Avenger of the most secret Crimes, among Men, consider'd even out of a State of civil Government, *Revenge* generally follows any Act of Wickedness, after it has been discover'd. For seeing it is the *Interest of all,* "That Crimes should be punish'd," any Person, that is *able,* has a *Right* to exact those Punishments, which a regard to the publick Good requires should be taken by *some body.* For, by the Supposition, all Inequality among Men being taken away, that Saying of the *Latin* Poet takes place, *I am a Man, and therefore no Calamity that befals Mankind seems to me indifferent.*[63]

Nor certainly can *Hobbes,* who *says,* "That every Man has in that State a Right of warring against all," justly deny him the *Sword of Justice* to punish Crimes. Nor do I see any just Reason why *he* (who teaches, that the *obligatory Force of Civil Laws* proceeds from the *Punishments* annex'd, and the Fear thence arising) should not allow some *Obligation* to accrue to the Laws of Nature, even to *external Actions,* either from the *Punishments* which Conscience foresees will be inflicted by *God;* or even from the *Punishments* which any *Man,* in a State of Nature, has a Right to exact from the Transgressor of Nature's Laws. Truly, the hands of so many Avengers were to be fear'd, and it were strange, if none of them were sufficiently furnish'd with Strength and Courage, so as to be both able and willing to revenge a Contempt of the common Good. But even *Hobbes* himself does elsewhere (*Leviathan, Chap.* 31. near the End) acknowledge, that we may observe such *natural Punishments;* and asserts, that they follow Crimes not by positive Appointment, but by Nature. *"There is* (saith he) *no Action of Man in this Life, that is not the beginning of so long a Chain of Consequences, as no human Providence is high enough to give a Man a Prospect to the End. And in this Chain, there are link'd together, both pleasing and unpleasing Events, in such manner, as he that will do any thing for his Pleasure, must engage himself to suffer all the Pains annex'd to it; and these Pains are the natural Punishments of those Actions, which are the beginning of more harm than good. And hereby it comes to*

(*Hobbes* is inconsistent with himself, in denying the foregoing Obligation of the Laws of Nature, in a State of Nature;)

---

63. [Maxwell notes the Latin] "Homo sum, humani nihil à me alium alienum puto." The line is from Terence, *Heautontimorumenos* [the self-tormentor], act 1, scene 1, verse 25.

pass, that Intemperance is naturally punish'd with Diseases, Rashness with Mischances, Injustice with the Violence of Enemies, Pride with Ruin, Cowardice with Oppression, negligent Government of Princes with Rebellion, and Rebellion with Slaughter; for seeing Punishments are consequent to the Breach of Laws, natural Punishments must be naturally consequent to the Breach of the Law of Nature, and therefore follow them, as their natural, not arbitrary, Effects."[64] But this same *Philosopher of Malmsbury*, altho he asserts a War of all against all in that State, hath entirely overlook'd *this Cause* of War, that *they might punish Crimes against the publick Good, or defend it against Invaders;* yet he sets all a fighting, *to take from others what they are either justly possess'd of, or lay claim to.*[65] And whereas the immediate effect of the Right to punish, for example, an Invader, be an Obligation to abstain from that Crime, *Hobbes* does indeed acknowledge the *Cause, viz.* that all have a Right to punish, by acknowledging their Right to War, but does not see the *Effect, viz.* the Obligation thence *arising,* or rather *discover'd.* He *acknowledges* almost all *Virtues* to be *necessary to Peace* and mutual Defence, and that Men do agree, that this State of *Peace* is *good,* and that *War* (in which is included the Right of punishing Offences) has a *natural Connexion* with the *neglect of moral Virtues;* and *yet he does not see,* that *Men* are *obliged,* for *fear* of that War as of a *Punishment,* to the *outward Acts* of those same Virtues, whose *inward Acts* only will not preserve Peace and mutual Defence, which Nature dictates are to be pursued. Compare *Chap.* 3. § 27. with § 31.[66]

64. Hobbes, *Leviathan,* ch. 31, p. 243. Maxwell has simply quoted the English text of *Leviathan* here, and Barbeyrac follows him (*Traité Philosophique,* p. 79, n. 5). However, Cumberland's Latin text (*De Legibus Naturae,* p. 45) draws attention to an important change between the English and Latin editions of *Leviathan.* Cumberland quotes Hobbes's Latin edition from "There is no action of man" to "suffer all the pains annexed to it." He then notes that in the English edition, Hobbes comments that "these pains are the natural punishments of those actions, which are the beginning of more harm than good." Hobbes not only removed this sentence from the Latin, but he also truncated the paragraph, thereby removing an extensive discussion of natural punishments. Curley's edition does not note this change; see Hobbes, *Leviathan* (1668), p. 172.

65. Hobbes, *On the Citizen,* 1.11–12, p. 29.

66. Ibid., 3.27, p. 53: "In the face of an inordinate desire for an immediate good, most men are disinclined to observe the laws given above, however well they recognize

§XXVII. But because, from this *general consideration of all things,* I have briefly *shewn,* "That it is necessary to the common Good, that all Rationals should constantly desire, that the *use* of *Things* and the mutual *Services* of *Men,* at least for the time in which they may be of advantage to particular Persons, should be *divided* or look'd upon as their Property"; and also, "That this Dictate of Reason declares *Rewards* to those who *observe* it, and *Punishments* to those who *violate* it; and that the same is *necessarily impress'd* upon the Minds of Men, and has therefore *God,* the Author of all natural Effects, for its *Author* and *Enforcer,*" in which the whole *Power* of a *Law* is contain'd; it will not be improper to examine likewise briefly *Hobbes's* Assertion, concerning *the Right of all Men to all Things:* for as we think, that the Foundation of universal Justice, and consequently of all Virtue, is establish'd by our Doctrine; so we are of opinion, that the same is entirely overthrown (as far as in him lies) by these his contrary Notions. *Hobbes* affirms, That *"in a natural State"* (that is, without the civil Authority) *"every one has a Right to all Things";* which he thus explains, that *"every one has a Right to do whatsoever, and against whomsoever, he pleases,"* or *"to have and to do all things,"* as he says in the Conclusion of that Article.[67] That this monstrous License is necessarily contain'd in the Law of Nature, he in the same place endeavours to prove, from what he had advanc'd in the *ninth Article,* and in the rest, from the *seventh* to the end of the *Annotation* subjoin'd to the *tenth;* which because I think not worth while to transcribe word for word, the Reader is desir'd attentively to consider, whether I have not justly reduc'd their whole force into this Syllogism. *In a State of Nature every one has a Right to, or may lawfully have, all things, and do all things against all, which he himself shall judge necessary to his own Preservation.* But *every one will judge it necessary to his own preservation, to have all things, and to do all things against all.* Therefore *every one has a Right to, or may lawfully, do thus.*[68]

Upon a mistaken Notion, of all Mens Right to all Things, which is here examin'd;

---

them." Cf. 3.31, p. 55: "All men easily recognize that this state [of war] is evil when they are in it; and consequently that peace is good."

67. Ibid., 1.10, p. 28.
68. Ibid., 1.7–10n, pp. 27–29.

But lest any one, perhaps, should not have *Hobbes*'s Treatise at hand, and to avoid Suspicion, that I have not fairly stated his Argument, I will transcribe the Abridgment of this Reasoning of *Hobbes*'s, which he himself has set down in these words, in his *Annotation* upon *c*. 1. §. 10. *"Every one has a right to preserve himself, by* Art. 7. *Therefore he has a right to make use of all the means necessary to that End, by* Art. 8. *But the Means necessary are those, which he shall judge such,"* by Art. 9. *Therefore he has a Right to do, and to possess all things, which he himself shall judge to be necessary to his own Preservation. "It is therefore by the Judgment of the Doer, that what is done, is either rightfully or wrongfully done; it is therefore rightfully done. Therefore it is true (which I propos'd) that in a State of Nature every one has a right to do all things against all,* &c."[69] From that last Consequence, *"Every one has a right to do and to possess all things, which he himself shall judge necessary,* &c. *therefore every one has a right to possess and to do all things against all"*; it is manifest, that this *Minor* Proposition is to be understood: *But to possess all things, and to do all things against all, every one will judge necessary to his own Preservation;* for otherwise the *Conclusion* would not follow from the given *Major*. But both the *Premises* of that *Syllogism* are false; and, in the first place, that *Minor* which is understood, which he seems to presume to be so evident, that he does not so much as mention, much less prove it; unless perhaps he thinks it sufficiently prov'd, from what he had said in the 7th §, That *"every one is carry'd to the Desire of that which is good to himself, and that by a natural Necessity, not less than that by which a Stone is carry'd downwards";*[70] for I do not *see*, even tho this be granted, "Why every one should judge every Good to be necessary to himself." Certainly *Hobbes* himself elsewhere (*c*. 1. § 4.) grants concerning some, that they think otherwise, in these words; *"For another, according to natural Equality, permits to the rest all those things which he claims to himself, which is the Part of a modest Man, and one who rightly estimates his own Strength."*[71] Certainly, if he judges according to right Reason, who permits to others

69. Ibid., 1.10n, pp. 28–29.
70. Ibid., 1.7, p. 27.
71. Ibid., 1.4, p. 26.

like things with himself, whosoever will arrogate all things to himself, as necessary to his own Preservation, can acquire no right to himself by such his irrational Judgment; for *Hobbes* himself has defin'd *"Right to be a Liberty of using our natural Faculties according to right Reason."*[72] Therefore no one will have a Right to disturb that natural Equality, which he had but just before confess'd that right Reason dictates. But if Individuals judg'd according to *right Reason,* at the same time that they *determin'd,* "That a plenary Disposition, Use, and Enjoyment, of all Things and Persons, according to their several Wills, tho perfectly contrary to one another, was necessary to the preservation of each particular Person"; *it might be concluded,* "That the matter were so"; for the matter is always as right Reason pronounces it. But, on the contrary, the *Nature,* both of all Bodies and of Motion, and common *Experience,* testify, "That it is impossible that any body" (much less that all) "should at once be subject to so many contrary Motions, as there would be contrary Wills of Men, concerning its Use; and therefore that that is, in the Nature of Things, *impossible,* which *Hobbes* supposes each particular Person to judge, according to right Reason, *necessary."*

§XXVIII. My Readers now, I suppose, perceive the Reason, why I rank'd that common Observation, that *the Powers and Uses of things are limited,* amongst the Notions chiefly necessary to the Knowledge of the Laws of Nature: for hence both a fundamental *Error* of *Hobbes* is *detected,* and a most useful *Truth* is *inferr'd,* "That both the Uses of Things, and Services of Men, are necessarily to be divided, or to be determin'd to one Person for one time, if we design they should effect any thing at all; and consequently, if we would promote the publick Good": Hence also, when many have a like Right to Things to be enjoy'd in common, the *first Occupant* has always the *Preference.*[73]

[margin note:] And which he endeavours to support by a groundless Supposition, That every Man has a Right to what he himself shall judge necessary to the Preservation of his Life,

---

72. Ibid., 1.7, p. 27.

73. Cumberland's property theory favors the first occupant following Grotius, *De Jure Belli ac Pacis,* II.2.2; see also Parkin, "Probability, Punishments, and Property: Richard Cumberland's Sceptical Science of Sovereignty" in Hunter and Saunders, eds., *Natural Law and Civil Sovereignty* (2002), pp. 76–90.

And so much may suffice *concerning the Minor of the foregoing Syllogism,* that it contradicts the most general Notions upon which Laws are founded; but the *Major* of that *Syllogism* is more diligently defended by *Hobbes,* and is by us therefore more at large to be confuted. But it cannot be done here so pertinently, because the Nature of this *Right* cannot be so distinctly understood, unless the Knowledge of the *Law* of Nature be first suppos'd. Wherefore *Hobbes* seems to have *transgress'd* the *Rules* of *Method;* who, altho he openly acknowledges, that by the Name of *"Right,"* he understands a *"Liberty left by the Laws";* [74] yet *supposes* it in Men, and sets forth to them its vast extent, *before* he explains even *Natural Laws:* and yet it is certain, that, without respect had to them as *prior,* what Right is cannot be understood; which very thing has given occasion to many of his *Errors.* But that *Hobbes* has thus transgress'd, may be understood from his Definition, who has defin'd *"Right"* to be *"A liberty of using the natural Faculties according to right Reason";* which is the very Law of Nature, by him not yet explain'd, *c.* 1. § 7. [75] Notwithstanding, because this *Syllogism* is before us, we will briefly consider how he proves the *Major,* in order to make the Falshood of it more evidently appear. His Proof of it, reduc'd by me into the Form of a *Syllogism,* stands thus: *Every one has a Right to possess all Things, and to do against all what the Judge shall have judg'd necessary to the Preservation of every one's Life:* But *what he himself shall judge necessary, that the Judge judges necessary to his Preservation; for he himself is the Judge of those things which are necessary to his own Preservation,* Art. 9. Therefore, &c. The Sense of the *major Proposition* is contain'd in these words, which are found *Art.* 10. *"But we suppose himself Judge, whether these things conduce to his Preservation or no; so that those things are to be look'd upon as necessary, which he himself judges to be such. And by* Art. 7. *Those things are,*

---

74. Hobbes, *On the Citizen,* 14.3, p. 156.

75. Ibid., 1.7, p. 27. Hobbes's intention, much clearer in *Leviathan,* is to distinguish between laws and rights. Cumberland argues that it is impossible to define right without reference to law. The argument revolves around the concepts of subjective and objective right, reflecting Hobbes's skepticism on the one hand and Cumberland's optimism about knowledge of an objective order in nature on the other.

and are esteemed to be, according to the Law of Nature, which necessarily conduce to the defense of a Man's proper Life and Limbs."[76]

But I affirm that *Major* to be false, (I.) Because *Life* it self is to be parted with for a *greater good,* such as the *Salvation of a Man's Soul,* the *Glory of God,* and the *common Good of Men.* These are not to be given up, altho it were necessary to the Preservation of Life. (2.) Because a *Judge* may in the State of Nature *falsly* affirm those things to be necessary, which really are not necessary. Nor can any *Reason* be given, "Why in a State of Nature the Sentence of a Judge should have power to confer a Right upon any one, if that Sentence disagrees with the *Rule according to which Judgment ought to be given.*" But the *Laws of Nature,* and the *Nature of Things,* whence they are drawn, are the *Rule of Judgment in that State;* so that it will come to the same thing, which of these two we take for the Standard of Judgment. No State can be imagin'd, in which there is either *no Rule of Judgment,* or wherein *things* immediately *become* such, as the *Mind* shall *rashly determine.* The *usefulness* of things to the preservation of human Life, much more their *Necessity* to that End, depends upon the *natural Powers* of things, nor can be chang'd at the *Pleasure of Men.* If any one, in a State of Nature, should have judg'd *Wolfsbane* to be a wholesom Herb, or even necessary to the Nourishment of his Body, and should therefore have gorg'd himself with its Juice, it will not therefore become wholesom Nourishment, but will kill him, notwithstanding the Opinion of the Judge to the contrary. Nor is the *Efficacy* of those things *less determin'd,* which are *good* or *evil* to the whole *collective Body* of Men, whether they be *voluntary human Actions,* (concerning which the Laws of Nature, or moral Philosophy pronounces,) or whether they be the *natural Powers* of Meats and Drugs, (in which Medicine instructs us;) nor are they chang'd by the Opinions of Men, however they may be Judges, from whom no Appeal is permitted. According to the *same* unalterable Laws of Motion act all those *universal Causes,* which at once profit or hurt *many,* as doth any *partic-*

Which ought to be parted with for a greater Good; Nor does his mistaken Judgment of the Means necessary to that End, alter the unalterable Nature of Things.

---

76. Ibid., 1.10, p. 28.

ular Cause, Wolfsbane for instance, when it takes away the Life of *one* only.[77]

The Rise of
Hobbes's Error,
"That a mis-
taken Judg-
ment, in a
State of
Nature, confers
a Right," pro-
ceeds from the
obligatory
Force of even
the unjust Sen-
tence of a civil
Judge, for Rea-
sons which will
not hold in a
State of
Nature.
§XXIX. But this *Error* of *Hobbes,* concerning the Force of that Sentence (which falsly pronounces *a Dominion over all Things and Persons to be necessary to Self-preservation*) to give any Persons such a prodigious Right, has arisen hence, that in civil Society he observ'd, "That the *Sentence of the supreme Judge bound the Subjects,* however it may have been given contrary to what the Nature of the Case requir'd." But this (which is supported only by a *probable* Foundation) has been introduc'd by the *Consent* of Parties, to put an *End* to *Contentions* in civil States. Nor is the Sentence of a Prince of so great efficacy, as to make things in their own Nature *impossible,* or *not necessary* to the Preservation of the Life of any Person, *become necessary* to that end.[78] It does indeed *transfer Property,* which Subjects are oblig'd not to resist; for all Subjects are oblig'd to acknowledge the *supreme Judge* (whenever there is occasion) as an *equal Arbitrator* to all, and in Law-suits are understood to have subjected themselves to his Arbitration. This Judge is supposed to be chosen out of the most *skilful Lawyers,* so as to be *able,* and to be under the *Obligation of an Oath,* so as to be *willing,* to give Sentence according to the known *Laws,* the *Allegations,* and the *Evidence.*

But all *think* with themselves, "That this conduces more to the common Happiness, That a *few* should suffer that Evil, which may follow from an *unjust Sentence,* (which will sometimes happen, notwithstanding the above-mention'd Precautions,) than that Strifes should never be ended, but by *Wars.*" So that a greater care of the *publick* Good, than of the Life of any *particular* Person, may be suppos'd as the Foundation of this Prerogative granted to the ruling Powers in *States.*[79] But in a *State*

---

77. Wolfsbane (*Aconitum napellus*) was a well-known poison reputed to be derived from the saliva of Cerberus (Pliny, *Natural History,* XXVII.4). It was also used therapeutically from the eighteenth century onward.

78. Cf. Cicero, *De Legibus,* I.xvi. 43–45.

79. Cumberland includes a small addition in his own manuscript copy: "Thus one may never presume that men might have accorded to any supreme Judge the power to ignore the natural causes of the public good, or to replace them, as it might please

of Nature, (which *Hobbes* supposes and defines to be the *Condition of Men out of civil Society,*) it is manifest, that *these* Considerations can have no place: for where *every one is a Judge,* there *no Skill* or *Probity* can be suppos'd, by which the Judge excels others; *no Power* of citing Witnesses, and of doing those other things which are requisite to come at the exact Knowledge of a Cause; *as is the Case of civil Judgments.* There is *no Agreement* of all in the *State of Nature* to be suppos'd, by which particular Persons should trust both themselves, and such things as are necessary to them, to the publick determination and integrity of supreme Powers. Nor is there at all any Reason, why this great Privilege of the chief Magistrates should be indulg'd to particular Persons in a State of Nature, however ignorant and wicked. On the contrary it is evident, that the State of Nature affords no other *final Determination* of any doubtful Case, except that *Evidence* which arises from *Things* themselves, or from *Testimony,* by which the Mind of Man is freed from all Scruples, and is fully satisfy'd that it is not deceiv'd; and that there could be *no end of a Dispute* among several, unless one Part willingly came into the Opinion of the other, being thereunto moved, either by the weight of *Reason,* or thro' an *Opinion* of the other's *Knowledge* and *Veracity:* for this is evident from the Nature of *Judgment,* (of which we are every one of us conscious within our own Breasts,) that its Doubts cannot be clear'd by any *coercive Power,* but by *Arguments* only, and that they are all deduc'd from *the Nature of Things,* or from *the Authority of the Teacher,* which the Learner receives as authentick. Nature acknowledges a Distinction between *true* and *false* Judgment, *right* Reason, and that which is *corrupted;* and *Truth* and *right Reason* have this Privilege, that Man has a *natural Right* to do those things which they command; for the very Definition of *Right* declares it to be nothing else but *a Liberty of using our natural Faculties according to right Reason:*[80] But *Error,* or a *false Judgment* of the Mind, whether it be concerning things necessary to support Life, or other matter of Practice, gives *no one a Right* of doing

---

them, with others which are not adequate." Cumberland, Trinity College MS.adv. c.2.4, p. 51.

80. Referring to Hobbes's definition in *On the Citizen,* 1.7, p. 27.

that which he falsly thinks necessary to be done, in order to preserve his Life: for the Reason of him who is in an Error, is not right; nor can any one use his Faculties according to right Reason, (which is to act by Right,) whilst he acts according to Error, which contradicts it. It is therefore a gross *Error* of *Hobbes,* when he *teaches,* "That all things are to be look'd on as necessary to any Man's Preservation in a natural State, which he himself judges necessary; and that therefore every one has a Right to all things, and to do any thing against every Man." But it was particularly a shame for *Hobbes* to commit such a Mistake in this *Matter,* or in this *Place:*

First,[81] Because it was absurd to ascribe to any Man in a *State of Nature,* that which is the peculiar Privilege of a *civil State,* even there where he pretends to treat with the greatest *accuracy* of the *difference* of these two States:

Secondly, Because he boasts to have demonstrated that to be *necessary,* which is naturally *impossible, That the same Body should be mov'd towards parts diametrically opposite, according to the opposite Wills of Men;* for that Conclusion will justly cause the truth of the Premisses to be suspected:

Thirdly, Because every thing that is *particular* to *Hobbes* in *Politicks* falls to the ground, when this Foundation is taken away; for that *State of War* vanishes, whose necessary Connexion with a *State of Nature* he hath hence inferr'd, *Art.* 12. where he hath rashly *concluded,* "That every one, from his own arbitrary Opinion, has a Right to invade all others; and that likewise every one has a Right of resisting, whence War ariseth."[82] All the rest likewise fall to the ground, which he thinks he has demonstrated from these Principles: but there will be a more convenient Opportunity for refuting these, when I shall have more fully propos'd better, Principles, whence both the *Laws of Nature* take their Rise, and a *Liberty* is left within the Bounds prescribed by them.

By means of which Error, *Hobbes* proposes Means   I will only *mention* this by the way, "That *Hobbes* has propos'd too *narrow* an *End* on this first Head now under examination, *viz.* the mere Preservation of *Life* and *Limbs";* for *Men* may be very miserable, tho

81. The numbering here is added by Maxwell.
82. Hobbes, *On the Citizen,* 1.12, p. 29.

these were safe. "The *Means* by him requir'd are likewise too *narrow, viz. only Necessaries,* c. 1. § 8."[83] For this World, whose Inhabitants we are born, and which first offers it self to our Consideration, supplies us with things innumerable, which solicit the Mind to the acknowledging and honouring its *first Cause;* and which, with regard to our selves, are subservient to the *Perfections* of the *Mind,* and do not only preserve the *Life* of the *Body,* but also contribute sufficiently to its *Health, Strength, Activity, Beauty,* and *Ornament.* All these, as well as the Necessaries of Life, do afford both Matter to the *Laws of Nature,* directing us in their Use, and Room for the exercise of *Liberty,* according to right Reason. But seeing these are manifest, from so superficial an Observation, that *Hobbes* could not be ignorant of them, any one may easily conjecture, for what cause he assign'd no *larger* Bounds to *Right* and the *Laws of Nature,* than the Preservation of this frail *Life;* as if Men, like Swine, had Souls given them only, instead of Salt, to preserve the Body from Putrefaction;[84] and in the mean time, to obtain so *diminutive* an *End,* has given every one *all* things as *means necessary;* so that here he has been as faulty in *excess,* as there in *defect:* nor can any one more shamefully transgress the Rules of right Reason, than by *neglecting* the *best* End, and by looking on things *impossible* as means *necessary.*

that are impossible, as necessary to obtain an End, which is too narrow.

§XXX. Vain is Mr. *Hobbes's* Attempt to maintain or prove this absurd *Right of all Men to all Things,* from that primitive holding things in *common,* which some *Philosophers suppose,* and some *Histories* have affirm'd:[85] For besides that Mr. *Selden* hath taught, and *prov'd* from the divine Donation, *Gen.* i. 28. "That private Dominion was a most acknowledg'd Right from the days of *Adam,*" as you may see in his *Mare*

Nor can such a Right of all Men to all things be prov'd, from an original holding all things in common;

83. Ibid., 1.8, p. 27.
84. Cf. Cicero, *De Natura Deorum,* II.lxiv; *De Finibus,* V.xiii.
85. Hobbes, *On the Citizen,* 14.9; Latin *Leviathan,* ch. 17, p. 107, n. 2: "The histories of ancient Greece teach the same thing also, that where there were no authorities except the paternal, theft, on land and sea, was a trade not only lawful, but also, provided they abstained from cruelty and from the tools of agriculture, honorable."

Clausum, l. 8. c. 4.[86] it is certain, that both *Philosophers* and *Historians* thought, "That the use of such an *universal Right* had so much in it of the nature of *Property,* that what any one had seiz'd for himself, it were an Injury in another to force from him." This may be explain'd by an *Example* us'd by *Cicero.* Altho the *Theatre* be *common,* it may justly be said, that the *Place* which any one has taken possession of, is *his.*[87]

Nor from the Power of Individuals. But no Mortal, before *Hobbes,* ventur'd to assert such a *Right of every one to all things;* which, if you will believe him, contains in it self a Right of reigning over all, coeval with their very Nature;[88] that is, from their *Infancy;* altho, according to the same Person, it be founded in *Power: Which* destroys all Property in another, so that it is *impossible* to invade that which is another's, and lawful to claim every thing to himself:[89] *Which* makes it lawful to lie with every Woman, to break the Faith pledg'd to another: *Which* makes it lawful to wage War against all, and therefore to kill any Person, even the most innocent: *Which* leaves every Determination of disputed Cases, to every Man's proper arbitrary Judgment, and Children at liberty to honour their Parents or not.[90] He in the mean time forgot, that he had said elsewhere, *"That it cannot be understood, that a Son can exist in the State of Nature";*[91] and that, therefore, neither has the Right proper to this State any place in Sons. Of a-piece with this, is what he has added in the end of *c.* 14. § 9. That *"there is no occasion to give Testimony, whether true or false, in a State of Nature, because there are there no publick Courts";*[92] as if a *private Judge* had no *occasion* for Testimony, in order to give his Award, where he hath

---

86. Genesis 1.28–29; Selden, *Mare Clausum* (1635), I.4 [Maxwell copied Cumberland's mistaken reference to VIII.4], p. 11–15.

87. Cumberland refers to Grotius, *De Jure Belli ac Pacis,* II.2.2, and the Ciceronian allusion is to *De Finibus,* III.xx.67.

88. Hobbes, *On the Citizen,* 15.5, p. 173.

89. As Barbeyrac notes (*Traité Philosophique,* 88, n. 4), it is true that the passage states that individuals have a right to all things from power, but Hobbes suggests (*On the Citizen,* 9.2) that no individual has this power from infancy because they are under the power of the parent. Cf. Pufendorf, *De Jure Naturae,* I.6.9.

90. Hobbes, *On the Citizen,* 14.9, p. 158.

91. Ibid., 1.10n, pp. 28–29; Cf. 14.9, p. 158.

92. Ibid., 14.9, p. 158.

been chosen Umpire between Persons at Variance; or, as if a *false Testimony* in such a Case were *not criminal,* (as contrary to the common Good,) altho there were yet no Civil Laws; such as he there contends the Precepts of the second Table of the Decalogue to be. Here may be added that of *Hobbes,* which he sometimes expresly acknowledges, That *"all Violation of the Laws of Nature consists in the false Reasoning, or in the Folly of Men who do not see,"* (and why not as well, of Men who do not observe?) *"their Duties toward other Men, necessary to their own Preservation."* [93] And he acknowledges that the Laws of Nature, in the State of Nature, do oblige in the inward Court, or that of Conscience; [94] therefore they at least oblige to pass a *true Judgment,* that all Things, and a Dominion over all Persons, are not necessarily requir'd to the Preservation of every one. But if every one is under an Obligation *so to judge,* vain will be the Judgment of him whose Sentiments are *contrary;* nor can that prodigious Right over all things accrue to him from so gross an Error. To be brief, there can be no Right of acting contrary to the Law of Nature, or the Dictates of right Reason, because *Right* is defin'd to be *a Liberty of acting according thereto.* But right Reason, as I have shewn, points out the necessity of coming to a division of Things; and, according to *Hobbes's* own Confession, forbids the retaining a Right to all Things, *c.* 2. § 3. [95]

§XXXI. Let us therefore proceed to examine, what other Arguments *Hobbes* has brought to establish this his wild Doctrine: He suggests, *"That what any one does in a State merely natural, cannot be injurious to any Man; because Injustice toward Men supposes human Laws, such as in that State are not."* [96] Yet he grants that even then, Men may sin against God and the Laws of Nature; but he in vain and without proof *assumes* what is most *false,* "That an Injury against Man supposes human Laws." For from the Dictates of right *Reason,* altho they be the natural Laws of

[margin note:] Another Error of *Hobbes,* by which he endeavours to support a Right of every Man to every thing in a State of Nature, is, "That Right and Wrong depend upon human Laws."

93. Ibid., 2.1n, pp. 33–34.
94. Ibid., 3.27, p. 54.
95. Ibid., 2.3, p. 34.
96. Ibid., 1.10n, p. 28; cf. Pufendorf, *De Jure Naturae,* I.7.13; I.8.1.

God only, accrues to *Man* a *Right* to those things, which *Reason* has dictated to be *granted* to him by *God*: As for example, "The innocent Person has a Right to his Life, to preserve his Limbs entire, and to necessary Sustenance, without which it is well known, that he cannot be subservient to the common Good." Therefore an *Injury* is done him, if any one, upon *Hobbes's* Principles, shall maim or kill him, in pursuit of his Claim of all things: for *every Opposition to, or Violation of, another's Right,* is an *Injury,* by what Law soever that Right accrued to the other; but much more, if that Right was yielded him by the *divine* Laws, than if by any *human* Law or Compact. *Hobbes* indeed *supposes,* "That no one can injure another, but after he has transferr'd by compact his own Right of doing what he pleases." But this *supposes* that it has been *prov'd,* "That a *Right of doing what he pleases* belongs to every one"; which I have prov'd to be *impossible.* Therefore in vain he seeks a Support to his tottering *Foundation,* from this *Consequence,* which wholly depends upon the *Supposition* (which I have overthrown) of *every Man's Right to all Things.* Even *Hobbes* himself, altho he asserts here, and more openly c. 3. § 4. *"That no Injury can be done to any one, with whom we have not enter'd into compact";*[97] yet elsewhere more justly, and as the Truth it self requires, he has most expresly taught, *"That it is injuriously done, whatsoever is done contrary to right Reason."*[98] Seeing all *grant,* "That to be rightfully done, which is not done against right Reason"; we ought to *think,* "That injuriously done, which is contrary to right Reason"; and so he there acknowledges, *That* to be a *Law.* You observe he does not here require a transferring our Right to another, before an Injury can be done. Now seeing he acknowledges these *Dictates of Reason* to be *divine Laws,*[99] I desire that he will *shew,* "What hinders, but that these may confer upon every one such a Right to Life, as without Injury cannot be taken away, or how any one can have a Right to oppose and violate an-

97. Hobbes, *On the Citizen,* 3.4, p. 45.

98. Ibid., 2.1, p. 33: "However, all men allow that any act not contrary to right reason is right, and therefore we have to hold that any act in conflict with right reason (i.e. in contradiction with some truth reached by correct reasoning from true principles) is wrong."

99. Cumberland may be referring to *On the Citizen,* 15.3, pp. 172–73.

other's Right": For every Man's *Right* is a *Liberty granted by right Reason*, which can never allow, that Men speaking or acting by its Prescription, can contradict or *oppose one another*. It will be in vain for him to say, that the Injury is done to *God only*, seeing only *his* Laws are violated; unless he shew, that these Laws of *God* cannot confer on *Men* a Right to their Life and its Necessaries, nor prohibit others to violate the Right so granted.

This however I here thought fit to *add* by the by, "That if an *Injury* consists only in the *Violation* of *Compacts* transferring Right, then no Injury could possibly be done to *God*, according to *Hobbes*'s Principles, altho his natural Laws, both concerning the Cultivation of Peace amongst Men, and concerning the Worship which ought to be paid himself, should be violated by Crimes of the deepest Dye, and even by Blasphemy it self": for Man is *suppos'd*, "Not to have enter'd into a Compact with God, to yield Obedience to his Laws";[100] nay, he openly *declares, c.* 2. § 12, 13. "That a Compact cannot be enter'd into with God, except as he has thought fit, by the sacred Scriptures, to substitute in his Place certain Men, with an Authority to consider and accept of such Compacts."[101] God therefore and Men are in such a State, according to *Hobbes,* that *without Injury* Men may be *Enemies to God,* and have a Right (as the *Giants* are fabled to have done)[102] to make war upon him, and to hate him. God indeed will have a Right (according to *Hobbes*'s Principles) to kill such, which he might with equal Justice have done, tho they had not sinn'd. But they, who so reject all Reverence towards God, as not to submit to his Precepts, nor fear his Threats, are not look'd upon as his *Subjects,* but his *Enemies,* or as living without the Limits of the KINGDOM OF GOD, whom he may at pleasure invade, as he hints, *c.* 15. § 2.[103] But, in my Opinion, even *Atheists* and *Epicureans,* who deny

100. Hobbes, *On the Citizen,* 2.12, p. 37.

101. Ibid.

102. Cumberland refers to the wars of the giants against the gods of Olympus reported in Pseudo-Apollodorus, *Bibliotheca,* I.6.1, and mentioned in numerous classical sources.

103. Hobbes, *On the Citizen,* 15.2, p. 172: "Nor do we count Atheists, because they do not believe that God exists." Cf. Pufendorf, *De Jure Naturae,* III.4.4.

a Providence, are *oblig'd* by the Law of Nature, (which is sufficiently promulg'd, altho by them neglected and deny'd,) to *obey God;* and they are Subjects by *Birth,* not *Compact,* and may therefore be *punish'd* by God for their Crimes as rebellious Subjects, and not *invaded* only, as Persons born without his Jurisdiction. But this by the by.

Nor does War, as *Hobbes* supposes, necessarily arise from the Passions.

§XXXII. Let us now consider, if you please, what the same Author has advanc'd in his *Leviathan,* towards the establishing this *Right of every one to all Things;* for he there endeavours to infer it from different Principles. However, I cannot but observe, that *Hobbes* is no less *inconsistent* with *himself,* than with *all others* in this Point, which is the Foundation both of his Morality and Politicks. For, in his Treatise *de Cive,* he deduces the *War* of every Man against every Man, from this Right of every Man to every Thing, as from a *Cause,* which made it both *lawful* and *necessary.*[104] Whereas, in his *Leviathan,* he first affirms the State of *Nature* to be a State of *War;* and thence infers a *Licence* to do *every* thing in that State, as will appear from considering the *Thirteenth Chapter,* and comparing the former part thereof with this in the Close. *"To this War"* (saith he) *"of every Man against every Man, this also is consequent, that nothing can be unjust; the Notions of Right and Wrong, Justice and Injustice, have there no place. Where there is no common Power, there is no Law; where no Law, no Injustice. Force and Fraud are in War the two cardinal Virtues,* &c."[105] *There* he affirm'd, that the Invasion of the one Party, and the Resistance of the other, were both just, whence a War must needs arise *just* on *both* sides. But *here* he refers the Original of this War to the Nature of the *human Passions,* little sollicitous about the Right of commencing it; and, War once suppos'd, he affirms (without proof) that it will follow, *That there is nothing unjust, That there is no Property,* &c. This Reasoning in the *Leviathan* is more popular, but less

---

104. Hobbes, *On the Citizen,* 1.12, p. 29.

105. Hobbes, *Leviathan,* ch. 13, p. 78 (see also p. 78, n. 9). Maxwell quotes the English text, but Cumberland follows the Latin, which omits "Where there is no common power, there is no law; where no law, no injustice." Cumberland, *De Legibus Naturae,* p. 58.

conclusive; for it is acknowledg'd by all judicious Writers, that a *War* must first be prov'd *just,* before it can *justify* any Proceedings against the Enemy; nor are *all* things *lawful,* even in the *justest War.* The *Law of Nature* must therefore first be acknowledg'd; whence we may determine, whether the War to be undertaken be *just,* or at least *permitted* by right Reason, before we can infer the *lawfulness* of those things, which are necessary in the carrying on such War. And this is so evident, that even *Hobbes* himself, tho in the *latter* part of this Chapter he contends, that, in a State of Nature, there is no Distinction between Just and Unjust; yet in the former Part of it he endeavours to *prove,* "That this Power of waging War ought to be allow'd to every Man in that State, as necessary to Self-defense";[106] which is equivalent to *saying,* "That such a War is just or lawful." Wherefore he is inconsistent with himself, even in the same Chapter; for whatever Argument proves, that *any* thing is *Just* and *Lawful* in a *State of Nature,* proves that there is a *Distinction* between *Lawful* and *Unlawful* in that State, and supposes the Obligation of some Law, by whose Permission, at least, that War may be licens'd: which is the chief Point I would establish, and which *Hobbes* (as we have seen) expresly denies, when he affirms nothing to be Just, or Unjust.

Let us examine by what Arguments he would prove a *War* of *all* against *all* to be *necessary* or *lawful.* In his *Leviathan,* he has not that close and compact way of Reasoning, which he aims at in his Treatise *de Cive.* However, he refers the Original of War to three principal Causes, *Competition, Defense,* and *Glory.*[107] And he affirms, that it must necessarily take its Rise from these *Passions.* War from Competition arises from the *Hope* of Gain: A defensive War, in which we prevent others by Force or Fraud, proceeds from *Fear,* lest others should usurp a Dominion over us; and we wage War to acquire Fame, from a *Desire* of Glory.

But I care not to transcribe all his unconclusive Reasonings, in order, from these *Affections,* to persuade the *necessity* of a State of *universal War;* he that pleases may turn to them in the Author himself. I think it

106. Hobbes, *Leviathan,* ch. 13, p. 75.
107. Ibid., p. 76.

sufficient to give this general *Answer:* "That Men are not necessarily led or *compell'd* by these Passions, but that both these, and all other Passions *may* be temper'd and *guided* by *Reason* and Counsel; so that it is false, that they hurry Men by a natural and irresistible Force to such a War; and the Reasoning is weak, which thence concludes it *lawful*." In human Passions, what is produc'd in Man by a *Necessity* arising from the Impulse of *external Objects,* cannot be forbid by any *Law* of Nature, because Laws direct only such Actions as are in our power. But those Passions, whence *Hobbes* would infer the *Necessity,* and consequently the *Lawfulness,* of *War,* are of such a kind, (because they look into Futurity, and that often at a great distance,) as depend upon the Reason and Counsel of Men, and consequently may by these be *govern'd.* Even *Hobbes* himself elsewhere openly owns, That *"those who cannot agree concerning the present"* (because of their contrary Appetites) *"may yet agree concerning the future, which is the Work of Reason; for Things present are perceiv'd by the Senses, Things future by Reason only."* [108] And hence he acknowledges the Agreement of Mankind in this, (which is the Summary of the Laws of Nature,) *that Peace is to be sought after.* He is therefore *inconsistent* with *himself,* when in the *Leviathan* he sets them at War from those Affections, which depend upon Reason taking a prospect of Futurity, thro' the whole Course of Life.

What is more, in the Close of this very *Thirteenth Chapter,* he acknowledges Men to have those *Passions* which have a *peaceable* Tendency, which are, *Fear,* especially of a violent Death, the *Desire* of the Necessaries and Comforts of Life, and the *Hope* of obtaining them by Industry. These Passions, if narrowly examin'd, are certainly the same with those, of which he had but just before affirm'd that they compell'd Men to War. This is the same *Fear* with that before-mention'd, lest others should lord it over us at pleasure, and should, in consequence, rob us of Life, whenever they so thought fit; by which Fear he had before affirm'd them to be prompted, to secure themselves by preventing and invading others. The like may be said of the *Desire* of Glory, which may

---

108. Hobbes, *On the Citizen,* 3.31, p. 55.

be reckon'd among the Necessaries of Life, and also of the *Hope* of Gain. And thus *Peace* and *War,* according to *Hobbes,* are Effects of the *same* Causes. Certainly, if any thing in these Affections be absolutely necessary, it ought carefully to be examin'd on both sides, in order to find out, whether they more powerfully incline human Nature to *Peace* or *War;* which *Hobbes* has no where in his Writings done. Yet it is no less *absurd* to affirm any thing concerning the State of *Man,* and his natural *Inclination* to future Actions, from the *sole* Consideration of those things which incline him to *War,* without examining those things which persuade him *rather* to *Peace,* than it would be to affirm, which way a *Balance* would *incline,* from the knowledge of the Weight thrown into *one* Scale only. But when I have compar'd, as diligently as I can, the Causes of these Effects, and the Forces of the Powers on each side, both as they are natural *Motions* arising from the *Impulse* of *external Objects,* and (in some measure) depending upon the *Constitution* and Frame of a human *Body;* and also, which is of much greater Consequence, as they are *excited* and *govern'd* by *Reason,* taking a prospect of Man's whole future Existence: They seem *more* powerfully to persuade universal Benevolence, and that *Peace,* which may reasonably be expected from the Exercise thereof, than that *War* of all against all; in which, according to *Hobbes's* own Confession, is *"continual Danger of violent Death, and a Life solitary, poor, brutish, and short";* [109] in which therefore no Safety can with Reason be expected.

§XXXIII. The only Appearance of Difficulty in this Question, is, "That a perfect Security of procuring to our selves all kinds of Happiness is not to be obtain'd, tho we should promote the common Good and Peace, by the Exercise of universal Benevolence; and that, because of the unbridled Passions of some others, who, thro' Folly and Rashness, will not propose to themselves the same End." But this will appear no Difficulty, if we *consider,* "That we can do nothing with respect to Men,

Hobbes's Objection, That perfect Security of all possible Happiness is not, by the practice of Benevolence, to be obtain'd,

109. Hobbes, *Leviathan,* ch. 13, p. 76.

Answer'd, by
proving it the
most effectual
means of Hap-
piness in our
power, and
therefore to be
chosen.
which will *more effectually* secure our Happiness"; or, (which comes to the same thing,) "That it is evidently impossible to obtain that perfect Security from all Misfortunes, proceeding from the unbounded Desires of Men; and that it is therefore necessary that we should be content to do that, among all those things which are in our power, which will be most effectual to the procuring this End." That is, that, by constantly *promoting the Happiness of all,* we should first bring them over to some degree of *Friendship,* and then to *civil* or *religious Society,* as effectually as we can; and that afterwards, by the same Benevolence, we should continue them in that State. Whatever is short of, or contrary to, this Endeavour, is so far short of, or contrary to, our utmost Endeavours to promote our own and the common Happiness of all, by those means which, by the Light of Nature, we know to be the most effectual. By this Method we sollicit to our *Aid* and *Defence all rational Beings,* whose joint Happiness is that common Good we are in pursuit of, who will therefore concur with us in the same Views, except they be *blinded* by some *Passion,* and have so far divested themselves of their Reason. If, thro' any Inconstancy of Mind, we neglect this End, or *hurt* any *one innocent* Person, it is evident, that *all* are, in some measure, neglected and provok'd; for *every one* will have just reason to fear the *same* Evil at our hands, which we have done to the *Innocent.*[110] And this *Hobbes* himself was aware of, in his Explanation of Compassion upon his own Principles, in his Treatise *of Human Nature.*[111] In short, the *Force* of these Passions, *Hope, Fear, &c.* which may incline Men either to Peace or War, is to be estimated from the Force of those *Causes,* which excite those Passions in Men; for, since these *Causes* are *Things good* or *evil,* which our Reason judges *possible* or certain, in consequence of the Actions of other rational Agents, we can no otherwise know the Force of those Causes, than by considering the Nature of those Agents. Wherefore the

110. Barbeyrac (*Traité Philosophique,* p. 94, n. 1) detects in Cumberland's Latin an allusion to one of Publius Syrus's *Sententiae:* "Multis minatur, qui uni facit injuriam." He that injures one, threatens many.

111. The title refers to the English translation (1650) of *The Elements of Law* (1640), 9.10.

present Question, when we are in search after a Rule of Action pointed out by Nature, is brought to this short Issue, whether, (without any regard to Civil Government,) it be manifest to Men, from such Knowledge of the Nature of God and other Men as is easily attainable, that they shall *better* consult the Happiness and Security of all, and of themselves in particular, by *universal Benevolence,* (which includes *Innocence, Fidelity, Gratitude,* and all the other Virtues,) than by *Hobbes's* "*Anticipation*" (explain'd by him in this Chapter) as *"The most reasonable way for any Man to secure himself in this Diffidence of one another; that is, by Force or Wiles to master the Persons of all Men he can, so long, till he see no other Power great enough to endanger him?"* [112] I affirm it to be evident, that whoever best consults both his own Happiness, and that of others, will compose and settle all those Passions, which may stir up needless Quarrels and Disturbances, such as *vain Hopes, Fears, &c.* Nor is it less evident, that *rational Agents* are the principal *Causes* of such *Happiness.* Wherefore he takes the best Measures to obtain this End, who most effectually *reconciles* these Causes to himself, which he does, who accommodates himself to their most prevailing and natural *Principles of Action, viz.* the Power and the Will of acting according to Reason, by pursuing that Happiness only, which is connected with, and subservient to, the Happiness of *All.* Hence all may conspire and co-operate with us to the same end, securely, and without prejudice to their rational Desire of obtaining their own Happiness.

No one can rationally desire or expect, from *external* Causes, greater degrees of Happiness, than what may proceed from the nature of *other rational Causes,* (between whom and him the dependence is mutual,) and which is therefore consistent with that Happiness of them all, which they all naturally desire. But it is manifest, that this common Good of *all* is greater than the Good of any *one,* or of a *few,* as the Whole is greater than a Part; and that the like Sentiments in all other rational Beings, are the necessary result of the nature of Things.

112. Hobbes, *Leviathan,* ch. 13, p. 75.

Upon these Principles, those rational Beings, who have so far cultivated their own Understanding, as to know certainly that *this* common
Good is the *greatest,* and that the adequate Causes thereof will effect the
greatest Happiness of each Individual which is *possible* in Nature, will
most assuredly pursue the same End with us, and will therefore be ready
to assist us. Nor are these Principles of living happily so *difficult to know,*
but that we may reasonably presume them, both understood and approv'd of, by *almost all* other rational Beings; or, at least; that they may
be *all instructed* to believe these Principles, except it appear evidently,
that they have entirely given themselves up to the Conduct of *unreasonable Passions.* These *Propositions* seem to me to have the *greatest Evidence,* little different from that of mathematical Axioms. "The good of
the Whole, is greater than the good of a Part. The Causes, which most
effectually preserve and perfect a Whole, or Aggregate, whose Parts mutually require one another's Assistance, do in like manner preserve and
perfect the Parts thereof." The Aid of those, who do not acknowledge
such first Principles of acting rationally, is either not to be sought after;
or, if necessary, it is to be procur'd by the Assistance of those who do
acknowledge them. On the contrary, *Hobbes's Anticipation* endeavours
to *compel* all others to things evidently *impossible* to be done, which they
would therefore be as unwilling to undertake, as unable to execute; for,
upon that Principle, *every* particular Person would endeavour to force
all, to obey him only as his sovereign Lord. But since such Dominion
of every particular Person is in direct opposition to the like Dominion
of all others, it is no less impossible, that several such Dominions should
at once take place, than that the *Motion* of the *same* Body should at once
have a thousand *contrary* Directions. It is *equally* absurd to suppose, that
Men should attempt such Impossibilities, after they clearly understand
them to be such, as it is that they should effect them. These Observations, drawn from the *nature* of rational Beings, and from the *practical
Principles* of a right Judgment, (which all rational Beings, as such, are
endow'd with,) prove, that universal Benevolence is a *more* effectual
means of Happiness, than *Hobbes's* Method of *Anticipation.* I shall offer
more that may be reduc'd to this Head, where I designedly treat of *Human Nature.*

§XXXIV. I shall confirm what I have said, by the addition of only *two Observations,* confirm'd by the concurring *Experience* of all Ages.

Likewise, universal Experience confirms Men's general Tendency, rather to Acts of Benevolence, than Malevolence.

First, Bordering States enjoy a *greater* Security and sweeter Fruits of Peace, by means of Alliances, which subsist only by Fidelity and some degree of mutual *Benevolence,* than when they are at open *War,* and practising upon one another by Force or Fraud.

Secondly, Even in *civil Society* there are numberless Cases, in which the Authority and coercive Power of the State cannot exert themselves, in which, however, we frequently observe, that Men *mutually* obey the Laws of *Innocence, Fidelity, Gratitude,* and all the other Virtues, and much less frequently presume upon a liberty of hurting others, than is usual in a State of War. No one has greater Security, that his Life or Possessions shall not be wrested from him by the *Perjury* and false Testimonies of his Fellow-Subjects, than what arises from the *Fidelity* of Men, the Violation whereof the civil Magistrate can rarely detect or punish. But it is needless to add more in answer to what *Hobbes* has advanc'd, of the necessity or lawfulness of warring against all, from the *nature* of the *Passions.*

In pursuit of the same Point he advances a *new Argument* in these words: *"The Desires and other Passions of Men are in themselves no Sin: No more are the Actions that proceed from those Passions, till they know a Law that forbids them; which, till Laws be made, they cannot know; nor can any Law be made till they have agreed upon the Person that shall make it."* [113] I answer, that Actions forbid by right *Reason,* (which is the natural *Law of God,*) are *Sins;* tho Men do not *see* this *Legislator,* nor *make* him their *Governor;* provided it sufficiently *appear* to them, that he has a *Right of Dominion* over all, and that he has *enacted* those *Laws.* Both which *Hobbes* elsewhere often acknowledges. Altho here he affirms, that Men are not *bound* by Laws, to which they themselves have not given their *consent.* Certainly, since *Sin* is the *Transgression of a Law,* if it be prov'd that there are *Laws of Nature,* the Transgression of them will be truly a Sin, tho none had consented to the Authority of God enacting

113. Ibid., p. 77.

them. But because I have before prov'd this in a summary way, and shall do it more at large hereafter, there is no occasion to insist upon it here.

Which Hobbes offers to disprove; by pointing out what the Dictates of Reason are, from the practice of Animals void of Reason;

However, I will not dismiss this Article of his *Thirteenth Chapter,* before I have advertis'd the Reader, by how strenuous an Argument *Hobbes* has confirm'd this his Position, of *the Right of War of all against allout of the Bounds of civil Society;* which, in the last Edition, he has added to the rest, near the Close, in these words. *"But why am I at the pains to demonstrate to Men of Learning, what even Dogs themselves are not ignorant of, who bark at those who approach them, by Day at Strangers only, but by Night at all?"* [114] Notably argu'd! The Rights of Nature (that is, the Power granted by right *Reason*) are to be learn'd from the Example of *Dogs void of Reason;* they *bark at all that approach them in the dark;* therefore it is lawful for Men, in a State of Nature, to *murder all,* even their familiar Friends, whom they meet with by *Day.* Let *Hobbists* rather learn to warn others, by their harmless barking, to be upon their guard; but let them not, as he has instructed them, attack the unguarded by Force or Wiles: Let them learn to watch before their own Doors; but let them not invade the Rights of others. But it is time to dismiss such Levities.

And by falsly asserting, "That Justice cannot be the Quality of a Man existing alone in the World."

What he afterwards adds to the same purpose, has more of *Subtilty* in it. *"Justice and Injustice are none of the Faculties either of the Body or Mind: If they were, they might be in a Man that were alone in the World, as well as his Senses and Passions: They are Qualities that relate to Men in Society, not in Solitude."* [115] But what he would insinuate is *false,* if it be understood of a *Society form'd by human Compact.* I own indeed, that *external Acts* of Justice for the *most part* respect *others,* (tho it is possible for a Man to be injurious to himself;) but the *Propension* or *Will,* to give every one his own, (in which the Nature of Justice consists,) both may and ought to be in a Man in *Solitude.* Were there but *one* Man in the World, he might be dispos'd to allow others, whenever they should be created, equal Rights to those he claim'd to himself. Nor is there any reason, why such an Inclination should not be call'd *natural,* tho it could not produce *external Acts,* in a Man existing *Single.* As *Hobbes* himself

114. Ibid., p. 77, n. 6.
115. Ibid., p. 78.

(I believe) will not deny Man's *Propension to propagate his Species* to be *natural,* as he is an *Animal,* tho he were suppos'd alone, as *Adam* was before the Creation of *Eve.*

§XXXV. *Lastly,* because *Hobbes's* whole *Hypothesis* is built upon this *one Principle;* and (as I believe) he perceiv'd, that this *Right of every Man's warring against all,* and of arrogating every thing to himself, was *not* very *consistent* with the true Definition of *Right,* which he himself had given in the Passage above quoted, therefore in the beginning of his *Fourteenth Chapter* of the *Leviathan,* he has given a different Definition of *natural Right,* thus: *"The Right of Nature is the Liberty each Man hath to use his own Power as he will himself, for the Preservation of his own Nature."* [116] *Now* truly, by the Name of *Right,* is to be understood, not the Liberty of acting according to *right Reason,* or any Law of Nature; but of acting any thing, *as he will himself.*

But lest *Hobbes* should seem too inconsistent, in order to reconcile him to himself, I will discover the truth of this Affair, which is, that by the Name of *"right Reason,"* he before understood, in his Treatise *de Cive, "every Man's own Opinion,"* (as appears from his Note on *c.* 2. § 1.)[117] not excepting what is most absurd, and contradictory to the Judgment of the same Person at another time, as well as to that of all others; and in *this Sense,* indeed, right Reason is consistent with every Man's own Will: But neither *right Reason,* nor *Right,* are thus *pliable* to every Man's pleasure. These are as *inflexible* as the *Beam of the Balance* is suppos'd to be; for *right Reason* consists in a *rigid conformity with Things them-selves,* whose Natures are *invariable,* as I shall hereafter prove at large; and *Right* extends it self no farther than *right Reason permits,* or pro-nounces to be *consistent* with that *End,* which it proposes to all rational Agents. It is in vain, and without example, to affirm that any one has a *Right* to do those things, which are neither *allow'd* nor *permitted* by any *Law.* There is no doubt, but that Man has a *natural Power,* or *Will,* which he himself may *determine* to act which way he pleases. But when we are enquiring into the *Right* of Acting, the *Question* is, "Which,

Lastly, Hobbes, in order to support his Hypotheses, gives absurd Definitions of Right, and of Right Reason.

---

116. Ibid., ch. 14, p. 79.
117. Hobbes, *On the Citizen,* 2.1, pp. 33–34.

among those Actions which are in our *power,* are *lawful?"* Any Answer
to this Question, without respect had to some *Law,* at least that of *Nature,* is absurd. Any one *can* either hang, or throw down a Precipice,
either himself, or any other innocent Person; yet no one will affirm, that
any one has a *Right* to do these things, because *Right* and *right Reason*
which directs it, respect a good or true *End,* namely, that Happiness
which is attainable consistently with the Rights of others, and the *Means*
subservient to that End. But the *Will* of Man may *rashly* depart from
both these. All others, if at any time they call *Liberty* by the name of
Natural Right, understand a Liberty *allow'd* and guarded by the *Laws
of Nature.* But if *Hobbes* pretends that he has a Licence to call such a
Liberty of acting any thing at pleasure for Self-preservation, by the name
of *Right,* (tho no one beside himself ever used that Word in this Sense,)
because Philosophers are at liberty to limit the Significations of Words
according to their own Definitions; this will be a sufficient *Answer:* Allowing his confining *that* Word to *that* Sense, in which he *alone* uses it,
(for others are not oblig'd to make use of that Word in the same Sense;)
it is incumbent upon him to *prove,* "That such a liberty of acting whatever he thinks fit for his own Preservation, *does,* or ever *did, exist in that
State";* or, "That there is nothing to *forbid,* and, consequently, to hinder
Men so to act, laying aside the Consideration of *Civil Laws."* I *affirm,*
"That, even in *that* State, there are certain *Dictates* of right *Reason,*
which God suggests, by the *Nature of Things,* to the Minds of Men,
which *denounce* most grievous *Punishments* attending them, who attempt any thing, tho for their own Preservation, *contrary* to the common
Good." Nor is this a bare Assertion, I prove it undeniably.

   Hobbes no otherwise proves, that such a Liberty, as what he calls *Right,*
is granted us, than by affirming, that *we cannot will to act otherwise;*[118]
which is *contrary* to every Man's manifest *Experience.* For my own part,
I profess, that I *can will* to act otherwise, and believe, that great Numbers
have *willingly* laid down their Lives for the common Good. So *weak* is
this *Foundation,* which supports *all* the rest of his *Morality* and *Politicks;*
so that *all those Arguments,* which I offer, in order to establish the *Law
of Nature,* as it respects the Good of others, will prove that, even before

---

118. Ibid., 1.7, p. 27.

the erecting *Civil Government,* it was *not lawful* for any one to preserve himself by the *Violation* of that *Law:* And they render ineffectual and ridiculous that *unbounded Right* asserted by *Hobbes,* which it will never be *lawful* to use, except when a Man's Will is *conformable to the Law,* and consequently *limited.*

But to what purpose take I so much pains to prove this *Right of acting arbitrarily against all,* vain? since even *Hobbes,* tho in contradiction to himself, acknowledges almost as much; for he allows (*c.* 1. § 11.) *"That this Right is unprofitable."*[119] He himself, who had concluded the immediate foregoing Article with affirming, *"That Profit is the Measure of Right,"*[120] does yet here immediately affirm, *"That this Right,"* which he had taken so much pains to establish, *"is unprofitable."* Nay the very words, *Right* (as he himself has defin'd it) and *unprofitable,* (which he has join'd to Right in the Margin of that Article,) are *inconsistent;* for in both places he defines *"Right"* by *"An Use of Liberty":* but he affirms, upon the same Subject, that no Use of Liberty consists in what is *"unprofitable."* But *right Reason* does not use to tack together such *contradictory* Notions, nor is so regardless of Futurity, as to affirm that War to be necessary to every one's Preservation, which it will immediately perceive to be destructive to all: Therefore *Hobbes's Reason,* by which he endeavours to establish these Opinions, is *not right.*

Remark on Chapter I

I think our Author is abundantly *too general* in this *Chapter of the Nature of Things;* and that he should either here, or in his *Chapter concerning Human Nature,* or in that *concerning Good,* have shewn more *particularly,* *"How* the most of our *Enjoyments* are *general* or *extensive* in their Use," and, *"That publick* and *private Happiness* are so *interwoven,* that

---

119. Ibid., 1.11, p. 29: "But it was of no use to have a common right of this kind. For the effect of this right is almost the same as if there were no right at all. For although one could say of anything, this is mine, still he could not enjoy it because of his neighbour, who claimed the same thing to be his by equal right and with equal force."

120. Ibid., 1.10, p. 28.

the very Actions which promote the private Interest of any particular Person, do in all, at least in all common Cases, necessarily tend to the Advantage of the Publick: *That* our *Possessions* of all Kinds, our Lands, our Houses, our Money, are all *enjoy'd* by many": And, *"That* it is *not possible* to *confine* them to the Use of *one.*" The very *Clothes* we wear are, in some measure, *common* in their Use: Nay, the very *Food* we eat is *not confin'd to one,* but returns to its Parent Earth, and there contributes to the growth of those Vegetables, which may, perhaps, serve for the Nourishment of the Inhabitants of the most distant Countries. Nay, the very individual Particles of *Air* we breathe, are *not our Property,* but perform the same kindly Office to Thousands. Our *bodily Labour* too is always *general* in its Use: We can't so much as plant a Tree, or manure a Field, but Thousands reap the Fruit of our Labours; and tho our *Labour* be most *extensive* in its Use, yet we are utterly *unable, without Assistance,* to *provide* for our selves the most *simple Necessaries of Life.* The most ingenious Mechanick would not, perhaps, be able of his own proper Labour, to furnish himself out so much as a commodious Garment. *Who,* that but reflects upon the Number of Hands that one single Garment must pass thro', before it becomes fit for Use, and upon the Number of curious Arts that contribute to its Perfection, (a competent Knowledge in none of which can be attained without the Industry of some Years:) *Who,* I say, that yields but the least Attention to these things, can doubt of our *Dependence,* nay, of the *Necessity* of our Dependence, on one another?

These things, which I but hint at, are, I think, worthy of the most serious Contemplation; and were they but fully laid open to our View, we should have a clearer insight into the *Beauties* of the *moral World,* and be at once fill'd with Love and Admiration of its Author.

The Force of the Reasoning, that is built upon the Observations that are above hinted at, may be thus express'd. It *appears,* from those *Observations,* "That the publick Good is, in the greater Number of Cases, most plainly connected with private Advantage. Therefore we have reason to believe, from the *Uniformity* of Nature, that there is the *like* Connexion in those other Cases, wherein, from our Short-sightedness into the Consequences of Action, we can't perceive it with so great Evidence."

Of Human Nature, and Right Reason.

By the Word [*Man*], I understand *an Animal endow'd with a Mind;* and   Man defin'd,
Hobbes himself, in his Treatise *of Human Nature,* acknowledges the
Mind to be one of the principal Parts of Man.[1] Natural Philosophers,
both antient and modern, *Des-Cartes, Digby, More,* but especially *Seth
Ward,* in opposition to *Hobbes* himself, have sufficiently proved the *dis-
tinctness* of the *Mind* from the *Body,* under which all the Animal Faculties are compriz'd;[2] so that I should but light a Candle to the Sun at
Noonday, in offering to add to their Arguments. However, I cannot but
take notice, that *Hobbes* has unluckily stumbled at the Threshold of his
Treatise *de Cive,* in reducing the Faculties of human Nature to four
Kinds, *bodily Force, Experience, Reason,* and the *Passions:*[3] For beside,
that the first of these, *bodily Force,* contains all the rest, in his Opinion,
who acknowledges no other *Force,* but that of *Body;* it is contrary to all
Use of Words, to call *Experience a Faculty* of our Nature; whereas it is
properly to be reckon'd among those things, which are *accidental* to our

---

1. Hobbes, *Humane Nature: or, The Fundamental Elements of Policy* (1650), 1.5,
p. 3. Cumberland mistakenly attributes Hobbes's comment to 1.3. Note that this work
is the first English version of Hobbes's *Elements of Law* (1640).

2. Cumberland refers to Descartes, *Les Passions de l'Ame* (1649); Digby, *Of the
Immortality of Man's Soul* (1644); More, *The Immortality of the Soul* (1659); and
Ward, *In Thomae Hobbii Philosophiam Exercitatio Epistolica* (1656). [Maxwell] "Dr.
Samuel Clarke having, in my opinion, set the *Immateriality* of the *Soul,* and its Distinctness from the Body, in the best light, of any Writer I have met with; I have, in
the *Appendix* to this Treatise, given his Reasoning upon that Head in as succinct a
manner as was consistent with Perspicuity."

3. Hobbes, *On the Citizen,* 1.11, p. 21.

Senses, both internal and external, of which *Memory* is sometimes the Effect, tho it is not it self Memory, as it is by him defin'd, in his Treatise *of Human Nature,* Page 36.[4] Nay further, it is well known, that things we have experienc'd, do sometimes slip out of our Memory: But, if by the word *Experience,* he understands a *Habit acquir'd by Experiments,* it is a mistake to reckon it among the *Faculties;* except he would reckon *Geometry,* a Knowledge of the *Law;* and other Sciences, both Theoretical and Practical, amongst our *Faculties,* because they are Habits. But this is not a Matter of sufficient importance to dwell longer upon: Let us rather a while consider the foregoing Definition of *Man.*

As Animal.   By the word [*Animal*] I understand, what the Philosophers agree is to be found in Brutes, the Powers of receiving Increase by *Nourishment,* of *beginning Motion,* and of *propagating their Species;* and I also willingly so far allow them a *sensitive* Power, as we may bestow the Name of *Sensation*[5] (in which I see no Absurdity) on the *Motions* impress'd on the Organs by the Objects, and thence transmitted, by the Nerves appropriated to the Senses, into the Brain, and sometimes thence communicated to the Muscles, where they excite *Motion,* or to the Heart or Lungs, and perhaps to other Intestines, by means whereof various *Affections* are excited. However, I suppose the Power of observing or distinctly *perceiving* these *Motions* to be *peculiar to the Mind,* so as freely to *contemplate what* in them, for example, determines the Figure of the Object, *what,* a Situation in the Object, different from that which is in the Retina; *what,* its Magnitude, *what,* its Motion; *what* in the Surface thereof, or *what* Refraction in the Medium, does so diversify the Motions of Light, as to exhibit all the various *Phaenomena* of Colours: for I do not see, what in the corporeal substance of the Brain can *separate* from one another all these (crowding at once into the Eyes, by means of the same percussion of the Rays of Light;) *compare* them with one

4. Hobbes, *Humane Nature,* pp. 35–36.

5. [Maxwell] "Tho *Motions,* impress'd upon the Organs of Sense, may *occasion Sensation,* yet *no Motion,* of any kind, *is Sensation:* If it were, Matter, which is capable of all kinds of Motion, would be capable of Sensation and Thought. But for a Proof, that Matter is incapable of Thought, I refer the Reader to Dr. *Clarke*'s Reasoning in the *Appendix.*"

another, and *distinguish* them; or what should hinder them from appearing always *confused,* as they are perceiv'd in the *Camera Obscura,*[6] or in the bottom of the Eye of an Animal, whence they naturally rush at once into the *Thalami* of the Optick Nerves, which penetrate the inward substance of the Brain. But these are Matters of physical Consideration.

To the *Mind* we ascribe *Understanding* and *Will;* to the *Understanding* we reduce *Apprehending, Comparing, Judging, Reasoning,* a *methodical Disposition,* and the *Memory* of all these things, and of the Objects about which they are conversant: To the *Will* we ascribe, both the simple Acts of *chusing* and *refusing,* and that Vehemence of those Actions which discovers it self in the *Passions,* over and above that emotion or disturbance of the Body, which is visible in them.

In the *Memory* of Propositions, Theoretical and Practical, consist *Habits,* as well *Theoretical,* which are distinguish'd by the Name of *Sciences,* as *Practical,* which are called *Arts.* Here *Ethicks,* which is the *Art of Living,* or of directing the whole of all human Actions to the best End, comes under Consideration.

Endow'd with Mind.

§II. Here it may be proper to take some notice of the *various Manners* of particular *Nations;* nay, and of most *Men* too: for various Habits are acquir'd, partly from *diversity* of *Disposition* or natural Genius, more prone to Habits of some sorts than others; partly from the *Temper* of the *Body, Climate, Soil, Education, Religion, Fortune,* and kind of *Business* about which Men are employ'd. From Manners, thus procur'd, arises to Men as it were a *second Nature;* they are therefore to be con-

(Whence variety of Manners proceeds. See ch. 5. § 9.)

---

6. [Maxwell] "A *Camera Obscura* is a darken'd Chamber, into which the Light is let only by one little Aperture in one Window; in which Aperture or Opening, if one or more Glasses, of proper Figures, be plac'd according to the Rules of Opticks, and the Light passing thro' them falls upon a Sheet of white Paper, *&c.* at a proper distance, the Images of those external Objects which could be seen by the Eye thro' the Aperture, will be very distinctly delineated upon the Paper in their proper Figures and Colours, especially if the Sun shine upon the Objects, whose very Motions also, if they be in motion, will be represented. If the Rays of Light pass in at the Aperture thro' one Glass only, the external Objects will appear inverted; if thro' two Glasses of proper Figures, and properly apply'd, the external Objects will appear erect."

sider'd in the *framing Laws,* and that so far, that very *antient* Laws, tho *not* in all respects, if consider'd in themselves, the *best,* ought nevertheless to be *retained,* were it but upon this account, that Men long accustom'd to them would not readily suffer better to be substituted in their stead, without publick Commotions, and, consequently, greatly *endangering the Rights of all.*

Man (notwithstanding *Hobbes*'s Assertion to the contrary) is rational, and fitted for Society, by Nature.

I thought it also proper to observe here by the way, that I, (as all other Philosophers do,) in the following enquiry into the Laws necessarily connected and agreeing with *human Nature,* always understand or suppose human Nature as it is in *adult* Persons, who have a *sound Mind* in a *sound Body;* so far, at least, as is necessary to the exercise of *Reason* and *Virtue:* for Laws are not framed for *Infants, Ideots,* or *mad Men;* nor of such do we form Societies; nor therefore ought we, from their *irregular* Appetites and Actions, to form a Judgment of the Rights and Inclinations of *human Nature.* Tho, I think, whatever we perceive in them (after Maturity) agreeable, whether to the animal or rational Nature, *that* we may look upon as a Proof, that such Actions are *very natural* to Men; so in them we may perceive, both an expectation of *Compassion* from Men, and a *Sympathy* to be accounted for upon Principles which I shall afterwards explain, by which they rejoice with those that rejoice, and weep with those that weep. In vain therefore does *Hobbes,* (explaining the Reason why, in opposition to the Opinion of most Philosophers, he affirm'd Man not to be Ζωον πολιτικὸν,[7] which he translates, *"An Animal form'd by Nature for Society,"*) bring this Proof for his Opinion, that since *"civil Societies are Leagues, whose* Obligation *Infants and the unlearned are ignorant of; and whose* Usefulness *is not understood by those"* (whom he afterwards affirms to be *"very many, perhaps the Majority, thro' distemper of Mind, or want of Discipline) who have not experienc'd the Damage arising from want of Society: Whence it comes, that those cannot, and these care not to enter into Society; yet these, both Infants and Adult Persons, partake of human Nature, therefore Man is not made apt for Society*

---

7. Aristotle, *Politics,* I.2.

by Nature, but by Discipline." [8] This is the Substance of *Hobbes's* Annotation, these the words, tho somewhat contracted for brevity's sake. I at present pass by his *false Supposition,* "That *Societies* are *Leagues";* and that he sets *Discipline,* which entirely accommodates it self, and is *subservient,* to *Nature,* in *opposition* to Nature; for whatever we *learn* from others; they draw from their own *Nature* and that of the Universe. I here also *affirm,* "That *Experience* it self (for want whereof he accuses the Generality as unfit for Society) is resolv'd into *Nature,* which, without doubt, teaches whatsoever Experience testifies to be true." Altho many acquire most of their Knowledge by *words* of *arbitrary* Appointment, yet the *Ideas* or *Sense* affix'd to these words, and *Connexion* of these Ideas, in which all *Truth* consists, are from *Nature;* whence they are the *same every where,* tho Languages differ. *Hobbes,* it seems, forgets here, where he sets *Experience* in *opposition* to *human Nature,* that he had before made it one of its Faculties. I would only *observe,* "That all Philosophers and Writers of Politicks, tho they were neither ignorant nor forgetful, how *unqualify'd, Infants,* and adult Persons of *distemper'd Minds,* were for forming Leagues, or doing the Duties of *Society,* have thought *Man* form'd by *Nature* for that, which, when come to years of *Maturity,* he was *prompted to by Nature,* except something *preternatural,* such as all *Distempers* of the Mind are, interpos'd." The Observation of *Juvenal* is well known,

8. Hobbes, *On the Citizen,* 1.2n, pp. 24–25: "But civil Societies are not mere gatherings; they are Alliances [*Foedera*], which essentially require good faith and agreement for their making. Infants and the uninstructed are ignorant of their Force, and those who do not know what would be lost by the absence of Society and unaware of their usefulness. Hence the former cannot enter Society because they do not know what it is, and the latter do not care to because they do not know the good it does. It is evident therefore that all men (since all men are born as infants) are born unfit for society; and very many (perhaps the majority) remain so throughout their lives, because of mental illness or lack of training [*disciplina*]. Yet as infants and adults they do have a human nature. Therefore man is made fit for Society not by nature, but by training." The quotation here is a translation of the passage quoted in Maxwell's footnote in Latin.

Nunquam aliud Natura, aliud Sapientia dicit.

Nature does not teach one thing, and Wisdom another.[9]

And *Aristotle* (*Politic.* I. *c.* 2.) affirms, that *"we ought to judge of Nature from her Intention or perfect State";* [10] and it is certainly a childish Inference, favouring more of the *Grammarian* than the *moral Philosopher; "Men are born Infants, therefore they are born unfit for Society."* This is much of a-piece with *Hobbes*'s accounting (in his Physicks) for the Noise of *Thunder* from the breaking of *Ice,* which, in spite of Staticks, he suspends in the Air in the middle of Summer.[11] Altho the word *Nature* be deriv'd from *Nascor* [to be born,] yet it is well known, that by *human Nature* we mean that *Force* of *Reason,* whose first *Rudiments* only are to be found in new born *Infants.* So *Man* is by *Nature* fitted for *propagating* his Species, which yet neither an *Infant,* nor one whom *Distemper* hath render'd *impotent,* is capable of, nor *any* Person without the help of a *Woman.* So likewise, we call the *Powers* of *Plants* and *Fruits* to afford us both *Nourishment* and *Medicine, natural,* which yet are not to be found in them, upon their *first Appearance* out of the Earth or Trees, but then only, when the Sun and Rain have brought them to *Perfection,* and they have escap'd the Malignity of blasting Winds: but that Reason, nay right Reason, is a Faculty of human Nature, and therefore natural to us, *Hobbes* himself acknowledges in these words, *"Right Reason therefore is a kind of Law, which may be call'd natural, since it is no less a part of human Nature, than any other faculty or affection of the Mind."* [12] Yet the same *Hobbes* elsewhere denies this very thing; *Leviath.* c. 5. p. 21. where he says, *"Reason is not, as Sense and Memory, born with us, nor gotten by Experience only, as Prudence is, but attained by Industry."* [13] Let him free himself, if he can, from Contradiction. I will not therefore waste my time in proving what is self-evident; especially when I had before affirm'd

9. Juvenal, *Satires,* XIV.321.
10. Aristotle, *Politics,* I.2.
11. Hobbes, *Problemata Physica* (1662), ch. 6, pp. 90–93.
12. Hobbes, *On the Citizen,* 2.1, p. 33.
13. Hobbes, *Leviathan,* ch. 5, p. 25.

expressly, that I consider'd the Nature of *Man* come now to *Maturity,* at which time Nature *usually* confers upon him the use of *Reason.*

§III. I shall think that I sufficiently prove my Point, when I have made it *appear,* "That human Nature suggests certain Rules of Life, in the same manner that it suggests the Skill of Numbering." All *Men,* when come to *Maturity,* except they labour under some *Distemper* of Mind, *of their own accord* reckon things by *Numbers,* adding, subtracting, multiplying, and dividing them, if the Numbers be small, without any Rules of *Art.* The Sentiments of all Nations are *necessarily* the *same,* concerning the *Sum* of two Numbers found by *Addition,* and concerning their *difference* by *Subtraction,* how much soever they may *differ* in the *Names* and Characters by which they express the Numbers, which every Nation fixes for it self *arbitrarily.* It seems to me, that all, in the same manner, under the same conduct of Nature, *necessarily* acknowledge, (1.) *That the Good of all rational Beings is greater than the like Good of any part of that aggregate Body;* that is, *That it is truly the greatest Good:* and (2.) *That in promoting the Good of this whole Aggregate, the Good of Individuals is contain'd and promoted:* Also, (3.) *That the Good of every particular Part requires the introducing and settling of distinct Property in such Things, and such Services of rational Agents, as contribute to the common Happiness;* that is, *such as are necessary to testify the Honour we pay to God, or to preserve the Life, Health, and Faculties of every particular Man.* In these three Propositions we shall find the Seeds and Force of all the Laws of Nature to be contain'd. Skill in *Numbering* is much assisted by *Industry,* by *artificial Characters,* and by their *Places:* but these very Helps we owe to *Nature,* as to their Original; nor can they ever cause that, which without Art we know to be true and of necessary use in Life, to become false or useless. "Whatever Assistance we may procure from *Art,* the whole *Effect* is to be ascrib'd rather to *Nature* than to *Art.*" Just as, after the Art of Cookery has fitted Meat for Nourishment, no one will deny, that we are nourish'd by the Power of Nature, otherwise Life it self were not natural.

This I think proper to premise as a *Postulatum,* which, I believe, no one will think unreasonable, "That the Mind of Man, and every Faculty

Which suggests the Law of Nature in the same manner as it does the Art of Numbering;

The Mind is necessarily

determin'd, in
forming simple
Apprehensions,
in chusing
Good, and
refusing Evil in
general.

thereof, especially the Intellectual, is prone to such Actions as are proper thereto, as often as Occasion is offer'd, and Matter suggested, either from without, or from the Body united to it." It is confirm'd by continual *Experience,* "That the *Mind* (whenever Light, Colour, or Sound, is presented to it thro' the Senses, the Eyes, for example, or the Ears) is immediately *apt to observe* what is *offer'd."* And the Case is the same, in observing painful or pleasant Sensations, taking their rise from the inward State of the Body. *Simple Apprehensions,* the more *obvious Comparisons of Ideas among themselves,* and *certain Judgments* or Propositions thence form'd, are in some sort *necessary;* the *evident Connexion* between Causes and Effects does also *lead* Men to *form Propositions* affirming that Connexion; and they *involuntarily* return upon the Mind, when any *occasion* is offer'd from the inward force or vigor of the *Memory;* nor can the *Will* at all put a *stop* to such Actions, tho it may indeed *promote* them. For we can *excite* our selves to *recollect* those things which had almost slipt out of the Memory, and attentively to *consider* what our Senses had observ'd, and diligently to *form Comparisons* and *Propositions* from Ideas compar'd among themselves, to form *Syllogisms* from Propositions compar'd, and from these to infer *new Conclusions.* Every one come to *maturity,* in *proportion* to the natural *vigor* of his Mind, is by the same Nature *spontaneously* carry'd on to such Operations, at once with the greatest *pleasure,* and with absolute *necessity.* Into *this natural Impulse,* I would resolve most of those Propositions, which I call the *natural Dictates of Reason,* (namely, the primary and self-evident ones;) as also those *Acts of the Will,* which are conversant, either about *Happiness in general,* that is, about the whole sum of all possible good Things; (for there is in this Case no occasion for the Judgment to deliberate and compare, because Happiness is, as defin'd by *Cicero, "A Collection of all good Things";*)[14] or about those several *parts* of our Happiness, which are desirable for their *own sakes;* such are Wisdom, Health, the seeing a Light not too strong, and such other agreeable Sensations as come in our way. Nor do I suppose that *Hobbes,* the great *Patron* of all kind of *Necessity,* will contradict me here, who hath affirm'd, that all *"Concep-*

14. Cicero, *Tusculan Disputations,* V.x.28–29.

tions are nothing really but Motion *in some internal substance of the Head; which Motion proceeding to the* Heart, *if it help the vital Motion, is called* Delight, Contentment, *or* Pleasure; *and, with reference to the Object,* Love. *But when such Motion* weakeneth *or* hindereth *the vital Motion, then it is called* Pain; *and in relation to that which causeth it,* Hatred, *which the* Latins *express sometimes by* Odium, *and sometimes by* Taedium; and that *this Motion* is also a Sollicitation, *or Provocation, either* to draw near *to the thing that pleaseth, and is then called* Appetite, *or to* retire *from the thing that displeaseth, and is then called* Aversion." *Human Nature,* p. 69, 70.[15] I do not indeed perceive any such Power of the material World over our Minds, that necessarily determines them by mechanical Principles; yet I concur with all Philosophers, that I know of, in *affirming,* "That the first Apprehensions of Things, and the desire of Good and aversion from Evil in general, are necessary": for the innate Activity of the divine Nature of the Mind, permits it not to be perfectly idle; nor can it do any thing else than (as occasion offers) *understand, chuse, refuse,* and *determine* certain *Motions* of the Body, in order to obtain what it has chosen.

§IV. But because the *Laws of Nature* enjoin those things only, which proceed from *innate Principles of Action,* it is therefore proper to take a thorow view of the *State* and *Power,* both of the *Mind* and *Body, separately* and *jointly,* that it may thence appear, for what kind of Action Man is *fitted* by his *inward Frame.*

There are most evident *Indications,* that the *Mind* has much *greater Powers,* and is created for much *nobler Purposes,* than only to *preserve the Life of one inconsiderable Animal;* which I shall now endeavour to explain.

And here, in the first place, I must not omit its *spiritual, incorporeal,* and *God-like Nature,* which is capable of a better Employment than that of the Soul of a Swine, instead of Salt, to preserve a Carcass from Rottenness: For it may and ought to be *observ'd* in general, "That Powers of the Mind, far inferior to those which we find in Man, are sufficient

A distinct enumeration of those Powers of the human Mind, (which has greater Powers than what are necessary to preserve the Life of the Body,) which dispose Men, beyond other Animals, to enter into Society with God, and other Men;

---

15. Hobbes, *Humane Nature,* 7.1–2.

to preserve Life for a long time"; which is evident in *long-liv'd Brutes,* nay, and in *Trees,* as the *Oak,* whose long continuance in a flourishing State is even *without Sense,* much more *without Reason:* Nay, "That the *Sagacity* of our *Mind* does not consist in discovering what kinds of *Nourishment, Medicines, Exercise,* &c. are most *conducive* to our *long continuance* in this State," for even the best Physicians are strangely at a loss in these Particulars; but, "That it rather excels in those *Qualities,* which relate to the *Knowledge* and *Worship* of a *Deity,* and to *Acts moral and civil."* But Dr. *Ward,* now Bishop of *Salisbury,* hath excellently manag'd this Argument, beyond any other, whether antient or modern, Philosopher, and vindicated it from the Objections of Mr. *Hobbes.* [16]

Nevertheless, it is necessary to lay before the Reader some *Powers* and *Actions* of the *Mind,* whence it may *appear,* "That it is *naturally fitted* to become a Member of the *greatest Society,* (consisting of all rational Beings with God at their head,) and that it neglects its *principal use,* and loses the *best Fruits* of its natural Disposition, if it *do not enter* therein"; and that for a *better Reason,* than we affirm that the *Earth* (which here spontaneously produces Ears of Corn, and there Fruit-Trees) is *naturally fit* to encourage and reward the Industry of the Tiller; for Soils have their different natural Dispositions. The human Faculties are so fitted for Society, that it *appears,* (1.) "That all Men can both *know* and *observe* the Laws of Nature, which must in the first place be *evident,* because otherwise both the Admonitions of others, and our own Endeavours would be vain: (2.) That the Observance of those Laws is in it self *pleasant* and grateful; that the Precepts which point out to us such a Method of Action, for this very reason that they lead us to things naturally pleasant, promise a *Reward* to Obedience; and that a suitable Practice brings along with it no inconsiderable *Advantage,* namely, that *Pleasure* or part of our Happiness, which is necessarily contain'd in such natural employment of the human Faculties, as leads to the best End we can propose in Life, and to the fittest Means to attain it": for all *exercise of natural Powers,*

16. Cumberland is probably referring to Ward's *A Philosophicall Essay Towards an Eviction of the Being and Attributes of God* (1652) and his lengthy refutation of Hobbes, *In Thomae Hobbii Philosophiam Exercitatio Epistolica* (1656).

especially of the *highest Order,* in which we neither miss our aim, nor turn out of the direct Road, is *naturally pleasant;* nor can we conceive any other pleasure in *Action,* except what arises from Actions of *this kind.*[17] *Freedom from Evil,* and from Uneasiness, and *grateful Impressions* of some kinds, may be effected in us by *external* Objects;[18] but no other Pleasure can take its rise from *within our selves,* than what either immediately or mediately depends upon such kind of Actions as I have now been describing. This is the *only* Happiness to which *moral Philosophy* directs us; nor can we be instructed how to obtain that, which in no sort depends upon our own Actions and Faculties. Hence it *follows,* "That the *more things* there are in the human Faculties, fitted for the knowledge and observance of the *Laws of Nature,* and consequently for the Practice of Virtue, *so much greater* are the *Rewards* annex'd to such Actions of the Mind, or, a Happiness so much the greater and more peculiar to Man, may be obtain'd by acting *virtuously*": For *each Faculty* is render'd *happy,* by those *Actions* tending to *promote the publick Good,* to the exercise whereof it is fitted by *Nature;* for I shall *shew* hereafter, "That Happiness's proceeding necessarily from such Actions as take their rise from Nature, is a most evident natural Proof, that it is the Will of the first Cause to oblige Men to such Actions, or that he enjoins them by his Law."

I have selected as fittest for my purpose,

First, Right Reason, and the Standard of its Rectitude;

Secondly, Universal Ideas, (such, for example, as that of human Nature in general,) and the *Judgments* or *Propositions* thence arising concerning the Properties agreeing or disagreeing with those *Ideas,* and *general* or undetermined Acts of the *Will* agreeable to, and consequent upon, such Judgments. Hither also is to be referr'd the *power* of appointing *arbitrary*

Which Powers are,
1. Right Reason.
2. The Power of forming universal Ideas, Judgments from them, and consequent Voli-

---

17. Barbeyrac (*Traité Philosophique,* p. 111, n. 4) suggests that Cumberland alludes to the classical discussion of pleasure in motion and pleasure in rest, referring to Diogenes Laertius, *Lives,* X.136, and Cicero's distinction between *voluptas in motu* and *voluptas stabilis* in *De Finibus* II.x.29–32, II.xxiii.75–77.

18. Barbeyrac (*Traité Philosophique,* p. 112, n. 5): "The deliverance from some evil, and a certain peace of mind, or even perhaps some not disagreeable impression, may come to us from without."

tions, and of representing these Ideas by arbitrary Signs, *i.e.* Words.

Signs, such as words spoken or written, accommodated to such universal Ideas, Propositions and Volitions. For *Speech,* because it is a help to the *Memory* and *Reason,*[19] is rather subservient to *Virtue,* than *Vice; to Society,* than *Sedition.* Hence arises the *power* of forming general *Rules of Life* or Action, from Ideas of Actions[20] agreeing in their general Nature with the Idea of human Nature: But such Propositions are more easily *remember'd,* if they be express'd in *Words* accommodated to this purpose, and to the Ideas of the generality of Mankind, and be applied by *common Consent* to express them. Thence are form'd Rules common to many, or *publick Laws,* which, as the State of Affairs happens to require, may be enacted, abrogated, or alter'd: As a Physician may justly prescribe to the same Patient, at different times, sometimes a slenderer, sometimes a more plentiful, Diet, now Restoratives, and then evacuating Medicines.

3. The Knowledge of Number, Measure, and Weights.

Thirdly, The *knowledge of Number, Measure, and Weights,* and consequently the power of collecting many Particulars (lesser good Things, for example) into one Sum, and comparing the same with one another, according to their *Difference* and mutual *Proportion.* Hence Man can discover the chief Good, that is, the *Collection* of all good Things, and a *comparative* Good, perceiving one Good to be greater or less than another; and can subtract some from others; and is able to estimate the Proportion between things equally and unequally Good. To direct such Actions in such manner, as that they may best promote the best End, is the business of all the Laws of Nature.

4. The Power of observing and establishing Order.

Fourthly, The *Power* (nearly related to this) of either *observing Order* already established, or of *establishing* it, in the Conduct of our Affairs, and of knowing of how great moment it is in uniting several Powers, in order to produce the same Effect, especially the *common Good,* as we may observe in modelling an Army or Common-Wealth. Whilst I was more attentively considering this Subject, I *imagin'd,* "That the best way

19. Maxwell correctly translates the original but failed to note that Cumberland corrects the sentence in his errata. The sentence should read: "In addition speech, because it is a help to. . . ."

20. [Maxwell] "That is, such Actions as are productive of natural Good to Men."

of distinctly knowing the *Nature* and *Force* of *Order,* was to consider it in the most *simple Matter,* that shews its most *simple Effect.*" But I no where meet with Order in a more simple Matter, nor a more simple Effect thence demonstrable, than that Geometrical *Order* of *right Lines* and *compounded Motions,* whence *Descartes* has demonstrated (*Geom.* 1. 2.) that his Geometrical Curves might be generated.[21] For he has there *prov'd* from Analytical Principles, "That the Nature and Properties of a Line describ'd by compounded Motions, is not subject to accurate Calculation or Demonstration, unless all the other Motions, in subordination to one another, be regulated by *one.*" What he has observ'd concerning a *Line,* the most simple Effect of compounded Motions, holds equally true in *all Effects, depending upon the Concurrence of many Causes;* namely, that it is necessary, that, among such Causes, some should be regulated by others in a certain Order, and *all* by *one* supreme Power; otherwise it will be *uncertain,* what Effect will follow from their Concurrence; and so either *no End* will be procured by the *common Assistance* of them all, or by Means which we know not, whether they be *proper or no.* By means of *this Knowledge,* and from the *Train of subordinate Causes,* which we perceive by our Senses, the Mind comes to a more distinct Knowledge of a *first Cause,* which is God the Governor of the World, who is able to *foresee,* what will be the Effects of the power of all rational Agents, placed and acting in a known Subordination; both which Considerations will have a natural Tendency to persuade Men, to consider themselves, both in their Thoughts and Actions, as subordinate Members of the most enlarg'd Society, in which all are contain'd, as it were in the KINGDOM OF GOD.

Fifthly, From these arises that exalted Privilege belonging to the Mind of Man, of great force to establish and preserve this Society, namely, the *Power of the Mind, to raise, stop, and moderate the Passions,* and to direct them to desire greater Good, and to avoid greater Evil, than what any other Animal is capable of knowing; because we comprehend good

5. The Power of the Mind, to raise, stop, and moderate the Passions.

21. Descartes, *La Géométrie* (1637), I.2.

Things, both *more in number,* and *universal as to extent,* their *Sums,* and their *orderly Series;* and we are conscious, that we can *divert* our Minds from such Thoughts and Affections as respect only our own private Good, and *fix* them upon the Care of the Publick Good, in which *Liberty* principally consists. I will not meddle with the Disputes about Liberty, which have been handled by others. This seems to be *beyond all Controversy,* "That the Nature of Man has so much Liberty, that he is determin'd to nothing (in external Actions, such as are Contracts, their Observation and Violation) without using his own Judgment, in forming which he may call in the Aid, not of the Senses only, but of the Memory; and to consider, Is this which I am going to do, consistent with the publick Good, which except it be preserv'd unviolated, the Happiness of particular Persons cannot be secur'd? Is this consistent with the well-grounded Motives of Virtue? *&c.*" I have observ'd that even *Hobbes*'s Politicks do, and that justly, suppose this *Postulatum,* "That Men may agree among themselves, or covenant, to transfer their Rights to another Person, for the common Good, (*c.* 5. §. 6.)"[22] tho elsewhere he *contends,* "That they can regard nothing but their own private Good." But since there is naturally in Men so large and noble a *Faculty,* which can both *comprehend* and *pursue* that vast Good, the *greatest united Happiness of all rational Agents,* the Reader will easily judge, whether the *greatest Happiness of every particular Person* does not consist in the perpetual vigorous *Exercise of that Faculty.* I do not contend that this *Faculty* is any thing *distinct* from the Powers of the *Understanding* and the *Will:* It is sufficient, if from the *Concurrence* of them the *Power* I have mention'd, arises. Every one sees, how immediately this Power of the Mind *disposes* or qualifies *Men* to *restrain* themselves from any sudden Sally of *Passion,* and to *conform* their *Manners* to the *Laws,* first of Nature, then of the Society; and, consequently, to establish at once the greatest and strictest Society of all rational Beings. Concerning *right Reason* and *universal Ideas,* I think proper to treat more *at large;* it will be sufficient to handle the *rest briefly.*

22. Hobbes, *On the Citizen,* 5.6, p. 72.

§V. We must treat of *right Reason* the more *particularly,* both because what is *right* discovers both *it self* and what is *crooked;* it holding the same *Rank* in *Morality,* that *Health* does in *Physick,* the knowledge whereof is *prior* and *more distinct* in the Order of Nature, than the Theory of *Diseases:* and because *Hobbes* agrees with other Philosophers, that it is the *Rule of human Actions,* even before *Civil Laws* are fram'd; (See *de Cive,* c. 2. §. 1. and the *Annotation.*)[23] And, if he will be consistent with himself, we shall not differ much with him about its *Definition.* For *c.* 2. §. 1. in a Parenthesis (which he seems to place there for a Definition) he hints, that it is *"Truth inferr'd from true Principles by right Reasoning."*[24] But I think that, in *this Argument,* the notion of *right Reason* is somewhat *more extensive;* for it comprehends, as well *first Principles,* or self-evident Truths, as *Conclusions* thence form'd. The *Etymology* of the Word [*Ratio*] favours this Sense, which implies only a *Proposition,* that is *rata,* i.e. certain, unchangeable, and agreeable to the Nature of Things, whether it be self-evident, or prov'd by the help of an inference. *Custom* also, which is the Rule of Language, favours the same Sense of the Word; for all acknowledge the most evident Propositions, (such as "It is impossible for the same thing to be, and not to be at the same time") for the Dictates of Reason, no less than those which require proof. Nor do I believe that *Hobbes* himself will oppose this *larger* Sense of the Words. I agree, however, with him, that by *right Reason* is not to be understood an *infallible Faculty,* (as he affirms many, but I know not who, to understand it;) but yet by it is to be understood a Faculty, *not false* in these Acts of judging. Nor is it properly understood to be an *Act of Reasoning,* (as he too rashly asserts,) but an *Effect of the Judgment;* that is, *true Propositions treasur'd up in the Memory,* whether they be *Premises* or *Conclusions,* of which some that are *practical* are called *Laws;* for Actions are compar'd with these, in order to examine their *Goodness,* not with those Acts of Reasoning which discover them; yet I willingly allow, that these Acts of Reasoning are also included in the Notion of *right Reason.*

Of right Reason, (which consists, as well of self-evident Truths, as of Conclusions thence deduced, and stored up in the Memory;)

23. Ibid., 2.1, p. 33.
24. Ibid., 2.1n.

Of which, not
every Man's
proper Reason,
but the Nature
of Things, is
the Standard.

But that which he immediately adds in the *Annotation,* (in order to give a Reason, why, in *his Definition of right Reason,* he lays down *"every Man's proper Reasoning as the Standard"*) is most false. *"Out of civil Society, where no one can distinguish right Reason from wrong, except by making a Comparison with his own, every Man's proper Reason is to be esteem'd, not only the Standard of his own Actions, which he does at his own peril, but also the measure of other Mens Reason with respect to his Affairs."* [25] For, *out of civil Society,* any one may *distinguish right Reason,* without *making a Comparison with his own.* Because there is a *common Standard,* by which every Man's own Reason (or Opinion) and that of others, is to be try'd, namely, the *Nature of Things,* as it lies before us, carefully to be observ'd and examin'd by all our Faculties. That is the Rule with which all, both Premisses and Conclusions, are to be compared, whether form'd by me or by any other Man, or by the Common-wealth it self, after it is form'd. For it is most *certain,* "That the *Truth* or Rectitude of *Propositions* concerning Things and Actions, present or future, consists in their *Conformity with the Things themselves,* concerning which they are form'd." For since all our *Ideas,* or simple Apprehensions of Things, are the *Images* of those *Things,* (and the Truth and whole Perfection of Images consist in their exact Correspondence to the Objects they are design'd to represent;) and since *true Propositions* are the *joining, by Affirmation, of Apprehensions impress'd upon the Mind by the same Objects,* or the *separating, by Negation, of Notions representing different Objects;* it is necessary, that their Truth and Rectitude should entirely depend upon their Conformity with the Things themselves; as all agree, that the Truth of simple Apprehensions is to be deduced from that Standard.

This therefore is *beyond Controversy,* "That the Man who judges of Things otherwise than they are, does not judge according to right Reason, or does not make a right use of his Judgment; but that he pronounces according to right Reason, who affirms or denies, as Things really are."

25. Ibid.

§VI. Nor is it *material* in this case, *"Who* it is that judges otherwise than the Thing really is, whether a *sovereign*, or a *subordinate*, Judge"; because the *Truth*, or Rectitude, *of a Proposition in no respect depends upon the Order established amongst Men*, but only upon the *Agreement thereof with the Things*, concerning which a Judgment is made. Nor is it any Proof of the contrary, that there are some Mathematical *Propositions*,[26] and others of like kind might be invented, which may be called *true*, tho there be *nothing in Nature*, to which they are *conformable*. For such conditional Propositions, because they pronounce *nothing concerning Things without the Mind*, are *not* to be *compar'd with them*; for their *Truth* consists only in an *Agreement* among the *Terms*, of which they are compos'd; and that is all which is to be look'd for in this Case. But these are of no use in human Life, except we find something external done, or possible to be done, which differs in nothing considerable from our Ideas.[27] If their *Subject*, or something extremely like it, *cannot exist*, the Propositions are trifling, and are only *equivocally* called *true*. For the *Truth of Propositions*, which consists only in the Agreement of the Terms, if the Terms themselves *cannot exist*,[28] is *not of the same nature* with that, which affirms the Agreement of Terms, *possible*, at least, if not *present* or *future*. The former kind of Truth is perfectly useless. However, let this Point be determin'd as it will, this is *clear*, "That a Proposition, whose Subject does or will exist, that is, whose Subject is conformable to Things without the Mind, which either now are, or hereafter shall be, does require, that what is affirm'd of that Subject should be conformable to the same things; and that therefore the whole ought to agree with the Nature of

Wherefore such Propositions only are true, as agree with the Nature of Things.

26. [Maxwell] "Such as Demonstrations concerning *imaginary* Worlds or Systems would be."

27. [Maxwell] "Thus, tho there are perhaps no Bodies in the World exact Spheres or Cubes, such as are the Subjects of Mathematical Demonstration, and tho the Curves in which the Planets revolve, are not perfect Ellipses; yet such Spheres, &c. as we meet with, differ so little from those which are exact, that the Difference is of no consequence in human Life, in Surveying, Gauging, Astronomy, &c."

28. [Maxwell] "If the Terms *cannot exist*, I do not see, that any thing can be demonstrated concerning them; for example, what can be demonstrated of a *Square Circle?*"

Things without us"; which is the principal Point I at present contend for.

It is also *certain*, "That *every particular Man*, and his *Right* over Things and Persons, whatever it may be, is not something *merely chimerical* and fictitious, but to be consider'd as something *real*, and existing without the Imagination": *because* the *Rights* of particular Persons relate to the *use of Things*, and to Effects grateful to Men; and therefore the *Truth* of Propositions, or of the Dictates of Reason, concerning them, does necessarily consist in their Conformity to the *State of Things;* which is what I would lay as a Ground-work, in order to overthrow *Hobbes*'s Fundamentals: for it hence immediately *follows*, "That contradictory Propositions, concerning the Right of any two to the same Things or Persons, cannot be the Dictates of right Reason"; which is the Foundation of *Hobbes*'s Scheme.

An Explanation of practical right Reason, which points out the end, and the means thereto;

§VII. I think it proper to *observe* here, by the way, "That by the *Dictates of practical Reason*, I understand *Propositions, which point out either the end, or the means thereto, in every man's power";* for all Practice is resolv'd into these: and, "That *practical Reason* is then called *Right*, when it determines truly, or as the thing is in it self, in Propositions declaring what is every man's best and most necessary *End*, and what are the most proper *Means* of obtaining it"; or (which comes to the same thing) which pronounces, according to *Truth*, *what* Effects of our own Counsel and Will will render our selves and others *happy*, and *how* we shall, with the greatest certainty, *produce* them; just as in *Geometry*, that *speculative Reason* is *right*, which affirms a Quantity, which *is* really in its own Nature *greater, to be greater*, than another. And that *practical Proposition* is *right*, which teaches that method of constructing Problems, which if we pursue, we shall *really produce the effect propos'd.* Nor is an *Opinion*, or Proposition of this kind, *truer*, when affirm'd by a *King*, than when by a *Subject*. Since then all *right Reason* is conformable to those *things*, about which we have form'd a Judgment, since *each* thing is, in its nature, but *one*, and uniform with it self; it *follows*, "That right Reason in one cannot dictate that, which contradicts right Reason, concerning the same things, in any other Person."

From this Principle follows that Precept of universal use, concerning the Actions of all Men, *That human Actions ought to be uniform and consistent with themselves, thro' the whole course of every Man's Life;* and that he cannot act always agreeably to right Reason, who, as *Horace* expresses it, And is uniform and consistent,

> *Aestuat, & vitae disconvenit ordine toto.*

Fluctuates, and disagrees with himself thro' the whole course of Life.[29]

It is included in the Notion of a *true Proposition,* (a practical one, for instance,) and is consequently a necessary Perfection of a Man forming a *right Judgment* in that Affair; that it should *agree with other true Propositions* framed about a *like* Subject, tho that like Case should happen at *another time,* or belong to *another Man:* And therefore, if any one judge, "That his Act of taking to himself the Necessaries of Life, not yet possess'd by any other, would promote the common Happiness"; it is necessary that the *Judgment,* "That the like Action of another in like Circumstances, would equally conduce to the same End," must be undoubtedly right. Whoever therefore judges *truly,* must judge the *same* things, which he thinks truly are lawful to *himself,* to be lawful to *others* in a *like* Case. In the same manner, whatever Assistance any Man *rightly* and truly believes, he may or ought to demand according to right Reason, it is *equitable,* and consequently a Dictate of right Reason, that he should think, that *any other* in *like* Circumstances *justly* may or ought to demand the *like* help from him. Forming like Judgments in like Cases, whether our own, or those of other Men.

The reason of *Hobbes's* making so gross a *Blunder* in this Argument, was, because he did not *observe,* "That there was the *same* Standard to *all,* by which the Reason of every one is to be tried, whether it be right or no"; namely, the *Nature of Things,* especially, of the *End* necessary to all rational Beings, and of the *Means* naturally leading thereto.

§VIII. We may observe here, by the way, how *honourable Hobbes's* Sentiments are concerning *God,* ruling naturally by the Dictates of Reason; (To which sight Reason,

---

29. Horace, *Epistles,* I.1.97.

and conse-
quently to
God, its
Author,
Hobbes
imputes Con-
tradictions;
that is, that God, instructing Men in the Laws of Nature by the Dictates
of right Reason, does enjoin *Contradictions;* that he *first* tells us, "We
must fight against all, and so engages Men in a War, in which all that
fall, are *unjustly* murder'd on both sides, because they claim only their
own Rights"; that *afterwards,* "By the same right Reason he forbids War,
and commands us to relinquish those very things, which yet he affirms
are *justly* to be retain'd, and defended by the Sword, because they are
Rights": For he must necessarily ascribe to *God* all those *Contradictions,*
which he imputes to the *right Reason* (as he calls it) of Men, contra-
dicting one another with relation to the Necessaries of Life; for he affirms, that *"God rules by this Reason, as by a Law,"* [30] and consequently,
that *he permits* all those things which *Reason permits;* and *teaches* that all
those things may be done consistently with his Laws, which *right Reason
has taught* may be done, by natural Right. For *Hobbes* himself does not
extend *"Right"* (where he purposely defines it) beyond *"the Liberty of
using our Faculties according to right Reason."* [31]

It is hence *evident,* "That *God,* according to *Hobbes,* first gives a Right
to invade the Properties of all others, that *his right Reason* includes a
Licence to commit any Crimes, and then involves all Men in the Miseries
of a destructive War." But after he has render'd Men miserable by the
Evils of *Wickedness* and *War,* he points out a somewhat better road to
Justice, such at least as may be sufficient to avoid the Punishment of the
civil Power; and then at last endeavours to bring over wretched Mortals
to *such a Peace,* as that Justice would establish.

Whereas right
Reason judges
alike in all.)
That *Reason,* which I acknowledge as *Right,* first examines all the
Parts, both of our own and others Happiness, and foresees, at a great
distance, the *Causes* thereof that are lodg'd in our own Power; then,
perceiving them in their own Nature so interwoven, that a *prudent* care
of our own Happiness cannot be separated from the pursuit of the Hap-

---

30. Hobbes, *On the Citizen,* 15.8, p. 175: "Since the *Word of God* (God reigning
through nature alone) is defined simply as right reason; and since the laws of Kings
can only be known from their Word, it is evident that the laws of God reigning
through nature alone are the only *natural laws.*"

31. Ibid., 1.7, p. 27.

piness of others, that is, of the common Society of all rational Beings, it determines, that the *strictest Justice* is to be cultivated, with respect both to *God* and *Men,* and presages, that the Fruit thereof shall be a most happy *Tranquillity.* By the same Reasoning it foresees, that the Actions of Men, who *arrogate each all things to himself,* or are guilty of such Practices, will involve all in *War* and extreme *Calamities;* and that so evidently, that there need not for Information be made so rash and fatal an Experiment. Therefore it will never allow a Right to act in such a manner; but, on the contrary, it will command Men to *contract Friendships,* to *establish civil Government* where it is wanting, and to *preserve* it when establish'd; that not only those Miseries of War, which it forsees may arise from the Folly of some Men, may be avoided, but the greatest Assistances to the most perfect Virtue and Happiness be procur'd. *Hobbes* therefore thought that this would be done, (and that necessarily too,) because he did not *observe,* "That there was the same Rule (the Nature of Things) for all, by which the Reason of all ought to be tried, whether it be right or no."[32]

Here, I think, the fundamental *Corner-Stone* of the *Temple of Concord* is laid by *Nature;* for hence is deriv'd that *Law of Nature* uniting all rational, or wise, Beings (for Reason in perfection is Wisdom)[33] among themselves, and with God as the wisest; which is thus express'd, *Whoever determines his Judgment and his Will by right Reason, must agree with all others, who judge according to right Reason in the same Matter.* Whence it also follows *conditionally,* (which I shall afterwards prove from proper Principles,) "If any right Reasoner, any wise Person, shall assign to each his proper Office, in order to the publick Good, all others who judge rightly, shall approve of the Distribution." But of this more hereafter.

32. Cumberland provides a manuscript replacement for this sentence: "Hobbes on the other hand is reduced to having to affirm generally that all the maxims of true reason, even on the effects of natural causes, and on the properties of numbers and figures, however varied they might be, are indeed maxims of true reason in a state where the sovereign approves them, but they are not so in another state, where the sovereign, through *folly* or *ignorance,* rejects and contradicts them." Cumberland, Trinity College MS.adv.c.2.4, p. 88.

33. Following Cicero, *De Legibus,* I.7.

How to pre-
vent false Rea-
soning. §IX. I shall hereafter *observe*, "That, in order to preserve our *Reason right*, we ought not only to avoid *false Deductions*, but especially the *rash Admission* of any thing as *self-evident*, without proof." And we ought to *take care*, in the first place, "That our *simple Ideas* be both *clear*, from strong and frequent Impressions of the same thing known in various Circumstances; and *distinct*, by a separate Observation of the Parts singly; and *adequate* also (as far as we can) by the Assistance of the Memory and Understanding, added to the Discoveries of Sense." It is to be *observ'd*, "That in these *external Impressions* there can be *no Falshood*, properly so called." The *Unwary*, indeed, take *occasion of judging falsly*, from the Distance, the Refraction, or the tinging of the Rays of Light in the Eyes of Persons infected with the Jaundice: but if all things in the *Medium* between the *Organ* of Sense and its *Object* be consider'd, as they ought, before we pass a Judgment, (to this Head is to be referr'd the Temper of the Blood, that of the Animal Spirits, and the Brain;) we may *avoid* falling into *Error*. In the *Medium* are the *partial Causes*[34] of the Impressions made, and they are therefore necessarily to be consider'd. What is more, before we determine any thing concerning the *Sameness*, and Connexion, or the *Diversity*, and Opposition of the *Terms*, they are most carefully to be *compar'd* with one another; and we ought to take care, especial care, when we contemplate the *first* and most *universal Truths*, *not* to give our *Assent* to any Proposition, without the strongest and most inevitable *Necessity*; for *Truth* depends not on our *Will*, but upon the *Connexion of Things*, and of those distinct *Ideas*, which are impress'd upon us by Things; but what we *perceive*, we *necessarily perceive*, whenever the *Faculty* is *attentive*, altho that *Attention generally* depends upon our own *Will*: and upon *this Rule* depends the *main Point* now in *dispute*. For *since* the whole *Truth* of *affirmative* Propositions consists in the *Connexion* of two *Terms*; and *since* these are *naturally* connected, because both Terms are imprinted upon the Mind by the *same* thing, and are evidently Representatives of one and the same *Thing* under different Respects; it is *evident*, "That *Truths* depend, not upon the *Will* of Men imposing and connecting Names arbitrarily, but upon

---

34. [Maxwell] "That is, those Causes, which give occasion to Error."

the *Natures of Things* delineating their own Representations upon the Mind. But whatever *Motions* are impress'd upon us by the Nature of Things, are *necessary,* and proceed from the *first Mover,* the Author of Nature; so, consequently, do all those Ideas, which, impress'd upon the Senses and Imagination by a Motion evidently *natural,* represent *practical Truth* to the Mind, concerning Actions most conducive to the common Good. Truths of this kind are *natural Laws,* as I shall hereafter prove; and their Impression upon the Mind is the Inscription and *Promulgation* of Laws; and they may for the *same* reason be affirm'd to be by the first Mover imprinted upon us, (by means of the Nature of Things;) that *speculative Axioms* (such as, "Lines drawn from the Centre to the Circumference of the same Circle are equal") may be truly affirm'd to be necessarily planted in our Minds by the First, thro' the intervention of Second, Causes. Justly therefore may we ascribe to the Law of Nature the words of *Demosthenes,* which *Marcian,* in the *Pandects,* has inserted into his general Description of *Laws,* that it is *"The Invention and Gift of God."*[35] They, who do not acknowledge the Proof of a *Deity* from the Necessity of a *first Mover,* (which *Hobbes* however acknowledges,)[36] take away the most *antient,* and, in my Opinion, the *strongest,* Prop of *Religion.* Nevertheless, if they own the Proof of a God from that *Order* which is visible in the World, the mutual Relations of Things, and the Beauty thence arising, or from this, that they perceive so many of them design'd by Nature for our Use, as their *final Cause,* they will be oblig'd, by this our Argument, to acknowledge *God* as the *Author* of all *necessary Impressions.*

§X. This *Observation,* concerning the *Truth of simple Apprehensions,* or of all natural Impressions, seems to me of so great importance, that I will venture thence to *conclude,* that "Neither does our own Nature, nor that of Things without us, ever necessarily or unavoidably determine us to form a false Judgment, nor, consequently, to chuse or act amiss"; which always proceeds from the Uncertainty or Error of the *Understand-*

To which we are never necessarily determin'd, Judging, Willing, or Acting, wrong, being owing only to an Abuse of Liberty;

35. Justinian, *Digest,* 1.3.2.
36. Hobbes, *Leviathan,* ch. 12, p. 64.

ing. Whatever, at any time, we judge, chuse, or act, contrary to those
Notices, which a thorow Examination into the Nature of Things affords;
that I think wholly owing to a hasty, *rash,* and unseasonable *Use of Liberty,* which is generally deluded thro' the Sollicitation of a *present Advantage,* and incites the Judgment to determine Points *not yet sufficiently*
clear'd up. "All Truths, (even in Morality,) which are *unchangeable* and
never deceive, are owing to *Nature,* and to a *Necessity* of assenting to
things *evident.* And to Nature *they only* (exclusive of *Errors*) are to be
ascrib'd, if we would not be injurious, to our own *Faculties,* no one of
which ever necessarily determines us to embrace a Falshood; to natural
external Agents, that cannot deceive; and, to *God* himself, to whose Nature it is a Contradiction to suppose him willing to deceive us." We *thus*
determine upon these Points, on better Authority, than *Physicians,* who
call only those Motions of the Humors, for instance, *Natural,* which
tend to the Preservation and Health of the Individual, calling the rest,
which tend to Disease and Death, *Preternatural;* and with Reason, because by *Nature* here they understand the Nature of the *Individual,*
whose Preservation is the End of their Art: Yet they will not deny the
most fatal Alterations of the Humours, to be according to the *universal*
Laws of Nature. But, in Man, the *Error* of the *Judgment,* and *Perverseness* of the *Will,* are neither agreeable to the Nature of the *Individual*
endeavouring its own Perfection, nor proceed from any necessary influence of *things external* upon him; but first from mere *Inadvertency* and
Rashness, afterwards from *Habits* or *Example,* the Imitation of himself
or others. *Hobbes* is therefore very unfair, who proposes whatever Transaction he has observ'd among Cabals of Villains, as a momentous Discovery in human Nature, and a Foundation of a new Set of Politicks.

And human
Judgment act-
ing most agree-
ably to Nature,
whom it
approaches
nearest to
Necessity.

I am of Opinion, that not only *speculative Axioms,* but the first Principles of *moral Habits* are thus *necessary.* It is sufficient, indeed, that those
Dictates which determine many *particular* Actions, as they are circumstanc'd, are supported by *probable* Reasons, such as the Weakness
of our Mind, which cannot examine all things present, much less foresee
all the Consequences of the present Action, can attain, whilst urg'd by
an *immediate* Necessity of Acting. Those things which proceed from

Examination and cautious *Deliberation*, from *Experience*, and the faithful *Testimony* of competent Witnesses, such are Civil Laws and Precedents, or Cases adjudg'd in Courts of Judicature, make the *nearest* Approaches to *Necessity*. We ought therefore to form a Judgment of the *Inclination* of human Nature from *these*, rather than from the *rash* Actions of Men. For Deliberation, Experience, and all the other helps to discover Truth, do continually bring us *nearer* to that State of Mind, by which, because of the Influence of Things upon it, it *cannot* think otherwise than it does think, which is the Case, when it judges from the *Evidence* of Sense, or clear *Demonstration:* And thus the *more necessary* and unavoidable any Judgment is, so much the *more natural*, or approaching to what is natural, it is to be esteem'd. *Hobbes*, on the contrary, forms a mistaken Judgment of *human Nature*, from *rash* Actions, as absurdly, as if we were to judge of the *Nature of a Tree*, from the fungous or mossy *Excrescencies* sometimes growing to its Bark.

§XI. 2. Next comes under Consideration, that peculiar *Power* of the human Mind, by which it forms *universal Ideas*, omitting those Accidents, by which particular things are distinguish'd. Hence arises a great help to the *Memory*, and consequently to *Prudence* thence arising; nay, to every *Virtue*, as connected therewith, and to every *Action* and *Habit*, which ministers Steadiness, Beauty, and Happiness, to human Life. For the Mind can easily apply to *innumerable* Individuals and their various Circumstances, Properties agreeing to *one* or a few Natures consider'd in themselves, whether those Properties respect their inward Frame, or their Causes and Effects: Hence all *Sciences* take their rise, as compos'd of Universals. By the help of these, *Abstracts*, and the chief Heads, of *Natural History* are easily collected; whence (to omit other Advantages) we readily learn what things are necessary, to preserve and perfect, both our own Nature and that of others. In like manner the Precepts of *Arts*, since they too are universal, compendiously instruct, by what means any Persons, whose Faculties are capable of them, shall or may attain the Ends by them propos'd. So Logick, Physick, Ethicks, (or the Art of Morality,) the Arts of Navigation and Architecture, do not instruct *one* par-

2. Of universal Ideas,

ticular Person only, how *Aristotle,* for example, shall direct his *Reason,* in *one* Affair, to the Discovery of Truth; or *Hippocrates* preserve, or recover, *his own* Health; or *Palinurus* reach *one* Port only; but they instruct *all* Artists *without distinction:* They consider the *End,* and, consequently, the propos'd Good of every Man *in general,* chusing, and prescribing the use of, *Means* as *general;* and, therefore, both they who teach, and they who learn, these Arts, first contemplate these general Precepts. Which proves, by the way, that Men not only *can,* but that in all Arts it *is* their *universal Practice,* to respect a *general* Good, earlier than *their own:* Altho nothing hinders, but that *Hippocrates,* applying his general Precepts to a particular Case, may preserve his own Health, for instance, as well as that of others; and *Vitruvius* may build himself a House, as he had done before for others. It is of this further Advantage to observe these universal Ideas and Propositions, both Speculative and Practical, which are naturally form'd by the Mind of Man, because from such universal Notions are form'd *Unchangeable,* and consequently in some Sense *Eternal,* Rules of human Action. In the following Sheets, I shall lay before the Reader many such Propositions or Rules, whence he may distinctly perceive, what those universal Notions are, of which they are form'd; and how peculiar they are to the Mind of Man; and how much they promote Religion, civil Government, and the Peace and Commerce of different Nations.

And Speech, which is compos'd of Words, which are the arbitrary Signs of universal Ideas.

But first I must make a few *Observations* on the Power and Inclination of the Mind of Man to form *Words,* spoken or written, and other *arbitrary Signs,* by help of which it may either *recollect,* or *communicate* to others, its Notions, both universal and particular. This remarkable Difference, between Men and other Animals, contributes much both to the forming and preserving *Societies:* The great *Agreement* observable among Men, in the use of such Signs, will easily be accounted for, if we consider (as becomes *Christians*) what the sacred History *informs* us, "That all Mankind have sprung from one Original,"[37] so that *Eve* might,

---

37. [Maxwell] "It is observable, that those Nations have the fairest Complexion, who live near the Poles, and that they generally grow darker, as they approach nearer the Equinoctial, so the *Swedes, English, French, Spaniards,* and the Natives of *Barbary,*

without Difficulty, have used words in the *same* Sense that *Adam* first appointed them, and their Posterity might suck in their Signification with their Mother's Milk. But if *Hobbes* would rather consider them in *his State of Nature,* as suddenly sprung out of the Earth (like Mushrooms) of full Growth, and without any Relation to one another;[38] even in *that* Case Reason would persuade them, that *many,* (namely, all those who wanted to maintain a mutual Intercourse,) might agree in the *same* words, or other Signs, to express the *same* things. Nor was it at all of any Consequence, who *first* express'd this Idea or Thing by that Sign; but it would greatly concern them all, to agree among themselves in some *common Marks* of their Ideas, by help whereof *each* particular thing might be *made known* to all. Hereby each Person, by communicating his Observations to others, is enabled to "Improve their Minds with a *further* Degree of *Knowledge";* so that the Experience and Endeavours of the

---

grow gradually of a more dusky Hue, each than the other, which is evidently owing to the greater Heat of Climate. The Natives of *Africa,* who live between the Tropicks, have receiv'd the deepest Dye, beyond either those of *America* or *Asia* in the same Latitude, which is probably owing to one of *two* Causes, or to both conspiring; either, 1. Certain subterranean Exhalations, whither of the mineral Kind, or others, which may be peculiar to those Parts of *Africa:* Or, 2. A greater Heat in those Parts of *Africa,* than what is to be found in *Asia* and *America* in the same Latitude. The Inland Parts of *Africa* are the worst water'd Countries we know; for the Vapours, which, in form of Dew, Rain, *&c.* moisten the Earth, do, most of them, fall to the Ground, before they can reach them, lying at so great a Distance from the Ocean, whence those Vapours are exhaled. Also the Soil of those Parts of *Africa* is generally more sandy than the correspondent Parts of the other Quarters, which greatly increases the reflected Heat; to which more of the Heat we feel is owing, than is generally imagin'd, as appears from this, that Snows lie long unmelted on the Tops of high Mountains, under, or very near, the Equinoctial, the direct Heat of the Sun, even there, being often not sufficient to melt them. Therefore the Parts of *Asia* and *America,* which lie between the Tropicks, are more temperate than those of *Africa* in the same Latitude, as not being so sandy, as receiving more Rain, *&c.* and abounding more with Rivers, with which *South-America* is mighty well supply'd. Beside, the Line cuts *Asia* among the Islands, and in such Parts of the Continent, as being near the Sea, are much refreshed with Breezes from thence. It is therefore, for these Reasons, to me highly probable, that the Colour of the Negroes, which is immediately owing to a *Mucus* between the inner and the outer Skin, is remotely owing to the Climate they inhabit, and that the Whites and Blacks are all come from the same common Stock."

38. Hobbes, *On the Citizen,* 8.1, p. 102.

present Age may point out to the succeeding ones a *shorter* way to Prudence and Happiness, and by a *more easy* Method produce in them all kinds of *Virtue;* hereby Men are inabled to *"Debate* concerning Covenants, and Laws, to be made," to *"Promulgate* such as have been agreed upon," to *"Examine,* whether they have been observ'd"; to "Produce and receive *Testimonies";* and to "Give *Judgment* according to the Proofs." *Hobbes* himself will not deny, both that these things are *peculiar* to human Nature, and that they fit Man for *Society.*

Of the Reflex Acts of the Mind, and of Conscience. §XII. Shall I not reckon among the Perfections of the human Understanding, that it can *reflect* upon it self? *Consider* its Habits, as Dispositions arising from past Actions? *Remember* and *recollect* its own Dictates, and compare them with its Actions? *Judge* which way the Mind inclines? And *direct* it self to the Pursuit of what seems fittest to be done? Our Mind is conscious to it self of all its own Actions, and both can, and often does, observe what Counsels produced them; it naturally fits a *Judge* upon its own Actions, and thence procures to it self either *Tranquillity* and Joy, or *Anxiety* and Sorrow. In this Power of the Mind, and the Actions thence arising, consists the whole force of *Conscience,* by which it *proposes* Laws to it self, *examines* its past, and *regulates* its future Conduct. Nor appear any Traces, in other Animals, of so noble a Faculty. Great are the Powers of this Principle, both to the Formation and Increase of *Virtue,* to the erecting and preserving *Civil Societies,* both among those who are not subject to the same Civil Power, and among Fellow-Subjects. And, indeed, the principal *Design* of this *Treatise* is to *shew,* *"How* this Power of our Mind, either of it self, or excited by external Objects, forms certain universal practical Propositions, which give us a more distinct Idea of the utmost possible Happiness of Mankind, and pronounce by what Actions of ours, in all Variety of Circumstances, that Happiness may most effectually be obtain'd." For *these* are the *Rules* of Action, *these* are the *Laws* of Nature.

I will here add nothing to what I have already mention'd of the Knowledge of *Number, Measure, Order, Free-Will,* &c. altho these be both peculiar to Man, and are very material in the present Argument.

§XIII. I will now apply my self to the Consideration of the *Human Body,* in which I meet with several things worthy of Observation for my present Purpose, which are usually neglected, or at least omitted, by others who have handled this Argument.

Indications enforcing universal Benevolence, from a Survey of the human Body, considr'd.

For, since the *Life, Health,* and most perfect State, of the human Body, which can be acquir'd, (every thing else being regarded according to its Value or Dignity,) is part of that *End* which right Reason proposes to its self, and its *Powers* and various Uses are *Means* highly useful to the whole Man, both to procure the Improvement of the Minds of Individuals, and to promote the common Good; it is impossible, but that the Consideration thereof must suggest somewhat useful to direct us in the *Choice* of the supreme End, and in the *Application* of the Means; but in Dictates concerning that End, and the Means conducing thereto, does the whole of the Law of Nature, whose original and principal Parts I here propose to enquire into, consist.

In the first place, I think that this may be affirm'd universally, That *whatever* (1.) *demonstrates,* from the divinely-contriv'd Make of our Body, "That the whole possible Happiness of Man depends upon many Causes, the chief whereof are Rational; and that, therefore, it cannot reasonably be expected but in conjunction with the common Happiness"; *whatever* (2.) *proves* further, "That every one can, by the proper Power of his own Body, effect somewhat, by which this common End may be promoted, and the Assistance of others procur'd, and that, by his Endeavours of this kind, every Man will procure to himself the greatest Happiness in his Power": *That demonstrates* certainly, "That the Nature of the human Body affords a sufficient Indication of our Obligation to such Endeavours." And this will appear plainly, from the Consideration of *natural Obligation,* and of *Law,* which I shall afterwards explain.

Further, the *more evidently* and constantly the Manner and Method is pointed out, according to which it is necessary, in order to our own Happiness, that we should co-operate with others to procure the common Happiness; and the *greater* any one's Powers are, or the *stronger* his Inclination to such Actions; so much the *easier* it is to pay this Debt due to the Publick, and the Crime the *greater,* which is committed by the Breach of the Commandment; and from hence our clearer and *stronger Obligation* to such Actions may with the utmost Certainty be inferr'd: For these Reasons I thought it proper to propose some *Indications* of this kind, taken from the human Body. The Observation and Sagacity of others will add more, or will pursue these Hints further.

In the human Body are to be consider'd, (1.) What belongs to it as *Body;* (2.) What it has, as a Body *endow'd with Life and Sense,* like other Animals; (3.) What are *peculiar to it self.*

I. As a Body in General,

I. It has these things in *common* with all other *Bodies.*

1. Having its Motions, necessary for its Preservation, dependent upon, and limited by, the Motions of other Bodies, especially those of other Men.

1. That all *its Motions,* and consequently those which preserve its Life, Health and Strength, (whose Preservation each Person proposes to himself as a principal part of his End,) proceed from the *first Mover,* and are necessarily complicated with, and in some measure depend upon, innumerable Motions of *other corporeal Parts* of the same System. Among these are chiefly to be consider'd the *Bodies of other Men,* and their Motions which can limit ours, and are govern'd by Reason, which we have just ground to hope may be brought to concur with our Reason.[39]

2. Being equally able to promote those Motions in other human Bodies, which are equally necessary for their Preservation.

2. That *its Motion* (as that of all other Bodies) is *propagated* far and wide, and does *not perish,* but *concurs* with other Motions to *perpetuate* the Successions of Things, or to preserve the Whole. And as the *first Observation* instructs us, "That our private Good depends upon common Powers"; so this *second Observation* proves, "That the Powers of particular Persons may be of publick and most extensive Advantage." The *former* forbids, "To hope for the Happiness of particular Persons separately from the Good of the Whole," and consequently points out "The common Good" as "The fruitful Cause of private Happiness": the *latter* shews, "That the Pursuit of the common Good will not be in vain, because it conspires with the Endeavours of the whole Universe." In *both* these complicated Motions, namely, *that,* by which almost all Things

39. [Maxwell] "Because right Reason is the same in all rational Agents, as having but one and the same invariable Standard, the Nature of Things, *See* § 5."

concur in some measure to the Preservation of any particular Body for some time, and *that,* by which any particular Body concurs with others to the Preservation of the whole System, a certain *Order* is preserv'd, by which some Motions are *determin'd* by others in a continued Series, and all are *govern'd* by the continued circular Motion of the whole System. I need not any particular *Hypothesis* concerning the System of the World, to prove what I have advanc'd concerning the necessary *Order,* and the *Powers of complicated Motions;* for these are demonstrated from geometrical Principles, which no *Hypothesis* can hurt. Tho a Contemplation of this kind may at first seem merely *speculative,* yet it is not without its *Use* in *human* Affairs; for hence we *know* distinctly, and from general Principles, "How necessary a certain Order among Causes which act by a corporeal Force, is, that many of them should conspire to produce any Effect foreknown and design'd in the Mind." It further *shews,* "How we may judge with Certainty, which Cause has contributed more, which less, to the Effect design'd." Whence the *value* and *worth* of *Causes,* with respect to any Effect, is fix'd and *determin'd* by their proper and natural Force; and, consequently, we are *instructed* by the very Nature of Things, both, "Which Causes are *more highly* to be valued, upon account of what they have already effected," and, "The Aid of what Causes we ought *chiefly* to sollicit, in order to procure what we farther desire." We thus come to *know,* "That those Causes, which Philosophers call *Universal,*[40] (such as the Motion of the Aetherial Fluid, &c.) but chiefly the first of them, God, are the principal Sources of the common Good, which we either all enjoy, or which we expect from the Nature of Things." We thus also *know,* "That Motions of Bodies ever so little subject to the Determination and Direction of the human Will, (to omit the Consideration of those which are exempted from it,) when govern'd by the universal Benevolence of all rational Beings towards all, are the

---

40. [Maxwell] "That is, such Causes, as concur with others to the producing many Effects of different Kinds; such as Universal Gravitation, the Solar Heat, &c. The *Aetherial Fluid,* or *Materia Subtilis* of *Des-Cartes,* which our Author gives as an instance of this Kind, is rejected as a fictitious Substance, since the introducing the *Newtonian* Philosophy."

principal Causes of the publick Happiness of all, whence is deriv'd the private Happiness of each." For *universal Benevolence* is the Spring and Source of every Act of *Innocence* and *Fidelity,* of *Humanity* and *Gratitude,* and, indeed, of all the *Virtues* by which Property and Commerce are maintain'd. They are govern'd by it, as particular Motions are determin'd by the universal Motion in the System of the World; or as all the Functions of the Spirits, Bowels, Vessels, and Limbs, in the Body of an Animal, proceed from the general Motion of the Blood. If we embrace this Opinion, from a thorow Examination of the Nature of Things, it will doubtless oblige us *to pay Obedience to all the Laws of Nature,* and to take diligent care, that the same be paid by *others:* This is the utmost we can do, to make our selves, as well as others, happy; nor can Reason propose to any one a greater End.

§XIV. However, in this *Comparison* of the *Aggregate of Mankind,* as they act by a corporeal Force, with the *natural System of Bodies,* I am not ignorant of this wide *Difference* between them, "That the Effects of Systems merely corporeal, are perform'd, not without Contiguity between the Bodies moving and moved, for the most part without Sense, but always without the interposition of Counsel and Liberty; whereas Men act often at a considerable distance, and make much use of their Reason and Liberty." It is, nevertheless, likewise *evident,* (1.) "That the corporeal Force of all Men, when it is exerted, is subject to the same Laws of Motion with other Bodies"; and, (2.) "That the force and necessity of Subordination between the Motions arising from Man, is the same with that which is among those of any other Bodies"; whenever many Men co-operate to any Effect which relates to others, (which they daily practise more than any one can "be well aware of":) with respect to these *two Points* only, I propos'd the foregoing Comparison; which, therefore, was made and apply'd justly. I will, upon this occasion, venture to go farther and *affirm, "That,* because Men have frequent Opportunities of meeting, by which they mutually profit or hurt one another, and many ways of doing, by Words or Actions, good or harm to Persons at a great distance, especially, if Men form Schemes for the Conduct of their Lives, (which it is certain every one naturally and constantly does, because every

Marginal note: Knowledge, and the Use of Signs, in Mankind, consider'd as a corporeal System, supplying the want of Contiguity in communicating Motion.

one desires that all his future Existence should be happy";) I will venture to *affirm,* I say, *"That* the whole Race of Mankind ought to be consider'd as one System of Bodies, so that nothing of any Moment can be done by any Man, relating to the Life, Fortune, or Posterity of any one, which may not some way affect those things which are alike dear to others; as the Motion of every Body, in the System of the World, communicates its Motion to many others, especially neighbouring ones." For that vast Privilege of extensive *Knowledge,* with which Men are endow'd, *supplies the want of Contiguity,* which is requisite in other Bodies, to the *Communication of Motion;* for Men are *excited* to Motion by the least *Signals,* whether Natural or Arbitrary, by which they quickly *perceive* what has been, or ought to be, done by other Men at the greatest distance. What is more, they *retain a Memory* of those things, done either to themselves or those who are dear to them, and by it are *excited* to take the first Opportunity of Retaliation; they are also naturally *provident,* and presage, from what has been done to others, what is to be expected by themselves, and those they love; and this *induces* them to many things, with a view to prevent Evils, and to create a probable Prospect of very remote future Advantages. This *Remembrance* of Things past, and *Foresight* of Things to come, are the Reason why Men, at a distance, are *more* mov'd by what is done to others, than inanimate Bodies are by the Motion of *neighbouring* ones, which act nothing, except they be *present:* for from these they immediately and justly *conclude,* "That being *like* in Nature and Condition, with respect to Necessaries, they also are to expect *like* things." Thus they cannot but be *affected* with those Actions of any towards others, which, if often repeated, or copied after by others, naturally work a considerable *Change* (either for the better or the worse) in the Condition of Men in general.

I own, however, that *all are not equally affected* with such Actions, but some more, some less, according to their *different degrees of Sagacity,* in apprehending the Causes or Hindrances of the common Good. Nor is the *Influence* communicated from some Men to others, by such Actions as respect the common End of all, for that Reason *less natural,* than that between Bodies of the same System with respect to *natural Motions,* which are communicated to more subtle and fluid Matter in a greater, to grosser Matter in a less, degree. It is sufficient, that "To *perceive* in Men a Likeness of Nature and Condition with respect to Necessaries," and "To *infer* from what is done to others, what we are to hope or fear will be done to our selves," are Acts, *Natural* and Universal, and not of *less* Efficacy to *influence* Men, than mutual *Contact* between Bodies moving and moved, is to *communicate Motion* among the Parts of a corporeal System. I will infer no more from hence, than what is otherwise evident, and seems to be naturally accounted for upon these Principles, that all Men may hence *learn,* "That their Security from Evils, and their whole Prospect of Assistance from others, in their pursuit of Happiness, necessarily depend upon the voluntary Assistance of many, who do not less stand in need of many others, that it may be well with them." Whence we are immediately oblig'd to *acknowledge,* "That the mutual good Offices of all are useful to all." Just as natural Bodies in the same System cannot perform their Motions, unless other Bodies concur with, and give place to, them.

From the Necessity of mutual Offices it *follows* necessarily, "That he that would, to the utmost of his Power, provide for his own Happiness, must, according to the measure of his Ability, procure to himself the Benevolence and Assistance of all others." Every one may easily know, that he has *Power* to confer upon others *Assistance* and innumerable good Offices, and to *conspire* with the whole System of rational Beings to the same End, and in pursuit of the common Good: but, on the contrary, that he can no more *compel* so many Causes, which are *singly* of force nearly *equal* with himself, to lend him their Assistance, and at the same time to relinquish and neglect all natural Endeavours to promote such things as are necessary for themselves, than *one* Pound Weight can, in a just Balance, raise a Weight of *some thousand* Pounds in the opposite Scale. For all *Struggles* between Men, by *force* merely *corporeal,* are perpetually determin'd according to the natural *Laws of Motion;* all which Laws *Wren* and *Huygens* have shewn how to exhibit by the Beam of a Balance, suspended either upon a single Center, or upon two Centers at equal distance from the Center of Gravity.[41] Nor is the *Cunning* or Craft

41. [Maxwell] "The *Author* is here *proving,* 'That in all Struggles between Men,

of any one above all the rest, of so great *Powers* as to *force* the Beam, which is depress'd by the real Necessities, *Powers,* and Counsels of a great Number, toward the *common Good,* to incline to the contrary Part, that is, to the *private Advantage of any particular Person.* Wherefore it cannot but *appear* evident, from the general Nature of *human Power,* "That we can more surely procure its *Assistance,* by *promoting the common Good,* than by *Force* and *Fraud,* or a savage Rapaciousness"; to which, according to *Hobbes's* Doctrine, (in the Epistle dedicatory to his Treatise *de Cive,*) even *good* Men must have recourse in a *State of Nature;*[42] and their natural Right to preserve themselves, makes it *no Vice.*

§XV. Our *Opinion* seems to be much *illustrated* by the general Principles of *Mechanical Philosophy,* (the only Principles *Hobbes* himself seems to me to agree to,) which *inculcate* this principally, as necessary in every *Hypothesis,* "That the Motion of the corporeal World, dispersed thro' the several Parts thereof, is preserv'd by that mutual Communication, Cession, Acceleration, or Retardation, of all Motions, which the Powers and Impulses of every particular Body, reduced to an exact Calculation, require: yet so, That the Motion of the whole System about the common Center, (which is compos'd as a whole, of the Motions of every particular Body added together,) is preserv'd always without In-

Which is illustrated from the known Laws of Matter and Motion.

---

by force merely corporeal, the greatest Force must as certainly prevail, as in a Balance that Scale in which the greatest Weight lies, must certainly preponderate,' which he proves thus. *All such Struggles* are according to those Laws of Motion, which take place in the Shock of two Bodies meeting; which Laws of Motion *Wren* and *Huygens* have shewn to be truly exhibited by a Balance, whose Beam, in some Cases, is suspended upon one Center, the Center of Gravity; in other Cases, upon two Centers, each of which is at equal distance from the Center of Gravity. That the Reader may the better understand this, I have subjoin'd what *Wren* and *Huygens* have said upon this Subject, to which our Author refers." Maxwell (p. 117n) includes an extract from Wren's discussion of the laws of collision from the Royal Society journal *Philosophical Transactions* 43 (1668/69), pp. 867–68 and Huygens's contribution to *Philosophical Transactions* 46 (1669) pp. 925–28.

42. Hobbes, *On the Citizen,* Dedicatory Epistle, sect. 2, p. 4: "But between commonwealths, the wickedness of bad men compels the good too to have recourse, for their own protection, to the virtues of war, which are violence and fraud."

terruption or Alteration, and determines and adjusts the Motion of all its Parts." *All* Bodies have the *same* Power and Necessity to continue in Motion, which is in each *proportionable* to their *Quantity of Matter,* or their Bulk and Solidity compar'd together: but even *this* Force is subordinate, in every *particular* Body, to the Motion of the *whole* System; and is therefore it self, as well as the whole, preserv'd by that which determines it. Thus the Motions of particular Bodies agree with the general Motion of the Whole, and are subservient thereto; and that *general* Motion of the System *governs* and *preserves* the Powers of all *particular* Bodies, in the most effectual manner, by the Nature of things consider'd, either together, or each by it self; which Nature consists in perpetual Motion and Change. All things are so *order'd,* "That not the smallest Quantity of Matter nor Motion may be lost," which is demonstrated from *Mechanical Principles;* and universal *Experience,* and the most authentick Histories of past Times, *witness,* "That the same Kinds of Animals are perpetuated, and their Numbers rather increas'd than diminish'd, notwithstanding the fierce Passions of some few Animals." In this *Perpetuity* of *Matter* and *Motion,* and of the *Kinds* of all things continued by a Succession of Individuals, consists the Preservation, or *natural Good,* of the *material Universe,* which is promoted, according to the unchangeable Laws of Motion. Nor can any sufficient Reason be *assign'd,* "Why the Preservation of *Mankind* should not be look'd upon as establish'd and continued by the force of Causes *equally* certain and natural, as the Successions of any *other Animals,* which entirely depend upon the *unchangeable* Nature of the material World, and the *necessary* Laws of Motion, since they perfectly *agree* in all that is *essential* to an *Animal.*" Certainly the Conjunction of the *Mind* with the *Body,* very often makes its Condition *better* than that of Brutes, but *never worse;* which will be evident to any one who considers, what *Advantages* the Body receives from the Conduct of *Reason,* which abundantly *compensate* some *Mischiefs,* which happen to the Body thro' the *Error* of the Mind: nay, it is certain, that the *Errors* of the Mind about Food, Pleasure, and other things which relate to the care of the Body, proceed from hence, that the Mind, *regardless* of the Admonitions of its own *Reason,* gives way to the Appetite, and the *corporeal* or animal *Affections.*

These *Observations,* concerning the *necessary Causes* of the Preservation of the *corporeal Universe,* and (to omit other things) of the several *Kinds of Animals,* and consequently of *Mankind,* make such *Impressions* upon the Minds of Men, as these which follow, and conduce much to our present purpose, *viz.*

Whence it appears, that the common Good is the noblest Effect possible, and inseparable from that of particular Persons.

1. That the *Preservation* (or common Good) *of Mankind* is a matter not only *possible,* but that it depends upon so many Causes, so certainly determin'd, that we have the greatest reason to believe, that it will undoubtedly *be perpetuated,* notwithstanding the malevolent Endeavours of any to the contrary.

2. That this Effect is both in its own nature the *most noble,* and *most closely united* with the *Preservation,* and possible *Happiness,* of *every Individual.*

3. That the Matter and Motion of all *particular Bodies,* and, consequently, of Men themselves, is, in some measure, naturally and necessarily subservient, whether they will or no, to the Preservation of the *corporeal Universe,* (which includes human Bodies,) namely, as every particular Body is determin'd in its own Motion, by the general Motion of the whole System, by which it is perpetuated.

Does not the *Nature* of Things, and consequently *God* its Author, powerfully persuade and *command* an Endeavour to promote the common Good of Mankind, *by every Indication* they give, that it is both a *possible* Effect, and the *greatest;* and also *more closely united* with the private *Happiness of every one,* than any other Effect which we can foresee as possible, and *by making us* in some degree to *promote* it *necessarily,* even then when we give way to our natural Affections, and oppose it to the utmost of our Power? Is it not evident, that he acts most *agreeably to practical Reason,* and to the imprinted Ideas of the Causes of both publick and private Good, who *promotes* the first Attempts of *corporeal Nature,* and exalts them to a greater height, by the *additional Force of the human Mind?*

But this seems to be sufficiently evident to all, especially because the whole *Operation of the Mind,* necessary to compleat human Happiness, may be deduced from what I have said concerning the manner in which the corporeal World is preserv'd; for it consists in these *two Things,*

Which is effected by the Subordination and balancing of Powers.

(1.) That the Endeavours of all particular Persons toward their own Preservation be made *subordinate* to such Endeavours or Actions as are evidently necessary to the Preservation of the Whole. (2.) That by this Method those Powers of all Individuals, necessary for Self-defence, be so *pois'd,* that no one can be destroy'd by any other, to the hazard and damage of the Whole. Something like these is observable in the Motions of the *Mundane* System, which arises from the Plenitude of the World,[43] and the Contact of Bodies, and therefore extends it self to them all. It is the work of the Mind and Reason to *observe,* "That every one's proper Happiness depends in a *nobler* manner upon the *voluntary* Actions of other *rational Agents,* even at a great distance"; and therefore to *take care,* "That all human Actions do in like manner contribute to the common Good of all rational Beings; as the Motions of all Bodies contribute to the Preservation of the corporeal System." This we shall effect, if these *two Things* which I have now mention'd, be observ'd in all voluntary Actions which respect others. Thus therefore we are *instructed* by the *Nature* of things, "How to promote the common Happiness, and our own, which is necessarily included therein": which is the same as to *say,* "We are *taught* what Actions are *commanded* by the *Law of Nature.*" And certainly all *prudent* Persons, in all kind of *Deliberations,* where Civil Laws take no place, or leave the matter to every Man's own Determination, naturally fix their Eyes on these things, and can *agree* among themselves upon these things only, which serve to promote the *common* Good of the *Parties consulting,* and so to *balance* the Powers of all, that it may be every one's Interest, that no one have Power to oppress another. Thus, among all *neighbouring States,* who are not subject to the same Government, this is the chief *View* in all Embassies, Covenants, and Leagues, so to *balance* the Powers of every particular

---

43. [Maxwell] "This *Hypothesis,* asserting the Plenitude of the World, or denying any Vacuum therein, is a fundamental Principle of the *Cartesian* Philosophy, and embrac'd by our Author, in whose time that Philosophy prevail'd much; but has since been disprov'd by Sir *Isaac Newton;* which, however, does not in the least affect our Author's Reasoning, which stands equally firm in either Case: For, whenever he makes use of an Hypothesis, it is only in order to illustrate, but not to prove any thing, to which Purpose the contrary Hypothesis would have serv'd as well."

State by mutual Assistance, that it should be *difficult* for them to *destroy* one another, but sufficiently *easy* to *preserve,* and, in some measure, enrich, themselves, which was the End of first erecting Civil States.

§XVI. In like manner, at the first *Establishment* of any *Commonwealth,* the *Powers* of all Orders and Parts are *mutually balanc'd* with the greatest Exactness, and are all subjected to the *supreme Power,* so as to be able mutually to assist, but hardly to hurt, one another. Nay, further, the *Preservation* of the Commonwealth, both from seditious and internal Evils, and from foreign Invasion, is only a *continued Establishment* of the same Balance of Power, and proceeds from Causes plainly alike. Moreover, whenever *new Laws* are to be *enacted,* or *old* ones to be *amended,* or receive an *equitable* Construction, all wise Men will ever have recourse to the Principles I have mention'd; and, universally, in all Cases where *civil Laws* are *silent,* or *cannot* bring a seasonable *Relief,* or where they allow a *Liberty* of acting, to Persons, whether in a publick or private Station, (which Cases, as *Hobbes* himself owns, are almost innumerable,)[44] *natural Rules* of human Actions can be taken from nothing else, than from the Consideration of the *common Good,* as the *End,* and from the Advantage of preserving that *Balance* of Power, which either *Nature* hath made, or the Constitution of the *Commonwealth* hath establish'd.

Which is illustrated from the Consideration of the Nature of Government,

Tho' I own, that the Power of *Order* and of conspiring to one common End, and also the Necessity of a *Balance* of Power in all Parts of any System, in order to the Preservation of the Whole, both may be, and usually are, observ'd in the Frame, whether Natural or Artificial, of such things especially as are most obvious, without any Skill in *Mathematicks,* and the *mechanical Philosophy* of the System of the World; in like manner, as much is discover'd concerning the *Numbers* and *Magnitudes* of Things, without any other *Arithmetick* and *Geometry,* than what is learn'd by common *Experience* only, without the Help of Books: *Yet* I thought it proper, in this stricter Research into the Nature of Causes, where we are endeavouring to obtain an *exact* Knowledge of the whole Matter, sometimes to have recourse to those *Sciences,* in which

And of the System of the World, without assuming any particular Hypothesis.

44. Hobbes, *On the Citizen,* 13.15, pp. 150–51.

these Notions are most distinctly explain'd, and in so general a manner, that they may, with great Advantage of *Illustration,* be thence easily ap-ply'd. So it is usual to have recourse to the *artificial* Rules of Arithmetick and Geometry, when any *Difficulty* arises relating to those Things, whose Number or Measure we have guess'd at by the Help of *natural Sagacity* only, or when we have occasion for an *exact* Computation. I chose to *illustrate* the present Argument by the *Example* of the *System of the World;* both *because* some *general,* tho confus'd, *Notion* thereof is *always* present to the Minds of *all,* and imprints upon them some *Idea* of the *greatest End,* the common Good, and of mutual Assistance, as the only *Means* to obtain it; and *because,* from those *general Motions* of the Sys-tem of the World, (of which only the Learned frame a distinct Idea,) the Powers, Orders, and Limits, of all *lesser Motions,* as from the most general Causes, are deduced; so that, in this Enquiry into *Causes,* we can never stop, till we arrive at the *First Causes* among those which are *cre-ated,* which lead us immediately to *God.* But let it suffice, to have hinted these things in general; from them it easily *appears,* "That those Powers, which, consider'd either singly or jointly with others, are very unequal, may yet be conveniently enough balanc'd among themselves in the same System, to the Preservation of the Whole." I thought it proper, not to make use of any *particular Hypothesis,* with respect to the System of the World; both *because* the *Resemblance* between the Manner and Causes, by which this material World and Mankind are preserv'd, does *not extend* it self to *all Circumstances,* (which is not necessary, in order to the Mind's learning something, which may be of publick Advantage;) and *because* what I have advanc'd is so *manifestly true,* that it must be admitted in *every Hypothesis:* Lastly, *because* to have added *more,* was *not necessary* to those who are *conversant in Natural Philosophy,* and to *others* it would be unacceptable, and seem *impertinent.*

II. As a Body, endow'd with Life and Sense, like other Animals. §XVII. II. *That Power* and *that Necessity* of being *subservient* to the Mo-tions of innumerable other Bodies, which I have shewn, from the general Nature of *Matter* and *Motion,* to be in *all Bodies,* as long as they continue in Motion, are found likewise in *human Bodies,* and seem to *persuade,* and readily incline, each particular Person to lend his Assistance to Mankind. But if to these we add those things which *distinguish* the Nature of *Animals* from *other Bodies,* they will *more strongly incline* us, and will lay before us a sufficient Reason, why we should be chiefly sollicitous to assist those of our *own Species,* with little *comparative* regard to *other* Bodies.

Bodies *Animate* are distinguish'd from *Inanimate,* by that Temper of Parts, and Configuration of Organs, which are sufficient for *Nutrition, Generation, Sensation, Imagination, Affections,* and *voluntary Motions;* and all unanimously agree, that, by these Actions, all kind of Animals endeavour their own *Preservation,* and *Perfection,* or Happiness, for the time appointed by the universal Causes of the World. Nor is it difficult, in some measure, to explain the Power and Causes of this *Endeavour,* from the Observations of Anatomists and Physicians, on the Circulation of the Blood and other useful Juices, and on the spreading of the Nerves thro' the whole Body of Animals, together with what Natural Philosophers have thence deduced, concerning the Causes of Hunger and muscular Motion; but it is not worth while to insist upon the Proof of Truths universally acknowledg'd; from these, as allow'd us by our Adversaries, it will be proper to draw some Inferences, which may make for our present Purpose. Such are,

First, "That, from the same inward Frame of Animals, which determines them to Self-Preservation, there are beside afforded manifest *Indications,* that their behaving themselves innocently and beneficently towards Animals of the same Species, is necessary to their own Preservation and happiest State": and then,

Secondly, "That, from the Concurrence of the same internal Causes, Animals cannot but be sensible of, and retain in Memory, these *Indications.*" The *former* of these summarily includes the *Precept* and the *Sanction* of the Laws of Nature; the *latter* respects their *Promulgation,* or the manner by which they become known: Therefore both these must be explain'd in their proper order.

In the *first* place it offers it self to our Observation, "That the Bodies of each Animal are contain'd within very narrow Limits, and that the time of their possible Duration is but small"; which is a sufficient *Indication,* that *each* has occasion for a *few* things only, in order to its Wel-

Whence the first *Indication* to Benevolence is this, That Men, being Animals of the

same kind with
other Men,
have therefore
their Appetite
of Self-
preservation
limited in like
manner; which
is therefore
very consistent
with a Permis-
sion to others
of the same
Species, to pre-
serve them-
selves likewise.

fare; or that, if some sort of *concurrence of many things* be necessary, it is no other, than what may at the *same time* be communicated to *many.* Hence they are by Nature induced to desire but *few* things for themselves *separately,* and to desire those things *in common* with others, whose Use may *conveniently* be *common* to many, such as Air and Light. The same Surface of *Skin,* which in every Animal *limits* the spreading and circulation of its *Blood,* by the same Power, sets *Limits* to those *Necessities,* which urge it to *Self-preservation.* All the Necessities of the Body are enclos'd within the Circumference of the Circle describ'd by the Blood of that Animal: Those *few* things which are sufficient to *fan* and *repair* this vital Fluid, are sufficient to the Preservation of *Life, Health,* and *natural Strength.* The *Quantity* of that *Juice* is very *small,* which, by twitching the Stomach and Throat of an Animal, excites *Hunger* and *Thirst;* and it therefore needs *no great Quantity* of *Meat* and *Drink* to rebate its force. Lastly, the *Capacity,* of those Vessels in which the Nourishment is prepar'd and fermented, of the Chyle-Vessels, and of the Veins and Arteries receiving it, is fill'd by a *Quantity* so determin'd and *small,* that I believe it evident, that no Animal, even of the Brute-kind, ever fell into *Hobbes's* Error, so as to think *all* things necessary to its own Preservation.

It is hence *evident,* from the *inward Frame* of Animals, "That it is necessary to their Preservation, that they take to themselves only a *few* things, to satisfy their Hunger and Thirst, and to repel the inclemency of the Weather, and leave the rest of fruitful Mother Earth's abundant Productions to those others, to whom they may be useful." Thus the *Quantity* of the *Bodies* of Animals, which is *naturally limited, limits* their *Appetites,* to seek only a *few* things necessary for themselves, leaving the rest to the use of others; whence *naturally* arises some kind of *division of Things,* among several Animals, in which is laid the *Foundation* of that Concord and *mutual Benevolence,* which we are inquiring after. For on this very account, that *Self-Love,* which is natural to Animals, is *limited* and satisfy'd in the manner I have now shewn, there is *no inducement* to their *opposing* the Preservation of others, either by debarring them from a free use of what is not necessary to themselves, or even by refusing to lend them their Labour, when it is of no further use to themselves;

but they are rather, on the contrary, thence *dispos'd* to *assist* others; whether from the *Pleasure,* tho it were not suppos'd very great,[45] which they receive from the Society of others, and the present Happiness thence arising; or from the *Hope* of their afterwards rewarding them with the like Assistance. *Animals* (I believe) are sensible, I am sure *Men* cannot be ignorant, that when once they have provided themselves with *Necessaries,* there remains nothing that can be of greater Advantage to them, than *Tranquillity,* and the *Society* of Animals of their *own Kind,* which can be procur'd or preserv'd, only by *Benevolence* towards them.

§XVIII. We may take the *second Indication,* from the Effects of the *Senses, Imagination,* and *Memory,* when they are employ'd about Animals of the *same kind;* for those Impressions, which, made upon the Senses of Animals, discover others to have a Nature very like their own, passing immediately into the Brain (where they go by the Name of *Imagination*) dispose them to Affections towards those of their own kind, like those they bear towards themselves, and that from the Constitution of their own Nature. Here I will industriously avoid all Controversies, concerning the *Knowledge of brute Animals,* of what *Kind* it is, and of the manner *how the Affections are mov'd by the Imagination;* I take this only for *granted,* "That the Imagination excites the Affections," and "That a like Imagination (as such) excites like Affections." The latter is a Consequence of the former; whence I would *infer* only thus much,

Secondly, That Likeness of Images, by which Animals of the same Species are represented, disposes them to Affections, like to those, by which they are inclin'd to their own Preservation.

45. [Maxwell] "I am of Opinion, that the Author here, in supposing the Pleasure, which Brutes receive from the Society of one another, not very great, means no more, than that it is very small, when compar'd with the Pleasures of Society among Men. For we have good reason to believe, from the Uniformity which we perceive in the Works of Nature, which we are acquainted with, that the Pleasures of Benevolence, as well among Brutes as Men, are the greatest and most refin'd of any which they enjoy. If it be *objected,* 'That the Pleasures of Benevolence are probably in different degrees, in proportion to the Usefulness of Society among them, but that Society is much more useful among Men than Brutes;' it may be *answer'd,* 'That to Bees, Ants, and some other Species, Society is as useful, in proportion to their Sources of Pleasure, as to Mankind.' And in most other Species it is also of great use. I believe, it will appear from a following *Note,* concerning the Behaviour of Men towards Brutes, that the Inquiry is not altogether unworthy of Regard."

"That a known Likeness of Natures, when discover'd, does somewhat promote Benevolence among those who are alike, except it be join'd with some unlikeness more strongly enforcing Enmity." To this it is owing, that Animals cannot wholly *forget others of the same Kind,* whilst they *remember themselves.* For *like* Animals (as far as they are such) are represented under the *same Image;* they also cannot but know, that they are subject to *like Hunger* and *Thirst* with themselves; and that they are therefore *equally* urg'd by Nature, to seek *Nourishment* for themselves; and that therefore it is *pleasing* to them, when they are permitted a free use of it, or when they are assisted in procuring it. Because Animals have perpetually such Images of others of the same Kind, and some benevolent Efforts thence necessarily arising from the Condition of their Nature, it *follows,* "That their *natural Disposition* is so far *thwarted,* as any thing *contrary* to such *natural Efforts* proceeds either from *Madness* or *Pleasure,* or any violent *Desires* or *Passions":* As all look upon it as a Distemper, and *praeternatural Disposition* of a Dog, who, thro' Rage or Madness, is unusually excited to bite every other Dog he meets. Nor can I see any Reason, why all kinds of *Affections,* which so *disturb* the Oeconomy of any particular Animal, as to hurry it on to Actions *destructive* to Animals of the *same Species,* (such as Malevolence, Envy, violent Fits of Anger, &c.) should not be look'd upon as certain *Distempers* of the Blood, and Brain perhaps, and somewhat a-kin to the Rage of a mad Dog. Such Affections are attended with manifest *Symptoms of Distempers,* an overflowing of the bilious Juices, a dangerous Effervescence of Blood, a Jaundice-Colour, Paralytick Tremblings, and other such Effects, well enough known to Physicians. Nor is raging *Anger* against Animals of the same Species, the *only Passion* which turns to a *formal Disease;* an excessive *Fear* of them is no less *Praeternatural;* that is, it is no less different from that Manner of all Animals, which arises from their natural and found Disposition; and, like other Distempers, it *prejudices* their *Health* by reducing them to Sadness, Solitariness, and unseasonable Watchings, with the other Symptoms of a predominant Melancholy, which *hastens* untimely *Death;* nor can any Measure or Bounds be set to this Fear, which is rooted in a false Imagination and Opinion, that all other Animals of the same Species, are naturally and necessarily inclin'd, to hurt, and fight against, them.

The Condition of such Animals, (and such *Hobbes* feigns all Men in a State of Nature,) is perfectly like the wretched State of those, who are seiz'd with a *Hydrophobia;*[46] they are afraid of Water and all Liquids, without which, (tho they sometimes hurt *accidentally,*) Life cannot be supported. And as this Opinion proceeds *not* from the *Nature* of the *Water,* but from an *Imagination disturb'd* by the Bite of a mad Dog, so it proceeds from a *distemper'd* Brain and *Imagination,* that any Animal is afraid of its whole Species, when in reality there is nothing pleasanter to those whose Brain is not disturb'd. It is too well *known* to need Proof, "That *Animals,* if by any Accident they have for some time been separated from others of the *same Kind,* as soon as they have come within sight of one another, even at a distance, immediately *rejoice,* shew their Joy by Gestures, run to one another, and with Pleasure eat, drink, and play together, but very seldom fight with one another; and, if at any time they happen to fight, that immediately after a Victory, for the most part obtain'd without any Damage, the same Animals herd again very lovingly and peaceably together." But because it is *evident,* "That the *Causes* of their thus *peaceably associating* and agreeing with one another, which are *essential* to Brutes, are plainly *necessary;* nor other than those, by which their Blood, Spirits, Brain and Nerves, are preserv'd in a *sound State";* it thence *follows* evidently, "That the Health of every one of them cannot be separated from an Inclination to associate friendly with those of the same Species, but is easily and naturally preserv'd therewith"; which was what was to be prov'd from this *second Indication,* which is common to all kinds of *Animals,* and consequently to *Men.*

§XIX. Near of kin to this is the *Third Indication,* taken from the *Pleasantness* of those *Affections, which are conversant about Good common to many:* This is of near Affinity with the precedent, because the Rise, and all the Powers, of the *Affections,* depend upon the *Imagination.* Natural

Thirdly, The Love Animals bear to those of their own Species, is a pleasant Affec-

46. Cf. Hobbes's use of the hydrophobia metaphor, *Leviathan,* ch. 29, p. 215.

tion, and its Exercise therefore closely connected with that Self-love, which is common to all Animals.

Philosophers very well *know,* "That the Motion of the Blood and Heart, which is necessary to Life, is befriended by Love, Desire, Hope and Joy, especially when conversant about a *great* Good; whence the Arteries and Veins are fill'd with better and more flowing Juices, brisker Spirits are produced, and the whole Circulation, and consequently all the animal Functions, perform'd with greater Ease." Nor is it less *evident,* "That the Good, which is known to extend it self to very many, (among which the Animal it self, concerning which we speak, is comprehended,) will upon this very account appear the *greatest.*" Wherefore *it self* will necessarily be much *befriended* by those very Affections, by which it *befriends other Animals* of the same kind with it self:[47] And for this very Reason, that it has *naturally* a perfect *Sense* of this *Effect* in it self, it will have a strong *Propension* to those *benevolent* Affections, as very *useful* to, and intimately united with, its own *Preservation,* and a *natural Reward* will follow such Affections. I affirm'd indeed, that *every Animal* perceives this agreeable Effect, or the *Pleasure* of such Passions; yet the *manner how* these Passions have this friendly Influence, is unknown to *most Men,* who are ignorant of natural Philosophy, much more is it above the Knowledge of *Brutes:* It is, however, sufficient, to excite the *Inclinations* I have mention'd, that they are sensible of the *Effect.* On the *contrary,* "In Envy, Hatred, Fear and Grief, the Motion of the Blood is retarded, and the Heart is clogg'd, so that it contracts, and expels the Blood, with difficulty; whence the Countenance of Man becomes pale, and numberless Mischiefs, in the whole Animal Oeconomy, but especially in the Functions of the Brain and Nerves, follow; such are the Distempers usually ascrib'd to the Spleen and Melancholy." This Matter belongs properly to the Consideration of *Physicians;* I therefore willingly resign it to the Skilful in that Art, who are daily industrious to adorn it with noble Discoveries for the Good of Mankind. I will, however, transcribe one

---

47. [Maxwell] "To what the Author has said upon this Head, may be *added,* 'That those who live to an healthful old Age, are, for the most part, remarkable, for an easy Chearfulness of Disposition, but that a natural unconstrain'd Chearfulness is always accompanied with Benevolence, is, I believe, sufficiently testify'd by every one's Experience.'"

extraordinary Case, from *Harvey's Anatomical Exercitation concerning the Circulation of the Blood,* which will be a noble Illustration of what I have advanc'd. "I knew" (says he) *"a high-spirited Man, who, thro' Anger and Indignation conceiv'd for an Injury, join'd with an Affront, receiv'd at the Hands of a powerful Person, so kindled with Rage, that, Envy and Hatred continually increasing for want of Revenge, and the strong Passion which rankled in his Mind being disclos'd to no one, he fell at length into a strange kind of Distemper, and was miserably afflicted with a great Oppression and Pain, both of his Heart and Breast, so that receiving no Relief from the Advice of the most Skilful, he fell, after some Years, into a scorbutick Habit of Body, which threw him into a Consumption, of which he died. He had some Ease, only as often and as long as the whole Region of his Breast was compress'd. His jugular Veins were swell'd, as thick as a Man's Thumb, with a Pulse high and strong, as if each of them were it self the Aorta, or great descending Artery, and appear'd like two oblong Aneurisms;*[48] *when I had dissected the Body, I found the Heart and Aorta so distended, and stuffed with Blood, that the Size of the Heart and Cavities of the Ventricles were as great as those of an Ox."* [49] Whence we may observe, that such Passions obstruct the Motion of the Blood in the small Branches of the Arteries, which are dispers'd thro' the Brain; and that vast Mischiefs arise thence to the Heart, and consequently to the whole Animal, with dire Symptoms of Distempers, whence Life it self (common to Man with other Animals) is greatly endanger'd. It is hence *evident,* "That the very Nature of an Animal, and of the Passions, admonishes Men, that it will be of Advantage to them, to be of a benevolent Disposition towards others, all, if possible"; since fierce Hatred against one Man brought so great Mischiefs to the Cherisher of the Passion.

§XX. Next follows the *fourth Indication* of the same thing, which is taken from hence, "That Animals are incited to *endeavour the Propagation of their own Species,* by the force of the same Causes, which pre-

Fourthly, The same is prov'd, from their natural Propen-

---

48. [Maxwell] "An *Aneurism* is a Tumour, form'd by the inward Coat of an Artery's being broke, and the Force of the Blood's distending the outward Coat."

49. Harvey, *Exercitatio Anatomica de Circulatione Sanguinis* (1649), pp. 89–90.

sion, to propa-
gate their Spe-
cies, and rear
their Off-
spring.
serve the Life of every Individual, so that these Two are connected by
Tie evidently natural." Hence it is, *that,* Animals of the same Species
but, *different Sexes are united,* by a strong Friendship, whence they perform to one another many mutual good Offices, and *that Offspring is
propagated,* which they love and cherish as their own Blood, except
something very unusual happens to change their natural Inclinations.
But those things, which so *rarely* happen, ought not to be brought *into
the account,* when we are taking a Survey of the ordinary and *regular*
State of Nature. The Connexion is very close between the *Propagation
of the Species,* and that *natural Affection,* which excites to an Endeavour
of nourishing the young when brought forth. *Preservation* is only a kind
of *continued Generation* of a thing; therefore the *same* natural Causes
will incline an Animal to *both:* But it is evident, that their Offspring
cannot be preserv'd, except Animals of the same Kind mutually *cultivate
Peace* or Benevolence. Therefore they naturally desire, that this Benevolence may be of as long *Continuance,* as they wish to their Offspring:
in such a *Benevolence,* which is *extensive* and *durable,* consists the *Pursuit
of the common Good* of the whole Species, in proportion to the Capacity
of the Animal, which, indeed, if Man be excepted, is but of a small
reach, and not at all provident. Yet that *low* degree of *Sagacity,* which
all *Animals* are possess'd of, is sufficient to enable them, to provide for
themselves and their *Young,* by the exercise of some kind of *Benevolence*
towards Animals of the same Kind. Because I *hinted,* "That the natural
Love of their Offspring, proceeds from the same Causes, which incline
Animals to propagate their Species," I must *shew,* "That this *Inclination*
is *essential* to Animals, whose Powers are come to their greatest *Perfection,* and that it flows from the same Causes, which are necessary to the
Preservation and Perfection of every Individual": Whence it *follows,*
"That it is necessary, that Animals should, along with their own Welfare,
endeavour the Continuation of their own Species, and, consequently,
promote the common Good." And this is evident, from the manner in
which Animals are *form'd,* and *nourish'd:* for it is certain, (as *Harvey* has
observ'd,)[50] that the *same Causes* which, in the Womb or Egg, form the
Parts requisite to the *Nourishment* of the *Individual,* (as the Stomach,

50. Harvey, *Exercitationes de Generatione Animalium* (1651), exert. 69, pp. 305–14.

Heart, &c.) do likewise form the *spermatick Vessels,* and *difference of Sexes,* in the first rough-draught of Animals. From the *same Mass* of nutritious Juice mingled with the Blood, *part* goes into *Nourishment, part* into *Seed* for propagating the Species. The whole Circulation of the Blood, and every thing instrumental thereto, as the muscular Force of the Heart, and the Contrivance of the Valves in the Veins, is at the same time subservient to the *private* Nourishment of the Individual, and to the *publick* Good by propagating the Species, whilst it sends off the Materials of the Seed to the spermatick Vessels. Lastly, whatever any of the Bowels, or other Parts of the Body, perform towards preserving the *natural State of the Blood,* at the same time tends to preserve the *Life of the Individual,* and, remotely at least, disposes to the *Procreation of Offspring,* which is hinder'd by every great Disorder of the Blood.

I might here expatiate very largely; but, lest I should be too prolix, I thought it proper to leave the Remainder of what belongs to this Subject, to be farther pursued by such Readers as are skilful in *Natural Philosophy* and *Medicine,* and to be apply'd, by a Parity of Reason with what I have already suggested, to the forming a *Rule of Manners* from the *Indications of Nature,* I will add only this, that it is very *evident,* "That Animals are in the manner above-mention'd inclin'd to the *Love* of the *other Sex,* and of their *Offspring,* and thus divest themselves of a contracted *Selfishness,* which when they have once laid aside, they are easily induc'd to proceed still *further* in the *Love of others,* till at last, upon account of their *Likeness of Nature,* it takes in *all of the same Species";* and, consequently, that the *Observation* of common Experience has its Foundation in the common Nature of Animals, "That Men are more inclin'd to Peace after begetting Children, and that their natural Propension to beget Children disposes all to the Love of Peace."

I must here, however, take notice of that common *Evasion,* by which many are wont to *elude* this and other *Indications* taken from *natural Inclinations,* whence human *Reason* may learn the *Law of Nature,* "That, altho it often happens that, by means of these Inclinations, many are profited, yet they all proceed from the Love of our own Pleasure only, and, consequently, that all the Actions flowing from hence have no other End, and that they therefore discover no thing but mere Self-Love."

I *answer,* 1. It is evident from what I have already said, that I do not

(All our Actions cannot be resolv'd into a principle of Self-Love; and, tho they could, that would not take away the Obligations to promote the common Good.)

take any *Indication of a Law of Nature,* obliging to promote the common Good, from the *End* which Animals propose to *themselves;* I affirm nothing concerning their *Intentions.*

2.[51] It cannot be prov'd, that Animals, in those *voluntary* Actions, by which they *actually* promote the Good of *others,* as well as *themselves,* do not *alike* intend and *will both.* It is certainly much more probable, that *both* Effects are *equally intended;* since it is so in *all* those *Cases,* where Men act *deliberately;* for they *intend* to produce *all the foreseen Effects* of their Actions, tho some of them *move* them to Action much *more strongly* than others, and *delight* them much *more,* after the Action is over; yet *every thing* which they *intend* to effect, is justly call'd an *End* of Action.

3. Supposing, but not granting, that Animals sought their *own Preservation and Happiness only,* as their *End,* and that they exercis'd *Benevolence* towards other Animals of the same Kind, as the *Means,* naturally and perpetually necessary to that End; yet even *this Supposition* would prove, that there was an *Indication* from *Nature,* "That the common Good of the whole Species was to be promoted," and thence would arise an *Obligation* to the use of *Means* so *necessary,* which would be *no less valid* than our Obligation to the *End* suppos'd, *viz.* Self-preservation. For the *Obligation* is the *same* to the necessary *Means,* and to the *End* it self. And this *Obligation* is *equally valid,* with any which can arise from the *Punishments of Civil Laws,* which can inflict nothing greater than *Death,* and which these *Objectors* contend, is by far the *greatest,* or rather the *only* real *Obligation* we lie under. For this Reason therefore, among many others, *Hobbes's* Argument is vain, who (that he might take away all *natural Obligation* to promote the *common* Good) endeavours to resolve all *natural Propensions* tending thereto, into a Desire of preserving or of *pleasing one's self only.* So, partly in his Treatise *of human Nature,*

---

51. [Maxwell] "The Author seems too complaisant to *Hobbes* in this Point. 'Tis certain, we often desire the Good of others, without ever considering it as the means of private Good, or having any such selfish Intention, as is evident in the *Natural Affections of Parents Toward Their Children, Friendship, Patriotism.*"

(Chap. 9. § 10, 15, 16, 17.)[52] partly in that *de Cive* (Chap. 1. § 2.) he affirms, not only that the *Love* by which Animals are inclin'd to the *Propagation* of their Species, but also, that the *natural Affection,* with which they embrace and rear their Offspring, and all *Charity* towards others, and *Compassion* towards the Afflicted, arise from hence, "That Animals, by these Actions, *either seek some Advantage to themselves, or, at least, that they may think magnificently of their own Powers, or have a good Opinion of themselves,*"[53] which is *Hobbes's* Definition of *Glory;* but, beside that the inward Force of these *Affections,* and their *Effects,* by which they are much *more* serviceable to *others,* than to the Agents *themselves,* are an evident Proof of the contrary; and that those Animals, in which these Affections are vigorous, are *sensible* enough of *this,* and therefore cannot but *intend greater Advantages to others than to themselves:* If it be *granted,* "That these Affections are necessarily in Animals, that they may make themselves happy by certain Advantages and this imaginary Glory," nevertheless the *Obligation to Actions advantageous to others* would remain, lest they should in any respect be *wanting to themselves,* in those things which he supposes to be *naturally* and *necessarily,* and, consequently, perpetually *desir'd.* For it is impossible, but that they must be influenc'd by the *Hope* of enjoying these Advantages, and by the *Fear* of losing them, if those Actions, which respect the Good of others, be neglected; and *Hobbes* acknowledges, that *natural Obligation* takes place, where human Liberty is restrain'd by *Hope* or *Fear, de Cive, c.* 15. § 7.[54] This Reasoning seems to me conclusive against *Objections* upon *Hobbes's* Principles. In what consists the Nature of *moral Obligation,* I have elsewhere explain'd; I will here only *add,* "That in the true Rules of Morality, whence natural Obligation arises, so diminutive an End as the Preservation of one Man only, is not regarded, but the common Happiness of all rational Beings." On the contrary, *Hobbes* proposes this *little End* as the *Rule* of all *human Actions,* with this View, that they may

---

52. Hobbes, *Elements of Law,* 9.10, 15, 16, 17. These sections deal with pity, lust, love, and charity.

53. Hobbes, *On the Citizen,* 1.2, pp. 21–25.

54. Ibid., 15.7, pp. 174–75.

neglect any Actions whatsoever, and any natural benevolent Propensions, whensoever they shall not seem to make for their own *private Advantage,* altho in reality "The Desire of the publick Good testify'd by outward Actions, is always a Means necessary to the chief Happiness of every particular Man"; which yet most, who are blinded with Self-Love, are generally ignorant of.

Lastly, Not to dwell too long upon the Solution of this *Objection,* it is to be consider'd, that I have drawn my Conclusion, not from *voluntary* Actions, whose Ends are various in different Animals, and in the same Animal at different times, but from such Actions and Inclinations as are evidently *necessary,* which are in Animals even *not conscious* of them, and sometimes *opposing* them; and which, as I briefly hinted, proceed from the very *Frame* and *Temper* of their *Bodies;* for it is not owing to their *chusing* and desiring to preserve themselves, but to the *natural* Contraction of the Heart, that the Blood is sent off to the spermatick Vessels, and the Seed thence separated and brought to Perfection, whence arise in all Animals, venereal Inclinations, and a *Desire of begetting and preserving Offspring.* For both Appetites are Effects of the same Cause: Just as from the same matter an Animal is at first form'd, and for some time nourish'd and grows in the Egg or Womb; yet of *these things* the Parents are so *little conscious,* that, tho they concur, as *Instruments* to the Production of the *Effect,* yet they know not before their Offspring comes into the World, whether what they have begotten be *Male* or *Female,* whether it receives its *Nourishment* by the *Mouth* or *Navel,* or both: Nay, whether it is at all nourish'd, or whether it *lives* or no. It is hence *evident,* "That, in the forming and nourishing the *Foetus,* Animals are not *directed* by their *Knowledge* foreseeing the Effect or End, much less by the Prospect of *preserving* their own *Life* by this Method, for that is rather *weakened* by the *Propagation* of the Species; but that these *Actions* are done by them *without Deliberation,* and that the *Propensions* to these Actions are in a *high Degree necessary":* In these Actions Animals are plainly like Plants, which, tho they are *void* of *Sense* and all *Prospect* of an *End,* yet do not draw in Nourishment for *themselves alone,* but produce Seed for the *Propagation* of their Species. And as in Eggs are contain'd both the Body of the Chicken, and proper Nourishment for it, till it becomes strong enough to procure its Food elsewhere, and to digest it; so also in Seeds, beside the small Bud, (which is the rough-draught of a future Plant,) is contain'd also a fit Substance, which, after moistening, and a certain kind of Fermentation arising from a proper Heat, insinuates it self into the tender Roots of the Bud, which it nour-ishes till it has got Strength enough to imbibe Nourishment out of the neighbouring Earth. But afterwards, when the *Foetus* is born, Animals perceiving, that an *Animal like themselves* is form'd from their own Blood, by the Concurrence of their own natural Powers, they are in-wardly *dispos'd not to destroy* it, by any *Act* or voluntary *Neglect* of theirs. What I have now advanc'd, is well enough known to *natural Philoso-phers;* which if any one desires to see more distinctly explain'd, he may consult *Harvey* and *Highmore of Generation,* and *Needham* in his learned Treatise *of the Formation of the Foetus.* [55] These few Observations are sufficient to *prove* "That a strong Tendency, not only to propagate their Species, but to nourish it when propagated, arises from the very Frame and natural Disposition of Animals (nay, and of Plants too) which proceeds from universal and determin'd Causes." What is more, it is well known from *Experience,* "That these *Propensions* grow *stronger* in Animals by *Age* and *Practice,* so that any Accident thwarting these, produces in them strong Resentments." Hence Mankind shed those *Tears,* which fall in case of *disappointed Love,* of *Barrenness,* or *Loss of Children.* Therefore one may easily *infer,* from these, and innumerable other like Instances which daily happen, "That the ordinary State of Animals would, for the most part, be very disagreeable to 'em, unless (to the best of their Power) they enter, by Benevolence towards others of the same Species, into a friendly Society with them, by whose Assistance they may beget Offspring, and rear them as safely as possible."

Lastly, The *whole Frame* of Animals, (because it is the necessary Cause of their usual Functions and Actions,) plainly *indicates,* "That from the *same* internal Causes proceed both *Actions* in order to *Self-preservation,* and *Affections* of so great *Benevolence,* as are sufficient for a friendly As-

Fifthly, Benevolence among Animals of the same Species, prov'd from the intire

55. Harvey, *Exercitationes de Generatione Animalium* (1651); Highmore, *The History of Generation* (1651); Needham, *Disquisitio Anatomica de Formata Foetu* (1667).

Frame of
Animals. sociation with other Animals of the same Species": for these *two* are
generally exerted by *all* Kinds of Animals, altho it happens sometimes,
but rarely, thro' *Ignorance* or *irregular Passions,* that they hurt either
themselves or *others* of the same Species. Therefore, because *Concord*
among them is much *more frequent* than *Discord,* it *follows,* "That the
natural and *internal* Causes of Concord are *stronger,* or that their Nature, without the Assistance of civil Society, does more strongly incline
them to this Affection than to Discord"; which is the principal Point I
contend for. For (unless it appear, that the *Animal Nature* in *Men* is
fiercer or less inclinable to Peace than the same in *Brutes*) this is sufficient
to prove, that in all *Deliberations* upon future Events (in which we can
only reckon upon what happens for the *most part*) we may *conclude* in
general, "That a peaceable Association with others will be more agreeable
to our natural Inclinations, and that the same is more probably to be
expected in others, than the contrary, tho in some Cases it may happen
otherwise." As any one may with truth affirm, that it is more agreeable
to the Nature of a Die, that a Six should not be thrown at the first Cast,
than that it should; because there are five possible Cases inconsistent with
this Cast, and but one that favours it. That *Brute* Animals act, for the
most part, benevolently with others of their own Kind, is easy to prove,
by taking a View of all those things, which I have in the *first Chapter*
shewn to be requisite, that any thing may be said to be subservient to
the publick Good of any Species.[56] They generally abstain from mutually hurting one another.[57] *Juvenal* has long since observ'd what makes
much for our present Purpose.

――― Mollissima corda
Humano generi dare se natura fatetur,

56. See Cumberland, *A Treatise of the Laws of Nature,* 1.24, 25.
57. [Maxwell] "Goodness of Temper, and Proneness to Society, mutual Aid, and
Compassion, tho in a weaker Degree, yet is observable among all Brutes toward their
own Species. Where Animals of the same Species are found prone to fighting, they
are such as do not continue in their natural State, but are pamper'd and artificially
fed by Men. And, this too happens only among some few Species, and will not continue, if they are restor'd to their natural manner of Feeding."

Quae lacrymas dedit. Haec nostri pars optima sensus.
Plorare ergo jubet casum lugentis amici,
Squaloremque rei, pupillum ad jura vocantem
Circumscriptorem, cujus manantia fletu
Ora puellares faciunt incerta capilli.
Naturae imperio gemimus, cum funus adultae
Virginis occurrit, vel terra clauditur infans,
Et minor igne rogi. Quis enim bonus & face dignus
Arcana, qualem Cereris vult esse sacerdos,
Ulla aliena sibi credat mala? separat hoc nos
A grege mutorum, atque ideo venerabile soli.
Sortiti ingenium, divinorumque capaces,
Atque exercendis, capiendisque artibus apti
Sensum à coelesti demissum traximus arce,
Cujus egent prona, & terram spectantia. Mundi
Principio indulsit communis conditor illis
Tantum animas, nobis animum quoque, mutuus ut nos
Adfectus petere auxilium, & praestare juberet,
Dispersos trahere in populum, migrare vetusto
De nemore, & proavis habitatas linquere silvas;
Aedificare domos, Laribus conjungere nostris
Tectum aliud, tutos vicino limite somnos
Ut collata daret fiducia: protegere armis
Lapsum, aut ingenti nutantem vulnere civem;
Communi dare signa tuba, defendier iisdem
Turribus, atque una portarum clave teneri.
Sed jam serpentum major concordia: parcit
Cognatis maculis similis fera. Quando leoni
Fortior eripuit vitam leo? quo nemore unquam
Expiravit aper majoris dentibus apri?
Indica tigris agit rabida cum tigride pacem
Perpetuam: saevis inter se convenit ursis.

Juven. Satyr. 15.[58]

---

58. Juvenal, *Satires,* XV.131–64. Cumberland quotes only lines 159–64. (Maxwell highlights the original quotation in italics.)

Compassion proper to Mankind appears,
Which Nature witness'd, when she lent us Tears.
Of tender Sentiments we only give
Those Proofs: To Weep is our Prerogative;
To shew by pitying Looks, and melting Eyes,
How with a Suff'ring Friend we Sympathize!
Nay, Tears will ev'n from a wrong'd Orphan slide,
When his false Guardian at the Bar is try'd:
So tender, so unwilling to accuse,
So oft the Roses on his Cheek bedews,
So soft his Tresses, fill'd with trickling Pearl,
You'd doubt his Sex, and take him for a Girl.
B'Impulse of Nature (tho to us unknown
The Party be) we make the Loss our own;
And Tears steal from our Eyes, when in the Street
With some betrothed Virgin's Hearse we meet:
Or Infant's Fun'ral, from the cheated Womb
Convey'd to Earth, and Cradled in a Tomb.
Who can all Sense of Others Ills escape,
Is but a Brute at best in Human Shape.
This natural Piety did first refine
Our Wit, and rais'd our Thoughts to Things Divine:
This proves our Spirit of the Gods descent,
While that of Beasts is prone and down-ward bent.
To them but Earth-born Life they did dispense,
To us, for mutual Aid, Coelestial Sense;
From straggling Mountainers, for publick Good,
To rank in Tribes and quit the Salvage Wood;
Houses to build, and them contiguous make,
For chearful Neighbourhood and Safety's sake;
In War, a common Standard to erect,
A wounded Friend in Battle to protect;
The Summons take of the same Trumpet's Call
To sally from one Port, or man one publick Wall.
But Serpents now more Amity maintain!
From spotted Skins the Leopard does refrain;
No weaker Lion's by a stronger slain.

Nor, from his larger Tusks, the Forest Boar
Commission takes his Brother Swine to gore.
Tyger with Tyger, Bear with Bear you'll find
In Leagues Offensive and Defensive join'd.
English'd by Mr. Tate.[59]

What is more, they behave *more mildly* toward those, with whom they have *herded for some time;* and the Practice of the *Storks,* who feed their disabled Parents, in which are to be found some Footsteps of *Gratitude,* is notorious.[60] In all these is observable a *limited Love,* both of *themselves* and their *Offspring,* and they are inclin'd to do several *mutual good Offices,* not trifling ones only, as when they play together, but very considerable, as when they assist one another against a common Enemy; and they *signify* their *Expectation* thereof, by a particular kind of *Voice,* by which most Animals, when sensible of approaching Danger, call others to their Assistance. These things are (if you consider the *Substance* of the Actions) the *same* with those which I have affirm'd to be necessarily included in the *care of the publick Good,* which, indeed, are perform'd very *imperfectly* by *Brutes,* yet in proportion to that *slender Knowledge,* which they use about things necessary to *their own Preservation.*

§XXI. If we inquire into those *Causes,* which are so interwoven into the Frame of *Animals* as to become part of their *Nature,* and which determine them generally to such a Conduct, besides those whence I have taken the foregoing *Indications,* the following are *peculiar* to them, as they are distinguish'd from *inanimate* Bodies. First, their *Frame,* as being made up of Parts very different, needs *more* things for its Preservation, than *Minerals* or *Plants* do. For the Blood, and other Liquors necessary to Life, as the Lymph, Bile, Pancreatick Juice, and perhaps a Nervous Fluid, and Animal Spirits, are so perpetually subject to Change

Sixthly, Benevolence is inforc'd among Animals of the same Species, by their numerous wants, and the most probable Method of relieving them, from natural Assistance.

59. The translation comes from Nahum Tate's contribution to John Dryden's *The Satires of Decimus Junius Juvenalis* (1693), pp. 303–5.

60. Pliny, *Natural History,* X.xxxii.63 [Maxwell incorrectly cites X.23]: "Storks nourish their parents' old age in their turn"; Solinus, *Polyhistor,* ch. 40: "Storks show extraordinary loyalty; indeed see how much time they spend in bringing up their young, the young supporting them as much in turn."

and Perspiration, that there is continual Occasion for *new Recruits,* and also for *Exercise, Rest, Sleep, Watching,* and moderate *Affections,* to *restore* to a just Temper what has been *chang'd,* or *repair* what has been *spent.* Hence arise very uneasy Sensations of *Hunger, Thirst,* and various *Diseases,* and these excite them to search for, and try, the most convenient Methods of acquiring *Nourishment, Medicine,* and other Helps, such as an Estimate of their own Powers, and a Knowledge of things about them shall suggest. But they are conversant with nothing *better known* to them, than Animals of their *own Species,* of whole *Powers* and *Necessities* they make an easy Estimate from their *Likeness to their own,* and, from the same Likeness of Nature, they conceive some Hope of their *Love* and *Assistance.* The Cause of that *Hope* is, *partly,* because *like Things* usually beget *like Images* of themselves, and, consequently, *like Affections* (except there arise some great Impediment, such as *Passion, Error,* a very *disagreeable unlikeness, &c.*) causing them to embrace other Animals of the *same Kind* with themselves, with the *same Love* as themselves: *Partly,* because they foresee great and innumerable *Evils* arising from *Discord* and Contention, but that *scarce any Good* can be *thence* expected. For *Equality of Strength,* or many Accidents which may set a *smaller* Power upon a *level* with a *greater,* (such as Sleep, Weariness, Diseases, the Confederacy of several weaker Powers, various accidental Advantages arising from the Place, by means whereof the weaker may overcome the stronger,) will give them frequent Opportunities of *mutually* hurting or killing one another. For if *contending Powers* by any means become *equal,* they are to one another mutually, as *Weights counterpoising* one another, of which each can with-hold the other from the lower place, to which it tends, and neither of them can reach the Place, to which it-self tends. Such are the *Mischiefs* arising from the *Contention* of *one* Animal with *another* of *equal* Power, tho *each* were at Peace with *all the rest.* But if each *One* should wage War with *all the rest,* there would be so frequent Contests with Forces *vastly superior,* that there would remain no *Hope* of Life to any. To be brief, it is *probable,* "That, even in the Judgment of Brutes, it is better, where there is plenty of all things necessary to the Preservation of every Individual, amicably, as occasion offers, to share in the Use of Things, and assume only what is at present necessary, than to expose themselves to the Hazards of perpetual War, in order to acquire Plenty of Things not necessary." But in the *Will* to *allow* such a *Division* of Things and mutual Services, and to *preserve* it after it is made, is contain'd the *Sum* of all *Actions,* by which the *common Good* of every one's Species is procur'd; wherefore "Even *Brutes* themselves, in some measure, perceive the *Connexion* between their own *Preservation,* and Actions contributing to the *common Good* of their Species, and for this Reason act *benevolently* to one another"; which was to be prov'd. I will add only this, that all those things which I have observ'd in Animals, are to be consider'd *jointly,* as concurring to *enable* and *incline* Animals to promote the *common Good* of their own Species, and that so *strongly* and *constantly,* that, except Animals comply therewith, they will *want* a great part of their *Happiness,* (which consists in the gratifying of their natural Inclinations,) and will *find* a *Grief* arising from this Struggle of *vain Passions,* which oppose those most *natural Principles of Action,* whose Force depends upon no Delusion of the Imagination; and are therefore justly distinguish'd from those Passions which I call'd *vain,* because they proceed from a deluded Fancy. It is with this View, that I inquir'd into the *Causes* of this *Benevolence towards Animals of the same Species,* which by the help of *Reason* may be rais'd to a *greater* Degree of *Pefection.*

§XXII. *Hobbes* was not ignorant, that this was no way consistent with his Principles, and therefore he abounds with such Insinuations as these to the contrary: That *"Men are fiercer than Bears, Wolves, and Serpents";* that *"Their natural State is a State of War of All against All,"* that *"Among them there is no such thing as publick Good or Evil, before the Establishment of civil Government,"* and that *"Therefore there is no Knowledge or Desire of such Good."* I have elsewhere cited the Passages in which he has advanc'd this Doctrine;[61] but here falls properly under Consideration a Passage in his *Leviathan, Chap.* 17. (which is agreeable to what he advances, *de Cive,* c. 5. § 5.) where he thus *objects* to himself, *"That certain*

Hobbes's Objections against the Argument, drawn from the Association of other Animals, answer'd,

---

61. Hobbes, *De Homine,* 10.3; *On the Citizen,* 1.13.

living Creatures, as Bees and Ants, live sociably one with another"; [62] and he asks, What hinders but that Men may do the same? He reduces his *Answer* to six Heads; of which the Substance is this.

1. *"Men are continually in competition for Honour and Dignity, which these Creatures are not."* [63] I *reply;* "That *civil Honours* (about which Contentions sometimes arise) have *no* place in a *State of Nature,* or before the establishing civil Government among Men, and that, therefore, they cannot contend about them in a State of Nature, (concerning which is the present Question,) more than *Brute* Animals." In the next place, *"true Glory,"* of such Honour as can be attain'd out of civil Society, according to *Cicero's* Definition, is *"The concurrent Praise of good Men, and the incorrupt Voice of those who form a true Judgment of eminent Virtue."* [64] But the *Pursuit of the common Good* comprehends *all Virtues,* and thence only is procur'd the *Praise* of *good* Men. *War,* and that against all, is so far from being an *Effect* of the *Desire* of such *Honour,* that, on the contrary, Men are *by this Motive excited,* beyond other Animals, to the Exercise of all the *Virtues,* which *Hobbes* himself owns to be necessary *Means* of the common *Peace. Leviath.* 15. [65]

2. He *answers,* 2dly. That *"Among all those Creatures, the Common Good differs not from the Private, and being by Nature inclin'd to their Private, they procure thereby the Common Benefit. But Man, whose Joy consisteth in comparing himself with other Men, can relish nothing but what is eminent."* [66] To this I *answer;* "That we are oblig'd to *Hobbes,* that he has *unawares acknowledg'd,* that there is such a thing as the publick or *common Good,* out of civil Society, and that this is really procur'd by *Brutes* themselves." Elsewhere he affirms the contrary; see his Treatise *de Homine,* c. 10. in the latter end. [67] I am of *opinion,* "That the *Knowledge*

62. Hobbes, *Leviathan,* ch. 17, p. 108; *On the Citizen,* 5.5, p. 71.

63. Ibid.

64. Cicero, *Tusculan Disputations,* III.ii.3–4.

65. Hobbes, *Leviathan,* ch. 15, p. 100.

66. Ibid., ch. 15, p. 108. Maxwell quotes the English version. There is a minor difference in the Latin version quoted by Cumberland, for which see *Leviathan,* p. 108, n. 4.

67. Hobbes, *De Homine,* 10.5, p. 60.

of the *publick Good,* disposes Men to *Peace* and *Virtue,* as in its own Nature *amiable,* and the strongest *Security of private Good."* Its *differing* (in *some* Cases) from the *private Good* of *some* Particulars, is not a sufficient Reason, why Men should *war* amongst themselves, rather than *Bees* or *Ants,* whose *common* Good is distinguish'd from the *Private* in the *same* manner. What he adds concerning *Men,* if it be taken *universally,* as the Words seem to import, is most *false* and groundless; unless, perhaps, he sends us to that general *Demonstration,* as he calls it, of such Matters, which he hints in the Preface to his *Leviathan;*[68] *Hobbes,* truly, knew *himself,* and that with respect to *his own* Possessions, he relish'd nothing but what was *Eminent,* upon comparing himself with other Men, and thence he concludes, that *all others* are in the *same* Sentiments. But he ought to have shewn something in the *Nature of Things,* or of *Men,* that imposes a *Necessity* upon all Men to form *such* a Judgment. All who reason justly, know certainly, from their *natural Wants* and the *Use of Things,* what Judgment to pass upon their *own Affairs,* whether they relish them or not, and in what degree, *without comparing* them with those of other Men. They are *foolish* or *envious* Persons, who take pleasure only in the *Excess* of their own Enjoyments above those of others. But if he would have his Assertion understood, with *Limitation* to *such* Men only, he does not assign a *sufficient Cause* of a *universal War* of All against All, but only of some accidental Contention rais'd by the *Foolish* and *Envious,* which the Reason or Force of wiser Men may easily restrain from hurting All.

3. He *answers,* 3dly. That *"These Creatures, having not (as Man) the Use of Reason, do not see, or think they see, any Fault in the Administration of their common Business: Whereas amongst Men it is otherwise: Hence War."*[69] To which I thus *answer;* "That this Reason suggests nothing to hinder Men from living peaceably with one another, tho they were subject to no civil Government; in which case their *natural Propensions to universal Benevolence,* and all the *Laws of Nature,* would take place, not-

---

68. Hobbes, *Leviathan,* Introduction, pp. 4–5.
69. Ibid., ch. 17, p. 108.

withstanding any thing here alledg'd to the contrary."[70] Nor does he offer any thing which proves, but that such Men may agree among themselves to *erect* Civil Government, (for the Causes of such hindrance are what we at present inquire into;) he only objects what may hinder the *Preservation* of Government already *establish'd* by Consent alone. Let *Hobbes* look to it, whether or no what he here asserts concerning the Temper of the Generality of Mankind, will not *as effectually* unsettle the Foundation of Peace, in a Commonwealth establish'd by his fictitious UNION. *"Among Men"* (saith he) *"There are very many that think themselves wiser, and able to govern the Publick better, than the rest; and these strive to reform and innovate, one this way, another that way, and thereby bring it into Distraction and Civil War."*[71] Do not Men, *so dispos'd,* usually *violate* the *Compacts* they have mutually enter'd into, and break into Civil War? It is farther to be *consider'd,* "That *human Reason* does much *more effectually* promote *Peace* and *Concord,* by discovering numberless *Delusions* of the *Imagination* and *Passions, than Discord,* by its own *Fallibility,* in such Things as are always necessary to the common Peace, which are but *few,* and very *evident."* Farther, "Men don't immediately make War, as soon as they think they see any Fault in the Administration of the Publick"; the *same Reason,* which *discovers* the Fault, also *admonishes* them, that many things are to be borne with for Peace-sake, and *suggests* several Methods, by which the redressing such Grievance may be peaceably attempted. I *appeal* to your Judgment, *can-*

---

70. Maxwell, as Barbeyrac notes (*Traité Philosophique* p. 152, n. 8), in an attempt to make sense of the confused original, makes Cumberland say something odd: Replying to Hobbes's accusation that conflict is caused by individuals assuming they know better than others how common business is to be transacted, Maxwell's translation stresses that men will find it easy to live together even without civil government, whereas the logic of the original passage is to emphasize that even without civil government, there is nothing to suggest that their natural propensions to benevolence and the law of nature would prevent them from transacting common business, notwithstanding anything Hobbes says to the contrary. Cumberland, *De Legibus Naturae,* p. 125: "Rationem hanc nihil suggere quò minus hominess pacatè inter se agerent, si nullam esset regimen Civile cui subjicerentur; quo casu propensiones naturals ad benevolentiam universalem, legèsq; naturae omnes locum haberent, his non obstantibus."

71. Hobbes, *Leviathan,* ch. 17, p. 108.

did Reader, whether *Reason* makes the Condition of *Man worse* than that of *Brutes?* Does not *Hobbes* rather form an *unjust* Judgment of Men, who *accuses* their *Reason* of all the *Miseries* arising from *War* and *Discord,* and for this Reason contends, that *Men* live *less peaceably* with one another, than irrational *Brutes?* But this whole Answer of *Hobbes's* is nothing to the Purpose. The *Question* is, "Concerning the Obligation of the Precepts of right Reason, *before the erecting of Government":* The *Answer* is, "That the Reason of many Men is so erroneous, as to *dissolve Governments* already erected."

4. He asserts, 4thly. That *"Men cannot live sociably with one another as Bees, &c. because those Animals want that Art of Words, by which some Men can represent to others, that which is Good in the Likeness of Evil, and Evil in the Likeness of Good, &c. discontenting Men, and troubling their Peace at their Pleasure."*[72] Truly, because it *sometimes happens,* that Seditions are rais'd by the help of the false colouring of Speech; therefore Men, because they *can* make such use of Speech, *certainly will* not preserve Peace among themselves. Here is evidently no Consequence. For he ought to *prove,* "That Men *necessarily,* or at least *certainly,* have the *Will* to use, and that *constantly,* such *seditious* Speeches as tend to raise War"; especially, since there are so many Causes, both *within* and *without* them, that *rather* persuade them to cultivate *Peace.* He ought likewise to *prove,* "That such Speeches *necessarily,* or at least *always,* have so great an Effect upon *all* or *most* of their Hearers, as to ingage them immediately in *War."* For "They may, perhaps, be too *sharp-sighted,* to suffer themselves to be *imposed* upon by rhetorical varnish." It is *possible,* "That they may rather listen to the *peaceable* Speeches of the *Prudent,* supported by *more solid* Arguments." It is *possible,* "That they may rather weigh the *importance of Things,* than the empty *Sound of Words";* to which they certainly have a *natural Tendency;* for they well know, that *Words* will not feed or defend them from Injuries, but that *Actions,* pro-

---

72. Ibid. Cumberland paraphrases Hobbes's Latin to reveal Hobbes's concerns about the instability of language. For discussion, see Skinner, "Hobbes on Rhetoric and the Construction of Morality" in Skinner, *Visions of Politics* (2002), vol. III, pp. 87–141.

ceeding from *mutual Benevolence,* will. What hinders, but that the Persuasion of *good* Men may *prevail,* which the *Reason,* both of the *Speaker* and *Hearer,* and the very *nature of Things* themselves, favour? Why may not the Tongue of the *Ambassador of Peace* prevail above that which sounds the *Trumpet of War?* All *cautious* Person regard diligently, rather what others *do,* than what they *say;* and, beside, take care, that the *Power* of those whom they *trust* be so *balanc'd,* that they may not be *able* to hurt them, without their own great *Peril.* But, if the Reader further considers, how great Force *Words,* both spoken and written, are of, to the making of all *Contracts,* and to the preserving the Memory of *Laws,* (by which *two* subsists all peaceable *Society;*) I doubt not, but that he will *agree* with me, "That they have a much *greater Tendency* to *establish,* than *banish,* Peace, and that they are, therefore, to be reckon'd among the *Advantages* of Mankind, and not among those things, which make Men *more inhuman* than *Brutes* themselves."

5. *Hobbes* urges, *"Irrational Creatures cannot distinguish between Injury and Damage, and, therefore, as long as they be at ease, they are not offended with their Fellows. Whereas Man is then most troublesome, when he is most at ease: for then it is that he loves to shew his Wisdom, and censure the Actions of them who govern the Commonwealth."*[73] The *Antithesis,* or Opposition, here *insinuates* thus much; "That Men are of a *less peaceable* Disposition than Brutes, because they distinguish between *Injury* and *Damage.*" I am of a very different *Opinion,* "That Men *more patiently* bear Damage done them by other Men, provided it be not *injuriously* done, and that all Distinction between these two, is founded in the Knowledge of *Right* and *Laws,* which I readily acknowledge, to be proper to Man alone." But I utterly *deny,* "That this *Knowledge* inclines Men to *violate Peace,* or to *trample* upon the *Laws,* and the *Rights* of *others* like their own." I *acknowledge,* indeed, "That Men *may* violate the Rules of Justice thro' unbridled *Passions,* notwithstanding this Knowledge"; but the Knowledge of the *Difference* between those things, which are done *rightfully* and *injuriously,* can never make Men *more prone* to injure others. But they will envy others, (as the *Antithesis* insinuates,) and will *"Love to shew*

73. Hobbes, *Leviathan,* ch. 17, pp. 108–9.

*their Wisdom, by censuring the Actions of them who govern the Common-
wealth.*" It is certainly very *injurious,* "To impute to *all* Mankind the
Faults of a *few,* and that *without Proof,*" except that, perhaps, he has
found such Affections in *himself,* and has thence concluded, that they
are natural to *all* Men; for, in the Preface to his *Leviathan,* he recom-
mends this Method of knowing Mankind, to Rulers and all others, affirming, that *"There is no other Proof of such Matters";* but he admonishes
us to examine, *"Whether these things agree with our own Thoughts."*[74]
With mine they certainly do not agree. Provided I am happy, tho others
be happier, I envy them not; I shall lose nothing by it. I believe human
Nature more modest, than to delight in censuring Princes. He must be
long *harden'd* in *Wickedness,* who will venture upon *Rebellion,* which is
a Complication of innumerable Acts of Murder, Plundering, Sacrilege,
and, in short, of all kinds of Villany. But *Hobbes* very improperly imputes that Crime to Man, in his suppos'd *State of Nature,* which State,
according to his *Hypothesis,* is previous to the Establishment of Civil
Government.

6. Let us now see, whether, in his *last Answer,* he brings any better
Proof, that Mankind is less apt than Brutes, to a mutual Agreement. *"The
Agreement"* (says he) *"of these Creatures is Natural, that of Man is by
Covenant only, which is Artificial; and, therefore, it is no wonder, if there
be somewhat else requir'd (besides Covenant) to make their Agreement constant and lasting, which is a common Power to keep them in awe, and to
direct their Actions to the common Benefit."*[75] I *answer;* "That the *natural
Causes,* which are woven, as it were, in the Constitution of human Nature, as they are Animals, and which induce them to agree in the Exercise
of mutual *Benevolence,* are plainly *equal* to those, which are found in
any *other Animals";* for instance, in Oxen, Lions, Bees; and this I have
already endeavour'd briefly to prove:[76] I will afterwards prove them to
be *greater.*[77] *Hobbes* cannot shew any thing *wanting in Man,* that is the

---

74. Ibid., Introduction, p. 4.
75. Ibid., ch. 17, p. 109.
76. Cumberland, *A Treatise of the Laws of Nature,* ch. 2., sections 17–21.
77. Ibid., sections 23–31.

Cause of such peaceful Agreement as is *found in Brutes.* What he adds, that it is from *Covenant* among Men, and therfore *artificial,* may perhaps deceive the Vulgar, but will easily be refuted by Philosophers. For these *Covenants* are form'd by the Power, both of the *animal* and *rational Nature.* Certainly, "If Men had neither enter'd into Covenants, nor made any use of their Reason, the common Nature of Animals of the same Kind, would, nevertheless, be of as great Efficacy among them, to procure their Agreement in cultivating mutual Benevolence, as far as among all Brutes of the same Species"; now such an *Agreement* among Brutes there is, which is acknowledg'd to be *natural.* What therefore hinders, but that, after *Reason* and the Use of Speech are added to Men, that *Agreement* may still continue to be *natural? Reason* does not destroy *natural* Endeavours and Propensions to Concord, nor is an Agreement which is natural, *less firm* or *durable,* because it is express'd in *Words:* As the desire and use of Nourishment cease not to be natural Actions in Man, tho he signify this Appetite by Words, and by his Reason appoint the Place, Time, and Kind of Food to be taken. Besides, *Hobbes* himself, sometimes, acknowledges *Reason* to be a Part of *human Nature,* and a *natural* Faculty,[78] and all others (that I know of) constantly acknowledge the same; whence it *follows,* "That any *further Agreement* or *Society,* which *Reason* persuades to establish by *Covenants,* proceeds from the *rational Nature* of Man; and that it may therefore be justly called *Natural,* tho it be much firmer, and bound by more Ties, than can be met with among Brutes." It will *appear* also, "That *Agreement,* proceeding from *Reason,* is therefore *more properly* called *Natural,* if we consider that *practical Reason* is wholly determin'd by the *Nature* of the *best End* we can propose, and of the *best Means* we can use": And *further,* "That *nothing else* is effected by the whole Process of *Reason,* than that those *Propensions to Concord* with others of the same Kind, which are natural to all Animals, (but exert themselves in Brutes in a very confused and improvident manner,) are *directed* to their *adequate Object,* namely, all rational Beings; and that every Action is, under its Conduct, exerted in the best *Time, Place, and other Circumstances,* which can be imagin'd."

78. Hobbes, *On the Citizen,* 1.1, p. 21; 2.1, pp. 32–34.

Thus that taking of *Meat* or *Drink* may justly be called *most natural,* which both, in *general,* takes its *Rise* from the *Constitution* of the *Animal,* and, in all *particular* Cases, is most perfectly *directed* by *Reason,* taking care of the Animal's Health, without any Error in Diet. These Precepts of regulating Diet, whose Efficacy and Truth Reason observes from the Nature of Things, may also properly be called *Art:* For *Art* is a *Habit directing Actions, as the Nature of the End and Means points out:* Yet such a *Habit* may justly be called *Natural* to a *rational Agent,* as consisting of Parts or Precepts so *few,* and so *obvious,* that they may be easily learn'd from the *Nature* of *Things, without teaching,* or so much as *intending* it; as Brutes collect the manner of regulating themselves, with respect to their Food, from Experience only; and even Plants, without Sense, much less Art, without Error extract from the Earth agreeable Juices only, for their Nourishment. *Habits,* properly so call'd, are the *first Principles of Arts,* and indeed *essential Parts* of the Arts, to which they belong; so that upon this account, perhaps, they may be called *Artificial;* but, because they are always learn'd *without Art,* they are by all acknowledg'd to become known *naturally;* and they, who write concerning Arts, do not *teach,* but *suppose,* them. Thus the Skill of adding *small* Numbers, and Right Lines, together, so as to make a Sum; and a like Subtraction in little or well known Quantities, may be called a *Habit,* and an *essential part* of Arithmetick and practical Geometry; yet Teachers of Mathematicks *suppose* their Scholars to have acquir'd this Skill by their own *natural Parts,* without Instruction, and, consequently, that it is plainly *natural. Euclid* therefore, in those common Notions, which he calls *Axioms,* supposes *"Equal Quantities added to, or taken from, Equals,"* and that it is known, that *"Their Sums, or Differences, will be equal."* The Reason of my observing which, is only to make it *evident,* "That some Skill of acting (adding, for *instance,* or subtracting) is at once an essential Part of an Art, and yet may be perfectly natural to Man, as a reasonable Creature." Wherefore I think *Hobbes* has not done right, in affirming, that the *Agreement* among *Men,* which is express'd in *Covenants,* is *Artificial,* in such Sense as to be oppos'd to *Natural.* I do not deny, that those *Words,* in which Covenants are express'd, proceed from *arbitrary* Appointment: But that *Consent of Minds,* relating to mutual

Offices of Benevolence, of which Words are only the Signs, is wholly *Natural.* But in that *Consent of Minds* to exchange good Offices consists the whole *Nature* of a *Covenant,* and from thence flows all its *obligatory* Force. The *Knowledge* also, and the *Will,* of appointing some Signs, by which such *Consent* may be mutually *declar'd,* is so easy and obvious to Man, without Instruction, that it may justly be called *Natural,* tho the use of some Signs *rather* than others, be *arbitrary,* (for so I would chuse to call it, rather than *artificial.*) To be brief, the *Agreement* express'd by *Covenants,* (especially about the most general Acts of Benevolence, of which, only, we treat in an Inquiry into the Laws of Nature,) ought either not to be called *Artificial,* or if it be so called that Term is to be taken in such Sense, as to be consistent with, not oppos'd to, what is *natural,* as if such Agreement were less constant or lasting, as *Hobbes* would have it. For the signifying a natural Agreement by Words, contriv'd by some kind of Art, does not make it less firm or durable.

It therefore remains firm, what at first I *advanced,* "That there are in Men, for this very reason, because they are Animals, at least such benevolent Propensions, as are to be found in other Animals, towards those of the same Species," which, I have taken notice, do in several Cases observe the chief Heads of the *Law of Nature,* in *proportion* to their *Knowledge.*

And retorted.   I thought it worth while, to examine *separately* these *Answers* of *Hobbes's, partly,* that the Reader might see, how gross an *Error* he is forc'd to defend, in his Attempt to deface the *Indications* of the *Sanction* of the *Laws of Nature,* taken from *natural Inclinations: Partly,* because I have observ'd, that all these Particulars, whence *Hobbes* would infer, that Man is *more malevolent* toward his own Species, and more unsociable, than *Brutes,* may, with great Advantage, be *retorted* upon himself, as the clearest *Indications,* that Man is by *Nature* fitted for *greater Benevolence* toward those of his own Species, than any *other* kind of *Animal* is. For, 1. He loves *Honour,* which flows naturally from such Benevolence. 2. He knows more perfectly the Influence of the *publick Good,* towards securing his own *private Happiness.* 3. He has the Use of *Reason,* which disposes him equally, either to *obey* or to *command,* as occasion offers. 4. He knows how, by *proper words,* to give, both an *Edge* and *Beauty* to the Force of his *Reason.* 5. He understands a *Law,* by means whereof he distinguishes an *Injury,* from a *Damage* done without Injury. 6. Lastly, to this Agreement, once made amongst Men, not *Nature* only imparts *Constancy,* but *Art,* the Assistant of Nature, communicates, by means of *writing,* many *Preservatives* against even less probable Accidents, and gives it a *Continuance* beyond the Age of Man. However, I will not insist longer upon explaining these things more particularly in this place, but leave it to the Reader's unbyass'd Judgment, whether *Hobbes's Answers,* or these *Retorsions,* be juster? or, whether these things, *peculiar* to Man, do not rather *promote* benevolent Inclinations, which, it is evident, are perpetually united to the *Animal* Nature, than *extirpate* or *weaken* them?

§XXIII. My Method requires, that I now take into Consideration some things, which are *peculiar to human Bodies,* in order to discover, whether these do not dispose Men, *more* than other Animals, to the Exercise of mutual Benevolence, and, consequently, to the forming more friendly Societies than *they* do? This will come *more pertinently* to be consider'd in *this* place, *because* even these things belong to them as *Animals;* and therefore they are to be consider'd, not as of any Efficacy by themselves, but as co-operating with what I have before observ'd *common* to them with other Animals, whence, from their *united* Force, we may expect an Effect of the *same Kind,* but *greater* and *more certain.* I, therefore, thought it proper to range these Particulars in *such* Order, that they may easily be referr'd to the *same* Heads, which we have but now perceiv'd to *indicate,* "That the same Formation and Structure of Parts, which inclines all Animals to preserve themselves, inclines them also to Benevolence towards others of the same Species."

Lastly, Benevolence is enforced, 1. From those Particulars, which are peculiar to a human Body; such are those which assist the Fancy and Memory, and, consequently, Prudence. (This falls under the Head of the foregoing second *Indication,* § *18.*)

I find nothing *peculiar,* remarkable in a *human Body,* to refer to the *first Indication,* which is taken from the *limited Quantity* of its Parts; but there are many Particulars, which may be referr'd to the *second,* which is taken from the Powers or Effects of the *Imagination* and *Memory,* in which a human Body excells the Bodies of other Animals. To these is to be premis'd this general *Observation,* "That, whatever increases the Powers of the *Fancy* and *Memory,* or makes them of longer

Continuance in Man, than in other Animals, that all contributes much to their learning many things, from natural and common Experience, relating to the Causes (subject to their Power) of both their own and the common Good, and therefore contributes to their greater Stock of *Prudence,* which will both inable and incline them to direct their Actions in pursuit, both of their own and the publick Good, which two are, from the Nature of Men, inseparably united and intervoven." But whatsoever tends to increase this kind of Prudence, equally disposes to the Practice of all *moral Virtues,* that is, to the Observance of all the *Laws of Nature.*

This being premis'd, I will, out of *Anatomical* Writers, and also from my own Observations, and those of others, take notice of some things *peculiar* and remarkable in a *human Body,* which contribute to the enlarging and strengthening the *Fancy* and *Memory* in Men, which *singly* consider'd are of *little* Advantage, but if *survey'd* as *united* among themselves, and with those things which are common to Animals of all kinds, and also in *Subordination* to the divine Powers of the Mind, of which these parts of our Body are the proper Instruments, they seem to afford *great* Light to the present Argument.

The human Fancy and Memory are assisted by, 1. The *Brain,* which, in proportion to the Bulk of his Body, is much *greater* in Man, than in any other kind of Animal: 2. *Greater Quantity of Blood and animal Spirits* thence form'd, and their *greater Purity,* from the erect Posture of the Body; a *greater Vigor* and *brisker Motion,* by means of a freer Passage into the Brain, thro' the unbranch'd Tubes of the Carotid Arteries: The *longer Continuance,* both of *Childhood,* in which great Plenty, both of Things and Words is treasur'd up, and of *Manhood,* in which our former, and our later, Observations are with greater Judgment rang'd under their several Heads, is of particular use to the *Memory.* I will enlarge a little upon each of these, to set the whole in a clearer Light.

Under this Head are consider'd, 1. The Brain, much greater in Man, than in other Animals, By the *Brain,* I here understand all that white Substance, which is contain'd in the Membranes within the Skull, which is sometimes divided into the *Brain,* properly so called, and the *Cerebellum,* of which *Bartholin* writes thus. *"The Bulk of the human Brain is remarkable, in proportion to the Body,* as Aristotle *has observ'd. And a Man has generally*

twice as much Brains as an Ox, to the Quantity of four or five Pounds."[79]
Hence, I think, we may thus reason. The weight of a middle-siz'd human
Body amounts not to more than a fourth Part of the weight of an Ox,
and yet has a Brain twice as large, to govern so little a Body; it hence
follows, that he has eight times the Quantity of Brain, to govern an equal
Quantity of Body. I have found the Bodies of large Sheep, and of Hogs,
to equal, in weight, a human Body; and that their Brain weighs, but
about the eighth Part of the Brain of a Man. But what other Inference
can we draw from so great a Disparity, in this matter, between these
Animals, than that Man is so form'd by Nature, that the *Influence* of his
Brain, on the Government of his Actions, may be much *greater* and more
conspicuous? It is certain, (to omit other Uses of the Brain, common to
Man with other Animals, upon account whereof no Reason can be assign'd for the *excess* of Weight,) that Man, by the help of this part, 1st.
Observes sensible Objects more accurately, and *examines,* (besides other
Effects of less Consequence,) how much all those things, which are in
our Power, can bring of *Good* or *Evil* to Men singly or jointly consider'd.
2dly. Because all the Nerves take their Rise from the Brain, or from the
spinal Marrow, which is only the Substance of the Brain continued, it
is evident, that *all voluntary Motions of the Body are directed and govern'd
by means of the Brain.* This may more clearly appear, from what *Willis*
has observ'd of the Origin of all the Nerves, which are us'd in voluntary
Motion, from the Brain properly so called. From these Observations it
naturally *follows,* "That both the greater Quantity and Force of the
Brain, which are visible in Man, are naturally of use to him, to direct
the various Actions or Motions thence depending, with more circum-
spect Deliberation, Counsel and Care, which are the peculiar Offices of
the Brain."[80] But this can no otherwise be effected, than by proposing
to himself the *greatest End,* (which is the *common Good* of the Universe,
but of rational Beings especially,) and, in the best manner, procuring the

in proportion
to the Bulk of
his Body.

---

79. Bartholin, *History of Anatomy* (1668), III.3, pp. 133–34; the report of Aristotle
refers to *De Partibus Animalium,* II.7.

80. Willis, *Cerebri Anatome, cui accessit nervorum descripto et usus* (1664).

assistance of the *best means,* that is, by procuring to himself the Favour of all rational Agents, by an active *Benevolence.* Certainly, a *more simple Apparatus* of Organs, such as is found in Trees, is sufficient for the *Preservation* of one *Individual;* (for most of them flourish longer than the Age of Man;) nay, is sufficient for the *Propagation of the Species,* in which is contain'd somewhat of the common Good. Therefore *so great a Quantity of Brain,* with so many admirable Instruments thereto pertaining, (such as the Organs of all the Senses, and of voluntary Motion,) must be design'd for *nobler Uses.* In some Birds and Fish, the bulk and weight of the Brain is not greater, but sometimes less, than that of the Eyes, (which, with many other Anatomical Observations, was first communicated to me by my worthy Friend, that learned and successful Physician, Dr. *Hollings;*)[81] yet even *these* want not *Understanding enough,* to live peaceably with those of their own Species. How much *less* can it be *wanting* to *Men* in general, (consistently with their Happiness,) who have the *largest Organs* for acquiring *Knowledge;* especially, since the greatest part of human *Happiness* consists in the Use of the Brain, in order to the attainment of *Truth* and the greatest *Good?* To this Head belongs what *Willis* has deliver'd, that, in the Dissection of the Body of one who was a *Fool* from his Birth, he discover'd nothing amiss in the *Brain,* but that it was extremely *small:* And in the Anatomy of a *Monkey* he observ'd, that the *Brain* differ'd but little from that in a Dog or Fox, except that, in proportion to the Bulk of its Body, it was much *greater,* and its *winding Passages larger,* whence this Animal makes nearer Approaches than the rest, to the Understanding of Man.[82]

2. The greater Quantity, Purity, and Vigour, of the Blood and Animal Spirits.

§XXIV. *Secondly;* In the human Body are observable the *Quantity, Purity,* and *Vigour,* of the *Blood* and *Animal Spirits* thence form'd, *greater* than are to be found in Brutes, which may justly be reckon'd among the Helps of the *Fancy* and *Memory,* and, consequently, of *Prudence* it self. The Quantity of Blood varies, for several Reasons, in all Animals, and,

81. For Hollings, see introduction, n. 38.
82. Willis, *Cerebri Anatome,* ch. 26, pp. 184–91.

consequently, in Man. *Charlton, Lower,*[83] and other Anatomists, have observ'd, that it is rarely more than 25, or less than 15, Pounds, therefore its Weight may be estimated, at a Medium, at 20 Pounds. If, therefore, we suppose the Body of such a Man, freed from Blood, to weigh 200 lb. (which exceeds the Weight of a middle-siz'd Man,) the Blood will be to the rest of the Body, as 1 to 10, or it will be the eleventh part of the Body of a living Man. *Glisson's* Computation is not much wide of this, who affirms the Blood to be the twelfth part of the whole human Body.[84] But in a Sheep, Calf, and Hog, I have often found, that the Blood is, in proportion to their bloodless Body, as 1 to 20, or, at most, to 18. Hence we may *infer,* "That the Blood of a Man is to his Body, almost in a *double* Proportion to that of Beasts." But, in Fish and Birds, the Proportion of the Mass of Blood to the Bulk of their Bodies, is still far less. Anatomists likewise agree, that Man's Blood is *warmer* than that of other Animals. From the *Plenty* and *Heat* of the *Blood,* it is obvious to collect the *Plenty* and *Briskness* of the *Spirits.* I thought proper to add here this one *Remark,* "That I affirm nothing of the Form of the *Spirits,* whether it be *Aerial* or no," which I perceive is oppos'd by *Harvey*[85] and his Followers; but that by that Name I understand the *most active Parts of the Blood,* thence convey'd into the *Brain,* to assist the Imagination and Memory, and also into the *Nerves* and *Muscular Fibres,* there to be subservient to the Motions of the Animal, such as *Harvey* himself does not deny. The manner *how* the Spirits, or more active Parts of the Blood, are *separated* from the rest, has not yet, perhaps, come to the Knowledge of those curious Inquirers into Nature, the learned in Physick. It is sufficient for my present purpose, that they are almost unanimously *agreed,* "That the Blood, whose more spirituous, or active, Parts have been in some measure freed from the rest by Fermentation, is convey'd to the Brain, that there the Spirits may be thorowly separated or distill'd." This further, only, I would *observe,* in order to my present Argument, that it is easily intelligible. "That the greater Quantity of Brain and Blood in

83. Walter Charleton (1627–1707); Richard Lower (1631–91).
84. Glisson, *Anatomia Hepatis* (1654), ch. 7, pp. 77–90.
85. William Harvey (1578–1657), discoverer of the circulation of the blood.

Man may produce greater Plenty of Spirits in him, than in other Animals," *however* it is *effected* in either.

Further, it may not, perhaps, be wholly impertinent, to take notice of what Dr. *Glisson,* our learned Physic-Professor, has observ'd in *rickety* Children, that the *Head* grows *greater,* thro' the wasting of the other Parts; and that, at the same time, the *Understanding* is *inlarg'd,* in *proportion* to the *Brain,* by means of the affluence of a *greater* Quantity of *Blood.*[86] Nor ought it to be omitted, that the *Posture* of our Body, which, when we are awake, is generally *erect,* contributes somewhat to this effect. For, *hence,* we are not only symbolically *instructed,* to contemplate *higher* Causes, which have an equal Influence upon all Men every where, and so upon this whole sublunary World, which has been observ'd by many of the Antients;[87] but, *hence* also, the *Brain* of Man is *dispos'd* to produce *greater Plenty* of *brisker* Spirits, whence we are naturally qualify'd the better, to execute all the extensive Duties of Reason; which are all discharg'd by a friendly Association with other rational Beings. The reason why I am of Opinion, that this *Situation* of the human *Brain* contributes somewhat to the Production of *more,* and *more active,* Spirits, is drawn from *statical Principles,* accommodated to the Functions and Situation of the Arteries and Veins, belonging to the human Head; the Influence of which Principles, tho they may to many seem impertinent, and foreign to our present purpose, appears to me to be extended thro' the whole material World; and, consequently, to have no inconsiderable Effect upon human Bodies. It seems to me, that, while the whole Mass of Blood rushes into the *Aorta,* by the impulse receiv'd from the Contraction of the Heart, all its Parts do not receive an *equal* degree of Velocity from that Impulse, because of their *difference* of Magnitude, Vigure, Solidity, and Motions, which are in the different Parts of the Blood; (which is a Liquor consisting of very *heterogeneous* Parts, which have *different* Motions, as they are *fluid,* as they are *warm,* as they are

86. Glisson, *De Rachitide* (1650), pp. 15–16.

87. Barbeyrac (*Traité Philosophique,* 164, n. 3) indicates Cumberland's likely sources: Ovid, *Metamorphoses,* I.84; Cicero, *De Legibus,* I.ix; *De Natura Deorum,* II.lvi.

fermented, and as they are more or less *heavy,* in proportion to their *Bulk;* but that some of them are, for these Reasons, mov'd more *swiftly,* which I therefore take leave to call, the brisker and *lighter Parts of the Blood.* Hence I think it probable, that a great Number of these Particles free themselves from the gross ones in the windings of the Arteries, and may with greater ease mount upwards by force of the Pulses perpetually re-new'd, by which an *unequal* degree of *Velocity* is communicated to the *different Particles* of the Blood; to the Active, a greater; to the Gross, a less degree. Hence I imagine, that the Blood is somewhat *brisker,* which rises in the narrow *ascending* Trunk, than that which passes into the wider *descending* Trunk, thro' which the grosser and heavier Blood is forc'd with greater ease. From the ascending Trunk, the *yet purer* Blood passes into the *Carotidal* and *Vertebral Arteries,* whence the Brain is sup-ply'd with Materials for forming the *Spirits.* I do not think, that the Difference is *great,* between the arterial Blood which passes thro' the Head, and that which passes thro' the lower Parts of the Body; but I thought, that even the *minutest* Things, which seem'd deducible from *clear* and universal Principles, were not to be wholly pass'd over in *si-lence,* when they came pertinently in my way. I will therefore add another Observation, of a like kind, concerning the *perpendicular Situation* of the *Veins* belonging to the *Brain,* which favours the *quicker Circulation* of the Blood, descending by its own Gravity; the Branches of the Jugular and Vertebral Veins are hereby quickly emptied, and way the sooner made for a Tide of fresh Blood, from the Carotid and Vertebral Arteries, which would otherwise be retarded by the Resistance of the venal Blood. From the happy Concurrence of these two Causes, that is, from the *ascent* of the more spirituous Blood, in the *Arteries* allotted to the Brain, and from the precipitate *Descent* of the same Blood, (after the Spirits are separated) in the *Veins,* thro' the *erect* Situation of a human Body, the Consequence will be a *swifter* Circulation of the Blood in the *Head,* than in other Parts of the Body, or than is in the Heads of other Animals; and, from the *swifter* Circulation, fresh Blood is *more quickly* supply'd, whence *greater Plenty of Spirits* is separated.

To confirm the *Ascent of the more spirituous Blood, by the Arteries of the Head,* I might easily bring many Arguments, and those taken from the *more frequent Obstructions* in the Region of the *lower Belly*, arising from impurer Blood; from the swelling, and sometimes *bleeding*, of the *haemmorhoidal Veins*, which Distemper (in my Opinion) peculiar to Man, seems to proceed, in part at least, from the *erect* Posture of his Body; but I study Brevity. The Reader, who desires more to this Purpose, may consult what *Lower* has writ in his learned Treatise *de Corde, cap.* 2. from *Pag.* 133 to the end of the *Chapter,* most of which (tho intended by him for another purpose) may, by the judicious Reader, be easily adapted to the present Argument.[88] Nor is it any *Objection* to what I have advanced, that some *long-neck'd Birds* walk with their *Heads upright.* It may be granted, that, in them too, the lighter and more spirituous Blood, by that means ascends; yet, from hence, no great Advantage to their Understanding is to be expected, because they have very little, of either Blood or Brain, in proportion to the Bulk of their Body. Moreover, so small a Quantity of Blood, tho it were not spirituous, might ascend thro' their Carotid Arteries, by a gentle impulse of the Heart's Contraction, because they are so very slender, that they partake much of the Nature of Capillary Glass Tubes, in which common Water, especially if heated, ascends, as it were spontaneously, to the height of several Inches.

I should now take notice of the *swifter* Motion of the *Blood* into the *human Brain,* proceeding from this, that the *Carotid Artery* is *not divided* in *Man,* as in most *Brutes,* into a great many Branchings and Windings like Net-work, which check the Motion of the Blood in them; whereas, in Man, it flows in one large and open Channel, till it enters the Brain; whence all its Parts, and, consequently, the Spirits themselves, must necessarily be mov'd with greater Force, its whole Circulation be sooner perform'd, and room sooner made for the Admission of fresh Blood. All which contribute much, to the *greater briskness and plenty of the Spirits.* But *Willis,* and *Lower,* have treated this Matter so fully, and accurately, that they have left no room for our Industry, and ought themselves to be consulted, as Originals.[89] It is sufficient for me, to have apply'd these

88. Lower, *Tractatus de Corde* (1669), 2.2, pp. 132–50.
89. Willis, *Cerebri Anatome;* Lower, *Tractatus de Corde.*

Observations, borrow'd from them, to my present Argument. This, however, I think proper to *add*, "That, tho in the *human Head* there are so *many Helps* to the *Imagination* and *Memory*, which are of great Service to the *Mind*, these are no way sufficient, to resolve the above mention'd Operations into the *mechanical Powers of Matter and Motion*." On the contrary, I think *Malpighius's Observation* very just, "That, the better we understand the nature and functions of the Brain, the *more* we shall despair of the Possibility of explaining the Operations of the Mind by its Motions." See *Malpigh. de Cerebri cortice*, cap. 4.[90]

§XXV. I now proceed to the *last help*, to the *Memory*, and, consequently, to *Prudence;* this Advantage Mankind usually enjoy beyond other Animals, which proceeds from our ordinary *length of Life*. The *Power* of our *Memory* is certainly *wonderful*, which comprehends some *Thousands* of *Words*, above a *Million* of Sentences or *Propositions* thence form'd, and an *almost infinite* Variety of *Things* and *Actions*, observ'd within the Compass of our Life. Which, however *short* it is, if compar'd with that *Eternity* we hope for, or with the *long* Lives of the *Antediluvian Patriarchs*, which we learn from sacred History, is yet much longer, than that of most other Animals we know. They sooner come to Maturity, and generally decay sooner, so as not to reach sixty or seventy Years, the usual Limits of the Life of Man. It is also providently *contriv'd* by Nature, "That the *Memory* of *Children* should be *retentive*, by means whereof, before we become fit for transacting Business, we *retain* much concerning *God* and *Men*, the Causes of the common Good, and of that Happiness we hope for"; and thence *learn*, "How necessary it is, both to pursue this greatest *End*, and to exercise a most extensive Benevolence towards them as the only *Means* to obtain that *End*." Yet *Hobbes*, in this Article as well as in others, prefers Brutes to Men; and in his *Leviathan*, *chap*. 3. where he treats of *Prudence*, he asserts thus. *"There be Beasts, that at a Year old, observe more, and pursue that which is for their Good more prudently, than a Child can do at ten."* [91] I, who have often, with

3. Longer Life.

90. Malpighi, *De Cerebri Cortice* (1666), ch. 4.
91. Hobbes, *Leviathan*, ch. 3, p. 14.

wonder, observ'd, the *Contrivance* of *Children* in their Plays, the *Pertinence* of their *Answers* to Questions, and their remarkable *Happiness* of *Memory* in learning Languages, have never met with any thing in Brutes comparable thereto: I therefore leave it to the Reader's Judgment, whether this be not affirm'd by *Hobbes,* with more *Ill-nature* than *Truth* and *Ingenuity.* He frequently *acknowledges,* "That many Years *Experience,* especially after we come to Years of Discretion, naturally produces *Prudence";*[92] yet he *sees not* "The advantage, which Men, in this particular, have over Brutes, whose *Life* is *shorter,* whose *Understanding improves* but very *little* by time, and who *cannot* so easily *communicate* to others, what they have learn'd by Experience, especially at a considerable *distance* of Time or Place, as Men can, and usually do, to their great *increase* of *Prudence* and mutual *Happiness.*"

Secondly, There are some things which, (1.) enable him better to rule his Affections, (This and the following § may be referred to the third Indication, § 19.) §XXVI. Having dispatch'd what relates to the human Imagination and Memory, let us now consider those Properties of a human Body, which seem more nearly to respect the *Government,* and *Determination of the Affections* to pursue, rather the *Good,* than *Hurt* of others. At present I *suppose,* and lay down as a foundation, what I have observed in the *third Indication,* taken from the common nature of Animals, "That those Affections, which are employ'd in pursuit of Good, do naturally more befriend and delight all Animals, in which they reside, and that they therefore incline to these Affections, as more conducing to the Preservation of their own Life, with the same necessity, that all Principles of Action, essential to them, are determined to preserve, rather than destroy, Life and Health." This being suppos'd, there are *two* peculiar properties of a human body, which ought to *incline* them, with a diligence *greater* than that of other Animals, to *govern* their *Affections;* of which the *first enables* them, *better* than other Animals, to effect it; the *second renders it more necessary* to the *Health,* and, consequently, to the *Life,* of Man, that he should govern his Affections, than it is to other Animals. If, in either Article, any thing seems not sufficiently proved to the Reader, let

92. Ibid. Cumberland may also be thinking of arguments in ch. 5, p. 26; ch. 8, p. 40; ch. 13, p. 74–75; ch. 46, p. 454.

him remember, that what I add here is more than is necessary to my Argument, which is otherwise sufficiently prov'd; and that it may be of some use, here to recount these things *peculiar to Man,* that others, at least, may more happily explain their uses. I make no question, but that they serve other purposes also: yet I think it probable, that they are not ineffectual to those noble ends, which I have hinted. And they are these, (1.) A *Plexus Nervosus peculiar to Man;*[93] (2.) The *connexion* of the *Pericardium* with the *Diaphragm,* and a like *communication* between the *Nervus Diaphragmaticus* and the *Plexus Nervosus peculiar to Man,* which is chiefly subservient to the *Praecordia.* With respect to these, I think proper, only briefly to sum up the observations of *Anatomists,* and to accommodate to my present purpose, what they have advanced in general, concerning the Affections hence depending. It is *evident,* "That the *strongest Passions* of Men are employ'd about those things, which are the *Objects* of *Laws,* whether *natural* or *civil*"; for the business of these, is to settle and preserve *Property,* both in Things and in human Services, than which nothing moves Men more strongly; therefore it is not to be *doubted,* but "That all those things in a human body, which naturally serve to *excite* or *allay* the *Passions,* have a considerable share in settling and defending a distinction of Property, in which the whole *matter* of the *Laws of Nature* consists."

I will begin with transcribing, from *Willis,* a few things concerning the *Plexus Nervosus peculiar to Man.* The Reader, if he has the Author by him, may consult himself, and receive it with greater pleasure at first hand, where he may find what is here describ'd, represented to his view in the *ninth Plate.*[94] "*The* Plexus Nervosus peculiar to Man, *is about the middle of the Neck, in the Trunk of the intercostal Nerve, which, beside the Fibres sent off into the Blood-vessels and Gullet, and those small Branches, which it sends into the Trunks of the Nervus Diaphragmaticus, and of the*

as a Plexus Nervosus *peculiar to Man.*

93. [Maxwell] *"Plexus Nervosus,* is a great number of minute complicated Branches of the Nerves."

94. Maxwell includes the illustration mentioned from Willis, *Cerebri Anatome,* plate 9, p. 223. Cumberland was not able to include the plate in the 1672 edition of *De Legibus.*

A. The Nerves of the fifth Pair, with its two Branches *A. A.* the upper of which tending straight forwards, distributes shoots into the Eyes and Face, into the Nose, Palate, and the upper part of the whole Mouth; beside, it reflects two shoots *a. a.* which are the two roots of the intercostal Nerve: The other lower Branch of the fifth Pair tending downwards, is dispers'd into the lower Jaw and all its Parts.

a. a. Two shoots sent down from the upper Branch of the fifth Pair, which meeting together with the other shoot *b.* reflected from the Nerve of the sixth Pair, constitute the intercostal Trunk *D.*

B. The Nerve of the sixth Pair tending straight forwards into the Muscles of the Eyes, out of whose Trunk a shoot *b.* which is the third root of the intercostal Nerve, is reflected.

b. The third root of the intercostal Nerve.

D. The trunk of the intercostal Nerve consisting of the three aforesaid Roots about to pass into the *Plexus Ganglioformis.*

E. The Original of the *Par vagum,* consisting of many Fibres.

G. The principal Branch of the *Par vagum,* lost in the neighbouring *Plexus Ganglioformis.*

H. The upper *Plexus Ganglioformis* of the *Par vagum,* which admits a shoot *K.* out of another neighbouring Plexus of the intercostal Nerve.

i. A shoot sent from the *Plexus cervicalis* of the intercostal Nerve into the trunk of the *Par vagum.*

K. The lower Plexus of the *Par vagum,* from which many Nerves proceed for the Heart and its Appendix.

l. A shoot sent to the *Plexus Cardiacus.*

m. Nervous Fibres distributed into the Pericardium and the Vessels hanging to the Heart.

n. The left recurrent Nerve, which, being reflected from compassing about the descending Trunk of the Aorta upwards to the *Cartilago scutiformis,* imparts in its ascent many shoots **** to the *aspera Arteria,* and at length meets with a shoot *h,* sent from the *Plexus Ganglioformis.* This returning back from the knot of reflexion, sends some shoots toward the Heart.

L. The recurrent Nerve in the right side, which, being reflected much higher, binds about the axillary Artery.

O. A branch sent down from the trunk of the *Par vagum,* in the left side towards the Heart, one shoot of which presently becoming forked, compasses about the trunk of the Pneumonick Vein; the other, attaining the hinder Region of the Heart, is dispersed into many shoots, which cover over its surface: A like Cardiack branch sent out of the trunk of the other side, meets with this.

p. The shoot of the aforesaid branch going about the Pneumonick Vein.

q. Another branch of the same imparting to the Heart many shoots which cover over its hinder surface, turned back beyond their proper Situation.

r. r. r. Small shoots sent out of the trunk of the *Par vagum,* which are inserted by a long tract to the Gullet.

S.S.S. Many shoots cut off, the branchings of which being distributed into the Substance of the Lungs, variously streighten and bind about the Blood-vessels.

Γ. The middle or Cervical *Plexus Nervosus peculiar to Man,* is placed nigh the middle of the Neck, in the trunk of the intercostal Nerve.

δ. A branch out of the second vertebral Pair, going into this Plexus, whereby this communicates with the *Nervus Diaphragmaticus* in its first Root.

εε. Two branches from the same Plexus into the Trunk of the *Nervus Diaphragmaticus.*

ζζ. Many nervous Fibres which come from the *Plexus Cervicalis* into the recurrent Nerve and into the Blood-vessels, and are also inserted into the *aspera Arteria* and Gullet.

θ. A shoot from the same into the trunk of the *Par vagum.*

X. Another shoot into the recurrent Nerve.

χχ. Two shoots sent down towards the Heart, which another branch *Δ* follows, arising a little lower: These being carried downwards between the Aorta and the Pneumonick Artery, meeting with the like branches of the other side, constitute the *Plexus Cardiacus Δ.* out of which the chief Nerves proceed which are bestowed on the Heart.

Δ. *Plexus Cardiacus.*

μ. The loop or handle going from the same, which binds about the Pneumonick Artery.

ν. The lower loop binding the Pneumonick Vein.

Ξ. The intercostal Nerve demersed into the cavity of the Thorax, where it binds the axillary Artery.

ξξξξ. The four vertebral Nerves sent down into the *Plexus Thoracicus,* the uppermost of which binds the vertebral Artery.

ooo. Three branches sent down from the *Plexus Cardiacus,* which cover the anterior Region of the Heart, as the Nerves *p. q.* going from the trunk of the *Par vagum,* impart branchings to its hinder part.

ϖ. The vertebral Artery bound about by the vertebral Nerve.

sss. Nervous shoots covering the anterior Region of the Heart.

ττ. Shoots and nervous Fibres distributed to its hinder part.

Θ. The *Plexus Thoracicus,* into which, beside the intercostal Nerve, four vertebrals are inserted; the uppermost of these in its descent binds about the vertebral Artery.

T. The *Nervus Diaphragmaticus,* a shoot of whose root *δ.* comes to the *Plexus Cervicalis,* and a little lower two other branches from the same Plexus *εε.* are reach'd out into its Trunk. This communication is proper to Man.

φ. The other root of the Diaphragma, from the second and third brachial Nerve.

χ. The lower trunk of the *Nervus Diaphragmaticus* being removed out of its place, which, in its proper Situation, passing through the cavity of the Thorax without any communication, goes straight forward to the Diaphragma, where, being stretched out into three shoots, it is inserted into its muscular part.

Par Vagum, and into the recurrent Nerve, detaches, beside, on each hand, two Branches toward the Heart, which are joined by another rising somewhat lower, and these, at length, meeting more from the other side, form the Plexus Cardiacus; thence proceed both those remarkable Branches of Nerves spreading over the Region of the Heart, and those nervous Loops, which gird the pneumonick Artery and Vein," (the principal conveyance of the blood, whence the spirits, which contain the first seeds of the Passions, break forth) *"and the same intercostal Nerve afterwards winds about the subclavian Arteries, before the rise of the vertebral Arteries, which convey the Blood to the Head. The intercostal Nerve, by these Branches, supplies the Place of an extraordinary Courier, communicating, to and fro, the mutual Sensations of the Heart and Brain. By means of this Communication, the Conceptions of the Brain affect the Heart, and move the Vessels thereof along with the Diaphragm, whence the motion of the Blood, and the Respiration, receive various Alterations, and the State of the Spirits, which are thence to be form'd, is somewhat chang'd."* He farther adds, *"That the Thoughts, relating to Acts of the Will or Understanding,"* (in which the Powers of Prudence, and the Virtues, are conspicuous,) *"may be duly form'd, it is necessary, that the torrent of Blood in the Breast be kept within bounds, and the inordinate motions of the Heart be restrained, by the Nerves, as by Reins, and be reduc'd to regularity."* He observ'd also, *"in the Dissection of one who was a Fool from his Birth, that the foresaid Plexus Nervosus was very slender, and attended with an unusually small Train."* And, moreover, he observed *"in a Monkey"* (which Animal makes the nearest Approaches to human Sagacity and Passions) *"some Branches sent off to the Heart and its Appendix, from the intercostal Nerve, before its insertion into the Plexus Thoracicus,"* (as he calls it,) *"which is different from what it is in other Animals."* [95] I will transcribe no more from him upon this head. It is sufficient to have *shewn*, "That Man is naturally furnish'd with these

---

95. Willis, *Cerebri Anatome*, ch. 26, pp. 184–91. The lessons drawn from this passage were popular among Cumberland's contemporaries. Samuel Parker uses it to the same effect in *Tentamina Physico-Theologica de Deo* (1665), pp. 79–98, 100–108, 116–20, 138–39; see also his *A Free and Impartiall Censure of the Platonick Philosophy* (1666), p. 66. Robert Sharrock also used Willis in *De Finibus Virtutis Christianae* (1673), pp. 114–15.

Instruments, (beside the Powers of his Mind, and, perhaps, yet other undiscover'd Properties of the Brain,) for the *Government* of his *Affections,*" which would not be *foreign* to our present Purpose, tho something of the *same kind* were to be found in *Brutes,* conducing to their living *peaceably* among themselves. But, since these things are *peculiar to Man,* it cannot but *suggest* to his *Mind,* "That it is its Province, *diligently to attend the Helm* committed to its care, and to *steer skilfully.*"

§XXVII. We are, in the *second* place, to consider the *connexion between the Pericardium and Diaphragm,* (which is not at all to be found in other Animals,) to which I thought proper to add the *Communication between the foresaid Plexus Nervosus peculiar to Man, and the Nervus Diaphragmaticus;* because, as *Willis* has observed in the same Place, *two,* and sometimes *three,* Nerves are inserted, from this *Plexus,* into the *Nervus Diaphragmaticus:* Nor is it to be omitted, that, from the same *intercostal Nerve,* in which the aforesaid *Plexus* is found, *innumerable Branches* are spread thro' all Parts of the *lower Belly,* so that the *Heart,* in some measure, *communicates* with them *all.*

I should be too *prolix,* if I endeavoured to *enlarge upon all these particulars,* and it would be *rashness,* to offer to determine the use of *each* of these Nerves, which to me seems not yet sufficiently discover'd. It is sufficient for my present Argument, to make a *few Observations* concerning their *general use,* in which *Anatomists* are *agreed,* which is, (1.) That they serve to begin, or stop, motion; (2.) That they convey to the Brain Sensations of Pain or Pleasure, from the Parts in which they are inserted; (3.) That those Nerves, with which they are complicated, sympathize with them. These Particulars being *suppos'd,* I *assume* what is evident from innumerable Experiments, "That our Heart and Diaphragm, and all the Bowels of the lower Belly, the Stomach, for instance, the Liver, Spleen, Spermatick Vessels, &*c.* are variously affected in all violent Passions about Good or Evil, whether our own or another's; especially, when our own Concerns are found involv'd, from the nature of Things, with those of others, which, because of the known likeness of the Condition of all Men, is always easy to observe." It is *evident,* "That the *Nerves* inserted in these Bowels, are the *Instruments* of these

(2.) Make Man's Government of his Passions *of greater Importance* to him, as the connexion of the Pericardium with the Diaphragm, and other Causes, which render his risques greater than those of other Animals, in violent Passions.

Motions, perhaps, not without the *Concurrence* of the *arterial Blood."* Hence I *infer,* "That the Heart of Man is, in such Passions, *more* affected than that of other Animals"; *because* it communicates or sympathizes with the other Bowels, by that connexion, peculiar to Man, of the Nerves and Pericardium, which I have mentioned; and *because* both his Heart and other Bowels, in every kind of Passion, are mov'd by the Influence of a more powerful Brain, and the Impulse of more active Spirits. And, because the *Heart,* and the *Blood* circulated by means thereof, is the Fountain of *Life* and *Health,* and, in consequence, of all the *Pleasure* we enjoy; those *Passions,* which *assist,* or *retard,* its *Motion more* powerfully in *Men* than *Brutes,* must necessarily *affect us more* than they do *them,* whose Hearts do not so many ways communicate with their Bowels: Beside, their *Brains* are *more sluggish;* and their *Spirits,* whether in the Blood or Nerves, are *fewer* and *less active.* How much it conduces to our present Argument, that, from the very *Structure* of our *Body,* we are continually *admonish'd* of the *necessity* of *governing* our *Affections* with a strict hand, they will easily understand, who *consider,* "That all the Virtues, and the whole Observance we owe to the Law of Nature, are contain'd in the Government of those Passions, which are employ'd in settling or securing every Man's Property."

But, because I have observ'd, from *Anatomists,* beside those *general Phaenomena,* concerning which I have treated, *two particular* ones, *peculiar to Man,* accurately explain'd from this Connexion between the Heart and other Bowels, which are *Laughing* and *Sighing,* I presently imagin'd, that these are *Symptoms* of our *two principal Passions,* that of a profuse *Joy,* this of *Grief;* and that all the rest of our Affections are like these; so that we may hope, from a Parity of Reason, that, in time, their Symptoms too may in like manner be explain'd. I therefore resolv'd briefly to explain, and to apply to my present purpose, these, as Specimens of what I have before asserted, only in general Terms.

First, therefore, I observe from *Willis,* in the *Chapter* before quoted, that, from the above-mention'd *Communication, between the Plexus Nervosus peculiar to Man, and the Nervus Diaphragmaticus,* the true Cause appears, why *Risibility* is *a Property of human Nature;* which is, because the Diaphragm, as well as the Heart, is affected with the pleasing Motion

of the Imagination, and is drawn upward by the Intercourse of the
Nerves proceeding from this Plexus, and is excited to repeated Heavings
as it were; whence, because the Pericardium is joined to it, the Heart it-
self and the Lungs are likewise mov'd; then, because the same Intercostal
Nerve is continued upward with the Nerves of the Jaws, when once the
Laugh is begun in the Breast, the Posture of the Mouth and Countenance pathetically corresponds thereto. *Willis* has more upon this Head.
What *Lower* delivers upon this Subject, differs somewhat from this, but
yet may be reconcil'd with it: The Place is worth the Reader's Inspection.[96] I *observe,* to my present purpose, "That *Laughter* gives a most
agreeable *Relish* to *human Life,* and, especially, to *friendly Society,* but is
of *little* or *no use* in *Solitude,* or in such *Affections,* as are conversant about
any *great Evil,* as in Anger, Envy, Hatred, Fear; and is, therefore, to be
reckon'd amongst those things, which frequently make human Conversation *more agreeable,* but seldom the *contrary.*" Because this Motion,
repeated at proper Intervals, is wonderfully *agreeable,* and strongly
throws off all *Uneasiness of Grief,* we may *conclude,* "That human Nature, (on this very account, that it is fitly fram'd to procure its own Preservation,) is inclinable to this sweetner of Society, which is peculiar to
Man; and that therefore, in this respect also, there is a *natural Connexion*
between our *Care of our-selves,* and a *Desire to please others.*"

   The *Sigh,* tho' it be not peculiar to Man, is yet more frequently observ'd in him; nor is it, that I know of, in other Animals reckon'd among
the Signs of Grief or Melancholy; however, it is *more prejudicial* to the
Heart in *Man,* than in *other Animals,* because of the Connexion between
his *Pericardium* and *Diaphragm,* by whose Motion it is produc'd; for
the Motion of the *Heart,* so necessary to the Life of Man, is *disturb'd*
by that extraordinary Motion of the *annex'd Diaphragm.* The Inconvenience of *Sighing,* when seldom, is but small; but, if frequent and of
long Continuance, it wonderfully tires the Heart, and disqualifies it for
its Functions. This Evil is near a-kin to that Distemper, which is call'd
the *Hiccough,* which, (as *Lower* has rightly observ'd,)[97] tho' it generally

---

96. Lower, *De Corde,* ch. 2, p. 90.
97. Ibid., ch. 2.

takes its Rise from the Stomach, to which it is prejudicial, is properly an
Affection of the Diaphragm; and which, tho' it hurt but little, when its
Stay is short, yet, when it is of long Continuance, and is attended with
other Symptoms, (which Physicians are acquainted with from the *Aph-orisms of Hippocrates,*)[98] is often a Harbinger, and partly a Cause, of
Death.

Whilst I was considering a *Sigh,* as an Effect of Grief, a probable
Conjecture (as it seems to me) came into my Mind, concerning the
Cause of *Tears,* which is one of the Effects of Grief, and almost proper
to Man alone. I am of *Opinion,* "That in *Grief* the *Motion* of the *Blood,*
in the Extremities of the Veins and Arteries in the Head, is somewhat
obstructed, so that it cannot so freely circulate as before," (nor are we
without other Proofs of this Obstruction in this Passion,) "in which case
the *Lachrymal Glands*" (for whose Explication we are indebted to
Steno)[99] "can make a *more plentiful Secretion* of the *Serum* from the
Blood, and empty it, by their Passages, into the Eyes." I took the first
Hint of this Conjecture, from that noble *Experiment* of *Lower,* in which,
after he had tied the Jugular Veins in a live Dog, all the Parts above the
Ligature swell'd prodigiously, Tears flow'd plentifully, and Spittle as co-piously, as if in a Salivation. Read the Experiment, useful upon many
Accounts, in its Author, in the *Chapter* above quoted, and I believe, my
Conjecture will not seem improbable: But, perhaps, *Man alone weeps,*
either because his *Blood* is *more obstructed* in *Grief,* in proportion to the
Size of his *Brain,* and the *Quickness* of his *Apprehension;* or because his
Blood, being *more copious* and *warm,* and of *swifter* Circulation in the
Head, cannot suffer such *Obstructions,* without the *Secretion* of a salt
Humour from the Glands, which breaks forth in Tears. However, if in
Grief there were no such Obstructions in the Brain as we suppose, yet,
if in that Passion the *Blood* either became *too thick* to find an easy Passage
thro' its usual Windings; or if, on the contrary, it were *more rarify'd,* or
its *Velocity* ever so little *increas'd* from the Heart toward the Head, be-

98. Hippocrates, *Aphorisms,* sect. III.
99. Niels Stensen, or Steno (1638–86), published detailed descriptions of the lach-rymal glands in *Observationes Anatomicae* (1662).

cause it does not find a *proportionably* freer Passage, thro' its winding
Canals, into the Veins, the *Arteries* must of Necessity *swell,* and there
will be the same reason of the watery Parts breaking forth in Tears, as if
such Obstructions, as I suppos'd, had oppos'd its Course, which might
easily be prov'd from *hydrostatical Principles.* However this happens, the
breaking forth of Tears, in these Obstructions, is an *Indication,* "That the
Health of *Man* is *more* endanger'd from giving way to Grief, than that
of *other Animals";* for the Lachrymal Glands will scarce suffice for evacuating the *whole Serum,* after it has made an Eruption in some other Part
of the Head, tho some Ease may arise from this *Partial* Evacuation. The
clouding the *Fancy,* and the *Symptoms* of various *Diseases,* which usually
follow, according to the various Circumstances, and Temper of Body,
of the Persons *grieving,* especially in those of a melancholy Disposition,
make it evident, that *all* the *ill* Consequences of *Grief* are not carry'd
off by *Tears,* which are seldom shed by Men come to Years. Yet it is
remarkable, that a *Stag,* whose Blood, especially when heated and accelerated by the Chace, approaches near to the State of human Blood,
when he cannot make head against the Fury of the Dogs bearing in upon
him, and sees Death approaching, *bursts forth into Tears.*

But, to cut these Speculations short, I will conclude with this *Remark,*
that it is *evident,* by the manifold Experience of all, "That human Passions, if not restrain'd by Reason, give Birth and Increase to several Distempers, especially Hypochondriacal, to which Man is subject, more
than other Animals; but that the same Passions, under the Conduct of
Reason, make Men hale, brisk, lively, and fit for all Duties." And, therefore, as we would lead our Lives *pleasantly,* we must *endeavour* to *govern*
our *Passions,* whether their *Causes* be now at length *discover'd* to us, or
whether they remain yet *unknown,* in whole or in part.

From this *Effect,* which we *certainly know* sufficiently, arises a *Necessity* of finding out some *Rules of Reason,* by which they may be *confin'd*
within certain Bounds; but *those Rules* are the *same* with those, which
command us to employ our *Affections,* only about the *Means* conducing
to the best and *greatest End,* or the common Good. But the Means to
this End, in the Power of Man, are only those *free Actions,* by which is
either *made* or *preserv'd* such a *Division* of Things and human Services,

as most conduces to the *Happiness* of *all*. And these Rules are the very *Laws of Nature*, as I shall afterwards shew; and such Actions are Acts of *universal Justice*, or of *Virtue conformable to such Laws*. Wherefore, from the Premises, I may *conclude*, "That all those Properties of a human Body, which effect, either that he is *better* able to govern his Passions, or that to do so is *more necessary* to him than to Brutes, do very much conduce, both to his *Knowledge* of the Laws of Nature, and to his *inclining*, in some measure, to the doing those things, which they enjoin."

Thirdly, Mankind are more particularly influenc'd to Benevolence, by their more uninterrupted Inclinations to beget, and, consequently, to rear, their Offspring, than are to be found in other Animals. (This is to be referr'd to the Head of the fourth *Indication, § 20.*)

§XXVIII. What remains will be soon finish'd. With respect to the *fourth Indication,* common to *all Animals,* taken from their *Propension to propagate their Species,* a *human* Body has this only (that I have observ'd) *peculiar* to it, which is, "That its venereal Inclinations are not limited to certain Seasons of the Year, as in most other Animals, but are, in some sort, perpetual." Hence it is, that most Men find it necessary to *marry,* and hence proceeds a *strong Desire of propagating their Species;* whence are inseparable, *Appetites,* and also *Covenants,* relating to the *Maintenance* and *Government* of their *Families.* And because the *Uninterruptedness* of this Propension, and its Consequences, proceed from the *greater Activity* of the *human Blood,* and the *greater Force* of the *spermatick Vessels,* they must necessarily be proportionably *greater* in *Men* than *Brutes;* his *Care* therefore must be *greater,* to *support* and *govern* his *Family;* and this necessarily *supposes* the *Knowledge* of the *Laws of Nature,* and some *Inclination* to observe them. For no *Provision* can be made for a Family, without settling and preserving some *Division* of Things and of mutual Services, for that purpose. But when this is once *understood* and *approv'd of* in the Care of *one* Family, the *Parity of Reason* is so evident, in those things which are *equally* necessary to the Happiness of *other* Families, that it cannot be, but that the *Necessity* of such a *Division,* must in like manner be *understood,* nor can any sufficient *Reason* be assign'd, "Why it should not in like manner be *approv'd of* by, and so extend it self to, *all* Mankind." But in the *Knowledge* and *Approbation* of such a *Division,* necessary for the Good of all, is contain'd the *Knowledge* and *Approbation* of the *Law of Nature.* Meanwhile, the *manner,* how the seminal and active Particles of the Blood excite the Idea and Appetite of Procreation, is to be explain'd by *natural Philosophers* upon some physical *Hypothesis;* for since these *Particles,* thro' their *minuteness,* fall *not* under the Observation of our *Senses,* their particular *Effects* and *Motions cannot* be methodically *explain'd* from *Observation* and Natural History. From the beginning I determin'd to abstain from such *Hypotheses;* let every one take that, which is most consistent with his own *Observations* and *Reason.* It is sufficient for my Purpose to have *shewn,* "That natural Affection, or the Appetite of preserving and educating Offspring brought into the World, is only a continued Appetite of begetting it, or causing it to exist, which includes an Opposition to those Causes, which hinder its Existence." But of this enough already. However, this I think proper here to *add,* "That, because the Offspring of Man continues *longer* weak, and in need of the help of its Parents, it is certain, that, thro' length of Time, and frequent *repeated* Acts of their Love, that Affection grows *stronger* in Parents; so that the longer they have bestow'd Pains upon their Education, they with less Patience bear any Evil, but especially Death, happening to them; and so the very *Difficulty* of forming Men, in order to the common Good, because it is overcome by Hope founded in their Nature, causes Parents to set about it with a *greater* Earnestness and Industry, and daily to give much greater Proofs of their natural Affection, than what are any where to be met with in other Animals."

All the *Indications,* deduc'd from this Head, are the *more carefully* to be observ'd, *because* into it finally is to be *resolv'd,* both the reciprocal *Love of Children toward their Parents,* and the *Benevolence of Relations* toward one another, which will, at length, extend it self to a *Love of all Mankind;* when once we come to *know,* from the most authentick Histories, (the only means antient Facts can be known by,) "That *all Men* are descended from the same *common Parents.*"

§XXIX.[100] To the *last Indication,* taken from the *entire Frame of Animals* and their *united Actions,* is to be referr'd the *Consideration,* "That the

Fourthly, From the Considera-

100. Maxwell breaks up Cumberland's original section XXVIII to provide a tidier break between topics. This involves inserting a new section (XXIX) at the beginning

Bodies of Men are generally more fitted, for discharging the Offices of
friendly *Society;* and, that the manifest Effects of a *stricter Union* among
Men than *Brutes,* is visible in *civil Government,* which has *always* taken
place, over the *whole* habitable World, at least under Heads of Families."
Yet I *confess,* "That this is not to be ascrib'd *wholly* to the Frame of their
Bodies, as in Brutes, but in much *greater* measure to the governing *Mind,*
which in Man sits as it were at the Helm." In this place we are not so
much to consider the *Privileges* of some *particular Parts,* as the apt *Disposition* of them *all,* with respect to one another, by which they are better
enabled to mutual Assistance, of which Disposition it is more easy to
perceive the *Effects,* than to *explain* wherein it consists. It is, however, to
be *observ'd,* "That almost *all* these *Parts* are somewhat *more powerful,*
by their being influenc'd by a *larger Brain,* by a *greater* quantity of *Blood*
and *Spirits,* and a *Heart more under command,* by means of Nerves peculiar to it-self." Yet I thought it proper, to take notice of something
remarkable in *two Parts* of a Man's Body, (by which he is better fitted
for friendly Society,) the *Countenance* and the *Hand.*

Of the *Countenance,* Cicero has long since *observ'd,* "That it is to be
found in no other Animal; their Faces not making near so many *Discoveries* of their *Thoughts* and *Affections.*"[101] These Discoveries are of
singular *use,* in beginning and keeping up an *Intercourse* among Men,
but in *Solitude* are of *no use* at all. These *Signs,* what they are, we all
perceive, but can hardly distinctly *express;* yet these are very conspicuous,
the *Blush* in *Shame, Paleness* in *Fear* and *Anger.* These *two* owe their
being *visible* in Man, to the *Transparency* of the *Scarf-skin* of his Face,
so that the greater or less *Quantity* of Blood, which lies under it, and its
various *Motions,* are easily perceiv'd. From the same *cuticular Transparency,* peculiar to Man, proceeds great part of that extraordinary *Beauty,*
which is conspicuous in the *human Countenance,* which is of great Efficacy in procuring *Good-will* among Men, and was, therefore, not to be

---

of paragraph 3 of p. 151 of the 1672 edition. The effect adds an extra section to the
translation and complicates the relationship with the section numbers of the original
text until the end of the chapter.

101. Cicero, *De Legibus,* I.ix.

pass'd over in silence. For hence we see, not only that *agreeable Mixture* of the bright Colour of the Blood with that of the Skin, but its various *Motions,* according to the Variety of the Passions: a very agreeable Spectacle! To these may be added *Laughter* and *Weeping,* (whose Causes peculiar to Man I have already hinted,) Symptoms of Passions, of great use to give a *Relish* to *Society,* and to banish *Savageness* of Temper. All other *Diversities of Countenance,* (which can hardly be enumerated,) according to the *Diversity of Passions,* arise, either from the various *Motions* of our *Blood,* which may, in some measure, be perceiv'd by the change of Colour in the outer Skin of the Face, or from the *Motions* of the *Muscles* belonging to the Eyes and the rest of the Face, which are excited by the Nerves of the fifth or sixth Pair, which owe their Original to the Intercostal Nerve, and so communicate more immediately than others, with the *Plexus Nervosus peculiar to Man.* Hence it is, that in the Nature of *Man alone* is founded that common Observation, *"The Countenance is the Image, the Eyes the Index, of the Mind."* [102] Moreover, that remarkable *Diversity of Face,* by means whereof, among so many Millions, scarce two can be found alike, is of vast use in *forming* and *preserving Societies;* for hence all may be easily *distinguish'd* from one another, so that every one may discern, with whom it is that he hath made any Covenant, or transacted any Affair, and Men may give certain Testimony, concerning those things, which any one has done, said, or attempted; which would be impossible, were there not something in the Faces of Men, by which they might be distinguish'd from one another.

The Make of the human *Hand,* consider'd with its Arm, is very particular;[103] and its various Powers, with respect to Agriculture, Planting, Architecture, whether in building Houses, Fortifications, or Ships, and all other kinds of mechanical Contrivances, would be almost useless, unless Men mutually assisted one another, and enter'd into friendly Society. I had not any Opportunity of dissecting an *Ape,* or *Monkey,* to compare, in every particular, their *Fore-feet,* which resemble our *Hands,*

and the Hand.

102. The phrase comes from Cicero, *De Oratore,* III.lix: "vultus est animi imago indices oculi."
103. Cf. Cicero, *De Natura Deorum,* II.lx.150–52.

with the dissected Hand, Arm, and Shoulder of a Man. But, without dissecting them, it is evident, both that no Effects of so great *Dexterity* are produc'd by those Animals, as appear in the Works of Man abovemention'd; and that the *Muscles,* both in the Extremity of the human Hand, Arm, and Shoulder, are *stronger,* in proportion to the Bulk of their Body, and the *Joints* much *more pliable* every way. It is also evident, that, in Man, the *Bone* of the *Arm,* properly so called, which reaches from the Shoulder to the Elbow, is very *long,* so as to exceed in length the Bones of the *Cubit,* which terminate in the Wrist, and that the said Bone of the Arm is so *conveniently inserted* into the *Scapula,* (which is plac'd upon the Back, and not so forward, as in Brutes,) and *govern'd* by its *Muscles,* that the *Hands* may by that means be *extended more widely* from one another, and even so turn'd backward, as to be able to *grasp a great Bulk,* or *lift a great Weight.*[104] By this very particular, and truly mechanical, contrivance of Nature, it is, that a Man's Hand is not only fitted for *many* more *Motions* and Operations, but that it has much *more Strength,* both in sustaining and carrying Weights, and in communicating Motion to other Bodies. For, when the Hand is to sustain and carry a great Weight, the Hand, with the Weight it holds, is so let down along the side, by the Motion of the Joints of the Arm, as to be at the least distance possible from the *Line of Direction;*[105] whence it is, that the Weight is poiz'd, with the smallest Force, upon the *Center of Gravity* of the whole Aggregate, compounded of our Body and the Weight to be sustain'd. And this they perform *spontaneously,* who are perfectly *ignorant* of the Doctrine of the *Center of Gravity,* being taught by Experience only; which were not possible, except the Hand were so conveniently fitted to the Shoulder, and to the upright situation of the Body. On the *contrary,* when our Hand is to communicate Motion to a lighter Body, (to a Stone, for *instance,* to be thrown, a Hammer, or any other Instrument;) it is from this convenient Frame of our Hand, that we learn

104. Cumberland's manuscript is corrected to read "introrsum" (inward) rather than "retrorsum" (backward). Maxwell translates the error with its rather odd effect.

105. [Maxwell] "The *Line of Direction,* is that right Line, which may be conceiv'd drawn from the Center of Gravity, to the Earth's Center."

to raise it; whence, because it is farther distant from the Center of its Motion, it moves more swiftly, and exerts a greater Force. As in a longer Sling, because of the greater distance from the Center of its Motion, a greater Force (*caeteris paribus*) is communicated to the Stone to be slung. The Center of Motion, whence the distance of the Hand, and, consequently, the increase of Force, is to be computed, is not always in the Articulation of the Bone of the Arm into the *Scapula*, (whence, however, the Stroke of a Man would receive an additional Force, greater than what is to be met with in other Animals,) but in many Cases, as when the whole Body, and, consequently, the Shoulder it self, is, in striking, mov'd along with the Arm, the Center of Motion is in the Foot on which we stand, and the distance is to be computed from the Foot to the elevated Hand, if we would understand the degree of Acceleration, and the Force thence arising. Thus a *new* and *further Strength* is added to that of our Hands, as *peculiar* to Man, as his *erectness* of Stature. And it is further to be observ'd, that the elastick Force of the many Muscles, spread almost thro' our whole Body, do both conspire to begin such Motions, and concur with the foresaid distance from the Center of Motion, to accelerate them, when once begun. These *Instruments of greater Power* may, indeed, be made use of for *Slaughter,* and other mischievous Purposes, against other Men: Yet I think it *evident,* "That all those things, which inlarge the Power of all Men in general, provided a due Equality or Balance be preserv'd, are Arguments to persuade each to use his Power, rather to assist, than to hurt others, and, consequently, to *recommend* that *mutual Benevolence,* which I endeavour to establish"; this is prov'd, Step by Step, in the following *Propositions.*

§XXX.[106] 1. *A Power of hurting others, balanc'd by an equal Power in them to hurt,* (in Defence or Revenge,) *does not afford a proper Motive to any one, who with Caution provides for his own Security, to endeavour to hurt others.* For it is manifest, because the *Forces* of the Powers are suppos'd *equal* on each side, that, so far, no Reason is assign'd, why the Scale should *incline* one way, rather than the other. On the *contrary,* because,

Notwithstanding these Advantages peculiar to Men, their Powers, how great soever, being nearly equal, afford

106. Section XXIX in the 1672 edition.

much stronger
Arguments to
Benevolence
than Malevo-
lence.

if they fight, it is certain, that *both* the contending Parties *may be kill'd* or maim'd, and it is also certain, that *neither* of them can *gain as much* by the *Victory,* as he who is *kill'd* in fight *loses,* nor as much as he *hazards,* who commits his *Life* to the *Chance* of War; it is *both* their *Interest,* "Not to engage." The hazarding my Life deprives me of more Good, than can accrue to me from this, that my Enemies Life is in equal Danger; nor is *his Security* therefore the *greater,* because *my Life* is *insecure;* but hence *both lose* something which *neither gains.* Nay, if we, for a while, lay aside the Consideration of *Life* and *Health,* and regard only our *outward Possessions,* it is *certain,* "That the Conquerors do not get all the Conquer'd lose, and that they acquire greater Advantages, who cultivate Peace, by which they may enjoy their own."

2. *A Power of helping others, balanc'd by an equal Power in them of helping, suggests to every one a proper Motive, to desire to help others, especially, when it is certain, such Assistance may be given without Damage to our selves.* For a *possible Compensation* partakes of the Nature of *Good,* and is, therefore, a *sufficient Motive* to influence the Will of Man, especially, when, for the most part, we *lose nothing* by our Beneficence, (the Compensation whereof is at least possible,) which can deserve to be brought into the Account. From comparing this with the former *Proposition,* it is *evident,* "That the Consequences (tho they should be suppos'd equally contingent) of Power, determin'd to act benevolently, have a *greater* Force to influence the Mind, *foreseeing* these Consequences, to Benevolence, than the Consequences of Power, determin'd to act malevolently, have to influence the Mind that way"; which is sufficient for my present purpose. For the Mind is chiefly influenc'd by the *foreseen* Consequences of its own Actions. In the *former case,* we foresee it *possible,* "That we may bring Evil upon others"; and we see it *equally possible,* "That we may suffer Evil from them": *on each side* there is an *equal Evil,* but nothing which may *allure* the Will, which always *inclines* to the *greater Good:* In the *latter case,* we foresee *Good,* which we are capable, both of *doing* and *receiving,* but *no damage* to draw back the Scale leaning this way; it is *not,* in this case, so much as *possible,* that *both* should *lose* any thing by Actions of this kind, and here *more accrues to the one,* than is *taken from the other.* I can benefit others by *Innocence,*

by *Humanity,* by *performing Covenants* in support of the common Good; yet, if I duly consider every thing, I *lose nothing* thereby; nay, by thus acting, I *gain* inward *Strength* and *Pleasure,* and the *Hope* of a plentiful *Return;* which yet, how small soever, can scarce be so small, as what by such Actions I deprive my self of, to bestow upon the Publick. For, if I am consider'd, not only as every one is, *alone,* but also *without* the *Benevolence, Peace,* and *Assistance,* of others, I have so very *little,* that I am *not sufficient* to supply my own *Wants,* but am, on all sides, so surrounded with extreme Necessity, that I can hardly make my Condition *worse* by *serving* others, which will be plainly understood by him, who considers the State of Man in a War of all against all, on all sides *unjust.* There is no occasion to *assert* with *Hobbes,* "That such a *War* is *just* and *necessary,* by means of the *right Reason* of every *particular* Person, judging all things to be *necessary to himself,* before the Establishment of civil Society"; since we may grant to him, that it may be very useful to *consider,* "How great *Evils* may proceed from *universal Injustice,* and the *mistaken Judgments* of any Number of Men, arrogating each every thing to himself." But this is widely distant from *Hobbes's Error,* who has *taught,* "That the right Reason of all, living out of civil Society, necessarily leads all into these Evils, so as to leave to Reason no Power of doing Good, beside what proceeds from the Authority of civil Government." I, on the contrary, *affirm,* "That it is impossible, that right Reason should teach us to arrogate all things to our selves only; nay, that it commands us, to agree benevolently to make and preserve a Division, by which every one acquires some Property; and that, as for many other reasons, so also, because it easily foresees Floods of Evils, that threaten all, and, consequently, every Individual, upon this one Supposition, that each regarded himself only, and with a Desire insatiable arrogated all things to himself." The *two precedent Propositions* prove my Point, if the *Power of each* be consider'd, as *balanc'd* by the *Power of one* other Person only. But the Matter will become yet more evident, if we consider,

3. That *the Power, in any single Person, of hurting others, is far exceeded by the Power of many, or of all, by which they defend themselves, or revenge an Injury:* And, 4. That *the Power of any one, by which he may benefit others, is far exceeded by the Power of Requital, which is in many, or in all.*

For *these Considerations* will most strongly *persuade us,* to determine our Powers, how great soever, rather to *benefit,* than to *hurt* others. Nor can it be *imagin'd,* "That the Powers of *all* will be always so *divided,* that *one* will in this War fight only with *one";* and by what Accident soever it happens, that an *unequal* Number of a side engage in the Combat, two against one, for *Instance,* this will carry on the War to the *more certain destruction* of that Person; and, if at first an *equal* Number engage of a Side, they may be reduc'd to an *Inequality* by the Death of one. But thus much seems abundantly sufficient to *prove,* "That the very Powers of Men, whilst they are suppos'd nearly equal, rather suggest Arguments for mutual Benevolence, than for attempting mutual Destruction." It has been already *prov'd,* "That the other Particulars, which I have shewn to be *peculiar to human Nature,* enforce the same *more strongly."*

(*Hobbes* falsly asserts, that Men generally refuse equal Conditions of Society, and he argues from accidental and partial Causes, instead of necessary and universal ones.)

§XXXI.[107] Here, Reader, I desire it may be *observ'd,* "That *Hobbes* has no where offer'd any thing, in this manner *natural* and *essential* to the *Mind* or *Body* of Man, which can suggest to any one a *necessary Argument,* or can otherwise *necessarily determine* Men, that *each* should claim *all* things to himself alone"; but that he sometimes imputes it to the *Passions,* which I have already disprov'd; sometimes, that he says only in general, That *"They will not bear equal Conditions of Society, tho they desire Society it self."*[108] I *answer,* "That, altho there are some Men, who sometimes will not accept of necessary and *equal Conditions of Society,* yet, neither the *Nature* of all *Things,* nor of *themselves,* teaches or determines them to *refuse those Conditions.* The Manners, which a *few* sometimes fall *rashly* into, and from which the Conduct of most others, and often of themselves too, differs, are not to be *imputed* to the *Nature of Man,* nor of the *Universe;* but as those *Manners* themselves are *Contingent,* so they have a *contingent Cause,* which is the *rash Determination* of their *Free-will.* He, who would affirm any thing to be *Natural,* ought

107. Section XXX in the 1672 edition.
108. Hobbes, *On the Citizen,* 1.2n, p. 25: "For even those who arrogantly reject the equal conditions without which society is not possible, still want it."

to consider the *constant, necessary,* and *essential Powers* and Tendencies of all *things,* especially, of *Man,* by which his *Life,* and ordinary *Happiness* are *preserv'd;* rather than those *accidental Irregularities,* by which they are *weaken'd:* For it is *certain,* "That, while we live and are in health, the Causes of Life and Health are stronger, than those which, by their Irregularity, disturb us; and that, therefore, an Estimate is to be made of our Nature from *those,* not *these.*" The reason is the same, in pronouncing concerning all Mankind, or all Ages of all Men, which succeed one another, like the Parts of a River. As to the *Manners* of Men, it is *generally,* tho *contingently, true,* "That they will accept equal Conditions of Society," which is evident from *Experience,* because we *see,* "That such *Societies* have been long ago voluntarily form'd *every where* by them, and that they are *preserv'd oftener* and *longer,* than they are *dissolv'd";* but to be willing to maintain civil Society, or to preserve Peace with another State, is only a constant and continued Will to establish it. Nay it is sometimes more difficult to continue, than at first to form, a Society; yet that *Difficulty* is *overcome* by almost all, thro' the Powers of their *Reason* and *Nature.*

Lastly, the *Nature of Man* does not comprehend only his *Mind* and *Body,* which are his essential Parts, but also the *Union* of *these* two to one another. And, therefore, I thought it proper to *observe,* "That Men may *hence* also be led to the *Knowledge* and *Desire* of a *Good common* to many, nay, and of *Society* and *Government,* and that these are agreeable and *grateful to the Will of the first Cause.*" For we perceive in our selves, that our *Body* is *naturally,* and, consequently, at the *divine Appointment,* not only *united* to our *Minds,* but also, that, in most acts of the Memory, Affections, and Motions, especially Muscular, it is subject to their Government. And *hence,* as by an Idea or Plan of Polity, inseparably united to the Mind, we are continually *admonish'd,* "How many *different* things, because of the *mutual Assistance* which they afford, are necessarily to be consider'd as *one* Aggregate, whilst we are in pursuit of the Causes of a happy Life; how necessary it is, that, among our Parts, *some* should be *determin'd* by *others:* Of how great *Advantage* the mutual *Order* of Parts is, and how *necessary* the *orderly Concurrence* of *many Causes* is to almost all *Effects* grateful to our Nature: Of how great *use*

The Advantages of Society, and convenient Subordination, and consequently of Government, may be shown from the natural Union of the Mind with, and Dominion over, the Body.

the *mutual Offices* of Parts are, and how *pernicious* the *Separation* of some from others, is, which threatens *Death.*" Having thorowly treated of these, I proceed next to the Consideration of GOOD, the *greatest Good,* which is any way in our Power to attain.

General Remarks on Chapter II

It is highly *probable,* "That Men are more *nearly equal* in natural Disposition to *Benevolence,* than is generally imagin'd, and that the *Difference* chiefly arises from *Habit.*"

If this Disposition depends so much upon *Habit,* surely every Person has the greatest reason, to use all the Industry in his power, to *improve* it, which, I believe, might, in great measure, be effected, by a strict regard to the *little common Occurrences of Life,* which are, for the most part, wholly disregarded, as trifling, and of no import. Of the many *Incidents* in Life, which may be used, either to the *Blasting,* or *Nourishment,* of this amiable Disposition, I shall only mention *one,* which seems to me of the greatest consequence, and the least regarded; and that is, *our Behaviour to one another in Company.* No Man who *considers,* "That the *Strength* of any *Habit* depends upon the *Strength* and *Number* of the *Acts* which constitute that Habit, and that we have the most frequent occasions in *conversation,* of acting in a good or ill-natur'd manner"; I say, none who considers these things can *doubt,* "That our Behaviour in Company is of the last consequence, towards the settling a Habit of Benevolence, or avoiding the contrary Disposition." I believe no Man, who would but seriously reflect, that, by every little piece of *ill-natur'd Raillery,* or *malevolent Contradiction,* that Disposition of Mind, upon the Strength of which the whole Happiness of his Life does in a great measure depend, could take *pleasure* in giving another *Uneasiness.* The *Politeness* of the *higher Ranks,* which chiefly consists in being *agreeable,* and avoiding every thing which may give Pain to any of their Company, is, in my opinion, no inconsiderable reason, why *Good-nature* is to be found more frequently among them, than those of the *lower Degrees,* among whom there is little else to be found, but *Rudeness* and *Rusticity.*

There is also another very considerable use to be made of this *Observation,* "That Benevolence principally consists in Habit," which regards the *Education* of Childhood and Youth. It is most *certain*, "That this *flexible* Age is the most proper for laying the Foundations of *Habits*"; and yet it is, with regard to *Benevolence*, almost wholly *neglected*. I believe there can be *no other Reason* assigned, "Why all our Dispositions, which are approv'd of by Reason, except Benevolence, gather Strength and flourish, as the Person grows in Years and Understanding; and that this, the most amiable, the most noble, of all, does wither and decay." I say, there can hardly be any other tolerable Reason assign'd for this, than what may be drawn from the above-mentioned Observation. For, tho the *Reason* of an *enlarg'd, well-inform'd* Mind does perfectly approve of the highest Benevolence, yet, there are many, of so *little, narrow,* souls, as to take in nothing but the *present:* And as a small degree of Understanding may make a *cunning,* but not a *wise,* Man; so it generally makes a Man *selfish,* but never *prudent.*

General Remarks on Chapters I and II

In the first and second Chapters, most of what the Author says, tends to *shew*, "That Benevolence contributes to the common Good; and that, from the *Nature of Things,* and from *Human Nature,* in particular, it appears, That it is the Will of the Author of Nature, that Men should, in general, assist one another; because he hath framed Man in such a manner, and hath adapted the Nature of Things to the Constitution of Man in such a manner, as that Man, partly from the Instinct of *Benevolence,* but, chiefly, from *Self-Love,* in consulting his own Advantage, acts in many cases for the Good of others." What can be collected chiefly for his purpose, from these things, is, in my opinion, *this,* "That, from what we know of Nature, it plainly appears, That God is a most benevolent Being; and that, in most grand cases, he hath plainly connected private with publick Good; and that, therefore, we have good reason to believe, from the uniformity of Nature, that private Happiness is in all cases perfectly connected with the publick Good, even in this Life; altho we are often so short-sighted, as not fully to perceive that *connexion:* Or, that, if private Happiness is not perfectly connected with publick Good in this Life, it is by superadded Rewards and Punishments in another."

Of Natural Good.

Natural Good is defin'd, and divided into Good, proper to one, and common to many.

Good, is that which preserves, or enlarges and perfects, the Faculties of any one Thing, or of several. For, in these Effects, is discover'd that particular *Agreement* of one thing with another, which is requisite to denominate any thing *good,* to the Nature of this thing, rather than of others.[1]

In the Definition of *Good,* I chose to avoid the Word [*Agreement*], because of its very uncertain Signification. Nevertheless, those things, whose Actions or Motions *conduce to the Preservation,* or Increase, of the Powers of other things, consistently with the nature of the Individual, may justly be said to *agree* with them. For we do not otherwise use to judge, whether the Nature or Essence of any thing agrees with another, or no, than by the *Effects* of the Actions thence proceeding. The *Effects* are what disclose the hidden Powers and inward Constitution of all things; these strike our Senses, and afford us a Knowledge of those things, whence they flow. In *Actions* are laid the *Foundations* of all Respects or Relations, to explain which, is almost the whole Business of *Philosophy.* So that is *Good* to *Man,* which preserves or enlarges the Powers of the Mind and Body, or of either, without Prejudice to the other. *"That is Good to any thing, which preserves it,"* says *Aristotle, (Pol.* 1. 2. c. 1.) speaking of Cities.[2]

---

1. A definition drawn from Aristotle, *Politics,* II.2, and one echoed by many of Cumberland's latitudinarian contemporaries. See, for example, Wilkins, *On the Principles and Duties of Natural Religion* (1675), p. 12.

2. Cumberland's reference is misleading; the quotation comes from Aristotle, *Politics,* II.2, 1261b9–10.

What I affirm concerning any *one* particular thing, I would have understood concerning a *Series* of many things, in which some things *profitable* are inseparably *connected* with others that are *hurtful;* in which case, those things which *hurt,* are to be compar'd with those that *profit,* and the *whole* is to be denominated from the *prevailing* Power, whether of hurting or profiting.

Good of this kind, of which we form an Idea, without the Consideration of any *Laws* whatsoever, I call *natural Good;* both because it respects the *Nature* of a thing, a Brute, for *instance,* or a Tree, whose Powers are capable of Preservation and Increase; and, beside, such is the Effect of such kind of Beings,[3] nay, of the Earth it self, that they may be *subservient* to the *Preservation* of *their own Natures,* or even of *ours,* or to our Improvement by farther Knowledge.

It is distinguish'd, by its *greater Extensiveness,* from that *Good,* which is called *Moral,* which is ascrib'd only to such *Actions* and *Habits* of rational Agents, as are *agreeable to Laws,* whether *Natural* or *Civil,* and is ultimately resolv'd into the *natural common Good,* to the Preservation and Increase of which alone all the Laws of Nature, and all just civil Laws, do direct us. Of *Moral* Good, more hereafter; let us now turn our Thoughts, for a while, to that which is *Natural.*

Having *shewn,* "That neither the *Notion,* nor the *Name,* of *Good,* does confine it to him only, who *thinks* or *speaks* of it, but that it may likewise relate to *every other Man,* nay, and to *all other Animals,*" (to say nothing of *inanimate Beings,* which are capable of Preservation, or further Perfection, consisting in the Order or Motion of their Parts;) we must proceed to the Consideration of those *Aggregates,* which may be form'd of *many,* nay of *all, Animals of the same Species;* I add, and of *all Beings making use of Reason,* how much soever they may otherwise differ, such as *Man* and *God.* For, as the Mind considers them under an indefinite Notion, equally applicable to all, it can also unite them into *one* general Body, in order to discover what is Good or Evil for it, which we shall therefore call the common or *publick Good* or *Evil* of *Mankind,*

Such Actions and Habits of moral Agents, as may be subservient to the common natural Good of all, are enforc'd by Laws; and, when such Acts or Habits are embrac'd, upon account of their agreement with moral Rules, they are call'd morally Good.

---

3. [Maxwell] "That is, such kind of Beings, as, having neither Reason nor Will, are incapable of Laws."

or even of *all rational Agents;* and can likewise judge, of the *diverse good* or *evil* things propos'd, which is *possible* or *impossible, greater* or *less.* Nor, in most Cases, is this very *difficult* to determine, at least in *general;* for, since they *all* have the *same* Nature, when we know wherein the Happiness of any *one* consists, we thence know, what kind of Happiness is to be sought for by *every* Individual. For it is *evident, "That* those natural Perfections of the *Mind,* and that Health and Vigour of *Body,* in which the whole Happiness of *one* consists, do also comprehend, when universally extended, all the Happiness of *all,*[4] consequently, both the *different Degrees* of *Happiness,* and the *nature* of *Means* generally necessary to each, in order to attain it, may be equally apprehended in relation to *all: That* all require Nourishment, for *instance,* Exercise, Sleep, &c." *because* such things are necessary to each, and the whole is the same with all its Parts: *hence* also, "Whatever adds any thing, tho but to *one part* of this whole, without changing, and, consequently, without hurting the *rest,* that increases the *whole,* which is compos'd of that, and the other Parts." He who does Good to *one* Man, without hurting any other, may justly be said to do Good to the *whole* Aggregate of Mankind, which may with reason *encourage* every one of us, from the Consideration of the publick Good, "So to take care of our selves, as not to hurt any other Person."

(Hobbes's Opinion concerning Good, stated, §II. I *own,* therefore, "That to be call'd *Good,* which *agrees* with another, and, consequently, that the *Term* is *Relative";* but it is not always *referr'd* to the *Desire,* nor always to that *one Person only,* who desires it. In these *two* Points *Hobbes* has often *err'd* grosly, (tho he sometimes comes out with the Truth, in Contradiction to himself;) and on these *fundamental Mistakes* is supported most of what he has writ amiss, concerning the Right of *War of all against all,* in a *State of Nature,* and a Right of exercising *arbitrary Power,* in a *State of civil Society.* Concerning *Hobbes's* Opinion, that any thing is therefore call'd Good, because it is desir'd.

---

4. [Maxwell] "The Author means, That we can as well compute the degrees of Happiness arising from any State or Circumstances of others, or of a whole Species, as we can the degrees of Happiness, from like Circumstances, enjoy'd by our selves."

See *De Homine,* cap. 11. § 4. *"All things* (saith he) *which are desir'd, are, as such, call'd by the common Name of Good, and all things which are shun'd, Evil,* &c. *whereas different Persons desire and shun different things, it must needs be, that many things which are good to some, should be evil to others,* &c. *Therefore Good and Evil are Correlatives to Desire and Aversion."*[5] Of a Piece with which, is what he has written in his Treatise *of Human Nature,* where he teaches, that *"That Motion, wherein"* he thinks *"our Conceptions of Things consist, passes from the Brain to the Heart, without any Intervention of Judgment, and there,"* (says he,) *"As it either helpeth or hindreth its vital Motion, is said to please or displease. And every Man, for his own part, calleth that which pleaseth and is delightful to himself, Good; and that Evil, which displeaseth him. Insomuch, that while every Man differeth from other in Constitution, they differ also from one another,"* (naturally, and therefore necessarily, and, according to his Opinion, in a State of Nature, unblameably; why not so in civil Society, where, the soundest Philosophers think, natural Necessity takes away Fault?) *"Concerning the common Distinction of Good and Evil."*[6] And says he, *"Such is the Nature of Man, that every one calls that Good, which he desires for himself, Evil, which he avoids. It therefore happens, thro' the Diversity of Affections, that what one calls Good, another calls Evil; and that what the same Man now calls Good, he presently calls Evil; and that he looks upon the same thing to be Good for himself, and Evil for another; for we all estimate Good and Evil, from the Pleasure and Uneasiness it creates to us."*[7] This, he contends, arises, *not* from a Fault of the *Will,* which may be avoided, *but* from the *Nature* of Man, and that it is therefore necessary and perpetual, and, before civil Laws are fram'd, *blameless.* In his *Leviathan,* chap. 6. he expresses himself in like manner, and adds, *"These words of Good, Evil, and Contemptible, are ever used with respect to the Person that useth them, there being nothing simply or absolutely so; nor any*

5. Hobbes, *De Homine,* 11.4, p. 62.

6. The first section of this quotation ("That Motion . . . displease") paraphrases Hobbes's *Humane Nature* (the English version of the *Elements of Law*) 7.1, p. 69. The second half (beginning, "And every Man . . .") quotes 7.3, p. 71.

7. Hobbes, *On the Citizen,* 14.17, p. 162.

common Rule of Good and Evil, to be taken from the Nature of the Objects themselves, but from the Person of the Man, (where there is no Commonwealth;) or, (in a Common-wealth,) from the Person that representeth it; or from an Arbitrator, or Judge, whom Men, disagreeing, shall by consent set up, and make his Sentence the Rule thereof."[8]

and confuted
by the Author,

I, on the *contrary,* am of *Opinion,* "That things are *first judg'd* to be *Good,* and that they are *afterwards desir'd,* only so far as they *seem Good:* That any thing is therefore *truly* judg'd *Good,* because its *Effect* or Force *truly helps Nature:* That a *Private* Good, is that which profits *One; Publick,* which is of advantage to *Many; not* because it is *desir'd* from *Opinion,* whether true or false; or *delights,* for this or that Moment of time." The *Nature* of *Man requires,* "That *Reason,* examining the *Nature* of *Things,* should, from the *Evidence* thence unalterably arising, *first determine* and judge what is *Good,* (whether in relation to our selves, or others) *before* we *desire* it, or are delighted therewith": And it is the Part of *Brutes* only, "To *measure* the *Goodness* of *Things, or of Actions, by Affection* only, *without* the Guidance of *Reason.*" Men of *brutish* Dispositions, experience in themselves such a way of acting, and are *pleas'd* with being told by *Hobbes,* That this is *agreeable to Nature:* Out of this Set of Men, the number of his Followers is increas'd. It is, however, more *certain,* "That a Mad-man suffers a real Evil, tho he be wonderfully pleas'd with his own Madness"; and, on the contrary, "That a Remedy is good for the Patient, tho he should ever so obstinately refuse it."

and contra-
dicted by
Hobbes him-
self,)

And even *Hobbes* himself sometimes relapses into a just way of thinking, and, *tho* he elsewhere most frequently *inculcates,* "That any thing is Good or Evil at the Pleasure of the supreme Powers, or of any private Person, without any respect had to the Good of Civil Society"; *yet, Leviath.* chap. 30. where he reckons it among the Duties of a supreme Governour, that he should frame good Laws, he plainly affirms, *"That all Laws are not Good, tho they are for the Benefit of the Sovereign";* and he defines *"Good Laws"* to be such, *"as are needful for the Good of the People, and withal perspicuous."*[9] Behold the *Good of the People,* which

8. Hobbes, *Leviathan,* ch. 6, pp. 28–29.
9. Ibid., ch. 30, p. 229.

is certainly common to Many, acknowledg'd by himself, as the *End,* which *ought* to be propos'd by the Legislator! But the End is supposed to be first *known,* and, consequently, its Nature *determin'd,* before the Law have *prescrib'd* to the People, what is Good or Evil. So also, *Leviath.* chap. 6. he defines *"Benevolence and Charity"* to be a *"Desire of Good to another":* Nor do I believe he would have *defined* this Affection, if he had *not* thought it *possible.* In the *English* Edition of his *Leviathan,* he acknowledges this *Affection,* when it extends itself to *all* Men, to be *"Good-Nature":* But in the *Latin* Edition he has omitted this; I suppose, as not consisting with his other Opinions.[10] For the *nature* of *Good,* and the *efficacy* of *Things,* to the Preservation and Perfection of the Nature of one or more Persons, is perfectly *determin'd,* and is to be estimated from the *agreement* of *Things* with all the *Faculties* of human Nature, or the *Principles*[11] of those Faculties; taking likewise into Consideration, either the *whole* Course of *Life,* or its *better part: not* from any *unreasonable Affection,* and transient Motion of the Blood, either somewhat promoted or retarded, from a superficial Apprehension of Things.

§III. It is of the last consequence, to *establish a well-grounded and irrefragable Notion of Good;* because, if this totters and wavers, we must, necessarily, be fluctuating and uncertain in our Opinions of *Happiness,* (which is the greatest Good of every particular Person;) and of the *Laws of Nature;* and of *particular Virtues,* Justice, *&c.* which are nothing else, but the means of obtaining that Good, and, in some respect, the Causes, in part, thereof.

The Necessity of establishing the true Notion of Good.

Altho, because of something *peculiar* in the *different Constitutions* of Men, it sometimes *happens,* "That the same Nourishment or Medicine is prejudicial to one, which to most is harmless, or, perhaps, wholesome";

Men agree in the general nature of Good, and in

10. Ibid. The English text reads: *"Desire* of good to another, BENEVOLENCE, GOOD WILL, CHARITY. If to man generally, GOOD NATURE." In the Latin edition, the last sentence, as Cumberland rightly observes, is dropped, probably because it opens the possibility of a generalized standard of good, which works against the relativism of his other definitions.

11. Cumberland and Bentley have amended "principiis" to "praecipuis" (particulars).

the *principal*
Branches of
the Law of
Nature con-
cerning it.

the *like* to which we may *observe*, "In the *Genius* and *Manners* of *Na-tions*,[12] some widely differing from others in some particular Establish-ments"; *yet,* this no more destroys the *Consent* of Men in the *general Nature of Good,* and its principal Parts or Kinds, than a light *diversity*

12. [Maxwell] *"Diversity of Manners,* in *various Nations,* and *Ages,* may be thus accounted for:

"1. From different Opinions of *Happiness,* and of the most effectual means to obtain it. Thus, in one Country, where there prevails a *couragious Disposition,* where *Liberty* is accounted a *great Good,* and *War* an *inconsiderable Evil,* all insurrections in defence of Privileges, will have the appearance of *moral Good* to our *Sense,* because of their appearing *benevolent;* and yet the *same Sense* of *moral Good* in *Benevolence,* shall, in another Country, where the Spirits of Men are more *abject* and *timorous,* where *Civil War* appears the *greatest natural Evil,* and *Liberty* no *great purchase,* make the same Actions appear *odious.* So, in *Sparta,* where, thro' contempt of Wealth, the Security of Possessions was not much regarded, but the thing chiefly desir'd, as *nat-urally good* to the *State,* was to abound in a *hardy shifting Youth; Theft,* if dextrously perform'd, was so little odious, that it receiv'd the countenance of a Law to give it impunity. But in these, and all other Instances of the like nature, the Approbation is founded on *Benevolence,* because of some real, or apparent, tendency to the *publick Good;* and Men *differ* upon these Heads, only from mistaken Computations of the *Excess* of the *natural Good,* or evil *Consequences* of certain Actions; but the Ground on which any Action is approv'd, is still some Tendency to the *greater natural Good* of others, apprehended by those who approve it. In the same manner, we may account for *strange Cruelties* practis'd toward the *Aged,* or *Children,* in certain Countries, but under some Appearance of *Benevolence;* such as to secure them from Insults of En-emies, to avoid the Infirmities of Age, which, perhaps, appear to them greater Evils than Death, or to free the vigorous Citizens from the Charge of maintaining them. A Love of Pleasure and Ease may, in the immediate Agents, be stronger in some Instances, than *Gratitude* towards Parents, or *natural Affection* to Children. But it is still a sufficient Proof of their *natural Affection,* that such Nations are continued, notwithstanding all the Toil in educating their Young. We know, very well, that an appearance of *publick Good* was the Ground of Laws, equally barbarous, enacted by *Lycurgus* and *Solon,* enjoyning the killing the deform'd, or weak, to prevent a bur-densom Crowd of useless Citizens.

"2. The next *Ground* of *Diversity* in *Sentiments,* is the *Diversity* of *Systems,* to which Men, from foolish Opinions, confine their *Benevolence.* It is *regular* and *beau-tiful,* to have *stronger Benevolence* towards the *morally good* Parts of Mankind, who are *useful* to the *Whole,* than toward the *useless* or *pernicious.* Now, if Men receive a *low* or *base Opinion* of any *Body* of Men; if they imagine them bent upon the *De-struction* of the *more valuable* Parts, or but *useless Burdens* of the Earth; Benevolence it self will lead them to neglect the Interests of such, and to suppress them. This is the Reason, why, among Nations, who have high Notions of *Virtue,* every Action toward an *Enemy* may pass for *just;* why *Romans* and *Greeks,* could approve of making

of Countenances takes away the *Agreement* among Men, in the common *Definition of Man,* or the *Resemblance* that is among them, in the Conformity and Use of their principal Parts. There is no Nation, which is not *sensible,* "That our *Love of God,* and *Observance of the Laws of Nature,* in Instances which shall be just now mention'd, afford both *present* Pleasure, and a well-grounded Hope of *future* Happiness." And this *Hobbes* himself somewhere confesses, as *de Cive,* cap. 15. § 9. and the following;[13] tho elsewhere he affirms, That the Honour due to God consists in Fear only, and an Opinion of his Power; as in *Leviath.* Part I. chap. 10, 11.[14] There is no Nation, which is not *sensible,* "That *Gratitude* towards Parents and Benefactors, is *beneficial* to *all* Mankind." No *difference of Constitution* causes any one to *imagine,* "That it is not for the *Good of the Whole,* that the *Lives,* Limbs, and Liberties of particular *innocent* Persons should be *preserv'd*"; and, therefore, the Murder of the Innocent is every where prohibited. What Man is of so *particular a Taste,* as "Not to think it *good* for single *Families,* and, consequently, for all *Nations,* that the Faith of the *Marriage-bed* be preserv'd *unviolated?*" And the *same* may be said of the *Right of using* and enjoying those outward Things, which are *necessary* to Life, Health, Fame or Honour, the Education of Children, and the cultivating Friendship. In judging of the *Goodness* of *these Things,* to take care of which is the whole Business of the Laws of Nature, and of most Civil Laws, *all Men every where agree,* as much as *Animals* do in the Motion of the Heart, and Pulse of the

---

those they call'd *Barbarous, Slaves.* To this Fountain is owing all Party-zeal, Rage, and Bigotry.

"3. A third *Ground* of Diversity of *Manners* is, *false Opinions* of the *divine Will,* producing *Idolatries, Superstitions, Murders,* &c. from a mistaken Sense of Virtue and Duty. *See this Passage more at large, in the* Inquiry into Beauty and Virtue. *Part* II. § 4. *Ed.* 2*d.*" Maxwell refers to the second edition of Hutcheson, *An Inquiry into the Original of Our Ideas of Beauty and Virtue* (1726).

13. Hobbes, *On the Citizen,* 15.9, pp. 175–76. This section is only tangentially related to Cumberland's case, dealing as it does with defining honor as a subjective appreciation of power and goodness. This perhaps explains why it is not quoted.

14. Hobbes, *Leviathan,* ch. 11, pp. 62–63. Cumberland also refers to ch. 10 of *Leviathan,* but the issue is not discussed there. Hobbes does discuss fear as the root of religion in ch. 12.

Arteries, or all *Men,* in their Opinion of the Whiteness of Snow, and the Brightness of the Sun. Even *Hobbes* himself acknowledges, that Civil Laws teach the same thing; *"That in all Cases omitted by Civil Laws,"* (which he acknowledges to be *"Almost Infinite,"* (c. 14. § 14) and may produce infinite Disputes,) *"The Law of natural Equity is to be follow'd."* [15] He therefore grants, that the *Laws of natural Equity* may be *discover'd,* without the help of the *Laws of the State,* and that *more Cases* may be sufficiently *determin'd thereby,* than are determin'd by *civil Laws,* which are not *"Almost Infinite."* This is all I *contend for* at present, "That since Rules of Equity are, naturally, so well known, that no Men, of common Understanding, differ about them." On the other hand, I freely *grant,* "That there are many things *indifferent,* or concerning which human Reason cannot universally pronounce, that it is necessary to the common Good, that the Matter should be transacted this way rather than that." In such cases, the *different Constitutions* of different States *take place,* which, altho they might, *without a Crime,* have been *oppos'd, before* they were enacted into Laws; yet, *after* once they have been establish'd by publick Authority, are to be most religiously *observ'd,* both out of *Conscience* toward God, whose Vicegerents Magistrates are, and for the *publick Happiness* of the *Subjects,* which is chiefly secur'd by the *supreme Authority's* being preserv'd *unviolated.* For it evidently *conduces more* to the *publick Good,* "That the Opinion of the Magistrates should prevail; in things indifferent and doubtful, and that the Subjects should take that for Good, which seems such to the supreme Power, rather than eternal Broils should continue among them, whence may reasonably be expected Wars and Murders, which are, without all question, Evil." [16]

It is a Mistake in *Hobbes* to assert, That §IV. There is another *Error* of *Hobbes,* concerning *Good,* which is, that *"The Object of the"* human *"Will is that, which every Man thinks good for*

---

15. Hobbes, *On the Citizen,* 14.14, p. 161.

16. Cumberland's admission of a positive role for an arbiter may reflect the debate over the role of the magistrate in religion, a live issue in the discussion of toleration during the period and one that framed much of the discussion of Hobbes in the later 1660s. See Parkin, *Science, Religion, and Politics,* ch. 1.

himself." [17] Which he thus expresses elsewhere, *"Every one is presum'd to pursue his own Good, naturally; that which is just, for Peace only, and by Accident."* [18] What is *just,* respects the *Good of others,* which he does not think any Man seeks, unless from a *Fear* of those *Evils,* which arise from a *State of War.* Of a Piece with these Passages, are the places above quoted out of him; and numberless others, scatter'd thro' his Writings, insinuate the same thing. Upon this is grounded that Passage, *"Whatever is done voluntarily, is done for some Good to him who wills it."* [19]

Man pursues only his own private Good.

All these Passages have this one Tendency, to prove, *that* "Men are so fram'd, that it is contrary to their Nature, and, consequently, plainly *impossible, that they should desire any thing but their own Advantage, and their own Glory."* [20] *That,* therefore, since it is evident, that every one can more effectually obtain these things, by Dominion over, than by Society with, others, "All naturally desire such Dominion, and are, consequently, led into a State of War against all, for the sake of obtaining it"; *that* "They are with-held from War, and forc'd to accept the Conditions of Society, by Fear only." But if we examine what led him into an *Opinion,* so *contrary* to that of *all Philosophers,* I can see nothing, but that one *Hint,* which he affords, by the Bye, in the same *Section,* where he explains *"Nature"* by *"The Affections planted in every Animal, till by inconvenient Consequences, or by Precepts, it is effected, that the desire of things present is check'd by the remembrance of things past."* He judges of *human Nature,* and the adequate *Object* of the *Will,* from those *Affections,* which are *previous* to the use of *Reason,* to *Experience,* and to *Discipline,* such as are found in *Children* and *Mad-Men;* see his Preface to his Treatise *de Cive.* [21] But I, as well as all other Philosophers, that I know of,

---

17. Hobbes, *On the Citizen,* 1.2, p. 23.

18. Ibid., 3.21, p. 52.

19. Ibid., 2.8, p. 35.

20. Ibid., 1.2, p. 23: "For since a society is a voluntary arrangement, what is sought in every society is an Object of will, i.e., something which seems to each one of the members to be Good for himself. Whatever seems Good is pleasant, and affects either the organs (of the body) or the mind. Every pleasure of the mind is either glory (or a good opinion of oneself), or ultimately relates to glory; the others are sensual or lead to something sensual, and can all be comprised under the name of advantages."

21. Ibid., preface to the readers, p. 11.

think, "That we are to take an Estimate of the *Nature of Man,* rather from *Reason,* (and that therefore the Will may extend it self to those things, which Reason dictates to be agreeable to the Nature of any Person;) since such *irrational Affections* are to be look'd on, rather as *Perturbations* of the Mind, and, consequently, as *Preternatural*"; which even *Hobbes* himself, since the publishing his Book *de Cive,* confesses in his Treatise *de Homine.*"[22] I also own it *possible,* thro' an *Abuse* of his *Freewill,* "That a Man (thro' his own Fault) of a narrow Soul, may consider *nothing beside himself,* and may therefore desire almost nothing, but what he judges *profitable to himself*"; but I could never observe any Symptoms of *such* a Will, in any Man, except in *Hobbes* only. Others are certainly of a more *generous Disposition,* "Who do not think that alone to be Good, which is such to themselves; but *whatever* conduces to the Preservation and Perfection, to the Order and Beauty of Mankind, or even of the whole Universe, as far as we have any Conception of it; *that* they think Good, *that* they will and desire, *that* they hope for, for the future, and rejoice in, when present." Nor see I any thing to hinder, but that what I judge agreeable to any Nature, I may desire should happen to it; nay, that I should endeavour, as far as in me lies, that it should be effected. But whatever any Faculty (and, consequently, the Will) can be employ'd about, is included in the *adequate Object* of that Faculty. To this appertains that Precept of *Aristotle,* concerning Legislators, *"It is the Duty of a good Law-giver, to consider how his Country, and all Mankind, and every particular Community, may live honestly, and enjoy all possible Happiness."*[23] And elsewhere, *"That is uniformly right, which conduces to the Advantage of the whole Commonwealth, and to the common Good of all its Members."*[24] For what *Aristotle* asserts, in this last place, concerning the Laws of the State, "That in them, not the Good of a part, but of the whole, is to be taken care of; which is to be look'd upon as the mea-

---

22. Hobbes, *De Homine,* 12.1, p. 67: "They [the emotions] are called perturbations because they frequently obstruct right reasoning."

23. Aristotle, *Politics,* VII.2, 1325a7–11. Cumberland quotes in Greek, *De Legibus Naturae,* p. 169.

24. Aristotle, *Politics,* III.7, 1283b40–43.

sure of Right by the Legislator"; this sufficiently instructs us, if the *whole World* be consider'd, as *one* State, what is *universally Right,* and, consequently, ought to be intended in the *Laws* of the Universe, or of *Nature.* For, since *every Legislator* is only a *Man,* and he both can, and ought, to *provide* for the *publick Good,* that being the end for which he is appointed, what hinders, but that we may allow it, to be in *other* Men's Powers, to do the *same?*

Nay, this may be demonstrated *à priori,* to those, who acknowledge the Nature of the *Will* to consist, in the *Consent of the Mind with the Judgment of the Understanding, concerning things agreeing among themselves.* For it is *certain,* "That the Understanding is capable of judging, what promotes the Good of others, as well as what promotes our own"; nor is there any *Reason,* "Why we cannot will those same things, which we have judg'd to be good." (Nay, it is hardly possible, that we should not will those things, which we have judg'd to be good.) But it is to be *observ'd,* "That, whatever a Man can will, he can also resolve to effect the same, as far as it is in his Power." *Good* thus *will'd* by us, is said to be *intended,* and, by virtue of this *Intention,* it assumes the complete Nature of an *End:* Therefore the *common Good* of the Universe may be an *End propos'd by Men.* And, because that is the *greatest Good,* which we can will, the Understanding, forming a *right* Judgment, will affirm *such* a Volition, to be *more* necessarily and essentially connected with the *Perfection* of Men, possess'd with a just Notion of the publick Good; than the Volition of any *smaller* Good. But, for the present, it is sufficient to have *prov'd,* "That the *common Good* may be the *End of Man,* and the *principal* one too; provided it be prov'd, to be *greater* than any other Good." But, whether any Man be *oblig'd* to pursue this End, we shall afterwards *discover,* when we inquire, concerning the *Obligation of the Laws of Nature.* Here I will only add, that *Hobbes* himself, in the *Latin* Edition of his *Leviathan, Cap.* 31. in the last *Section,* contradicts all that he had advanc'd, concerning Man's seeking, *only,* his own proper Good; and does not only acknowledge, that the *publick Good* may be regarded, but openly declares, that he hopes his *Leviathan* will, sometime or other, be serviceable to that End. His words are these, *I do not despair, but that hereafter, when Princes shall have more attentively consider'd their Rights, and Professors their Duty, and that of Subjects, this very Doctrine, softned by Custom, shall, sometime or other, be commonly receiv'd, to the Benefit of the Publick.*"[25] Here, truly, he presages, that his Doctrine, tho not yet establish'd by Princes, shall, hereafter, promote the *publick* Good; and insinuates, that it is adapted to the Good (not of one State only, but) of *all* the *Nations* in the World. Of the Falshood of which, tho I am abundantly convinc'd, yet it is a sufficient Proof, that his Thoughts were sometimes employ'd about this End, and that he knew it might be sincerely intended, otherwise he would, not only, not intend it, but he would not so much as pretend, that he had intended it.

What is more; That *to please others,* is naturally *pleasant,* and consequently seems *good,* to Man, may be prov'd from *Hobbes* himself, because in his Treatise *of Human Nature,* Chap. 9. § 15. he plainly *asserts,* "That even venereal Pleasure is, partly, a pleasure of the Mind, taking its Rise from this, That we are sensible we please another."[26] But it is highly *absurd,* "That he should acknowledge a *Pleasure* of the Mind to arise hence, that something grateful is done to *one* Person only, and that in a Matter of the *smallest Consequence,*" when in the mean time he will not *acknowledge,* "That the Mind of Man receives a *greater Pleasure* from this, that we at once *more highly* gratify *many* in *more important Matters,* when we benefit both their Minds and Bodies, in procuring the common Good, by Fidelity, Gratitude, and Humanity, even when we are not subject to the same civil Power."

Lastly, in his Treatise *de Homine, cap.* 11. § 14. where he purposely inquires, among good Things, which is greater, and which less, he plainly declares, that the Good, which is a Benefit to many, is greater (other Considerations being equal) than that which is so to few.[27]

General Remarks on Chapter III

It would have been very proper for the Author in this Chapter, to have briefly enumerated or compar'd the chief of the human Pleasures.

---

25. Hobbes, *Leviathan,* ch. 31, pp. 244 and 244, n. 15.
26. Hobbes, *Humane Nature,* 9.15, pp. 105–6.
27. Hobbes, *De Homine,* 11.14, p. 66.

What follows, (taken from *Wollaston's Religion of Nature,* Sect. 2.)[28] seems here pertinent.

Prop. I. *Pleasure is a Consciousness of something agreeable, Pain of the contrary; and they are proportionable to the Perceptions and Sense of the Subjects, or Persons affected with them.* (See Observations on this Proposition, in a *Note* on *Chap.* 5. § 6.)

Prop. II. *Pain consider'd in it self is a real Evil, Pleasure a real Good.*

Prop. III. *By the general Idea of Good and Evil, the one* [Pleasure] *is in it self desirable, the other* [Pain] *to be avoided.* What is here said, respects mere Pleasure and Pain, abstracted from all Circumstances, Consequences, &c. But because there are some of these generally adhering to them, and such as enter so deep into their Nature, that unless these be *taken in,* the full and true Character of the other cannot be had, nor can it therefore be known what *Happiness* is, I must proceed to some other Propositions relating to this subject.

IV. *Pleasure compar'd with Pain may either be equal, or more, or less: also Pleasures may be compar'd with other Pleasures, and Pains with Pains.* Because all the Moments of the Pleasure must bear some respect, or be in some *Ratio* to all the Moments of Pain: as also all the degrees of one to all the degrees of the other: and so must those of one Pleasure, or one Pain, be to those of another. And if the degrees of intenseness be multiply'd by the Moments of duration, there must still be some *Ratio* of the one Product to the other.

That this Proposition is true, appears from the general Conduct of Mankind; tho in some Particulars they may err, and wrong themselves, some more, some less. For what doth all this Hurry of Business, what do all the Labours and Travels of Men tend to, but to gain such Advantages, as they think do exceed all their Trouble? What are all their Abstinencies and Self-denials for, if they do not think some Pleasures less than the Pain, that would succeed them? Do not the various Methods

---

28. Wollaston, *The Religion of Nature Delineated* (1722), pp. 23–29.

of Life shew, that Men prefer one sort of Pleasure to another, and submit to one sort of Pain rather than to have another? And within our selves we cannot but find an indifference as to many things, not caring, whether we have the Pain with the Pleasure obtain'd by it, or miss the Pleasure, being excus'd from the Pain.

V. *When Pleasures and Pains are equal, they mutually destroy each other: when the one exceeds, the Excess gives the true Quantity of Pleasure or Pain.* For nine degrees of Pleasure, less by nine degrees of Pain, are equal to nothing: but nine degrees of one, less by three degrees of the other, give six of the former *net* and *true.*

VI. *As therefore there may be true Pleasure and Pain: so there may be some Pleasures, which compar'd with what attends or follows them, not only may vanish into nothing, but may even degenerate into Pain, and ought to be reckon'd as Pains; and* v. v. *some Pains, that may be annumerated to Pleasures.* For the *true Quantity of Pleasure* differs not from that *Quantity of true Pleasure;* or it is so much of that kind of Pleasure, which is *true* (clear of all Discounts and future Payments): nor can the *true Quantity of Pain* not be the same with that *Quantity of true* or mere *Pain.* Then, the Man who enjoys three degrees of such Pleasure as will bring upon him nine degrees of Pain, when three degrees of Pain are set off to balance and sink the three of Pleasure, can have remaining to him only six degrees of Pain: and into these therefore is his Pleasure finally resolv'd. And so the three degrees of Pain, which any one endures to obtain nine of Pleasure, end in six of the latter. By the same manner of computing, some Pleasures will be found to be the loss of Pleasure, compar'd with greater: and some Pains the Alleviation of Pain; because by undergoing them greater are evaded. Thus the Natures of Pleasures and Pains are varied, and sometimes transmuted: which ought never to be forgot.

Nor this neither. As in the Sense of most Men, I believe, a *little* Pain will weigh against a *great deal* of Pleasure: so perhaps there may be some Pains, which exceed all Pleasures; *that is,* such Pains as no Man would choose to suffer for any Pleasure *whatever,* or at least any that we know of in this World. So that it is possible the difference, or excess of Pain, may rise so high as to become immense: and then the Pleasure to be set against that Pain will be but a Point, or Cypher; a Quantity of no Value.

VII. *Happiness differs not from the true Quantity of Pleasure, Unhappiness of Pain.* Or, *any Being may be said to be so far happy, as his Pleasures are true, &c.* That cannot be the Happiness of any Being, which is bad for him: nor can Happiness be disagreeable. It must be something, therefore, that is both *agreeable* and *good* for the Possessor. Now present Pleasure is for the present indeed agreeable; but if it be not true, and he who enjoys it must pay more for it than it is worth, it cannot be for his Good, or good for him. This therefore cannot be his *Happiness.* Nor, again, can that Pleasure be reckon'd Happiness, for which one pays the full Price in Pain: because these are quantities which mutually destroy each other. But yet since Happiness is something, which, by the general Idea of it, must be desirable, and therefore agreeable, it must be some kind of Pleasure: and this, from what has been said, can only be such Pleasure as is true. That only can be both agreeable and good for him. And thus every one's Happiness will be as his true Quantity of Pleasure.

One, that loves to make *Objections,* may demand here, whether there may not be Happiness without Pleasure; whether a Man may not be said to be happy in respect to those Evils, which he escapes, and yet knows nothing of: and whether there may not be such a thing as *negative* Happiness. I *answer,* an Exemption from Misfortunes and Pains is a high Privilege, tho we should not be sensible what those Misfortunes or Dangers are, from which we are deliver'd, and in the larger use of the Word may be styled a Happiness. Also, the Absence of Pain or Unhappiness may perhaps be called negative Happiness, since the meaning of that Phrase is known. But in proper speaking Happiness always includes something positive. For *mere* Indolence resulting from Insensibility, or joined with it, if it be Happiness, is a Happiness infinitely diminish'd: *that is,* it is no more a Happiness, than it is an Unhappiness; upon the confine of both, but neither. At best, it is but the Happiness of Stocks and Stones: and to these I think Happiness can hardly be in strictness allow'd. 'Tis the Privilege of a Stock to be what it is, rather than to be a miserable Being: this we are sensible of, and therefore, joining this

Privilege with our own Sense of it, we call it Happiness; but this is what it is in our manner of apprehending it, not what it is in the Stock itself. A Sense indeed of being free from Pains and Troubles is attended with Happiness: but then the Happiness flows from the *Sense* of the Case, and is a *positive* Happiness. Whilst a Man reflects upon his negative Happiness, as it is called, and enjoys it, he makes it positive: and perhaps a Sense of Immunity from the Afflictions and Miseries every where so obvious to our Observation is one of the *greatest* Pleasures in this World.

VIII. *That Being may be said to be ultimately happy, in some degree or other, the sum Total of whose Pleasures exceeds the Sum of all his Pains:* or, *ultimate Happiness is the Sum of Happiness, or true Pleasure, at the Foot of the Account.* And so on the other side, *that Being may be said to be ultimately unhappy, the Sum of all whose Pains exceeds that of all his Pleasures.*

IX. *To make itself happy is a Duty, which every Being, in proportion to its Capacity, owes to itself; and that, which every intelligent Being may be supposed to aim at, in general.* For Happiness is some Quantity of true Pleasure: and that Pleasure, which I call true, may be consider'd by itself, and so will be justly desirable (according to Prop. II, and III.) On the contrary, Unhappiness is certainly to be avoided: because being a Quantity of mere Pain, it may be consider'd by itself, as a real, mere Evil, &c. and because, if I am oblig'd to pursue Happiness, I am at the same time oblig'd to recede, as far as I can, from its contrary. All this is self-evident. And hence it follows, that,

X. *We cannot act with respect to either our selves, or other Men, as being what we and they are, unless both are consider'd as Beings susceptive of Happiness and Unhappiness, and naturally desirous of the one and averse to the other.* Other Animals may be consider'd after the same manner in proportion to their several degrees of Apprehension.

But that the Nature of Happiness, and the Road to it, which is so very apt to be mistaken, may be better understood; and true Pleasures more certainly distinguish'd from false; the following Propositions must still be added.

XI. *As the true and ultimate Happiness of no Being can be produced by any thing, that interferes with Truth, and denies the Natures of Things: So neither can the Practice of Truth make any Being ultimately unhappy.* For that, which contradicts Nature and Truth, opposes the Will of the Author of Nature; and to suppose, that an inferior Being may, in opposition to his Will, *break through* the Constitution of Things, and, by so doing, make himself happy, is to suppose that Being more potent than the Author of Nature, and, consequently, than that very Being himself, which is absurd. And it is also absurd to think, that by the Constitution of Nature and Will of its Author, any being should be finally miserable, only for *conforming* himself to Truth. As if God had made it natural to contradict Nature; or unnatural, and therefore punishable, to act according to Nature and Reality. Which must come to pass, either thro a defect of Power in him to cause a better and more equitable Scheme, or from some *delight,* which he finds in the Misery of his Dependents. The former cannot be ascribed to the first Cause, who is the Fountain of Power; nor the latter to him, who gives so many Proofs of his Goodness and Beneficence.

XII. *The genuine Happiness of every Being must be something, that is not incompatible with or destructive of its Nature, or the superior or better part of it, if it be mixt.* For instance, nothing can be the true Happiness of a *rational* Being, that is inconsistent with *Reason.* For all Pleasure, and therefore be sure all clear Pleasure and true Happiness must be something agreeable (Prop. I.): and nothing can be agreeable to a reasoning Nature, or (which is the same) to the Reason of that Nature, which is repugnant and disagreeable to reason. If any thing becomes agreeable to a rational Being, which is not agreeable to Reason, it is plain his Reason is lost, his Nature deprest, and that he now lists himself among *Irrationals,* at least as to that Particular. If a Being finds Pleasure in any thing *unreasonable,* he has an *unreasonable* Pleasure; but a rational Nature can like nothing of that Kind without a Contradiction to itself. For to do this, would be to act, as if it was the contrary to what it is. Lastly, if we find hereafter, that whatever interferes with Reason, interferes with Truth, and to contradict either of them is the same thing; then what has been said under the former Proposition, does also confirm this: as what has been said in proof of this, does also confirm the former.

XIII. *Those Pleasures are true, and to be reckon'd into our Happiness, against which there lies no Reason.* For when there is no Reason against any Pleasure, there is always one for it, included in the Term. So when there is no reason for undergoing Pain (or venturing it), there is one against it.

Obs. There is therefore no Necessity for Men to torture their Inventions in finding out Arguments to justify themselves in the Pursuits after worldly Advantages and Enjoyments, provided that neither these Enjoyments, nor the means by which they are attained, contain the Violation of any Truth, by being unjust, immoderate, or the like. For in this Case there is no reason why we should not desire them, and a direct one, why we should; *viz.* because they are Enjoyments.

XIV. To conclude this Section, *The way to Happiness and the Practice of Truth incur the one into the other.* For no Being can be styled happy, that is not ultimately so: because if all his Pains exceed all his Pleasures, he is so far from being happy, that he is a Being unhappy, or miserable, in proportion to that Excess. Now by Prop. XI. nothing can produce the ultimate Happiness of any Being, which interferes with Truth: and therefore whatever doth produce that, must be something which is consistent and *coincident* with this.

Two things then (but such as are met together, and embrace each other), which are to be religiously regarded in all our Conduct, are *Truth* (of which in the preceding Sect.) and *Happiness, that is,* such Pleasures, as accompany, or follow the Practice of Truth, or are not inconsistent with it: (of which I have been treating in this). And as that Religion, which arises from the Distinction between moral Good and Evil, was called *Natural,* because grounded upon Truth and the Natures of Things: so perhaps may that too, which proposes Happiness for its End, in as much as it proceeds upon that difference, which there is between true Pleasure and Pain, which are Physical (or *Natural*) Good and Evil. And since both these unite so amicably, and are at last the same, here is *one* Religion which may be called natural upon *two* accounts.

Of the practical Dictates of Reason.

I must begin this Chapter with observing, that *not all the Actions of Men are grounded upon the Dictates,* or upon *Notions equivalent to the Dictates, of Reason.* For *our first Apprehensions,* and *certain Motions of the Spirits,* or Imagination, sometimes also *muscular Motions,* as the winking of the Eyes, or a sudden starting back from our Friends, seem to be effected *without any Dictate of Reason;*[1] also, *most Actions of Infants,* as Comparing, Judging, *&c.* concerning things pleasant and hurtful, by which, nevertheless, their Treasure of Knowledge is increas'd: And, perhaps, the *Desire of Good in general* may be reckon'd among these.

> All human Actions are not voluntary and, consequently, do not suppose practical Dictates of Reason.

For the Author of Nature has so *fram'd* us, "That, *in our Childhood,* we, even *unwillingly,* perceive many things by our Senses, and firmly retain them in Memory, and judge by a *spontaneous* Comparison, whether some are greater than others, like or unlike, profitable or hurtful"; but, above all, (because we are always present to our selves, and from the particular Frame of our Mind, reflecting upon it self,) "We are *necessarily* conscious of the Acts of our Understanding and Will, and how much we have it in our Power, to excite, and govern, certain Motions of our Body," which are, therefore, usually call'd *voluntary;* and, therefore, we *necessarily* know by experience, "What Actions of these Faculties bring us Harm, or Benefit and Perfection," with which Knowledge, Desire and Pursuit, or Aversion and Avoidance, are *naturally* connected. Further, we easily *perceive,* by a Parity of Reason, (without any

> How the practical Dictates of Reason are form'd.

1. Barbeyrac (*Traité Philosophique,* p. 194, n. 1) suggests that Cumberland's classical source for this discussion is Seneca's *De Ira,* II.iv.1–2.

other Guide than *Nature*,) "That the *like*, both Advantages and Disadvantages, accrue to, and are perceiv'd by, *other* Beings also, as far as
they *resemble* us, either in Mind, or Body, or both." Hence we draw some
Conclusions, concerning Actions acceptable to God, but many more,
concerning such as are advantageous, and disadvantageous to Men.

When we have attain'd to a *Maturity of Reason*, we take into *Consideration* the *whole* of our *Life*, or the whole future exercise of all our
Powers; and, *because* a greater Number of Actions, probably future, and
also of good Effects, which we hope for from thence, presents itself now
at once to our Mind, than formerly; and a longer Train of Events, which
are to succeed in order, and mutually depend upon one another, is contemplated by the Mind, now come to a ripeness of Judgment: *Therefore*
the Mind calls in, to the Assistance of the *Memory*, not single Words
only, but Propositions, distinctly exhibiting the Connexion of our Actions of all Kinds, with their natural Effects. These *Propositions* are called
Practical, nor is it necessary, that they should be pronounc'd in the Form
of a *Gerund*, "*This*, or *that, ought to be done*," as some *Schoolmen* teach;
because that *Fitness*, which is express'd by a *Gerund*, wants Explanation,
which is to be fetch'd, either from the necessary *Connexion* of the *Means*
with the *End*, or from the *Obligation of a Law*. The Obligation of Laws
is *not* yet to be suppos'd *known* by those, who are in *quest* of their *Original*. And the necessary *Connexion*, between the *Means* and the *End*, is
sufficiently express'd, in the *Connexion* of them, as of *Causes*, with their
design'd *Effects*.

Moreover, as we *approach Manhood*, it is natural for us, to *compare*,
with one another, the *Powers* of several *Causes*, to produce the like Effects, as also the several *Degrees of Perfection* of those *Effects*, from which
Comparison we form a Judgment, that this is *greater*, or *less* than, or *equal*
to, that. Hence, for *example*, we *conclude*, "That *some* of those *Actions*,
which are in our Power, can contribute *more* than others, or *most* of all,
to our own *Happiness*, and that of others." Such kind of practical Propositions, I call *comparative Dictates of Reason*.

It is not necessary for us, who only inquire into the *Formation* of the
Laws of Nature, to assert, that *such Dictates*, even after we know that
they have the Force of Laws, *do always determine* Men to Action; it is

sufficient, that they tell us, *how we ought to determine.* For, concerning the *Power, which determines us to Action,* there are different Opinions, and I care not to engage in the Dispute. All, however, I think, *acknowledge,* "That a practical Dictate of Reason is previously necessary to our deliberate Acts, and does, in some manner, direct the Determination of our future Actions." Nevertheless, the *essential Parts* of a *practical Dictate,* and its *Form,* require, in the next place, to be more attentively consider'd; for thence its *Formation,* in our Mind, will more easily be apprehended.

A *practical Proposition* is, sometimes, thus express'd. "This possible human Action" (universal Benevolence; for *instance*) "Will chiefly, beyond any other Action at the same time possible, conduce to my Happiness, and that of all others, either as an essential part thereof, or as a Cause, which will, some time or other, effect a principal essential part thereof." It is sometimes express'd, in the *Form* of a *Command.* "Let that Action, which is in thy Power, and which will most effectually, of all those which thou can'st exert, promote the common Good in the present Circumstances, be exerted"; often also, in the *Form* of a *Gerund;* "Such an Action ought to be done." In my Opinion, *these several Forms* of Speech, relating to the Law of Nature, mean the *same thing,* whether the Understanding *judges this best* to be done, or *commands* it, or tells me, in the *Form of a Gerund,* that I am bound to do it. For the Understanding (which in this Affair is call'd *Conscience*) sufficiently hints the *natural Obligation,* when it *says,* "This is best to be done, both for your self and others." For, in *omitting* what is declar'd *best* for me, it is thence evident, that *I bring mischief* (which may be called *Punishment*) upon my self. If the Dictate be consider'd, under the Form of a *Command,* the same thing is inculcated, by representing every Man's own Understanding, as a *Magistrate* deputed, and authorized, to make Laws: Which, because it sounds somewhat *metaphorically,* is, therefore, *less philosophical;* it is useful however, because the Comparison has a very just Foundation in Nature. The Form of a *Gerund* teaches the same thing; but as an inferior Judge, or *Counsellor,* admonishing concerning a Law already made, and requiring a Conformity of the future Action therewith. The *first* manner is most becoming a *Philosopher,* which, if

Three Forms of practical Dictates of Reason,

Compar'd.

we consider the *Form,* appears a *speculative Proposition;* if the *Force,* a *Practical,* as teaching the natural Foundation of Obligation. The *second* best becomes a *Sovereign* Prince; the *third,* a *Divine.* But they may all be us'd promiscuously, provided we retain in Mind the Distinction, such as it is, between these Forms. The *Nature* of Things *represents* to the Mind, what is *best* to be done. The *Mind,* considering the Government of Things, does, from the Idea of God, conclude, that he wills, or *commands,* them to be done, and, in his Name, imposes the Command on it self, in the second Form. In the third, it reflects upon the two former, and pronounces, that an *Action agreeable to that Command,* will be *just;* the contrary, *unjust.*

A fourth Form, §II. There is also another manner of expressing the Laws of Nature, as *thus,* "This, or that, possible Action is most agreeable to human Nature." But the Sense is doubtful; for, (1.) *Human Nature,* either signifies the *particular nature* of the Agent, and then it is not expressive enough of what ought to be consider'd before Action: For, not the Happiness of one particular Person only, but the greatest common Good, ought to be regarded. Or, (2.) *Human Nature* respects *all Men,* and so God is not taken into Consideration. But, if, in either of these Notions, the publick Good is, by consequence, implied, this Form of speaking is coincident Coincident with the first, which is therefore to be preferr'd, because it is free from with the first, this Ambiguity. Again, it is doubtful, to what the Expression [*is agree-* which is less *able*] relates: For, (1.) An Action may be said to *be agreeable to any Nature,* ambiguous, when it is agreeable to the *Principles* of *acting,* such are Faculties, Habits, and Objects, either treasur'd up in the Memory, or solliciting to Action from without; and to these Heads may be reduced the practical Dictates of Reason, (that is, Propositions, which are the Rules of Action,) whose Terms, having taken their Rise from Objects, are retain'd in the Memory, and are, by the Mind, form'd into Propositions, whereby they determine our Actions, and constitute Habits. (2.) An Action may be said to *be agreeable to human Nature,* when its *Effects preserve,* or *improve,* the *Nature* of one or more Men. This latter Sense coincides with the Form 1 first propos'd, which is free from Ambiguity: And the first Sense of the *Agreeableness* of Actions, may, for the most part, be reduced thereto. For *practical Propositions,* which are among the *internal Principles of Action,* relate all to the *Desire* of an *End,* the chief principally, and to the *Use* of the *Means.* Those Propositions, which relate to the Desire of the *ultimate End,* pronounce only to *this Purpose,* "This is, in its own Nature, Good, or a part of human Happiness, and that the greatest possible in the present Circumstances." Those, which determine concerning the *Means,* inculcate only *thus,* "This conduces to the obtaining such Good, and that the most effectually in the Case propos'd." And *these Forms* of speaking *coincide* with the *first.* The *first Form* is to be *preferr'd,* because this manner of resolving a Proposition, concerning the *Agreeableness* of an Action, is not, for the most part, obvious to the Understanding; and, beside, what I aim at, *is,* "To *explain* the *manner* of *forming* these first *Dictates* of Reason, with which Actions *ought to agree";* wherefore it is not sufficient to our purpose, to *say,* "That an Action is agreeable to Dictates *already form'd,* such as, alone, are the immediate Principles of human Actions." It may not, however, be useless, to remark, that we may truly *affirm,* "That all good Actions, or *Virtues,* do perfectly and essentially *agree* with the Notion or Idea of a *rational Agent,* whose Reason has ripen'd into Prudence, whither it naturally tends." For *Prudence* necessarily includes, both the *Desire* of the best and *greatest End,* which is within the reach of any one's Faculties, and the *Prosecution* of the same, by the *most effectual means.* The *greatest End* is the *common Good* of all rational Agents, and the *Consent* of all, to give *mutual Assistance* toward obtaining that End, is the *most effectual means* of promoting it. In Actions pursuant to such *Consent,* consists all Religion and Virtue. And it may be presum'd, even before Compacts are enter'd into, that all will agree, that *this* is the greatest End, and *this* the only Means plainly necessary, because *no Cause* can be assign'd to human Actions, of mutual Assistance, *beside* the *Consent* of the Will.[2] Therefore, if we reckon such

2. Barbeyrac (*Traité Philosophique,* p. 198, n. 1) suggests that this sentence lacks the reference to rational ideas required by the subsequent sentences and suggests that Cumberland's sentence should have read, "Nulla praeter consensum INTELLECTUS ET voluntatis esse potest causa." It could be argued that Cumberland presupposes that the consenting will is rational and that Barbeyrac's correction here is pos-

Dictates of Reason, (which, whilst they are stored up in the Memory, determine us to Action,) among the *inward Principles of human Actions,* (which we may very justly do, since they contain in themselves the whole Essence and Force of *Habits,*) then it may, truly and agreeably to what we have said, be *affirm'd,* "That every thing is *Just,* which agrees with these *Principles,* and the *Laws* of a *rational Nature.*"

Whether the
Law of Nature
be sufficiently
promulg'd. §III. We are next to *consider,* especially with respect to the *first,* which is Nature's *principal Form* of proposing its Laws, "Whether that *Law,* or practical Proposition, be taught, or *promulg'd, with sufficient clearness,* when its *Terms,* (and consequently their *Connexion,* or the Truth of the Proposition,) are *obvious,* and as it were expos'd to the View of those Men, who are *willing* to *attend* to the *Consequences* of their own *Actions?*" Or, "Whether we are to think, that Nature has *not with sufficient Plainness declar'd* such a Truth, so as to *oblige* those, who, thro *Wickedness,*[3] or other *Cares* with which they distract their Mind, *do not compare* these *Terms* with one another, nor form such *practical Propositions,* for the future Direction of their Actions"? The *former Opinion* seems to me the more *probable,* because whoever shews me a Triangle, shews me with sufficient evidence, that the two sides of a Triangle are longer than the third, altho he does not form the Proposition for me. It is, however, incumbent upon me, in this Treatise,[4] to *prove,* (1.) "That the *Terms* of the Laws of Nature are, as things are fram'd, in the same manner *clearly* enough laid before the Minds of Men." (2.) "That the *Minds* of Men are in like manner *excited,* by their own Nature, or by their Union with the Body and the rest of the System of the World, to *consider,* abstract, and compare, those Terms among themselves, and thence to *form Prop-*

---

sibly superfluous. Neither Cumberland nor Bentley amended this passage in the corrected copy.

3. Barbeyrac (*Traité Philosophique* p. 198, n. 1) indicates that Maxwell, in translating *injuriam,* has translated a printer's error. The word should be *incuriam* (negligence), and this does sit more naturally with the rest of the sentence.

4. [Maxwell] "The Author considers these two Points in the following Chapter."

ositions for the Conduct of their Actions; and that, therefore, all Persons, in their Senses, *retain* such Propositions in their Mind, tho sometimes blended with what is impertinent or false, and thereby obscur'd."

The *Terms* of those practical *Propositions,* which are called the Laws of Nature, are such *human Actions,* as are capable of being *guided* by Counsel or *Reason;* and which, after they are exerted, do jointly contribute to the greatest Happiness of *all* rational Agents, and to *our own* in particular. Such Actions are commonly divided, justly enough, into, (1.) The *Elicit* (that is, the proper and immediate) Acts of the Understanding and Will, and, consequently, of the Affections, (at least so far as the stronger Affections have place in the Mind itself;) and, (2.) The *Imperate,* which are exerted, in the Body, by the Power of the Mind.

§IV. But, before we consider these Laws more particularly, it will be worth while, to insist somewhat longer, on treating of the nature of *practical Propositions,* and first to shew their great *Affinity,* or Agreement in meaning, whether they be Absolute or Conditional, with *speculative Propositions.* 2dly, That, in them all, the *Effect* is look'd upon as the *End; Actions* in our Power, as the *Means.* The Nature of the practical Dictates of Reason illustrated by a Comparison of them with mathematical Practice.

In order to which we are first to observe, that those are properly called *practical Propositions,* which *declare the Origin of an Effect from human Actions,* which Definition I think proper to illustrate by Examples. Such is this in *Arithmetick,* "The Addition of Numbers forms the Sum," or, "The Subtraction of one Number from another, leaves their Difference." So in *Geometry,* "The Practice, prescrib'd in the first Proposition of *Euclid*'s *Elements,* will effect an Equilateral Triangle," is, a practical Proposition, pronouncing concerning the Effect of a certain Series of human Actions. Practical Propositions,

Moreover, the Mind certainly *understands* the *Truth* of such a *practical Proposition,* in the *same manner* it does that of any *Theorem,* which is, by *considering* its *Terms,* of which one includes the other. So the Truth of this *Proposition,* "The Construction of a whole Equilateral Triangle is made, by constructing and uniting all its Parts," is known after the same manner with this *Theorem,* "A whole Equilateral Triangle is the same, with all its Parts united among themselves." which are near of kin to Theorems,

consider the
Effect as the
End, Actions
as Means.

It comes to the same thing, if the *Construction* of this *Whole* be consider'd as the *End,* and the *several Motions,* by which the three sides of that Triangle are form'd and fitted to one another, are consider'd as the *Means* necessary to that End. The *same Proposition,* as to Sense, may be *otherwise* thus *express'd.* "It is necessary to the Construction of a whole Equilateral Triangle, that all its sides be form'd, and mutually join'd, after the manner prescrib'd by *Euclid,* or some equivalent Method." For, truly, the *End* is the *Effect intended,* and all the *Causes,* effecting a proper Union of all the Parts, include at once all the *Means.* What we have already said about the *Construction,* may be very easily accommodated to these other Operations,[5] the *Preservation* or *Perfection,* of any Whole, which needs such Operations. Seeing the *Preservation* of any thing, is only the *continuing those Actions, by which it was first form'd.* Hence this *practical Proposition,* "It is necessary, in order to procure the Preservation of the whole System of rational Agents, as far as in us lies, that we should preserve, as much as possible, all its Parts, and their Union among themselves, (such as the Perfection of such a System requires.)" This, I say, has a *like* Evidence with that *Theorem,* which *affirms,* "That the Whole is the same with all its Parts united." And in *that* Proposition, rightly understood, I will prove are contain'd the *Foundations* of all natural Laws. What I have offer'd, concerning the *Conversion* of *Euclid's* first *Problem* into a *Theorem,* I would have, by a *Parity* of Reason, understood *universally.* For nothing hinders, but that "The *Solution* of all those things may be perfectly propos'd in *Theorems,* which are usually sought after in the Form of *Problems.*" Therefore *Archimedes,* in his *second Book of the Sphere,* plainly *professes,* "That, of Problems, whose Solution consists of Propositions directing Practice, he form'd Theo-

---

5. The original Latin text here is "ad operations conservantium," which Maxwell has translated as "to these other operations, the Preservation." Bentley and Barbeyrac felt that the operations under consideration in the passage were linked to preservation and perfection, and sought different solutions to make the parts of the sentence agree. Bentley's solution is the neatest. He amends the text to "operationis conservationem." See Barbeyrac, *Traité Philosophique,* p. 200, n. 1.

rems." And *Ramus,* in Imitation of him, in his *Geometry,* converts all
Euclid's Problems into *Theorems.*[6] And in *specious Arithmetick,* (the happiest art of solving Problems,) at the end of the Operation is always
produc'd a *Theorem,* pointing out the Solution of the *Problem.*

Nor is it to be doubted, but, as *Des-Cartes, Vieta, Wallis,* and others,
have successfully taught an expeditious Method of solving *Problems* in
pure Mathematicks, (Arithmetick and Geometry,) by *Theorems* algebra-
ically invented and exhibited: so also *Problems* might be solv'd, in the
same manner, in *mixt Mathematicks;* not in Astronomy only, (which
Ward has excellently perform'd,) but also in Mechanicks, Staticks, &c.
and in great part of natural Philosophy.[7]

Yet farther; the science of *Morality* and *Politicks,* both can, and ought
to, *imitate* the *Analytick Art,* (in which I comprehend, not only the Extraction of Roots, but also the whole doctrine of specious Arithmetick
or Algebra,) as the noblest Pattern of Science.

(1.) By *delivering the Rules of its Practice, and the whole Substance of
its Art, in a few universal Theorems.* Where I think proper to *observe,*
"That its *certainty* is *no more weaken'd,* or *usefulness lessen'd,* because we
cannot exactly determine what is fit to be done, in our external Actions,
with relation to a Subject *involv'd* in a vast Variety of Circumstances;
than the *Truth* or *Usefulness* of *Geometrical* Principles, about measuring
Lines, Surfaces or Solids, is *overthrown,* because neither our Senses, nor
Instruments, will enable us, to form without us a Line *exactly* strait, or
a Surface *perfectly* plane or spherical, or a Body, *in all respects,* regular."
It is sufficient, that we *approach so near* to Exactness, that what we *want*
of it, is of *no consequence* in Practice. We may attain a *like Degree of
Exactness,* in *Morality,* by the help of its Principles. I *confess,* however,
"That *those things* which, in *Morality,* are granted, or *assumed* as known,
such as GOD and MAN, their Actions and mutual Relations, are *not so*

6. Euclid, *Elementa Geometriae;* Archimedes, *De Sphaera et Cylindro,* II; Ramus,
Arithmeticae (1555).

7. Cumberland refers to Descartes, *La Géométrie* (1637); Vieta, *Canon-
Mathematicus* (1571) and *In Artem Analyticum Isagoge* (1591); Wallis, *Arithmetica Infinitorum* (1656) and *De sectionibus conicis tratatus* (1655); Ward, *Astronomia Geometrica* (1656).

exactly known, as *those things,* which in *Mathematicks* are *assum'd,* in a fix'd determinate Proportion or Quantity; and that, therefore, the *Conclusions* thence drawn must labour under the *same want of Exactness."* Yet the *Method,* the *Rules* of Operation, and the *Manner* of drawing Consequences, is the *same.* Nor is *Exactness* necessary for the Uses of Life; as neither is it requir'd, in the Practice of measuring Planes and Solids.

(2.) *As Algebra,* by *beginning with,* and supposing, the most compounded and *involv'd Aequations,* where the known Quantities are mingled with the unknown, then diligently *comparing* among themselves the several *Terms,* does at length discover some simple *uncompounded* thing, of which the *compounded* parts may be compos'd, and which, consequently, leads us to the *Knowledge* and Explanation of the *unknown* Quantities, by the *known. So,* likewise, *moral Philosophy begins with* contemplating an *End very intricate,* and *Means variously involv'd.* For the *End* is a Collection of all those good things within our Power, which are capable of adorning the Kingdom of God, the whole System of intelligent Agents, and its several Parts. The *Means,* by which this End is to be obtain'd, are all our possible free Actions, about what Object soever. And, from an *Equality suppos'd* between these *two Ideas,* as between the Powers of the *Cause,* and their adequate *Effect,* are to be drawn all moral *Rules,* and all virtuous Actions enjoin'd by them. It is evident, that these Things are *equal,* because the End is the intire *Effect* to be produc'd, and all our possible Actions make up the intire *efficient* Cause. But in this consists the *Art of Life,* "To consider every *publick Good* in our Power, and all our *particular Actions,* and their Order, (by which some may prepare Matter for, or add Force to, others,) with such Attention and Care, that having, at length, *trac'd* out the *most easy* Actions, which may serve to promote to that End, by their Help we may *proceed* to the *more difficult,* and, *at last, reach* those utmost and *most intricate* bounds of our Faculties." And *this* Practice perfectly corresponds to *that* of Algebra.

(3.) *As Algebra supposes* the Quantity *unknown,* and yet *sought* after, in *some sort* already *known,* by a certain Anticipation of the Mind, and expresses it by a proper *Character,* and is thus enabled to exhibit its given

Relation to the *known Quantities,* by means whereof it-self at last *becomes known: So Ethicks,* also, forms *some kind of Idea* of the *End* or Effect propos'd; by the help of those *Relations,* which it bears to our Operations *in some measure known,* (at least in general,) it *distinguishes* it by the name of the *chief Good,* or of Happiness, from other Objects, altho' it *knows,* "That it does not yet exist," and altho' it does *not* distinctly *know,* "What shall at last be the Effect of our Operations, and of the Concurrence of Things without us"; whence it may justly be called *Unknown:* But, by the help of those *Actions* and *Faculties,* to which it is *related,* as the Effect to its Causes, and on which, consequently, it most certainly intirely depends, it at last gradually *becomes known.* Hither also is to be referr'd, that, *whereas* the End propos'd by every one, is that intire and greatest Good, which he can procure to the Universe, and to himself in his station, it *follows,* "That the End is to be conceiv'd as the greatest Aggregate, or Sum, of good Effects, most acceptable to God and Men, which can be effected, by the greatest Industry of all our future Actions." It often *happens,* (and we ought to endeavour that it should happen as often as may be,) "That the good Effects of our Power increase in a Geometrical Progression"; (as in increase arising from Interest upon Interest, or in Husbandry, or Merchandizing, when every year the increase of the former is added to the main Stock;) *whence* arises a vast increase, both of publick and private Happiness, beyond what can be distinctly foreseen.

(4.) Since it is *manifest,* "That *Man,* without the Concurrence of *God,* can contribute *nothing,* without that of *other Men, almost nothing,* toward the common Good (the Glory of God, and Happiness of Men;)" but on the *contrary,* "That by any Action entering into, or preserving, *Society* with God and Men, any one may contribute much (comparatively speaking) to the publick Good": The Judgment of *Reason* must, therefore, necessarily *determine* Man to such Actions, as tend to the forming or preserving *such Society.* But *little,* or *nothing,* is transacted in Society among Men, which does not depend upon the Knowledge of *Numbers* and *Measure;* and, therefore, if all *Questions,* concerning *Practice,* were handled *accurately,* they might be *reduced* to *mathematical* Evidence and Certainty; such are the determining the *Value,* both of

Things and human Labour or Actions, either by comparing them among themselves, or with a third Thing, *Money*, of which also there are various Species; to reduce the Values of which to the most known and convenient Denomination, there is need of *Arithmetick*, either Natural or Artificial. To this Head are to be reduced, the *Calculation* of *Prices* in all *Commerce*, the *Computation* of *Time*, the *investigating* the *Proportion* of every Man's *Profit*, or *Loss*, in *Partnership*. It would be endless, to attempt enumerating the *Uses* of *Mathematicks* in *Tacticks*, in *Navigation*, in the Contrivance and Application of all Kinds of *Engines*, in *Surveying*, and in *Building*, whether Houses, Ships, or Fortifications. It is sufficient, in few Words, to *affirm*, "That in *all Affairs*, whether *private* or *publick*, Mathematicks is the principal *Instrument* of *Certainty* and *Justice* in Action, wheresoever *Exactness* is requisite." Which I do not advance, with a view to *commend Mathematicks*, (which is needless,) but to demonstrate the *Certainty* of the Rules of Life and *Morality*, upon this Account, that *Natural Prudence* almost always makes Use of the *Assistance* of a *Science* that is *certain*, or of *self-evident Principles*. To this *Head* also, I think, may be *referr'd*, "That, whereas we know not what shall hereafter happen, we may, nevertheless, know what is *possible:* And things *possible* may be *compar'd* among themselves; and it may be *certainly* known, not only, which of *two possible* Things will be of *greater* or *less Value*, when they do happen; but, also, which of them may be produc'd by *more*, which by *fewer, Causes*, that do now, or shall soon, exist. But that is *more probable*, which may happen *more ways*, and its *Chance* or Expectation is of *greater Value*." Now it is of great *Consequence*, in the Management of Affairs, "To know certainly the *Probability*, and *Value*, of the *Hope* of the several Things, or Effects, we have occasion to consider." For *such* is the condition of human Life, that we must lay out *almost* our *whole Labour*, our *Expence often*, nay expose *Life* it-self to *Danger*, for the *Hope* of such Things, as conduce to the Preservation or Happiness of our-selves, or of others, altho' that Hope be *probable* only, *not certain;* even in Affairs of *Peace*, such as Agriculture, Merchandize, &c. much more in the *Chance of War*. That skill of investigation by *Analysis*, which all Men exercise *naturally*, teaches how to weigh these things very well; how the Value may be farther ascertain'd by *Analysis,* improv'd by *Art,* the famous *Huygens* hath finely shewn in his *Calculations of the Chances of the Dice,* which you may find at the End of *Schooten's Miscellaneous Mathematical Exercitations.*[8]

It is an *Observation* pertinent to this *Head,* "That, *as in Matters of Prudence* we must *sometimes try several Ways, before we can know certainly, whether the Affair shall succeed,* according to our Wish, in this or that manner? Or whether we can at all obtain what we hop'd for? *So,* also, *in Algebraick Investigations, sometimes various Comparisons,* sometimes various Divisions, and other Kinds of Reduction, are to be *tried, before we can solve the Problem* propos'd." It would not be impertinent here, to proceed farther, in tracing the *resemblance* between these *Arts,* in shewing, how the *Method* of Operation in *both,* does sometimes discover the *Supposition* built upon, to be *false* or *impossible,* not much less usefully, than it discovers another *Supposition* to be *true* or *possible:* And, moreover, by shewing, how *negative Signs* resemble *Motions contrary* to the Motion design'd, and how the *Labours of different Men, conspiring* to the same Effect, are correspondent to a *compounding of Motions, concurring* to form one and the same Line. But, since such matters are not very obvious, and the Resemblance is seldom carried on throughout, I thought it *properer* to stop here, whither those, who are but superficially conversant in Mathematicks, or who have a genius happily form'd by Nature for Science, may go along with me; *than,* by Comparisons with Things little known, to obscure, instead of reflecting light upon, Morality.

General Remarks on Chapter IV

Tho' the Nature of future Contingencies will not admit of a *Demonstration,* "That any particular virtuous Action will be more for the Advantage of the Agent upon the whole in this Life": Yet a Man of an enlarged Understanding may, in most moral Actions, have an *intuitive Knowledge,* that it is *highly probable,* "The Action will be for his Advan-

---

8. Huygens, *Tractatus de ratiociniis in aleae ludo* in van Schooten, *Exercitationum Mathematicarum libri quinque* (1657), vol. V.

tage," altho' he has not a precise Knowledge of the *Degree* of the Probability, or Value of the Chance. And perhaps it is *not impossible* to the *human* Capacity, to determine even the *exact* Degree of Probability in most *moral* Cases of Action, tho' this wou'd be a Work of very *great Difficulty,* most Cases being *exceedingly complicated.* An exact *Enumeration* and *Comparison* of our *Ideas* of *Pleasure,* would be a great Step towards this Work. Tho' this would be of great Use in Morality, yet we may with Pleasure observe the *Benevolence of the Deity,* "in giving us so great a Knowledge of the Consequences of Action, without any great Pains or Labour, as that, in most Cases, we may have a certain Knowledge of the Probability, *That the Action will be for the Advantage of the Agent upon the whole,* tho' we have not an accurate Knowledge of the Degree of the Probability." And this is sufficient to influence Action. For any Probability of Advantage, whatever the Degree of it be, if it be sufficient to overcome our natural Indolence and Inactivity, is sufficient to determine us to Action, upon a calm and thorough Deliberation.

Of the Law of Nature,
and its Obligation.

Having prepar'd the Way for all that is to follow, I shall begin this Chapter with the Definition of the Law of Nature.[1] *The Law of Nature is a Proposition, proposed to the Observation of, or impress'd upon, the Mind,*

The Law of Nature defined.

---

1. This definition has attracted much critical attention owing to the existence of a variant text in some copies of the first (1672) edition of Cumberland's work. The first, shorter, version of the definition reads, "Lex Naturæ est propositio naturâ rerum ex voluntate primæ causæ menti satis apertè oblata vel impressa, quæ actionem agentis rationalis possibilem communi bono maximè deservientem indicat, & integram singulorum fœlicitatem exinde solùm obtineri posse." The second, "corrected," printed version reads after "impressa": "actionem indicans Bono Rationalium communi observientem, quam si præstetur præmia, sin negligatur pœnæ sufficientes ex Naturâ Rationalium sequuntur" (p. 185). This is followed by a section that has no counterpart in the original (in Maxwell's translation, herein, "The former Part" to "anything to the contrary," p. 331). Linda Kirk is undoubtedly correct to suggest (*Richard Cumberland and Natural Law*, p. 79) that Cumberland revised this passage, and the crowding of the longer version on p. 85 of Cumberland's text suggests that it was a late revision. However, Kirk goes further and argues that the different versions reveal that Cumberland vacillated between a proto-utilitarian formula, by which moral obligation arises from the good consequences of rational actions, and a "conventional," voluntarist account that stresses rewards and punishments of a divine legislator. Knud Haakonssen ("The character and obligation of natural law according to Richard Cumberland" in Stewart, ed., *English Philosophy in the Age of Locke* [2001], pp. 35–41) has suggested that a conflict between the two versions is inadmissible on the basis of Cumberland's own assertions, especially in 5.3 where Cumberland argues that although the initial definition seems to omit the concepts of commanding, forbidding, punishing, and rewarding, "nevertheless I acknowledge that [the law of nature] to have all those powers." My own work on Cumberland suggests that there was, as Kirk perceived, a tension between a naturalist (utilitarian) and voluntarist

with sufficient Clearness, by the Nature of Things, from the Will of the first
Cause, which points out that possible Action of a rational Agent, which will
chiefly promote the common Good, and by which only the intire Happiness
of particular Persons can be obtain'd. The former Part of this Definition
contains the *Precept,* the latter, the *Sanction;* and the Mind receives the
Impression of both, from the *Nature of Things.* "Those *Rewards* and *Pun-*
ishments are *sufficient,* which are so *great* and so *certain,*[2] as to make it

---

account, but that the whole point of *De Legibus* was to reassert the connection between
voluntarism and naturalism, i.e., to demonstrate that natural law could carry all of the
formal qualities of law that Hobbes had denied. Cumberland's revision simply removed
a hostage to interpretative fortune (Parkin, *Science, Religion, and Politics,* p. 108n). Maxwell offers what Barbeyrac calls "un mélange assez bizarre" (*Traité Philosophique,* p. 209,
n. 1) in that he reproduces the first definition entire, ignoring the amended passage after
"impressa" and then joins it to the second section of the corrected version beginning
"Huius definitionis." It is possible that Maxwell felt that to reproduce the long version
involved some repetition of the discussion of sanctions and opted for a combination
that covered all of the ideas discussed in the two variants. Barbeyrac translates the corrected version in the belief that this represented the author's intentions. Translated from
the Latin (following Linda Kirk) this runs as follows: "The law of nature is a proposition
presented to or impressed upon the mind clearly enough by the nature of things from
the will of the first cause pointing out the action which will promote the good of
rational beings and whose consequences, from the nature of rational beings, will be
rewards if it is performed and sufficient punishments if it is neglected." Kirk, *Richard
Cumberland and Natural Law,* 31.

2. [Maxwell] "The following *Observations,* from Mr. *Wollaston,* (in his *Religion
of Nature,* sect. II) seem here pertinent.

"*Pleasure is a consciousness of something agreeable, Pain of the contrary.*

"*Obs.* 1. *Pleasures and Pains are proportionable to the Perceptions and Sense of their
Subjects, or the Persons affected with them.*

"*Obs.* 2. *Whatever increases the Power of Perceiving, renders the Percipient more
susceptive of Pleasure or Pain.* Among the principal Means, by which Perceptions and
the inward Sense of Things may be heighten'd and *increas'd,* is *Reflexion.* All Perceptions are produc'd in time; Time passes by Moments; there can be but one Moment present at once; and therefore all present Perceptions, consider'd without any
Relation to what is past or future, may be look'd upon as momentaneous only. In
this Kind of Perception the percipient perceives, as if he had not perceived any Thing
before, nor had any thing perceptible to follow. But in Reflexion there is a repetition
of what is past, and an Anticipation of that which is apprehended as yet to come;
there is a *connexion* of past and future, which by this are brought into the Sum, and
superadded to the present or momentaneous Perceptions.

"*Obs.* 3. *The Causes of Pleasure and Pain are relative Things: And in order to estimate
truly their Effect upon any particular Subject they ought to be drawn into the Degrees of*

evidently *conduce* to the intire *Happiness* of *particular* Persons," (which the Nature of Things, both compels them to desire, and makes possible for them to obtain,) "if they continually *promote* the *public Good*, more

---

Perception in that Subject. When the Cause is of the same Kind, and acts with an equal Force, if the Perception of one Person be equal to that of another, what they perceive must needs be *equal.* And so it will be likewise, when the Forces in the producing Causes and the Degrees of Perception in the Sentiments are *reciprocal.* For (which doth not seem to be considered by the World, and therefore ought the more particularly to be noted) if the Cause of Pleasure or Pain should act but half as much upon A, as it does upon B; yet if the Perceptivity of A be double to that of B, the Sum of their Pleasures or Pains will be *equal.* In other Cases they will be *unequal.* As, if the *causa dolorifica* should act with the same *impetus* on C with which it acts upon D; yet if C had only two Degrees of Perception, and D had three, the Pain sustain'd by D would be half as much more as that of C; because he would perceive or feel the Acts and Impressions of the Cause more by so much. If it should act with twice the Force upon D which it acts with upon C, then the Pain of C would be to that of D as 2 to 6: *i.e.* as one Degree of Force multiplied by two Degrees of Perception, to two Degrees multiplied by three of Perception. And so on.

"*Obs. 4. Mens respective Happinesses or Pleasures ought to be valued as they are to the* Persons themselves, *whose they are; or according to the Thoughts and Sense, which* they *have of them:* Not according to the Estimate put upon them by other People, who have no Authority to judge of them, nor *can* know what they are; many compute by different Rules; have less Sense; be in different Circumstances; or such as Guilt has render'd partial to themselves. If that Prince, who having Plenty and Flocks many, yet ravish'd the poor Man's single Ewe lamb out of his Bosom, reckon'd the poor Man's Loss to be not greater, than the Loss of one of his Lambs would have been to him, he must have been very defective in moral Arithmetic, and little understood the Doctrine of Proportion. Every Man's Happiness is *his* Happiness, what it is to him; and the Loss of it is answerable to the Degrees of his Perception, to his Manner of taking things, to his Wants and Circumstances.

"*Obs. 5. How judicious and wary ought Princes, Lawgivers, Judges, Juries, and even Masters to be!* They ought not to consider so much what a stout, resolute, obstinate, harden'd Criminal may bear, as what the weaker Sort, or at least (if that can be known) the Persons immediately concern'd can bear: *that is,* what any Punishment would be to them. For it is certain, all Criminals are not of the former Kind; and therefore should not be used as if they were. Some are drawn into Crimes, which may render them obnoxious to public Justice, they scarce know how themselves: Some fall into them through Necessity, Strength of Temptation, Despair, Elasticity of Spirits and a sudden Eruption of Passion, Ignorance of Laws, want of good Education, or some natural Infirmity or Propension: And some, who are really innocent, are opprest by the Iniquity or Mistakes of Judges, Witnesses, Juries, or perhaps by the Power and Zeal of a Faction, with which their Sense or their Honesty has not permitted them to join. What a Difference must there be between the Sufferings of

than if they *attempt* any thing to the *contrary.*" And whereas *Privations* are best understood by means of their opposite *Positives,* Actions and Omissions contrary to this End, and the Mischiefs connected with them, seem by this Method to be both discovered and prohibited. For *"Right"* (or strait) *"shews what is crooked, as well as what is strait."* That which takes the *shortest* Way from the given Term, or State of Things, to this End, is called *Right,* by a Metaphor taken from the Definition of a *right Line,* in use among *Mathematicians.* An Action, attaining the most desireable Effect in the quickest Manner, takes the shortest Way to this End. Therefore it is Right. And that very Comparison, by which such Action is discover'd, supposes all things so consider'd, that it is known, both what will less conduce to the End, and (with much greater Ease) what would obstruct the effecting it.

It is a true Proposition.
I will now consider the Particulars of the Definition given. *A Proposition*] Viz. a *true* one, as what follows will make evident. This Word seem'd more simple and *plain* than the Phrase, *The Dictate of right Reason,* which yet comes to the same thing, when all Ambiguity in the Ex-

---

a poor Wretch sensible of his Crime, or Misfortune, who would give a World for his Deliverance, if he had it, and those of a sturdy *veteran* in Rognery; between the Apprehensions, Tears, Faintings of the one, and the Brandy and Oaths of the other; in short, between a tender Nature and a Brickbat!

"Obs. 6. *In general, all Persons ought to be very careful and tender, where any other is concern'd.* Otherwise they may do they know not what. For no Man can tell, by himself or any other way, how another may be affected.

"Obs. 7. *There cannot be an equal Distribution of Rewards and Punishments by any stated human Laws.* Because (among other Reasons) the same thing is rarely either the same Gratification, or the same Punishment to different Persons.

"Obs. 8. *The Sufferings of Brutes are not like the Sufferings of Men.* They perceive by Moments, without Reflexion upon past or future, upon Causes, Circumstances, &c.

"Time and Life without Thinking are next Neighbours to *nothing,* to No-time, and No-life. And therefore to kill a Brute is to deprive him of a Life, or a Remainder of Time, that is equal to little more than nothing: Tho' this may perhaps be more applicable to some Animals than to others. That, which is chiefly to be taken Care of in this Matter, is, that the Brute may not be killed unnecessarily; when it is killed, that it may have as few Moments of Pain as may be; and that no young be left to languish. So much by the Way here." Wollaston, *The Religion of Nature Delineated* (1722), pp. 23–25.

pression is taken away. Nor did I think it proper, to make use of the word *Oration* for the Genus, as *Hobbes* has done,[3] lest any should in a Mistake imagine, that the use and knowledge of Words, or any *arbitrary Signs* whatsoever, were *essential* to a *Law*. The Knowledge (or Ideas form'd in the Mind) of *Human Actions,* of Consequences good or evil to human Nature, but, especially, of *Rewards* and *Punishments* naturally connected with such Actions, and those Ideas reduc'd into the Form of *Practical Propositions,* such as I have describ'd, are all that is *essential* to a *Law*. Such Ideas may be produc'd, by Observation, in the Minds of those who are born *Deaf,* tho' they form no notion of the sound or force of Words; and so the Laws of Nature will become known, even to them.

By Nature] It was proper, to mention the *efficient* Cause in this Definition, because we were not inquiring into the Definition of a *Law* in *general,* but of the *Law of Nature,* which Word denotes the Author or *efficient* Cause. Imprinted by the Nature

The Nature of Things] Does not only signify this LOWER WORLD, whereof we are a Part, but its Creator and supreme Governor, GOD. For, to our forming a true Judgment of Actions necessary to the publick Good, conspire (1.) the *World without us,* especially, those Men with whom we have to do, who, as Objects, excite us to think of, and consider, them; (2.) *ourselves,* both as parts of Mankind, and as free Causes of our own Actions; (3.) *God,* as the common Cause, and supreme Governor of all Things, whose Authority comes often into consideration. of Things

It is *certain,* "That only true Propositions, whether speculative or practical, are imprinted on our Minds by the Nature of Things"; because a *natural* Action points out that only which *exists,* and is never the Cause of any *Falshood,* which proceeds wholly from a *voluntary Rashness,* joining or separating Notions, which Nature has not join'd or separated. If therefore the *Terms* are *connected* by *Nature,* a *true affirmative Proposition* may be form'd of them. The *Terms* are *connected,* when the *different Ideas* (for the most part inadequate or incomplete) of an *Object* are imprinted upon the Mind, by the *same* Object view'd in *different* Lights,

---

3. Hobbes, *On the Citizen,* 3.33, p. 56, where Hobbes suggests that laws, properly speaking, are utterances of one who commands. Cf. *Leviathan,* ch. 15, p. 100.

or compar'd with different Things. It is hence easy, to form a Judgment of *true negative Propositions.* It is, therefore, with great justness, that these Laws or Propositions are ascrib'd to *Nature,* since Nature exposes to the Observation of the Mind, both the *Terms* of those Propositions, and the *Connexion* of those Terms.

on our Minds,   Farther; *"Rational Agents* are so fram'd, that, whilst they continue in this State, they are *led, by Necessity of Nature,* to perceive or *apprehend* the Terms of these Propositions; nay, are also *inclin'd, by an inward Propension,* to *compare* them, so as to frame affirmative Propositions of those which agree, negative, of those which disagree; nay farther, *so* to compare two Propositions among themselves, *as* to draw from these, as *Premises,* a third in the Form of a *Conclusion."* The Nature of a rational Agent exacts, that *self-evident* Propositions (especially, concerning the Consequences of our own Actions, relating to our own Happiness, or that of others) be form'd, such are the *primary* Laws of Nature; and from them be deduced other Propositions or *Conclusions,* which may be call'd the *secondary,* or less obvious, Laws of Nature.

from the Will   We cannot doubt of the *Nature of created Beings,* but that both
of the first   Things external, exciting Thoughts in us, and our Mind comparing these
Cause,   Thoughts, are the *Causes of necessary Truths.*[4] As to the *Nature of the Creator,* there will remain no doubt, but that he too is to be look'd upon as the *Cause of those Truths,* if we seriously consider, both what has been already said, and what we now think proper to *add;* which is, "That all Truth is from the first Cause of those Things, in which it is founded, and the uncorrupt Effect or Work of God, without any Tincture from the preternatural Stain of Mankind." Therefore, if any *true Proposition declares,* what ought to be done, it *declares* so *from God.* Nor is it more *certain,* "That those *natural Things* are form'd by God, to produce their *natural Effects,* the Sun, for *Instance,* to enlighten the Air, and Rain to moisten the Earth"; than "That such Propositions as *naturally regulate* our Actions, are given to us by God *for that very Purpose."* For that *Regu-*

---

4. [Maxwell] "Created Beings are the second Causes of necessary Truths, the Creator, the first Cause of them."

lation is the *only* Effect they can have, and that they do *necessarily,* from their own inward Nature.

"That Proposition is propos'd, or imprinted by the Objects, with *suf-* *ficient plainness,* whose *Terms,* and their natural *Connexion,* are so ex- pos'd to the Senses and Thoughts, by obvious and common *Experience,* that the Mind of an *adult* Person, not labouring under any *Impediment,* if it will *attend* or take Notice, may easily observe it." Such, for *Example,* are these Propositions; *"That* a Man may be kill'd, by a profuse Loss of Blood, by Suffocation, by Want of Food, &*c. That* Life may for some time be preserv'd by Air, Nourishment, and Cloathing: *That* the mutual Assistance of Men contributes much to a happy Life."

with sufficient Clearness.

But, if any one has a Mind to add, to these Reasons, another from the *Effect,* and will *affirm,* "That the Laws of Nature are so called, be- cause they supply its Necessities, and are the principal Means of per- fecting it," I will not contradict him; because the same Person, and, much more, different Persons, may have different Reasons for *imposing* the same Name on Things.

§II. But, because the *Law* or *Right* (for these Words are there used in the same Sense) *of Nature* is defin'd in another Sense by the *Civilians,*[5] both in the *Pandects,* and *Institutions, Lib.* I. *"That which Nature has taught all Animals";*[6] and they thus distinguish it from *"the Law of Na- tions, which all Nations use, and which natural Reason establishes among*

(*Justinian's* Definition of the Law of Nature, oppos'd, by Authority,

5. [Maxwell] "The *Civilians* universally acknowledge, 'That the Division into the *Law of Nature,* and that *of Nations,* according to *Justinian's* explication, is only the explaining two different senses of the same Word;' the former, *improper* and *Meta- phorical,* as Naturalists use the word *Law,* to denote *those uniform Effects, which are observ'd in the Motions of Bodies.* The latter is *proper.* By the *Laws of Nature,* the Emperor understands only *uniform Instincts observ'd in all Animals,* by the *Law of Nations* he denotes, what our Author, with most Moderns and Ancients, calls the *Law of Nature.* Some later Writers, by the *Laws of Nations,* understand *that Branch of the Law of Nature, which relates to sovereign States or Princes,* or those Conventions about certain Privileges of Ambassadours, about Goods taken in open War, and cer- tain Limitations of the Methods of Hostility, to which, perhaps, antecedently to Conventions express or tacit, there would have been no obligation."

6. Justinian, *Digest,* I.1.1.3; *Institutes,* I.2.

all Men":[7] I think it proper, to *oppose* to so *great* an *Authority,* both an *equal Authority,* and *Reason,* which is of *greater Authority* among Philosophers. As to the First, the same *Justinian, (in Instit. Lib.* 2.) treating of *Property,* expresses himself thus. *"We acquire a property in some things by the Law of Nature, which, as we are inform'd, is call'd the Law of Nations."*[8] Behold, how here the *Law of Nature* does with him signify the same Thing with the *Law of Nations,* which he defines in the same manner, as to sense, that we do the Law of Nature! And *Cicero* also, who, as to proper *Latin,* will not give Way, even to the Emperor, in the *third Book* of his *Offices,* has made use of these two expressions, as signifying the *same* thing, *"By Nature, that is, by the Law of Nations."*[9] And, as part of the Law of Nature, he reckons the Precepts of Religion, which are peculiar to Man, and not common to him with other Animals.[10] Hence it appears, that these *antient* Authors us'd the *Law of Nature* and *of Nations* in the *same* sense; so that it would be superfluous to prove, by Reason.) that *modern* Philosophers us'd the same way of speaking. The *Reason,* why I affirm the *Laws of Nature* to be *proper to Man* alone, is this, because they are *Propositions* concerning consequences depending upon the influence of actions, or *Determinations* of the Judgment compounding or dividing Terms, whose chief *Authority* depends upon this, "That they are known to proceed from God." And I meet with nothing to *convince* me, "That Brutes form Propositions," such as these especially, "and regulate their Lives by them," much less can they *know,* "That they are imprinted upon them by God."

which
points out §III. I am not ignorant of what *Modestinus* affirms, *"The Law has power to command, forbid, permit, punish,"*[11] to which may also be added, *to reward.* And yet I have mention'd none of these, *in the Definition* of the *Law of Nature,* which, nevertheless, I acknowledge to have all those

---

7. Justinian, *Digest,* I.1.1.3; *Institutes,* I.1.
8. Justinian, *Institutes,* II.1.1.
9. Cicero, *De Officiis,* III.v.23.
10. Cicero, *De Inventione,* II.xxii.65.
11. Justinian, *Digest,* I.3.7.

powers.[12] For they *all* seem to follow from this *one,* wherein their whole force consists, *the pointing out of those Actions, which are most conducive to the Common Good.* Philosophy, and those Notices, which are impress'd upon us by external Objects, shew, of what *Kind* those actions are, and what they do. These expressions, *to command,* &c. seem more adapted to the *Style of Magistrates,* when they signify their Will, than to the *simple Indications* afforded by Things; from which, however, the whole *force* of Commands, Prohibitions, Punishments, and Rewards, is easily deduc'd.

For, "after the supreme *Governor* of the World has *declar'd* plainly, that he WILLS the Publick Good; he plainly *commands,* by pointing it out, what promotes that, and, by that Command, evidently *forbids* contrary Actions or Omissions. And he, whose *Will* it is, that *every Man's particular Happiness,* and peace of Conscience, should *depend* upon his endeavours to perform these things, and upon the *publick Happiness,* in which it is contain'd, hath decreed a certain *Reward* to such Actions, as procure the Common Good, and hath added the sanction of a *Punishment* to contrary Actions; which is, his Want of that part of the Publick Good, which would have fallen to his share, if he had endeavour'd to promote it." The Law of Nature may be said to *permit* those things, which it discovers, *not* to be necessarily *requisite* to the Common Good, and *yet* to be *consistent* with it. If such things were *unnecessarily* restrain'd by Rulers, it is plain, that *Nature* would be *hurt,* which *consists* in such motion, as tends to perpetual Variety. *Positive* Rewards and Punishments will be considered hereafter. All these points will be better understood, after I have explained the *nature* and *causes* of the *Publick Good.* *(and, by doing so, commands, forbids, rewards, punishes, permits)*

The following words insinuate the *subject Matter* of the Laws of Nature, which are such Actions as the *Schoolmen* call *Human;* those, for *Instance,* which we can govern by *Counsel,* and which are, therefore, *not* either *Necessary, nor Impossible.* For the Law of Nature, or *"Reason,* weighing the powers of Nature, cannot propose to us that which is *impossible,* as an *End,* nor prescribe the making use of such *Means,* as *exceed* *that possible Action*

---

12. This sentence supports the suggestion that the allegedly utilitarian definition in 5.1 is in fact conventional. See n. 1 above.

the limits of our power"; because both would be vain, and inconsistent with our faculties. But Reason is plainly averse to *vain* attempts and inconsistencies.[13] For, *tho'* it may happen, thro' an unforeseen concurrence of external causes, that affairs (in this Life) may succeed very prosperously with those, who have neglected to use the best means in their power to promote their own happiness: *Yet,* because such Effects are, with respect to us, *purely contingent,* and do but *rarely happen,* it is evident, that our Reason, or Judgment, does not advise, much less does the Law of Nature command, any such Actions. This, however, Natural Reason *teaches* evidently enough, "That it will much more probably promote our Happiness, that we should act for a *foreseen End,* and by the *best Means* in our power adapted to that End, than that, laying aside Counsel, we should commit our-selves to *uncertain chance.*" Nor does the *Law of Nature* promise greater Happiness, than what arises from a *rational* behaviour toward God and Man, beyond what can be hop'd for from a Life, whose conduct is committed to *rashness* and *chance.* The *ground* of this *greater hope* is founded upon this, "That our *Reason* will *not hinder* the accession of such good things, as may come to us from any other quarter, without our care, but *will add* thereto all those, which it can effect or obtain from God and Men." Beside, I would exclude from the title of *Human Actions,* those, which throw the whole affair upon *Fortune,* without the least *probable* cause of hoping for a good, rather than an evil Event.

(*i.e.* Series of Actions)   The *Action,* here describ'd, is to be understood *universally,*[14] not the action of one Man only, nor those of a Day; but all the human Actions of all Men, thro' their whole Life, ought to be directed to the Common Good of all. I chose to treat expresly of the actions of *Men only,* because they are well known to us by daily Experience; and, if the Law of Nature leads us at all to philosophize, concerning the actions of *God* or *Angels,*

---

13. Barbeyrac (*Traité Philosophique,* p. 213, n. 3) suggests a similarity with Marcus Aurelius, *Meditations,* V.17.

14. [Maxwell] "It can not only be *prov'd,* 'That a course of Virtue is most for a Man's advantage,' but that perhaps in most common Cases 'every single virtuous action is most for the advantage of the Agent, be his preceding or following actions what they will.'"

it is to be deduc'd from an *analogy* or resemblance, founded on Human Actions.

The words [*of a Rational Agent*] plac'd in the Definition, are *indefinite,* and are, therefore, applicable to any Man whomsoever; for *Example,* to the *first Man,* yet alone; and then the Common Good would be, whatsoever would be acceptable to *God* and *Him.* But this *indefinite* proposition, connecting those things which are in nature necessarily connected, amounts to, or is in sense, an *Universal; i.e.* after more than one Man is suppos'd, it extends to all and every one, taken jointly or severally. This I thought proper to mention, for this reason, because the *most known* Laws of Nature, which direct to the practice of Justice and Charity among Men, *suppose* them to have *increas'd* to some Number; and do chiefly aim at this point, to manifest to them, by what *mutual actions* they may make one another most happy. The *Laws of Nature* therefore speak, as *Civil Laws* usually do, *to many at once.* Hence the Lawyers call the Law, a *common command;*[15] and we have an account, that *Solon* (if I remember right) expresly provided for it by a *Law,* "That no Law should be made for the case of any particular person."[16] Beside, the *joint* endeavours and Actions of *many* may effect something *considerable* toward the common Good; and, therefore, the truth of this *Proposition,* "Fidelity, Gratitude, natural Affection, or the Innocence of *all* or *many,* conduces to the Publick Good," is more evident, than that such Actions in *any single* person should have the same effect.

of a (i.e. Every) Rational Agent.

§IV. "The *principal, and most distinguishing, Character* of the Laws of Nature, is taken from the *Effect* of those Actions they prescribe, which is, the *Publick Good.*" That it should be so, the matter it-self requires. For, *since* the *Nature* of Actions, which are the Objects of Laws, is best perceiv'd by their *Effects; since* these Laws, as being Propositions, and, consequently, form'd of Ideas combin'd among themselves, are *distinguish'd* from all Laws of different kinds, by their *Objects,* the inward

which will chiefly promote the Common Good.

15. Justinian, *Digest,* I.3.1: "Lex est commune praeceptum."
16. Barbeyrac (*Traité Philosophique,* p. 214, n. 6) suggests that this reference comes from Aeneas Gazaeus, a fifth-century Platonist, who quotes Solon in his *Theophrastus.*

nature of the Laws themselves must be seen in the *Effects,* to which they *direct.*

This, the greatest End of human Actions,   The *Effect* (as the Idea thereof, preconceiv'd in the Mind, first moves a Rational Agent to intend the producing it, and afterwards limits his actions in order thereto) is called the *End.* All agree, that whoever acts *deliberately,* must (1) propose an *End* to himself, then (2) search out, chuse, and apply the *Means,* by which it may be obtain'd. "Therefore *Laws,* perfectly fitted to a *Rational* Nature, must both point out the *best End,* and the *most suitable Means* for obtaining it." Wherefore, in the given Definition, for the *End,* I propose the *Publick Good,* (in a more extensive sense than *Ulpian,* who defines the *Publick Good* "*That which conduces to the benefit of the Roman state, and consists in sacred Rites, Priests, and Magistrates*"; [17] for my notion of it includes the *Good of all Men,* and the *Honour of God,*) which is certainly the greatest End, which can possibly be propos'd by us: For the Means, I propose *all those Actions, which are in our power, and, in the given circumstances, are most effectual to obtain that End.*

is here consider'd as their Effects,   But, because the words, *End* and *Means,* are of very doubtful signification, and suppose the *free,* the *mutable,* intention of a rational Agent, which can *never be certainly known;* and because they, consequently, present to our Minds a matter *not so proper for Demonstration;* I thought it fit, *without changing* the matter in hand, to consider it *under another notion;* that is, because the *connexion* is more *conspicuous,* and perfectly *inseparable,* between *Efficient Causes,* and their *Effects;* and continual experience and frequent observation plainly discover, *what* Effects will follow Causes assign'd; therefore "I have laid down in the Definition, the *Publick Good* as the *Effect,* our *Actions* and *Powers,* from which any thing of that kind is hop'd for, as the *Efficient Causes.*"

and Morality thereby render'd more Demonstrable.   "By this means, *Moral* and *Political Questions* are converted into Terms in use among *Natural Philosophers,* Whether these Efficient Causes can produce this Effect, or no? And to *Questions thus express'd,* an *Answer* may be given, which is *capable of Demonstration,* from the formerly-observ'd efficacy of human Actions, consider'd, both by themselves, and in concurrence with other Causes, not unlike those at present

---

17. Justinian, *Digest,* I.1.1.2.

suppos'd." *Altho'*, while we *deliberate*, we may truly be called *Free*, and the future effects of our Actions, with respect to that *Liberty*, may, with great propriety, be called *Contingent; yet*, after we have *determin'd to act*, the *connexion*, between our *Actions*, and all the *Effects* thence depending, is *necessarily* and plainly natural, and, therefore, *capable of Demonstration;* we may observe this in *Mathematical operations*, which are *not less free* than any *other human actions*. Therefore, "*as* a long series of consequences, beyond the expectation of such as are not vers'd in such matters, concerning the mutual proportion of Lines or Angles, may be demonstrated from this, That a few Lines have been drawn according to Geometrical Rules: *So*, from the principles of Natural Philosophy, may be demonstrated many Effects of a Human Action, communicating a known motion to a Body in a known system of other Bodies; and, consequently, often, what will prejudice the Life of Man, the soundness, intireness, and power of beginning Motion (in the use of which consists Liberty, as it is oppos'd to external restraint) in his Members, or even the Goods which he possesseth; or what, on the contrary, will benefit any one Man, or many." A rational inquiry into Nature hath *demonstrated*, (if I am not mistaken,) "That *all the changes of all Bodies*, even Human, which are produc'd by external Causes," (for determinations, arising from the inward Liberty of the Will, must be excepted,) "whether they are for the better or the worse, are *produc'd*, according to those *Theorems* concerning Motion, which are investigated and demonstrated by a Geometrical Analysis." I confess, they are but *few* things, tho' of *great moment*, which have yet been produc'd upon this Subject: Yet a method has been shewn, of subjecting all Motions, however complicated, to a Geometrical Calculation, and of finding out all Theorems, concerning Lines, Figures, and the determinations of Motion thence arising; and, consequently, (since the whole Nature of Body is to be resolv'd into its Extension, Figure, and variously-compounded motions;) "a general Method is discovered, of reducing all the effects of Body to Demonstration."[18] I take Notice of these Things by the way, only that I might *shew*, "in what *method* we must proceed, to come at *a perfect demonstra-*

18. Cumberland is following Descartes' description of *mathesis universalis*, for which see n. 10 in ch. 1.

tion, from the *necessary connexion of the Terms,* of those things which are well enough known, from common observation and continual experience, to exist in Nature, and to depend mutually on each other, as *Causes* and *Effects,"* and which others endeavour to deduce from other natural principles. Such are those *Actions,* by which Men usually *destroy,* or *preserv* the *Lives, Liberties,* and *Fortunes* of others.

Virtue and the only Good. §V. Upon this head, the *Stoicks* are to be reprehended, who *affirm'd,* "nothing to be *Good,* but *Virtue;* nothing *Evil,* but *Vice.*"[19] For, whilst they endeavour to establish the transcendent Goodness of Virtue, and the egregious Evil of Vice, they, incautiously, intirely take away the *only reason,* why *Virtue* is *Good,* and *Vice, Evil.* For Virtue is therefore Good, (and in truth it is the greatest Good,) because it determines Human Actions to such effects, as are principal parts of the Publick *Natural Good;* and, consequently, tends to improve in all Men the Natural perfections, both of Mind and Body, and to promote, as much as possible, the Honour of God, by imitating the Divine Beneficence. Further, seeing one part of *Universal Justice* (which is Virtue it-self conspicuous among Men) consists in *Innocence,* that is, in restraining Murder, Theft, &c. it is *manifest,* "That they can give *no reason of the Law prohibiting such Injuries,* unless they acknowledge, that such actions, as the *robbing* an Innocent person of his Life or Goods, (by which Life is preserv'd,) are *Evil,* or hurtful to one or more, *antecedently to all Laws,* and, consequently, without respect to *Virtue,* which consists in *paying obedience to Law.*"

Good and Evil antecedent to Civil Laws. Whether this be denied by *Hobbes,* or no, I know not; for he openly allows, that there is a *Damage* in such actions, and that it is *Evil* to him who is thereby the sufferer, in these words. *"In the Commonwealth, if any one hurts another, with whom he has enter'd into no Compact, he damages him, upon whom he has brought the Evil; he injures him only, who has*

---

19. Again, Cumberland demonstrates the compatibility of his work with Stoic sources. For the contemporary authority for these ideas, see Lipsius, *Manuductio ad Stoicam Philosophiam* (1604), II.20.

the power of the Common-wealth." [20] Elsewhere he as expressly contends, That *"Civil Laws are the Rules of Good and Evil, and that, therefore, what the Legislator hath commanded, is to be esteem'd Good; what he has forbid, Evil; and that it is seditious to say, that the knowledge of Good and Evil belongs to private persons."* [21] I would willingly *reconcile* these passages, by *distinguishing* a word of doubtful Signification, and supposing, that *Evil* in the former passage signifies *that which is hurtful to Nature;* but in the latter, *that which disagrees with the Laws.* But I am afraid, this way of reconciling him to himself will not please him, because from this concession may be *inferr'd,* "That some things may be known, before the declaration of the Law, to be Evil, or hurtful, either to a single person, or to a multitude, and thence *some Civil Constitutions* may be prov'd *Evil* or hurtful to the People." To avoid this inconvenience, he *determines,* "That no Definition, no Reasoning, in all Mathematicks, Natural Philosophy, or Politicks, should be acknowledg'd, unless approv'd by the Civil Powers." [22] Truly, what he denies of *"Christ, that he came into the World to teach Logick,"* [23] that he contends belongs to the Prerogative of Monarchs and all supreme Powers. They, truly, are rais'd to the Throne, to teach Logick and other Natural Sciences. O happy times, not ours only, but even all times of all Nations! All Kings and Republicks have perpetually philosophiz'd; and the Decrees of them all have been acknowledged Axioms, however they may have contradicted, either themselves, or one another. But let him reconcile these his inconsistencies more happily himself; and, at the same time, I intreat him to remove this *scruple,* "How all effects (beneficial and hurtful, good and evil) of Natural Agents, and even of Men themselves, are *necessary:* And yet it depends upon the *mutable* Will of Princes, to *determine,* whether these

20. Hobbes, *On the Citizen,* 3.4, p. 45.
21. Ibid., 12.1, pp. 131–32: "For it has been shown that the civil laws are the rules of good and evil . . . and that therefore one must accept what the legislator enjoins as good, and what he forbids as evil. . . . When private men claim for themselves a knowledge of good and evil, they are aspiring to be as Kings. When this happens the commonwealth cannot stand."
22. Ibid., 17.12, pp. 214–15.
23. Ibid.

same effects be *Good* or *Evil*"? Which are *two Fundamental doctrines* of his, tho' they are in *direct contradiction to one another*. What is more; the latter opinion is inconsistent with those things, which are necessarily and essentially requisite to Society, and acknowledged by *Hobbes* himself for Laws of Nature (*cap. 3 de Cive*) such as, the *rejecting a right over all* things and persons, *keeping Faith* in Compacts, and *Gratitude*.[24] Certainly, if any Prince should enact general Laws *contrary* to these, in order to *establish his State,* he would do it with the *same Success,* as if he should decree the use of *Poison,* or of Air and Garments infected with the Plague, for *preserving the health of his Subjects.* For the force and efficacy of such methods do, with as great certainty, introduce the Evils of Discord, Murder, Robbery, and the like, among Men, as Poison or the Plague corrupts the Blood. *Xerxes* may lash the *Hellespont,*[25] but it will not obey him; nor will things *hurtful* change their Natures, and become *profitable,* in *obedience* to the Decrees of *Princes.* Suppose a Law, commanding the Subjects of any State, to *kill* one another, without any regard to Sex, Age, or Actions by them done; to *break* all *Compacts;* to be universally *ungrateful:* Suppose it universally obey'd, and see, whether it would not immediately introduce a *general Slaughter,* (notwithstanding any obligation of *Conscience* to the contrary, which he would *seem* to acknowledge, only to impose upon the unwary;) till at last only One surviv'd, whom now elated with the murder of the rest, no fear of a greater power (the only obligation acknowledg'd by *Hobbes*) would restrain from killing his Prince, whom we may, without absurdity, suppose less strong than his Subject. Let him likewise *shew,* "How all his Philosophy is *Demonstrative,* and necessarily true, when as yet it has been *confirm'd by no Prince* whomsoever; but on the contrary, many of his opinions (particularly that concerning *Necessity,* in opposition to *Freewill*) are *condemn'd* by almost all Princes professing *Christianity.*"

Whatever his real Sentiments may be, it is not very material; yet it is a more favourable construction to *judge,* "That he was either *deceiv'd* by the ambiguity of the words, *Good* and *Evil,* or was *willing to deceive*

24. Ibid., ch. 3.
25. Herodotus, *Historia,* VIII.35.

his unwary Readers"; than to *believe* him come to that pitch of Madness, "as to think *natural Good* and *Evil* (that is, such Actions, especially Human, as benefit or hurt the Bodies or Minds of Men, singly or collectively) are *not determin'd* by their own *Nature,* to produce their natural effects, but *advantage* or *prejudice us,* merely at the *Pleasure of Princes.*

§VI. We may, therefore, *suppose* the following sensible *Phenomena,* which are confirmed by constant Experience, if not already demonstrated, are capable of being demonstrated from the Principles of Natural Philosophy, (whose business it is, to discover and demonstrate the Causes and Effects of such things;) "That Men, *by* a proper course of Diet, *by* mutual Benevolence, *by* permitting every one by his own labour to acquire things necessary for Life and Health, *by* Innocence and Beneficence, *by* observing Compacts, *by* Gratitude to our Benefactors, *by* a particular Affection for our Children and Kindred, both in the ascending and descending Line" (who are distinguish'd from others by that peculiar character of a Sameness of Natural Principles deriv'd from one and the same fountain;) that *by* such methods (I say) "Men formerly were of mutual advantage, and that, the more they pursue the like Methods, they will hereafter be of the greater advantage to one another, both with respect to the health and strength of the *Body,* and the Knowledge, Prudence, Joy, Tranquillity in every state, and well-grounded Hope of the *Mind,* even in Death it-self." On the *other Hand,* "That, from actions of a contrary kind, arise Errors and grievous Anxieties of *Mind;* to the *Body,* loss of Limbs, Distempers, the inconveniencies of Hunger and Thirst, and to many Men Death it-self"; *Evils,* which, by using our power otherwise, might have been prevented. *Wars* arise from *Discord, Drunkenness, breach of Faith,* &c. as from their *natural causes.* Hence *Massacres, Plundering of Goods,* and *Burning of Houses,* arise as necessarily and *naturally,* as Men *die* in consequence of the *Plague;* or as the *ruin* and swallowing up of a *City* sometimes proceeds from a great *Earthquake;* so that *both* are *equally natural,* and *equally* publick *Evils.* In the same manner, a *well-regulated Diet,* mutual *Concord, Fidelity* and *Gratitude,* are as truly *natural* and publick Advantages, as are *uncorrupted Air,* or the *benign influence of the Sun,* which are beneficial to all. For

The *Principles*
of Human
Actions, as
naturally Good
or *Evil,* as are
their Effects.

the powers of these dispositions (tho' they lie *scatter'd* among particular persons) may be *jointly consider'd,* and they are truly natural causes, affecting the *whole body* of Mankind, or a *considerable part* thereof: Just as the several *seeds* of *Animals* and *Plants,* tho' Nature hath assign'd to *each* their *peculiar place,* wherein *only* they exert their powers, may, nevertheless, be *consider'd jointly;* and it may truly be affirm'd of them, that they are *Principles* and necessary Causes of *Life, Increase,* and innumerable other effects in *Plants* and *Animals.* For the *whole collection of Effects* is no less necessarily *connected* with the *whole collection of Causes,* than *particular Effects* are with their *particular Causes.*

It may, therefore, be look'd upon as *certain,* "That Propositions of eternal truth may be form'd concerning the *Effects* of *external Human Actions,* whether *virtuous* or *vicious*": And, on the *contrary,* "That from the *Effects* of human Action, hurtful or beneficial to particular persons, but especially to many, it may be known, whether the *internal practical Principles* were advantageous or prejudicial, that is, *naturally Good* or *Evil.*"

The difficulty of calculating future effects, arises from mixture of concurrent causes. All the *difficulty of foreseeing,* "whether a good or ill Effect will follow from any *Action suppos'd,*" arises *hence,* "That it is generally *not known,* what *Concurrence* there will be of *other causes* with that." For hence it may happen, that what at first seem'd to have a good tendency, may afterwards have a bad effect. As *Mathematicians demonstrate* the Genesis of Lines and Figures from natural Motion, *abstractedly consider'd;* several things are with ease *demonstrated,* concerning Human *Actions and their Effects,* under the same *abstract* and general *consideration.* Hence it is *evident,* "That the greatest *perfection* of *Moral* and *Political Prudence,* consists in a through *Knowledge* of the *circumstances, concurring* with Human Actions to produce their *effects,* or *obstructing* them; whose principal part is an intimate Knowledge of those particular persons, with whom we are to act *in conjunction,* or whom we are to *oppose,* as well with respect to their Understanding and practical Principles, as their peculiar turns of Affection; as also with respect to their Friends, Servants, Possessions, and assistance from the State, now Commonwealths are founded."

§VII. This is the *Sum* of what I have said, "That the consideration of our Powers and *Actions,* as *Causes,* and the *End* desir'd, as the *Effect,* seems the most convenient general method of resolving moral Rules into the *Phaenomena,* or appearances, of Nature"; which ought to be the principal scope, both of a Writer upon the Law of Nature, or of him who would live according to it. For certain Actions, and their Object, (which in this case is one or more Men,) being suppos'd, *Natural Philosophy* will *discover,* "whether the Preservation and Perfection of the Object, which is *Good;* and its Corruption or Damage, which is call'd *Evil,* will ensue." By this means, in order to *foresee* what *Effect* will follow, we bring under our view and deliberation, all we know of the nature of *our Powers,* and of other *Causes co-operating* with us, as also of those persons, who are to be the *Objects* of our Action.

But the consequence of our *considering* and *comparing,* among themselves, the *various Effects,* which would follow the *various Actions* in our power, is this, that we shall take sufficient care of these Two things, (1.) That we alwaies propose a *possible* End (or Effect,) and, of those which we can attain, the *best:* (2.) That we apply those Actions as *Means,* which are the most suitable and *adequate* Causes of the foreseen intended Effect. In these *two* consists the *Whole of Moral and Political Prudence.* The *Dictates of Prudence,* directing Human Actions every where to the Greatest Possible Good of all rational Agents, are the very *Laws of Nature.* When these procure the *assent* of any Man's *Understanding,* and so actually *determine* his *Will,* that they *influence* his *Actions,* and, being treasur'd up in his *Memory,* return upon proper occasions to determine him, they are the *Habit* of *moral Virtue.* If to these Dictates of Prudence there be any thing added, which respects the *particular constitution* of any *State,* or the *Publick office* and *Private affairs* of any *Person* therein, they then become *Civil, Political,* or *Private Prudence,* according as that addition requires. But, perhaps, I have already said too much upon this head in this place.

§VIII. I proceed, more fully to explain the [*Common*] (which also I call the Publick) *Good.* By these words I understand "the Aggregate or sum

[*Common*]
Good, the End
or the Effect of
the Law of
Nature.
of all those good things, which, either we can contribute towards, or are necessary to, the Happiness of *all* rational Beings, consider'd as collected into one Body, each in his proper order." For I consider *God,* and all *Men,* upon account of some resemblance in *Reason,* or an intelligent Nature, as represented under *one Notion,* which is extended to every particular by the word, *All.* 'Tis easy for every Man, to form an Idea of *rational Being in General,* and to conceive the meaning of the word, *All.*

Both which are above the capacity of *Brutes,* who can neither *Abstract from Particulars,* nor *cast up Sums,* much less perceive that *Agreement in Nature,* which is between *God* and *Man.* For which reason, amongst others, "They cannot regard the *Common Good,* and are, therefore, incapable of *Virtue,* and of *Society with Men,* which is founded in the consideration of the Common Good."

Altho' I *affirm'd,* "That the Common Good of rational Beings is immediately regarded in the Laws of our Nature," I would not however, *deny,* "That they extend our care to things of inferior Nature, to things irrational and corporeal"; They oblige us, for *Example,* to *feed Animals, sow Vegetables,* and *till* the very *Ground,* as far as these Actions *promote the Honour of God,* and *Happiness of Men;* but, while we are so imploy'd, the *perfection* of these things is not *properly,* at least not *ultimately,* sought after; their *use,* and concurrence with our Actions towards the Good of rational Beings, is the thing *intended.*

For, in examining Nature, we *observe,* "That *all* Bodies are govern'd by God, the SUPREME RATIONAL AGENT": And, whilst we experience, that, at the command of our Judgment and Will, our Muscles and many neighbouring Bodies are moved, we *see,* "That *our own Bodies,* and, by means of them, very *many others,* are necessarily determin'd by *Human Reason*"; and thus, by the constitution of the Universe, we find the *subordination* of Bodies, one to another: For the Mind cannot but conceive some *order,* between that which *determines* and those things which *are determined,* so that what determines must be *before,* what is determin'd must be *after,* in acting. But it is our interest, to observe the order *settled by Nature,* and by *that means,* as far as lies in our power, to promote our own perfection. Whence I may justly *conclude,* by the way, "That he, who *seeks* the chief *Good* of *rational* Agents, *seeks* the *Good* and *order of the whole World;* and that, from the slightest observation of the natural Determinations of Motion, some *notion* of *Order* and *dependence* is produc'd in the Mind; which regular Dependence, as it proceeds from the judgment of a rational Mind, is properly called *Government.*" Wherefore, since we are perfectly conscious of such manner of proceeding within our-selves, and, by the natural assistance of our Senses, we see the like transacted without us; we may truly *affirm,* "That we have receiv'd the Idea of *Order* and *Government* from *Nature.*" So much may suffice for the word *Publick* or *Common.*

§IX. By the word [*Good*] plac'd in the Definition, I understand, "That which by the Philosophers is usually call'd *Natural* Good, and, which I have already defin'd, with respect to *Created Beings,* as *that which preserves, or renders them more perfect or happy:* With respect to the *Divine Nature,* as being completely happy in himself, *what is grateful or pleasing to him*"; i.e. by *Analogy* or resemblance, because what things we perceive to preserve or perfect us, those we call grateful to us, that is, they leave the Mind in a state of Tranquillity and Joy. Now, though it is inconsistent with the infinite perfection of God, that he should be preserv'd or render'd more perfect; yet, because *Tranquillity, Joy,* or *Complacency,* may be conceiv'd separately from *Imperfection,* these may safely be ascrib'd to the *Divine Majesty.*

Of [*Good*] Natural, with respect both to the Creatour and his Creatures.

But, to return to Man, his *Natural good things,* or Advantages, are of two kinds,

Those things which are Naturally Good and belong to Man, subdivided into advantages of the Mind,

(1) Those, which adorn and chear the *Mind,* the foundation of all which seems to be laid in such things as perfect the Knowledge and *Judgment,* to which if the *Will* consents, it is likewise perfect.

(2) Those, which preserve and increase the powers of the *Body.* For *publick* good things are the *same* with the good things of *particular* persons; and, from a true Idea of *any Man's* Happiness, may easily be deduc'd, by Analogy, the happiness to be sought after for *any Civil State,* or even for *all Men* jointly consider'd. For a Society, compos'd of *particular* persons, is only then happy, when *each* of its members, especially

Body.

the principal ones, have their *Minds endow'd* with the natural *perfections* of the Understanding and Will, and their *Bodies sound,* and with vigor ministring to their Minds.

The Reader is to *observe,* "That I have called these things *Naturally Good,* in that sense, in which these words, as being of a more extensive signification, (and, consequently, more general and first known in the order of Nature,) are distinguish'd from things *Morally Good";* for these are only *voluntary actions conformable to some Law,* especially, that of Nature. Therefore Good is not to be taken in this sense, when it is inserted in the Definition of the *Law of Nature,* because it is absurd, to Define any thing, by what supposes the thing Defin'd, already known. There are *many things Naturally Good,* that is, such as contribute somewhat to the Happiness of Man, which are *not Morally Good,* as being either *not voluntary* Actions, or *not commanded* by any Law: such are an enlarg'd Understanding, the ornaments of the Sciences, a tenacious Memory, strength of Body, the assistance of external Possessions, &c. On the contrary, I am of *opinion,* "That *no action* of the Will is enjoin'd or recommended by the Law of Nature, and, consequently, *Morally Good,* which does *not,* in its own nature, *contribute* somewhat to the *Happiness of Men."* The *Moral* Philosopher *supposes,* "That it is known from *Natural Philosophy* or Experience, what preserves or increases the powers of the Mind, and what renders Life more vigorous and lasting; and that, above the rest, some Human Actions, which are distinguish'd by the name of *Virtues,* contribute much to these effects, and that all these Actions are very consistent with one another." The *Mind of Man,* conscious of its power to perform such Actions, observing these things, in particular instances or examples belonging to it-self or some other known person, *concludes,* "That such kind of Actions will make all Men happier, or, at least, consist with the happiness of all Men." Such *general Conclusions* are *Laws of Nature.* So, from the observ'd *resemblance* between Human Bodies, and from the experienc'd *advantage* of Meats and Drinks, of Sleep and Exercises, and of the whole *Materia medica,* are form'd *general Aphorisms,* with relation to *Diet* and *Medicine,* in use among *all* Nations; tho' many *medicinal precepts,* according to the *variety* of *Soils* and *Climates,* may vary, and indeed *are various,* as the Civil

Moral Good.

Laws of different States. When, afterwards we act in pursuance of these Conclusions, and, upon comparison, find our actions conformable to them; beside the previously known appellation of *natural* Goodness, there accrues to these actions this, that they are *morally* Good, from their conformity with the Laws of Nature already enacted.

I will add nothing here, concerning the word [*possible*], which I inserted, because the utmost bounds of Obligation to action, never exceed the limits of the Faculty oblig'd. Altho' the words 'Publick Good' have a great sound, no man is oblig'd to promote it beyond his ability.

The word [*chiefly*] shews, that the *Affirmative* Laws of Nature, or those enjoining Action, are *Comparative* Dictates of Reason, and prescribe the *best* action, we can either think or say, is in the given circumstances in our power; *alwaies* the *Best*.[26] It is, however, to be observ'd, That what is *equal to the Best,* may justly be called the *Best,* and, when we can perceive no material difference, we may act either way. In such cases, the Law of Nature has left us at Liberty.

Now I have here describ'd *Affirmative* Laws only, because *Negative* Laws may easily be thence deduced; and Nature, which consists wholly in things *Positive,* seems to imprint *immediately* these only.

§X. The last words of our Definition *implied,* "That the Law of Nature alwaies declares those actions only, which tend to promote the Publick Good, sufficient to procure the intire and chief Happiness of particular agents"; and they *express* "The *Sanction* of these Laws, which is discover'd from the *happiness* annex'd to their *observance,* and the *misery* consequent upon their *violation.*" I *affirm'd,* "That the *intire and chief happiness* possible was aim'd at in them," because all men naturally and necessarily desire, not any part only thereof, but the *whole* which seems possible to them, according to the will of the First Cause. And this desire is highly *rational,* and evidently *more* conducing to our perfection, than the desire of any *less* Good. To this it is owing, (which is of great importance with respect to *Universal Justice,*) that *no proposition* is to be

The last words, concerning [the necessity of promoting the Common Good, in order to intire private happiness,] explain'd.

26. Cumberland quotes the phrase in Greek. Possible sources are Epictetus, *Enchiridion,* 52, or Marcus Aurelius, *Meditations,* III.6.

look'd upon as a *Law of Nature*, which declares what sort of actions can procure bodily Pleasure, Wealth, Honours, or any other *portion* of Happiness, *for a time*, but *those only*, which certainly foreshew, by what methods, we may procure the *greatest quantity* of all good things, especially the *Greatest*, which may render our *Minds perpetually* Happy. It is, for this reason, *necessary*, "That we should deliberate and determine with our-selves, not with respect to any small parts of our Life, (for example, what we ought to do to-day, in order to spend this day happily,) but with respect to our whole life to come, what will conduce *alwaies*, and in *all circumstances*, to our perpetual Happiness." Because in the whole series of actions, to be perform'd thro' the whole course of our future life, is contain'd, as in its cause, that whole Happiness, which is or will be in our power, which we naturally desire. "Almost all the Crimes of Wicked Men arise hence, that they regard only Corporeal and Immediate Pleasures, and regulate their actions accordingly, not at all solicitous about those, which respect the Mind, or which are not to happen, till after a long series of Actions."

These words [*the happiness of particular agents*, &c.] *insinuate*, "That some part of those good things, which are, by the will of the First Cause, as it were laid up at the Creation for the *Common Happiness*,[27] is by the same act allow'd and given to *particular persons* in the ordinary preservation of the World, and, therefore, that the measure of each one's share may be adjusted by Human Reason, in that proportion, which particular persons bear to the whole collective Body of rational Agents." As the Heart, by the same Circulation of the mass of Blood, preserves the Life of the whole *Animal*, and distributes a justly-proportioned nourishment to *every Member*. Only there is this *difference*, "That, by the Members of the Body, their proportion is imbib'd *without Reason*: But, in Men, the judgment of *Reason*, considering each man's proportion, claims to itself that share of good things, which is consistent with the welfare of the Whole."

27. Barbeyrac (*Traité Philosophique*, p. 226, n. 1) notes that there should be an ampersand instead of a comma here. Maxwell follows the text.

§XI. Before I come to *consider,* "What kinds of actions are necessary to the Publick Good, or consistent with it," I thought it necessary to *shew* these *Two* things,

(1.) That, in this our Definition, are contain'd (at least, by an easy consequence, may be thence deduced) all those things, which are *requisite to the general nature of a Law;*

(2.) Also those things, which are *peculiar to the Law of Nature.*

As to the *First,* that Passage of *Modestinus,* before cited out of the *Digests,* comes pertinently into consideration; *"The force of a Law is to command, forbid, permit, punish,"*[28] to which also may be added, in some Laws, *to confer rewards:* In these words are certainly contain'd, what some express by the *Metaphorical* words of *Obliging* and *creating a Duty. Obligation* is defin'd by *Justinian "That bond of the Law, by which we are tied with the necessity of paying any thing, according to the Laws of that State to which we belong."*[29] Where it is to be *observ'd,* "That he respects the Laws of his own State only, that of *Rome;* whereas *Papinian,* with much greater reason, acknowledges a *Natural Obligation* (distinct from the *Civil,*) *which is supported by the bond of Equity only":*[30] As also, "That it breeds *obscurity,* that he uses *Metaphorical* words, which are generally of *doubtful* meaning." For those words, *bond* and *tied,* are not more easily understood, than *Obligation,* which is to be defin'd. But, if we consider the matter attentively, this is plainly *insinuated,* "That Punishments, and also Immunities and Privileges, are annex'd to the Laws, by the authority enacting them; and that Men, partly from the prospect of Good arising from obedience, partly from the fear of Evil from disobedience, are determined, or at least in some measure moved, to act as the Laws prescribe." For no other necessity determines the mind of Men to act, than that of shunning apparent Evil, and of obtaining apparent Good. All (that I know of) acknowledge this *Necessity,* which is consistent with the *freest* power of inquiring into the goodness of things, to be essential to Human Nature. Therefore the whole force of *Obligation*

> The Law of Nature has the whole force of a proper Law.

> The obligation of a Law arises from the Legislator's annexing Rewards and Punishments to it.

---

28. Justinian, *Digest,* I.1.1.3.
29. Justinian, *Institutes,* III.14.
30. Justinian, *Digest,* XLVI.3.95.4.

is this, *That the Legislator has annex'd to the observance of his Laws, Good; to the transgression, Evil; and those Natural, in prospect whereof men are moved to perform actions, rather agreeing than disagreeing with the Laws.*

The Greatest Good, and Evil, connected with our Actions observing, or violating the Law of Nature.

The *good* Things, connected with the *observance of the Laws of Nature,* are the very same, which compose mens chief happiness, and, therefore, they are evidently the *Greatest:* Those *Evils* also, which are the consequence of a state in perpetual *opposition to those Laws,* are those, which produce the *greatest Misery.* The *connexion* of these with Human Actions, is *Natural* and *Necessary,* that is, does not *wholly* depend upon the pleasure of sovereign Powers; (tho' in every Civil State *some part* of these Rewards and Punishments are dispensed according to the will of the Governors;) but, if there were *no Civil Government,* they would *partly* follow from the *nature of the actions,* and *partly* be necessarily added by *private persons:* And, now that Civil Government is every where set up, the well-known *necessity* of preserving that Nature, which is common to all Political societies, every where *determines Rulers to exact Punishments and confer Rewards,* tho' with some diversity in different times and places.

This Connexion is either Immediate or Mediate.

§XII. But, because this is the *chief debate in this controversy,* I must *shew,* more accurately, "The *Connexion* between *all the actions* of every particular person, directed (as far as may be) thro' the whole course of Life, to *promote the Publick Good,* and the *greatest* possible *happiness* and perfection of Each." And it is twofold, (1.) *Immediate,* (2.) *Mediate,* upon account of Good procur'd, by such actions, from Men, nay, from God himself.

1. Immediate Happiness consisting in the due exercise of all our Faculties about the Common Good.

I intend to treat *first* of the *former,* because it is a *reward* of Virtue, *inseparable* from the very action, and the most easily *demonstrable,* as being *present,* not liable to *uncertain* chances of *Futurity,* nor *intangled* in that *multiplicity of Causes,* on which *Future* Rewards depend. The *immediate connexion,* between every man's greatest *happiness* of Mind, that is in his power; and the *actions,* which he performs to promote most effectually the common Good of God and Men, consists in *this;* "That these are the very *actions,* in the exercise and inward consciousness whereof, every man's *Happiness* (as far as it is in his own power) consists." The *same actions consider'd,* "As distinguish'd, from all others of a different kind, by their Objects and most extensive external Effect," are call'd *Actions promoting the Publick Good:* But, *consider'd,* "As the exercise of the Agent's greatest powers, or as his greatest perfections, producing Tranquillity and the greatest Joy to him from a consciousness of them," are called the *greatest Happiness* he can procure to himself. After the same manner, as we perceive a *connexion,* between the *Health* and unimpair'd Powers of the Body, and its *Actions;* both Natural (relating to nourishment and generation,) and Animal.

I suppose what follows in this *Paragraph,* known from the study of Nature, or learn'd by Experience, (1.) in *General,* "That it conduces to the natural perfection of the Mind of Man, that his Faculties, of *Understanding* and *Will,* be conversant about Objects of all kinds, especially, about God and Men." For they have a nature *resembling,* or analogous to, the *Mind of every Man,* and, so far, capable of being known from our own Actions, of which we cannot but be conscious; and, beside, most of their actions very *nearly affect our-selves;* and they (as acting according to right Reason) may be *mov'd* by our Actions, to concur with us in promoting our Happiness. *{This evinced from some Observations concerning (1.) the Perfection of the Mind in General,}*

(2.) In *Particular,* that there are requir'd to the perfection of the *Understanding* (1.) "That it *abstract* Universal Ideas from particulars, and compare them with others, and observe, that their necessary Attributes belong to other individuals we meet with"; for *Example,* that, from a Knowledge of it-self, abstracting what is peculiar, it may learn the Essential Properties of the Rational, or Animal, &c. Nature; and, among other things, observe, in all, some endeavours to their own preservation and perfection. (2.) "That it *search* into the *productive* and *preserving Causes* of things, in some measure, dependent upon our power." (3.) "That it *form like Judgments in like cases,* and alwaies *agree with it-self,* after once it has form'd a right Judgment." (4) "That it *deduce,* not *speculative Propositions* only, but *practical* ones also, from known Principles." (5.) That it *follow the order of Nature,* as occasion requires, sometimes in the *Analytick,* sometimes in the *Synthetick* method. *{(2) the perfection of the Understanding in particular, and}*

To this head[31] is to be reduc'd that known Axiom, That *the perfection of a rational Agent requires, that he should resolve upon the End before the*

---

31. [Maxwell] "This is an instance of the Analytick method."

Means: Or, that he should consider, as throughly as he can, the Effect propos'd, before he makes use of Means to produce it. And that, therefore, he should *first* propose to himself the *End* of his whole future Life, *before* he can reasonably enter upon *Actions;* the influence whereof, as of Means or Causes, may affect his whole Life, and render it more or less happy. We shall easily perceive the *use* of this *observation,* in what follows, where we shall *see,* "That all and every one of our actions may increase the whole of our Happiness, nay, that they must necessarily, either improve or diminish it; and that Reason enjoins a Uniform direction of all our future actions to this End."

Nay, the *Synthetick* method of considering the intire trayn of our voluntary Actions, comes to the *same* thing. For, if *voluntary* Action be consider'd in *General,* without respect to this or that particular case, "Its *Object* and Effect is *Good,* even the most diffusively extensive, whether acceptable to the Doer, or to any others whomsoever." The other Property of *Voluntary* Action in *General,* is, "The *Avoiding* all manner of *Evil,* whether it be Evil to one, or to many, whether it thwart our own Good, or that of others." Our *Acts of the Will,* whether *Chusing,* or *Refusing,* according to the degree of Good or Evil, and other circumstances, are call'd by the names of several *Passions,* on the one hand, of *Love, Desire, Hope, Joy;* on the other, of *Hatred, Fear, Aversion, Grief.* At length, we *proceed* "To the consideration, of particular actions, both those, which may be perform'd at present, and those, which will probably be exerted hereafter; and, of that *Order among those actions,* by the assistance whereof arises (as it were the Sum of a Geometrical Progression) the greatest Sum of good things, which can be done, or enjoy'd, thro' the whole course of Life." This is call'd *every Man's Happiness, or chief Good.*

Of the Will.   I judge it requisite to the natural *perfection* of the Human *Will,* "That it follow the most *perfect Reason,* both in its *calmer resolutions,* which are simply call'd *Desires* and *Aversions;* and in those more *vehement* ones, which usually go under the name of *Passions.*"

Hence we may *perceive,* "That Actions, *contrary* to these, are *Imperfections* and *Diseases* of the *Mind,* as Lameness, or Paralytick and Convulsive Motions are Symptoms of *Diseases* of the *Body.*" Such are the

Assents given to contradictory Propositions, because it is certain, that one member of a Contradiction must be false: *Unlike Judgments in like Cases,* &c.

§XIII. I have no inclination, very curiously to *inquire,* "Whether the *Happiness* of Man be an Aggregate of the most vigorous *Actions,* which can proceed from our Faculties; or rather a most *grateful Sense of them,* join'd with Tranquillity and Joy, which by some is call'd *Pleasure.*" These are inseparably connected, and *both necessary* to Happiness. This I will affirm, that we have nothing more in our power, towards making ourselves happy, than *Actions:* And that Actions are incapable of any other *Augmentation,* than what is to be perceiv'd in *their own inward Vigour,* and the natural *excellency of the Object* or Effect. Therefore, seeing the Common Good of God and Man is the greatest and most excellent Object we can imploy ourselves about; (for the Happiness of every one contains his Perfection, and the Common Good unites the Happiness of all;) our most *vigorous Actions* respecting that *Object,* and the *Complacency* arising from the *consciousness* of them, will, beyond any thing in our power, render us the most *Happy.* Most of the wiser Philosophers placed, both the *Happiness* and *Virtue* of the *Human* Mind, in *Action,* or in the right use of both its Faculties, which *Plutarch* has compriz'd in a few Words, *"Happiness consists in right reasonings ending in a steady disposition of Mind."* [32] Yet all do not sufficiently *explain,* "about what object and effect all these Actions conducing to Happiness, are immediately and adequately to be imploy'd." For, to assign *Happiness,* as *that Object* or *that End,* is not satisfactory. For, since *Happiness* itself is a certain Aggregate, whose parts we are continually enjoying, and itself is confess'd to *consist in Action;* to say, *We act for Happiness,* is to say no more than that, *We act, that we may act.* When we say that, *the Object and Effect of those our Actions which render us happy, are the Honour and Glory of God,* we say, indeed, something; but, instead of the *whole,* we express *part* only, of the *Object* about which *They* are conversant, who live well and happily. It may indeed be *affirm'd,* "That the *Knowledge*

The same prov'd from hence, that, "Happiness consisting in the vigorous employment of our Faculties on their noblest Objects"; God and Man, whose Common Good we pursue, are such.

32. Plutarch, *De Consolatio ad Uxorem* (in *Moralia*), 611a.

of our-selves and others, and also *Charity* and *Justice* towards Men, may be *deduced* from the Study of *God's Glory.*" But the Knowledge and Love of our-selves and other Men *include a natural Perfection,* (in possession whereof some part of Human Happiness consists,) essential and proper to themselves, which we can come to the Knowledge of, *without deducing* it from *God's Honour.* Nay, we seem *first* to know and love *Man,* before the Mind raises it-self to the knowledge and love of *God,* whose *Being,* and amiable Goodness are *discovered* from his *Works,* and chiefly from *Man.* Be it, therefore, *concluded,* "That *God* and *Men* are the immediate and intire *Object,* what is grateful and *good to Them* is the *Effect,* of those Actions, which are principally conducive to our Happiness." Certainly, there cannot be a *greater* Object of Beatifick Actions, than what comprizes *all* Things and their mutual Relation to one another, nor can that Object be consider'd under a notion more *General, Perfect* and *Pleasant,* than that by which it is represented in these Words, the COMMON GOOD. For, beside that *Good* is as extensive as *Being,* and so takes in all Individuals, especially Rational; there is this further consideration, that it does not only respect the internal and *essential Perfections* of things, but all those *Ornaments,* which can afterwards accrue to them, whether consider'd singly in themselves, or in whatever Relation: And beside; Beings are consider'd only as they are capable of *Doing* or *Receiving Good,* when *voluntary* Actions, relating to them, are *directed by Laws:* Hence it is, that the infinite Extent of such an Object, calls forth, exercises and suffices, the whole force of the most capacious Faculties, and delights the same with perpetual Pleasure, (for nothing can be pleasanter than Happiness.) Surely he is *stupid,* whom the Sight, even of *Trees and Herbs flourishing* in Spring and Summer, does not much more *delight,* than when Winter has carried off their Bloom and Verdure. But he has intirely *divested himself of Human Nature,* who, foreseeing in his mind the *greatest Happiness* which would arise from the observance of the best Laws, is not greatly *delighted* with the prospect and hope thereof. It is looked upon as a Fault in the *Eye,* if a Person in the Jaundice sees every thing ting'd with *his own Colour* only, or if nothing but a Man's *own Image* were always presented to his Sight; much more is it an Imperfection and unhappiness of the *Mind,* to imploy its thoughts upon the Preservation of *One only Body united to it-self,* and to neglect all others.

§XIV. However it is *certain,* "That Nature has furnish'd almost all Men of sound Mind and Body with such Powers, that, *without any detriment to themselves,* they may do many things of *great advantage to others,* which would be of *little* or *no use to themselves";* such as, "To counsel others in the preservation of their Life or Health, to shew the way to him that knows it not, &*c.*"[33] If such *Powers* are *not exercised* upon proper occasions, they are *vain,* and a perpetual *reproach* to their owner; like an uncultivated field, and seed spoil'd thro' neglect, which, sown, would have commended and rewarded the Husbandman's care and pains. For *to act* (which we certainly do, when we serve others) contributes more to our Health and Pleasure, than *to be wholly idle;* for, by *Exercise,* we *recollect* what we can do, which is a Pleasure to the Able; we *preserve,* and often augment, our *Faculties;* and *strengthen* those *Habits,* which render us expert in Acting: Without Acting, both the Habits would be lost, and the Faculties themselves grow languid.

The Pleasures of Beneficence further shewn.

It is *evident,* "That *no Action relating to others* can be *consistent* with those necessary and right *Actions conducing to our own Good,* unless the *Practical Dictates of Reason,* by which we are determin'd to *that Action,* be plainly *conformable to those,* by which we are directed in *pursuit of our own Happiness,* that is, unless they enjoin us to *desire such things to them as to our-selves."* For we must of necessity desire *like things,* to *things* which are necessarily judg'd *alike, i.e.* of equal importance to the Whole; unless the *Understanding judges Falsly* or *Inconsistently,* or the *Will resist its Judgment;* either of which *destroys* that Internal *Peace,* that is necessary to Happiness. Hence we desire to others, *equally* Innocent or Useful, *equally* Free or Bound, &*c. like* Advantages as to our-selves. And such Judgments are so essential to the Understanding, that whoever acts accordingly, acts *agreeably to his* Intellectual *Nature.* And what is *agreeable to Nature,* gives it *Pleasure.* This hinders not, but that from

---

33. The quotation here echoes Ennius in Cicero, *De Officiis,* I.xvi.50–51.

Generation,[34] in *Families,* and from *Compacts,* in Civil *States,* may arise an *Inequality,* or Superiority of some over others.

Further; because it is very *agreeable* to the Mind of Man, to *succeed* as much as possible, in what he labours to obtain, and *vain* Endeavours are extremely *disagreeable;* therefore, He will be much more happy, in bestowing his pains in benefiting, than in endeavouring to hurt, *Many.* For most Men will very willingly accept of, and *second,* our *Benevolent* Endeavours, who, if they should perceive us endeavouring to *hurt* them, would vigorously *oppose* us; so that attempts of that kind would generally be *in vain.*

Those Enjoyments, which are *necessary* to the preservation of Life, are therefore *more distinctly known,* and desir'd, by all, because necessary Causes are *naturally* connected with their Effects, and can only be deduced from them: And their deduction and application to their Effects, is very *agreeable* to the Mind of Man, which is always in pursuit of the *greatest Certainty.*

Further; greater *Knowledge,* and *Sagacity,* and *Industry,* are requir'd to *preserve* and *perfect* Human Nature, for *Example,* than to *destroy* and *corrupt* it; which may be easily effected by mere *Neglect* or *Ignorance,* and is often effected by the Strength of very weak Men, or perhaps of some other most despicable Animal. But the prosecution of the Publick Good (which contains every Good of every Man, and consequently is the greatest) requires the greatest *Wisdom;* and the least *Folly* may in some measure lessen, and disturb it. But I suppose *Wisdom* to be much *more natural, than Folly, to any Rational Nature.* Our Volitions, therefore, and external *Endeavours to promote the Publick Good,* must needs be naturally more perfect, grateful and *agreeable* to that same *Rational Nature;* unless, perhaps, some *Error* of the Judgment, or Habit arising from Error, and consequently Evil, have been introduc'd into the Mind; which may make what is *hurtful* to Nature, *seem acceptable* to it, as too much Drink appears to one in a Dropsy, or a Fever. For it is *certain,* "That the

---

34. [Maxwell] "Consider'd as the Foundation of the Relation between Father and Son."

inward and natural *perfection* of the *Will,* or of the Man, consists in Willing what the *Wisest* Understanding (most perfectly comprehending the most and the best of things) shall have *most truly* determin'd, to be *most highly beneficial* to the *most* and *best* of *Beings.*" Consent and *Harmony* between the actions of the same *Man,* (one of which, (the Act of the Understanding,) is acknowledg'd to be right and perfective of Nature;) are better proofs of a *right disposition* of Mind, than their *Disagreement,* by which a Person is at variance with, and opposes, himself: Therefore, where the *Understanding* is suppos'd to *act most perfectly,* (which is, when it considers, and puts together, the most and best Objects, in such a manner, that thence, in Idea, arises the best state and order of the Universe, wherein all, Rational Beings especially, enjoy the happiest and most convenient Peace and Agreement;) there a *Will perfectly right must of necessity approve such a Judgment.* And, consequently, since it is the Business of *both* Faculties, to determine our Actions, whether *Immanent* or *Transient,*[35] when they are dispos'd as above, (*i.e.* are *Right*) they must determine us to do *as much Good,* and to *as many,* as we *can.* That the Care of the Common Good, as of the greatest End, implies actions of this sort (*i.e.* Beneficent and Consistent,) is too evident to need proof: As also, that the Internal Perfections of our Mind require us to employ all our Faculties, in their natural and proper order, in an active and vigorous pursuit of Good; of the *Good of the Noblest Beings,* with whom we are concerned; of the *Greatest Good* of all those Beings.

§XV. This *Reason,* by which we have prov'd the *Happiness of the Will to consist in the most extensive Benevolence,* is greatly confirm'd by *Experience,* which gives us vast *Pleasure* in the acts of *Love, Hope* and *Joy,* whether employ'd about our own Good, or that of others. *These* Affections are Essential Ingredients of *Happiness;* they bring *Pleasure* along

These Reasons confirm'd by Experience.

35. [Maxwell] *"Immanent* Actions of the Mind, are such as terminate within the Mind itself, such as all Acts of the Understanding; *Transient,* such as produce Effects without the Mind, such as those acts of the Will, which begin Motion, or produce any Effect without the Mind."

with them, and we find *them* continually mov'd by the *Happiness of others.* He, therefore, robs Man of great part of his Happiness, who deprives him of that most pleasant affection of *Love* and *Benevolence* towards others, and of that *Joy*, which arises from their Happiness. *Our own* Advantages can afford but *small matter of Joy;* the Subject will be exceedingly *inlarged,* if we are delighted with the Happiness of *every other person.* For *This* to *That* will bear the *same Proportion,* which the *Infinite* Happiness of God and of all Mankind has to the *scanty imaginary* Happiness, with which the *Goods of Fortune* can supply *one* Man, and him too, *Envious* and *Malevolent.* For, certainly, *no virtue* can adorn his *Mind,* who has *divested* himself of all *Benevolent Affections* toward Mankind. Nay, *Hatred* and *Envy,* which fill the Mind of him who regards *his own Good only,* are necessarily accompanied with *Trouble* and *Sadness, Fear* and a *Solitary State,* which are evidently *inconsistent* with a *Happy Life.* If we examine our Faculties separately, we shall perceive, after we have arriv'd at Man's Estate, that they grow, as it were, *Prolific,* and too great, to be confin'd and exercised about ourselves only. The *Understanding* has a strong *Natural Propension,* to make itself Master of those things, which may be useful to *others* as well as to *ourselves.* Hence all the Sciences, which have been found out by great application of Mind, and made Publick for the Common Benefit, have taken their rise. The pleasanter Affections of the *Will* (which are conversant about Good) such as Love, Desire and Joy, in the rational use whereof consists our chief Happiness, are seldom found in a *Timon,* a Man-hater.[36] 'Tis certain, they can neither be *frequent,* nor afford *much* Pleasure, unless we are diligent in our endeavors after the Good of *many,* Common *Reason* enjoins us to exert all our Faculties in pursuit of the *Publick* Good, as the most effectual method of obtaining *our own* Happiness. When we have added to the Common Stock by our greatest Industry, we may take out our own share with Innocence, and enjoy it with Pleasure.

§XVI. Because much of what I have to say concerning *Morality,* depends upon what I am now laying down, I will add more to the same purpose.

Private Good cannot be the

---

36. From Lucian's dialogue, *Timon the Misanthropist.*

Since it is certain, from the Nature of the *Will* and of voluntary Action, that the effecting the *Greatest Good* is the *Greatest End* prescrib'd by *Reason;* That Good must either be the greatest *Common* Good (wherein I include whatever is consistent with it,) or the greatest *Private* Good, which every Man can desire or propose to himself as Possible, and to which he directs all his Actions. For the Good of any *particular Family* or *Commonwealth,* is either not yet suppos'd to be consider'd; or, if it be consider'd, it is press'd with almost the same Consequences with the prosecution of the Private Good of any *particular person.*

Reason will not suffer, that the greatest *Private* Good should be propos'd as the *ultimate End.* For, since that *Action* is certainly *Good,* which will lead directly, or the shortest way, to that *End,* which is truly *ultimate;* supposing *different ultimate Ends,* whose Causes are *opposite, Actions* truly *Good* will be in *mutual opposition* to one another, which is impossible. For *Example;* if right Reason instructs *Titius,* that his greatest Happiness, which he is to pursue as his ultimate End, consists in the enjoyment of a plenary Property in the Possessions, and an absolute Dominion over the Persons, of *Seius* and *Sempronius,* and of all others: Right Reason cannot dictate to *Seius* and *Sempronius,* that their Happiness, the object of their pursuits, consists in the enjoyment of plenary Property in the Possessions, and Dominion over the Person, of *Titius,* and of all others. For these contain a manifest Contradiction; and, therefore, one only of these Dictates can be suppos'd true. But, since there is no, Cause, why the Happiness of one of these should be his ultimate End, rather than the Happiness of another should likewise be his ultimate End; we may conclude, that Reason dictates to neither, that he should propose to himself his own Happiness only, as his greatest End, but to every one, rather his own in conjunction with the Happiness of others; and this is that *Common Good,* which we contend is to be sought after. For that only is *that one End,* which is consistent with, and most promotes, the greatest possible *Happiness of every particular person.* In that End, alone, can agree, both *natural Instinct,* regarding *its own,* and *Reason,* respecting the *Common Good.*

It is, certainly, essential to the perfection of Practical Reason, or of *Prudence,* (in what subject soever it be seated,) "That to all, who are to be guided by right Reason, one only End be propos'd, as a Common Standard of Good and Evil to all"; or, "That all Rational Agents should intend one and the same Effect"; whose essential *parts* and *causes,* whether they contribute to its Existence, Preservation, or Perfection, are called *Good;* and those which *hinder its Existence,* &c. *Evil.* Otherwise, the Terms, *Good* and *Evil,* will be *uncertain,* and altogether Equivocal, signifying *differently,* when they are made use of by *different* persons; and whatever is *called Good by one,* because it answers his particular purposes, That all *others will call Evil,* because it is not subservient to their desires; which is *inconsistent with the design of Speech,* which is the communication of Knowledge. But if these *words* be applied to *signify* those things, which are of *common benefit* to Mankind, they have a *determin'd meaning* of great advantage to all.

I add further; if *any one* would regard his own Good only, and endeavour to *force all* Rational Agents to carry on that only, as the chief end they ought to pursue, he would be able to *effect nothing,* but, perhaps, draw down his own *destruction* upon himself. For it is evidently *impossible,* "That *all,* both Things and Persons, should be order'd according to the Wills of *all* particular persons willing things contrary." The *effect* of every *volition* upon things *external,* is some determination of *Local Motion;* as is evident in the taking of Nourishment, Cloathing, Attendants, &c. But *contrary determinations* of the Motions of Natural Bodies *mutually destroy* one another. For, if any Body were at the same time mov'd toward opposite points, it must of necessity be in different places at the same time. But, if it is impossible for every particular Person, to subject all Persons and Things to himself, that Reason, which proposes this end to *every one,* which can happen to *one only,* would, oftener than a Million of times, propose an impossibility, and, once only, what was possible; and, therefore, any one may easily calculate, whether that Reason were Right or Erroneous. Others have both their Natural *Powers,* and Innocent *Appetites,* which, whether we will or no, they will obey; they have *Reason* also, which, directing them to pursue greater things than the pleasure of any one Man, they will by all means follow; and *Strength,* to defend themselves with ease from the overbearing of one or a few; so that he must needs be a *Mad-man,* not a Reasonable

Creature, who could not foresee these consequences, but would attempt, by force of arms, to assert to himself that prodigious Right, which Mr. *Hobbes* maintains every Man has over every Thing and Person. He himself defines *"Right"* to be *"a Faculty of acting according to right Reason."*[37] Now I should call that *Practical Reason* only, *Right,* which directs us to endeavour after things *possible* only, and not ingage us in the fruitless, if not destructive, attempt of gaining an Universal Dominion over all Things and Persons. See his *Chap. 1. §. 10, 12.*[38] *On the contrary,* when any one *serves the Publick,* he *never loses his labour;* his Power, though it perhaps, *immediately,* reach but *one* only, is often, in its *consequences,* useful to *many;* and, sometimes, when we expected no other fruit of our Beneficence, than that *Joy* which arises in our minds from the prosperity of others, brings ourselves home a plentiful Harvest.

Further; to study, and *endeavour after the Common Good* of all Rational Beings, superadds to the attempts of an Innocent Self-love, many noble Actions in favour of Objects like our-selves, and thereby begets and compleats a *Habit of Love towards Mankind,* of which Philanthropy the Love of our-selves is but a finall Portion. I suppose every one seeks *his own* Good, and that *to act in pursuit thereof,* adds to the *perfection* of his Nature. Therefore, *to act in like manner* with respect to others, (among whom is God by far more excellent than himself,) will add a *perfection of the same nature* with that, which consists in acting in pursuit of one's own Good; namely, *a Joy arising from the Harmony and Agreement of our Actions.* For it is more pleasing to the Mind of Man, to observe agreement in it-self and its own actions, than in Musical Notes and Geometrical Figures. As 'tis a *Perfection* of the Human Mind, to form *like Judgments,* so is it, to entertain *like Affections,* concerning *like Things.* To have *contrary Judgments of like Things,* implies a *Contradiction,* and is a kind of *Madness,* and, in Speculation, is shunn'd as a Disease of the Mind. In Practice, it argues as great an imperfection, and is a direct contradiction, in cases perfectly alike to have different Judgments, and different Volitions, according as my-self or another is con-

Benevolence to all Rational Beings is necessarily connected with our own most perfect Estate.

---

37. Hobbes, *On the Citizen,* 1.7, p. 27.
38. Ibid., 1.10, 12, pp. 28–30.

cern'd. Nay, *since* every one's Nature, as always intimately present, is fully known to himself; *since,* from thence, the Nature of other Men is not less known, as to those essential and general things, in which all agree, and in which, both our own Right, and that of others to the means necessary to the preservation of Life, is founded; it *follows,* "That he, who, with respect to a like Right, determines otherwise in another man's case than in his own, contradicts himself in a most known matter, which lies perpetually before him." And such a *Contradiction,* above all others, greatly *hurts* the Soundness, Peace, and *Contentment,* of the Mind in its Actions; as *Uniformity* in these Matters *produces* the greatest *Tranquillity.*

The Common Good, the only End, in which Mens equal Claims to Happiness can unite.

§XVII. To this *Head* it belongs, "That whoever has judg'd any Actions necessary to his own Happiness, cannot, with Reason, but consent, that any other should judge, in like manner, the same Actions necessary to his Happiness, and, in pursuance of that Judgment, put them in execution." Therefore, if any one takes an exact survey of what is contain'd in those *practical Propositions,* which determine every Man to endeavour his own preservation, he will perceive something that *dictates Self-preservation to others as well as himself,* and that will hinder him from *opposing* any *others* in the *same pursuit.* For, in this Proposition, "It is lawful for Human Nature (in *Hobbes*) to take those things which will preserve, and perfect its Faculties," is included, as Antecedent in Nature, this *indefinite* Proposition, (which, by the necessary relation of Identity in the Terms, becomes Universal, and, therefore, holds equally true in all cases;) "It is lawful for Human Nature (in any person) to take, or to do, those things, which will preserve and perfect its Faculties." Let *Hobbes* tell me, what the addition of a *proper name* does, toward making the former Proposition a *more evident* Dictate of Reason, that is, a Law of Nature, than the latter, which affirms the same with respect to *every one?* But, if he *assert,* "That every one thence acquires a Right to act at pleasure," (as he contends *Chap.* 1. §. 10.) because I have already shewn the Absurdities thence arising,[39] I think it sufficient to make this *reply,* "That the *application* of such a general Law to the Nature of any *par-*

---

39. See Cumberland, *A Treatise of the Laws of Nature,* 1.28.

ticular person (*Hobbes* for instance) can neither immediately, nor by good consequence, contradict a *like application* of it to *any other* person: Nor can *any one's Right* or Liberty, allow'd by *any Law,* extend so far, as to make it *lawful* to *oppose* those things, which the *same Law commands* to be done by *others.*" Nay, without doubt, any person's delighting in a good Law, and inclination to Uniformity in Action, and Reverence to the Law-giver, will influence him to assist others in observing the same Law, as far as he can without any prejudice to himself; the *effect* of which will be, "That every one will promote the Common Good, who, with due deliberation, considers the Principles enjoining Self-preservation."

The following Reasoning, in the form of a *Syllogism,* will finish this Argument, and prepare the way to what follows relating to the *Mediate,* or more remote, Effects of Benevolent Actions. "Those Actions of ours, which make us perfectly conscious, That we have, to our power, contributed to the Happiness, both of our-selves and others, do affect us with the most pleasing Joy, and, therefore, render us happy. Actions promoting the Publick Good effect this, Therefore, &c." The *Major* is taken from the Definition of our Happiness (as far as it is in our own power;) and, therefore, needs no Proof. The *Minor* is very easily prov'd, by considering, that Human Nature is such, that it cannot but be perfectly conscious of its own deliberate Actions; and we alwaies suppose every Wise person, studious of the Common Good, to act in such a deliberate manner. But he cannot neglect his own Happiness, who wisely endeavours to profit that Whole, of which he himself is a Part. His care of the *End* will cause him to preserve and increase all his own Powers and Perfections, because they are the only *Means,* by which he can attain that End. Nor can any thing *more effectually* procure him the favour and *concurrence* of God, of Men, and of all the most operative Causes, in his endeavours to promote *his own* Happiness jointly with that of *others.* For what can *more effectually* procure him the assistance, both of God and Men, than such *sincere Affections* and Endeavours of doing things acceptable to all? Certainly, since there is *nothing greater* in Human Faculties, *nothing greater* can be expected from Man, by God or Men. Lastly, among the Rewards, *immediately* connected by Nature with our Endeavours to promote the Publick Good, is to be reckon'd that manifold

Pleasure, which arises from the exercise of all those *Powers* and Inclinations, which I have shewn at large to be implanted in Human Nature, and to be chiefly fitted for this very purpose, in the *Chapter concerning Human Nature,* whither I refer the Reader.[40]

2. The *Mediate* connexion of Happiness with acts of Universal Benevolence, is upon account of Advantages procured by such Actions from God and Men.

§XVIII. Let us proceed to consider the good Effects, we may, with *certainty,* expect from *God,* and, with greater *probability,* hope to obtain from *Men,* by a continual course of Universal Benevolence, than by arrogating to our-selves all things by Fraud or Force. We shall be able, *more distinctly,* to foresee the consequence, if the *whole state of Life be, in both cases, compar'd,* than if a *few Actions only;* and to those who deliberate upon future Actions, of which they must *of necessity chuse one,* 'tis sufficient to shew, when *Demonstration cannot be had* on either side of the Question, that on this lies the *more probable expectation of the greater Good.* Upon this account it was, that *Seneca* long ago complain'd, and not without reason, *"That Men, tho' they deliberated concerning parts of their Life, did not deliberate concerning"* (the uniform conduct of) *"the*

The Good or Bad Actions of Men will *probably* gain the Favour or Hatred of other Men;

whole."[41] If they did this, they could not but *see* most evidently, "That the Man, who, disregarding the Rights of God and all other Men, alwaies arrogated all things to himself, and made himself, alone, the only End of all his Actions, must be hateful, both to God and all Men, and must needs pull down Destruction upon himself." *On the contrary,* "That He, who, by Love and Obedience to God, by Innocence and Benevolence towards all Men, sought his own Happiness, in consistence with that of others, and in dependence upon their Concurrence, acts more advisedly, and may very justly hope for better success." Altho' the judgment we make of the *future* Actions of other Men, whose Favour we endeavour to procure, be *probable* only, yet, because it has the *greatest Evidence* we can obtain about such *Future Contingencies;* and, because the necessity of affairs requires, that the Mind, taking a Prospect of the future Actions of Men, should not remain in a *state of perfect Indifference,* but must incline to believe, that rather such Actions shall come to

40. Ibid., 2.17, 2.19.
41. Seneca, *Epistulae Morales,* LXXI.2–3.

pass than others; hence it is, that it is *more reasonable,* to do that, which will *more probably* turn to our increase of *Happiness;* than either, by do-ing nothing, neglect all opportunities of procuring to our-selves the as-sistance of Men, or, by attempting Men by Force or Fraud, commit our Hopes to the uncertain Chance of War. For, among *Future Contingen-cies,* some are much *more probable* than others; and the Hope of *Those* is of much *greater Value* than that of *These.* And *Reason,* supported by *Experience,* knows how to *ascertain the Difference* between the values of *this* and *that* Hope, and reduce it to an exact Mathematical Calculation, (which *Huygens* has made evident in his reasonings upon that subject in his Treatise *of the chances of the Dice.* [42]) Therefore the same *right Reason* will *command* us, where greater Certainty cannot be obtained, to *chuse that way,* which, upon account of the Assistance of other Men, *most probably* leads to Happiness.

Hence we may *conclude,* "If we cannot procure the external Neces-saries and Conveniences of Life, by deserving as well as we can at the hands of all; that, then, those Advantages are to be reckon'd among those things, *which are not in our Power";* and this is the *Foundation* of that Rule of the Law of Nature, "What we cannot do lawfully, is to be reckon'd amongst Impossibilities."[43] This, in the Matter before us, is therefore with more safety injoin'd, because it is most *certain,* that, "by acting for the Good of the Whole, the main point is insured." For, by this course, we shall do, both *all* that is *in our own Power,* and what is of the *greatest Importance* toward making our Life happy, as I have already shewn: And the *Favour of God* (the supreme Disposer of all things) *will most certainly be procured,* as I shall presently make appear, from Principles acknowledg'd, both by *Hobbes* and *Epicurus.* For, since *Men can pay nothing more than Love,* and the consequences thereof, to-ward all Rational Beings, (the Head whereof is God,) it is most evident by the Light of Nature, that *he owes nothing more,* because we cannot be oblig'd to Impossibilities; and, therefore, that nothing more than Love is requir'd of him. Now no One who *acknowledges,* from the Light

most certainly the Favour or Displeasure of God.

42. Huygens, *Tractatus de ratiociniis in aleae ludo.* See ch. 4, n. 7.
43. Cumberland's formula recalls Justinian, *Digest,* 28.7.15.

of Nature, "That God is the Governour of the World," will ever *deny*, "That those, who have *perform'd their Duty* toward God and Men, shall find themselves highly *favoured* by Him." Reason, therefore, may *dictate*, "That Innocence and Benevolence are the most effectual Means of promoting our own Happiness, as well as that of other Men"; tho' we cannot *demonstrate*, "That They will act with Benevolence and Gratitude towards us, and be faithful in the Observance of their Compacts."

This prov'd
from two
Topicks. §XIX. I will briefly lay down what I have to say upon this Head. Every Man's *Obligation*, to act in pursuance of the Common Good of all, (which is the Summary of the Laws of Nature,) becomes known by those methods, by which we *know*, "That God, the First Cause of all Things, wills that such Actions should be performed by Men"; or, "That, in his ordinary Government of this World, he has so order'd or adjusted the Powers of all things, that such Actions should be rewarded, and the contrary punished."

It is of *no consequence,* whether this Distribution of *Rewards* and *Punishments* be made *immediately,* or put off for a time; provided, that *interval* of Time be *compensated* by the *greatness* of the Rewards and Punishments; and the *Reasons for believing* that Compensation, manifestly, *outweigh* all grounds of suspecting the *contrary.*

Waving, in the present Argument, the consideration of *Revelation* made by the Prophets in the Scriptures, the *Will of God,* in these matters, is *naturally known,* (1.) From those his *known Attributes,* which, in the order of distinct Knowledge in the *Synthetick* way,[44] go before and incline his Will, to put these things in execution, and may, therefore, be consider'd as *Causes* of his Willing and Acting thus. (2.) From the *Effects,* arising from his Will before determined so to act. Of this *latter* Method of knowing the Divine Will, I have said somewhat already, and more remains yet to be spoken. On the *former* I shall insist more sparingly, because our Adversaries will hardly grant any thing relating thereunto, and all the Attributes of God are to be deduced by us in the *Analytical*

44. [Maxwell] "Arguing *à Priori,* from the Cause to the Effect."

Method, from his Effects.[45] I have, however, thought fit to suggest the little that follows.

We must needs conceive, that *the Framer of the World is endow'd with Reason, Wisdom, Prudence, and Constancy.* For "these are Perfections, which, in some degree, we are sensible of in ourselves (his Workmanship;) nor is it possible, that any Perfection should be found in the Effect, which is not contained in its Cause. *But* these Perfections are prior to such a Will as we are now inquiring about, and, as it were, lead to it. *Therefore* we know such a Will to be in God." The *Minor* is prov'd by this, That the *Practical Right Reason of Man,* and the consequent *Volition,* must, of necessity, *agree with the Judgment and Will of God,* in respect to the *same Object.* For the Judgments of *both,* as being *Right,* must *agree with the same thing,* and, consequently, *with one another.* The thing, concerning which ought is determined by the *Practical Judgment,* is either the *End,* or the *Means* to the End, concerning both which is determin'd, *which is Best.* Wherefore *God will determine the same End and Means* to be best, which the *Reason of any Man truly judges to be so.* The Matter will become plainer by an *Example.* If any *Man rightly judge,* "That the Common Good of All, who act according to the Rule of Reason, is a greater Good than the Good or Happiness of one Man," (and this is no more, than to judge the Whole to be greater than its Part;) there is no doubt, but that *God thinks the same.* And it will come to the same thing, if it be *affirm'd,* "That the Happiness of All is greater than the like Happiness of any smaller Number." But "that Happiness is the greatest, which is greater than any other assignable." Nor is it a different Judgment, that by which we *affirm,* "The greatest Happiness of all Rational Beings is the greatest or chief End, which any Rational Agent can pursue." For a possible End is nothing else, than that Good or Happiness, which any one may propose to himself to pursue. Therefore there is no room to *doubt,* but that we shall *here also have God's Concurrence.* For, since He himself is *Rational,* and it cannot be conceiv'd, how he can act *rationally, without* proposing an *End* to himself, nor can there be a *greater* End than the aforesaid *Aggregate of all Good* Things; we

1. From the Knowledge of those things, which, as it were, antecedently incline Him to act thus, The Perfection of His Understanding and Will.

---

45. [Maxwell] *"A Posteriori,* from the Cause to the Effect."

cannot but think, he judges this to be the best End he can propose to himself. Nor is it to be doubted, but that the most *perfect* Being will *pursue* that *End,* which he has *rightly judg'd* to be the *best,* all Circumstances rightly consider'd. For no reason can be assigned, why he should *stop short* of it; nor can the most *perfect* Will act *without* Reason, much less, *against* it. For, altho' here the Obligation of a Law *properly so called,* which proceeds from the Will of a Superior, has no place, yet that *Perfection,* which is Essential to Him, and Invariable, will invariably *determine* his *Will,* to *concur* exactly with his omniscient *Understanding.* For it implies a Contradiction, that the same Will should at once be Divine or most *perfect,* and *disagree with the most perfect* Dictates of the Divine Understanding. But *supposing,* "That God proposes to himself the Common Good, as an End," the *consequence* is easy, "That he Wills, that Men should pursue the same End."

It is *evident,* "That the distribution of *Rewards* and *Punishments* among Men, is absolutely necessary, and the *most certain Means,* to *lead* them to consent and *concur* with the Divine Will, in promoting this End, and to *deter* them from Actions *contrary* thereto." God, therefore, Wills such Rewards and Punishments, as he knows *sufficient* to secure this End; he *Wills,* I say, both to *decree* them, and actually to *distribute* them, as occasion requires. Whence may be *inferr'd,* "That, if any thing, necessary to this End, be wanting in this Life, it will be supplied by God in a Life to come." And upon *this ground,* chiefly, it was, that the *Heathens* formed their *Presages* of the Happiness, or Miserie, of Men departed this Life, according as their Actions were Good or Evil. But this may be easily *learned* from their own Writings.

§XX. I chuse *the rather* to observe, that, from what I have prov'd concerning the *Reason* and *End* of God, may be *demonstrated,* "That Benevolence, Justice, Equity, and those other Attributes, which have any Analogy with Human Virtues, are actually to be found in God and in his actions; and that it is, therefore, his Will to govern Men by Precepts guarded with Rewards and Punishments"; *because* it thoroughly overthrows *Epicurus's* Notion, *That the World is not govern'd by Providence.* For it is manifest, both that all these Attributes have a view this way, and,

[margin note:] From whence whom are deduced his Moral Attributes and Providence;

besides, that the whole affair of *Government* (or Divine Providence, for which we contend) consists in this only, that we know of, "That the Common Good of all Rational Beings should be promoted by the most proper Means." Which will appear more clearly, from what shall afterwards be laid down, concerning the *Virtues* and *Civil Government.*

Here I have thought proper to add only thus much; in vain do the *Epicureans* ascribe to God *Happiness* and *Majesty,* unless they acknowledge in him *Wisdom,* or *Prudence,* and *Justice,* and, consequently, *every kind of Virtue.* For all the Virtues *spring* from *Prudence,* (which directs to the Best End by Proper Means,) as from their Fountain, which *Epicurus* has acknowledg'd:[46] And they are all only *integral parts* of Universal *Justice.* But there can be *no Happiness, no Majesty,* nor even Dignity, in any Rational Agent, if he has *not Prudence,* nor any Virtue Analogous thereto.[47] Nor can there be any *Prudence,* except the *best End* be chosen, and the *Means* most suitable thereto; nor can these be *chose,* if they are not, in their own Nature, fixt and *determin'd:* That is, if nothing be good, before it is chose, and one End be no better than another, nor any Means more conducive than the contrary, to that End. For *Example,* if the Publick Good be not greater than any Private; and if Innocence, Fidelity, Gratitude, &c. are not properer Means to attain this End, than Cruelty, Perfidiousness, and Ingratitude. Certainly *Power,* how great soever it may be imagin'd, if it be consider'd *without Wisdom* and *Justice,* has in it *no more* of *Happiness* or *Majesty,* than what is to be found in a *Mass of Lead* of infinite Weight; for Weight is equivalent to any Power, as those skill'd in Mechanicks very well know. This Reasoning is yet of more Force against the *Epicureans,* because they themselves, if we may believe *Gassendus,* or even *Velleius,* who, in *Cicero,* defends their opinions, acknowledge the Happiness of the Gods to consist in this also, *that they rejoice in their own Wisdom and Virtue.*[48] But there is

46. Diogenes Laertius, *Lives,* X.132.

47. Barbeyrac (*Traité Philosophique,* p. 244, n. 3) suggests Seneca, *Epistulae Morales,* XCV, as a possible source here.

48. Cumberland refers to Gassendi's *Philosophiae Epicuri Syntagma* (1649); the reference to Velleius comes from Cicero, *De Natura Deorum,* I.viii–xx.18–56.

left no *Subject* for them to work upon, except they own, that they take care of that *chief common End,* and the *Means* leading thereto. Take them away, and the *name* only of Wisdom, or Virtue, or Deity, *remains,* the *thing* itself is *gone.*

also from his
being the First
Cause. §XXI. Of near affinity with this *Argument,* drawn from the *Divine Attributes,* is that which is taken from the notion of a *First Cause,* the first notion Men learn of God from his Works; for that *implies,* "That all Creatures, but especially Rational, have receiv'd their Existence, and, consequently, all the Powers essential to their Nature, from his Will." Now, because it is certain, that the *Common Good of Men* signifies nothing else, but the *Preservation of their Nature, and the most flourishing State of their essential Powers;* the Mind of Man cannot but conclude it far more *probable,* "That the same invariable Will, which gave Men *Existence,* would will rather their Continuance and Happiness, so far as is consistent with the necessary nature of the rest of the System, which he made at the same time, than that they should be thrown down from that State, in which he himself had plac'd them, without any real necessity, which can arise only from a regard to the preservation of the Whole." For I suppose it *known* from true Principles of Natural Philosophy, "That the natural Vicissitudes of Things, their Generation and Corruption, always rise from the Laws of Motion, by which the whole System of the World is preserv'd." It must certainly proceed from the *same* Goodness, "To cause Men to be," and, "To cause them to be preserv'd and assisted, according to the condition of their Nature, as far as the Welfare of the Whole permits." But, because neither the *Understanding* of Man can *conceive,* nor the *Power* of Man *effect,* any thing *greater* relating to the Creatures, than what regards the Preservation of Mankind, he must of necessity think, that this is the *greatest* affair God Wills them to take care of. And, doubtless, seeing he *commits the care of this to Man,* he will *reward* his *Fidelity* and *Diligence,* and will *punish* his *Perfidiousness* or *Sloth.* Thus, from this *Will to create,* is discover'd his *Will to preserve* and protect Man, and, from hence, our *Obligation* to be *subservient* to the same Will so known.

Almost in the same manner we collect, that it is the *Will of God,* "That

Men should honour Him."[49] Because it was his *Will,* that there should be so many *Proofs* of his *Perfections,* in the Creation and Preservation of this System which we inhabit; and that Men should be so form'd, that, if they would but *exert* the powers of their own *Understanding,* they *could not but observe* these things; he *Will'd,* that they should both *know* and *acknowledge,* what he *is.* And, because he *Will'd,* that *Men* should be *Rational,* that is, consistent with themselves, and averse to all contradiction, he *Wills,* that their *Words* and *Actions* should keep pace with their *Thoughts* concerning his *Perfections,* that is, he Wills, that they should *Worship* and *Honour* Him.

49. [Maxwell] "It ought not to be said, as some say, 'That God demands Honour of us *merely* out of Goodness to us.' For God, consider'd as Imperial over the Universe, is necessarily the Law of true Religion. The Duties of Religion are founded upon his being God, which, supposing our Existence, is to be unto us a sovereign Liege-Lord. These Duties are founded upon the Rights of his Godhead (which are singular, proper, incommunicable, inviolable, unalienable, and essential to his being God,) upon the immutable Nature of Good and Evil, Right and Wrong, Gratitude and Justice, and *his Interest as well as our Interest.* The religious acknowledgment of his Rights is the Interest of his Pleasure, Honour, Service, of his Kingdom and Government, and of his being God. If we make not a religious acknowledgment of them, if we oppose them, this is a doing him the most real and deadly Displeasure and Injury, it is a denying and bereaving him of his Subjects and Service; a fighting against God, a vilifying him, and pouring Indignities upon him, a despoiling him of his Worth and Excellence, and of his Attributes and Perfections, a deposing, dethroning, and undeifying him. Therefore it is *God's Interest,* that we should do him Honour. Kings and Parents do not require, that their Subjects and Children should honour them, merely for that Party's Benefit, but for the Publick Interest. Can it be imagin'd, that *merely* for our Benefit he forbids us, *to vilify and undeify him, and to make him a Lyar?* That his Honour and Interest is subordinate and merely subservient to our Advantage. For what is Man to God, or the Creature to the Creator? As his Honour is his Interest, and he is infinitely superiour to us, so his Interest is transcendent to ours; agreeably to the order of the *two great Commandments,* the *first* of which requireth our superlative Love for God, the *second* enjoineth the Love of our Neighbour in due Equality with our-selves. So our *Lord's Prayer* allotteth the *second* place to the Matters of our Benefit in the three last Petitions, *Our Bread, the Forgiveness of our Sins, and the leading us not into Temptation:* But the three *first* Petitions are, *Thy Name be hallowed, thy Kingdom come, thy Will be done.*" Maxwell is keen to reinforce Cumberland's point that religious worship is not simply a transactional arrangement in return for benefits received.

§XXII. The *second* method of knowing that God *Wills,* "That Actions conducing to the Common Good of Rational Agents should be perform'd by Men"; or, that he wills, "That such Actions should be honoured with Rewards, or the contrary restrain'd by Punishments," is taken from the *Effects* of this Will, that is, from the *Rewards* and *Punishments* themselves, which, by means of the inward Constitution of all Men, and of this whole System of the World, fram'd *by the appointment of the Divine Will,* are the *natural* and ordinary *consequences* of Human Actions; and do render Men, either miserable by Evil, or happy by Good. For it is not to be doubted, but that God, who has *so establish'd* the natural Order of all things, that the Consequences of Human Actions, with respect to the Actors themselves, *should be such;* and who has *caus'd,* that these ordinary Consequences may be *fore-known,* or expected, with the highest probability, by them; *Will'd,* that, before they prepar'd for Action, they should *consider these things,* and be determin'd by them, as by Arguments contain'd in the *Sanction* of the Laws.

Such kind of Effects are, those *Internal* Pleasures of Mind, which accompany every noble Action intended for the publick Good; and, on the contrary, those Fears and Anxieties of Mind, which, like Furies, pursue the Wicked: And also those *External* Rewards and Punishments, by which other Rational Agents, according to the Dictates of right Reason concerning the best End and Means, preserve Mankind from Destruction, and promote the common Happiness. For, since as many as form a *true judgment* concerning the *Greatest End* and the *Means* of obtaining it, (*viz.* That the *common Good* is the *greatest End* which can be propos'd, and that *Rewards* and *Punishments* are the *Means* conducing thereto,) are *determin'd* to those Practical Judgments, by the *Nature* of those *things* about which they deliberate, whose *impressions* upon the Human *Understanding* are perfectly *necessary;* and, since the *Connexion* between *necessary Causes* and all their *Effects* proceeds from the *First Cause;* it *follows,* "That those Dictates of right Reason, by which any Men resolve upon the necessity of distributing Rewards and Punishments in order to the common Good, proceeds from God." That is, "All Men are determin'd by God, by the intervention of the Nature of Things, to judge *both,* that the common Good is the Best End, or the Greatest Good,

From our knowledge of those Effects which suppose this Will, viz.

the Internal Pleasures and Pains, or External Good and Evil, which accompany the pursuit or violations of the Common Good.

which can be obtained, and in which all men may naturally agree, as that which contains (as far as the Nature of all Things will permit) the private Happiness of all particular Persons: *And,* that it is likewise necessary, as the Means to this End, that every one take as much care as possible, that Rewards and Punishments be distributed, by which Actions in pursuance of this End may be encouraged, and the contrary restrain'd.

But, since in those *Propositions, concerning* the Best End and the Means leading thereto, or *concerning* the Greatest Good and its Causes, which are within the power of Men, are contained all those Conclusions which we call the *Laws of Nature,* it *follows,* "That all those Laws are, together with the aforesaid Propositions, imprinted upon the Minds of Men by the Will of the First Cause; and, therefore, that he will'd, that Rewards and Punishments should be distributed, according as these Practical Dictates of Reason suggest, as far as can be done by Men": Whence the *Conclusion* is, "That every such Punishment, and every Reward, so distributed, is distributed according to his Will, and that they are all Effects and Declarations of the Divine Will"; which when known, Men cannot be ignorant of their Obligation thence arising. It is further *manifest,* "That the same God, alwaies consistent with himself, who will'd, that Men should secure, to the utmost of their power, the Common Good by Rewards and Punishments, will also take care, where the Power of Men does not sufficiently defend it, to protect it by his own Power. *[margin: are the Effects of his Present Will, and the Declarations of his Future.]*

I thought it proper, to insist the longer upon this Argument in this Treatise, because I hop'd my *Antagonists,* who are so *intent upon their own Preservation,* would the *more willingly* acknowledge its Force; and, because the *Nature of Things* seem'd to propose *many Proofs* of this matter, which requir'd a very particular Explication. I, therefore, resolve *Moral Obligation,* (which is the immediate *Effect* of Nature's Laws,) into their First and Principal *Cause,* which is the *Will* and Counsel of *God* promoting the Common Good; and, therefore, by Rewards and Punishments, *enacting* into Laws the *Practical Propositions* which tend thereto. Mens *care of their own Happiness,* which causes them to *consider,* and be *moved* by, Rewards and Punishments, is no *Cause of Obligation;* That proceeds, wholly, from the *Law* and the *Lawgiver:* It is only a *nec-*

essary Disposition in the Subject, without which the Rewards and Penalties of the Law would be of no Force to *induce* Men to the performance of their Duty.[50] As Contact is necessary in the Communication of Motion from Body to Body; tho' Force impress'd be the only Cause of that Motion.

It ought, also, in confirmation of this Point, to be *consider'd,* "That the Obligation lies upon them too, whose Mind is so stupid, that they wholly neglect the Divine Will, and the Sanction thereby annex'd to the Law." I must *add,* "That the *Care of* preserving and perfecting *our-selves,* which is *natural* and inseparable from Man, and that which is *superinduced* by right Reason, and, which I acknowledge, has some place among the *Motives* to good Actions, tho' not a *Cause* of our *Obligation* to them, are both wholly from God." From thence it *follows,* "That the force of this Care detracts nothing from his Authority or Honour, and that it ought to have its due Influence."

However, *his own* Happiness is an extremely-*small* part of that End, which a truly-rational Man pursues, and bears only that *proportion* to the *whole* End, (the Common Good, with which it is interwove by God the Author of Nature,) which *one* Man bears to the collective Body of *all* Rational Beings, which is less than what the smallest grain of Sand bears to the whole Mass of Matter. Because God (between Whom and Man there is no Proportion) is reckon'd among Rational Beings, and the Care of the Publick Good includes in the first place, his Honour, and then the Happiness of all Men, which exist at present, or shall exist hereafter.

The Obligation, however, of the Laws of Nature is §XXIII. Lastly, to prevent all Suspicion, that I imagin'd the *Obligation of the Laws of Nature,* which I have deduc'd from the *Will* of the First Cause, to be *Arbitrary* and *Mutable,* I have thought fit to *add,* "That,

---

50. This passage makes clear Cumberland's theory of obligation. A common misunderstanding is that Cumberland was proposing that rewards and punishments in themselves were a source of obligation. As Cumberland states, obligation arises from a knowledge of the law and the lawgiver alone. Rewards and punishments can provide a clue to the nature of God's will, but they do not oblige of themselves.

laying aside the Consideration of the Divine Command, the Exercise of Benevolence, and, consequently, of all the Virtues, does as naturally and necessarily produce the private Happiness of every Rational Agent, and the common Happiness of All, as any Natural Cause produces its Effect, or a Necessary Mean its End"; that is, as two and two make four, or as the Operations prescrib'd by Geometry and Mechanicks solve the propos'd Problems. A *Necessity* this so *Immutable,* that neither the *Wisdom,* nor the *Will* of God can be thought *capable* of appointing a *contrary* Law or Constitution, *whilst the Nature of Things remains such as now it is.* It is, however, certain, that *every Human Action* and Effect, and, consequently, *Arithmetical* and *Geometrical* Operations with all their Effects, *depend* upon the *Will* of the *First Cause.* Our whole inquiry is concerning the *Existence* of the Laws of Nature, and of their Obligation, which must intirely be *deduced* from the Will of the First Cause; I mean *that Act of his Will,* (and that only, as will appear by what follows,) *by which the Powers, Actions, and Natures, of Rational Beings exist.* Wherefore any *Mutability* in the Obligation of the Laws of Nature, is so far from being hence to be inferr'd, that, on the contrary, it has been my chief aim to *prove,* "That it is not possible, without manifold Contradictions, that God should at the same time will, that Rational Agents should be such as they are, and that they should not be oblig'd by those Laws of Nature, which we shall afterwards lay down." This is the only Method, by which any thing can be prov'd *impossible to God;* for he can do any thing, which does *not imply a Contradiction.* But, if any one imagines, that He can make *contradictory Propositions be at the same time true,* by parity of Reason it may be true, *That he cannot do so;* and therefore the Assertion is *vain.* All considerate Persons, therefore, I believe, will think, that I have prov'd the *Law of Nature* sufficiently *immutable,* when I have *shewn,* "That it cannot be chang'd without Contradiction, whilst the Nature of Things, and their actual Powers, (which depend upon the Divine Will,) remain unchang'd." And this I sufficiently prove, when I make it *appear,* "That both the common Happiness of *All* proceeds from the natural efficacy of the Actions of universal Benevolence, and that the Happiness of *particular Persons* is naturally inseparable from the *Common,* with which all are bless'd." *Partly,* because the Happiness

immutable, the Natures of Things remaining as they are.

of the particular Parts is not, in reality, distinguished from the Welfare of the Whole: *Partly,* because we in some measure render our-selves happy by those Actions, by which we benefit others, and, as far as in us lies, thereby determine them to a grateful Return. *Thus* it is, that Actions of publick Benefit naturally reward their Authors: Whereas contrary Actions no less naturally pull down Punishments and Destruction upon their Contrivers.

§XXIV. I will now (having discarded that Right of every Man to every thing, and the War thence arising, which, as I have shewn, *Hobbes* in vain endeavours to establish) *assume* that, which, forced by the glaring truth of the Matter, he *grants,* "That there follows War and the Destruction of All, upon the violation of those Dictates of Reason, which forbid, that any one should claim to himself a Right to all things, and which command to perform Compacts, &c. in observing which Dictates all Virtues consist." I say, that *these Evils* of War are *truly Punishments* inseparably united with such Crimes, by the Will of the supreme Governour, when he settled the order of the Universe. From this, that the *Mind* of Man is *forewarn'd* by the Nature of Things, and, consequently, by God its Author, of the Punishment connected with such an Action, the *Obligation* to abstain from such Action, is *publish'd;* or the Mind is sufficiently forbid, so to act; and the Prohibition is so much the *plainer,* as it appears, that the Action will be hurtful, as well to others, as to its Author.

In my *Opinion,* "The Common Good" (under which I comprehend the Honour of God, and the greatest Happiness of Mankind) "is pleasanter than even Life itself, and, alwaies, to be preferr'd before it"; and, *therefore,* "Those Evils, which either detract from the Honour of God, or endanger the greatest Perfection of Human Minds, are to be esteem'd a greater Evil, than the loss of any one's Life." Whence I reckon it amongst the *Natural Punishments,* that the Violation of the Laws of Nature is attended with, that it *hurts* the principal *Faculties* of the Transgressor, introduces *Folly* and *Error* into the Understanding, and a *perverse Choice* of Evil under the Appearance of Good.

These Evils more particularly deduc'd, and shewn to be Punishments.

But, because Reasonings *of this kind,* as depending upon *much Reflexion* on our own Minds, do not *so sensibly affect* the *Minds* of those, who have of a long time, studied only the Safety or Delights of their *Body,* I think it proper to lay before *them* those *external Evils,* which *Hobbes* acknowledges proceed from the Violation of the Precepts of Virtue, the necessary Means to Peace,[51] and to consider *them* as a Punishment annex'd to the Laws of Nature by the Author thereof, that thus, by Instances frequently obvious to Sense, I may *prove,* "How the Mischief, which redounds to those who are Enemies to the Publick Good, by the natural Establishment of Physical Causes, but principally by the Intention of Rational Agents, is properly and truly a Punishment, and an Indication, that the Author of Nature has establish'd that Law, the Violation whereof was so punish'd." By the same Reasoning it will *appear,* "That all Advantages, which are the Fruits of that Peace and Concord, which are establish'd by the pursuit of the Common Good, become truly a Reward, and prove the obligatory Force of a Law to be given by God to the affirmative Precepts of Virtue." Afterwards it will hence easily appear, *how* those Things *Good* or *Evil,* with respect to our Minds, which may be foreseen as the Consequences of our Actions or Omissions relating to the Common Good; and also, *how* the *Joies* and *Griefs* proceeding from our Sense of the Happiness or Misery of others; *point out, to what kind of Actions we are oblig'd.* "The Mind of Man, by these steps, may at length easily raise itself, to have some Notion or Taste of that most delightful Joy, which arises from the Consciousness, that in Practical Principles our Mind agrees with the Mind or Will of God, the most Benevolent Being; and to conceive the Bitterness of that Grief, which arises from the Consciousness, that our Thoughts and Affections are directly opposite to those of God, conspicuous in his Government of Men." In *these Joies* is the *highest pitch* of our *Happiness,* in *these Griefs* consists the *most wretched Misery.* And, therefore, I affirm, the *Dictates of Reason* do *hence* chiefly receive their power of *Obligation.* Wherefore, seeing they obtain all the *Force* and Efficacy of a *Law,* from the *Will of*

Whence we may easily proceed to a further Proof of the same kind, from the Joies and Griefs arising in the Mind, from a Consciousness of our Consent with, or Dissent from, the Benevolent Will of God.

51. See ch. 1.27ff.

God joining so great *Rewards* to their *Observance,* and *Punishments* to their *Violation,* there is no reason to refuse them the appellation of *Natural Laws.* But it is proper to begin with Instances sensible and confess'd.

§XXV. It is *manifest,* from the very *Terms* themselves (as the *Logicians* call them) well understood, "That so great an innundation of Evils, from War or the less cruel Enmities of every Man against every Man, would overflow Mankind, that, for the Preservation of the Whole, it is necessary to seek Peace"; but the *Means* necessary to obtain *Peace,* are, To permit to others those things which are necessary for them, Faithfully to observe Compacts, To behave ourselves Gratefully and Beneficently to all, and To practice all the other Virtues, which (if they be throughly consider'd) all promote the Common Good. These Truths, even *Hobbes* himself acknowledges, as appears *de Cive,* c. 1. §. 15. c. 2. §. 3. & c. 3. §. 1. and the following; and he repeats the same in the *Leviathan,* but deduces them from the care of *Self-preservation* only;[52] *Publick Good,* at least before the establishment of Civil Societies, he does not acknowledge. Mean-while he most diligently *inculcates* this, "That a War of All against All, in which there are no grounds to hope for Safety, will follow from those Actions, by which any one claims to himself a Right over all Persons and Things, as being contrary to those plainly necessary Means to Peace, which are usually celebrated under the Name of *Virtues.*"[53] It is most *certain,* "That Men, in all States, are forc'd by *Self-preservation,* to oppose and punish those, who would force from them, however Innocent, either their Life or the Necessaries thereof."[54] But, for this very Reason, that *these Evils are inflicted upon others, at the command of right Reason, upon account of Actions prejudicial to Mankind,* they are *Punishments,* and those *Practical Propositions,* which teach, that it is necessary to Peace, "That we should do to others, what we would that they should

Marginal note: The Evils inflicted on others, at the command of right Reason, for Actions hurtful to Mankind, are properly Punishments, and the Sanctions of a Divine Law.

---

52. Hobbes, *On the Citizen,* 1.15, p. 31; 2.3, p. 34; 3.1, pp. 43–44; *Leviathan,* chs. 14–15.

53. A paraphrase of the arguments in *On the Citizen,* 1.10–13.

54. Ibid.

do unto us,"[55] have this *Punishment annex'd,* by the Author of our rational Nature, to their *Violation,* and are hence known, to obtain the intire force of *Laws:* Nor are, now, any more to be look'd upon, as *mere Practical Propositions,* which one may use or neglect to use with Safety, (such as those that teach the Construction of Mathematical Problems;) they are *properly Laws,* and claim to themselves the Obedience due to Laws.

Here (as in the Laws of Civil States) the *Obligation* of the Law is discover'd, from its *Sanction* by Rewards and Punishments; the *Right* of guarding the Laws of Nature by such Sanctions, is to be resolv'd into the *natural Authority of God,* in right of which he exercises an universal Dominion: The real *Goodness* of these Laws becomes known, from the natural and necessary *Connexion* of the *Actions commanded,* with the preservation or increase of the *Common Good:* Almost in the same manner, as the *Right* of annexing Penalties to Civil Laws is resolv'd into the *Authority of the chief Governours,* and their *Goodness* into the *Fitness* of the Actions commanded, to promote the *Common Weal.* For *Example,* that universal Proposition, which we have premis'd concerning the force of Benevolence towards all Rational Beings, to procure the Happiness of the Benevolent, naturally obliges Men to such Benevolence, upon this *account,* "That the Ruler of Mankind has given them natural means of knowing, that he himself is so inclin'd toward the Common Good, and has so constituted the order of Nature, that they, who endeavour to promote the Common Good, shall thereby, not only have the concurrence of the Natural, but gain the favour of those Rational, Agents, which can contribute to their Happiness," (which assistance is also a *Natural Reward:*) And they, who act otherwise, shall, by such Actions, excite against themselves the causes of their Destruction.

As many *learn* the *Laws* of their own *Country,* not from the Laws themselves publish'd in Writing, or from the Mouth of the Legislators, but from the judgment of their *Reason* concerning the proper Causes of the Publick Good, and from the *Observation* of those Things, which

---

55. Cf. Hobbes's use of the Golden Rule (Matthew 7.12) in *On the Citizen* 3.26, p. 53, and also *Leviathan,* ch. 15, p. 99.

they perceive to be publickly rewarded, permitted, or punish'd; *so,* what are the *Laws* of a *Rational Nature,* or of the Kingdom of God, we *learn* first, by a diligent *consideration,* what things are necessary to the Happiness of all the Subjects, and to the Honour of God, the Sovereign of that greatest State; and afterwards by *observing,* how naturally and necessarily Men are inclin'd, to restrain those who pursue contrary Measures.

It is not to be *doubted,* but "That the First Cause commanded that Punishment to be inflicted, which right and necessary Reason commands to be inflicted"; for that is intirely determin'd by the *nature of things* exactly weigh'd, and, consequently, by God the *Maker of all Things.* We may likewise *infer,* "That God decrees Rewards to such Actions, as the right Reason of Man decrees Rewards to"; and *also,* "That it is his Will, that those Propositions, concerning Actions contributing any thing to the Common Good, should obtain the force of Laws, which he has honour'd" (beyond other True and Practical Propositions, Geometrical, for *Instance*) "with Rewards and Punishments thus establish'd."

God will certainly punish such crimes as escape Human Knowledge, and those that Human Power is too weak to restrain.
Further; if God teaches Men to *judge,* "That it is necessary, both to the Common Good and the Private Good of particular Persons, that all violations of the Peace should be, when they come to know of what evil consequence they are, restrain'd by Punishments"; we may clearly *gather* by a *Parity* of Reason, "Not only that he himself so judges, and Wills that Men should do so too; but also, that he makes the same judgment on all Actions equally hurtful, which Men either do not know, or cannot punish." For it is most *certain, That* every *Right Judgment,* and consequently the Divine, determines *alike* concerning *Cases* wholly *alike;* and *that* the most secret Actions cannot be conceal'd from him: And *that,* therefore, there can be *no Reason,* why he should *forbear to pass a Judgment* upon them, as Men are often oblig'd to do, left by a *rash* Judgment they should hurt the Innocent." This reasoning is obvious to all, whence they cannot but *think* with themselves, "That God has appointed Punishments to their secret Crimes," and, "that he will avenge the insults upon the Weak." For there is no reason to doubt, but that he will *pursue this End,* the Common Good, in which both his own Honour and the

Happiness of all Rational Beings is contain'd. For a greater End there cannot be; and a less End cannot be taken for the Greatest, by him who judges truly. Thus the Pangs and Obligation of *Conscience* take their Origin from the Government of God.

§XXXVI. But let us return to the *Punishments inflicted by Men,* for violating the conditions necessary to Peace; more things concerning the *Obligation,* which we have prov'd from thence, remaining to be explain'd. For it is to be observ'd, that, altho' such Crimes *sometimes* escape *unpunish'd* by Men, yet we may truly affirm, that they are *determined by Nature* and right Reason to *punish* them, as far as lies in their power; and that it is therefore *by accident only,* that they sometimes permit *wicked* Persons to escape *unpunish'd.* So other Effects, which we either do or suffer to be done, thro' natural *Ignorance* or *Weakness,* are imputed rather to *Chance* than to human *Nature,* and are usually reckon'd by wise Men among those things which *rarely happen.* Now *right Reason,* while it delivers the Precepts and Rules of Action, will *never advise* us to place our *Hopes* in *such* Events, or expect the Means of Happiness from thence. On the contrary, it will tell us the *safest* way to Happiness is by Benevolent Actions, which, upon this very account, is more particularly acceptable to God and agreeable to our own Nature; in which we need neither fear the *Divine Vengeance,* which neither the Force nor Stratagems of Men can elude; nor the *Punishments threatened by Men,* which ought to be consider'd, at least, as *probable.* Concerning these, however contingent, right Reason concludes thus much with certainty, that, *as Advantages, contingently future only, have a certain determinate Value,* and contain in themselves the *real nature of Good,* which wise Men, from the observation of the Causes upon which they depend, know how to estimate at a certain Price to be paid at present; (This is done daily in the purchase of Reversions, and in other like cases:) *So* also *Future Contingent Evils,* (among which the Punishments Reason teaches to inflict upon all who are hurtful to the Innocent, ought to be reckon'd,) *are to be estimated as Evils present and certain, but somewhat less.* So the *Hazard* of losing Life, Health, Expence, and Pains, (all which happen in human affairs,) every where, with Reason, increases the Price

Human Rewards and Punishments, foreseen as probably, tho' not certainly, future, may be justly rated at a certain present value, and are therefore properly said to lay us under an Obligation, and are sufficient Motives of Action.

of Labour; and is therefore *compensated* at a *certain* and *present Rate,* no less than a present and certain Evil accruing and Gain ceasing. Wherefore, natural right Reason plainly *teaches,* "That the Hazard of imminent Punishment may be rated as a present and certain Evil, tho' it sometimes happens, that the guilty Person may avoid it"; which, however, will be *lessen'd,* according to the *Degrees of Hope,* which any one, from a through knowledge of all Circumstances, has of *escaping* those Punishments. Let therefore that *Punishment,* to the Hazard of which the Invader of another's Property exposes himself, be suppos'd somewhat less than it would be if it were *actually* inflicted, as soon as the Crime were committed; that is, let *as much be subtracted* from the Greatness thereof, *as Reason prescribes* upon this account, that it is *uncertain,* whether it will be inflicted or no; and yet there will *remain more Evil,* than can be *compensated* by the unjust Gain: That *Excess* then of Evil is a Penal *Sanction* to the Dictate of Reason, which forbids the Invasion of another's Property.

'Tis of great importance to this Argument, to *observe,* "That natural Reason instructs all Men, even out of civil Society, so to enhance the Punishments of Crimes, that, tho' much should be detracted from them upon account of uncertain Execution, the present estimated Evil of the foreseen Punishments should much overbalance the Gain expected from the Crime." This is manifest, both in the *Punishments,* which are by either Party *inflicted by the right of War*[56] for smaller Injuries done those, who are not subject to the same Civil Government; and in those Cases, in which *Civil Laws* permit the *Punishment* of the Crime to the *Discre-*

---

56. [Maxwell] "I question, whether this *increasing* of *Punishment,* because of the *uncertainty,* should take place in the State of Nature, or among *Independent States,* tho' it is just that it should in any *one State.* The reason of the *Difference* is probably this. In the natural Equality of Men, or among sovereign States, the Balance of Power is generally kept so even, that there is no great probability, that the just Side shall prevail, in External Force, against the unjust; and, the severities of the one will provoke the like severities of the other. But, in a well-regulated State, there is still much greater Probability of *Justice* in the Sentences of the Judges, and of *Superior Force* to support the Just Cause. The want of these circumstances in the State of Nature, shews the reasons of our preferring the more Human Methods of War, to the more Cruel, which once prevailed."

tion of the Subjects aggriev'd; for *Example,* the Vengeance on those, who by night break open other Mens Houses, or who rob upon the Highway.[57] In such Cases Men are, in some measure, reduc'd to *Hobbes's* State of Nature, and, in that, even *smaller Crimes are punish'd capitally:* Nor unjustly, for, because the Civil Magistrate is often unable to come to the knowledge of such Crimes, they often escape unpunish'd; therefore, whensoever Punishment can be taken, it is taken most heavily, that, by how much the more they are *embolden'd, from the Hope of frequent Impunity,* so much the more they may be *check'd by the fear of the severest Punishment.* And this seems to me the true Reason, *why* such *Revenge* as appears *very horrible,* is sometimes *necessary* in *War;* And *why,* even in *Civil States,* more *grievous Punishments* are inflicted, than would be requisite, if *all Crimes* that are committed, were *immediately* judg'd and punished. For these Reasons I think it *evident,* "That the *foreseen Hazard,* especially of more grievous Punishment, (altho' the Certainty of its future Execution could not be known,) has a constant and perpetual *power of determining the Will,* to avoid all deliberate Actions, against which those Punishments are threaten'd." *In like manner;* "The foreseen Probability of a very great Good, is a proper Weight to determine Men to those Actions, which may be any way instrumental in procuring it." Or, to explain the *Metaphor,* these considerations furnish an Argument *concluding necessarily,* "That a Practice conformable to the Law is one of the causes of that compleat Happiness we naturally desire," which is sufficient to infer an Obligation. For the *Natural Obligation* of the Laws of Nature leaves those who are *oblig'd,* at *liberty to act otherwise* at their own *peril:* It furnishes only a *proper Argument,* to induce the Person oblig'd, to act or to forbear, as Reason or the Law commands him.

§XXVII. Here, lest I should be thought to *use Words* in a *Sense different* from what is *usual,* I shall briefly shew, that what I have said is implied in the received Definition of *Obligation.*

The Nature of Moral Obligation explain'd, and *Justinian's*

---

57. Cumberland's argument here has interesting parallels with Locke's treatment of the same issue in the *Two Treatises on Government,* II.19; cf. Pufendorf, *De Jure Naturae et Gentium,* II.5.17, 18.

Justinian gives this Definition of it, *"Obligation is that Bond of the Law, by which we are tied with the Necessity of paying any thing, according to the Laws of our State."* [58] It is evident, that what is said of *"payment"* and *"his State"* is *special,* and ought, therefore, to be omitted in the *general* notion of Obligation, after which we are inquiring; and that the rest that goes before in the Definition, is indeed *general,* but somewhat *obscure* from Metaphors; for the *Mind* of Man is not properly *"tied with Bonds."*

There is nothing which can superinduce a *Necessity* of doing or forbearing any thing, upon a Human Mind deliberating upon a thing future, except Thoughts or *Propositions* promising Good or Evil, to ourselves or others, consequent upon what we are about to do. But, because we are *determin'd, by some sort of natural Necessity, to pursue Good foreseen,* especially the Greatest; and to *avoid Evils;* hence those Dictates of Reason, which discover to us, that these things will follow from certain of our Actions, are said to lay upon us *some kind of Necessity* of performing or omitting those Actions, and to *oblige* us; because those Advantages are necessarily connected with our Happiness, which we naturally desire, and our Actions are evidently necessary to the attainment of them.

I, therefore, think, that Moral Obligation may be thus universally and properly defin'd. *Obligation is that Act of a Legislator, by which he declares, that Actions conformable to his Law are necessary to those, for whom the Law is made.* An *Action* is then understood to be *necessary to a rational Agent, when it is certainly one of the Causes necessarily requir'd to that Happiness, which he naturally, and consequently necessarily, desires.* Thus we are oblig'd to pursue the Common Good, when the Nature of Things (especially of Rational Causes,) expos'd to our Observation, discovers to our Minds, that this Action is a Cause necessarily requisite to compleat our Happiness; which, therefore, naturally depends upon the pursuit of the Common Good of all Rational Agents; as the Soundness of a Member depends upon the Soundness and Life of the whole Animated Body; or, as the Strength of our Hands cannot effectually be preserved, without first preserving that Life and Strength, which is diffus'd thro' our whole

58. Justinian, *Institutes,* III.14.

Body. For every Man's proper Happiness does no less naturally depend upon the influence of the First Cause, and the mutual assistance of other Rational Agents, which is to be procured by the pursuit of the Common Good, than the Hand depends upon the rest of the Body; altho' the Dependence of one Man upon others consists in *fewer particulars,* and is often *more remote,* and, therefore, *not alwaies so evident:* I have *shewn before,* "That the prosecution of the Common Good is essentially requisite to every one's Happiness"; by *proving,* "That in such Actions consists the most happy State of our Faculties"; *here* we *learn,* "That by these Actions its Preservation and further Perfection may most effectually be procured from God and Men." But we *resolve* all into those *voluntary* Acts of the *First Cause,* by which he has *determin'd* the *Measure* of our Faculties, and their proper *Happiness* thence arising; and by which he has plac'd and continues us depending *in such a System,* upon other Rational Causes. For *these* things being *establish'd,* the *Foundation* and natural *Discovery* of our *Obligation* are necessarily *establish'd,* and *thence* arise, with the same Necessity, first our *Knowledge,* and then our actual *Obligation.*

It amounts to the same thing, when we *say,* "That the Obligation is an Act of the Legislator," or of the First Cause; as if in this place we had *call'd* it, "An Act of the Law of Nature." For the Legislator obliges by the Law sufficiently promulg'd, and he sufficiently promulges it, when he *discovers* to our Minds, "That the prosecution of the Common Good is the Cause necessarily requisite to that Happiness, which every one necessarily desires."

Upon *discovering* this, all Men are *oblig'd; whether* it be of so great Weight with them, as perfectly to incline their Minds to what it persuades; or *whether* what is alledg'd in favour of the contrary Opinion, weigh more. Those Bodies, which, thro' a *Fault in the Balance,* are raised by a smaller Weight in the opposite Scale, are yet in themselves heavier, or have a greater tendency toward the Center of the Earth.

It is to be observ'd, that those *Arguments,* which prove our Obligation, in this case would *certainly prevail;* unless the *Ignorance,* turbulent *Affections,* or *Rashness* of Men, like the *Fault in the Balance,* oppos'd their Efficacy; as discovering, beside *Rewards* and *Punishments mani-*

fested or express'd, that *others greater* (if there be occasion) will be *added* at the pleasure of the supreme Governour of the World.

The *Obligation* to promote the Common Good, as a necessary *End*, being once settled, it will hence follow, "That the common *Obligation* of all Men, to pursue the Dictates of Reason concerning the *Means* necessary thereto, is likewise known."

The Sum of all these Dictates is contain'd in our *Proposition*, "concerning the Benevolence of each Rational Agent towards All"; from whence 'tis evident, that a War of each against All tends to the Common Destruction, and cannot by any method be a Means conducing to the Happiness of All, or even be consistent with the Means necessary to that End; and, therefore, can neither be enjoin'd, nor permitted, by right Reason.

§XXVIII. Altho' I have suppos'd, That *every one* necessarily seeks *his own* greatest Happiness, yet I am far from thinking that to be the intire and *adequate* End of *any one*. I was willing to *assume*, what my Adversaries would *allow*, in order to carry them farther with me, if it were possible: For, *as* the Frame of our Body cannot subsist, or enjoy Health, except the great System of Bodies about us contribute somewhat to this Effect; nor can any one, rightly understanding the Nature of Things, wish that it were otherwise, because he knows it to be impossible: *So* the intire Happiness of every particular Man naturally depends upon the Benevolence of God, and of other Men; but neither can the *Benevolence of God* toward any one be separated from his regard to his own *Honour;* nor the *favourable inclination of others towards us,* be disjoin'd from their *care of their own Happiness;* nay, we must needs acknowledge this to be stronger in them, than their *Affection* towards us: Wherefore it is impossible, that he who duly *considers the Nature of Rational Beings,* should desire that they should assist us, except their own Preservation were at the same time taken care of; and, therefore, he *cannot propose* to himself *his own Happiness,* separately from that of others, as his *adequate End.*

But let us distinctly consider, what I have but now briefly hinted; and, First, no one, who acknowledges the Divine Providence to be sufficiently prov'd from the Nature of Things, can *deny*, "That every Man's Hap-

Margin note (left): Every Man's own Happiness, tho' necessarily sought by him, is not his *Adequate* End of Action.

Margin note (left): But jointly (1.) with the Honour of God,

piness depends upon the Benevolence of God, as upon a Cause necessarily requisite." But, who can ground his Expectations of the Divine Favour upon right *Reason,* except he sincerely render God that Honour, which he has *Reason* to believe acceptable to Him? Hence the various Precepts of *Religion;* hence the Precepts of *Justice,* and of *every Virtue* that can be mutually exercised among Men, are shewn to be *Means* necessary to every Man's *Happiness,* and therefore to *oblige* every Man; because it is most *certain,* "That the Governour of the World is by no Means honour'd, except all his innocent Subjects be justly and kindly treated, according to the Conditions necessary to the Preservation of Universal Peace"; that is, as all the Virtues prescribe.

§XXIX. What I have *hinted,* beside, "That every Man in some measure depends upon the Benevolence of other Men," I believe to be most true; but not so obvious, but that it requires the attentive Consideration of what I shall presently offer, and perhaps of other matters, which every one's Experience may easily suggest to him. and (2.) the Happiness of Men.

As *First,* "That every Man's Happiness consists in a great Collection of many Good Things, and that it is not sufficiently safe, unless we provide for the Future long before, and reconcile to ourselves, as far as in us lies, all the Causes, which can contribute any thing to this Effect." This makes way for the *Concurrence of innumerable Causes,* so that there is scarce any part of this Visible World, but what may be in some measure *useful to every one;* much less is there *any Man,* who neither was, nor is, nor may be, *contributing,* something at least, to our *Preservation* or *Perfection. For* (after Mankind is suppos'd to become numerous) "No-one can be imagin'd, whose Happiness and Pleasures of Life do not immediately depend upon two (at least;) each of these two stands in need of other two, in order to live happily." *In like manner,* "Every Nation wants the Commerce of two other Nations, and others are likewise necessary to these." By proceeding in this manner we shall *find,* "That every one assists every one." It is *not* however *necessary,* minutely to *consider,* "What Benefit we receive from every Individual"; it is sufficient that we perceive, that *all contribute somewhat* to the Common Stock, which ought to be *compensated by us with like pains* bestow'd upon the Publick.

Such kind of human Actions as these, seem to me fitly to be compar'd to the general Motions of Bodies Natural, which at once contribute to many Effects.

It is in the *next place* to be consider'd, "That the Word *Benevolence* is taken by me in the largest Sense, so as to include the lowest degrees of *Innocence, Fidelity, Gratitude,* or any kind office of *Humanity* perform'd by others to us." Any one has it in his power, but at his own Peril, a thousand waies to create to others innumerable Troubles spreading themselves far and wide; if Men act otherwise, and stop short of that wild Malevolence, which threatens War, that is, all the greatest Evils to All, it is to be attributed to some degree of Benevolence. Whatever is done, which in its own Nature ever so little conduces to the preservation of Peace and a general Good-Will among Men, that protects many from most grievous Evils, and is, therefore, of great Advantage.

It were endless to attempt recounting all the particular *Advantages,* which accrue from a *Benevolence* of each towards All. It is very well known, that they who have *least in their power,* benefit others; either by the *Exchange* of Things or Services, or by *observing Compacts,* or by giving us reason to place a *Confidence* in them, even without Compacts, or by the *Examples* which they afford (if not of great Exploits, yet) of *Industry, Patience* or *Innocence.* These things are consider'd by Men, even *without* any respect to *Civil Government,* and extend their *influence* over the *whole Earth.* The very *Imperfections* and *Infirmities* of Men, so far as they naturally *excite Pity,* and *point out* the necessity of *Government,* do strongly *persuade* all to concur in instituting and preserving it, and are, therefore, of considerable *use to all,* as they any way contribute to the vast Advantages of Society. I own, however, that the *Advantage* is *but small,* which each receives from many, especially the *more remote,* but we give them in *return* only a *like share* of the effects of our Industry; yet even *these cannot with safety be neglected,* because the *whole Happiness,* and that not small, of particular Persons, grows out of such *minute* offices of Humanity included in the care of the Common Good, almost in the same manner *as* this most beautiful *Frame* of the Material *World* arises, from the regular Motions and Figures of the *minute* Particles of Matter. But, having in the Chapter concerning *Human Nature* enumerated many particulars, which *demonstrate,* "That Men have, from *Nature,* both Power and Inclination to do good Offices to others, provided they are consistent with their own Happiness"; the little I have mention'd may warrant my supposing it at present as sufficiently *prov'd,* "That Men, of all Created Beings, are the principal Causes, upon which every one must acknowledge his present and future Happiness upon Earth necessarily depends." For the same reason there is no occasion to add here any thing farther, to *shew* "the Unreasonableness of expecting, that Men should willingly labour to make those happy, whom they know to be in themselves *Malevolent, Perfidious, Ingrateful, Inhuman";* or the Reasonableness of taking it *for evident,* "That others will concur to restrain or destroy such by condign Punishments."

§XXX. It is to be *observ'd,* "That there is so strict a mutual Dependence among all Rational Beings, that it admonishes Man, thro' the whole course of Life, of the Vanity of imagining, that he has sufficiently provided for his own Happiness, tho' he have performed all the offices of Humanity to one Person, or for one Time; if he has at pleasure broke thro' them, with respect to another Person, or at another Time." This is evident, *not only* from what I have now been saying, *viz. Because* the Happiness of every particular Person perpetually depends, *immediately* indeed upon *Many,* but *remotely,* and with respect to smaller Matters, upon *All* who regard the Common Good: *But also because* the same Common *Father of All,* the First Cause, takes *care of All:* And *lastly, because* whatever any one of these, from the Dictates of right Reason, wills should be done to himself or others, That do all, who are truly Rational, will necessarily and alwaies, so far as they come to the knowledge thereof.[59] *For* "all, (both God and Men) who think justly of the same thing, agree."

The Law of Universal Benevolence obliges, with respect to all Persons, and at all Times, the Weak as well as the Strong; in Private, as well as in Publick.

Hence it is, "That to deny any one his own," that is, those Necessaries without which he is incapable of promoting the Common Good, "is to

59. [Maxwell] "Because every Person, who is truly rational, will assist every other Person, how weak soever, in favouring and promoting his reasonable Desires and Expectations; so far as it comes to their Knowledge, and as they have it in their Power."

act in prejudice to the Common Benefit, and contrary to the Opinion and Will of all who judge rightly"; whence it *follows,* "That every one, in a state of Equality here suppos'd, has a Right, and is excited, to punish such Invasion, as Opportunity offers, which all Men can never long be without, but God never; against whom no Place of Concealment, nor Power, nor even Death itself, can defend the Wicked."

Which Observation I make chiefly with this view, that it may thence *appear,* "That the *Obligation* to study to promote the Common Good (which is the Summary of the Laws of Nature,) which is discover'd naturally by the Punishments and Rewards annex'd to Actions, according as they are contrary, or suited, to this End, is evidently *perpetual,* and *binding in all Circumstances;* and, therefore, a sufficient Motive to Universal Justice and Benevolence, as well in Secret as in Publick, with respect to the Weak as well as to the Strong." For, *since* it is hence *evident,* "That all who are perfectly Rational are united among themselves, because right Reason, wherever it is, is alwaies consistent with right Reason, and because the Causes of their Common Happiness are the same"; and *since* it has been also specially *shewn,* "That He, whoever he is, who is about to do any Act, hurtful or beneficial to others, does so depend upon other Rational Beings, that all that Happiness he necessarily seeks, is to be received from their Concurrence, or at least free Permission, as the Reward of past, or Encouragement of future Benevolence": It *follows,* "That his Right can be denied to no-one, how weak soever, even in Secret, without so far slighting and lessening the Publick Good, and thereby provoking all who have it truly at heart, (that is, all who are truly Rational in Practical Matters,) to refrain such Invasions of another's Property by Punishments." For the *Common Good* is the *only End,* in the pursuit whereof *all Rational Beings can agree* among themselves; because it comprehends the *greatest possible Happiness of all;* and it is most certain, that only *that* Practical Reason is true, which discovers to *all* an *End* and *Means,* in which *all* who make a true Judgment *can agree;* and that those, therefore, act according to true Practical Reason, who have this End at heart, and make use of the Means necessary thereto. Hence we may *conclude,* "That the Reason of God, which seeth all Things, and of all truly Rational Men, are upon the watch to discover every Invasion of another's Right, that is, every Injustice, even out of Civil Society; so that there remains not the least hope of escaping the Knowledge of God, and but very little of deceiving the Sagacity of Man": *And,* That, after Wickedness is discover'd, God and Men will neither want the Will nor the Power, to ward off the intended Injury, or to punish that which has been committed."

§XXXI. In a word, the *Invader of another's Right,* in that he opposes Reason, conspiring in all to promote the Common Good, *forsakes Truth,* and so far deprives himself of the innate Beauty of Practical Right Reason; and, by admitting one Practical Error, *makes way for innumerable* in the same kind; and delivers himself up to the *conduct* of his blind *Passions,* among Precipices innumerable. All these *Consequences,* both because they are Evil, and because they follow the Evil Action in the ordinary course of Nature establish'd by God, are justly called *Punishments.*

Not only the External, but *Internal,* Causes of our Happiness conspire to produce the same End by the same Means, viz. perpetual and universal *Benevolence* towards all Rational Agents.

"In every Deliberation concerning our future Actions 'tis necessary to consider, what other Rational Agents will think of them," *because* (beside that they form the most noble Class of Beings,) they are the principal and *Universal Causes,* necessarily and perpetually requisite, of that Happiness which we aim at by Action: For the greatest diligence in procuring the Concurrence of such Causes, is above all and alwaies necessary to every Man, who would provide for his own Happiness according to the Dictates of Reason. I call those *Universal Causes,* which concur to many Effects, and of other kinds, beside that which is the subject of the present Inquiry. I don't believe it necessary to be at much pains to *shew,* "That all the Necessaries to Happiness are dispos'd according to the Will of God and Men"; to procure which, their Concurrence or free Permission is no less requisite, than the rising of the Sun to dispell the darkness of the Night. It may be sufficient to take notice, that, *as* in the *Sciences,* those Propositions, which explain the most *general Causes* or Properties of Things, (the Laws of Motion, or the Properties of Triangles, for *Example,*) imply no contradiction in particular Cases, tho' they be there much diversified: *So* in *Practice,* the care of procuring the Favour of the *Universal Causes,* (Rational Agents, suppose, jointly consider'd,) can never be laid aside, much less oppos'd, by him, who in reality and with right Reason pursues their natural Effect, which is his own Happiness: *On the contrary,* the care of gaining the First and most necessary Causes, prepares the way to, and directs and governs, the use of the Inferior when acquired; as the knowledge of General Truths assists the Judgment of the Skilful in forming Conclusions in all variety of Cases, and continually leads them to farther Discoveries.

The *help then of other truly Rational Beings,* (that is of *God,* and *such Men* as concur in promoting the Common Good,) being thus found to be the most universal *external* Means to our Happiness (a *Means* in the first and principal Place and at all Times necessary;) it immediately *follows,* "That *Nothing* ought to be committed against *any* one, *secretly* or *openly,* thro' the whole course of Life, by which we may be depriv'd of this Help; that is, that we ought *never to invade another's Right,* but, on the contrary, endeavour by all methods to procure this Assistance perpetually to our-selves."

It *happens* likewise most favourably, "That *within us* nothing can more intimately and abundantly promote our Happiness, than the most enlarged *Contemplation* and Love of, and Joy in, such Things and Actions as are acceptable to *God* and *such Men,* the *noblest Objects"*: Now all these acts of Justice and Beneficence, by which we endeavour to please both God and Men, are the Effects, the Fruits, of that Universal Benevolence, which I inculcate; which will therefore naturally, by the most powerful Persuasive (that of Benevolent Actions) both implore and obtain the assistance of all Rational Beings; and, consequently, most happily unite the *Internal* and *External* Causes of our Happiness, and give rise to Virtue, Religion and Society. This *Reason,* (by which 'tis asserted, that we should in the *first* place take care to procure the Favour of the first and principal Causes of the End desired,) is indeed most *General,* and *agreeable to the Rules of Logick,* (which are prior to those of Morality;) but does not therefore *agree the less with Experience* and the natural Order of human Operations, which is sometimes very justly objected against some Logical Subtilties unskilfully applied to Practice.[60]

60. [Maxwell] "Such as those Arguments by which it is offered to be prov'd, That a Traveller, ignorant of the Situation of the Country, and without a Guide, coming

§XXXII. To make this appear yet more evident, I will *illustrate* this whole Matter, by considering, first, the *Opposite* Case, next a *Parallel* Case.

To the perpetual pursuit of the Common Good, (by which, to the best of our power, we ingage in our favour the most universal Causes of our Happiness,) is *oppos'd* every wilful neglect thereof; by this therefore we leave in the hand of God or Men, wholly to take away our Happiness, or to diminish it to such a degree, as to their right Reason shall seem necessary to deter us or others (by way of sufficient Punishment) from a like Neglect.

What is more; he who by a neglect of such Universal Benevolence neglects those Universal Causes, which I have mentioned, of his Happiness, alwaies *substitutes others less effectual* in their place, perhaps his own Force or Cunning, or the Assistance of a few like himself; hence the Mind forms new Rules of Practice, which do not satisfy, because of their inward Deformity, that is, because they are not equally rational, or fit to produce the End propos'd; and yet perplex and *disturb the Mind by their Opposition to the former.* They moreover presently beget in us and those that imitate us, a most mischievous off-spring, I mean most restless *Passions,* and *Vices* most destructive of Peace, such as Hatred, Envy, Fear, Sorrow, Inhumanity, Pride, &c. which (as is fabled of the Viper's brood[61]) eat thro' their Mothers Bowels. For he who perseveres in such measures, brings upon himself certain *Destruction,* both *from within* and *without;* but, if he returns from that to a right Mind, he finds his Happiness so impair'd in *both Respects,* that he cannot doubt, but that it had been better for him never to have laid aside the Care of the Publick Good. He that comes to himself will certainly take less Comfort (to say no worse) from the Remembrance of his past malevolent Actions: He will have less reason to hope for and expect a future happy Progress; either in the Improvement of his *internal Faculties* already hurt, (which might have been strengthen'd by constant well-doing,) or in the acqui-

Benevolence prov'd the necessary means to Happiness, *first,* by shewing the *Opposite* Practice naturally and unavoidably to tend to Misery.

---

to a Place, where the Road parts into two, equally fair, and equally probable to be the right, will stand still, and not proceed either Way, which is contrary to all Experience."

61. Herodotus, *Historia,* III.9.

sition of *external Assistances* from those he had offended, which he has reason to expect more sparingly for the Future. And *these Evils follow necessarily,* whether the Offenders will or no, from every wilful Neglect of perpetually soliciting the Favour of God and Man. Wherefore we may *conclude,* from the Punishment naturally annex'd to this neglect, "That the Duty (of always endeavouring by Benevolence to obtain the Favour of God and Men,)" which I undertook to prove from the consideration of its *Opposite,* "ought in no case to be omitted." And even *Hobbes* himself *acknowledges,* "That such Evils may be said to be Punishments divinely inflicted, if we acknowledge God the Author of Nature," *Leviath. Chap.* 28. in the sixth Consequence, which he has deduc'd from his Definition of *Punishment.*[62]

Secondly, by considering a *Parallel* Case of the Necessity 1. of the moderate Influence of the Sun to Human Life, compar'd to the Divine Favour.

§XXXIII. "That the engaging these universal and principal Causes of Human Happiness in our favour, ought to be our principal and perpetual Care, in order to obtain the End desir'd," remains now to be *shewn* by the help of an *Example,* or *like Practice* in the affairs of Life and Health, which they are very careful of, who disregard Justice and Probity. And this I shall do with this *view* only, "That the Force and Scope of the foregoing Reasoning may more evidently appear," for no rational Person will expect a strict Proof in such Comparisons.

All acknowledge the Powers of the *Sun* and *Air* to be very great, and absolutely necessary to the Preservation of Human Life. These are those universal Causes, which, beside numberless other Effects, claim in this the principal Share. Yet so, that they require the Concurrence of many other Causes in some sort subordinate; such are a just Temper of our Body, a justly-proportion'd Configuration of its Parts, a healthful Soil, a sufficiency of Nourishment and Cloathing, and mutual Human Assistance, which yet all depend upon those Universal Causes. For the Rays of the *Sun* do daily produce such Alterations and Dispositions to productions of all kinds, in the Earth, the common Mother of all, in Plants and Animals, which are raised and nourished by her, and in the vital Blood of Man, drawn from the Juices of Plants and Animals, that all,

62. In fact the reference is to Hobbes, *Leviathan,* ch. 27, pp. 204–5.

who with moderate Attention search into the Causes of Things, must readily confess the Sun, above any other created Being, the most universal Cause of all those Changes so necessary to Life, which we experience in our-selves. Seeing therefore the Dependence of the Life of Man upon the moderate Influence of the *Sun,* is in some measure Analogous to the Dependence of Human Happiness upon the *Divine Favour;* it *follows,* "That the Necessity of procuring to our-selves God's Favour by Benevolence or Universal Charity, (which comprehends all, both Religious Worship and Justice,) is taught by the *same* Reason, that teaches the necessity of inhabiting such Places as enjoy the benefit of the Sun's Influence." The *same* Reason likewise *forbids* "Rendering our-selves obnoxious to his Wrath by acts of Wickedness," that *forbids* "Continuing in such Places, where those Assistances to our innate Heat cannot be had, which here we daily receive from the Sun," or that *teaches* us, "To withdraw from those excessive Heats of Climates and Seasons, by which the Sun exhales and dissipates in too great a degree our Blood and vital Spirits."

§XXXIV. But, leaving this part of the *Comparison,* as having no occasion to treat at large of *Natural Theology,* let us proceed to that other Branch of it, which is taken from the *Air,* which is so necessary to the Life of Man, that from thence I thought it proper to shadow out the Dependence of every particular Person upon the surrounding Multitude of other *Men;* and I shall insist the longer upon this Comparison, because hence may be illustrated the mutual Offices of Men, which I have chiefly undertaken to explain.

2. Of the Air, compar'd to mutual human Offices.

How necessary *Air* is to the Life of Man, even the Vulgar, from Experience, readily acknowledge; and Philosophers have more plainly demonstrated by instructive Experiments, which they have found out. This has been prov'd by means of Animals endow'd with Blood, which immediately died in the Air-Pump (the Honourable *Robert Boyle's* most ingenious Contrivance) upon the Air's being exhausted.[63] Dogs, dis-

---

63. The experiments referred to were carried out by Robert Hooke in 1659 and are recorded in Robert Boyle's *New Experiments Physico-Mechanical* (1660).

sected by the Learned Mr. *Hook,* testify the same; who after the *Aspera Asteria* was cut through below the Epiglottis, and the Ribs, Diaphragm and Pericardium were cut away, liv'd above an Hour by the help of fresh Air blown into the Lungs by the help of a pair of Bellows.[64] It is therefore certain, in the Judgment of all, that the Air is one of the necessary Causes of Life, and that which is healthful is therefore every where sought; altho' all its essential Properties, and the Manner of its acting upon us, be not yet fully discover'd. *In like Manner* (supposing many Men to exist together out of Civil Society, endow'd with natural Powers sufficient to assist, or to hinder one another from enjoying the Necessaries of Life, and consequently Life it-self, which is the soundest Part of Mr. *Hobbes*'s suppos'd *State of Nature;*) it is *certain,* "That they could not live out the Time appointed by Nature, unless they so far at least consented to one another's Welfare, as to abstain from mutual Harms, and to permit to every one the Use of those Necessaries which Nature has produc'd": This *Agreement* therefore is necessary almost *in the same Manner* as the Use of the *Air* is to Life, and includes some kind of Benevolence, greater certainly than *Hobbes*'s *State of War;* for it both regards the End of Benevolence, and, as it is a voluntary Act about Means naturally fit, regards their Use also. Nay, farther, every one will necessarily consider his own Powers, as able to contribute something to the Happiness of many, and will accordingly apply them to that purpose, when he perceives that by so doing he will not lessen, but rather enlarge his Power, his own Faculties being improv'd by Exercise, and new foreign Assistance gain'd, at least reasonably hop'd for, in Compensation; thus in this Agreement alone will be contain'd, not *Innocence* only, but *Beneficence,* which two make up *both* Tables of Universal *Benevolence,* and of the Law of Nature.

For this Reason therefore, because such Agreement is necessary to every one, we ought always to endeavour, as much as possible, to obtain it from Men; tho' we no more understand the inward Constitution of Men, than of the Air; nor can we foresee all that, whether Good, or

---

64. This gruesome experiment was performed before the Royal Society in October 1667. It was recorded in *Philosophical Transactions,* 2 (1667), pp. 539–40.

Harm, which may arise from their Society: As in like Manner we are ignorant, what draught of Air is perfectly Healthful, and which will bring along with it a contagious Distemper; yet we know, that certain Death is the Consequence of Respiration stopt, but that the Continuance thereof is, for the most part, a vast advantage to Life.

Farther; that Universal Influence of other Men upon every Man's Happiness makes it *requisite,* "That we should be so diligent in procuring their favour, (wholly neglecting, or willingly provoking, no one) as never to suffer our-selves to be carried off from thence to other Methods of acquiring, and to particular or partial Causes of, Happiness, (for *Example,* Gain, Glory, or Pleasure;) tho', in their proper Places, (due regard being had to the most general Causes,) they are not without their Use." For no Man in his Senses will *so* throw himself into the Depth of the Sea, in pursuit of those most pretious Treasures, which lie scatter'd here and there, in the Bottom thereof, *as* to deprive himself of the necessary Use of Air, and, consequently, of Life it self. For they know it to be extremely foolish, to provide for only a few Occasions of Life, and, in the mean while, to neglect the whole of future Happiness, and the necessary Causes thereof, and, consequently, *Life it-self.* Wherefore, the *same Reason,* which instructs us to direct our Organs of Respiration, (which, in some measure, may be obstructed or excited at the command of our Will,) and the other voluntary Motions of our Body, that we may always, as far as in us lies, enjoy the Use of wholesome Air, will *also* teach us to regulate all our inward Affections, and outward Actions, that regard other Men, with that *Humanity,*[65] that, to the utmost of our Power, we may cause them all to entertain and refresh us with *their Benevolence,* so Necessary to *our Happiness.*

We are cautious, not to fill the Air of our Houses with noxious Steams and Vapours, but especially, that this perpetual Nourishment, both of our own Lives and that of others, may not be corrupted with Pestilential or other contagious Effluvia; which is a faint Resemblance of *Innocence,* and teaches the necessity thereof in all our Actions.

The Air, which we have drawn into our Lungs, we immediately

---

65. Cumberland (*De Legibus Naturae,* p. 253) uses the Greek term here.

breathe back again; or, if a small Portion thereof be retain'd for some little time, for the refreshing *our* Blood and vital Spirits, it is afterwards, along with the Blood it-self and vital Spirits, as it were with *Interest,* restor'd by insensible Perspiration to the *common* Mass of Air; this *reciprocal* Natural Motion, which is intermixt with somewhat Voluntary, thus resembles *Gratitude,* and points out its Necessity for the Good of the Whole.

And because, not only *everyone's* Blood and vital Spirits are nourished by this Air, but that also a *procreative* Juice, subservient to the Continuation of the Species, is thence perfected by Organs appointed by Nature to that End, a limited care of *our-selves* and our *Posterity,* is by the same Method pointed out.

Moreover; because the Powers of Man, recruited by Respiration, are naturally applicable to the Common Use of All;[66] and the Air it self, which we breathe back out of our Lungs, is restor'd for the Common Good of All; we, by *Respiration,* shadow out some slight touches of *Humanity.* But this natural Action, so far as it is a Motion *merely Mechanical,* perform'd by Brutes and Men asleep, is only a *mere Shadow* of these *Virtues:* Yet this *Shadow* exactly represents all the particular Branches of *Living-Virtue,* and their mutual Connexion, with their *Real* Motions, or Effects; which will appear evidently to those, who compare what I have now said, with what I had before advanc'd concerning Actions necessary to the Common Good: And they will moreover be of opinion, that *Virtue* is nothing but an *habitual Will to obey the Laws of Nature,* which injoins Actions necessary to that End. But so far as *Respiration* itself, and other *Acts common to Brutes,* are guided in Man by *Reason,* if they are perform'd with a perpetual regard to the noblest End, the Common Good of the KINGDOM OF GOD, in which is included the Honour of God the Governor, and the Happiness of Men his Subjects, then at

---

66. Maxwell follows Cumberland's Latin (*De Legibus Naturae,* p. 254: "ad communem omnium usum," p. 254), but Barberyrac (*Traité Philosophique,* pp. 268–69, n. 2) thinks that the text is corrupt at this point, the sentence referring to the common use of all the parts of the body, and a variant he follows in his text ("l'usage commun de tous les Membres de nôtre Corps"). This does seem to make better sense of Cumberland's developing analogy of the benefits accruing from respiration.

length these Actions become true *Virtues;* as Feasts and Fasts become *religious Exercises,* when they are observ'd to *religious Purposes.*

Finally; not to be tedious in pursuing this *Comparison,* I will add this only, in which there seems to be a *farther mutual Correspondence* between them. "Altho' the mutual Benevolence of Men and the free Use of the Air be *General* and *Necessary* Causes, the one of Life, the other of Happiness; yet *neither* is the Total, or" (to use a *School-term*) "the *Adequate,* Cause of the Effect;[67] for many things beside are requisite to secure Life and Happiness, but nothing that can exclude these Causes; also the determinate Influence of *neither* to produce the desir'd Effect, is throughly *known,* and *neither* is intirely in the *Power* of those who need them": Hence it is, that having taken all possible care about them, we are not therefore *certain* of obtaining the desir'd Effect, without the *Concurrence* of other Causes, which are *not in our Power* to influence. Yet this ought not to deter any one from the Pursuit of Virtue, or Universal Benevolence; because we see, that a *Reason,* in all respects *alike,* persuades no-one to throw away the Care of breathing wholesome Air, and betake himself to places infected with such a deadly pestilential Contagion, that not one of a Million can escape thence with safety. Such an *infected* Air were like a *State of War* of each against all; and such a State necessarily follows, wheresoever the Common Good is not taken for the Rule of Action, but every one proposes to himself *his own Good* only, as the *End* of all *his own* Actions, and the *Measure* of all *other Mens.*

This only can be *inferr'd* from those *Evils,* which sometimes happen to the *Followers of Virtue,* "That all degrees of Happiness cannot always be obtain'd by our whole Power, even when perfectly regulated by the best Moral Precepts." It is, however, *certain,* "That by obeying them we shall do every thing that is in our Power, to procure the Happiness of Life," which is all that Morality, or practical right Reason, undertakes to perform. And hence we shall reap this *Advantage,* "That we shall most surely escape numberless Calamities, which many bring upon themselves by their Vices, and by Patience surmount those we cannot avoid." Mean-while *we* enjoy a sound and serene Mind in Fortitude and Tran-

(The Evils which happen to the Good, prove only all Degrees of Happiness not to be in our Power, whereas all that are, are to be obtain'd by Virtue only.)

---

67. The "School-term" is *causa adequata, De Legibus Naturale,* p. 255.

quillity, which, thro' a most pleasing Reflexion upon good Actions, will render us Happy in present Joy, and the Hope of a future Reward. Whereas, *on the contrary, they* who, neglecting the Pursuit of the Common Good, slight the Favour of God and Men, in neglecting the principal Causes upon which, both their Being and Happiness necessarily depend, wittingly undermine the Foundations of their own Happiness, and convert that Friendship, which they themselves know to be necessary to them, into most deserved Hatred. Whence they must unavoidably dread Punishment, and when they perceive inevitable Evils coming upon them, acknowledge themselves the Authors of their own Calamities, and upbraid themselves with most shameful Folly, that *they* would live to themselves alone, who were by no means self-sufficient.

From hence inferr'd, That we can never, with impunity, neglect God or Men in our pursuit of Happiness.

§XXXV. I have thus far treated of these Things, only to *shew;* "That the most useful Precept concerning Method, *That we ought to form Conclusions Universal, as well as True, concerning Universals,*[68] takes place also in the Rules of Human Practice," (which lay down the Art of procuring Happiness;) "and that, therefore, the Universal Causes thereof" (*God,* and *Men,* or the Aid of Rational Agents) "ought *universally* to be regarded, and their Favour sought, at *all* times, in *every* place, &*c. never* wholly neglected, much less provoked; which will certainly be the Case, if in *any* Circumstances, tho' in *private,* or but *seldom, any thing* be committed in prejudice of the Publick Good." The Pleasure in Vice is but of *momentary* Duration; but Injuries committed against God, or Men, endure *for ever. Tenacious* is the *Memory* of the Sinner himself, which both upbraids him with his Crime, and often betrays him against his Will: *Tenacious* also is the *Memory* of those, whom the Infringer of the Publick Good has offended; which, if there be no present opportunity, may minister to future Revenge, or commit the Retaliation to late Posterity. But above all, *God* is *not forgetful* of Crimes, even when he *defers* Punishment. From these Considerations, and others, which are

---

68. Maxwell cites Cumberland's Greek quotation in a footnote, "Γένιχα γενιχως," a formula possibly taken from Aristotle's treatment of the subject in *On Interpretation.*

obvious to every one, we may *conclude,* "That Reason, duly considering all the necessary Causes of Human Happiness, can never pronounce, That any Thing can be committed against the Common Good by any one, without lessening those Causes, and, consequently, destroying some part of his own Happiness."

Let us now *shew,* "That from the foresight of this Penalty on the one hand, and a probable Expectation of Retribution on the other, Men may know their Obligation to do nothing prejudicial to the Common Good; but, on the contrary, to endeavour to deserve the Favour of Others by all kind of Benevolence." Whence will be *deduced* their *Obligation* to *exercise* all Acts of *Virtue,* (which are only Universal Benevolence variously diversified;) and to *shun* all *Vices,* whose Nature cannot be unknown, when the Virtues are known. For, since the *avoiding* such *Punishments,* and the *obtaining* such *Rewards,* are contained in the essential Idea of that *Happiness* Nature lays us under the necessity of seeking; as being a Collection of every Good, which we can obtain: All acknowledge, that *Motives,* or Arguments to *inforce* the Observance of *Laws,* may be drawn from hence. But the *intrinsick Force*[69] *of all those Arguments, with which the Legislator* (God) *uses to enforce Universal Benevolence,* is, in my opinion, all that is meant by the *Obligation of Laws:* The *Rewards* annext to Universal Benevolence by the *right Reason of Men,* chiefly *oblige,* because they promise, beside the Favour of Man, the Friendship of the *Chief of Rational Beings,* GOD, the Supreme Governour of the World. The *Punishments* they inflict by the same Reason, are both *Parts* of the *present,* and most certain *presages* of the *future,* Divine Vengeance. For RIGHT REASON in God *cannot differ* from the same in Men: Which that saying of *Cicero* (1. *de Legibus*) shews to have been well enough known by the *Light of Nature,* where he thus expresses himself with respect to God, *"That to whom Reason is common, Right Reason is common."*[70] Nor can I conceive any thing, which could *bind*

69. [Maxwell] "The *intrinsick* Force of these Arguments consists in the *necessary* Connexion, according to the establish'd Course of Nature, between Virtue and Happiness, Vice and Misery."

70. Cicero, *De Legibus,* I.vii.22.

the Mind of Man with any *Necessity,* (in which *Justinian's* Definition places the Force of *Obligation,*[71]) except *Arguments* proving, that Good or Evil will proceed from our Actions; of which since the greatest is the Favour or the Wrath of GOD, their Connexion with our Actions sufficiently shews, what it is which *his Authority* commands, wherein consists the true *Nature of Obligation.*

It is however necessary to *remember,* "That all those things, Good or Evil, which, at the Divine Appointment, are evidently connected, in the Nature of Things, with such free Actions as respect either the Common Good or Hurt, are to be esteem'd *Rewards,* or *Punishments"*: Whether that *Connexion* be *immediate,* as when any Action, honourable to God, or beneficial to Men, is perform'd, it carries with it its own Reward, by that inward Pleasure, which every one experiences upon such occasions: (Let us take, for *Instance,* useful Contemplations, or Acts of Love towards God, or Man; or, on the other hand, Envious, Wrathful, or Malicious Dispositions, which are immediately connected with uneasiness and anxiety of Mind:) Or, if the *Connexion* be *not immediate,* when a Series of Causes, whether necessary, or free, intervenes between our Actions and the Good, or Evil, that follows them; thus, by the appointment of Rational Beings, (God or Men,) are Positive Rewards or Punishments connected with human Actions. That God will distribute such after this Life, the natural Reason, even of those who wish the contrary, is throughly sensible.

But it ought to be our *principal Care,* "Not to take our measure of the Sanction of the Law of Nature, only from the outward and contingent Rewards and Punishments of this Life." For this would be, to neglect the *greatest* Evidences of its Obligation, whence the step would be easy, to slight the *Law it-self;* and, if we did any good, only from the Hope or Fear of *these* Advantages or Disadvantages, it were the sign of an abject and *mercenary* Spirit. But, if you seek also that internal Reward with which the Mind is bless'd, and the everlasting Favour of God, while you co-operate with him in promoting the Publick Good; there can

71. Justinian, *Institutes,* III.13.

never be hence wanting to you a sufficient Spur to Virtue, and you shall avoid all Suspicion of Mean-Spiritedness.

These following are certainly *honourable* Rewards, *always* connected with the Practice of Virtue.

1. A *fuller Knowledge of God and Men,* the most noble Causes, not of your Happiness alone, but of the Common Happiness of all Rational Beings. And whilst you study to do things acceptable to God and Men, upon whom we depend, you will perceive, that you draw every Virtue from the Sourses of the Being, Preservation, and Perfection of Human Nature, which can never be exhausted.

2. The *Conformity of our Nature with the Divine,* consisting in an imitation of the Divine Goodness, conspicuous in his Providence over all his Subjects.

3. The *Dominion of your Reason over your Passions, and all your voluntary Motions.* It is hence evident, that Piety and Justice, (which consist in what I have been just laying down,) their Improvements and immediate Effects, (that Joy and Tranquillity, which arise from an inward Sense of them,) are the *principal* Part of the Reward of Virtue. Thus may the Opinion of the *Stoicks* and others, who would have *Virtue sought for its own sake,* be reconcil'd to Truth.[72] For this Reward I acknowledge to be so *intimately* connected with it, as to be *inseparable* from it by any Misfortune whatsoever. But, because this Reward may be *distinguish'd,* in Thought at least, from Virtue, and is *proper* to it, and may be *foreseen* as a *Reward,* it seem'd necessary to consider it under the Notion of a *Sanction* annex'd to that Practical Dictate of Reason, which prescribes the Pursuit of the Common Good, (or the Practice of all manner of Virtues;) and by this *particular Mark* this Dictate is *distinguish'd* from all other Practical ones, which are *true* indeed, but *not necessary* to be observ'd by all. Such are the Propositions about the Solution of Arithmetical and Geometrical Problems, which are not *Universal Laws,* because they want *such a Sanction.* For a *Law* is a *practical Proposition con-*

---

72. For examples of this position, see Marcus Aurelius, *Meditations,* V.6, VII.73, IX.42; XI.4; Diogenes Laertius, *Lives,* VII.94; Epictetus, *Discourses,* III.7.

*cerning the Prosecution of the Common Good, guarded by the Sanction of
Rewards and Punishments.*

Lastly, The Reader may observe, That I do not deduce the *Obligation*
of Laws, from this kind of Sanction, (I have assign'd, another efficient
Cause, another End, far greater;[73]) I explain only that part of the Definition, which affects the Necessity of such pursuit of the Common
Good, in order to the Private Happiness of every particular Person; from
which Necessity it is, that Actions commanded by the Laws are call'd
Necessary. An *absolute* Necessity cannot here be understood, such as is
in Mechanical Motions, but *relative* and upon *supposition,* with *respect*
to some effect, if we would produce it. In that most Universal Law,
which I chiefly consider, concerning the pursuit of the most General
Good, the Honour of God join'd with the Happiness of Men, it is evident, that the Action commanded, is not necessary to any superior or
greater Effect, since no such there either is, or can be. It is also manifest,
that, if this Pursuit be said to be necessary to the producing *this very
Effect,* the Proposition will be Identical,[74] and will propose no incitement
to Action; therefore the Pursuit or Production of this Effect (as far as we
are able) is to be look'd on as necessary to some *lesser Effect* thence depending; that is, in order to procure, by the Assistance of all Causes, our
own Happiness, which we are justly suppos'd to desire. The Proposition,
understood so, does most powerfully excite to Action. However, I most
readily acknowledge, that, after this Obligation is *made known* to us
from the *Effects,* as above, it is much *confirm'd* by considering the *Efficient Cause* from which I have deduc'd it, that is the Will of the First
Cause. For it is thence certain, both that the infinite *Wisdom* of God
has approv'd of those Laws and their Sanction, and that *all* the Divine
Perfections *conspire* to the same Effect. For there can never be any *Dis-*

73. In footnotes Maxwell briefly glosses each term to reinforce Cumberland's argument that such sanctions are not the cause of obligation. The cause is the divine
will whose end is the common good of all, not just the good of individuals.

74. [Maxwell] "An Identical Proposition is that, which affirms any thing of it-self,
as *Happiness is Happiness.*"

agreement between the Will of God and his other Perfections. Wherefore, these all will encourage Men to *hope* for *greater* Rewards, and will afford sure *Presages* of *greater* Punishments, to confirm the Sanction of these Laws, and the necessity of Obedience.

The *Original,* as well of all *Ignorance* about the Law of Nature, as of *Negligence* in observing them, seems to me to be this, "That most Men do not sufficiently *consider,* either what are the genuine *Parts* of their own and others Happiness, and what *Proportion* there may be between them, so as to understand, which contains in it more, which less, Good; or that afterwards they do not consider their genuine *Causes,* and which Cause contributes more, and which less, to this End, or Effect." *Hobbes's* Principles, according to which he thinks Men should govern themselves in the State of Nature, are faulty in both respects, both, because they propose an End too mean, the Preservation of Life and Limbs, neglecting the Perfections of the Mind, and hope of Immortality: And, because he *alledges,* "That the Power of Rational Causes (God and Men) to restrain all Invasion of Right, is ineffectual, without the Declaration of the supreme Civil Authority." Whereas, tho' I willingly acknowledge, that they are much strengthen'd by Civil Society, yet I *affirm,* "That, supposing no Civil Government were erected, there is no necessity to pursue our own Happiness, by first invading others, either by Force or Fraud, that is, by entering into a State of War; but that there is reason abundantly sufficient, arising from the Nature of God and Men, why we should rather be desirous to solicit all Rational Beings, by Universal Benevolence, and, consequently, by all manner of Virtue, to Peace, Benevolence, and lastly, to Society, both Civil and Sacred."

§XXXVI. Having explain'd, as briefly as I could, the Substance of my Opinion, concerning the *Nature and Original of Natural Obligation,* I thought it necessary to obviate *two Scruples,* which might disturb Minds of the *better* sort. 1. That the *Punishments* of Vice seem *uncertain,* and the *Rewards* of Virtue *not well enough known,* so as to be sufficient Declarations of Natural Obligation, and the Will of the First Cause. 2. That according to this Opinion it might seem, that the *Common Good* is post-

The Cause of Mens not observing the Laws of Nature;

Two Objections against the foregoing Notion of Moral Obligation, propos'd.

pon'd and *subordinate* to the *Private* Happiness of every particular Person.[75] I shall shew, that my Opinion is liable to neither of these Objections.

Object. I. The Rewards and Punishments of the Law of Nature are too uncertain.

As to the *First,* which suggests the *Uncertainty* of the *Connexion* of Rewards and Punishments with Actions publickly useful or hurtful, I make the following Reply. Let us begin with the Connexion of *Punishment* with *Wickedness,* of which we shall treat more at large, because it is the more difficult affair, and what respects the *Reward* of *good* Actions may thence be easily judg'd of.

Answer. Not so; The Punishments not uncertain, for

(1.) Altho' *some wicked Actions* may escape *some kind of Punishment,* that is, such as is inflicted by *Man,* yet even these Crimes do not wholly go *unpunished;* and, therefore, there is not wanting an *Obligation* arising from the consideration of this Punishment, which *cannot be avoided.*

1. Struggles of Conscience, Fears of Divine and Human Punishment, Greater Corruption, Tortures of Envy and Malice, are Unavoidable Punishments of Wickedness.

For it is impossible to separate from the Crime all degrees of *Anxiety of Mind,* arising from the struggle between the sounder Dictates of Reason, which enforce our Duty, and those rash Follies which hurry Men on to Wickedness: There likewise ensue *Fears* (which cause present Grief) of *Vengeance,* both *Divine* and *Human,* and an *Inclination* to the *same Crimes,* or even *worse;* which, because it hurts the Faculties of the Mind, seems to me that it ought to be also reckon'd among Punishments: Even the very *Malice* and *Envy,* which are essential to every Invasion of another's Right, do necessarily and naturally *torture* every malevolent Mind; and so the wicked Man drinks deep of the poyson'd Draught of his own Mixture.[76]

II. The Expectation of contingent Evils is equal to a present Evil, and may therefore in Reason be esteem'd a certain Punishment; for

(2.) Whoever will prudently consider, what he has done, or is about to do, to the Prejudice of others, must of necessity consider and estimate those Punishments, which are not the certain, but the contingent only and probable, Consequences of bad Actions. Seeing therefore I have already *prov'd,* "That the Chance of a future contingent Evil is of a determinate present Value"; it *follows,* "That such Evil, (which, in as much

---

75. [Maxwell] "See the Answer to this Objection in the 45th and following Sections of this Chapter."

76. "And so the wicked Man . . .": a version of a quotation attributed to Attalus by Seneca in *Epistulae Morales,* LXXXI.22–23.

as it may be inflicted with the Approbation, at least, of the Supreme
Governour of the World, is to be look'd upon as a Divine Punishment,)
is an Argument made use of by Him, to persuade his Subjects, not to
expose themselves to so great Danger, for the sake of any Advantage,
which may accrue from injuring another; and, therefore, certainly
obliges all those, who weigh, as Reason directs, every Impediment of
their Happiness." This *Consequence* is sufficiently plain, from what I
have already laid down, concerning the nature of *Obligation.*

I am now briefly to *shew,* "That the Consideration of Human Actions
hurtful to other Rational Beings, necessarily leads the Mind of Man to
the Prospect of great Danger from that Punishment, which there is the
greatest reason imaginable to fear, tho' we cannot certainly foresee, what
the Event will be." This will be evident from what follows.

In the *first* place it is *manifest,* "That all Human Actions hurtful to
others, as such, have in them the Force of a *meritorious Cause,* sufficient
to incite every other Rational Agent, those especially who have been Sufferers by them, to restrain by Punishments, to the utmost of their Power,
those who have injur'd other innocent Persons." This inciting, impulsive, Force is not Fictitious and Imaginary, but altogether as Real, as any
Impulse from external Objects upon our Senses. I confess, this impulsive
Force alone is not sufficient to inflict Punishment on the Offenders, and,
therefore, Punishment does not always follow such Incitement, such
Provocation to it: But, *because* whoever would act reasonably, must consider the Force, and all the Effects of his Actions, but principally, how
far they may influence other Rational Beings, in defence of the Common
Good, to punish, or not, I thought *fit* to make this *Observation. Desert*
is justly reckon'd among, and joined with, partial, assisting Causes, such
as *Invitation* of *Objects,* the *Temptation* of *Opportunity,* the *Authority*
of an *Adviser,* or Persuader; and, therefore, ought not to be neglected,
because our Mind is hence led to *consider,* "That the Efficacy of our own
Actions may be join'd with that of many other Causes, in the Production
of great Effects, which could not be hoped for, from any or all of those
Causes, singly or separately consider'd." And for this Reason that *Paradox,* which I just now advanc'd, is most true, "That whoever will consider, in such manner as Prudence directs, our noxious Actions, must,

the Mind of
Man cannot
avoid expecting
many contin-
gent Evils, as
Consequences
of his Evil
Actions; for

(1.) they
deserve, and
incite to, Pun-
ishment.

of necessity, take into consideration those probable Punishments, which the Concurrence of external Causes renders not necessary indeed, only contingent." It is certain, that by *Innocence* we shall not pull Mischief down upon our own head: By *Injuries* we give being, at least to one, and that the *first* Cause of our Destruction;[77] we lay down a Motive, an Incitement, to others to contribute to that Effect. And how *probable* their Concurrence is, we may conclude from what follows. I must first add a few Remarks concerning other Effects of wicked Actions, which render their Punishment *more certain.*

(2.) They are infinitely Productive of other evil Actions, prejudicial to both Publick and Private Happiness.

§XXXVII. It is in the *second* place *certain,* "That every Action proceeding from Malevolence towards others, has a natural endless Tendency to produce other Malevolent Actions of the like kind, thwarting the Common Happiness, and consequently diminishing that of the Malevolent Person himself," (which upon many accounts depends upon the Common Good:) *Partly,* because it paves the way to *evil Habits,* and a corruption of Manners: *Partly,* because it lays him under a sort of Necessity, *to defend one Wickedness by another;* what is begun by Fraud and Covertly, comes to be finish'd by Force and open Violence: *Partly* also, because the *contagious Example* infects others far and wide. And it is *evident,* "That, the more Malevolence gains ground, the more openly all things tend to a State of War, which is but too productive of severe Punishments, and threatens Destruction, not less certain to the Leader in Wickedness, than dreadful to all."

(Mr. *Hobbes's* Acknowledgment of the Calamities consequent from his State of War, employ'd to overturn his Method of deducing the Laws of Nature.)

Altho', therefore, the *Fear of a War of each against all,* on all sides *Just,* be wholly *Vain,* as being what, I have already prov'd, can never happen; yet any One, suppos'd to live out of Civil Society, may *with the greatest reason fear to raise up* by his own Wickedness, and unite against himself in a *just War,* the Forces of *many,* either to preserve their own Property, or to take *Vengeance* for Injuries offered. He may also *fear the overwhelming* his *Confederates* with himself, (if perhaps he has drawn over many to his Defense,) in the Calamities of an unjust War. Nay, if he chances

77. [Maxwell] "This first or leading Cause, the *Motive,* is what *Logicians* call the *Procatarctick* Cause."

to come off Conqueror, which is more than he had reason to expect from the Justice of his Cause, he has *reason to fear,* lest his *prosperous Wickedness stir up Others,* in hopes of the *like* Success, in *like* manner to *invade his Rights.* We may most *evidently perceive,* both from the consideration of Human Nature, and from the observation of those things which pass daily among bordering Nations, that *Wars* may draw their *Original* from such like *Causes* as *these.* It is *likewise evident,* that these Wars are *no less prejudicial* to the preservation of *particular* Persons, than if they owed their Original to *Hobbes's* fictitious Right of every Man to every Thing. Wherefore, when he *contends,* "That the Calamities of *his* State of War affords, not only a sufficient, but a necessary, Reason, to incline all Men every where, laying down the Arms they had taken up, to submit themselves to Absolute Government, and to whatever Laws their Governours please to impose upon them";[78] he will be *inconsistent* with himself, if he will *not allow,* from a Parity of Reason, "That a Prospect of a War no less dangerous, which may arise from the Invasion of the Rights of Others, or from any kind of Wickedness, may be a sufficient Motive to the same Men, to abstain from unjust Actions, or such as oppose the Common Good, and mutually to cultivate, from the beginning, Peace, and all its friendly Offices, towards one another; and, consequently, never to attempt that War, which he dreams of, of each against all." For it is a most *evident Dictate of right Reason,* "That the same Evils of War, certainly foreseen, are sufficient to deter Men from entering into War, which are able to dissuade them from continuing War already begun."

If "These pernicious Effects of unjust Actions, which recoil upon the guilty Person, are understood to be necessarily connected with the Guilt, by Virtue of that Order among all Things, which the First Cause, and Supreme Governour of the World has appointed," they are justly to be look'd upon as *Punishments appointed by God.* And "That Proposition, which, according to the determination of the Nature of Things, (and consequently of the Author of Nature,) pronounces that Action, not to be Good, or Eligible, which at once both hurts Others, and pulls down Mischief upon our own head," will be a *Law of Nature,* sufficiently *dis-*

---

78. A paraphrase of the argument in Hobbes, *On the Citizen,* ch. 5.

covering it-self to be such by these *Characters,* 1. That the subject Matter thereof are Actions of Publick Mischief or Advantage (the proper Subject of Laws); 2. That it has a Sanction, a Punishment, annex'd by the Supreme Governour of the World.

I agree with Hobbes, "That the Prospect of the Evils of War may conduce much, to the causing Men mutually to perform toward one another the Offices of Peace, by the exercise of all kinds of Virtues"; but I do *not allow,* as he has done (*de Cive, C.* 1. §. 10.) "That every Man has a Right of waging War, in order to support his Claim to every Thing."[79] I consider only the *Possibility* and the *Consequences* of a *War,* just on one side, unjust on the other. *Before* I would venture to *affirm* any thing, concerning the *Right* to do any Action, especially to *wage War,* I first *consider,* what Things are necessary to necessary Ends, and thereby settle the Nature of *Property:* I *acknowledge* the *Nature of Things* has immutably determin'd, what Things are *necessary:* I have *shewn,* "That, not those Things only are naturally determin'd, which are necessary to *particular* Persons singly considered, but those also, which are necessary to *many,* or even to all, jointly consider'd": Moreover, I have by the way *demonstrated,* "That those Propositions which truly, that is, agreeably to the determination of Nature, declare, *what* kind of Human Actions are necessary to the Common Good of Mankind, and *what* are inconsistent with that End, are *Laws of Nature";* I have *collected* the Sum of them into *one* general Proposition, and have *reduc'd* to a *few* Heads the *particular Precepts* enjoined thereby; and, in *these particulars,* I have sufficiently *differ'd from* Hobbes. And now, when I treat of *Obligation,* which is the proper Effect of Laws, and becomes known to our Senses by the Rewards and Punishments consequent upon the Observance and Violation of those Laws, and is, therefore, a proper Evidence, that they are Laws; I may *assume* what *Hobbes* himself has with reason *granted,* provided I take care to avoid the many Errors he has intermixt therewith. But that I have sufficiently taken care of, both by what I have but now said, and by *maintaining,* "That this just War, of which I now treat, is the Effect of the Laws of Nature, and of the Nature of Rational Agents

79. Ibid., 1.10, p. 28.

acquainted with those Laws, which, in order to defend Themselves and their Property, and to restrain Aggressors, will have recourse to Arms, which are therefore just, because they are in this Case necessary Means to the Common Good." Whereas Mr. *Hobbes supposes,* "A War just on all Sides, both of the Invader and Resister, before the Laws of Nature, upon which Justice is founded, are established; their business being," as he endeavours to prove, "To propose the Means necessary to avoid this War, which," according to his Doctrine, "Is at the same time just on all Sides, and destructive to All."[80] But of this elsewhere.

§XXXVIII. It is *sufficient for our present Purpose,* what, I believe, no Man in his wits will deny, "That any Invasion of another's Property does naturally tend much to the stirring up Strife and kindling War": And, "That right Reason dictates this to every Man, that greater Damage is to be apprehended from this open'd Sluice of all Evils, than can be compensated by the hope of the trifling Advantage, which can be procur'd by the Injury, especially in that State, where no Civil Government is suppos'd, which might restrain Anger and Revenge within some bounds; and where one Contention may breed others without end; and the least Strife may bring Life in danger." It is most *certain,* "That as soon as a Duel is commenc'd upon an equal foot, where each of the two has an equal Hazard of Life and Death, the Hope of the Life of each becomes but of half its former Value." As if any One should hold close twenty Shillings in one Hand, in the other, nothing; and should give his Choice to a Person ignorant of what was done, to take what was contain'd in which Hand he pleas'd; it is certain, that such a Gift, or the Hope thereof, before the Choice made, is worth ten Shillings, that is, half the whole Sum exposed to Hazard, which in this Case is, as it were, in an even uncertain Balance. And, for this reason, it is likewise *certain,* "That Reason, rightly weighing Things, would not permit any One to throw his Life into such Hazard," (altho' our Lives were as much at our own disposal, as the Money in our pockets,) "Except for the Gain of that, the uncertain Hope whereof is equal to half the Value of our Life"; or, which

He, who, by invading another's Property, commences an unjust War, has no Prospect of any Advantage equal to Life, the Loss of which he hazards in the Quarrel.

---

80. Ibid., 1.12, 13, 15, pp. 29–31; 3.33, pp. 56–57.

comes to the same thing, "For the sake of that, whose certain Gain is worth the certain Loss of Life." The Invader of another's Property has scarce a certainty of gaining any thing to compensate so great a Hazard, so great a Loss. The Life of the Conquered vanishes into Air, wholly useless to the Conqueror. Those Goods, which, because they were really *necessary to him* he called *his,* will *not* be in like manner *necessary to the Conqueror,* nor will they therefore, in this State, become *his Property.* For I justly *suppose,* "In a State where all Things are in Common, both that Nature has liberally afforded as much as is necessary to every particular Person, where human Industry has not been wanting, and that those Things which are truly *necessary to any one,* are *not* likewise *necessary to any other.*" The latter is a Consequence of the former. But the certain Acquisition of those Things, which before were not, nor do now become, necessary by the Death of the conquer'd Person, is not of so great Value, as that it ought to be purchas'd by the certain Loss of Life. But, after the Victory, in that State of Community which *Hobbes* supposes, they will still remain Common to all; so that, beside the Hazard of Revenge which may be taken by Others, there accrues nothing to the Conqueror.

(*Hobbes's* Prospect of Security by preventing others by Force or Fraud, in a State of Nature, is absurd.)   That Security, which, according to *Hobbes,* is gain'd, in this State, by preventing others, either by Force or Fraud, is either of no Value, or, at least, not of so great.[81] For, in our Deliberation, whether we shall invade others, and give them a just Cause of War, or no, they are of necessity suppos'd Innocent, and such as would not take Arms, unless they were forced by an Attempt to deprive them of Necessaries, or, at least, have not as yet had recourse to Arms: But, where there is no reason for Fear, Security ought not to be purchas'd at the Hazard of Life. Much less would any Man in his senses think a War against all, a way to secure himself.

In this Inquiry, *concerning the Obligation of the Laws of Nature, and the Prospect of Punishments to be apprehended from violating them by Invasion of another's Right,* I have affirm'd Men are necessarily *suppos'd Innocent:* both, *because* we allow, that it is lawful to punish the *Guilty*

81. Ibid., 5.1, p. 69.

by the Loss of Goods, or of Life it-self; and, *because* it is a mad Rashness to suppose Men, who have shew'd no Signs of Malevolence towards us, entertain a Will to hurt us, and, for that reason, either by Force, or Fraud, to set upon and kill them, that we may be secure from them, which yet is the Sum of Natural Right, according to *Hobbes;* and also, *because* I think it may be collected from *Hobbes's Hypothesis,* tho' he often contradicts it. For he *supposes,* in his *State of Nature, several Persons as rais'd out of the Earth at the same Time, and of full Growth,* C. 8. §. 1.[82] I ask, Does right Reason dictate to these, as soon as they come in sight of one another, that they should mutually *cultivate* the Offices of *Peace,* that is, behave themselves Benevolently, Faithfully, and Gratefully; or that they should *rather rush into a War* of every Man against every Man? Is their State, when they have not as yet done, or determin'd to do, to one another, either Good or Harm, that of *Peace* or *War?* I affirm it to be *Peace,* and that *all* Men are as yet to be look'd upon as *Innocent,* and that Reason dictates, that they should *preserve* this *Peace,* by trusting others, and faithfully discharging the Trust that is repos'd in themselves, by Gratitude and Beneficence in their external Actions: And that, *partly,* because such Actions are in their own Nature most pleasant, and in some measure bring their own Reward along with them; whereas the contrary Actions, as they are necessarily accompanied with Hatred and Envy, so they are inseparable from Grief, which is essentially connected with those Affections; which was my *first* Reason:[83] *Partly,* because whoever is Malevolent towards others, and denies to them their reasonable Demands, hazards the engaging himself in a War, whose Consequences, I am sure, are very Penal; which is my *second* Reason,[84] which I now handle. What is more, since *Hobbes* acknowledges, that it is the *first Law of Nature* in the State of Nature, *"That Peace is to be sought after";*[85] and likewise teaches, *"That Right is natural Liberty left by the Laws,"*[86] it necessarily

---

82. Ibid., 8.1, p. 102, where Hobbes deploys his notorious "mushroom men" metaphor.
83. [Maxwell] "See the second Paragraph of the precedent Section."
84. [Maxwell] "See the third Paragraph of the precedent Section."
85. Hobbes, *On the Citizen,* 2.2, p. 34.
86. Ibid., 14.3, p. 156.

follows, "That Man in this State has no Right to act contrary to the Law of Nature, *by* rushing into War, before it appears, that he cannot enjoy Peace; or *by* arrogating to himself a Right to all Things, since the Law of Nature forbids a Man to exercise such a Right, even tho' he were supposed once to have had it," both which *Hobbes* hath taught.[87] His *Subterfuge,* sought from thence, "That these Laws do not oblige to external Acts for want of Security," is elsewhere by me examin'd;[88] here I *affirm* only thus much, "That they have no obligatory Force, and, consequently, that they have nothing in them of the Nature of Laws, if they respect not external Actions." Because it is impossible to cultivate Peace with others, or to depart from one's Right, by any *internal* Action; for these are *transient* Actions in their own Nature, that is, they have a relation to Men *without us.* But, if he *answer,* "That these are *improperly* call'd Laws," as he insinuates (*De Cive. C.* 3. §. 33.) I thus *reply,* "That those Arguments which I have already advanc'd, and which I shall presently offer, do prove them *properly* Laws." However, with respect to *Hobbes,* this is a necessary *Consequence;* if there be *no Laws,* properly so called, in a State of Nature, there are *no Rights,* properly so called; hence this *Right,* suppos'd by him, of every Man to every Thing, and to wage War with all, are *improperly Rights,* and *improper Foundations* of Morality and Politicks. For they are not more *properly* Rights, than they are the Concessions of Laws *properly* so call'd; nor are there any other Laws in that State, beside those of Nature. Wherefore, if the Laws of Nature are not *properly* Laws, neither are the Rights of Nature *properly* Rights;[89]

87. Both Cumberland (*De Legibus Naturae,* p. 269) and Maxwell cite *De Cive* 2.23 here, but this seems to be a misprint; *De Cive* 2.3 is the passage that actually refers to the continued exercise of natural rights being opposed to the law of nature. Hobbes, *On the Citizen,* 2.3, p. 34.

88. [Maxwell] "In the fiftieth and following Sections of this Chapter."

89. In his own copy, Cumberland strikes out the last (abusive) sentence of the section and replaces it with the following: "But such rights, which are improperly so called, however drawn together and united they might be, also improperly, to constitute the civil government, could never result in a right of sovereignty. Yet, in matters of politics, one always supposes that there are sovereign rights, properly so-called: and Hobbes himself has to attribute them, in a proper sense, to all civil states; otherwise he is only spouting empty phrases." Cumberland, Trinity College MS.adv. c.2.4, p. 270.

and *Hobbes,* when he lays these down as the Principles of Moral Philosophy and Politicks, is but *improperly* a Philosopher, *improperly* a Polititian; and all these Conclusions, which depend upon these Premises, and which *Hobbes* would pass upon the World for strict Demonstrations, are but *improperly* demonstrated.

§XXXIX. But these Contradictions are tedious. Let us, therefore, proceed to the *third* Reason, on account whereof the Transgressors of the Laws of Nature may justly fear Punishment. This is taken from that *Rational Nature,* which is common to God with Men, and which is the *immediate Cause* of inflicting *Punishment:* Of which thus much is *certain,* whence every Man cannot but presage to himself what will follow.

3. Reason inclines God and Men to punish all Acts of Malevolence.

It is *certain,* "That right Reason (and consequently the Divine) declares it to be a necessary Means in order to the Common Good, that Punishments be appointed to such Human Actions as are inconsistent with it, the Sharpness and reasonable Fear of which may restrain the Malevolent." Whence it is *manifest,* "That right Reason licenses the punishing such, and that they are, therefore, liable to Punishment, whensoever others have it in their Inclination and Power to inflict it."

It is, moreover, *certain,* "That all who have the Common Good at heart" (in the Number of which are God and all good Men), "and all beside, whose Interest it is, that no-one's Rights should be invaded" (under which are compriz'd almost all, even bad, Men), "are actually willing to inflict Punishments upon those, whom they have found, either to have perpetrated such Actions, or even to have discover'd an Inclination to have perpetrated them."

What is more; altho' the Will, both of God and Men, sometimes leaves room for Pardon, it is, nevertheless, *certain,* "That Reason so far every where takes place, with respect to the Common Good," (because it is every one's Interest, that it should be sufficiently secur'd,) "that there should never be given so great Incouragement to hope for Pardon, but that it may appear plainly, that it were better, not to transgress, and not to stand in need of Pardon." For the Reason of all does inviolably *require,* "That such Actions as are inconsistent with the Common Good of all, should be guarded against by such Punishments as are sufficient to secure it, and that no Punishments are sufficient, if there remains a greater Probability of Pardon than Punishment."[90] Hence Reason *dictates* it as necessary, "That all hope of escaping Punishment should be *much* outweigh'd, partly by the *frequency* of the Punishments, partly by their *sharpness*": For a *small* Difference between the causes of Fear and Hope will be scarcely discernible. It is *necessary,* "That the prospect of Impunity should be taken away, *rather* by the *frequency* than the sharpness of such Punishments as are actually inflicted": *Because,* by this Method, a *proportion* between Crimes and their Punishments will be better observ'd, and there will be no room left for that *Complaint,* "That the Punishments of some are unjustly enhanc'd, on purpose that others, guilty of the like Crimes, should escape unpunish'd": Lastly, *because* nothing can be inflicted by Man beyond *Death;* but Death, tho' it were *certain,* seems *not* to me to be a *sufficient Punishment* for their Crimes, who have bereav'd of Life *many,* or such as were *greatly serviceable to the Publick,* and have, beside, put them to horrid *tortures:* Common Reason would forsake its office, that is, would act contrary to Reason, if it should neglect such things; and Men, unless they punish'd them, would, by the prospect of Advantage arising from unpunish'd Crimes, as it were hire the Wicked to injure them.

90. [Maxwell] "Tis true, that the *Roguish,* and consequently, the *Inconsiderate,* part of Mankind are, generally, IN FACT not deterr'd from the Commission of Villainy, if they think the Probability greater of escaping, than of suffering, Punishment; how great soever the Punishment is, with which they are threaten'd, if they are detected, and brought to Justice. Yet, IN REASON, and to one who balances the Motives *for* and *against* any Action deliberated upon, the Motives may be stronger against committing a Crime, than for committing it, tho" the Probability were greater of escaping, than of suffering, the Punishment threatened. For *Example;* Suppose a Man stealing *three* Pounds, is threaten'd by the Law with a *sevenfold* Restitution, that is, with a Fine of *Twenty-one* Pounds, and that the Chance of his escaping, is to that of his suffering, Punishment, as *four* to *three,* or that he has four Chances for escaping, and three for suffering, Punishment. That Fine of twenty-one Pounds, threaten'd with such a degree of Probability, is equal to *nine* Pounds certain; and, consequently, the *Motive to Steal* is but as *three,* but the *Motive not to steal* is as *nine,* that is, is thrice as great as the former; and, consequently, in Reason, sufficient to deter, tho' no regard were had to any other Consideration, than barely to the Punishment threaten'd by the *Civil* Power."

But, if it be doubted, not whether Rational Agents *will*, but whether they *can*, apprehend and punish those that transgress against the Common Good, it immediately *occurs*, "That nothing can shun the Divine Knowledge and Power." Nor is it to be doubted, but that the Will of God *inclines* to do that, which *right*, and consequently, the *Divine Reason* has determin'd to be necessary to the chief End.

It were easy to *prove*, with respect to Men, whilst they are consider'd as out of a State of Civil Society, in a State of Equality, according to *Hobbes's Hypothesis*, since in that case none could claim a Property except in things necessary to him-self,[91] "That there would be room for fewer Crimes, and that they could be more easily discover'd, and punish'd without difficulty; especially, if several should mutually agree to restrain the Malevolent, whose Wickedness would, in this case, be look'd upon as equally dangerous to all."

Since, therefore, it is the *Interest* of all, that they who oppose the Common Good, by violating the Laws of Nature, should be punish'd; *since* Nature has endow'd Men with an eminent *Sagacity*, beyond other Animals, by which they may discover latent Criminals; *and* does also strongly spur on all with a desire of *Glory*, (of which other Animals are insensible,) to restrain the common Enemies; *then* are there the *greatest Reasons* to *fear* Punishments, and but very *small Hope* of *avoiding* them.

§XL. I am weary with insisting so long upon the *Proofs* of *Obligation*, taken from *Punishment* or the Hazard thereof; especially, because those Advantages or *Rewards*, which are connected with the pursuit of the Common Happiness, (altho' they are not generally reckon'd among the essential Ingredients of a Law, and Proofs of Obligation;) yet to me seem *clearer* and *prior Proofs* of the *Divine Will*, than the Punishments most certainly consequent upon the contrary; and these come now under our Consideration. I *suppose* here, as before, "That all Connexion or Concatenation between Causes and their Effects, in Nature, proceeds from the Will of the First Cause." For the *same Reason*, which *proves* the Things themselves to have been made by a First Cause, *demonstrates* all

Neither are the Rewards, or positive Advantages of pursuing the Common Good, uncertain.

---

91. See Cumberland's views on property, 1.22–23; 7.

the Order or natural Connexion among them, to proceed from the same Cause. For which Reason, even here, where it is *disputed,* "whether it is the Will of the First Cause or no, to govern the World by the Practical Dictates of Reason, or Natural Laws," it may be taken for *granted,* "That both the good and bad Effects of Human Actions are always in consequence of the Will of the First Cause."

This prov'd by shewing, 1. That greater Advantages follow Virtue, than what can, with Reason, be expected from the contrary Practice.

Two things are here briefly to be consider'd. I am to *prove* from the known Order of Nature, 1. "That Advantages follow such Actions, and those so great, that we cannot with reason hope for equal from the opposite Vices." 2. "That the so obtaining these Advantages; is a sufficient Natural Discovery of the Divine Will's commanding such Actions."[92] Nor will it be necessary here to use many words, because what would here be pertinent, may easily be collected from what I have laid down concerning Punishments, as from *Opposites parallel'd* or compar'd together.

(1.) Security from the foregoing Punishments.

In the *first* place, therefore, I reckon among these Advantages, "A *Security* from pulling down those Mischiefs, which we shall otherwise bring upon our-selves, which I have just now prov'd, most frequently to fall upon the Wicked"; nor need they be repeated here. Only this I think fit to *add,* "That the shunning and fear of Evil does in the same manner express the pursuit and acquisition of Good, as two Negatives make an Affirmative."[93] For *Evil* denotes *the want of that Good, which Nature*

---

92. [Maxwell] "See the Proof of this in the 44th § of this Chapter."

93. Cf. Introduction, sect. 14, where Cumberland also deploys Cicero's refutation of the Epicurean position; Cicero, *De Finibus,* II.x.32. [Maxwell] "There are many Evils, of which we have as positive Ideas, as of the good Things opposite; our Aversion from Evil is as positive an Action, as our pursuit of Good: Pain is no more shunn'd from desire of opposite Pleasure, than Pleasure is desir'd from Aversion from Pain. Both are positive Sensations; nor can we suppose any *Negative Ideas.* The Word, *Incidence,* is Negative, and may denote a State, without either Pleasure, or Pain: But Negative Ideas are not Intelligible, much less are they the Objects either of Desire, or Aversion. When we compare any State of Pain, with a State of Freedom from that Pain, the latter does, from the Contrast, become very pleasing and agreeable; whereas, did we consider it barely in it-self, and without any regard to the opposite State, there would be scarce any discernible Pleasure therein; or, at most, none so great, as to raise a desire sufficient to influence an Endeavour after it. Hence it happens, that there is, for the most part, not only an Aversion from the present Evil, but a Desire of the

requires, and the *shunning* of *that* is in reality the *pursuit* of *Good,* which is only therefore express'd by the *avoiding Evil,* because, tho' most are *not sufficiently careful* of those *Good* things which they *Enjoy;* yet they are *strongly excited* to *pursue,* or *defend* them, when they either *feel* or *fear* the *Loss* of them. However, tho' such *negative Ideas,* and Words denoting them, be in use among Men, yet that which compells them to act, is really a *positive Good,* the procuring, or continuing whereof is hop'd for, from the removal of the contrary Causes. *Privations* and *Negations* do *not move* the Will of Man; nor does it upon any other account chuse to *avoid Evil,* than as that implies the *Preservation* of some *Good.* Whatever *Force* is usually attributed to *Punishments,* or *Natural Evils,* in exciting Men to avoid them, that is wholly to be resolv'd into the attractive *Influence* of those Advantages, of which they would be depriv'd by Punishments, or Evils. All those things, which are said to be done for *fear* of *Death,* or of *Poverty,* would more properly and Philosophically be said, to proceed from the *love* of *Life,* or of *Riches.* Death could not take place, had not Life preceded; nor could *that* be fear d, except *this* were first desir'd. The Reason is the *same* in *all* Evils, and, therefore, in all voluntary Actions, the Love or Pursuit of Good necessarily precedes the shunning Evil. Every *Motion,* indeed, is promiscu-

---

opposite State, which rises in Proportion to the Degree of the Aversion. But, as the Impression of Pain upon the Mind, is generally more deep and lasting than that of Pleasure, the Emotion of Mind excited by the former is proportionably more strong and violent than that occasioned by the latter: Hence, in case of present Pain, the Aversion does often in so great Measure ingross the Attention, that the Desire of the opposite State is scarce discernible. From this Cause, as I take it, proceeds their Opinion, who think that the Aversion from Evil does, of it-self, for the most part, influence the Volition of the Means to avoid the Evil then hated, without any desire of a State of Freedom from that Evil accompanying it. On the contrary, the Mind is sometimes so much taken up about the Means, that its Attention is diverted from the Evil it seeks to avoid: The Volition of every of which Means is immediately preceded by a Desire. Hence it happens, that many think there is no Aversion from Evil at all, distinct from the Desire of Good; and that the only Emotion of Mind, which influences Action, is Desire. Whether Desire always accompanies Aversion; or whether it sometimes does not accompany it, according as we happen to think of a State of Freedom from the present Evil, I will not determine: But that we often think of the Happiness of the opposite State, and consequently desire it, I think is certain."

ously *denominated*, sometimes from the Point *whence* the Motion begins, sometimes from that *toward which* it tends; yet, certainly, it is *distinguish'd*, or receives the most perfect Limitation of its Nature, from that Point *toward which* it tends. In *voluntary Motions* there is a particular Reason, why they should rather be *denominated* from *Good*, for they not only *tend to Good*, but are first *excited by it*.

The *first Reason* of my making this *Remark*, is, "To oppose that *Assertion* of *Epicurus*, which places the *chief Pleasure*, (which with him is the chief Good and End,) in the *absence of Pain*": [94] A-kin to which seems the Opinion of Mr. *Hobbes*, who asserts, "That Men seek Society from their *fear of Evil*"; whereas the *hope*, at least, of *Good* thence arising is easily perceiv'd; nor can any *greater Good* be requir'd in this State of Human Affairs, than what *Society* affords, since that *Dominion* of each over all, which *Hobbes* imagines to afford a Good, greater than that of Society, is evidently *impossible*. See *de Cive*, C. 1. §. 2.[95]

The *next Reason*, and, indeed, the principal One, of my making this *Remark*, was, to *evince*, "That the *Proofs of Obligation*, drawn from the Advantages and *Rewards*, which are the Effects of pursuing the Common Good, have altogether the *same Force* with those, which are usually taken from *Punishments*"; tho' the Common Herd of Mankind, in their confus'd way of Thinking, are more sensible of these. If any one were desirous to form a *distinct Idea of the Force of Punishments*, I am of opinion, that it must be reduced to the *natural desire of preserving and increasing our Happiness*. For, as such *speculative Conclusions* as are demonstrated by a Reduction to that which is *Absurd*, or *Impossible*, from

94. For this argument, see Diogenes Laertius, *Lives*, X.139.

95. Hobbes, *On the Citizen*, 1.2, 21–25. It was a common move for Hobbes's critics to associate him with Epicurus and Epicureanism, and there was some justification for this given Hobbes's close relationship with the neo-Epicurean philosopher Pierre Gassendi. That said, there were important differences, not least in terms of Hobbes's more Stoic position on free will and determinism. For the relationship between Hobbes and Epicureanism, see L. Sarasohn, "Motion and Morality: Pierre Gassendi, Thomas Hobbes and the Mechanical World View," *Journal of the History of Ideas* 46 (1985), pp. 363–80; Sorell, "Seventeenth-Century Materialism: Gassendi and Hobbes," in Parkinson, *The Renaissance and Seventeenth-Century Rationalism* (1993), pp. 235–72.

the *supposition of the contrary,* may *much better* and more naturally be *deduc'd directly* from Definitions, or the *Properties thence arising:* So also *Practical Conclusions,* which would determine us to act in a certain manner, because of *Evils following from the contrary Actions,* are *much better prov'd* from the *Good thence directly flowing,* especially, if it be the greatest. Certainly, the best Abridgment of *Ethicks* is the *Idea* of that true *Happiness* which is attainable by every one, and of all its *Causes* methodically dispos'd. For hence, both the Force and *Consequences* of Human Actions, and also their proper *Order* is immediately perceiv'd, so that nothing is wanting, which may direct and *influence the Will.*

Altho' *Human Legislators* seem not to enter into this Method, making *frequent* use of *Punishments,* but very *rarely* of *Rewards;* nevertheless, if we throughly examine the matter, we shall *find,* "That all Civil Laws are contrived, recommended, and enacted, sometimes also alter'd, relax'd, or even abrogated, and all with respect to this End, *Happiness,* in as much as it may be promoted by Civil Society." This I might easily *prove* by numberless Instances, out of the *Civil Law,* or even from *our own.* Nay, and the *Reason* of the Law it-self, whence Laws are Interpreted, and even sometimes Corrected, has a respect to the *Common Good.* I will cite only one Law from *Modestinus,* *"No Reason of the Law, or favourable Interpretation of Equity, permits, that what was profitably introduc'd for the Advantage of Men, should by a harsh Interpretation be severely stretch'd to their Prejudice."* [96] Here it is implied, that both *Laws* and *Equity* chiefly respect the Advantages of Men, under which *two* are compris'd all the Means of Happiness which can be obtain'd by the help of Laws. And these are indeed Rewards sufficiently great for our Obedience to the Laws. But, because *Protection* from Injuries, and the *Security* thence arising, with the *other Advantages* of well-constituted Governments, are common to *all Subjects,* and flow from obeying *all the Laws* together, therefore it was not proper to propose these great Advantages in any *one* Law: But *every particular Law,* if the scope thereof be well consider'd, brings along with it its *own Reward.* Obedience to them all, has for its Reward, the Sum of all those Advantages, which are procur'd and pre-

---

96. Justinian, *Digest,* 1.3.25.

serv'd in any State by the force of Government. The avoiding and fear of any Misery that may be avoided, if at any time it proceeds from clear and distinct Knowledge, is subsequent to, and deriv'd from, the Knowledge of Happiness that may be attain'd.

Wherefore, even upon this account the *Method* of the antient *Philosophers,* who *taught,* "That the Virtues, and their Rules, the Laws of Nature, were to be cultivated as Means necessary to Happiness, the constant Aim of all Men," is far *more excellent* than that of *Hobbes,* who would *have them,* "To be only the Conditions of Peace to be made, or of finishing a certain War of every Man against every Man," which no-one in his senses would ever undertake; he would rather preserve Peace, as being always esteem'd by him, a Part, or a Means, of acquiring and preserving Happiness.

For *Peace* does *not* necessarily *presuppose War,* nor ought to be defin'd by the removal thereof, as *Hobbes* defines it,[97] to favour that *Hypothesis,* which he design'd afterwards to establish. For it is *that State, in which Rational Agents enjoy among themselves the Advantages of Concord and mutual good Offices;* and *War* ought to be defin'd by the *removal of Peace:* As *Health* is evidently to be defin'd, *not* by the *absence of Diseases,* but *Disease,* by its *contrariety to Health. Nature* has always the *first place;* with it are immediately *connected,* both the *Causes* preservative thereof, and its *Effects,* or unhurt Operations; *afterwards* is gain'd, by *comparison* with these, the distinct *Knowledge* of *Diseases,* and of every thing opposite to Nature. Health is not desir'd, that we may avoid the Painfulness of Diseases, but for its own sake: So Peace is sought after, for the sake of the consequent Advantages, not, that we may avoid the Mischiefs of War. But this is no proper place for further Inquiries of this *kind;* it is sufficient, that, among the good Effects of Virtue, is reckon'd *Security,* both from *inward Evils,* such as unruly Affections, a restless Conscience, &c. and from *outward Punishments,* which, in *Hobbes's* State of Nature, are called *Wars,* which the Wicked pull down upon themselves. These, good Men are free from, tho' from *other Causes* they sometimes *suffer* Grievances, to which *others* are *likewise* liable.

97. Hobbes, *On the Citizen,* 1.12, pp. 29–30.

§XLI. Let us now proceed to those *greater Rewards, which, being inti-* *mately and essentially connected with the Common Good, Nature promises,* *and certainly bestows on those who cultivate it.* They are the *internal Per-* *fections of the Mind,* all the *Moral Virtues,* all the Benefits of *Natural* *Religion;* a Life equal to it self throughout, by means whereof a wise Man is always consistent with himself; Tranquillity of Mind; and what arises from a grateful Consciousness of all these, a *Joy,* which is both uninterrupted, and, because its rise is in our-selves, affects and satisfies the most inward Recesses of the Soul. Out of a desire of Brevity, I have, as it were, crowded all these together; 'tis the *unanimous Opinion,* of even the very *Heathens,* and of the most *disagreeing Philosophers,* "That in these, incomparably the greatest Pleasures are situated, and that they are intimately connected with Human Happiness."

(2) Greater Rewards, aris- ing within the Mind it-self;

I might here easily *shew* "The wonderful Agreement between the *Per-* *ipateticks,* the old and new *Academy,* and even the *Epicureans* them-selves"; tho' *some* taught *Virtue* to be the *only Good; others,* only the *chief* *Good; some,* that it was it-self the very *End; others,* that it was the most proper and absolutely-necessary *Means* to the obtaining it. This even *Epicurus* himself frequently inculcates, both, in what he affirms *con-* *cerning the Wise Man,*[98] and in his *Maxims.*[99] What is more, he has ap-prov'd of it by his own Example, (at least if any credit is to be given to his last Words, which to me seem to be but a Rant;) for he affirms, *"That* *he endur'd the Torments of the Stone, and of an Ulcer in his Bowels, which* *were so exquisite, as to be incapable of an increase of Pain; yet that he look'd* *upon that Day as happy, by means of that Joy of Mind, which arose from* *the Remembrance of his Reasonings and Inventions."* The Reader, if he pleases, may find these his Words in the Epistle to *Idomenes* in *Laer-* *tius.*[100] Certainly, tho' there be something of Boast in these Words, they, at least, prove thus much, that he openly *acknowledg'd,* "That, from the true Knowledge of Nature, and from a Life spent under the Conduct of Reason, proceeded a *great Joy* of Mind, which might afford Comfort

(with Respect to which there has been a wonderful Agreement among all Sects of Phi- losophers, *Epicurus's* not excepted;

98. Diogenes Laertius, *Lives,* X.117–21.
99. Ibid., X.139–54.
100. Ibid., X.22; Cicero, *De Finibus,* II.xxx.96.

to a Man afflicted with the most violent Agonies, and, as a Reward, might excite the Minds of Men to Virtue." He *contends*, "That Virtue alone is inseparable from Pleasure,"[101] and with him *Pleasure* is only another Name, for the *chief Happiness*. But, if these things are acknowledg'd by a *Philosopher*, who, of all others, has made the *greatest Blunders* in the pursuit of natural Knowledge, (as perceiving no *Foot-steps* of the Divine *Wisdom, Goodness*, and *Providence*, in so surprizing a Disposition and Usefulness of all Things;) How much *greater Pleasures* are they sensible of, in the Paths of Virtue, and pursuit of the Common Good, who, from a more through consideration of the very *long* and *regular Train* of natural *Causes, concurring* to produce the most beautiful *Effects*, contriv'd and executed with the most consummate Wisdom and greatest Power, can with ease *demonstrate*, "That it is impossible, that this Universe should spring from *Epicurean* Principles; but that it is necessarily requisite, that a Divine Power and Wisdom should preside over the Motions and Dispositions of Natural Affairs, especially those relating to Man?" Hence they will immediately *perceive*, "That God himself continually attends the Preservation of the Universe," (which is the Common Good,) and (as I have prov'd,) "That he commands Men, according to their Abilities, to promote the same"; whence they will immediately perceive a most grateful *Harmony* between *their* Actions and the *Divine*: From the *Perception* of this Consent with God, necessarily results a most agreeable *Joy* and *Tranquillity* of Mind, as under his safe Protection, accompanied with great *Hopes* of receiving *Immortal Happiness* at his bountiful hands.

the Principles of whose Natural Philosophy, by which he endeavour'd to banish the Belief of a Providence, are briefly refuted.)

Epicurus's Sect alone, among all the *Philosophers, denied*, "That God took care of the Universe," and, consequently, "That he favour'd the cause of Justice among Men," which comes to the same thing: Of which this seems to me the Reason, because (as *Cicero*, in the Person of *Possidonius*, often hints in his Treatise *of the Nature of the Gods*,[102]) he *intended* "in words only to acknowledge, but in reality to deny, a Divine Nature": And, therefore, what he has affirm'd concerning the Gods, was

101. Diogenes Laertius, *Lives*, X.138.
102. Cicero, *De Natura Deorum*, I.xliv.123.

only to avoid Odium and Danger. Among many things which led him into this wicked Error, *this* seems to me, *not* to have been the *least,* "That his knowledge of Nature, in confidence whereof he had the Rashness to deny a Divine Providence, was but very mean and superficial."[103] Altho' I am not ignorant, that *Gassendus* has labour'd much in his defence;[104] yet, notwithstanding, it is *evident,* "that his Natural Philosophy must be resolv'd into certain Principles, which assume many Suppositions not to be granted; which yet, if they were granted, would not be sufficient to establish this most beautiful System which we behold." For he *supposes,* "All Things to be compos'd of Atoms moving thro' the Void with a double natural Motion, one Perpendicular, the other Inclining, and that they owe their Motion to an innate Gravity."[105] As if *Gravity* were any thing *distinct* from *Motion,* or a Conatus to Motion, downward; or, as if the *Cause* thereof were *not to be inquir'd into.* But I will insist no longer upon the reciting such Opinions, the bare recital of which, in an Age of so great Discoveries, is a sufficient Confutation. He was a perfect Stranger to the *Laws of Motion,* nor did he sufficiently consider that remarkable *Order, Connexion,* and *Dependence,* which is conspicuous in those innumerable complicated Motions, whence the uninterrupted Revolutions of all kinds of Productions and Changes in this System proceed; yet in these, and in the Proportions of Figures and Motions thence arising, consists almost the whole Beauty of this Material System, in the investigating whereof are chiefly employ'd the Powers of the most excellent natural Disquisitions, or rather of Mathematicks, (for the Knowledge of these exalted Sciences is nearly allied.) But it is *confess'd,* "That *Epicurus* was so utter a Stranger to Mathematicks, that he was not sensible of the Spherical *Figure* of the *Earth,* contending,

---

103. Cumberland follows the critique of Epicurean philosophy in Cicero, *De Finibus,* I.iv.17–21.

104. Cumberland refers to Gassendi's works on Epicurus, including the *Animadversiones in Decimum Librum Diogenis Laertii, qui est de Vita, Moribus, Plascitisque Epicuri* (1649), the *Philosophiae Epicuri Syntagma* (1649), collected with his works in the *Syntagma Philosophicum* (1658).

105. The main classical sources for Epicurus's theories are Diogenes Laertius, *Lives,* X.40–42; Lucretius, *De Rerum Natura,* II.216.

that it was a Plain," which is easily refuted from the first Elements of Geometry.[106] Who then would expect any thing Rational from this Man, concerning the *whole System of the World,* and the most beautiful Order that is between its more remarkable Parts and Motions, whence both the Existence of the First Mover, and his Providence in the Government of them, may be demonstrated? It certainly to me discovers the greatest *Stupidity* of Mind in him, that he *affirms,* "So curious a Texture of all Plants and Animals to have arisen from a casual concourse of Atoms without any conduct of Reason." I could *rather believe,* "That Cities adorn'd with Edifices and Temples, set forth with Columns and other Furniture, displaying, or even exceeding, all the Ornaments of *Vitruvian* Architecture, were fitted up by a confus'd jumble of Materials, proceeding from an Earthquake."[107] But the extravagance of his Notions out-did even it-self, when he *affirm'd,* "That the Human Mind, and consequently, even Reason, Wisdom, and all Arts and Sciences, ow'd their Original to a fortuitous concourse of the same Atoms, without the help of Reason." And these Absurdities must first be believ'd, *before* you can *learn* from his Natural Philosophy, "That the Precepts of Religion and Justice are not discover'd to us from the Nature of Things govern'd by the Divine Will; and *before* the Hope of an ample Reward for the Observance of them, and the Dread of Divine Vengeance upon those who violate them, could be razed out of the Minds of Men."

But it is now time to dismiss *Epicurus* and his Herd, tho' lately increas'd.[108] There is, however, something in his *Maxims,* which openly *acknowledges,* "That the Just Man gains this point of Happiness by his Virtue, that of all Men he enjoys the greatest Tranquillity, or freedom from perturbations of Mind."[109] Nor is it to be wonder'd at, that *he* would *not acknowledge* the Divine Reason and other Perfections to in-

---

106. Gassendi, *Philosophiae Epicuri Syntagma,* vol. I, p. 672ff.

107. Cumberland is glossing a passage in Cicero, *De Natura Deorum,* II. xxxvii.94.

108. Cumberland is referring to the revival of Epicureanism. For the impact of Epicureanism in England, see Mayo, *Epicurus in England 1650–1725* (1934); Kroll, *The Material World: Literate Culture in the Restoration and Early Eighteenth Century* (1991). The phrase "Epicurus's Herd" comes from Horace, *Epistulae,* I.iv.15, 16.

109. Diogenes Laertius, *Lives,* X.144.

terest themselves in Human Actions, *who denied,* that they were visible in the Formation and Preservation of the Universe. His esteeming it necessary to *deny* "such Divine Interposition in the forming and preserving the World," that Men might neither hope for, nor fear, any thing from God, upon account of their Actions; sufficiently *shews,* "That he thought the Hope of a farther reward for Justice, and the Fear of Punishment, was no less rational, than it is certain, that the World is form'd and govern'd by the Divine Reason." But, since this has been evidently prov'd by others, I shall pursue it no farther, content to have brought my Argument to this Issue. It is certainly *prov'd* sufficiently, "That such a Proposition is a Law of Nature, which is prov'd to have receiv'd the Sanction of Rewards and Punishments from that Cause, which has establish'd the Connexion between all Causes and their Effects in the System of the World."

§XLII. Mean-while the judicious Reader will *observe,* "That I reckon all the Virtues, and that perfection of Mind which accompanies them, among the happy Consequences, or natural Rewards, of Universal Benevolence." But *they* are, as I shall afterwards shew, after the *same manner* the *Consequences* of that *practical Dictate of Reason* which enjoins them, *as* the *Skill* of demonstrating and constructing the various Cases in any general Geometrical Problem, *follows* from the *Knowledge* of the general Method of solving that Problem; in the use of which, however, it is well known, that an *attentive Mind* is requisite, which may diligently mark all those Particulars in which the several Cases differ; for otherwise it may easily slide into *Error.* However, because *all* the several *Virtues* are the *Parts* of this diffusive *Love,* and the several *Modes* of practising it, and therefore, in reality, all taken together, constitute it, (as Parts the Whole;) I acknowledge, "that *Virtue* is great part of its own Reward," and do declare, that much of that Happiness, which we seek after, is contain'd therein. This I understand in the same sense as we say, "that *Health* is great part of that Happiness sought by Animals." *That* is a state of Mind fit for rightly performing its Functions; *this* is a correspondent condition of the Body: *Both* States imprint a pleasing Sense of themselves upon the Mind, and thence produce a certain gentle un-

Virtue it-self the Principal, both Cause and Part of Happiness.

interrupted Joy, even when other matters succeed less happily. I care not in this Argument to *distinguish* between this *Health of Mind,* and the Consciousness, or *Enjoyment* thereof by *Reflexion,* since Nature has so intimately united these two, that the free Exercise of the Virtues, and the Perception or inward Sense thereof, are inseparable: *Nor* will I *contend* with them who would rather call *"Virtue* the immediate efficient Cause of Formal Happiness," provided they *agree* in the *Thing,* "That it both enriches Man in his present Condition with an essential and noble part of Happiness, and paves the way to the future Acquisition of that greater Happiness, towards which it raises his Hopes." For nothing hinders, but that the *same Thing* may be a *Part* of a *Whole* whose Parts exist *successively,* (such as Human Happiness is,) and, nevertheless, an *efficient Cause* of *other Parts* of the *Same Whole,* which are afterwards to exist; just as the same Man may be a Part of the *Roman* State, and the Father of a Son, who will afterwards be a Member of the same State.

Which is therefore a Proof from Nature, and the strongest possible, that it is the Will of God, that we should practise Virtue.

Much has been advanc'd by *Philosophers,* especially the *Stoicks* and *Academicks,* which with strength and perspicuity *demonstrates,* "That the *Virtues* necessarily bring Happiness along with them, as essentially connected therewith": Which I did not think fit to transcribe, as being what the Learned are already sufficiently acquainted with. It is sufficient, that I readily acknowledge them to be the *principal Parts* of Human *Happiness,* so that neither without them can any Man (tho' abounding with all other Advantages) be Happy: Nor, if he posesses them, can he be miserable, however unfortunate. They are therefore, upon account of their own *intrinsick Perfection, worth the pursuit,* tho' they were *enjoin'd by no Law* of Nature; which I would have been at more pains to prove, but that I find it not only granted, but prov'd at large by *Torquatus* in *Cicero de Fin.* even when he is defending *Epicurus's* Doctrine.[110] What I would *infer* from these Reasonings or Concessions of *Philosophers,* is, "That we have a proof, from Nature, that virtuous Actions have a Reward annex'd to 'em by the Will of the First Cause; and, therefore, that it is the Will of the same Cause, that Men, whom he has instructed how to

110. Cicero, *De Finibus,* I.ix–xxi.

foresee the Rewards consequent upon such Actions, should act so as to obtain that foreshewn Happiness." In *this discovery* of the Divine Will consists the *Promulgation of the Law of Nature,* and thence directly flows *Natural* and *Moral Obligation.* And this is what even those *Philosophers,* who taught *Virtue to be the chief Happiness,* seem *not sufficiently* to have *regarded.* For, in my opinion, it adds *vast weight* to the *Arguments* drawn from the *Pleasures* consequent upon *virtuous Actions,* if they be consider'd as *Rewards* annex'd to *Virtue* by the Will of the *First Cause,* for that very purpose, that He might *discover* to Men, that it is His *Will,* "That they should rather do those things which he has honour'd with Rewards natural and easily foreseen, than Actions of a contrary kind, which are known to lead Men to Destruction naturally, in that Scheme of all Things which he has establish'd.

God's constantly and naturally rewarding any Actions, is the plainest and most effectual Method, that can be by natural Signs, of persuading to such Actions, and authentically declaring, that he has commanded them. No-one in his senses expects from God, in the *ordinary* course of Nature, *arbitrary Signs,* such as Words spoken or written, in order to *promulge* his Laws. *Nor, if he afforded such, could we so certainly come at the Knowledge of their Signification, as we understand the Force of a Reward to incline the Minds of Men to do such things, as they perceive to be thereby honour'd.* It is from *Conjectures* not perfectly demonstrative, that we *collect,* in our Childhood, what others *mean* by those *Words,* which Men use among themselves: Yet these are generally *sufficient to explain* to us the Meaning of *Civil Laws.* What is more; I have observ'd many of *such a Disposition,* "That they would willingly part with the Perfections of their Minds, and be content to want that share of Happiness, provided they might indulge their favourite Passions; who yet, after once it sufficiently appears, that the Divine Will has, by Rewards and Punishments, establish'd a Law which restrains those Passions, and calls upon them otherwise to bestow their Pursuits and Labour, reverence and observe it; and readily conjecture, that greater Good or Evil may, by the Interposition of the Divine Will, follow from their Actions, than what can be distinctly foreseen." For the smallest Hint, provided it be certain, of the Will of the SUPREME LORD OF ALL, is of the greatest Weight among all, who are

A Proof superior to what can be given by any arbitrary Signs.

truly Rational; because whatever is of the utmost Importance may be justly expected, both from his Favour, and from his Anger.

Whence Reason promises Good Men, Happiness, not in this Life only, but in a future Immortal State.

Among *these Rewards* is *that happy Immortality, which natural Reason promises to attend the Minds of Good Men, when separated from the Body.* For it perceives the *Mind,* as exerting more noble Powers, to be a Substance of a *different* kind from the *Body,* and is sensible of its *firm Resolution* of practising perpetual Benevolence, and, consequently, all the *Virtues.* Now it is *evident,* "That Substance will enjoy a happy Immortality, which upon account of the Diversity of its Nature, is not hurt by the Death of the Body; and which still enjoys the charming Remembrance of its former Virtue, and is ready to lay hold of all Opportunities, which an endless Duration will afford, of practicing Virtue." For it *appears* from what I have already said, which is confirm'd by all Experience, "That the Happiness of Good Men is inseparable from the Remembrance and Exercise of Virtue." But it is sufficient for me briefly to have hinted this, which has by others been handled more at large.

(3.) All the Advantages of Civil Society.

§XLIII. In the *third* and last place, *all the various Advantages of Political Societies come to be reckon'd among the Rewards naturally consequent upon endeavouring to promote the Common Good:* For they are at first establish'd, and afterwards preserv'd, with that view. *States,* indeed, have a *particular* respect to their *own Subjects;* yet so, that their Rulers take an especial Care, *not to injure,* violate Faith, or refuse any office of Gratitude, or Humanity, to those who are *without their State;* to *these Heads* are reduc'd the principal *Rights of Peace and War;* which, by the Intervention of the supreme Powers are by all good Subjects observ'd, with respect to those of all other Nations. I shall elsewhere, if there be occasion, shew more at large, that the Reason of *forming all States* is to be drawn from *this Principle.* Even Mr. *Hobbes* himself in many places *grants,* "That the Advantages of Societies are great, and that they can neither be establish'd nor preserv'd, unless the Precepts of most Virtues be incorporated into, and confirm'd by the Authority of, the Laws of the State";[111] so that it would be superfluous to add more here upon that

111. E.g., Hobbes, *Leviathan,* ch. 26.

head. This *Remark,* however, it may not be improper to make here, "That to *this Class* I reduce all those Advantages of Society, which, altho' they be not always enjoin'd by all, and are consequently to be look'd on as Contingent, are yet such as may with some probability be expected." Such *Contingent* Advantages are of *no contemptible Value* in this Argument; such are *Plenty* of Necessaries, *Security* of Life, *Honours, Riches,* a happier *Education* of Youth, a greater share of *Learning,* &c. These indeed fall *not* to the share of *All,* at least, *not equally,* from the Advantages of Society. Yet I am of opinion, that *All* do thence enjoy a much *greater share* of such Benefits than they could obtain, if Men did not study to promote the Common Good, and *no Civil Societies* were form'd, but that all liv'd in that Brute-like State, to which *Hobbes* contends, that the right Reason of Individuals would reduce all, before Societies were erected. It is *necessary,* "That we should set a value upon such contingent Advantages, when we deliberate upon those Affairs, which we are to transact with other Men"; *because* all Effects which we can *hope* for from such free Agents, by our behaviour toward them, are in their own Nature Subject to such *Contingency.* So that either we are *not to hope* that any Good can be obtain'd from them, which is contrary to all Experience; or we must *set some value* upon that Civil Good, which is liable to many Hazards. As for my own part, I so highly prize the Advantages (I have enumerated) which flow immediately from Civil Society, but draw their Original from the Observance of the Law of Nature by pursuing the Common Good, that I sincerely believe, even the Loss of Life (which the Laws of Nature sometimes oblige us to lay down for our Country[112]) is abundantly recompensed, and even surmounted by

112. [Maxwell] "It may be *objected* against our Author's Scheme, That there are some Actions for the Good of the Publick, which, Revelation tells us, are Duties, which, nevertheless, don't appear, from the Light of Nature, to be enforced with Rewards and Punishments. Such are the laying down Life for the Good of our Country, or in Case of Persecution, for what we believe a true Religion. To this I *answer,* That we can scarce conceive it possible for the Constitution of Things to have been so fram'd, as that from the natural Consequences of Action in this Life, a Rational Agent would have had a sufficient Motive to lay down his Life upon any Occasion whatever: Unless the Nature of Things were so contriv'd, as that the Consequences of avoiding that Action would render Life less eligible, than Non-existence; or, at

them. A liberal Education, Learning, the Security arising from Government, the agreeable Intercourse of Mankind, and all other Ornaments which we owe to mutual Assistance, are what make Life worth enjoying; therefore, after we have for several years reap'd these Advantages, from the Benevolence of our Fellow-Subjects promoting the Publick Good, they would make no unreasonable demand, should they command us to restore, or lay out for their benefit, that Life which was at first receiv'd, and afterwards often preserv'd, by their means. Nay, after all, we should still be Debtors to our Native-Country, or Fellow-Citizens, tho' in some uncommon Cases, and when our Country is in the utmost Necessity, we should, at their Desire, repay that Life, which it gave us, and which it daily and perpetually preserv'd.

There are few who would hurt others upon account of their observing the Precepts of the Law of Nature, and therefore to guard them, smaller certain Rewards, or obscure Hints of greater ones, will be sufficient. But, because many Persecutions arise, in opposition to those Articles, which are peculiar to the *Christian* Faith, or Discipline; therefore, to strengthen *Christians* it was necessary, that the Resurrection, and the Glory of the Kingdom of Heaven, should be reveal'd, lest *Christians should be of all Men most miserable.* [113]

---

least, so far inferior in Happiness to that future State of Existence, which from the Light of Nature, we have hope of enjoying, so that the Excess of Happiness of the latter, would, upon a rational Deliberation, be sufficient to overbalance the Excess of Certainty of the former. And our Author asserts, and I think with Reason, That Things are so constituted, that it is certain, that what the Nature of Things would admit of for our Happiness, our Creator has given us, namely, such inward Dispositions and Propensities of Mind, as have sometimes produced such noble Actions, as are above-mention'd. But, let natural Reason, amongst the Bulk of Mankind, should not have been sufficient to have perform'd these Heroick Acts of Virtue, and, because Passion, not temper'd by Reason, is always fickle and unsteddy, the Author of our Being, in the overflowing of his Bounty, has given us a supernatural Revelation of his Will, to fill up the Defects of Nature, and compleat our Happiness; which Assistance of Revelation, that it is sufficient, the innumerable Army of Martyrs, of each Sex, is an undeniable Proof."

113. Cumberland here echoes St. Paul, I Corinthians 15.19: "If in this life only we have hope in Christ, we are of all men most miserable."

§XLIV. Having now *prov'd* what I *first* propos'd, "That those Human Actions which promote the Publick Good, obtain the greatest Advantages for their Reward";[114] the *second* remains to be dispatch'd, "That the conferring these Advantages, or Rewards, by the Appointment of the First Cause, is a sufficient Proof from Nature, that God wills or commands, that Men should in all their Actions perpetually pursue the Publick Good." Because I think I have sufficiently prov'd this already, where I treated of *Punishments,* and of that *Happiness* of the Mind, which is united to Virtue, I shall here contract the Force of that Reasoning into one *Syllogism.*

II. That such Advantages are a natural Declaration of God's commanding such Actions, in pursuit of the Common Good.

The supreme Governor of the World, or First Rational Cause, by whose Will things are so dispos'd, that it is with sufficient clearness discover'd to Men, that some Actions of theirs are necessary Means to an End, which Nature determines to pursue, wills, that Men should be oblig'd to those Actions, or he commands those Actions.

But things are so dispos'd by the Will of God, that it is sufficiently discover'd to Men, that the Pursuit of the Common Good is such a Means to an End plainly necessary to them, by Nature determining them to the Pursuit thereof, namely, their Happiness, which is contain'd in the Common Good, and can with Reason be expected from thence only.

Therefore it is his Will, that they shall be oblig'd to this Pursuit, or to such Actions as flow from thence: That is, he enjoins Universal Benevolence, which is the Sum of the Laws of Nature.

The *Major* is taken from that Definition of Obligation, which I have before establish'd. The *Minor* is now prov'd. Therefore the *Conclusion* holds good. I am to advertise the Reader, that by *their Happiness* I here mean their true and intire Happiness; which comprehends all the attainable Perfections both of Mind and Body, and extends it-self, not to the present Life only, but to that which is to come, as far as it may be known by the Light of Nature. Likewise by *those Actions which are suppos'd to be the Means of this Happiness,* I understand, principally, the intire Series of Actions thro' the whole course of Life, which may promote that End; tho' every single Action, necessary to procure any part

114. Cumberland refers us back to the start of the discussion at 5.40.

of that true Happiness, is by this Argument prov'd to be commanded by the Author of Nature. It is *necessary* to this constant and solid Happiness (which I treat of) of particular Persons, "That every Rational Being should come to some resolution within himself, concerning some constant Tenor of his Actions looking that way." Such is the natural Constitution of all those Causes, upon procuring the Concurrence whereof that Happiness depends, that the *right Reason* of Men (namely, that which is agreeable to the Nature of Man, and promises the desir'd Effect from Causes which will certainly produce it) can *discover no other Action* of ours *effectual* to produce this *End,* but this only, "That, to our power, we should procure to ourselves the Favour of God and Men by Universal Benevolence." Or, which comes to the same thing, the *Nature* of God and Man rightly consider'd *discovers* this, "That every one uses the best Method in his Power, to procure his own Happiness" (which is a part of the Publick Happiness) "who constantly promotes the Common Good": And therefore it is *necessary,* "That he should thus act, if he would use his utmost Endeavours to make himself Happy." All who form a right Judgment of the Nature of God and Men, in which are contain'd the Causes of the Happiness of every particular Person, *may agree* in this consistently with the care of their own Happiness; and they are mov'd or solicited by sufficient Discoveries from Nature, and, consequently, from its Author, that they should *actually agree,* "That this Proposition is perpetually true, and the perpetual Rule and Law of Action." Altho' it may *sometimes,* but very rarely, *happen,* "That *some particular Person* may obtain for a time some greater Advantages, than what are consistent with the Common Good"; yet because, "If the whole course of Existence be taken into consideration, greater Happiness may be obtain'd by neglecting those Advantages, than by pursuing them," *that Person* cannot reckon them among the Parts of his greatest possible Happiness. Under this *one* most general *Dictate* is comprehended all *Philosophy Moral, Civil,* and *Oeconomical,* all true *Prudence,* and every *Virtue.* By this Method we shall best consult the Interest, both of others, and ourselves; nor shall we disturb the Order of Nature, by making all Things *subordinate to ourselves,* which was the *second* Objection.

§XLV. I will now proceed to the Solution of that *Objection* which *sug-gests,* "That the Effect of my Method of deducing the Laws of Nature, is, that the Common Good, and, consequently, the Honour of God, and the Happiness of all other Men, will be postpon'd to the Happiness of every particular Person, and be made subservient thereto, as to the chief End." Far be it from me to advance any such Doctrine. On the contrary, I here endeavour to establish, what overthrows the very Foundation of that Opinion, because I have *asserted,* "That no Man has a Right to Life, or to the Necessaries thereof, but so far as the Life of every Man is either a Part, or a Cause, of the Common Good, or at least consistent with it." But I will here distinctly shew the *Consistency* of these things.[115]

Obj. 2. That by the Author's Method the Common Good (the Honour of God, as well as the Happiness of other Men) is postpon'd to the Happiness of every particular Person.

Answ. No; for

---

115. [Maxwell] "This *Objection* against our Author and some other Moralists, is very unjust; 'tis perhaps true, that 'No Action can be called Virtuous, so far as the Agent is excited to it by Private Interest, or Self-Love.' And yet it is plainly impossible for any Moralists to set other Motives to Action before Men, but these from Self-Love. These Motives will not excite Benevolent Affections directly, since no Man can love another, only out of intention to obtain private Good to himself: But Benevolence is really Natural to all Men, and the only Reason why it does not excite them to act for Publick Good, is this, That upon some false Views they imagine their private Interest would be oppos'd by it. Remove these false Views, and Benevolence, when the seeming Obstacle is remov'd, must influence Men: Nay, Self-Love must conspire with it, to excite to the very same Actions. Moralists indeed may do this to raise Benevolent Affections, (which perhaps we cannot call proposing Motives to Action,) viz. *represent* Objects as morally Good. Such Representation does necessarily raise Benevolent Affections. This our Author has done in his Representation of the Goodness of the Deity, and the Constitution of Human Nature, in opposition to the Odious and Horrible Idea *Hobbes* has given of both. This our Author's Scheme, tho' it raises Mens Attention to their Actions, first from regard to their Private Interest, does not necessarily represent all Virtue, as only the Effects of Self-Love, or intended ultimately for private Good.

"According to our Author's Scheme, Private and Publick Good never interfere, but are perfectly connected, and the same Actions are productive of both.

"If it be *objected,* 'That, by our Author's Scheme, the Force of moral Obligation consists in Rewards and Punishments:' I *answer,* 'That, consistently enough with our Author's Scheme, Benevolence does morally oblige, as well as Rewards and Punishments.' For the only Obligation to Action, which Human Nature admits of, is the Influencing of the Human Will: But Benevolence influences to Volition, as well as the Determination of the Understanding, with regard to the greater Good. It may

I. The Rational
pursuit of a
Man's own
Happiness
obliges him to
pursue the
Common
Good, the
Honour of
God, and the
Happiness of
other Men.

First then I am to *observe,* "That natural Obligation is not discover'd by Man in the same Order, in which it is founded and establish'd in Nature by the Author thereof." We are under the necessity of first using the *Analytical* Method, by rising from those *Effects* which immediately affect us, to various and very complicated *second Causes,* 'till at length we arrive at the *First.* But we are by no means injurious to him, if at the End of our inquiries we *acknowledge,* "That all those *necessary* Effects which we had before observ'd, ow'd their Original to his Will; and, if we refer to him all that Perfection, which we had taken notice of in them." So, with respect to our present Subject, we *have* first "some Knowledge of our own Nature, and of the Necessity of some things to its Happiness, and of some plainly natural Propensions and Endeavours to obtain such Necessaries." We then *observe,* "That some free Actions of ours are, whether we will or no, naturally oppos'd and restrain'd, as far as in them lies, by those with whom we have to do; while others of our Actions (such as are beneficial to others) are chearfully recompens'd with reciprocal Affection"; we further *perceive* "ourselves so fram'd by Nature, that we incline, with out deliberation, *to repel Force with Force,* and, *to return Like for Like*";[116] nor does the most consummate Reason

---

therefore, with as much Reason, be allow'd me to *say,* 'That the Force of moral Obligation consists in our Love of the Deity, and of our Fellow-Citizens,' as to the *Objector,* 'That it consists in the Rewards and Punishments, with which the Laws of Nature are enforc'd.' The *Truth* being, 'That both Benevolence and Self-Love morally oblige;' sometimes each operating singly, but, for the most part, both jointly concurring in exerting their Power, with regard to the same Action.

"If it be *objected,* 'That, according to our Author's Scheme, the Principle of self-Love is more strong and uniform than that of Benevolence.' Or, 'That we have a stronger and more constant Desire of our own Happiness, than of the Happiness of others.' I *answer,* 'That I don't see, that our Author has advanc'd any thing from which it particularly follows, That we desire our own Advantage more strongly than that of others.' However, I am of Opinion, that it is so in most People, and that it is not inconsistent with Virtue: Nevertheless, I believe there are some, of so exalted and generous a Disposition, as to entertain as great, nay, a greater, Desire of the general Good of Mankind, than of any private Advantage; and that a Desire of doing things that are pleasing and agreeable to the Will of God, proceeding from a pure disinterested Benevolence, is, in some, more vehement and forceable, than any particular Affection for private Good."

116. Cf. Seneca, *De Beneficiis,* IV.16–17.

dictate otherwise. From innumerable and perpetual Observations of this kind, and others that I have before suggested, the Mind of Man becomes *persuaded*, "That the Benevolence of each towards all paves the way to the Rewards and Happiness of all other Men alike; and that so much the more, by how much it is the more diffusive." When afterwards the Mind *considers*, "That this is all effected by the most provident Author of Nature," it cannot *doubt*, "But that he would have this regarded by Men, as it really is, to be a sufficient Argument afforded by the supreme Governor of the World, to incline them to the exercise of Universal Benevolence": That is, (as I have shewn,) as a *Proof* of our *Obligation*, and a certain *Mark* of the *Law* enjoining it. Altho', therefore, this be *last* discover'd, yet *here* the Obligation of the Laws of Nature takes its *first* Rise, namely, from the *Discovery* of the WILL OF GOD, whom, from his Works, we had learn'd to be a most perfect Being, the Cause of all Things, upon whose Pleasure depends the whole Happiness of All, and consequently our own, concerning which we are naturally most solicitous. The *Obligation arises* no otherwise from the *Love of our own Happiness*, than the *Truth* of Propositions concerning the Existence of Things natural, and of their First Cause, which is thence discover'd, *arises* from the Credit given to the *Testimony of our Senses*. Yet no-one would *say*, "That we, therefore, preferred our *Senses* to the whole World, and to God himself"; since we readily *acknowledge*, "That *their very Existence*, and all their Use, depends upon God as their First Cause, and upon the System of the World, as upon Causes subordinate to him." That is *first* in Nature, at which we arrive *last* in this *inverted* Method of Reasoning. Therefore, *altho'* this Method of coming at Knowledge, be evidently natural and very common; *altho'* our Passions also, and several Appetites, are excited according to the discoveries we make of Good and Evil; *yet* we may not, therefore, *thence* affirm, what is most worthy to be known, or amiable above all other things. But, *as* by the help of our *Senses*, we learn some very general Principles, (as for *Example*, the most universal Theorems of *Arithmetick* and *Geometry*,) whereby we may successfully *correct* those Errors, which the generality are wont to imbibe from *misapprehended Sensations; in like manner*, from the *Love of our own Happiness*, under the conduct of *Prudence*, all who are truly Rational attain such a *Knowledge* of Natural Things and of God himself, and such *Affections* towards his Honour, and the Common Happiness of all, as either prevent or *root out* all *perverse Self-Love:* Those, (or at least some of those,) first Natural and Necessary Appetites, which we suppose in Men, of procuring their own Preservation and Happiness, are confin'd within a very narrow compass, and are perfectly free from *Fault;* as our simple Sensations, with respect to the proper objects of our Senses, under proper Regulations, are free from *Error.*[117] Which were it otherwise, there would be no hope left, either of *knowing* Nature, or of *conforming* our Actions to the Laws of Nature; but a fruitless and perpetual *Scepticism* would be necessarily introduc'd into the place of *Science,* and a *casual Determination* of our Actions into that of *Prudence,* and the regular Conduct of our Passions; and there would be no difference between the Wise Man and the Fool.

Because, from the *Knowledge* and *Love* of those *Effects,* which immediately affect us, our Mind, by natural methods, comes to *know* and *love* all those various *Causes* upon which we depend, especially those Causes which are *Rational;* which *recommend* themselves to our *Understanding* and *Passions,* not only upon account of the *Effects* which they produce, but also of the *Resemblance of their Nature to our own;* it is *evident,* "That those first *Notions* which we form of ourselves, and *Inclinations* towards our own Happiness, are only, as it were, *Steps* to the *Knowledge* of more exalted Objects, and to *Affections* more diffus'd and more intense, in proportion to that Goodness and Perfection which we discover in other Objects." It is certainly too *plain* to need proof, "That the Degrees and *Measure* of our *Love* do *not* depend upon the *Order of Time,* when the Objects begin to be known or lov'd; *but* upon our Judgment of that *Measure* of natural *Goodness,* which we discover in Persons and Things." I have *prov'd,* in the Chapter *concerning Good,* "That any thing is esteem'd *good,* not with respect to ourselves only," which alone *Hobbes* acknowledges in a State of Nature, "but upon account of the Influence it has in preserving or perfecting others, especially that Aggregate Body, which is compos'd of all Rational Beings." This *Goodness*

117. Cf. Cicero, *De Finibus,* V.ix.24.

or Happiness will readily be acknowledgd to be *greater* in all Mankind, than in any single Person; but in God by far the *greatest;* he will, therefore, be *amiable above all* Things.

The *whole Matter* therefore is reduc'd to *this Point;* we are *excited* by the *Love of our own Happiness,* (which we look upon as a thing that may be effected,) to *consider* those *Causes* upon which it depends; those especially, which have the principal share in effecting it, and which are inclin'd, according as we behave, to increase or diminish it; such are *God* and all *other Men.* Upon a through examination of the *Nature* of these Causes, we *observe* in them a Perfection and Goodness, or an *aptness to preserve* and *improve* the State of the Universe, evidently *like* to what render'd us amiable to ourselves; but in God we perceive it infinitely *greater.* Farther; we find that *every one* of them is no less *determin'd by its own Reason,* to pursue those things which are agreeable to its *own Happiness,* than we ourselves are; so that there is evidently *no Reason,* "Why we should either desire or expect, that all should be subservient to us, rather than to others, or themselves."

§XLVI. There is but *one way of reconciling all Rational Beings to all and every one,* so far as the Frame of the Universe permits; and *that* Reason suggests from the *Knowledge of a Sum* or Aggregate of Particulars, a Knowledge peculiar to Rational Beings, namely, *That all should agree in and pursue one End, the Common Good.* This every particular Person may easily do, because the Nature of every Rational Agent is possess'd of an *Understanding* in some measure comprehending it, and of a *Will* inclinable to pursue it. For by this means the Happiness of Individuals will be provided for, in the best manner that the Nature of Things permits; for each Individual is a Part of the Community: But that Happiness which any one may *rashly* hope for, which is *inconsistent* with the *Happiness of the Aggregate Body* compos'd of all Rational Beings, is *impossible,* as being *inconsistent* with the determinate *Force of Causes much more powerful* than the Will of him, who aims at such Happiness; and, therefore, cannot be rationally propos'd.

The only way of reconciling all Rational Agents being, That all should agree in and pursue one End, The Common Good.

This I would chiefly have *observ'd,* "That, tho' the Care of *our own Happiness* led us to *consider* the Nature of Rational Causes; yet that *Reason* which is essential to all, and the natural Determinations of their *Will* to pursue their possible Happiness; and all that *Perfection* and *Goodness,* which we perceive in them relating to the State of the Universe, do both *enable* them to propose to themselves this Common End, and *make it necessary,* "That they should resolve actually to pursue it, if they would come to any rational Resolution concerning their own Practice." For *that* is the only End, in pursuit of which all *can conspire;* and it is most *certain,* "That no Method of Action can be propos'd according to right Reason, in which all cannot agree." Therefore there arises a *necessity* from the common Nature of Rational Agents, that every one, by the exercise of *Universal Benevolence,* should always seek the *Common Good,* and *his own* only as a *Part* thereof, and consequently *subordinate* thereto, which is the Sum of the Law of Nature.

Altho' the Nature of all other Rational Beings, among which every Man may reckon his own, discovers to us, what, in the present System, is necessary to be done, in order to obtain an End, greater than our own Happiness, which End will yet bring along with it the fullest Enjoyment of that, so far as it can be obtain'd; *yet because* in this System of Rational Beings, there is but one Author, Preserver, and Lord of All, at whose pleasure all that is necessary to the Happiness of all others is principally dispos'd; and the Necessity of pursuing this End, and of exerting suitable Actions, as the Means to attain it, does, consequently, proceed from his Will made known to us by his Works: "The Obligation to such Actions is justly ascrib'd to his Will alone, as commanding them."

In the *Analysis* of the *Question* which we propose, "concerning the Method of acquiring the Happiness of any particular Person in any given Circumstances," it *happens,* (what may perhaps seem strange to many, tho' very usual in *Geometrical Analysis;*) "That at the End of the Inquiry is found, not only that which was at first sought after, but also other matters relating to the Subject, about which the Proposer of the Question was not at all solicitous." For,

First, there comes out an Answer, or *general Solution,* which is not suited to the Circumstances of that one Person only, but of any other, as equally depending upon God and other Men; nay, whole Nations are directed by the same method to their Happiness. This Universal Benevolence, and all those Precepts which are contain'd in the Care of the

Common Good, do oblige, both every Man, and whole Nations, for the same reason that they are to be observ'd by any one, as is evident upon consideration.

Secondly, it appears from the same *Analysis, how the Question* (which was propos'd without any Limitation) *must be limited,* to make the Solution possible and certain. For it is *requir'd,* "That the Happiness propos'd by any one be such, as may be consistent with the Nature and determinate Inclinations of other Rational Causes, whose force is greater"; that is, "That it be consistent with, and subservient to, the Honour of God, and the Common Good of Men." Whoever would propose to himself any other Happiness, is *admonish'd* by this Solution, "that his desire is to be look'd upon as an impossible Problem, and therefore to be wholly rejected." I forbear mentioning *Geometrical Examples* of such Solutions, because they are familiar to the skilful in the Analytick Art, and to others they would be ungrateful, and seem too foreign to our purpose. And this may serve for the *First* Part of our Answer to the propos'd Objection.

§XLVII. I add *Secondly,* "That the End of the Legislator, and also of him who fulfils the Law of Nature, is far greater and more excellent, than the avoiding that Punishment, or the obtaining that Reward, whence the Law receives its Sanction, and which is what immediately affects every Subject; though the Obligation of every Subject to yield Obedience be indeed, immediately, discover'd by those Rewards and Punishments." For the *End,* that is, the Effect directly intended by *both,* is the *Publick Good,* the Honour of the Governor, and the Welfare of all his Subjects. But these are manifestly *greater* than the *Happiness* of any *single Person,* who pays Obedience to the Law. No-one does truly observe the Law, unless he sincerely propose the same End with the Legislator. But, if he directly and constantly aim at this End, it is *no diminution* to the *Sincerity* of his Obedience, "that, at the Instigation of his own Happiness, he first perceiv'd, that his Sovereign commanded him to respect a higher End." Laws would receive the *Sanctions* of Rewards and Punishments *in vain,* "unless the Consideration of them might be effectual, to incline those Subjects, whose Happiness they increase or diminish, to a sincere

2. The End of the Legislator, and of the Observer of the Law of Nature, is far greater than the Sanction, which regards the Private Happiness of any Individual.

and intire Obedience." For *such a Sanction* is added to the Law for this *very Purpose,* "That it might incline the Subjects to pursue a greater End

than every one his own Happiness." Therefore, when *Moral Writers* speak of *every Man's Happiness* as *his ultimate End,*[118] I would willingly *interpret* them in this sense, "That it is the chief End among those, which respect the Agent himself only"; and I doubt not, but that every *Good Man* has an End, that is, intends an Effect, that is greater, namely, the Honour of God, and the Increase of other Mens Happiness. I conceive the *one chief End* or best Effect, to be compos'd of our own Happiness, and that of all other Rational Beings, (which we endeavour as opportunity offers.)

Our present *Inquiry* is, *not* that common one of the antient *Philosophers,* "which of several good Things possible is greater, and, therefore, more industriously to be pursued"; but, supposing Human Happiness is made up of the Concurrence of many good Things of different kinds, and may be successively enjoy'd thro Man's whole natural course of existence, the *Question* is, whilst we are in pursuit of a continual Succession of such Advantages, or even greater; "Whether the Nature of Rational Causes, on which depends the Hope of this Happiness, requires, That I should procure their Favour by preferring the Common Good of all to my own private Happiness, and by considering that only as a Part of the Common Happiness, which cannot be procur'd; unless that of the Whole be preserv'd intire?" *Or,* "Whether the Nature of Rational Causes does rather admonish, that I should endeavour to secure my-self by preventing others, by Force or Fraud, as if they naturally regarded the Good of themselves alone, and were therefore my Enemies?" This is plainly enough Mr. *Hobbes's* Doctrine, *De Cive* C. 5. §. 1.[119] But I apprehend such a *natural Benignity* in Rational Agents, as inclines them to befriend all others, provided they will concur with them to promote the Common Good. The *Cause* of this Benignity is, "That all, the more Reason they

118. Cf. Aristotle, *Nicomachean Ethics,* I.7.

119. Hobbes, *On the Citizen,* 5.1, p. 69: "Each man's hope therefore of security and preservation, lies in his using his strength and skill to stay one step ahead of his neighbour either openly or by stratagems."

are endow'd with, are the more ready to consent to this End, as the greatest of all, and to judge, that their own Happiness can be best promoted by this method only":[120] Whence it *follows,* "That every one of these is inclinable, either by Words or Actions to propose this End to others, and to enforce it by Persuasion, as soon as there is an opportunity of meeting, and that no one can rationally with-hold his Consent"; so that we *ought not* to presume of any one, that he would refuse to consent to this End, except we have sufficient Proof, that he hath divested himself of right Reason; but *ought* to treat all others, as if they had expressly concurr'd with us in such Consent. But on this very *account,* "that any one resolves with himself to pursue the Common Good, preferably to that of any particular Person," he proposes to himself an *End* compos'd of *his own* Happiness and that *of others,* and obtains some Part of it, whenever he benefits either others or himself, ever so little, without hurting any other Person.

Upon this occasion it may be very pertinent to *observe,* "That an *End* is not that only, which any Rational Agent enjoys," (His own proper Happiness for *Instance,*) "but all the whole Effect, which he wittingly, willingly, and designedly produces, or endeavours to produce." And hence those things which we *advisedly* do, that we may profit or please others, are no less justly to be esteem'd *our Ends,* than that inward Happiness, with which we are formally blessed. That *internal Happiness* of any one seems to me upon no other account to be called *his End,* than "as all the Parts thereof are *Effects,* towards which, as points in view, our Actions and Affections are *directed by Reason."* Nor can any Reason be assign'd, why *"other Effects,* towards which, as certain Aims plac'd with-

[Marginal note:] The End of a Rational Agent is, not only his own Happiness, but every Effect, which he intends to produce: His *principal* End is that which limits all his Actions, in pursuit of his *other* Ends.

120. [Maxwell] "The Benignity of Human Nature is in part only, not wholly, resolvable into Conclusions of Reason. We have kind Affections, wherever there is no opposition of Interest, even before any Reasoning, in the same manner in which we love our-selves, tho' generally in a weaker degree. Our Benignity, in nearer Ties, sometimes continues, where there is opposition of Interest, as toward Off-spring and Friends, whose Ease and Pleasure we sometimes study more than our own, and without intention of our own. Reason indeed, as our Author excellently explains, does confirm and direct both these Affections."

out us, such kind of Actions and Affections are *directed by the same Reason,* may not for the same Cause be called *Ends.*"

Farther; among such Ends, that is justly look'd upon as *Chief,* upon account whereof, according to the Dictates of right Reason, we willingly limit our Operations relating to all other Ends whatsoever, even those which respect our own Happiness. But from the consideration of the Common Good, as our intire and adequate End, and of our own Happiness as a small Part thereof, we determine all those Operations which respect our-selves. *Therefore* I make the *Common Good* the *chief End* in that Method, which I here prescribe to Human Actions.

The Proof of the *Minor* is evident from what I have advanc'd in the *First Chapter,* where I *prov'd,* "That the Measure of good Things every one is intitul'd to, and may rationally seek, is no otherwise to be determin'd and settled, than by that Proportion he bears to the System of all Rational Beings, or to the whole natural KINGDOM OF GOD." Perfectly in the same manner as the Nourishment fit for the Preservation and Increase of each particular Member in a healthful Animal is determin'd, by that Proportion which it bears to the most flourishing State of the whole Body.

§XLVIII. We are necessarily led, to make this *Limitation* of the Happiness we hope for, by those Principles I have laid down, representing God and other Men, as the *voluntary* Causes thereof, so that it is necessary for us, (the Nature of God and Men requiring it,) to procure their *Favour,* by gratifying them in all things, as by far the greatest and *principal Parts* of the whole natural Community, before we can with reason expect their *Assistance,* which is plainly *necessary to our Welfare.* For, "In acting for an End, it is perfectly repugnant to Reason, to hope for, or intend, any other Effect, than what is determin'd from the Nature of all those Causes, especially the principal ones, which concur thereto." And, therefore, "Since the principal Causes of our Happiness are other Rational Agents, beside ourselves, only such a Measure thereof ought to be expected, as the Will and Reason of such Causes, which are naturally necessary thereto, will permit." For, *altho'* in the *Investigation* of *Causes* (as in the *Solution* of *Problems*) we begin at the *Effects,* of which we have, for the most part, only a *confus'd* Idea, or barely wish for, (which is every one's possible Happiness, in our general Conception of it,) *yet* (having finish'd the *Analysis,* and *distinctly* discover'd and rang'd in our Minds the Consequences, as well as their immediate Effects,) in Action we proceed *Synthetically,* from weighing, and considering, and procuring the Assistance of particular *Causes,* (God, for *Instance,* and Mankind, which precede in the Order of Nature,) to those good *Effects* relating to the publick Happiness, which may be obtain'd by their Powers and natural Tendencies concurring with our Endeavours. Just as in the Construction of Geometrical Problems, we use a regular *Synthesis,* (which the *Analytick* Method had before discover'd,) which, from the real or suppos'd Position of Points, or drawing of the most simple Lines, and their known Properties, throughly determines the Nature of the Effect desir'd.

Let us *illustrate* this whole matter by an easy *Geometrical Similitude.* One has occasion to *find* out a *Mean Proportional* between two given Lines; he presently makes an *Analytical* Inquiry into the *Causes* by which that may be determin'd, and *finds,* "that by the *Circumference of a Circle,* whose Diameter is the Sum of the two given Lines, the business may be most conveniently done."[121] Here then *another Operation,* and that *greater* than the drawing one strait Line, namely, the Mean Proportional wanted, is offer'd to the consideration of our Geometrician. The two given Lines are to be connected, and the middle Point is to be found out in the Line compos'd of them both. With this Center, and the Distance thence measur'd to either End of the compound Line is to be describ'd a Circle, from whose Circumference a Perpendicular let fall upon the Point of Connexion of the two Lines, will finish the affair. It is *evident* in this *Construction,* "That the *Synthetick* Method is requisite; and that the Operations of our *Geometrician* are not directed *only* by a respect had to the Length of *that right Line* which he seeks, *but also* by the consideration of the Nature of the *Center, Diameter, Circumference,* and *Perpendicular* to be let fall upon the given Point": For "from the *Natures* or Definitions of these, and their mutual *Relations,* the *Efficacy* of the

This illustrated by the Geometrical Method of finding and a Mean Proportional

121. Euclid, *Elementa Geometriae,* VI. Prop. 13.

Practice to obtain the End desir'd, is *demonstrated*"; from them is also *prov'd,* "That the same Construction is sufficient to determine the Length, not of this one Line only, but of innumerable others of the like kind, which may perhaps be of use to others"; because that Diameter may be divided in any Point thereof into two other right Lines, between which the *same Circle* exhibits a *Mean Proportional,* which, upon another Occasion, may perhaps be of use to *some other,* or to *himself. In like Manner,* all particular Men, in their natural search after Happiness, *first discover,* "That the Object of their Pursuit ought to be a determinate Measure of Good, *proportionable* to their Wants, which is somewhat distincter than their Idea of the Happiness they are in search of." *Afterwards* they make a stricter Inquiry into (the Causes, whence such Good is to be hop'd for, and proceeding in their *Analysis* from the next immediate Causes, to those which are more remote from us in the System of Things, are led by Nature to *understand,* "That all the Rational Agents about us are to be regarded as Causes upon which we in some measure depend, and are accordingly to be made our Friends by Universal Benevolence." Wherefore this *Analysis instructs* us, "That a *greater End* is to be pursued, than what *at first offer'd* it-self to our view, as what, from the Nature of the Universe, (of which we are a Part,) our own greatest Happiness is necessarily connected with; and, therefore, we must either pursue it in conjunction with that nobler End, the Publick Good, (the Honour of God and Happiness of Mankind;) or throw away all hopes thereof, founded in the Nature of Things." These discoveries thus made by the *Analysis* of those Causes, the Mind applies it-self to the prosecution of that *nobler End,* (in which our own Happiness is abundantly contain'd,) and ranks and rates all Causes, according to the *Measure* of the Powers and Inclinations it finds in them with respect to this End. Hence, since it perceives that *God* and *Men,* both *can* and *will* contribute *most* to this End, as *their* Common Good is the *End;* it acknowledges, that *their* Powers are the Causes, or *fittest* Means thereto; and therefore it unites it-self to them and makes use of them, in a manner agreeable to their *Rational* Nature and Dignity, that is, either by *proposing* to them some things to be done which may conduce to this End, or by *consenting* with them in such Actions as they convince us to be *necessary,* or at least discover to be *permitted* without prejudice to this End. Since all these things are done for the sake of this *noblest End alone,* it *follows,* "That we, thro' our whole Train of Action, and, consequently, thro' our whole Course of Life regulated according to this method, will *unite* ourselves to those Causes, which we know most able and willing to promote that End, that is, God especially, and Good Men; and *prefer* the greater Parts of this End, before the lesser; Publick Advantages, for *Example,* before Private, &*c.*" that is (to pursue the *Parallel*) when we proceed to operation, we shall in the first place take care to find out the *Center* and first Principle of that most noble Problem which is propos'd, and to keep our *due distance* from it; that is, we shall have an Eye to *God,* and those Discoveries of his Will, which are visible in his Works, afterwards considering those *particular Men,* which every way *encompass* us, as the infinite Points of the *Circumference,* and preserving inviolably that Order and Situation of all, which is establish'd by the First Cause, by the help of a *Circular Motion,* or of *Benefits mutually exchang'd,* we at length find out a *happy Opportunity,* as the *Point of Connexion* of the two Lines, in which what is sufficient for us may be allow'd without Injury to others; and so the Measure *proportionate* to our Condition, that we may promote the Good of the whole System, is *limited* by all others *around* us, as the Length of the *Mean Proportional* inquir'd after, is *determin'd* by the *Circumference.* Mean-while it is owing to this most noble *Motion of reciprocal Beneficence,* that others reap *like,* and often, as occasion offers, *greater* Benefits, than those we obtain for ourselves; as by drawing the *same Circle,* not only a *Mean Proportional* may be found out between two given Lines, but also *like Mean Proportionals* between infinite other Lines, into which the same Diameter may be divided; and those *Means* useful to others may be often *greater* than that we have occasion for. Lastly; the Power, *Perfection,* and Rank of the *Circle* among Figures, is not *valued* by the *skilful Geometrician* from any *single* Effect, but from *all* its Effects united, or from the Construction of all Problems, which may be any way solv'd by it. *In like manner,* every *Rational* Person will *value* the *Perfection* and inward Force of the *First Cause, and of all Mankind,* not only from that Influence upon *his own* Happiness he discovers in them, but from that prodigious *variety* and *greatness* of Effects, which have hitherto proceeded, or may hereafter proceed, from these Causes; but especially from the Good of the Universe, or the Common Happiness of all Rational Beings, which is daily preserv'd, and even increas'd, by their Powers. For the only Measure of Power, is the Sum of all its Effects, and, therefore, the Power of Beneficence is to be estimated from the Aggregate of all the Benefits thence arising. And the natural *Rank* among Beneficent Causes, is according to the *Measure* of their Beneficence, so that the *less Beneficent* may, with respect to this Attribute, be called *Inferior*, or Subordinate, to the more Beneficent; as in an increasing or *ascending Series* of Numbers, the *smaller* are called *Inferior*.

§XLIX. It is hence *manifest*, "That our Minds are sufficiently instructed, from the Natures and essential Powers of Things, how to form a just Judgment or Estimation of the *Goodness, Order*, and *Dignity* of Things; and that, not from their Relation to ourselves little Mortals, but to the whole collective Body of Rational Beings, or to that whole SOCIETY, of which GOD is the HEAD; altho', perhaps, the first *Inducement* to a more strict *Inquiry* into the Nature of all Things, was a regard to *our own Happiness*."

It is likewise *evident*, "That, if we will *compare* the Parts of that greatest End, of which I have been treating, and contemplate their *Order* among themselves, that Part of the End will be *Superior*, which is grateful to the Nature of the more perfect Being. So that the *Glory of God* is *Chief, then* follows the *Happiness of many Good Men*, and *Inferior* to this is the *Happiness of any particular Person*."

Among the *Means* to this End or *Causes* of this Effect, each will claim a *greater* Share of *Esteem, Love*, and *Care*, as it is *more Effectual* to obtain that End; whence the *first Place* will here be given to *God*, the *next* to the Assistance of the *most* and *best Men*; but any *particular* Person, (and consequently, he that deliberates with himself upon his own Affairs,) will take up with the *lowest Place*, if he act agreeably to the Nature of Things.

And thus, I think, I have abundantly remov'd all Suspicion of any Consequences from *my Method*, which might prefer the Happiness of any single Person, to the Honour of God, or the Publick Good.

> The Natures of Things are not to be estimated from any one *particular*, but from their adequate Effect.

But lest any one should *take offence,* "That even the First Cause and all Mankind should be consider'd as the Means to that noblest End, a small Part whereof is the Happiness of any particular Person"; I think it proper here openly to *affirm,* what I have often hinted, "That these Words, [*End*] and [*Means*], are only external Denominations ascrib'd to *Effects* and *Causes,* so far as they proceed from the Deliberation and Intention of Rational Agents": Any *Effect* propos'd by them is call'd an *End,* and any *Cause,* whose force contributes any thing towards it, is call'd the *Means.* But such *extrinsick* Denominations are neither the proper Measures of the *intrinsick* Perfection of Things, nor of that *Esteem* they are in with others. For it is *obvious,* "That neither God, nor the Body of Mankind, lose ought of their Dignity or Honour, by voluntarily contributing to the Happiness of an Inferior."

The Words, [*End*] or Effect, [*Means*] or Cause, are only *external* Denominations, no way measuring the *inward* Perfection of Things.

"A particular Effect may be far inferior to its Cause, and is generally so reputed"; and therefore the *particular End,* at which a Rational *Agent* aims, may be *less noble* than himself. It is sufficient, if his whole or *adequate End* be agreeable to his *Dignity.* However, the *Honour* of *superior* Causes is sufficiently provided for, even when they condescend to the *lowest* Effects, both because they do it *voluntarily* and *deliberately,* and because there is *no other Method* of procuring their Assistance, but by consenting *voluntarily* to serve their *Interest,* in denying to ourselves whatever is dearest to us, if at any time the Publick Good so requires.[122]

Every particular Effect is Inferior to its Cause.

Farther; that great Joy, in which great Part of the Happiness of every particular Man consists, is founded in the *Consciousness,* of our having endeavour'd in our past Life, and of our firm Resolution and Disposition of endeavouring for the future, to please both God and Men; and in a sincere *Will* to contribute to, and rejoice in, the Happiness of all

---

122. [Maxwell] "When it is *objected,* 'That Virtue is intended for the Pleasure of the Agent, and, consequently, that all Ends are subordinate to Private Good;' it is to be *consider'd,* 'That in virtuous Actions the Intention of Agents is the Good of others, or Pleasing the Deity from Gratitude, either without Intention of Private Good, or with this Intention only as concomitant to some kind Affection—. There is a plain difference to be made between the natural Tendency of an Action to make the Agent Happy; and the Design which the Agent had in doing it, or that which he chiefly desir'd to be effected by his Action. Private Good is not in this sense the Design, at least not the sole Design, of virtuous Actions.'"

others. So that it is impossible, that he who seeks *such* Happiness to himself, should be found guilty of *selfishness*. For in this manner he *repays* others the Happiness he has receiv'd from them, as a River returns into the Ocean the Waters it has thence receiv'd.

(Hobbes denies, That the Laws of Nature, in a State of Nature, oblige to external Actions, and that for want of Security.) §L. Having, as I hope, at length *remov'd* those *Difficulties,* which seem'd to *weaken* some Part of *my Method* of deducing the Laws of Nature, and their Obligation; let us now proceed to *examine Hobbes's Principles,* by which "he endeavours to *destroy intirely all Obligation of the Laws of Nature to external Actions,* and so leaves them only the Name of Laws, and that but improperly; and allows every one a Right in the State of Nature to violate them at pleasure, that is, as often as the Authority of the State is either silent, or can be evaded."[123] He offers only one Reason in the Places referr'd to, for wholly denying their Obligation, in that State, to external Actions; Because *"we cannot be secure, that others will observe them, in those things which respect our Preservation";* Hence he infers, *"That every one's whole Hope of Security consists in this, that he should prevent his Neighbour by his own Force or Contrivance, either openly*

---

123. Hobbes, *On the Citizen,* 3.33 [Maxwell's translation]: "The Law of Nature is not, properly speaking, a law"; ibid., 3.27 [Maxwell's translation]: "Because most Men are apt, thro' an unjust Desire of present Advantage, to neglect the Observance of the aforesaid Laws, (namely, of Nature,) tho' known to them; if perhaps any, more modest than the rest, should practice the equitable and beneficent Dictates of Reason, whilst others practis'd the contrary, their Practice would be most absurd; for they would not thereby procure to themselves Peace, but sure and speedy Destruction, and those who observ'd the Laws of Nature, would become a Prey to those who did not observe them. We must not therefore imagine, That Men are oblig'd by Nature, (that is, by Reason,) to the Practice of all those Laws, among Men who do not likewise exercise them. We are, however, oblig'd to a Disposition to observe them, whensoever the Observing of them shall seem to conduce to their design'd End. We may therefore conclude, 'That the Law of Nature obliges at all Times, and in all Places, in the *internal Court,* or that of Conscience, not always in the *external Court;*' but only then, when it is consistent with our Security'; ibid., 5.1 [Maxwell's translation]: "Every one's prospect of Security and Self-preservation is owing to this, That he should prevent his Neighbour, by his own Force or Cunning, Openly or by Wiles"; ibid., 5.2 [Maxwell's translation]: "It is a common Observation, *That in War Laws are silent;* and it is true, as well of the *Law of Nature,* as of *Civil Laws,* if we do not respect the inward Disposition, but the outward Actions."

or treacherously." This is *that unanswerable Argument,* which he thinks strong enough to *break* intirely the whole *Force* of the *Laws of Nature,* out of the bounds of Civil Society. For, tho' he would *seem* to leave them some Power, to oblige in the internal Court of *Conscience* to the Study of Peace, it is evident, that he expresses himself thus, only to throw a *Mist* before the *Eyes* of his *unwary* Reader; for, since almost all the Laws of Nature relate only to *external Acts,* and impose only *these Commands,* "Not to arrogate all things by such Acts, but to abstain from hurting the Innocent, to observe Compacts, make grateful Returns for Benefits receiv'd," &c. he must be blind who does not see, that the Force of these Laws is wholly taken away, where he contends, that *external* Actions contrary to these may be *lawfully* done, as in the Places above quoted, and *Chap.* 14. §. 9.[124] and elsewhere. I answer therefore,

First, "That there is *no Necessity of Security,* (especially such as is free from all Cause of Fear,) that others shall likewise observe the Laws of Nature, in order to *oblige* us to *external* Actions in conformity to them." The *Will of the First Cause,* when discover'd, by which he adds his *Sanction* to these Laws enjoining external Action, is in it self a *sufficient Cause of Obligation* to such Actions; and whilst that continues, the Obligation cannot be taken away; (the Divine Will, with respect to this, may be known by those Methods, which I have already explain'd;) altho' the Manners of many are so deprav'd, that they often return Evil for Good.

That Reason insufficient: For

1. Perfect Security is not necessary, to make an Obligation valid; and

This will be made clearer by a *Comparison* with the *Obligation of Civil Laws,* by which Mr. *Hobbes* himself will not deny, that all Subjects are bound to *external* Obedience. Now, tho' all Men are not subject to the *same Human Government,* they are all Members of the great SOCIETY OF RATIONAL AGENTS, WHOSE GOVERNOR IS GOD. And it is *obvious,*

is not afforded by Civil Government, whose Laws are confess'd to oblige to external Acts; and

---

124. Ibid., 14.9, p. 158: "For the natural law did give rise to obligation in the natural state, where, first, nothing was another's (because nature gave all things to all men), and it was consequently not possible to encroach on what was another's; where, secondly, all things were in common, for which reason also all sexual unions were licit; where, thirdly, it was a state of war, and hence licit to kill; where, fourthly, the only definitions were those of each man's own judgement, and that would include the definition of the honours due to parents; finally where there were no public courts and therefore no practice of giving testimony whether true or false."

"That they who are subject to the *same Human Government,* cannot be perfectly *Secure,* either that their *Fellow-Subjects* will observe the Laws of the State, by abstaining from Rebellion, and all Invasion of another's property, or that their chief *Governor* will be both *able* to punish the Transgressors of his Laws, (especially when Factions happen to be powerful,) and *willing* to take the greatest care he can of the Publick Good." The *most Cautious* of those, who have *thrown off* all sense of *Religion,* *think,* "If it be *probable,* that the Magistrate both can and will secure the Authority of his Laws, by protecting the Obedient, and punishing the Disobedient, that there is all the *Security necessary to oblige* us to observe those Laws." *Men of Piety* towards God, (who are incomparably the best Subjects,) do indeed go farther, and *think* "The *Obligation* of Civil Laws sufficiently *firm,* altho' both the *Power* of the Magistrate should be *suspected,* and his *Will* prove *defective,* with respect to many points of his Duty, provided that from their Obedience they procure to themselves Tranquillity of Mind, and a well-grounded Hope of the Divine Favour"; or (in a word) "whilst the *natural* Proofs of *Obligation* to promote the Common Good remain *unshaken.*" From this *Comparison* it is therefore *evident,* "That, if *Hobbes's* Reasoning were conclusive, all *Obligation* of *Civil* Laws would at the same time be *destroy'd*"; and it is impossible, but that their *Force* should be *enervated* by all Principles, which *destroy* or lessen the *Force* of the *Laws of Nature,* because in these is founded, both the *Authority* and Security of *Civil Government,* and the *Energy* of *Civil Laws.*

is an Impossi-
bility.

    I add; Whoever requires absolute or *perfect Security,* concerning *future Human Actions,* whether in a State of Nature, or under Civil Government, requires an *Impossibility;* for the Actions of Men are in their own Nature *Contingent.*

2. There is a
greater compar-
ative Security
in the State of
Nature, by
observing its
Laws in our
External
Actions, than

§LI. *Secondly,* if by *Security* be meant a *State of greater Freedom from fear and hazard of Misery;* I *affirm,* (and the Proof appears from what I have said concerning the Indications of Obligation,) "That God has manifested to all, that, even out of Civil Society, he will be freer from all kind of Evils consider'd together, who shall constantly observe the Laws of Nature by external Actions, than he, who, according to Mr. *Hobbes's*

Doctrine, shall aim at Security to himself, by endeavouring to prevent all others by Force or Fraud";[125] and *therefore,* "this comparative Security is afforded by God to all, even consider'd in a State of Nature." *by entering into Hobbes's State of War.*

We must, however, when we *compare* the Dangers or *Security* of the *Just* (such are they only, who observe the Laws of Nature, even in their external Actions) and of the *Unjust,* in order to observe which of them has the *greatest* Security, take into the account, *not only* those *Evils,* which *both* are liable to from other *Men; but* those *also,* which the *Unjust* bring upon themselves, by an *inconstant* and *inconsistent* manner of Life, by *irregular* Affections, Envy, Anger, Intemperance, *&c.* and those *beside,* which may with reason be fear'd from *God.* Nor are these to be compar'd in *one* Case, or in a *few* Circumstances only, but in *all* Cases and Circumstances which can happen through the *whole* course of our Existence: For it is otherwise impossible we should form a true Judgment, which State of Life, whether *uniform* Justice, or Injustice in all its *inconsistent Forms,* be *most secure.* I have already *prov'd,* "That their Condition is the Happiest, who steddily observe the Law of Nature in all their Actions"; and I will not repeat the Proof. *In the Comparison, all Evils and Dangers should be taken into the account.*

However, I thought fit here to *add,* "That Mr. *Hobbes* himself, (altho', where he treats of the Security requisite to the Observance of the Laws of Nature, he insists wholly upon Security from the Invasion of other Men, and contends, because that is not to be had, that therefore no-one is oblig'd to external Acts of Justice, but that every one has a Right to all Things, and a Right of Warring against every one, *Chap.* 5. §. 1.[126]) elsewhere, as it were forgetting himself, acknowledges some things, but very sparingly, which prove him sensible of a *sufficient Obligation, even to an external Conformity with the Law of Nature,* lest we should fall into other Evils, beside those which may be apprehended from the Invasion of Men." As for *Example,* when he endeavours to *prove,* "That we ought to keep Faith with all," (*De Cive C.* 3. §. 2, 3.) he gives this *Hobbes, inconsistently with his own Scheme, acknowledges some Things, that shew our Obligation to observe the Law of Nature in external Actions, viz. That they who do otherwise,*

125. Ibid., 5.1, p. 69.
126. Ibid.

1. fall into a
Contradiction

Reason, That *"he who breaks his Compact, falls into a Contradiction"*; which he acknowledges to be an *absurdity in Human Practice.* [127] Since therefore, in this *Instance,* he allows it to be *better,* not to break, than to break, a Compact, *lest we fall into a Contradiction;* what reason is there, why we may not *infer Universally,* "Concerning every Law of Nature, and its Obligation, even to external Actions, that it is better, not to violate it by any external Actions in the State of Nature, than to violate it; because the Violation thereof necessarily brings along with it a Contradiction and Absurdity in Practice?" For whoever diligently considers the Nature of all Beings, especially Rational, must acknowledge, that all his possible Happiness naturally *depends* upon the Common Happiness, as upon its adequate Cause; and he wills, therefore, to seek them both *jointly:* But, whensoever he *breaks* any Law of Nature, he wills to *separate* his own Good from that of the Publick, which implies a *Contradiction,* and raises a Civil War in the breast of Man, and miserably disturbs his Tranquillity. That Misery is no contemptible Part of the Punishment naturally inflicted for Crimes, and destroys the *Security* of the Criminal.

2. bring on
themselves
Punishments
annex'd by
God to such
Violation in
the ordinary
Course of
Nature.

Of a piece with this is what he *acknowledges* (*Leviath. Chap.* 31. §. last but one), "That there are Natural Punishments, with which, Transgressions of the Laws of Nature are punish'd in the ordinary Course of Nature"; and in the *English* Edition he expressly acknowledges them to *proceed from God;* so *Violence is punish'd by foreign Force, Intemperance by Diseases,* &c. In the *Latin* Edition this Passage is somewhat maim'd; yet there he acknowledges *Natural Punishments.* [128] But, if these Punish-

127. Ibid., 3.2, p. 44: "Therefore either one should keep faith with every one or one should not make agreements, that is, one must either declare war or maintain a firm and faithful peace"; ibid., 3.3, p. 44: "He who is compelled by arguments to deny an assertion he had previously upheld, is said to be reduced to *absurdity;* in the same way he who, through weakness of will, does or fails to do what he had previously promised by *agreement* not to do or not to fail to do, does a wrong, and falls into a contradiction no less than someone in the schools who is reduced to absurdity."

128. Hobbes, *Leviathan,* ch. 31, p. 243: "Having thus briefly spoken of the Naturall Kingdome of God, and his Naturall Lawes, I will adde only to this Chapter a short declaration of his Naturall Punishments. There is no action of man in this life, that is not the beginning of so long a chayne of Consequences, as no humans Providence, is high enough, to give a man a prospect to the end. And in this Chayn, there are

ments follow the Violations of the Laws of Nature by external Actions, from the inseparable Connexion of Things appointed by God, without all doubt *these Laws will oblige Men to external Actions* conformable to them. For *Punishment cannot be inflicted* upon any one for an Action to which he was not *oblig'd;* and Security is in vain fought for by preventing others by Force or Fraud, if God has appointed a Punishment to such an Invasion.

§LII. Altho' the *Security* of Just Men were to be *estimated* from the consideration of those *Hazards* only, which might be expected from other *Men,* (which, however, is very false;) I think it *evident,* "That there remains more Security to all Just Men, consider'd thro' all the parts of Life, than to all Unjust Men who would seek for Security, according to *Hobbes's* Advice, by preventing others by Force or Fraud, if all Circumstances relating to them be likewise consider'd." Nor do some Examples to the contrary prove it to be otherwise; two Sices have been often thrown at the first Cast of two Dice, tho' it is certain, there are 35 Chances to that one.[129]

Because I have before prov'd this at large, I will here add only *two* Arguments, which bear particularly hard upon Mr. *Hobbes.*

The *first* of these is suggested by the *Presumption of Civil Laws* in our own and all other States; which shews, what Rulers think of Human Nature. *Every Man is presum'd to be good, 'till the contrary be prov'd from*

Tho' Security were to be estimated, in relation only to Hazards from Men; the external Observance of the Law of Nature were a more probable way of obtaining it, than a violent or fraudulent Prevention of others.

1. From the Presumption of Civil Laws, "That Men are

---

linked together both pleasing and unpleasing events; in such manner, as he that will do any thing for his pleasure, must engage himself to suffer all the pains annexed to it; and these pains, are the Naturall Punishments of those actions, which are the beginning of more Harme than Good. And hereby it comes to passe, that Intemperance, is naturally punished with Diseases; Rashnesse, with Mischances; Injustice, with the Violence of Enemies; Pride, with Ruine; Cowardise, with Oppression; Negligent government of Princes, with Rebellion; and Rebellion, with Slaughter. For seeing Punishments are consequent to the breach of Lawes; Naturall Punishments must be naturally consequent to the breach of the Lawes of Nature; and therefore follow them as their naturall, not arbitrary effects." The Latin edition omits everything from "Diseases" to the end of the passage, replacing it with "&c. & tales sunt quas voco Poenas Naturales." ["of such kind are called natural punishments"]. Cf. Hobbes, *Leviathan* (1668), p. 172.

129. Huygens, *Tractatus de ratiociniis in aleae ludo,* Prop. 9.

some Action sufficiently testified. But, because Mr. *Hobbes* every where *affirms,* "That the Reason of the State, or of the supreme Magistrate, only is right and true"; *he* must needs *acknowledge,* "That other Men ought not to be esteem'd so grossly wicked, that we should kill them, tho' yet innocent, for our own Security." They ought rather to be reckon'd so *good,* that we may *safely* keep Faith and Peace with them; *safer* certainly, than by rushing into a War against All. This *Presumption* is of greater force against *Hobbes,* because *he* resolves that Security, which he acknowledges to be found sufficient in Civil States, into those Punishments, by which the Magistrates restrain all Invaders of the Rights of others. Now it is certain, no Punishments are inflicted in any Government, but according to the Sentence of Judges, who always give Judgment according to this *Presumption.* Either therefore this *Presumption* is *true,* and, consequently, *fit to direct Actions* in the State of Nature, or there is *not even in Civil States a sufficient Security* afforded, by Punishments inflicted only according to this *Presumption;* and, consequently, even *Civil Laws do not oblige to external Actions,* and so all States would be dissolv'd. But we *experience,* "That Publick Judgments, given according to this Presumption, do for the most part secure the Life of Man; much more certainly, than if they presum'd all who were brought before their Tribunal to be publick Enemies, and adjudg'd them all to Death, by *Hobbes's* method of *Anticipation.*" Whence it *follows,* "That even the private Judgments of particular Persons made concerning others, according to this Presumption, do conduce more to the Security of *All,* than that rash Presumption of *Hobbes's,* which persuades to prevent all others by Force or Fraud."

2. From hence,
that *Hobbes's*
Universal War
is the necessary
Consequence
of an Universal
Violation of
the Laws of
Nature in
external
Actions. §LIII. The *second Argument* which *proves,* "That the Violation of the Laws of Nature, by external Actions in order to prevent others, affords less Security, than an exact Observance of them," is brought from this; "that from hence," as *Hobbes* himself confesses, "will necessarily follow a War of each against all"; and the *Consequence* is undoubted, if all would take his advice, "that such a War would be inevitable, tho' it were no where Just." This War once suppos'd, he very justly *acknowledges,* "That all would immediately be most miserable, and quickly be de-

stroy'd"; whence I *infer,* "That in vain is Security sought or hop'd for in this Method," contrary to *Hobbes*'s Doctrine, who tells us, *De Cive. C. 5. §. 1. and Leviath. Chap.* 13. That, *"While Men are afraid of one another, no Body can have a better Security, than by Prevention, so that every one should endeavour to oppress all others either by Violence or Fraud, while there are any remaining to be afraid of,"* that is, 'till there remains not one Man but himself, and the Earth is become the common Sepulchre of all the rest.[130] No Man can procure *Aid* in this State, because mutual *Compacts,* by which only one can enter *Society* with others, will *oblige no-one* to external Actions in this State, *de Cive. C. 2. §. 11.*[131] There is, therefore, *no Security* by this method of *Anticipation:* And therefore, if there be but the *least Security* in the Nature, Reason, or *Conscience of Men,* or, if but even a *few* of them do *ever so little* incline to promote the *Common Good,* (in which their own Happiness is contain'd,) they will *spare* the *innocent* and *benevolent* Person, who endeavours by outward Actions to deserve well of them all, and so *his Security* will be *greater* than can be expected by *Anticipation,* because that is certainly *none at all.*

Nay, *Hobbes* himself acknowledges, *"There may be one at least in his State of Nature, who, according to natural Equality, will permit to others the same undisturb'd Enjoyment of all Things which he claims to himself."*[132] Now, if but a *few such* Men should *associate* themselves by mutual *Compacts,* which they will acknowledge *valid* for the sake of that *Common Good* they all endeavour to promote, *those few* will easily defend themselves from *all others at Enmity* and War amongst themselves.

That *Hobbes* did not *perceive,* "That those numberless Evils of a State of War of each against all, are sufficient to deter all in a State of Nature from that mad desire of preventing all others," is very *surprizing;* because

Hobbes gives every Man a Right to commit Treason,

130. Cf. Hobbes, *Leviathan,* ch. 13, p. 75.

131. Hobbes, *On the Citizen,* 2.1, p. 37: "In the state of nature agreements made by a contract of mutual trust . . . are invalid if a just cause for fear arises on either side."

132. Ibid., 1.4, p. 26: "One man practises the equality of nature, and allows others everything which he allows himself; this is the mark of a modest man, one who has a true estimate of his own capacities."

he has asserted *nothing else* beside the *Evils* of such a War, to *deter* Men, who have already erected themselves into a Civil State, from *Treason* and *Sedition,* by which the State is dissolv'd, and all Obligation of Civil Laws is taken away. For he contends, *"That the Sin, which by the Law of Nature is Treason, is a Transgression of the Law of Nature, not of the Law of the State—and therefore, that Rebels and Traitors are punish'd, not as bad Subjects, but as Enemies of the State, not by Right of Empire, but by Right of War."* [133] I take notice here by the way only, that those *two Laws,* that of the *State,* and that of *Nature,* are too crudely and *rashly set in opposition* to one another. Nay, it is dangerous, and tends to *Sedition,* to *affirm,* "That Treason is not a Transgression of the Law of the State, and that Rebels are not punish'd as evil Subjects, by Right of Empire"; but I will not here insist any longer upon this Point.[134] I *ask* of Mr. *Hobbes,* "Whether this Punishment to be inflicted by Right of War, namely, Death, or the Hazard thereof, be a sufficient Proof, that the Law of Nature concerning keeping Compacts, and, in consequence, abstaining from Treason, is obligatory as to external Actions?" If he *denies* it, he allows a Right to commit Treason; and leaves no natural Proof, by which that Law can be known to oblige Subjects to abstain from Rebellion. If he *affirms,* "That this Punishment sufficiently proves the Obligation of Subjects to observe Compacts by external Actions," let him *tell* me, "Why the same Punishment, to be inflicted in a State of Nature by a like Right of War, does not sufficiently prove a like Obligation to observe Compacts by external Actions with all others out of Society?" And the Reason is the same, with respect to all the other Laws of Nature. *Hobbes* is confus'd upon this Head; for in the *Latin* Edition of his *Leviathan,* in the last Consequence drawn from his Definition of *Punishment,* he expresses himself thus, *"Harm inflicted upon one that is a declar'd Enemy, falls not under the Name of Punishment, because Enemies are not Sub-*

---

133. Ibid., 14.21, p. 166: "The sin which is the crime of treason by natural law is a transgression of natural, not civil, law."; Ibid., 14.22 (166): "It follows from this that *rebels, traitors* and others convicted of treason are punished not by *civil right,* but by *natural right,* i.e. not as *bad citizens,* but as *enemies of the commonwealth,* and not by the right of government or dominion, but by the *right of war.*"

134. Cumberland takes up the topic in 9.14.

jects: Altho' they had formerly been Subjects, yet, if they afterwards profess themselves Enemies, they suffer, not as Subjects, but as Enemies. From whence it follows, that, if a Subject shall by Fact or Word, wittingly and deliberately, deny the Authority of the Representative of the Common-Wealth, (whatsoever Penalty hath been formerly order'd by the Law for Treason,) he may be lawfully made to suffer by an arbitrary Punishment, as an Enemy, seeing he hath now profess'd himself an Enemy of the State."[135] In these Words there are *many Passages* deserving *Censure,* which yet all follow from what he had before advanc'd in his Treatise *De Cive,* in the Place above quoted[136]: I will take *notice* of a *few* of them only. 1. He *contradicts himself,* when, in the *Beginning* of them, "He does not comprehend under the Name of Punishment the Evil inflicted upon an Enemy," and at the *latter End* affirms, "That a Rebel, who has already declar'd himself an Enemy, is punish'd, as an Enemy, by an arbitrary Punishment": For an arbitrary Punishment is comprehended under the Name of Punishment. 2. It deserves *Censure,* "That he would not have the Evil inflicted on an open Enemy called Punishment." For it *follows,* "That the Evil inflicted upon a Rebel for Treason, because he has already declar'd himself an Enemy of the State, is not Punishment." Certainly *Punishment* is nothing else than *Evil inflicted for the Transgression of the Law;* and he that denies *Evil inflicted* to be *Punishment,* denies it to be *inflicted for a Crime,* or Transgression of the Law; and *insinuates,* "That an Enemy, and consequently a Rebel, who is now become an Enemy, does not suffer for a Crime, or that he has either not broken any Law, or that he has not, for the Breach thereof, deserv'd Punishment." And, truly, since all *Enemies* are in *Hobbes's State of Nature,* he speaks agreeably to his own *Principles,* if he says they are *not guilty of any Crime;* because they have a *Right* to do any thing: But *Rebels,* according to his Doctrine, are *Enemies,* and, therefore, they are *not* to be *charg'd* with

---

135. Cf. Hobbes, *Leviathan,* ch. 28, pp. 205–6. Cumberland is right to suggest that Hobbes confuses the argument in the Latin edition by arguing that rebellious subjects are punished. Cf. *Leviathan* (1668), p. 148. The English edition consistently argues that enemies cannot be punished as such.

136. Hobbes, *On the Citizen,* 14.21, 22, p. 166.

any *Crime.* Yet they may be *put to Death Arbitrarily,* but *not punish'd,* unless you would, with *Hobbes,* contradict what was said before. So unavoidably does *Hobbes free Rebels* from the Punishment and Guilt of their *Crimes,* who *allows* "to Enemies of all kinds a Right to all Things"; and *denies,* "that the Laws of Nature" (whereof Treason is one Transgression) "oblige to external Actions." And *he allows* "no proper Punishment of Rebellion," *who denies,* "that the Evils of War, into which any one hath thrown himself by violating the Laws of Nature, are Punishments"; and *who contends,* "that Hostile Anticipation, by Force and Fraud, which gives rise to such War, is the readiest way to Security." I think, however, that I have *prov'd,* "That the external Acts of Innocence, Fidelity, Gratitude, and the Aids which they procure, afford any one greater Security out of Civil Society; and that it is therefore better for all, even in a State of Nature, to abstain from invading others, than to endeavour to prevent them by Force or Fraud."

Farther; *Hobbes* Himself *acknowledges,* "That such *comparative Security* is *sufficient* to oblige to external Acts of Obedience to be paid to the Laws, not of Nature only, but also to all those of the State"; for, where he purposely describes this *Security,* he has these Words; *"Nothing else can be contriv'd for this Purpose,"* (namely, sufficient Security,) *"but that every one should procure to himself sufficient aid, by which the Invasion of one another should be render'd so dangerous, that each should think it more adviseable to keep Peace, than make War."* [137] It is evident, that *this Security* is *not perfect,* but that all its force consists in this, that, if the Dangers on both sides be *fairly compar'd* with one another, it may *appear less hazardous,* to keep Peace, than make War. *Altho'* I readily *grant,* "That those Aids which may be procur'd in Civil Society by means of that Fidelity, which most Subjects are wont to yield their Magistrates, do generally render the Invasion of a Fellow-subject much more hazardous"; *yet* I *affirm,* "That, without this Assistance of Civil Aid, there is sufficient Reason, why every one should think it more adviseable to abstain from Invading others, than to engage in a War against all, for the sake of such things as are not necessary." *Hobbes* must needs *own*

137. Ibid., 5.3, p. 70.

"the Danger arising from such a War, greater than all other Dangers," and *therefore* "sufficient to deter any one, in a State of Nature, from invading others"; *because,* upon his Principles, "the Prospect of Evils threatening all from such a War, is the only Reason which deters all, after they have enter'd into Civil Society, from trampling upon the Laws of the State, as well as of Nature, and from dissolving all States by Rebellion, and so relapsing into a State of Nature."

§LIV. I see nothing that *Hobbes* can *reply* to this, except he will shelter himself under that *Principle* peculiar to himself, which I have already refuted; *namely,* "In this State every one is a Judge of his own Actions, whether they are done according to Right and Justice, or not: But he will affirm concerning the Violation of the Laws of Nature, That they are made in order to his own Preservation, and with the View of procuring Peace. Therefore they are rightfully made."[138] Thence is deriv'd what he adds, That *"The Notion of Just and Unjust in the State of Nature, is not to be taken from the Actions, but from the Design and Conscience of the Agents. What is done thro' Necessity, or a desire of Peace, or for Self-preservation, is rightfully done."*[139]

If "every Man be the sole Judge of Right and Wrong in his own Actions," then *Hobbes's Distinction,* "That the Laws of Nature oblige to Internal, but not to External, Actions," is *vain.*

1. If he will abide by that Opinion, I thus *answer,* "That, if this Principle could be depended upon, whoever had no Inclination to observe the Law of Nature in *external* Acts, needs not have recourse to this Distinction, which supposes him oblig'd to observe it in *internal* Acts only, that is, in the Approbation and Desire of his Mind." For, since the *Person himself is Judge,* he may with equal safety *allow,* "That the Law obliges to external Acts," and then either deny the *Fact,* or say, it was *no Violation of the Law of Nature.* For it is evident, That the Sentence of a Judge

---

138. Ibid., 1.10n, pp. 28–29: "Each man has a right of self-preservation (by article 7), therefore he also has the right to use every means necessary to that end (by article 8). The necessary means are those that he shall judge to be so himself (by article 9). He therefore has the right to do and to possess everything that he shall judge to be necessary to his self-preservation. In the judgement of the person actually doing it, what is done is rightly done, even if it is a wrong, and so is rightly done. It is therefore true that in the natural state, etc."

139. Ibid., 3.27n, p. 54.

concerning *Fact,* is of no less validity than concerning *Right,* or the Law. It can as well make an *unjust Fact,* a *Just* one, or *no Fact* at all; as it can do what he says it does, give a Man a *Right to do any thing against any one,* for this reason only, *because,* "Since he himself is Judge, he thus determines concerning his Right, and concerning the use of things necessary to his own Preservation." A cautious Deduction of the Laws of Nature is evidently in vain, whilst Mr. *Hobbes's Man* continues in *his State of Nature.* For *every Determination of his concerning things necessary to the Preservation of his Life,* is a *Law,* and gives him a *Right* to do any thing, altho' that very Determination should contradict a thousand others affirm'd by himself.

2. *Secondly,* I *suppose,* what *Hobbes* himself *supposes* in this Deliberation, "That the Man has not yet come to any arbitrary and rash Resolution, but that he now doubts, and would make a cautious inquiry, *whether* it were better to keep Peace, or make War?" That is, supposing others to have an equal, or not much different Right, *"Whether* it would more probably contribute to his Happiness, Government being not yet settled, to cultivate Peace with others, by permitting them to enjoy all natural Advantages equally with himself, by lending them his Assistance, when it can be done conveniently; in a word, by acting according to the Laws of Nature?" Or *rather* "slighting the equal or proportional Right of others, to begin or continue against all indifferently an offensive War, in order to subject every thing to himself?" Truly, if I have any Judgment, the *Question* is not very difficult; for a Man of moderate Understanding will easily *perceive,* "That there can be *no Safety* in so unjust a War, which one wages against all; but that there is *some,* tho' doubtful, *Hope* founded in the Dictates of Reason teaching all, *that an universal Proposal and Pursuit of the Common Good as their End, would promote the Common Happiness,"* and consequently, "that of all particular Persons." This is likewise confirm'd by *Experience.* We have Instances of it in all *bordering States,* who can sometimes continue in Peace for a long time together, (as it is the Interest of all, so to do,) tho' they have no common Superior but God.

Hobbes denies, "That the Laws of Nature, even that of observing Compacts, obliges the Rulers of different States to external Actions conformable to them." His Words are express, *"The State of Independent Governments, with respect to one another, is a State of Nature, that is, of Hostility. Nor, if they cease to fight, is it therefore to be called Peace, but a Breathing-time; in which each Adversary, watching the Motions and Countenance of the other, judges of his Security, not from Compacts, but from the Force and Councils of his Adversary."* [140] And elsewhere thus, to the same purpose; *"What else are most Republicks but so many Camps mutually guarded and fortified against one another; whose State (because they are restrain'd by no common Power, notwithstanding the Intervention of uncertain Peace, like a short Truce) is to be esteem'd a State of Nature, that is, a State of War?"* [141] And again most expressly, to the same purpose, *"That Compacts of mutual Faith, in a State of Nature, are vain and invalid; for, since by the Contract something is to be perform'd on both Sides, if either fear, that the other will not perform what he has promis'd, he is not bound to perform what he himself had covenanted to do first. But, whether his Fears be just, that the other will not perform, he who fears is himself the Judge."* [142] Whence, according to his *usual manner,* he would *conclude,* "That he justly fears, whensoever he fears." But this reason is so *general,* that, if it have any force, it would *conclude,* "That Compacts, not only in which nothing has been perform'd on either part, are invalid; but also those, in which any thing of moment remains yet to be perform'd by each Party." *For* "He, who has no mind farther to perform his Contract, need only fear, (he may do it justly, since himself is Judge,) that the other will falsify his Promise; his reason therefore, which is always right, will not enjoin him to perform his Compact, but that will be plainly of no validity." His requiring in the *Note,* a *"new cause of Fear,"* [143] does not hinder Compacts to be invalid, if the Reason he brings in §. 11. holds good; for the *Fear* of another's Non performance arises either from the

140. Ibid., 13.7, p. 144–45.
141. Ibid., 10.17, p. 126.
142. Ibid., 2.11, p. 37.
143. Ibid., 2.11n. [Maxwell's translation]: "The Fear cannot be thought just, unless there appear some new Cause of Fear, from some overt Act, or other Signification of his Will, that the other Party does not design to perform his Part. For that Cause, which could not prevent his contracting, ought not to prevent his performance."

remembrance of *the evil Disposition of Mankind,* which he who now fears had not sufficiently consider'd before the Compact; or he takes any the most *innocent Act* of the other for a *sufficient Proof of his Intention, not to perform.* Nor is there any thing in a State of Nature, which can make a *fearful* Man perfectly *secure* of the Fidelity of others, so as to *oblige* him to perform his Contract, which is an *external Action,* as *Hobbes* himself affirms, *Chap.* 5. §. 1, 2. and *Chap.* 7. §. 27.[144] *"All Hope,"* says he, *"of Security is plac'd in the Power of preventing others by Force or Fraud."* [145] This is that *notable Discovery,* in which *Hobbes excels* even his Master *Epicurus,* who thought he had sufficiently subverted *Justice,* when he *asserted* in his *Maxims,* "That there was no Justice among those Nations, who either could not, or would not, enter into mutual Compacts, neither to give nor receive Damage; but left the Force of Compacts unshaken, tho' no common Governor presided over both Nations."[146] *Hobbes* ascribes even this *Force* to his darling Passion, *Fear,* "That in a State of Nature," (such as is that of different States,) "it may justly violate Compacts of mutual Faith."

The Security of Ambassadors, of Commerce, of the Rights of Hospitality, and of Leagues, is detroy'd by Hobbes.

§LV. From this *Doctrine* it is easy to deduce the *greatest Inconveniences to all Mankind.* The *Safety of Ambassadors,* how innocent soever, is immediately *destroy'd.* The whole *Force of Leagues* between Princes and different States, is *taken away; Hobbes* expressly pronounces them "vain and invalid." Finally, all *Security of Merchants,* and, consequently, all *Commerce,* with the *Rights of Hospitality* necessary to Travellers, are intirely overthrown; and there remains *no Security to small States* from the Power of the Greater. *Consequences,* all contrary to daily *Experience;* for we daily see Leagues enter'd into, to be perform'd at a distant Time, which are therefore *"Compacts,"* as he calls them, *"of mutual Faith."* Nay, Ambassadors, Merchants, and other Travellers into foreign States, are

---

144. Ibid., 5.1–2, pp. 69–70; ibid., 3.27 [Maxwell copies Cumberland's mistaken reference in *De Legibus Naturae,* p. 134], p. 54.

145. Hobbes, *On the Citizen,* 5.1, p. 69; see also Cumberland, *A Treatise of the Laws of Nature,* 5.50 above.

146. Diogenes Laertius, *Lives,* X.150, maxim 33, 36.

safe enough, altho', according to *this Doctrine,* they are *Enemies,* and have put themselves in the Power of Foreigners: For *Hobbes* reasons thus, *"That Foreigners, as being stronger, may* justly *compel these being weaker to give Security for their future Obedience," (except they would rather die;)* and that *"nothing can be thought of more absurd, than by letting him go, to make him at once both strong and an Enemy, whom you have weak in your Power."* [147] These Words, *"Security for their future Obedience,"* plainly enough *insinuate* what he afterwards expressly declares, "That no Security seems to him sufficient, but that *Union,* by which Men become Members of the same State, and in all things subject to the same Government";[148] which how ill it agrees with the Rights of Ambassadors and of Commerce, every one sees. But, if all Ambassadors and others who Travel abroad, both could rightfully, and would, subject themselves to others in all respects; *no Law of Nature* (according to *Hobbes's* Doctrine) *could oblige* Foreigners to any *external Acts* of Benevolence, but it would be free for them to *chuse,* "Whether they would signify by any external Act, their acceptance of this Surrender, or would rather feast their Eyes with the Blood of Innocents." These Consequences, I suppose, will not move Mr. *Hobbes,* or those his Disciples, who are throughly instructed in the more hidden Mysteries of his Philosophy. For these, and innumerable other such, *Corollaries* they both plainly perceive, and earnestly desire: However, I thought it proper slightly to glance at them, and expose them to view, that they whose Tastes are not yet so throughly de-

147. Hobbes, *On the Citizen,* 1.14, pp. 30–31: "And the victor may *rightly* compel the vanquished (as a strong and healthy person may compel the sick or an adult an infant) to give a guarantee of future obedience, unless he prefers to die. For since the *right* of protecting ourselves at our own discretion proceeds from our danger, and the danger arises from equality, it is more rational and gives more assurance of our preservation if we make use of our present advantage to build the security we seek for ourselves by taking a guarantee, than to attempt to recover it later with all the risks of conflict when the enemy has grown in numbers and strength and escaped from our power. And from the other side it is the height of absurdity, when you have him in your power in feeble condition, to make him strong again as well as hostile by letting him go."

148. Ibid., 5.5–8, pp. 71–73.

prav'd may try, whether their Reason, and every thing Human about them, is not shock'd at such monstrous Opinions.

Innumerable Advantages, both to private Persons and to States, without the Influence of Civil Society, from observing the Laws of Nature.

My present View is only to *prove* from the Actions of Men, as from Effects known by Observation and constant *Experience,* "That there generally accrue greater Advantages, both to every particular Person (abstractedly from the Influence of Civil Society,) and to different States, from Innocence, Gratitude, Fidelity, Humanity, and other Virtues enjoin'd by the Law of Nature, than from Violence, Ingratitude, Perfidiousness, and other Vices thereby forbid; that our natural Obligation to observe these Laws in our external Actions, may evidently appear, not only from the intrinsecal Pleasures of Virtue, but from these Advantages, as from a natural Reward; and from the opposite Evils annex'd as Punishments to such Actions, by the very Nature of Men." We see great Numbers, who are *not particularly Interested, run voluntarily to extinguish a House a-fire,* without any constraint of the Civil Laws. We see daily, *Lies, Frauds, Oppression,* that have never been brought before, much less punish'd by, a Court of Judicature, render their Authors so odious, often so contemptible and wretched, that the very *Disgrace* and the *Difficulties,* and *want of Friends,* consequent thereon, are justly reckon'd among their *Punishments.* It has also often happen'd, that they, whose Crimes have justly render'd them odious, have *prefer'd Death to Life with Infamy;* and that others (wickedly enough inclin'd) *abstain* from many *Crimes,* merely to *avoid Infamy:* In like manner we may observe, that *Obedience to the Laws of Nature* obtain'd in *Heathen Rome* the name of HONESTAS, from that *Honour* which most are wont to confer upon good Men, without the Injunction of Civil Laws. Innumerable are the Advantages, which, without the Authority of the Laws, at the pleasure of *private Persons* only, daily accrue to the Innocent, Grateful, Faithful, and Benevolent, rather than to the Wicked, (as in the *Contracts* of *doing Business for them gratuitously, being Bound, or giving Pledges for them, of Lending them without Interest,* and of *Partnerships with them;* or *in taking Care of their Families as Executors,* or even *in making them their Heirs or Legatees:*) and these sufficiently *shew,* "That Men naturally incline to reward Virtue." As for *different States,* which are perfectly in a State of Nature, it is evident, 1. Tho' sometimes *Wars* happen between them, that they are *not* therefore *on both Sides just,* which both the contending Parties confess, tho' one Side only can justly wage War.[149] And 2. which I here chiefly regard, That no-one ever yet saw, or has met with it in the most antient Records, that *All States waged War against All,* which yet *Hobbes* boasts that he has demonstrated.[150] 3. Nay, we see that *many States* have for *many Years* most religiously *observ'd Leagues of mutual Faith with other States,* to the Improvement and carrying on in time of Peace, a Commerce very advantageous to both sides, and that they have *mutually assisted one another,* as occasion requir'd in War, tho' they thereby expos'd themselves to *Danger.* This is so notorious, that it would be superfluous to quote Examples from History, since there has scarce ever been any considerable War carried on, but that on one side at least, if not on both, *Confederates* from other States have *undergone some part of the Hazard.*

§LVI. To this, if any one thinks fit to *reply,* "That this is done, in order to balance in some measure the Powers of different States, for fear they themselves should at length be destroy'd by the overgrown Greatness of any one"; I *answer,* "That in this place I inquire concerning *Fact* only, whether it be usual for Men, in a State of Nature, to do good Offices to one another, and to perform Compacts of mutual Faith, even when ac-companied with Hazard"; and that, from this *Fact* allow'd, I would *infer,* "That like Things may in like Cases with probability be expected from Men; and that, therefore, *Compacts of mutual Faith,* even in that State, are not in vain; and that he does not act unreasonably, who first performs what he covenanted to do." I prove this *Fact,* and draw this *Inference,* in order to *shew,* "That one Man may reasonably do the first good Office to another (tho' subject to a different State,) and lies under no necessity to invade him, as a threatening Beast of Prey." *Hobbes* indeed *alledges,* "That *one Man is a Wolf to another,*" (except they be both under the same Civil Government,) in a *stricter sense* than that of the *Proverb;* so that, in our first Intercourse with others, we should necessarily be as Savage

No State should either be establish'd or preserv'd by such Men, as Mr. Hobbes contends that all men are.

---

149. Grotius, *De Jure Belli ac Pacis,* II.1.
150. Hobbes, *On the Citizen,* 1.12, pp. 29–30.

as Brutes. (see his Epistle Dedicatory to his Treatise *De Cive.*[151]) But this Expression is in the Epistolary manner, too soft, too full of Compliment. He tells us afterwards, where he is Philosophizing strictly, "That *Man exceeds Wolves, Bears, Serpents, (who are ravenous only to satify their Hunger, and upon Provocation,) in Rapacity and Cruelty.*"[152] I look upon these *Expressions* as *unjust Reproaches* of Mankind, (whether justly or no, let any Reader of Humanity judge,) and contrary to all Experience. Yet upon these Principles has *Hobbes* built all his *Politicks.*

And, if they were true, it were evidently *impossible,* "To reduce such Beasts of Prey, always thirsting after the Blood of their Fellows, into a Civil State." For *Hobbes's Method* of effecting this by *Compacts,* "by which each Individual is said to transfer to the Magistrate his Right of resisting," will effect nothing. For *such* Animals cannot be *so* contain'd within the bounds of their Duty, by the *Conscience* of Compacts or Promises, but that they would immediately re-demand and resume the Power before conferr'd upon the Prince. But, if the *greatest Part* of the Subjects have a mind to make *void* those *Compacts,* by which they had constituted a Prince, the whole *Force* of restraining by *Punishments* the Violation of plighted Faith, vanishes; on account of which *Force* only, *Hobbes* contends, that Compacts are *binding* in *Civil Society,* which in a State of Nature did not oblige to external Actions. If Men were as *Faithless* as he represents them, they *could* contribute no Power to the Prince whom they had chosen, either to punish Rebellion against himself, or Injuries done his Subjects; and, therefore, according to *his* Principles, a State would almost as soon be dissolv'd for *want of Security,* as

---

151. Ibid., Dedicatory Epistle, p. 3, quoting the proverb from Plautus, *Asinaria,* 2.4.88: "There are two maxims which are surely both true: *Man is a God to Man,* and *Man is a wolf to Man.* The former is true of the relations of citizens with each other, the latter of relations between commonwealths. In justice and charity, the virtues of peace, citizens show some likeness to God. But between commonwealths, the wickedness of bad men compels the good too to have recourse, for their own protection, to the virtues of war, which are violence and fraud, i.e. to the predatory nature of beasts."

152. Hobbes, *De Homine,* X.3, p. 59.

it had been establish'd, and all would relapse into that State of War, which he pretends to be Natural.

It is *necessary,* "That Compacts should oblige to those external Acts, which gave and continue to the Prince the Power of punishing the Transgressors of his Laws." *But* "these Compacts cannot receive this obligatory Force from the Prince already establish'd and continued." For the Powers of the Cause are prior to the Powers of the Effect produc'd by that Cause; it is *therefore necessary,* "that the Force of those Compacts, by which a State is establish'd, should be resolv'd into something prior, both in Nature and in Time, to that Power of punishing, which a State has after it is establish'd." Nor can any *adequate Cause* of such an *Effect* be found, except the *Nature* of *Men,* and the *Will* and *Nature* of the *First Cause* thence in some measure *discover'd.* If *these* be not sufficient to produce in the Mind of every Man, a knowledge of, and reverence for, the Laws of Nature; and to model even his outward Behaviour to Innocence, Fidelity, and Gratitude; it is in vain to expect that a *bad Man* will become a *good Subject.* When the Foundation is undermin'd, the Building, however elegant, rais'd thereon, falls to the ground; and vitiated Chyle can never become healthful Blood.[153] So much may suffice for the *Definition* and *Obligation of the Laws of Nature* in General.

§LVII. I will here lay before the Reader the *Substance* of what I have advanc'd upon this Head, reduc'd into *one Proposition,* in imitation of *Euclid's Data,* (which are best adapted to Practice,) *That, it appearing manifestly from the Nature of Things, that the Common Good of Rational Beings is the greatest Good in the Power of Man; and that the diligent Pursuit thereof will be naturally rewarded with the greatest Happiness attainable by each particular Person, and, on the contrary, that the neglect thereof will be punish'd with Misery proportionable: it appears evidently, That it was the Will of the First Cause, to oblige Men to a diligent Pursuit of that Good:* Or, which comes to the same Thing, *There is given a Promulgation*

Upon Hobbes's Principles, the obligatory Force of Compacts cannot be accounted for.)

From the foregoing Data is concluded, That there is given one Fundamental Law of Nature, That the Common Good of Rational Beings is to be promoted.

---

153. Descartes uses the same structural metaphor in *Meditations,* I.2. The view that blood is made from chyle was derived from Galen and was developed by seventeenth-century anatomists such as Harvey.

of the first and most general Law of Nature. Or thus briefly, *There being given a Knowledge of the necessary Dependence of the Happiness of particular Persons, upon the Pursuit of the Common Good; it appears evidently, That each particular Person is oblig'd to pursue that Good.* This *Proposition* is prov'd evidently, from the bare *Definitions* which I have already given of the *Law of Nature,* and of *Obligation.*

The Phenomena of Nature relating to that Proposition reduc'd into one Lemma.

That all these Things are *Given* or appear manifestly, which are *suppos'd* in the *Subject* of this *Proposition,* I have abundantly *prov'd* from the *Phenomena* of the Nature of all Things, and especially of Man; the Sum of which is contain'd in this Fundamental *Lemma. He who, as far as is in his Power, best consults the Good of the whole Body of Rational Agents, does, likewise, best consult the Good of those Parts of that Whole, which are essential thereto, and receive all from its Influence; and, consequently, of himself in particular: Because, for the most part, it is in the Power of any one to contribute more to the flourishing Condition of his own Mind and Body, without hurting others, than to that of any other; and this increases the Happiness of the whole aggregate Body.*

The Lemma prov'd, as to the external Causes of Happiness.

It is very well *known,* "That the Happiness, especially the *External,* of every Individual, depends upon the Aid, or at least upon the Permission, of almost all other Rational Beings, at least remotely, and in part." We find by *Experience,* "That the Will of the First Cause has so *complicated* all the Parts and Powers of the System of the World, that there is nothing which may not give either Force or Opposition to any other Body whatsoever, either now or hereafter." This *Complication* is yet more conspicuous in *Human Powers,* because their Faculties are more *extensive,* upon account of the additional Force, which the Powers of our *Mind* give to our *Bodily Motions.* I cannot *illustrate* this Point better, than by a *Comparison* with a *Balance.* It is evident, that the smallest Particles of a Weight laid in one Scale, contribute something to the Counterpoizing an equal Weight, how great soever, laid in the opposite Scale; it adds both Force to its own Side, and Opposition to the contrary. *So,* in Nature, according to the *Aristotelian Hypothesis, every Particle of the Earth* contributes something to the *Poizing* the whole Earth upon its Center: Or, if the *Cartesian Hypothesis* seem more Philosophical, every Part of this *Vortex,* in which we are whirl'd, is, as it were, in a

Balance reverse, upon account of the *Centrifugal Force* of all the Parts; and, in Proportion to its quantity of Matter and Motion, contributes somewhat to that Equilibrium or Poize between the Parts of the whole System jointly consider'd, by which the whole System is preserv'd.[154] *In like manner Politicians* are wont to consider the Powers of *different States,* as *counterpoizing* one another; to which it is owing, that they are not able to destroy one another. *Just so,* if *particular Men* be consider'd without any Common Governor, to which they are subject, (which is the Case of different States,) yet there is a certain *Proportion* between those *natural Powers* of Defence and their *natural Necessities:* And the *same Arguments,* which move *different States* to exercise *mutual Commerce,* and to *confederate* against Common Enemies, and to endeavour to prevent one's destroying the rest, would likewise prevail with Individuals to enter into *Compacts,* by which their mutual Happiness may be both secur'd and increas'd.

The *Resemblance* between the Cases and Conditions of *all Men,* is plainly *Natural;* and it is equally *Natural* for them to reason from the *Dangers,* as well as from the *Advantages,* which they observe happen to those *like themselves,* to *like Events* which may happen to *themselves* also. Hence all are mov'd with *Hope* and *Fear,* by means of what happens to those in *like Circumstances,* and unavoidably think, that he *threatens* them with immediate Danger, whom they see *invade the Innocent;* and look upon the Foundations of *their own Security* to be *destroy'd* by him, who breaks thro' the bonds of *Compacts,* or of *Gratitude.* It is no less *Natural* to a *Man,* to be *mov'd* with an Argument drawn from the *likeness of Cases,* than it is *Natural* for *Bodies,* to be *mov'd* by a *stroke,* or a *weight;* for to *Man, Reason* is equally *Natural.* Nor would it be difficult to *prove,* "That all our Reasoning, with respect to Futurity, (by which only, deliberate Human Actions are regulated,) is drawn from such a Resemblance between Causes and their Effects, past and future." The *Condition,* therefore, of their *Nature* will *incline* Individuals, to preserve Innocence, keep Faith, and exercise Gratitude. By *these Methods* the

---

154. For the Aristotelian hypothesis, see Aristotle, *De Caelo,* II.14; Cumberland refers to Descartes' theory of vortices from the *Principia Philosophiae* (1644).

Powers of some will of necessity be *counterpoiz'd* by others; and some *Friendships* will be establish'd, on which the Foundations of *Societies* may be laid. *These Methods of acting* may happen, indeed, to be *slighted by some for a time,* and in some *particular Instances;* but it is certain, whenever they do so, they divest themselves, even of *Reason* it-self, or of the far better part of Human Nature. And the *same Principles return* to them, as certainly as repuls'd *Nature* (that is, Reason blinded for a time) *returns,* or as they return to themselves.[155] *Reason* therefore, which is *Natural,* led by the *natural Resemblance* of Men, *inclines* Men for the most part, (for the general Principles of Reason for the most part prevail among them,) to *assist* one another *mutually,* but especially to *repay,* to the utmost of their Power, the *Benefits* which they have receiv'd at the hands of others. I have laid down these *Observations,* in order to *shew the Reason,* "Why I consider'd all Mankind as one Whole, whose Parts are in some measure connected, by an obvious Resemblance of Nature and Necessities; and that there is a Probability of procuring Friendship among them, especially after one has begun, by Benevolence, to deserve well at their hands."

As to the *internal* Causes of Happiness. §LVIII. The *Truth* of the foregoing *Lemma,* altho' it be made *manifest* from these and other foregoing *Observations,* with respect to the *outward* Helps of Human Happiness, appears yet *more clearly* in those parts of our Happiness, which lie principally *in every Man's own Power;* that is, in a Tranquillity of Mind consistent with it-self in all things, in the Government of the Passions, and the pleasing Reflexion upon good Actions, or a Joy, that it has with its utmost endeavours pursu'd the best End, by the properest Means; and in a well-grounded Hope of the Divine Favour.

Other Advantages, which we cannot procure by Benevolent Actions, are *excluded,* as *things not in our Power,* by the very Words of the *Lemma,* whose Truth therefore they cannot render uncertain, tho' they them-

155. Barbeyrac (*Traité Philosophique,* p. 328n) suggests that Cumberland is alluding to Horace's "Naturam expellas furca, tamen usque recurret" ("Though you drive nature out with a pitchfork, she will still find her way back"), *Epistles,* I.x.24.

selves be uncertain. For it is not to be *expected,* "That things *impossible* to Man should be *natural Rewards* of Human Actions promoting the Common Good": It is abundantly sufficient to *prove,* "That the Author of Nature would oblige us to promote the Common Good"; *because* "He has ascertain'd the Rewards I have mention'd; and has beside given a greater Certainty, that we shall, by this Method, procure the Benevolence and Assistance of Men, than that we should secure our-selves by attacking all others by Force or Fraud." These Effects of the Actions of other Men, are in their own Nature *contingent,* and, therefore, Human Reason performs its part, if it directs us to make that Choice, which will *most probably* happen. The value of a *probable* Gain is *certain,* (as is evident, not only in *Games of Hazard,* but also in *Agriculture, Merchandize,* and in almost every thing, about which Human Industry is employ'd;) and this is the *natural Reward* of the more *prudent Choice.* Altho' therefore he who has aim'd at securing himself by *Hobbes's* Methods of *Force* and *Fraud,* may *sometimes escape Mischiefs,* which Prudence would rather expect should have *overwhelm'd* him; or may even *procure some Advantages,* which he who acts more prudently may *fall short of;* yet these Events do not prove, that his *Reasonings* were more *Just,* nor that Nature *generally* bestows these Rewards upon such Actions. Just as it *may happen,* "That he who has undertaken to throw two Sices at the first Cast with two Dice, may get the better of him who laid an equal Wager, that he would not do it"; yet it is *demonstrable,* from the *Nature* or cubical Figure of a *Die,* "That the odds are 35 to one; and that *therefore* the Expectation of the one is worth so much more than that of the other; and that this *difference* between the Value of the Chances may be justly esteem'd as the Advantage or natural *Reward* of the more *prudent Choice.*"[156] The like Judgment is to be made of Damage, in the Nature of Punishment, sustain'd by an imprudent Choice. But, if an *Illustration* from *Nature* would be more agreeable, (tho' here the matter cannot be reduc'd to exact Calculation,) it is at hand. The Stomach and Intestines by digesting the Nourishment, the Liver by separating the Bile, the Heart

---

156. Another reference to Huygen's *Tractatus de ratiociniis in aleae ludo;* see also ch. 4, n. 7, and ch. 5, n. 42.

by its Contraction and Dilatation, are of immediate use to the *Health of the whole Body,* and at the same time preserve *their own sound State* in the best manner they are able: Yet it *may happen,* thro' the Disease or Defect of other Parts, that they may be defrauded of their due Nourishment, without any Fault of their own. But, because that will *more certainly* be effected, if they be wanting to the whole Body, the *Preservation they generally gain* by performing their Offices, is a kind of Image of a *Natural Reward,* and may therefore serve to *illustrate* our purpose.

The knowledge of this Lemma imprinted on our Minds, by the Will of the First Cause,

But, *because* the knowledge of this most certain *Lemma,* as that of all other Truths concerning Causes and their natural Effects, is imprinted upon the Mind of Man from the Nature of Things, by the Determination of the First Cause; it is *evident,* "That His Will discovers this Truth to us."

who therefore persuades to Universal Benevolence,

Farther; Since the assent given to this *Lemma* naturally *persuades* and *inclines* us, to procure the Publick Good; it is equally *true,* "That the First Cause persuades the same thing in this manner." There is no danger of our making the *First Cause* the *Author* of any Evil, whilst we esteem him the Cause of Natural and *Necessary* Effects only. For all *Moral Evils* come thro' the Interposition of Human *Ignorance, Inadvertency,* or *Rashness,* arising from the *Abuse* of our *Liberty.* "The First Cause, *therefore,* persuades whatever the Judgment of Right, that is, True Reason persuades, concerning what is necessary to obtain this chief End by the properest Means."

nay commands it.

But "His *Admonition,* who *persuades* by Arguments drawn from the greatest *Rewards* and *Punishments,* which he himself, who is superior to all in Wisdom, Goodness, and Power, has annex'd to our Actions, according as they are agreeable or disagreeable to his Admonitions, is a *Law*"; and for this very reason, "He who thus *persuades* is a *Law-giver.*" What the *Roman* Senate judg'd was *best to be done,* tho' it did not pass into a Law, *thro' a defect* in the Number of those who were conven'd, or in the Place, or in the Time, or because of the Interposition of a Tribune, claim'd the respect due to *Authority,* as *Dion Cassius* declares, *Lib.* 5.[157] How *much rather* ought that to be look'd upon as enforc'd by

---

157. Cassius Dio Cocceianus, *Roman History,* LV.3.1–6. Cumberland's reference is incorrect.

Authority, which the First Cause has, *without any defect,* discover'd as *best to be done* for the Common Good, and establish'd by the Sanction of Rewards and Punishments, altho' by the Nature of Second Causes, which he himself has limited and determin'd? For his Will, for this very Reason, that it is the *First,* is the *Supreme* Cause, the *Wisest, Best,* and *most Powerful;* for *other Causes* can have nothing but what they *receiv'd* from him: And, because of his *Infinite Perfection,* his *Will cannot disagree* with the Dictates of his *Understanding.*

From what I have laid down it is easy to *shew,* "How the Laws of Nature, defin'd as above, have the Power of *Commanding, Forbidding, Permitting,* &c." Nor is it difficult to *reconcile my Definition* with those to be met with in the *most approv'd Authors,* by a proper Interpretation of those doubtful Expressions, which they have made use of. But these Points I thought fit to leave to the Industry of the Reader.

General Remarks on Chapter V

The *Nature of Things* in the Natural World is so exactly *fitted* to the *Natural Faculties* and Dispositions of Mankind, that were any Thing in either *otherwise* than it is, even in *Degree,* Mankind would be *less Happy* than they now are. Thus the Dependence of all natural Effects upon a *few simple Principles* is wonderfully Advantageous in many respects. The *Degrees* of all the *sensible Pleasures* are exactly suited to the Use of each: So that, if we enjoy'd any of them in a greater Degree, we should be less Happy; for our Appetites of those Pleasures would by that means be too strong for our Reason; and, as we are framed, tempt us to an immoderate Enjoyment of them, so as to prejudice our Bodies. And where we enjoy some of them in so high a Degree, as that it is in many Cases very difficult for the strongest to regulate and moderate the Appetites of those Pleasures, it is in such Instances where it was necessary to counterpoize some Disadvantages, which are the Consequences of the pursuit of those Pleasures. Thus the pleasing Ideas, which accompany the Love of the Sexes, are necessary to be possess'd in so high a Degree, to balance the Cares of Matrimony, and also the Pains of Child-bearing in the Female Sex. The same may be said of our *Intellectual Pleasures.* Thus, did we receive a greater Pleasure from Benevolence, Sloth would be encouraged by an immoderate Bounty. And, were the Pleasures of our Inquiries into Truth greater, we should be too speculative and less active. It seems also probable, That the Degree of our Intellectual Capacity is very well suited to our Objects of Knowledge; and that, had we a greater Degree thereof, all other Things remaining as they are, we should be less Happy. Moreover; it is probably so adapted to the inward Frame of our Bodies, that it could not be greater, without either an Alteration in the Laws of Nature, or in the Laws of Union between the Soul and Body. Farther; were it much greater than it is, our Thoughts and Pursuits would be so spiritual and refined, that we should be taken too much off from the sensible Pleasures. We should, probably, be conscious of some Defects or Wants in our Bodily Organs, and would be sensible, that they were unequal to so great a Capacity, which would necessarily be follow'd by uneasiness of Mind. And this seems to hold in the Brute Creation. For methinks it would be for the Disadvantage of a Horse, to be endued with the Understanding of a Man. Such an unequal Union must be attended with continual Disquietudes and Discontents. As for our *Pains,* they are all either *Warnings* against Bodily Disorders, or are such as had we wanted them, the Laws of Nature remaining as they are, we should either have *wanted* some *Pleasures* we now enjoy, or have possessed them in a *less Degree.* Those Things in Nature, which we can't reconcile to the foregoing Opinion, as being ignorant of their use, we have good reason from *Analogy,* to believe are really Advantageous and adapted to the Happiness of the Intelligent Beings of the System; tho' we have not so full and compleat a Knowledge of the intire System; as to be able to point out their particular Uses. From these Observations we may *conclude,* "That all the various Parts of our System are so admirably suited to one another, and the Whole contrived with such exquisite Wisdom, that, were any Thing in any Part thereof in the least otherwise than it is, without an alteration in the Whole, there would be a less Sum of Happiness in the System, than there now is." From this it *follows,* "That whatever would have added to our Happiness, consistently with the other Parts of our System, the Author of Nature has given us." But we can't imagine it impossible to Infinite Power, consistently with the other Parts of our System, to order the Consequences of Human Actions, and the Human

Sourses of Pleasure in such a manner, as that Private should be perfectly connected with Publick Good. *But* this would contribute much to the Happiness of Mankind. *Therefore* there is such a Connexion. This Argument from *Analogy,* tho' it is not a *Demonstration,* yet it is very strong, and obtains a very firm Assent. Our Belief, that the Human Bodies we daily see, are actuated by like Minds with our own, is founded upon the like Reasoning; together with numberless other Instances of Belief, which are so strong as not to be accompanied with the least *Doubting.*

The Argument taken from the Benevolence of God, and express'd in this manner, is, I think, inconclusive.

A perfect Connexion between Private and Publick Good would be for our Advantage. God is infinitely Benevolent. Therefore he has made such a Connexion.

For this Argument will equally conclude, that he hath given us all possible Happiness. We have not a Knowledge of the Divine Motives to Action. But, if we would indulge our-selves in Conjectures of that kind, it is probable, That he takes pleasure, not only in the *Happiness* of his Creatures, but in the *variety* of their Happiness; and that he therefore hath created a great number of Systems, the Inhabitants of each of which differ from those of another, both in the *Kind* and *Degree* of their Happiness.

II. I am of opinion, that the Author's Scheme would have been more compleat, had he included *Benevolence towards Brutes. First,* because we can't imagine, but that the Deity takes pleasure in the Happiness of all his Creatures, that are capable thereof. Neither can it be said, that the Benevolence of the Deity does not extend to them, because they are incapable of Law, and, consequently, of Rewards and Punishments. For it is *highly probable,* "That there are Species of Beings, whose Happiness does as much exceed ours upon the whole, as ours does that of the lowest Brute." Farther; it is to me utterly inconceivable, that a Being, who is pleas'd with a great Degree of Happiness in another Being, shou'd not, from the same Constitution of Nature, be also pleas'd with a lesser.

The *second* Reason for our Benevolence towards Brutes, is, that a merciful and compassionate Behaviour towards them, feeds and cherishes that natural Disposition; whereas a barbarous and cruel Treatment of those Creatures must undoubtedly have some Effect, to harden our Temper, even against Rational Beings. Every Man that examines his own breast, will find the same tender and benevolent Disposition, tho' in a lesser Degree, towards the lowest and most imperfect Being, that is capable of Sensation, as towards those of his own Species.

The *third* Reason is, that it adds to our own Happiness. A truly Benevolent Man receives pleasure, even from the Happiness of the Brute Creation. Nevertheless, it seems probable, that our Custom of killing them for Food, and of using their Labour in a moderate and merciful manner, is consistent with Benevolence, and agreeable to the Will of the Deity, because it is highly probable, that such a practice contributes to the Happiness of the whole of the sensitive System, which comprehends both Men and Brutes; besides, that Man seems to be form'd by *Nature* a *Carnivorous* Animal, see *Barbeyrac* (in his Notes on *Puffendorf*) upon this Head.[158]

III. I shall subjoin the *chief Advantages of Benevolence,* that are mention'd by our Author, together with several others, that he has not taken notice of, that the Strength of his Reasoning may appear more forceable and collected.

Acts of Benevolence are accompanied with *Pleasure,* but the contrary Actions with *Pain.* By the former is gain'd the *Good Will,* by the latter, the *Evil Will* of others. The former begets *Self-approbation,* and the latter *Self-condemnation.* By the smaller Faults against Benevolence, there is a Habit contracted, or at least the contrary Habit broken; and the Person becomes wavering and unsettled in his Actions, and for the most part guided by a narrow and short-sighted *Self-Love.* In the Execution of Benevolent Designs others concur, and by that means the Agent is *seldom disappointed;* but the Case is just the reverse in contrary Actions. Benevolence is an additional *Spur* to the Acquisition of *Knowledge,* and constant Industry is seldom excited by a bare Ambition. Benevolence has very *frequent,* almost perpetual, Occasions of Gratification, and that in the most common Affairs of Life; whereas the selfish Pleasures are *small in number,* of *short duration,* and *infrequent,* if compar'd with the

---

158. Barbeyrac himself (*Traité Philosophique,* p. 332) suggests looking at his edition of Pufendorf, *Le Droit de la Nature et des Gens* (1706), III.4, 5; IV.

Pleasures of Benevolence. By Actions of Malevolence there is a Habit of *Indifference,* with regard to the Happiness or Misery of others; for by Custom we not only become hard and insensible, with regard to the Misery of others, but we gain a Habit of thinking so much upon ourselves and our own Happiness, that our Thoughts are thereby engross'd and taken off from a regard to the Happiness of others. Therefore the Pleasure, which accompanies the Actions of Benevolence of a vitious Man, is far *short* of that, which accompanies the Benevolence of the habitually Virtuous. As the Pleasure of Benevolence is lessen'd by a contrary Habit, so it is much *increas'*d by a *Habit* of Benevolence. The Benevolence of the virtuous Man extends much *farther* than that of the Vitious; for the latter is so weak, that it seldom extends farther, than the Circle of his Acquaintance, whereas the former extends to all Mankind, and not only to his Contemporaries, but to latest Posterity. And for this reason also their Pleasures in Benevolence are vastly different. The truly Benevolent enjoy, even the selfish Pleasures with greater Advantage, from a Consciousness that they give Pleasure to others.

The Contemplation of the Happiness of others, especially of those of superior Rank, often occasions Envy and *Discontent,* which arises from a reflexion upon our own Condition compar'd with that of others, whom we think more Happy. But to a truly Benevolent Man the Happiness of others gives real *Delight,* which takes up the Attention, and prevents the Sorrow and Uneasiness of the Malevolent. Many Actions which produce private Pleasure, are also productive of the Good of the Publick; so that in those Actions the Benevolent Man has a *double* Pleasure. The Malevolent Man not only wants all the above-mention'd Advantages, but wherever the Benevolent, as such, receives Pleasure, he receives real positive Pain.

The Benevolent are at *Peace* with all Men, and enjoy the Advantages of good-Neighbourhood, not only in the common Offices, but often in extraordinary Cases; whereas the Malevolent not only want all those Advantages, but are disquieted by Feuds and Animosities, and do often suffer Injuries from their Enemies. One Offence generally introduces many others, either to defend or hide it; and one Malevolent Contention naturally introduces others, by which the Enmity is increas'd.

The *Tranquillity of Mind,* which arises from *Self-approbation* is constant and uninterrupted, and disposes the Mind for the Enjoyment of all its other Pleasures, whereas most other Pleasures are of a short duration. And to a Man, who upon sedate Reflexion does not approve of his own Actions, his Pleasures are pursued in a broken, turbulent, and interrupted manner, and as it were by a War within a Man's self; and, when past, give Uneasiness, when reflected on.

Of those Things which are contain'd in the general Law of Nature.

Having already *establish'd* the general Precept *to promote the Common Good,* it seems proper in what follows, to *explain* 1. What those Things are, which we comprehend within the *Common Good?* 2. What Actions any way tend to *promote it,* and are, therefore, directed by this Law?

Two Questions propos'd.

As to the *First,* it may be sufficient to make the few following *Additions* to what I have already laid down in the Chapter *concerning Good.* Since the *Parts* of that *System,* whose Good we here chiefly consider, are *God* and *Men,* it *follows,* "That all those Things come under this Head, which are contain'd in the *Honour,* or *Glory of God,* and in the whole compass of the *Happiness of Men,* or what Things soever tend to the *Perfection,* either of their *Minds,* or *Bodies.*" But, because the aggregate Body of *Mankind* (as are generally such collective Bodies) is most naturally resolv'd, first into its greater Parts, these afterwards into smaller Ones, and those at last into the least of all; namely, first into different *Nations,* then into *Families,* and lastly into *Men* consider'd *singly;* for the same Reason, those Things which are good for Mankind, are, some of them, profitable to *whole Nations,* or to *many such,* or to them *all;* such are the Points about which *Moral Philosophy,* and the *Law of Nations,* (which two are very nearly related,) are conversant; others are profitable to a *single State,* or to those who live under the *same Civil Government,* which are the Subject of their *Civil Laws;* others respect the Advantages of only *one Family,* with respect to which the Rules of *Oeconomy* prescribe: Lastly, there are other Advantages proper to *one Man*

The first answer'd.

The Common Good comprehends the Honour of God, and the Good of Men, *viz.* of

Na- } collec-
tions } tively,
} singly;

Fami- }
lies, } singly.
Men, }

only, which are the Subject, as of *Logick,* and the *Regimen of Health by Diet,* so of all the abovementioned *Arts;* of *Ethicks,* as it limits the Actions of particular Persons regarding their own private Advantages, by the respect due to the Good of *all rational Beings,* namely, the Honour of God, and the Rights of all other Men; of *Civil Laws,* as they limit every one, with respect to the Good of the *State;* of *Oeconomical Rules,* with regard to the Care of their *Family.* Yet one general *Law of Nature* at once provides, both for the *whole* System of rational Beings, and its *Parts,* according to the Proportion which they bear to the *Whole.*

The Good of the *Greater Society* ought to limit the Power and Actions of the Less.

§II. It seems to have given *Occasion* to many *Errors,* "That some believ'd it the whole business of *Ethicks,* to instruct Man consider'd in a *solitary State,* without any respect to others"; whereas *universal Justice,* which is the Summary of all the Moral Virtues, almost wholly *relates to others:*[1] Nay, if the Matter be throughly examin'd, it is *evident,* "That true *Ethicks* instructs Men to enter into, and keep up, the most enlarg'd Society with God and all Men." Many of its Precepts do indeed *abstract* from the Consideration of *Society,* both *Civil* and *Sacred,* that is, are not limited to either; yet their *Influence* extends to *every Society,* and confers upon them all their chief Force and Ornament. For it is to be *observ'd,* "That all *lesser Societies,* their Powers and Actions, are *limited* with respect to the Good of the *Greater* and more worthy Society." Thus *States* are oblig'd to enjoin nothing contrary to the *Law of Nations,* by which I understand those *Natural Laws, by which the Actions of all States and private Men toward all of what State soever, are directed;* or (if they are not yet consider'd as reduc'd into the Form of a State) such Laws of Nature as inforce an innocent Behaviour toward the Innocent, and Fidelity and Gratitude: In like Manner, neither are *Civil Laws,* by which the safety of the State is secur'd, to be violated, in order to promote the Advantages of a *Family,* much less of any *one Man.*

---

1. Cumberland's original use of Greek at this point (*De Legibus Naturae,* p. 326), αλλότριον αγαθον, identifies Cumberland's source as Aristotle, *Nicomachean Ethics,* V.1.17.

§III. The Mind, while it rightly pursues these Advantages, proceeds wholly in the *Analytick Method,* from Things more compounded, to those that are more simple; that is, its *first* and principal Regard is to the *Whole,* the *Parts* are its *second* Care. Nor do they lose by this Method, they all reap their *proportionable* Share of Happiness from the Happiness of the Whole. For the *Whole* is nothing else but the *Parts consider'd jointly, and in their proper Order and Relation to each other;* and, consequently, "The Good of the Whole is nothing else but Good communicated to all the Parts, according to their natural mutual Relation." Therefore, when it is *requir'd,* "That regard be first had to the Whole," nothing more is intended, but "That we take Care in the *first Place,* that Fidelity, Gratitude, and the other Bonds of mutual Assistance, by which the Union and Order of *all* is establish'd and preserv'd, be not violated." For by these, as by Blood-Vessels and Nerves, dispers'd thro' the whole Body, the *Parts of Mankind,* like Members of the same Body, are *united* among themselves, and perform their *mutual* Offices; whether they be Members of the same State, or no. By means of these Ties, *we* often gain Wisdom by the Counsels and Prudence of *others,* become better by *their* Virtues, are enabled by *their* Strength to procure and preserve such Things as are of use to our-selves, and are enriched by *their* Wealth. But, *because* it is *obvious,* "That those Perfections of the Mind, which are distinguish'd by the Names of the *intellectual and moral Virtues,* and also the *Powers* of the *Body,* and *Riches,* are those Advantages, in Plenty whereof the *Happiness* of *each particular* Person is commonly and justly suppos'd to consist"; it *follows,* "That all these are *common* Advantages composing the *Publick* Happiness, when by observing *Compacts,* by *Gratitude, Humanity,* &c. they are thrown into the *Publick* Fund. He, I confess, encreases the *common* Stock of Happiness, who benefits even *one,* without hurting any *other;* but this cannot be *deliberately* done, without taking care, that the *Rights of others be not violated;* nor will this be taken care of, except we have *universal Benevolence,* which regards the Rights of God, of other Nations, our native Country, and Family; in all which consists the common Good of the Whole: This, therefore, must be taken care of, if we would *innocently profit one;* and the Care thereof will lead us to the Consideration and Observance of *all* Laws,

The Good of the Whole *is nothing else but Good communicated to all the* Parts, *according to their natural mutual Relation.*

(not Natural only, but Positive, which are promulged, whether Sacred, or Civil.) For it is certain, that *all* good Laws, nay, and *all* wise Admonitions of Parents, and Counsels of Philosophers, respect the *same* ultimate End; and do therefore, in *proportion* as they are *more* or *less necessary* to this End, and *more* or *less evident* from the Nature of Things, *partake* of the Force of natural Laws, or *fall short* thereof.

The Author's Method proper, however Societies were first form'd.

§IV. Lastly, if any one should *find fault*, "That I suppose the collective Body of all Mankind distinguish'd into different Nations, States, and Families, without explaining their Origin out of a confus'd Chaos." I *answer*, 1. That it is not necessary to suppose so confus'd a State of Mankind, in order to explain the Origin of States and Families; nay, that, in the Judgment of Reason only, it is most *probable*, "That Mankind, and, consequently, all States and Families, have descended from one Man and one Woman,"[2] and that, therefore, all Authority derives its Original from that which is most Natural, the PATERNAL. 2. That, though *no mutual Relation* were suppos'd among all Mankind, yet my Method is sufficient to account for the Original of all, both greater and lesser, Societies; because it is naturally *evident*, "That it is both a necessary and principal Means to procure the Common Good, that the collective Body of Mankind, (if they were not all willing to form one State, which we do not perceive at present to be the Case,) should be divided into different Political Societies, all subordinate to God alone; and that these should be distributed into lesser Societies and Families; that by that means some Things should become the Property of particular Persons, to be by them laid out upon the Publick, according to the Rules hereafter to be deliver'd": *Just as* if we should consider, in an *unhatch'd Egg*, the Condition of Matter and Motions of Particles, necessary to form the Animal; it is manifest, that *this only* is wanting to the common Perfection of them all, "That they should be form'd into the distinct Parts of an Animal, and then to each should be assign'd their proper Offices, subservient to the sound State of the Whole." But as *Physicians* suppose the Parts of Animals already form'd, so *Moral Philosophers* suppose Societies

2. [Maxwell] "See Note on Chap. 2. §. II" [see ch. 2, n. 2].

already establish'd. Yet what I have laid down concerning the Origin of Dominion over *Things* necessary,[3] laying aside the Knowledge of those Things which are deliver'd in Scripture, does in the same Method explain the Original of Dominion over *Persons,* both Paternal over Families, and Civil over States; and, in consequence, the fundamental Principles (*which only* Reason can reach) of the Rights necessary in every Society.

§V. To the *second Question,* namely, "What Actions tend to promote the Common Good," I give this general *Answer.* In my Opinion, "All Human Actions, as they can be regulated by Reason, Counsel, or any introduc'd Habit, as Means to the Common Good, do contribute to, or are Part of, the Pursuit thereof." And they are either *Acts* of the *Understanding,* or *Will* and *Affections,* or *Acts* of the *Body* determin'd by the *Will.*[4]

The *second Question* answer'd. With respect to the *Kind* of Actions which promote the Common Good, they are all such as can be directed by Reason, *&c.* as Means to that End.

First then it is *enjoin'd* by the *Law of Nature,* (which commands us to pursue, to the utmost of our Power, the Common Good,) "That we should exert the natural Powers of our Understanding about all Things and Persons, which we can any way direct to this End, in order to acquire that Habit of Mind, which above all others conduces to it, and is called Prudence." Its *Foundation* lies in a true *Knowledge* of all *Nature,* but especially the *rational* Part thereof; its chief *Parts* are a Knowledge of the *chief Ends,* (of which the *greatest* is that we are inquiring after,) and a practical Knowledge of the *Means* conducing thereto. For the whole thereof consists in giving assent to the practical Dictates of Reason. To the acquiring both these Parts are subservient the Operations of the Mind, 1. *Invention,* which consists in the Observation of Things present, and the pertinent Recollection of Things past: And 2. *Judgment,* whether *Intuitive,* or *Discursive,*[5] which consists in the Deduction and methodical Ranging of Truth: We may hence *infer,* "That Nature rec-

Hence is enjoyn'd in the Understanding *Prudence* in all Kinds of Actions relating to God and Man.

---

3. Cf. Cumberland, *A Treatise of the Laws of Nature,* 1.21, 22.

4. Maxwell cites Cumberland's Latin in a footnote: *"Actus Eliciti"* and *"Actus Imperati."*

5. Maxwell cites Cumberland's Latin in a footnote: *"Noeticum"* and *"Dianoeticum."*

ommends to us the Use of true *Logick"*; and we may hence also *under-stand,* "In what sense are naturally commanded those Acts and Habits, which in the *Invention* are called, *Sagacity in investigating, Wisdom in deliberating, Caution, Presence of Mind, Subtilty,* or *quickness of Apprehension;* and in the *Judgment, Clearness in Judging, Rectitude in Determining,* &c.[6] If the Judgment is supported by artificial Arguments, it is called *Science;* but, if it makes use of sufficient Testimony, *Belief*."[7] All these, so far as they are in the Power of particular Persons, and are necessary to the chief End, are commanded by that Law.

From Prudence arise 1. *Constancy of Mind,*   §VI. The immediate, most general, and essential *Effects* of *Prudence,* are 1. *Constancy of Mind,* by which we adhere without wavering to its Dictates, as being of *unchangeable* Truth, and fitted to all Circumstances. For there is a kind of *Immutability* in the *practical Judgment,* concerning the best End and Means, and in the *Will* consequent thereupon, which proceeds immediately from the Perception of the *immutable* Truth of those practical Propositions, which relate to the End and the Means necessary. *Prudence* bears the same relation to *Inconstancy,* that *Science* does to the giving *assent to contradictory Propositions* at the same time.

And its various Modes, *Fortitude* and *Patience.*   Constancy in the Prosecution of this great End, in opposition to foreseen Dangers and Difficulties, is *Fortitude;* the same continuing under present Evils, *Patience.*

6. Cumberland's original Greek terminology follows Aristotle's discussion of the components of prudence in *Nicomachean Ethics,* VI.10–13; *Eudemian Ethics,* V.9–12.

7. [Maxwell] "In the Original here is evidently some Word wanting, answering to *Fides,* and which should be the nominative Case to *Dicitur,* as *Fides* is to *Appellatur:* Which Word wanting appears plainly by the Sense to be *Scientia* (probably omitted by the Fault of the Transcriber of the Manuscript for the Press) or some other Word signifying *SCIENCE,* which I have accordingly inserted." There is no correction in Cumberland's own copy, and Barbeyrac (*Traité Philosophique,* p. 338n) is right to suggest that Maxwell's addition has damaged the sense of the text. Cumberland's original simply appears to be drawing a distinction between judgment based upon artificial arguments (intelligence, good sense) and judgment based upon sufficient testimony (belief), without requiring the mention of science at all; Cumberland, *De Legibus Naturae,* p. 329: "In Judicio συγεσις, γιώμη &c. si artificialibus nitatur argumentis, dicitur; at si Judicium idoneo nitatur testimonio, Fides appellatur."

2. *Moderation* is "an effect of Prudence restraining our Affections and Endeavours within those Bounds, which are most suitable to the Goodness of the End, and the Necessity or Usefulness of the Means." But, because Prudence always directs the Mind to pursue the best End *intire,* or in all its Parts, and to use *all* the necessary Means; therefore true Moderation is inseparable from *Integrity,* and from *Diligence,* or *Industry.* I suppose in the foregoing Description of Moderation, that it is both known and *allow'd,* "That the most intense Affections and most earnest Endeavours of Men relating to the chief End, and the Means principally necessary to that End, are commanded by the general Law of Nature": This being granted, by discovering the *Proportion* between *any other End* and the *Chief,* and also between the Use and Necessity of *any other Means,* we discover the *Proportion,* that ought to be between our *Affections* and *Endeavours* in those Cases. 2. *Moderation,* which comprehends *Integrity,* and *Diligence,* or *Industry.*

From this Moderation, which I have prov'd *consistent* with the greatest *Earnestness* about the best End and Means, differs nothing (in my Opinion) that *Mediocrity,* (which the *Peripateticks* celebrate as the Essence of all Kinds of Virtue,[8]) provided it receive a favourable Interpretation. I own, Moderation is more conspicuous in Acts of the *Will* and *Affections;* yet, because the *discovering* and determining the *Measure* and Proportion, which is essential thereto, is a power proper to the *Understanding;* and beside, because some *Measure* is to be fixt to the *Inquiries* of the Understanding, lest Doubt and Caution should degenerate into perpetual Scepticism; and lest a diligent Endeavour to search out Causes should turn to impertinent Curiosity; I thought it proper to shew, that Moderation was enjoin'd here, and from them to pass to those Acts of the *Will,* which are enjoin'd by the same Law. (Moderation the same with the celebrated *Mediocrity* of the *Peripateticks.*)

§VII. They may all be comprehended in the general Name of the most extensive and operative BENEVOLENCE. For this exerts itself in all kinds of *Affections* and *Endeavours* to effect Things acceptable both to *God* and *Men,* or to remove Things disagreeable to either of them. It belongs In the Will is enjoin'd *Universal Benevolence;*

8. Aristotle, *Nicomachean Ethics,* II.6–9.

(from a Con-
currence of
which with
Prudence,
arises *Equity*.)
to the same Benevolence, to endeavour that *nothing* be done *contrary* to
the Common Good, and to *correct* and amend it, if there has; hence
Equity is an essential Branch of this Virtue; by *Equity* I mean, "A Will
prepared by the Rules of Prudence to correct those Things, which were
determin'd by the Law, or civil Judicature, perhaps otherwise than the
Nature of the Common Good in such Circumstances requir'd." For it
often happens, that by means of *Expressions too general,* or some *human
Weakness,* even in Legislators and Judges, which cannot provide for all
possible Cases, Rulers miss that Mark at which they sincerely aimed. But
the Love of the Common Good *requires,* "That" (after they have more
exactly consider'd the Circumstances of the present Case, than was possible for them, when they beheld it at a Distance,) "they should amend
those Things, from a more perfect Knowledge of the Circumstances now
in full View, which had been less happily establish'd, with respect to the
same Circumstances view'd more imperfectly from afar."

From this Law of Nature, *equitable Judgment* derives all its Authority,
and, therefore, this is the true Foundation of *Equity;* nor is it impertinent
to mention it in this Place; tho' I own, that its most remarkable Use in
correcting *Civil* Laws, cannot here be so distinctly explain'd, the establishment or original of Civil Laws having not been yet explain'd. Yet,
because it has other Uses, in Cases where Civil Laws are *Silent,* and in
the *making* Civil Laws, which ought to be *equitable,* it was not in this
Place to be pass'd over in Silence.

And the *Gov-
ernment of the
Passions,* which
are
§VIII. The *Sum* of what I have hitherto advanc'd comes to *this,* "That
a PRUDENT BENEVOLENCE toward all Rational Beings, fulfils the most
general Law of Nature." This will propose the *best End* to our *Affections*
and Endeavours of all Kinds, and prescribe that *Measure* to them, which
will be most *effectual* to the obtaining that best End, which, upon this
Account, is naturally their best Measure.

here accounted
for;
There is no Necessity, (tho' many seem to think otherwise,) that we
should assign a *distinct* Virtue to the Government of *every* Affection,
since the *same* Care of attaining any End will cause us, to *love* those
Things which promote it; to *desire* them, if absent; to *hope* for them, if
they seem probable; to *joy* in them, when present: And on the contrary,

to *hate* those Things which stand in opposition thereto; to *shun* them, when absent; *fear* them, when probable; and *grieve,* when they are present. Therefore, if we seek that End which the Law of Nature directs, and our Care to acquire it be conformable to the same Law, the Motions of all our Affections, (as what depend thereon from the Condition of Human Nature,) will naturally be in proportion to that Care, unless the Understanding be blind, in distinguishing their particular Objects, or Causes; which yet that due Love (that is suppos'd) of the End, will move every one to endeavour to prevent as much as he can.

This same Universal Benevolence, as it *restrains* and *corrects* in us all voluntary Motions opposite to the Common Good, those especially, by which we would prefer our own private Advantages to those of the Publick, comprehends *Innocence, Gentleness, Repentance, Restitution,* and *Self-denial:* As it includes a constant effectual and avow'd *Intention* to do Good, it will cause us to think *favourably* of others, which is *Candour;* and both to *promise* and *perform* good Offices to others, which is *Fidelity.* The same Benevolence, because it *loves,* in a *greater* Measure, known *Causes* of the common Good, will make Men *highly Grateful.* For *Gratitude* is nothing else than "Benevolence heighten'd towards those, who have been first Benevolent to us," nor does it oblige any one, unless when the Benefit is conferr'd without injuring another: It excites us to repay Benefits receiv'd, to our Power, but without Prejudice to the Publick Good. *[margin: and those Virtues, which respect the special Laws of Nature, Innocence, Gentleness, Repentance, Restitution, Self-denyal, Candour, Fidelity.]* *[margin: Gratitude;]*

Finally, the same Universal Love, tho' it endeavours to do Things acceptable to *all* the Parts of the System of Rational Beings, will, in an *especial* manner, regard those who both can and will *most profit* the whole Community, (such are *God,* and they who *preside* over Things Civil and Sacred by his Appointment;) or who, by the Condition and State of our Nature, may be *most profited* by us, as every one can be of greatest Benefit to *himself* and *his own Family,* to his Posterity and Kindred. *[margin: Our Duty to our God, our Governors, our selves, and our Family.]*

In these *few Heads* are contain'd the *Primary Special Laws of Nature,* and the fundamental *Principles* of *all* Virtues and *all* Societies, whether Sacred, Civil, or Oeconomical; it is likewise shewn, how the *same* Affection toward the Common Good is *naturally* sufficient for *all* these Offices, because it *naturally opposes contrary* Motions, and *assists* Affections, which are *Causes* and *Parts* of it-self.[9] Whence it is evident, that the same Law which enjoins this Affection, does at the same time command, that *Motions opposite* thereto should be restrain'd with our utmost Efforts; that the *Causes* conspiring therewith should be assisted; and that all the *Parts* of its proper Object, those especially now mention'd, should be regarded.

The Distinction explain'd between Actions *necessary* and *indifferent*, in which there is room for *Liberty*, and the interposition of the supreme Powers by *positive Laws.*

§IX. *Lastly,* I thought it proper to *suggest* in this Place, "That the Distinction between Actions *necessary* and *indifferent* takes its Rise from the Relation, which they naturally have to the Effect, or End propos'd by this Universal Law." Those Actions, without which it is impossible to obtain the End propos'd, are *necessary.* Those, to which there are others equivalent, or equally effectual to promote this *End,* are *Indifferent;* as concerning which the Law of Nature does not determine, whether we ought to act after this, or that Manner, solicitous only, that we contribute as much as we can to the Publick Happiness by some Method or other. In these Cases there is room for the greatest *Liberty;* and also for *Positive Laws,* contracting such Liberty within narrower Bounds.[10] I, usually in

9. Barbeyrac (*Traité Philosophique,* p. 342, n. 3) identifies a fault in the original text, which also escaped Bentley. The original has "& [idem affectus] causas partesque sui affectus juvat." Barbeyrac suggests that the copyist may have mistranscribed "sui affectus" for "sui objecti." This gives Barbeyrac's more plausible rendering: "and because it assists the causes capable of procuring the good that is its object, and the parts of which that good is composed."

10. [Maxwell] *"Indifferent* Actions, in this Explication, are indeed *one part* of the Materials of *Human Laws,* but not the *only Subject* of them. For as the Civil Laws order a particular Form for the Prosecution, or Defense of Rights given by the Law of Nature, in that Manner which is most convenient for the Society, and not intirely Indifferent; so they particularly determine the Obligations arising from the Constitution of the Society, which often are not Indifferent: And, in order to the regular Defense, or Prosecution of Rights, or even the Management of our Goods, make some general Limitations of some Points, which in the Whole are most convenient, different from what was determin'd by the Laws of Nature. An Instance will explain this. The *Law of Nature* requires, 'That no Contract shall be valid, if one of the Parties, by reason of Child-hood, could not understand what he was doing;' and also requires 'That Men of full Understanding should have the Administration of their own Affairs.' Now 'tis impossible for *Courts* to make particular Inquiries into the Abilities of every Youth; 'twas therefore necessary to determine a precise Age, which

my own Mind, *illustrate* this *Distinction* between *necessary* and *indifferent* Actions, by *comparing* them with the Methods of Practice subservient to the Construction of Geometrical Problems. Of these, some are so necessary, that the Construction of a Problem is impossible without them: Yet, in many Questions, various Methods of constructing the given Problem, without transgressing the Rules of Geometry, offer themselves; so that the Geometrician is at liberty, to use this, or that Method of Construction; yet still with this Limitation, that, whatever Method of Practice he follows, he must observe certain Rules, necessary to bring him in the end to the same Solution. As it is *free,* now that the Earth is *well-peopled,* for a Man to live *Single,* or *Married;* yet our equal Obligation in both States, not to violate, but pursue, the Common Good, lays us in either, under the Restraint of certain Laws.

§X. I have *not,* however, thought it *necessary,* "To reduce all those Particulars, which I have prov'd to be contained in one General Law, into the Form of Laws of Nature, and so to lay them before the Reader." Every Reader may, by his own Skill, form the Law enjoyning the Acquisition, and Exercise (always in order to promote the Common Good,) of *Prudence, Constancy, Moderation, Benevolence,* &c. provided he remembers, that their *Form,* made evident from the Appearances of Nature, is *this,* or to this Purpose. *The first Cause of Nature would have it known to all, that it is necessary to the common Happiness, and to the private Happiness of every particular Person, which is to be expected only from the Prosecution of the Common Good, That every one ought to pursue it with Prudence, Constancy,* &c. or, *a Law being given to prosecute the Common Good according to our Abilities; a Law is likewise given, commanding Prudence, Constancy, Fidelity,* &c. Nor is there a different Reason of the Laws

How to reduce any moral Virtue to the Form of a Law of Nature.

---

should, in the Whole, be most expedient, by excluding as few Persons of ripe Judgment, and yet including as few of unripe Judgment, as possible. It cannot be called wholly *Indifferent,* where the Bounds shall be set, whether at the Age of 10 Years, or 30, or 40. 'Tis plain, from universal Experience of civilized Nations, that the former would be too early, and the latter, too late; that, consequently, between 20 and 25 is really most convenient, and not an Arbitrary or Indifferent Decision; excluding few Men of Judgment, and including as few without it, as possible."

commanding us to *plight* and *keep Faith,* and to *practice Gratitude;* for these also take place in our Actions towards *all* Rational Beings whomsoever. There are many other Human Actions, which, tho' they promote the Good of the whole Society of Rational Beings, are yet immediately and in a peculiar Manner *appropriated* to certain Parts thereof; the Origin, therefore, of *Property* and *Dominion* (in a somewhat larger sense of the Words, than what is in use among the *Civilians*) is next to be enquir'd into.

ਊ CHAPTER VII ਊ

Of the Original of Dominion,
and the Moral Virtues.

As the *Animal Oeconomy* is *truly,* tho' *not sufficiently,* explain'd by saying, That the whole Fabrick of the Body is supported by the continual *Circulation* of the *Blood; so* the *Society* of all *Rational Agents* is *truly* said to be preserv'd by a *Circulation* of *Good Offices* for the benefit of the Publick; yet is *not sufficiently* explain'd, 'till it be shewn what Kind of Actions are necessarily to be assign'd to the chief Parts of that Society, and allotted to the peculiar Uses of these Parts respectively, in order to obtain that End; *as* to a distinct Explanation of the Nature of *Animals* it is requisite to shew, *what proportion* of the Blood should circulate thro' the Brain, and upper Parts of the Body, what thro' the lower, as the Liver and Hypochondria, and *how* the Nourishment should be distributed to the other, at least to the more noble, Parts of the Body.

It ought, however, to be observ'd, That, *as* the Vessels, which convey the Spirits and Nourishment to *one Part,* are not subservient to the particular Benefit of *that Part alone,* but also to the Well being of the *Whole* at the same time, since every Part of the Body is of some Use to the Whole: *so* those Things, which become the Property of the *particular Parts* of this Society, do not cease to be subservient to the *Whole* in the most advantageous Manner.

§II. The Original of *Right* over *Things* and *Persons,* (which I take leave to call by the Names of *Property* and *Dominion,*) seems deducible in the following manner from what I have already said. It has been *prov'd,*

Margin notes:

A Comparison between the Animal Oeconomy, and the Society of all Rational Agents, in order to illustrate the Origin of Dominion and Property.

The Origin of Property and Dominion over Things and

Persons, is deduc'd from the Law of Nature, commanding the making and preserving a Division of Rights.

"That in the Common Happiness are contain'd, both the highest Honour of God, and the Perfections, both of the Minds and Bodies of Men"; moreover, it is well *known* from the Nature of Things, "That, in order to these Ends, are necessarily requir'd, both many Actions of Men, and Uses of Things, which cannot, at the same time, be subservient to other Uses"; from whence it *follows*, "That Men, who are obliged to promote the Common Good, are likewise necessarily oblig'd to consent, that the Use of Things and Labour of Persons, so far as they are necessary to particular Men to inable them to promote the Publick Good, should be so granted them, that they may not lawfully be taken from them, whilst the aforesaid Necessity continues; that is, that those Things should, at least during such time, become their Property, and be called *their own.*" But such Necessity *continuing* by reason of the *Continuance* of *like* Times and Circumstances, a *perpetual* Property, or Right to the Use of Things, and to the Assistance of Persons necessary, will follow to each Person during Life. Farther; if the *same* Thing (as Lands, or Trees) can promote the aforesaid End for *several* Days, or Years, the *same Reason,* which gave a Right to them the *first* Day, will give a *like* Right the *following* Day, and so on, whilst Things continue as they were. And, by such Steps as these, does Reason lead Men to consent to the settling a *plenary Dominion* over *Things,* and at length also over *Persons,* or such *Labours* of Persons as are necessary to the Common Happiness. For the Obligation (which I have already demonstrated) to prosecute the *End, obliges* likewise to the absolutely-necessary *Means,* namely, the Consent of every Individual to some *Division* of Things and Human Labour; because it is *impossible,* "That the same Thing, or the Labour of the same Man, can serve the contrary Wills of many Men." For the *Things* which we make use of, and the *Members of Men,* by which their external Labour is perform'd to the Benefit of others, are *Bodies,* and therefore *limited* at any one Time to one Place, and therefore their *Motion,* by which they can be subservient to any one, is at any given time directed to *one Point only;* hence it *is,* "That the same Nourishment and necessary Cloathing, which preserves the Life of one Man, cannot at the same time perform the same Office for any other"; tho' remotely indeed, or by the Intervention of the Assistance of that Person, it may be useful to many. It is,

therefore, *evident*, "That the Nature of Things discovers, that it is necessary to the Happiness, Life, and Health, of every particular Person,
upon which all other Advantages depend, that the Uses of Things should
be limited, at least for a time, to particular Persons exclusive of others."
It is hence further *evident*, "That the same is likewise necessary to the
Common Happiness of All, because the Whole is not distinguish'd from
all its Parts taken together." *Lastly,* it is *manifest* by a *parity of Reason*,
"That this Limitation, made for a time, ought necessarily to be continued thro' all succeeding Times, in order to obtain the same End, either
in the same Things, or in others equivalent." But in this *continued Limitation* of Things and Human Labour, which are necessary to the Life
and Health and intire Happiness of Individuals, is contain'd the whole
Essence, Force, and Efficacy, of *Property* and *Dominion*, tho' it may be
cloathed with some additional Circumstances by *Civil Laws. Nature*,
therefore, evidently *teaches*, "That a Dominion over Things and Persons
ought necessarily to be settled for the Common Good of All," (if it be
suppos'd, that it was not settled at the very Beginning;) or *rather*, "That
it should be received and continued as already settled by the First Cause."

§III. These Things are thus reduc'd into the *Form* of a *Law of Nature.*

The Nature of Things made by the First Cause, plainly discovers, That Here reduc'd
it is his Will, that all voluntary Actions of Rational Agents, which are nec- to the Form of
essary to the establishing and preserving a Property in Individuals to some Nature,
*Things, or Persons, should be absolutely necessary to the enjoyn'd Pursuit of
the Common Good; and, therefore, that all Rational Agents are oblig'd by
the same Law, (by which they are oblig'd to promote the Publick Good, as
far as in them lies,) and the same Rewards and Punishments, to establish (or
acknowledge) and preserve some kind of Property, or Dominion.* Or thus
briefly, *There being given a natural Law to procure the Common Happiness
of All, there is given a natural Law, to establish and preserve, to particular
Persons, Properties in those Things, which are evidently necessary to the Happiness of Individuals, as well in Persons and their Actions necessary to mutual Assistance, as in other Things.*[1]

1. [Maxwell] "See *Carmichael*'s and *Barbeyrack*'s *Puffendorf* upon this Head of

consisting of two Parts, relating to the Rights of God and Men.

In this Law are contain'd these *two* Parts: 1. Let there be given to *God* such Things as are his: 2. To *Men* likewise such Things as are theirs: Both are necessary to be done, that God's *Honour* may be preserv'd to him, and that those Advantages may be preserv'd to Men, by which they may preserve and perfect themselves, and be useful to all others; *both* which are *contain'd* in the End propos'd, the *Common Good.*

What is intended by the Words *Property,* or *Dominion* in this Argument.

I chose to use those indefinite Words [*some kind of Property, or Do-minion,*] because I readily *acknowledge,* "That Nature does not always discover it to be necessary, that such kind of Property as consists in an *intire* Division of Things should be establish'd"; all that is *essential* to true Property, or Dominion, is, "That any one should have a Right se-cur'd by Law, to possess or dispose of certain Advantages, in a Thing, for *Example,* an undivided Field, which we use and enjoy in Common with others, and from which others have no Right to exclude us." If any one will contend, that this word *Property,* or *Dominion,* is *improperly* us'd in this Case, I will not dispute with him about *Words,* being solic-itous about the *Thing* only. *Grotius* acknowledges *"such a Restriction of the universal Right to be instead of Property."* [2] I chose this Word, because I could not find one more convenient to *signify,* "That the Prosecution of the Common Good requires such an Appropriation of some Things to particular Persons, as makes it unlawful for others to deny them to them, or take them from them"; and that I might by this Method *shew,* "That Mr. *Hobbes's* War, which would necessarily arise from his imagi-nary Right of every one to every Thing, was not lawful." It is *certain,* "That in the best regulated States many Things are possess'd by many in Common, and that some of these have a Right to a greater Share of the Profit than others, and that they peaceably enjoy it"; and it is no question, but that the *same* may happen, when by *Abstraction* of Mind we suppose the Removal, or *Non-existence,* of *Civil* Power. *Such Right*

---

the *Original of Dominion* upon which our Author is very *General."* Maxwell refers to Gershom Carmichael's lectures on Pufendorf, published as *Supplements and Ob-servations upon Two Books of Samuel Pufendorf's On the Duty of Man and Citizen* (1724); see also Pufendorf, *De Jure Naturae,* IV.4.

2. Grotius, *De Jure Belli ac Pacis,* II.2.2. no. 1.

(to the use and disposal of Things, and to some human Assistance,) which can be taken from no-one, without violating the Respect due to the Law of Nature, and to God its Author, I call by the Name of *some kind of Property,* or *Dominion.*

§IV. To these Things thus explain'd, I thought it proper to *add,* "That the *Law of Nature,* which I have now laid down, is the very same that enjoins *Universal Justice.*" For it enjoyns nothing but what is contain'd in *Justinian's* Definition of *Justice,* when rightly explain'd, which runs thus. *"Justice is the constant and perpetual Will to give every one his Right."*[3] Now I have affirm'd, that all voluntary Actions are to be directed by the Law, which enjoins consummate Prudence, and, in consequence, Constancy, Moderation, Benevolence, &c. I have, therefore, taken sufficient Care, that the Will employ'd about these be both *Constant* and *Perpetual.* What he affirms ought *"to be given to every one,"* that I alledge respects *all Rational Beings,* and therefore *God* himself.[4] Hence I affirm, That some Things ought to be look'd upon as belonging to *God,* others to *Men;* some Things as *Sacred,* others as *Profane.* Lastly, I thus understand that *Right is to be given,* that whatsoever has been made *any one's Property,* either by God, or Man, should be acknowledg'd, and reserv'd to them inviolably; and besides, that we should consent that those Things, which have *not become any one's Property,* should, in such Manner, be *distributed* amongst All, as may best conduce to the establishing and preserving the *Common Peace* and *Happiness* of All. The Words of the *Definition* may be thus conveniently explain'd; and it certainly belongs to the *same* Virtue and Disposition of Mind, to *divide* Things and human Services for the Common Good, and to *keep up* their *Division* for the same End; to *make* the *Division,* and to *consent* to it when made. Wherefore the *same* general Law of Nature commands *either* of these Actions, that, namely, which the present State of Affairs shall require, in order to that End, which it commands should be chiefly regarded.

(*Justinian's* Definition of *Justice* supposes this Law.)

3. Justinian, *Institutes,* I.i.

4. For the Ciceronian lineage of these comments, see Cicero, *De Finibus Bonorum et Malorum,* V.xxiii. 65–66; *Tusculan Disputations,* I.xxxvi and III.xvi.

Justice enjoins
Repentance
and Restitu-
tion.

We may further *add,* "That the same Law does clearly enough direct Men to *Repent,* and to make *Reparation of Damages,* as far as we can, if in any Thing we have transgress'd the Law." For, in the Laws of *Nature,* the Letter is not regarded, as is generally the Case in *Positive* Laws, but the *most effectual* Prosecution of the End propos'd: The Publick Good is *best obtain'd* by unerring Justice, but *next* by Repentance and Restitution, in case of Transgression, which often happens thro' human Frailty.

From this Law
is prov'd the
Justness of the
Distinction
between
Things, or Per-
sons Sacred,
and those
appointed to
Common Use.

§V. Here opens a spacious Field of Inquiry, 1. Concerning the *Right of God* over Things and Persons, and concerning the Manner *how* Men discover that such Right belongs to him: 2. Concerning the *Dominion of Men,* or those Things which are ours, either by a common Right of All, or our own particular Right; which are the Subject of the two Tables of the *Decalogue,* and of which *Grotius* treats at large.[5] The *First* I pass over, to avoid falling into *Theological Disputes;* and the *Second,* lest the present Treatise should swell to *too great* a Volume. However, I think proper to *observe,* "That this general Law establishes some difference between Things and Persons which are consecrated to *God,* and those which are allow'd for the *common Uses of Men.*" For it is an *Effect* of this Division of Dominion, "That, beside the *universal* Dominion over all Things which belongs to God, which is consistent with a subordinate Property of Men in the same Things, there should, beside, be some Things *peculiar* to God, both among *Persons,* as Kings and Priests; and among *Things,* as Times and Places, as being consecrated to him." And *further,* "That from this Fountain are deriv'd all good Laws, which limit, or direct, Men in Things to be set apart for God"; such are those, by which some *Privileges* are granted them; or, on the contrary, by which some *Measure* is prescrib'd to Things, which (to use a Law-Term) may fall into *Mort-Main:*[6] I think it sufficient to mention these Things by the way, because my chief Aim is to *shew,* "That all Right acquir'd by

5. Grotius, *De Jure Belli ac Pacis,* II.2.
6. *Mort-main:* Inalienable ownership, from Old French and medieval Latin for "dead hand."

us, either over *our-selves,* which is called *Liberty;* or over *Things* by Occupancy, or by Division; or in *Persons* distinct from ourselves, by Pater-
nity, Consent, or Forfeiture; is granted to us by the Will of the First
Cause, establishing that primary Law of Nature, enjoyning the Prosecution of the Common Good." For hence is *prov'd* by an *Induction of
Particulars,* "*That* every Right of Men is deduc'd from that Law, and
that by the same Law the Rights of all particular Persons are so limited,
that no-one has a Right to violate the Publick Good, or to take away
from any other, who has not hurt the Community, either Life, or those
Things which are necessary to enable him to promote the Common
Happiness."

§VI. Altho' I have adapted these Things (the Nature of *Laws,* properly
so call'd, requiring it) to the Condition of Rational *Creatures,* yet I have
taken care, that every Thing should be so laid down, as that they might
all be ascrib'd to God in such an ANALOGICAL Manner, as the *Observance*
of the *Laws* of Nature is ascrib'd to him, when he is by all acknowledg'd
Just, Liberal, Merciful. Certainly, no-one in his Senses can *imagine,*
"That the FIRST CAUSE is bound by any Laws, if Laws be taken for practical Dictates (or Rules of Action) receiving the Sanction of *Rewards*
and *Punishments* from the Will of a *Superior";* from whence it follows,
That no-one can imagine his *Dominion* over the Creatures to be founded
in, or regulated by, a *Law* in *that* Sense. On the contrary, no-one can
think honourably of God, who does not *acknowledge,* "That his Wisdom proposes to him the best End, namely, his own Honour, and the
Happiness of other Rational Beings, by the Use of that Understanding
and Will which is natural to them; and that the same Wisdom requires,
as the Means necessary to this End, that Necessaries, at least, be so
granted to each Individual, that it should not be lawful to violate them."
But this is to prescribe and establish the distinct Rights of Individuals,
or *Dominion.*

    Nor is there less necessarily *included* in the *Perfection* of the Divine
Nature, "A *Will* to pursue this best End by proper Means, in concurrence with infinite Prudence," in which *Concurrence* the greatest Benevolence is included. *Because* it is necessary to the supreme Honour of

*The Divine
Dominion is
deduc'd from
the Dictate of
the Divine
Wisdom,*

*approv'd of by
his Will;*

God, and to the Preservation and Perfection of the whole System of Things, that God should govern and dispose all Things, according to the Counsel of his own Understanding, his own Wisdom *cannot but* dictate this to him: Nor can there be suppos'd in him a *Will dissenting* from this Dictate of his own *Wisdom.*

which is Analogous to a Natural Law.

It is further *evident,* "That the Dictate of the Divine Understanding concerning the End, and the Means conducing thereto, is *Analogous to a natural Law,* and that the Necessity of his continuing to Will perfectly, that is, agreeably to his Infinite Wisdom, does in Effect *far surpass* all the Sanctions of a Law by Rewards and Punishments."[7] *Consequently,* "All his Actions will be conformable to the Dictates of his Understanding, concerning promoting the best End, the Common Good, and may be called *Just,* for the same Reason those *Dictates* are allow'd to have the force of *Laws.*" And, in like manner, his Power of disposing of all Things, as he shall think fit, in consistence with this End, and the Means necessary, may be called the RIGHT OF GOD, or his Dominion over Things and Persons, from all Eternity, proceeding (as I have shewn) from his essential Perfections, as from a natural Law. Upon the maturest Deliberation, I can find nothing to hinder, but that this *Dictate* of the Divine Understanding, *It is necessary for the Common Good, that the most full and supreme Power of governing all Creatures should be assum'd by God, and reserv'd to him,* has the full *Force* of a *Law,* and may, therefore, be a solid Foundation for the *Divine Dominion;* unless, perhaps, it be *objected,* "That it is not enjoin'd by, nor has receiv'd a Sanction from, any *Superior*": But to give it the essential Force of a Law, it is *sufficient,* "That it is a true Proposition formed by the supreme and most perfect Being, concerning the best End, and the Means necessary thereto," tho' it proceed not from a *Superior,* which in this Case is *impossible.* Whereas this *Dictate* is in itself *most perfect,* (containing an evident Truth concerning the noblest Subject,) and has for its *Author* a Being infinitely *superior in Perfection* to all others, that can exist: It cannot need an *external Recommendation* from another *Author,* and it must as little need

---

7. Cf. Pufendorf, *De Jure Naturae,* II.1.3, II.3.5–6.

a *Sanction* by Punishments to be inflicted by another, because the *intrinsick Propension* of the Divine Will, to advance this greatest Good, will not suffer him to violate this Dictate. For, if it were *suppos'd*, "That the Divine Will had departed from the best End, and the Means necessary to it," he would at the same time be *suppos'd* "to have fallen from his infinite Perfection," (for he would have been more Perfect, if he had not so departed;) that is, he would be *suppos'd* "to have laid aside his Deity," which implies a *Contradiction*. The Dictates, therefore, of the Divine Understanding, do in the *same Manner* pass into Laws, binding him by the *Immutability* of his own Perfections, *as* we use to say, that the Oath of God is ratified, when he swears by himself, or by his own Life; that is, by his *immutable* Perfections, which will endure for ever.[8]

However, *this Dominion* over All, which we assert God reserves to himself, is on this Account *free* from all suspicion of *Injury*, because "No Law can be imagin'd *prior,* which can be thereby *violated,* and no *reason of Competition* can be produc'd on the Part of the *Creatures,* who can yet be only considered as *possible,* whose future *Existence,* and all their future *Right* to any kind of Dominion, depends intirely upon the *Bounty* of the Divine Will." Further; the very *End,* in order to which I affirm'd it necessary, that God should take to himself the Exercise of this Dominion, namely, the *Common Good,* has so full a View to the *Happiness* of the *Creatures,* that no-one (except thro' his own *Fault*) can be *hurt* by this, or any other Means necessary to the Prosecution thereof.

[margin: and is free from Injury to any;]

Lastly; I think this resolving the *Divine Right* into such a Dictate of the Divine Understanding, and the other *incommunicable* Perfections of his Will, ought, *therefore,* to be admitted, *because* "No Creature, from an Opinion of his own Wisdom, or Goodness, much less Power, can ever arrogate to himself, from this Example, a right of Dominion over

---

8. Cumberland adopts the quasi-voluntarist "middle way" between voluntarism and intellectualism detailed in Suarez, *De Legibus ac Deo Legislatore* (1612), II.2.4, and taken up by several English writers; Culverwell, *An Elegant and Learned Discourse of the Light of Nature* (1651), p. 65; Parker, *An Account of the Nature and Extent of the Divine Dominion and Goodnesse* (1666), pp. 150–51.

other Creatures." Whereas, on the contrary, *"Hobbes's* Resolving the *Di-vine Dominion* into his *irresistible Power,* so evidently leads Men to seek Dominion over others by Force, or Fraud, by Right, or Wrong, that I doubt not, but that it was invented by him, and ascrib'd to God, for that End only, that it might countenance his pretended *Right of all Men to all Things."* 9

I may here *add,* "That the *Law of Nature,* properly so called, (which takes place in the Minds of Men, and which, because of the Will of God, whom we discover to be the supreme Governor in the Manner above-mention'd, *obliges* Men to pay him *Honour* and *Worship,*) may be justly said to give him this *Right of Dominion,* as it *obliges* us to *ac-knowledge* that Right in him, and *voluntarily* to offer him the same." For it is *evident,* "That, if we would *propose* to ourselves this *noblest End,* as we ought, we could not in a more *prudent* Manner promote it, than by giving the Glory of *Commanding* to *God,* and by reserving to *ourselves* only the Praise of *Obedience,* and so a *Right* to Things and Persons, in *Subordination* to him, and to the Common Good." For it is *apparent,* "That this *subordinate Right* to the Use of many Things, and of human Aid, is plainly *necessary* to support the *Lives* and *Powers* of Men, and, consequently, to all that *Worship* and *Honour* which they can give to *God* in this Life"; the IMMORTAL GOD, however, standing *not* in the least *need* of these Things, and, therefore, *not requiring* them, except for the more liberal *Support* of those who in a *more particular Manner serve* and *represent* him upon Earth, namely, Civil Magistrates and the Ministers of Holy Things.

§VII. Before I had *universally* and *distinctly* consider'd the Original of *all* Dominion and Right whatsoever, I *us'd,* indeed, as most others do, "to deduce the Divine Dominion intirely from his being the Creator": *For* I thought it *Self-evident,* "That every one was Lord of his own Pow-ers," which are little different from the *Essence* of any Thing, and that, *therefore,* any *Effect* must be *subject* to him, from whose *Powers* it receiv'd

---

9. Hobbes, *On the Citizen,* 15.5, pp. 173–74; Cf. Pufendorf, *De Jure Naturae,* I.6.10.

its whole Essence, as is the case in *Creation,* by which the whole Substance of the Thing is produc'd into Being.

But, because all *Dominion* supposes some *Right,* and all Right is a Power granted or permitted by some *Law,* at least Analogically such; therefore, the Law *granting* or *permitting Dominion* ought *first* to be acknowledg'd. But Law there is none prior to the *Natural* Law, or that *Dictate* of the Divine *Wisdom,* concerning the *Best End,* and the *Means* thereto *necessary,* which is perfectly *agreeable* to the *Law of Nature,* and may *Analogically* be called, the LAW OF THE DIVINE ACTIONS; I, therefore, came to this *Conclusion,* "That the Dominion of God is a Right, or Power, given him by his own Wisdom and Goodness, as by a Law, for the Government of all those Things which ever have been, or shall be, created by him." In the Divine *Wisdom* is necessarily contain'd "a Dictate to pursue the best End by the necessary Means"; and in the *Goodness,* or Perfection, of the Divine Will is by a like Necessity included "a ready Consent to promote the same": And these, by a natural *Analogy,* answer to a *Ratification* of this eternal *Law,* whence the *Divine Dominion* may take its *Original.*

deducing it from the Dictate of the Wisdom of God, in concurrence with his Goodness.

Nor can any one justly *complain,* "That the Dominion of God is contracted within *too narrow Limits* by this Explication, which amounts to this only, that no Part thereof consists in the Power of doing any Thing contrary to the best End, the Common Good, that is, his own Honour, and that Happiness of other Rational Beings, which both the Nature of Things made by himself admits of, and to the procuring whereof the Faculties given them by himself are fitted." For it is *plain,* "That infinite Wisdom and Power can dispose of all Things and Men after infinitely-different Manners, yet so, that in each of these Ways the Common Good of the whole System might be equally obtain'd." And it is *as plain,* "That perfect Liberty does not consist in the Power of doing better, or worse, but in the Power of equally doing for the best, whether God confers his own Benefits more abundantly upon these, or others, respect being always had to the best End." We ought, however, to be cautious, lest we *imagine,* "That nothing is consistent with this End, which our Understanding does not comprehend, in what Manner it can promote it"; for we know, that the *Weakness* of our Mind is *not able* to comprehend an *End so great*, nor can reach that *infinite Variety of Means*, which can be fitted by God to the procuring of it; and we shall afterwards learn much concerning these Things, of which we are at present ignorant. Thus, for *Instance*, we know in *general*, that *all* the Parts of an Animal are *some way useful* to it, tho' we do not yet *distinctly* and throughly understand the Use of many Parts, as the *Spleen, Brain*, &c. However, because the Perfection, both of the Divine Understanding and of his Will concurring therewith, is *intrinsecal* to God himself; it is evident, that his Dominion, explain'd in this Manner, is not understood to be receiv'd from *without*, nor to be *less Eternal* than those *Perfections*, from which it is *discover'd* and demonstrated by us, *rather* than properly *deriv'd*. The Question concerning the Original of the Divine Dominion, must needs be thus understood, for no Man in his wits would search for a *Cause*, properly so called, of a Right that had *no Beginning*.

I hope the Reader will pardon this *Digression*, which I have not made without reason, because it seem'd almost *necessary*, "To give some Account how a Right of imposing those Laws upon Men, which are the Subject of our present Inquiries, belongs to God," which might be better grounded than what *Hobbes* has propos'd, where he *contends*, "That the irresistible Power of God gives *him* (and consequently *any other*) a Right to do any Thing, without any respect to the Common Good." I, on the contrary, (by shewing that the Care of the chief Good, by Means naturally sufficient and necessary, is necessarily included in the Perfection of the Divine Nature, as it is Rational,) have pointed out that fundamental Principle, whence it may be *demonstrated*, "That Universal Justice, and, consequently, every Moral Virtue requisite in a Governor, display themselves in God above all others," just in the same Manner, that I shall in what follows *prove* "Men are oblig'd to the Exercise of the same." For *that* being what I have undertaken to explain in *this Treatise*, I resolv'd not to insist upon the *Disputes* which may be raised, concerning the *Right of the Deity* over his Creatures.

§VIII. Let us, therefore, now resume the Consideration of the Law lately discover'd, which *commands*, "That Necessaries, at least, be allow'd to all without Violation"; that is, "That they become their Properties, at

What Regulations the Law of Nature laid Men under, in

least for the Time they continue necessary to 'em, whence they are called *their* Rights." The Reason of my proposing that Law in such *general* Terms, as I have used, *was,* "That the same Rule might oblige and direct Men, as well in that State which may be suppos'd *prior* to, as in that which follows, the Division of Things and mutual Offices made by consent." In the *former* State it obliges only to a *limited Occupancy* and Use of Things and human Assistance, such as may be consistent with the Convenience of others: *Such* may be imagin'd the State of our *First Parents,* if *nothing* were suppos'd divinely *Reveal'd* of the Power of the Husband over the Wife. a State suppos'd *prior* to a plenary Division of Property by Consent.

And, in *this State, many* Things may be suppos'd to have happen'd, which would demonstrate it the *Interest* of all, "to make by consent a Division of Things and mutual Offices"; such as the *Disputes* of many, where it was not very evident, what was necessary to each; and the *Sloth* of some neglecting to cultivate the Common Fields, and the like. In such Cases, the *Laws* concerning the End and the Means necessary, being applied to the *given Circumstances,* would oblige to a *further Division* of Property, and the *same Laws* would oblige, both them and those who should be born after them, to *preserve* this Division, so highly conducive to the Common Good. After this Manner their Rights will be *gradually* settled, to each particular Man, Family, City, State, and that, both over Things and the Services of Men; whence will arise the Rights of *Commerce* and *Friendship,* and also the Rights of *Government* in Families, and States, both in Things Sacred and Civil. The Reasons, from the Nature of Things, enforcing the coming to such a Division.

§IX. Of the *making this Division,* I will not say much, because we all find it *ready made* to our Hands, in a Manner plainly *sufficient* to procure the best End, the Honour of God, and the Happiness of all Men, if they be not wanting to themselves. I will, therefore, *offer* only in few Words, That, "wherever such a Division is farther necessary, and a Difference arises between them, whose necessity requires that it should be made," It is *evident,* "That it tends more to the Common Happiness, to entrust the Division to the Arbitration of any prudent Man, who has no Interest to favour either Party, than to commit the Event to Force, or Fraud." For it is more probable, that *any one's Reason* will prescribe The present Methods for making such a Division; when it is necessary, and the Parties cannot amicably agree it among themselves: Namely, by *Arbitration,* or *Lots.*

that Method which is consistent with the known End, the Common Good, than that either of them should by *blind* Force hit that *Mark,* at which *neither Aims:* For I agree with *Hobbes* in *supposing,* "That, in such a War, each Party seeks only his own Safety in Victory." *But,* "If it so happen, that the disagreeing Parties can agree upon *no Umpire,* it will be more reasonable to leave the Division, or the whole Property of the Thing in Dispute, if it cannot be divided, rather to *Chance* than to *War"; because* "In War both Parties may perish, and so fall short of the End propos'd, which cannot happen, if the Affair be committed to Chance."[10]

Upon what Reason the Rights of Primogeniture and First Occupancy are grounded.

I mention this, by the way, in order to shew the *Reason,* "Why we ought to acquiesce in some Methods of disposing of Things and Employments, which partake more of *Chance* than of *Rational Choice";* such are, beside casting Lots, *Primogeniture,* and *First Occupancy.*

It is unjust, to attempt any innovation in the present settlement of Property.

"The *same* Reason and Law of Nature, which commands the *establishing* a distinct Dominion over Things and Persons, commands also *more evidently* to *preserve* them inviolable, now that they are establish'd and prov'd by *Experience* to answer the design'd End." For it is *evident,* "That the Division of Dominion, which we find made by our Ancestors, and establish'd by the Consent, or Permission, of all Nations and States, has been sufficient for the Procreation and Preservation of all that now exist, and to the Procuring all that Happiness, which we now see Mankind possess'd of; and, beside, that it affords such Intercourse among Men, such Opportunities of mutual Assistance, that all may attain greater Degrees of Happiness, both in this Life and a future."

It is beside *manifest,* "That the Happiness we now enjoy, and have the greatest Reason to expect from the present Division, is greater than any prudent Man could hope to obtain, by violating and overturning all settled Rights, Divine and Human, and endeavouring to introduce a new Division of all Property, according to the Judgment, or Affections, of any one Man whatsoever."

For it is *obvious,* "That this is an Undertaking, to which the Understanding of no one Man, or Assembly of Men, is equal"; and it is easy

10. Cf. Pufendorf, *De Jure Naturae,* III.2.5.

to *foresee*, "That the Opinions of so many Men would differ so widely upon this Head, that all would immediately be reduc'd to a State of War and Misery." Wherefore, "A Desire of Innovation in Things pertaining to Property, is unjust, because it is inconsistent with this Law, which is inseparable from the Common Good." I do, therefore, not only highly approve (with *Grotius*) of that Sentence of *Thucydides, "It is just for every one to preserve that Form of Government in the State, which has been deliver'd down to him."* [11] But I am of Opinion, that what he has affirm'd of *one State* only, ought to be extended to the great Society of all Rational Beings, (which I call the KINGDOM OF GOD;) and that it ought not to be limited only to the *Form of Government,* which contains the Division of the principal Offices in the Administration, but extended universally to the *Division of Things:* And in this Latitude I assert it *Just,* "To preserve inviolably the antient Division of Dominion over Things and Persons, both among different Nations, and in particular States." For Experience has shewn *it* conducive to the best End, and no Laws of Nature can be conceiv'd, which, consistently with this End, could prohibit *such a Division*'s being at first made; *That,* therefore, could be injurious to no-one. But the *same Reason,* which first *oblig'd* Men to *make* this Division, (since they who rightly judge must unavoidably *agree,*) will also *oblige* their Successors to *approve* and confirm the same.

I own, indeed, That the various Vicissitudes of Human Life and Actions, do necessarily introduce various *Alienations* of *antient Rights,* and many *new Regulations* concerning them; but, because all *Conveyance* of Rights and new Regulations are made by the *Will* of them, to whom they were (at least Mediately) *at first* granted, the *antient* Division of Property is still preserv'd, for this very *Reason,* "That their Will is observ'd." For it must be *suppos'd,* "To have been the Intention of the Authors of the first Division, along with the Property to have conferr'd a Power of conveying it, and of making many new Regulations, with respect, both to the first Possessors, and to their Successors." For *Dominion* contains a *Power to dispose* of that Thing, or Labour, which is Ours, but

Of transferring Property by Compacts, whose Obligation,

11. Thucydides, *The History of the Peloponnesian War,* VI.89; Grotius, *De Jure Belli ac Pacis,* II.4.8.

a Compact consists in the *Consent* of two concerning such *Disposal;* the same Law, therefore, ratifies such *Compact,* which gives a Man *Power to dispose* of that Thing, or Labour, which is his.

and Limita-
tions, are
deduced from
the same Law.

But, because this Power, or the *Dominion* it-self, which is conferr'd on any, is only in order to the *Common Good,* it *follows,* "That no Compact (whose Obligation is intirely owing to that) can oblige any One to such Things as are inconsistent with that End, or which are forbid by the Law of Nature"; and, consequently, both the *Obligation* and *Restrictions* of Compacts are deriv'd from the *same* Fountain.[12]

From the same
Law is deriv'd
the Obligation
to *Beneficence*
and *Gratitude;*

§X. A Dominion over Things and Persons being establish'd, from the General Law of Nature, *particular Persons* have somewhat of their own to *Give,* or to *Promise,* Absolutely, or upon Condition. A *Property* in Things is *suppos'd,* before there is any room for *keeping Faith.* For, seeing the very *same Reason,* that establishes Dominion, in which the Power of bestowing is included, namely, the Common Good of all Rational Beings, but of those especially, to whom this Power is allow'd in any particular Case, *renders a free Gift valid;* it is, evidently, the perpetual *Will* of God, and of all Authors of Dominion subordinate to him, "That Men should in all Giving and Receiving aim at this End, without which the Law of Nature would allow no place for such Actions." *Wherefore,* "He who accepts of a Benefit, is understood, by the very Action, to have consented to accept it under this Limitation, and upon this Condition, that it should be better for the Publick, but especially for his Benefactor."

---

12. [Maxwell] "There are certain Affairs, in which 'tis necessary for the Publick Good, that Men should be constituted *valid Disposers;* such as concerning their *Labours* and *Goods:* Concerning the disposition of these there are many general Laws, both of Nature and Revelation, but scarce any special Laws, determining any precise Quantities, or Proportions of either. These General Laws leave all Men *valid Disposers,* since they leave all precise Determinations to their own Prudence. Now, to know whether we are oblig'd by a Contract, we are only to inquire, whether the Parties were *valid Disposers,* or not: for Men are often obliged to observe very foolish Contracts, when they are *valid Disposers,* and by such Contracts others do acquire external Rights. But no Man can be a *valid Disposer,* so as to oblige himself to any Violation of the Honour of God, or perfect Right of another."

But *this Consent* includes a kind of *tacit Compact,* "To return the Benefit, as occasion offers," in which the whole Force of *Gratitude* displays it-self: And, beside, *such Consent* is only "an Approbation of the general Law, to promote the Common Good, and to settle Dominion, or Prop-erty, for that very End"; Gratitude, therefore, is hence clearly enough enjoin'd. It is "Another's giving, of his own, what we were not intitled to," that lays us under *Obligations of Gratitude* to him, and makes us know, and acknowledge, his Benevolence.

To proceed; the *Measure* of our Property being fix'd and determin'd by its respect to the Common Good, (as I have already shewn,) we hence learn the *Limits* of a laudable *Self-love:* For we must always, in providing for our-selves, "Abstain from invading another's Property," and take care, "That we promote the Publick Good." This limited Self-love displays it-self chiefly in *Temperance, Frugality* and *Modesty.* *to a limited Self-love (including Fru-gality, Temper-ance, and Chastity;)*

Lastly; the *same Law* of Nature, which distributes Property, and the *same Justice,* (or Will to preserve Property so distributed to each,) which takes care, both of our selves and others (as I have shewn) does farther *enjoin* and *limit* the *natural Affection of Parents towards their Children,* which is highly subservient to the Common Good. Our *Children* are something compounded of *our-selves and others;* and it is therefore nec-essary, that the Virtue, by which we are inclin'd to the Care of *our-selves and others,* should in a particular Manner regard those, in whom we our-selves are, as it were, united and mix'd with others, and both Branches of the Object of this Virtue meet. To this is owing that eminent *Care of Posterity,* which all States manifest in their Laws concerning the Suc-cession to the Goods, and often to the Employments, of the Deceased. *to a limited Natural Affec-tion;*

From what has been said upon this Head, it is obvious to any One.

1. That *Beneficence* towards others, the Obligation and Faith of *Com-pacts, Gratitude, Temperance, Frugality, Modesty, Natural Affection,* can-not be clearly explain'd, unless a *Division of Property,* by which what is ours may be distinguished from what is anothers, be *first establish'd,* or suppos'd.

2. That the *same General Law,* by which this *Division* is made and preserv'd, obliges Men to the Exercise of *all these Virtues,* and to *all oth-ers,* that are either contain'd in them, or may be deduc'd from them.

to the Laws of
Nations and of
Civil Societies,
whether they
regard Sover-
eigns, or Sub-
jects.
§XI. *Lastly;* all particular Moral Rules, or Laws; as well those, by which the *Rights of different Nations* are guarded from mutual Invasion; as those, by which the *Authority of the Supreme Powers* is founded and pre-serv'd from the Attempts of the Seditious, and the *Rights of Subjects* are protected from the Violence of the Powerful; are deriv'd from the same Command to distribute and settle *Property,* with a view to the Common Good.

I *affirm'd,* "That Civil Authority was founded on this Command," because it is *evident,* "That the establishing Civil Government is a much more effectual Means to promote the Common Happiness of Mankind, and to preserve Peace, than an equal Division of Things, which is in-consistent with Civil Dominion." Yet *Hobbes contends,* "That such an *equal* Distribution of all Things and Rights is commanded by the *Law of Nature,*" and would have natural *Equity* to consist in this; led, truly, by the likeness of Words, as became him, who is frequently inculcating, *"That all Reasoning depends upon Words."* This Doctrine of the equal Distribution of Property, he gradually instills, *Lib. de Cive. Cap.* 3. *a* §. 13. *ad* 19.[13] Which I care not to spend time in refuting, both because he has nothing there which can deceive a prudent Man, and because the very Foundation, on which all the rest is built, *"That it is necessary to promote Peace, that Men be look'd on as equal,"* §. 13. does not seem even to *Hobbes* himself, a Means proper to that *End,* "The procuring Peace and Security," but he requires the establishing a *coercive Power,* which must immediately destroy such an *equality,* as is evident from his *Fifth Chapter.* It is, however, dangerous to *teach,* "That an equal Distribution is commanded by the Laws of Nature," because, by his own Confession, they are wholly *Unchangeable,* C. 3. §. 29.[14] and, therefore, according to his Principles, an *unequal Distribution* of Dominion, altho' it be ab-solutely necessary to a Monarchical Constitution, can *never be Lawful,* because it is contrary to the Laws of Nature.

13. Hobbes, *On the Citizen,* 3.13–18, pp. 49–51.
14. Ibid., 3.29, p. 54.

§XII. I ought rather to *observe*, "That the Division of all Kind of Property, or Dominion, is by me deduc'd from a Law, which does not suppose the Erection of any Civil Government, and, therefore, depends not upon the Will of the Civil Magistrate, and is, consequently, a Rule proper to direct the Actions of different States, and impose Restrictions which are not to be broke thro', even by Princes." *Because* "such a Law only, can guard those Things that are necessary to the Happiness of every One, from the Invasion of all Others"; it *follows*, "That Peace amongst all can be establish'd, only by such a Law, and that it actually will be establish'd, as far as can be done by Virtue of a Law, and the Power, or Right, thence granted to Men"; nor can more be desired. *On the contrary,* "If Property may be arbitrarily settled and unsettled by the sole Will of the Supreme Powers in every State, and the Nature of the Best End, or of the Common Good, and of the Means naturally leading thereto, fixes no Rule," (as *Hobbes* every where teaches,[15]) "Which even their Wills are obliged to obey in external Actions," there is *no Law* to restrain States from perpetual War; *no Law* to oblige the Rulers of States to seek the Publick Good of their Subjects, and to preserve them their Rights by external Acts; (for their Will, which only, *Hobbes* acknowledges for a Law, may lead them to the contrary:) *No Law* to forbid a Faction, powerful enough to overturn the State, to commit Treason. For, on this very Account, that a Faction is suppos'd too Powerful for the State, there is *no* longer any *coercive Power* in the State, either to protect the Obedient, or to punish the Disobedient; and, therefore, according to *Hobbes's* Principles, there is *no Security* to be had, such as is necessary to oblige to the Observance of the Laws of Nature, (for *Example,* to keep Faith,) by external Actions, and, therefore, this Law will *not oblige,* but it will be lawful to dissolve that State, which was founded upon Compact: And, therefore, any State may be crumbled into Parts less and less without end, and that *lawfully,* according to *Hobbes's* Doctrine; because *no Law,* of Force in that Case, will be violated; not the *Law of Nature,* which for want of Security, in that Case, will not oblige to external Actions, (so he tells us *de Cive, Cap.*

*It is *necessary,* "That the *forming* and preserving States be enjoin'd by a *Natural Law,* obliging to the Performance of *External* Actions, *before* the Foundations of such States." Hence, not receiving its *Force* from the *Magistrate,* it *binds him* indispensably, as also *all Nations,* with respect to one another.*

---

15. For Hobbes's views on property, see *On the Citizen,* 12.7, pp. 136–37; *Leviathan,* ch. 18, p. 114; ch. 24, pp. 160–63.

3. §. 27;[16]) nor the *Law of the State,* because they are not violated by Rebellion, or Treason, according to his Assertion, *c.* 14. §. 21.[17]

The same Law of Universal Justice teaches to acknowledge and preserve *Natural* Governments;

and, after these Patterns, to establish *Civil* Government:

Gives the Dictates of Reason the Force of Divine Laws;

and leaves room for Positive Laws by God and Men;

all which must be plainly promulg'd;

§XIII. This Law of Universal Justice (which I have laid down, for this Reason, that it lays the Foundation of Dominion Divine and Human, both over Things and Persons, in the Respect due to the Common Good,) teaches us to acknowledge and preserve all *Government* establish'd *naturally,* (such as is that of God over all Creatures, and of Parents over their Children:) And by this Means chiefly does this Law provide for the Necessities of Human Nature, and admonishes us, where they are wanting, to erect the most convenient *Forms of Government* according to these *Patterns,* and to preserve *Peace* with them who are not under the same Civil Power. Hence it is, that the *Dictates of Reason,* (naturally, that is, from the *Will of the First Cause* establishing the Nature of Things,) laying down many clear and general Precepts concerning the Common Good, are justly esteem'd *Divine Laws:* And that large Room is left for *Divine Revelation,* or *Human Authority,* to superadd, in order to the same End, *Positive Laws,* (as they are called,) which shall, in the given Circumstances, be our special Rule of Action.[18]

Moreover; these general *Laws of Nature,* concerning the Care of the Publick Good, and the settling and preserving Dominion, *require,* "That both God and Men take care, whenever they please to enact any *Positive* Law, to give *sufficient Evidence* of their doing so"; for such Discovery is

---

16. Hobbes, *On the Citizen,* 3.27, pp. 53–54.

17. Ibid., 14.21, p. 166. Here Hobbes argues that treason is an offense against natural law rather than civil law, because civil law presupposes obedience.

18. Cumberland manuscript addition: "It is from the natural laws, inasmuch as they establish the estate of God, that flows the obligation on men to obey the precepts revealed in the Gospel. Consequently it is on them that the strength of the ecclesiastical power also depends originally, which power is immediately inferred from the precepts and examples that are to be found in the books of the New Testament. It should not be suggested that the primitive basis of this power is the authority of every Civil Government, since we are also obliged to recognise it in all states to which the laws of the Gospels are sufficiently published: but we must relate it to the Natural Laws, or the Right of Men, which, according to Roman jurisconsults, encompass the precepts of natural religion." Cumberland, Trinity College MS.adv.c.2.4, p. 355. The Roman law reference can be found in Justinian, *Digest,* I.1.2.

necessary to the *Promulgation* thereof, without which no-one can be oblig'd. Hence it is necessary, that, "if God would command any Thing   and also consistent with the
Laws of
Nature.
by a Revelation," it must first appear *plain,* "That the Command is perfectly consistent with his unchangeable Laws known from Nature." For
it is *certain,* "That the Divine Reason cannot contradict it-self." And it
is farther *required,* "That his Will to enforce this new Law be discover'd
to those for whom it is enacted, by enabling his Messengers to foretel
future Contingencies without Mistake, or Deceit, or else to work true
Miracles." Hence also *Human Legislators,* when they enact Laws, do in
the first Place *declare,* "that they tend to the Publick Good," and, therefore, have the same View with the Laws of Nature; and then *add* "some
Signs, or Testimonies, to make it known, that they have been actually
promulg'd by their Authority."

Of the Moral Virtues in particular.

The Author proceeds to a particular Description of the more *limited Moral Virtues.* Having explain'd the *Original of Dominion,* and, by the way, declar'd its *Progress* thro' all Society, whether Sacred, or Civil, or between different States, or between the different Parts of the same Family; I will now "proceed to a particular Description of the more *limited Moral Virtues."* Something upon this Head I have *already suggested* in the foregoing Discourse, where I have *shew'd,* "That they were contain'd as *Parts* in that Universal Benevolence enjoyn'd by the Law of Nature." But, because these Virtues are properly conversant only about such Matter, as is, *of right, in our own Power;* and because in these there is a distinction between *Debts* and *Gifts,* between *Superiors* and *Inferiors,* between *different States,* and between the *several Members of the same State,* and between the *Parts of a Church,* or *Family;* it was necessary to lay down something, in general, concerning the *Original* of *Dominion* over Things and Persons, whence all these *different Relations* arise; and that it was to be deduc'd from Principles, which did not *suppose* any Obligation to the *special* Acts of the Virtues.

All Obligation to the exercise of Moral Virtues, arises immediately from *this,* "That such Actions are commanded by the Law of Nature." First, then, we are to *observe,* that, *"As Universal Justice* is a Moral Perfection, to which we are therefore oblig'd, because such a Will, or Inclination of Mind, is commanded by the *Universal Law* of Nature, enjoining the settling and preserving to every one his Rights; *So* we ought to possess all *particular Virtues,* or we are therefore oblig'd by them, because they are commanded by some *particular Law* of Nature, which is contain'd in that Universal One, which I have mention'd." They are indeed, in their own Nature, *Good,* tho' there were *no Law,* because they conduce to the *Good* State of the Universe: But *Moral Obligation,* and the Nature of a *Debt* thence arising, is unintelligible without a respect to a *Law,* at least, of Nature. Nay, farther; the very Honour, from which Actions are distinguish'd by the Title of [*Honestas*] *laudable* Practice, or are called *Honourable,* seems wholly to come from *this,* "That they are *prais'd* by the Law of the supreme Ruler, discover'd by the Light of Nature, and *honour'd* with the greatest Rewards, among which is to be reckon'd the concurring *Praise* of Good Men."[1] And justly they are called *naturally* Lawful and Honourable, because the Law, which makes them such, does not depend upon the Pleasure of the Civil Power, but arises necessarily, in the Manner already explain'd, from the very *Nature* of Things, and is altogether *unchangeable,* whilst Nature remains *unchang'd.*

§II. The *special* Laws of the Moral Virtues may, after this Manner, be deduc'd from the Law of *Universal* Justice. *There being a Law given, which fixes and preserves the Rights of particular Persons, for this End only, That the Common Good of all be promoted by every one, all will be laid under these two Obligations, in order to that End:* 1. *To contribute to others such a Share of those Things which are committed to their Trust, as may not destroy that Part which is necessary to themselves for the same End:* 2. *To reserve to themselves that Use of what is their own, as may be most advantageous to, or at least consistent with, the Good of others.*

From the Law requiring the settlement of Property, in order to the Publick Good, are inferr'd the Duties 1. Of *Giving* to others. 2. Of *Receiving* to our-selves, those Things, which are either necessary, or highly serviceable, to this End.

In order to *explain* these Laws, it is to be *observ'd,* "That *others* and *our-selves* are Terms, which, in every one's Mind, divide the whole System of Rational Beings; and may, indifferently, be referr'd to God and Men"; *whence* both "his Honour is to be regarded by Men in the consideration of the Common Good"; and he himself may be understood, by an easy Analogy, "to act towards other Rational Agents, according to the Rules of the Moral Virtues." The *former* Law, which commands us "to regard others in order to the Common Good," enjoins *Liberality,* and the *Virtues of common Conversation*[2] in a strict Sense, (for in a large

1. The language here echoes Cicero's discussion of true glory from *Tusculan Disputations,* III.ii.3.
2. Maxwell cites Cumberland's Latin in a footnote: *"Virtutes homileticae."*

Sense every part of Universal Justice promotes *Conversation* with others;) the latter Law enjoins *Temperance* and *Moderation* about those Things which are to be reserv'd to our-selves, so as may best enable us most effectually to promote the Publick Good, of God and all Mankind, and, in a particular Manner, of our native Country and Family.

All the Virtues, Parts of Universal Justice, and consequently *connected,* but not *confounded.* In *both* Laws, *both* Members of the Division, that is, the Whole, of which we *our-selves* and *others* are Parts, comes into consideration; and, *therefore,* "All the Virtues prefer the Publick Good before the Private Advantages of any one, tho' some of them may be said to regard one Part of that Whole, more immediately than another." For this Reason some may perhaps *think,* "That these parts of Justice, and, consequently, all the particular Virtues, are not sufficiently distinguish'd from one another, but *confounded.*" But whoever throughly considers the Matter will *see,* "That their mutual natural *Connexion,* and the *reciprocal* Assistance which they mutually afford to one another, and to the Common Happiness, can hardly otherwise be more conveniently express'd." And, therefore, no-one can *say,* "that these Virtues are confounded," who would not accuse *Nature* it-self of *Confusion;* because she provides for the Health of the *whole* Body, and of a *particular Part,* by the *same* Motions of the Blood, and by the *same* Arteries and Veins. Thus, for *Example,* the Animal Nature performs these *two Offices* by straining the Blood thro' the Vessels of the Liver: 1. It prepares fit Blood (which would otherwise produce a Jaundice) for *all the other Parts,* being in the mean time not forgetful of nourishing the Liver it-self: 2. It nourishes the *Liver,* at the same time not forgetting the other Parts. Thus the *Publick* Office of the Liver is naturally *interwove* indeed, but *not confounded,* with the *Private.*[3] These *two Offices* may be *understood distinctly,* and some *Peculiarities* may be ascrib'd to *each* of them thus consider'd; and this is sufficient to *prevent Confusion.* Yet these two Offices *cannot* be actually *separated* from one another in a *healthful* State, or whilst Nature remains undisturb'd. So neither can the *subordinate Virtues* be really *di-*

---

3. Cumberland's knowledge of the functions of the liver appears to come from Glisson's *Anatomia Hepatis,* cited in ch. 2, n. 83.

vided from one another, *consistently with Justice,* or the Publick Good; yet there is *no Confusion,* whilst each may be consider'd *separately,* by its respect to those Parts, which it *immediately* regards, tho' they all *ultimately* promote the Good of the Whole. The *ultimate End* and Effect of both Laws, and, consequently, of all the Virtues enjoin'd by them, is one and the *same;* but the *immediate Ends* which they regard, and *Effects* which they attain, are no less *various,* than are the several Parts of the System of Rational Agents, each of which may be provided for, in order to the greatest Good of the Whole.

§III. Hence we may understand the *Reason,* "Why the Minds of Men do not always very *explicitly* view and intend the *Common* Good, even when they act according to the rule of Virtue": 'Tis *this,* "The *immediate* Object of their Pursuit is *some Part* thereof, but which they otherwise very well know, to be perfectly *consistent* with its *other Parts,* and *necessary* to the Composition of this *Whole."* But in *every* act of Virtue there are many Things which *prove,* "That the Care of the Common Good is never laid aside." *For,* in these, *Care* is always taken, "That every one confine himself within the Bounds of his own Rights, and invade not those of another." *But,* "Rights cannot be consider'd as so limited, without some respect to the Rights of others; and, consequently, to the Good of all others, on account of which the Properties of all are limited." All *States,* and their *Founders,* "acknowledge that general Division of Rights and Property, whereby certain Things are appropriated to God as Sacred, and their proper Bounds are assign'd to other Nations"; *by* their acknowledging their own Territories to be bounded, *by* their practising Religion, and entering into Leagues and Commerce with other States. *Private Persons, because* they subject themselves to, and govern themselves by, the Laws of their own Country, "whilst they give themselves up to the Practice of Virtue, of necessity do so far consent with their own and other States, that such general Division of Dominion is necessary to the Good of the Whole." Lastly; *because* in *every Virtue* the Mind is dispos'd to give their Rights to God and to all Men, to Foreigners, to Members of the same State, to those of the same Family; and

The Minds of Men, in the Practice of all the Virtues, are always conversant, tho' not always explicitly, about the Common Good.

that always in this Order, that the Rights of God should take the first Place, those which are common to all Nations the second, and the Rights of any particular State the third; those of lesser Societies, such as Corporations, Colleges, Families, following: *Hence* is easily *inferr'd,* "That their *principal* End is the *Common* Good of the whole System of Rational Agents"; *for* "this is not really distinguish'd from the Good of those Parts, consider'd in that Order, and mutually united by those Bonds, of Society."

Mediocrity consists in giving to no Part more or less, than a due regard to the Whole requires.

"From this *End,* and the Parts thereof consider'd in the *Order* now mention'd, is to be taken the *Measure* of all *Actions* and *Affections,* so that they may justly be said to be faulty thro' excess, or defect, if at any time they give more, or less, to any Part, than the Preservation of the Good of the Whole will permit." Thus may easily be found out a *certain* Measure of Action from stated and *known Rules,* namely, "The Laws which determine the Rights of God, of Nations, of that State under which every one lives, and of lesser Societies, and Individuals"; so that it is *without doubt,* "That all those Actions are within the Bounds of *Mediocrity,* which violate none of these Laws"; and *as certain,* "That every Action departs from thence, or is Vitious, that breaks any of these Laws." I *suppose* "these Laws to *agree* among themselves, so that the Rights of lesser Societies may in all Things be *consistent* with the Rights of the Superior; That, in Families, nothing can be rightfully enjoin'd, which contradicts the Laws of that State, of which they are Parts; in States, that nothing can be commanded rightfully, contrary to the Laws binding all Nations, (such are those concerning the Division of Dominion, or the not violating Property, concerning keeping Faith, &c.) And in these, that nothing contradict the Dominion of God over his Creatures." *For* "all the Force which inferior Laws have to oblige, is deriv'd to them, from the Force of the Superior; which Power of obliging must, therefore, be wholly wanting in those Laws, which contradict others of a higher Nature." *For* "an Inferior Power cannot abrogate the Law of a Superior; tho' it may variously limit the Liberty left by the Law of the Superior"; *because* the Power of further determining, in Cases undetermin'd by a Superior, is perfectly consistent with Subordination; nay, and is the chief Reason, why subordinate Rulers are appointed."

§IV. Having explain'd the *Measure* of that *Mediocrity,* which is usually requir'd in *Moral Virtues,*[4] it is easy to describe them *separately,* because their *Essence* consists in "the Inclination of the Will to obey the Laws deduc'd from the general Law of Justice." Let us, therefore, consider those *two former Laws,* which I have just now shewn to be deriv'd from the Law settling Dominion, or Property, for the Common Good.

The *former* of these *commands us, for this End, to communicate of our own to others in such Manner, that we may, nevertheless, reserve to our selves sufficient to pursue our own Happiness.* It is *obvious* enough that this is commanded, "Because it is evidently necessary to the Common Happiness, without which it is absurd to expect our own private Happiness," as I have already shewn at large. In this Law are contain'd, both a *Regulation* concerning "Gifts," for which either no Reward is expected, or where it is left wholly to the Will and Opportunities, of him who receives the Benefit; and also a *Precept* concerning "that less, but most useful, Benevolence, which is practis'd in all kind of Agreements, Compacts, and Commerce, in which we either promise, or perform, any Thing to others, under a Condition to be by them executed." We may bestow upon others, either our *Goods,* or our *Services,* or both. The *Will* to obey this Law is *conspicuous,* either in beneficent Actions, which are its proper Effects, and, therefore, *natural Signs* of it; or in the *voluntary Signs* of it. To the first Head belongs *Liberality;* to the Second, *the Virtues of common Conversation.*

§V. *Liberality* is *Justice conspicuous in Actions, bestowing gratis upon others what is our own.*[5] I make *Liberality* a Species of *Justice,* to *avoid* repeating the Definition of Justice, *viz.* A *Will to obey the Law of Nature,* and to *shew* by the same Word, "that the Necessity and true Measure thereof was to be taken from the Law." *For,* "every Part of Justice ought to be conformable to a Law; and all the Laws an Agent is subject to, (the Nat-

> From the former of the two Laws are deduc'd Precepts *1st.* Concerning *Gifts,* in which *Liberality,* and *2dly,* Concerning Conversation, in which the Virtues peculiar to that are conspicuous. The Virtues observant of the First Law, are,

> Liberality,

---

4. Cf. 6.7–8, where Cumberland links this position to the virtuous mean of Aristotelian moral theory.

5. Cumberland draws upon Aristotle's discussion of liberality in *Nicomachean Ethics,* IV.1.

ural and Positive Law of God, the Laws of Nations, Laws Civil and Municipal, and those of smaller Societies,) are to be consider'd, before his Action can be pronounc'd *Just,* or Virtuous." *For,* in all these, the best End, and the particular Parts thereof," (the Honour of God, the Peace and mutual Commerce of different Nations, the proper Polity of particular States, the Wealth and Security of smaller Societies, and of Families,) "are *regarded.*" And all, either Excess, or Defect in free Gifts is *forbid,* by which any of these is violated: "But such a free bestowing of Things and Services, as tends to establish and enlarge the particular Parts of this End in their proper Order, is *commanded.*"

(with the Virtues subservient thereto, But, *because* "it is impossible to support a liberal Expence, without an honest Endeavour to *acquire,* and to *preserve* our Acquisitions," *this* also is *commanded* by the Precepts and Admonitions deduc'd from the Consideration of the same End, and of the particular Parts thereof, consider'd in the same Order; and, *therefore,* "The same Liberality, which *principally* denotes a Will to expend, *subordinately* at least includes a Will obedient to the same Commands in Acquiring and Preserving": *That* is *Providence* and *Frugality;*) called *Providence,* or *Prudence,* and is oppos'd, both to *Rapacity,* and *improvident Negligence; this* is call'd *Frugality,* or *Parsimony;* which, on the one hand, is oppos'd to *sordid Niggardliness,*[6] and, on the other, to *Prodigality.* So *Providence* and *Frugality* may be defin'd *Justice in acquiring* and *in preserving,* and the same correspond to *Justice in laying out,* and are subservient to it.

and the different Branches of Liberality, as *Generosity,* *Liberality* is distinguish'd by *various Names,* according to the Variety of Objects, upon which it is exercis'd: For, if it exerts it-self in Things of signal Publick Use, it is call'd *Generosity,* or *Publick-Spiritedness;*[7] to which, on the one hand, is oppos'd the *Lavishness of the Ambitious;* and, on the other, the *Mean-Spiritedness of sordid Wretches.* Towards the Mis-

---

6. Cumberland's Latin phrase (*De Legibus Naturae,* p. 362) is "Sordidae Euclionum parcitati," a reference to the miser Euclio in Plautus' *Aulularia.* Cumberland adds a note in the manuscript mistakenly attributing the character to Terence, but this is corrected by Bentley. See also Barbeyrac, *Traité Philosophique,* p. 369, n. 2.

7. Cf. Aristotle, *Nicomachean Ethics,* IV.2.

erable, it is called *Compassion;* and towards the Poor in particular, *Alms-giving.* Toward Strangers it is called *Hospitality,* especially, if we entertain them in our Houses. In all these, the *Measure* of Beneficence is taken "from that which is most conducive *to* the various Parts of the chief End; *to* Piety, which establishes some kind of Society between God and Men; *to* mutual Assistance, Fidelity, and Commerce among various States; *to* Concord, and the other Duties of the Parts of the same State towards one another; and *to* the most flourishing State of lesser Societies and Families, which can be obtain'd consistently with *prior* Obligations." I have explain'd these Things the *more distinctly,* in settling the *Mediocrity,* or Measure, of this *first special Virtue,* "to supersede the Necessity of adding more, to discover the Method of deducing with the greatest Certainty, the true Measure of the following Virtues."

Compassion, Alms-giving, Hospitality:

§VI. Let us now proceed to *the Virtues of common Conversation,* which consist in Obedience to the same Law. I define them thus in General. *The Virtues of common Conversation are Justice, doing good to others by a Use of voluntary Signs subservient to the Common Good.*

And the *Virtues of common Conversation*

I have express'd the *End* in the *Definition, not* that it was *necessary,* because a respect to that is included in the general Notion of Justice, which aims thereat wholly; *but* for *Perspicuity.*

By *voluntary Signs* I understand, chiefly indeed *Speech,* but I respect also the *Gesture* and *Habit* of the Body, and all *Motions* of the Countenance, which make a *voluntary Discovery of the Mind. Gravity* and *Courteousness* observe a just Measure in all these. But with respect to Speech especially, *Taciturnity, Veracity,* (which in Promises is call'd *Fidelity,*) and *Urbanity,* keep us within due Limits. Of each of these in particular I shall treat briefly.[8]

I cannot better explain *Gravity* and *Courteousness,* than by considering, that all the various acts of *Justice* towards others, require, in the Agent, true *Prudence* and extensive *Benevolence,* as I have already shewn. But the Conversation of a Man, in which are conspicuous all the various

and, in particular, *Gravity* and *Courteousness,*

---

8. What follows draws upon Aristotle's account of the social virtues in *Nicomachean Ethics,* IV.6–9.

Signs of a just *Prudence,* is call'd *Grave.* And that, in which all the Marks of a sincere *Benevolence* shine, is call'd *Courteous.* Wherefore I would define *Gravity* to be *A Virtue of common Conversation which is distinguish'd by proper Signs of Prudence; Courteousness, A Virtue of common Conversation adorn'd with the Marks of great Benevolence.* These two are as *consistent* with one another, as *Prudence* and *Benevolence,* of which they are *Marks.* Hence the opposite Vices may easily be understood: To *Gravity* are oppos'd, on the one hand, a certain affected *Severity* and *Stiffness* of Manners, when one uses either *more* such Signs than the Nature of the End requires, or such as are *not proper* to promote, either the Honour of God, or the Happiness of Men, (which are the Parts of it;) or when one *neglects the Thing* it-self, whilst he industriously *affects the Signs* of it: On the other hand, *Levity,* which the Reader may easily understand, from the Description of the contrary Virtue, and opposite Vice. In like Manner are opposed to Courteousness and an obliging Civility of Manners, on the one hand, *Flattery,* or the soothing Arts of the Parasite; on the other, *Moroseness.*

But, because *Speech* is the *principal* Interpreter of the Mind, and *peculiar* to Mankind, therefore the Law of Nature commanding us, on proper occasions, to express a *prudent Benevolence* towards others, does, more particularly and expressly, prescribe to our Words a *Measure,* which various Virtues do observe with care. For, in the first place, we are enjoin'd to be sometimes *Silent;* namely, whenever the Reverence due to God, or to others our Superiours, requires it; or to avoid revealing, to any one's Prejudice, either the Secrets of the State, or of our Friends, or Family, or our own, when the concealing them will more effectually pro- *Taciturnity,* mote the Publick Good. *Taciturnity* pays Obedience to these Laws, which is *a Virtue of common Conversation, keeping Silence, when the Common Good requires it.* The Excess of this is an unseasonable Niggardliness of Speech, which greatly prevents the Communication of Knowledge, and the principal Advantages of Human Society. Again; we are sometimes by the same Law commanded to *speak* to others, when the Common Good requires it; there is no Name of any one Virtue, which can fully, in one Word, express the Obedience due to this Law: It may, perhaps not improperly, be called, a *Prudent Liberty of Speech,* or a just and due Liberty in Speaking, and consists in "a readiness of the Mind to express every Thing in Words, which Reason suggests may be any way advantageous to the Community of Rational Agents." The *Words*, about which this Law is conversant, either respect Things *past* and *present;* concerning which it *commands* us, in order to this End, "to declare the Matter as it is, so far as it is known to us," in which consists *Veracity:* or they respect Things *hereafter to be done* by us, with respect to which it *commands* us, "to promise such Things to others as "may turn to the Publick Advantage"; and that, either *without* a Condition, or *with* one, as the nature of the best End requires. "Promises, mutually agreed upon among several," form a *Covenant, Contract,* or *Compact,* to which is owing almost all the *Commerce* that is among Rational Agents. There is *no Name* of any *one particular Virtue,* which obliges Rational Beings to *make* such Promises, or Contracts, as may most effectually promote the Publick Good; but that Virtue, which *keeps* such Promises and Compacts, is every where celebrated by the Name of *Faith,* or *Fidelity.* They are Acts of the *same* Disposition of Mind, and of the *same* Virtue, to will the *making* such Compacts, and to will the *Observance* of them, when made. Nor is it *lawful* to *observe Compacts,* unless the *Performance* of the Thing *covenanted* be *Lawful,* that is, permitted by the Laws of Nature, as consistent with the Publick Good. It is so far from being true, that all *Justice* (which properly consists in the Observance of the Laws) may be resolv'd into *Fidelity in observing Compacts,* that, on the contrary, before it can be *known,* "Whether any Compact ought to be observed," it ought to be *certain,* That the Laws of Nature enjoin'd, or at least permitted, the making that Compact."[9] *Lastly,* "The greatest Benevolence is not express'd in our Conversation, except something *Pleasant* be seasonably intermix'd therewith, according to every One's Talent that way," which is what is called *Urbanity,* or Facetiousness. This Virtue is *limited* by all the Parts of the chief End, in the same Manner as the rest. For it is *enjoin'd Universally,* "That nothing be said, tho' it were but in Jest, which may diminish the Honour of God, or the Happiness of Mankind"; which we shall *observe,* "If we do not, by a base and wanton

Veracity,

Faith, or *Fidelity,*

Urbanity, or *Facetiousness.*

9. [Maxwell] "See note at the End of Chap. 7. §. 9" [ch. 7, n. 12].

Satyricalness, expose, to Contempt and Ridicule, the Laws of Religion; nor the Rights of Nations, nor of particular States, nor of smaller Societies, or Families, or of particular Persons." They who, by their *Jesting, transgress these Laws,* are justly tax'd with *Scurrility.* They, who in their own Conversation wholly *neglect,* or *condemn* in that of Others, innocent *Pleasantness* of Speech, fall into *Rusticity.* And so much may suffice for the *first special Law* deriv'd from the *general Law* of Justice, and for all its different Branches, together with their correspondent Virtues.

Virtues obser-vant of the sec-ond Law, are the several Branches of a limited Self-Love;

§VII. The *second special Law* of the Moral Virtues is thus deriv'd from the Law of *Universal* Justice. *There being given a Law (of Universal Justice) fixing and preserving the Rights of every particular Person for this End only, that every One may promote the Common Good of All, every One is oblig'd, in the second Place, so to consult his own Interest in the Use of his own Advantages, that they may be of the most Advantage to all Others, or at least may diminish no Part of their Common Good.* The *Meaning* of these Words has been *explain'd* just now, when I deduc'd the *two special* Laws from the *general* Law of Justice. This Law is *observ'd,* "When we limit our Love of our-selves, by the Bounds prescrib'd by Universal Justice, which gives to God and Men their several Rights." This *limited Self-love,* being enjoin'd in this Law of Nature, and that in order to the best End, cannot but be *Just* and *Laudable.* Nay, as I have *shewn,* "That some Rights ought necessarily to be given to *every One,* that it might be well with *All*"; [10] we may, by a *Parity of Reason, infer,* "The necessity of a Law commanding every one constantly to use his own Things in order to his own Happiness, where that is no way Inconsistent with, or Prejudicial to, the Happiness of the whole Community"; *for* "The Happiness of the Whole consists in the Happiness of all the Parts"; and *therefore* "The Care of the former being commanded, the Care of the latter also must of necessity be commanded therein"; nor can the Happiness of every One be procured by Others, if they neglect Themselves.

with regard, First, to our

Seeing "every Man's essential Parts are his Mind and Body," this Law is understood to *command* "The proper Improvements of both, in order

10. See ch. 8.2.

to the Common Good, and by Means agreeable to that End, that is, by making use of our own Rights over Things and Persons, and not invading those of others." I need not inculcate any Thing *particularly,* concerning the Method of *cultivating the Mind,* because it is the whole Business of "Moral Philosophy, and every Thing subservient to it, to instruct and improve and fit the Mind for this End." The *Care of our Body,* in order to this End, is commanded by those Precepts, or Laws of *Moral Philosophy,* the Observance whereof is distinguish'd by the Name of *Temperance.* For the *Moral Laws* concerning Meat, Drink, Sleep, Exercise, and Venereal Enjoyments, are distinguish'd from the *Precepts given by the Physicians* concerning the *same* Things, in *this,* "That all these Things, which *Physicians* prescribe only for the *Health* of particular Persons, the immediate End of Medicine, are in *Morality* directed to a *higher End.*" I, certainly, would not call him *Temperate,* that is, Virtuous, "Who most diligently observ'd all the Precepts of the Physician relating to the Preservation of Health, without any regard to the Laws providing for the Common Good, and, consequently, to the End propos'd by them." It is, however, sufficient to make Actions *Virtuous,* "If the Mind of the Agent has a general Inclination to do those Things, which are acceptable to God, and to all Men, proceeding from an habitual Intention to promote this End, and, consequently, from an Assent formerly given to such Practical Propositions and Laws." For the whole Force of *practical Habits* arises "from the Assent of the Understanding to Practical Propositions, formerly given, and still remaining in the Memory."

Essential Parts, the Mind and the Body.

§VIII. *Temperance* may, therefore, be defin'd, *Justice towards our-selves, employ'd in taking Care of our Body, in order to the Common Good. If* "any one, while he indulges his Body, is so far forgetful of his Mind, as to drown, or lessen its Powers, and render himself less qualified for Things Divine, or Human, Civil, or Domestick; altho' this may sometimes be done consistently with Health, and, consequently, with the Rules of the Physicians," he is *Intemperate.* For *Instance,* if any one breaks a Religious Fast, which may, consistently with Health, be either observ'd, or neglected; or fares so Luxuriously, but without loss of

Temperance in the Moderation of our Natural Desires, respecting the Preservation.

Health, as to waste his Fortune, and become unable to pay the Publick Taxes, he is certainly guilty of Intemperance. But "they who impair their Health by their pursuit of Pleasures, do not prejudice themselves only, but, in some measure, both their Friends and their Country, so far as their want of Health renders them less qualified to do Good to others." We may *estimate* this from the "Proportion Health bears to Life." *Civil Laws* (which take care of Matters of *greater* Consequence only) usually judge a *Self-Murderer* injurious, not to *himself alone,* but to the *Publick* also, which he robs of a *Subject;* and that Fact is justly reckon'd amongst the greatest Crimes. Every *voluntary Diminution of our Health* approaches to *this Crime* against the *Publick* Good, in the same *Proportion,* that the Value of *Health* lost does to the Value of *Life;* both the Health and Life being estimated, chiefly in relation to Publick Duties, the Execution whereof is in some Measure expected from *All.*

The Matter will become yet *plainer,* if we *consider* particularly, "That the Care of Our Body consists in the Moderation of our Natural Desires, which respect the Preservation, either of the Individual, or of the Species."

of the *Individual,* with respect 1. to Meats.

2. Drink.

3. Sleep.

4. Recreation and Exercise.

5. The Ornaments of Life.

To the Preservation of the *Individual,* belongs the *Desire* 1. *of Meats,* which *Abstinence* limits, with respect to the End aforesaid; to which are oppos'd, both a *keeping the Body too low,* and *Gluttony.* 2. *Of Drinks,* the desire of which is limited by *Sobriety,* to which is oppos'd *Drunkenness.* 3. *Of Sleep,* the desire of which is limited by *Watchfulness,* which shakes off the opposite *Drowsiness.* 4. *Of Recreations* and *Exercises,* the Virtue setting Bounds to which, has no proper Name (that I know of,) nor the Vices opposite thereto, either in Excess, or Defect. 5. *Of Ornaments* belonging to outward Decency, in Furniture, Cloaths, and Buildings; *Neatness* and *Elegance,* in Proportion to every Man's Fortune, observing a due Measure in these; which *Niceness* exceeds, and *Nastiness,* or *Slovenliness,* does not come up to.

Of the *Species,* with respect to *Chastity,*

§IX. *Lastly;* to the Preservation of the *Species* belongs the *Appetite to Venereal Enjoyments,* to which *Chastity,* from the same Rules, fixes Bounds, which *Incontinence* breaks thro'; whose various Kinds are too well known to need Enumeration. We may hence easily *perceive,* "How we may be many ways injurious to Others, in an intemperate indulging Ourselves; *both as* he who hurts himself, wounds a Member of a Family, of a State, of Mankind; which, whilst sound, is in numberless ways subservient to the Good of Others: *and as* hence follows some Neglect of Piety, and of all severer Studies, for which the *Intemperate* Person is wholly unqualified; which is a loss to the whole System of Rational Beings, which had a Right hence to expect some Advantage." Not to insist upon *this,* "*That* Men are incited to seize the Property of Others, to satisfy their own *Intemperate Desires; that Intemperance* raises the Price of Victuals, to the great Mischief of the Poor: What Mischief does not *Drunkenness* produce?"[11] The *publick Inconveniencies* which flow from *Incontinence,* are too *filthy* to be mention'd with Modesty, too *manifest* to need an Enumeration. It may be sufficient to *mention,* "That Crimes of this kind cannot be committed without a Partner," whence they cannot be confin'd to the breast of *One alone,* but are communicated to more; hence *Families,* and the Rights of *Succession* are *confounded;* whence the hidden Mischief spreads, and bears hard upon all those, who had a *Right* to *expect* any thing from the *abused Family,* or from the *Inheritance;* and thus by this Crime whole *States* are sometimes reduc'd to great *Streights,* and the Condition of *all Mankind* is made *worse.*

Nor is it less *manifest,* "That the Business and Tendency of the known Laws of Chastity,[12] both in a single and married State, is, not only to benefit the Minds and Bodies of the Chast; but to found new Families, to preserve old Ones, and to extend Friendships, rising from Affinity by Marriage"; whence arises a closer Union and Society between the Parts of the same State, and also between the Members of different States, and, consequently, of all Mankind.

For this Cause, in my Opinion, has *Natural Reason* instructed *almost*

---

11. In the original text, Cumberland (*De Legibus Naturae,* p. 369) italicizes the quotation, which is from Horace, *Epistulae,* I.v.16: "Quid non ebrietas designat?"

12. Maxwell departs from the Latin (*De Legibus Naturae,* p. 369), which has "civitatis" rather than "castitatis." Barbeyrac (*Traité Philosophique,* p. 376, n. 2) points out that, although the original text is not correct grammatically, it is closer to Cumberland's meaning. Cumberland is referring to the known laws of the state concerning the single and married condition.

all Nations, (since Mankind has been *multiplied* into numerous Families, and the Memory of their *Primitive Relation,* by descent from the same First Parents, came to have *little Influence* on them;) "To prohibit Marriage between the nearest Relations"; for *this very Cause,* I say, "That Marriages might unite and engage distant Families, whom Relation could not, into greater Friendships and Intimacies": For *Example;* Marriages between *Brothers* and *Sisters* are now forbidden by the Dictates of Reason consulting the Common Good of Mankind, by a *more widely extending* the Friendships of *Affinity,* which Marriages in the first Age of the World were *Lawful;* because *necessary* to propagate that Race of Men, and to raise those Families, which Reason now endeavours to *Preserve,* by *prohibiting* such Marriages, in order to *extend Friendships.*

Thus the *Sovereign Goodness* of the *same* End renders it *Just,* both to *grant* that Liberty in the beginning, and to *forbid* it afterwards, when the *State* of Human Affairs was *chang'd.*

and Affection in the Preservation and Education of our Posterity.

Lastly; because "The desire of preserving our Off-spring," which is call'd *Natural Affection,* is only a *Continuation* of that Appetite, by which Animals are inclin'd to *Procreation;* it is *evident,* "That Natural Affection ought to be both *excited* and *limited* by a respect to the same chief End, and the several Parts thereof": We ought, *so far,* to love our Children, *as* that conduces to the Honour of God upon Earth, and to the Happiness of all Nations, of our respective Countries and Families. It is *evident,* "That the Happiness of all Posterity depends upon the Care of Educating our Off-spring": And, *because* our Off-spring is a kind of Compound of Our-selves and Others, it is *plain,* "That our Care thereof affords a Specimen of the Virtues, which relate both to Our-selves and to Others."

Secondly, to the Goods of Fortune:

§X. But the due Care of Our-selves, in order to the Common Good, implies, *not only* the Consideration of those *Parts,* of which we are each of us compounded, the Mind and Body, of which I have already treated; *but also* of the *Means,* (even the remote Ones,) by which both Parts of us may be any way assisted; which the *Lawyers* call by the general Name of *our Goods* and *Rights* over Things and Persons, in plenty whereof consist every One's *Riches* and *Honours.*

Therefore the *same* Law of Nature, which *limits* our Will, and, con- Riches,
sequently, all our *Affections* toward *Our-selves*, by their relation to the
best End, will, for a *like Reason*, from the consideration of all the Parts
of this End, *limit* all our *Affections* about the acquiring and preserving
Wealth and *Honour*. For *these* are sought after by *all*, for no other reason,
than as *Means* to the Happiness of their Possessors; which I have *prov'd*,
"No-one is to look for in any other Measure, than what is subordinate
to, or at least consistent with, the Common Happiness of All." What I
have already, by the way, said concerning the Limitation of our Care of
acquiring and preserving Riches, as a necessary *Means*, in order to *Liberality*, may be sufficient to limit our Desires about them, as *Means* to
our *Happiness*.

All that I have to add upon this Head, is, in few Words to *admonish* and Honour;
my Reader, "That all are commanded by this Law to pursue Honours,
in *such Measure* only, and by *such Means*, as are not only consistent with
the *Health* both of *Body* and *Mind*, but also with a due Care of their
Family, lest we ruin that in pursuit of Honours; and with the Peace of
the *State*, lest any One should raise Himself to Dignities by seditious
Practices; with the Peace of other *Nations*, lest the Rights of Nations
should be violated, in order to swell our Titles; and *lastly*, with Piety
towards *God*, lest any one, to encrease the Glory of his Name, become
guilty of Profaneness against the Divine Majesty, or violate Things and
Offices Sacred."

The Will, when its Motions are agreeable to these Laws, has obtain'd *Modesty*,
that just Mediocrity, which ought to be observ'd in pursuing Honours,
and avoiding Infamy; the Virtue of such a Disposition is called *Modesty*,
which may be defin'd, *Justice toward our-selves, consisting in a pursuit of
Honours subordinate to the Common Good*. The same *Modesty*, "as it re- with its
Branches,
strains the Will from pursuing Things higher than what are consistent *Humility*, and
with this End," is call'd *Humility:* But, "as it raises the Mind to the Pur- *Magnanimity;*
The Vices
suit of the greatest Honours subservient to this End," is true *Magna-* opposite being
nimity. [13] I suppose every one *knows*, "That it belongs to the same Virtue, *Pride* (includ-
ing *Ambition*,
to acquire and preserve Honour, and to avoid and ward off *Infamy*." *Arrogance*, and

13. Cf. Aristotle, *Nicomachean Ethics*, IV.3.

Vain-glory)
and Pusilla-
nimity.

From these *Definitions* of the *Virtues,* the Nature of the *Vices opposite* is easily discover'd: For *Pride,* which displays it-self in *Ambition, Arrogance,* and *Vain-Glory,* is in direct opposition to *Humility;* as *Pusillanimity* is to *Magnanimity.*

All sorts of
Virtues respect
the Publick
Good: and
Man, acting
according to
them, pursues
that Good;
either in the
Synthetick way,
as does the
Private Man;

§XI. I have thus briefly consider'd all the Virtues, and made it *appear,* "That in each of them is contain'd some respect to the Common Good of Rational Beings," (which I take leave to call the City, or Kingdom, of God in the largest Sense;) "and that, whether they more immediately concern Others, or Our-selves, the greatest Good of all is always ultimately intended."

The Mind of Man, acting according to the Precepts of Virtue, prosecutes this Common Good, both in the *Synthetick,* and in the *Analytick,* Way.[14] A *private Person* imitates the *former* Method, when he so regulates his several Cares, that, *beginning* at *his own* proper Affairs, he does nothing in the Management of them, which the settling, the preserving, or advancing and improving his Family, does not persuade, or at least permit: In his Provision for his *Family,* he does nothing inconsistent with his greater Care to preserve the State: In his regard for the *State,* nothing but what is accommodated to, or at least permitted by, the Happiness of other Nations; which he is oblig'd, at least, not to diminish, and even to promote, as far as is in his Power. Lastly, in his pursuit of the Good of *Mankind,* nothing inconsistent with the Honour of the *Divine Majesty,* and the Preservation of the Rights of the Kingdom of God, in which are contain'd all Things both Divine and Human; and these several Rights he generally supposes already settled and appropriated.

or in the *Ana-*
lytick Method,
as do *Legisla-*
tors.

But they who *preside over others,* and have a Power to distribute such Rights, *begin* at their Regard to the *whole System,* and so rather pursue the *Analytick* Method. They think they sufficiently discharge their Duty to the whole Kingdom of God, by paying him, as Sovereign King,

14. Maxwell translates "genetico" as "Synthetick," but it is not clear that Cumberland wanted to contrast analytic with synthetic. The subsequent sentences indicate the suggestion that the mind of man prosecutes the common good both in terms of their construction and their analysis. See Barbeyrac, *Traité Philosophique,* p. 378, n. 1.

supreme Honours, and giving to all Nations, as his SUBJECTS, their several Rights over Things and Persons; the Regard due to the Rights of each several *Nation* is satisfied, by a just Care of the Rights of the several lesser Societies, Families especially, comprized in it; as the *lesser Societies* are sufficiently provided for, if the Goods and Interest of the several *Members* be taken care of. It was very easy and necessary, to use this Method in the *first Division,* or Settlement of *Property* over Things and Persons, when our First Parents (reserving to God his Rights) divided all other Things among their Children;[15] for the *Happiness of the whole Rational System* is that single *End,* in its own Nature the *best* and *greatest,* (because the Sum of all Good Things, and therefore Naturally better and greater than any Part thereof, that is, than any other Good,) which they who rightly *understand, cannot but* pursue; and the *Necessity* of pursuing it renders *Necessary* the Settlement of distinct Properties over Things and Persons, that is, gives Original, both to all *Laws,* and to the *Rights* every one derives from them. But, when we proceed from the Care of the Whole to the Care of the Parts, it is evident, that the *Analytick* Method takes place.

§XII. These *Laws* being establish'd, which regulate and bind the several Societies and Relations between God and Men, between different Nations, and also between the Members of the same State and Family, we have *undoubted Marks,* by which we can *judge* of *Piety,* and of all kinds of *Virtue;* so that their *Name* given to Actions overturning the Rights of Religion, of Nations, States, or Families, *need deceive no-one* hereafter. For it is *evident,* "That all the Parts of Universal Justice," (which I have

Hence Mankind are possess'd of an unerring Rule of Virtuous Actions.

---

15. [Maxwell] "This Supposition of a Division actually made by *Adam* and *Eve,* as it is not necessary to our Author's Scheme, so it is precarious. The Grant of the Use of all Things was not confin'd to them; so that the World was made *Negatively Common* to Mankind, so that any one might, without Consent of the rest, use what was not occupied, as we now may do with running Water and Air; and not *positively Common,* like a Theater, or Common of a Town, which cannot be appropriated without Consent of All, nor can be used by any, but the joint-Proprietors, without their Consent." Barbeyrac comments on this passage, *Traité Philosophique,* p. 378, n. 3.

briefly recounted,) "and all the Acts of every Virtue, are commanded by these Laws for the Common Good alone"; *for* "such Acts do," as is evident by constant *Experience,* "Naturally either give Honour to God, or promote the Peace and Happiness of different Nations, or benefit some State, or smaller Society, or some particular Person"; *but* "of these Parts, consider'd in this Order, is the Common Good wholly made up."

Wherein right Reason, prescribing *Mediocrity* in Human Actions, consists.

Farther; *hence* may very clearly be *explain'd,* "What is that right *Reason,* which enables the *Prudent* Man to prescribe that *Mediocrity,* which ought to be observ'd in Human Actions." For *it* consists wholly, in "such Practical Propositions, as propose to us the greatest *End,* and discover to us the proper *Means* in our Power, by which we may attain it." Now *they* are, "Those *Human Actions* that are *commanded* by the Laws, which found, preserve, and regulate, Religious Worship, the mutual Commerce of Nations, the Interest of States and Families; or *directed* by the Dictates of Private Men; provided such Laws and Dictates be agreeable to our Experience, concerning the *natural Efficacy* of Human Actions." Thus the *Means,* by which we may obtain or hinder our own Happiness, or that of others, are ultimately *resolv'd* into the *Natural Powers* of Actions to *help,* or *hurt,* Men, consider'd either singly, or jointly, as in a Family, or in one, or more Nations.[16] We *judge* of those Things which belong to, or are proper Expressions of, the *Honour of God,* by *Analogy* drawn from those Actions, which tend to *Honour Men.* And Experience no less evidently *teaches,* "what kind of Human Actions are beneficial or hurtful to most others"; than it *shews,* "what kind of Food nourishes and refreshes most Men, what on the contrary breeds Distempers and hastens Death."

All our Moral Knowledge is ultimately resolv'd into

[17]Nor do we *with greater difficulty learn* from Experience the Truth of these *Propositions,* "That it is necessary to the Common Good, that a distribution of Things and mutual Services should be made"; and,

---

16. [Maxwell] "In the Original it runs thus, [*Sic ultima tandem Resolutio fit in vires Naturales,* &c.] *Resolution* of what? The Word [*mediorum*] seems plainly to be wanting after [*Resolutio*] which, the Sense requiring it, I have accordingly supplied."

17. Section XIII of the Latin text begins here. Cumberland, *De Legibus Naturae,* p. 374.

"That it should be preserved, by acting, both with respect to Others and Ourselves, as the Preservation of Nations, single States and Families, whereof we are Part, requires": (From which all the Laws of Nature, and the Virtues proceed:) *Than we learn,* "That it is necessary to the Life and Health of an Animated Body, that Nourishment should be communicated to all its Parts, and that the Distribution made by Nature should be preserv'd by every Member so discharging its proper Office; that first the principal Parts, then the less Principal, and the Meanest, may have their Obstructions remov'd, their Decays repair'd, and their Growth continued, 'till they arrive at the Stature and Strength prescrib'd by Nature."

The truth in *both Cases* is *resolv'd* into these, or such like, *Propositions;* "That those Things which preserve the Whole, preserve all its Parts"; and "That the Preservation of the less Principal or subordinate Parts, proceeds from the Preservation of the Principal"; which, because they are *evident* from the *Definitions* of such Causes, may justly be said to be discover'd by the *Nature of Things* to our *Experience. For,* "Definitions are learn'd from our Experimental Knowledge of the Nature of Things."

[18]Farther; *as* the whole *Certainty* of the rules of *Medicine* and *Diet* proceeds from the *unchangeable* Efficacy of such corporeal Causes to produce their Effects in an Animate Body; *in like manner* all *Certainty* of those practical Propositions, which are Laws of Nature, and which compose *Moral Philosophy,* and determine the Nature of all the Virtues, proceeds from the *unchangeable* Influence of Human Actions, upon the Preservation or Damage of particular Men, of Families, of Commonwealths, and of all Nations.

Moreover; that *Variety* of Actions which is enjoin'd Men, with respect to their various Conditions, Families, Commonwealths, and other Circumstances, is *no more* inconsistent with that necessary and *constant* Care of preserving and perfecting all the Parts of the best End, which I have often enumerated; *than Diversity* of Diet in diverse Climates, Ages, and Constitutions, of Men, is inconsistent with that *constant* Care in all, of every where nourishing all their Members, and every where sat-

[Marginal notes:]

our Experience of the Powers of Natural Causes.
In this § is explain'd the *Manner* of naturally deducing these Dictates of Reason, by which all our Actions are regulated according to all the Virtues,

by an *unerring Method,*

in all *Variety* of Circumstances,

---

18. Section XIV of the Latin text begins here. Ibid.

isfying their natural Necessities, with relation to Hunger and Thirst, and Sleep, and of prescribing Bounds to their Exercises, their Venery, and their Affections, according as their several Natures require.

Tho' not to a Mathematical exactness,

In these, *as* in Things necessary to the Publick Good, we cannot attain our End, by acting any Thing at pleasure: But the Nature of the End sets some Limits, tho' our Understanding cannot reach *Mathematical Exactness* in settling them.

which is not necessary.

We take *sufficient Care* of our Life, without *Lessius's* Method of *weighing* our Food;[19] and, *in like manner,* we may *truly promote* the Publick Good according to our Power, tho' we cannot reach what is *exactly* best in all Cases; provided we endeavour, as far as we can, to reach it in all given Circumstances.

The Common Good is the proper Measure of every lesser Good and Evil, and of their comparative value;

§XIII. This I think necessary here to *add,* "That the *Common Good* of all Rational Beings, on this very account, that it is the Sum of all Things naturally Good, and, therefore, the greatest Good, is the *fittest natural Measure,* by a comparison of other good Things with which, we may safely pronounce, whether they be *Great,* or *Small;* and, therefore, whether they ought to have the *first Place* in our Desires, or should be *postpon'd* to others." The *same Measure,* by which we compare the Proportion that *good Things* bear to one another, affords likewise a true Standard for the measuring *Evils,* and therefore discovers, what is more, or less, to be avoided, or griev'd for. Hence we shall likewise *learn,* "what kind of Affections ought to prevail over others, and which should give way"; *since* it is *certain,* "that only *that* Measure of all our Affections is consistent with the Nature of a Rational Being, and of the Universe, *which* exactly corresponds to the true Valuation of those Things, Good and Evil, by which they are excited."

because it is naturally determin'd,

[20]*Because* the Government of our Affections is an affair of the utmost Importance, (as that from which every Virtue, and every Degree of Hap-

---

19. Cumberland refers to Leonard Lessius's *Hygiasticon* (1613), a popular treatise on preserving strength and achieving longevity.

20. Section XV of the Latin text begins here. Cumberland, *De Legibus Naturae,* p. 376.

piness in our own Power, proceeds;) and *because* That Government (as I have now hinted) depends intirely upon the Knowledge of the true Measure, according to which all Things, Good and Evil, are to be esteem'd Great, or Little; I therefore think proper, more largely to explain what I have just now *affirm'd,* "That the Common Good is this Measure," and, "That it is fix'd by the Nature of Things." This is evident, from what I have already *shewn,* "That the Common Good of all Rational Beings is the End, to the pursuit whereof all are naturally oblig'd." *But* "the End is more known than the Means, and is the Measure by which Rational Beings must (from the Condition of their Nature) rate the greater or lesser Goodness of all the Means"; *therefore,* "this being establish'd as the principal End, the Good of any particular Person will be a Means to the Good of the whole Rational System"; as the Soundness of any Member in an Animal, is a Means to the Soundness of the whole Animal.

Nor is it at all unusual, to find out the Quantities of Things by a *Measure greater than the Things to be measured,* with this only *Precaution,* "That the Measure be divided into Parts small enough, every one of which has a known Proportion to the Whole." For *Instance;* we may measure a Line shorter than the tenth Part of a Foot, by a two or three-foot Rule, provided this be divided into Feet, and the Feet into Twelve, a Hundred, or a Thousand, equal Parts: Just in the *same manner,* altho' the Common Good be by far the greatest, yet because its Parts, both the greater and the smaller, are known, and the Proportion of each of them to the Whole is sufficiently understood; we can, therefore, most commodiously determine by this Measure, both how great every Good is, and among good Things, which is Greater, or Less. *and divided into proper Parts;*

[21]The *Parts,* into which the Common Good, consider'd as a *Rule,* is divided, are, "All the Advantages of All, which are contain'd in the happiest State of the System of Rational Beings, and are subordinate thereto": Such are those which belong, to the Worship of *God,* or to Religion; to the Peace and mutual Assistance of *Nations;* and those which belong to the happiest Condition of *single States, Families,* and *by means whereof the Value of all Good and Evil,*

21. Section XVI of the Latin text begins here. Ibid., p. 377.

Persons, which can be procur'd by Human Industry; this *Order* of the Parts among themselves being preserv'd, in order to the Preservation of the Whole.

Farther; *as,* from a Division of a Rule into Feet, of a Foot into Tenth, Twelfth, or any other Parts, and of these into Hundredth Parts, and so on, the Proportion of the smallest Part to the Whole may become known: *So,* from the known Order and Proportion of the *several* good Things to one another, and of them *all* to the Common Good, the Proportion, of any Good assign'd, to that greatest Good, which is the Collection of all others, is easily discover'd. Thus, from the known Proportion of any true *Proposition* to *Science,* of Science to the *Tranquillity of the Mind,* and Government of the Affections, of this to the *Happiness of the Person,* of the *Person* to the *Family,* of the Family to the *State,* of the State to *all Nations,* and of these to the whole *System of Rational Beings;* it at length becomes *known,* "How much the Knowledge of one Truth contributes to the Good of the Universe." *Like to this* is the Method of valuing the Advantages of the Body; we estimate what Proportion, for *Instance,* the Soundness of the smallest *Member,* or the Benefit of a Garment, or Portion of Meat, bears to the Preservation of the *Body;* and may, by the like method, find out the Proportion of the Body to the *whole Man,* to the *Family,* to the *State,* and at length to the *Universe.* Lastly; the most Skilful in Mensuration, I mean the *Geometricians,* are wont to use this Method of determining the *Proportion* of Quantities, by comparing them with the *greatest,* to which they can be referr'd. The Reason of this Method can easily be accommodated to our present Purpose. 'Tis this; the *smallest* Quantities *escape* both our *Senses* and our *Understandings;* the *intermediate* Ones, between the Greatest and the Smallest, are *Infinite;* nor is there any Reason, why *one* of them should be taken for a Measure, rather than *another;* nay, the same Quantity is called both great and small; with respect to different Quantities: But the *Greatest* is but *One,* and is more obvious to our *Understandings* than the rest; it is, therefore, the *fittest to be taken for a Measure,* in which is *requir'd,* "That it should be a determinate Quantity, and better known." *Thus* the *Mathematicians* discover the Length of Lines inscrib'd in a Circle, by comparing them with the Diameter, which, of all the Lines inscrib'd, is the Greatest. And the determining the Sines, in the Table of Sines, by comparing them with the Radius, comes to the same Thing. For the Sines are the Halves of Lines inscrib'd subtending double their Arches, and the Radius is Half the Diameter. And it is *obvious,* "That Halves are in Proportion as their Wholes." *So also* the Regular Bodies are measur'd, by comparing them with the Sphere, which is the greatest Body, in which all the rest are inscrib'd.[22] But I care not to be tedious in such *Examples.*

The only *Reason,* why I have said thus much concerning the Measure of Good Things, is, "That we may esteem Good, or Evil, *Great;* not as it is more Helpful, or Hurtful, to *Our-selves only,* but as it adds more to, or detracts from, the *Common* Happiness: And, in comparing Good Things, may reckon that *Greater,* which is the greater Part of the *Publick* Happiness; that *Less,* which adds less to the *Common* Advantage." For from hence, I think, may be *drawn* "An universal Remedy for all irregular Affections, injurious to Others, or Destructive of our own Quiet, which generally proceed from too great a love of Ourselves." He, who esteems nothing a *Great* Good, but what contributes *much* to the Common Happiness, will never *inordinately* desire any Thing; and, consequently, will never so offend against the Publick Good, as to be disturb'd with the Conscience of any Crime; nor, if Human Affairs suffer by the Wickedness of Others, or by Causes superior to the Power of Man, will this rob him of his Tranquillity; partly, because he knows these Things to be out of his Power; partly, because, being well aware of that Inconstancy to which all Human Affairs are subject, he expects many such Events Daily; but especially, because it is certain, from the Experience of so many Ages, that the innumerable Revolutions of Human Affairs have left us the World in a better, rather than in a worse; State, whence we have just reason to hope, that it can hardly happen otherwise with our Posterity.

and, consequently, the Measure of all Affections conversant about them, may be naturally ascertain'd.

---

22. Section XVII of the Latin text begins here. Ibid., p. 378.

Corollaries.

From the pre-
cedent General
Law are
deduc'd,

Having drawn, from *Nature,* the most *general* Moral Precepts, and thence explain'd the Moral Virtues in *particular;* I shall now briefly *shew,* "How these most general Precepts, which I have deliver'd, may lead us to others more limited, and of more common Use"; for hence it will be *prov'd,* "That God hath both *promulg'd,* even those particular Laws, by Natural Signs, and given them the *Sanction* of Natural Rewards and Punishments": This I will make evident, by briefly considering the *Decalogue* and *Civil Laws.*

1. The
Decalogue,

The *Decalogue* is usually divided into *two Tables,* of which the *former* contains Precepts concerning our Behaviour toward *God,* the *latter,* toward *Men:* Both are fulfilled by *Love* toward God and Men. But it is *evident,* "That the Precept, which we have drawn from Nature concerning Universal Benevolence or the Pursuit of the Common Good, contains these two"; *because* it respects God, as the *Head* of the Intellectual System, and Men, as his *Subjects.*

Table the first,
containing the
Duties toward
God;

§II. The *first Table* is contain'd, particularly in *that part* of the Law of *Universal Justice,* by which I have prov'd we are *taught,* "That it is necessary to the Common Good, and, consequently, to the Happiness of each of us in particular, which can thence only be obtain'd, *To give, God what is his own,* that is, all things, in our Power, necessary to *maintain* and *express* our sense and acknowledgment of his *Supremacy over All,* and *beget* in others a *Conviction,* that it is the chief Interest of all, *That he have a Supereminent Dominion over All Things and Persons.*" That he *has* such Dominion, we may *perceive* from hence, "That he is the first

Free and Independent Cause of all Things." His *Right* to, or the Necessity of, such Dominion, in order to the Common Good, is *understood* from hence; "That he alone, both can and will most perfectly attain this End, who is indued with infinite *Wisdom,* comprehending all the Parts, and the properest Means, of this End; and a *Will,* because of its essential Agreement with his Wisdom, always embracing the best End, and the fittest Means; and lastly, with *Power,* which can never fail in the Execution of those Things, which his infinite Wisdom has once made the Object of his Choice."

Having discovered, from these *Natural,* and consequently *Eternal,* Perfections of God, this *Necessity* of the Divine Dominion, in order to the Common, that is, the Greatest, Good; the *Law of Nature* giving him that Dominion, in the manner I have already explain'd, is *discover'd.* For it is *manifest,* "That the *right Reason of God,* (which is to him a kind of Natural Law,) would from Eternity assume this Dominion, in order to that End"; and, "That the *right Reason of Man,* as soon as it exists and perceives this, will, of necessity, *concur* therewith"; *for,* because it is *Right,* it *cannot disagree* with the Divine Reason. But, there being *given a Law,* "To acknowledge the Divine Dominion," there are *given Laws,* "Commanding, toward him, the greatest Love, Trust, Hope, Gratitude, Humility, Fear and Obedience, and what other Sentiments and Affections are expressed, by Prayer and Thanksgiving, and hearing the Word of God; and, by consecrating Things, Places, Times, and Persons, to the Honour of him alone."

We are hence sufficiently *caution'd,* "Not to give any other *equal* Worship with him," which is forbid by the *First Commandment;* "Not to *liken* him to Men, or any other Animals, or ascribe to him any Bodily Shape," which is forbid in the *Second;* "Nor to provoke him to Anger by *Perjury,*" which is inculcated in the *Third;* we here also find an *Injunction,* "To allot a *fit Proportion of our Time* to his Worship," which is intimated in the *Fourth Commandment,* by the Example of the *Sabbath.*

§III. In like manner the *Second Table* of the Decalogue may be deduced from *that part* of the Law of Nature concerning *Universal Justice,* by

Table the Second, contain-

which I have *shewn,* "That it is commanded, (because it is necessary to the Common Good,) that a distinct Dominion over *Things* and *Persons,* and their *Actions,* should be settled and preserv'd inviolably among all Men; that is, that a Distribution should be made, wisely accommodated to the best End, and that the Distribution should be preserv'd, which we find so settled, by which Necessaries, at least, may be allow'd to every one, both to preserve himself and be of use to others, both which contribute to the Publick Happiness." This Division of Things, and Actions, or Human Services, to every one, is *therefore* necessary to this End, *because* "No-one can live, much less be happy, without the use of many Things, and the Assistance and voluntary Permission of many Men"; and *because* "The Welfare of all Mankind, which is most evidently connected with the Common Good, consists in the Welfare of particular Men." But, if we more narrowly *inquire,* "What is necessarily to be allow'd to *every one,* that it may be well with *all,*" the *result* will be this, 1. "That the Power of preserving Life and Limbs intire, is necessarily to be allow'd to every Man, whose Offences against the Common Good do not exceed the Value of his Life." This is enjoin'd by the *Sixth Commandment,* which, therefore, not only permits, but commands, a *limited Self-love.* 2. "That *Compacts,* consistent with the Common Good, must have full Force and Credit among All." Among such Compacts, *Marriage* is one of the most useful to Mankind; as that, in which all hope of Posterity, and support of approaching Old Age is contain'd. Therefore the *Seventh Command* enjoins every one, "To keep the Marriage-Bed unviolated"; and, thereby, promotes an *extraordinary Affection of every One towards his Off-spring,* which, by this Method, is *more certainly known.* 3. "That some Share in other Things, and in the Services of Men, is necessary to every one, to enable him to support his Life and Family, (which are allow'd him in the Laws foregoing,) and to promote the Common Good of others." It is, therefore, *necessary* to the Common Good, *both;* "That such Goods should be allow'd to every one in the first Division of Things," *and,* "That, after they are given, they should be preserv'd unviolated." This is enjoin'd by the *Eighth Commandment.* Farther; it *conduces* to the Publick Good, "That, not only the Actions, but the Words and Desires, of Men be restrain'd from hurting others in the

possession of those Things, which have been hitherto allow'd them."[1]
This Restraint is the business of the *Ninth* and *Tenth Commandments.*
In obedience to all these *Negative* Precepts consists *Innocence.*

§IV. It is farther *evident,* that it conduces to the Publick Good, *not only,*   Humanity,
"That we should *abstain* from hurting others"; *but,* "That we should,
upon proper Occasions, *assist* them by our Affections, Words, and Actions, in such Things as these Commandments insinuate the necessity
of, in order to that End"; and this is a representation, or description, of
the most diffusive *Humanity.* And thus the Publick Good is *provided for,*
by "Removing its Impediments, and placing in their stead Benevolent
Affections, which may extend themselves to all the Parts of the Rational
System, and give to every one what is necessary.

But *as,* according to the *Mechanick Philosophy,* the *Material System* is   Gratitude,
indeed preserv'd by a Motion communicated to all its Parts; but it is
necessary, that such Motion should *return into it-self,* and, by that means,
be *perpetuated:* In *like manner,* in the *Moral System,* a Universal Benevolence, once begun, is daily renew'd by the *reciprocal* Force of *Gratitude,*
and by its Aid, or even by a prospect or *hope* thereof, gains new Strength,
and an eternal Youth. It is, in it-self, *evident* enough, "That *Benevolence,*
rightly and in a peculiar manner, directed towards those who had been first
Benevolent to us," (which is the *Definition* of *Gratitude,*) "contributes
much to the *Perpetuity* of the Common Good." We may *understand,*
from what has been laid down in the former *Chapter,* "That Gratitude
is then *rightly dispos'd,* when it returns good Offices to a Benefactor,
without invading the Right of any Person, Family, State, much less of
Nations": And for this Reason I would not treat of it, 'till I had *prov'd,*
from the other *Commandments,* "That the Rights of others were in no
wise to be violated." This Virtue is enjoin'd in the *Fifth Commandment*
of the Decalogue: For, tho' Gratitude to our *Parents,* who are our first
Benefactors, next after God the common Parent of All, be there *more*
expressly enjoin'd; this *Example* instructs us, by *Parity of Reason,* "To
repay to all our Benefactors the Favours they have conferr'd upon us."

1. [Maxwell] "That is, in the foregoing Commands."

These few Precepts, in my Opinion, contain all *the Universal Laws of Nature;* and, applied to the Actions of different States, with respect to one another, limit also and settle all the *Rights of Nations.*

2. *Civil Government and Laws,* necessary to the Publick Good; and, therefore, prescrib'd by the Law of Nature, commanding us to promote this End.

§V. From this *abstract of the more General Laws of Nature,* the *Transition* is *easy* to the Consideration of those "Dictates of Reason, which direct all to the forming and preserving *Societies* with a Power, not only of *making* Rules, but *enforcing* them by Punishments." *For* "such Societies are necessary, to enforce the Observance of the Laws of Nature, to the Honour of God, and Happiness of Mankind, but especially of those, who are Members of such Societies." And, *therefore,* a Law of Nature being Given, "which commands us to promote the *End,*" a Law is likewise Given, "prescribing the Settlement and Preservation of so necessary a *Means* as *Society with Sovereign Power.*" The *Necessity* of this Means to this End, is easily *learn'd* from the common *Experience* of All, "in those Things which respect, the care of a Family, or the building a House, or the production of any other Effect, to which the different Services of several Persons are requir'd"; where we *percieve,* "that all our Labour is bestow'd in vain, except some *Command,* and others *Obey.*" For it is *evident,* "That the procuring the greatest Good the whole Society of Rational Beings is capable of, is an Effect *more complicated* and *intricate* than any of these now mention'd," *and,* "That it depends necessarily upon the concurrent Assistance of *every one,* by mutual Services of very different Kinds," *and,* "That it is therefore impossible to obtain such Effect, tho' foreseen and design'd, with *Certainty* and *Steddiness,* except a *Subordination of Rational Beings* be establish'd, and all obey GOD, as the *Supreme* and most Perfect Rational Agent, by observing those Natural Laws, common to all Nations, which I have explain'd.

This demonstrated from Mathematical Principles.

I am of Opinion, that this Reasoning, which is grounded on common and obvious Experience, *proves,* "the necessity of establishing *Order,*" to all Men not blinded with Prejudice. But, because my Adversaries in this Dispute are usually very importunate in demanding *Demonstrations,* I will endeavour to point out some Mathematical Principles, whence is universally demonstrated "the *necessity of a known Subordination* among any number of Corporeal Causes co-operating to the Production of an

Effect certainly foreseen and design'd": Such is the *Common Good*, in the Estimation of all who would obey the general Law of Nature. For I do not contend for any other *Necessity* of establishing Order, than what proceeds from the Necessity of this *End*. We *learn*, from the second Book of *Des-Cartes's* Geometry, "That the most simple Effects arising from compounded Motions (the Descriptions and Properties of Curve Lines) may be exactly known, and certainly produc'd, if the several Motions whence they arise, be so adjusted, that the Latter are *govern'd* by the Former, but by no means without such a Subordination."[2] And it is *certain*, "That the fix'd Determination of all kinds of Surfaces, which can thence be produced, as well as of Lines, requires the *same Subordination* of Motions," from which will *therefore* proceed "the certain Genesis of all kinds of Figures." But true Natural Philosophy (I mean, that which owes its Original to Mathematicks) *teaches*, "That all natural Effects are produc'd by *compounded Motions*, and the *Figures* of Bodies limited by a due *Subordination*." It will therefore farther *instruct* us, "That those natural Effects, by which the Industry of Men can *certainly* promote the Publick Happiness, must be produc'd by a *like Subordination* of the Motions proceeding from Human Bodies." It is *evident*, "That some bodily *Motions* of Men are requisite in every good Office, especially in the Aquisition, Use, and Alienation, of *Dominion over Things and Persons*, in which, all Justice is contain'd." It is *therefore necessary*, "To establish a *Subordination* among such Motions of theirs, and, consequently, among Men themselves, in order to their conspiring to produce *one* and the *same* Effect, *the Common Good*." But, whilst I attentively consider this somewhat tedious Deduction, I perceive it may be much *contracted* thus. "If the *smallest* Effect of compounded Motions, *the Description of a Geometrical Curve*, cannot be *certainly* perform'd without a *Subordination* of Motions; much less can so *complicated* an Effect of many Causes, as is the Common Good, be procur'd, in any *certain* Method, without such a *Subordination*."

Yet I would not reject the former Deduction, because it may perhaps

---

2. Descartes, *La Géométrie*, II.

be acceptable to some, to *see,* "That there is some kind of Connexion between Natural Philosophy and Civil Government."

Nevertheless, tho' the Necessity of establishing *Order,* "That many may successfully unite their Powers in bringing about any great Effect," may be *demonstrated* from such Principles, yet that Necessity was *not first learn'd* by Men from this Deduction, but from obvious daily *Experience* in the manner above hinted.

The first Beginnings of *Empire* are to be seen in a *Family.* The Power of the Husband over his Wife, of the Parents over their Children, and the just Bounds of Empire, are *all* drawn from the Relation, which they bear to the *Common Good,* as to their *End.*

§VI. Having prov'd the Necessity of Government *in General,* from its *End,* these Things may easily be applied, to prove the Necessity, both of *Domestick* and of *Civil* Government, in order to obtain the several *Parts* of the best End, first the Happiness of *Families,* next of particular *States,* and lastly of the *Universe.*

I will carry this *Geometrical Illustration* only thus much farther, "That, *as* in Geometry, tho' the first Example of Subordination is between *two* Motions, of which one is govern'd by the other; yet Order is most conspicuous and remarkable, when the Subordination is among *more* Causes: *So,* when we consider Human Affairs, tho' the first Example of Order and Government is between the *Husband* and *Wife,*[3] in which the Husband is by Nature Superior, as generally having a greater

---

3. [Maxwell] "The true Foundation of the Power of Husbands over their Wives seems this, That in a Society of two, 'tis necessary there should be in one the casting Voice: The generally greater Ability of Men for management of private Affairs does make it Prudent in any State, if they make a general Regulation, to lodge the casting Voice in the Man, where the Parties make no contrary Agreement. The Gospel has done no more. But in this Case I see not, why the old Axiom may not take place, *Provisio Hominis tollit provisionem Legis;* as well as in Jointures, Division of Estates, and many other Cases, where the Regulation of the Law is only to take Place, when the Parties have made no contrary Covenant. So the Woman, knowing the general Regulation, either Divine, or Civil, and yet contracting Marriage without reserve, does tacitly contract to submit herself. But, if any Woman, conscious of her Superiority of Sense, or Fortune, should stipulate the contrary, and the Man consent, she would have Right, by the Law of Nature, to the same Dominion, which now is in the Husband, according to the Custom of our Country; nor do I see that the Gospel would invalidate this Contract. Greater Strength of either Body, or Mind, is not universal in Men." Maxwell seems to be following Locke's argument here, *Two Treatises of Government,* II.82.

Strength, both of Body and Mind, and, therefore, contributing more to the Effect design'd from their Society, the Common Good of both in Things belonging both to God and Man; yet *Paternal Government* is more remarkable, after Children have been born of that former Society." Therefore, from the *Paternal Power* are we to take the Copy, and deduce the Origin, of *Power,* both *Civil* and *Ecclesiastical.* For, in order to that necessary End I have mentioned, *both* must have been lodg'd in the *First Father;* a *Family,* therefore, was the *first regular Society,* the *first Civil State,* and, at the same Time, the *first Church:* And as Families encreas'd in number, so did States and Churches. As these Things agree with the *Nature of Things,* and, consequently, with *right Reason,* which is thence deriv'd, so do they with the most Antient and Faithful *History,* I mean the *Mosaick,* which is also *Divine.*[4]

I must farther *observe,* "That Government, or the Civil Power, is naturally and necessarily *limited* by the same End, for which it is *establish'd.*" Every Means ought to be *fitted exactly* to its End, so as neither to fall short of, nor exceed, it. It is *therefore evident,* "That, in order to the Honour of God, and the Happiness of all Nations, no Government can be establish'd, that can have a *Right* to destroy these." But, since all Things, absolutely necessary to these Ends, are but *few* and very *evident,* and, as I have already shewn, clearly enough laid open in the *Decalogue,* the *Limits* of the Civil Power still remain very *extensive.* Nothing is *prohibited* the supreme Power, but the *Violation of the necessary Division of Dominion,* by which their Rights are distinctly assign'd to God, and Men; and the *overturning those other Laws of Nature,* for preserving which it is it-self founded, and to which the whole Security and Happiness of Rulers is owing. *Consequently,* from these Restraints nothing harsher is *commanded* them by the Author of Nature, than "Not to overturn the Foundations of their own Happiness and Dominion, nor to destroy themselves along with others, by opposing such Things as are

4. [Maxwell] "Parental Power is wholly upon a different Foundation from Civil, see Mr. *Locke* on Government. Nor does the *Mosaick* History assert such Power in Parents, much less in elder Brothers, as can be called Civil Power." See Locke, *Two Treatises of Government,* II.1–3; Cf. Pufendorf, *De Jure Naturae,* VI.2.10.

necessary to the Common Good." However, *because* "The Dictate of Reason, by which the establishing and preserving Government is commanded, is a Law of Nature," (as appears from what is already said;) it *follows,* "That it owes its Original to God," *and* "That the Limits I have mention'd, are assign'd by him only," which makes much for the *Honour* of Government.

Supreme Powers cannot lawfully be punish'd by their subjects.§VII. This is the *peculiar Privilege* of the supreme Powers, "That God has appointed, under himself, no *Coercive Power* to punish them, if they have transgress'd the Laws of Nature, with respect to their Subjects."[5] If this were the Case, for the *same* Reason "another Power ought to be set over this, to punish it, if it have unjustly punish'd that Power, which I have before suppos'd *Supreme*"; and for the *same* Reason "Powers Superior to the Supreme must be establish'd in an *infinite Progression,*" than which nothing can be imagin'd more *absurd.* We must, therefore, *stop* at those, upon whom the *supreme* Power is devolv'd, and they are not liable to any Punishment from *their own State.* They who endeavour to subject them to Punishment, do, by this very Action, as far as in them lies, *destroy the very Nature of Civil Government;* because, "they reduce those who are Supreme to the Condition of Subjects." For it is no less *inconsistent* with the Nature of Government, that in it *all* should be *Subjects,* than that in it *all* should be *Sovereigns.* The Nature of *Order* (which is essential to Government) necessarily *requires,* "That something should be *First,* and nothing before that": And, *therefore,* in the present Case it is *necessary,* "That, among Men in the same State, there should

---

5. [Maxwell] "There is nothing in this Section contrary to the Right of Resistance in Subjects, who have reserv'd to themselves certain Privileges in the Constitution of the supreme Power, or who see the supreme Magistrate openly counteracting all Ends of Government. This Resistance does not suppose the Subjects Superior to the supreme Magistrate, nor that they have a proper Right of punishing him, any more than the rising in Arms against an Independent State upon their Invading us, supposes us Superior to them, or having a Right, as Superiors, to judge, or punish them." Although Maxwell wishes to reconcile Cumberland's statement with the Glorious Revolution of 1688, Cumberland is unlikely to have supported such a position in 1672, and his argument explicitly endorses an account of passive obedience. Indeed, Cumberland's text is remarkable for the absence of any discussion of tyrannicide.

be some *First* Subject of Coercive Power, from whom it may be deriv'd to all others"; but it is *certain*, "That they who have receiv'd that Power from it, can thereby have no Right to punish the very Author of their own "Power." Yet this is *no Reason*, "Why they should not be punish'd by *God*, if those Powers, which are *Supreme among Men*, should transgress the Laws of Nature." For they are *Subjects* in the KINGDOM OF GOD, or in the Universe, who in a HUMAN KINGDOM are *Supreme*. Therefore it cannot be said, that they have a *Right* to do those Things, which they do *with Impunity from Men;* because *Right* signifies a Power granted by *every* Law, to which we are subject; and, therefore, Actions done *rightfully* cannot be punish'd by *any Legislator;* whereas the Crimes, even of *supreme* Powers, committed against the *Laws of Nature*, may be justly punish'd by the *Author of Nature.* By thus distinguishing between *Impunity from Civil Laws,* and an *absolute Right,* of which the Law of Nature, and the End or Design of Civil Laws, is the *Measure*, I think, that both *Caesar* has his Due, and that their Due is reserv'd, both to *God* and his other *Subjects*.

§VIII. How *large* an Authority may be given to the *supreme* Powers, within the Bounds of the Laws of Nature, he will easily discover, who *considers,* from what is already prov'd, "That they extend universally to things *Divine* and *Human,* of *Foreigners* and *Fellow-Subjects,* of *Peace* and *War*"; the *Consequence* of which is, "That the Magistrate, in order to pursue the Common Good, according those Laws, must be constituted Guardian of both Tables of the *Decalogue;* and have Right, with relation to *Foreigners,* to make War and Peace; with relation to his own *Subjects,* to make Laws, to Judge, Punish, confer Honours, publick Gifts, and all kind of Advantages." But, *because* the Publick Happiness of all Mankind, and of every single State, may (as far as Men can judge) be almost *equally* procur'd by Constitutions, Manners, and Laws, very *different;* and the Welfare of the Society permits a *various* distribution of Honours and Advantages, nay, of Pardons and Punishments, where the Persons concern'd are not differenc'd by their Merit; it is *evident*, "That innumerable Articles may be (as they usually are) with safety permitted to the *Discretion* of Rulers"; tho' they are *always* oblig'd to the Care of

According to the foregoing Principles, a very extensive Power is allow'd to Sovereign Powers.

the *chief End,* which is *unchangeable;* and to very many *Means,* which
are *naturally Necessary* thereto. And no Body can be ignorant of these
Things, who has *observ'd* "those *Changes,* which are daily made in the
Fortunes of Subjects at the Pleasure of Princes, *without* any remarkable
Prejudice to the State"; or who *compares* "the several Constitutions of
the Kingdoms or Republicks in *Europe";* and *perceives,* "That in each of
them prudent Men may live happily," *and,* "That all these States do so
mutually balance one another, by Commerce and Intercourse of various
kinds in Peace, and by mutual Assistance in War, that much is by each
contributed to the present Happiness of *Europe."* For, altho' it *wants
many Advantages,* and may justly *complain of many Disadvantages, Europe* will appear very *Happy,* "if we reckon and justly value all the Advantages we enjoy, of Society, whether between the Members of the
same State, or with Foreign Nations, and compare them with the Miseries which would follow, if all, according to *Hobbes's* Scheme, consulted
their own Interest only, and every one thence arrogated to himself a
Right to every Thing, and engag'd in a War against All." Now we ought
to reckon, as *Effects* of the Principles of Concord, and of a Propensity
to the Common Good, "all those Advantages which would be wanting,
if the Principles of Discord and unbounded Self-love only, prevail'd
among Men, of which kind are those, which *Hobbes* has advanc'd for
the Dictates of right Reason in a State of Nature."[6] Having shewn thus
much in *general,* it will neither be *necessary* to my present Purpose, "To
enter into a *particular* Explication of all the Rights of supreme Powers";
nor "To explain the various Forms of Government, and the Causes
whence they are form'd, or dissolv'd," (which belongs to *Polititians*) the
usefulness of our Principles in Civil Government will be abundantly
prov'd, if I briefly *shew,* "That *Hobbes's* Doctrine to the contrary, is so
inconsistent with the Establishment and Continuance of all States; that,
if that obtain'd, they could either never be form'd, or must, of necessity,
be immediately dissolv'd." This will appear in the *following Observations.*

---

6. Section IX of the Latin text begins here. Cumberland, *De Legibus Naturae,*
p. 390.

§IX. 1. *First;* "All those Reproaches *Hobbes* has thrown upon all Men are thrown also upon all supreme Powers, of what kind soever; and, consequently, upon all Kings, our own not excepted."

Hobbes's Principles overturn the Foundations of all Government.

For Kings do not *divest* themselves of Human Nature, when they *put on* a Crown. The Nature of Kings remains the *same,* "as if no State, or Kingdom had ever been erected upon the foot of *Hobbes's* Contracts." These are so far from changing the Mind of the Prince for the *Better,* that *Hobbes* openly declares, *"He is not oblig'd by them,"* de Cive Cap. 7. §. 12.[7] And thence infers, That *"Princes cannot injure their Subjects,"* how much soever they may *hurt* them. §. 14.[8] Therefore, whatever he has affirm'd as *naturally* and *necessarily* true of *all* Men universally, and laid down as the Foundation of his Politicks, That *"in Cruelty and Ravenousness they exceed Wolves, Bears, and Serpents, who are Ravenous no farther than to satisfy their Hunger, and do not Rage unprovok'd."*[9] And, That *"Nature has made them Unsocial, and inclin'd them to mutual Slaughter. " Leviath. Chap.* 13.[10] And much more to the same Purpose. All these *Reproaches,* I say, bear hard upon *Royal Majesty.* Who could *love* one whom he believ'd to be such? Who could *trust* such a one with his Life and Fortune and all his Hopes? Must not all of necessity be *afraid,* "That he will destroy them one by one?" They would have the same, or rather *greater,* reason to *shun* and esteem him an Enemy, *than any other;* because his *Inclination* to hurt, which *Hobbes* pretends necessary to all, would be *equal* to that in them, and his *Power* would be *greater,* because the Force of all is in him united.

1. Because they represent the Nature of Princes, as more Fierce and Cruel, than that of wild Beasts.

[11]All those *Arguments,* by which he endeavours to prove, "That Human Reason is wholly unfit for a Rule of Manners, as not discerning

And deny to all, and conse-

7. Hobbes, *On the Citizen,* 7.12, p. 96.

8. Ibid., 7.14, p. 97.

9. Hobbes, *De Homine,* X.3, p. 59.

10. The quotation translates the passage from Hobbes's *Leviathan,* printed in his *Opera Philosophica* (1668), ch. 13, p. 65: "Naturam hominess dissociavisse, & ad mutuam caedam aptos produxisse." The milder English version reads: "that nature should thus dissociate, and render men apt to invade and destroy one another." Hobbes, *Leviathan,* (1994), ch. 13, pp. 76–77.

11. Section X of the Latin text begins here. Cumberland, *De Legibus Naturae,* p. 391.

between Good and Evil, but only as we *desire that* to be done to us, and *shun this"*; do in the same manner *destroy* "the Dignity of Monarchs, and all Polity whatsoever. *We all"* (says he) *"rate Good and Evil by our proper Pleasure, or Pain."*[12] Therefore, if *Hobbes*'s Doctrine be true, *no-one,* not even a Prince, either *can,* or *will consider,* "what is profitable, or hurtful to others." And there would remain *no Reason* drawn from the Common Good, "why a Prince should be appointed, or continued," *because,* according to him (as I have shewn in the Chapter *concerning Good,*[13]) *"The Nature of Man,"* (not excepting the supreme Magistrate, whether Prince, or Council,) *"does not understand Good, or Evil, except with relation to the Person who uses those Words."* Therefore whatever the King commands as *Good,* is to be understood "Good to the King, or the Representative of the Common-Wealth." *Leviath.* C. 6.[14] But "not to the Common-Wealth it-self, much less to the Universe," such as others think those Actions to be, that promote, both the Honour of God, and the Happiness of Mankind. By *reasoning thus,* "he makes all Government unfit for the End for which it is desir'd, and thereby does but too plainly insinuate, That it ought wholly to be rejected."

Nor can this *Wound* given Sovereign Powers, be *heal'd* by the help of all those *Blandishments,* with which he afterwards sooths Rulers, namely, that *"That is Good, or Evil, Just, or Unjust, whatever they pronounce to be such, and that they make all Things Just by commanding them, Unjust by forbidding them."*[15] Whence it *follows,* "That they are infallible in such Judgments and Declarations, and that they have no occasion to ask the Opinion of Lawyers, or consult with Men of Experience, to inform themselves what will promote, or hinder the Happiness of their State." Nor will it avail, that he has defin'd *"A Crime, to be that only, which has been either done, or omitted, said, or will'd contrary to the Reason of the Common-Wealth,"* or, *"of the Representative of the Common-*

---

12. Hobbes, *On the Citizen,* 14.17, p. 162–63.
13. Cumberland, *A Treatise of the Laws of Nature,* 3.2ff.
14. Hobbes, *Leviathan,* ch. 6, pp. 28–29.
15. Hobbes, *On the Citizen,* 12.1, pp. 131–32.

Wealth,"[16] as he elsewhere explains himself: And that he has asserted, That *"his Reason is to be always esteem'd, Right by the Subject."* [17] Because he himself has affirm'd, That *"the Commands of States may be contrary to right Reason in matters of Religion;*[18] *and contrary to the Laws of Nature"* (in Human Affairs) *"which are the Dictates of right Reason."* [19] And has also depriv'd States of all Rules that might be taken from the Nature of Things, according to which States might rectify their Commands, since he has expressly asserted (*Leviath*. C. 6.) That *"there is no Common Rule of Good, or Evil, and Contemptible, to be taken from the Nature of the Objects themselves."* [20] And elsewhere he plainly enough *teaches,* "That he does not believe the Reason of the Common-Wealth to be really right Reason"; but that, in order to end Controversies, *"The contending Parties, by their own Accord, set up, for right Reason, the Reason of some Arbitrator, to whose Sentence they will both stand, or their Controversy must either come to Blows, or be Undecided, for want of a right Reason constituted by Nature."* *Leviath*. Chap. 5.[21] Where afterwards he compares *right Reason* to the *Trump* in playing at Cards, to which the Superiority is given, partly by the *Consent* of the Players, and partly by *Accident*.

[22]Upon this Head he is certainly so far *in the right;* "In Controversies which it is necessary to end, it makes for the Common Good, that the contending Parties willingly relinquish their Decision to the Reason of the Common-Wealth, and fully acquiesce therein." And this common and right Reason persuades; *because* it is *certain,* "That this Decision will either be right, or that a righter cannot be had, consistently with the Common Good." And this Reason is both evident enough, and is preferable to that given by Mr. *Hobbes* upon this account, that it *supposes,* "That there is somewhere among Men a practical right Reason; and gives

Hobbes's Argument is refuted, by which he endeavours to *prove,* "That we ought therefore to obey the Reason of the Common-Wealth, because there is no such

---

16. Ibid., 14.17, pp. 162–63.

17. Ibid., 2.1n, p. 33.

18. Ibid., 15.18, pp. 183–85.

19. Ibid., 6.13, pp. 81–84; 7.14, p. 97.

20. Hobbes, *Leviathan*, ch. 6, p. 29.

21. Ibid., ch. 5, p. 23.

22. Section XI of the Latin text begins here. Cumberland, *De Legibus Naturae,* p. 392.

thing as right Reason, or which can judge according to a Rule establish'd and enforc'd by the Nature of Things."

them such Directions, that they may either reach it exactly, or that which approaches nearest it, which is sufficient for all the purposes of Human Happiness and our Duty." But *Hobbes's* Reason *supposes,* "That there is no right Reason settled by Nature,"[23] and upon this Account *appoints* us, "To stand to the Reason of the Common-Wealth," as if that were Right, than which nothing can be affirm'd more absurd, or mischievous. For one of the *Premisses* so contradicts the *Conclusion* to be thence deduced, that it might much more justly be *inferr'd,* (upon supposition, that there were no right Reason settled by Nature,) "Therefore, we ought not to stand to the Reason of the Common-Wealth." This reasoning of *Hobbes* is so much the more dangerous, because it may easily lead the unwary, when they perceive the falsity of one of the *Premisses,* to suspect the useful *Conclusion* he would infer from thence; or the notorious Truth of the Conclusion may cause that most false Principle whence *Hobbes* infers it, to seem true. Mean while, nothing more *reproachful* can be said of Sovereign Powers, than, "That their Laws are not the Dictates of right Reason, but only to be taken for such, because they have now got the Supreme Power by their own Fortune and our Consent, but that other Laws in perfect Contradiction to all these would equally conduce to the Common Happiness, and might justly claim an equal Respect, if by chance of War, or the Success of cunning Counsels it should happen, that a Mad-Man should get uppermost, who would enact Laws favouring Universal Cruelty, Perfidiousness, Ingratitude, and the Lust of Rule over all Things and Persons." There is nothing which could more effectually encourage the most profligate Wretches to raise Rebellion, than the view of filling the Thrones of their deposed Sovereigns, and thereby procuring to their own wild Opinions, and depraved Affections, the Honour of being esteemed Actions of right Reason and Virtue.[24]

---

23. Hobbes, *Leviathan,* ch. 5, p. 29.

24. In the margin Cumberland added the following: "It follows from this, that the subjects need respect the laws of their sovereign no more than the fall of the dice; and that they would be acting just as reasonably if they allowed decisions to be made about their lives by any sort of blind fate, as if they subjected themselves to the judgement of princes whose reason can never be safely directed by the nature of things."

§X.[25] 2. *"Hobbes's* Doctrine of the *Right of every One, to every Thing, in a State of Nature,"* (which I have explain'd and refuted in the First *Chapter,*) "does not permit Men who have imbib'd it, to enter into Civil Society, and disposes them who have imbib'd it, whilst in a State of Society, to throw off all Obedience to Civil Laws," that is, (according to his own Exposition,) "To commit Treason."

2. *Hobbes's* Doctrine of the Right of every one to every thing, would not suffer any one to enter into Civil Society;

The former part of this Assertion is thus prov'd. Mr. *Hobbes,* if we may believe his Principles, (*de Cive, C.* 1. §. 7–10.[26]) demonstrates, "That every one has a Right to every Thing"; from *thence,* "That right Reason gives every one a Right to preserve and defend himself." Farther, he himself asserts, "That *a Right can be transferr'd only in this manner, when any one declares to another, by proper Signs, that it is his Will, that it should not hereafter be lawful for him to resist the other, who is willing to accept of this Right, as he might justly before resist him."*[27] But (he says) that *"No-one can be oblig'd, by such Compacts, not to resist another threatning Death, Wounds, or any other bodily Harm,"*[28] and that *"Every one retains a Right to defend himself against Violence,"* and that he does not transfer that to the Common-Wealth, *"When he consents to that Union, by which it becomes a Common-Wealth."*[29] Therefore, "If a Right to all Things, and to wage War against All, can be inferr'd from his Right to preserve and defend himself," I *affirm,* "He stills retains it, even against the Common-Wealth.

It were easy here to *prove,* "That every one, according to *Hobbes's* Principles, is judge, whether the Common-Wealth is about to inflict Death, or any other corporal Punishment upon him, and consequently, whether Rebellion be necessary to his Defence or no"; and to *shew,* "That that is a necessary Means to every one's Preservation, or Defence, which he, as the proper Judge, has pronounc'd to be such"; nay, *and* "That

---

The addition is deleted, but it is not clear whether by Cumberland or Bentley. Cumberland, Trinity College MS.adv.c.2.4, p. 393.

25. Section XII in the Latin text. Cumberland, *De Legibus Naturae,* p. 393.
26. Hobbes, *On the Citizen,* 1.7–10, pp. 27–29.
27. Ibid., 2.4, pp. 34–35.
28. Ibid., 2.18, pp. 39–40.
29. Ibid., 5.7, p. 72.

that right Reason, which had before taught, that all things were necessary to the Preservation of every One, cannot afterwards contradict it-self, and affirm that less is sufficient." But any *Reader,* who understands *Hobbes's* Doctrine, may make these *Objections* to it; nor do I see what *Hobbes* can reply. I therefore hasten to the *second* Part of my Assertion, which, I believe, will give *Hobbes* greater Displeasure.

and excites
Subjects to
Rebellion.

[30]This might be prov'd by the *same Argument,* by which I now *proved,* "That the Right of claiming all things to himself by War, cannot be transferr'd"; for thence it *follows,* "That every one, according to *Hobbes,* retain'd to himself a right of waging War against any one, and, consequently, against his own State, except it grant to each Man a Right to every thing, which yet is evident can be granted in no State." But let us rather have *Hobbes's* Sentiments in his own Words. He, from an unlimited Right of preserving and defending Themselves, has openly allow'd the Subjects a Liberty of defending Themselves with united Arm'd Force against the Sovereign Power of the State. *Leviath. Chap.* 21. he proposes the Question, and Answers it in these *Words. "In Case a great many Men together have committed some capital Crime against the Sovereign Power, for which they all, except they defend themselves, expect Death, Whether have they not the Liberty to join together, and assist and defend one another? Certainly they have. For they but defend their Lives, which the guilty Man may as well do as the Innocent. There was, indeed, Injustice in the first Breach of their Duty, but that they afterwards took Arms to defend themselves, is no new Crime."*[31] In the *English* Edition of the *Leviathan* he asserts the same things, but somewhat more boldly, for, instead of the last Clause, he inserts these two, *"Their bearing of Arms subsequent to it, tho' it be to maintain what they have done, is no new unjust Act, and, if it be only to defend their Persons, it is not unjust at all."*[32] I think, indeed, he was to be commended, that, in the *Latin* Edition he somewhat soften'd so

---

30. Section XIII of the Latin text begins here. Cumberland, *De Legibus Naturae,* p. 394.

31. Hobbes, *Leviathan* (1668), ch. 21, p. 109.

32. Ibid., p. 143. The change to the lines in the Latin edition is typical of several alterations that Hobbes made to tone down the argument of *Leviathan.*

wicked a Doctrine; yet even these *second Thoughts* seem destructive enough, and to breathe forth nothing less than *Rebellion*. For, let us imagine that *Capital Crime*, which he supposes many to have committed, to have been this; "Many had conspir'd together to kill the King, this Crime is brought to the King's Ears by some One that is privy to it; hence the Conspirators are afraid of that Death, which they deserve: It is lawful (says our Casuist) for them to take up Arms in their mutual Defence, and to do this, is no new Crime." But, I *think*, "such Conspirators, taking up Arms against their King, that they might ward off that Punishment they have deserv'd, wage an unjust War, and are truly guilty of Rebellion; and that they, therefore, by this Step add another Crime to their Conspiracy; altho' both Crimes are equally included in one general Name, and both be a Breach of Faith, it is nevertheless a new Crime, that is, it is another newly added to the First, and they increase their Crimes by every Act in Prosecution of this War. The taking up Arms against the Sovereign Power, endeavouring to bring Criminals to condign Punishment, tends to Sedition and Civil War. Nor, if this be permitted, can they be forbid to kill the King, offering to lay hands upon any of them"; which of how ill consequence it may be, I leave others to judge.

§XI.[33] 3. "Some things also, which he has advanc'd concerning the Laws of Nature, threaten all Civil Government with Ruin; particularly, what he has deliver'd concerning the Obligation of Compacts and Oaths."

3. *Hobbes's Doctrine of Compacts,*

It has a dangerous tendency to Governments, his *Assertion,* "That *Compacts*" (by which only, he has affirm'd, they are establish'd and preserv'd) "Do not oblige, except where Credit is given to him who promises." This is insinuated in his Definition of a Compact, *de Cive, Cap.* 2. §. 9. which he explains and applies, *Cap.* 8. §. 3, & 9. where he treats of the *Obligation of Slaves. "The Obligation"* (of Slaves) *"arises from Compact; but there is no Compact, where Credit is not given, as is evident from C. 2. §. 9. where a Compact is defin'd, to be the Promise of him who is believ'd. There is, therefore, along with the Benefit of Life pardon'd, join'd*

33. Section XIV in the Latin text. Cumberland, *De Legibus Naturae,* p. 396.

a Confidence, in which his Lord leaves him his corporal Liberty, so that, except an Obligation by the Ties of a Compact had interven'd, he might not only run away, but also deprive his Lord, who had sav'd his Life, of Life." [34] He adds more to the same Purpose, in the ninth *Section* of the same *Chapter,* where, explaining by what Methods Slaves may be freed from their Bondage, he at last affirms, *"That the Slave who is thrown into Chains, or any other way depriv'd of his Corporal Liberty, is thereby freed from that other Obligation of his Compact. For no Compact* (says he) *can take place, except where Credit is given to him who Covenants; nor can that Faith be violated, which is not given and receiv'd."* [35] Nay, he speaks more plainly, §. 4. of the same Chapter, *"Slaves, if they be thrown into Prison, or Chains, do nothing against the Laws of Nature, if they kill their Lord."* [36] All these Positions are advanc'd by him, in order to explain the Rights of Empire, or of *a natural Common-Wealth, which is acquir'd by Power and natural Force,* which he affirms, *"To be then establish'd, when Captives in War, or the Conquer'd, or those who distrust their own Strength, promise the Conqueror, or the Stronger, that they will serve him,"* as appears from the first *Sect.* of the same *Chapter.* [37] And it is notorious, from the most authentick Histories, that most of the Governments now in being have been set up in this manner. It is, therefore, of the *worst Consequence* to all those States, "That," (according to *Hobbes*'s Principles,) "immediately after a Prince has made any Discovery, that he does not give Credit to any of his Subjects promising him their Obedience, they should be freed from their Subjection, and, notwithstanding their Compacts, may, without any Violation of the Laws of Nature, lawfully kill their Prince. If a Subject be imprison'd, and can escape by breaking Prison, or corrupting

34. Hobbes, *On the Citizen,* 8.3, p. 103.

35. Ibid., 8.9, p. 105; cf. Pufendorf, *De Jure Naturae,* VI.3.6; Grotius, *De Jure Belli ac Pacis,* III.7.1, 6.

36. Hobbes, *On the Citizen,* 8.4, pp. 103–4.

37. Ibid., 8.1. In his note, Maxwell paraphrases Hobbes in Latin, which can be translated as follows: "The natural commonwealth (as distinguished from the commonwealth by institution) is acquired by natural power and strength . . . if, on being captured or defeated in war, or losing hope in one's strength, one makes (to avoid death) a promise to the victor or the stronger party, to serve him, i.e. to do all that he shall command."

his Keepers," according to *Hobbes*, "He is freed from his Covenant and Oath of Allegiance, and may raise Rebellion without a Crime."[38] These things are of the more *dangerous Consequence*, because the Signs are very *uncertain*, by which we *discern*, "Whether Princes believe us or no," and the *Caution* necessary to their Safety may make Men of *suspicious* Tempers easily *conclude*, "That they are not trusted, and that they are, therefore, freed from their Subjection." Nor may we take bare Imprisonment, or corporal Restraint, for a *sufficient Sign*, "That we are not trusted," (which *Hobbes* has asserted, but not prov'd;) *that* is *often intended*, "Only to secure the Innocent, perhaps in order to be examin'd, or to answer for smaller Crimes," but never as a *Sign*, "That it is the Will of the Prince, to set the Subject at Liberty from his Covenanted Fealty."

[39]Farther; "It overturns the Foundations of all States, what he asserts," That *"Compacts, in which the Parties contracting mutually give Credit to one another, neither Party performing any thing immediately, are invalid in a State of Nature, if a just Fear arise on either side,"*[40] that the other Party will not perform what he has promis'd. For it is *certain*, "The Compacts, by which Common-Wealths (according to *Hobbes*'s Scheme) were form'd, are made in a State of Nature, and that both Parties, that which is to take upon them the Governing Power, and therefore promises Protection, and that which promises Obedience, cannot immediately perform what they promise"; and, *without all doubt*, "The contracting Parties may afterwards fear being deceiv'd, and they will think this their Fear just, and therefore (according to *Hobbes*) it is just, because they themselves are the proper Judges, and there is no third Power able to compel both Parties to observe their Compacts." *Therefore*, "These Compacts are not valid"; and, *consequently*, "The Common-Wealth, which seem'd to be rais'd and supported by them, falls to the ground, like a Building upon an infirm Foundation." But this *short* Hint may be sufficient here, for I have already handled *at large*, in its proper Place,

---

38. Not a quotation from Hobbes, but an argument based upon the implications of *On the Citizen*, 8.3–4, pp. 103–4.

39. Section XV in the Latin text. Cumberland, *De Legibus Naturae*, p. 397.

40. Hobbes, *On the Citizen*, 2.11, p. 37.

this whole affair of the *Obligation of the Laws of Nature,* especially that which relates to *Compacts.*[41]

[42]Let us now proceed to *Hobbes's* Notion of *Oaths,* "which, in effect, destroys Civil Society, by destroying, or rendering ineffectual its greatest Security." *Chap.* 2. §. 22. He has this marginal Note, *"An Oath adds nothing to the Obligation of a Compact."* But, in the Text, he expresses himself more equivocally, *"That a simple Compact does no less oblige than that which we have confirm'd by an Oath."*[43] I readily own, "a Compact not confirm'd by Oath, is Obligatory." To which I add, that it is *thence certain,* "That God will punish the Breach of plighted Faith, according to the Prayers of him who takes a lawful Oath," *because,* "It is the Transgression of a natural Law, which God has enforced by a Sanction for the Common Good"; *and* "That this is *known* from the Nature of Things, so that there is no need of Revelation, or any Person standing in the place of God, to signify that God accepts to be Guarrantee of such a Vow," as *Hobbes* seems to insinuate.[44] However, an Oath introduces a *new* Obligation, *because* "then we owe Obedience to another Divine Law, by which we are forbid, under a new and most grievous Punishment, to invoke the Name of God rashly, and in confirmation of a Falshood." Nor is *Hobbes's* exception to the contrary, of any validity, when he affirms, that *"he who in an Oath renounces the Divine Mercy,"* unless he perform his Promise, *"does not oblige himself to any Punishment, because it is always lawful for him, to deprecate Punishment however provok'd,*

---

41. Cumberland, *A Treatise of the Laws of Nature,* 5.54.

42. Section XVI in the Latin text. Cumberland, *De Legibus Naturae,* p. 398.

43. Hobbes, *On the Citizen,* 2.22, p. 41.

44. Ibid., 2.12, 13, pp. 37–38: "From the fact that acceptance of the transferred right is a requirement of all gifts and agreements, it follows that no-one can make an agreement with someone who gives no sign of acceptance. . . . Nor can one enter into agreements with the majesty of God, nor be bound by a vow to him, except in so far as it has pleased him, through the holy scriptures, to make certain men his substitutes, with authority to review and accept such vows and agreements and to accept them as his representatives. Thus men who live in a state of nature, where they are not bound by any civil law, make vows in vain (unless they know by certain revelation that the will of God accepts their vow or agreement)."

and to take the benefit of God's Pardon, if it be granted."[45] For "even they,
who may lawfully deprecate Punishment, when they have deserv'd it,
are oblig'd, both to caution, not to deserve Punishment, and also to bear
it patiently, when they have." After all these things are duly weigh'd, I
beseech the *Reader* to consider, what firmness *Hobbes* has left in Civil
Society, who *contends,* "That an Oath adds no Obligation." Kings are
deceiv'd, and *vain* are the Laws enjoining Oaths of Fidelity to them. *In
vain* are their Privy-Counsellers, their nearest Attendants about their
Person, or their Arm'd Guards, sworn. Neither sworn Witnesses, nor
Judges, are at all the more oblig'd upon account of Oaths, in publick
Judicature. Mr. *Hobbes,* truly, has by a slight reasoning freed them from
all Obligation of this kind, and, with the same ease, has subverted all
Civil Government.

§XII.[46] 4. *"Hobbes's Doctrine, concerning the Original of Civil Power,
contains some Principles evidently inconsistent with the Stability
thereof."*

    4. His Original of Government inconsistent with its stability.

    Its Original, in a Common-Wealth form'd by *Compact,* according to
him, is this. Many, out of mutual Fear, transfer all their Rights to one
Political Person, (whether a single Man, or a Council,) by a *Compact*
of this sort made with all their future Fellow-Subjects.[47] *"I transfer my
Right to this Person, upon this Condition, that you will transfer your Right
to the same Person."* And to the same purpose, *Leviath.* C. 17.[48] As soon
as the Person design'd for Government has accepted of this, the
Common-Wealth is form'd. The other *two kinds* of Common-Wealths,
the *Despotick,* which is the Government of the Conqueror over the
Conquered, whose Lives are preserv'd, (who are call'd *Slaves;*) and the
Paternal, which is over Children begotten and educated, and, conse-
quently, preserv'd from that Death, which it was in the Power of the
Parent to have inflicted, he insinuates to be form'd by the *same Compacts;*

---

45. Ibid., 2.22, p. 41.
46. Section XVII in the Latin text. Cumberland, *De Legibus Naturae,* p. 399.
47. Hobbes, *On the Citizen,* 5.12, p. 74.
48. Ibid., 6.20, p. 90; *Leviathan,* ch. 17, p. 109.

not express'd indeed, but implied and understood; Reason (truly) *teaching*, "That Conquerors and Parents do not on other Conditions spare those Lives, which are once in their Power"; and the same Reason *commanding*, "both the Conquered and Children, to accept their Lives on these Terms." These Conclusions may easily be inferr'd, from what he says *Cap.* 1. §. 14. and *Cap.* 8. §. 1. &c. and *Cap.* 9. §. 2.[49] Therefore the whole matter is briefly resolv'd into a *conveyance of Rights by Compacts.*

But, if we inquire how, according to *Hobbes,* they *convey their Rights,* he informs us, *C.* 2. §. 4. He says, This is then perform'd, when any one *"declares it to be his Will, that it should no longer be lawful for him to resist the other, doing any certain thing, as he might before with Right resist him."*[50] Therefore Subjects, in *Hobbes*'s Scheme, in their Compacts with the Person going to take upon him the supreme Power, *promise* only this, "That they will not resist him Doing, or Commanding, any thing (consistent with Self-preservation.") And, from this *Principle Hobbes* justly *infers,* That *"the Obligation to yield unlimited Obedience does not immediately arise from the Compact, by which we have convey'd all our Right to the Common-Wealth."*[51] That Compact obliges only to a *Passive,* not to an *Active* Obedience. And, indeed, Civil Power will be very scanty, if by this Compact, to which it entirely owes its existence, no-one be oblig'd to *obey* it, only *not to hinder* the King, for *Example,* "from doing what he can with his own Hands." But (says *Hobbes*) *"from this Compact, indirectly, arises an Obligation, viz. thus, that, without Obedience, the Right of Empire would be vain; and, consequently, a Common-Wealth would not at all have been form'd."*[52] But I affirm, that this is a *juster Consequence,* "That *Hobbes*'s Compact to convey Right, which contains nothing more than a promise, *not to resist,* does not truly and sufficiently explain the Original of Civil Power"; *for* "such a Right of Empire is in vain con-

49. Hobbes, *On the Citizen,* 1.14, p. 38; 8.1, pp. 102–3; 9.2, p. 108.

50. Ibid., 2.4, pp. 34–35.

51. Ibid., 6.13, p. 82.

52. Ibid.: "The obligation to offer it [simple obedience] does not arise directly from the agreement by which we transferred every right to the commonwealth, but indirectly, i.e. from the fact that the right of Government would be meaningless without obedience, and consequently no commonwealth would have been formed at all."

ferr'd," so that (according to *Hobbes*'s own Concession) "a Common-Wealth is not formed by conveying that Right," *because* "no-one would be thereby obliged to yield Obedience to the Prince appointed." And, according to *Hobbes*'s Principles, "Right cannot otherwise be convey'd"; *because* "he, to whom any Right is to be convey'd, is suppos'd to have that Right before"; *for* "he has a Right to all Persons and Things," which yet he could not use, *because* "others had a Right to resist him"; *whence* "Compacts were, only to remove this Obstacle, that *The Right of Ruling over all*," which is *"in every one coeval with his Nature,"* (C. 15. §. 5.[53]) should exert it-self, when Impediments were taken away.

But let us pass by this *Difficulty,* and *grant,* "That *Hobbes*'s Subjects had, along with the Compact conveying their Rights, involv'd a Covenant to yield as much Obedience as was necessary, that the Right of Empire might not be wholly in vain." Yet still the Bounds of that Empire are *too narrow,* which is only *not vain, or null.* Besides; "since *Hobbes* obliges Subjects to no certain Measure of Obedience to be yielded to Sovereign Powers, but to so much only, that the Right of Empire may not be conferr'd in vain; and since this very Thing is to be deduced by themselves, by a consequence arising from Compacts about transferring their Rights"; of necessity he has left them *Judges* of this Question, "How much Obedience is necessary to be given, that the Right of Empire they have convey'd be not in vain?" *For* "they themselves can best judge of the End intended by themselves in making such a Compact"; nor can it be *known,* "whether any Act be vain, but by him who perfectly understands the End of that Action." But, how *dangerous* this would be in a settled Government, every one must see: For "Subjects will, at pleasure, set Bounds to their Obedience" *whereas* "the supreme Powers," as I have already shewn, "are to be limited by the Divine Laws only, which are not changeable by the Will of Man": And "Subjects are oblig'd by the same Natural Laws, to obey in all things not forbidden by an evident Law of Nature." The sagacious *Reader* will hence *observe,* "That the principal and direct Cause of Sovereign Power in every Common-Wealth, is, according to *Hobbes,* that imaginary Right to all Things,

53. Ibid., 15.5, pp. 173–74.

which he pretends Nature has given every one, and, consequently among the rest, to him who is design'd for Government." *And,* "That the Compacts of others, conveying their Right to him, only remove the Impediment, or Resistance of others, by which the Exercise of *that Right, coeval with the Nature* of the Sovereign, might be restrain'd": *And,* "That Fear is no otherwise the Cause of forming a Common-Wealth, than as it obliges to remove that Impediment": *And,* "That the Nature which he bestows on Man, more Savage than that of wild Beasts, is no otherwise necessary to the forming *Hobbes*'s Common-Wealth, than as it is the Cause of such Fear, that is, as a remote Cause, upon account whereof it may be necessary by Compacts to remove that Resistance of others, by which the Right of one to Rule over all was restrain'd." He *professes* this openly enough, where he discourses of the Original of the Right to punish a Subject. *Leviath. Chap.* 28. In the beginning, where he has these Words. *"It is manifest, therefore, that the Right which the Common-Wealth (that is, he, or they, that represent it) hath to punish, is not grounded on any Concession, or Gift of the Subjects. But I have also shew'd formerly, That, before the Institution of a Common-Wealth, every Man had a Right to every Thing, and to do whatsoever he thought necessary to his own Preservation; subduing, hurting, or killing any Man, in order thereto. And this is the true Foundation of that Right of punishing, which is exercised in every Common-Wealth. For the Subjects did not give the Sovereign that Right, but only in laying down theirs, strengthen'd him to use his own, as he should think fit, for the Preservation of them all, so that it was not given, but left to him, and to him only."*[54] It is *evident,* "That in this Power are contain'd, a Power to guard the Laws by Sanctions," *and* "To cause those Sanctions to be executed," *and* "To make War," *and, consequently,* "All the Sinews of Government." But what is this else than to *say,* "That all Rights of Empire may be overturn'd by all those Arguments, by which a Right of every one to every Thing is overturn'd," which *destroys* it-self by implying infinite *Contradictions,* and which I have prov'd in the *first Chapter,* not to be supported by any Reason?

To all which I will here add this *Remark* only; "That, upon these Prin-

54. Hobbes, *Leviathan,* ch. 28, p. 204.

ciples, any Enemy and Invader of a Foreign Dominion, has as good
Right to kill lawful Princes, as *Hobbes* allows Kings to punish their rebellious Subjects"; which may make Subjects *more remiss* in defending
their Princes from Foreign Invasion. An Enemy invades rightfully, *because* he has a Right to every Thing: And a Prince has no other Right to
punish a Rebel, than *because* in a state of Nature he had a Right to all
Things, and that Right is still left to him. Nay, a Subject (by *Hobbes*'s
confession) becomes an *Enemy* by Rebellion; but every Enemy has that
Primitive Right, as well as a Prince, "To punish every one at pleasure":
It *therefore follows,* "That a Rebellious Subject acquires, by his Rebellion,
the same Right to punish his Prince at pleasure, which the Prince has to
punish his Subject for any Crime whatsoever."

§XIII.[55] 5. "All those *Powers,* which, under the notion of *Rights,* he ascribes to supreme Powers, more than what other Writers concerning
Government acknowledge, must, of necessity, weaken the Power and
Firmness of Common-Wealths, if they were put in practice"; and he
himself, in other places, *denies* them those *same* Rights; whence we have
just Reason to *suspect,* "that he first inserted those Passages, only to *flatter*
them." I will give only *two* Instances, but those the Principal, 1. His
attributing to them a Right to make what Laws they please concerning
Property, Just and Unjust, Honest and Dishonest, Good and Evil. 2. His
declaring them free from all Obligation by Compacts.

On the *first* Head he writes thus. *"What a Legislator has commanded,
that we are to esteem Good, what he has forbid, Evil: He is the Legislator,
in whom the supreme Power of the Common-Wealth is lodg'd";* and a little
after, *"Before Common-Wealths were form'd, there was no Difference of Just
and Unjust, whose Nature relates to a Command, and every Action is in its
own Nature indifferent."*[56] *Except in Civil Life, there is no common Standard of Virtue and Vice to be found, which therefore can be no other, than
the Laws of every Common-Wealth. For"* (says he) *"the Laws of Nature,
after a Common-Wealth is establish'd, become part of the Laws of the*

(marginal notes)
5. The Power *Hobbes* ascribes to Princes, more than what other Philoso-phers have done, perni-cious Flatteries, particularly;

First, the pre-tended Right of making what Laws they please concerning Property, Just and Unjust, Good and Evil.

55. Section XVIII in the Latin text. Cumberland, *De Legibus Naturae,* p. 403.
56. Hobbes, *On the Citizen,* 12.1, pp. 131–32.

State."[57] Hence he defines *"a Crime, what any one has done, or omitted, said, or will'd, contrary to the Reason of the Common-Wealth, that is, contrary to the Laws."*[58] Numberless are the Passages in which he inculcates this Doctrine, especially *Cap.* 6. §. 9. which he closes thus, *"The Civil Laws are the Commands of him, who is invested with supreme Power in the Common-Wealth, with relation to the future Actions of his Subjects."*[59] Truly, Whatever he commands to be done, tho' it proceed from a sudden Fit of *Passion,* and *contradict* his own deliberate *written Laws,* is a *Law* nevertheless, and the *only Measure of Honesty.* For he affirms, *"That it cannot be exactly and certainly known, that the Laws promulg'd are enjoin'd by him who has the Sovereign Power, except by those who have received them from his own Mouth."*[60] To *apply such Laws,* that is, Arbitrary Commands, to particular Cases, is to *judge according to Laws,* as he affirms in the close of the same Section;[61] whether it be done, immediately by the Sovereign himself, or by any other, with whom the Power of promulging and interpreting these Laws is entrusted. But the great *Privilege* of Princes, which he endeavours to prove from hence, is this, "That they are incapable of committing a Crime," and, *consequently,* "that they can never be justly blam'd"; *because* "they are not subject to the Laws of the State," for *"no-one can be brought under an Obligation to himself,"* as he asserts *C.* 12. §. 4.[62] And, *therefore,* "they cannot invade the Property of another"; for, *since* "their Will is the Law, whatever they will, is their legal Property; they can be guilty of no Dishonesty"; *because* "that only is Dishonest, which they forbid, whose Will is the only Measure of Honesty"; *but* "they forbid themselves nothing," *nor* "can any one be brought under an Obligation to himself."[63] And it is insidiously said by *Hobbes,* "That the Ruling Powers are not bound by Civil Laws," because in truth there are many Civil Laws made, *only* to regulate the Actions of Subjects,

----

57. Hobbes, *De Homine,* XIII.9, p. 75.
58. Hobbes, *On the Citizen,* 14.17, p. 163.
59. Ibid., 6.9, p. 79.
60. Ibid., 14.13, p. 160.
61. Ibid., p. 161.
62. Ibid., 12.4, pp. 134–35.
63. Ibid.

which, consequently, bind them *only*. But the *principal Point* which *Hobbes* would here insinuate lies deeper, "That Rulers are neither oblig'd by the Laws of Nature, nor by any others Reveal'd by God." He has directly asserted, *"That the Laws of Nature are not properly Laws,"* [64] and therefore are not properly Obligatory, except as they are part of the Laws of the State, (as I have already shewn;) and *"That it is impossible, that Civil Laws can contradict the Laws of Nature."* [65] He has also laid down *both the Premises* of this *Syllogism,* and left the *Conclusion* to be drawn by any one that pleases. "The Sovereign Power is not oblig'd by Civil Laws. The Precepts of the second Table of the Decalogue are only Civil Laws," *Cap.* 14. §. 9. *Cap.* 6. §. 16. *C.* 17. §. 10.[66] *Therefore* "the Sovereign Power is not oblig'd by those Precepts of the Decalogue," (which are really Laws of Nature.) Elsewhere he *affirms,* "That the whole Body of the sacred Scriptures are in no other respect Laws, than as they are incorporated by the Sovereign Power into the Laws of the State, (which he may change at pleasure;)" and, *therefore,* "the Commands of Scripture do not oblige the Supreme Powers." *Leviath. C.* 33.[67] By *these Arguments,* truly, *Hobbes* has taken care, (out of his great Veneration for all Sovereign Powers,) to *prove* "they are wholly unblameable," (how wicked soever all others may think them;) nay, "that they are most Just and Holy," *because* "their Actions are conformable to their own Will, and therefore always agree with that, which is the only Rule of Action." Whereas I am of *Opinion,* "That nothing more Reproachful can be said of Princes; nothing, which could expose them so much to the Hatred

---

64. Ibid., 3.33, pp. 56–57.

65. Ibid., 14.10, pp. 158–59: "Since therefore the obligation to observe those laws is older than the promulgation of the laws themselves, because contained in the actual formation of the commonwealth, natural law commands that all civil laws be observed in virtue of the natural law which forbids the violation of agreements. For when we are obligated to obey before we know what orders will be given, then we are obligated to obey universally and in all things. From this it follows that no civil law can be contrary to natural law except a law which has been framed as a blasphemy against God (for in relation to Him commonwealths themselves are not *sui juris,* and are not said to make laws)."

66. Ibid., 14.9, p. 158; 6.16, pp. 86–87; 17.10, pp. 213–14.

67. Hobbes, *Leviathan,* ch. 33, pp. 250–61.

of all, both their own Subjects and Foreigners; and consequently nothing, which would so surely deprive them of the Good-Will of all, which is the greatest Security of Rulers." For this *Apology* for Princes professedly *allows* all those *Charges,* which their bitterest Enemies usually draw up against them. "That their Actions are not at all regulated by any certain Rules, or Laws, taken from the Nature of the best End, and of the Means naturally fitted to that End"; and, therefore, *That they are wholly lawless.* He openly professes, That he cannot otherwise vindicate them from the Crimes laid to their Charge, than by endeavouring to *shew,* "That their Actions ought not to be reduced to the Standard of the Laws of Nature, or of the Scriptures, in that sense, in which others are oblig'd to obey them; but that they are Rules to be warp'd to the pleasure of Princes, so as to have no other meaning, than what they are pleas'd to put upon them; and that, by this method only, they can be justified from those Crimes, which seditious Spirits, for the most part falsly, lay to their charge." Without doubt, all *Good* Princes will reject such a Defense, as no less false, than reproachful. And among the *Bad,* there is not one so perfectly profligate, who would not suffer and desire, that some, at least, of his Actions should be tried by some certain Rule besides his own Will; and, therefore, would justly spurn at this Defence by Mr. *Hobbes.*

[68]Moreover, whilst *Hobbes* endeavours, by this method, to *free* Princes from all imputation of *Fault,* he is most highly *injurious* to them; *because* "at the same time, he deprives them of all Praise, arising from Wisdom and Justice." *For* "those Virtues (and, consequently, all others which flow from them) are conspicuous in such Actions only, as are govern'd by certain Rules taken from the Nature of the subject Matter, about which they are conversant." *Practical Wisdom* consists in the *Skill of designing an End, or Effect, in its own Nature worth our Pains, and of chusing and applying means naturally sufficient to produce the design'd Effect.* And *Universal Justice* is nothing else than a *constant Will agreeing with that Wisdom, which designs the best and greatest End,* the Common Good, as I have already shewn. *No Praise,* therefore, is due to Princes for the Prac-

---

68. Section XIX begins here in the Latin text. Cumberland, *De Legibus Naturae,* p. 406.

tice of any Virtue, "if they themselves both act, and command others to act, according to *Hobbes's* Doctrine, without any respect to the Nature of the End and the Means." No Prince is reckon'd *Wise*, or *Just*, "for doing whatever chances to come into his Thoughts, or to be his Will, without any regard to the Nature of God and Men, and of those things which may be applied to their Service." If every Action were *Wise*, and *Just* and *Good*, for no other *Reason*, but "because the Prince Will'd it," there would remain *no difference* between *Nero*, whom the Senate condemn'd as an *"Enemy of Mankind*," and *Titus*, to whom they gave the Title of the *"Delight of Mankind"; no Praise*, by which to distinguish *Tiberius* and *Caligula* from the two *Antonines*, the Pious and the Philosopher.[69] All the Actions of each of these Emperors were *equally* agreeable to their own Will; and were, therefore, according to *Hobbes*, *equally* Good, Just, and Honest. But Mankind can never be so blinded, as not to *see*, "That the Safety of any particular Common-Wealth, (and, consequently, that of all Nations,) is a natural Effect, not of every Action of the Prince, or the Subjects, but of a due Search and Application (in Laws, Judicature, and the whole publick Administration) of those natural Causes, which are proper to preserve the Lives, Fortunes, and Minds of Men, in a perfect State." *These Causes* are no other, than such Actions as I have already prov'd, to be commanded by the Laws of Nature; namely, "A voluntary *Division* of Things and mutual Services, by which may be assign'd and preserv'd to each, at least, what is necessary to the Preservation of Life and Health, and the Improvement of the Mind; the Exercise of all the *Virtues*, and the Establishment of *Civil Government*, where it is wanting, or the Preservation of it, where it is already established." And, therefore, unless Sovereign Powers *frame* their *Laws*, and *administer publick Affairs* in such a manner, as to make it *evident*, "they have a view to this End and apply Means some way suitable thereto"; Subjects will of necessity *lessen* their Reverence for the Laws. *For* "Men, as being Rational, and in some measure endued with the Knowledge of Truth, do naturally and necessarily set a great Value upon that alone,

---

69. For Nero's reputation, see Pliny, *Natural History*, VII.45; for Titus, see Suetonius, *Vitae duodecim Caesarum*, XI.1.

which appears to be greatly Valuable; and therefore they set the greatest Value upon, and pay a sort of Divine Veneration to, that publick Administration of Affairs, which they see promotes the Publick Good, which is by much the greatest Effect of Human Industry." But, *because,* on the contrary, "it is below the Dignity of the meanest of the People, to act without respect to an End, or to take improper Measures, even in Affairs of the smallest Consequence; and it is much more beneath the Dignity of Princes, to act wholly by a blind Impulse, without any care of the common Safety, by means naturally adapted to this End, in matters of the greatest Consequence; where the Interest of the whole Common-Wealth is concern'd"; *therefore,* "Men cannot so highly esteem the Laws of Princes, in which they plainly perceive any thing inconsistent with the Means necessary to this End, which are contain'd in the Laws of Nature, already explain'd." Nevertheless I own, "That, where the same good End may be obtain'd by Actions of diverse kinds," (such Actions are called *Indifferent,*) "it is not to be expected, that any weighty Reason should be given, why one indifferent Action is commanded, rather than another." It is *sufficient,* "if the proper End may be obtain'd by the Method commanded." For *such* a Command is *truly rational;* nor is Obedience to such a Command less rational, whether in Affairs *Ecclesiastical,* or *Civil.* I *own* farther, "that it is not necessary, that the whole Reason of every Law should be particularly explain'd to all"; it is *sufficient,* "if they are not inconsistent with, or may any way serve to promote, the chief End, and the Means necessary thereto"; and, therefore, Princes usually *Preface* their *Laws* with *Reasons,* briefly drawn from the *Publick Good,* and the known *Rules of Equity,* as appears from many of the *Constitutions* of *Justinian* and *Leo* in the Body of the Civil Law, and in most of our own *Acts of Parliament.* But, on the contrary, to *teach* openly, *"That* it is owing only to the Command of the Common-Wealth, or of the Law, that any Action is Good, and the contrary, Evil; and *that, therefore,* the most useful Actions, if not commanded, conduce nothing to the Publick Good; and *that* it cannot be foreseen by the Legislators, that a good Effect will naturally follow from them," (all which follow from Mr. *Hobbes's* Doctrine;) this were to make the *Government* of Sovereigns, and the *Obedience* of Subjects, *equally* brutish and unreasonable; *either* of which Assertions is a Reproach to them *both,* and threatens the Ruin of the Common-Wealth. For, if every thing were Good, for this *Reason,* "that it is commanded by the Prince"; he would have *no occasion* for a Council, in order to *deliberate,* by what means the Safety of the Common-Wealth might *best* be provided for: Any Means would be *best* for this *Reason,* "that it was commanded." *For* "the same Power, which can make Actions *Good,* can give them any *Degrees* of Goodness; and, consequently, make any Actions to be the *best,* or ser-viceable, beyond all others, to the Common-Wealth." The Prince, who thinks his Commands *thus* Effectual, would *in vain consult* with Men of Experience. He will always believe *his own Method* of Government, however rash, to be the *best,* which he will find by experience to be of the *worst Consequence,* both to Himself and his Subjects.[70]

This Doctrine is the *more pernicious* to Princes, *because* "It at once hurries them on to Rashness in Action, and destroys all hope of cor-recting in their Laws, whatever, thro' human Frailty, may be found amiss in them." For *Hobbes* has taken away all *Standard* of Good and Evil, except the single *Will* of Sovereign Powers; and has, therefore, left *no Rule,* by which *That,* when *Wrong,* may be set *Right.* Yet we see, that all States and Princes every where candidly and freely *own* in subsequent Laws, *"That* they have observ'd many Things not sufficiently provided for in former Laws"; *and,* "That they themselves have learn'd by expe-rience, that many things are prejudicial to the Common-Wealth, which they before were of opinion would be of publick Benefit"; *consequently,* they openly *acknowledge,* "That they have discover'd, from the natural Effects of Human Actions, what kind of Actions will be publickly Use-ful, or Good"; and, *therefore,* "That they cannot make all such Actions Good, as they are pleas'd to command." To this Head belongs all *amend-ment* of Civil Laws, and of Judicial Sentences given in pursuance of

---

70. Cumberland manuscript annotation: "Experience, drawn on the nature of the effects necessarily produced by human actions, teaches all men, that the surest way is to deliberate with people educated by long observation of what has happened, for having noted the natural results of such and such an action which has already oc-curred, they usually foresee those of similar actions which are to occur." Cumberland, Trinity College MS.adv.c.2.4, p. 408.

them by Equity and the known Rules of the Law of Nature. For which there would be *no Room,* "If Civil Laws only, (or the Will of the Prince made known by them,) were the Rule of Action." But it is *certain,* "That no Common-Wealth can subsist long, where such Equity is excluded": And, therefore, in *all* Common-Wealths we know, "Many things are left to the decision of Equity, in a manner different from what the Laws determine." Wherefore Princes themselves every where *reject* this *Privilege,* which *Hobbes* allows them.

[71] *Lastly;* "*Hobbes contradicts* himself upon this Head, and deprives Common-Wealths of what he had before allow'd them." So C. 6. §. 13. after he has given *Examples* of unjust Commands, with respect to which he denies, that the Subject is oblig'd to obey the Common-Wealth, as in case of a Command to kill himself, his Prince, or his Parent, he proceeds thus. *"There are many other Cases, in which what is commanded, being unlawful to some, but not to others, the latter may justly obey, but not the former; and that consistently with the absolute Right granted to the Sovereign Power. For the Right is in no Case taken away from him, of putting those to Death, who shall refuse Obedience. But they, who thus put Subjects to Death, altho' they do it by a Right granted from him who had Authority to do so, yet using that Right, otherwise than right Reason requires, sin against the Laws of Nature, that is, against God."*[72] In this Passage I observe, 1. That *Hobbes confesses,* "Some things are unlawful to some, tho' they are enjoin'd by the Will of the Supreme Power, or by the Laws of the State"; whence it *follows,* "That the Laws of the State are not the only *Standard* of what is Lawful," which he has elsewhere affirm'd. 2. That he *confesses,* "That *Sovereigns,* when they punish Subjects for disobeying their Laws, may *sin* against right Reason, the Laws of Nature, and God"; tho' he has elsewhere *affirm'd,* "That their Commands *cannot* contradict the Law of Nature, because their Subjects have covenanted to yield them *absolute* Obedience."[73] 3. It implies a *Contradiction,* where he *affirms,*

---

71. Section XX begins here in the Latin text. Cumberland, *De Legibus Naturae,* p. 409.

72. Hobbes, *On the Citizen,* 6.13, p. 83.

73. Ibid., 14.10, pp. 158–59.

"That they can use their Right otherwise than right Reason directs." *For* "No one can have a Right to act contrary to right Reason," *because Hobbes* himself defines *"Right"* to be *"The Liberty which every one has to use his Natural Faculties according to right Reason."*[74] And elsewhere he teaches, That *"Sovereign Powers may many ways sin against the rest of Natures Laws, as by Cruelty, Injustice, Reproach, and by other Crimes, which are not properly Injuries,"*[75] that is, are no breach of Compact.

I shall presently[76] inquire into this last Crime.[77] Here I shall only *take notice*, "That he confesses that the Wills of those who have the Right of making Laws may be corrupted by many Vices," whence it *follows*, "That he prescribes some certain Rule of Action, even to Sovereigns," and *consequently*, "That he does not leave every thing to their Will": Whence I *infer*, "That Subjects are certainly no less oblig'd by such Laws of Nature"; and *therefore*, "That all their Actions ought not to be in Obedience to the Will of their Sovereigns, unless they would chuse to sin against God in Obedience to Man." And thus much *Hobbes* himself has own'd, where he treats of the Duties which are owing to Men. To the same purpose he acknowledges, where he treats of the Commands of Natural Reason, about the Worship and Respect due to God. For after he had affirm'd, *"That Obedience is to be given to the Common-Wealth, commanding us to worship God by an Image,"* (that is, openly commanding Idolatry,) and other gross Absurdities of that Kind, he confesses, That *"such Commands may be contrary to right Reason, and, therefore, may be Sins in those who command them";*[78] and he acknowledges, That

---

74. Ibid., 1.7, p. 27.

75. Ibid., 7.14, p. 97: "There are however many ways in which a *people*, a *council of optimates* and a *Monarch* can sin against natural laws, by *cruelty*, for example, or by *unreasonableness*, by *insolence* and by other vices, which do not come under the strict and accurate signification of *wrong*."

76. [Maxwell] "In the following Paragraph, and to the end of the Chapter."

77. [Maxwell] "Breach of Compact."

78. Hobbes, *On the Citizen*, 15.18, pp. 183–85: "For instance, if an order were given to worship God in the form of an image in the presence of people who believe that to do so is a sign of honour? Certainly it must be done. . . . For although such commands may sometimes be against right reason, and are therefore sins in those who command them, yet they are not against right reason nor sins in subjects."

"*Common-Wealths are not at their Liberty, nor can be said to make Laws, with respect to God*"; and, *consequently,* "That they have no Right to make Laws, to the dishonour of God."[79] Whence I *infer,* "That the Reason of the Common-Wealth, is not *always* Right," and, *consequently,* "That it is not *always* the Measure of what is Good, Honest and Just; but *then only,* when it is conformable to the Nature of those Things, or Actions about which it is conversant"; and, therefore, That *Hobbes contradicts* himself, elsewhere (*C.* 14. §. 17.) defining "*Sin*" to be nothing else, than "*what is contrary to the Reason of the Common-Wealth.*"[80]

Secondly, The pretended freedom of Supreme Powers, from all Obligation by Compacts to their Subjects.

[81]There remains to be consider'd the *second* Instance of exorbitant Power, which *Hobbes* gives to Sovereigns, which is not so extensive as the former, and might have been comprehended under it: But, because *Hobbes* has handled it *a-part,* and because it is press'd with Absurdities *peculiar* to it-self, I thought it proper also to consider it *distinctly,* namely, *That Sovereign Powers are bound by no Compacts to any One.* It is incumbent upon me to *shew,* "That this pretended Right of theirs, does in reality lessen or destroy their Power, and that he is not here very consistent with himself." This is affirm'd by him in general terms *C.* 7. §. 14. and is inferr'd from what he has advanc'd §. 7, 9, 12. of the same *Chapter,*[82] in which he speaks of *Compacts with their Subjects* only, by which he denies Princes are obliged, and therefore concludes, "They can do no Injury to their Subjects."

This is an Opinion before unheard of, new out of Mr. *Hobbes's* Mint. For *Epicurus,* from whom he has borrow'd most of his other Sentiments, *altho'* "He has much weakened Justice in its other Parts, allowing them no other Force, than what they receive from the Faith of Compacts," *yet,* "Would have this unshaken in every State."[83] Let us then hear

79. Ibid., 14.10, p. 159.

80. Ibid., 14.17, pp. 162–63.

81. Section XXI begins here in the Latin text. Cumberland, *De Legibus Naturae,* p. 411.

82. Hobbes, *On the Citizen,* 7.14, p. 97: "Since it has been shown above (articles 7, 9, 12) that those who have obtained sovereign power in a commonwealth are not bound by any agreements to anyone"; 7.7, p. 95; 7.9, p. 96; 7.12, p. 96.

83. Cumberland, *A Treatise of the Laws of Nature,* 5.54.

Hobbes's Reason, by which he would support so extraordinary a Paradox. It is to be taken wholly from *C. 7. §. 7.* where he affirms, That *"The People*[84] *are bound by no Obligation to any Subject."*[85] *For* "The other Kinds of Sovereign Powers, the *Senate* in an Aristocracy, and a *Monarch,* receive all their Rights, according to *Hobbes*'s Doctrine, from the *People,"* and are, *therefore,* "Freed from the Obligation of Compacts, in the same manner with the *People."* Take it in his own Words from the Place last quoted, *"After a Common Wealth is established, if a Subject enters into a Compact with the People, it is void; because the People include, in their Will, the Will of that Subject, to whom they are suppos'd to be oblig'd, and, therefore, they can free themselves at pleasure, and, consequently, they are now actually free."*[86] The *force* of this Reasoning lies here. *Because* "A Subject has power to free any one from the Obligation of Compacts enter'd into with himself, by renouncing his own Right; and has conveyed all his Power to the People"; *therefore* "The People can free themselves from their own Compacts," and "What they *can,* they *will.*"

I *answer,* 1. No Reason can be brought to prove, that at the framing the Common-Wealth, the future Subjects agreed in this grant to the People, "That it should be in their Power to free themselves from all Obligation of Compacts they should afterwards make with the Subjects themselves": *For* "This is so far from being *necessary* to the forming a Civil Government, that it is wholly *inconsistent* with that End, for which it is form'd, *The common Happiness of all."* I own it is *necessary,* "They should renounce all Right, to compell those, whom they have invested with Sovereign Power." But there is *another Obligation,* by which the People are bound to observe Compacts enter'd into with their Subjects, the *Obligation of the Law of Nature,* which owes both its Authority and Sanction to God. "The Benefit arising from this, Subjects *can* safely reserve to themselves," and it is to be suppos'd, "That it is their *Will* to reserve it," because it is necessary to the common End. And truly I *believe,* "That it is neither lawful for Subjects to give their Sovereigns a

---

84. [Maxwell]: "In a Democracy."
85. Hobbes, *On the Citizen,* 7.7, p. 95.
86. Ibid.

Liberty to break their Faith, nor lawful for *Sovereigns* to *accept* it when offer'd," *because* "The Obligation to the Law of Nature cannot be dispens'd with"; by which, for the sake of the Common Good, both Parties are oblig'd by the Authority of God, to procure, as far as in them lies, that the Faith of Compacts be preserv'd inviolable.

2. I *answer,* That the Inference is false, by which *Hobbes* immediately draws his Conclusion. *"The People can free themselves by their own Will, therefore they are actually free."* The falsity of the Inference is hence evident, *because* "The Contradiction to *Hobbes's* Conclusion, may be inferr'd by a Consequence just as good, *Thus." The People can chuse, not to free themselves (from the Obligation of their Compacts) by their own Will, therefore they are not actually free.* In *neither* Case will the Consequence hold, from the *Power* to the *Will* in free Agents. The only *Reason* why, upon Mr. *Hobbes's* Principles, the former Conclusion should rather hold good than the latter, is this, "That he supposes all Mankind, and consequently Princes, cannot but Will what is Evil to others, if ever so little Power accrues thence to themselves." But I beseech the *Reader* to *observe,* "How *odious* to their Subjects, and consequently how *weak,* this would make Princes." Why might we not as well *infer,* "That it is the Will of the People, to neglect that Security which is necessary to the Subjects," *because* "They have a Power to do so?" And then every Common-Wealth would be dissolv'd immediately, *because* (according to *Hobbes, C. 6. §. 3, 4.*[87]) "No-one is supposed to have submitted himself, or to have stept out of a State of War against All, if he be not sufficiently secur'd by Punishments so great, that it would be evidently a greater Evil, to *hurt* a Subject, than *not to hurt* him." The Common-Wealth *can* indeed sometimes lawfully *dispense* with punishing a guilty Person. It were, nevertheless, of *mischievous* consequence thence to *conclude,* "That the State is *free* from all Obligation to punish the Guilty."

From what I have said, I think it is *plain,* "That *Hobbes* has *not* sufficiently *prov'd* this extraordinary Doctrine of his, which sets Sovereigns free from any Obligation, to keep Compacts they make with their Subjects." I have at the same time *prov'd* "It of *pernicious* consequence to

87. Ibid., 6.3, 4, pp. 77–78.

Common-Wealths." To which I will add only this, "That Sovereign Powers can neither be set up, nor preserv'd, by Men making use of their Reason, but for some End *common* to them All"; that is, unless it *appear,* "That their Government will be a means to promote the *Publick* Welfare, of those *especially,* by whom it is set up and preserved." But, because this is *future,* and depends upon the *Will* of the Sovereigns, it can no otherwise be *ascertain'd,* than from the *Promises,* or *Compacts,* (which may be confirmed by *Oath,*) of the Supreme Powers, and from their *Care* that they be *exactly observ'd. Hobbes,* therefore, having destroyed the *Obligation of such Compacts,* there remains *no Reason,* "Why Subjects should hope that Sovereigns would perform these Compacts"; there is likewise *no Reason,* "Why Sovereigns should trouble themselves about keeping their Promises," and so *all Reason is taken away,* "Why States should be either erected, or continued," and so *of course* "They fall to the ground." Nay farther; "That Subjects may have *no Security* left, from any thing their Sovereigns *can say,*" *Hobbes* advances, That *"An Oath adds nothing to the Obligation of Compacts," C.* 2. §. 22.[88] And *therefore,* "Where the Obligation of Compacts is *void,*" (which, according to *Hobbes's* Doctrine, is the case, where Princes Covenant,) "The Obligation of Oaths added to them, at Coronations and in some Leagues, will likewise be *void* and null." This makes the Condition *wretched,* not of *Subjects* only, but of *Princes* also; *for,* "If this Doctrine were true, their Subjects would *never* have *reason* to *believe* them, nor is there any method left, by which they *could assure* Men who deserv'd well at their Hands, that they should receive the Rewards they promised them." But in *these Circumstances,* (where there is no Faith, no prospect of Rewards,) the *Power* of Princes is *nothing,* and all the Sinews of Civil Government are cut asunder, by which they might move their Subjects to Fidelity, or Courage, in Peace, or War.

[89]Let us now *inquire* "What *Hobbes's* Sentiments are, of Compacts between *different States.*" This we may discover with ease, from what he

88. Ibid., 2.22, p. 41.
89. Section XXII begins here in the Latin text. Cumberland, *De Legibus Naturae,* p. 415.

before affirmed of the State of Nature, in which he *alledges*, "That the Laws of Nature do not oblige to external Acts."[90] *But* "To keep Faith, and to perform Compacts, is a Precept of the Law of Nature, and an external Act is here requisite." So he affirms *"That the Laws of Nature are silent in the midst of Arms,"*[91] (or in a State of War of every one against every one,) at least *"With relation to external Actions";* and, "That those *common Measures,* which are usually observed in War between Nation and Nation, are *not* to be looked upon, as what they are *obliged* to by the Law of Nature." He elsewhere (*C.* 13. §. 7.) gives a direct Answer to this Question, *"The State of Common-Wealths with respect to one another"* (says he) *"Is a State of Nature, that is, a State of War. Neither, if they leave off Fighting, is it therefore to be called Peace, but a Breathing-time, in which each Enemy, watching the Motion and Countenance of the other, judges of his own Security, not from Compacts, but from the Forces and Counsels of his Adversary. And this from the Law of Nature, as is shewn, Chap. 2. §. 11. from this, That Compacts are not Obligatory in a State of Nature, whenever a just Fear interposes."*[92] *"In all times"* (says he, *Leviath. C.* 13.) *"Kings, and Persons of Sovereign Authority are in a Posture of War."*[93] But *"What is a just Cause of Fear in the one Party,* That the other Party will not perform his Promise, *he who Fears, is the proper Judge,"* according to *Hobbes, C.* 2. §. 11.[94] And, *therefore,* "Any new Cause of Suspicion will be sufficient to make void any *Compact of mutual Trust,"* (such all Leagues between different States are,) as is *evident* from the Passages already quoted, compared with *Leviath. C.* 14.[95] *because,* truly, "There is no Power which can compell both States, to hinder one from deceiving the other." Upon these Principles has *Hobbes allow'd* "A Right to

90. Cumberland, *A Treatise of the Laws of Nature,* 5.50.

91. Hobbes, *On the Citizen,* 5.2, pp. 69–70: "It is a commonplace that *laws are silent among arms.* This is true not only of the civil laws but also of natural law, if it is applied to actions rather than to state of mind."

92. Ibid., 13.7, pp. 144–45; Cumberland silently corrects Hobbes's mistaken reference to 2.10 in *On the Citizen.*

93. Hobbes, *Leviathan,* ch. 13, p. 78.

94. Hobbes, *On the Citizen,* 2.11, p. 37.

95. Hobbes, *Leviathan,* ch. 14, p. 84.

Princes, to falsify their Faith to other Princes, whenever they please." This, tho' it *seem to flatter* them, under the appearance of Liberty, does *in truth greatly weaken* their Power, and leaves them hardly any Security. *For* "There is no State *Self-sufficient,* or that can support it-self against the united Force of all neighbouring States, except in Confederacy with other Nations, by means of Treaties of Commerce and of mutual Aid." And this *even those* Princes, who are most guilty of Breach of Faith, are *sensible* of. *For* "They no sooner *break* their Leagues with one State, or Monarch, than they find it necessary to *strengthen* themselves with *new* Alliances, to prevent being oblig'd to fight singly against all"; and so change their Leagues or Compacts, but do not reject all; and, by having recourse to the Faith of Others, *condemn* "their own Perfidiousness."

Farther; it is *evident* by common *Experience,* "That all States limit the Power of other States by the help of Leagues, and that it is a principal part of Political Prudence, to know the various methods of balancing the Power of their Enemies by Leagues." But these could *never take place,* "if *Compacts of mutual Faith* between different States, were not oblig-atory," according to *Hobbes*'s Doctrine. If these things were true, "our King,[96] when he was banish'd from his own Dominions, by a Rebellion prevailing in *Britain,* might justly have been put to death, (I mention it with Horror,) by the *French, Spaniards,* or *Dutch,* among whom he so-journ'd; and that after Friendship promis'd by Compacts." But God instructed them better by the Laws of Nature imprinted upon their Minds; tho' *Hobbes* at that very time publish'd, thro' *France* and *Hol-land,* his Doctrine favouring Perfidiousness, and boasted he had dem-onstrated it in his Treatise *De Cive,* and inculcated the same among the *English* by his *Leviathan.*[97]

Lastly; "If the *State of Common-Wealths,* with respect to one another, were necessarily a *State of Enmity,* and Force and Wiles were therein

96. Charles II.

97. *On the Citizen* was published in Paris in 1642, with the second edition ap-pearing in Amsterdam in 1647. *Leviathan* was published in London in 1651, the Latin version was published in Amsterdam with the 1668 edition of Hobbes's two-volume *Opera.*

Cardinal Virtues, as *Hobbes* teaches, *Leviath.* C. 13.,[98] there would be *no Intercourse,* or Commerce among them, which would deprive them all of many Advantages, they now enjoy." Princes would then receive *no Customs* arising from Traffick, and so would lose a great part of that Wealth, by which they are now strengthen'd; there would be *no safety,* nor indeed any *use* for *Ambassadors;* for it were vain to make Leagues, if the slightest Suspicion of Non-performance render'd them immediately void, as he affirms *Lev.* C. 14. These, truly, are the *glorious Privileges,* which *Hobbes* offers to Princes; these are the *Gifts and no-Gifts,* which he bestows on them. Yet he himself has justly render'd *suspected* his so great *Officiousness* to serve Princes, *because* he *avows,* "That to flatter others, is to honour them"; *because,* truly, "it is a sign that we stand in need of their Protection, or Assistance," (*Lev.* C. 10. P. 45. of the *Latin* Edition.[99]) But it is *obvious,* "That to say things which we believe to be false of any one, provided they seem great, is essential to *Flattery.*" Princes have, therefore, just ground to *suspect,* "that *Hobbes* has complimented them with such Powers, not because he believ'd them true, since he so often contradicts himself, upon that Head, but because they seem'd to be great, and he believ'd he did them Honour by Flattering."

6. Hobbes's Doctrine concerning Treason encourages subjects to commit that Crime.

§XIV.[100] 6. "*Hobbes's* Doctrine concerning *Treason,*" consider'd in company with the principal of his other peculiar Notions, "encourages Subjects to commit this Crime"; and, *therefore,* "tends openly to the Subversion of Civil Government."

For he affirms, That this Crime *"is a Transgression of the Law of Nature, not of the Civil Law."* And, consequently, *"those guilty of this Crime are punish'd, not by Right of Dominion, but by Right of War; not as bad Subjects, but as Enemies of the Common-Wealth."* [101] It is obvious hence to *conclude,* "That any Member of the State, may, by Rebellion, free

98. Hobbes, *Leviathan,* ch. 13, p. 78.

99. Ibid., ch. 10, p. 52.

100. Section XXIII begins here in the Latin text. Cumberland, *De Legibus Naturae,* p. 417.

101. Hobbes, *On the Citizen,* 14.21, 22, p. 166.

himself from the condition of a Subject, and transfer himself into a Hostile or Natural State." Hence it directly *follows,* "That this Rebel has recover'd his Natural Right to put his Sovereign, from whom he has revolted, to death, in like manner as his Sovereign has a Right to put him to death." For in a State of War, or *Hobbes's State of Nature,* the *Rights* are on both sides *equal.* It will farther *follow,* "That a Subject deserves no other Punishment for Treason, than that to which he is expos'd for defending his Right to the Necessaries of Life in a State of Nature." For *then* also he will be treated as an *Enemy,* by any other claiming to himself a Right *to all things.* Nay, *Hobbes* openly teaches (*Leviath.* C. 28.) That *"Harm inflicted upon one that is a declar'd Enemy, (tho' before subject to the Law,) falls not under the name of Punishment."* [102] Whence it *follows,* "That Rebels are not liable to any Punishment, tho' they are expos'd to the Calamities of the State of Nature." Farther; since there are numerous Civil *Laws* in most *States,* particularly our own, which have *enacted* most grievous *Punishments* against *Traytors,* nothing can be *affirm'd* more in opposition to the Laws, than "that they are not liable to Punishment, or that their Crime is no Transgression of the Laws of the State, which threaten them with Punishment." It is a ridiculous *Evasion* to say, That *"the Obligation is superfluous to that which we were before oblig'd to,* by the Law of Nature."[103] *Several* Bonds are certainly a *stronger* Tie than a *single* One. Beside; he himself has many ways attempted to *weaken,* or even to destroy, the *Obligation of the Law of Nature; and it was *therefore necessary,* "To have recourse to the assistance of Civil Laws"; that they, whom he had instructed to throw off all Reverence for the former, might be kept within some Bounds of Duty, thro' fear of the Civil Power. For it is *evident,* "That every thing, which weakens or destroys the Obligation of the Laws of Nature, especially, of that which commands *Fidelity in keeping Compacts,* does so far extenuate or take away the Sin in Treason; and does, consequently, allure Men to perpetrate that detestable Crime." Therefore, whether *Hobbes* will, or no, he solicites Men to be guilty of this Crime, as often as he *affirms,*

102. Hobbes, *Leviathan,* ch. 28, p. 205.
103. Hobbes, *On the Citizen,* 14.21, p. 166.

"That the practical Dictates of Reason are improperly called Laws, and are only Theorems, concerning such things as conduce to the Preservation of Men," as *Leviath. Chap.* 15. and *De Cive Chap.* 3. §. 33.[104] where he *says* indeed, "That, as they are enacted by God in Scripture, they are properly Laws"; but, if we *inquire* of him, "Whence the Holy Scripture is a Law?" He *answers Leviath. C.* 3. "That they to whom God has not supernaturally revealed, That the Scriptures are from him, are oblig'd by no Authority to receive them, except His, who is invested with supreme Power in the Common-Wealth; for He is the only Law-giver."[105] Hence it *follows,* "That the Law of Nature, even as contain'd in Scripture, is not properly a Law, except by the Sanction of the State." For, altho' he just before *acknowledges,* "That it is the Law of God, and of manifest Authority"; yet, because he would have this Authority to be no other, than what belongs to every Moral Doctrine, if true, he would *insinuate,* "That it is not sufficient to make them Laws properly so call'd, if they be not enacted by the Authority of the Common-Wealth." It will hence *follow,* "That Treason is not forbid by any Law properly so called," and *therefore,* "That it is not properly a Crime." *For* "the Law of Nature forbidding it," according to *Hobbes,* "is not properly a Law"; and, according to him, "this Crime is not a Transgression of the Law enacted by the Civil Power."

All those Passages also *favour this Crime,* where he *affirms,* "That the Laws of Nature," (for *Example,* this of keeping Compacts, by which Rebellion is forbid,) "do not oblige to external Acts," (for *Example,* do not forbid the external Act of Regicide;) "except sufficient Security be given to every one by the Civil Power, which can compell both Parties to obey the Laws of Nature, that they shall not be injur'd by any others," *C.* 5. §. 1, 2, &*c.*[106] But here he *teaches,* "That the Civil Power it-self can neither be constituted, nor preserv'd safe from Treason, except by virtue of the Obligation of the Law of Nature," which, if it does *not* reach even to *external* Acts, Princes will *not be secure* from Rebellion. Where-

---

104. Ibid., 3.33, pp. 56–57; *Leviathan,* ch. 15, p. 100.
105. Ibid., ch. 33, p. 259. Maxwell's reference in the text omits a "3."
106. Hobbes, *On the Citizen,* 5.1, 2, pp. 69–70.

fore he must needs *confess,* "That the Civil Power, and the Obligation
to obey it," (in the intire Violation whereof Treason consists,) "are supported by a Foundation, which he himself has taught to be of *no validity,*
but whilst it is *supported* by the force of *its own Effect.*" But it is *impossible,* "That the Effect can, before it exists, give strength to its Cause, by
which it must be at first produc'd, and afterwards preserv'd." But *whatever* invalidates the ground of the Obligation to Civil Obedience, *that*
lessens, or rather takes away intirely, the Crime in Treason, by which is
at once thrown off all Obedience to the Civil Power.

Lastly; "Men are animated to *Rebellion* by *Hobbes's* Principles, as they
allow *equally* all Rights of Empire, *to* those who have ascended the
Throne by Rebellion, or Regicide, as *to* Kings with the best Titles." This
is *evident,* because he openly declares, "That *from the natural Right of
every one to all Things, every one has a Right, coeval with his Nature, to
rule over All.*"[107] And, *therefore,* "whoever can any how shake off all superior Power, does, in so doing, remove all Impediment debarring him
of the Exercise of his Right"; and, after he has seiz'd the Throne, according to *these Principles,* "he shall be esteem'd rightfully possess'd of
it, and," *consequently,* "no Usurper." Hence it is that *Hobbes,* consistently
enough with his own Principles, *affirms,* "That, in time of Rebellion
and Civil War, there are two supreme Powers form'd out of one," *C. 6.
§. 13.*[108] The Author of the Civil War has by his Rebellion, truly, acquir'd
Sovereign Power over his Accomplices, and may rightfully defend himself and them against their Sovereign; as I have before shewn, from the
express Words of the *Leviathan.* Hence also he most *justly confesses,* in
the Epistle Dedicatory prefix'd to his *Leviathan,* That *"he defends the
supreme Powers, as the Geese, by their cackling, defended the* Romans, *who
held the Capitol"; for* "they favour'd *them* no more than the *Gauls* their
Enemies, but were as ready to have defended the *Gauls,* if they had been
possess'd of the Capitol."[109] The *Reader* may *compare,* (if he thinks it

---

107. Ibid., 15.5, p. 173.
108. Ibid., 6.13, p. 82.
109. Hobbes, *Leviathan,* Dedicatory Epistle, p. 2; the reference is to Livy, *History
of Rome,* V.47.

worth while,) the Epistle before his *English* Edition of the *Leviathan,* which was publish'd, when the Rebellion in *Britain* was at the height, and our lawful King banish'd, (where he professes this Doctrine more openly,) with the *Latin* Edition of the same, somewhat chang'd, where he thought it proper to insinuate the same Thing more covertly, after our most gracious Sovereign had recover'd his Rights.[110] What I have already said, seems to me a sufficient *Proof,* "That *Hobbes,* whilst he pretends with one Hand to bestow Gifts upon Princes, does with the other treacherously strike a Dagger to their Hearts."

FINIS.

---

110. Cumberland is referring to the slight changes Hobbes made to the Latin version of the dedication. In the English edition, Hobbes had written: "But yet, me-thinks, the endeavour to advance the civil power, should not be by the civil power condemned; nor private men, by reprehending it, declare they think that power too great." This is replaced with "But I see no reason why either side would be angry with me. For I do but magnify as much as I can the civil power, which anyone who possesses it wishes to be as great as possible." Hobbes, *Leviathan,* Dedicatory Epistle, pp. 1–2 and n. 4.

EDITOR'S NOTE

At the end of his own copy, Cumberland included an extra section in manuscript (Cumberland, Trinity College MS.adv.c.2.4, three leaves following p. 421). The original manuscript is in Latin, but Barbeyrac also translates the addition into French (*Traité Philosophique,* pp. 423–25). The text below gives an English translation of Cumberland's manuscript addition prepared for this edition.

§XXIV.[1] It seems quite clear, in my opinion, through the observations that I have made on many of Hobbes's principles, that whilst with one hand he offers them gifts, he holds in the other a sword ready to pierce their breast. Let us nonetheless add two other consequences which are born of these principles, equally pernicious to civil government and especially to the sovereignty of princes and monarchs. Firstly I say that princes could never be safe from the designs of their successors apparent. One always knows them, both by Hobbes's principles and by those of other politicians. But, following the doctrine of our philosopher, there is no law, which can properly be called such, which obliges these successors to abstain from killing the kings which they must succeed. For he destroys the obligation of the natural laws, and founds the authority of the Holy Scripture on civil law alone: But this law could have no sway with regard to the person who, having treacherously slain the reigning king, seized that very power that the deceased had; and who henceforth is subject to no penalty, unless he punishes himself, which situation no-one will think to fear. The consequence of this is particularly pernicious, not only for our king, whom God preserve from such attempts on his life, for all other monarchs of this world, and all those

1. The section number continues from the final section of the Latin edition (see ch. 9, n. 100).

who will succeed them, be it legitimately or by the crime in which
Hobbes encourages whosoever may wish to replace the reigning king.
These villainous successors will be exposed to the same danger from
those around them, who are just as entitled, by Hobbes's principles, to
commit all sorts of crimes. But the real maxims of true reason forbid
all that, as being contrary to the majesty of God, whose lieutenants
here below are the kings, and to the well-being of all peoples, and even
to the interest of those who commit such infamous deeds, by which
they call down upon themselves very great evils, amongst which is that
of which I have just spoken, which is included in part of the sanction
of natural law, which is to say, in that part which is associated with the
defense of murder, and above all the murder of kings. In his English
edition of *Leviathan,* Hobbes himself mentions the consequence with
which I am dealing here, of the danger to which he is exposing kings,
namely that of being killed by their successors.[2] But all that he says in
response, is that such an act is contrary to reason, 1. Because one could
not reasonably hope that in such a way the successor could immediately
make himself master of the kingdom; and 2. because he would teach
others, by his example, to undertake the same action against himself.
But here is my reply to that. It is clear that such a crime can very often
be committed successfully; especially if the successor has found a way
of including in his party many people who, imbued with Hobbes's
principles, and believing them to be proven, are persuaded that there
is no other actual law than the civil law, and that in the case in point,
there is nothing to fear from this law. As for our philosopher's second
response, I say that, when reason makes the successor envisage the identical danger to which he himself will be exposed by the person who
must follow him next, either it imposes this like a law that it prescribes,
accompanied by a sanction which is binding with regard to exterior
actions, quite apart from the fear of civil laws, or it does not impose it
in this way. If Hobbes means the former, he destroys his own principles,
and he recognizes a law with sufficient support from a natural sanction.
If the latter, he is in truth arguing consequentially, but then he is delivering up to the dagger of a successor the life of his king and that of
all other monarchs, since he leaves them no safety founded in actual

2. Hobbes, *Leviathan,* ch. 15, pp. 92–93.

law, which might shelter them from the murderous actions of their successors. These principles of Hobbes must therefore be abhorrent to all princes.

I note secondly that these same principles are destructive of the safety of all sovereigns, excepting one. And who should that be, that one sovereign? We know not: unless we may conjecture, that it will be the empire of the Turk. For the arguments of our politician seem to establish, that there can be no justice on Earth, whose laws are common to all men, unless we suppose that all kingdoms and states subject themselves to a single, common Sovereign. Either Hobbes's arguments prove that or they prove nothing. I am persuaded that they are very false, and thus that one can draw from them no well-founded conclusion. But those who believe them to be true, must also accept the conclusion that I have just indicated. Thus, all princes have no other recourse but to reject and condemn Hobbes's principles; unless they wish either to be perpetually at war with all others, or to be subjects of one powerful prince, that is the Turk, who is the one whom Hobbes may have had in mind as such. We must therefore believe one of two things, either that this philosopher wrote for the good of no prince or state, but recklessly poured out his wild imaginings, to corrupt the morals of all men; which is very likely: or that he desired to clear a path to universal domination for the Turk, for the destruction not only of Christianity, but also of all rights of property that subjects have over their goods. There are here certainly only the principles of the Muslims, with which Hobbes's opinions concur, in matters ranging from the fatal necessity of all human actions, to the absolute power of sovereigns. And his lessons on atheism are closely linked with the ideas of that political sect of Turks which, if I remember correctly, Ricaut, the modern author, calls the sect of the Muserim.[3]

Let us also note, that all that Hobbes wrote on the duties of sovereigns, in a chapter of his treatise *On The Citizen*,[4] is either false, or does not agree in any way with his principles. For, if the natural laws do not bind princes with regard to exterior actions, as he teaches, the princes are not obliged to do anything for the good of their people,

3. Rycaut, *The Present State of the Ottoman Empire* (1668), II.12, pp. 129–31.
4. Hobbes, *On the Citizen*, 13, pp. 142–52.

since, according to him, neither they, nor their subjects, were bound
by the natural laws to perform any exterior action, in keeping with it,
before the conventions drawn up for the establishment of civil societies;
and the princes themselves are in no way bound by these conventions,
nor in consequence since they were made. If Hobbes takes as true and
compelling the maxims that he prescribes for princes, it follows that
the natural laws, whence these precepts come, bind princes at least with
regard to exterior actions, but also to interior actions, or conscience,
independent of the weight of conventions constituted by the state. So
assuming this to be the case, all the foundations of Hobbes's thesis and
all the individual principles that he built on it, necessarily collapse.

APPENDIX:

CONTAINING

I. A SUMMARY of the Controversy between *Dr. Samuel Clark* and an anonymous Author, concerning *The Immateriality of Thinking Substance.*

II. A TREATISE concerning the Obligation, Promulgation, and Observance, of the Law of Nature.

LONDON:

Printed in the Year M. DCC. XXVII.

Appendix I

A Summary of
*The Controversy between Dr. Samuel Clark
and an anonymous Author, concerning the
Immateriality of Thinking Substance.*

That the *Soul* of Man is an *Immaterial Substance,* and, therefore, distinct
from the Body, has, in my Opinion, been set in a clear light by Dr. *Samuel Clark,* whose reasoning I shall, therefore, here transcribe, in his own
Words, from his *Defenses of an Argument made use of in a Letter to Mr.*
Dodwell, &*c.*[1]

Note; By Consciousness, *in the following Reasoning, the Reader may
understand, indifferently, either* the Reflex Act, by which a Man knows
his Thoughts to be his own Thoughts; (*which is the strict and properest
Sense of the Word;*) or the Direct Act of Thinking; or the Power or Capacity of Thinking; or (*which is of the same Import;*) simple Sensation;
or the Power of Self-motion, or of beginning Motion by the Will: *The
Argument holding equally in all or any of these Senses. And by* Individual
is understood the same with Undivided, *or* Single, *as oppos'd to* Specifick.

That *the Soul cannot possibly be material,* is demonstrable from the
single Consideration, even of bare Sense and Consciousness it-self. For

A Material
Substance
cannot think.

---

1. Maxwell refers to a sequence of works in which Samuel Clarke attacked Henry
Dodwell for his belief that the soul is naturally mortal before baptism. Clarke also
attacked Anthony Collins, who was soon embroiled in the debate. See Dodwell, *An
Epistolary Discourse, proving, from the Scriptures and the First Fathers, that the Soul is
a Principle Naturally Mortal* (1706). Clarke responded with *A Letter to Mr. Dodwell*
(1706) and several defenses of his arguments, passages of which are reproduced by
Maxwell.

Matter being a divisible Substance, consisting always of separable, nay
of actually separate and distinct Parts, 'tis plain, unless it were essentially
conscious, in which case every Particle of Matter must consist of innumerable separate and distinct Consciousnesses, no System of it, in
any possible Composition or Division can be an individual conscious
Being: For suppose three, or three hundred, Particles of Matter, at a
Mile, or any given Distance, one from another, is it possible, that all
those separate Parts should in that State be one individual conscious
Being? Suppose then all these Particles brought together into one System, so as to touch one another, will they thereby, or by any motion or
composition whatsoever, become any whit less truly distinct Beings,
than they were at the greatest Distance? How then can their being dispos'd in any possible System, make them one individual conscious Being? If you suppose God, by his infinite Power, superadding Consciousness to the united Particles, yet still those Particles, being really and
necessarily as distinct Beings as ever, cannot be themselves the Subject,
in which that individual Consciousness inheres; but the Consciousness
can only be superadded by the Addition of Something, which, in all the
Particles, must still it-self be but one individual Being.

Suppose the smallest imaginable Particle of Matter, indued with
Consciousness or Thought, yet, by the Power of God, this Particle may
be divided into two distinct parts; and then what will naturally and consequently become of its Power of thinking? If that Power will continue
in it unchanged, then there must either be two distinct Consciousnesses
in the two separate Parts, or else the Power, continuing in the intermediate Space, as well as in the Parts themselves, must there subsist
without a Subject; or else, not the material Substance, but some other
thing, is the Subject of the Consciousness. If the Power of thinking will
remain only in one of the separated Parts, then either that one Part only
had at first the Power residing in it; and then the same Question will
return, upon the supposition of its being likewise divided; or else it will
follow, that one and the same individual Quality may be transferred
from one Subject to another, which all Philosophers, of all Sects in the
World, have always confess'd to be impossible. *If,* in the last place, it be
said, that, upon the Division of the Particle, the Power of thinking,

which was in it, will wholly cease; then it will follow, that That Power was never at all a real Quality inhering or residing in the Substance (in which mere Separaration of Parts makes no Alteration;) but that it was *merely an external Denomination,* such as is *Roundness* in a Globe, which perishes at its being divided. And this, I suppose, will be granted to be sufficiently absurd. The Soul, therefore, whose Power of thinking is undeniably one individual Consciousness, cannot possibly be a material Substance.

"Which Argument the Doctor has reduc'd to the following fifteen Propositions."[2]

I.

Every System of Matter *consists of a* Multitude of *distinct* Parts.

This, I think, is granted by all.

The several kinds of Qualities ascrib'd to Matter, considered.

II.

Every real Quality *inheres in some* Subject.

This also, I think, is granted by all: For whatever is called a *Quality,* and yet inheres not in any *Subject,* must either subsist of itself, (and then it is a *Substance,* not a *Quality,*) or else it is nothing but a *mere Name.*

III.

No individual *or* single Quality *of one Particle of Matter can be the* individual *or* single Quality *of another Particle.*

The *Heat* of one Particle is not the *Heat* of another. The *Gravity,* the *Colour,* the *Figure,* of one Particle, is not the same individual *Gravity, Colour* or *Figure* of another Particle. The *Consciousness* or *Sensation* of one Particle (supposing it to be a Quality of Matter) is not the *Consciousness* or *Sensation* of another. If it was, it would follow, that the same thing could be *Two* in the same sense, and at the same time, that it is but *One.*

---

2. Clarke, *A Second Defence of an Argument Made Use of in a Letter to Mr. Dodwell.* The passages can be found in Clarke, *The Works of Samuel Clarke D.D.* (1738), vol. 3, pp. 795–99.

Note; From hence may be drawn an evident Confutation of that absurd Notion, which Mr. *Hobbes* suggests in his Physicks (*Chap.* 25. *Sect.* 5.) that all *Matter* is essentially *endued with an obscure actual Sense and Perception,* but that there is required a Number and apt Composition of Parts, to make up *a clear and distinct Sensation or Consciousness.* For from this Notion it would follow, that the resulting *Sensation* or *Consciousness* at last, being but One distinct Sensation or Consciousness (as is that of a Man;) the *Sensation* or *Consciousness* of every one of the constituent Particles, would be the individual *Sensation* or *Consciousness* of All and Each of the rest.

IV.

Every real simple Quality *that resides* in *any* whole material
System, *resides* in *all the* Parts *of that System.*

The Magnitude of every *Body* is the Sum of the *Magnitudes* of its several *Parts.* The *Motion* of every *Body* is the Sum of the *Motions* of its several *Parts.* The *Weight* of every *Body* is the Sum of the *Weights* of its several *Parts.* The *Heat*[3] of every *Body* is the *Heat* of its several *Parts.* And the same is universally true of every *simple Quality* residing *in* any *System:* For residing in the *Whole,* and not residing in the *Parts,* is *residing* in a Thing, and *not residing* in it, at the same time.

These Qualities are always the Aggregates of Qualities of the *same Kind,* inhering distinctly in every part of the Material Subject.

V.

Every real compound Quality, *that resides in any whole material*
System, *is a Number of simple Qualities residing* in *all the* Parts *of
that System; some in one part, some in another.*

Thus, in the Instance of mixt *Colours,* when the Simples, *Blue,* suppose, and *Yellow,* make the *whole* appear *Green;* in this case, that *Portion* of

3. [Clarke] *"Note, by* Heat *here, is meant that* Motion *which causes in us the Sensation of Heat; by* Colour *that* Magnitude *and* Figure *which causes particular Rays to be transmitted to us, &c."*

the System, in which any one of the particular simple Qualities resides, is a *whole* System, with respect to that *Quality,* and the *Quality* residing in it, resides in the several *Particles,* of which that *Portion of the System* is constituted: And so of the rest.

VI.

Every real Quality, simple *or* compound, *that* results from *any whole material* System, *but does not* reside in it, *that is, neither in All its distinct Parts, nor in All the Parts of some Portion of it, according to the Explication of the two foregoing Propositions, is the Mode or Quality of some* other Substance, *and not of* That.

All sensible secondary Qualities, *Heat, Colour, Smell, Taste, Sound,* and the like, are of this kind, being in reality not *Qualities* of the Bodies they are ascrib'd to, but *Modes* of the *Mind* that perceives them. These Qualities, not really inhering in the Subject to which they are usually ascribed, but being indeed Modes excited, and residing in some other Subject, do not at all exist in that Subject to which they are usually ascribed, but in some other Subject.

VII.

Every Power, simple *or* compound, *that results from any whole material* System, *but does not* reside in it, *that is, in all its Parts in the manner before explained; nor yet resides in any* other Substance, *as its Subject; is no* real Quality *at all, but must either be it-self a real Substance, (which seems unintelligible) or else it is nothing but merely an* abstract Name *or* Notion, *as all* Universals *are.*

Thus the Power resulting from the Texture of a *Rose,* to excite in us the Sensation of Sweetness, is nothing but an *abstract Name,* signifying a particular Motion and Figure of certain parts emitted. For the Sweetness of a Rose is well known, not to be a Quality really inhering in the Rose; but a *Sensation,* which is merely in him that smells it, and a Mode of the *Thinking Substance* that is in the Man. And these Qualities, in no Sense wherein they can be ascribed to a System of Matter, are *individual*

Powers. They are Individuals, only as they are Modes of the thinking Substance that perceives them; but in the Bodies themselves, they are *only specifically,* not *individually,* single Powers; that is, they are only a Number of *similar Motions* or *Figures* of the Parts of the Body. Nay, they are not always so much as *specifically* single Powers. Thus compound Colours, as certain *Greens,* for Example, which are *individual Modes* in the thinking Substance that perceives them, may in the Objects be nothing but a Number of Figures or Motions *even specifically* different, namely, such as usually represent both *Blue* and *Yellow.* And the same may be said of *Heat, Light, Taste, Sound,* and all those others, which are called *sensible Qualities.* The Power of a *Clock* to shew the Hour of the Day, is nothing but one *new complex Name,* to express at once the several Motions of parts, and, particularly, the *determinate Velocity* of the last Wheel to turn round once in twelve Hours: Upon the stopping which Motion, by the Touch of a Finger or any other Impediment, without making any Alteration at all in the Number, Figure, or Disposition of the parts of the Clock, the *Power* wholly ceases; and, upon removing the Impediment, by which nothing is restored but *mere Motion,* the *Power* returns again, which is, therefore, no new real Quality of the *whole,* but only the *mere Motion* of the *Parts.* The Power of a *Pin* to prick, is nothing distinct from its mere Figure permitting it to enter the Skin. The Power of a *Weight* in one Scale of a Balance, to ascend or descend, upon increasing or diminishing the Counterpoise in the other Scale, is not a *new real Quality,* distinct from its *absolute Gravity,* tho' it occasions a new *Effect,* there being no alteration at all made in the *Weight itself.* The *Power of the Eye to see,* is not a real Quality of the *whole Eye,* but merely an *abstract Name,* signifying a transmitting and refracting of the Rays of Light in a certain manner thro' its several parts; which Effect, by the Interposition or Removal of an opake Body, is destroyed or renewed, without any Alteration at all in the Eye it-self. A *Key,* by having many new Locks made to fit it, acquires a *new Power* of producing Effects, which it could not before; and yet no new real Quality is produced, nor any Alteration at all made in the *Key* it-self. And so, universally, of all Powers of this kind: These Qualities not really inhering in any Subject at all, but being mere *abstract Names,* or external Denominations, to express certain complex Ideas framed in our Imaginations; or certain general extrinsick and relative Effects, produced upon particular Systems of Matter by foreign Agents, or certain Dispositions of the particular Systems of Matter, requisite towards the producing of those Effects, such as are *Magnetism, Electricity, Attraction, Reflexibility, Refrangibility,* and the like. These have no real Existence, by way of *proper inhering,* in any Subject. If these Powers were any thing else, but *mere abstract Names,* they would signify Qualities subsisting without any Subject at all; that is, such as must themselves be distinct Substances, which is unintelligible.

VIII.

Consciousness is neither a mere abstract Name,
(*such as the* Powers *mentioned in* Prop. VII.) *nor a* Power of
exciting or occasioning different Modes in a foreign Substance,
(*such as are all the* sensible Qualities *of Bodies* Prop. VII.) *but a*
real Quality, truly and properly inherent in the Subject it-self,
the thinking Substance.

If it was a *mere abstract Name,* it would be nothing at all, in the Person that thinks, or in the thinking Substance it-self, but only a Notion framed by the Imagination of some other Being: For all those Powers, which are only *abstract Names,* are not at all in the *Things whose Powers they are called;* but are only *Notions,* framed in the Imagination, by the Mind that observes, compares and reasons about different *Objects without it-self.*

   If it was a *Power of exciting or occasioning different Modes in a foreign Substance,* then the *Power of thinking* must be, before, in that foreign Substance; and that foreign Substance alone would in reality be conscious, and not *This,* which excites the different Modes in *That foreign Substance:* For the Power that is in one Substance, of exciting different Modes in another Substance, pre-supposes necessarily, in that other Substance, the *Foundation* of those Modes; the *Power of thinking* is, beforehand, in that Being, wherein those Qualities excite or occasion *different Modes* of thinking.

It remains, therefore, that it must of necessity be a *real Quality, truly and properly inhering in the Subject it-self, the thinking Substance;* there being no other *Species* of *Powers* or *Qualities* left, to which it can possibly be referred. And this indeed is, of it-self, as evident by every Man's Experience, as it can be render'd by any Explication or Proof whatsoever.

IX.

No real Quality *can result from the* Composition *of* different Qualities, *so as to be a new Quality in the same Subject, of a* different Kind *or* Species, *from all and every one of the* component Qualities.

If it could, it would be a *Creation of something out of nothing.* From compound *Motion* can arise nothing but *Motion:* From *Magnitudes,* nothing but *Magnitude:* From *Figures,* nothing but *Figure:* From Compositions of *Magnitude, Figure* and *Motion* together, nothing but *Magnitude, Figure* and *Motion:* From *mechanical Powers* nothing but *mechanical Powers:* From a composition of *Colours,* nothing but *Colour,* which it-self (as appears by Microscopes) is still the *simple Colours* of which it was compounded. From Mixtures of *Chymical Liquors,* nothing but *Ferments,* which are only mere Motions of the Particles in mixing, such Motions, as arise from placing of *Iron* and a *Loadstone* near each other. *Gravity* is not a Quality of Matter, arising from its Texture, or any other Powers in it; but merely an *Endeavour* to *Motion,* excited by some foreign Force or Power. *Magnetism* or *Electricity* are not new Qualities, resulting from different and unknown Powers; but merely Emission of certain Steams of Matter, which produce certain determinate Motions. Compositions of *Colours* can never contribute to produce a *Sound,* nor Compositions of *Magnitude* and *Figure* to produce a *Motion;* nor *necessary and determinate Motion,* to produce a *free and indetermined Power of Self-motion;* nor any *mechanical Powers* whatsoever, to produce a *Power not mechanical.* And the same must of necessity hold universally true, of all Qualities and Powers whatsoever, whether known or unknown; because otherwise, as hath been before said, there would in the Compound be something created out of nothing.

X.

Consciousness, *therefore, being a real Quality,* (Prop. VIII.) *and of a kind* specifically different *from all other Qualities, whether known or unknown, which are themselves acknowledged to be* void of Consciousness, *can never possibly result from any Composition of such Qualities.*

This is as evident from the foregoing Propositions, as that a *Sound* cannot be the Result of a Mixture of *Colours* and *Smells;* nor *Extension* the Result of a Composition of parts *unextended;* nor *Solidity* the Result of parts *not solid,* whatever other different Qualities, known or unknown, those constituent parts may be supposed to be endued with.

XI.

No individual Quality *can be transferred from one* Subject *to another.*

This is granted by all.

XII.

The Spirits *and* Particles *of the* Brain, *being* loose *and in* perpetual Flux, *cannot, therefore, be the Seat of that* Consciousness, *by which a Man not only remembers things done many Years since; but also is conscious that* he himself, *the same* individual conscious Being, *was the Doer of them.*

This follows evidently from the foregoing.

XIII.

The Consciousness *that a Man has at one and the same time, is* one Consciousness, *and not a* Multitude of Consciousnesses; *as the* Solidity, Motion *or* Colour *of any piece of Matter, is a multitude of distinct* Solidities, Motions *or* Colours.

This is granted by all, who deny that the Particles of the Brain, which they suppose to constitute a conscious Substance, are themselves each of them conscious.

XIV.

Consciousness, *therefore, cannot at all reside in the Substance of the* Brain *or Spirits, or in any other* material System, *as its* Subject, *but must be a Quality of some* immaterial Substance.

This follows necessarily from the foregoing Propositions compared together: For, since every possible Power of Matter, whether known or unknown, must needs be either, First, A *real Quality* of the Matter to which it is ascribed; and then it must inhere in the several distinct parts: Or, Secondly, A Power of exciting or occasioning certain *Modes* in some *other Subject;* and then it is truly the Quality, not of the *Matter,* but of that *other Subject:* Or, Thirdly, A *mere abstract Name* or *Notion* of what is, properly speaking, no real Quality at all, and inheres in no real Subject at all: And Consciousness is acknowledged to be none of these: It follows unavoidably, that it must of necessity be a Quality of some immaterial Substance.

XV.

Difficulties that arise, afterwards, concerning other Qualities *of that* Immaterial Substance, *as, whether it be* extended *or* unextended; *do not at all affect the present Argument.*

For thus even abstract mathematical Demonstrations; as those concerning the *infinite Divisibility of Quantity,* the *Eternity of God,* and his *Immensity,* have almost insuperable Difficulties on the other side: And yet no Man, who understands those Matters, thinks that those Difficulties do at all weaken the Force, or diminish the Certainty, of the Demonstrations.

What follows, is the Sum of Objections *that have been made to the foregoing Reasoning, and of the* Answers, *that have been given to those Objections by* Dr. Clark.[4]

---

4. Clarke, *A Third Defence of an Argument Made Use of in a Letter to Mr. Dodwell,* in Clarke, *Works,* vol. 3, pp. 825–27.

It is Objected, That there are some real Qualities, truly and properly inhering in the Subject to which they are ascribed; which yet are not, like Magnitude and Motion, Sums or Aggregates of Powers or Qualities of the *same Kind,* inhering distinctly in the several Parts of the Subject: And that, therefore, *thinking,* though it be not an Aggregate of the Powers of the *same kind,* may, nevertheless, be a real Quality inhering in Matter. Objections against the foregoing Reasoning,

That numerical *Powers,* or *particular and individual Modes,* are such real inherent Qualities, residing in a System of Matter, without inhering distinctly in its several Parts; in contradistinction to *generical Powers,* such as *Magnitude* and *Motion,* which the *Objector* acknowledges to be the Sums of the Magnitudes and Motions of the several Parts.

That, for Instance, the Power of the *Eye* to contribute to the Act of Seeing; the Power of a *Clock,* to shew the Hour of the Day; the Power of a *Musical Instrument,* to produce in us harmonious Sounds; the particular Figures, such as *Roundness* or *Squareness;* and particular or individual *Modes of Motion,* are such *numerical Powers,* not at all resulting from any Powers of the *same kind,* inhering in the parts of the System: And that Thinking, therefore, in like manner, not being an Aggregate of Powers of the *same kind,* may yet inhere in a System of Matter, as one of those *numerical* or *individual Modes* of some *generical Power.*

That, upon this Supposition, of *Thinking* being a *numerical Mode* of some *generical Power* of Matter, it may be conceived, that *as the Roundness of a Body is not the Sum of the Roundnesses of the Parts;* nor the *Squareness* of a Body, the Sum of the *Squarenesses* of the Parts, nor *the Power of a musical Instrument to cause an harmonious Sound, the Sum of the Powers of the same kind in the Parts singly considered;* nor any particular *Mode of Motion,* the Sum of the same *Modes of Motion* in all the several Parts; so the *Consciousness* that *inheres in a System of Matter,* may yet *not be the Sum of the Consciousnesses of the Parts.*

That the Argument, therefore, drawn from *Consciousness* not being made up of *several Consciousnesses,* concludes no more against the Possibility of its residing in a System of Matter, than the like Argument would *conclude against the Possibility of the Existence of* Roundness, *or any other* numerical Mode in a Body.

For *Roundness no more consists of several Roundnesses, than Thinking or Consciousness does of several Consciousnesses.*

And *Roundness is as specifically different from other Figures,* of which it may be composed, *as Consciousness is from a circular Motion.*

So that *Sensation* may be conceived to be *in the parts of an Animal's Body, just as Roundness is in the parts that compose a round Body: Each part has as much of Sensation, singly consider'd, as each part of a round Body has of Roundness: And when the parts are duly disposed, whole Thinking is performed, as whole Roundness exists by the Conjunction of parts.*

For *Consciousness, being supposed to be a real numerical Power, such as Roundness is, may result from the Composition of different Qualities, as Roundness does from different Species of Figure: and is consequently a new Quality in the same Subject, of a different kind or Species from all the component Qualities considered together.*

Wherefore, *tho' Consciousness be a real Quality, and different from all other Qualities, whether known or unknown, which are themselves acknowledged to be void of Consciousness; yet it may result from such Qualities, as, singly considered, are void of Consciousness;* In like manner as *Roundness is a real Quality specifically different from other Qualities void of Roundness, and yet may be the Result or Composition of such Qualities.*

That Consciousness may be considered particularly, as an individual *Mode* or *Species of Motion.*

For, as nothing more *goes to the Composition of Roundness, than the Conjunction of several Particles, not singly indued with Roundness;* so, upon *this Supposition,* nothing more needs *go to the Power of Thinking, than the Conjunction of several Particles, not each indued with that Species of Motion called Thinking.*

Answered.

To this (says Dr. *Clark*) I answer, as follows.[5]

Every real Quality of any material System, resides distinctly in the several parts of the

It is absolutely impossible, that any real Quality should truly inhere in a System of Matter, without being the Aggregate of a Number of Qualities, residing distinctly in the several Parts of the System, and being always of the *same* kind with the whole that results from them. For, as the *Substance it-self* of a System of Matter is nothing but a Sum of its

5. Ibid. Maxwell's extract contains passages from pp. 825–53.

parts, existing distinctly and independently from each other, and the
whole cannot but be of the *same kind* with the parts that constitute it;
so no *Power* or *Quality of the Substance* can be any thing else, but the
Aggregate of the Powers of the several Parts: and that Aggregate, without
a Creation of something out of nothing, cannot but be of the *same kind*
with the Powers that constitute it. If the Parts of the Substance be *similar,* the System it-self is an *uniform* or *homogeneous* Substance: If the
Parts be *dissimilar,* then the Substance is *difform* or *heterogeneous;* but
still always of the *same kind* or *kinds* with the parts that compose it. In
like manner, if the Powers of the several Parts of the System be *similar,*
the Power of the whole will be a *simple* and *uniform* Power: If the Powers
of the several Parts be *dissimilar,* the Power of the whole will be a *compound difform* Power; but still always necessarily of the same *kind* or
kinds, with the Powers of which it is compounded. Since therefore you
acknowledge *Thinking* to be a Power not compos'd of a multitude of
Thinkings; and 'tis evident (as shall in the Sequel be made fully appear)
that no Power void of thinking can be made of the same kind with the
Power of thinking, so as to be Parts of it, and that from a Composition
of them the Power of thinking may arise; it follows, that *Thinking* is
not made up at all of Parts, and consequently, that it cannot reside in a
Substance, that consists of distinct and independent Parts, such as all
Matter is confessed to be.

System, the
Qualities of
the parts being
of the same
kind with that
of the whole.

To suppose any real Power or Quality arising from, or belonging to,
any *whole* System of Matter without belonging to the *several Parts* of
which that Whole consists, is an express Contradiction: 'Tis supposing,
either an *Universal* to exist without *Particulars,* or an *Effect* to be produced without a *Cause,* or to have more in it than was in the *Cause,* or
that a *Quality* is, by the Power of God, made so to arise out of nothing,
as to be superadded to a *Subject,* and to subsist without inhering in that
Subject, to which it is, at the same time, supposed to belong.

For, if the whole, or Result, be *specifically* different from all and every
one of the particular Powers contributing to it; as *Thinking* manifestly
is, from all the Powers of Particles not indued with *Thought,* it is certain
that such a *particular* Power is a *Whole* bigger than *all its parts;* a *Whole*
that contains something in it, besides all and every one of its *Parts;*

which is, evidently, an *Universal* without *Particulars.* As if it were asserted, that a *Smell* and a *Colour* could be joined together to make up a *Sound;* or, as if *Hardness* and *Figure* could be the Particulars contributing to constitute a *Motion.*

Tho' the different Powers, in the single and separate Parts of a System of Matter, (as for Instance, their Magnitude, Situation, Figure and Motion,) may, by uniting in one Operation or Power to operate, be the cause of the Existence of another Power of the *same Species,* which did not exist in the Particles, singly considered; that is, may constitute another Magnitude, another Figure, another Motion, than was in the single Particles; just as twenty different Numbers, added together, constitute a new Number, different from any of the Particulars: Yet those Powers cannot, without an evident Contradiction, be the cause of the Existence of any other Power of a *different Species,* (as *Thinking* is confessedly of a *different Species* from *Magnitude, Figure, Motion,* or whatever other Properties may belong to *unthinking* Particles of Matter;) for the same reason, as that the Addition of different Numbers in Arithmetick cannot, without a manifest Contradiction, be the Cause of the Existence of a Line or a Figure; or the mixture of Tastes constitute a Colour; namely, because thus the *Effect* would contain more in it than was in the *Cause;* that is, something would, without any Efficient, be produced out of nothing.

Because Wholes are nothing specifically different from their Parts;
That which has been apt to deceive Men, in this matter, is this; that they imagine Compounds to be somewhat specifically different from the things of which they are compounded; which is a very great Mistake; As when two Triangles, put together, make a Square, that Square is still nothing but two Triangles: And in short, every thing, by Composition, Division or Motion, is nothing else but the very same it was before, taken either in the Whole, or by Parts, or in different Place or Order, so as to excite in our Minds different *complex Notions,* and occasion new *abstract Names* of things, but by no means to produce any new real Quality in the things themselves, such as Consciousness is agreed to be, inhering truly and properly in the Subject it is ascribed to. For Instance: All possible Changes of *Figure,* are still nothing but *Figure:* Of *Magnitude,* but *Magnitude:* Of *Motion,* but *Motion:* All Compositions of *Magnitude, Figure* and *Motion* together, are still nothing but *Magnitude, Figure* and *Motion.*

The true State of this case seems, in brief, to be this. Sometimes we consider one and the same Quality of a thing, in different Circumstances and Respects, and with relation to other different things, which Relation may be changed, by the Alteration or Removal of those other things, and a new Effect be produced, without any Alteration at all of the thing it-self, or any of its Qualities; and yet, then, we give it a *new Name,* and are apt to think that *new Name* a *new Quality.* Sometimes we consider several distinct Qualities of different Parcels of Matter, together; and, because some new Effect is thereby occasioned in some other Being, we give the *imaginary Whole* a *new Name,* and think that *new Denomination* a *new Quality.* But with how little reason this is done, will abundantly appear by the following Instances. The same Particle of Matter, which makes a Point in the Surface of a *Globe,* may, by other Parts being shaved off, become the Point of the Angle of a *Cube,* without undergoing any Alteration it-self, and produce an Effect which it could not produce before: But is this truly a new *Quality* or *Power* in the Point it-self? *Blue* and *Yellow* Powder, mingled together, occasion a new Effect, and are called by a *new Name, Green:* But is this really a new *Quality* or *Power?* Is it not plainly the same two Qualities, which they had when separate, acting still distinctly, as appears in a Microscope?

That *particular and determinate degree of Velocity* in a Wheel, whereby it turns once round, precisely, in twelve Hours, is that which is called the *Power of a Clock* to shew the time of the Day; and, because such a determinate *Velocity of Motion* is made use of by us for the Measure of Time, and has an abstract Name given it to express that use, is it therefore a new *Quality* or *Power,* distinct from the *Motion* it-self? As the Number *a thousand* is the Sum of a great many *Numbers,* but cannot with any Sense be imagined to be a Composition of Sounds and Colours, so the *numerical Power of a Clock,* being it-self nothing but *Motion* and *Figure,* cannot be the Result of any other Powers in the Parts, but such as are themselves singly *of the same kind,* in the manner before explain'd; namely, *Motions* and *Figures:* And in like manner *my present numerical Consciousness,* if it were at all a Quality inhering in a System of Matter; tho' it need not indeed be the Sum of the *like individual Thoughts,* inhering in the several distinct parts of the System; yet it must be the Sum of *such* Powers in the Parts, as would themselves singly be of *the same*

and the mutual Relations of things to one another are not really Qualities of the things themselves:

As is evident from the Power of a Clock to shew the Hour of the Day,

kind, namely, *Consciousness* or *Thoughts.* It being equally, and for the very same reason, impossible that my Consciousness should be the Result of such Powers in the parts of my Brain, as are, *toto genere,* different from *Thinking;* (such as are *Figure* and *Motion,* and all other Powers which are void of Consciousness;) as that the fore-mentioned number *a thousand,* should be a Composition of *Sounds* or *Colours,* or of any thing else but *Numbers.*

When a *Weight,* in one Scale of a Balance, does, by taking one part of the Weight that was in the other Scale, begin to *preponderate,* which it did not before; Is this any *Quality* or *real Power* in the Weight that is not altered, different from what it had before?

of a musical Instrument to produce harmonious Sounds,   The *Power of a musical Instrument to produce harmonious Sounds,* is not indeed a Result from the like *individual Powers,* residing in the several Parts of the Instrument; any more than the *Circumference of a Circle* is made up of a Number of the *like whole Circumferences:* But, as the *Circumference of a Circle* is a Sum of a Multitude of *convex Arches of like Curvity,* but cannot be an Aggregate of *strait Lines,* or of *Cubick Bodies,* or of Arches of *unlike Curvity;* so the *Harmony* produced by a musical Instrument, being, it-self, in the Mind that perceives it, nothing but Sound; and, in the Instrument, and in the Air, and in the Organs of Sensation, nothing but a Motion of Parts, cannot be the Result or Composition of any other Powers, but what are themselves singly *of the same kind* in the several Subjects respectively; namely, in the Mind that perceives them, *Sounds* likewise; and in the Instrument it-self, and in the Air, and in the Organs of Sensation, *Motion of the Parts.* And in like manner *Consciousness,* if it were a Power inhering in a System of Matter, could not be the Result of any other Powers in the Parts, but *some sorts of Consciousness;* for the very same reason as the *Circumference of a Circle* cannot (as we before said) be an Aggregate of *strait Lines,* or of *Cubick Bodies;* nor an *harmonious Sound* a Composition of *Colours,* or of any thing else beside *Sounds.*

and of the Eye to see.   The *Power of the Eye to see,* is nothing else but such a Power as is in the *Object-Glasses* of Telescopes, of *transmitting* and *refracting* Rays of Light, so as to paint the Image of the Object in the bottom of the Eye. And this is evidently nothing but a Sum of Powers of the *same kind,* namely, Powers of *transmitting* and *refracting* of Rays, residing distinctly in the several Parts of the *Eye*, or of the *Glass*. Every part of the Eye *transmits* and *refracts* Rays, and those Rays paint several Parts of the Image: And the *whole Image* differs no otherwise from *all its parts;* nor that which you call the *numerical Power of the whole Eye*, from *the single Power of all its Parts;* than the Idea of *a Dozen* differs from the Idea of *twelve Units:* Which, if it be as great a Difference, as is between the Idea of *Consciousness,* and the Idea of a *Circular or any other Motion,* I confess I have lost my Understanding. Moreover, to shew the Unhappiness of chusing the *Power of the Eye to see* for an instance in the present Argument; even every *Part* of the Eye has the same Power as the *whole*, (differing only in *degree,*) of painting at the Bottom the *whole Image* of the Object. For, as each Half of a broken Object-Glass of a Telescope, or any Piece of it that retains the Polish on both Surfaces, will represent distinctly the whole Object, only with less Brightness and Luminousness than the whole Glass would do; so each part of the Eye, paints every part of the whole Object: And, if half of the Eye, or almost the whole Eye, be covered, so that you look only through a Pin-hole; still the whole Object is seen distinctly, even by that very small part of the Eye, and, consequently, the Power of the Eye is the same, both in the *Whole* and in *every Part.*

For the clear Explication of this whole Argument, and to vindicate the Notion from all the Objections, and pretended Instances brought to the contrary; it is to be observ'd, that the Terms, *Kind* and *Species,* and of the *same Kind* or *Species,* are very ambiguous Terms. [For the clearer Explication of the present Argument, the Ambiguity of the Words [kind] and [species], [of the same kind] and [of the same species] is cleared up.]

For Example: It is an evident Truth, that *All Circles of four Foot Diameter,* are of *one and the same kind* or *Species;* and this is what the Logicians call *Species specialissima.* It is true in another Sense, that *all Circles whatever,* are of the *same Species:* In another Sense, that *all curvilinear Figures,* are of the *same Species:* In another, that *all plain Figures, both strait-lin'd and curvilinear,* as oppos'd to Solids, are of the *same Species:* And in another, that *All Figures whatsoever, whether plain or solid,* are of the *same kind* or *Species,* as contradistinguished from Motion or Thinking, or from any thing else of a totally different kind. This is what they call the *Genus generalius.* And it is not true to say, that *Figure* and *Motion,* or *Figure* and *Colour,* or *Figure* and *Thought* are of the *same Kind;* because there is nothing common in their Ideas, by which they can be rank'd together; save only, as they are all comprehended, perhaps, under the mere abstract Name of Quality in general. Which makes it appear, by the by, with what Truth and Sense the Objector affirms, that *Roundness is as specifically different from all other Figures, as Consciousness is from a circular Motion;* That is, that a *Circle* differs as much from an *Ellipsis,* not only as it differs from a *Cube,* but even as much as it differs from the *Reason of a Man:* Or, as the Logicians would express it, that the *Species specialior* differs as much from the *Species* next and immediately superior to it, as it does from the *Genus generalissimum;* and not only so, but as it does also from any thing that is not so much as included even in *That Genus.*

In what Sense the Powers or Qualities of the whole, and of its parts, are said to be of the same kind;
 Now, to apply this to my present Question: When I affirm, that every real Power or Quality, inhering in a System of Matter, must, of necessity, be the Sum of Powers of the *same kind,* residing distinctly in the several Parts of that System; 'tis manifest, that by this Term, *of the same kind,* is not to be understood the *Species specialissima,* but some of the *Species generaliores.* For Example, When I say the *Magnitude* of a *Cubick Foot* of Gold, is the Sum of the *Magnitude* of its Parts; I do not mean to say, that it is a Sum or Aggregate of *Cubick Feet,* but of other *Magnitudes* which constitute a Cubit Foot, and which are of the *same kind* with it, in the Sense that *all Magnitudes* are of the *same kind,* and may be parts of one another: But *Magnitude* and *Motion,* or *Magnitude* and *Figure,* are not in any sense *of the same kind,* and cannot be part, one of another; neither can *Figure* or *Motion* be a *piece* of a *Thought.*

applied to the Objector's favourite Instance of the Roundness of a Globe,
 In like manner: When I say *Roundness* or *Globosity,* or any other Figure of a Body, must needs be the Sum of Qualities of the *same kind,* inhering in the several parts; 'tis plain I do not mean to affirm, that Globosity is made up of Globosities, any more than the Number *Twenty* is made up of *Twenties,* or the *Motion of a Cubick Foot* of Matter made up of the *Motions of Cubick Feet:* But that a *whole round Figure* must necessarily be made up of *Pieces of Roundness,* which are all of the *same kind* with it; just as the *Numbers,* which are Parts of *Twenty,* are of the *same kind* with the whole, and the Motions of the Particles of a Cubick

Foot of Matter, which are Parts of the Motion of the whole, are of the *same kind* with the whole Motion. But *Figure,* and whatever is not *Figure,* are not in any sense of the *same kind;* neither can any thing that is *void of Figure,* be part of any *Figure* whatsoever; nor any thing that is void of *Curvity* in particular, be part of a *round Circumference;* nor any thing that is void of that *particular Degree of Curvity,* which makes a Circle of a determinate Diameter, be part of the *Circumference of that Circle;* nor any thing that is *void of Thinking,* be a Part or Constituent of a *Thought.*

It is as evident, that the *superficial Roundness* of a *Globe,* is the Sum of its *convex Surfaces* of its outward parts; and its *solid Figure,* the Sum of all its *solid Parts, taken together,* considered like so many *concentrick Shells,* or any other Figures, which can be constituent Parts of the solid Content of a Globe; as it is that the *Motion* of a Globe, is the Sum of the *Motions* of its Parts. And the *convex Outsides* of its outward parts, and the *concentrick Roundnesses* of its inward parts, are as much of the *same kind* with the *whole Roundness,* or the *whole Globosity* of which they are Pieces, as the several distinct *Motions* or *Magnitudes* of its parts are of the *same kind* with the *whole Motion* or *Magnitude* which they constitute. For why is not a *Semicircle* of the *same kind* with the Circumference of a Circle; as much as the *Motion* or *Magnitude* of *half a Foot Cube* of Matter, is of the *same kind* with the Motion or Magnitude of the *whole Foot Cube?*

As the *individual Roundness* of a *Globe,* is a *numerical Quality* of that *individual Globe,* so the *Objector* can only say, that the individual Consciousness, which I find in my-self, at any particular Moment of Time, is a *numerical* Mode of some Power, inhering in that System of Matter, which constitutes my Brain. Now, as the *individual Roundness* of a *Globe,* is not indeed made up of a number of the *like whole Roundnesses,* (even as the Number *a Hundred* is not made up of *Hundreds;*) but yet must needs be made up of *such Figures* as are *Parts of Roundness,* nay, Parts indued with that *particular numerical Degree of Curvity or Roundness;* and cannot be made up of *strait Lines,* nor of any Figures which are *not Pieces* of *Roundness,* or *not Pieces indued with that particular determinate Degree of Curvity or Roundness:* So the *individual Conscious-*

ness, that I find in my-self, at any particular Moment of Time, (supposing it to be a Quality inhering in a System of Matter,) must be made up, though not indeed of a Number of the *very same Consciousnesses,* yet of such Powers, as are much of the *same kind* with that *numerical Consciousness,* as *Arches of Circles* are of the same kind with the whole *circular Circumference:* That is, it must be made up of *different* Consciousnesses indeed, but still of *Consciousnesses* only, and not *Motions* or *Figures* or any thing else, any more than the *Roundness* of a *Circle* can be made up of *strait Lines,* or of *Colours,* or *Sounds,* or any thing else besides *Pieces of circular Roundness. Every part* of the Circumference of a Circle is not only *not wholly void of Roundness,* but has really *as much Roundness* or *Curvity* (as much in *Degree,* tho' not as much of it in *Quantity*) as the *whole* Circle it-self has: And therefore Consciousness, in like manner, if it was a Quality answering to, or that could be compared with, the Roundness of a Circle; must consist of Parts, every one of which would have as much Consciousness (in Degree) as the whole.

It is evident, that no *whole* can possibly differ from *all its parts* in any thing else, but only in the abstract Name, the mere external Denomination of its being a *whole,* which is nothing at all in the thing it-self, but merely a manner of Conception, a Conjunction of Ideas in the Imagination of the Person that thinks upon it. *Thinking,* if it was the Quality of a System of Matter, that is, the *Sum* or *whole* of the Powers of its Parts; must differ from the distinct Powers of those Parts, no otherwise, than as the Idea of the Roundness of a *Circle* differs from the Idea of *two Semicircles joined together,* or as the Idea of *twice six,* differs from the Idea of the Number *Twelve.* If, therefore, *Thinking* was, as the *Objector* supposes, a Composition or Result of several Powers, and those Powers such, as were themselves *utterly void of Consciousness; Thinking* would be either a *mere outward Denomination,* and nothing at all really in the thinking Substance it-self; just as *a Dozen* is only a mere Name, and nothing at all different really in the thing it-self from *twelve Units:* or else it must unavoidably be a *Whole* bigger than *all its Parts;* that is, containing *all its Parts,* and *Thinking besides:* As a Cube would be *bigger* than *all its Parts,* if it were made up of Parts, that had none of them singly any *Magnitude at all.*

As nothing that is not *Curve* can have any *Tendency* towards *Curvity;* as nothing that is not *Colour,* can have any *Tendency* towards *Colour;* as nothing that is not *Sound,* can have any *Tendency* towards *Sound:* So nothing that is not *Consciousness,* can have any *Tendency* towards *Consciousness:* As it is plainly impossible, that any *Colour* should have any *Tendency* towards being any Sound, nor that any *Figure* should have any *Tendency* towards being any *Motion;* so it is likewise ridiculous to imagine, that any *Motion,* or any other Quality of Matter void of *Consciousness,* should have any *Tendency* towards being *Consciousness.* The Curvities of several little Arches, that constitute the Circumference of a Circle, are not properly *Tendencies* towards *Roundness,* but they are themselves, taken together, the whole Circle, or the *Roundness* it-self.

To the *Objection,* That a *Square* Figure may consist of Parts, that are none of them singly indued with any thing like *Squareness:* I answer, that the *Squareness* of the Figure of a Body, is a mere *external Denomination, a mere Relative, comparing together, in the Imagination, the Bounds of a Surface, the Situation of four strait Lines, with Respect one to another;* and has not properly any real Existence in things themselves, so as Consciousness is acknowledged to have in the Thinking Substance. And Roundness it-self, being considered in the same manner, might *this way likewise* afford a just Answer to the Argument drawn from thence. and to the Squareness of a quadrilateral Figure.

To prove the Absurdity of supposing *Consciousness* to be a *Mode of Motion,* I offer the following Arguments. Arguments to prove, that Consciousness cannot be a Mode of Motion;

I. Every *Mode* of any *Power* or *Quality,* is nothing else but *That Power* or *Quality,* of which it is a *Mode,* understood with some particular Limitation; that is to say, 'tis nothing but a *particular Instance* of that *general Power* or *Quality,* considered under this or that *particular Modification.* *Blue* and *Red,* and all other *Modes* of *Colour,* are nothing but several particular *Colours,* and can contain nothing in their Idea, beyond the *Genus* of *Colour. Acute* and *Grave,* and all other *Modes* of *Sound,* are nothing but several particular *Sounds,* and can contain nothing in their Idea beyond the *Genus* of *Sound. Circular* and *Triangular,* and all other *Modes* of *Figure,* are nothing but several particular *Figures,* and can contain nothing in their Idea beyond the *Genus* of *Figure.* In like manner, All *Modes* of *Motion,* are nothing else but *merely* particular *Motions,* and I.

cannot contain any thing in their Idea beyond the *Genus* of *Motion.* Now, if *simple Ideas* be the Foundation of all our Knowledge, and *clear and distinct Perception* of the *Agreement* or *Disagreement* of those Ideas, be the best and greatest *Criterion* of Truth, that our Faculties enable us to attain to; then it is as evident as any Truth in the World, that Consciousness cannot possibly be a *Mode of Motion.* For I have as *clear and distinct Perception,* that the Idea of *Consciousness* contains something in it, besides and beyond the *Genus* of *Motion,* as I have that it contains something in it beyond the *Genus* of *Figure.* The Idea of *Consciousness* is totally and *generically* different from the Idea of *circular Motion,* or an *elliptical Motion,* or any other *Mode of Motion* whatsoever, as it is from the Idea of a *Circle* or a *Cube,* or any other *Mode of Figure* whatsoever. I have, therefore, exactly the same *intuitive Certainty,* that *Consciousness* cannot be a *Mode of Motion,* as I have that a *Circle* or a *Cube* is not a *Thought,* or that an *Acute Sound* is not a *Purple Colour,* or that any one thing in the World is not another, whose Idea is the remotest and most different from it, that can be imagined.

Local Motion can have no other Effect upon any System of Matter, than only producing in it a different *juxta-position* of Parts: To which to ascribe Wisdom and Knowledge, nothing would be more absurd. For *unthinking* Particles of Matter, however put together, can have nothing thereby added to them, but a *new relation of Position,* which 'tis impossible should give *Thought* and *Knowledge* to them. *Lock*'s Essay, Book IV. Chap. 10. Sect. 16.

To this Argument it has been *objected;* That *we have no Idea of all the possible Modes of Motion;* that, though *we have,* indeed, *Ideas of the more simple Modes of Motion,* yet of the *very complex* ones *we have no Distinction in our Minds;* that, therefore, we *can no more prove or know, that* Thinking *is not one* of these more complex Modes of Motion, *than* we *can know, whether two things agree or differ from one another, that we have no Idea of at all;* that *it is not possible for us to say, that Thinking does not consist in the peculiar Motion of the Spirits in the Brain, till we have a particular Idea of the Motion of those Spirits, and an Idea of Thinking, as something distinct from a Mode of Motion;* that *Thinking has the Genus of Motion, by arising from Motion, by being varied by Motion, by pro-*

ducing other Motions, by having Succession, and Parts, and innumerable Modifications; that *no Idea of human Consciousness can be produced beyond the Genus of Motion:* that *saying we have an intuitive Certainty, that Consciousness cannot be a Mode of Motion, is only affirming the Question in Debate, which can signify nothing to any body that wants Conviction.*

In this is, at last, declared the fundamental Error (ϖρῶτον Ψεῦδος) of the *Objector's* whole *Hypothesis;* namely, that he intends to make *Thinking,* not a *real Quality,* but a *mere empty Name,* or *external Denomination,* such as I at first ranked under the *Third Head:* For the most complex Modes of Motion possible, whatever *Name* we call them by, are still nothing but Motions; and the *Name* we give them, is nothing but a *mere external Denomination. Thinking,* therefore, according to the *Objector,* being only a *very complex Mode of Motion* (or *of any other Quality of Matter,*) is nothing but a *mere external Name* or *Denomination* of that Mode.

Every Man has, within himself, the *Idea of Consciousness,* which, tho' he cannot *produce* (as the *Objector* absurdly requires,) that is, cannot *define,* nor *describe,* any more than the *Objector* can describe his Idea of any *Colour* or *Sound;* yet he as certainly knows *it* not to be any complex *Mode of Motion,* as the *Objector* knows his Idea of *Colour* not to be any complex *Mode of Sound;* which intuitive Certainty, if it be *only* a bare *affirming the Question in Debate* in one case, *and can signify nothing to any Body that wants Conviction;* 'tis so in the other likewise: And then there's an End of all human Knowledge, and no Man can pretend to know any one thing not to be any other.

Thinking has, indeed, *Succession and Modes,* and many other things, in common with *Motion;* but so has *every thing* with *every thing.*

We cannot, indeed, frame in our Minds distinct *Images* of the more complex Modes, as we can of the more simple ones: But are we not, nevertheless, equally certain, that they are alike *imaginable,* though our narrow Imaginations cannot comprehend them? And that, if we could represent them to our Imaginations, they would all appear as remote from the Idea of *Thinking,* as any one of them does? Because we cannot comprehend, in our Imagination, a distinct Conception of a *vast number in Arithmetick,* as we can a *small one,* do we not, therefore, know, but that a *vast Number* may possibly prove so different from a *small one,* as to turn into a *Plant* or an *Animal?* Because we cannot form, in our Minds, an *Image* of a Space *ten thousand Millions of Miles* square, as we can of *ten Foot* square; are we not, therefore, sure, that such a great Space may possibly be something, whose true Idea shall have no Similitude, no Relation, to Extension?

II.   II. If *Thinking* was any *Mode* or *Species* of Motion, it would follow, that *All Motion* would be some *degree* or *kind* of *Thinking:* For *Motion,* in the thing moved, excepting only the Difference of *Degrees,* of its Swiftness or Slowness, is a *similar Quality,* and has no Variety in it: All its different *Determinations, Modes,* or *Species,* being *nothing really* in the *Body it-self,* that is moved; but mere *abstract Notions,* or *external Denominations,* conceived *only in our Imagination.* For, moving with one Determination, or with another; from North to South, or from South to North, is *merely* relative, and not really a different thing from the Body moved, that one of these Motions should be *Consciousness,* the other not. In like manner, *circular Motion,* or *Motion in any other Figure,* is not any thing, really and truly inherent in the Body it-self, different from Motion in a *strait Line.* For the Determination of any Body, that *moves in a Circle,* is nothing else, at any given Point of Time, but a Determination to *move in a certain strait Line;* and, at another given Point of Time, to *move in another strait Line;* and so on: So that there is no such thing as a *circular Motion,* of any Particle of Matter, co-existent at once; but all Motion is, strictly and properly speaking, a similar and uniform Quality, *to wit,* a Body's *Going on* according to its Determination; which Determination is always in a strait Line, and causes the Body to go on actually in a strait Line, where it meets with no Resistance; and where it meets with Resistance, by Intervals, there to go on into new strait Lines successively, into which it is diverted by such Resistance; and where it meets with continual Resistance, there to go on in a curve Line, into which it is continually diverted: And every such *curvilinear Motion,* whether *circular* or of *any other Species whatsoever,* is but the Idea of a Number of successive Motions of a Body, never existent together; a pure *Ens Rationis,* or Operation of the Mind; which considering past Motion and future, and recollecting *the whole,* by the Memory and Fancy, calls

that whole, sometimes by one Denomination, and sometimes by another. How then can any of those *Modes of Motion* be the *Efficient* of
Thought, or (according to the *Objector's* Supposition) be themselves
Thought; when they are, evidently, nothing, but the *Effect* and *Product*
of it, *viz.* Ideas fram'd merely by the Imagination and Memory?

And the same, that has been said concerning the *Modes of Motion* of
a *single Body,* may, easily, be applied to the *Modes of Motion* of *any Number of Bodies,* in any *System* or *Composition* whatsoever. It being very
evident, that, if the *Progression* of *one Particle* of Matter *directly in a
strait Line,* be not *Consciousness* or *Thought;* the *like Progression* of *twenty
Particles* at the same time in strait Lines, cannot be *Consciousness* neither:
The Position of those Lines with respect to one another, which determines the particular *Mode of Motion* of the whole System, being merely
imaginary, relative, and comparative; a Figment only in the Mind or
Imagination, and not any thing really existing in the Bodies themselves,
at any one and the same Moment of Time.

In like manner, the *Impulse* also, or *Beating of one Particle of Matter
against another,* is a thing similar, and in all Cases alike; differing in nothing, but in the *Degrees* or Quantity of the Force: And, therefore, must
always, and in all cases, if ever in any case at all, be some *Degree* of
Thought. From whence it would follow, that there must be as many several
incoherent *Consciousnesses,* as there are Particles of the Brain or Spirits, or
of any other Matter in any System, that ever dash one against another.

With respect to this Argument, the Objector *allows, that every Motion
is a Degree of Thought, in that Sense,* wherein *it is proper to say, that every
Motion is a Degree of Fire,* &c. That is, he *allows* every Motion, to be as
much a Degree of the *Sensation itself,* of *Heat,* for Instance, or of any
other *Sensation* or *Thought* arising in the *Mind,* as it is a Degree of that
Mode of Motion in Matter, which excites in us such or such a particular
Sensation: Which is *allowing* every the slowest Motion of a *Needle,* to
be as much, and as properly, a Degree of *Pain,* as it is a Degree of *that
Motion,* which causes it to prick the Skin.

III. No particular *Mode* of any Power can contain under it so great   III.
a Variety of *Modes* as the superior Power it-self does; for the same reason
that *quadrilateral Figure,* which is a *Mode* of *Figure,* cannot contain un-

der it so great a Variety of *Modes,* as *Figure* in general does: And, therefore, if *Thinking* was a particular *Mode* of *Motion,* there could not possibly be so many *Modes* of *Thinking,* as there are of *Motion.* But, now,
on the contrary, 'tis evident, there are more *Modes* of *Thinking,* than
there are of *Motion,* because every *Mode of Motion* has a *Mode* of *Thinking* (an Idea) answering to it, and there are innumerable other *Modes* of
Thinking besides: *Thinking,* therefore, cannot possibly be a *Mode* of
Motion. [And the same Argument holds against the Possibility of its
being a *Mode* of *any other Power of Matter whatsoever.*] There are as
many *Ideas of Figure,* as there are *Figures;* and as many *Ideas of Motion,*
as there are *Modes of Motion;* and as many *Ideas of other things,* as there
are *other things* in the World, that *can be thought upon:* And all these
Ideas are Modes, and Sorts or Kinds of *Thinking.* Now, if *Thinking* is
a Power more various, more extensive, than *Motion,* 'tis manifest, that
it cannot be a *Mode* or *Species* of *Motion,* as *Roundness* is a *Mode* or
Species of *Figure.*

IV.   IV. "If it was the Motion" of the parts of a corporeal System, "on
which its Thinking" depends; "all the Thoughts, there, must be unavoidably accidental and limited," because each one of "the Particles,
that by Motion cause Thought, being in it-self without any Thought,
cannot regulate its own Motions; much less be regulated by the Thought
of the whole; since that Thought" of the whole, "is not the Cause of
Motion, (for then it must be Antecedent to it, and so without it,) but
the Consequence of it; whereby Freedom, Power, Choice, and all rational, and wise thinking or acting, will be quite taken away: So that
such a thinking Being, would be no better nor wiser, than pure blind
Matter; since to resolve all into the accidental unguided Motions of
blind Matter, or into Thought depending on unguided Motions of blind
Matter, is the same thing: Not to mention the narrowness of such
Thought and Knowledge, that must depend on the Motion of such
Parts. But there needs no enumeration of any more Absurdities and Impossibilities in this Hypothesis, (however full of them it be,) than that
beforementioned; since, let this Thinking System be All, or a Part of,
the Matter of the Universe; it is impossible, that any one Particle should
either know its own, or the Motion of any other Particle, or the whole

know the Motion of every particular, and so regulate its own Thoughts or Motions, or, indeed, have Thought resulting from such Motion." *Lock's* Essay, Book IV. Chap. 10. Sect. 17.

The same Arguments prove no less strongly, that it is not possible for *Thinking* to be a *Mode* of *Figure,* or of any other *known* Property of Matter; and, also, that it is not possible for it to be a *Mode* of any *unknown* Power of Matter, which in the general is void of Thinking: Because every *unknown* Power, which is *void of Thinking,* is as different from *Thinking,* as *Motion* it-self is, or *Figure,* or any other *known* Power; for the same reason, that a *Smell* or a *Taste,* or any other *known* or *unknown* Quality, which is *not a Colour,* must of necessity be as different from *Blue* or *Scarlet,* as the *Sound of a Trumpet* is. *or if any other Property of Matter, whether known or unknown.*

The Argument, drawn from the Divisibility of Matter, proves, that Matter is not a Subject capable of having the Power of *Thinking superadded* to it, even by the divine Omnipotence. And, if it be not, then recurring to the divine Omnipotence for the making out an Impossibility, is not *magnifying,* but *destroying* the Power of God. For the same reason, it is of no consequence, in the present Argument, what *Properties, unknown to us,* Matter may be indued with; *Thinking* cannot be the Result or Effect of any such, because it is inconsistent with one of its certainly known Properties. *Nor, since it would imply a Contradiction, is it possible, that the Power of Thinking should be superadded to Matter.*

Our being *tired with Contemplation;* the mutual *Reaction of our Ideas and Words;* our *Forgetfulness,* that follows upon certain *Defects* or *Discomposures* of the Brain, &c. do not prove, that the *Soul it-self* is a *bodily Organ;* but only, that it *acts upon,* and *is acted upon* by, bodily Organs; and is assisted by them, as Instruments in its Operations. Experience shews us, that the *Sight* is better'd by the use of good Telescopes, and the *Hearing* by Instruments of conveying Sounds; but not that those Instruments, therefore, *hear* or *see:* That all *Sensation* is better'd by good Organs of Sense; but not that the Organs themselves *are sensible:* That *Imagination* and *Memory* depend on the Brain; but not that the Brain *imagines* or *remembers.* The Organs of the Senses are intirely distinct from one another; but the thing, which perceives by those different Organs, is one and the same thing; one Thinking Being, which every Man calls *himself.* And this one Thinking Being has not some Powers in some *Our being tired with Contemplation; Forgetfulness upon Discomposures of the Brain, &c. do not prove the Soul it-self a bodily Organ.*

Parts, and other Powers in other Parts; some Actions in some Parts, and other Actions in other Parts; but all its Powers are the Powers of the Whole; and all its Actions are the Actions of the Whole. The Whole Thinking Substance sees both the whole Object, and every part of it; the same whole Substance hears every Sound, smells every Odour, tastes every Savour, and feels every thing, that touches any part of the Body. Every Imagination, every Volition, and every Thought, is the Imagination, Will and Thought, of that whole thinking Substance, which I call *my-self.* And if this one Substance (which we equally style the *Soul* or *Mind*) has no parts, that can *act* separately, it may as well be conceived to have none, that can *exist* separately, and so to be absolutely *indivisible.*

If the fleeting Substance of a material System were the Subject of Thinking, it would be impossible for us to preserve the Consciousness of our past Actions;

In answer to the foregoing *twelfth Proposition,* it is alledg'd; That, *in order to retain the Consciousness of an Action, it is only necessary to revive the Idea of it before any considerable Flux of Particles; and, by reviving the Idea of that Action, is imprinted afresh the Consciousness of having done that Action, by which the Brain has as lively an Impression of Consciousness (though it be not intirely composed of the same Particles) as it had the Day after it did the Action, or as it has of a Triangle, or any other new Idea not before imprinted on it. Consciousness of having done that Action, is an Idea imprinted on the Brain, by recollecting or bringing into view our Ideas, before they are quite worn out; which Idea continues in me, not only the Memory of the Action it-self, but that I did it. And if there is, every now and then, a Recollection of a past Action;* it may hereby be *conceived,* that *a Man may be conscious of things done by him, tho' he has not one Particle of Matter the same that he had at the doing of those things; without Consciousness being transferred from one Subject to another, in any absurd Sense of those Words.* And again: *If* Matter *can know at this Instant, that it thinks,* the Objector *can see no reason, why it may not remember To-morrow, what it thinks of to-day, though some Particles will be then wanting which it has at present: And, if it can remember at all, then the Memory of things may be continued, even after we have lost all the Particles of Matter that we had at the doing them, by continual intermediate repeating or imprinting afresh our Ideas, before they are quite lost or worn out.* But the Fallacy of this Reply is very evident: For to affirm, that *new Matter* perpetually added to a fleeting System may, by repeated Impressions and

Recollections of Ideas, participate and have communicated to it a *Memory* of what was formerly done by *the whole System;* is not explaining or *proving,* but begging the Question, by affirming an *impossible* Hypothesis: For how is it possible, That new Ideas, printed upon new Particles, should be a *Memory* of old Ideas, printed upon old Particles? But supposing, if it were *possible,* That the Memory, in general, of such or such an Action's having been done, might be preserv'd in the Manner supposed; yet it is a manifest Contradiction, that the *Consciousness* of its being done by *me, by my own individual self* in particular, should continue in me after my whole Substance is chang'd, unless Consciousness could be transferr'd from one Subject to another, in the absurdest Sense of these Words. For, to suppose, That one Substance should be conscious of an Action's having been done by it-self, which really was not done by it, but by another Substance; is as plainly supposing an individual Quality to be transferred from one Subject to another, in the most absurd Sense, as it is plain, that *Consciousness* is a *real individual Quality,* and different from bare *General Memory.*

If it be *answered,* That what we call *Consciousness,* is not a *fixt individual numerical Quality,* like the numerical Figure or Motion of a solid Body; but a *fleeting transferrible Mode or Power,* like the Roundness or Mode of Motion of Circles upon the Face of a running Stream; and, That the *Person* may still be the same, by a continued Super-Addition of the like *Consciousness,* notwithstanding the whole Substance be chang'd: This, I say, is to make *individual Personality,* to be a mere *external imaginary Denomination,* and nothing at all in Reality: Just as a Ship is called the *same Ship,* after the whole Substance is changed by frequent Repairs; or a River is called the *same River,* tho' the Water of it be every day new. The Name of the *Ship* is the same; but the *Ship itself* is not at all the same: And the continued *Name* of the River, signifies Water running in the same Channel, but not at all the *same Water.* So, if a Man, at Forty Years of Age, has nothing of the same Substance in him, neither material nor immaterial, that he had at Twenty, he may be called the same Person, *by a mere external imaginary Denomination;* in such Sense as the aforesaid Ship: But he cannot be really and truly *the same Person,* unless the same *individual numerical Consciousness* can be

And there would be no Principle of individual Personality in Man;

transferred from one Subject to another. For, the continued Addition or exciting of a like *Consciousness* in the new-acquired Parts, after the Manner supposed, is nothing but a Deception and Delusion, under the Form of Memory; a making the Man seem to himself to be conscious of having done that, which really was not done by him, but by another.

Nor Justice in rewarding or punishing a man, after a Change of his Substance. And such a Consciousness in a Man, whose Substance is wholly chang'd, can no more make it just and equitable, for such a Man to be punished for an Action done by another Substance; then the Addition of the like Consciousness (by the Power of God) to two or more new-created Men, or to any Number of Men now living, by giving a like Modification to the Motions in the Spirits of the Brain of each of them respectively, could make them all to be one and the same individual Person, at the same time that they remain several and distinct Persons; or make it just and reasonable, for all and every one of them to be punished for one and the same individual Action, done by one only, or, perhaps, by none of them at all. The *Objector* replies, *A Man who, during a short Frenzy, kills another, and then returns to himself, without the least Consciousness of what he has done, cannot attribute that Action to himself, and therefore the mad Man and the sober Man, are really two as distinct Persons, as any two other Men in the World, and will be so considered in a Court of Judicature.* Extraordinary Reasoning indeed! because, in a *figurative* Sense, a Man, when he is mad, is said not to be himself, and, in a *Forensick* Sense, is look'd upon, as not answerable *for his own Actions:* Therefore in the *natural and philosophical* Sense also, *his Actions* are not *his own Actions,* but another Persons; and the *same Man* is *really two distinct Persons.*

And it would be possible for two different Men at the same time to be the same Man. To say, that God's *Justice and Goodness* will not permit him to put any such inevitable Deceit upon Men, is nothing to the purpose: For, if it be but *naturally possible* for him to do that, which, upon Supposition of the Truth of the *Objector's* Notion, will be a *plain Contradiction;* this is a certain Demonstration, that the Notion is false. And I think it a *Contradiction plain enough,* to say, that God's impressing permanently upon an hundred Mens Minds, after the manner of the Representation of a Dream, the like Consciousness with that which I find in my own Mind, would make every one of them, to be, not Persons *like* me, but the *same individual Person* with my-self.

It is *Objected,* that, though *Consciousness* were allowed necessarily to infer *Indivisibility,* and *Indivisibility* to infer *Immateriality:* yet, even then, not *the Soul,* the *thinking immaterial Being,* but only the bare *immaterial Subject or Substance* it-self *would be proved to be naturally immortal;* since *Thinking is a Power which may commence after the Existence of its Subject, and may cease, its Subject still remaining:* It is *answered,* that the contrary is evidently true; namely, that, not only the *bare immaterial Subject,* but the *Subject* and the *Power* together, the *thinking immaterial Being* it-self, is hereby proved to be *naturally immortal:* Because, whatever Substance is wholly *indiscerpible,* is plainly by Virtue of that Property, not only it-self incapable of being destroy'd by any natural Power (for so also is the most *discerpible* Substance likewise;) but all its *Qualities* and *Modes* also, are utterly incapable of being affected in any measure, or changed in any degree, by any Power of Nature; for all real and inherent Qualities of any Substance, are either Modifications of the Substance it-self, or else Powers super-added and connected to the Substance, by the immediate Power of God; and, in either of these cases, 'tis manifest, no *Quality* can be altered by any natural Power, which is not able to affect and make some Alteration (in the Disposition of the Parts at least) of the Substance it-self; which, in an *indiscerpible* Substance, 'tis evident cannot be done. The *Soul,* therefore, the *whole conscious Being;* the *Power of Thinking,* as well as the *bare immaterial Subject or Substance it-self;* (whatever may be said concerning the *Power of God* in this Question;) will clearly, notwithstanding what any *finite* Power can do, of necessity be *naturally immortal.* The Truth of this Reasoning is evident, from what we cannot but observe, even in the *material World;* namely, that all the Changes, which are caused therein by any Powers of Nature, are nothing but Changes of the Order, and Disposition of the Parts of compound Bodies. The original and perfectly solid Particles of Matter, which are, (not indeed absolutely in themselves, but) to any Power of Nature, indiscerpible; are utterly incapable of having, not only their Substance, but even any of their Qualities or Properties altered, in any measure, by any Power of Nature: As is evident, from the Form or Species of those we vulgarly call simple or elementary Bodies, remaining always unalterably the same, and indued continually with the same Powers and Qualities.

The Indivisibility of a Thinking Substance infers necessarily, that its Power of Thinking can never be destroy'd by any Power of Nature;

Tho' they may
be acted upon
by other Sub-
stances.
I do not here mean, that *indiscerpible* Substances cannot be *acted upon
at all* by any Power of Nature. But, as the solid Particles of Matter may
be *acted upon,* and *struck* by each other, may be removed this way or that
way, upwards or downwards; all which make no real Alteration in them:
So an indiscerpible immaterial thinking Substance, tho' it may be transferred from one part of the Universe to another, tho' it may be *acted
upon* by a Multitude of things, tho' it may have different Ideas represented to it, tho' the Organs of the Senses may, at times, transmit different Species, or hinder them from being transmitted to it; yet all this
makes no real Alteration, either in the Substance, or its inherent Powers;
nor can its Power of Thinking be destroy'd or altered by these, or any
other natural Powers; any more than the *Mobility* or *Hardness* of the
original perfectly-solid Particles of Matter can be destroy'd, by any of
their Actings one upon another.

Immaterial
Substance may
be indivisible,
tho' it were
extended, tho'
whether it be
extended or
no, we are not
certain, nor is
it material in
the present
Argument;
It is *objected,* that *immaterial Substance,* also, may, *as well* as Matter,
be conceived capable of Division, and, consequently, incapable of
Thought; *supposing Extension not excluded out of the Idea of Immateriality.* I *answer:* That in *immaterial Beings* we do not know of any such
Properties, as any ways implies Discerpibility. It cannot be collected from
any Property we know of *them,* but that they *may* be such Beings, as
can no more be *divided* than *annihilated,* that is, whose whole Essence
may be necessarily *one,* and their Substance essentially *indivisible,* upon
the same ground as their Existence continues: Nay, the only Properties
we *certainly and indisputably* know of them, namely *Consciousness* and
its Modes, do prove (as hath been before shewn) that they *must necessarily*
be such *indiscerpible Beings:* As evidently as the *known Properties* of *Matter* prove it to be certainly a *discerpible Substance,* whatever other *unknown Properties* it may be indued with; so evidently the *known and
confessed Properties of immaterial Beings* prove them to be *indiscerpible,*
whatever other *unknown Properties* they likewise may be indued with.
How far such *Indiscerpibility* can be reconciled, and be consistent, with
some kind of *Expansion;* that is, what *unknown Properties* are joined
together, with these *known ones* of Consciousness and Indiscerpibility;
is another Question of considerable Difficulty, but of no Necessity to
be resolved in the present Argument. As the Parts (improperly so called)

of *Space* or *Expansion* it-self, depend upon each other for their Existence; not only because of its Infinity, but because of the Contradiction, which a Separation of them manifestly would imply, and they can therefore demonstrably be proved to be *absolutely indiscerpible;* so it ought not to be reckon'd an insuperable Difficulty, to imagine, that all *immaterial thinking Substances* (upon Supposition that Expansion is not excluded out of their Idea) may be so likewise.

In like manner, other Difficulties, that arise from any other Hypothesis concerning other Properties of immaterial indiscerpible Substance, as whether it acts *wholly separate,* or always in some *material Vehicle,* whether it *always actually thinks,* or no, and the like, affect only the particular Hypothesis, from which they arise.

No more than it is, whether they always act in a material Vehicle, or whether they always actually think or no.

Lastly, the foregoing Doctrine does not put the Souls of Men and Brutes upon a Level, with respect to future Rewards and Punishments.

Lastly, It is *objected,* That, by the foremention'd Argument, *all the sensible Creatures in the Universe are put in the same Condition with Man, and made capable of eternal Happiness, as well as he;* or else that, *to avoid this consequence, all those Creatures must be supposed, to be only mere Machines;* or else, *that their Souls shall be annihilated at the Dissolution of their Bodies;* And if so, *then the Proof of the natural Immortality of Mens Souls, from their Immateriality, tends not to prove, that their Souls shall really be immortal.* It is *answered,* That, though all sensible Creatures have certainly something in them that is immaterial, yet it does not at all follow, either that they must needs be annihilated upon the Dissolution of their Bodies, or else that they must be capable of eternal Happiness *as well as Man.* As their present subsisting implies not, that they must needs be capable of the *Expectations* and *Conditions* of eternal Happiness *as well as Man;* so neither does their future eternal Existence, if they should never be annihilated or reduced to a state of Insensibility, prove that they shall enjoy eternal Happiness, *as well as Man.* This is just such an Argument, as if a Man should conclude, that whatsoever is not exactly like himself, can therefore have no being at all: Or that all the Stars of Heaven, if they be not exactly like our Globe of Earth, cannot possibly be any Globes at all. Certainly, the omnipotent and infinitely wise God, may, without Difficulty, be suppos'd to have more ways of disposing of his Creatures, than we are at present let into the secret of. He may, indeed, if he pleases, annihilate them, at the Dissolution of their Bodies; (and so he might, if he thought fit, annihilate the Souls of Men; and yet it would be nevertheless true, that they are *in their own Nature immortal;*) or he may, if he pleases, without either annihilating them, or suffering them to fall into a State of Inactivity, dispose of them into *numberless* States, concerning the particular Nature of which we are not now able to make the least Conjecture. *So far Dr.* Clark.

The following Reasoning, upon the same Subject, is Mr. *Ditton's,* in his *Appendix* to his *Discourse concerning the Resurrection of* Jesus Christ.[6]

To argue *or* infer *one thing from another, is wholly irreconcilable to, and simply impossible to be effected by, any mere mechanical Laws.*

Thinking cannot be mechanical.

For, the same Parts of Matter, cohering together after the same manner, moving in the same Direction, and with the same Velocity, in the same Space or System, will continue to produce the very same Effect, whatever that Effect be, which was once produced by them. And, therefore, if Thought be the Result of any sort of Motion, Pressure, or Contranitency, of the solid, figured, divisible Parts of Matter; it is necessary, that in the Production of different sorts of *Acts,* of *Thought* and *Reflexion,* if all other Circumstances continue the same, the Circumstance of *Motion* should be some way diversified, either as to *Velocity,* or *Direction,* or both: And, *vice versâ,* if in different Acts of Thought and Reflexion, the Circumstance of Motion continue unvaried, as to *Velocity* and *Direction;* there must needs be some Variation in the other Circumstances. Suppose then, in order to diversify our Ideas or Modes of Thinking, that the Change is made in point of *Motion;* for it will come to the same thing, were the Change supposed in the *Solidity, Cohesion* or *Configuration* of the Parts of Matter. This *Change in the Motion,* whether with respect to the *Velocity* or *Direction,* must be by the Impulse of some *external Mover.* For they cannot change their own Condition, and throw themselves out of one Motion and Direction into another: This Mover must still be Matter, and must therefore be moved or acted on it-self, by some *prior* Mover, and so on *in infinitum.* And this must be the case of every individual Thought. But how absurd such an infinite Progression is, let the Philosophical Reader judge.

6. Ditton, *A Discourse Concerning the Resurrection of Jesus Christ* (1712), appendix.

If, to avoid this Difficulty, it be alledg'd, that *the Parts of Matter determine themselves to the Production of those Effects,* then All Matter is made active and self-moving, and indued with an innate Power of Thinking, which is as contrary to the *Supposition,* as it is to all *Experience* and *Philosophy.*

Appendix II

A Treatise concerning the Obligation, Promulgation, and Observance of the Law of Nature

CHAPTER I. The Obligation of the Law of Nature.

The *Law of Nature is a moral Law, discover'd to all Men by the Light of Nature.*

The *Jews* divide the Precepts of their Law into *"Intellectual"* and *"those which are received by Tradition."*[1] The former are such Precepts, as, tho' not written, the Understanding would find out; such as the Precept of honouring Parents, against Homicide, Theft, false Witness, Adultery, and such like.

So the *Fathers* of the *Christian* Church say. *"Before the Law of* Moses, *written in Tables of Stone, there was an unwritten Law, which was discovered by the Light of Nature.—Before the Jews receiv'd the Law, all Nations and the whole World receiv'd the Law of Nature.—That Law, which is written in the Heart, extendeth to all Nations, and no Man is unacquainted with it.—We have, in our-selves, a natural Discernment of the Good from the Evil.—What is the Law of Nature? Our Conscience hath given us plain Notice of it, and hath made the Knowledge of the Things that are honest, and that are otherwise, to be self-taught."*[2]

The *Civilians* sometimes, unwarily, extend the Law of Nature to irrational Animals; yet, when they define it properly and accurately, they

The Notion of the Law of Nature, according to the *Jews.*

Christian Fathers,

Civilians,

1. J. H. Hottinger, *Thesaurus Philologicus seu Clavis Scripturae* (1649), p. 546.
2. Tertullian, *Adversus Judaeos,* ch. 2.

do it agreeably to the Sense of the *Christian Fathers.* *"The Law of Nature is the Rule of right Agency, which Nature discovers, and flows from natural Affection and Reason."* [3]

Modern
Divines, and
School-men,

Modern *Divines,* and *School-men,* define it thus, *"The Law of Nature is that which proceedeth from the Institution of Nature it-self, and this is common to all."* [4]

and also of the
Heathen Phi-
losophers.

The learned Heathens define it *"Reason from the Nature of Things, which enjoineth the Things which ought to be done, and forbiddeth the contrary."* [5] By *Aristotle* it is call'd, *"The Law, which is common to all, that just and unjust, which is by Nature, and common to all."* [6]

The Notion of
the Law of
Nature is Two-
fold;

Therefore, the Law of Nature, according to all these Definitions, is, the true Moral Philosophy; *a Law of the great Morals of Nature's Institution.* But this great Law must be several Ways distinguish'd: For it must be consider'd, *under a two-fold Notion, in a three-fold Respect: In Respect of the Obligation, Promulgation, and Observance of it.*

First, in
respect of its
Obligation.

First, in Respect of its Obligation, it is of a two-fold Notion; for the Law of Nature signifieth *what is, in its own Nature, Law* to all intelligent Agents; and it is, also, Law to all intelligent created Agents, by an *Obligation from Authority.* But, antecedently to this Obligation from superior Authority, it is of an Obligatory Nature, and must be consider'd as *what is, in its own Nature, Matter of Law,* or of Obligation; for, that this Law is of this Nature, will appear, as from other Considerations, so from a due Explanation of the *Good,* which it requireth, and of the *Evil,* which it forbiddeth.

Of the Mean-
ing of the
Word, *Good.*

§2. Altho' Mankind are, by Nature, furnish'd with, and agree in, the true *Notions* of Good and Evil, Just and Unjust, Decorous and Indecorous; yet they are not of one Mind about the Application of those Names to the *Things* themselves, to which they belong; and this is the

---

3. Zouch, *Elementa Jurisprudentiae* (1629), pt. I, sect. 3; Selden, *De Jure Naturali et Gentium* (1640), I.8.

4. Sharrock, *De Officiis Secundum Naturae Jus* (1660), ch. 2; Suarez, *De Legibus ac Deo Legislatore* (1612), I.3.

5. Cicero, *De Legibus,* II.

6. Aristotle, *Rhetoric,* I.13.

matter of their *Disagreement.* There is no Appearance, indeed, of any considerable Disagreement, amongst the *ancient Philosophers,* touching the *Definition of Good:* But such a Disagreement there is in the *Christian Schools;* for the Metaphysicians, and learned Writers of Morality, are not agreed about the Notion of *(Bonum) Good,* the principal Source of which Disagreement is, an unavoidable Ambiguity in the Word.

For, sometimes, it is used *Ironically;* because Men are denominated *Good,* upon account of their Innocence and Harmlessness; hence, among the Heathen, it became a Term of Reproach, and, so us'd, it importeth Silliness. *O bone, ne tu frustrere,* Horat. Satyr. 2. *O bone, num ignoras?* Pers. Sat. 6. *Bone custos, defensorque Provinciae,* Cicer. 7. Ver. 10. *Ehodum, bone vir, quid ais?* Terent. Andr. 3. 5. 10.[7] But, except when the Name *Good* is thus us'd Ironically, it always denotes, *what is to be lik'd, and, in some Degree, commended,* either really for sufficient Cause and Reason, or in the Opinion of the Speaker; for so it signifies, even when it is connected with Vices and Crimes. As when we say, *A good Pickpocket, a good Flatterer,* it signifies one that is *dextrous* and *expert* at picking Pockets and Flattery. Usually *Good* signifieth *(Bonum utile)* the *profitable* Good, as every Tree, that is *good for Food, Gen.* 2. 9. So we say, *A good House, a good Field, good Advice:* And as usually it signifieth *(Bonum jucundum)* the *pleasant* Good; thus a *joyful* Day is call'd a *good* Day, *Esth.* 9. 22. Thus, also, we say, *a good Companion.* We say, *Security is good, Money is good,* a *Bargain, Tender,* or *Grant is good,* which is unexceptionable, and, so far, is to be lik'd. When we perform our *Promises,* we are said to make them *Good,* what is to be lik'd and allow'd of. If any Man's Property be taken away, or damaged, Restitution, or *Reparation,* is call'd *making it Good,* as what is to be lik'd, and allow'd of, as an Equivalent. When *Alexander* was dying, his Friends ask'd him, to whom he would leave the Kingdom; his Answer was (ἀρίϛῳ) *to the best Man,* namely, with Respect to military Fortitude, which was a Quality in the highest Esteem among the *Greeks,* with whom κακὸς signifies *a Coward.* Usually, *Things* are denominated *Good,* with respect to their

---

7. Horace, *Satires,* II; Persius, *Satires,* 6; Cicero, *In Verrem,* II.V.12; Terence, *Andria,* 3.5.10.

Size and Measure, which are to be lik'd, and *Persons,* with respect to their *Rank* and Degree in the World, in which Sense we say, *A good while, a good Way off, good Business, a good Estate, a good Price, Man of good Note, good Rank and Fashion, good Towns, a good Family.* Good, therefore, usually signifieth, with respect to Rank and Degree; for, in such sense, Equals are denominated as *Good;* and the *Best* Man signifies him, that is highest in Rank and Degree, who, with regard to Esteem, is most to be lik'd, and superiors are styl'd the *Betters.* So the superior in Strength and Power is, in that respect, the *better* Man. Amongst the Lawyers *[boni & legales homines] good and lawful Men* are those who are to be lik'd, and are unexceptionable in Law. *Well-born,* are those who are of a Rank to be lik'd, with respect to their Birth. *Bonus,* sometimes, signifies a *learned* Man. *"Viz. bonus & prudens versus reprehendet inertes."* Horat. in Arte Poet. 90.— *"Boni quoniam convenimus ambo, Tu calamos inflare leves, ego dicere versus."* Virg. 5. Eclog. *"Quandoque bonus dormitat Homerus."* Horat. in arte Poet. 73. *Bonus* sometimes signifies *propitious,* or *favourable. "Adsit laetitiae Bacchus dator, & bona Junc."* Virgil I. Aeneid. *"Sis bonus ô, faelixque tuis."* Virg. 5. Eclog. 6. *Bonus,* sometimes, signifies a *Benevolent* Man. *"Vir bonus, qui prodest quibus potest, nocet nemini."* Cicer. 3. Offic. *"Deus Optimus Maximus, optimus,* i.e. *Beneficentissimus,"* says *Cicero* 2. de Nat. Deor. 92, and 93. Sometimes a *virtuous* Man. *"—Nemo sine crimine vivit, Optimus ille, qui minimis urgetur."* Horat. *Bonus,* sometimes, signifies *Just,* as in the *Latin* Phrase, *Bonum & aquum.* We likewise say, *Good-nature, good Courage, a good Intention, Good-will, a good Old Age,* (that is, such as Men desire to reach,) *Anima melior,* that is, fitter; *"Hanc tibi Erix meliorem animam pro morte Daretis Persolvo."* Virgil. 5. Aeneid. 96.[8] So we likewise say, *Artes bonae, bonis avilus, a good Climate, a good Cause, a good Condition, a good Conscience, to take in good Part, a good Quantity, a good Event, a good Action,* that is, such as ought to be done, *good Fame* or *Name, Good-faith, a good Countenance, a good Family, a good Wrestler, Singer,* &c. *Good-liking, good*

---

8. Horace, *Ars Poetica,* 90; Virgil, *Eclogues,* 5; Horace, *Ars Poetica,* 73; Virgil, *Aeneid,* I; Virgil, *Eclogues,* 5, 6; Cicero, *De Officiis,* III; Cicero, *De Natura Deorum,* II.92–93; Horace, *Satires,* II.3; Virgil, *Aeneid,* V.96.

Parts, Memory, Judge, Judgment, Journey, good Right, good Reason, &c. In all which Instances, and in numberless more, which might be given, without any Exceptions, that I know of, *Good* always signifies *what is to be lik'd,* or approv'd of, in its Kind. Somewhat near the Use of the Name *Good,* as it is expressive of Rank and Degree, is a peculiar Use of it in our *English* Language, wherein Things are said to be *as good,* (without any Intention to say, that they are good) only to signify, that one Thing is little less than the other, not valuably or considerably deficient. For, when we have near finish'd any piece of Work, we say, *it is as good as finish'd;* when any Thing is well nigh gone, we say, *it is as good as lost;* and our Translators say of *Abraham,* Heb. 11. 12. *"Him as good as dead,"* to signify, that he was little less than dead.

The Metaphysicians Maxim is of great Truth and Certainty; *Every Being, as it is a Being, is Good.* Every Being, properly so call'd, hath, as its Nature is, a certain *Perfection* and Form, whereby it is, what it is. And as a *Being* is that which is of *some Kind,* so it is that, which is necessarily of a certain *Rank* and Degree amongst Beings, above Nothing, and better than such a Something, that is worse than Nothing, which is a Good, or Well-being. Existence may be so complicated, as to be, in several respects, worse than Non-Existence; for we love Existence as a Good, and, therefore, prefer not Being before Ill-being. But Existence is, of itself, better than Nothing and Non-existence, and must, therefore, be counted a *Good.* To which the Schoolmen add, That *Good, as an Attribute of Being, denotes that which is perfect.* Every Being is without Defect of its essential Perfections, which is well-being, and *that which is to be lik'd,* as this Word [Good] always signifies.

§3. Good and *Evil* so far depends upon *Perception,* that, if there were no Perception of them, they would be of no more Regard or Consideration, than if they were not at all. But, notwithstanding this *Connexion* between *Good* and *Perception,* it ought not to be thus defin'd; *"Good is that which is pleasant to a perceptive Life, jointly with the Preservation of the Perceiver."*[9] For the Nature and Notion of Good does not consist in

9. More, *Enchiridion Ethicum* (1668), I.4.

being pleasant, but *in being worthy to be pleas'd with.* This Definition of Good does not belong to the *Metaphysical Good* of Being in general, before describ'd; nor does it belong to *profitable Good,* as such, which is often painful and afflictive: Nor can it pretend to be the Definition of the *Good* of *Duty* and *Virtue,* as such; for nothing can be the Good of Duty and Virtue, which is good Practice, merely *as pleasant to a Perceptive Life, jointly with the Preservation of the Perceiver.* Intelligent Agents must not be *told,* "That nothing is good, but as it is pleasant to a perceptive Life, jointly with their Preservation." But they should be *told,* "That they ought to make the Things that are Good, the matter of their Pleasure; that there is sufficient Cause and Reason, why they should be pleased with them, and that, upon this Account, they are good." If nothing is good, but as it is *pleasant to Perception,* there can be no other Good in the Universe, than the *Good of Happiness:* Nor can the *Evil of Sin and Wickedness,* as such, be in the World, but only the *Evil of Infelicity.* But such Definitions of Good and Evil are defective and partial, and much too narrow, to be the Definition of *Good and Evil in general;* and there is the like Exception against another celebrated *Definition* of *Good,* That *"Convenience and Inconvenience, to some Body, are the Definitions of Good and Evil. Good is that which is convenient to the Nature of a Thing, or what is not hurtful, but really helpful to Nature."* And Bp. *Cumberland* himself has given in to this *Definition* of *Good,* which is not only *faulty,* but productive of many *Mistakes* in the *Contemplation of the Law of Nature.*[10] For,

Cumberland's Definition of Good, supposes the Nature of Things, not to be Good. (1.) The Nature of Beings is manifestly a *Good Antecedent* to what is *convenient* and *helpful* thereto, *preservative* or *perfective* thereof. But, if nothing is good, except only as convenient to the Nature of Beings, their Nature, even the Nature of rational Beings, must not be suppos'd, to be good; and, consequently, there can be no sufficient Reason for, or Obligation to, an universal Love, which is a Summary of the Law of Nature; for it is not possible, much less laudable, to love that which is not suppos'd to be good. The Notion of Good, therefore, must be so large and

10. Cumberland, *A Treatise of the Laws of Nature,* 3.1, 2.

general[11] as to take in the Nature of Beings, especially, of created rational Agents, and, more especially, the Nature of God, who must not be thought good, only as convenient to himself and to us, as some suppose, who yet style him *Goodness itself,* which Attribute would not belong to him, if he be good only *relatively.*

(2.) In our Elogies, both of God and Creatures, *Good* usually signifieth in such a Sense, as cannot be explain'd by *convenient.* For we pronounce an Angel, to be superlatively *good* and *excellent,* where superlatively *good* and superlatively *excellent* are Words of the same Signification, but superlatively *good,* and superlatively *convenient,* are not so. So when God is intitul'd, *The Supreme Good, the infinite and absolutely perfect Good,* the Attribute *Good* must mean his *Excellence.* If we should suppose, what is impossible, God to do any thing contrary and destructive to the Godhead; such an Evil would not be *merely* an *Inconvenience* to himself, and to the Creatures, but it would be a horrible *Wickedness* beside. Evil, therefore, is not merely an Inconvenience to himself and to Creatures, therefore Good is not merely a Convenience to these. Men, truly religious, are the Admirers and Lovers of the Deity, and adhere to it by their devotional Esteem and Affection, not merely as supposing it a Convenience to any, but also upon account of its own intrinsick Worth, Excellence, and Pulchritude. That *Good,* which is merely *relative,* which is good only as *convenient* to something, cannot be *absolutely* the ultimate and *final Good,* which the Deity is.

> 2. It is not agreeable to that Notion of Good, which God is.

(3.) If nothing be good, but *respectively* only, as convenient to Nature, there can be no other *ultimate* End of Things, but *Self* and a great *System of Selves,* the Aggregate of all rational Beings. Whatever is good, merely as convenient to something, must be convenient to some or all of these; and it may be either *natural Good,* or *moral Good.* If it be natural Good, that is convenient to all these, it is call'd the *common* or *publick Good* or *Happiness.* If it be *moral Good,* that is convenient to all these, it is call'd

> 3. It makes *Self* the ultimate End of all Agents.

---

11. [Maxwell] "The constituting, preserving, and perfecting Causes of Things or Men, are those Things, which we call Good. *Chap.* 1. § 20."

Moral Virtue, which moral Good is productive of the natural Good, and is a Means subservient to the common Good and Felicity. *"The common Good of all rational Agents is the greatest End.*[12] *Virtue is therefore good, because it determines human Actions to such Effects, as are principal Parts of the publick natural Good.*[13] *Moral Good is a kind of Profitable Good, which doth effect Delectable Good, the end of all our Actions, the Universal Good.*[14] *The general Preservation of Mans natural Good is the sole Root and Fountain of the moral: The universal Profit and Pleasure, the publick Happiness of human Life, giveth Being and Denomination to every Virtue and Vice; and the true Rules and Directions, to preserve and secure that Happiness, make the whole Volume, the Code and Pandect of the Law of Nature."*[15] The *Law of Nature,* according to this Scheme of it, is an Institution of mere publick *Self-convenience* as the *End,* and of mere publick *Self-convenience* as the *Means.* For the publick Happiness, as such, is nothing else but the common and publick Self-convenience, of which an *Aggregate of Selves,* and every *private Self,* in his publick Capacity, is the *ultimate* End. *"Happiness is the End of those good Things possess'd by Man, but Man is the End of Happiness; for we love our Happiness for our own Sake."*[16] What *Cicero* says of Pleasure, must be said of Happiness, *"We love it for the Sake of our-selves, but do not love our-selves for the Sake of it."*[17] Wherefore, according to this Scheme of the Law of Nature, which supposeth, that nothing is good, but as convenient to Nature, there can be no other End of Things, but natural Self, or an Aggregate of Natural Selves; nor can there be any other ultimate Reason of Things, but private or publick Self-conveniency. And this would really be the State of Things in the Universe, if the whole Universe of rational Beings were *Self-existents* and *Independents,* that combin'd of themselves into

---

12. Cumberland, *A Treatise of the Laws of Nature,* 4.2.

13. Ibid., 5.5.

14. Bright, *An Essay in Morality* (1682), pp. 14, 55, 57.

15. Bentley, *Of Revelation and Messias. A Sermon Preached at the Publick Commencement at Cambridge* (1696), pp. 14, 15.

16. Buridan, *Quaestiones in decem libros Ethicorum Aristotelis ad Nicomachum,* p. 49.

17. Cicero, *De Finibus,* V.

Society, merely for their common Happiness, and for their own Sake; or, if they were merely *political* Animals, that were so combin'd into Society by Nature. But in the *Kingdom of God,* a Kingdom of *Virtue* and of *Holiness,* they are not thus combin'd into Society, but they are link'd together by an Adamantine Law of *right* and *due Agency,* and, by this *legal Necessity,* they are *obliged,* not to be wicked, but to be holy and virtuous. They practise Righteousness and true Holiness, for other ultimate Reasons, than personal Self-respects, and they shun Sin, for other ultimate Reasons, than merely because it is a publick Nusance and Inconvenience. In the Kingdom of God, Holiness and Virtue do not exist merely for the sake of the publick Happiness, nor is the Holiness of God to be considered as a Means to that End, but the publick Happiness existeth for his Holiness and Rectitude of Will.

(4.) This Scheme of the Law of Nature, and its Definition of Good, because it *supposeth,* "That nothing is good, but as convenient to Nature, that Virtue is of the Rank of *profitable Good,* and is *no otherwise Virtue,* but as it contributes to this great End, the common Good of rational Agents," destroyeth the *Self-amiableness* and *Self-eligibleness* of Virtue, and the *Self-odiousness* of Sin and Wickedness. For it does not, nor can, acknowledge any other Beauty in Virtue, than the Fitness of it to this greatest End, *the common Happiness of rational Agents;* whereas, abstracting from all respect to Happiness or Misery, publick or private, *"a foul Action, because it is foul, ought not to be done,"* as *Cicero*[18] usually insisteth and inculcateth. Wickedness is to be shun'd, not only as a publick Inconvenience, but for its own intrinsick Turpitude, as all the *virtuous Philosophers,* in consort with *Christians,* agree, and that Sin, as such, is to be avoided with an infinite Aversion. *"To do an Injury is to be avoided for its own sake, whose Turpitude outweighs all Rewards encouraging to the Commission of Wickedness,"* saith *Seneca.*[19] It has been a *Question,* "Whether Justice be for Society, or Society for Justice? Do Men live in Society, merely that they may live justly? Or, do they live justly,

4. It destroys the Self-eligibleness of Virtue, which it degrades to the Rank of profitable Good.

---

18. Cicero, *De Officiis,* III.
19. Seneca, *De Beneficiis,* IV.15.

merely that they may live in Society?" Neither of these can be affirmed with Truth, but Men live in Society for Society-sake, the innumerable Benefits of it; and they ought to live in Society for Justice-sake, which obligeth Children to live in Society with their Parents, and rational Beings to live in Society with God. Justice, therefore, is, in part, for its own sake,[20] and, in part, for Society; and Society is, partly, for its own sake, and, partly, for Justice-sake. So Virtue is, partly, for Felicity, Holiness for Happiness: Felicity and Happiness are, partly, for Virtue and Holiness. For Virtue and Holiness design and endeavour the publick Happiness, and consist in the faithful Love of the Whole and its Interest; but, besides this Love of the publick Good, there is in all Men a good Disposition, a faithful Esteem and Love of Righteousness, and Hatred to Sin, for their own sakes. They practise Righteousness, ultimately, for Righteousness-sake, because of its own intrinsick Worth, Rectitude, and Pulchritude, *"for this sole reason, because it is decorous, right and just."*[21] So the virtuous Philosophers call that which is honest, *"Self-amiable, Self-laudable, Self-desirable."*[22] *"That which is right and just, is eligible, because it is such."*[23] There is more good in Justice, than, merely, a Subserviency to the publick Happiness, and, consequently, it is not good, merely as a Convenience to Nature; else it is nothing better than a Contrivance for living in Society, and for publick Convenience.

5. It introduces a Virtue, not truly moral, but merely politick and prudential. (5.) This Scheme of the Law of Nature, and its Definition of Good, introduceth an Institution of Morality, not truly moral, but merely politick and prudential. For it supposeth, *"That all the Acts of the Virtues are commanded, merely for the common Convenience of rational Agents; that the Dictates of Prudence, directing the Actions of Men to the publick Good, are the very Laws of Nature; that the Maker of the World must be suppos'd to be endowed with Prudence, in which there is a Volition of the best and greatest End, the common Good of all rational Agents, and a Pros-*

---

20. Cicero, *De Finibus*, III.
21. Ibid., II.
22. Ibid.
23. Iamblichus, *Protrepticus*, ch. 19.

ecution of it by the most effectual Means, in which sort of Acts all Religion and Virtue is contain'd."[24] The Maker of the World is suppos'd, from a Principle of *Prudence,* to will the greatest End, the common Happiness; and, from the same Principle of *Prudence,* also to contrive and enjoin the most effectual Means thereto, which are called the *"Acts of Religion and Virtue"*; and this his *prudential* Institution of End and Means is the Scheme of the Law of Nature, which, therefore, is not a *virtuous,* but a *political* Institution. For it is one thing, to institute Men to live well, only as to a *certain Interest;* and another thing to institute them to live well, *simply* and *absolutely.* A mere prudential Institution of Morality careth neither, for Virtue nor Vice, for living well nor living ill, as such and for their own sake, nor any further than as they promote or hinder the publick Convenience. As if one, who foundeth a Family, should prudentially institute the Members of it to demean themselves *humbly,* that they may live in *peace,* without caring, either for Pride or Humility, but only for the common Peace. So this Institution affirmeth, *"That the Laws of Nature, and all the Virtues, are nothing else but Means of obtaining the common Good."* It *supposeth,* "That Virtue is not good, but only as a Means to the common Happiness; and that Vice and Wickedness is not Evil, but as productive of publick Misery," as will further appear presently.

(6.) This Scheme of the Law of Nature, agreeably to its Definition of Good, supposeth, *"That the common Good or Happiness is the whole Rule and Measure of Virtue,"* as the adequate End is the Rule and Measure of the Means.[25] It supposeth, also, That there is no other Rule or Measure of endeavouring the common Happiness of rational Beings, but *"The Will determin'd to this supreme End and Good, to the utmost of its Power."*[26] The "eternal Happiness of the whole Universe ought to have the greatest Strength of Volition that can be, which is no less than in-

> 6. It contradicts this Truth, *That Virtue is the Rule and Measure of endeavouring the common Happiness of rational Agents.*

---

24. Maxwell attributes this to Cumberland, *A Treatise of the Laws of Nature,* but it is not a direct quotation.
25. A general reference to Cumberland.
26. Ibid.

finite."[27] Both which Propositions clash with this plain and certain Principle, *That Virtue is the Rule and Measure of endeavouring the common Happiness of rational Beings.* Which, including our own Happiness, may be sought, merely as an Interest, and, out of Interest, from a Principle of natural and lawful Self-love. But the common Happiness of rational Beings, must be sought also from a principle of *Duty* and *Virtue,* and, consequently, it must be sought, only in consistence with Virtue, nor otherwise than Virtue requireth. A Man may not violate Virtue, nor touch with Wickedness, no, not for the Happiness of the Universe. He may, in some degree, part with his own Happiness, which is part of the publick Happiness, and chuse his own Unhappiness, or several Inconveniences of Life; but no Man may chuse Wickedness in any degree, altho' himself only were the material Object of his Sin; so much *greater* and stricter are his *Obligations* with respect to *Virtue* than *Happiness.* To chuse Annihilation rather than Sin is a laudable Choice, and it is therefore laudable, because it is virtuous. When *Moses* wisheth his own Name *"blotted out of the Book of Life";* [28] when St. *Paul* saith, *"I could wish, that my-self were accursed from Christ, for my Brethren, my Kinsmen according to the Flesh";* [29] these holy Men, in some degree, with their own Unhappiness, for the sake of a more publick Happiness; but their wishing is not to be understood absolutely, but with this Restriction and Limitation, *so far as it is lawful and virtuous so to do.* Virtue, therefore, is the Rule and Measure of endeavouring, both our own, and the publick, Happiness. God himself promotes the publick Happiness, yet cannot be said to do it, *"to the utmost of his Power,"* but so far as it is *fitting* so to do. We are obliged to endeavour his Glory, which is one Branch, and the chief, of the publick natural Good; but such a kind of endeavouring it, which is not consistent with Virtue, true Holiness, and Godliness, is not acceptable, but criminal in his Eyes. No pious Frauds. No doing Evil, that Good may come thereof. We are oblig'd to endeavour the Unhappiness of rational Creatures, but so, as to endeavour the Unhappiness

27. Bright, *An Essay in Morality,* pp. 38, 64.
28. Exodus 32.32.
29. Romans 9.3.

of the Apostate Angels, and the Ruin of their Kingdom. And, if any Men be in the same State of Reprobation with the Apostate Angels, by notoriously sinning the *Sin unto Death,*[30] we are not obliged to seek their Happiness.

(7.) According to its Definition of Good, this Scheme of the Law of Nature condemneth the Philosophy of the *Stoicks, "Because, whilst they endeavour to establish the transcendent Goodness of Virtue, and the egregious Evil of Vice, they, incautiously, intirely take away the only Reason, why Virtue is Good and Vice Evil. For Virtue is therefore Good, (and in Truth it is the greatest Good,) because it determines the Actions of Men to such Effects, as are principal Parts of the publick natural Good, or Happiness."*[31] Agreeably whereto, it is affirm'd, *"That the best Compend of Ethicks is the Idea or Plan of that true Happiness, which is in every one's Power, and of all the Causes thereof, dispos'd in their natural Order."*[32] In this Scheme of the Law of Nature, nothing is counted *good* but *Happiness,* other Things, only as productive of Happiness; nothing is counted *evil,* but *Misery,* other Things, only as productive of Misery. *Virtue,* therefore, is *degraded,* to be of the same *Rank* with *Food,* Sleep, and Houses, that are good and necessary, as promoting the common Happiness of Mankind; which *Happiness* is generally suppos'd, to consist merely in *Pleasure;*[33] and, consequently, *Virtue* is suppos'd to be *good,* only as *subservient to Pleasure,* private and publick; therefore the only *Competition* between Vice and Virtue, must be touching the *Pleasure* which they afford: And this must be the only *Fault* of the Pleasures of *Sin,* they are *deficient* in matter of *Pleasure,* or clash with greater Pleasure, as a lesser Good with a greater; no *Vice* or Villainy is to be *discommended,* but only as *opposite to Pleasure,* in itself, or its Effects; and, if it were not opposite to Pleasure, it would not be a Vice, nor at all to be discommended, as

7. According to *Cumberland*'s Scheme, nothing is good but Happiness; other Things, only as productive of Happiness.

---

30. 1 John 5.16.

31. Cumberland, *A Treatise of the Laws of Nature,* 5.5.

32. Ibid., 5.40.

33. Ibid., 5.12, 13; Bright, *An Essay in Morality,* pp. 55, 90; Sharrock, *De Officiis,* ch. 1, n. 3; More, *Enchiridion Ethicum,* I.2; Stearne, *Anima Medela* (1653), I.13.

Epicurus said of Luxury. Vice and vicious Persons would be as good as Virtue and virtuous Persons, if the Nature of the Universe could be so contrived, that the former could be as subservient to Pleasure as the latter. Accordingly, the Goodness of Virtue and the *Law of Nature* is said to be *no otherwise,* nor any further, *unalterable,* than *"whilst the Nature of Things"* (that is, of Causes and their Effects) *"continues such as now it is."*[34] As the *same* Subserviency to Happiness, so the *same* Unalterableness, is ascribed to *Virtue* and to *natural Things,* (Victuals, Cloaths, Physick,) which are said to be *unalterably good,* that is, *tending to the Preservation and Happiness of Mankind.* The Immutability, therefore, of Virtue is not absolute, nor is it of an immutable Nature, in and of itself, as a Square and a Cube, but the Immutability which it hath, is owing to the unchang'd Nature of the Universe, to the Happiness whereof it is a Means subservient.

8. And Virtue is not good, as amiable, but as convenient.

(8.) This Scheme of the Law of Nature, agreeably to its Definition of Good, derives the *Necessity of Virtue* in Men, merely from *Necessity of publick Good,* which necessarily requires it, and from their being enjoin'd it, merely in Order thereto.[35] Man must practise universal Benevolence, Justice, Temperance, Chastity, only for this great End. According to this Maxim, the Virtues have nothing to recommend them, at least nothing to necessitate their Practice, but only their necessary Serviceableness to a *common Self-Convenience,* for which sole Reason the several Clans of Thieves and Robbers strictly practise Justice among themselves. As they practise it, because it is necessary to their common Good, and Injustice would be a grand Inconvenience to their System of rational Agents; so, if Mankind, in general, practise Justice, merely because it is necessary to their common Good, and Injustice would be a grand Inconvenience to their System of rational Agents, altho' their System, and the Good

---

34. Cumberland, *A Treatise of the Laws of Nature,* 5.23, 8.1.

35. Ibid., 5.48; 8.1; 2.7. [Maxwell] "Only for this noblest End, *Cumber.* c. 5. § 48. Because they conduce to the happy State of the Universe, *Ibid.* c. 8. § 1. For this End only, that the common Good of all be promoted by every one, *Ibid.* § 2, 7."

thereof, is of a different Nature from that of Thieves, yet is not their Respect to Justice and Injustice both of the same Kind?

But these Maxims not only destroy the *Self-Amiableness of Virtue,* and the *Self-Odiousness of Vice,* but their being *by Nature,* not *by arbitrary Appointment.* For let us suppose, that, antecedently to the Constitution of rational Agents, there was one only *solitary Rational* in being; this one solitary Rational, according to these Maxims, *cannot practise* any *Virtue,* nor is he, in his solitary State, capable, either of Virtue or Vice, which, therefore, are not *in themselves necessary.* Such they are not, according to these Maxims, after the Universe of rational Beings is constituted; they are necessary, only and merely, for the common Good of this constituted Universe, and by his Will, who, constituting this Universe, appointed them, only and merely, for the common Good thereof. They are, therefore, as arbitrary, as the constituted Universe, and as his Will and Appointment, in constituting the Universe. But whatever is in itself, in its own Nature, *Well-doing,* the *right* and *due Practice,* is, upon that Account and *for itself,* not merely for publick Good, indispensably necessary, upon that Account it is *commanded by God,* upon that Account it is *Virtue,* because it is *Well-doing,* and not, merely, because it is a promoting the common Good. *To endeavour the common Good of rational Beings,* is so far from comprehending all Virtue, that, unless our Endeavours to promote this common Good be *duly qualified,* it is *not Virtue,* but *Vice* and Crime. Such is all *Benevolence* and *Beneficence,* which is against Righteousness. *To benefit another* may sometimes be *ill-doing,* according to that of *Ennius* in *Tullie's Offices,* Book 2:

> *Benefacta male locata malefacta arbitror.*[36]

"I look upon Benefits misplac'd, to be evil Actions." All are not oblig'd to perpetual and universal *Benevolence* and *Beneficence* without Limitation; but all are oblig'd to *Righteousness* without Limitation; this, therefore, is Virtue, and the Rule of Virtue, which must rule and limit *our endeavouring to promote* the common Good of rational Agents. Therefore *Benevolence* is but a *Branch* of *good Life.* So the *Philosophers* sup-

---

36. Cicero, *De Officiis,* II.xviii.62.

pos'd, who so discoursed of Virtue, as to make Men the Admirers and Lovers of it for its own sake; and so *Christians* are Admirers and Lovers of the divine Image, *the Life of Righteousness and true Holiness.*

9. And the Sovereignty of God is not founded upon a sufficient Authority.

(9.) This Scheme of the Law of Nature, agreeably to its Definition of Good, deriveth the Dominion and *Sovereignty of God* himself, merely *"from the Necessity of publick Good, God did assume it to himself, because the common Good necessarily requir'd it."* [37] But, if the divine Dominion and Sovereignty over all Creatures is thus founded, it is not so well founded as human Sovereignties; for these are founded upon Necessity of publick Good, and also the Law of a superiour Sovereign, from whom they derive their ruling Authority. But the divine Dominion and Sovereignty is suppos'd to be founded, merely, upon Necessity of publick Good, and the Dictate of the divine Mind concerning it. Which Dictate can give no Authority, unless one can give Authority to himself, merely, by the Dictate of his own Mind; nor can it pretend to be a Law, unless one can make a Law antecedently to his Sovereignty and legislative Power; nor are any oblig'd to be subject to this assum'd Sovereignty, founded merely upon the Necessity of the publick Good, but by the great Law of endeavouring the publick Good, which, therefore, must be made antecedently to this Assumption of the Sovereignty, and, consequently, it must be made by one, that had no Sovereignty, no legislative Power. To this assumed Dominion and Sovereignty, assumed merely from Necessity of common Good and in order thereto, he cannot claim our Subjection, save only from Necessity of the common Good, and in Order thereto. But, if this is the whole of the divine Dominion and Sovereignty, he is far from having the most supreme Dominion possible, which the Deity must have; nor hath he the supreme governing Power *originally* and essentially, for he could not have it, if the common Good did not require it; it accrueth to him adventitiously and *derivatively;* he is not sole Owner of his own Dominion, nor is it independent or plenary; but all is the Publick's, the Publick is necessarily supreme Lord of all, for whatever Dominion God has, is *from the Publick,* from the Ne-

---

37. Cumberland, *A Treatise of the Laws of Nature,* 7.6, 7; 9.1, 2.

cessity of publick Good; *for the Publick,* for the sake of the Publick, and the Use thereof. But thus to derive his Dominion and Sovereignty from the Necessity of publick Good, is to say, that he must be God, merely because the publick Good requires it; for his Dominion and Sovereignty is his Godhead.

(10.) This Scheme of the Law of Nature, agreeably to its Definition of Good, makes God's Dominion and Sovereignty, *a subordinate and subservient Means to the publick Good.* For it *supposes* "all Rights and Dues to be deriv'd from the common Good, and to be Means subordinate and subservient thereto";[38] it *supposes,* "That the divine Dominion and Sovereignty is *in Order to the* common Good, and the *Means necessary to the obtaining thereof.*"[39] The Means are subordinate and subservient to the End; the End always excells the Thing which is to the End; the End is always desir'd for itself, the Means for the End, which are necessary, when the End cannot be had without them, not otherwise; they have their Goodness and Measure from it, and the Reason of them is taken from the End. The End has a greater Sovereignty in all Actions, than the Actor himself; he rules others, but the End rules him. The common Good of rational Agents, therefore, is highly dignified, because it is suppos'd, to be the *End,* the *best* and *greatest* End.[40] But, with respect to this, we must distinguish between a *made* and *unmade,* a *human* and *divine,* Sovereignty. If the Sovereignty is a human Sovereignty made by the People, or made by God for the People, altho' it has all the usual Rights of Sovereignty, yet it is necessarily, in the strict and proper Sense, *a subordinate and subservient Means to an End, the common Good.* But Things are quite otherwise, if the Sovereignty is unmade, and maketh the People, and is infinitely better than they; for such a Sovereignty is necessarily *unsubordinate,* and cannot be *the subordinate and subservient Means to any End,* but is, absolutely, as without an *Efficient,* so without any *Final* Cause. Whence a Judgment may be form'd; whether a pious

Marginal note: 10. But a subordinate and subservient Means to the common Good.

38. Ibid., 7.3, 6.
39. Ibid., 7.6.
40. Ibid.

Man would say, "That the common Good is a Law and End above God, that his Goodness is but a Means to it, that he is no further necessary, than in order to it; not so good, or great, or excellent, or amiable, or honourable, as the publick Good; nor are we to love him, or devote ourselves to him, or to adhere to him, so much as the common Good, in which we ought finally to acquiesce, which is thus exalted, even above God himself."

11. And only one half of the common Good is represented as such.

(11.) In this Scheme of the Law of Nature, agreeably to its Notion of Good, but *one half of the common Good* is represented, as such; for, by the common Good of rational Agents, it means only their *Happiness,* to which it renders *God* and *Virtue subordinate.* Whereas the common Good of rational Beings must be distinguish'd, into *the Good which is for them,* which is their *Happiness,* and into *the Good which they are for,* which is their *Holiness,* the Good of Virtue. "*That which is* absolutely *good, is every way superior to us, and we ought always to be commanded by it, because we are made under it: But that which is* relatively *good to us, may sometime be commanded by us. Eternal Truth and Righteousness are, in themselves, perfectly and absolutely good, and the more we conform ourselves to them, the better we are.*"[41] If the Deity, if Virtue and Righteousness, were only relatively good, as convenient and commodious to us, if they were merely for us, as their End, they must be look'd upon as Things merely subservient to our Pleasure, and must be esteemed and loved accordingly. But, because they are absolutely and in themselves good, superior to us and our Pleasure, therefore our Pleasure ought to be accommodated to them, and all rational Agents should take the highest Complacence in them, both for their own sake, their own Excellence, and for our sake, as being our true Excellence and Felicity. "*We love the Virtues for the sake, both of themselves, as being in themselves excellent and honourable; and of something else, that is, our Happiness.*"[42] So the *Pagans* philosophize at a more virtuous Rate, than those *Christian* Divines, who say, "*There is some first and chief Good, which a Man desireth for itself,*

41. Smith, *Select Discourses* (1660), pp. 159, 160.
42. Apuleius, *De Philosophia.*

and for it all other Things, which Good is the Good of Pleasure, or the delectable Good. For this Good only a Man enjoyeth. Of the Good of Honesty, Profit, Decorum, there is in itself no Enjoyment. Only the Pleasure which resulteth from it, or is conjoin'd with it, a Man can enjoy. The Evil, contrary to this Good, can be nothing else but Misery or Pain, and that perpetual. For there is no Man, who does not hate that at the highest rate, and all other Things upon the account of it."[43] With this Discourse of a foreign Divine, I will confront a better and more religious Discourse of a Divine of our own, "*Those are ignorant of the Nature of Sin, that imagine any Evil greater than it, or so great.* Cicero's *Saying, in the first Book of his* Tusculan *Questions, hath, without doubt, not a little of Truth in it.* Ne malum quidem ullum, cum Turpitudinis malo comparandum. *There is no Evil comparable to that of Sin.* Hierocles, *a sober Philosopher, and very free from the high-flown Humour and ranting Genius of the* Stoicks, *though he would allow, that other Things, beside Sin, may be* χαλεπὰ καὶ δυσδιάθετα, *very grievous and difficult to be borne, yet he would admit nothing besides, to be,* ὄντως κακὸν, *truly evil; and he giveth this Reason; viz. Because that certain Circumstances may make other Things Good, that have the Repute of Evil; but none can make this so. He saith, the Word* καλῶς (well) *can never be join'd with any Vice, but so it may with every Thing besides. As it is proper to say concerning such or such a Person,* νοσεῖ καλῶς, πένεται καλῶς *he is well diseas'd, he is well poor, that is, he is both these to good purpose, behaving himself well in his Sickness and Poverty, as he ought to do: But it can never be said,* ἀδικεῖ καλῶς, ἀκόλας αίνει καλῶς, *he doth Injury well, or he is rightly and as becometh him intemperate.*"[44]

(12.) In this Scheme of the Law of Nature, agreeably to its Notion of Good, the due Order of Reasoning and of our Obligations is inverted. For, antecedently to the Law of *endeavouring the common Good*, there is an Obligation upon Mankind, and therefore a Law, of conscientious Subjection and Obedience to the Authority of the Lawgiver. He would not make this Law for them, if they were not antecedently under such

12. And the Order of our Obligation is inverted.

43. Episcopius, *De Liber Arbitrio*, ch. 4.
44. Fowler, *The Design of Christianity* (1671), sect. 2, ch. 9.

an Obligation, if he could not claim Subjection and Obedience from them. Their *Subjection* to this the *supreme Lawgiver* is, therefore, the *first Law of Nature*. As all Governments, in the first Place, take care, to establish their Authority; and as a Man is bound to acknowledge *Subjection to the King,* before he is bound to obey the Law of endeavouring the common Good of the Kingdom: So Mankind are first oblig'd to consent, to be Subjects to God, and then, as his Subjects, to endeavour the common Good. The Order of their Obligations is not, to endeavour the common Good in the first Place, and so to be pious and virtuous towards God; but to be pious and virtuous towards God, and so to endeavour the common Good; for, if they endeavour the common Good, they are bound to do it, from a Principle of Piety towards God; and the Law of Nature is not Religion, if it does not oblige them to it. So in all our Actions Inquiry must be made, whether they be right in respect of Matter, Manner, Object, Measure, Principle, End, Circumstances, which sort of Inquiries would be impertinent, if Virtue is not Virtue, but merely as it is an Endeavour of the common Good. The Law of Nature instituteth Men, in the first Place, to be *the Well-doers, not the Evil-doers, the Righteous, not the Wicked,* and as such, Men have Rewards promis'd, and Punishments threaten'd in Laws; as such, they are justified or condemned in Law. Ethicks is the Art of living well, as to *Virtue,* and as to *Felicity.*

(13.) **And Laws have no Obligation, but their Sanction.** (13.) This Scheme of the Law of Nature, agreeably to its Definition of Good, seems to acknowledge no other Obligation of it, but merely from the Sanction of it, which is Self-Interest. *"The whole Force of Obligation"* (saith *Cumberland* [45]) *"is this, that the Legislator hath annex'd to the Observance of his Laws, Good; to the Transgression, Evil; and those natural: In Prospect whereof Men are moved to perform Actions, rather agreeing than disagreeing with the Laws. The Mind of Man is not properly tied with Bonds.* . . . [46] *I think that moral Obligation may be thus universally and properly defin'd. Obligation is that Act of a Legislator, by which he declares,*

45. Cumberland, *A Treatise of the Laws of Nature,* 5.11.
46. Ibid., 5.27.

that Actions conformable to his Law are necessary to those, for whom the Law is made. An Action is then understood to be necessary to a rational Agent, when it is certainly one of the Causes necessarily requir'd to that Happiness, which he naturally, and consequently necessarily, desires. I cannot conceive any Thing which could bind the Mind of Man with any Necessity, (in which Justinian's *Definition places the Force of Obligation,) except Arguments proving, that Good or Evil will proceed from our Actions.*[47] *Natural Rewards and Penalties, those Motives of Obedience, are the proper Sanction, to make the Law obligatory. For Obligation properly signifieth nothing, but laying a Necessity upon us, to act according to the Direction of the Law."*[48] So that, according to this Scheme, the Law-giver is suppos'd to *indicate* to Men, "That the endeavouring the common Good, or universal Benevolence, is a necessary Means to that End, which Nature has determin'd them to pursue, which is their own Happiness contain'd in the common Good, and that, if they do not so act, this will be pernicious to themselves." But, if this be the whole of the Law's Obligation, the Transgression of the Law is *not Unrighteousness, Sin,* and *Crime,* but only *Imprudence,* and *Infelicity,* for the Sanction of the Law importeth no other Evil. But the *Obligation* or Bond of the *Law* is the *jural Restraint,* which is express'd by *(Non licet) you may not do it;* but, because a bare *non licet* or prohibition is not sufficient to enforce the Law, therefore the *Sin* and *Punishment,* the *Precept* and the *Sanction* both concur, to make the *jural Restraint,* which must be thus fully express'd, *(Non licet impune) you may not do it with Impunity.* But, altho' Sin and Punishment are closely connected, yet the Obligation of *(non licet) it may not be done,* is distinct from the Obligation of *(Non impune) not with Impunity,* as Sin and Punishment are of distinct Consideration. But a Man is *bound,* both when he cannot do a Thing *without Sin,* and when he cannot do a Thing *without Punishment,* and *both* these *Obligations* are in *every Law,* and both concur to make the Obligation of it. But, because the Obligation of *non licet* is antecedent to the Obligation of *non impune,* the

47. Ibid., 5.35.
48. Parker, *A Demonstration of the Divine Authority of the Law of Nature, and of the Christian Religion* (1681), p. 60. This work adapted Cumberland's ideas.

Precept to the Sanction, and the Sin is made by the Law, the Law hath
so much Obligation, as to make the Sin, before the Penalty is enacted;
therefore the Law has an Obligation antecedently to the Sanction of it.
For every one is bound to avoid what is Sin, because none can have a
Right to do what is unrighteous, which is a Contradiction to the Law
of Religion (which is suppos'd to have its Name *a Religando,* which is
call'd [*Religionis nodus, vinculum Pietatis*] *the Tie of Religion, the Bond
of Piety*) cannot rationally be thought obligatory, merely from the Sanction of it; for to do any Thing contrary to the Holiness of the Deity, is
necessarily, and in itself, Sin. No ingenuous Man looks upon himself as
oblig'd to be grateful to his Benefactors, to love his Wife and Children,
or to love and honour his God and Saviour, merely by the Sanction of
Rewards and Punishments. Is there no Obligation upon Men from Right
and Wrong, due and undue, Sanctity and Sin, Righteousness and Wickedness, Honesty and Dishonesty, Integrity and Guile, Worthiness and
Baseness, Conscience or Crime, Virtue or Villainy, but merely from a
prudent Regard to their own Happiness? But, if a Man should be so
imprudent, as to discard all care and regard to his own Happiness, would
he be discharg'd by this Imprudence from all his Bonds and Fetters of
Obligation, and become loose and unbound, to live as he pleas'd? *Cicero*
asketh the Men of Prudence, if they were secure from the Sanction of
the Law, whether they would be dishonest or not?[49] If they say, they
would, let them (saith he) confess themselves wicked; if they say, they
would not, let them acknowledge, that all Things foul and base are to
be shun'd, because they are such. If a truly wise Man had *Gyges's* Ring,
*"He thinketh not, that he hath more License to Sin, than if he had it not.
We ought to be of this Persuasion, that, if we could be hid from all the Gods
and Men,"* (and, therefore, were secure from the Sanction of the Law,)
"yet nothing is to be done avaritiously, unjustly, libidinously."[50] The Vulgar
say, *I am bound in Duty, in Justice, in Gratitude, in Conscience;* and the
Schools say, "That the Obligation of the Law of Nature is a Bond of
Conscience." According to our *Author's* Scheme, a Man is oblig'd to

49. Cicero, *De Officiis,* III.ix.38–39.
50. Ibid.

choose to be annihilated for the Welfare of others, if the common Good did require it; which yet no Man can be oblig'd to do, out of regard to his own Happiness. Nor is it possible, to deduce a conscientious Obligation, merely from a *Politick and Prudential regard to our own Happiness.* But, because the Legislator annexes [*honum jucundum*] *delectable Good* to his Law, and, for the Sake of this, Men choose Virtue and Obedience; hence some infer, That *delectable Good* hath the precedence of [*bonum honestum*] *the Good of Virtue;* which Argument may be thus retorted. The Legislator annexes to his Law the Sanction of the *Good of Pleasure,* for the Sake of the *Good of Virtue,* which the Law enjoineth; this, therefore, is the principal in the Estimation and Intention of the Law-giver. Whose Will, if it be made known, is, without a Sanction, a Bond or Obligation upon us; for we owe Obedience thereto, and every one is bound to pay what he oweth.

(14.) The Law of Nature is certainly a *Matter of Conscience,* not of mere Policy and Prudence, not of mere civil Society, as it is made in this Scheme of it, which is a System of *human Policy and Prudence, modelling the Universe of rational Agents into a civil Society, by Consent and Agreement in their Politicks, for the common Happiness of civil Life.* The Universe of rational Agents is in a very divided State, but they are modell'd into one Society in this Scheme,[51] which is an Institution to civil Society, into which the whole Universe of rational Agents is suppos'd to be combin'd. Civil Society, being Civil-religious, is not without a sacred Society; for all Civil People have their Deity, their Religion, their Priests, and their *Sacra,* which must be in this great Civil-Society, which consisteth of the Under-rational Agents, and of God the Head-rational, which looketh like, but is not, a *Divine Society.* Into this Society the Universe of rational Agents is suppos'd to be combin'd, not by the Bands of Right and Due, but in the Methods of human Policy and Prudence, by one common Interest (their common Happiness) and by Consent and Agreement in their Politicks. The Universe of rational Beings is suppos'd to be united, in order to the common Good, which is the common End.

(14.) And the Law of Nature is not Matter of Conscience, but Prudence; not a spiritual, but a civil Institution.

51. Cumberland, *A Treatise of the Laws of Nature,* 6.2.

For God, in order to the common Good, assumeth to himself the supreme governing Power, and the under-rationals, for Necessity of common Good, do and must yield it unto him;[52] by which Agreement in Politicks they are related as *Rector* and *Subjects* in Society. Which Society, being of no higher Kind than Civil, the common Happiness (that is, the End of the Association) can be no more than the Happiness of Civil Life; and, consequently, the *universal Benevolence,* and the other Virtues, which are in this Scheme of the Law of Nature, are no other, than those of *Aristotle*'s and *Cicero*'s Institution. This, therefore, being not satisfactory, we are obliged to recede from it, and to give a different Account of the *Law of Nature,* and of the *Good,* to which it instituteth.

What follows from my Lord *Shaftesbury* seems to me so just, so rational, and so much in Confirmation of what I have been here advancing, that I have thought it proper to add the Force of his Reasoning to what I have laid down.

I have known a Building, which by the Officiousness of the Workmen has been so *shor'd,* and *screw'd up,* on the side where they pretended it had a Leaning, that it has, at last, been turn'd the contrary way, and overthrown. There has something, perhaps, of this kind happen'd in *Morals.* Men have not been contented to shew the natural Advantages of Honesty and Virtue. They have rather lessen'd these, the better, as they thought, to advance another Foundation. They have made *Virtue* so mercenary a Thing, and have talk'd so much of its *Rewards,* that one can hardly tell what there is in it, after all, which can be worth rewarding. For to be brib'd only, or terrify'd into an honest Practice, bespeaks little of real Honesty or Worth. We may make, it's true, whatever *Bargain* we think fit; and may bestow *in favour* what Overplus we please. But there can be no Excellence or Wisdom in voluntarily rewarding what is neither estimable, nor deserving. And, if Virtue be not really estimable in it-self, I can see nothing estimable in following it for the sake of *a Bargain.*[53]

If the Love of doing Good, be not, of it-self, a *good* and *right* Incli-

52. Ibid., 9.1; Introduction, sect. 24.

53. Shaftesbury, *Characteristicks of Men, Manners, Opinions, Times* (1714), I, pp. 97, 98.

nation; I know not how there can possibly be such a thing as *Goodness* or *Virtue*. If the Inclination be *right;* 'tis a perverting of it, to apply it solely to *the Reward,* and make us conceive such Wonders of the Grace and Favour which is to attend Virtue; when there is so little shewn of the intrinsick Worth or Value of the Thing it-self.

I have known it ask'd, *Why should a Man be honest in the Dark?* What a Man must be to ask this Question, I won't say. But for Those, who have no better a Reason for being *honest,* than the Fear of *a Gibbet* or *a Jail;* I should not, I confess, much covet their Company, or Acquaintance. And, if any Guardian of mine who had kept his Trust, and given me back my Estate when I came of Age, had been discover'd to have acted thus, thro' *Fear* only of what might happen to him; I should for my own Part, undoubtedly, continue civil and respectful to him: But for my Opinion of his Worth, it would be such as the PYTHIAN God had of his Votary, who *devoutly fear'd* him, and *therefore* restor'd to a Friend what had been deposited in his Hands.

> *Reddidit ergo* metu, *non* moribus; & *tamen omnem*
> *Vocem adyti dignam templo, veranique probavit,*
> *Extinctus tot à pariter cum prole domoq;*[54]

I know very well, that many Services to the Publick are done merely for the sake of *a Gratuity;* and that *Informers,* in particular, are to be taken care of, and sometimes made *Pensioners of State.* But I must beg pardon for the particular Thoughts I may have of these Gentlemens Merit; and shall never bestow my Esteem on any other than the *voluntary* Discoverers of Villany, and *hearty* Prosecutors of their Country's Interest. And in this respect, I know nothing greater or nobler, than the undertaking and managing some important Accusation; by which some high Criminal of State, or some form'd Body of Conspirators against the Publick, may be arraign'd and brought to Punishment, thro' the honest Zeal and publick Affection of a private Man.

---

54. Juvenal, *Satires,* XIII.204: "He therefore restored the money, through fear, and not from honesty; nevertheless he found all the words of the Oracle to be true and worthy of the shrine, being destroyed with his whole race and family and relations, however far removed."

I know too, that the mere Vulgar of Mankind often stand in need of such a rectifying Object as *the Gallows* before their Eyes. Yet I have no Belief, that any Man of a liberal Education, or common Honesty, ever needed to have recourse to this Idea in his Mind, the better to restrain him from playing the Knave. And, if A SAINT had no other Virtue, than what was rais'd in him by the same Objects of Reward and Punishment, in a more distant State; I know not whose Love or Esteem he might gain besides: But for my own part, I should never think him worthy of mine.[55]

As to the Belief of a DEITY, and how Men are influenc'd by it; we may consider, in the first place, on what account Men yield Obedience, and act in conformity to such a Supreme Being. It must be either *in the way of his* POWER, as presupposing some Disadvantage or Benefit to accrue from him: or *in the way of his* EXCELLENCY and WORTH, as thinking it the Perfection of Nature to imitate and resemble him.

If (as in the first Case) there be a Belief or Conception of a DEITY, who is consider'd only as *powerful* over his Creatures and inforceing Obedience to his *absolute Will* by particular Rewards and Punishments; and, if on this account, thro' Hope merely of *Reward,* or Fear of *Punishment,* the Creature be incited to do the Good he hates, or restrain'd from doing the Ill to which he is not otherwise in the least degree averse; there is in this Case (as has been already shown) no Virtue or Goodness whatsoever. The Creature, notwithstanding his good Conduct, is intrinsically of as little Worth, as if he acted in his natural way, when under no Dread or Terrour of any sort. There is no more of *Rectitude, Piety,* or *Sanctity* in a Creature thus reform'd, than there is *Meekness* or *Gentleness* in a Tyger strongly chain'd, or *Innocence* and *Sobriety* in a Monkey under the Discipline of the Whip. For, however orderly and well those Animals, or Man himself upon like Terms, may be induc'd to act, whilst the Will is neither gain'd, nor the Inclination wrought upon, but *Awe* alone prevails and forces Obedience; the Obedience is *servile,* and all which is done thro' it, merely *servile.* The greater degree of such a Submission or Obedience, is only the greater *Servility;* whatever may be the

55. Shaftesbury, *Characteristicks,* I, pp. 125–27.

Object. For, whether such a Creature has a good Master, or an ill one, he is neither more nor less servile in his own nature. Be the Master or Superiour ever so perfect, or excellent, yet the greater Submission caus'd in this Case, thro' this sole Principle or Motive, is only the lower and more abject Servitude, and implies the greater Wretchedness and Meanness in the Creature, who has those Passions of Self-Love so predominant, and is in his Temper so vitious and defective, as has been explain'd.

As to the second Case. If there be a Belief or Conception of a DEITY, who is consider'd as *Worthy* and *Good,* and admir'd and reverenc'd as such; being understood to have, besides mere Power and Knowledg, the highest Excellence of Nature, such as renders him justly amiable to All; and, if in the manner this Sovereign and mighty Being is represented, or as he is historically describ'd, there appears in him a high and eminent regard to what is good and excellent, a Concern for the good of *All,* and an Affection of Benevolence and Love towards *the Whole;* such an Example must undoubtedly serve (as above explain'd) to raise and increase the Affection towards Virtue, and help to submit and subdue all other Affections to that alone.

Nor is this Good effected by *Example* merely. For, where the Theistical Belief is intire and perfect, there must be a steddy Opinion of the Superintendency of a Supreme Being, a Witness and Spectator of human Life, and conscious of whatsoever is felt or acted in the Universe: So that in the perfectest Recess, or deepest Solitude, there must be *One* still presum'd remaining with us; whose Presence, singly, must be of more moment, than that of the most August Assembly on Earth. In such a Presence, 'tis evident, that, as the *Shame* of guilty Actions must be the greatest of any; so must the *Honour* be, of well-doing, even under the unjust Censure of a World. And in this Case, 'tis very apparent how conducing a *perfect Theism* must be to Virtue, and how great Deficiency there is in *Atheism.*

What the FEAR *of future Punishment,* and HOPE *of future Reward,* added to this Belief, may further contribute towards Virtue, we come now to consider more particularly. So much in the mean while may be gather'd from what has been said above; That neither this *Fear* or *Hope* can possibly be of the kind call'd *good Affections,* such as are acknowledg'd the Springs and Sources of all Actions truly *good.* Nor can this Fear or Hope, as above intimated, consist in reality with Virtue, or Goodness; if it either stands as *essential* to any moral Performance, or as *a considerable Motive* to any Act, of which some better Affection ought, *alone,* to have been a *sufficient Cause.*

It may be consider'd withal; That, in this religious sort of Discipline, the Principle of *Self-Love,* which is naturally so prevailing in us, being no-way moderated, or restrain'd, but rather improv'd and made stronger every day, by the exercise of the Passions in a Subject of more extended Self-Interest; there may be reason to apprehend, lest the Temper of this kind shou'd extend it-self in general thro' all the Parts of Life. For, if the Habit be such as to occasion, in every Particular, a stricter Attention to Self-Good, and private Interest; it must insensibly diminish the Affections towards Publick Good, or the Interest of Society; and introduce a certain Narrowness of Spirit, which (as some pretend) is peculiarly observable in the devout Persons and Zealots of almost every religious Perswasion.

This, too, must be confess'd; That, if it be *true Piety,* to love GOD *for his own sake,* the over-solicitous regard to private Good expected from him, must of necessity prove a diminution of Piety. For, whilst *God* is belov'd, only as the Cause of private Good, he is no otherwise belov'd, than as any other Instrument or Means of Pleasure by any vitious Creature. Now the more there is of this violent Affection towards *private Good,* the less room is there for the other sort towards *Goodness it-self,* or any good and deserving Object, worthy of Love and Admiration for its own sake; such as GOD is universally acknowledg'd, or at least by the generality of civiliz'd or refin'd Worshippers.

'Tis in this respect that the strong Desire and *Love of Life* may also prove an Obstacle to Piety, as well as to Virtue and publick Love. For the stronger this Affection is in any one, the less will he be able to have true *Resignation,* or Submission to the Rule and Order of THE DEITY. And, if that which he calls *Resignation* depends only on the expectation of infinite Retribution or Reward, he discovers no more Worth or Virtue here, than in any other Bargain of Interest: The meaning of his Resignation being only this, "That he resigns his present Life, and Pleasures, conditionally for THAT which he himself confesses to be beyond an Equivalent; *eternal Living, in a State of highest Pleasure and Enjoyment.*"

But, notwithstanding the Injury which the Principle of Virtue may possibly suffer, by the Increase of the selfish Passions, in the way we have been mentioning; 'tis certain, on the other side, that the Principle of *Fear of future Punishment* and *Hope of future Reward,* how mercenary or servile soever it may be accounted, is yet, in many Circumstances, a great Advantage, Security, and Support to *Virtue.*

It has been already consider'd, that, notwithstanding there may be implanted in the Heart a real Sense of Right and Wrong, a real good Affection towards the Species or Society; yet, by the violence of Rage, Lust, or any other counter-working Passion, this good Affection may frequently be controul'd and overcome. Where therefore there is nothing in the Mind capable to render such ill Passions the Objects of its Aversion, and cause them earnestly to be oppos'd; 'tis apparent, how much a good Temper in time must suffer, and a Character by degrees change for the worse. But, if Religion interposing creates a Belief, that the ill *Passions* of this kind, no less than their consequent *Actions,* are the Objects of a Deity's Animadversion; 'tis certain, that such a Belief must prove a seasonable Remedy against Vice, and be in a particular manner advantageous to Virtue. For a Belief of this kind must be suppos'd to tend considerably towards the calming of the Mind, and disposing or fitting the Person to a better Recollection of himself, and to a stricter Observance of that good and virtuous Principle, which needs only his Attention, to engage him wholly in its Party and Interest.

And as this Belief of a future Reward and Punishment is capable of supporting those who thro' *ill Practice* are like to apostatize from Virtue; so when by *ill Opinion* and wrong Thought, the Mind it-self is bent against the honest course, and debauch'd even to an Esteem, and deliberate Preference of a vitious one; the Belief of the kind mention'd may prove on this occasion the only Relief and Safety.

A PERSON, for Instance, who has much of Goodness and natural Rectitude in his Temper, but withal, so much Softness, or Effeminacy, as unfits him to bear Poverty, Crosses or Adversity; if by ill Fortune he meets with many Trials of this kind, it must certainly give a Sourness and Distaste to his Temper, and make him exceedingly averse to that which he may falsly presume the Occasion of such Calamity or Ill. Now, if his own Thoughts, or the corrupt Insinuations of other Men present it often to his Mind, *"That his* Honesty *is the Occasion of this Calamity,* and *that if he were deliver'd from this Restraint of* Virtue *and* Honesty, *he might be much happier":* 'Tis very obvious that his Esteem of these good Qualities must, in Proportion, diminish every Day, as the Temper grows uneasy, and quarrels with it-self. But, if he opposes to this Thought the Consideration, "That Honesty carries with it, if not *a present,* at least *a future* Advantage, such as to compensate that Loss of private Good which he regrets"; then may this Injury to his good Temper and honest Principle be prevented, and his Love or Affection towards Honesty and Virtue remain as it was before.

In the same manner, where instead of *Regard* or *Love,* there is rather *an Aversion* to what is good and virtuous (as, for Instance, where *Lenity* and *Forgiveness* are despis'd, and *Revenge* highly thought of, and belov'd) if there be this Consideration added, "That *Lenity* is, by its Rewards, made the cause of a greater Self-Good and Enjoyment than what is found in Revenge"; that very Affection of *Lenity* and *Mildness* may come to be industriously nourish'd, and the contrary Passion depress'd. And thus *Temperance, Modesty, Candour, Benignity,* and other good Affections, however despis'd at first, may come at last to be valu'd *for their own Sakes,* the contrary Species rejected, and the good and proper Object belov'd and prosecuted, when the Reward or Punishment is not so much as thought of.

Thus in *a civil* State or Publick, we see that a virtuous Administration, and an equal and just Distribution of Rewards and Punishments, is of the highest service; not only by restraining the Vitious, and forcing them to act usefully to Society; but by making Virtue to be apparently the Interest of every one, so as to remove all Prejudices against it, create a fair Reception for it, and lead Men into that Path which afterwards they cannot easily quit. For thus a People rais'd from Barbarity or despotick Rule, civiliz'd by Laws, and made virtuous by the long Course of a lawful and just Administration; if they chance to fall suddenly under any Misgovernment of unjust and arbitrary Power, they will on this Account be the rather animated to exert a stronger Virtue, in opposition to such Violence and Corruption. And even where, by long and continu'd Arts of a prevailing Tyranny, such a People are at last totally oppress'd, the scatter'd Seeds of Virtue will for a long time remain alive, even to a second Generation; e'er the utmost Force of misapply'd Rewards and Punishments can bring them to the abject and compliant State of long-accustom'd Slaves.

But, tho' a right Distribution of Justice in Government be so essential a cause of Virtue, we must observe in this Case, that it is *Example* which chiefly influences Mankind, and forms the Character and Disposition of a People. For a virtuous Administration is in a manner necessarily accompany'd with Virtue in the Magistrate. Otherwise it cou'd be of little effect; and of no long duration. But, where it is sincere and well-establish'd, there Virtue and the Laws must necessarily be respected and belov'd. So that as to Punishments and Rewards, their Efficacy is not so much from the Fear or Expectation which they raise, as from a natural Esteem of *Virtue,* and Detestation of *Villany,* which is awaken'd and excited by these publick Expressions of the Approbation and Hatred of Mankind in each Case. For in the publick Executions of the greatest Villains, we see generally that the Infamy and Odiousness of their Crime, and the Shame of it before Mankind, contribute more to their Misery than all besides; and that it is not the immediate Pain, or Death it-self, which raises so much Horror either in the Sufferers or Spectators, as that ignominious kind of Death which is inflicted for publick Crimes, and Violations of Justice and Humanity.

And as the Case of Reward and Punishment stands thus in the Publick, so, in the same manner, as to *private Families.* For Slaves and mercenary Servants, restrain'd and made orderly by Punishment, and the Severity of their Master, are not, on this account, made good or honest. Yet the same Master of the Family, using proper Rewards and gentle Punishments towards his Children, teaches them Goodness; and by this help instructs them in a Virtue, which afterwards they practice upon other Grounds, and without thinking of a Penalty or Bribe. And this is what we call *a Liberal Education* and *a Liberal Service:* The contrary Service and Obedience, whether towards God or Man, being *illiberal,* and unworthy of any Honour or Commendation.

In the Case of Religion, however, it must be consider'd, that if by the *Hope of Reward* be understood the Love and Desire of virtuous Enjoyment, or of the very Practice and Exercise of Virtue in another Life; the Expectation or Hope of this kind is so far from being derogatory to Virtue, that it is an Evidence of our loving it the more sincerely and *for its own sake.* Nor can this Principle be justly call'd *selfish:* For if the Love of Virtue be not mere Self-Interest, the Love and Desire of Life for Virtue's sake cannot be esteem'd so. But, if the Desire of Life be only thro' the Violence of that natural Aversion to Death; if it be thro' the Love of something else than virtuous Affection, or thro' the Unwillingness of parting with something else than what is purely of this kind; then is it no longer any sign or Token of real Virtue.

Thus a Person loving Life for Life's sake, and Virtue not at all, may, by the Promise or Hope of Life, and Fear of Death, or other Evil, be induc'd to practise Virtue, and even *endeavour* to be truly virtuous, by a Love of what he practises. Yet neither is *this very Endeavour* to be esteem'd *a Virtue.* For tho' he may intend to be virtuous; he is not become so, for having only intended, or aim'd at it, thro' Love of the Reward. But, as soon as he is come to have any Affection towards what is morally good, and can like or affect such Good *for its own sake,* as good and amiable *in it-self;* then is he in some degree good and virtuous, and not till then.

Such are the Advantages or Disadvantages which accrue to Virtue from Reflexion upon private Good or Interest. For, tho' the Habit of *Selfishness,* and the Multiplicity of *interested Views,* are of little Improvement to real *Merit* or *Virtue;* yet there is a Necessity for the Preservation of *Virtue,* that it should be thought to have no quarrel with *true Interest,* and *Self-Enjoyment.*

Whoever, therefore, by any strong Persuasion, or settled Judgment, thinks in the main, *That Virtue causes Happiness, and Vice Misery,* carries with him that Security and Assistance to Virtue which is requir'd. Or, tho' he has no such Thought, nor can believe Virtue his real Interest, either with respect to his own Nature and Constitution, or the Circumstances of human Life; yet, if he believes any Supreme Powers concern'd in the *present* Affairs of Mankind, and *immediately* interposing in behalf of the Honest and Virtuous, against the Impious and Unjust; this will serve to preserve in him, however, that just Esteem of Virtue, which might otherwise considerably diminish. Or should he still believe little of the *immediate* Interposition of Providence in the Affairs of *this present Life;* yet if he believes a God dispensing Rewards and Punishments to Vice and Virtue in *a future,* he carries with him still the same Advantage and Security; whilst his Belief is steddy, and no-wise wavering or doubtful. For it must be observ'd, that an Expectation and Dependency, so miraculous and great as this, must naturally take off from other inferior Dependencies and Encouragements. Where infinite Rewards are thus inforc'd, and the Imagination strongly turn'd towards them, the other common and natural Motives to Goodness are apt to be neglected, and lose much by Dis-use. Other Interests are hardly so much as computed, whilst the Mind is thus transported in the Pursuit of a high Advantage and Self-Interest, so narrowly confin'd within our-selves. On this account, all other Affections, towards Friends, Relations, or Mankind, are often slightly regarded, as being *worldly,* and of little moment, in respect of the Interest of *our Soul.* And so little thought is there of any immediate Satisfaction arising from such good Offices of Life, that it is customary with many devout People zealously to decry all temporal Advantages of Goodness, all natural Benefits of Virtue; and magnifying the contrary Happiness of a vitious State; to declare, "That, except only for the sake of future Reward, and fear of future Punishment, they would divest themselves of all Goodness at once, and freely allow themselves to be most immoral and profligate." From whence it appears, that in some respects there can be nothing more fatal to Virtue, than the weak and uncertain Belief of a future Reward and Punishment. For the Stress being laid wholly here, if this Foundation come to fail, there is no further Prop or Security to Men's Morals. And thus Virtue is supplanted and betray'd.[56]

Tho' the *disinterested Love of God* be the most excellent Principle, yet, by the indiscreet Zeal of some devout well-meaning People, it has been stretch'd too far, perhaps, even to Extravagance and Enthusiasm, as formerly among the *Mysticks* of the antient Church, whom these of

56. Ibid., II, pp. 54–69.

latter Days have follow'd. On the other hand, there have been those, who, in Opposition to this devout Mystick way, and as profess'd Enemies to what they call *Enthusiasm,* had so far exploded every thing of this ecstatick kind, as, in a manner, to have given up Devotion; and, in reality, have left so little of Zeal, Affection, or Warmth, in what they call their *rational Religion,* as to make them much suspected of their Sincerity in *any.* For, tho' it be natural enough for a mere political Writer to ground his great Argument for Religion, on the Necessity of such a relief, as that of a *Future Reward* and *Punishment;* yet 'tis a very ill Token of Sincerity in Religion, and in the *Christian* Religion more especially, to reduce it to such a Philosophy, as will allow no room to that other Principle of *Love;* but treats all of that Kind as *Enthusiasm,* for so much as aiming at what is call'd *Disinterestedness,* or teaching the *Love of God* or *Virtue* for God or Virtue's Sake.

Here, then, we have Two Sorts of People, who, in these opposite Extremes, expose *Religion* to the Insults of its Adversaries. For as, on one hand, 'twill be found difficult to defend the Notion of that high-rais'd Love, espous'd with so much Warmth by those devout *Mysticks;* so, on the other hand, 'twill be found as hard a Task, upon the Principles of these cooler Men, to guard Religion from the Imputation of Mercenariness, and a slavish Spirit. For how shall one deny, that to serve God by Compulsion, or for Interest merely, is *Servile* and *Mercenary?* Is it not evident, that the only *true* and *liberal* Service paid, either to that Supreme Being, or to any other Superior, is *that* "which proceeds from an *Esteem* or *Love* of the Person serv'd, *a Sense* of Duty or Gratitude, and a Love of the dutiful and grateful Part, as *good* and *amiable, in it-self?"* And where is the Injury to *Religion,* from such a Concession as this? Or what Detraction is it from the Belief of an After-Reward or Punishment, to own, "That the Service caus'd by it, is not equal to that which is *voluntary* and *with Inclination,* but is rather disingenuous and of the slavish kind?" Is it not still for the Good of Mankind and of the World, that Obedience to the Rule of Right should, some way or other, be paid; if not *in the better way,* yet, at least, *in this imperfect one?* And is it not to be shewn, "That, altho' this Service of *Fear* be allow'd ever so low or base: Yet RELIGION still being *a Discipline,* and *Progress* of the Soul towards Perfection, the Motive of Reward and Punishment is primary, and of the highest Moment with us; 'till being capable of more sublime Instruction, we are led from this *servile* State, to the generous Service of *Affection* and *Love?"*

To this we ought all of us to aspire, so as to endeavour, "That the *Excellence of the Object,* not the *Reward* or *Punishment,* should be our Motive: But that where, thro' the Corruption of our Nature, the *former* of these Motives is found insufficient to excite to Virtue, there the *latter* should be brought in Aid, and on no account be undervalu'd or neglected."

Now this being once establish'd, how can RELIGION be any longer subject to the Imputation of *Mercenariness?* But thus we know Religion is often charg'd. *"Godliness,* say they, *is great Gain:* Nor is GOD devoutly serv'd *for nought."*—Is this therefore a Reproach? Is it confess'd there may be *a better* Service, *a more generous* Love?—Enough, there needs no more. On this Foundation it is easy to defend Religion, and even that *devoutest Part,* which is esteem'd so great a Paradox of Faith. For, if there be in Nature such a Service as that of Affection and Love, there remains then only to consider of *the Object,* whether there be really that *Supreme-One* we suppose. For, if there be *Divine Excellence* in Things; if there be in Nature a *Supreme Mind* or Deity; we have then an Object consummate, and comprehensive of all which is *Good* or *Excellent.* And this Object, of all others, must of Necessity be the most amiable, the most engaging, and of highest Satisfaction and Enjoyment. Now, that there is such a principal Object as this in the World, the World alone (if I may say so) by its wise and perfect Order must evince. *Thus far the Lord* Shaftesbury.[57]

§IV. The Good, to which the Law of Nature, and the Discipline of Morality, instituteth, is the *good Life and Practice,* of which there are many Branches, the Notion whereof is compounded of Two Notions, *Beauteous-Beneficial.* As the Works of Nature, are therefore said to be *Good,* because the Make of them is *Beauteous-Beneficial.* *"For all the*

> That Good, to which the Law of Nature instituteth, is the *Beauteous-Beneficial.*

57. Ibid., II, pp. 271–74.

Parts of the World are so constituted, that they could not be better, either for Beauty or Usefulness."[58] The *Lacedemonians* had regard for both these, when they pray'd for *[oulchra cum bonis] Things good and comely.* The Antient Philosophers had regard to both these in their Definitions of Good and Evil. "*All the good things are those that are profitable, conducive, beauteous, comely, cognate; but the Evils are the contrary, those things that are hateful, noxious, incommodious, alien, uncomely, and foul.*" So Perfections in general, are ornamental, and useful, agreeably whereto the good Morals must be defin'd the *Beauteous-Beneficial.* "*The* Grecians, *most divinely*" (saith Judicious Mr. *Hooker*)[59] "*have given to the active Perfection of Men, a Name expressing both Beauty and Goodness* (καλοκ᾿ ἀγαθία) *because Goodness, in ordinary Speech, is for the most part applied only to that which is beneficial; but we, in the Name of Goodness, do here imply both.*" Good, therefore, in Morality, the good of Virtue, is τὸ καλοκ᾿ ἀγαθὸν *the Beauteous-Beneficial Life and Practice.* "Aristotle *teacheth that all the Virtues are compriz'd* τῇ καλοκ᾿ ἀγαθία, *in what is Beautifully-beneficent.*"[60]

Its Beauty; What is Beauteous is amiable, and is to be lik'd and lov'd; whence it is called τὸ καλὸν which signifieth it to be both *Beauteous* and *Good;* in both which Significations the Word is frequently us'd. Agreeably to this, the Nature of Good is to consist in these three things *in Modo, in Specie, in Ordine; in Measure, in Comeliness, in Order,* all which are certain Modes of Beauty.[61] "*The good of Honesty* [bonum honestum] *is laudable for its Beauty* and *Form.*[62] *Wherein appeareth an Ornament and gracefulness of Life, Temperance, Modesty, a quieting of Perturbations, and a due measure of things, which is* τὸ ωρέπον, *that which is decorous.*[63] *How*

58. Cicero, *De Natura Deorum,* II.

59. Hooker, *Of the Laws of Ecclesiastical Polity* (1594), I.

60. Maxwell's cryptic note [Casaub. Not. m. Matth. 22. 49] suggests Isaac Casaubon's contribution to *Novi Testamenti Libri Omnes recens nunc editi cum notis* (1587), but I have been unable to find the reference—Matthew 22 has only forty-six verses.

61. Aquinas, *Summa Theologica,* I. Qu. 5. Art. 5.

62. Cicero, *De Finibus,* II.

63. Ibid., *De Officiis,* I.

come we to understand what is Virtue? By seeing the Order and Decorum that is in it.[64] *Virtue is so graceful, that even bad Men approve of better things."*[65] Of the excellent Beauty of Justice *Aristotle* saith, "Neither the *Evening nor the Morning is so admirable.*[66] *Virtue sendeth its Light into the Minds of all, even they that are no Followers of it, yet see it."*[67] Virtue is an Honourableness, as well as Amiableness, of Practice, whence it hath the Name of *Honestas.* Vice and Wickedness is that which is *"foul, dishonest, indecorous, bad, flagitious, filthy,"*[68] that is, *Foulness* and *Deformity,* the *Crookedness* and *Obliquity* of Practice. The various Names, which the Philosophers, in concurrence with the generality of Mankind, have given to the virtuous practice, denote its Regularity and Beauty. τὸ εὖ, *that which is well,* τὸ δέον, *that which ought to be,* τὸ πρέπον, *that which is decorous,* τὸ ἴσον, *that which is equal,* τὸ καλὸν, *that which is fair,* τὸ ἁρμοζὸν, *that which is fit, congruous, proportionate,* τὸ Ὀρθὸν, *that which is right.*

We have all a Sense of what is *naturally graceful* and *becoming.* There is an Ear in Musick, an Eye in Painting, a Fancy in the ordinary things of Ornament and Grace, a Judgment in Proportions of all kinds; and a good Taste in most of those Subjects, which make the Amusement and Delight of the Ingenious.

How do we admire Beauty in the inanimate World, in Architecture, Musick, Stones, Metals, Vegetables, Mountains, Vales, Rivers; the terraqueous Globe, our whole solar System, and probably others like innumerable? Rising to the *animate* World, How do admire Beauty in a Dog, a Horse, a Hawk?

But, of all Beauties, the most delightful, the most engaging and pathetick, is that which is drawn from real Life, and from the Passions; such as the *Beauty of Sentiments,* the *Grace of Actions,* the *Turn of Characters,* and the *Proportions* and *Features of a human Mind.* What is the

64. Seneca, *Epistulae Morales,* C.
65. Ibid., *De Beneficiis,* IV.17.
66. Aristotle, *Nicomachean Ethics,* V.3.
67. Seneca, *De Beneficiis,* IV.17.
68. Cicero, *De Finibus,* III.

Beauty of Poetry, but, "In Vocal Measures of Syllables and Sounds to express the Harmony and Numbers of an inward Mind, and represent the Beauties of a Human Soul, by proper Foils and Contrarieties, which serve as Graces in this Limning, and render this Musick of the Passions more powerful and enchanting?"

Whoever has any Impression of what we call *Politeness,* is already so acquainted with the *Decorum* and *Grace* of Things, that he will readily confess a Pleasure and Enjoyment in every Survey and Contemplation of this Kind. Now, if in the way of Polite Pleasure, the *Study* and *Love of Beauty* be essential; the *Study* and *Love of Sympathy* and *Order,* on which *Beauty* depends, must also be essential in the same respect.

'Tis impossible we can advance the least in any *Relish* or *Taste* of outward Symmetry or Order, without acknowledging, that the proportionate and regular State, is the truly *Prosperous* and *Natural* in every Subject. The same Features, which make Deformity, create Incommodiousness and Disease. And the same Shapes and Proportions which make Beauty, afford Advantage, by adapting to Activity and Use. Even in the imitating or designing Arts, the *Truth* or *Beauty* of every Figure or Statue is measured from the Perfection of Nature, in her just adapting of every Limb and Proportion to the Activity, Strength, Dexterity, Life and Vigor of the particular Species or Animal design'd.

All *Beauty is Truth.* *True* Features make the Beauty of the Face, and *True* Proportions the Beauty of Architecture, as *True* Measures that of Harmony and Musick.

Thus *Beauty* and *Truth* are plainly join'd with the Notion of *Utility* and *Convenience,* even in the Apprehension of every ingenious Artist, the *Architect,* the *Statuary,* and the *Painter.* 'Tis the same in the *Physicians* Way. Natural Health is the just Proportion, *Truth,* and regular course of Things, in a Constitution. 'Tis the *inward Beauty of the Body.* And when the Harmony and just Measures of the rising Pulses, the circulating Humours, and the Spirits are disturbed or lost, Deformity enters, and with it Calamity and Ruin.

Should not this, one would imagine, be still the same Case, and hold equally as to the *Mind?* Is there nothing *there,* which tends to Disturbance and Dissolution? Is there no Natural Tenor, Tone or Order of the

Passions? No *Beauty* or *Deformity* in this *Moral* kind? or, allowing that there really is, must it not of consequence, in the same manner, imply *Health* or *Sickness*, Prosperity or Disaster? Will it not be found in this respect above all, "That what is Harmonious and Proportionable, is *True;* and what is at once both *Beautiful* and *True,* is, of consequence, *Agreeable* and *Good*"?

There is nothing more certain, than that a real *Genius,* and thorow *Artist,* in whatever kind, can never without the greatest Unwillingness and shame, be induc'd to act below his Character, and for mere Interest, be prevail'd with to prostitute his Art or Science, by performing contrary to its known Rules. Whoever has hear'd any thing of the Lives of famous *Statuaries, Architects,* or *Painters,* will call to Mind many Instances of this Nature. Or whoever has made any Acquaintance with the better Sort of Mechanicks, such as are real Lovers of their Art, and Masters in it, must have observ'd their Natural Fidelity in this respect. Be they ever so idle, dissolute or debauch'd; how regardless soever of other Rules; they abhor any Transgression *in their Art,* and would chuse to lose Customers and starve, rather than, by a base Compliance with the World, to act contrary to what they call the *Justness* and *Truth of Work.*

"Sir, (said a poor Fellow of this kind to his rich Customer,) You are mistaken in coming to me, for such a Piece of Workmanship. Let who will make it for you, as you fancy; I know it to be *Wrong.* Whatever I have made hitherto, has been *true Work.* And neither for your sake or any bodies else, shall I put my Hand to any other."

This is Virtue! *real Virtue,* and Love of Truth; independent of *Opinion,* and above the *World.* This Disposition transferr'd to the whole of *Life,* perfects a *Character,* and makes that *Probity* and *Worth,* which the Learned are often at such a loss to explain. For, is there not a *Workmanship,* and a *Truth* in *Actions?* Or is the *Workmanship* of this kind less becoming, or less worthy of our Notice; that we should not in this Case be as surly as the honest *Artizan,* who has no other Philosophy, than what *Nature* and his *Trade* have taught him?

Who can admire the *outward* Beauties; and not recur instantly to the *inward,* which are the more real and essential, the more naturally affecting, and of the highest Pleasure, as well as Profit and Advantage? Of which the *Roman Orator* thus expresses himself. "Honestum *is what may be justly Commended upon its own Account, tho' destitute of any Advantage or Reward; which what it is, cannot be so well understood from any Definition as from the common Sentiments of Mankind; from the Pursuits and from the Actions of the Virtuous, who do many things for no other Reason, but because it is Decent, Right, Honest, tho' they see no Advantage to ensue.*" The Men of Pleasure, who seem the greatest Contemners of this Philosophical Pleasure, are found often to confess her Charms; they can as heartily as others commend *Honesty,* and are as much struck with the Beauty of a *generous Part.* See Ld. *Shaftesbury's* Characteristicks Vol. 1. p. 135 &c. p. 142. p. 261, 262. Vol. 3. p. 182, &c. See also a further Explanation and Defence of these Principles by the Author of the *Inquiry into the Original of our Ideas of Beauty and Virtue.*[69]

Its Bene-
ficialness.
§V. *Virtue* is likewise the *good Life and Practice,* upon account of its *Beneficialness* and Utility, to which some have erroneously confin'd the Notion of *Good.* But, without confining thereto the Notion of *Good,* the Philosophers observe, "That Good, in common Acceptation, is Profit." Which is agreeable to the common Sense of Mankind; for we all desire Profit. In their private Capacity, Mankind are intent upon their private Profit, and in their publick Capacity, upon their common Profit; for Laws are made for the common Profit, which is the End of the Society. What is profitable and beneficial, useful and needful, altho' it be only wholesome, not sightly nor pleasant, for sufficient Cause and Reason ought to be liked, and is therefore *Good.* "*He is a good Man* (saith *Cicero*[70]) *who profiteth whom he can, is hurtful to none.*" The several Branches of Vice are *mischievous* and *maleficial,* simply and absolutely. In enormous Selfishness, Malevolence, Pride, Ambition, Fraud, Guile, Perfidiousness, Envy, Avarice, Circumvention, Wrath, Enmity, Calumny, Theft, Cruelty, Homicide, Profaneness and Contempt of God, and in all unjust and uncharitable Actions, there is a deadly Maleficent

69. Hutcheson, *An Inquiry into the Original of Our Ideas of Beauty and Virtue* (1726).
70. Cicero, *De Officiis,* III.

Deformity. The Definition, therefore, of the vicious *Life and Practice,* is the *foul and ill-favour'd maleficial;* as, on the contrary, the virtuous Life and Practice is the *Beauteous-Beneficial.* All the Branches of it are *absolutely beneficial,* and not only of Utility, but indispensible Necessity, to the Happiness of every one and of all. Thus *Purity* and *Charity* are, in Religion, inseparably connected, and the Connexion of them is a joining Beauty with Beneficialness. Now, tho' the *Beneficialness* of the good Life may, in a large Acceptation of Beauty, be call'd the *Beauteousness* thereof; yet, in the strict Acceptation, these are distinguish'd, as the Beauty of the Rose is distinguish'd from its Medicinal Virtue.

He, therefore, is the *good* Man, who is *voluntarily benevolent to others thro' goodness of Affection,* whence it will be proper to examine, which are the *good* and *natural,* and which the *ill* and *unnatural,* Affections, which I find already excellently-well done to my Hand by the noble Author lately quoted. *Charact.* Vol. 2. Pag. 22, &c.

In the first Place then, it may be observ'd, that if there be an Affection towards any Subject consider'd as private Good, which is not really such, but imaginary; this Affection, as being superfluous, and detracting from the Force of other requisite and good Affections, is in it-self vitious and ill, even in respect of the private Interest or Happiness of the Creature.

If there can possibly be suppos'd in a Creature such an Affection towards Self-Good, as is actually, in its natural degree, conducing to his private Interest, and at the same time inconsistent with the publick Good; this may indeed be call'd still a vitious Affection: And on this Supposition a Creature cannot really be good and natural in respect of his Society or Publick, without being ill and unnatural towards Himself. But if the Affection be then only injurious to the Society, when it is immoderate, and not so when it is moderate, duly temper'd, and allay'd; then is the *immoderate* degree of the Affection truly vitious, but not the *moderate.* And thus, if there be found in any Creature a more than ordinary Self-Concernment, or Regard to private Good, which is inconsistent with the Interest of the Species or Publick; this must in every respect be esteem'd an ill and vitious Affection. And this is what we commonly call SELFISHNESS, and disapprove so much, in whatever Creature we happen to discover it.

On the other side, if the Affection towards private or Self-Good, how-ever *selfish* it may be esteem'd, is in reality not only consistent with pub-lick Good, but in some measure contributing to it; if it be such, perhaps, as for the good of the Species in general, every Individual ought to share: 'Tis so far from being ill, or blameable in any sense, that it must be ac-knowledg'd absolutely necessary to constitute a Creature *Good.* For, if the Want of such an Affection as that towards Self-Preservation, be in-jurious to the Species; a Creature is ill and unnatural, as well thro' this Defect, as thro' the Want of any other natural Affection. And this no-one would doubt to pronounce, if he saw a Man, who minded not any Precipices which lay in his way, nor made any Distinction of Food, Diet, Cloathing, or whatever else related to his Health and Being. The same would be averr'd of one, who had a Disposition which render'd him averse to any Commerce with Womankind, and of consequence unfitted him thro' *Illness of Temper* (and not merely thro' *a Defect of Constitution*) for the Propagation of his Species or Kind.

Thus the Affection towards Self-Good, may be a good Affection, or an ill-one. For, if this private Affection be too strong, (as when *the ex-cessive Love of Life* unfits a Creature for any generous Act,) then is it undoubtedly vitious; and if vitious, the Creature who is mov'd by it, is vitiously mov'd, and can never be otherwise than vitious in some degree, when mov'd by that Affection. Therefore, if thro' such an earnest and passionate *Love of Life,* a Creature be accidentally induc'd to do Good (as he might be upon the same terms induc'd to do ILL) he is no more a good Creature for this Good he executes, than a Man is the more an honest or good Man, either for pleading a just Cause, or fighting in a good one, for the sake merely of his Fee or Stipend.

Whatsoever therefore is done which happens to be advantageous to the Species, thro' an Affection merely towards Self-Good, does not imply any more Goodness in the Creature, than as the Affection it-self is good. Let him, in any particular, act ever so well; if at the bottom, it be that selfish Affection alone which moves him; he is in himself still vitious. Nor can any Creature be consider'd otherwise, when the Passion towards Self-Good, tho' ever so moderate, is his real Motive in the doing that, to which a natural Affection for his Kind ought by right to have inclin'd him.

And indeed whatever exteriour Helps or Succours an ill-dispos'd Creature may find, to push him on towards the performance of any one good Action; there can no Goodness arise in him 'till his *Temper* be so far chang'd, that in the Issue he comes in earnest to be led by some immediate Affection, *directly,* and not *accidentally,* to Good, and against Ill.

For Instance; If one of those Creatures suppos'd to be by Nature tame, gentle, and favourable to Mankind, be, contrary to his natural Constitution, fierce and savage; we instantly remark the Breach of *Temper,* and own the Creature to be unnatural and corrupt. If at any time afterwards, the same Creature, by good Fortune or right Management, comes to lose his Fierceness, and is made tame, gentle, and treatable, like other Creatures of his Kind; 'tis acknowledg'd that the Creature thus restor'd, becomes good and natural. Suppose, now, that the Creature has indeed a tame and gentle Carriage; but that it proceeds only from *the Fear* of *his Keeper;* which is set aside, his predominant Passion instantly breaks out: Then is his Gentleness not his real Temper; but his true and genuine *Nature* or *Natural Temper* remaining just as it was, the Creature is still as *ill* as ever.

Nothing therefore being properly either Goodness or Illness in a Creature, except what is from *natural Temper;* "A good Creature is such a one as by the natural Temper or Bent of his Affections is carry'd *primarily and immediately,* and not *secondarily and accidentally,* to Good, and against Ill": And an *ill Creature* is just the contrary; *viz.* "One who is wanting in right Affections, of force enough to carry him *directly* towards Good, and bear him out against Ill; or who is carry'd by other Affections directly to Ill, and against Good."

When in general, all the Affections or Passions are suited to the publick Good, or Good of the Species, as above-mention'd; then is the *natural Temper* intirely good. If, on the contrary, any requisite Passion be wanting; or if there be any one supernumerary, or weak, or anywise disserviceable or contrary to that main End; then is the natural Temper, and consequently the Creature himself, in some measure, corrupt and *ill.*

There is no need of mentioning either *Envy, Malice, Frowardness,* or other such hateful Passions; to shew in what manner they are ill, and constitute an *ill* Creature. But it may be necessary perhaps to remark, that even as *Kindness* and *Love* of the most natural sort (such as that of any Creature for its Offspring) if it be immoderate and beyond a certain degree, is undoubtedly vitious. For thus over-great *Tenderness* destroys the Effect of Love, and excessive *Pity* renders us uncapable of giving succour. Hence the Excess of motherly Love is own'd to be a *vitious Fondness;* over-great Pity, *Effeminacy and Weakness;* over-great Concern for Self-preservation, *Meanness and Cowardice;* too little, *Rashness;* and none at all, or that which is contrary (*viz.* a Passion leading to Self-destruction) a *mad* and *desperate Depravity.*

We know that every Creature has a private Good and Interest of his own; which Nature has compell'd him to seek, by all the Advantages afforded him, within the Compass of his Make. We know that there is in Reality a right and a wrong State of every Creature; and that his right-one is by Nature forwarded, and by Himself affectionately sought. There being therefore in every Creature a certain *Interest* or *Good;* there must be also a certain End, to which every thing in his Constitution must *naturally* refer. To this End if any thing either in his Appetites, Passions, or Affections be not conducing, but the contrary; we must of necessity own it *ill* to him. And in this manner he is *ill, with respect to himself;* as he certainly is, *with respect to others of his kind,* when any such Appetites or Passions make him any-way injurious to them. Now, if by the natural Constitution of any rational Creature, the same Irregularities of Appetite which make him ill *to Others,* make him ill also to *Himself;* and if the same Regularity of Affections, which causes him to be good in *one* sense, causes him to be good also in *the other;* then is that Goodness by which he is thus useful to others, a real Good and Advantage to himself. And thus *Virtue* and *Interest* may be found at last to agree. So far Ld. *Shaftesbury.*[71] This *Cumberland* has set in a clear and a strong Light.

"*We ought* (saith *Gassendus* in his Treatise concerning the moral Philosophy of *Epicurus)*[72] *to admire the Contrivance of the most wise Author of Nature, who, because all Action, even the most Natural, such as Seeing*

---

71. Shaftesbury, *Characteristicks,* II, pp. 15, 16.
72. Maxwell is referring to Gassendi's *Philosophiae Epicuri Syntagma* (1649).

and Hearing, was in it-self laborious and troublesome, which Use makes so
familiar to us as to become insensible, hath therefore season'd every Operation
with the Blandishment of Pleasure, and that so much the greater, by how
much the Action it-self was more Necessary, whether to the Preservation of
the Species, or of the Individual. Animals would either not care, or they
would forget, or not take Notice, at what times it might be proper to prop-
agate, their Species, or to Eat and Drink for prolonging the Life of the In-
dividual, unless they were naturally spurr'd by an uneasiness exciting them
to such Operations, whose concomitant Pleasure takes that uneasiness away,
whence we are naturally allur'd to such Actions." This seems to be the true
Reason, why the Deity has made such Actions Pleasurable, as we ought
to do, were no such Pleasure connected with them.

Suppose a Brute possess'd of many good Affections, as Love to his
Kind, Courage, Gratitude, or Pity. If to this Animal Reason and Reflexion were added, it would at the same instant approve of Gratitude,
Kindness and Pity; and this would be *Virtue,* this would be the having
a Sense of Right and Wrong, when *Worth* and Honesty as such, were the
Objects of his Affection; which one may do, before they have any settled
Notions of a Deity, which early Youth, and the more unciviliz'd Nations,
do not much refine upon, who yet are not void of a just Notion of Good
and Evil, Right and Wrong.

If by Temper any one is passionate, angry, fearful, amorous; yet resists
these Passions, his *Virtue* is the greater, provided his resistance arise from
his Affection towards Virtue it-self, not from Self-Interest, as is already
prov'd. Yet Propensity to Vice is no ingredient in Virtue, or any-way
necessary to compleat a virtuous Character. If there be any part of the
Temper in which ill Passions or Affections are seated, whilst in another
part the Affections towards moral Good are such as absolutely to master
those Attempts of their Antagonists; this is the greatest *Proof* imaginable, that a strong Principle of Virtue lies at the bottom, and has possess'd it-self of the natural Temper. Whereas if there be no ill Passions
stirring, a Person may be indeed more *cheaply virtuous;* that is to say, he
may conform himself to the known Rules of Virtue, without sharing so
much of a virtuous Principle as another. Yet if that other Person, who
has the Principle of Virtue so strongly implanted, comes at last to lose

those contrary Impediments suppos'd in him, he certainly loses nothing in Virtue; but on the contrary, losing only what is vitious in his Temper, is left more intire to Virtue, and possesses it in a higher degree. So far Lord *Shaftesbury.*[73]

To it the Names of Praise and Commendation belong.

§VI. If the *Beauteous-Beneficial* is the *good Life and Practice,* the Names of *Praise and Commendation necessarily belong to it;* for what is Good, compriseth in it-self all Praise and Commendation: And to the contrary Life and Practice, the Names of Odiousness and Disgrace, of Infamy and Dispraise belong. *"What is dispraisable for it-self, is upon that account named Vice."*[74] And *"The Good of Honesty is that which maketh them Praise-worthy, that have this Good worthy of Praise."*[75] The Operations of Virtue are called the *laudable Operations.* To understand what is Virtue and what is Vice, a great Philosopher prescribeth a Young Man this Method. *"Consider what sort of Men it is, that you praise, when you are unbyas'd with any Affection: Is it the Just or the Unjust? The Just. Is it the Temperate, or Intemperate? The Temperate. Is it the Continent or Incontinent? The Continent."*[76] Virtue is, therefore, the *laudable Practice,* and thence it is, that all Mankind would be in some sort reputed Virtuous. *"For who is there that would not seem Beneficent? That doth not desire to be accounted good in the midst of all his atrocious Villanies and Injuries? That doth not put some colour of Right upon those things that he hath done most outrageously?"*[77]

The good Life and Practice is also *excellent* and *Productive of the Happiness of others;* otherwise it were not *Praise-worthy;* upon which account, ordinary self-regard for our own Happiness is not Virtue. *"To Love one's self, to Spare one's self, to get to one's self; what is there excellent in so doing?"*[78]

The good Life and Practice is also the *Honourable* and *Comfortable.* There is a *Dignity* in it, which exempts its Possessors from being *Vile,*

73. Shaftesbury, *Characteristicks,* II, pp. 37, 38.
74. Cicero, *De Finibus,* III.
75. Diogenes Laertius, "Zeno" in *Lives,* VII.
76. Epictetus, *Discourses,* III.1.
77. Seneca, *De Beneficiis,* IV.17.
78. Ibid., IV.14.

and affords Comforts of another sort than the Pleasures of Sin do; those Substantial vital Enjoyments, which are infinitely Comfortable.

The good Life and Practice is also the *true Perfection* of Man. As all Beings have their Perfection by their proper Virtue, which is their Nature raised to its Height, such as Sharpness of Sight is in the Eye, Quickness of Hearing in the Ear, Swiftness in the Feet; So the *good Life* and Practice is the proper Virtue of Man, raised to its Height and Perfection.

The good Life and Practice must not be thought merely a Publick self-Convenience, which is necessary for Men, only because of the necessity of their Affairs, but it is the doing what is *simply and absolutely convenient.* *"Wisdom is a doing what is convenient—As a Stage-player must not have any, but a certain Action; and a Dancer must not have any, but a certain Motion: So a Man must live not any, but a certain kind of Life, which we call Convenient and Consentaneous."*[79]

The *Beauteous-Beneficial* Life and Practice is likewise *Righteousness,* which is a threefold Comprehension of Duty, as *to God, to others and to our-Selves;* Piety towards God, Justice and Charity towards Men, and Sobriety, as to our-selves. Hence we may resolve a celebrated Question in Morality, *What is the Rule and Measure of Good and Evil, Just and Unjust?* For Righteousness is the Rule and Measure of Practice, all intelligent Agents must be regulated by it; but of Righteousness there is not properly any Rule or Measure but its own Nature, which is the *Beauteous-Beneficial Life and Practice, consider'd as that which ought to be.* This is the *Rule and Measure of Righteousness constitutively such.* But, beside this, there may be a Rule and Measure of Righteousness *evidentially and declaratively such.* The common Opinion is, "That right Reason is the Rule and Measure of Good and Evil." Which may signify, that the Discernments and Dictates of Reason are only *evidentially and declaratively* the Rule and Measure of Good and Evil; as a positive Law is, in Matters of positive Institution, *constitutively* the Measure of Good and Evil. In this latter Sense, the right Discernments and Dictates of Reason are not the Rule and Measure of Good and Evil, as they are not in such Sense, the Rule and Measure of Good Air, or Good Medicines.

The Rule and Measure of Good and Evil.

79. Cicero, *De Finibus,* III.

As things are not true, so neither are they right and good, because they are conformable to Reason: But Reason is therefore right and good, because it is conformable to the Things that are so. This, therefore, is not a good Definition; *That which is agreeable to a rational Intelligent Nature, as it is such, is Good; That which is dissentaneous or disagreeable to it, is Evil.* For *Good* is not to be accommodated to a *rational Nature,* but the rational Nature is to be accommodated to Good, and its Reason is then right, when it *rightly discerneth between Good and Evil.* Some suppose, that the *Happiness of the System of Rational Agents, is the Sole End and Measure of Good:* But this Opinion maketh Virtue to be Policy, rather than Virtue. The only Rule and Measure of Good and Evil is the *Beauteous-Beneficial Practice,* and the various means of discerning what is so; but the *common Happiness* of the whole, rightly understood, may be counted the *Measure* of it as it is *Beneficial.*

§VII. A Mistake, touching the Rule and Measure of Good and and Evil, of greater Importance than any of these, is this; "That the Arbitrary Will of God is constitutively the adequate Rule and Measure of Good and Evil, Just and Unjust, and that nothing is Good or Evil, but because it is commanded or forbidden." With which absurd Notion, Bp. *Taylor* falleth in, affirming, *"That nothing is just or unjust, of it-self, until some Law of God or Man doth supervene. God cannot do an unjust thing; because whatsoever he willeth or doeth, is therefore Just, because he willeth and doeth it, his Will being the Measure of Justice. It is but a weak Distinction, to affirm, some things to be forbidden by God, because they are unlawful, and some to be unlawful, because they are forbidden. For this last part of the Distinction taketh in all that is unlawful in the World, and therefore the other is a dead Member, and may be lopp'd off.* So Occham affirmeth *against the common Sentence of the Schools, (as his manner is,)* Nullus est actus malus, nisi quatenus a Deo prohibitus est, & qui non potest fieri bonus, si a Deo praecipiatur &c converso: *Every thing is good or bad, according as it is commanded or forbidden by God, and no otherwise."* [80] These Sayings are attended with a self-Contradiction, *"That it is actually and*

The Arbitrary Will of God is not the Rule and Measure of Good and Evil.

80. Taylor, *Ductor Dubitantium* (1660), II.1, no. 4, 52, 58.

indispensably necessary, that we love God, and that he cannot Command us to hate him."[81] And 'tis but reasonable, that they should contradict themselves, who contradict Common Sense, and contemplate *Goodness* at the same rate of Extravagance, that some others contemplate *Truth,* who affirm, "*That God indeed does necessarily conceive those Truths, which immediately relate to himself, his Nature, Essence, and Attributes: He was never indifferent as to these; but as for all other Truths, which are not God himself, these wholly depend upon the most free and arbitrary Determination of his own Will, and are only therefore true, because he appointed them to be so; and that there might, if God had so pleased, either have been none of these at all, or else quite different from what they now are.*"[82] If Truth is of so indeterminate a Nature, Good must be as Arbitrary, as some say, "*That by the mere Light of Nature, without Divine Revelation, it cannot be made appear, that there is any difference between Vice and Virtue; altho' we were assur'd, that there is a God. That nothing is Just and Good, but that only, which he commandeth, and for no other Reason, but because he doeth so.*"[83] They that discourse at this rate, are extremely deficient, either in their Reason, or in their Religion. According to this Scheme, Law is suppos'd to make Justice, whereas, without antecedent Justice, it is impossible, that there can be any made Law. For no Law can be made, but by one, who hath Right to be obey'd, and to whom Obedience is due: Right and due Obedience, and consequently Just and Unjust, is necessarily antecedent to any made Law. If nothing is Unrighteous, but by a made Law, Mankind must be consider'd, as perfectly at Liberty and un-obliged, antecedently to that Law; and, if we suppose them to be perfectly at Liberty and un-obliged, then that Law could not oblige them; for no Command or Prohibition can oblige them to Obedience, who are Persons perfectly at Liberty and unoblig'd. Nor can they oblige themselves by any Pacts or Covenants of their own making; for, if there be nothing in its own Nature Unjust, it cannot be in its own Nature an unjust thing,

81. Ibid., Rule 9, no. 12.

82. Poiret, *Cogitationum Rationalium de Deo* (1685), III.10; Descartes, *Epistolae* (1668), pt. I, no. 37.

83. Cuper, *Arcan Atheism,* II.10. I have not been able to identify this text.

to break their own Pacts and Covenants, but they may unmake them, as fast as they make them. And, consequently, if we suppose them, to be once perfectly at Liberty and unoblig'd, they must for ever continue, so, if there be nothing unjust in its own Nature. If nothing is, essentially and in its own Nature, unrighteous, there is nothing so bad, which God may not do, (lye and deny himself, condemn the Obedient and reward the Disobedient;) there is nothing so Wicked, which God may not command, (Atheism, Blasphemy, Demonolatry, Fraud, Cruelty;) and a System of Moral Truths, Virtues, and Duties, might be made, by Divine Appointment, just contrary to those which are now such; and, by arbitrary Will and Appointment, all manner of Wickedness would be Righteousness; Good would be Evil, and Evil Good: But, if Religion and Virtue were thus destroy'd, God himself would be destroy'd, for, *without Virtue, God is but a Name.* If God is essentially Good and Holy, a good and holy Nature and Life is essential to God; which is, therefore, not a mere Arbitrary Determination of the Divine Will. The several Attributes of Benignity, Mercy, Justice, Veracity, Faithfulness, and such like, as they are in God, are that which is essentially and in its own Nature Good; therefore they are so, as they are in Man.

Nor of Truth.   If God, by his free Appointment, did not make this Proposition to be a Truth, "A Being absolutely perfect is necessarily-existent"; it is a fond Imagination, to suppose, that by his free Appointment, the like self-evident Propositions are made Truths. The Mind clearly discerneth, that this is essential to the Whole, *to be bigger than the Part;* that it is essential to a Cause, *To be, in Order of Nature, before the Effect;* that it is essential to a plain Triangle, *To have its three Angles equal to two right ones;* these are therefore *necessary, unchangeable and eternal Truths.* But whatever the Mind clearly perceives to be repugnant to the essential Nature of Things, that she calleth *Impossible* and a *Contradiction,* which is as repugnant to Conception as it is to Reality, and which determines the extent, even of Power omnipotent; for it can do nothing that is a Contradiction or impossible.

Which are such antece-   §VIII. *Bonum Honestum* or Virtue is, not a mere Name, but hath its proper specific Nature, which is the *Beauteous-Beneficial Practice,* as is already prov'd; which it is as certain, that this Name, [*Virtue*] denotes, as that the Word [*Man*] denotes a *Rational Animal,* or that a *Square* signifies *a Plain Figure with Four equal sides and right Angles. Moral Good* is, therefore, the *Beauteous-Beneficial Practice* essentially and in its own Nature, and consequently it is *necessarily, unchangeably, eternally* so. "*Order, Measure, Comeliness, Pulchritude, Elegance, and Congruity of Parts, which no Animal but Man discerneth, Reason transferreth to the Mind, and thinketh, that they ought to be observed there, and the Observance of them is that which maketh that* Honestas, *which is in its own Nature laudable.*"[84] If therefore Beauty, Pulchritude, Order, Measure, Congruity, Proportion, are not wholly of Arbitrary Determination and Institution, not variable at pleasure, but of a fix'd determinate Nature; if in Pulchritude of Body there must be a certain Figure, Order, and Symmetry of Parts; if in a good and Virtuous Soul there must be such an orderly Subordination of Parts, as there is in a well-order'd City; hence it appeareth, that the Good in Morality, is that which is essentially and in its own Nature such, and is not a matter of Arbitrary Determination. In several instances, indeed, Mankind are of different Sentiments, touching what is graceful and handsome, regular and beautiful; yet none can deny, that the natural Position and Situation of the Parts of the Face is Beautiful, and that a Distortion of them is hideously ill-favour'd. Such Deformities of the Body are a faint resemblance of those of the Mind. And as the politer part of Mankind are extremely averse to any Filthiness or Deformity of Body; so in the truly-virtuous there is greater Aversion to any Vice in the Mind. "*Take not, says Temperance, whence it becometh not, Eat not, Drink not; sustain, endure, nay, rather die, than commit any thing contrary to Decorum.*"[85] So much for *Virtue* in its *Beauteous* Light.

The Good in Morality, as it is the *Beneficial* Kind of Practice, is that which is *Essentially and in its own Nature Good,* and is not of arbitrary Institution. "*Charity, Peace, Brotherly Love are Good, not only, because God hath commanded them, or willed us to follow them: But God, by his Law, doth will and command us to follow after those things, because they were*

dently to the Divine Appointment.

---

84. Cicero, *De Officiis,* I.
85. Sharrock, *De Officiis,* ch. 2, n. 9.

always Good, even before he willd or commanded us to follow them. The Time will never be, wherein Innocency, Brotherly-Love, Charity, Peace and Loving-Kindness shall be as displeasing to God, as Murder, Hatred, Malice, Cruelty and Uncharitableness hitherto always have been. He cannot enact a Law, either to authorize these or the like Practices, or to prohibit the contrary Virtues.[86] *Whoever thinks there is a God, and pretends formally to believe that he is just and good, must suppose that there is independently such a thing as Justice and Injustice, Truth and Falshood, Right and Wrong; according to which he pronounces that God is just, righteous and true. If the mere Will, Decree, or Law of God, be said absolutely to constitute Right and Wrong, then are these latter Words of no Significancy at all. For thus, if each Part of a Contradiction were affirm'd for Truth by the supreme Power, they would consequently become true. Thus, if one were decreed to suffer for another's Fault, the Sentence would be just and equitable. And thus, in the same manner, if arbitrarily, and without Reason, some Beings were destin'd to perpetual Ill, and others as constantly to enjoy Good; this also would pass under the same Denomination. But to say of any thing, that it is just or unjust, on such a Foundation as this, is to say nothing, or to speak without a meaning."*[87] If a City maketh Laws and Statutes, which seem to them profitable, yet, really, they may be pernicious; for Things are not profitable and hurtful, merely in our Opinion, but they are really and in their own Nature such; and a Law cannot make Things noxious to be wholesome. Theft, Adultery, falsifying Wills, (Crimes forbidden by the moral Law,) can never be made innocent or salutary by any Votes or Statutes, as the contrary Virtues cannot, by any Authority whatsoever, be made Evil. The Virtue of the *Eye,* or of a *Watch,* is their *Beauteous-beneficial* Properties, which is their Goodness and Perfection, and their Aptitude for their End and Use, and no other Properties can constitute a *good Eye* or a *good Watch:* So the Virtue of intelligent Agents is the *Beauteous-beneficial Life and Practice,* which is their Goodness and Perfection, and their Aptitude for their End and Use; and no other Life and Practice can

86. Jackson, *The Works of the Reverend and Learned Divine, Thomas Jackson* (1653), B. 10. th. 89. p.m. 3180.

87. Shaftesbury, *The Moralists, a Philosophical Rhapsody,* pp. 49, 50.

possibly constitute them good, or good Agents, that is, *the Well-doers, and not the Evil-doers.* Whence, in the Nature and Reason of the Thing, it is indispensably requisite in all intelligent Agents, and is to them *matter of Law or Obligation.* For *Law* or *Obligation* (in a large but very proper Sense) is nothing else, but a *Non licet,* or a Boundary to License. Thus, according to *Aristotle,* ὁ νόμος το μέσον, *Measure is Law,* ἡ τάξις νόμος, *Concinnity of Order is Law,* so *Plato* saith in his *Gorgias.* *"As the ordinate Dispositions of the Body are called Health: So this Name Law and Legitimate belongeth to the ordinate Dispositions and Ornaments of the Soul, (whence Men become Legitimate and Decorous,) which are Justice and Temperance."* The Rules of Musick, by which the Measures of Singing and Playing are determin'd were call'd by the *Greeks* Νόμοι, *Laws,* from those Bounds which the Musicians of old prescrib'd for the tuning of Voices and Instruments, they observing in every *Nomus, its proper Intention. "They were call'd Nomi* (Laws) *because in every one of them it was not lawful to transgress the prescrib'd* (νενομισμένον) *sort of Intention."* [88] If the old Musicians had prescrib'd no Rules of Musick, yet there would be unavoidably Laws of Musick in their own Nature such, without the Observance whereof there could be no Singing or Playing well: So in the Discipline of Morality, if no Law were made by a Superior Authority, yet some Practices would be notic'd to the Mind *as Well-doing, that cannot be left undone without Crime,* and the contrary *as Evil-doing,* which Notices are necessarily Laws, as being *Boundaries to License.* Human Practice must be the *Good,* in one Sense; it must be the *Beauteous-beneficial,* or it cannot be the *Good,* in the other Sense, *that which is to be lik'd.* Nothing is done, as it ought to be, unless it be well done, and a Mechanick Work is not well done, unless it is *Beauteous-beneficial;* the Works and Doings of Men, therefore, ought to be of that Character.

§IX. The Beauteous-beneficial Life and Practice is *Righteousness,* not only in respect of the Agent, as being what he ought to do, but in respect of the Objects, as being that which ought to be done to them, and a giving them what is their Right and Due. *Jus suum cuique tribuit.* There-

The good Life and Practice is the just Practice towards all the Objects of Practice.

88. Plutarch, *De Musica* (in *Moralia*), pp. 1132, 1133.

fore this Life and Practice may not unfitly be call'd, *the just Life and Practice,* (the opposite to the injurious,) which, being a Debt unto all, is, therefore, the Good of Duty to all, and such Duty, as is not of arbitrary Appointment, but is *natural and necessary Justice,* that which, in its own Nature, is Right and Due, Just and Good; the Rights and Dues of the Universe of Rational Agents being *Necessary, Immutable,* and *Eternal.* For such are the Right and Dues of God, of the natural Relations of Parents and Children; and that the Rights and Dues of Mankind in general are such, will appear by considering a Summary of the Philosophers Discipline of Virtue. Moral Philosophy, in the first place, adjusteth the Rates of Things, allotting to all Things that Measure of Esteem, which belongs to them: And, in the next place, it takes care, that the Bent of the Soul about them (wherewith the Actions must accord) be ordinate, proportionate, and agreeable to the Dignity of the Things. Whence the virtuous Life necessarily becomes *Beauteous;* for Order, Measure, Congruity, Proportion and Symmetry are Beauteous things, and the Rectitude of the Soul, in duly valuing and affecting the things Divine and Excellent, and duly depreciating the Vile, is also a Nobleness of Nature, an Excellency and Pulchritude of the Soul: Hence, also, the virtuous Man reapeth this inestimable *Utility* and *Benefit,* he escapeth those Snares, whereby Men are drawn to the vile and maleficent Practices. For the vitious Opinions that Men have of secular Honour, Riches and Pleasure, are the Fountain of the greatest Part of flagitious Practices. Therefore, towards Man, *do those Things which are according to his Dignity,* which Valuation is his Due. Accordingly, he is so valued in the *Beauteous-beneficial Life,* which consisteth in observing an Equality between Man and Man, *another Man and one's self,* without any inordinate Partiality or warping to our own side. If another Man must be rated according to his Dignity, he must be rated, compar'd *with Self;* and, therefore, must be of *impartially-equal* Consideration and Regard, and must have an *impartially-equal* share in the Distribution of our Esteem and Affection; and, consequently, another Man must be *another self.* He is such in Constitution and Condition, and it is, therefore, necessarily his Due, to be such in our internal and external Practice, our Will and Actions; therefore these great Laws, *Whatsoever ye would, that Men should do to you, do ye even so to them; Thou shalt love thy Neighbour as thy-self,* (which are the summary of Justice and Charity to our Neighbour,) are in the Nature and Reason of the Thing, Matter of *Duty* and *Justice,* of *Law* and *Obligation;* such is the Gratitude of a Beneficiary towards his Benefactor, who hath merited it, and whose Right and Due it is; and, in the Nature and Reason of the Thing, it is the Right and Due of a Righteous Person, and therefore matter of Law, to be justified, not condemn'd: So to be free from any intended Hurt, is the Right of an innocent Person. Therefore, to hate him and bear him ill-will, to bear any evil Passions against him, evil Thoughts of him, malignly to censure him, proudly to despise him, to speak against his Credit, to do him Prejudice in Soul, Body or Possessions, is against his Right and Due, and is, essentially and in its own Nature, *Injury* and *Injustice.* And, in general, we must pronounce touching every Man, that whatever cannot be denied him, without repugnance to the *Beauteous-Beneficial Practice,* is necessarily his Right and Due.[89] Whence Rights and Dues accrue unto Men by Contract, and the several sorts of Contracts amongst Men are so many Settlements of Rights and Dues, because no Man may break Faith, or be faithless in his Dealings, which is a gross repugnance to the *Beauteous-Beneficial Life and Practice,* as is also the denying Alms to an Honest Poor Man, which is, therefore, a sort of Due to him. *Prov.* 3. 27. So if a Man denieth Necessaries to his own Soul and Body, if he doth not order them well, and keep them in Chastity and Temperance; if he prostituteth, hurteth, diseaseth and destroyeth them, if he taketh not an ordinate care of his Welfare, of his Reputation and Maintenance in this Life, and of his future Felicity, his Practice is a Repugnance to the *Beauteous-Beneficial,* he denieth to himself, what he may not deny to himself, and what cannot be denied to any one of Mankind, without being injurious and unjust towards him.

We should do all things no otherwise, *"than as if Justice it self did them";*[90] Justice regardeth Things, as they are in themselves without partial Regard to this or that Person. If, upon a true Judgment of Things,

89. [Maxwell] "Grotius says otherwise"; *De Jure Belli ac Pacis,* II.11.3.
90. Marcus Aurelius, *Meditations,* XII.24.

another appeareth to deserve any Love of Complacence, Praise and Honour, as much as my-self, Justice saith, he ought to have an equal share of it. If the Temporal and Eternal Concerns of another be equally valuable with mine own, I am not equally (or well) affected, if they be not of *impartially-equal Regard* with me. So the Good of Two, being twice as much as the Good of One, is to be, ordinarily, so far preferr'd before the Good of One. Justice saith, if an Owner leaveth his Ground uncultivated for many Years, it is fit he should lose it; if any will not Work, neither shall he Eat: But what a Man getteth by his honest Labour and Industry, of Right and Due belongeth to him and is his *Property.* Such Dictates of Justice introduc'd *Dominion* and *Property* amongst Men. For, altho' there is much of Irregularity and Confusion in Human Affairs, and Power ordinarily prevails against Right; yet it is not to be suppos'd, that Property was introduc'd among Men, merely by *Division* of the Earth, and by *Occupancy* (arbitrarious and fortuitous,)[91] or merely by *positive Law;*[92] but upon Grounds and Reasons of Justice. When a Dish of Meat is brought to the Table, before it is cut up, and every Man has taken his Share, then what part one hath taken to himself, that is not common to the rest, but is proper to him. But this Property is not *merely* from Occupancy or Possession, or Division by Consent; it ariseth from this Ground and Reason of Justice; *to every Man, that hath not forfeited it, of Right and Due belongeth* (altho' not this or that particular share, yet in general) *a share of the Food which the Earth affordeth; and his Occupancy or Seizure of this or that particular Piece of Food at the common Table, is a particular Determination and Limitation of his general Right, and an Inclosure made thereby, which none may invade without Leave.* This Similitude is easily applicable to the Original Partition of the Earth, and the Accommodations thereof, and to the introduction of Property; for, antecedently thereto, the Founder of the Earth had made a Donation of it to Mankind; and, when they divided the Earth by Occupancy, (for so they divided it,) this their Occupancy was an Inclosure made by a particular Determination and Limitation of their Rights in

91. Grotius, *De Jure Belli ac Pacis,* II.2.
92. Selden, *Mare Clausum* (1635), I.5.

general to some Part of the Earth, and some of its Accommodations, for their Place, Food and Raiment; Nor can there be any such Community of Things, wherein every one must not have his peculiar Place and Share of Food and Raiment, distinct and apart from all others. Therefore Natural and Necessary Justice, in a great degree, introduced *Property* of Goods amongst Men, and made them *Owners,* who, doubtless, have Right, to transfer their Rights, and to alienate their Property by Donation or by Contract; upon which account, as well as by the Obligation of keeping Faith, Contracts become Settlements of the Rights and Dues of Men usually, they lose and forfeit their Rights and Dues by a change of their Qualifications; for so Men forfeit their Estates and Lives into the Hands of Justice; the due Objects of Favour become worthy of Punitive Displeasure; as on the contrary, he that is an apt and worthy Object of punitive Justice to-day, may be a fit and due Object of Clemency to-morrow. And who does not applaud and honour such *Beauteous-Beneficial Practice?* Nature constraineth us to love those, in whom Liberality, Beneficence, Justice, Fidelity, and such other Virtues appear; because *Bonum Honestum,* of it-self, and for its own sake, is pleasing, and by its Beauty, is moving and taking to the Minds of Men.

§X. The Good in Morality, that is the *Beauteous-Beneficial* Life and Practice, and the just Practice, is, in conjunction therewith, *the living socially.* The Obligation that is upon rational Beings to this *social Life and Practice* as such, (to live in Society, and to live the good Life in Society, and to be of a social Disposition and Practice,) may seem to be of mere arbitrary Appointment, because it must be deduc'd from the Creation of the Universe, which was Arbitrary. Yet, notwithstanding this Deduction of it, it must be denominated a *natural necessary Obligation;* For, altho' the Creation of the Universe was Arbitrary, yet, supposing this Creation, the rational Beings that were made, were necessarily of Right and by Obligation Gods Subjects and Servants; they were therefore made to be in Society with him, the Citizens of his Kingdom, *the Parts of this Whole;* and, consequently, they were made for the Whole, to constitute and conserve it, and for the Common Good thereof. Of this Whole the *Pagan* Theologers mistaken Account of the Universe is

The good Life and Practice is the social.

an Image and Resemblance. They look'd upon the World as the common City of Gods and Men, and every one as a Part thereof, which naturally and necessarily inferreth, that we ought to prefer the common Utility before our own. So Holy Men live and lay down their Lives for the Interest of the Kingdom of God, which is the truly Noble and Illustrious Whole, and the Interest thereof is the truly noble Common Good, to which all the Parts are to cooperate and be subservient. If they were made to be Parts of this Whole, and to promote the Commonweal thereof, they were necessarily made for the *Holy-social* (or the God-social) Life and Practice, which chiefly consists in the *Holy-social Practice of Love,* or the Practice of the *Divine Love.* The Holy-social Life and Practice is also necessarily the *Just Practice* towards all in their Social Capacity; the *Holy-social Duty to God,* (universal Piety, without which there is no living in Society with him;) *the Holy-social Duty to our Fellow-Citizens,* and *to our-selves,* who are also Parts of the Whole, whence, by prejudicing our own true Perfection and Felicity, we are injurious to the Whole. To which Holy-social Practice Rational Creatures are oblig'd, not merely by one solitary Obligation, but by innumerable necessary Obligations, from the Nature and Reason of Things, conjoin'd with the necessary Constitution of the Universe. For how innumerable are their Obligations from thence, to be and live in the State of Society with God and his Liege People, as his Servants and Subjects? To Piety, and all the Branches of universal Piety? How many and great Obligations have the regenerate and Divine Family to Unity and Concord, to a special Love and Kindness towards the Fellow-Citizens of the Holy Empire, that are Members of the same Mystical Body, animated by the same Holy Spirit, Children of the same Heavenly Father, so nearly related to him, so highly belov'd by him, and that are Co-heirs of the same Inheritance? How many and how great Obligations are there upon every one of them, not to live only or chiefly for *self,* but that their Care and Concern be for the Interest of the Whole, and for themselves as Parts of the Whole? The Law of the Kingdom of God, therefore, must be consider'd as the *Law of Nature,* that is, not of mere arbitrary Appointment; but the whole of it is what is in its own *Nature* (supposing the Constitution of the Universe) *necessarily* and *immutably* Matter of Law, Duty, and Justice. We cannot doubt, but it may be denominated, so far and in such Sense, the *Law of Nature.*

There is great Analogy and Resemblance between the *Human-social* and the *Holy-social* Life and Practice; for, altho' the World of Mankind is not properly a Polity as the City of God is, yet they are the Aggregate of several Polities, Families, Cities, and Kingdoms, every one of which is an Image of the City of God. The Civil-social Virtue requireth, that the Parts of them be subservient to the Whole, and co-operate to the Good thereof, else their Practice is not the social; nor is their Practice the Human-social, but destructive to Society, if it is not in some sort, the *Just Practice* towards the Deity. *"For it is more possible for a City to subsist without a Foundation, than that a Polity should consist, if the Opinion of the Gods be taken away. If you go about the Earth, you may find Citys without Walls, Letters, Kings, sumptuous Houses, without Riches, Money, Theatres and places of Exercise: But an Atheous City, a City without a Temple, Prayers, Oaths, Vaticinations, Sacrifices for procuring Good and averting Evil, none ever saw, or will see."*[93] The Human-Social Practice is the *just Practice* towards various special Relations, Sovereign and Subject, Parents and Children, Brethren, Husband and Wife, Master and Servant, (the Nature of which Relations is necessarily a Law to those that live in Society with such Relations,) and in general towards all, that all that are Fellow-Citizens, who could no more support Society, if they refuse and rob one another of their Rights, than an Animate Body could subsist, if the Members did so by one another. In every Polity, therefore, the *just Practice,* towards Fellow-Citizens in general, is indispensably necessary, as being the only social Practice, which social Practice is not to be confin'd to the particular Polities of Men; for there is no living the Good Life without exercising towards Mankind in general the Beauteous-beneficial Practice, (Innocence, Inoffensiveness, universal Benevolence, Beneficence, Justice and Equity, Mansuetude and Peaceableness, Veracity, Fidelity, Candor and Humanity;) nor without exercising towards them the *just Practice;* for every Man is a Citizen of this World, hath his Rights and Dues, with respect to the universe of Man-

---

93. Plutarch, *Adversus Colotem* (in *Moralia*), p. 1125.

kind; and, till he hath made a Forfeiture, it is necessarily his Right and Due to have a place upon Earth, and a portion of its Accommodations, and not to be prejudic'd by any in his Life, Liberty, or other secular Concerns. Mankind, therefore, are related to one another as Fellow-Citizens (tho' not in the strict Polical Notion) and as Human-Societists, whence they are oblig'd to the human-social Life and Practice towards one another. As every particular Country is a part of the World, which is every Man's Country, so every particular Man and Nation is a part of this great Nation, (which are all one Kindred, Family and Tribe,) a Part of this Whole, and is for the Whole, to promote its Good, but no farther than it is consistent with, and so as to render it subordinate to, the Interest of a far greater and better Whole.

The Law of Nature Immu-table, Eternal, Universal. §XI. The Law of Nature therefore, besides that it is impos'd by a superior Authority, appeareth to be a comprehension of what is, in its own Nature, matter of Law or Obligation, antecedently to that Authority; whence these three honorary Attributes necessarily belong to it, *Immutability, Eternity, Universality,* which *Cicero* hath conjoin'd. "*All Nations are at all times within the Extent of one Law sempiternal and immutable.*"

(1.) In opposition to its *Immutability,* which is generally acknowledg'd by Philosophers, Lawyers and Divines, some dispute (or rather loosely declaim), "*That the Law of Nature can be dispens'd with by Divine Power.*"[94] But these will have (what none will allow them) *an altering the case and a changing the matter,* to be a dispensing with the Law. They have alledg'd nothing, that looks like an Argument, save only these few Matrimonial Cases, *The dispensing with Polygamy, and permission of Divorces in the Old-Testament, and the dispensing with the Law against the incestuous Marriage of Brother and Sister in the beginning of the World.* But these Matrimonial Cases are weak Allegations; for it is not certain, how far they are determin'd by the Law of Nature, and how far they properly belong to positive Law. The *Objector* himself affirmeth, "*That*

94. Taylor, *Ductor Dubitantium,* II.1, n. 9, p. 200.

the Marriage of Brother and Sister is unlawful only, because forbidden by positive Law.[95] But the Lawyers say, *"Those are incestuous Marriages, which are prohibited by Nature."* And it is more reasonable to suppose, that all the Laws in Scripture against *Incest* are, not absolutely, but in a degree and measure, greater or lesser, Laws of Nature, or Branches of the Law of Nature, at least the slenderer and remoter Branches thereof: Of which sort is the Law against setting the younger before the first-born, *Gen.* 29. 26. and 48. 18. *Deut.* 21. 16, 17. which must be reputed, in some sort, a Branch of the Law of Nature, because the doing otherwise is ordinarily in the Nature of the Thing an Incongruity; yet is not such an Incongruity, but that it may be outweigh'd by a greater Good or Congruity, and in such a Case the Law is not obligatory, or not Law; so the Law, against the Marriage of Brother and Sister must be reputed, in some sort, a Branch of the Law of Nature, because the doing otherwise is ordinarily, in the Nature of the Thing, an Incongruity; yet not such, but that, in the beginning of the World, it was outweigh'd by a greater Good and Congruity, that all Mankind might issue from a common Parent; and, among the *Jews* also, it was outweigh'd by a greater Good, as in case a Brother died without a Child; and in such a Case the Law was not obligatory, or not Law. The Reasons, why certain degrees of Kindred were forbidden to marry, I suppose may have been the following. Probably, in these Laws some regard was had to the inlarging Friendships in the World, by Alliances. Probably, some regard was had to the bettering the Breed of Mankind; for it is commonly observ'd, that without *crossing the Strain* (as it is called) the Breed of some Animals is not Good. *Parents* and *Children,* (the right ascending and descending Line,) *Mothers-in-Law* and the *Husbands Children, Uncles* and *Nieces, Aunts* and *Nephews,* cannot marry without some (greater or lesser) violation of a certain Sanctity (greater or lesser), which superior natural Relations have, and of a Religious distance which it requireth, to be observ'd; for as the antient *Greeks* call'd our Parents Θεούς (Gods), so they call'd our Parents Brethren Θείους (Divine), as *Simplicius* upon *Epictetus* observeth: Probably, another Reason of the Prohibition might

95. Ibid., II.2 n. 24; Selden, *De Jure Naturali,* I.6.

be, that, were not the Marriages of so near Relations prohibited, the intercourse and familiarity between them is so great, that Chastity, among them, could not generally be otherwise preserv'd, than by the restraint of that Horrour, which generally attends such Mixtures, which are thereby the most effectually prevented that is possible. And, touching all the prohibited degrees of Kindred, we may affirm, that, for this Reason, they may not marry, because in the Nature of the Thing there is an Incongruity (more or less), which is (more or less) discern'd by common Reason, as the Reasons above-mentioned (and perhaps others which may be assign'd) make appear; and so far as there is such an Incongruity, there is a moral Turpitude in Incest. But this Incongruity ceaseth in case of a greater Good and Congruity, whence there is no difficulty in the case of *Cain's* marrying his Sister. And as for the *Polygamy* and *Divorces,* that were permitted in the times of the Old-Testament, they were repugnant, indeed, to the primitive Institution of Marriage in Paradise, to which our Saviour has reduc'd us, but seem not to have been contrary to the Light of Nature, or any Law which it revealeth; for it discovers nothing of the Creation of one Man and one Woman only in the beginning of the World, nor their Paradisaical State, nor the establishment of the conjunction of one Male and one Female, in single Wedlock, at the beginning. But, from the permission of Polygamy and Divorces, there is great Reason, to infer the Imperfection of the Institution of Piety in the Old-Testament-Times, and that the famous Ancestors of old *Israel,* who practised Polygamy, (altho', in the main, real and spiritual Religionists, yet) were in great Degree secular kind of Pietists; and that God, for increasing their Seed, dispens'd with his own Institution of Marriage: But no just Inference can be made from thence, that the *Law of Nature* can be dispens'd with by Divine Power.

(2.) The *Eternal Law* is of various acceptation. The *Pagan* Theologers call *Themis the Eternal Law,*[96] whereby they mean *the universal Law* prescrib'd to the World and unintelligent *Nature,* which observeth a settled Law and Order. In the School of the *Stoicks* there is a two-fold Eternal

---

96. Pighius, *Themis Dea* (1568), p. 13.

Law,[97] the one merely *providential,* (as when they say, *omnia aeternae legis imperio fieri,* all things are by Law, Fate, or providential Decree;) the other *moral and preceptive,* called by *Cicero sempiterna Lex,* which is the eternal Mind or right Reason of *Jove,* consider'd as commanding some things to be done, and prohibiting others.[98] This two-fold Eternal Law of the *Stoicks* conjoin'd into one, is *the Eternal Law* of the *Schools;* for their Eternal Law is, *"Ratio gubernativa totius Universi in mente divina existens,"*[99] Reason existing in the Divine Mind as governing the whole Universe. The *Stoicks* look'd upon their morally-Preceptive Eternal Law as *the Law of Nature,* and, therefore, look'd upon the Mind and right Reason of *Jove* (commanding and forbidding) as the *primary* and *original* Law of Nature, the Mind and right Reason of Man commanding and forbidding (a derivative from the eternal Mind of *Jove*) they look'd upon as the *secondary* and *derivative* Law of Nature. So *Cicero,* agreeably to their sense, saith, *"Lex nihil aliud est nisi recta & a numine Deorum tracta Ratio, imperans honesta, prohibensque contraria";*[100] Law is nothing else but right Reason, deriv'd from the Gods, commanding things virtuous, and forbidding the contrary. So the Schools say, *"Lex naturalis est quaedam participatio legis aeternae in rationali creatura,"*[101] The Law of Nature is a certain Participation of Law Eternal in a rational Creature. Right Reason is represented as the Law of Nature *constitutively;* and this Law is suppos'd to exist from Eternity: But, as we do not acknowledge, that right Reason is in such sense Law, so neither do we suppose, that the Law of Nature is in such sense denominated *the Eternal Law:* But it is so denominated, in the same sense that necessary Propositions are denominated *Eternal Truths.* And they are so denominated, not to signify, that such Propositions existed from Eternity, and had a Truth from Eternity as so existing; or that the *Truth of the Thing,* which they express, mentally or really existed from Eternity: But the sense is, that, supposing

97. Lipsius, *Physiologia Stoicorum* (1604), I, diss. 12.
98. Cicero, *De Legibus,* II.
99. Aquinas, *Summa Theologica,* 1a. 2ae. Qu. 91, art. 1.
100. Cicero, *Phillippicae,* XI.
101. Selden, *De Jure Naturali,* I.8.

those Propositions to exist, which cannot but be Truths (necessary Truths), they are Truths of eternal Necessity. They are *Eternal Truths,* not as being Truths which cannot but exist, (as some say, that they necessarily exist in an eternal Mind,) but as being Truths, which cannot but be Truths, there is an eternal Necessity of their being Truths. As these Verities, *Eternal Truths,* are of *eternal immutable Necessity,* and there is an impossibility of their being otherwise: So the Laws of Nature are *Eternal Laws,* as being of *eternal immutable Necessity,* and it cannot be, but they must be the things that are the just, the right and the good. In such sense they are Laws that had no beginning, but *always were,* according to the saying of *Antigone* in *Sophocles,* who having buried her Brother *Polynice,* and being accus'd of doing it against the Laws, she made answer, that, altho' she had offended against the Laws of *Creon,* yet she had committed no Offence against the unwritten Law, which is not of late or yesterday's standing, but *always was. "These are not matters of to-day or yesterday, but they ever live, and none knoweth their Date, or from whence they came."* [102]

(3.) A third honorary Attribute of the Law of Nature is the *Universality* of it, and that in several respects. In respect of the *Universe of Mankind,* it is *the Law universal.* The Matters of it are call'd by the *Greek* Writers κοινα των α᾿νθρώπων δίκαια. *"the common Rights of all Men."* [103] And the Lawyers say, *"All People that are governed by Laws, have a proper civil Law of their own, and the common Law of all Men besides."* [104] So *Aristotle* saith, *"I distribute Law into that which is proper, and that which is common; for there is that which all Men suppose a common Just and Unjust, which is by Nature such, and is immutable."* [105]

But the Law of Nature is not only universal in respect of the Universe of Mankind, but in respect of the vast Universe of rational Creatures. Agreeably whereto *Empedocles* sang of natural Justice; *"It is extended*

---

102. Aristotle, *Rhetorica,* I.13, 15.
103. Selden, *Mare Clausum,* I.3.
104. Selden, *De Jure Naturali,* I.3.
105. Aristotle, *Rhetorica,* I.13.

through the vast Aether, and the infinite Regions of Light.[106] *Celsus* having said from *Pindar, "that Law is the King of all,"* *Origen* answereth, that, if he meaneth the Law of Cities, this is false; for all are not under the Rule of that Law; but *Christians* acknowledge a Law, *"that is by Nature King of all,"* *"The true Law* (saith *Cicero) is right Reason, congruous to Nature, diffus'd into all, constant, sempiternal, which calleth to Duty by commanding, and by forbidding deterreth from Villany."* If right Reason is the Law of Nature (as *declaratively* it is;) or, if the Law of Nature *"is the Force of the Intellect, whereby we discern those things that are in themselves good, from those that are in themselves evil";*[107] or, if it is *Lex vera impressa mentibus,* a Law impress'd upon intelligent Minds; it cannot be a Law wholly appropriate and peculiar to the Universe of Mankind, but is necessarily *the Law of the vast Universe of Men and Angels.* So in the School of the *Stoicks* the Law of Nature is, *"The Law of the Universe, one Law the common Reason of all intelligent Beings, the Reason and Law of the most antient City and Polity."*[108] For they argue, *"That Reason, which prescribeth what is to be done, and not to be done, is common to us all; if that, then Law; if so, then are we Fellow-Citizens, and the World is as a City."*[109] So *Cicero* argueth, *"They that have Reason in common, have right Reason in common, which is a Law; therefore Men are thus consociated with the Gods, they are of one common Law, and consequently they are of the same City or Polity."*[110] But supposing, right Reason to be Law, that all rational Beings have something of it, and, consequently, that they have something of one Law; yet they have not one Law, as Citizens of the same City; for rational Beings are not Fellow-Citizens, and of the same Society as Rationals, but as a special kind of Rationals, (as *Salts* that associate are those of the same kind), *divine, diabolical,* or *human.*

The Law of Nature, therefore, is the Comprehension of what is *in its own Nature Matter of Obligation, and ought to be,* abstracted from the

---

106. Ibid.
107. Selden, *De Jure Naturali,* I.8.
108. Marcus Aurelius, *Meditations,* VII.9; II.16.
109. Ibid., IV.4.
110. Cicero, *De Legibus,* I.

preceding Authority of Command of the *subsequent* Sanctions of Rewards and Punishments.

CHAPTER II. The Promulgation of the Law *of* Nature.

The Law of Nature, with respect to its Promulgation, is the Comprehension of our natural Notices of what is Law.

The *divine moral Law* is thus far the *Law of Nature,* it is *the Comprehension of what is in its own Nature Matter of Law,* and this is the Law that is notic'd by the Light of Nature, yet it may not be called the Law of Nature without Distinction and Limitation of Sense. For the Law of Nature, according to its true and usual Definition, is this moral Law, *only as it is notic'd by natural Light;* so that the Law of Nature, considered with respect to the Promulgation of it, must be defined, *The Comprehension of our natural Notices of what is Law.* These natural Notices are of two sorts, (so that the Law of Nature is of a two-fold Notion, as in respect of the *Obligation* of it, so in respect of the *Promulgation* of it;) for some of them have only *the Verity of natural Notices,* others have not only the Verity, but the *Notoreity of natural Notices,* which, therefore, have a greater Promulgation. By *Nature* here I understand *Mundane Nature,* or *the natural Constitution of the World,* especially of our-selves, which, in the first place, noticeth the *Being of God,* whose Existence is Law.

Our natural Notices of what is Law, are from the Existence of God notic'd by Nature.

§1. Mundane Nature (that Comprehension of the Works of the Creation) clearly noticeth to Mankind the Existence of God, which is written in this great Book, or Volume of the World, in Capital Letters, to be seen and read of all Men. *"For the invisible things of him, from the Creation of the World, are clearly seen, being understood by the things that are made, even his eternal Power and Godhead,"* Rom. i. 20. *"There is no Speech nor Language where their Voice"* (the Voice of the Heavens and the Heavenly Bodies) *"is not heard : Their Line"* (or loud Voice rather) *"is gone out thro' all the Earth, and their Words to the End of the World,"* Psal. xix. 3, 4. If we ask, whence it is, and whose doing it is, that there is such an admirable System as our Eyes behold, with all the Excellencies and Conveniences, the Parts, Furniture, and Inhabitants thereof? In answer thereto universal Nature proclaimeth, *the great God formed all things.* Such is the Origination of things in Theism, wherewith Atheism thus far agreeth, they both suppose, *That a thing cannot be made by itself,* (for then it must be existent before it is existent;) *that it is impossible that all things should be made; that if at any time there was nothing, there never could have been any thing,* (for something cannot come from nothing;) *that something was, from Eternity, unmade, increate, self-existent, and absolutely independent.* Thus far there is no Disagreement between the Atheists and the Theists (or Religionists;) the only Matter in Debate, is, whether this *acknowledg'd eternal Something* (which is *necessarily increate, necessarily existent,* and *absolutely independent*) is such an eternal Something as the *Religionists God* or whether it be only *universal Matter,* or the *material World,* as the Atheists suppose.

Matter *cannot be the self-existent Being.* The self-existent Being, having the Reason of its Existence within it-self, and in its own Nature, as it has existed always, so it exists every-where, always and invariably the same; its Necessity, being *absolute,* is *uniform,* with respect to *all Time* and *all Place,* absolute Necessity being every-where and always alike, admitting of no Change, no Variety; the Properties of such a Being, being as necessary as the Being it-self, to which they belong; which is, therefore, incapable of suffering any Change. But universal Matter, or the material Universe, is not such a Being. For, 1. If Matter were the self-existent Being, it must, according to the foregoing Reasoning, exist every-where, and a *Vacuum,* with respect to it, would be impossible; but if there be no *Vacuum,* how is it possible that there should be any *Motion?* or, whence arises the different *specifick Gravities of Bodies?* or how could Bodies be *rarify'd* and condens'd? or, how could the Parts of it be actually separated from one another? All motion is rectilinear, till its Determination be chang'd; but, upon the supposition of a *Plenum,* in case of any Motion, the Protrusion, and consequently the Resistance, would be infinite. The Motion of the Planets and Comets prove a *Vacuum.* "Against filling the Heavens with fluid Mediums, unless they be exceeding rare, a great Objection arises from the regular and very lasting Motions of the Planets and Comets in all manner of Courses through the Heavens. For thence it is manifest, that the Heavens are void of all sensible Resistance, and by consequence of all sensible Matter.

"For the resisting Power of fluid Mediums arises partly from the At-

Matter is not the self-existent Being.

trition of the Parts of the Medium, and partly from the *Vis inertiae* of the Matter.[1] That part of the Resistance of a spherical Body which arises from the Attrition of the Parts of the Medium is very nearly as the Diameter, or at the most, as the *Factum* of the Diameter, and the Velocity of the spherical Body together. And that part of the Resistance which arises from the *Vis inertiae* of the Matter, is as the Square of that *Factum*. And by this difference the two sorts of Resistance may be distinguish'd from one another in any Medium; and these being distinguish'd, it will be found that almost all the Resistance of Bodies of a competent Magnitude moving in Air, Water, Quick-silver, and such like Fluids, with a competent Velocity, arises from the *Vis inertiae* of the Parts of the Fluid."

"Now that part of the resisting Power of any Medium which arises from the Tenacity, Friction or Attrition of the Parts of the Medium, may be diminish'd by dividing the Matter into smaller Parts, and making the Parts more smooth and slippery: But that part of the Resistance which arises from the *Vis inertiae,* is proportional to the Density of the Matter, and cannot be diminish'd by dividing the Matter into smaller Parts, nor by any other means than by decreasing the Density of the Mediums. And for these Reasons the Density of fluid Mediums is very nearly proportional to their Resistance. Liquors which differ not much in Density, as Water, Spirit of Wine, Spirit of Turpentine, hot Oil, differ not much in Resistance. Water is thirteen or fourteen times lighter than Quick-silver, and by consequence thirteen or fourteen times rarer, and its Resistance is less than that of Quick-silver in the same Proportion, or thereabouts, as I have found by Experiments made with Pendulums. The open Air, in which we breathe, is eight or nine hundred times lighter than Water, and by consequences eight or nine hundred times rarer, and accordingly its Resistance is less than that of Water in the same Proportion, or thereabouts; as I have also found by Experiments made with Pendulums. And in thinner Air the Resistance is still less, and at length, by rarifying the Air, becomes insensible. For small Feathers falling in the

1. Maxwell quotes at length from the second edition of Newton, *Opticks* (1717), p. 339ff.

open Air meet with great Resistance, but in a tall Glass well emptied of
Air, they fall as fast as Lead or Gold, as I have seen tried several times.
Whence the Resistance seems still to decrease in proportion to the Density of the Fluid. For I do not find by any Experiments, that Bodies
moving in Quick-silver, Water or Air, meet with any other sensible Resistance than what arises from the Density and Tenacity of those sensible
Fluids, as they would do, if the Pores of those Fluids, and all other
Spaces, were filled with a dense and subtile Fluid. Now if the Resistance
in a Vessel well emptied of Air, was but an hundred times less than in the
open Air, it would be about a million of times less than in the Quick-
silver. But it seems to be much less in such a Vessel, and still much less
in the Heavens, at the height of three or four hundred Miles from the
Earth, or above. For Mr. *Boyle* has shew'd that Air may be rarefied above
ten thousand times in Vessels of Glass; and the Heavens are much emp-
tier of Air than any *Vacuum* we can make below. For since the Air is
compress'd by the weight of the incumbent Atmosphere, and the density
of Air is proportional to the Force compressing it, it follows by Computation, that at the height of about seven *English* Miles from the Earth,
the Air is four times rarer than at the Surface of the Earth; and at the
height of 14 Miles, it is sixteen times rarer than that at the Surface of
the Earth; and at the height of 21, 28, or 35 Miles, it is respectively 64,
256, or 1024 times rarer, or thereabouts; and at the height of 70, 140, 210
Miles, it is about 1000000, 1000000000000 or 1000000000000000000
times rarer; and so on."

"Heat promotes Fluidity very much, by diminishing the Tenacity of
Bodies. It makes many Bodies fluid which are not fluid in cold, and
increases the Fluidity of tenacious Liquids, as of Oil, Balsam and Honey,
and thereby decreases their Resistance. But it decreases not the Resistance of Water considerably, as it would do, if any considerable part of
the Resistance of Water arose from the Attrition or Tenacity of its Parts.
And therefore the Resistance of Water arises principally, and almost intirely, from the *Vis inertiae* of its Matter; and by consequence, if the
Heavens were as dense as Water, they would not have much less Resistance than Water; if perfectly dense, or full of Matter without any
Vacuum, let the Matter be never so subtile and fluid, they would have a

greater Resistance than Quick-silver. A solid Globe in such a Medium would lose above half its Motion in moving three times the length of its Diameter, and a Globe not solid (such as are the Planets) would be retarded sooner. And therefore to make way for the regular and lasting Motions of the Planets and Comets, 'tis necessary to empty the Heavens of all Matter, except perhaps some very thin Vapours, Steams or Effluvia, arising from the Atmospheres of the Earth, Planets and Comets, and from such an exceedingly rare Aethereal Medium as we described above. A dense Fluid can be of no use for explaining the Phaenomena of Nature, the Motions of the Planets and Comets being better explain'd without it. It serves only to disturb and retard the Motions of those great Bodies, and make the Frame of Nature languish: And in the Pores of Bodies, it serves only to stop the vibrating Motions of their Parts, wherein their Heat and Activity consists. And as it is of no use, and hinders the Operations of Nature, and makes her languish, so there is no evidence for its Existence, and therefore it ought to be rejected." *Newt.* Opt. Eng. Edit. 2d. p. 339, & *seq.*[2]

As to *Rarefaction* or *Condensation* and the *different specifick Gravities of Bodies,* the same Author reasons thus in his *Principles,* drawing these Corollaries from *L. 3. Prop. 6. Corol.* 1.[3] "Hence the Weights of Bodies do not depend upon their Forms and Textures. For, if they could be varied with their Forms, they would be greater or less, according to the difference of Forms, in an equal Quantity of Matter; which is altogether contrary to Experience. *Corol.* 2. All Bodies about the Earth gravitate towards the Earth, and the Weights of all Bodies, which are equally distant from the Earth's Center, are as the Quantities of Matter in their Bodies: This is the Quality of all Bodies, upon which we can make Experiments, and, therefore, by Rule the third, is to be affirm'd of all Bodies whatsoever. If the Aether, or any other Body whatsoever, were altogether destitute of Gravity, or did gravitate less, than in proportion to the quantity of its Matter: Because (according to the opinion of *Aristotle,*

---

2. Ibid., pp. 339–43.
3. Maxwell translates from the third edition of Newton, *Principia Philosophiae* (1726), p. 402ff.

Des Cartes, and others) it differs from other Bodies, only in the Form of
the Matter, the same Body might, by the change of its Form, gradually
be converted into a Body of the same constitution with those, which
gravitate most in proportion to the Quantity of Matter; and, on the
contrary, the most heavy Bodies might gradually lose their Gravity, by
gradually changing their Form. And, therefore, the Weights would depend upon the Forms of Bodies, and might be chang'd with them, contrary to what is prov'd in the foregoing Corollary. *Corol.* 3. All spaces are
not equally full. For, if all spaces were equally full, the specifick Gravity
of that Fluid, with which the Region of the Air would, in that case, be
fill'd, upon account of the most perfect Density of the Matter, would
not be less than the specifick Gravity of Quick-silver, or Gold, or any
other the most dense Body; and, therefore, neither Gold, nor any other
Body whatever, could descend in the Air: For Bodies specifically lighter
do not at all descend in Fluids. But, if the Quantity of Matter in any
given space, might be diminished by any Rarefaction whatever, what
hinders, but that it might be diminish'd infinitely? *Corol.* 4. If all the
solid Particles of all Bodies are equally dense, nor can be rarefied without
Pores, there is a *Vacuum.* I call those Bodies equally dense, whose Powers
of Inactivity (*Vires inertiae*) are as their Magnitudes." *Fourthly,* if there
can be no *Vacuum,* I cannot see how any Part of Matter could be divided
from that which is next adjoining, any more than it is possible, actually
to divide the Parts of absolute Space from one another, which in the
Continuum were at no distance from one another, one beginning where
the other ended; but such separating the Parts of Matter must infer Va-
cuities between. As for the Figures of the Parts of Bodies, upon the supposition of a *Plenum,* their Surfaces must be, either all Rectilinear, or
Concavo-Convex, the Concavities of the one exactly fitting the Con-
vexities of the other, otherwise they could not adequately fill Space: But
that all Bodies are so figur'd, we do not find true in Fact. Lastly, the
denying a *Vacuum* supposes what is impossible for any one to prove to
be true, *That the Material World has no Limits.* Thus we see, that *Matter*
is not *infinite* or *commensurate with Space,* as it must be, if it were the
self-existent or a necessarily existing Being; in which case it must be both
Uniform and *Invariable,* as well with respect to its Modes and Properties,

as to its Substance; and, consequently, it must be a Contradiction to suppose, that it ever did, or could, exist in any other manner, than that, in which we see it now to exist. But we know, that it has undergone and continues to undergo perpetual Changes and Alterations in all its Parts that we are acquainted with. We plainly perceive, that it is no Contradiction or Absurdity, to suppose, that the World were in some respects otherwise than it is; that the kinds of Animals or Plants, &c. were more or fewer than they are, and that there were more or fewer Individuals of any Kind than there now are; that there were a greater or less Quantity of Motion in the World than there is, and the like. If the material World existed necessarily, it were impossible for it to exist in any respect otherwise than it does; but we can easily conceive it existing otherwise, which we could not do, if it were impossible for it to exist otherwise, for we cannot conceive Impossibilities. As for *Uniformity,* which is necessarily connected with *Necessity of Existence,* we see no such thing in Matter, but the reverse. Farther; necessary Existence, which is itself the greatest Perfection, does in itself include all possible Perfections; otherwise, there might be some Perfection in a dependent Being, which an Independent Being might want; which to suppose, were absurd. But how can that Being have *all Perfections,* which has *no Power,* and is perfectly Passive, as is the case of Matter, which always continues in that state of Rest or Motion, in which it is once plac'd, till it receives some external Impression? The self-existent Being must *actually* have all possible Perfections. Whatever Perfections Matter may have, it seems not to be *sensible,* that it has any. Understanding is certainly a Perfection, which therefore, surely, Matter must have, if Matter were self-existent; and, consequently, *all Matter* would be *Intelligent,* which is so far from being true, that no Matter is *Intelligent,* or can Think.[4]

§2. *If there be no God, every thing in the World is Mechanical, according to the Laws of Mechanism, of Matter and Motion. But every thing is not*

If there be no God, all is

---

4. [Maxwell] "See the Argument upon this Head in the foregoing part of this *Appendix.*"

Mechanical; therefore there is a God. The *Minor* in this *Syllogism,* which I think is all in it that can be controverted, is thus prov'd.

First; there must be a *First Mover,* and, therefore, *a Beginning of Motion,* which could *not* be *Mechanical.* If Motion be Essential to Matter, it must be a Contradiction to suppose Matter or any part of it, at Rest, equally as to suppose it Indivisible, Unextended, or Penetrable. But it is no Contradiction to suppose Matter, or any part of it, at Rest; therefore Motion is not Essential to Matter. We can form an Idea of Matter at Rest, but we can form no Ideas of Contradictions or Impossibilities— If Motion be necessary to Matter in the Nature of the Thing, this Necessity must be Uniform and act Uniformly, in all Matter, absolute Necessity being always and every where the same. Now this Motion cannot be suppos'd to have any particular determination to move any one way, rather than the contrary, for what shall determine it, to move one way rather than another? But every Motion must have a particular Determination; for an equal Tendency to move every way, is being at Rest. If Matter move necessarily, it must move necessarily with some particular Direction, because without a Direction it cannot move at all, and then that necessary Direction must be unchangeable, as also its Velocity, both which are contrary to all Experience. If Motion be Essential to Matter, then all Matter must have the same Direction, or each independent Part must have a particular and independent Direction of its own, each of which is contrary to Experience. If Matter be the self-existent Being, it must exist in every point of Space, and then whither could it move; or how would the Motions of the different and even contrary Determinations be practicable?

Secondly; Gravity is not Mechanical, but must be owing to the actual incessant Concurrence of an Immaterial Being. It is not the Matter of the Sun, that causes the Earth to gravitate towards it; because nothing can act, but where it is. Whatever it is, that is the immediate Cause of Gravity, it is something that acts as freely, and as powerfully upon the central parts of all the solid Substances we know, as upon the superficial; for the interior parts of a solid Globe of Gold gravitate as much as the exterior, nor will beating it out into a thin Plate encrease its Gravity at all, which it must necessarily do, if the immediate Cause of Gravity did

Mechanical; but all is not Mechanical, therefore there is a God.

1. Motion must have had a Beginning, which could not be mechanical.

2. Gravity is not Mechanical.

not act as strongly upon the inward as the outward Parts of the Gold, which is not easily conceivable, if that Cause were a material Fluid, how subtile soever; but, supposing it, as some do, an extremely subtile elastick Fluid, surrounding all gross Bodies, increasing in its Density directly as the Squares of the Distances increase, whose Parts, endeavouring to recede from one another, impell neighbouring Bodies to move that way, where they find the least Resistance, that is, towards the great and gross Collections of Matter, such as the Sun, Stars and Planets, in the neighbourhood of which this subtile elastick Fluid is more rare, and consequently less active; *what supports the Tortoise,* and causes the Parts of this elastick Fluid to recede from one another, and is the Cause of that their Motion mutually Receding from one another? Nothing mechanical, certainly, can be the beginning of this, more than of any other Motion.

"This Gravitating Power acts upon Bodies equally, when they are in the most violent Motion, and when they are at Rest; as the Celerity of Descending Bodies with us, and Celerity of the Comets in the Heavens, Geometrically computed, do particularly shew. Now this is absolutely impossible; that any Mechanical Pressure or Impulse from a Body, let its Motion be never so swift, or its Pressure never so strong, should equally accelerate another Body, when at Rest, and when in Motion; it being a known Law of Mechanism, that a Body in Motion impells another at Rest, with its whole Force; but one in Motion, which it overtakes, with only the excess of its own Velocity above the others; as is most obvious also on the least Reflexion." *Whiston's* Astronomical Principles, p. 45.[5]

3. Nor the Cohesion of Matter.

Thirdly; The Cause of the *Cohesion* of the Particles of *Matter* is also *Immechanical.* It cannot be a *Material Vinculum,* which connects them; for then the Question recurs, What keeps the Parts of the *Vinculum* together? And the Pressure of a circumambient Fluid will by no means salve the Phaenomenon.

4. Nor Elasticity.

Fourthly; That *Power,* by which some Particles of Matter, Air for Instance, *mutually repell* one another, which is the Cause of *Elasticity,* is

5. Whiston, *Astronomical Principles of Religion* (1717).

also as *Immechanical,* as that Power, by which all Particles of Matter mutually tend toward one another.

Fifthly; *The Frame of the solar System is not Mechanical.* See Fig. IV.

"The Comets, by reason of their great Number, and great Distance of their Aphelia from the Sun, where they are long detain'd, must needs be somewhat disturb'd by their mutual Gravitations towards one another, and have their Eccentricities and times of their Revolutions, sometimes a little encreas'd, sometimes diminish'd. Whence it is not to be expected, that the same Comet should revolve exactly in the same Orbit, and in the same periodical Times. It is sufficient, if there do not happen greater Changes, than what may arise from the Causes aforesaid.[6]

"And hence a *Reason* is assign'd, *why* the Comets are not comprehended in the Zodiack, as the Planets are; but deviate therefrom, and are carried by various Motions towards all Parts of the Heavens. And that for this End, that, in their Aphelia, where they move most slowly, they might be mutually at the greatest Distance, and their mutual Attraction might be the weakest. For which reason the Comets, which descend the lowest, and therefore move slowest in their Aphelia, ought to ascend the highest.

"The Comet, which appear'd in 1680, in its Perihelion was not a sixth part of the Sun's Diameter distant from the Sun; and, upon account of that near Approach to the Sun, and some Density of the Sun's Atmosphere, it must meet with some sensible Resistance, and be somewhat retarded, and approach nearer to the Sun; and, by continually making nearer Approaches every Revolution, it will at last fall down to the Body of the Sun. And also in its Aphelion, where it moves slowest, it may sometimes be retarded by the Attraction of other Comets, and for that reason fall into the Sun. Thus the fix'd Stars, which gradually decrease by the emission of Light and Vapours, may be recruited by Comets falling into them, and their Fires being repair'd by the addition of new Fuel, by means thereof they may blaze out afresh, and so pass for new Stars. Such kind of fix'd Stars then are those, which appear suddenly and all

6. Maxwell translates material from Newton's *Principia,* pp. 525–30.

at once with a very great Brightness, but afterwards by degrees disappear. But those fix'd Stars, which appear and disappear periodically, and whose Increase of Light is gradual, but seldom or never exceeding that of the Stars of the third Magnitude, seem to be of a different kind, and, by revolving upon their own Axes, to turn toward us, periodically, a bright and a dark side. Those Vapours, which proceed from the Sun and fix'd Stars and Tails of Comets, may fall, by their Gravity, upon the Atmospheres of the Planets, and be there condens'd, and converted into Water and moist Spirits, and may afterwards pass gradually by a gentle Heat into Salts, and Sulphurs, and Tinctures, and Mud, and Clay, and Potters Earth, and Sand, and Stones, and Corals, and other terrestrial Substances.

"The Hypothesis of Vortices is press'd with many Difficulties. That each Planet, with a Radius drawn to the Sun, may describe Areas proportional to the Times, the Periodical Times of the Parts of the Vortex ought to be in a Duplicate Proportion of their Distances from the Sun. That the Periodical Times of the Planets may be in a sesquiplicate Proportion of their Distances from the Sun, the Periodical Times of the Parts of the Vortex ought to be in the same Proportion of their Distances. That the lesser Vortices, which roll round *Jupiter, Saturn,* and the other Planets, may be preserv'd, and swim undisturb'd in the Vortex of the Sun, the Periodical Times of the Parts of the solar Vortex should be equal. The Revolution of the Sun and Planets upon their Axes, which ought to agree with the Motions of the Vortex, differ from all these Proportions. The Motions of the Comets are exactly regular, and observe the same Laws with the Motions of the Planets, and cannot be explain'd by Vortices. The Comets are carried by Motions very Eccentrical toward all Parts of the Heavens, which, upon the supposition of Vortices, is impossible.

"Projected Bodies, in our Air, meet with no Resistance but that of the Air. The Air being taken away, as it is in Mr. *Boyle's* Air-Pump, the Resistance ceases, seeing soft Down and solid Gold fall, in such a Vacuum, with equal Velocity; and the case is the same in those Celestial Spaces above the Earth's Atmosphere. All Bodies ought to be mov'd most freely in those Spaces, and, therefore, the Planets and Comets ought perpet-

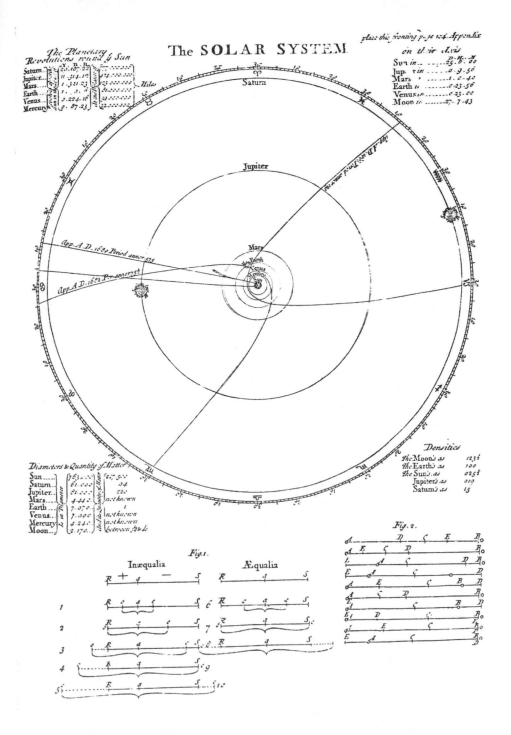

The SOLAR SYSTEM

place this fronting page 124 Appendix

ually to be revolv'd according to the Laws already explain'd, in Orbs, such in Kind and Position, as we have suppos'd. They will, indeed, be retain'd in their Orbits by the Laws of Gravity; but *they could by no means acquire such a regular position of their Orbs by those Laws.*

"The six Primary Planets revolve round the Sun in Circles concentrical to the Sun, with the same Direction of their Motion, and, very nearly, in the same Plain. The ten Moons (or secondary Planets) revolve round the Earth, Jupiter and Saturn, with the same Direction of their Motion, and very nearly in the plain of the Orbs of the Planets. And *all these regular Motions have not their rise from Mechanical Causes,* seeing the Comets are carried in Orbs very Eccentrical, and that very freely thro' all parts of the Heavens. By which kind of Motion the Comets pass very swiftly and easily thro' the Orbs of the Planets, and in their Aphelia, when they move more slowly and are longer detain'd, they are the most remotely distant from one another, and their mutual Attraction by much the weakest. This most elegant System of the Planets and Comets could not be produced, but by and under the Contrivance and Dominion of an Intelligent and Powerful Being. And, if the fix'd Stars are the Centers of such other Systems, all these, being fram'd by the like Counsel, will be subject to the Dominion of *One;* especially seeing the Light of the fix'd Stars is of the same Nature with that of the Sun, and the Light of all these Systems passes mutually from one to another. And *He* has placed the Systems of the fix'd Stars at immense Distances from one another, *lest they should mutually rush upon one another by their Gravity.*

"He governs all Things, not as THE SOUL OF THE WORLD, but as THE LORD OF THE UNIVERSE; and, because of his Dominion, he is wont to be called (παντοκράτωρ) UNIVERSAL EMPEROR. For GOD is a Relative Word, and hath a Relation to Servants; and THE DEITY is THE EMPIRE OF GOD, not over his own Body, as is the opinion of those who make him the Soul of the World, but over his Servants. THE SUPREME GOD is a Being Eternal, Infinite, absolutely Perfect; but a Being, however Perfect, without Dominion, is not Lord God. For we say, My God, your God, the God of *Israel,* God of Gods, and Lord of Lords; but we do not say, My Eternal, your Eternal, the Eternal of *Israel,* the Eternal of Gods; we do not say, My Infinite, or my Perfect. These Titles have no

Relation to Servants. The Word [God] frequently signifies Lord,[7] but every Lord is not God. The Empire of a Spiritual Being constitutes God; true Empire constitutes the true God; Supreme, the Supreme; Feigned, the Feigned. And, from his true Empire, it follows, That the true God is Living, Intelligent, and Powerful; from his other Perfections, that he is the Supreme, or supremely Perfect. He is Eternal and Infinite, Omnipotent and Omniscient, that is, he endures from Eternity to Eternity, and he is present from Infinity to Infinity; he governs all Things, and knows all Things, which are done, or which can be done. He is not Eternity and Infinity, but he is Eternal and Infinite; he is not Duration and Space, but he endures and is present. He endures alwaies, and is present every where; and, by existing alwaies and every where, he constitutes Duration and Space, Eternity and Infinity. Whereas every Particle of Space is ALWAIES, and every indivisible Moment of Duration is EVERY WHERE, certainly the Framer and Lord of the Universe shall not be [*nunquam, nusquam*] NEVER, NO WHERE. Every sensible Mind is, at different Times and in the different Organs of its Sense and Motions, but one and the same individual Person. There are successive Parts in Duration, and co-existent Parts in Space; neither of these are compatible to the Person of Man or to the Thinking Principle in him; much less can they be ascrib'd to the intelligent Substance of God. Every Man, as a sensitive Being, is one and the same Man, during his whole Life, in all and each of the Organs of his Senses. God is one and the same God alwaies and every where. He is Omnipotent, not VIRTUALLY only, but also SUBSTANTIALLY, for Power, without Substance, cannot subsist. In him are contain'd and mov'd all Things, but without being mutually affected. God is not at all affected by the Motions of Bodies; nor do they suffer any Resistance from the Omnipresence of God. It is confess'd,

---

7. [Maxwell] *"Pocock* derives the Word [*Deus*] from the *Arabick* Word [*du*] (in the Genitive Case, *di,*) which signifies *Lord. Hence the chief Magistrate in* Algiers *is called the* Dey. And in this Sense Princes are call'd *Gods. Ps.* 84. 6. and *Joh.* 10. 45. and *Moses* is call'd the *God* of his Brother *Aaron,* and the *God* of King *Pharaoh,* (*Exod.* 4. 16. and 7. 1.). And in the same Sense the Souls of Princes decess'd were, of old, by the Heathen call'd *Gods,* but falsly, because they had no Dominion." Maxwell refers to Pocock, *Specimen Historiae Arabum* (1650).

That the Supreme God exists Necessarily, and by the same Necessity he exists ALWAIES and EVERY WHERE. Whence he is all similar, all Eye, all Ear, all Brain, all Arm, all the Power of Perceiving, Understanding, and Acting; but after a manner not at all corporeal, after a manner not like that of Men, after a manner wholly to us unknown. As a blind Man has no Notion of Colours, so neither have we any Notion of the Waies, by which the most Wise God perceives and understands all Things. He is wholly destitute of all Body, and of all bodily Shape; and, therefore, cannot be seen, heard, nor touch'd; nor ought he to be worshipp'd under the representation of any thing corporeal. We have Ideas of his Attributes, but we know not at all what is the Substance of any thing whatever. We see only the Figures and Colours of Bodies, we hear only their Sounds, we touch only their outward Surfaces, we smell their Odours, and taste their Savours; but we know not by any Sense, or reflex Act, their inward Substances; and much less have we any Notion of the Substance of God. We know him, only by his Properties and Attributes, and by the most wise and excellent Structure of Things, and by Final Causes; but we adore and worship him upon account of his Dominion. For we worship him, as his Servants; and God, without Dominion, Providence and Final Causes, is nothing else but Fate and Nature. There arises no Variety in Things, from blind Metaphysical Necessity, which is always and every where the same. All Diversity, in the Creatures, could arise only from the Ideas and Will of a necessarily-existent Being. We speak, however, allegorically, when we say, That God sees, hears, speaks, laughs, loves, hates, despises, gives, receives, rejoices, is angry, fights, fabricates, builds, composes. For all Speech concerning God, is borrowed, by Analogy or some Resemblance, from Human Affairs, not a perfect Resemblance indeed, of some sort however. And so much concerning *God,* of whom to discourse from Phaenomena, belongs to Experimental Philosophy.

"Hitherto I have explain'd the Phaenomena of the Heavens and of our Sea by the *Power* of Gravity, but I have not at all assign'd the *Cause* of Gravity. This Power, however, arises from some Cause, which penetrates even to the Centers of the Sun and Planets, without any Diminution of its Force, and which *acts not in proportion to the Quantity of the Surfaces* of the Particles upon which it acts, (*as Mechanical Causes use to do,*) but according to the Quantity of *solid* Matter; and whose Action is every way extended to immense Distances, decreasing always in a Duplicate Proportion of those Distances. Gravity towards the Sun, is compos'd of the Gravities towards each Particle of the Sun, and decreases from the Sun-ward, accurately in a Duplicate Proportion of those Distances, as far as the Orb of Saturn, as is evident from the Rest of the Aphelia of the Planets; and as far as the remotest Aphelia of the Comets, if their Aphelia also rest. But I have not yet been able to deduce the Reason of these Properties of Gravity from Phaenomena, and I do not form Hypotheses. For whatever is not deduced from Appearances, is to be term'd an HYPOTHESIS; and Hypotheses, whether Metaphysical, or Physical, or of occult Qualities, or Mechanical, have no place in Experimental Philosophy. In this Philosophy Propositions are deduced from Appearances, and render'd General by Induction. So the Impenetrability, Mobility, and the Force of Bodies, and the Laws of Motion and of Gravity have become known: And it is enough, that Gravity really exists, and acts according to the Laws explain'd by us, and suffices for all the Motions of the Heavenly Bodies, and of our Sea." Sir *Isaac Newton's* Principia. Ed. 3. p. 525, &c.

"For rejecting a DENSE AETHEREAL FLUID, we have the Authority of the oldest and most celebrated Philosophers of GREECE and PHOENICIA, who made a Vacuum and Atoms, and the Gravity of Atoms, the first Principles of their Philosophy; tacitly attributing Gravity to some other Cause than dense Matter.[8] Later Philosophers banish the consideration of such a Cause out of Natural Philosophy, feigning Hypotheses for explaining all things mechanically, and referring other Causes to Metaphysicks: Whereas the main business of Natural Philosophy is, to argue from Phaenomena without feigning Hypotheses, and to deduce Causes from Effects, till we come to the *very first Cause, which certainly is not Mechanical;* and not only to *unfold the Mechanism of the World,* but chiefly to *resolve these* and such-like *Questions.*

"What is there in Places almost empty of Matter; and whence is it,

---

8. Newton, *Opticks,* pp. 343–45.

that the Sun and Planets gravitate towards one another, without dense Matter between them? Whence is it, that Nature doth nothing in vain; and whence arises all that Order and Beauty, which we see in the World? To what End are the Comets, and whence is it, that Planets move all one and the same way in Orbs concentrick, while Comets move all manner of ways in Orbs very eccentrick, and what hinders the fix'd Stars from falling upon one another? How came the Bodies of Animals to be contriv'd with so much Art, and for what End were their several Parts? Was the Eye contriv'd without Skill in Opticks, and the Ear without Knowledge of Sounds? How, do the Motions of the Body follow from the Will, and whence is the Instinct of Animals?[9] Is not the Sensory of Animals

9. [Maxwell] "The *Instinct,* as it is called, in Animals, is truly wonderful; and can be nothing less than the Contrivance of a Wise and Powerful *Providence,* for the Preservation of Individuals and the Propagation of the Species. Upon this occasion, I shall here only take notice of some common Actions in Birds. Two Gold-finches, for *Instance,* who never had young ones, make it their first care, after Coupling, to make, in a convenient Place, a convenient Nest; which they know how to build, the first time they go about it, with as much Art and Regularity, as if they had before built an hundred. They begin with twisting little Sticks with Fibres of Plants, which they cover with Moss on the outside, to defend it against the Rain; and garnish it within with Hay and Hair, and a kind of Cotton, soft and warm, of which they make their Bed. In this the Female lays her Eggs, which she keeps warm, by sitting upon them, and spreading a little her Wings, in order to cover them. Tho' Hunger prompts her to go out, she will not leave them, till the Male be ready to take her place, left the Eggs, growing cold, should become addle and produce nothing. When the young Ones are hatch'd, the Male and Female are continually busied in bringing them Worms, which they never eat themselves, and which they equally divide in sufficient Quantities to each; who fail not to open their Mouths out of a desire to receive it; and, from the beginning, always keeping their Nest clean; at proper time, betaking themselves to the open Air and to shift for themselves. Who taught them at first to make a Nest with so much Art, and exactly after the same manner, as all others of their kind do? Who declared to them, that the Female had Eggs in her, and that she should quickly lay them, and that it would be necessary for her and the Male, to cover them alternately with all possible Care, and that, after a certain time, those Eggs would bring forth young ones? Who inform'd them, that they should not feed their young with Seeds, upon which they live after they are grown big; but that they should chuse out for them such Insects, as were most easy of Digestion? Who taught these young ones to open their Bill, almost as soon as they come out of the Shell, to take their Food, and to keep their to Bed so clean? Where is the Artificer among Men, who is so ingenious, as to make a House so well contriv'd and of so regular a Symmetry, as if he were the most skilful Architect? or what Man can provide for an unforeseen

that Place, to which the sensitive Substance is present, and into which the sensible Species of Things are carried through the Nerves and Brain, that there they may be perceiv'd by their immediate presence to that Substance? And these things being rightly dispatch'd, *does it not appear from Phaenomena, That there is a Being, incorporeal, living, intelligent, omnipresent,* who, in infinite Space, as it were in his Sensory, sees the Things themselves intimately, and thoroughly perceives them, and comprehends them wholly by their immediate presence to himself: of which Things the Images only, carried through the Organs of Sense into our little Sensoriums, are there seen and beheld by that which in us perceives and thinks. And, tho' every true Step made in this Philosophy brings us not immediately to the Knowledge of the First Cause, yet it brings us nearer to it, and on that account is to be highly valued." Sir *Isaac Newton's* Opticks." Ed. 3. p. 343, 4, 5.

"When Spirit of Vitriol poured upon common Salt or Salt-petre makes an Ebullition with the Salt and unites with it, and in Distillation the Spirits of the common Salt or Salt-petre comes over much easier than it would do before, and the acid part of the Spirit of Vitriol stays behind; does not this argue, that the Alcaly of the fix'd Salt attracts the acid Spirit of the Vitriol more strongly than its own Spirit, and not being able to hold them both, lets go its own? And when Oil of Vitriol is drawn off from its weight of Nitre, and from both the Ingredients a compound Spirit of Nitre is distilled, and two parts of this Spirit are poured on one part of Oil of Cloves or Caraway Seeds, or of any ponderous Oil of

---

Event, as they for their Eggs and young? Is it credible, that Beasts should partake of so excellent Prerogatives, and that the wonderful Things, which we admire most in them, should be the Effects of their *Reason* and *Knowledge?* If this be so, how can the surprising Things which they do, be reconcil'd to their other Actions, in which they appear to be altogether Brutes? How comes It, that they are so much superior to Man, only in what concerns their Preservation and the Propagation of their Kind, and so much inferior in all other Things? Must not all this, and every thing of the like kind, call'd Instinct, in Animals, be ascrib'd to the Care and Contrivance of a Wise, a Powerful, and a good Providence? For these Actions have too plain Marks of Wisdom, to be the Effects of a blind Cause; nor can it be a supereminent Reason, which these Brutes are endow'd with above Rational Animals, they being, in other matters, so stupid."

vegetable or animal Substances, or Oil of Turpentine thicken'd with a little Balsam of Sulphur, and the Liquors grow so very hot in mixing, as presently to send up a burning Flame: Does not this very great and sudden Heat argue, that the two Liquors mix, run towards one another with an accelerated Motion, and clash with the greatest Force? And is it not for the same reason, that rectified Spirit of Wine poured on the same compound Spirit flashes; and that the *Pulvis fulminans,* composed of Sulphur, Nitre, and Salt of Tartar, goes off with a more sudden and violent Explosion than Gun powder, the acid Spirits of the Sulphur and Nitre rushing towards one another, and towards the Salt of Tartar, with so great a violence, as by the shock to turn the whole at once into Vapour and Flame? Where the Dissolution is slow, it makes a slow Ebullition and a gentle Heat; and where it is quicker, it makes a greater Ebullition with more Heat; and where it is done at once, the Ebullition is contracted into a sudden Blast or violent Explosion, with a Heat equal to that of Fire and Flame. So when a Drachm of the above-mention'd compound Spirit of Nitre was poured upon half a Drachm of Oil of Caraway Seeds *in vacuo;* the Mixture immediately made a flash like Gun-powder, and burst the exhausted Receiver, which was a Glass six Inches wide, and eight Inches deep. And even the gross Body of Sulphur powder'd, and, with an equal weight of Iron Filings and a little Water, made into Paste, acts upon the Iron, and in five or six Hours grows too hot to be touch'd, and emits a Flame. And by these Experiments compared with the great quantity of Sulphur with which the Earth abounds, and the warmth of the interior Parts of the Earth, and hot Springs, and burning Mountains, and with Damps, mineral Coruscations, Earthquakes, hot suffocating Exhalations, Hurricanes and Spouts; we may learn that sulphureous Steams abound in the Bowels of the Earth and ferment with Minerals, and sometimes take fire with a sudden Coruscation and Explosion; and, if pent up in subterraneous Caverns, burst the Caverns with a great shaking of the Earth, as in springing of a Mine. And then the Vapour generated by the Explosion, expiring through the Pores of the Earth, feels hot and suffocates, and makes Tempests and Hurricanes, and sometimes causes the Land to slide, or the Sea to boil, and carries up the Water thereof in Drops, which by their weight fall down again

in Spouts. Also some sulphureous Steams, at all times when the Earth
is dry, ascending into the Air, ferment there with nitrous Acids, and
sometimes taking fire cause Lightening and Thunder, and fiery Meteors.
For the Air abounds with acid Vapours fit to promote Fermentations,
as appears by the rusting of Iron and Copper in it, the kindling of Fire
by blowing, and the beating of the Heart by means of Respiration. Now
the above-mention'd Motions are so great and violent, as to shew, that
in Fermentations the Particles of Bodies which almost rest, are put into
new Motions by a *very potent Principle,* which acts upon them only when
they approach one another, and causes them to meet and clash with great
violence, and grow hot with the Motion, and dash one another into
pieces, and vanish into Air, and Vapour, and Flame." *Newt.* Opt. *Eng.*
Ed. p. 353, 4, 5.

"The Parts of all homogeneal hard Bodies, which fully touch one
another, stick together very strongly. And for explaining how this may
be, some have invented hooked Atoms, which is begging the Question;
and others tell us that Bodies are glued together by Rest, that is, by an
occult Quality, or rather by nothing; and others, that they stick together
by conspiring Motions, that is, by relative Rest amongst themselves. I
had rather infer from their Cohesion, that their Particles *attract one another by some Force,* which in immediate Contact is exceeding strong, at
small distances performs the chymical Operations above-mention'd, and
reaches not far from the Particles with any sensible Effects.

"All Bodies seem to be composed of hard Particles: For otherwise
Fluids would not congeal; as Water, Oils, Vinegar, and Spirit or Oil of
Vitriol do by freezing; Mercury, by Fumes of Lead; Spirit of Nitre and
Mercury, by dissolving the Mercury and evaporating the Flegm; Spirit
of Wine and Spirit of Urine, by deflegming and mixing them; and Spirit
of Urine and Spirit of Salt, by subliming them together to make Sal-
armoniac. Even the Rays of Light seem to be hard Bodies, for otherwise
they would not retain different Properties in their different Sides. And
therefore Hardness may be reckon'd the Property of all uncompounded
Matter. At least, this seems to be as evident as the universal Impenetrability of Matter. For all Bodies, so far as Experience reaches, are either
hard, or may be harden'd; and we have no other Evidence of universal

Impenetrability, besides a large Experience without an experimental Exception. Now, if compound Bodies are so very hard as we find some of them to be, and yet are very porous, and consist of Parts which are only laid together; the simple Particles which are void of Pores, and were never yet divided, must be much harder. For such hard Particles being heaped up together, can scarce touch one another in more than a few Points, and therefore must be separable by much less Force than is requisite to break a solid Particle, whose Parts touch in all the Space between them, without any Pores or Interstices to weaken their Cohesion. And how such very hard Particles which are only laid together and touch only in a few Points, can stick together, and that so firmly as they do, without *the assistance of something which causes them to be attracted* or press'd towards one another, is very difficult to conceive.

"The same thing I infer also from the cohering of two polish'd Marbles *in vacuo,* and from the standing of Quick-silver in the Barometer at the height of 50, 60 or 70 Inches, or above, when ever it is well purged of Air and carefully poured in, so that its Parts be every where contiguous both to one another and to the Glass. The Atmosphere by its weight presses the Quick-silver into the Glass, to the height of 29 or 30 Inches. And *some other Agent* raises it higher, not by pressing it into the Glass, but by making its Parts stick to the Glass, and to one another. For upon any discontinuation of Parts, made either by Bubbles or by shaking the Glass, the whole Mercury falls down to the height of 29 or 30 Inches.

"And of the same kind with these Experiments are those that follow. If two plane polish'd Plates of Glass (suppose two pieces of a polish'd Looking-glass) be laid together, so that their sides be parallel and at a very small distance from one another, and then their lower Edges be dipped into Water, the Water will rise up between them. And the less the distance of the Glasses is, the greater will be the height to which the Water will rise. If the distance be about the hundredth part of an Inch, the Water will rise to the height of about an Inch; and if the distance be greater or less in any Proportion, the height will be reciprocally proportional to the distance very nearly. For the attractive Force of the Glasses is the same, whether the distance between them be greater or less; and the weight of the Water drawn up is the same, if the height of it be reciprocally proportional to the height of the Glasses. And in like manner, Water ascends between two Marbles polish'd plane, when their polished sides are parallel, and at a very little distance from one another. And if slender Pipes of Glass be dipped at one end into stagnating Water, the Water will rise up within the Pipe, and the height to which it arises will be reciprocally proportional to the Diameter of the Cavity of the Pipe, and will equal the height to which it rises between two Planes of Glass, if the Semidiameter of the Cavity of the Pipe be equal to the distance between the Planes, or thereabouts. And these Experiments succeed after the same manner *in vacuo* as in the open Air, (as hath been tried before the Royal Society,) and therefore are not influenced by the Weight or Pressure of the Atmosphere.

"And if a large Pipe of Glass be filled with sifted Ashes well pressed together in the Glass, and one end of the Pipe be dipped into stagnating Water, the Water will rise up slowly in the Ashes, so as in the space of a Week or Fortnight to reach up within the Glass, to the height of 30 or 40 Inches above the stagnating Water. And the Water rises up to this height by the Action only of those Particles of the Ashes which are upon the Surface of the elevated Water; the Particles which are within the Water, attracting or repelling it as much downwards as upwards. And therefore the Action of the Particles is very strong. But the Particles of the Ashes being not so dense and close together as those of Glass, their Action is not so strong as that of Glass, which keeps Quick-silver suspended to the height of 60 or 70 Inches, and therefore acts with a Force which would keep Water suspended to the height of above 60 Feet.

"By the same Principle, a Sponge sucks in Water, and the Glands in the Bodies of Animals, according to their several Natures and Dispositions, suck in various Juices from the Blood.

"If two plane polish'd plates of Glass three or four Inches broad, and twenty or twenty five long, be laid, one of them parallel to the Horizon, the other upon the first, so as at one of their ends to touch one another, and contain an Angle of about 10 or 15 Minutes, and the same be first moisten'd on their inward sides with a clean Cloath dipp'd into Oil of Oranges or Spirit of Turpentine, and a Drop or two of the Oil or Spirit be let fall upon the lower Glass at the other end; so soon as the upper

Glass is laid down upon the lower, so as to touch it at one end as above, and to touch the Drop at the other end, making with the lower Glass an Angle of about 10 or 15 Minutes; the Drop will begin to move towards the Concourse of the Glasses, and will continue to move with an accelerated Motion, till it arrives at that Concourse of the Glasses. For the two Glasses attract the Drop, and make it run that way towards which the Attractions incline. And if when the Drop is in Motion you lift up that end of the Glasses where they meet, and towards which the Drop moves, the Drop will ascend between the Glasses, and therefore is attracted. And as you lift up the Glasses more and more, the Drop will ascend slower and slower, and at length rest, being then carried downward by its Weight, as much as upwards by the Attraction. And by this means you may know the Force by which the Drop is attracted at all distances from the Concourse of the Glasses.

"Now by some Experiments of this kind, (made by Mr. *Hauksby*,) it has been found that the Attraction is almost reciprocally in a duplicate Proportion of the distance of the middle of the Drop from the Concourse of the Glasses, *viz.* reciprocally in a simple Proportion, by reason of the spreading of the Drop, and its touching each Glass in a larger Surface; and again reciprocally in a simple Proportion, by reason of the Attractions growing stronger within the same quantity of attracting Surface. The Attraction therefore within the same quantity of attracting Surface, is reciprocally as the distance between the Glasses. And therefore where the distance is exceeding small, the Attraction must be exceeding great. By the Table in the second Part of the second Book, wherein the thicknesses of colour'd Plates of Water between two Glasses are set down, the thickness of the Plate where it appears very black, is three eighths of the ten hundred thousandth part of an Inch. And where the Oil of Oranges between the Glasses is of this thickness, the Attraction collected by the foregoing Rule, seems to be so strong, as within a Circle of an Inch in diameter, to suffice to hold up a Weight equal to that of a Cylinder of Water of an Inch in diameter, and two or three Furlongs in length. And where it is of a less thickness, the Attraction may be proportionally greater, and continue to increase, until the thickness do not exceed that of a single Particle of the Oil. *There are therefore Agents in*

Nature able to make the Particles of Bodies stick together by very strong Attractions. And it is the Business of experimental Philosophy to find them out.

"Now the smallest Particles of Matter may cohere by the strongest Attractions, and compose bigger Particles of weaker Virtue; and many of these may cohere and compose bigger Particles whose Virtue is still weaker, and so on for divers Successions, until the Progression end in the biggest Particles, on which the Operations in Chymistry and the Colours of natural Bodies depend, and which by cohering compose Bodies of a sensible Magnitude. If the Body is compact, and bends or yields inward to Pression without any sliding of its Parts, it is hard and elastick, returning to its Figure with a Force rising from the mutual Attraction of its Parts. If the Parts slide upon one another, the Body is malleable or soft. If they slip easily, and are of a fit size to be agitated by Heat, and the Heat is big enough to keep them in Agitation, the Body is fluid; and if it be apt to stick to things, it is humid; and the Drops of every fluid affect a round Figure by the mutual Attraction of their Parts, as the Globe of the Earth and Sea affects a round Figure by the mutual Attraction of its Parts by Gravity.

"Since Metals dissolved in Acids attract but a small quantity of the Acid, their attractive Force can reach but to a small distance from them. And as in Algebra, where affirmative Quantities vanish and cease, there negative ones begin; so in Mechanicks, where Attraction ceases, there a repulsive Virtue ought to succeed. And that there is such a Virtue, seems to follow from the Reflexions and Inflexions of the Rays of Light. For the Rays are repelled by Bodies in both these Cases, without the immediate Contact of the reflecting or inflecting Body. It seems also to follow from the Emission of Light; the Ray, so soon as it is shaken off from a shining Body by the vibrating Motion of the Parts of the Body, and gets beyond the reach of Attraction, being driven away with exceeding great Velocity. For that Force which is sufficient to turn it back in Reflexion, may be sufficient to emit it. It seems also to follow from the Production of Air and Vapour. The Particles, when they are shaken off from Bodies by Heat or Fermentation, so soon as they are beyond the reach of the Attraction of the Body, receding from it, and also from one another with great Strength, and keeping at a distance so as some-times to take up above a million of times more space than they did before in the form of a dense Body. Which vast Contraction and Expansion seems unintelligible, by feigning the Particles of Air to be springy and ramous, or rolled up like Hoops, or by any other means than a repulsive Power. The Particles of Fluids which do not cohere too strongly, and are of such a smallness as renders them most susceptible of those Agi-tations which keep Liquors in a Fluor, are most easily separated and rar-ified into Vapour, and in the Language of the Chymists, they are volatile, rarifyed with an easy Heat, and condensing with Cold. But those which are grosser, and so less susceptible of Agitation, or cohere by a stronger Attraction, are not separated without a stronger Heat, or perhaps not without Fermentation. And these last are the Bodies which Chymists call fix'd, and being rarified by Fermentation, become true permanent Air: those Particles receding from one another with the greatest Force, and being most difficultly brought together, which upon Contact cohere most strongly. And, because the Particles of permanent Air are grosser, and arise from denser Substances than those of Vapours, thence it is that true Air is more ponderous than Vapour, and that a moist Atmosphere is lighter than a dry one, quantity for quantity. From the same repelling Power it seems to be that Flies walk upon the Water without wetting their Feet; and that the Object-glasses of long Telescopes lie upon one another without touching; and that dry Powders are difficultly made to touch one another so as to stick together, unless by melting them, or wetting them with Water, which by exhaling may bring them together; and that two polish'd Marbles, which by immediate Contact stick to-gether, are difficultly brought so close together as to stick.

"And thus Nature will be very conformable to her self and very sim-ple, performing all *the great Motions of the heavenly Bodies by the Attrac-tion of Gravity which intercedes those Bodies, and almost all the small ones of their Particles by some other attractive and repelling Powers which in-tercede the Particles.* The *Vis inertiae* is a *passive Principle* by which Bodies persist in their Motion or Rest, receive Motion in proportion to the Force impressing it, and resist as much as they are resisted. *By this Prin-ciple alone there never could have been any Motion in the World. Some other*

Principle was necessary for putting Bodies into Motion; and now they are in Motion, some other Principle is necessary for conserving the Motion. For from the various Composition of two Motions, 'tis very certain that there is not always the same quantity of Motion in the World. For if two Globes joined by a slender Rod, revolve about their common Center of Gravity, with an uniform Motion, while that Center moves on uniformly in a right Line drawn in the Plane of their circular Motion; the Sum of the Motions of the two Globes, as often as the Globes are in the right Line described by their common Center of Gravity, will be bigger than the Sum of their Motions, when they are in a Line perpendicular to that right Line. By this Instance it appears, that Motion may be got or lost. But by reason of the Tenacity of Fluids, and Attrition of their Parts, and the Weakness of Elasticity in Solids, *Motion* is much more apt to be lost than got, and *is always upon the Decay.* For Bodies which are either absolutely hard, or so soft as to be void of Elasticity, will not rebound from one another. Impenetrability makes them only stop. If two equal Bodies meet directly *in vacuo,* they will by the Laws of Motion stop where they meet, and lose all their Motion, and remain in rest, unless they be elastick, and receive new Motion from their Spring. If they have so much Elasticity as suffices to make them rebound with a quarter, or half, or three quarters of the Force with which they come together, they will lose three quarters, or half, or a quarter of their Motion. And this may be tried, by letting two equal Pendulums fall against one another from equal heights. If the Pendulums be of Lead or soft Clay, they will lose all or almost all their Motions: If of elastick Bodies, they will lose all but what they recover from their Elasticity. If it be said, that they can lose no Motion but what they communicate to other Bodies, the consequence is, that *in vacuo* they can lose no Motion, but when they meet they must go on and penetrate one anothers Dimensions. If three equal round Vessels be filled, the one with Water, the other with Oil, the third with molten Pitch, and the Liquors be stirred about alike to give them a vortical Motion; the Pitch by its Tenacity will lose its Motion quickly, the Oil being less tenacious will keep it longest, but yet will lose it in a short time. Whence it is easy to understand, that if many contiguous Vortices of molten Pitch were each of them as large as those which some suppose to revolve about the Sun and fix'd Stars, yet these and all their Parts would, by their tenacity and stiffness, communicate their Motion to one another, till they all rested among themselves. Vortices of Oil or Water, or some fluider Matter, might continue longer in Motion; but, unless the Matter were void of all Tenacity and Attrition of Parts, and Communication of Motion, (which is not to be supposed,) the Motion would constantly decay. *Seeing therefore the variety of Motion which we find in the World is always decreasing, there is a necessity of conserving and recruiting it by active Principles,* such as are the *Cause of Gravity,* by which Planets and Comets keep their Motions in their Orbs, and Bodies acquire great Motion in falling; and the *Cause of Fermentation,* by which the Heart and Blood of Animals are kept in perpetual Motion and Heat; the inward Parts of the Earth are constantly warm'd and in some places grow very hot; Bodies burn and shine, Mountains take Fire, the Caverns of the Earth are blown up, and the Sun continues violently hot and lucid, and warms all things by his Light. For *we meet with very little Motion in the World, besides what is owing to these active Principles.* And if it were not for these Principles, the Bodies of the Earth, Planets, Comets, Sun, and all things in them would grow cold and freeze, and become inactive Masses; and all Putrefaction, Generation, Vegetation and Life would cease, and the Planets and Comets would not remain in their Orbs.

"All these things being consider'd, it seems *probable* to me, that *God in the Beginning form'd Matter* in solid, massy, hard, impenetrable, moveable Particles, of such Sizes and Figures, and with such other Properties, and in such Proportion to Space, as most conduced to the *End* for which he form'd them; and that these primitive Particles being Solids, are incomparably harder than any porous Bodies compounded of them; even so very hard, as never to wear or break in pieces: No ordinary Power being able to divide what God himself made one in the first Creation. While the Particles continue intire, they may compose Bodies of one and the same Nature and Texture in all Ages: But should they wear away, or break in pieces, the Nature of Things depending on them would be changed. Water and Earth composed of old worn Particles and Fragments of Particles, would not be of the same Nature and Texture now, with Water and Earth composed of intire Particles, in the Beginning. And therefore that Nature may be lasting, the Changes of corporeal Things are to be placed only in the various Separations and new Associations and Motions of these permanent Particles; compound Bodies being apt to break, not in the midst of solid Particles, but where those Particles are laid together, and only touch in a few Points.

"It seems to me farther, that these Particles have *not only a Vis inertiae,* accompanied with such *passive Laws* of Motion as naturally result from that Force, but also that they are moved by certain *active Principles,* such as is that of Gravity, and that which causes Fermentation, and the Cohesion of Bodies. These Principles I consider not as occult Qualities, supposed to result from the specifick Forms of Things, but as general Laws of Nature, by which the Things themselves are form'd: their Truth appearing to us by Phaenomena, though their Causes be not yet discover'd. For these are manifest Qualities, and their Causes only are occult. And the *Aristotelians* gave the Name of occult Qualities, not to manifest Qualities, but to such Qualities only as they supposed to lie hid in Bodies, and to be the unknown Causes of Gravity, and of magnetick and electrick Attractions, and of Fermentations, if we should suppose that these Forces or Actions arose from Qualities unknown to us, and uncapable of being discovered and made manifest. Such occult Qualities put a stop to the Improvement of natural Philosophy, and therefore of late Years have been rejected. To tell us that every Species of Things is endow'd with an occult specifick Quality by which it acts and produces manifest Effects, is to tell us nothing: But to derive two or three general Principles of Motion from Phaenomena, and afterwards to tell us how the Properties and Actions of all corporeal Things follow from those manifest Principles, would be a very great step in Philosophy, though the Causes of those Principles were not yet discover'd: And therefore I scruple not to propose the Principles of Motion above mention'd, they being of very general Extent, and leave their Causes to be found out.

"Now by the help of these Principles, all material Things seem to have been composed of the hard and solid Particles abovemention'd, variously associated in the first Creation *by the Council of an intelligent Agent.* For it became him who created them to set them in order. And if he did so, *'tis unphilosophical to seek for any other Origin of the World, or to pretend that it might arise out of a Chaos by the mere Laws of Nature,* though being once form'd, it may continue by those Laws for many Ages. For while Comets move in very excentrick Orbs in all manner of Positions, *blind Fate could never make* all the Planets move one and the same way in Orbs concentrick, some inconsiderable Irregularities excepted, which may have risen from the mutual Actions of Comets and Planets upon one another, and which will be apt to increase, *till this System wants a Reformation.* Such a wonderful *Uniformity in the Planetary System* must be allowed the Effect of *Choice.* And so must the *Uniformity in the Bodies of Animals,* they having generally a right and a left side shaped alike, and on either side of their Bodies two Legs behind, and either two Arms, or two Legs, or two Wings before upon their Shoulders, and between their Shoulders a Neck running down into a Back-bone, and a Head upon it; and in the Head two Ears, two Eyes, a Nose, a Mouth, and a Tongue, alike situated. Also the first *Contrivance of those very artificial Parts of Animals,* the Eyes, Ears, Brain, Muscles, Heart, Lungs, Midrift, Glands, Larinx, Hands, Wings, Swimming Bladders, natural Spectacles, and other Organs of Sense and Motion; and the *Instinct* of Brutes and Insects, can be the effect of nothing else than the *Wisdom* and *Skill* of a powerful ever-living *Agent,* who being in all Places, is more able by his Will to move the Bodies within his boundless uniform Sensorium, and thereby to form and reform the Parts of the Universe, than we are by our Will to move the Parts of our own Bodies. And yet we are *not* to consider the *World* as the *Body of God,* or the several *Parts* thereof, as the *Parts of God.* He is an uniform Being, void of Organs, Members or Parts, and they are his Creatures subordinate to him, and subservient to his Will; and he is no more the Soul of them, than the Soul of a Man is the Soul of the Species of Things carried through the Organs of Sense into the place of its Sensation, where it perceives them by means of its immediate Presence, without the Intervention of any third thing. The Organs of Sense are not for enabling the Soul to perceive the Species of Things in its Sensorium, but only for conveying them thither; and God has no need of such Organs, he being every where present to the Things themselves. And since Space is divisible *in infinitum,* and Matter is not necessarily in all places, it may be allow'd, that God is able to create Particles of Matter of several Sizes and Figures, and in several Proportions to Space, and perhaps of different Densities and Forces, and thereby to vary the Laws of Nature, and make Worlds of several sorts in several Parts of the Universe. At least, I see nothing of Contradiction in all this.

"If Natural Philosophy in all its Parts, by pursuing this Method, shall at length be perfected, the Bounds of Moral Philosophy will be also enlarged. For so far as we can know by Natural Philosophy what is the First Cause, what Power he has over us, and what Benefits we receive from him, so far our Duty towards him, as well as that towards one another, will appear to us by the Light of Nature. And no doubt, if the Worship of false Gods had not blinded the *Heathen,* their Moral Philosophy would have gone farther than to the four Cardinal Virtues; and, instead of teaching the Transmigration of Souls, and to worship the Sun and Moon, and dead Heroes, they would have taught us to worship our true Author and Benefactor, as their Ancestors did under the Government of *Noah* and his Sons, before they corrupted themselves." *Ibid.* P. 363, &c.

What can be more just than the *Conclusions* drawn by this great Philosopher from the Phaenomena of Nature; *viz. That the World owes not its being such as it is, to Mechanism, Chance, or Necessity; but to the Will of a Wise and Powerful Being, who first form'd, and continually governs, the same;* in opposition to those Atheists who hold, with *Epicurus* and others, that the present Frame of Nature had a Beginning, but not from God? And does he not, with equal Strength of Reason, conclude, *That Motion is, of it-self, continually decreasing;* and, *That this Frame of Nature does, of it-self, tend to Decay, Confusion, and Ruin;* and, consequently, *That it could not, of it-self, have subsisted from all Eternity;* which is, at present, the more prevailing Opinion among Men of Atheistical Principles?

The Formation of Animals is not Mechanical. Of this Truth there are several Indications; but I shall here make use only of the following Observation and Reasoning of Dr. Pitcairn, in the Beginning of his *Dissertation of the Circulation of the Blood in Animals, before and after Birth.*

6. The Formation of Animals is not Mechanical.

"I am confident, nothing in Life can be found more useful, or more agreeable to the Mind, inquiring into the Original of Things, (known only to God, the Author of All,) than to have found out, and be convinc'd, that the first Rise of Animals is owing to God himself. For 'tis now known, from the Law of Circulation, that the Blood is receiv'd by, and propell'd from, the Heart of an Animal alternately; for which reason, neither Heat, nor any Ferment, nor Liquor, however charg'd with Spirits or Salts, or any other Power constantly and not alternately impress'd, expels the Blood or nutritious Juice, from the Heart or its Neighbourhood; otherwise, when once propell'd, it would never return back to the Heart, that Force perpetually opposing it, as not being alternately impress'd. But the Force, which is alternately communicated to the Heart, does not proceed from the Womb of the Mother; for whatsoever goes from the Womb to the Heart of an Embryo, is discharg'd into its Ventricles, and not into the Ducts of its Fibres, by which it is contracted; and beside, the Heart of an Embryo will still continue its Contraction, and the Blood its Circulation, tho' freed from the Uterus. Therefore the moving Force is to be deduc'd from some part of the Embryo. For the Law of Circulation shews, that nothing can be remitted to the Heart from any part in an Animal, that was not first sent to that part from the Heart along with the Blood; and we have shewn, that the Secretion of Fluids in an Animal, (whether they return to the Heart or not,) are perform'd by means of Circulation opposing the secernible Fluid to the secretory Orifices equal in Magnitude to the Particles to be secern'd; and that there is no other Mechanical Reason of Animal Secretion: and, therefore, that there do not only exist secretory Vessels, and others, before any assign'd Secretion; but also, that the Secretion of those Powers return'd to contract the Heart, is perform'd before any assign'd Constriction of the Heart, or any Circulation of the Blood is begun; or that the Contraction of the Heart propelling the Blood to the part secerning the Body or Powers for the contracting the Heart, is perform'd before any Secretion, or return and communication of the contracting Powers. Farther; Circulation teaches us, that the Medullary Substance of the Brain and Spinal Marrow are the Parts, from whence the Power, which alternately expels the Blood, is communicated to the Heart: Nor, by the

Changes and Metamorphoses common to some kind of Animals, are the Powers, or Relations of Powers, alter'd, whereon their Life and Circulation depend; so that the Communication between the Heart and Spinal Marrow is not chang'd. Whence it follows, that the Heart, Brain, and Spinal Marrow, have the same mutual Dependence by the same Powers operating after the same manner, which was the same at the first Contraction of the Heart, as in any subsequent one. For which Reason, the Powers of the Heart and Brain were form'd at the same time, and exist together; and, therefore, *no Animal is produc'd Mechanically.*" [10]

§3. *The World is a System or Whole, whose Parts are design'd and contriv'd mutually for one another;* which plainly proves it to have been fram'd by *a Being powerful, wise, and good.* I shall here close my Quotations of Arguments to prove the Being of a God, with one upon the Head now laid down, taken from Lord *Shaftesbury's* Characteristicks Vol. 2. P. 282, &c. where he introduces one talking to his doubting Friend, in the following Words.

> The World is a *System* or *Whole,* whose *Parts* are design'd and contriv'd mutually for one another; which plainly proves it to have been fram'd by a Being Powerful, Wise, and Good.

"O my ingenious Friend! whose Reason, in other respects, must be allow'd so clear and happy; how is it possible that, with such Insight, and accurate Judgment in *the Particulars* of Natural Beings and Operations, you shou'd no better judge of the Structure of Things *in general,* and of the Order and Frame of NATURE? Who better than yourself can shew the Structure of each Plant and Animal-Body, declare the Office of every *Part* and *Organ,* and tell the Uses, Ends, and Advantages to which they serve? How, therefore, should you prove so ill *a Naturalist* in *this* WHOLE, and understand so little the Anatomy of *the World* and *Nature,* as not to discern the same Relation of Parts, the same Consistency and Uniformity in *the Universe!*"

"Some Men, perhaps, there are of so confus'd a Thought, and irregularly form'd *within themselves,* that 'tis no more than Natural for them to find fault, and imagine a thousand Inconsistences and Defects in this *wider Constitution.* 'Tis not, we may presume, the absolute Aim or In-

---

10. Maxwell translates from Pitcairne, *"Dissertatio de Circulatione Sanguinis in Animalibus Genitis et non Genitis"* (1713).

terest of the Universal Nature, to render every private-one infallible, and without defect. 'Twas not its Intention to leave us without some Pattern of Imperfection; such as we perceive in Minds, like these, perplex'd with froward Thought. But you, my Friend, are Master of a nobler Mind. You are conscious of better Order *within,* and can see Workmanship and Exactness in yourself, and other *innumerable Parts* of the Creation. Can you answer it to yourself, allowing thus much, not to allow all? Can you induce yourself ever to believe or think, that where there are Parts so variously united, and conspiring fitly within themselves, *the Whole* it-self shou'd have neither Union nor Coherence; and where inferior and private Natures are often sound so perfect, *the Universal-One* shou'd want Perfection, and be esteem'd like whatsoever can be thought of most monstrous, rude, and imperfect?"

"Strange! That there shou'd be *in Nature* the Idea of an Order and Perfection, which NATURE her-self wants! That Beings which arise from *Nature* shou'd be so perfect, as to discover Imperfection in her Consti-tution; and be wise enough to correct that Wisdom by which they were made!"

Nothing, surely, is more strongly imprinted on our Minds, or "more closely interwoven with our Souls, than the Idea or Sense of *Order* and *Proportion.* Hence all the Force of *Numbers,* and those powerful *Arts* founded on their Management and Use. What a difference there is be-tween *Harmony* and *Discord! Cadency* and *Convulsion!* What a differ-ence between compos'd and orderly Motion, and that which is ungov-ern'd and accidental! Between the regular and uniform Pile of some noble Architect, and a Heap of Sand or Stones! Between an organiz'd Body, and a Mist or Cloud driven by the Wind."

"Now as this difference is immediately perceiv'd by a plain Internal Sensation, so there is withal in Reason this account of it; That whatever Things have *Order,* the same have *Unity of Design,* and they which con-cur *in One,* are Parts constituent of *one* WHOLE, or are, in themselves, *intire Systems.* Such is a *Tree,* with all its Branches; an *Animal,* with all its Members; an *Edifice,* with all its exterior and interior Ornaments. What else is even a *Tune* or *Symphony,* or any excellent Piece of Musick, than a certain *System* of proportion'd Sounds?"

"Now in this which we call the UNIVERSE, whatever the Perfection may be of any *particular Systems;* or whatever *single Parts* may have Proportion, Unity, or Form within themselves; yet, if they are not united all in general, *in* ONE *System,* but are, in respect of one another, as the driven Sands, or Clouds, or breaking Waves; then there being no Coherence in *the Whole,* there can be inferr'd no Order, no Proportion, and, consequently, no Project or *Design.* But, if none of these Parts are Independent, but all apparently united, then is the WHOLE *a System* compleat, according to one *Simple, Consistent,* and *Uniform* DESIGN."

"Here then is our main Subject, insisted on: That neither *Man,* nor any other Animal, tho' ever so compleat a *System* of Parts, as to all *within,* can be allow'd in the same manner compleat, as to all *without;* but must be consider'd as having a farther relation abroad to *the System of his Kind.* So even this System of his Kind to *the Animal-System;* this to the World (our *Earth;*) and this again to *the bigger World,* and to *the Universe.*"

"All Things in this World are *united.* For as the *Branch* is united with the *Tree,* so is the Tree as immediately with the *Earth, Air,* and *Water,* which feed it. As much as the fertile *Mould* is fitted to the Tree, as much as the strong and upright Trunk of the *Oak* or *Elm* is fitted to the twining Branches of the *Vine* or *Ivy;* so much are the very *Leaves,* the *Seeds,* and the *Fruits* of these Trees fitted to the various *Animals.* These again to one another, and to the *Elements* where they live, and to which they are, as Appendices, in a manner fitted and join'd; as either by *Wings* for the Air, *Fins* for the Water, *Feet* for the Earth, and by other correspondent inward Parts, of a more curious Frame and Texture. Thus in contemplating all on Earth, we must of necessity view *All in One,* as holding to one common Stock. Thus too in the System of the bigger World. See there the mutual Dependency of Things! the Relation of one to another; of the Sun to this inhabited Earth, and of the Earth and other Planets to the Sun! the Order, Union, and Coherence of *the Whole!* And know (my ingenious Friend) That by this Survey you will be oblig'd to own the UNIVERSAL SYSTEM, and coherent Scheme of Things, to be establish'd on abundant Proof, capable of convincing any fair and just Contemplator of the Works of Nature. For scarce wou'd any one, 'till he had well survey'd this universal Scene, believe *a Union* thus evidently demonstrable, by such numerous and powerful Instances of mutual Correspondency and Relation, from the minutest Ranks and Orders of Beings to the remotest Spheres."

"Now, in this mighty UNION, if there be such Relations of Parts one to another as are not easily discover'd; if on this account the End and Use of Things does not every where appear, there is no wonder; since 'tis no more, indeed, than what must happen of necessity: Nor could Supreme Wisdom have otherwise order'd it. For in an Infinity of Things thus relative, a Mind which sees not *infinitely,* can see nothing *fully:* And since each particular has relation to all in general, it can know no perfect or true Relation of any Thing, in a World not perfectly and fully known."

"The same may be consider'd in any dissected Animal, Plant, or Flower; where he who is no Anatomist, nor vers'd in Natural History, sees that the many *Parts* have a relation to *the Whole;* for thus much even a slight View affords: But he who like you, my Friend, is curious in the Works of Nature, and has been let into a Knowledge of the Animal and Vegetable World, he alone can readily declare the just Relation of all these Parts to one another, and the several Uses to which they serve."

"But, if you would willingly enter farther into this Thought, and consider how much we ought, not only to be satisfy'd with this our View of Things, but even to admire its Clearness; imagine only some Person intirely a Stranger to Navigation, and ignorant of the Nature of the Sea or Waters, how great his Astonishment would be, when finding himself on Board some Vessel, anchoring at Sea, remote from all Land-prospect, whilst it was yet a Calm, he view'd the ponderous Machine firm and motionless in the midst of the smooth Ocean, and consider'd its Foundations beneath, together with its Cordage, Masts, and Sails above. How easily would he see *the Whole* one regular Structure, all things depending on one another; the Uses of the Rooms *below,* the Lodgments, and Conveniences of Men and Stores? But, being ignorant of the Intent or Design of all *above,* would he pronounce the Masts and Cordage to be useless and cumbersome, and for this Reason condemn the Frame, and despise *the Architect?* O my Friend! let us not thus betray our Ignorance;

but consider where we are, and in what a Universe. Think of the many Parts of the vast Machine, in which we have so little insight, and of which it is impossible we should know the Ends and Uses; which instead of seeing to the highest *Pendants,* we see only some *lower Deck,* and are in this dark Case of Flesh, confin'd even to *the Hold,* and meanest Station of the Vessel."

"Now, having recogniz'd this uniform consistent Fabrick, and own'd the *Universal System,* we must of consequence acknowledge a *Universal* MIND; which no ingenuous Man can be tempted to disown, except thro' the Imagination of Disorder in the Universe, its Seat. For can it be suppos'd of any one in the World, that, being in some Desart far from Men, and hearing there a perfect Symphony of Musick, or seeing an exact Pile of regular Architecture arising gradually from the Earth, in all its Orders and Proportions, he should be persuaded that at the Bottom there was no *Design* accompanying this, no secret Spring of *Thought,* no active *Mind?* Would he, because he saw no Hand, deny the Handy-work, and suppose that each of these compleat and perfect Systems were fram'd, and thus united in just Symmetry, and conspiring Order, either by the accidental blowing of the Winds, or rolling of the Sands."

"What is it then should so disturb our Views of *Nature,* as to destroy that Unity of Design and Order of *a Mind,* which otherwise would be so apparent? All we can see either of the Heavens or Earth, demonstrates Order and Perfection; so as to afford the noblest Subjects of Contemplation to Minds, like yours, enrich'd with Sciences and Learning. All is delightful, amiable, rejoicing, except with relation to *Man* only, and his Circumstances, which seem unequal. Here the Calamity and Ill arises; and hence the Ruin of this goodly Frame. All perishes on this account; and the whole Order of the Universe, elsewhere so firm, intire, and immoveable, is here o'erthrown, and lost by this one View; in which we refer all things to ourselves; submitting the Interest of *the Whole* to the Good and Interest of so small *a Part.*"

"But how is it you complain of the unequal State of Man, and of the few Advantages allow'd him above the Beasts? What can a Creature claim, so little differing from 'em, or whose Merit appears so little above 'em, except in *Wisdom* and *Virtue,* to which so few conform? Man may be Virtuous; and by being so, is Happy. His Merit is Reward. By Virtue he deserves; and in Virtue only can meet his Happiness deserv'd. But, if even *Virtue* it-self be unprovided for, and *Vice* more prosperous be the better Choice; if this (as you suppose) be in the Nature of Things, then is all Order in reality inverted, and Supreme Wisdom lost: Imperfection and Irregularity being, after this manner, undoubtedly too apparent in the Moral World."

"Have you then, e'er you pronounc'd this Sentence, consider'd of the State of *Virtue* and *Vice,* with respect to *this Life merely;* so as to say, with assurance, When, and How far, in what Particular, and how Circumstantiated, the one or the other is *Good* or *Ill?* You who are skill'd in other Fabricks and Compositions, both of Art and Nature, have you consider'd of the Fabrick of *the Mind,* the Constitution of the Soul, the Connexion and Frame of all its Passions and Affections; to know accordingly the Order and Symmetry of the Part, and how it either improves or suffers; what its Force is, when naturally preserv'd in its sound State; and what becomes of it, when corrupted and abus'd? 'Till this (my Friend) be well examin'd and understood, how shall we judge either of the Force of *Virtue,* or Power of *Vice?* Or in what manner either of these may work to our Happiness or Undoing?"

"Here therefore is that INQUIRY we should first make. But who is there can afford to make it as he ought? If happily we are born of a good Nature; if a liberal Education has form'd in us a generous Temper and Disposition, well-regulated Appetites, and worthy Inclinations, 'tis well for us; and so indeed we esteem it. But who is there endeavours to give these to himself, or to advance his Portion of Happiness in this kind? Who thinks of improving, or so much as of preserving his Share, in a World where it must of necessity run so great a hazard, and where we know an honest Nature is so easily corrupted? All other things relating to us are preserv'd with Care, and have some Art or Oeconomy belonging to 'em; this which is nearest related to us, and on which our Happiness depends, is alone committed to Chance: And *Temper* is the only Thing ungovern'd, whilst it governs all the rest."

"Thus we inquire concerning what is good and suitable to our Appetites; but what Appetites are good and suitable to us, is no part of our

Examination. We inquire what is according to *Interest, Policy, Fashion, Vogue;* but it seems wholly strange, and out of the way, to inquire what is *according to* NATURE. The Balance of EUROPE, of Trade, of Power, is strictly sought after; while few have heard of *the Balance of their Passions,* or thought of holding these Scales even. Few are acquainted with this Province, or knowing in these Affairs. But were we more so (as this *Inquiry* would make us) we should then see Beauty and Decorum here, as well as elsewhere in Nature; and the Order of the Moral World would equal that of the Natural. By this the *Beauty of* VIRTUE would appear; and hence (as has been shewn) *the Supreme* and *Sovereign* BEAUTY, the Original of all which is Good or Amiable."

"But, lest I should appear at last too like an *Enthusiast,* I chuse to express my Sense, and conclude this *Philosophical Sermon,* in the Words of one of those antient *Philologists,* whom you are us'd to esteem. *For Divinity it-self,* says he, *is surely Beauteous, and of all Beauties the brightest; tho' not a beauteous Body, but that from whence the Beauty of Bodies is deriv'd: Not a beauteous Plain, but that from whence the Plain looks Beautiful. The River's Beauty, the Sea's, the Heaven's, and Heavenly Constellation's, all flow from hence, as from a Source Eternal and Incorruptible. As Beings partake of this, they are fair, and flourishing, and happy: As they are lost to this, they are deform'd, perish'd, and lost.*"[11]

§4. *The Origination of Things in Theism is in such Order, which is Natural and Possible: But Atheism inverteth it, beginning at the wrong End, and deduceth things in such an Order, as is Unnatural and Impossible.*

Atheism inverteth all natural Order, and deduceth the Origin of Things in an impossible Manner.

That an Universe of imperfect Beings should issue from *a Being absolutely perfect,* is no more Unnatural and Impossible, than that a Poet should make a Verse, or the Sun produce Vapours: But that an Universe of Beings of great Perfections (Vital and Intellectual, Natural and Moral,) should be produc'd merely by Matter (which is of all things the most Imperfect,) is as Unnatural and Impossible, as that the Verse should make the Poet, or the Vapours should produce the Sun. That Nonsense should generate Sense, and the imperceptive Stupidity of Matter should

11. Shaftesbury, *Characteristicks of Men, Manners, Opinions, Times,* II, p. 282ff.

produce perceptive Life, Cogitation, Reason, and Understanding; that the Ascent of Things should be upwards, from Matter producing all the higher Orders of Beings, of manifold Species and Ranks, of various Kinds and Degrees of Perfection, (Inanimate, Animate, Vegetative, Sensitive, Rational;) that the greater Plenty of Perfection should be the Product of the greater Penury, is, in the Judgment of common Sense, plainly Impossible; as if the Matter of an House should, without an Architect, build it-self into an House, and furnish it with Inhabitants, providing them with all Accommodations.

Mankind are
not Self-
existent.

§5. *The Self-existence of Mankind from Eternity is an impossible Supposition.* No rational Man, or Men, now in being, can possibly be of this Opinion, that he or they are Self-existent; and so it was in all Generations that are past. Nor could they be Existent from Eternity; for, since each in the Succession had a Beginning, the Whole must have had a Beginning.

"An *infinite* Succession of Effects will require an *infinite* Efficient, or a Cause *infinitely Effective.* So far is it from requiring *none.*"

"Suppose a *Chain* hung down from the Heavens of an *infinite* Height, and, tho' every Link of it gravitated towards the Earth, and what it hung upon was not visible, yet it did not descend, but kept its Situation; and upon this a Question should arise, *What supported or kept up this Chain:* Would it be a sufficient Answer to say, that the *first* (or lowest) Link hung upon the *second* (or that next above it), the *second,* or rather the *first and second together,* upon the *third,* and so on *ad infinitum?* For what holds up the *Whole?* A *Chain* of *ten* Links would fall down, unless something able to bear it hinder'd: One of *twenty,* if not stay'd by something of a yet greater Strength, in proportion to the increase of Weight: And, therefore, one of *infinite* Links certainly, if not sustain'd by something *infinitely* Strong, and capable to bear up an *infinite* Weight. And thus it is in a Chain of Causes and Effects tending, or as it were *gravitating,* towards some End. The last (or lowest) depends, or (as we may say) is *suspended* upon the Cause above it; this again, if it be not the First Cause, is suspended, as an Effect upon something above it, &*c.* And, if they should be *Infinite,* unless (agreeably to what has been said) there is some Cause upon which all hang or depend, they would be but an infinite Effect without an Efficient: And to assert there is any such thing would be as great an *Absurdity*, as to say, that a Finite or *little* Weight wants something to sustain it, but an infinite one or the *greatest* does not. Suppose a Row of blind Men, of which the last laid his Hand upon the Shoulder of the Man next before him, he on the Shoulder of the Man next before him, and so on, 'till the foremost grew to be quite out of sight; and somebody asking, What Guide this String of blind Men had at the Head of them, it should be answer'd, that they had no Guide, nor any Head, but one held by another, and so went on *ad infinitum*, would any rational Creature accept this for a just Answer? Is it not to say, that Blindness, in an infinite Progression, could supply the Place of Sight, or a Guide?" *Wollaston's* Religion of Nature delineated. *P.* 67, 68.[12] This is equally applicable to the Proof of the Necessity of a *First Mover*.

That *our Earth is of late Formation*, appears from the late Invention of Letters and Arts, the known Plantation of most Countries, the gradual Decrease of Mountains, and gradual Increase of Mankind. The Earth is of late Formation.

§6. *"If any Man"* (says *Cicero* L. 2. de N. D.[13]) *"should carry to* Scythia *such a Sphere as* Posidonius *made, that doth but represent the Motion of the Planets, who amongst these Barbarians could doubt but that such a Sphere was made by Reason?"* No Man is so mad as to think, that an artificial Sphere, an excellent Book, or a magnificent Building, were made by themselves merely by the mechanical Motion of their own Materials; yet what mean and contemptible Pieces of Artifice are all artificial Spheres, Books, and Buildings, compar'd with the Stars and Planets, the immense and goodly Volume and stupendious Structure of the visible World? The Parts whereof relate to certain Operations and Uses, to which they are admirably fitted; and they relate to one another, and are aptly combin'd into one harmonious habitable World, wherein *Artificialness* and *wise Design* are every where visible; such Artificialness and The Proof of a God from Final Causes in the World Inanimate,

12. Wollaston, *The Religion of Nature Delineated* (1722), pp. 67–68.
13. Cicero, *De Natura Deorum*, II.

wise Design; such Order and Regularity, as the contemplative Mind of Man can never fathom, nor sufficiently admire; and which plainly demonstrateth, that things were not left to the blind Agitation of Matter, (which cannot Model, Distinguish, Proportionate, nor do things in Number, Weight, and Measure, nor do them so well as the greatest Reason can do no better,) but that there is a Maker of all Things, who well understood what he had to do, is of immense Wisdom, Goodness, and Power, and that the World is, in all the Parts of it, the Work of a *Wonderful Providence.* Such is the *Light* of the Sun and Heavenly Bodies; and such is our *Earth,* with its diurnal Revolution to make the Succession of Day and Night; and its annual Revolution about the Sun, with its Axis so inclin'd, but always parallel to it-self, as regularly to bring about the 4 Seasons of the Year, with so nearly equal a distribution of Light and Heat thro' the Whole; having its Surface cloath'd with Green; being a Terraqueous Globe, involv'd in a convenient Atmosphere, furnish'd with copious Stores of Water, with various Sorts of *Minerals, Animals* (in all respects suited to their Elements,) *Vegetables* (of admirable Contexture, many of them of exquisite Beauty, and others of as great Use,) with all Sorts of Seeds or Seminal Principles, (which are also propagated for continuance of the Species.) It is not probable, that any of these had been, if there had been no higher Cause of Things, than the undirected Agitation of Matter, which knoweth no Beauty, Order, Regularity, or Final Cause. No Reason can be assign'd, why any of them are, but only from the Final Cause (it is for *the Best,* that they should be so;) and from the Wisdom of the Creator of all Things, who design'd them for End and Use. For who can doubt, but the Parental Nature, which hath furnish'd Animals with Organical Parts for the Reception, Mastication, Digestion, and Distribution of Food, hath also provided the Herbs and Grass, and Plants, and their Fruit, to be their Food and Physick, and that they were made for this End and Use? That the Feet were made for Walking, the Hands for Working, the Eyes for Seeing, and that Light and Eyes were design'd for one another? *Who is it then, that hath suited and adapted this to that, and that to this? That hath made the Fruits of the Earth for Animals, Animals for Men, as the Horse for carrying him, the Ox for ploughing, the Dog for hunting and keeping House?*

It must be an intelligent Cause, (not senseless Matter,) that diversified
the Matter into such innumerable Species of Beings as this World consisteth of, (all which are of regular Idea, and have their Specifick Natures
and Properties;) that instituted a beauteous Order and gradual Subordination of them (of Plants to Animals, and Animals to Men;) that adjusted the Growth of Animals, determin'd their Stature, gave them their
Beauty and their Usefulness, their distinction into Male and Female,
(which are manifestly design'd, the one for the other,) made some of
them *Oviparous,* and others *Viviparous,* some with *Wings,* and others
with *Fins,* of which differences amongst Animals no Mechanical Cause
can be assign'd, but a Reason may be assign'd from the Final Cause,
which sheweth, that they were not so made without Reason. Which also
appeareth from the Fabrick of the Bodies of Animals, of the Formation
and Organization whereof it is Madness to pretend to give a Mechanical
Account (why the Brains and Lungs, the Nerves and Membranes, the
Veins and Arteries, the Bones, Joints, and Ligaments, the Valves and
Fibres, were so fram'd and situated,) in which we find nothing unfit,
nothing in vain, and the Artifice that is in them so amazingly exquisite
and elaborate, that all the Works of Human Art are but a Bungle, if
compar'd with the Body of an Animal. That the rudely-agitated Matter
can form it-self into Clocks, Engines of War, and Musical Instruments,
is much more credible than that it can form it-self into the Bodies of
Animals. And, if one should suppose, that the undirected Agitation of
the Particles of senseless Matter did of old, of their own accord, spin
themselves into Threads; these Threads, of themselves, did weave themselves into Pieces of Cloth (of numerous Kinds); that these Pieces of
Cloth did make themselves into Garments of Thousands of regular
Shapes hugely different, and also into some Hundreds of the same
Shape; and that when those Garments were worn out, the Matter, of its
own accord, should make it-self into new ones exactly like the former
(altho' the odds are infinite to one, that it does not twice hit upon the
same Form); this would be a much more credible Hypothesis, than the
Atheistick Hypothesis touching the Origin of Animals; that the rudely-
agitated Particles of Matter did, of their own accord, form themselves
at first into certain *Stamina* of the Parts of Animals, next into Organical

Parts, and next into perfect Animals of numerous and hugely-different Kinds, and into a great Number of Individuals of several Kinds, which are propagated from one Generation to another, with as great regularity as the Body of an Animal is form'd, which consists of a vast variety of Parts and Organs, of exquisite Size, Situation, Temper, Texture, Connexion, Distinction; every Animal is form'd with such Organs as are suitable to it, its Organical Parts are admirably fitted for their several Functions, and these Functions are such as the Oeconomy of the Whole requireth (Mastication, Deglutition, Concoction, Fermentation, Chylification, Sanguification, Separation, Percolation, Respiration, Nutrition, Generation, Local Motion, various Sensation, and other Functions of Life;) the Parts of an Animal and their Functions constitute one orderly Oeconomy of the Whole; therefore they were made by an intelligent Contriver, who had the Whole in his Mind, and design'd the Good thereof. The several Parts of it are the Wonders of his Divine Art; for such is that astonishing Organ the Eye, which is of so curious a Structure and so many Excellencies, and so admirably fitted for its Function and Office, that every one who will not shut the Eyes of his Mind, cannot fail to discern, that it was made by a Divine Artist, for the Use of Seeing. Not less wonderful, tho' not so much expos'd to view or taken notice of, is the Organ of Hearing, the Ear. Such is the *rete mirabile* in the Brain; the Fabrick of the *Aspera Arteria,* which is cover'd with the *Epiglottis,* and is smooth in that part, which toucheth the *Oesophagus;* the bending of the *Arteria Aorta* a little above the Heart, and the Fabrication of the *Valves* of the Blood-Vessels; the most numerous concurrent Organs for the enlarging and contracting the Breast in Respiration; *"About which Motions,"* as Dr. *Willis* observes, *"the Mechanick Artifice of the Creator, which is plainly adapted to Mathematical Rules, we cannot sufficiently admire."* And who can chuse but admire that wise and useful Provision of temporary Parts, and of Nutriment, which Provident Nature maketh for the *Foetus* during the time of Gestation? What we have said of the Bodies of Animals, is in great Degree, applicable to Plants, in which the Root, the Stalk, the Flower, the Seed, with their numerous constituent Parts (the Skin, Cortical Body, Vessels, Fibres, Covers, Pith, Radicle, Lobes, and such like) and even the Claspers, Thorns, Hairs,

Globulets, are admirably fitted for an Use and Purpose, some Service of the Plant, and are manifestly design'd thereto.

Atheism can give no account of the Origination of Mankind, or indeed of any Animal; for those Accounts, which the old Atheistick Philosophers gave of it, are as gross Absurdities as the Fictions of the Poets. Such is the Conceit of *Anaximander,* [14] That the first Men were generated in the Bellies of Fishes, and were there nourish'd, 'till they were able to help themselves, and then they were cast upon dry Land. Which ridiculous Conceit is as wise as that of *Epicurus,* [15] That the Slime of the Earth, being heated, there grew out of it certain Wombs or Bags, wherein the first Men (and other Animals) were form'd; for whose Nourishment these Wombs drew out of the Earth a Milky Liquor; and these being excluded from their Wombs (the Earth still affording them Milk) and Adult propagated their Kind. So *Democritus* suppos'd, That Men at first were generated out of Water and Slime. But, if Mother Earth thus produc'd Mankind at first, it is much, that in so long a time, there were never since any of the like Productions, (seeing she observeth fix'd and determinate Laws, and is constant in observing them,) and that now Mankind cannot be generated, but by Propagation from their Kind. As the King of *Siam* ask'd the *French* Missionaries, [16] If the Sun in *Europe* was the same with theirs in the *Indies?* So we must ask the *Epicureans,* If their Child-bearing Earth was the same with ours? For our Earth is as unfit for Child-bearing, as Fishes for engendering Human Flesh. That which formerly seems to have given any a Handle for this wild Conceit, is, with certainty, discover'd to be a Mistake, by Experiments and Microscopical Observations. They thought that Vermin, at least, proceeded frequently from Putrefaction, and that sometimes Animals of a higher Order were produc'd by the Slime of *Nile* expos'd to the Rays of the Sun, no one Instance of which has been sufficiently vouch'd. On the contrary, it is now, I think, universally agreed by all Natural Philosophers, that every Animal proceeds from an Egg, that was before produc'd

Atheism can give no Account of the Origination of Mankind.

14. Plutarch, *Symposium,* VIII.8.
15. Lucretius, *De Rerum Natura,* IV.
16. Compte, *Memoirs and Observations* (1697), p. 487.

by another Animal of the same Species; as every Vegetable is, in like Manner, produc'd from its proper Seed. Were it otherwise, how comes it about, that we see no Instance, in any Age or Country, of either Animal or Plant arising of a new Species? And as the Earth hath no Seminal Principles for Human Productions, nor any Faculty of conceiving with Child; so, if any Nurslings were committed to her Care, she must necessarily expose them, and could not educate them. If of old she afforded Milk, she could not thereby originate Mankind, unless she could also contrive and form Human Bodies; nor would her *Nutriment* signify any thing, unless she could also furnish them with all the wonderful *Organs of Deglutition, Nutrition, and Concoction;* their Tunicles, Muscles, Glands, Fibres, their Shape and Situation, their Dilatation and Contraction, opening and shutting, Faculties of Digestion, Retention, Expulsion, the Commixtures and Secretions that are made in them, with the Causes of them, the Peristaltick Motion of the Intestines, their Valves to hinder Regurgitation, their Convolution, Corrugation, and Cells, their wonderful Intertexture (the Mesentery,) and the Net-work that covereth them; the Lacteal Vessels, with their Insertion into the Intestines, and their Valves, wherein a superlative Wisdom of Parental Providence appeareth. From these Legends of the old Atheistick Philosophers, it appeareth, (and I do not find their Successors among the Moderns have a-whit mended the Matter,) that the *Philosophy of Atheism* is the merest *Credulity* in the World, and that they are of all Persons the most Guilty of what they are so apt, at every turn, to object to their Adversaries, *an irrational, absurd, and implicit Belief.* The *Atheist's Creed,* and *Believing,* That this Frame of Nature (which appears most evidently, to consist of the *Wisest* Means fitted to the *Best* Ends, by a most *powerful* Intelligent Agent,) does not owe its being what it is, to *Design,* is as unreasonable and foolish, as if a Man should *believe* in all the Stories of *Witches* and *Apparitions* that ever were invented, all the *Fables* of the Poets, *Paradoxes* of the *Stoicks,* and the *Fables* of *Aesop,* in a literal Sense, all in one. *"But this is the principal Wisdom of our Times: It is an easy Matter to deny any Thing, that thou mayst be counted Wiser than others,"* as *Cardan* complain'd in his Time.[17]

17. Cardan, *De Rerum Varietate,* XVI.92.

§7. The Soul of Man is of such a Nature, that it cannot be deriv'd from Matter, whence it appears, that God is the Maker of it, and of the World. For such are the Faculties and Operations of the Mind of Man, *Sensation, Cogitation, Imagination, Memory, spontaneous Motion, Self-consciousness, Self-reflexion, Understanding, and the noble Operations of Reason, Liberty of Will, and Agency,* that are plainly incompetible to *Matter* in general, and to an Organiz'd Human Body in particular. *See the first Part of this Appendix.* No Effect can transcend the Perfections of its Cause: But these Faculties and Operations are certainly great Perfections, that far transcend Matter with its Modifications. *Spontaneous Motion* (our immitting and directing the Animal Spirits into the Muscles, in order to Local Motion, by an Act of Volition, upon consulting and deliberating within ourselves touching Good and Evil,) is an Act of *free Self-determining Agency;* whereas all the Motions of Matter (in respect of it-self) are purely necessary, and according to certain Laws of Motion. A Body cannot act but necessarily, as it is caus'd to act by some other; that is in Propriety of Speech, it cannot act at all: Atheism, therefore, that maketh Man nothing more than a mere Corporeal Machine, bereaveth Mankind of that Liberty of Agency, whereby they are capable of deserving Praise or Dispraise, Rewards or Punishments, and thereby destroyeth Laws and Government. Our Consciousness of Liberty is as strong a Proof of its Existence, as it is possible for us to have of the Existence of any thing; therefore all the Cavils brought against the Possibility of Liberty, are as vain and idle, as the Metaphysical Subtleties brought by some *against* the Possibility of Motion, or of a swifter Bodies overtaking a flower at a distance before it, when we have perpetual Experiments to the contrary; *against* the infinite Divisibility of Quantity, when we have Demonstration for it; or *against* the Possibility of an Eternal Duration already past, and come to an End, tho' it be as certainly so, as that there is a Duration present. The reasoning Mind also inquireth into the Natures and Causes of Things, maketh a judgment of them, and rectifies the Errors of Sense; its Cogitations are not confin'd to the Objects of Sense, it searcheth into recondite and mysterious Things, contemplates Things purely intelligible, reckoneth and numbereth; and the Natures and Essences of Things, that are Universal and beyond the reach of the Senses, are its Objects of Science. The Soul herself exerteth

And from a more particular Consideration of the peculiar Frame of Man, his Powers and Properties:

the second Notions, and because a Corporeal Substance can have no Perceptions but only Corporeal Impressions, therefore these *second Notions* of the Mind, which are no Corporeal Impressions, are a certain Proof, that there is an Incorporeal Substance in Man. Not only the *Logical* and *Mathematical* Terms, but our ordinary Terms of Language, (as Relation, Difference, Good, Evil,) have a certain Meaning and intelligible Notion, but no Phantasm or Image belonging to them. The intelligent Mind withstandeth the Hurry of Passion, the Inveiglements of Sense, the Impostures and Tricks of Fancy; she compareth the Phantasms of Sense and Imagination, and judgeth of them, formeth Propositions, maketh Deductions, and cannot but form those Propositions called *common Notions,* which she knoweth to be *Eternal* Verities, without any Information from Sense.

In Human Nature, degenerate as it is, there are such Moral and Religious Endowments, such laudable Qualities and Properties, such a kindly Sort of Instincts and Inclinations, that plainly speak its Divine Original, and give Attestation to the Existence of God. For who doth not approve and applaud Beneficence, Faithfulness, and Justice? And who doth not detest Maliciousness, Fraud, and Injustice? A common Goodness of Nature, Humanity, Ingenuity, Gratitude, Sociableness, Friendship, a singular Affection towards near Relations, and Civil Virtue, is common to Mankind in general, and was found in great Plenty, even in the *Heathen* World. Atheism, therefore, is monstrously unnatural, which, together with the Existence of God (Parental Nature,) discardeth all good Nature, all Obligation to it, any Institution to it by the Author of Nature, and any such Instincts in Man's Nature. *"A Father is nothing, a Son is nothing,"* (Atheists make no account of Natural Relation and Affection,) *"with them Affection to our Off-spring is not Natural."* [18] *"You Epicureans suppose, that Men would not be benign and beneficent, if they were not weak,"* (if it were not merely out of Self-Interest, as fearing or needing others,) *"not acknowledging any Natural Love or Affection."* [19] Atheism, therefore, is destructive of common Goodness of Nature,

---

18. Epictetus, *Discourses,* I.23; II.20.
19. Cicero, *De Natura Deorum,* II.

which is manifestly implanted in Men by Parental Nature, whence the Ants have their Prudence, the Bees their Polity and sexangular Cells, the Birds their Contrivance in building their Nests, and their Care of their Young. There could have been no such Goodness in Man's Nature, as now there is, if God was not the Author of Nature; Nor would there be such Civil Virtues, as there are amongst Men, if God was not the Maker and Governor of Mankind, and if Man was not made Social by God. In such Sense *Cicero* may be understood to say, and to say well *"Mind, Fidelity, Virtue, Concord, whence could they come among Men, but from above?"* [20]

The Wisdom and Goodness of Parental Providence is seen in the Usefulness of those Instincts of Nature, called the *Passions,* which are implanted in Man and other Animals; for the substantial Happiness of Life consisteth in them, thereby Man hath a little Kingdom within himself, consisting of Subjects and Sovereign; the Passion of *Veneration* is requisite in Government; *Anger,* for the Exercise of Fortitude; *Commiseration* is for succouring the Afflicted; *Fear,* for avoiding Danger; and all the other Passions are of great Use, which sheweth that Nature had a very Wise and Designing Author; and some of them, as the Passion of *Devotion,* are plain Indications, that Man was made for Religion. Mankind are by Natural Instinct, in some sort, the devotional Suppliants of an invisible superior Power, and have so strong a Propension to Religion, that they will rather worship Rivers, Trees, and a Red Cloth, than live without a Religious Worship, of which the Deity alone is the due Object. And as there would not have been such a natural Appetite as Hunger, if there had been no Meat, for Nature doth nothing in vain: So, if there had not been a God, there would not have been in Man a Natural Propension to Religion. Mankind hath also *Natural Conscience,* which is a Consciousness of Duty and of Sin, of well and evil Doing, with respect to an invisible superior Power. The *Fear of Conscience* is one of their Natural Passions, and upon violating the Dictates of their Conscience they have naturally a Remorse, and a Presage that some penal Evil will befal them from an invisible superior Power, because of the

20. Ibid.

moral Evil which they have done; and upon well-doing, according to
their Conscience, they have naturally a Hope and Confidence of their
Safety and Prosperity, and that doing well they shall fare well. If any
seem to themselves, to have extinguish'd the Sense of Conscience, usually they find the contrary, that they have only laid it to sleep, and that
when Troubles and Dangers come, it awaketh like a sleeping Lyon. Or,
if there be any that have totally extinguish'd it, these have manifestly
extinguish'd the Light of Nature, and have done such Violence to their
Minds, as is done to the Sensories of the Body by a violent Disease,
whereby Sensation is destroy'd. *Natural Conscience* implieth, that there
is in Man the Faculty called [*Liberum Arbitrium*] *Free Will,* (else it would
be Folly, for Men to be troubled for their Evil doings,) and that there is
a Law of Nature, a natural *Ethicks* and Discipline of Morality, a Well-
doing and Evil-doing, Duty and Sin, antecedently to any Human Institution, which is a plain Truth, and plainly subversive of Atheism.

As the *Natural World* is a well-made System, so is the *Human World,*
or World of Mankind, as it consisteth of Societies, lesser and greater
Polities, that are beauteous and useful Structures. These give an Attestation to the Existence of God; for none else can reasonably be suppos'd
to be the Founder of them; and they shew, that Man is made and *design'd* for Society, whence the Existence of God appeareth. The Atheists,
that discard the Existence of God, discard therewith the Natural Sociableness of Man, and not without great Reason; for that God existeth,
and is the Maker of Man, is as evident, as that Man is made and design'd
for Society. And it is evident, that Man is so made; for he is not only
Sociable towards those of his own Kind by kindly Natural Instinct and
Inclination, as the Brutes are; but he is capable of proper Laws and Government, of cultivating the Common Good, and of Arts needful for
Human Society. He hath the Power of Speech, which would be in vain,
if Man was not design'd to live in Society. His natural Passions of *Veneration, Glory, Shame,* manifestly relate to Society. So doth the thin Skin
of his Face, thro' which his Thoughts and Passions make a discovery of
themselves; the Beauty of his Countenance; the Differences of Mens
Countenances in vast variety, whereby they are known, one from another; and the different Qualifications of Men, some being Magnani-

mous, others of softer Temper, some being fitted for the Pen, others for the Plough, some to command, others to obey, that the Welfare of the Whole might be provided for, *by that which every Joint supplieth.* Mankind are born in Families, constitute and live in Families, in which there is a constant Cohabitation of both Sexes for their mutual Help and Comfort, for the Propagation of their Species, and to take care of their Off-spring, (which continueth weak and feeble much longer than that of the Brutes, and therefore requireth a constant Cohabitation, and continual Care of the Parents;) these Family-Societies are plainly by the Order and Design of Nature, Mankind are manifestly design'd to live in Family Societies, the first elementary Societies, which therefore derive their Origin from Parental Providence, which also continueth the different Sexes of Animals, Male and Female, in due Proportion throughout all Ages of the World. *"And, because Solitude is intolerable to every Man, even with an infinite Abundance of Pleasure, hence it is plain, that we are naturally design'd for a Conjunction and a Community."*[21] Mankind are by Nature design'd and necessitated, to live in Society, in which there is no living without a *God* and *Providence,* a *Life to come,* and a *Religion.* For there can be no Good of Virtue in Human Life, if there be no Religion; nor any thing to restrain Men from any Heart Villainy, or any secret Villainy, or any Villainy that they can commit with Safety and Impunity in this World, nor from any Villainy, save only so far as they want an Opportunity to commit it. The Religion of an Oath must be out of doors. None can have the Right of Authority and Sovereignty, nor can others be under a conscientious Obligation to Subjection and Obedience. Princes cannot be conscientiously oblig'd to keep Faith with their Neighbours, or to govern their Subjects with Wisdom and Justice, or to stand to the Compacts or Covenants, which they make with them, nor can themselves have any Security from Assassination and Violence; *"for Strength must be the Law of Nature."*

§8. *The Antients report an universal Consent of Nations touching the Existence of a Deity.* Some Modern Travellers say otherwise, and make an   From the Consent of Nations;

---

21. Cicero, *De Finibus,* III.

Exception of some barbarous unciviliz'd Nations, at the Bay of *Soldania,* in *Brasil,* and the *Caribee* Islands, in *New-found-Land* and *New-France,* the Natives whereof are said to live without any Acknowledgment of a God, and Sense of Religion. But, altho' these Savages are so extremely degenerate into Brutishness, that they scarce deserve to be reckon'd amongst Mankind; and, if they live without Civil Government, they must be acknowledg'd hugely anomalous and dissonant from the Nations; yet it is great Rashness and Unadvisedness to believe the Reports of their total Irreligion. For some of these Reporters contradict themselves, as *Johannes Lerius* manifestly doth; others of them are contradicted by other Travellers, that were better acquainted with these Savages, and better understood their Sentiments. It is possible, that some Persons among them may live in the total Neglect of a God, and a Religion; that those who have but little of Political Government, which they cannot, however, be wholly without, have but little Religion; and that the Universality of them make no great shew of any Religion: And this seemeth to be all the Truth that is in the Story. The Existence of a Deity hath certainly the general Consent of Nations to recommend it, and it is so evident, that the World of Mankind have always stood convicted of the Truth of it; it may justly be reckon'd one of their common Notions; and, because it is the commonest Sense of Mankind, it must be accounted true in the Judgment of common Sense, and according to the Light of Nature. Had it been wholly an arbitrary Fiction or Imposture, it is not possible, that there could have been so universal an Agreement, both touching the Existence of a Deity, and also the Properties and Attributes of a Deity, and that these Notices and Opinions should not wear away and vanish, (as Impostures do, that in process of Time are discover'd,) but continue firm and immoveable, throughout all Countries and Ages. No Cause can reasonably be assign'd of this so Universal a Consent, but Nature, *Universal Mundan Nature, and the Nature of Man.* "*Seeing this Opinion is not establish'd by any Institution, Custom, or Law, and among all without exception a firm Consent doth continue, it must necessarily be understood, that there are Gods, we having implanted, or rather innate, Notices of them; but that, about which there is a Consent of All by Nature, must necessarily be true.*"[22] The Belief of the Soul's Immortality, and of a Life to come, which is the general Sense of Mankind, and which inferreth the Existence of a Deity, both issue from the same Cause, and are the eminent Branches of Natural Religion, which is a Property of Man's Nature.

§9. To these evident Notices of God from Nature, we may annex *extraordinary and special Providences.* For, altho' Providence is a somewhat lubricous Argument, the ways of governing Providence being Various and Mysterious; and altho' this sort of Providences are no *sensible Miracles,* nor can so easily be distinguish'd as they, from what is done by the mere Agency of a second Cause: Yet there are several Occurrences in Human Affairs, that, in fair and reasonable Construction, must be accounted *Special Providences,* and carry the Marks of a Divine Hand. Such is the Dispersion of the *Jews,* and their continuing a distinct People in their Dispersion, a thing that hath no Parallel in History; the portentous Presignifications that have usher'd in calamitous Wars; strange Deliverances of good Men, and of Societies of good People; strange Discoveries of Plots and Murders; remarkable Judgments, that have befallen Persecutors and Tyrants, and other wicked Grandees of the World; signal Answers of Prayer, the Decay and Ruin of many great Families for their Injustice, and prophetick Dreams. The sudden Rise of the *Macedonian,* and Ruin of the *Persian* Monarchy, was plainly an Act of Divine Providence; the *Heathen* Poets and Historians, with great reason, ascribe it to Fate, for *Darius* was manifestly blinded in his Conduct, when he fought with *Alexander.* The Greatness of the *Roman* Empire was decreed by Fate, saith *Machiavel;* and the Ruin of it was by a Divine Fate, for the barbarous Northern Nations that laid it waste, acknowledg'd, that their Invasion of it was not of themselves, but that *they were divinely impell'd thereto.* The Justice of Providence is very visible in those Temporal Judgments, that have a conformity or resemblance to the Sin, that was the Cause of them. The Issue of many Wars and Battles hath been

and from extraordinary and special Providences.

---

22. Cicero, *De Natura Deorum,* I.

determin'd by some special Providence. The Impunity, in this Life, of some Men outrageously wicked, is not so great an Objection against Providence, but that some remarkable Instances of its Justice may reasonably move an ingenuous *Pagan,* to make such an Acknowledgment, as *Manlius Torquatus* made, when, finding *Annius* lying dead at the foot of the Steps of the Temple of *Jupiter Capitolinus,* (after an insolent Speech he had made against the *Romans,*) he cried out, *"Est coeleste numen, es, magne Jupiter!"* *There is a God in Heaven, thou art, O mighty Jupiter!* [23] The Lord is known by the Judgments that he executeth, as he is by Mundane Nature.

The Knowledge of the Being of God noticeth the Law of Nature to Mankind.

§10. If the Existence of God is naturally noticed to Mankind, a Law of Religion and Virtue, which is the Law of Nature, is naturally notic'd unto them; for to be the Sovereignty of God to us is necessarily the Law of our *Subjection* and *Service* unto him, and of that Universal Righteousness, that we sin not against him. But this Natural Notice of the Existence of God, and of a Law of Religion and Virtue, is of a two-fold Notion. For the Existence of a Deity (Supreme Deity) in general, and a Law of Religion and Virtue in general, hath *the Notoreity of a natural Notice to the World of Mankind;* whence they are necessarily oblig'd to all that Religious Subjection and Service, Honour and Worship (internal and external), which Sanctity and Piety is the Comprehension of, and which is manifestly and in its own Nature Piety and God-service, a virtuous and honorary Congruity unto God. If he is notic'd to them, as of Right and Due *the Sovereignty of God to them,* they must necessarily have this Notice, that they are of Right, and by Obligation, his Subjects and Religionists, that are bound to give unto him the Rights and Dues of his God-head, which is a terrible Prohibition to them, not to live in Atheism (speculative or practical), Profaneness, Neglect, Oblivion, or Contempt of God and his Service, not to alienate themselves from him, or be Evil-doers towards him, Injurious, Unthankful, and Unworthy, not to disparage and vilify, not to put Disgraces and Contumelies upon him, not to deny his Sovereignty and Attributes, (by not making a vir-

---

23. Livy, *Ab Urbe Condita,* VIII.6.

tuous and honorary Acknowledgment of them,) not to give his proper
Honour to another, deifying Abominations, and thereby blasphemously
reproaching God, which was a principal Crime of the *Heathen* World,
which swarmed with Idols and fictitious Deities, yet *knew God,* (had the
true God notic'd to them,) γνωϛὸν τοῦ θεοῦ *that which may be naturally
known of God* was notic'd to them, *was manifest in them* (in their
Minds,) *for God had shew'd it unto them.*[24] His Truth therefore, (his practical Truth, namely, these Notices and Instructions, Rules and Precepts,
which concern the Service of God,) is not unknown to them, as the
Apostle affirmeth. His Truth and their Duty could not but be notic'd,
if the Existence of the Sovereignty of God was notic'd unto them;
knowing this, they could not but know, in great degree, that just and
agreeable Worship and Service, which they ow'd unto him, and that
Man must be Religious towards God. Not only *singly,* but *in Society,*
Man must be Religious towards God, (the publick religious Worship in
Assemblies and Societies of Men, being highly honorary to God, and
beneficial to Man;) and seeing God is naturally notic'd unto all Men, as
a Sovereign Power over them, that superintendeth their Affairs and
Ways, is just in his Government, and will reward or punish them, as they
are *Well-doers* or *Evil-doers,* (so that they cannot be ignorant, that they
must fare as they observe or violate the Truth which is notic'd unto
them,) it is manifest, that they are under the Obligation of *Non licet
impune,* that they may not with Impunity be Evil-doers; and that a necessity of living the good Life, and of Universal Righteousness, is
notic'd, to all Men by the Light of Nature, which noticeth the Existence
of God. The *Heathen* World that walk'd in Impieties and Impurities,
yet knew the judgment of God, that Men ought not to be Evil-doers, and
that they which do such Things are Evil-doers, and worthy of Death.[25] "Ver-
ily there is a God, that heareth and seeth what we do, who will deal with
every Man, as he is well or ill deserving,"* saith an *Heathen* Comedian.[26]

24. Romans 1.18–21.
25. Romans 1.32.
26. Plautus, *Captivi,* 2.2.

The Law of
Nature is dis-
cern'd by natu-
ral Reason.

§11. *The Law of Nature is notic'd to Mankind by the Nature of Well and Evil-doing, as understood by the Mind, and discern'd by our natural Reason and Understanding.* As every Man hath the Existence of God externally notic'd unto him, and as the Mind of Man of it-self discerneth *the Well and Fit* that is in external Nature: In like manner what is *Good* and *Evil*, *Right* and *Wrong*, is (in good degree) notic'd to every Man, and the Mind herself discerneth, what is the *Beauteous-beneficial*, and the *Foul-maleficial* Practice. The Mind is of such a Frame, that she naturally and rightly noticeth unto all Men, touching some things, that they are of such a Nature, that they cannot be done, and touching other things, that they cannot be left undone, without the Guilt and Crime of being Evil-doers; and that their being such is contrary to the Mind of God, and subjecteth them to his punitive Displeasure: As on the contrary, their being Well-doers is according to the Mind of God, and intitleth them to his Favour and Rewards: And *the System of these natural Notices is the Law of Nature.* It may here, therefore, be not improper to consider the Objections against this Notice of the Law of Nature.

Objections
against this
Proof of the
Law of Nature
answer'd.
1. Objection,
That it suppo-
seth, without
Proof, the Leg-
islative Power
of Reason.

§12. The first Objection against this Proof of the Law of Nature, is, *That it supposes, without Proof, the Legislative Power of Reason,* which is not to be suppos'd. *"Reason is not the Law, or its Measure; neither can any Man be sure, that any thing is a Law of Nature, because it seems to him hugely reasonable, neither, if it be so indeed, is it therefore a Law. For Reason can demonstrate, and it can persuade, and invite, but not compel any thing but Assent, not Obedience, and therefore it is no Law."* [27] 'Tis true, that mere Reason is not Law, but Reason, complicated with what is Law, is necessarily Law. For as right Reason noticeth what is the *Well-doing* and the *Evil-doing,* it is complicated with what is, in its own Nature, matter of Law. And as it noticeth, that the *Well-doing,* and the *being Well-doers,* is according to the Mind of God, and the *Evil-doing,* and the *being Evil-doers,* is against the Mind of God, it is complicated with what is Law, by a superior Authority. The Laws of Nature must be consider'd, not as

27. Selden, *De Jure Naturali*, I.7; Taylor, *Ductor Dubitantium*, II.1, n. 30.

the Dictates of mere right Reason, but as the Dictates of *conscientious right Reason.*

§13. A second Objection against this Account of the Law of Nature, is, *That the Proof of its Legislation from God is wanting.* This Objection *Cumberland* hath sufficiently answer'd. However, the Doctrines and Practices of the *Heathens* (which have been particularly set forth in the *Introductory Essays*) *shew,* "That their Reason wanted a Rectification; that the perfect Revelation and Legislation from God, adapted to all Mankind, are the Laws of supernatural Revelation; and that (altho' Mankind by considering the Nature of any Practice may, and ordinarily do, know whether it be a Branch of the Law of Nature, yet) Men need the Aids of supernatural Revelation, to better their Knowledge of the Law of Nature."

2. Objection, That the Proof of its Legislation from God is wanting.

§14. A third Objection against this Account of the Law of Nature, is, *an uncertain Notice of the Morals of it,* of Religion and Virtue; for they suppose, that right Reason is that which noticeth to Mankind the Virtuous Morals, and is the noticing Rule thereof. But according to the *Pyrrhonians* and *Scepticks,* there is no Truth in the Reasonings of Men.[28] "The Professors of right Reason (the Philosophers) were hugely different touching Good and Evil, and the great Principle of conducting Life, *the Chief Good;* what some account a Principle or Conclusion evidently true, others, no less intelligent, account extremely false; some of them believ'd the worst Crimes to be Innocent, as *Theodorus* the Philosopher allow'd of Adultery, Theft, Sacrilege; *Plato* allow'd Adultery and Community of Wives, so did *Socrates* and *Cato; Zeno* and *Chrysippus* approv'd of Incest, and so did the *Persians.* So that we may well say as *Socrates* in *Plato's Phaedrus; When we hear the Name of Silver or Iron, all Men that speak the same Language, understand the same Thing: But, when we speak of Just or Good, we are distracted into various Apprehensions, and differ from each other, and from ourselves.* Every Man maketh his Opinions to be Laws of Nature, if his Persuasion be strong and violent. And

3. Objection, That the Notices of Reason are an uncertain Guide, about which Men are not agreed.

28. Selden, *De Jure Naturali,* I.7; Taylor, *Ductor Dubitantium,* II.1, n. 31.

some are Atheists that believe no God, nor any thing to be dishonest, which they can do in Private, or with Impunity. Some have believ'd, that there is nothing in it-self Just, and only regarded what is profitable, so did *Carneades,* and so did *Aristippus.* And it is not sufficient to say, some Persons are unreasonable, unless we first know some certain Rule and Measure of Reason. Now we cannot take our Measures of Reason from Nature; or, if we do, we cannot take the Measures of Nature from Reason. If we judge of what is natural by its Conformity to right Reason, we cannot judge of right Reason by its Conformity to what is natural." Thus Reason is made use of against it-self, various Reasons are alledg'd to shew the uncertainty of the Notices of Reason in Moral Matters. But, as was said of the *Milesians* of old, *"The* Milesians *are no Fools, but they do the same things that Fools do":* So they that are not Irrational, yet sometimes argue at an unreasonable rate. For the Dissent of *Pyrrhonians* and *Scepticks* doth it signify any thing, to destroy the certainty of Reason? Or the Dissent of Atheists, to destroy the certainty of the Existence of God? The Name of *Theodorus* was not *the Philosopher,* but *the Atheist,* and *Aristippus* was of no better Character. The *Philosophers* were not the genuine Professors of right Reason, but generally they were extravagant unpopular Humorists, that affected to maintain Paradoxes. *Heraclitus* held, that contradictory Propositions are consistent. *Zeno Eleates* held, that Motion is impossible; and *Anaxagoras,* that Snow and Coal are of the same Colour. If any one should alledge these absurd Paradoxes of the Philosophers, to destroy and impair the certainty of Logick and external Sense, such Allegations would not signify any thing, such Uncertainties do not make an Uncertainty; and the Allegation of their absurd Conceits, touching Moral Matters, signifies as little, to destroy or impair the evident Certainty of the Notices of right Reason, and the Morals of the Law of Nature. Of which we must affirm.

1. *So great a Certainty there is in the Law of Nature,* that there is no invincible Difficulty in the Whole of it, or the Science of it, as there is in other Sciences, Metaphysicks, Natural Philosophy, nay, in Mathematicks it self, in which there are invincible Difficulties. But the Science of *Universal Righteousness* hath no such invincible Difficulty in it, as rendereth it impossible for Mankind, to arrive at an evident Certainty,

touching the whole of it. For it must be suppos'd, that they that are oblig'd to *fulfil all this Righteousness,* may have an evident Certainty, touching what it is, as several Righteous Men have had; that this *whole Duty of Man* is not a thing incomprehensible by Man; for then it could not be the *whole Duty of Man,* nor could it be taught or learned.

2. *So great a Certainty there is in the Law of Nature,* that none can innocently be grossly Ignorant of, or mistake, any of the Morals of it, but it is their Sin and their Crime; so the Polytheism, Idolatry, Unchastity, and bloody Spectacles, which were the Practice of the *Heathens* in their Night of Ignorance, was their Sin and their Crime. By their Reason God had notic'd to the World of Mankind in general, the Knowledge of Himself, his Truth, and their Duty, which is the Law of Nature; so far the Truth was not unknown to them: But they were not Sincere, Upright, and Faithful towards it, holding the Truth in Unrighteousness; whence they were involv'd in Atheous Ignorance, which was their deadly Sin, and their Crime, and no excuseable invincible Ignorance, but an Effect of their Unfaithfulness and Insincerity. Their Polytheism does not prove, that Mankind have but uncertain Notices touching the Unity of the God-head: Nor does the Philosophers allowing Adultery and Incest prove, that Mankind have but uncertain Notices of the Law of Nature. It is certain, they had better Notices, and, if these better Notices were not to them evidently certain, yet they would have been evidently certain, if they had been Sincere and Faithful; so great a Certainty there is in the Notices of the Law of Nature. Would it not have been evidently certain to *Carneades,* that there are things in themselves Just, if he had not been a Villain? To be a sound Moralist towards God and Man, is not a business of abstruse and subtile Speculation, but of Sincerity, Faithfulness, and Integrity; it is not so much in the Head and a piercing Judgment, as in the Heart and a Rectitude of Will; nor is it so requisite to be a Philosopher, as to be Honest, and duly Conscientious.

3. *So great a Certainty there is in the Law of Nature,* that there is a certain Rule of right Reason in Morality, which is the Beauteous-beneficial Practice. If the Mind noticeth or dictateth what is the right Practice, this is necessarily right Reason; if therefore she noticeth or dic-

tateth touching the *Beauteous-beneficial* Practice, that this is to be done, and touching the *Foul-maleficial* Practice, that this is not to be done, this is right Reason. And there is no more difficulty in discerning what is right Reason in Morality, than there is in discerning, what is the *Beauteous-beneficial,* and what is the *Foul-maleficial* Practice. Now, it is as evident and certain, that the Virtues, commonly so call'd, are the *Beauteous-beneficial* Practice, and the Vices, commonly so call'd, are the *Foul-maleficial* Practice, as it is evident and certain, that hating and hurting, is not helping, that to be a Lyar is not honourable, that the *Soldanian* Diet of Guts and Garbage is not cleanly, and that *Thersites* is not handsome.

4. *So great a Certainty there is in the Law of Nature,* that a great part of it is of unquestionable Evidence and Certainty, with Mankind in general, and is ascertain'd by the *Consent of Nations;* with respect whereunto the *Lawyers* define the *Law of Nature.* *"That which natural Reason hath settled among all Men. That which is alike observed amongst all People or Nations. The natural Laws are those, which are alike observ'd in all Nations."* [29] *"The Consent of all Nations in every Thing is to be reputed a Law of Nature,"* saith *Cicero.* [30] So *Aristotle* defineth the Law of Nature, *"That which hath every where the same Force, as Fire alike burneth here and among the* Persians." [31] The Law of Nature therefore is of a larger and narrower Acceptation; the one the more *comprehensive,* the other the more *famous.* In the more *comprehensive* Sense it is that whole System of Law, which a just Providence requireth the Observance of from all Mankind, antecedently to supernatural Revelation, which hath the *Verity* of natural Notice. But, in the *narrower* and *more famous* Sense, it is only that part of the Law of Nature, which hath the *Notoreity* of natural Notice, the common Acknowledgment of the World. But, as Miracles are not a sufficient Proof of the Divinity of a Doctrine, unless, upon impartial Examination, the Nature of it appeareth to be Divine: So the Consent of Mankind, alone, is not a sufficient Proof touching any Morals, that they

---

29. Selden, *De Jure Naturali,* I.6–8.
30. Cicero, *Tusculan Disputations,* I.
31. Selden, *De Jure Naturali,* I.6–8.

are Laws of Nature, unless, upon impartial Examination, they appear to
be in their own Nature Good or Evil, and therefore of themselves Matter
of Law. But, if any Morals are receiv'd or acknowledg'd by the common
Consent of Nations, as Branches of the Law of Nature, and upon impartial Examination they appear to be in their own Nature Good or Evil
(agreeably to the general Acknowledgment of Mankind,) of such Morals
we have the greatest Assurance imaginable, that they are Branches of the
Law of Nature. For they are so in the Judgment of common Sense, to
Notoreity, and so as to be common or general Notions; and they must
be grossly plain and evident Branches of the Law of Nature, that have
the general Acknowledgment of Mankind, in this their degenerate
Condition. This general Agreement concerning them, their firm Continuance throughout all Ages, the impossibility of eradicating them out
of the Minds of Men, plainly demonstrate, that they are not from any
arbitrary Institution of Man, but are natural Notions; that the Mind is
of such a Nature as to notice them, and the Soul of Man is naturally
dispos'd to the Belief of them. The Consent of Nations, therefore, both
demonstrateth the Existence of the Law of Nature, and is in part a certain Notice of the Morals of it. It demonstrateth the Existence of the
Law of Nature, for it appeareth from the Consent of Nations, that there
is a just Providence, which requireth of all Men, that they be the Well-
doers, not the Evil-doers; and that a System of Morals, which are in their
own Nature Well-doing, are *naturally* and *convictively,* even to the *Notoreity* of a general Acknowledgment, notic'd to Mankind. The certainty
of noticing the Morals of the Law of Nature from the general Consent
of Nations, hath many Objections made against it. But they are made
without a due Clearness and consistency of Discourse, and without any
considerable Strength of Reasoning. For sometimes it is said, *"That a
Body of the Law of Nature is not to be look'd for from the Consent of Nations,"* which no Man will contradict.[32] Sometimes it is said, *"That the*
Hebrew *Doctors do not unwisely, to make no reckoning of the Consent of
Nations in the Designation of the Law of Nature";*[33] and *"That the Law*

32. Ibid., I.6.
33. Ibid.

of Nations is no Indication of the Law of Nature.[34] Which are Positions hugely extravagant, maintain'd by Reasons extremely insignificant. For what if all Nations are not known? If some known Nations are Savages, and in great degree live without Law? If in some other known Nations, some of the grossest Immoralities have been commonly practis'd and authoriz'd? What signify these Exceptions to the invalidating this great Certainty; *That the Existence of the Law of Nature hath the Consent of Nations, and the general Acknowledgment of Mankind, as also several great Moralities, particular Branches of that Law, which is an Indication, that they are of the Law of Nature?* If a judicious *Heathen* Lawyer *Paulus* saith,[35] that Theft is prohibited by the Law of Nature; if *Ulpian,* another of the same Character, calleth it (*Naturae turpe*) an Action of natural Turpitude, there are few but will look upon these Sayings as considerable Indications, that the Prohibition of Theft is of the Law of Nature; how much more ought they to think so, if the Generality of Mankind say so? The *Persians* practis'd and authoriz'd an incestuous Mixture with their own Mothers, and *Antiochus Soter* married his Father's Wife: But such incestuous Mixtures were against the general Sense of Mankind, as we learn not only from the Poets, and from *Cicero,* but from a better Author, 1 *Cor.* 5. 1. which ought to be look'd upon as an Indication, that they were against the Law of Nature. *"The Nations differ about their Superstition, but what Nation is there, that does not like and love Mansuetude, Benignity, and a grateful Mind? And that doth not vilify and hate the Proud, the Malitious, the Cruel, and the Ungrateful?"*[36]

5. In written Laws, both Divine and Human, there is such uncertainty, that Men are of various Opinions touching their Interpretation, and touching what is the Sense of those Laws, what is Just and Good (according to the Saying of *Socrates* to *Phaedrus,*) and every one thinketh that his own Opinion is Law; yet this uncertainty does not hinder, but that there is an evidently certain Interpretation of these written Laws: So there is a Diversity of Opinions touching what is right Reason, Just

---

34. Taylor, *Ductor Dubitantium,* II.1, n. 28.
35. Grotius, *De Jure Belli ac Pacis,* I.1.10.
36. Cicero, *De Legibus,* I.

and Good, according to the Law of Nature, such uncertainty there is in it; yet this does not hinder, but that there is an evidently certain right Reason (in Moral Matters) well and evil Doing, according to the Law of Nature: Touching which the Differences of Mankind would not be very great, if they were duly conscientious. *"Let no Man pretend, that through Ignorance he neglecteth Virtue, or because he hath none to shew him the Way, for we have Conscience a sufficient Teacher."* [37] *He hath shew'd thee, O Man, what is good,* Mic. 6. 8.

§15. A fourth Objection against this Account of the Law of Nature, is, *the Supposition of Innate Ideas, Notions, and Principles, which it involveth.* The antient Writers look upon the natural Law, as an innate Law (*Nata Lex,* as *Cicero* calleth it) as a natural Inscription or Impression upon the Minds of all Men; and the Apostle manifestly favoureth this Notion of it, *Rom.* 2. 14, 15. For, altho' he doth not say, that the Moral Law is written in the Heart of the *Gentiles,* yet he saith, *That the Law, as to the Work of it, is written in their Hearts* (their inward Man) *and that they are a Law unto themselves,* as to the Work of the Law, which is to indicate, direct, dictate, command, and forbid, to judge, *Joh.* 7. 51. to criminate or accuse, *Joh.* 5. 45. to convince and condemn, *Jam.* 2. 9. The Apostle affirmeth, that the Law in some sort (as to the Work of it) is written in the Heart of the *Gentiles,* and consequently, in some respect, it is *the Law written in the Minds of Men,* as the antient Moralists style it. They suppose it to be written in the Soul as having τὸ ἡγεμονικὸν, *the leading part,* τὸν ὀρθὸν λόγον, *right Reason,* τὸ συνειδὸς, *Conscience,* τὸ κριτνίριον φυσικὸν, *that natural discernment whereby we distinguish Good from Evil.* This is their Sense, as appeareth from their Accounts of it, and this is all that they mean, when they speak of a Law naturally written and impressed upon the Soul, *"That right Reason"* (which is the Law of Nature) *"is innate to the Soul, and written or implanted in her."* [38] They suppose, that it is *Innate* or *Natural* to the intelligent reasoning Mind, to understand and reason rightly, in some degree at least, touching the Matters

---

37. Vossius, *Historiae de Controversiis quas Pelagius,* III, pt. 3. theses 10.
38. Hierocles, *In Aureum Pythagoreorum Carmen Commentarius,* p. 107.

of Morality, and consequently to form those *Notices* or *Dictates,* which
are the Law of Nature. In this Sense they suppose it *Innate, a natural
Inscription or Impression,* and in this Sense we ought to assert *innate Ideas,
Notions, and Principles,* that are not adventitious. For all Arts and Sciences had their Origin from Nature, all Mankind are by Nature, in some
degree, *Logicians* and *Mathematicians,* in some degree they are born
such, and in the like degree they are born *Moralists* and *Religionists.* The
Design and Business of Arts and Sciences, is only to make up what is
begun in Nature. It is innate, therefore, to the Mind of Man, to form
Logical, Mathematical, Religious, and *Moral Ideas, Notions,* and *Principles,* which are not adventitious *Notices* or *Evidences.* It is innate in a
Child to grow up to be a Man in Mind and Understanding, as well as
Stature of Body; and, consequently, it is innate to him, to grow up to
understanding the common Notions, which is essential to one who un-
derstandeth at the rate of a Man. *Reasoning* is certainly innate to the
reasoning Mind; and, if the Mind is, by natural Constitution, *Religious*
as well as *Rational,* Religious Reasoning must necessarily be innate to
her. Her innate Reasoning implieth, that the *Method* of Reasoning is
innate to her, which is to form Ideas, to compare them, to make a Judgment of them, to make Deductions of Causes from Effects, of Effects
from Causes, of Consequents from Antecedents, and of Conclusions
from evident Principles. In this Method of Reasoning the Mind findeth,
that it is natural and innate in her, to form those Propositions call'd the
common Notions, to think of them, and to think them true, that they
are not in her as adventitious Notices and Evidences; but *they are as much
innate in her, as it is innate to Man, to be actually a Rationalist and a
Religionist,* and, therefore, she calleth them innate Notions and Principles. As she hath an innate *Power,* so (being made both *Rational* and
Religious) she hath an innate *Propension,* to notice and dictate the *common Notions,* which are hereby distinguish'd from adventitious Notices
and Evidences. Because of this *innate Propension,* they are *self-taught, by
an untaught Gift of Nature,* nor can the Mind disbelieve them, without
doing Violence to her-self. This *innate Propension* appeareth from the
general Consent, that hath been amongst Mankind, in good degree,
touching the Laws of Nature. For in all Ages, without any Philosophical

Disquisitions about them, or any abstruse Inquiries into the Causes or Reasons of them, Mankind had the Knowledge of them. Which plainly sheweth, that they deriv'd this their Knowledge of them, from one great Universal Teacher, and that they were notic'd and dictated to them from an innate Propension of their own Minds. Of the *common Notions* that are *speculative,* we must affirm, that the Mind, merely by her *innate Power of distinguishing* between True and False, *hath, virtually at least, the Notice of them,* and the Discernment of the Truth of them, *without needing any adventitious Notice or Evidence.* Of the *common Notices* that are *practical,* we must affirm, that the Mind, merely by her *innate Power of distinguishing* between well and evil Doing, *hath, virtually at least, the Notice of them,* and a Discernment of their Obligation, *without needing any adventitious Notice or Evidence.* These are, therefore, justly counted *Ideas, Notions,* and *Principles,* that are *innate* to us, not in every Sense, but so as is explained, which seems to be intirely the Sense in which the Antients understood them; and, in such Sense, innate Ideas, Notions, and Principles, may and ought to be asserted against all Objections that are made against them.

1. Against innate Principles in general, it is argu'd, *"Infants and Ideots do not know them, therefore they are not imprinted on their Minds."* [39] But how vastly remote and distant is this Argument from concerning innate Ideas and Principles in the genuine Sense of asserting them? Alike remote and distant is this other Reasoning. *"If these suppos'd innate Principles were native Characters and Impressions, they would appear fairest and clearest in Naturals, in Children, Ideots, Savages, and illiterate People, being of all other the least Corrupted by Custom or borrow'd Opinions."* For it is not imaginable, that the Principles of Science and of Law, and the Dictates of right Reason should appear fairest and clearest in them, that are almost totally devoid of Reason; nor do Infants know them, 'till they come to the Use of Reason. But the Objector proceeds and affirms; *"It is utterly false, that the Use of Reason assisteth us in the Knowledge of these Maxims, or that Children know or assent to these Maxims, as soon as they come to the Use of Reason; some time after during a Man's Life, they may*

Objections against innate Principles, answer'd 1. Objection, Infants and Ideots do not know them.

39. Locke, *Essay Concerning Human Understanding,* I.1.27.

be assented to, and so may all other knowable Truths." All Mankind call these *common Notions,* the *Dictates of right Reason;* the Use of Reason, therefore, assisteth us in the Knowledge of these self-evident Maxims: Which are not of the Condition of other knowable Truths, (that may be known or not known by Mankind;) but the Notice of the common Notions is essential to such Rationalists and Religionists as all Men are by Nature. And proportionably as common Reason displayeth it-self in Mankind in their Growth from their Non-age, these common Notions are discover'd, and, as they have the Use of Reason in a greater degree, they are discover'd in a greater degree.

2. Objection, Thieves and High-way-men do not own them.

2. Against innate Principles it is argu'd; *"That Thieves and High-way men do not own Faith and Justice as Principles; the Principles of Morality, therefore, are not own'd by all Men,"* (have not universal Consent,) *"therefore they are not innate."* But they know very little, who do not know, that Thieves and High-way-men, many of which are educated in the *Christian* Religion, do ordinarily own *Faith* and *Justice,* as to the *Notice, Conviction,* and *Dictate* of their own Minds, which they sin against. It is argu'd also; *"That there are no Practical Principles wherein all Men agree, (not any Practical Truth that is universally receiv'd without Doubt or Question,) therefore none innate."* But, if Mankind universally desire their own *Felicity,* if they are universally *Social,* there is an universal Agreement of Mankind in great practical Principles; and such an Agreement implyeth and inferreth their Agreement in a great number of practical Principles. But the Hypothesis of innate Ideas and Principles does not require, that there should be any practical Truth universally receiv'd, without Doubt or Question by Mankind. It is enough to justify that Assertion, if all Men have Notices and Dictates of practical Truth, that are innate. And of these we must affirm, that, as to be actually a Sinner, is innate to every Child of Man in a degree of prevalent Tendency that way; to be actually a Rationalist, a Logician, an Arithmetician, a Societist, is innate to every Child of Man in a degree of prevalent Tendency that way.

3. Objection, A Reason may be requir'd of every Moral Rule; they are therefore not

3. It is argu'd; *"That not one Moral Rule can be produc'd, whereof a Man may not justly demand a Reason, and therefore it is not self-evident, as every innate Principle must needs be."* But may a Reason justly be demanded of the great Rules and Principles of Morality, which cannot be

denied without a Contradiction? *The Good is not to be hated, but is that* self-evident nor
which is to be lik'd and chosen: The Evil is not to be lov'd, but is that which innate.
is to be dislik'd and avoided. The Beauteous-beneficial Kind of Practice is
the Good, the Foul-maleficial Kind of Practice is the Evil. The Good is the
Well-doing, the Evil is the Evil-doing. The Well-doing is Righteousness (the
Right-doing), the Evil-doing is (the Wrong-doing) Unrighteousness. To be
an Evil-doer, is Vice and Crime. That which cannot be done without Vice
and Crime, is not allowable, may not be done. None can have a Right to do
the Wrong, that which is Unrighteousness, nor may do that which ought not
to be done. It is necessarily Wickedness and Crime to be a Doer of Unright-
eousness. To be a Criminal or Malefactor, is not lawful or tolerable, but
punishable. Innocence, Piety, Order, Aptitude, Congruity, and Proportion,
in our Practice, is Beauteous. The sincere Benevolence is Goodness of Will
and Affection. To reverence the Elders, to keep Faith, to do to others as we
would be done to, is the Beauteous-beneficial Practice. The Malevolent Na-
ture and Practice is the Evil. Guile and Hypocrisy is Villainy. To act the Part
of an Enemy to a Friend, to design Evil to the Innocent, to condemn the
Righteous, are the Foul-maleficial Practice. The great Rules of Morality
are as self-evident, as the Principles of the speculative Sciences. *Luk.* 12.
57. *"Why even of yourselves judge ye not what is Right?"*

4. The Objector saith; *"I cannot see, how any Man should ever transgress* 4. Objection,
the Moral Rules with Confidence and Serenity, were they innate and stamp'd If Moral Prin-
upon their Minds. If any can be thought to be naturally imprinted, none, ciples were
innate, Man
I think, can have a fairer pretence to be innate than this, Parents preserve could not
and cherish your Children. But have there not been whole Nations, and those transgress
them with
of the most civiliz'd People, amongst whom the exposing their Children, and Confidence
leaving them in the Fields to perish by Want or wild Beasts, hath been the and Serenity.
Practice, as little condemn'd or scrupled as the begetting them? It was fa-
miliar and uncondemn'd Practice amongst the Greeks *and* Romans, *to*
expose, without Pity or Remorse, their Infants." But whether Moral Rules
be *extrinsecally* imprinted upon the Mind (from a Book, a Teacher, or
the Frame of the World,) or whether they be imprinted in the way of
innate Principles, the Case is the same, as to the Possibility of transgressing them *with Confidence and Serenity.* If Men can with Confidence
and Serenity transgress any Moral Rules, that are imprinted upon their

Minds, they may so transgress those, that are impress'd in the way of
innate Principles. And nothing is more usual than for Men, with Confidence and Serenity to transgress the Moral Rules imprinted upon their
Minds; for the *Jews* and *Papists* transgress this Commandment, *Thou
shalt not kill;* and so the *Protestants* transgress these Moral Rules, *Be not
drunk with Wine, Let there be no Divisions among you.* There is no Sect
of Religionists, that doth not violate some Moral Rules, imprinted on
their Minds, with greater Confidence and Serenity than the *Greeks* and
Romans expos'd their Children; for, altho' the Objector hath some to
bear him company in his Exaggerations of their inhuman Practice, yet
it is certain, there are several Mistakes in his Account of it. For, as the
exposing Children was condemn'd[40] amongst the *Aegyptians,* and the
Germans,[41] so among the *Greeks* it was severely prohibited by the *Theban*
Law. *Aelian,* who was a *Roman,* altho' he wrote in *Greek,* saith of this
Theban Law, which made the exposing an Infant, Capital, *"It was a Law
of the greatest Rectitude and Philantrophy."*[42] *Isocrates* condemneth these
Crimes in other Cities, and vindicateth his own City from them. The
Greeks and *Romans* were far from being totally devoid of natural Love
and Tenderness to their Children (commonly call'd by them σοργή) and
usually there was a Mixture of Kindness and Tenderness in their exposing their Infants, as there was also in their Pawning and Selling them.
For these their Practices were not with design to have their Children
destroy'd, but preserv'd. They had this Law of Nature, *Parents preserve
and cherish your Children,* not only imprinted upon their Minds, *but
upon their Bowels;* yet because of Poverty or Want, and to avoid the
Burden of them, they often kill'd some of their Children, insomuch that
the Emperor *Constantine,* to prevent the killing their supernumerary
Children, made a Law for their relief. But those Parents that were more
Parental than to kill their Children, chose rather to expose them (as the
lesser of the two Evils,) not with a design to have them destroy'd, but

40. Wits, *Aegyptiaca* (1683), I.5.
41. Lipsius notes in book V of his edition of Tacitus, *C. Corn. Taciti Annalium
et Historiarum* (1574).
42. Aelian, *Varia Historia*, II.7.

that some might shew Pity on them, take them up, and educate them. There was, therefore, a Mixture of Humanity and Pity in the *Pagans* exposing their Children; and, doubtless, it was from a Principle of *Heathen* Piety, and great respect to their aged Parents, that some barbarous Nations kill'd them, when they grew very Old, accounting it ignominious to be decrepit;[43] and others sacrific'd and ate them, accounting this the most honourable Burial, to entomb them in their own Bowels. So the *Mahometans,* from a Principle of mistaken Piety and Devotion, have a great Veneration for Distracted Men and Leud Miscreants that have the Garb of Asceticks, and give them an universal License to do any thing, even to lie with their Wives, accounting the Children they beget, Holy.[44] But, considering these and the like Instances of the Paradoxical Nature of the World's Piety, our Objector should not have ask'd, *"Where are those innate Principles of Justice, Piety, Gratitude, Equity, and Chastity?"*[45] But, in all reason, he ought to have ask'd, *Where are they not?* For the Principles of Piety and Virtue in general we find all the World over, the World of Mankind are agreed in them; but it is with this difference, *what one Party of Men call Virtue and Piety, another Party calleth Vice and Impiety.* And with great Reason; for with unregenerate Mankind many Enormities have the repute of Virtue, or at least of sinless Practices. Which is not for want of the innate practical Principles, *"But this is the Cause of all Evils unto Men, they have not skill to accommodate and apply the common Notions* (τὰς προλήψεις, τὰς κοίνας ἐννοίας) *to particular Matters of Practice."*[46] They know the true *Notions* of Good, Justice, Virtue, and Piety, and that they ought to chuse and practice them: But are often grossly unacquainted with what is *materially* so. Whence it is too possible, for a whole Nation to allow the Transgression of a Practical Rule, which is imprinted on their Minds; for they may do it from a false Opinion of *Well-doing,* as the Church of *Rome* alloweth (and more than alloweth) the Transgression of the second Command-

---

43. Isocrates, *Panathenaicus,* p. 444.
44. Sharrock, *De Officiis,* ch. 3, n. 5.
45. Locke, *Essay,* I.2.9.
46. Epictetus, *Discourses,* III.16.

ment. And they may do it from an Opinion of the Necessity of Affairs, as the Church of *Rome* hath allow'd Stews, and the *Persians* allow'd the grossest Incest from an extravagant Affectation of *Magianism.*

Nam Magus ex matre & gnato nascatur oportet.

Whence it is easy to a Judgment of this remaining Part of our Objector's Argument; *"That no practical Rule, which is any-where universally, or with publick Approbation or allowance, transgress'd, can be suppos'd innate. It is impossible to conceive, that a whole Nation of Men should all publickly reject and renounce what every one of them certainly and infallibly know to be a Law; for so they must, who have it naturally imprinted on their Minds."* From the Necessity of Affairs, and an Opinion of greater Good, the *Greeks* and *Romans* in some degree, and but in some degree, tolerated the Transgression of this Law, *Parents preserve your Children:* But they were far from publickly rejecting and renouncing it; the Transgression of it was not uncondemn'd amongst themselves, and from themselves it appeareth, that they had it deeply imprinted in their Natures. *"Nature"* (saith *Cicero*) *"impelleth Men, to love those that they have begotten, and ingendereth in them a special Love to their Off-spring, and taketh care to make Provision for Wife and Children, which are counted dear, and ought to be taken care of."*[47] There is nothing more that is worth considering in our Objector's Discourses against innate practical Principles, save only his Demand of a Catalogue of them, which is like the Demand, made by our Adversaries of the Church of *Rome,* of a Catalogue of Fundamentals.

Objections against the innate Idea of God.

5. Our Objector disputeth against *the innate Idea of God,* and therein some others of the Learned agree with him. But by this innate Idea they mean, *"An original Notion and Proposition that God is, actually imprinted on us antecedently to all use of our Faculties. An anticipating Principle, engraven upon our Souls before all Exercise of Reason."*[48] Such an original

47. Cicero, *De Finibus,* I; *De Officiis,* I.
48. Bentley, "A Confutation of Atheism from the Structure and Origin of Humane Bodies," pt. I, pp. 5, 6; published in *The Folly and Unreasonableness of Atheism* (1693).

Notion or Proposition needeth not to be confuted by any operose Reasonings; for in so absurd a Sense I know not who ever held it, being a Notice of God by Reason, antecedent to all use of Reason, which is Nonsense and a Contradiction. But a Prolepsis or Anticipation concerning God, rightly understood, is only antecedent to the Argumentative Deductions of Reason, as other common Notions are; it is a natural and spontaneous Exertion of Reason, *"An innate Notion to all Men,"* whereby we mean, *"that it is innate to the Mind of Man, to suggest and notice to him the Existence of a Deity in general"* (an invisible Sovereign Power over us, an Object of Religious Worship,) *"not without noticing to him the true God and his Service."* As it is also innate to the Mind of Man, to suggest and notice to him *a future State of the Soul, and Rewards and Punishments there;* both which are prime Dictates and Suggestions of the Mind, made Rational and Religious, and prime Branches of natural Religion. *So far the Soul of Man is naturally Christian.* But against the innate Idea of God, some incredible Stories of some Savage Nations, that live in total Atheism, are objected; in answer to which I will add nothing to what I have already said upon this Head, except the following Quotation from Lord *Shaftesbury.* "It must certainly be something else than *Incredulity,* which fashions the Taste and Judgment of many Gentlemen, whom we hear censur'd as *Atheists,* for attempting to Philosophize after a newer manner than any known of late. For my own part, I have ever thought this sort of Men to be in general more credulous, tho' after another manner, than the mere Vulgar. Besides what I have observ'd in Conversation with Men of this Character, I can produce many anathematiz'd Authors, who, if they want a true *Israelitish* Faith, can make amends by a *Chinese* or *Indian* one. If they are short in *Syria,* or the *Palestine;* they have their full measure in *America,* or *Japan.* Histories of *Incas* or *Iroquois,* written by Fryars and Missionaries, Pyrates and Renegades, Sea-Captains and trusty Travellers, pass for authentick Records, and are *Canonical,* with the *Virtuosos* of this sort. The *Christian* Miracles may not so well satisfy them; they dwell with the highest Contentment on the Prodigies of *Moorish* and *Pagan* Countries. They have far more pleasure in hearing the monstrous Accounts of monstrous Men and Manners; than the politest and best Narrations of the Affairs, the Governments, and Lives, of the Wisest and most Polish'd People."[49]

It is objected also, that an innate Idea of God is not requisite. *"A Man, by the right Use of his natural Abilities, may, without any innate Principles, attain the Knowledge of a God, and other things that concern him."*[50] *"Without any such primitive Impression, we may easily attain to the Knowledge of the Deity, by the sole Use of our natural Reason."*[51] It is possible, that, without any original Impression, Men, by the sole Use of their Reason, might discover, *that there is a God,* as Propositions in *Euclid* have been found out and discover'd: And it must be acknowledged, *"That they who made the Discovery, had made a right Use of their own Reason."*[52] But it must be acknowledg'd also, that an εὔριχα had well become them upon so wonderful and important a Discovery; and it is great pity that, amongst the Inventors of useful Things, their Names are not recorded, who first made this momentous Discovery, *That there is a God.* Men, by the sole Use of their Reason, *may* discover, that there is a God; but there is much of *peradventure* and *hap-hazard,* whether Mankind discover the Being of God, or not. For we are told, that, *"if Men do not make Inquiry into the admirable Contrivances that are in the World, they may live long without any Notion of such a Being."*[53] It is more than probable, therefore, that the Generality of Mankind (who do not Philosophize) will be universally Atheists, as void of any Notion of God, as the Soul is suppos'd to be originally, by them that style her, *Tabula abrasa, a blank Sheet of Paper.* Without innate Principles, or primitive Impressions, it is possible, that Men may attain the Knowledge of a God; but is it not possible, that they may not? *"That they may live long without any Notion of such a Being?"* In which tract of time, they must necessarily have no Conscience, nor any Law, or *"Work of the Law,"* nor any *"Thoughts accusing or excusing,"* they must necessarily be Atheists with-

49. Shaftesbury, *Characteristicks,* I, p. 345.
50. Locke, *Essay,* I.3.12.
51. Bentley, "A Confutation of Atheism," p. 5.
52. Locke, *Essay,* I.3.10.
53. Ibid., I.3.23.

out being Rebels, without the Guilt of the *Heathen,* who when *"they knew God, did not glorify him as God, nor lik'd to retain God in their Knowledge";* and they must necessarily be ungodly and unrighteous, *"without holding the Truth in Unrighteousness."* It must be suppos'd, that God made them, without making them Religionists; for as Men cannot be said, to be made Philosophers, merely because by their natural Abilities they may become Philosophers; so neither can they be said, to be made Religionists, merely because by their natural Faculties they may become such. Are they not born by Nature Atheists, if they have no innate Idea of God, no primitive Impression, *"if they may live long without any Notion of such a Being?"* That Mankind may be by Nature Religionists, innate Idea is requisite, *"A necessary and innate Notion, which is naturally in every Rational, without a Human Teacher or operose Deductions of Reason,"* as an Antient well expresseth it. This legitimate innate Idea of God, is incumbred with no valuable Objections, but it is possible that those Objections may be made against it, that are urg'd against an erroneous innate Idea of God and primitive Impression, therefore we will briefly consider them.

First, it is argu'd, *"That such an Impression taketh away the Commendableness and Rewardableness of Faith, by rendering the Belief of a God irresistible and necessary."* [54] But our legitimate innate Idea of God is not liable to this Objection; for, altho' it is innate to the Minds of all Men, to notice to them the Existence of God, as a Principle of natural Religion, yet they may be Atheists: But it will be very hard, if not impossible, to be thorough-pac'd Atheists; and so some wise Men have thought, that the Fool who saith in his Heart, there is no God, *"rather saith it by rote to himself, as that he would have, than that he can throughly believe it, or be persuaded of it."* [55] The Commendableness of *Faith* is not taken away in any such case, where there is place for a virtuous Disposition; whence, altho' the Apostle *Thomas* had the Evidence of Sense (which may seem to necessitate Assent) for our Saviour's Resurrection, yet his Faith was commendable and rewardable. In his Case there was

---

54. Bentley, "A Confutation of Atheism," p. 5.
55. Bacon, "Of Atheism" in *Essays* (1601).

place for virtuous Disposition; whence *the Watch,* and from them the Chief Priests, altho' they had the Evidence of Sense as well as he, yet being devoid of his virtuous Disposition, continued in Unbelief, *Matth.* 28. 11. Evidence of Sense, Evidence plainly Mathematical, will not *necessitate Assent* in such Cases, where a requisite virtuous Disposition is wanting, and a powerful Interest and Inclination is against it, of which *Transubstantiation* may be an Example.

Another Argument against an erroneous innate Idea of God, is drawn from the Apostle's Preaching to the *Athenians, Act.* 17. 27. *"of seeking the Lord, if happily they might feel after him and find him."* Whence this Inference is made, *"That it requireth some Industry and Consideration, to find out the Being of God by the Light of Nature."* [56] This Inference being part of a Dispute against an innate Idea, must mean thus; *That the finding out the Being of God by the Light of Nature, is merely by Industry and Consideration, exclusively of an innate Idea;* which is no just Inference from the Apostle's Text, whose Scope is not, to exhort the *Athenians* to seek and find out the Being of God; nor did he preach to them as to *Atheists,* or such Heteroclites, that had not made the Discovery, but as to *Pagan Theists,* who had *Gods* too many; nor doth *seeking after the Lord and finding him,* signify the finding out this Proposition, *That there is a God;* nor are all those who have found out this Proposition, such as have found out God in the Apostle's Sense. But he considereth the *Athenians* as Aliens from the true God, and from knowing him; he exhorteth them, therefore, *to seek the Lord, to feel after him, and find him,* which is to come out of their *Heathen* State, to know him so, as to become his Religionists. To find out the Being of God, the Existence of a Deity, this needed not *"a seeking the Lord with Meditation and Study";* [57] their innate Notion of the Being of God, and the obvious Phaenomena of Nature, made them a sort of Theists; but to be in *Theism of Religion and Condition,* This was the thing which requir'd a seeking the Lord with Meditation and Study; and, because they were without it, therefore they were a *Hea-*

---

56. Bentley, "A Confutation of Atheism," pp. 1, 6.
57. Ibid, p. 7.

thenish Atheistical Kind of Theists, and the true God was to them a Stranger-Deity.

§16. The *Stoicks* define *Duty, A Practice agreeable to the natural Constitutions.*[58] So the Apostle supposeth Sodomy, Bestiality, and other *Heathen* Pollutions, were Crimes against the Law of Nature, because they were repugnant to the Order and Constitution of Nature, to the manifest Institution of the great Author of Nature, and to the natural Use of Things, *Rom.* 1. 26, 27. *"Men and Women chang'd the natural Use into that which is against Nature."* The *Heathen* Idolatry was against the Nature of Creatures, that were deified by it, and upon this account also it was a Crime against the Law of Nature; it was repugnant and injurious to the Dignity of Man made after God's Image, to fall down before Stocks and Stones, with all manner of submissive and lowly Adoration. As Idolaters sin against their own Dignity, *So he that committeth Fornication, sinneth against his own Body,* (and therefore against his own Dignity,) prostituting it, and making it so abominably Vile, as to make it the Member of an Harlot, 1 *Cor.* 6. 15, 16, 17. Fornication was manifestly forbidden, because of the Turpitude which such things have, when they are out of a certain Orbit, within which they ought to be confin'd, and without which they are foul, criminal, shameful Contaminations, repugnant to that graceful and ornamental Purity and Chastity, which is the Honour and Ornament of the Body and of the Reason, 1 *Thes.* 4. 4. The sensual Excess of Drunkenness is in like manner manifestly repugnant to the natural Use of Things, the Honour and Dignity of Man, (indeed to common Civility, Gravity, Modesty, Discretion.) For whereas Man is naturally a beauteous, noble, and cleanly Animal, there is no Beast of the Field so Beastly as a Drunkard, a most foul, nasty, noxious, and mis-shapen Animal, with staring distorted Eyes, a fetid Breath, a stammering bauling Tongue, leud Demeanour, and, as *Chaucer* telleth him, *"Thy Face is turn'd into a new array."* His Trade is gorging, surcharging, disgorging, and *"shameful Spewing is upon his Glory."* The Life of Sensualists is opposite to the regular Frame and Constitution of Man,

The law of Nature is notic'd to Mankind by the Nature of Things.

---

58. [Maxwell] "Officium est actio naturalibus constitutionibus conveniens."

which consisteth in the Sovereignty and Rule of his Intellectual Rational Nature, and the Subjection of the Sensitive; for in them Animal-sensitive Nature is predominant and beareth the Sway, and the Head is, where the Heels should be. Whence evil Men are reproach'd with the Names of brute Animals, Wolves, Dogs, Foxes; with being Brutes in the Shapes of Men, which are Monsters in Nature. All Vices are repugnant to Nature, the Nature of Things; all of them are inordinate. Inordinate Self-love, Self-magnifying, Fear, and Care, inordinate Anger, and all *"inordinate Affections* (Col. 3. 5.) *the Lust of the Flesh, the Lust of the Eyes, and the Pride of Life"* (the Summary of all Wickedness) are Vitious and Criminal, because of their Inordinacy; for they are Nature grown Unnatural, Enormous, Disproportionate, and like a Musical Instrument out of Tune. Gross Irreverence to a Prince, Ingratitude to a Benefactor, insulting a Friend, are Repugnancies and Incongruities to the Object; and such is the justifying the Wicked, the befriending Sin, the profaning that which is Holy, all Impiety towards God, the minding Private Interest, and slighting the Publick, the taking Care of the Body and neglecting the Soul, to which, in worth, the World bears no Proportion.

The Instincts of Nature, §17. The Law of Nature is, in some degree, notic'd by *the kindly Instincts that are in Nature,* which is below Reason, Will, and Choice. So Nature, in the narrow Sense, usually signifies the natural unintelligent Agents Nature. *"The Antients call'd the Passions Natural and devoid of Reason."*[59] In this Notion of Nature, Custom is said to be a second Nature, or an acquir'd Nature. Nature in this Notion, Nature in the Universe, altho' she acteth not electively or with intention, but fatally, yet she doth nothing in vain, but all for Ends and Uses. As Nature blindly operateth in the great World, so in Animals and in Men, in whose Animal Nature, as in brute Animals, there are blind Instincts, which are not the Law of Nature, and ought to be in subjection to Reason (as Reason to God) which they usually rebel against, and dethrone. The Animal Nature in Man is full of inordinate Concupiscence, which is not so Nature, as not to be *vitious Nature;* for the Nature of Man is sadly out of Frame by it.

59. Cicero, *Academicae Quaestiones,* I.

Nor is it Nature, as being Natural to the Soul of Man, but it is extraneous and adventitious, and requireth a Purgation. Nor is it kindly and agreeable, and in such Sense natural to the Soul, *"But consider, if Virtue and Sanctity be not more kindly and pleasant."* [60] Yet a Nature it is, as being the Animal Nature, and so far the Nature of Man; it is now, in a certain degree, his innate Constitution, and it is the specifick Nature of the Carnal and Mundan Family; whence the Apostle saith of inordinate Concupiscence (the Lust of the Flesh, the Lust of the Eyes, and the Pride of Life), *"it is not of the Father, but it is of the World,"* 1 *Joh.* 2. 16. It is of the World, as it is lapsed, and become this wicked World.

But, if this Animal Nature be consider'd, as it is *Nature,* but *not vitiated Nature,* the kindly Instincts of it are Notices of the Law of Nature, and contradict the Atheists Politicks, that are founded upon Slanders of Mankind, (whereby it appeareth, how highly well they deserve of Mankind,) *That natural Relations are nothing, that there is nothing of Honesty, Justice, or Philanthropy, in human Nature, no natural Charity, or Friendliness, that Man is not sociable by Nature,* (as Brute Animals are, that have a sort of Benevolence for those of their own kind,) *but that all Benevolence is either from Fear or Feebleness.* If these unnatural Abusers of Nature and worst of Impostors teach, *That nothing is Just or Unjust in the State of Nature; that every Man by Nature hath a Right to every Thing* (whatever his Appetite inclineth to,) *and whatsoever one doth to another it is no Injury;* so that a Son may lawfully kill his own Parents, and the Innocent may be tortur'd to all extremity: the innate Humanity and natural Affection, that is in Mankind, the natural Affections of *Gratitude* and *Commiseration* that are in Human Nature, contradict these lewd and wicked Maxims; and this other ill-natur'd Maxim also, *That Man seeketh that which is Good for himself, as the only Object of his Desires,* is contradicted by Nature, for Ants, Bees, and Storks do some things for the sake of others. *"The Inclination to Goodness is implanted deeply in the Nature of Man; insomuch that if it issue not towards Men, it will take unto other living Creatures; as is seen in the* Turks, *a cruel People, who nevertheless are kind to Beasts, and give Alms to Dogs and Birds: Insomuch as*

---

60. Marcus Aurelius, *Meditations,* V.9.

Busbequius *reporteth, a* Christian *Boy in* Constantinople *had like to have been ston'd for gagging in Waggishness a long-bill'd Fowl."* [61] Many Instincts of Nature instigate to what is manifestly a sort of Goodness or Well-doing, and these are Indications, that the being devoid of them, and the Practice which is contrary to them, is criminally Unnatural. Such is the Instinct to common *Modesty,* call'd by the Atheists *Foolishness,* and the Instinct to *natural Affection, Rom.* 1. 31. Such is the Instinct of Nature to an ordinate regular *Self-love,* Desire of our own Good, Self-preservation, Well-being, and Felicity, and an Aversion from the contrary. *Naturâ enim sibi quisque amicus est,* "for every one by Nature is a Friend to Himself," was a common Saying. *"No Man ever hated his own Flesh"* (without being criminally Unnatural) *"but loveth and cherisheth it,"* Ephes. 5. 29. Nature instigateth Mankind to take care of themselves and their Off-spring, so making a natural Society, Kindred, and Friendship, and taking care of the Conservation of the Species, and to extinguish and controul these Instincts, is criminally Unnatural. In disposing of their Estates, Men rightly suppose themselves oblig'd to proportion their Kindness to others, to their Degree in Nearness to themselves, as the kindly Instincts of Nature incline them. *"There are various Degrees of Society and Conjunction among Mankind; and as every one is nearer, so ordinarily he is to have a greater Share of our Kindness with its Effects."* [62] The Instincts of Nature to Religion and Society, by shewing the Design of the great Author of Nature, are manifestly Notices of the Law of Nature.

and the Sense of Conscience.

§18. The Law of Nature is notic'd by the *Sense of Conscience,* the peaceful and joyous Sense of Innocence and Well-doing, and the dolorous, torturing, Sense of Guilt. *Conscience* is certainly of this Definitive Notion, it is *the Mind as conscious of Duty and of Sin,* and so far it is the same with *the Practical Mind.* For Conscience denoteth that which is *conscious* in a Man, as such; it denoteth therefore, the Mind as conscious, and it must necessarily denote the Mind as *conscious of Duty and of Sin,* because

---

61. Bacon, "Of Goodness," in *Essays.*
62. Cicero, *De Officiis,* I.

nothing else in Law or Religion is matter of Conscience. Those Passions of the Mind as conscious of Duty and Sin, *The Stings of Conscience, the Mind's Satisfaction and Complacency in itself, (which is Peace and Quiet of Conscience,) and Repentance,* are the *Conscience* in Man; therefore the Conscience is the Mind of Man, as conscious of Duty and Sin. Of Conscience, so defin'd, there are two Branches; the one *Directive,* which respecteth Duty and Sin not yet done, (which is call'd *the practical Understanding* and *Synteresis,* or System of common practical Notions;) the other is *Reflexive,* which respecteth Duty and Sin already done; and from both these Branches of Conscience, but chiefly from the latter, Conscience hath its Name. *Conscientia* signifieth *Consciousness of our Doings,* sometimes the Consciousness of others, but most usually our own Consciousness. So *Tacitus* saith of *Nero,* that he fell in Love with *Acte,* "*Having taken two young Men into Consciousness of his doing.*"[63] So *Cicero* saith, that *Epicurus* Philosophiz'd in such a manner, "*That there is nothing so foul, which he seemeth not willing to do for Pleasure-sake, if Men be not conscious thereof.*"[64] But most usually *Conscientia* signifieth our own *Consciousness* of our own Doings. As when *Cicero* saith, "*Every one's flagitious Doing exagitateth him and affecteth him with Madness: His evil Cogitations and Consciousness of Mind terrify him.*"[65] "*The Consciousness of a well-spent Life and the Remembrance of many Well-doings is most pleasant.*"[66] "*The Consciousness of a right Will is the greatest Consolation of incommodious Affairs.*"[67] "*In the very Consciousness of Well-doings there is Fruit enough of our Labours.*"[68] The same Author somewhere says, "*I use not so much to rejoyce in any thing as the Consciousness of my Duties.*"[69] In these Sayings and such like, *Conscientia* is rightly render'd *Consciousness,* as appeareth from many parallel Sayings of the antient Writers.[70] From

---

63. Tacitus, *Annales,* XIII.
64. Cicero, *De Finibus,* II.
65. Cicero, *Pro Sextus Roscio Amerino Oratio.*
66. Cicero, *De Senectute,* I.iii.9.
67. Cicero, *Ad Familiares,* VI.4.
68. Maxwell notes *Philippics,* V, but the passage does not occur there.
69. Maxwell is referring to Cicero, *Ad Familiares,* V.7.
70. Sharrock, *De Officiis,* ch. 1, n. 11; Taylor, *Ductor Dubitantium,* I.1, R. 2, n. 9.

whose usual Phraseology it is manifest, that *Conscience* has its Name
from *Consciousness* (the Mind's Consciousness of well and evil Doing),
whence it must be defin'd, *the Mind as conscious of Duty and of Sin.*
Agreeably to which Definition of *Conscience,* the usual Distributions of
Conscience may easily be understood and explain'd. For, if the Mind,
as conscious of Duty and Sin, is uncriminal, this is *the good Conscience:*
If it be criminal, this is *the evil Conscience.* As conscious of Duty and
Sin, the Mind may be quiet or troubled: The one is a *quiet,* the other a
troubled Conscience. If the Mind is tenderly conscious of Duty and of
Sin, this is a *tender Conscience:* If Senseless and not apt to check, or to
check but feebly, this is a *stupid Conscience.* And what is an *erroneous,
doubtful, scrupulous Conscience,* but the Mind conscious in general of
Duty and of Sin, and erroneous, doubtful, or scrupulous, touching some
particular Matters of Practice? The Notion of Conscience in the New-
Testament, (where the Name occurreth no less than 32 times,) is the
Mind as conscious of Duty and of Sin. When the sacred Writers speak
of being *convicted* by our own Conscience,[71] of being *condemn'd* by
it, of the *Testimony of our Conscience,* and *our Conscience bearing Witness,*
of *commending ourselves to every Man's Conscience,* and *being made manifest in their Consciences,* and *having no more Conscience of Sins;* Conscience signifies as in profane Authors, *the Consciousness of our Mind, the
Mind as conscious of Good and Evil.* To do any thing *for Conscience-sake,
for Conscience towards God,* is to do it as *conscious of Duty to God, and
of Sin against him, Rom.* 13. 5. 1 *Pet.* 2. 19. Some ate things offer'd to an
Idol with *Conscience of the Idol,* as conscious of Duty and religious Worship to the Idol, 1 *Cor.* 8. 7. their being so conscious of Duty and of Sin,
was their sinful Weakness, and therefore their Conscience was weak,
1 *Cor.* 8. 7. and it was also render'd criminal by the Practice of Idolatry.
So the Mind of ungodly Infidels, as such, is defiled, and their Conscience
is defiled by their deadly criminal Practice, *Tit.* 1. 15. *Christians* were at
liberty, to eat what was offer'd unto Idols, *asking no Question for*

71. John 8.38; Wisdom 15.13; Titus 3.11; I John 3.20; Romans 2.15, 9.1; II Corinthians 1.12, 4.2, 5.11; Hebrews 10.2.

Conscience-sake,[72] (asking no Question upon account of their own Minds Consciousness of Good and Evil:) But they might not eat it under this Notion, as Idols Meat, in the apprehension of those who made Conscience of a Worship of Idols, but were bound to abstain, because of their Conscience (their Consciousness of Good and Evil;) for, if they did in such manner externally symbolize with them, their Liberty would be *judged* (construed and interpreted) by their Conscience (their Consciousness of Duty and Sin) who made Conscience of the Worship of Idols. How then could a *Christian* think it a reasonable Thing, to symbolize with them? *Christians* have not only a Conscience, but *the good Conscience;*[73] which is sometimes called *a Conscience void of Offence,* sometimes *a pure Conscience.* And, because by Virtue of Christ's Sacrifice, uncondemnably Sinless and Guiltless, as to the Mind, Soul, and Conscience, therefore they are said to have *their Hearts sprinkled from an evil Conscience, Heb.* 10. 22. to have their Conscience purg'd from dead Works (those deadly Works, that were deadly Crimes and deadly Pollutions, *Heb.* 9. 14.) and Christ's Sacrifice is said to make them *perfect as pertaining to Conscience, Heb.* 9. 9. For they are perfect as to the Expiation of Sin, or are perfectly expiated by Christ's Sacrifice, being made by it uncondemnably Sinless and Guiltless, as to the Mind, Soul, and Conscience. In one place more of the New-Testament mention is made of *Conscience,* but it is of a superlatively evil Conscience, for the Apostle speaketh of a *Conscience seared with a hot Iron,* 1 *Tim.* 4. 2. Such is the Conscience of an habituated atrocious Criminal. The Phrase may signify, that his Conscience is deeply maculated with the Marks of his Crimes; it may signify, that he is of a branded stigmatiz'd Conscience, an infamous Villain; and the Phrase may allude to fear'd cauteriz'd Flesh, and therefore may signify, that he is become insensible as to his Conscience, and is so far harden'd in his Villainy.

At this monstrous Pitch of Wickedness they are arriv'd, that have overcome their checking and controuling Mind, that can commit gross

72. I Corinthians 10.25, 27, 28, 29.

73. Acts 23.1, 24.16; I Timothy 1.5, 19; 3.9; Hebrews 13.18; II Timothy 1.3; I Peter 3.16, 21.

and flagrant Sins without Reluctance or Regret, Remorse or Shame, and perpetrate notorious Wickedness with an Opinion of its Generosity, Gallantry, and Bravery. So the Philosophers distinguish between ἀκρασία *Incontinence*, and ἀκολασία *Intemperance*.[74] *"In Incontinence the Man keepeth his Judgment right, but is carried away by the Appetite, that is too strong for Reason."* But of *Intemperance* they say, *"It addeth a vitious Judgment to a vitious Appetite, and it destroyeth the Sense of the Sins."* The Man *"from his whole Soul inclineth and consenteth to his sensual Pleasures,"* and such *commit Uncleanness with Greediness,"* Ephes. 4. 19. How far Men may thus degenerate, to be past feeling, having the Mind clouded, and the Conscience deaded, is best known to them that make the desperate Experiment: But in some of the greatest Monsters for Wickedness amongst the *Heathen,* (*Tiberius, Caligula, Nero,*) the Sense of Conscience was so far from being extinguish'd, that in the height of their Greatness, and in an affluence of Prosperity and sensual Pleasures, they found the Rebukes and Lashes, the Anguish and Terrors of their own guilty Minds unavoidable. Whence the Historian observeth, that *"if the Minds of Tyrants were laid open, the Verberations and Laniations might be seen."*[75] By the Vultur gnawing *Ixion's* Liver were meant the Torments of an evil Conscience. By their *Erinnyes, Eumenides, Furies,* the *Heathens* meant the Horrors and Terrors of a guilty Mind. They found that certain gross Sins did sensibly wound their Consciences, which also wounded them, convicting and condemning them, and scourging them with silent Strokes, disquieting them with Anguish and Pensiveness, with doleful Fears and sad Presages; and this Sense of Guilt in their own Minds was a manifest Notice and Indication to them, to look upon those Practices as Wickedness, and to avoid them as such, which did clash with the Frame of their Minds, and brought so many and so great Evils of an evil Conscience upon them. By internal Sense and Experience they found, they had a Conscience *bearing them Witness,* acquitting and comforting, or accusing and condemning them; they found a difference be-

---

74. Plutarch, *De Virtute Morali* (in *Moralia*), pp. 445, 446; Casaubon, *Persii Flacci Satirarum,* pp. 249, 250.

75. Grotius, *De Veritate Religionis Christianae,* I.

tween Well-doing and Evil-doing in general, that some Practices were peaceful and pleasant to their Mind, as harmonious and agreeable thereto, and that others they could not dispense with; whereby the Duties of Honesty and Justice were notic'd to them, to be Laws inviolable, and they were warn'd of a future Judgment. They found that Sin had another Face, after the Commission of it, than it had before, and that the only way to Peace, was, not to sin against their Consciences.[76]

CHAPTER III. The Observance of the Law of Nature.

§1. As in respect of its *Obligation* and *Promulgation*, so, in respect of its *Observance,* the Law of Nature is of a two-fold Notion. For, abating an additional restriction which is in its Definition (that limiteth it to the Notices of the Light of Nature), the Law of Nature is intirely the same with the Divine Moral Law. The Law of Nature therefore must be consider'd, as also the *Mosaick* Moral Law must be, both as it is of *Civil-religious,* and as it is of *Spiritual-religious,* Observance. The one constituteth the *Civil-religious,* the other the *Spiritual-religious,* People. The one is necessary to Civil-religious Society, the other is Righteousness and true Holiness, which alone is available to constitute Men Righteous as to their Soul-Interests.

The Observance of the Law of Nature, two-fold.

§2. The Law of Nature, because of this different Observance of it, is an Institution of *Spiritual-religious Virtue and Duty,* in order to Mens *Soul-interests,* and also an Institution of *Civil-religious Virtue and Duty,* in order to their *secular* and *Civil* Interests, as the Apostle considereth the *Mosaick*-moral Law. 1 *Tim.* 1. 9, 10. *"The Law is not made for a righteous Man, but for the Lawless and Disobedient, for the Ungodly and for Sinners, for the Unholy and Profane, for Murderers of Fathers and Murderers of Mothers, for Man-slayers, for Whore-mongers, for them that Defile themselves with Mankind, for Man-stealers, for Liars, for perjur'd Persons."* As a Philosopher is far from supposing, that a Virtuous Man's proper In-

The Law of Nature, or the Moral Law, is a Civil-religious Institution, promoting the Welfare of Civil Society, in order to the Preservation and Happiness of Temporal Life;

76. Tacitus, *Annales,* XIV.10.

stitution of Virtue is not made for a Virtuous Man: So, if the Apostle had consider'd the Moral Law, as the Law of Righteousness and true Holiness, he would not have said, that *it is not made for a righteous Man;* for it is his proper Institution of Righteousness, *Rom.* 2. 13. and 8. 7. and 13. 8, 10. *Jam.* 2. 8.–11. But as the Philosophers say of the Civil Law of the Common-Wealth, *"It is not made for the Good,"*[1] it is not needful to make such Laws for them: So the Apostle saith of the Civil-religious Law of the *Jews,* it is not made for a righteous Man, as necessary to be made for him, but for the Lewd and Flagitious, that by the Authority of the Law they may be disciplin'd with the Civil-religious Morals, re-strain'd from violating them, or punish'd, if they do violate them. The *Mosaick* Law, as it was the Law of the *Judaical* Common-Wealth, that Political Law, was an Institution of Civil religious Virtue and Duty, and of Civil-religious Observance. Whence a young Man telleth our Saviour (*Matth.* 19. 20.) that he had always observ'd the Moral Precepts of the Law; and the Favour which our Saviour had for him, sheweth, that he spake nothing but Truth; for, as to the Civil-religious Observance of the Precepts of the Moral Law, he was train'd up to Virtuously, that he had kept them from his Youth. So the Apostle in his *Judaical* Religion, *touch-ing the Righteousness which is in the Law* (consider'd as a Civil-religious Institution of Civil Societists) *was blameless, Phil.* 3. 6. Such also is the Law of Nature, as it is the Law of Civil Societists, merely in order to their secular Interests. For the Civil Law of every Nation, in great part, consisteth of the Law of Nature, which Civil Law is a Civil-religious Institution, (an Institution of Civil-religious Virtue and Duty, and of Civil-religious Observance,) and, consequently, the Law of Nature whereof it consisteth, is of the same Character. Such a Civil-religious Institution as the Civil Lawyers Discipline, which is defined by them-selves, *The Knowledge both of Divine and Human Things, the Science of Just and Unjust.* This sort of Religion and Virtue, necessary for Human Society and Civil Life, Human Laws institute, and, inconsort with them, the Law of Nature doth the same. As a Civil-religious Institution, and for the Conservation of Human Life, the Law of Nature had an agree-

1. Grotius, *Annotationes in Novum Testamentum* on I Timothy 1.9–10.

able Observance, among the Virtuous Popular *Pagans;* for their Observance of it was (in their way of Religion) Civil-religious; which was *Virtus civilis, non vera, sed verisimilis, quae ad veras virtutes, aeternamque beatitudinem non profecit,* Civil Virtue, not the True, but a Resemblance thereof, wholly ineffectual to make the Soul truly Holy and eternally Happy.[2]

§3. But the Law Natural and *Mosaical* is the Law or Religion of Soul-interests, *"for so the doers of the Law shall be justified,"* Rom. 2. 13. *"The Commandment was ordain'd to Life,"* Rom. 7. 10. When a young Man ask'd, *Good Master, what shall I do, that I may inherit Eternal Life?,* Christ answer'd, *If thou wilt enter into Life, keep the Commandments,* which he reckoneth in their Order. The Commandments of the Law, therefore, were such, and that by the Purpose and Design of the Law-giver, who intended to lead Men to Life and eternal Salvation. In like manner *Luk.* 10. to a Lawyer that asked, *What shall I do to inherit Eternal Life?* Christ answer'd, *What is written in the Law, how readest thou?* Signifying plainly, that the Law was given as the way of obtaining Eternal Life. The Moral Law, therefore, Natural and *Mosaical,* is not merely a Civil-religious Institution, but an Institution of Religion and Virtue, in order to Life Eternal, which may therefore properly be call'd, *The Law-religion touching Soul-interests.* Our Saviour, in his Discourse with the Lawyer, expresseth the very Terms (the Condition and premiant Part of the Sanction) of this Law-religion; for he having repeated to our Saviour the grand Precepts of the Moral Law, touching the Love of God and Man, our Saviour replyeth to him, *This do, and thou shalt live.* Therefore, if the Moral Law, Natural and *Mosaical,* is a Settlement or Covenant of Life Eternal, it is necessarily also a Settlement of Condemnation and of Death, Spiritual and Eternal. Therefore, if the Moral Law hath this tragical Effect, in the Sense of the New-Testament, if the Design of a Saviour was to redeem Mankind from the manifold Evils brought upon them by the Moral Law, it must be thought a Premiant and Penal Settlement of the Soul-interests of Men. Nor is it possible, that it can be a *Holy*

and also a Spiritual-religious Institution, in order to everlasting Happiness and Life Eternal.

---

2. Vossius, *Historiae de Controversiis quas Pelagius,* III, pt. 3, theses 8 and 11.

Spiritual Law, as the Apostle styleth it, unless the Sanction of it be the Settlement of the Spiritual and Soul-interests of Men. From whence it followeth, that *Life* and *Death,* as they are the Sanction of the Law, must be understood in a two fold Notion, the one *Civil-religious,* the other *Spiritual-religious,* the one of which is Figurative of the other; therefore Life must signify *secular Prosperity* as premiant to *Civil-religious* Obedience, and *Life Eternal* as premiant to the *Spiritual-religious* fulfilling the Law.

The Moral Law is a Law of Spiritual-religious Morals, and Spiritual-religious Observance.

If the Moral Law, Natural and *Mosaical,* is the Law or Religion of Soul-interests, it is necessarily, in the preceptive Part of it, an Institution of the *Spiritual-religious* Morals, and of *Spiritual-religious* Observance, which belongeth to it, as it is *the Holy Spiritual Law, Rom.* 7. 12, 14. Such a kind of Law requireth, that Men be truly Spiritual kind of Livers (not of the wicked and carnal Kind,) and that they live the holy Spiritual kind of Life, which is the Righteousness and true Holiness of the inward Man, and the Spiritual-religious Observance of the Law. The Law is Spiritual, both in respect of the Life and Practice, and in respect of the Virtue and Duty which it requireth; for it requireth the holy Spiritual Life and Practice, and the Spiritual-religious Virtue and Duty, which are the same Things, but with this difference; the Holy Spiritual Life and Practice is contradistinguish'd to Carnality and Wickedness of Life and Practice; but the Spiritual-religious Virtue and Duty is contradistinguish'd to the Civil-religious, which, if alone, is but a Carnality of Religion and Virtue. Such was the Religion and Virtue of *the Jews after the Letter, that serv'd in the Oldness of the Letter,* being totally devoid of the Holy Spiritual Life, and therefore they were under the Curse of the Holy Spiritual Law, for all that are under the Letter, are under the Curse. They are in their Carnality of Life and Practice, and in their Carnality of Religion and Virtue, and are a Family of Virtuous People, and of Religionists, opposite to the Spiritual and Divine Family of regenerate Religionists, in whom the Righteousness which the Holy Spiritual Law requireth, is fulfilled (in the main, tho' not in the rigour of it,) *Rom.* 8. 4. and 13. 10. Regenerate *Christians,* that *walk not after the Flesh, but after the Spirit* (live the Holy Spiritual Life) fulfil the Righteousness of the

Law; the Law is therefore the Institution of the Spiritual-religious Duty and Virtue. None are the Doers of it, and of the Righteousness which it requireth, but they that belong to the New-Testament, that have the Law, not written on Tables, but in their Hearts by an intimate and faithful Love of God and of Righteousness, which is the Spiritual-religious Observance of the Law. To do the Commandments of the Moral Law from servile Fear of Punishment, which is to do them against one's Will, is not to be a Well-doer. The Law is not observ'd, but by the Love of God and of Righteousness, and delight in Things Spiritually good, and by that equitable Charity, which doeth to all, as we our-selves would be done to. And, if the Life of Divine Charity is the only genuine Observance of the Law, it is necessarily of Spiritual-religious Observance. The *Christian* Moral Law is of Spiritual-religious Observance, and the *Mosaick* Moral Law is of the same Nature; for our Saviour in his Sermon on the Mount, which is the *Christian* Moral Law, is said to have *perfected* and *filled up* the *Mosaick* Moral Law upon this account, because what was obscurely implyed therein, our Saviour hath clearly and distinctly explain'd. That part of his Moral Law, wherein he seemeth to dilate, extend, and fill up the *Mosaick* (using the Phrase, *But I say unto you*) is in the main, nothing else but the Contents of the *Mosaick* Moral Law, clearly unfolded, and *so as to be chang'd into Christianity.* The Law of Nature, therefore, is of various Acceptation; for the whole Divine Moral Law, *without restriction to Natural Light,* (the whole System of that Moral Law, of which there are Notices by the Light of Nature,) is sometimes called *the Law of Nature.* And by confining it to the Notices of Natural Light, this large Acceptation of it is made narrower; for it is not to be suppos'd, that the Light of Nature, so fully and perfectly noticeth the Moral Law, as the *Mosaical* Scripture doth.

As the Summary of what the Law of Nature, or the Moral Law, requireth, is *the good Life,* and Well-doing or Universal Righteousness: So it appeareth, that the good Life must be distinguish'd into two Kinds, the *Civil-religious,* and the *Spiritual-religious.* The Civil-religious good Life maketh a flourishing State, or Civil Society, and a Civilly-good People. The good Life of the Virtuous *Pagans,* who *did by Nature the*

Things contain'd in the Law, cannot be thought of a better Character than the Civil-religious, which is only *a bad kind of good Life,* which continueth Men in the State of Death; for *the Divine Moral Law* is not only a *Law of external good Deeds, and of a carnal Commandment,* but also a *Spiritual Law.*

FINIS.

Appendix 1

Richard Cumberland's Original Dedication to
De Legibus Naturae

The Author's Dedication.[1]

To the Right Honourable Sir Orlando Bridgman *Knight and Knight Baronet, Lord High Chancellor of* England, *Keeper of the Great Seal, and of his Majesty King* Charles *the Second's most honourable Privy Council.*[2]

My most noble LORD,

The two Reasons which chiefly prevail with all Authors, who dedicate Books, are either, *First,* the Importance of the Subject; or, *Secondly,* The particular Situation and Circumstances of the Author himself. Both these Reasons prevail with me to address this Performance to your Lordship.

For since *the Laws of Nature,* the Subject-matter of this Work, are the Solid Foundations of that Equity which your Lordship, from your

---

1. Richard Cumberland's original dedication (Cumberland, *De Legibus Naturae,* A3r–a2r), translated into English by the Rev. John Towers for his edition of Cumberland, *A Philosophical Enquiry into the Laws of Nature* (1750), Appendix, Part IV, pp. 83–85. The references in square brackets occur as marginal notes in Cumberland and Towers.

2. Orlando Bridgeman (1606–74) was made Lord Chancellor in 1667. Educated at Magdalene, Cambridge, Bridgeman went on to become a lawyer and M.P. for Wigan and was knighted in 1640. At the Restoration he was made a baronet and presided over the trial of the regicides. Bridgeman fell from office after refusing to endorse Charles II's Declaration of Indulgence in 1672. For full details of Bridgeman's career, see *The Dictionary of National Biography* (Oxford: Oxford University Press, issued various years).

own innate Disposition, so fondly admire; and since in the *High Court of Chancery,* where, by the Royal Favour of our most gracious Sovereign, you preside as supreme Judge, it must appear a Piece of unpardonable Injustice in me, to have sought after any other Patron.

In this controversial Treatise, however, we do not only discourse upon the Maxims of Equity in particular, but upon Religion, upon Justice, and upon Civil Government in general.

These Principles, which your Lordship holds in the highest and dearest Esteem, are, as we complain, attacked by Mr. *Hobbes.*

For, altho' this Gentleman, at some times, allows the Dictates of Reason, which concern these Points, to be impressed upon every human Mind, by Almighty God, as Rules of Action [*De Cive,* ch. 4. Sect. 1.]; yet he, notwithstanding this Concession, obstinately denies any such Dictates to lay an Obligation upon outward Acts, conformable to these Dictates [*De Cive,* ch. 3. Sect. 27]: Or, that they are, in any Propriety of speaking, *Laws,* unless they first be established upon Civil Authority [*De Cive,* ch. 5. Sect. 2, 5.]: And, unless they first are guarded by the Sanctions of the Civil Magistrate [*De Cive,* ch. 6. Sect 3.]. In short, he utterly denies that any such Laws are the Concern of those who are not Members of the same Civil Community.

These are the prevailing Opinions, the ruling Principles, the Κυρία Δόξα of Mr. *Hobbes;* and, from which his most fundamental Maxims are deduced. Hence he concludes [*Leviathan* in English, Chap. 26. pag. 143], that in all the several Constitutions of Civil Government, from the highest to the lowest, one with another, the Members of one Community may act as they please by the Members of any other; all being, as he says, in a perpetual State of War, notwithstanding that the Compacts of mutual Faith and Fidelity be as binding and obligatory as possibly can be devised.

From hence, he peremptorily insists upon it, That all Men lawfully may take away Life, with the Necessaries and Comforts thereunto belonging, from all Men, provided they be in a State which he imagines and calls *natural;* or, provided they be not Members of the same Civil Community.

Whereas we, on the contrary, maintain, That these Principles are not only repugnant to the Divine Authority over the external Acts and Behaviour of Mankind, and which Natural Religion dictates; but we also affirm this Conclusion to follow as a direct Consequence from his Principles, That Almighty God has not laid an Obligation upon any Man to the external Acts of Justice and Fidelity, without which it is, in the Nature of Things, impossible for any peaceable Society or Intercourse amongst Mankind to subsist.

For, taking away the Sanction of that Obligation, which these Dictates of Reason derive from the Authority of Almighty God, it is no Matter of Wonder if Mr. *Hobbes* cannot produce any other Tye of Obligation binding enough to restrain the unbounded Liberty of Mankind.

For all Civil Authority, as being inferior to the Divine Authority of the Laws of Nature, becomes weak and helpless, unless aided by Nature's Laws, which lay the Obligation upon outward Acts, as the wise Foundation, and the well-connected Security of such Authority.

But, besides this: He is not satisfied totally to demolish the Foundations of Civil Society and Laws, unless he can overset and change Laws, even after they were written and established, to favour every Vice according to the Humour of his *Leviathan.*

In order, therefore, that Lawyers may have no Business at all upon their Hands, he introduces armed Force, as the Interpreter of Law, which is, with Sword in Hand, to cut short all knotty Points. And, he openly declares, in the very same Chapter of his Book called the *Leviathan,* That our Judges of the English Common Law are not Judges but Lawyers [*Leviathan* in English, Pages 143 and 147].

Since, therefore it is so well known, my Lord, to all the World, how zealous you have always appeared in the Cause of Piety, Religion and Justice, you justly claim the first Right to this Treatise: Because, you constantly and propitiously promote that universal Good of the whole Community, under which [*universal Good*] are contained Religion and universal Good-will, and in these we shall find comprehended all the Laws of Nature.

Your Lordship's Piety towards God, is fully demonstrated from your

Bounty to his Church, by endowing the Episcopal See of *Chester* with Land, as also many Parishes with Glebes, for the Accommodation of resident Curates.[3]

You, my Lord, in one capacity, exercise and practice Benevolence to Mankind in general, as a Member of the Privy Council, (where the grand Concernments of universal Trade and public Treaties are transacted) and where your Lordship most religiously reveres the Laws of Nations, of Public Contracts, of Public Peace; and where, in all Consultations, you utterly abhor and abominate even every the least Appearance of, Invasion upon Property.

In your Lordship's other Capacity, you likewise shew yourself a steady, faithful Subject to that Constitution of Government under which you are born, and for the Support of which (in *Lucan's* Character of *Cato*) you delighted to stand, when it was even overcome and oppressed.

Victrix causa Diis placuit, sed victa Catoni.[4]

Neither would your Lordship submit to an usurping Tyrant, altho' in actual Possession, and at a Time when Mr. Hobbes avowedly maintained and openly supported, as Doctrines, that this usurped Power, and a quiet Submission to it, were lawful [Leviathan in English, at the Conclusion, pag. 300].

In short, the Subject Matter of this Treatise apologizes best for me; and, to speak ingenuously, is the original Source of this Dedication.

As to the AUTHOR; it is sufficient to say, That he lies under Obligations to your Lordship as his Patron, which he with Pleasure and Gratitude acknowledges: And, that the Production of his Studies and Labours belong of Right to you, he being, in a Manner, born under your Lordship's Roof.[5]

---

3. Bridgeman's father, John (1577–1652), was Bishop of Chester; and Bridgeman maintained active links with the diocese.

4. Lucan, *Pharsalia,* I.128: "The victorious cause was pleasing to the Gods, but a lost cause to Cato."

5. Cumberland became Bridgeman's client in 1667. This patronage was decisive in Cumberland's promotion to two posts, the vicarage of All Saints and the rectory of St. Peter's, both in Stamford, Lincolnshire.

I have, indeed, these further Views in dedicating this Book to your Lordship, that it may prove more acceptable to Men of Letters, who rise and flourish under your Lordship's Protection;[6] and because I am, in my Conscience convinced, that this Treatise will be most highly acceptable to your Lordship's Sons, who inherit their Father's Virtues.

What now only remains is, humbly to ask Pardon, that I have presumed to declare publicly, those Acts of Goodness which you liberally performed for the Good of the Church with all possible Secrecy.

I have not addressed myself to your Lordship with the least View towards Flattery, but from an inward Persuasion, that your great Liberality will redound to the Glory of the *Reformation,* and shine as an Example illustrious enough for men of the highest Figure and Fortune to behold, admire, and as truly worthy of their own Imitation.

Above all, I beseech your Lordship's Pardon for having detained you too long from Affairs of the first Importance. I therefore now retire to my daily Supplication, which is, That God may, as long as possible, preserve your Lordship a Blessing to his Church, to our gracious Sovereign, to these Realms, and to us all: *All Mankind.*

> I am, MY LORD,
> Upon Many Accounts,
> Your Lordship's most obedient,
> And most devoted humble servant,
>
> R.C.

---

6. Bridgeman acted as patron to several intellectuals and writers, notably John Wilkins, Hezekiah Burton, and Thomas Traherne.

Appendix 2

Hezekiah Burton's "Address to the Reader"

The Reverend Doctor HEZEKIAH BURTON's
ALLOQUIUM AD LECTOREM:
OR,
A short Admonition to the Readers of this Philosophical
Enquiry, &c. *Translated into* English *by* J.T.[1]

I beg the Favour of the learned Readers to take Notice, that our Author, in this his *Philosophical Dissertation,* did not study to captivate the Fancy with enticing Words, nor with the laboured Refinements of Rhetoric.

He did not waste his Time and Pains in collecting far and near, elegant Turns of Expression, nor in modelling the Harmony of his Periods.

As his Readers, however, are not, on the one Hand, to walk in the Flower-gardens of Oratory; so, neither are they, on the other, to tread the thorny Ways of dry Schoolmen, nor travel a dreary Journey thro' the wild Thickets of Briers and Brambles only. They will not find in our Author Monkish Barbarisms; and but few, if any, Terms of Art, as they are commonly called, neither, in short, will he ensnare them with the Fallacies of Sophistical Reasoning.

Our Philosopher does not cherish such rigid, austere, Stoical Principles; neither does he abominate all kind of Elegance with such an Ab-

---

1. Hezekiah Burton's "Address to the Reader" (Cumberland, *De Legibus Naturae,* "Alloquium ad Lectorem," A3r-b1r), translated into English by the Rev. John Towers for his edition of Cumberland, *A Philosophical Enquiry into the Laws of Nature* (1750), Appendix, Part IV, pp. 86–88.

horrence, as to place the whole Value of his Performance upon a careless, wild Neglect: And yet, he cannot be ranked in the Class of what are termed *your finished Men, your nice, polite, courtly Authors. He does not set up for so absolute an Admirer of* Cicero, neither did he exert all his Talents in pleasing those, who place the whole Value of Writing in Language and Expression: He values Expression, indeed, so far, as to understand his own Meaning himself, and convey the full Sense of it to others. And, since he could not be exact in every minute Article, he would not neglect the most material.

[Objection] "But, his Attention being closely engaged upon his Subject, like all those who chiefly study the main Point, he appears in a Negligence of Style, and in a Sort of an Undress."

[Answer] In order to clear him from this kind of Imputation, he entrusted me with his Manuscript. Whether thro' Inability or Idleness, or (which is pretty much the same Thing) thro' many other Avocations and trifling Kinds of other Business, I certainly have not fully executed the Task by some expected of me.

I must therefore intreat the Readers, to take off every Imputation of this Kind from our Author, and to lay it at my Door.

Now as to that most heinous Offence which I have committed against the grammatical Folks (which to be sure is an Offence no less than capital) I acknowledge myself deservedly worthy of their severest Indignation and Punishment.

If none of these Excuses, in short, can plead my Pardon, I must appeal to Scioppius,[2] and the other critical, strict Judges of the *Latin* Tongue; I will call them to my Assistance, who never refused Patronage to such Votaries as invoke their Aid. These Gentlemen are, to be sure, the high and mighty Judges, who have a Right to ascertain and vindicate the just Forms, and proper Modes of Expression.

It is the usual Practice of these Critics, and with the whole Weight of their Authority, to transplant and naturalize foreign Phrases. Now they will, beyond all Doubt, strenuously maintain, That a plain stile is

---

2. Kaspar Schoppe, or Scioppius (1576–1649), was the author of several Latin pedagogical texts.

agreeable to a Philosophical Subject; because it is the easiest, and the most naturally adapted to handle every such Subject well.

Take heed therefore, my good Readers, and be advised by me, not to find Fault with our Author's Stile, lest ye proclaim and wage War publicly with the whole Herd of Critical Grammarians.

There is also another Caution necessary, and that is, not to expect in this Treatise any witty Points, satyrical Turns, or facetious Jokes, either in the Thought or in the Expression. Because, our Author was, to be sure, an utter Enemy to all that Kind of Confutation; and from which Sort of Reasoning, in such numberless Instances, he so heavily reproaches his Adversary, and would never have spared him, but that he did not care always to give a Loose to his just Indignation.

It is the most difficult Thing in the World, to refrain from Satyr, in treating that rude, barbarous Philosophy, which lays the Foundations of all Irreligion, Injustice, Villainy, and even Rebellion itself.

However, our Author, who is of a most beneficent Nature, chose to use a gentle, mild Expression, and that upon many Accounts:

First, He was fully resolved to treat Mr. *Hobbes* with Humanity and Gentleness, not only upon Account of his great Learning; but, more especially, because Mr. *Hobbes,*—poor Gentleman! is now emaciated, and almost quite sunk beneath the Weight and Infirmities of Age.[3]

Secondly, Because, our Author imagines it equally barbarous, to declaim with bitter Invectives against a dying old Man, continually under the dreadful Apprehensions of Death, as to insult over the last Remains of a departing Soul, or to torture the Manes of the Dead.

Thirdly, Because, our Author employed a great deal of his Time and Pains in mathematical Studies, from which Kind of Studies he learned a Simplicity and Purity of Expression, quite disengaged from rhetorical Ornaments, and free from all Points of Wit.

Fourthly, No possible Reason can be assigned, why our Author should not use this plain Manner of Writing, altho' upon a Subject different from Mathematics.

For the Case is pretty much the same, in writing upon other Subjects,

---

3. In 1671 Hobbes (1588–1679) was 83 years old.

as upon those of Mathematics. You seldom find Authors, well principled in the mathematical Science, mistaken in Point of Reasoning; unless, perhaps, it happens, now and then, that a mathematical Scholar may grow somewhat mad: A melancholy Instance of which we have in Mr. *Hobbes!*

That our Author, therefore, might investigate and trace our Truths of the most Importance and Difficulty, and fairly lay these Truths before his Readers in a clear, regular Stile, he judged, that reasoning upon a moral Subject with mathematical Demonstration, could the better banish from his Thoughts and Writings the uneven and turbulent Irregularities of an unsettled Genius.

In a Word, to avoid Prolixity, whoseover will cavil at this Book (as a jejune, barren Performance, without any Spirit, Wit or Beauty) ought to consider, that our Author's sole Intent was, to discover and lay the most weighty Truths open in the clearest Manner, and confirm them by the most conclusive Demonstrations; which, if he has not effectually performed, we may despair of ever seeing such a Work well executed, even unto the End of Time.

This Caution, however, I give you, by the Bye, That whatsover Commendation I most deservedly bestow either upon our Author or upon his Performance, not to understand it as if I would pre-engage your Favour by too early, hasty an Encomium.

Every one is at all the Liberty in the World (notwithstanding any Thing that I have said to the contrary) to judge for himself: But with this Proviso, that he first reads over, with Patience and Attention, the Book itself; and that he thoroughly understands it; and then, when this is done, he may (but yet with Candour and Impartiality) pass Sentence upon it.

Whatever ignorant, malevolent, invidious Scoffers object against our Author, or his Performance; whatever muttering Noises, by way of Contradiction, lazy Sophists may snarl out against it; whatsoever little Cavils Atheists, and the Enemies to God and Man, we shall esteem, rather praise than reproach.

The best of Men will, to be sure, behave themselves with Candour;

and they all, even to a Man, will take upon themselves the Defence of that Cause [*the common Good*] which our Author defends. Nay,—I have no Doubt upon me, but that this Book will be acceptable to all, except the very worst of Men, especially since the main Design of this Undertaking is to prove, That every Individual, to the best of his Abilities, must promote the common Happiness of All.—And, unless I am mistaken in my Conjecture, the present Generation will highly commend, and Posterity, with Wonder and Surprize, esteem our Author. For, if I have the least Judgement at all, this Book is written, not only for the present Age, but for endless Ages to come.

Go on, therefore, O thou most excellent Author, according to that boundless, diffusive Benevolence with which thou art blessed! Go on, I say, to deserve the best Gratitude from the whole human Race! That is, go on and communicate to ALL, those most excellent Precepts which you yourself have traced out:—Precepts which truly may be called your own,—Precepts incessantly flowing from your own Mind, as from a Fountain of the clearest, purest, best Ideas: And,—may the whole Universe reap the blessed, most delicious Fruits of your Learning, your Wisdom, your Integrity.—Fruits which very few,—too few, indeed, as yet, either feel, taste or understand.

And now—by way of Conclusion—I address myself to all, the whole rational System of created Agents, and who, upon Principles of *Universal Benevolence,* are my Parents and Brethren. I address myself to you all, as many as ye be, altho' in Number passing Numeration, diffused and spread over the whole Expanse of boundless Space, whether ye be *Indians,* or *Scythians,* or *Africans,* or the Inhabitants of Regions and Countries as yet unknown; whether ye be more widely different on your Sentiments of Religion, in your Notions and Affections, than in Situation and Place. I address and beseech you all, with Care and Observance, to peruse *The Holy Bible,* and this admirable Book of our Author, if happily, by any Means, these two most excellent Books of divine Instruction happen to fall into your Hands—Hearken to your own Reason,—Hearken to your own Experience,—Hearken unto your own Senses,—All silently admonishing and pronouncing Instructions—

Hearken, in a Word, to Universal Nature, with one Voice declaring, That nothing is more humane, more lovely, more amiable, more perfective of human Nature: That nothing more nearly resembles the Nature of God, than *Benevolence* universally extended and exerted towards *All.*

All these Monitors with a clear, with an audible Voice, (A Voice by the deep Ear of Meditation heard) and with one Consent declare, That a Good-will, the most diffusive and boundless, is the first Principle, the just Measure, and the only sure Rule of all our Duty: That is the ultimate End of all our Actions; the amplest Reward the Fulness of Hope can reach: And—in short,—that it is Man's chief Good.

To what exorbitant Degrees of Excess, or to what Ends and Purposes, therefore, shall we, a wretched Race of stupid, absurd Mortals, indulge our Hatred and Malice, our Envy and Jealousy, our Simulation and Dissimulation?

Let us rather, having laid aside Malevolence, Anger, Wrath, and an Over-violence of Self-love [*Nimia φιλαντία,*] provoke one another to Love, to a Love unfeigned, to a Love without End and without Bounds towards *All.*

By these Means we shall arrive at the highest, most exalted State of human Happiness, where we shall consult and act, not only the Good of ourselves, and of our own Flesh and Blood: Not only the Good of those who agree with us in Opinions and Sentiments: Not only the Good of our Friends and Countrymen, but *the Good of All,* let that *All* be as many, as numberless, as Imagination can conceive. *Rare is the Happiness of such an Age!* A Golden Age scarce to be found! When ALL, with their highest their purest Affections, and with their best-united Endeavours will promote the Happiness of ALL.—O Blessed Time!—O most amiable Age!—Let us, my Brethren, as much as in us lies, press forward to so blessed a State.—And—that—our most bountiful God, the one eternal Fountain, Prototype and original Parent of Love, would assist our own Endeavours, and (having purged all Rancour and Malignity of Envy and Malice from our Souls) plentifully pour into our Hearts and Minds his holy Spirit, his Mankind-loving Spirit. That we *All,* all who inhabit the universal Frame of Nature, may firmly unite and be linked together by indissoluble Bonds of beneficent Affection. And this, from the inmost Recesses of a sincere Soul, is my fervent Prayer, who am, with ardent Zeal,

Your truly Benevolent,

HEZEKIAH BURTON

SELECTED BIBLIOGRAPHY

Published Works of Richard Cumberland

De Legibus Naturae Disquisitio Philosophica, in qua earum Forma, Summa Capita, Ordo, Promulgatio, & Obligatio è Rerum Natura Investigantur; quinetiam Elementa Philosophiae Hobbianae, cùm Moralis tum Civilis, Considerantur & Refutantur. London, 1672.

De Legibus Naturae . . . editio secunda. Lübeck-Frankfurt, 1683.

De Legibus Naturae . . . editio tertia. Lübeck-Frankfurt, 1694.

De Legibus Naturae . . . Dublin, 1720.

An Essay Towards the Recovery of the Jewish Measures & Weights, comprehending their monies; by help of ancient standards, compared with ours of England. London, 1686.

Les loix de la nature, expliquées par le Docteur Richard Cumberland . . . Traduits du Latin, par Monsieur Barbeyrac . . . Avec des notes du traducteur. Translated by Jean Barbeyrac. Leiden, 1757.

"The Motives to Liberality Considered." In *The English Preacher,* ix. London, 1774.

Origines Gentium Antiquissimae; or, Attempts for Discovering the Times of the First Planting of Nations. In several tracts. London, 1724.

A Philosophical Enquiry into the Laws of Nature: . . . Wherein also, the Principles of Mr. Hobbes's Philosophy, . . . are examined into, and confuted. Translated by John Towers. Dublin, 1750.

Sanchoniatho's Phoenician History, translated from the First Book of Eusebius de Praeparatione Evangelica. With a continuation of Sanchoniatho's History by Eratosthenes Cyrenaeus's Canon. London, 1720.

Traité Philosophique des Loix Naturelles, ou l'on recherche et l'on établit, par la Nature des Choses, la forme de ces Loix, leurs principaux chefs, leur ordre, leur publication & leur obligation: on y refute aussi les Elémens de la Morale & de la Politique de Thomas Hobbes. Traduit du Latin par Monsieur Barbeyrac,

. . . avec des notes du traducteur, qui y a joint celles de la Traduction Angloise. Translated by Jean Barbeyrac. Amsterdam, 1744.

A Treatise of the Laws of Nature. By the Right Reverend . . . Richard Cumberland, Lord Bishop of Peterborough. Translated by John Maxwell. London, 1727.

Other Works Referenced in the Text and Notes

Acosta, Joseph. *Historia Natural y Moral de las Indias.* Barcelona, 1591.

Airy, Osmund. "Sir Orlando Bridgeman." In *The Dictionary of National Biography.* Edited by L. Stephen and S. Lee. Oxford: Oxford University Press, 1917, 1226–28.

Aristotle. *Nicomachean Ethics.* Translated by H. Rackham. Cambridge, Mass.: Loeb, 1926.

———. *On the Heavens.* Translated by W. K. C. Guthrie. Cambridge, Mass.: Loeb, 1939.

———. *Politics.* Translated by H. Rackham. Cambridge, Mass.: Loeb, 1942.

Arminius, Jacobus. *Orationes.* Leiden, 1611.

Augustine. *The City of God.* Translated by R. W. Dyson. Cambridge: Cambridge University Press, 1998.

Bacon, Francis. *De Augmentis Scientiarum.* London, 1623.

Bartholin, Thomas. *History of Anatomy.* London, 1668.

Bentley, Richard. *The Folly and Unreasonableness of Atheism.* London, 1693.

———. *Of Revelation and Messias. A Sermon Preached at the Publick Commencement at Cambridge.* Cambridge, 1696.

Boyle, Robert. *New Experiments Physico-Mechanical.* London, 1660.

Bright, George. *An Essay in Morality.* London, 1682.

Brocklesby, Richard. *An Explication of the Gospel—Theism and the Divinity of the Christian Religion.* London, 1706.

Buridan, John. *Quaestiones in Decem Libros Ethicorum Aristotelis ad Nicomachum.* Paris, 1513.

Buxtorf, Johannes. *Lexicon Talmudicum et Rabbinicum.* Basel, 1639.

Cardano, Girolamo. *De Rerum Varietate.* Basel, 1557.

Carmichael, Gershom. *Natural Rights on the Threshold of the Scottish Enlightenment: The Writings of Gershom Carmichael.* Edited by James Moore and Michael Silverthorne. Indianapolis: Liberty Fund, 2002.

Casaubon, Isaac. *Persii Flacci Satirarum.* Paris, 1605.

Cicero. *De Finibus Bonorum et Malorum.* Translated by H. Rackham. Cambridge, Mass.: Loeb, 1914.

———. *De Natura Deorum and Academica.* Translated by H. Rackham. Cambridge, Mass.: Loeb, 1933.

———. *De Oratore. De Fato.* Translated by H. Rackham. Cambridge, Mass.: Loeb, 1942.

———. *De Republica and De Legibus.* Translated by C. W. Keyes. Cambridge, Mass.: Loeb, 1928.

———. *Letters to Friends.* 2 vols. Translated by D. R. Shackleton Bailey. Cambridge, Mass.: Loeb, 2001.

———. *On Duties.* Translated by W. Miller. Cambridge, Mass.: Loeb, 1913.

———. *Philippics.* Translated by W. C. Ker. Cambridge, Mass.: Loeb, 1969.

———. *Tusculan Disputations.* Translated by J. E. King. Cambridge, Mass.: Loeb, 1927.

Clarke, Samuel. *The Works of Samuel Clarke D.D.* 4 vols. London, 1738.

Collins, Anthony. *A Discourse of the Grounds and Reasons of the Christian Religion.* London, 1724.

Compte, Louis le. *Memoirs and Observations Topographical, Physical, Mathematical, Mechanical, Natural, Civil, and Ecclesiastical. Made in a late journey through the empire of China.* London, 1697.

Cory, Isaac P. *Ancient Fragments.* London, 1832.

Crinitus, Petrus. *De Honesta Disciplina.* Paris, 1508.

Cudworth, Ralph. *The True Intellectual System of the Universe.* London, 1678.

Culverwell, Nathaniel. *An Elegant and Learned Discourse of the Light of Nature.* Edited by Robert A. Greene and Hugh MacCallum. Indianapolis: Liberty Fund, 2001.

Darwall, Stephen. *The British Moralists and the Internal "Ought."* Cambridge: Cambridge University Press, 1995.

Della Casa, Giovanni. *Galateus de Moribus.* Oxford, 1653.

Descartes, René. *The Philosophical Writings of Descartes.* 2 vols. Edited by J. Cottingham. Cambridge: Cambridge University Press, 1985.

Digby, Kenelm. *Of the Immortality of Man's Soul.* London, 1644.

Dio Cassius. *Roman History.* 9 vols. Translated by E. Cary and H. B. Foster. Cambridge, Mass.: Loeb, 1914.

Diogenes Laertius, *Lives and Opinions of Eminent Philosophers.* 2 vols. Translated by R. D. Hicks. Cambridge, Mass.: Loeb, 1925.

Ditton, Humphrey. *A Discourse Concerning the Resurrection of Jesus Christ.* London, 1712.

Dodwell, Henry. *An Epistolary Discourse, proving, from the Scriptures and the First Fathers, that the Soul is a Principle Naturally Mortal.* London, 1706.

Dryden, John. *The Satires of Decimus Junius Juvenalis.* London, 1693.

Epictetus. *Discourses.* Translated by W. A. Oldfather. Cambridge, Mass.: Loeb, 1925.

Eusebius. *De Praeparatio Evangelica.* 4 vols. Edited by T. Gaisford. Oxford: Oxford University Press, 1843.

Ficino, Marsilio. *Platonis Opera Omnia.* Florence, 1484.

Forbes, Duncan. *Hume's Philosophical Politics.* Cambridge: Cambridge University Press, 1975.

————. "Natural Law and the Scottish Enlightenment." In *The Origin and Nature of the Scottish Enlightenment.* Edited by R. Campbell and A. S. Skinner. Edinburgh: John Donald, 1982, 186–204.

Forsyth, Murray. "The Place of Richard Cumberland in the History of Natural Law Doctrine." *Journal of the History of Philosophy* 20 (1982): 23–42.

Fowler, Edward. *The Design of Christianity.* London, 1671.

Gassendi, Pierre. *Animadversiones in Decimum Librum Diogenis Laertii.* Paris, 1649.

————. *Syntagma Philosophicum.* Paris, 1658.

Glanvill, Joseph. *The Way to Happiness.* London, 1670.

Glisson, Francis. *Anatomia Hepatis.* London, 1654.

————. *De Rachitide.* London, 1650.

Greaves, John. *Anonymus Persa De Siglis Arabum & Persarum Astronomicis.* London, 1648.

Grotius, Hugo. *Annotationes ad Vetus Testamentum.* Paris, 1644.

————. *De Jure Belli ac Pacis.* Paris, 1625.

————. *De Veritate Religionis Christianae.* Paris, 1627.

Grotius, William. *De Principis Juris Naturalis Enchiridion.* The Hague, 1667.

Haakonssen, Knud. "The Character and Obligation of Natural Law According to Richard Cumberland." In *English Philosophy in the Age of Locke.* Edited by M. A. Stewart. Oxford: Oxford University Press, 2001, pp. 29–47.

————. "Moral Philosophy and Natural Law: From the Cambridge Platonists to the Scottish Enlightenment." *Political Science* 40 (1988): 97–110.

————. *Natural Law and Modern Philosophy.* Cambridge: Cambridge University Press, 1996.

Hammond, Henry. *A Paraphrase and Annotations upon All the Books of the New Testament.* London, 1659.

————. *A Paraphrase and Annotations upon the Books of the Psalm.* London, 1659.

Harvey, William. *Exercitatio Anatomica de Circulatione Sanguinis.* London, 1649.

————. *Exercitationes de Generatione Animalium.* London, 1651.

Hierocles. *De Providentia & Fato.* London, 1673.

————. *Hierocles upon the Golden Verses of the Pythagoreans.* Translated by J. Norris. Oxford, 1682.

Highmore, Nathaniel. *The History of Generation.* London, 1651.

Hobbes, Thomas. *Elementorum Philosophiae Sectio Prima de Corpore.* London, 1655.

————. *Elementorum Philosophiae Sectio Secunda de Homine.* London, 1658.

————. *Humane Nature: Or, the Fundamental Elements of Policy.* London, 1650.

————. *Leviathan with Selected Variants from the Latin Edition of 1668.* Edited by E. Curley. Indianapolis: Hackett, 1994.

————. *On the Citizen.* Edited and translated by Richard Tuck and Michael Silverthorne. Cambridge: Cambridge University Press, 1998.

————. *Problemata Physica.* London, 1662.

————. *Thomae Hobbes Malmesburiensis Opera Philosophica.* 3 vols. Amsterdam, 1668.

Hochstrasser, Timothy. *Natural Law Theories in the Early Enlightenment.* Cambridge: Cambridge University Press, 2000.

Hoffman, Christian. *Umbra in Luce sive Consensus et Dissensus Religionum Profanorum.* Jena, 1680.

Hoornbeek, Joannes. *Pro Convincendis et Convertendis Judaeis Libri Octo.* Leiden, 1655.

Horace. *Satires, Epistles, Ars Poetica.* Translated by H. R. Fairclough. Cambridge, Mass.: Loeb, 1926.

Hottinger, Johann Heinrich. *Thesaurus Philologicus seu Clavis Scripturae.* Zurich, 1649.

Hulsius, Antonius. *Theologiae Judaicae.* Breda, 1653.

Hunter, Michael. *Establishing the New Science: The Experience of the Early Royal Society.* Woodbridge, England: Boydell, 1989.

———. *Science and Society in Restoration England.* Cambridge: Cambridge University Press, 1981.

Hutcheson, Francis. *An Inquiry into the Original of Our Ideas of Beauty and Virtue.* Indianapolis: Liberty Fund, 2004.

Hyde, Thomas. *Historia religionis veterum Persarum.* London, 1700.

Iamblichus. *De Mysteriis.* Edited by T. Gale. London, 1678.

Jackson, John. *A Defence of Human Liberty.* London, 1725.

Jackson, Thomas. *A Treatise Containing the Originall of Unbeliefe.* London, 1625.

———. *The Works of Thomas Jackson.* Edited by B. Oley. London, 1653.

Justinian. *Corpus Juris Civilis.* 4 vols. Edited by T. Mommsen and P. Kreuger. Berlin: Wiedmann, 1968.

Juvenal. *Satires and Persius.* Translated by G. G. Ramsay. Cambridge, Mass.: Loeb, 1918.

Kirk, Linda. *Richard Cumberland and Natural Law.* Cambridge: James Clark, 1987.

Kroll, Richard F. *The Material World: Literate Culture in the Restoration and Early Eighteenth Century.* Baltimore: Johns Hopkins, 1991.

Lessius, Leonardus. *Hygiasticon.* Antwerp, 1613.

Lightfoot, John. *A Commentary upon the Acts of the Apostles.* London, 1645.

———. *Horae Hebraicae et Talmudicae.* Cambridge, 1664.

Lipsius, Justus. *C. Cornelii Taciti Annalium et Historiarum.* Antwerp, 1574.

———. *Iusti Lipsii Opera Omnia.* Wesel, 1675.

———. *Physiologia Stoicorum.* Antwerp, 1604.

Locke, John. *An Essay Concerning Human Understanding.* Edited by P. H. Nidditch. Oxford: Clarendon, 1975.

———. *Two Treatises of Government.* Edited by P. Laslett. Cambridge: Cambridge University Press, 1970.

Lord, Henry. *A Display of Two Forraigne Sects in the East Indies.* London, 1630.

Lower, Richard. *Tractatus de Corde.* London, 1669.

Lucan. *The Civil War (Pharsalia).* Translated by J. D. Duff. Cambridge, Mass.: Loeb, 1928.

Lucretius. *De Rerum Natura.* Translated by W. H. D. Rouse and M. F. Smith. Cambridge, Mass.: Loeb, 1975.

Ludolf, Hiob. *A New History of Ethiopia.* London, 1682.

Maffeius, Joannes Petrus. *Historiae Indicae.* Antwerp, 1605.

Maimonides, Moses. *De Idolatria.* Edited by G. Vossius. Amsterdam, 1641.

Malpighi, Marcello. *De Cerebri Cortice.* Paris, 1666.

Marcus Aurelius. *Marcus Aurelius Antoninus, the Roman Emperor, his Meditations concerning himselfe.* Translated by M. Casaubon. London, 1634.

———. *Markou Antoninou tou autokratoros ton eis heauton.* Edited by T. Gataker. London, 1653.

Marsham, John. *Chronicus Canon Aegypticus, Ebraicus, Graecus, et Disquisitiones.* London, 1676.

Mayo, T. F. *Epicurus in England 1650–1725.* Dallas: South West Press, 1934.

Mede, Joseph. *Clavis Apocalyptica ex Innatis et Institis Visionem.* London, 1627.

———. *Diatribae. Discourses on Divers Texts of Scripture.* London, 1642.

Montaigne, Michel de. *Essays.* Translated by John Florio. London, 1603.

Moore, James, and Michael Silverthorne. "Gerschom Carmichael and the Natural Jurisprudence Tradition in Eighteenth-Century Scotland." In *Wealth and Virtue: The Shaping of Political Economy in the Scottish Enlightenment.* Edited by I. Hont and M. Ignatieff. Cambridge: Cambridge University Press, 1983, pp. 73–88.

More, Henry. *Divine Dialogues.* London, 1668.

———. *Enchiridion Ethicum.* London, 1668.

———. *The Immortality of the Soul.* London, 1659.

Moyle, Walter. *The Works of Walter Moyle.* 2 vols. Edited by T. Sargent. London, 1726.

Münster, Sebastian. *Biblia Hebraica.* Basel, 1534–35.

Needham, Walter. *Disquisitio Anatomica de Formata Foetu.* London, 1667.

Newton, Isaac. *Abregé de la Chronologie de M. le Chevalier Newton.* Paris, 1725.

———. *Opticks.* London, 1717.

———. *Principia Philosophiae. Editio Tertia.* London, 1726.

Ovid, *Metamorphoses.* Translated by A. D. Melville. Oxford: Oxford University Press, 1986.

Ovington, John. *Voyages to Suratt in 1689.* London, 1696.

Palafox y Mendoza, Juan de. *The History of the Conquest of China.* London. 1676.

Palladini, Fiametta. *Discussioni Seicentesche su Samuel Pufendorf.* Bologna: Il Mulino, 1978.

———. *Samuel Pufendorf: Discepolo di Hobbes.* Bologna: Il Mulino, 1990.

Parker, Samuel. *An Account of the Nature and Extent of the Divine Dominion and Goodnesse.* Oxford, 1666.

———. *A Demonstration of the Divine Authority of the Law of Nature, and of the Christian Religion.* London, 1681.

———. *Disputationes de Deo et Providentia Divina.* London, 1678.

———. *A Free and Impartiall Censure of the Platonick Philosophy.* Oxford, 1666.

———. *Tentamina Physico-Theologica de Deo.* London, 1665.

Parkin, Jon. "Probability, Punishments and Property: Richard Cumberland's Sceptical Science of Sovereignty." In *Natural Law and Civil Sovereignty.* Edited by Ian Hunter and David Saunders. Basingstoke, England: Palgrave, 2002, pp. 76–90.

———. *Science, Religion and Politics in Restoration England: Richard Cumberland's* De Legibus Naturae. Woodbridge, England: Boydell, 1999.

Pétau, Denis. *Opus de Theologicis Dogmatibus.* Paris, 1644.

Pighius, Stephanus. *Themis Dea.* Antwerp, 1568.

Pitcairne, Archibald. "Dissertatio de Circulatione Sanguinis in Animalibus Genitis et non Genitis." In *Dissertationes Medicae.* Edinburgh, 1713.

Plato. *Republic.* Translated by D. Lee. Harmondsworth, England: Penguin, 1974.

Pliny. *Natural History.* 10 vols. Translated by H. Rackham. Cambridge, Mass.: Loeb, 1938.

Plotinus. *Enneads.* 7 vols. Translated by A. H. Armstrong. Cambridge, Mass.: Loeb, 1969.

Plutarch. *Moralia.* 16 vols. Translated by F. C. Babbitt et al. Cambridge, Mass.: Loeb, 1927.

———. *Parallel Lives.* 11 vols. Translated by B. Perrin. Cambridge, Mass.: Loeb, 1914–26.

Pocock, Edward. *Specimen Historiae Arabum.* Oxford, 1650.

Poiret, Pierre. *Cogitationum Rationalium de Deo.* Amsterdam, 1685.

Popkin, Richard H. *The History of Scepticism from Erasmus to Spinoza.* Berkeley: University of California Press, 1979.

Porphyry. *Select Works of Porphyry.* Translated by T. Taylor. Frome, England: Prometheus Trust, 1999.

Prideaux, Humphrey. *The Old and New Testament Connected in the History of the Jews and Neighbouring Nations.* London, 1717.

Pufendorf, Samuel. *De Jure Naturae et Gentium.* Lund, 1672.

———. *Elementorum Jurisprudentiae Universalis.* Translated by W. A. Oldfather. Oxford: Clarendon, 1931.

Purchas, Samuel. *Purchas his Pilgrimage.* London, 1619.

Rycaut, Paul. *The Present State of the Ottoman Empire.* London, 1668.

Sanderson, Robert. *XXXIV Sermons.* London, 1671.

Sarasohn, Lisa. "Motion and Morality: Pierre Gassendi, Thomas Hobbes and the Mechanical World View." *Journal of the History of Ideas* 46 (1985): 363–80.

Schneewind, Jerome B. *The Invention of Autonomy.* Cambridge: Cambridge University Press, 1998.

Schneider, Hans. *Justitia Universalis.* Frankfurt: Klosterman, 1967.

Schooten, Frans van. *Exercitationum Mathematicarum Libri Quinque.* Leiden, 1657.

Scott, W. L. *The Conflict between Atomism and Conservation Theory 1644–1860.* London: Macdonald, 1970.

Selden, John. *De Diis Syris Syntagma II.* London, 1617.

———. *De Jure Naturali et Gentium.* London, 1640.

———. *Mare Clausum.* London, 1635.

Seneca. *Epistulae Morales.* 10 vols. Translated by R. M. Gummere. Cambridge, Mass.: Loeb, 1920.

———. *Moral Essays,* 3 vols. Translated by J. W. Basore. Cambridge, Mass.: Loeb, 1928.

———. *Naturales Quaestiones.* Translated by T. H. Corcoran. Cambridge, Mass.: Loeb, 1971.

Shaftesbury, Anthony Ashley Cooper, 3rd Earl of. *Characteristicks of Men, Manners, Opinions, Times.* London, 1711.

———. *The Moralists, a Philosophical Rhapsody.* London, 1714.

Sharrock, Robert. *De Finibus Virtutis Christianae.* Oxford, 1673.

———. *De Officiis Secundum Naturae Jus.* Oxford, 1660.

Skinner, Quentin. *Visions of Politics.* 3 vols. Cambridge: Cambridge University Press, 2002.

Smith, John. *Select Discourses.* Edited by J. Worthington. London, 1660.

Sorell, Tom. "Seventeenth Century Materialism: Gassendi and Hobbes." In

The Renaissance and Seventeenth Century Rationalism. Edited by G. H. R. Parkinson. London: Routledge, 1993, pp. 235–72.

Spencer, John. *De Legibus Hebraeorum Ritualibus.* Cambridge, 1685.

Spencer, William. *Origenis Contra Celsum.* London, 1658.

Stearne, John. *Anima Medela.* London. 1653.

Stewart, Larry. *The Rise of Public Science: Rhetoric, Technology and Natural Philosophy in Newtonian Britain 1660–1750.* Cambridge: Cambridge University Press, 1992.

Suárez, Francisco. *De Legibus ac Deo Legislatore.* Coimbra, 1612.

Suetonius, *The Lives of the Caesars.* Translated by J. C. Rolfe. Cambridge, Mass.: Loeb, 1914.

Taylor, Jeremy. *Ductor Dubitantium.* 2 vols. London, 1660.

Tenison, Thomas. *Of Idolatry.* London, 1678.

Thucydides. *History of the Peloponnesian War.* 4 vols. Translated by C. F. Smith. Cambridge, Mass.: Loeb, 1919.

Truman, Joseph. *A Discourse of Natural and Moral Impotency.* London, 1675.

Tuck, Richard. "The 'Modern' Theory of Natural Law." In *The Languages of Political Theory in Early Modern Europe.* Edited by A. Pagden. Cambridge: Cambridge University Press, 1987, pp. 99–122.

———. *Natural Rights Theories: Their Origin and Development.* Cambridge: Cambridge University Press, 1979.

Vossius, Gerardus. *Historiae de Controversiis quas Pelagius.* Leiden, 1618.

Wallis, John. *Arithmetica Infinitorum.* Oxford, 1656.

———. *De Sectionibus Conicis Tratatus.* Oxford, 1655.

Walton, Brian. *Biblia Sacra Polyglotta.* London, 1657.

Ward, Seth. *Astronomia Geometrica.* Oxford, 1656.

———. *In Thomae Hobbii Philosophiam Exercitatio Epistolica.* Oxford, 1656.

———. *A Philosophicall Essay Towards an Eviction of the Being and Attributes of God.* Oxford, 1652.

Whiston, William. *Astronomical Principles of Religion.* London, 1717.

Wilkins, John. *On the Principles and Duties of Natural Religion.* London, 1675.

———. *Sermons Preached upon Several Occasions by the Right Reverend Father in God, John Wilkins.* London, 1682.

Willis, Thomas. *Cerebri Anatome, cui Accessit Nervorum Descripto et Usus.* London, 1664.

———. *Pathologiae Cerebri et Nervosi Generis Specimen.* Oxford, 1667.

Windet, James. *De Vita Functorum Statu.* London, 1663.

Wollaston, William. *The Religion of Nature Delineated.* London, 1722.

Wright, M. R. *Empedocles: The Extant Fragments.* New Haven: Yale University Press, 1981.

Zouch, Richard. *Elementa Jurisprudentiae.* London, 1629.

INDEX

authority for natural law, 249–250, 251, 260; civil government's need for, 753–756; God as author of natural law, 302–308, 501–502; Hobbes on, 249–250, 303–307, 753–756

Baal/Bel, 32, 63–64, 122, 126, 183
Babylonians, 37–42. *See also* Chaldeans
Bacchus, 88, 125, 130
Bachanalia, 188
Bacon, Francis (Lord Verulam), 252, 931n55, 936n61
balance, hypotheses regarding, 640–641
balance of powers theory, 400–402
Balbo, 131
Balbus, 118, 130, 152
Banians, 36, 37
baptism, natural mortality of soul prior to, 759n1. *See also* immateriality of thinking substance
Barbeyrac, Jean: actions promoting common good, 656n7, 660n9; animals, human benevolence toward, 648; Cumberland's manuscript addition used in, 753; human nature, 373n17–18, 436n87, 518n27; moral virtues, 697n12, 700n14, 701n15; natural law and moral obligation, 496n1, 504n13, 505n16, 539n47, 568n66, 642n155; nature of things, 329n54, 330n55, 332n59, 336n64, 346n89, 354n110; reason, 481n1, 486n2, 486n3, 488n5; translated edition of *De Legibus* produced by, xix; use of translation in this edition, xx
beauty, 264, 829–834, 897
Beelzebub, 46
Bel/Baal, 32, 63–64, 122, 126, 183

Bellona, 51
Belshazzar, 40
benefactors, obligations toward, 329
beneficial nature of good life and practice, 834–840
benevolence: advantages of, 648–650; animals, benevolence of humans toward, 647–648; animal tendency toward, 358; defined, 292–293, 297–298n8; dominion and property rights, 678–679; equality of human power to hurt or help each other, consequences of, 455–458; gravity and courteousness as moral virtues, 691–692; happiness derived from, 322, 525–528, 557–559; human powers of, 525–527; human tendency toward acts of, 357–359, 369–371; Maxwell on, 645–650; moral philosophy and, 297–300; natural law as to practice of (*see* common good, promotion of); necessity for happiness, 322; species of, 312n32; universal, prudent benevolence and promotion of common good, 657–660. *See also* natural good
Bentley, Richard: civil laws and civil government, 723n24; common good, 802n15; editions of *De Legibus,* xix; general law of nature, things contained in, 660n9; innate ideas, 928n48, 930n51, 931n54, 932n56–57; natural good, 467n11, 486n2; reason, practical dictates of, 488n5
Berosus, 40
Bible. *See* Scripture
blood and animal spirits, 434–439, 568, 639, 663
bodies, corporeal. *See* human bodies
Boyle, Robert, 565, 863, 870

This book is set in Adobe Garamond, a modern adaptation by Robert Slimbach of the typeface originally cut around 1540 by the French typographer and printer Claude Garamond. The Garamond face, with its small lowercase height and restrained contrast between thick and thin strokes, is a classic "old-style" face and has long been one of the most influential and widely used typefaces.

Printed on paper that is acid-free and meets the requirements of the American National Standard for Permanence of Paper for Printed Library Materials, z39.48-1992. ∞

Book design by Louise OFarrell
Gainesville, Florida
Typography by Apex Publishing, LLC
Madison, Wisconsin
Printed and bound by Edwards Brothers, Inc.
Ann Arbor, Michigan